THE ROUGH GUIDE TO
CALIFORNIA

This twelfth edi
Nick Edward

ROUGH
GUIDES

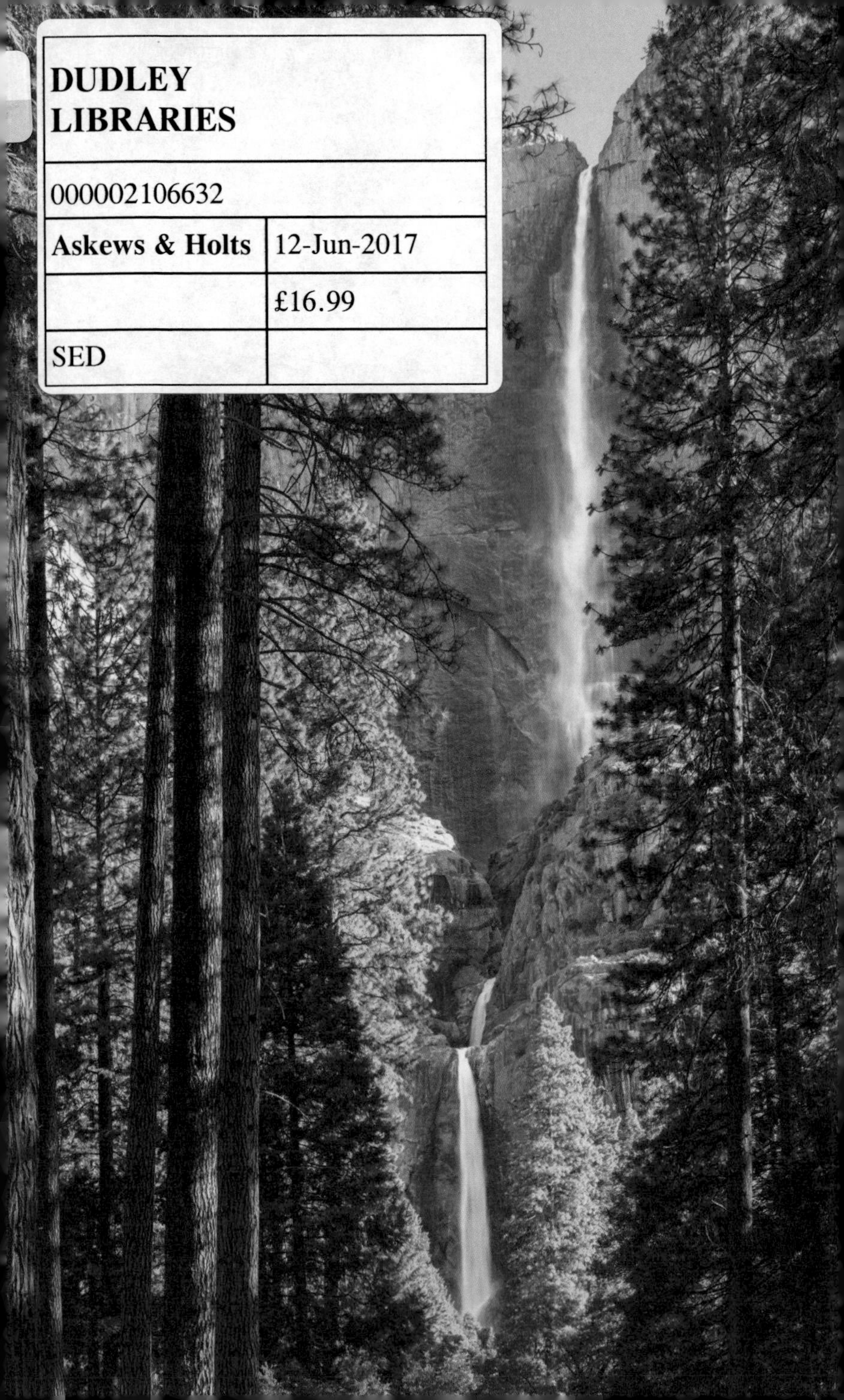

Contents

Introduction to
California

Few regions of the world have been as idealized and mythologized as California – and yet it seldom fails to live up to the hype. The Hollywood glamour, surf beaches and near-endless sun of the Southern California coast are rightly celebrated, but from here you're only a few hours' drive from majestic snowy mountains (and even ski resorts), Wild West ghost towns and barren deserts pocked with Joshua trees. Further north, boutique wine regions mix with primeval redwood forests, wild seascapes and the engaging metropolis of the Bay Area, with singular San Francisco as its hub. The Golden State's almost-unequalled diversity is packed into nearly 164,000 square miles – an area nearly twice the size of Great Britain – and yet California ranks as only the third largest state in the US, after Alaska and Texas.

To outsiders – and even a certain percentage of its residents – California represents the ultimate "now" society, where urban life is lived in the fast lane, conspicuous consumption is often paramount and, in some circles, having the right hairstyle, wardrobe and income is crucial. And while there's a bit of truth to this stereotype of the state's infamous superficiality, the fact is that California's staggering scope of cultures and lifestyles, determined as they are by everything from socio-economic factors to simple geography, could never allow for a single statewide identity to take root. The state's rich and ongoing penchant for invention and, moreover, re-invention underscores how there's far too much going on here for one single California to exist.

In one state you have the great metropolis and home of the movies Los Angeles, Beverly Hills and Disneyland, but also the staggering natural wonders of Yosemite National Park, towering redwoods and primitive rock carvings left by Native Americans. In the south, the unforgiving, mythical landscapes of the Mojave Desert and Death Valley contrast with the golf courses, resorts and Coachella festivities of Palm Springs, while the big names of Silicon Valley – Facebook, Google, Apple – lie short rides away from the isolated coast of Big Sur. You can sip your way through the vineyards of Napa, visit the abandoned mines of Gold Country and climb the snowcapped peaks of the Sierra Nevada, where bears and pumas roam.

California may well have a strong focus on the here and now, but it also has a fascinating past. Hunter-gathering Native American tribes had the place largely to themselves until Spanish missionaries arrived from modern-day Mexico and began building a string of missions from 1770 onwards. Contact was minimal and on a small scale until the Gold Rush of the 1840s and 1850s – a period that bestowed California its "Golden State" moniker. People of all social and political stripes flocked here, a pattern that has continued ever since and which has undoubtedly contributed to making this one of America's most polarized states, home to right-wing bastions such as Orange County and San Diego and yet also a principal source of America's most dynamic left-wing movements: environmentalism, women's liberation, and gay and immigrant rights. Some of the fiercest protests of the 1960s took root here, and in many ways this is still the heart of forward-looking America, as California continues to set the standard in terms of progressive action and social tolerance.

Put simply, this is a place that can be all things to all people. Whatever you want California to be, you'll find it somewhere; and no matter what you expect, it'll always surprise you.

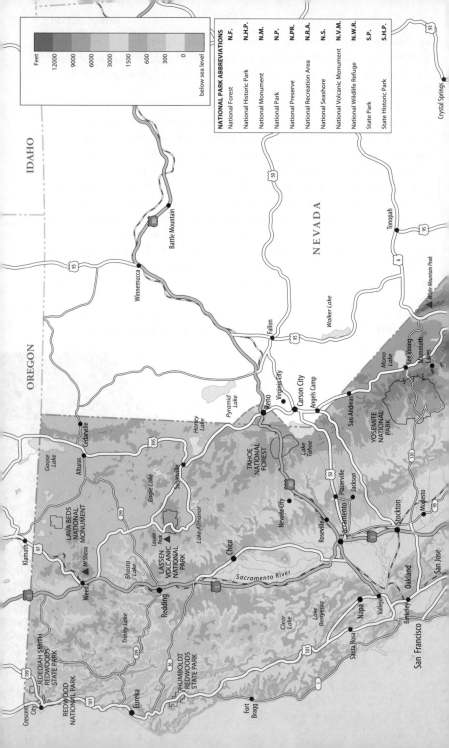

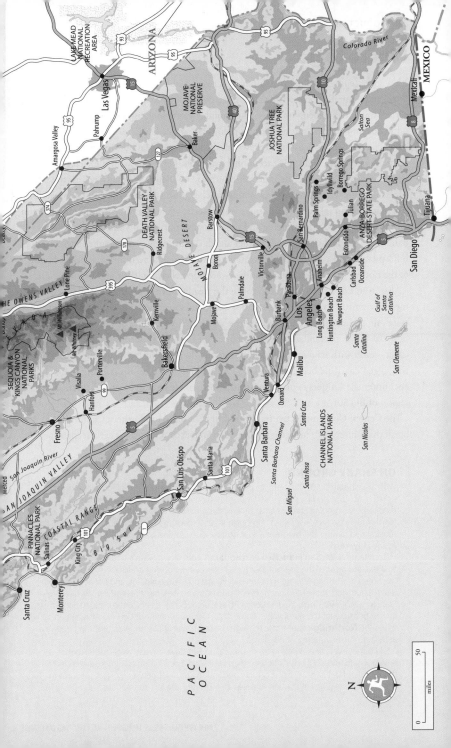

Where to go

It's worth keeping in mind that distances between California's main destinations can be huge, and naturally you won't be able to see everything on one trip. In a state that's so varied, much will depend on the kind of holiday you're looking for. You may well start off in **Los Angeles**, the second-most populous city in the US (after New York), a vast, sprawling metropolis boasting Hollywood, the beaches of Malibu, the bars of Sunset Strip, Venice Beach and some exceptional museums, beginning with the Getty Center. From here, you can make the short trip south to **San Diego**, set snugly against the US/Mexico border with its broad, welcoming beaches, world-famous zoo and laidback vibe. Alternately, head inland to California's vast **deserts**, where the resort community of **Palm Springs** invites poolside lounging and other languid pursuits; if you'd rather explore national parks, **Joshua Tree** and, further afield, **Death Valley** – as its name suggests, an inhospitable landscape of volcanic craters and windswept sand dunes that becomes one of the hottest places on earth in summer – are unparalleled in their arid beauty.

Also from Los Angeles, you can make the steady journey up the **Central Coast**, a meandering run that traces the Pacific's gorgeous shoreline and takes in some of the state's most dramatic scenery. Along the way, you'll visit a few of California's liveliest mid-size cities, particularly Santa Barbara, San Luis Obispo, Monterey and Santa Cruz – each with its own character and markedly different from one another. Along the jagged coastline between San Luis Obispo and Monterey on twisting CA-1, you'll encounter the uniquely epic homestead known as **Hearst Castle** and the park-rich region of **Big Sur**.

The Central Coast marks the transition from Southern to Northern California – a break that's more than just geographical. **San Francisco**, California's earliest metropolis

---

ON SHAKY GROUND

With an estimated 500,000 tremors detected annually in the state, California is a seismic time bomb, bisected by the most famous faultline in the world, the **San Andreas**, which runs loosely from San Francisco to Los Angeles and marks the junction of the Pacific and North American tectonic plates. Although it has a fearsome reputation, it's not, in fact, the most active fault at the moment – that honour goes to one of its connected faults, known as the **Hayward**.

Despite the 1906 **San Francisco earthquake**'s notoriety, it wasn't actually the quake itself that levelled most of the city, but a careless homeowner cooking breakfast on a gas stove at the time; the ensuing fire raged for three days, razed 28,000 buildings, and left at least 3000 dead. Since then, there have been several significant quakes, most recently in 1989, when San Francisco again shook during the **Loma Prieta**, named after its epicentre close to Santa Cruz and responsible for the horrifying collapse of an Oakland double-decker highway, and in 1994, when the **Northridge** quake tore through the north side of Los Angeles, rupturing freeways and flattening an apartment building.

Of course, everyone's waiting for the so-called **Big One**, a massive earthquake that, it's feared, could wipe out Los Angeles or San Francisco. Speculation has intensified over the last couple of decades, as experts have pegged the interval between major ruptures in the southern reaches of the San Andreas at 140 years: the last such quake was Fort Tejon in 1857.

Author picks

We've traversed California's soaring mountains, sinuous coast, wide-open deserts and ebullient cities to bring you our favourite Golden State places. Scream your head off on a rollercoaster, enjoy urban vistas from quiet hillside gardens and soak your bones in a mineral-water-filled tub deep in the desert – all in one visit to this remarkable state.

Lush hillside paths Laid out in wooden planks and brick, San Francisco's parallel Filbert and Greenwich steps cling to the steep eastern flank of Telegraph Hill and provide a dizzying combination of fragrant honeysuckle and roses, lovely gardens, extraordinary bay views – and even a giant flock of wild parrots. See p.442

Film among the spirits Summer weekends at Los Angeles' romantic (and slightly creepy) Hollywood Forever Cemetery see crowd-pleasing movies such as *Pulp Fiction* and *The Graduate* shown under the stars; there's even a photo booth themed according to each week's film. **See p.82**

Ale ahoy Along the wild Mendocino shore, Fort Bragg's North Coast Brewing Co. produces some of California's finest craft beers, including its celebrated Red Seal Ale; stop by en route to the redwoods for a brewery tour, pint and hearty pub meal. **See p.621**

Year-round outdoors playground The Lake Tahoe region is California's best place for winter pursuits, while the rest of the year sees exceptional opportunities for kayaking, rafting, boating and beach-going, as well as hiking the Tahoe Rim Trail, which circles the azure lake for 165 miles. **See p.568**

Thrillseekers' paradise Six Flags Magic Mountain boasts its share of superlatives: the world's tallest and fastest looping rollercoaster and highest drop tower ride (among many others), to say nothing of its staggering line-up of coasters that range from classic wooden to ultramodern "5th dimension". See p.120

High desert soaking Just inside California in remote Mono County, Benton Hot Springs is the place to head to after a day of Mammoth Mountain skiing or Eastern Sierra hiking, where outdoor tubs are filled with mineral-rich water under a starry desert sky. See p.280

> Our author recommendations don't end here. We've flagged up our favourite places – a perfectly sited hotel, an atmospheric café, a special restaurant – throughout the Guide, highlighted with the ★ symbol.

and today its proud second city, is quite different from Los Angeles down the coast: it's the West Coast's most compact, romantic and European-styled city, where Victorian houses cling to a series of steep hills that tumble down to water on three sides. From the San Francisco Bay Area, you have access to some of the state's most extraordinary scenery, not least in the national parks set to the east, far across heavily agricultural **San Joaquin Valley**. **Yosemite**, where powerful waterfalls cascade into a sheer glacial valley immortalized by Ansel Adams – and countless others – in search of the definitive landscape photograph, is the unquestioned highlight of the Sierra Nevada mountains; south from here are the huge parks of **Sequoia** and **Kings Canyon**, while to the north you'll find an intriguing mix of inviting Gold Rush-era towns such as Nevada City and the year-round resort of **Lake Tahoe**.

North of the San Francisco Bay Area, the population thins drastically and the landscapes change yet again. The climate is wetter up here and much more akin to that of the Pacific Northwest states of Oregon and Washington; as a natural result, the valleys are that much greener and flanked by a jagged coastline shadowed by towering **redwoods**, the tallest trees in the world. Though many visitors choose to venture no further than the **Wine Country** of Napa and Sonoma valleys on weekend forays from the Bay Area, it's well worth taking time to explore the state's northernmost regions, which are split distinctly in two. The coastline is simultaneously rugged and serene, guarded by mighty forests best enjoyed in **Redwood National Park** and a series of adjacent (and equally enjoyable) state parks. The region's interior, meanwhile, is dominated by the lofty peaks of majestic **Mount Shasta** and burly **Lassen Peak** – a volcano-scarred land that's as different from the stereotype of California as you could imagine.

EPICUREAN CALIFORNIA

The rich diversity of California's food and wine holds many contradictions. Los Angeles is the land of protein bars, salads and the faddy diets of wannabe actresses and models, but it's also known for its burgers and the innovative pizza of Wolfgang Puck. In Northern California, the San Francisco Bay Area spawned the state's signature California cuisine, a style of cooking that emphasizes the use of seasonal ingredients; it's also the birthplace of the ever-popular, enormous slab known as the Mission-style super burrito.

CELEBRITY CHEFS

California cuisine got its start in Berkeley in the early 1970s, when **Alice Waters** began preparing French recipes using the best local ingredients she could find, adjusting the menu of her restaurant, *Chez Panisse* (see p.504), according to the seasons; Los Angeles' **Wolfgang Puck** of *Spago* (see p.135) helped further popularize the cuisine. Other celebrated California chefs include **Michael Mina** and **Gary Danko**, each of whom has an eponymous restaurant in San Francisco, and **Thomas Keller**, whose *French Laundry* in Napa Valley's Yountville (see p.604) is widely considered the finest restaurant in the US.

BURRITOS AND BURGERS

California invented its own take on Mexican cuisine called **Cal-Mex**, a style that is often less saucy than the better-known Tex-Mex and incorporates plenty of vegetables and seafood. The hand-held monstrosity known as the **super burrito** (see p.471) became the state's signature Cal-Mex item by the 1980s, two decades after it was first concocted in San Francisco's Mission district. The worldwide popularity of the **hamburger**, meanwhile, can be traced to mid-century Southern California, where the McDonald brothers capitalized on the region's burgeoning car culture by opening their first drive-in restaurant in San Bernardino in 1940. These days, *In-N-Out Burger*, another Southern California-born chain, is widely loved for its made-to-order burgers and hand-sliced fries.

FRUITS OF THE VINE

California is by far the largest and most famous wine-producing state in the US, its vintners the first to prove that great wines could be made outside Europe. A variety of regions around the Golden State consistently turn out superb wines, from the celebrated vineyards of Napa and Sonoma, further south to the Santa Cruz Mountains and down to Santa Ynez Valley near Santa Barbara.

When to go

California's climate is as varied as its landscape: in **Southern California**, count on full days of sunshine between May and October, and warm, dry nights – though Los Angeles' notorious **smog** is at its worst when temperatures are highest, in August and September.

Along the **coast**, mornings can be hazily overcast, especially in May and June, though you can still easily tan – or burn – under grey skies. In winter, temperatures drop, but, more importantly, weeks of rain can cause massive mudslides that wipe out roads and hillside homes. Inland, the **deserts** are warm in winter and unbearably hot (42°C is not unusual) in summer; desert nights can be freezing in winter, when it can even snow. For serious white stuff, though, head to the **mountains**, where hiking trails at the higher elevations are blanketed with snow from November to June: skiers can take advantage of well-groomed slopes among the Sierra Nevada mountains and around Lake Tahoe.

The **Northern California** coast is wetter and cooler than the south, its summers tempered by sea breezes and fog, and its winters mild but damp. **San Francisco**, because of its exposed position at the tip of a peninsula, can be chilly all year, with summer fog often rolling in and chasing off what may have started as a pleasant day. Head across the bay to Oakland and Berkeley, however, and you'll often be back in the sun.

AVERAGE TEMPERATURES AND RAINFALL

	Jan	April	July	Oct
DEATH VALLEY				
max/min (°F)	66/39	89/62	118/86	92/61
max/min (°C)	19/4	32/17	48/30	33/16
rain (inches/mm)	0.4/10	0.1/3	0.0/0	0.1/3
EUREKA				
max/min (°F)	55/41	57/44	63/53	61/48
max/min (°C)	13/5	14/7	17/12	16/9
rain (inches/mm)	5.9/150	2.9/74	0.2/5	2.4/61
LAKE TAHOE				
max/min (°F)	41/15	53/26	79/40	62/26
max/min (°C)	5/-9	12/-3	26/4	17/-3
rain (inches/mm)	6.9/175	2.5/64	0.5/13	2.2/56
LOS ANGELES				
max/min (°F)	68/48	73/54	84/65	79/60
max/min (°C)	20/9	23/12	29/18	26/16
rain (inches/mm)	3.3/84	0.8/20	0.0/0	0.4/10
SAN DIEGO				
max/min (°F)	66/50	69/56	76/66	74/61
max/min (°C)	19/10	21/13	24/19	23/16
rain (inches/mm)	2.3/58	0.8/20	0.0/0	0.4/10
SAN FRANCISCO				
max/min (°F)	56/43	64/48	71/55	70/52
max/min (°C)	13/6	17/9	22/13	21/11
rain (inches/mm)	4.5/114	1.2/31	0.0/0	1.0/25

FROM TOP YOSEMITE NATIONAL PARK; LOS ANGELES; DEATH VALLEY NATIONAL PARK

27

things not to miss

It's not possible to see everything that California has to offer in one trip – and we don't suggest you try. What follows is a selective taste of the state's highlights, from its bustling beaches to its deserted Gold Rush outposts. All highlights are colour-coded by chapter and have a page reference to take you straight into the Guide, where you can find out more.

1 BIG SUR
Page 388

Enjoy Pacific Ocean views from the secluded beauty of Big Sur's approximately ninety miles of rocky coastline.

2 HISTORIC ROUTE 66
Page 248

Cruise a stretch of the original Mother Road as it cuts across the Mojave Desert, home to the atomic-era Modernism of *Roy's Motel & Café* and the classic Americana of the *Wigwam Motel*.

3 SAN FRANCISCO PRIDE
Page 483

In late June, the San Francisco Pride parade takes over the city's Castro district and Civic Center in colourfully exuberant fashion.

4 HEARST CASTLE
Page 380

Of all California's lavish dreams, none quite rivals William Randolph Hearst's monument to himself, which boasts a Mudejar cathedral façade.

5 SEQUOIA NATIONAL PARK
Page 312

The trees after which this park is named are the world's largest – and some of the oldest – living things.

6 PALM SPRINGS MODERNISM
Page 215

The verdant desert oasis of Palm Springs features some of the nation's greatest examples of mid-twentieth-century Modern architecture, best sampled on a guided tour.

7 HIKING MOUNT WHITNEY
Page 273

Trek to the top of the tallest mountain in the contiguous US, which caps the knife-edge ridge of the mighty Sierra Nevada range.

8 RIDING A CABLE CAR
Page 438

No visit to San Francisco is complete without a ride on one of these antique trolleys – the best means of scaling the city's punishing hills.

9 BALBOA PARK
Page 161

San Diego's staggering collection of museums, lush greenery and evocative Spanish Colonial buildings provides a wealth of opportunities for exploration.

10 TUFA TOWERS OF MONO LAKE
Page 291

Marvel at the fluffy, sand-castle-like tufa spires that have frothed up from below the surface of this ultra-saline body of water.

14

11 YOSEMITE VALLEY
Page 332

California has no shortage of stunning geology, but nothing surpasses Yosemite Valley, where the humbling and awe-inspiring monoliths of El Capitan and Half Dome await.

12 RAFTING, ON THE KERN RIVER
Page 303

The Kern River offers some of the most exciting whitewater rafting anywhere in the country.

13 VENICE BEACH
Page 105

Los Angeles comes to play at the sun-soaked promenade between Santa Monica and Venice, home of surfers, muscle-men and street performers.

14 CHOLLA CACTUS GARDEN
Page 232

One of the high points of any trip to Joshua Tree National Park is this cactus garden, part of a circular hike that takes in the unique "jumping" cholla.

15 SURFING
Page 106

From the gargantuan waves at Mavericks to the hot-dogging longboard heaven of Malibu, California's consummate pastime can be enjoyed year-round all along its coast.

16 THE COAST STARLIGHT
Page 353

The best – and often, only – way to view the stunning 100-mile-long coast between Santa Barbara and San Luis Obispo is by train.

15

16

17

18

19

17 LAVA BEDS NATIONAL MONUMENT

Page 662

The eerie black volcanic landscape and massive network of nearly 750 lava tubes are also the site of some grim history.

18 MEXICAN FOOD

Page 471

Duck into a roadside taquería to enjoy one of the state's signature cuisines.

19 GETTY CENTER

Page 100

This massive art museum is a trove of Grand Masters, sculpture and decorative arts, set on a hillside with sensational views of Los Angeles.

20 REDWOOD NATIONAL PARK

Page 632

The tallest trees in the world – some nearly 380ft high – preside over this dramatic national park, home to Roosevelt elk, black bears and hiking trails leading through serene groves.

21 DISNEY HALL

Page 143

Although Frank Gehry's architectural marvel was designed in 1987, sixteen years passed before it was finally built; today, this inspired sculptural creation serves as the monumental home of the Los Angeles Philharmonic.

20

24

25

26

27

Itineraries

The following three itineraries take in much of what makes California so special, from the state's electrifying major cities to its formidable mountains, serpentine coastline and arrestingly beautiful deserts. Be sure to budget at least ten days (if not more) to fully enjoy each route, as the vastness of the Golden State is best absorbed leisurely.

CLASSIC CALIFORNIA ROAD TRIP

Explore a broad swathe of California with this grand tour that visits a host of landscapes: urban, coastal, mountains and deserts.

❶ Los Angeles Visits to world-class museums, Venice Beach and Universal Studios, are among the countless attractions spread about this sprawling megalopolis of 18 million. **See p.54**

❷ Central Coast Wind your way up CA-1, with stops in the vibrant towns of Santa Barbara, San Luis Obispo and Santa Cruz, leaving time for Hearst Castle and Big Sur. **See p.348**

❸ San Francisco Spend a few days exploring this unique city's distinct neighbourhoods, with side-trips to nearby redwood forests, elephant seal breeding grounds and the Wine Country. **See p.416**

❹ Gold Country Head east across San Joaquin Valley to the charming Gold Rush-era towns of the Sierra foothills. **See p.536**

❺ Yosemite Gaze slack-jawed at the magnificent granite domes, crashing waterfalls and titanic sequoias protected in this world-famous national park. **See p.329**

❻ Eastern California Get a glimpse of pioneer life, photograph Mono Lake's bizarre tufa towers and see the world's oldest trees. **See p.252**

❼ Death Valley Experience the otherworldly landscapes of the hottest place on earth – an arid region of narrow canyons and, at its higher elevations, fragrant pine forests. **See p.258**

❽ Joshua Tree Freakish trees, sensual boulders and the nightly howl of the coyote make camping in this popular desert national park a real treat. **See p.228**

❾ Palm Springs Sip a cocktail by the pool at a stylish resort and ride the tram up 10,834ft San Jacinto Peak. **See p.208**

BEST OF THE COAST

Trace a southbound route along the Pacific Ocean to take best advantage of roadside lay-bys and unimpeded vistas.

❶ The far north The roughhewn coast of Del Norte and Humboldt counties is an otherworldly region of fern-lined canyons, fog-enveloped beaches and stands of soaring redwoods. **See p.586**

❷ Mendocino to Marin By turns wild and luxurious, the inviting coasts of Mendocino, Sonoma and Marin counties include the extraordinary Point Reyes National Seashore and the precious weekend-getaway town of Mendocino. **See p.533 & p.614**

❸ San Francisco The City by the Bay's entire west side is bound by a long and sandy shore, with a northwest corner that's an enclave of bluff-top trails and the evocative ruins of bygone amusements. **See p.416**

ABOVE JOSHUA TREE NATIONAL PARK

❹ Santa Cruz and Monterey Freewheeling Santa Cruz and family-friendly Monterey boast seaside rollercoasters and a top-tier sea-life museum. **See p.407 & p.394**

❺ Big Sur This storied, nearly 100-mile stretch of rocky shore has inspired innumerable artists and writers; it's also the southernmost home of coastal redwoods. **See p.388**

❻ Southern California The south's sun-drenched coastline stretches from the yawning sands of Malibu to party-central Mission Beach in San Diego. **See p.106 & p.171**

CALIFORNIA HIGH COUNTRY

From 10,000ft peaks only a couple of hours' drive from central Los Angeles to the wild and remote mountains in the northwest of the state.

❶ San Jacinto Mountains Access 10,834ft San Jacinto Peak via the popular Palm Springs Aerial Tramway from the east, or take in the pine-covered slopes of this so-called Sierra of the South at the charming mountain town of Idyllwild. **See p.212 & p.219**

❷ Southern Sierra Nevada Encompassing the eastern reaches of Sequoia and Kings Canyon National Parks as well as the staggering 14,497ft Mount Whitney, the southern section of this range is its most rugged: no highway crosses it. **See p.312 & p.270**

❸ Central and northern Sierra Nevada With the glacier-carved grandeur of Yosemite, Lake Tahoe's cobalt-blue water and a free-falling eastern escarpment, this is an incomparably gorgeous high country that's accessible year-round. **See p.329 & p.568**

❹ Cascade range California is home to the southernmost region of this dramatic volcanic range that stretches 700 miles up into Canada; Lassen Peak and colossal Mount Shasta are both unmissable sights. **See p.644 & p.653**

❺ Klamath Mountains The remote Klamaths in Northern California are penetrable on a 285-mile loop along a trio of beautiful, river-hugging state highways (CA-299, CA-3 and CA-96); keep your eyes open for Bigfoot. **See p.631**

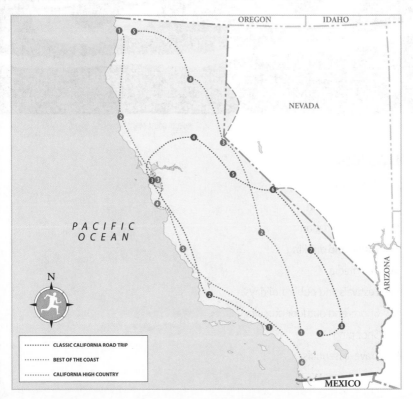

OREGON IDAHO

NEVADA

PACIFIC OCEAN

N

ARIZONA

- - - - - - CLASSIC CALIFORNIA ROAD TRIP
- - - - - - BEST OF THE COAST
- - - - - - CALIFORNIA HIGH COUNTRY

MEXICO

DRIVING ROUTE 66

Basics

Getting there

The second largest state in the continental US, California presents an easy target for both domestic and international visitors. All the main airlines operate daily scheduled flights to San Francisco and Los Angeles from all over the world, and the state is easily accessible by road and rail too. California is a year-round destination but fares tend to be highest over summer (June–September) and around Christmas.

Flights from the UK and Ireland

There are **nonstop flights** from London to Los Angeles and San Francisco (both 10hr 30min–11hr) with British Airways (Ⓦbritishairways.com), American Airlines (Ⓦamericanairlines.co.uk), United Airlines (Ⓦunited.com), and Virgin Atlantic (Ⓦvirgin-atlantic.com); Norwegian (Ⓦnorwegian.com) fly nonstop from London to LA only and Thomas Cook Airlines (Ⓦthomascookairlines.com) operate a nonstop flight from Manchester to LA. Other flights are often advertised as "direct" because they keep the same flight number but actually land elsewhere first. The first place the plane lands is your point of entry into the US, which means you'll have to collect your bags and go through customs and immigration formalities there, even if you're continuing on to California on the same plane. Most other routings involve a change of aircraft.

Britain remains one of the best places in Europe to obtain flight **bargains**, though fares vary widely according to season, availability and inter-airline competition. Fares, including taxes, can be as little as £350 return with indirect budget carriers such as Wow Air, rising above £1000 in high season, especially for nonstop flights.

Aer Lingus (Ⓦaerlingus.com) fly direct from Dublin to Los Angeles and San Francisco with refuelling stops in Boston or Chicago. Expect to pay €520 to €1200. Flights via London may cost less, but you pay slightly more tax.

"**Open-jaw**" tickets can be a good idea, allowing you to fly into LA, for example, and back from San Francisco for little or no extra charge. This makes a convenient option for those who want a **fly-drive** deal, although there are usually surcharges for dropping the car off in a different city. Many airlines also offer **air passes**, which allow foreign travellers to fly between a given number of US cities for one discounted price.

Packages – fly-drive, flight-accommodation deals and guided tours – can work out cheaper than arranging the same trip yourself, especially for a short-term stay. The obvious drawbacks are the loss of flexibility and the fact that most schemes use hotels in the mid-range bracket, but there is a wide variety of options available.

Flights from the US and Canada

Most domestic flights are likely to take you to one of the following international airports: **Los Angeles** (airport code LAX), **San Francisco** (SFO), **Oakland** (OAK), **San Jose** (SJO) or **San Diego** (SAN). Some flights use smaller airports in the vicinity of those metropolitan areas and you can also fly direct to one of the minor cities such as Sacramento or Reno (in Nevada) for the Lake Tahoe region.

Flying is the most convenient and sometimes the cheapest way to travel within the US and Canada. Return prices midweek in summer on the major airlines start at around $350–400 from New York and other eastern seaboard or Midwest cities, and $650–700 from Toronto and Montréal. What makes more difference than your choice of carrier are the conditions governing the ticket – whether it's fully

A BETTER KIND OF TRAVEL
At Rough Guides we are passionately committed to travel. We believe it helps us understand the world we live in and the people we share it with – and of course tourism is vital to many developing economies. But the scale of modern tourism has also damaged some places irreparably, and climate change is accelerated by most forms of transport, especially flying. All Rough Guides' flights are carbon-offset, and every year we donate money to a variety of environmental charities.

refundable, the time and day, and, most importantly, the **time of year** you travel.

In addition to the big-name scheduled airlines, a few lesser-known carriers run no-frills flights, which can prove to be very good value, especially if you have a flexible schedule and can put up with a few delays; try **JetBlue** (W jetblue.com) or **Frontier Airlines** (W flyfrontier.com), for example, who can often get you across the country and back for around $300, if booked well in advance.

Flights from Australia, New Zealand and South Africa

If you are coming from Australia or New Zealand, there's very little price difference between airlines and no shortage of flights, either via the Pacific or Asia, to Los Angeles and San Francisco. Most flights crossing the Pacific are nonstop, with twelve to fourteen hours' travel time between Auckland/Sydney and LA, though some include stopovers in Honolulu and a number of the South Pacific islands. If you go via Asia (a slightly more roundabout route that can work out a little cheaper), you may have to spend the best part of a day (or a night), in the airline's home city.

Flights from **eastern Australia** to Los Angeles, the main US gateway airport, tend to start at around Aus$1000 in low season, or more like Aus$1200 in summer. Flying from **western Australia** can add around Aus$300–400. Seat availability on most international flights out of Australia and New Zealand is limited, so it's best to book at least several weeks ahead.

From **New Zealand**, the cost of flying from Auckland or Christchurch to LA or San Francisco ranges from roughly NZ$1200–1700 across the year.

From South Africa, transatlantic flights from Cape Town or Johannesburg are not as expensive as they used to be, costing around ZAR15,000–18,000 to LA or San Francisco, depending on the time of year.

Round-the-world tickets

If you intend to take in California as part of a world trip, a **round-the-world** (**RTW**) ticket can work out far more economical than booking separate flights. The most US-oriented are the 28 airlines making up the Star Alliance network (W staralliance.com), which offers three to fifteen stopovers worldwide, with a total trip length from ten days to a year. Another option is One World (including Qantas, American and British Airways; W oneworld.com), which bases its rates on the number of continents visited,

allowing three to six possible stopovers in each. RTW **fares** from London are often the best value: expect to pay around £1600 for a basic itinerary, more like £2500 for something quite comprehensive. Set aside around Aus$3600–4500 from Australia, NZ$4000–5000 from New Zealand, and ZAR25,000–35,000 from South Africa. If you're starting in the UK, consider the Escapade group (Virgin, Singapore Airlines and Air New Zealand; W thegreatescapade .com), who offer more limited routing possibilities but great prices, starting around £1300.

Trains

If you are willing to pay for extra creature comforts and have the time and inclination to take in some of the rest of the US on your way to California, then riding **Amtrak** (T 800 872 7245, W amtrak.com) may be just the ticket. The most spectacular train journey of all has to be the **California Zephyr**, which runs all the way from Chicago to San Francisco (50hr 10min; departs 2pm daily) via the exquisitely scenic Rockies west of Denver and the mighty Sierra Nevada, as it traces the route of the first transcontinental railroad. It actually terminates in Emeryville, where you change onto a bus for the twenty-minute ride into San Francisco. Two other useful services are the **Texas Eagle** (63hr 50min; departs 1.45pm daily), which also starts in Chicago and travels through chunks of the Midwest and Southwest before eventually arriving in Los Angeles, and the **Coast Starlight** (see p.353), which covers all of the West Coast between Seattle and Los Angeles.

Amtrak **fares** can be more expensive than flying, though **off-peak discounts**, special deals and passes (all detailed on the website) can make the train an economical and appealing choice. If you want to travel in a bit more comfort, costs rise quickly – **sleeping compartments**, which include meals, small toilets, and showers, start at around $400 per night for one or two people, including three meals.

Buses

Travelling by **bus** is the most tedious and time-consuming way to get to California but can save you a lot of money if you don't mind the discomfort. **Greyhound** (T 800 231 2222 and T 214 849 8100, W greyhound.com) is the main long-distance operator and has an extensive network of destinations in California. An alternative, in every sense, is the San Francisco-based **Green Tortoise** bus company (see p.33).

AGENTS AND OPERATORS

Abercrombie & Kent worldwide ☎ 800 554 7016, Ⓦ abercrombiekent.com. Well-tailored, somewhat upmarket tours worldwide with a handful in California.

American Holidays Northern Ireland ☎ 028 9099 6797, Republic of Ireland ☎ 01 673 3855, Ⓦ americanholidays.com. Package tours to the US, including California, from Ireland.

Backroads worldwide ☎ 800 462 2848, Ⓦ backroads.com. Cycling, hiking and multisport tours.

Bon Voyage UK ☎ 0800 316 3012, Ⓦ bon-voyage.co.uk. Flight-plus-accommodation deals all over California.

Contiki Travel UK ☎ 0808 281 1120, Ⓦ contiki.com. West Coast coach tours aimed at 18–35-year-olds willing to party.

Flight Centre Australia ☎ 133 133, Ⓦ flightcentre.com.au; New Zealand ☎ 800 243 544, Ⓦ flightcentre.co.nz; South Africa ☎ 0877 405 000, Ⓦ flightcentre.co.za; UK ☎ 0800 587 0058, Ⓦ flightcentre.co.uk. High-street agency frequently offering some of the lowest fares around.

Kuoni UK ☎ 0800 540 4786, Ⓦ kuoni.co.uk. Flight-plus-accommodation-plus-car deals featuring the big cities, beaches and national parks. Special deals for families.

Mountain Travel Sobek worldwide ☎ 888 831 7526, Ⓦ mtsobek.com. Hiking tours in the California mountains.

North South Travel UK ☎ 01245 608 291, Ⓦ northsouthtravel .co.uk. Friendly, competitive travel agency, offering discounted fares worldwide. Profits are used to support projects in the developing world, especially the promotion of sustainable tourism.

STA Travel Australia ☎ 134 782, Ⓦ statravel.com.au; New Zealand ☎ 0800 474 400, Ⓦ statravel.co.nz; South Africa ☎ 0861 781 781, Ⓦ statravel.co.za; UK ☎ 0333 321 0099, Ⓦ statravel .co.uk; US ☎ 800 781 4040, Ⓦ statravel.com. Worldwide specialists in independent travel. Also does student IDs, travel insurance, car rental, rail passes and more. Good discounts for students and under-26s.

Trailfinders UK ☎ 020 7368 1200; Ireland ☎ 021 464 8800, Ⓦ trailfinders.com. One of the best-informed and most efficient agents for independent travellers.

Travel CUTS Canada ☎ 800 667 2887, Ⓦ travelcuts.com. Canadian youth and student travel firm.

Travel.com.au Australia ☎ 1300 130 481, Ⓦ travel.com.au. Efficient online travel agency offering good fares, hotels and car rental.

TrekAmerica UK ☎ 0333 220 1560, Ⓦ trekamerica.com. Touring adventure holidays, usually small groups in well-equipped 4WD vans.

USIT Republic of Ireland ☎ 01 602 1906, Ⓦ usit.ie. Ireland's premier student travel centre, which can also find good non-student deals.

Virgin Holidays UK ☎ 0344 557 4321, Ⓦ virginholidays.co.uk. Packages to a wide range of Californian destinations.

Entry requirements

Citizens of 38 countries – including the UK, Ireland, Australia, New Zealand and most Western European countries – can enter under the **Visa Waiver Program** if visiting the United States for a period of less than ninety days. To obtain authorization, you must apply online for **ESTA** (Electronic System for Travel Authorization) approval before setting off. This is a straightforward process – simply go to the ESTA **website** (Ⓦ esta.cbp.dhs.gov), fill in your info and wait a very short while (sometimes just minutes, but it's best to leave at least 72 hours before travelling to make sure) for them to provide you with an authorization number. You will not generally be asked to produce that number at your port of entry, but it is worth keeping a copy just in case, especially in times of high security alerts – you will be denied entry if you don't have one. This ESTA authorization is valid for up to two years (or until your passport expires, whichever comes first) and costs $14, payable by credit card while applying. When you arrive at your port of entry you will be asked how long you are staying and sometimes to prove that you have an onward ticket and adequate funds to cover your trip. The customs official may also ask you for your address while in the US the hotel you are staying at on your first night will suffice. Each traveller must also undergo the US-VISIT process at immigration, where your fingers are digitally scanned and a digital headshot is also taken for file. All passports need to be **machine readable** but that is now standard procedure.

Prospective visitors from parts of the world not mentioned above require a valid passport and a non-immigrant **visitor's visa** for a maximum ninety-day stay. How you'll obtain a visa depends on what country you're in and your status when you apply; check Ⓦ travel.state.gov. Whatever your nationality, visas are not issued to convicted felons and anybody who owns up to being a communist, fascist or drug dealer. On arrival, the date stamped on your passport is the latest you're legally allowed to stay. The Department of Homeland Security (DHS) has toughened its stance on anyone violating this rule, so even **overstaying** by a few days can result in a protracted interrogation from officials. Overstaying may also cause you to be turned away next time you try to enter the US. To get an **extension** before your time is up, apply at the nearest Department of Homeland Security office, whose address will be under the Federal Government Offices listings at the front of the phone book. INS officials will assume that you're working in the US illegally, and it's up to you to convince them otherwise by providing evidence of ample finances. If you can, bring along an upstanding American citizen to vouch for you. You'll also have to explain why you didn't plan for the extra time initially.

US Customs

Upon your entry to the US, customs officers will relieve you of your **customs declaration form**, which you receive on incoming planes, on ferries and at border crossing points. It asks if you're carrying any fresh foods and if you've visited a farm in the last month.

As well as food and anything agricultural, it's prohibited to carry into the country any articles from such places as North Korea, Iran, Syria or Cuba, as well as obvious no-nos like protected wildlife species and ancient artefacts. Anyone caught sneaking drugs into the country will not only face prosecution but be entered in the records as an undesirable and probably denied entry for all time. For **duty-free allowances** and other information regarding customs, visit ⓦcbp.gov.

CONSULATES IN CALIFORNIA

AUSTRALIA
Los Angeles 2049 Century Park E, 31st Floor, CA 90067 ☎310 229 2300, ⓦdfat.gov.au/missions.
San Francisco 575 Market St, Suite 1800, CA 94105 ☎415 644 3620.

CANADA
Los Angeles 550 S Hope St, 9th Floor, CA 90071 ☎213 346 2700, ⓦinternational.gc.ca.
San Francisco 580 California St, 14th Floor, CA 94104 ☎415 834 3180.

NEW ZEALAND
Los Angeles 2425 Olympic Blvd, Suite 600E, Santa Monica, CA 90404 ☎310 566 6555, ⓦmfat.govt.nz.

SOUTH AFRICA
Los Angeles 6300 Wilshire Blvd, Suite 600, CA 90048 ☎323 651 0902, ⓦwww.dirco.gov.za/losangeles/index.html.

UK
Los Angeles 2029 Century Park E, Suite 1350, CA 90067 ☎310 789 0031, ⓦgov.uk/government/world/usa.
San Francisco 1 Sansome St, Suite 850, CA 94101 ☎415 617 1300.

Getting around

Although distances can be great, getting around California is seldom much of a problem. Between the major cities and some of the smaller towns there are good bus links and a reasonable train service, but to see much of the state you will need a car.

By car

Throughout most of the state, **driving** is by far the easiest way to get around. Los Angeles, for example, sprawls for so many miles in all directions that your hotel may be fifteen or twenty miles from the sights you came to see. Away from the cities, points of interest are much harder to reach without your own transport; most national and state parks are only served by infrequent public transport as far as the main visitor centre, if at all. What's more, if you are planning on doing a fair amount of camping, renting a car can save you money by allowing you access to less expensive, out-of-the-way campgrounds.

Car rental

Expect to pay anything from $120 to $250 per week to **rent a car**. Unless you have got a cheap fly-drive deal, car rental rates are often cheaper from city locations than airports and it's worth checking the wider urban area of the city you want to rent from; you might, for example, find a car up to $100 per week cheaper from Richmond than from San Francisco or Oakland. Always be sure to get free unlimited mileage and be aware that leaving the car in a different city than the one in which you rent it will incur a **drop-off charge** that can be $200 or more. However, some companies do not charge drop-off fees within California itself, so check before you book if you're planning a one-way drive. If you intend to venture **outside California**, enquire if there are any limitations; some companies don't allow travel beyond Nevada or into Mexico, while others simply ramp up their insurance charges, which are typically $12–20 per day.

Drivers **under 25 years old** who wish to rent a car may encounter problems, and will probably get lumbered with a higher than normal insurance premium — and if you're under 21, it's unlikely you'll be permitted to rent at all. Car rental companies will also expect you to have a **credit card**.

The **American Automobile Association**, or AAA (☎800 222 4357, ⓦaaa.com), provides free maps and assistance to its members and to members of affiliated associations overseas, such as the British AA and RAC. If you **break down** in a rented car, call one of these services if you have towing coverage, or ring the emergency number provided by the rental company. Note that cars invariably have automatic transmissions.

CITY-TO-CITY DISTANCES

Distances between cities in miles.

	Los Angeles	Sacramento	San Diego	San Francisco
Bakersfield	115	272	231	297
Eureka	694	314	800	272
Los Angeles	-	387	116	412
Monterey	335	185	451	116
Palm Springs	111	498	139	523
Redding	551	164	667	223
Sacramento	387	-	503	87
San Diego	116	503	-	528
San Francisco	412	87	528	-
San Jose	367	114	483	45
Santa Barbara	95	406	211	337

RV rental

Campervans and **mobile homes**, usually known as **RVs** (recreational vehicles) in the US, have been popular with domestic tourists for some years now. The largest and most expensive ones really are like houses on wheels, with water pipes for showers and electrical wiring that can be connected to the mains at campsites via RV **hookups**.

If you wish to **rent** one of these vehicles, there are numerous companies that can arrange one for you. Unlike cars, they do not usually come with unlimited mileage, so an estimate of the distance you expect to travel is factored in when booking. For a week in California with 1000 miles, you can expect to pay from around $800 for a van-sized camper, up to well in excess of $2000 for a monster mobile home. Bear in mind that these vehicles are gas guzzlers, so **fuel costs** will be high, and insurance premiums also add to the price. However, savings in accommodation costs will offset that to some extent.

One thing to be aware of is that most rental companies do not allow drivers arriving on trans-atlantic flights to pick up their RV for at least twenty-four hours after landing.

Insurance

When you rent a vehicle, read the small print carefully for details on the **Collision Damage Waiver (CDW)** – sometimes called a Liability Damage Waiver (LDW) or a Physical Damage Waiver (PDW) – a form of **insurance** which usually isn't included in the initial rental charge. Americans who have their own car-insurance policy may already be covered (check before you leave home), but foreign visitors should definitely consider taking this option. It specifically covers the car that you are driving, as you are in any case insured for damage to other vehicles. Smaller companies may offer low-cost CDW that still leaves

you liable for, say, the first $500 of any claim. Before stumping up for their optional Personal Accident Coverage (or similar), consult your travel insurance policy, which may cover you for a certain amount of rental vehicle excess, eliminating the need for this extra cost. Alternatively, your **credit card company** may cover your rental when you use its card for the transaction; however, policies can vary widely, depending on the company, and there may be strict limitations on the liability coverage offered, with collision coverage even less common. European residents can also cover themselves against such costs with a reasonably priced annual policy from Insurance4CarHire (Ⓦ insurance4carhire.com).

CAR RENTAL COMPANIES

Advantage Ⓦ advantage.com
Alamo Ⓦ alamo.com
Avis Ⓦ avis.com
Budget Ⓦ budget.com
Dollar Ⓦ dollar.com
Enterprise Ⓦ enterprise.com
Hertz Ⓦ hertz.com
National Ⓦ nationalcar.com
Payless Ⓦ paylesscar.com
Rent-A-Wreck Ⓦ rentawreck.com
Thrifty Ⓦ thrifty.com

RV RENTAL COMPANIES

Camper Travel USA Ⓦ campertravelusa.com
Cruise America Ⓦ cruiseamerica.com

Rules of the road

Foreign nationals from English-speaking countries can drive in the US using their **full domestic driving licences** (International Driving Permits are not always regarded as sufficient). Driving in the US is **on the right**. Once you have rented a vehicle, you'll find that **gas** (petrol) is fairly cheap compared to Europe, though California is one of the more expensive states for it; a self-serve US gallon (3.8 litres) of **unleaded** cost around $2.80 at the time of writing, depending on the location of the gas station. In California, most gas stations are self-service and you always have to prepay; full-service pumps, where available, often charge upwards of 30¢ extra per gallon.

There are several **types of roads**. The best for covering long distances quickly are the wide, straight and fast interstate highways, usually at least six-lane motorways and always prefixed by "I" (eg I-5). Even-numbered interstates usually run east–west and those with odd numbers north–south. Drivers **change lanes** frequently; in California, you are also permitted to stay in the fast lane while being overtaken on the inside, although common courtesy dictates that slower drivers stay to the right. A grade down, and broadly similar to British dual carriage-ways and main roads, are the **state highways** (eg Hwy-1) and the **US highways** (eg US-395). In rural areas, you'll also find much smaller county or rural roads, sometimes topped with dirt or gravel, or even more challenging forest service roads, for which you may need a four-wheel-drive vehicle.

The maximum **speed limit** in most of California is 65mph, with some freeways allowing 70mph. Lower limits – usually around 35–55mph and 20mph near schools when children are present – are signposted in urban areas. If the **police** do flag you down, don't get out of the car, make any sudden movements, or reach into the glove compartment, as they may think you have a gun. Simply sit still with your hands on the wheel; when questioned, be polite and don't attempt to make jokes. Speeding fines usually start at around $200.

> ## ROAD CONDITIONS
>
> The California Department of Transportation (Caltrans) operates a toll-free **24-hour information line** (☎ 800 427 7623) giving up-to-the-minute details of road conditions throughout the state. Simply input the number of the road ("5" for I-5, "299" for Hwy-299, etc) and a recorded voice will tell you about any relevant weather conditions, delays, detours, snow closures, and so on. From out of state, or without a touch-tone phone, road information is available on ☎ 916 445 1534. You can also check online at ⓦ dot.ca.gov.

As for other possible violations, US law requires that any **alcohol** be carried unopened in the boot (US "trunk") of the car – **driving under the influence (DUI)** is a very serious offence (see p.48). At inter-sections, one rule is crucially different from many other countries: you can turn right on a red light (having first come to a halt) if there is no traffic approaching from the left, unless there is a "no turn on red" sign; otherwise red means stop. Stopping is also compulsory, in both directions, when you come upon a school bus disgorging passengers with its lights flashing, and not doing so is regarded as a serious infraction. Blinking amber lights indicate that you should cross the intersection with caution but do not need to come to a complete stop. And at any intersection with more than one **stop sign**, cars proceed in the order in which they arrived; if two vehicles arrive simultaneously, the one on the right has right of way. Three other rules to be aware of: it is illegal to park within ten feet of a **fire hydrant** anywhere in the US; when **parking on a hill** in California, your wheels need to be angled towards the kerb if you're parked downhill, and if you're parked uphill, your wheels need to be angled towards the left; and California motorcycles are allowed "**lane-splitting**" – riding the line between cars in traffic – an unnerving experience for drivers not used to seeing choppers passing a few inches away.

By train

California is well covered by the **Amtrak rail** network (☎ 800 872 7245, ⓦ amtrak.com), thanks to the number of routes available and the Amtrak Thruway buses that bring passengers from the many rail-less parts of the state to the trains. The train is more expensive than Greyhound – for example, $59 one-way between Los Angeles and San Francisco (by way of Oakland or Santa Barbara and a bus connection) – but most major cities are connected and the carriages rarely crowded, though delays can be frequent since Amtrak shares rail lines with commercial freight carriers.

Probably the prettiest route is the **Coast Starlight**, which runs between Seattle and Los Angeles and passes some of the most attractive scenery in the state, from an evening trip around Mount Shasta to coastal views between San Luis Obispo and Santa Barbara. Shorter in-state routes include the **Pacific Surfliner**, which connects San Diego to San Luis Obispo; **Capitol Corridor**, from Sacramento to San Jose; and the **San Joaquin**, connecting Oakland to Bakersfield across the San

Joaquin Valley. Other routes – Southwest Chief, Sunset Limited, Texas Eagle – connect to places such as Chicago, Texas and New Orleans.

By bus

If you're travelling on your own and making a lot of stops, **buses** are the cheapest way to get around. The main long-distance service is **Greyhound** (ⓣ800 231 2222, ⓦgreyhound.com), which links all major cities and many smaller towns. Out in the country, buses are fairly scarce, sometimes appearing only once a day; as a result, you'll need to plot your route with care. But along the main highways, buses run around the clock to a fairly full timetable, stopping only for meal breaks (almost always fast-food dives) and driver changeovers.

It used to be that any sizeable community had a Greyhound station; now in some places, the post office or a gas station doubles as the bus stop and ticket office, and in many others the bus service has been cancelled altogether. Note that advance reservations, either in person at the station or on the toll-free number, are useful for getting cheaper tickets but do not guarantee a seat, so it's still wise to arrive in good time and join the **queue** at busy stations.

An **advance online fare** from Los Angeles to San Francisco can cost as little as $20. Though long-distance travel by bus is inefficient, it's the best deal if you plan to visit a lot of places. To plan your route, pick up the free route-by-route **timetables** from larger stations, or consult Greyhound's website.

Bear in mind that fair distances can be covered for very little money – if also very slowly – using **local buses**, which connect neighbouring districts. It's possible, for example, to travel from San Diego to Los Angeles using Metrolink and Coaster systems for around $10–20, but it'll take all day and at least

three changes of bus to do it. Then there's always the hippie-ish **Green Tortoise** (ⓣ800 867 8647, ⓦgreentortoise.com), which offers various itineraries around the state and beyond (most multi-day trips within California $100–450), and also runs every Sunday from June to late September between San Francisco and LA on the **Hostel Hopper** route ($42 one-way).

By plane

Air travel is obviously the quickest way of getting around California, and less expensive than you may think. Airlines with a strong route structure in the state include Alaska, American, Delta, Northwest, Southwest, Spirit, United and Virgin America. At **off-peak times**, flights between Los Angeles and San Francisco can cost as little as $45 one-way, though they will require booking 21 days in advance. If you're flying between other cities, such as Sacramento and San Jose or Santa Barbara and San Diego, bear in mind that a stopover in Los Angeles or San Francisco may be necessary, even if it means flying twice the distance.

By bike

In general, **cycling** is a cheap and healthy method of getting around all the big **cities**, though hilly San Francisco will test your legs. Even cycling in Los Angeles has its appeal, mostly along the beaches and in the mountains. Some cities have cycle lanes and local buses equipped to carry bikes, strapped to the outside. In **rural areas**, certainly, there's much scenic and largely level land, especially around Sacramento and the Wine Country.

Bikes can be **rented** for $20–50 a day, and $125–250 a week from most bike stores; local visitor centres will have details. Apart from the coastal fog, which tends to clear by midday, you'll encounter few **weather** problems (except perhaps sunburn), but remember that the further north you go, the lower the temperatures and the more frequent the rains become.

For **long-distance cycling**, a route avoiding the interstates – on which cycling is illegal – is essential, and it's also wise to cycle **north to south**, as the wind blows this way in the summer and can make all the difference between a pleasant trip and a journey full of acute leg aches. Be particularly careful if you're planning to cycle along Hwy-1 on the Central Coast since, besides heavy traffic, it has tight curves and dangerous precipices, and is prone to fog.

HITCHHIKING

Hitchhiking in the US is generally a **bad idea**. We do not recommend it, though it is practised commonly enough by hikers seeking access to Sierra trailheads and in certain parts of Northern California. In Southern California, standing anywhere near a highway is highly risky.

If you're camping as well as cycling, look out for **hiker/biker campgrounds** (around $5 per person/night), which are free of cars and RVs and are dotted across California's state parks and beaches. Sites are allotted on a first-come, first-served basis, and all offer water and toilet facilities but seldom showers. For more information, check with the Adventure Cycling Association (☎ 800 755 2453, ⓦ adventurecycling.org), or the Sierra Club (see box, p.330).

Accommodation

California offers the visitor an array of accommodation options, from flashy hotels in the big cities to quaint B&Bs that ooze character, from roadside motels to rustic cabins in the more rural parts of the state. Costs are higher than the US average but those on a budget can stay at hostels in the big cities, and the climate is generally conducive to camping.

Typical room rates in motels and hotels start at $55 per night in rural areas offseason, more like $80 in major cities. Prices can easily double during the peak summer season and major holidays, though discounts may be available at slack times. Unsurprisingly, the sky's the limit for luxury hotels, where exclusive suites can easily run into four figures. Many hotels will set up a third single bed for around $15–25 extra, reducing costs for three people sharing. For lone travellers, on the other hand, a "single room" is usually a double room at a slightly reduced rate at best. A dorm bed in a hostel usually costs $20–40 per night, but standards of cleanliness and security can be low, and for groups of two or more the saving compared to a motel is often minimal. In certain parts of the US, camping makes a cheap – and exhilarating – alternative, costing around $12–35 per night. For alternative, online methods of finding a room, try ⓦ airbnb.com and the free hosting site ⓦ couchsurfing.com.

Wherever you stay, you'll be expected to **pay in advance**, at least for the first night and perhaps for further nights, too. Most hotels ask for a credit card imprint when you arrive, but some still accept cash or US dollar travellers' cheques. Reservations – essential in busy areas in summer – are held only until 6pm, unless you've said you'll be arriving late. Note that some cities – probably the ones you most want to visit – tack on a **hotel tax** that can raise the total price for accommodation by as much as fifteen percent.

Hotels and motels

Hotels and **motels** are essentially the same thing, although motels tend to congregate along the main approach roads to cities, around beaches and by the main road junctions in country areas. High-rise hotels predominate along the popular sections of the coast and are sometimes the only accommodation in city centres.

In general, there's a uniform standard of comfort everywhere, with all rooms featuring one or more double or queen beds, plus bathroom, cable TV, phone, fridge, a coffee-maker and maybe a microwave. The budget places will be pretty basic and possibly run-down but an extra $10–15 will get you more space, modern fittings and better facilities, such as a swimming pool and/or gym. Most hotels (and the better motels) provide a **complimentary breakfast**. Sometimes this will be no more than a cup of coffee and a soggy Danish pastry, but it can also be a sit-down affair likely to consist of fruit, cereals, muffins and toast. In the pricier places, there may be a hot buffet.

Enormous roadside signs make finding cheap hotels and motels pretty simple and you'll soon become familiar with the numerous **chains**, such as

ACCOMMODATION PRICES

The price quoted in accommodation reviews represents the rate for the **cheapest available double room in high season** (mostly the summer between Memorial and Labor days, plus major holidays such as Christmas or local festivals). At other times you'll usually be able to stay for a lower price than the one given. Breakfast is included in the price, unless stated otherwise; we've noted down places where it is particularly good. For youth hostels we give the price for a dorm bed.

Econolodge, Days Inn and Motel 6. For mid-priced options try Best Western, La Quinta and Ramada, though if you can afford to pay this much there's likely to be somewhere with more character to stay. Bear in mind that the most upscale establishments have all manner of services which may appear to be free but for which you'll be expected to **tip** generously in a style commensurate with the hotel's status.

Discounts and reservations

During **off-peak periods**, many motels and hotels struggle to fill their rooms and it's worth **haggling** to get a few dollars off the asking price. Staying in the same place for more than one night will bring further reductions, and motels in particular offer worthwhile discounts (usually ten percent) for seniors and members of various organizations, particularly the American Automobile Association (AAA). Members of sister motoring associations in other countries may also be entitled to such discounts. You could also pick up the many **discount coupons** which fill tourist information offices and look out for the free *Traveler Discount Guide*. Read the small print, though – what appears to be an amazingly cheap room rate sometimes turns out to be a per-person charge for two people sharing and limited to midweek.

Bed and breakfasts

Staying at a **bed and breakfast** in California is mostly a mid-range to luxury option. Typically, the bed-and-breakfast inns, as they're usually known, are restored buildings and grand houses in the smaller cities and more rural areas, although the big cities also have a few, especially San Francisco. Even the larger establishments tend to have no more than ten rooms, often without TV and phone but with plentiful flowers, stuffed cushions and a quaint atmosphere. Others may just be a couple of furnished rooms in someone's home, or an entire apartment where you won't even see your host. Victorian and Romantic are dominant themes; while selecting the best in that vein, we've also gone out of our way to find those that don't conform.

While always including a huge and wholesome **breakfast** (five courses is not unheard of), prices vary greatly: anything from $85 to $300 depending on location and season. Most bed and breakfasts charge between $100 and $180 per night for a double, a little more for a whole apartment. Bear in mind, too, that they are frequently booked well in advance and even if they're not full, the cheaper rooms may already be taken.

As well as the B&Bs listed in the Guide, there are hundreds more throughout the state, many of them listed on **accommodation websites** such as B&B Travel (Ⓦ bbtravel.com), the California Association of B&B Inns (Ⓦ cabbi.com) and Select Registry (Ⓦ selectregistry.com).

Hostels

At an average of around $30 per night per person (somewhat higher in San Francisco and in Santa Monica in LA), **hostels** are clearly the cheapest accommodation option in California other than camping. There are two main kinds of hostel-type accommodation in the US: the internationally affiliated Hostelling International – USA hostels, and a growing number of independent hostels aligned with assorted umbrella organizations.

Altogether California has around twenty **Hostelling International – USA** hostels (**HI** in accommodation reviews; Ⓦ hiusa.org), mostly in major cities and close to popular hiking areas, including national and state parks. Most urban hostels have 24-hour access, while rural ones may have a curfew and limited daytime hours. HI hostels don't allow sleeping bags, though they provide sheets as a matter of course. Few hostels provide meals but most have **cooking** facilities. Alcohol and smoking are banned.

Dorm rates at HI hostels range from $25 to $33 for members. **Membership** is international, though people typically join in their home country, which will cost the equivalent of $20–30 annually. Non-members pay an additional $3 per night for the first six nights at an HI hostel, at which point membership is granted – a cheaper option than joining upfront. Particularly if you're travelling in high season, it's advisable to make **reservations**, either by contacting the hostel directly or booking online at least 48 hours in advance. Alternatively, Ⓦ hihostels .com helps you reserve certain big-city and gateway hostels through your home organization. San Diego, LA and San Francisco hostels can be booked this way.

Independent hostels now number around fifty and are concentrated in the big cities. They're usually a little less expensive than their HI counterparts and have fewer rules, but the quality is not consistent; some can be quite poor, while others are wonderful. In popular areas, especially LA, San Francisco and San Diego, they compete fiercely for your business and offer airport and train station pick-ups, free breakfasts and free bike rental. There is often no curfew and, at some, a social atmosphere is encouraged with barbecues and keg parties. Their independent status may be due to a

TOP 5 PLACES TO STAY

Carter House Inns Eureka (see p.627)
HI-Pigeon Point Lighthouse
The Peninsula (see p.521)
Inn at Benton Hot Springs Benton Hot
Springs (see p.280)
Majestic Yosemite Hotel Yosemite
National Park (see p.334)
Mt Ada Santa Catalina Island (see p.130)

failure to measure up to the HI's strict criteria, yet often it's simply because the owners prefer not to be tied down by HI regulations.

Keep in mind that hostels are often shoestring organizations, prone to changing address or closing down altogether. Similarly, new ones appear each year; check the notice boards of other hostels for news or consult hostel websites, a good one is ⓦhostels.com.

Campgrounds

California **campgrounds** range from the primitive – a flat piece of ground that may or may not have a pit toilet and water tap – to others that are more like open-air hotels, with shops, restaurants and washing facilities. In major cities, campgrounds tend to be inconveniently sited on the outskirts, if they exist at all.

When camping in **national and state parks**, as well as **national forests**, you can typically expect a large site with picnic table and fire pit, designed to accommodate up to two vehicles and six people. It is usually a short walk to an outhouse and drinking water. Note that sites fill up quickly and it's worth reserving well in advance (see opposite). Campgrounds outside the parks are often less busy, and the facilities are usually marginally better; some of the more basic campgrounds in isolated areas will often be empty whatever time of year you're there.

Prices vary accordingly, ranging from nothing for the most basic plots, up to $35 a night for something comparatively luxurious, and more like $40–50 if you want to hook your RV up to electricity, water, sewage and cable TV. For comprehensive listings of these, check out ⓦcalifornia campgrounds.org and Kampgrounds of America (ⓦkoa.com). Often rural campgrounds have no one in attendance (though a ranger may stop by), and if there's any charge at all you'll need to pay by posting the money in the slot provided.

Look out too for **hiker/biker** or **walk-in** campgrounds, which, at around $5 per person per night, are much cheaper than most sites but only available if you are travelling without a motorized vehicle. **Backcountry camping** (see p.43) is invariably free but sometimes requires a permit.

CAMPING RESERVATION CONTACTS

National Forests and National Parks ☎ 877 444 6777,
ⓦ recreation.gov.
State Parks California State Parks Reservations ☎ 800 444 7275,
ⓦ reserveamerica.com.

Eating and drinking

It's not too much of an exaggeration to say that in California – its cities, at least – you can eat whatever you want, whenever you want. On every main street, a mass of restaurants, fast-food places and coffee shops vie for your business. Be warned, though, that in rural areas you might go for days finding little more than diners and cheap Chinese or Mexican joints.

California's cornucopia stems largely from its being one of the most agriculturally rich parts of the country. Junk food is as common as anywhere else in the US but the state also produces its own range of high-quality, often organic, produce. You'll rarely find anything that's not fresh, be it a bagel or a spinach-in-Mornay-sauce croissant, and even fast food won't necessarily be rubbish.

California is also one of the most **health-conscious** states in the country and the supermarket shelves are chock-full of products that, if not fat-free, are low-fat, low-sodium, low-carb, zero-transfat, caffeine-free, gluten-free and dairy-free. The same ethic runs through the menus of most restaurants, though you needn't worry about going hungry: portions are universally huge and what you don't eat can always be "boxed up" for later consumption – no shame involved even in a high-class establishment.

Breakfast

For the price, on average $8–12, **breakfast** is the best-value and most filling meal of the day. Go to a diner, café or coffee shop, all of which serve breakfast until at least 11am, with many diners serving them all day.

The breakfasts themselves are pretty much what you'd find all over the country. **Eggs** are served in a variety of styles, usually with some **meat** – ham, bacon or sausages – and generally accompanied by some form of potatoes, toast or a muffin. **Waffles, pancakes** or **French toast** are typically consumed swamped in butter with lashings of sickly-sweet maple syrup, though you may be offered **fruit**.

Lunch and snacks

Between 11am and 3pm you should look for the excellent-value **lunchtime set menus** on offer – Chinese, Indian and Thai restaurants frequently have help-yourself buffets for $8–10, and many Japanese restaurants give you a chance to eat sushi much more cheaply ($9–15) than usual. Most Mexican restaurants are exceptionally well priced at any hour: you can get a good-sized lunch for $6–8. In Northern California, look out for seafood restaurants selling **fish'n'chips**: the fish is breaded and then fried, while the chips are chunky chipped potatoes rather than matchstick French fries. A plateful is about $8–10. Look as well for **clam chowder**, a thick, creamy shellfish soup commonly served for $5–7, sometimes using a hollowed-out sourdough cottage loaf as a bowl for a dollar or so more.

As you'd expect, there's also **pizza** ($12–18 for a basic two-person pizza) available from chains like *Pizza Hut*, *Round Table* and *Shakey's*, or from local, more personalized restaurants. Delis usually serve a broad range of salads from about $5, ready-cooked meals for $7–10 and a range of **sandwiches** which can be meals in themselves: huge French rolls filled with a custom-built combination of meat, cheese and vegetables. **Bagels** are also everywhere, filled with anything you fancy. **Street stands** sell hot dogs, burgers, tacos or a slice of pizza for around $3–5, and most shopping malls have stalls selling ethnic fast food, often pricier than their equivalent outside, but usually edible and filling. There are **Mexican** chains too, like *El Pollo Loco*, *Del Taco* and *Taco Bell*, which sell tacos and burritos from only $2. And of course the burger chains are as ubiquitous here as anywhere in the US: best to seek out the few *In-n-Out* franchises if possible, with the burgers all made to order and as delicious as you'll find.

TOP 5 PLACES TO EAT

Bestia Los Angeles (see p.131)
Le Cheval Oakland (see p.496)
Moonstone Grill Trinidad (see p.631)
Nepenthe Big Sur (see p.393)
Swan Oyster Depot San Francisco (see p.469)

Restaurants

Even if it often seems swamped by the more fashionable regional and ethnic cuisines, traditional **American cooking** – juicy burgers, steaks, fries and salads (invariably served before the main dish) – is found all over California. Cheapest of the food chains is the nationwide *Denny's*, although you'll rarely need to spend much more than $15 for a filling feast at any of the lower budget joints.

By contrast, though, it's **California cuisine** – American recipes with added touches of European (especially French) flair, an emphasis on presentation and the use of locally sourced ingredients – that's raved about by foodies on the West Coast, and rightly so. Restaurants serving California cuisine build their reputation by word of mouth; if you can, ask a local enthusiast for recommendations or simply follow our suggestions, especially in Berkeley, the recognized birthplace of California cuisine. Meals usually cost at least $30 per head, and often a lot more. Although technically ethnic, **Mexican** food is in effect an indigenous cuisine, especially in Southern California. What's more, day or night, it's the cheapest type of food to eat: even a full dinner with a beer or margarita will only cost around $15 at all but the more upmarket establishments. Californian Mexican food makes more use of fresh vegetables and fruit than in Mexico but the essentials are the same: lots of rice and pinto beans, often served refried (ie boiled, mashed and fried), plus chopped veg and a choice of meat. The accompanying **tortilla**, a thin maize or flour-dough pancake, comes in various forms: wrapped around the food and eaten by hand (a **burrito**); filled and folded (a **taco**); rolled, filled and baked (an **enchilada**); or fried flat and topped with a stack of food (a **tostada**). One of the few options for vegetarians is the **chile relleno**, a mild green pepper stuffed with cheese, dipped in egg batter and fried. Veggie burritos, filled with beans, rice, lettuce, avocado, cheese and sour cream are another option.

Other ethnic cuisines are plentiful, too. **Chinese** and **Indian** restaurants are everywhere and can often be almost as cheap as Mexican if you go for the buffet lunches and dinners, often only about $10. **Thai**, **Korean**, **Vietnamese** and **Indonesian** food is also available and generally fairly cheap. Moving upscale, you find **Italian**, which can be pricey once you explore specialist Italian regional cooking, and **French**, which is seldom cheap and rarely found outside the larger cities. Expect to pay $25–50 per head.

Drinking

In freeway-dominated Los Angeles, the traditional neighbourhood bar is as rare as the traditional neighbourhood. There are exceptions, but LA bars tend to be either extremely pretentious or extremely seedy, neither good for long bouts of social drinking. On the other hand, the San Francisco Bay Area is consummate boozing territory, still with a strong contingent of old-fashioned bars that are fun to spend an evening in. Elsewhere in the state you'll find the normal array of watering holes.

To buy and consume alcohol in California, you need to be 21 and bars almost always have someone at the door **checking ID**: you'll probably need to be into your thirties before getting waved through automatically. Alcohol can be bought and consumed any time between 6am and 2am, seven days a week in bars, clubs and many restaurants. Some **restaurants** only have a beer and wine licence, and quite a few allow you to bring your own bottled wine; the corkage fee may be up to $10–15. You can buy beer, wine or spirits more cheaply and easily in supermarkets, many delis and, of course, liquor stores.

American **beers** fall into two distinct categories: wonderful and tasteless. The latter are found everywhere: light, fizzy brands such as Budweiser, Miller, Coors and so on; the alternative is a fabulous range of **microbrewed beers**, which are becoming increasingly popular. Head for one of the many listed brewpubs and you'll find handcrafted beers such as crisp pilsners, wheat beers, full-bodied hoppy ales and stouts on tap; they are pricier but much better than the national brews. Bottled microbrews, like Chico's hoppy Sierra Nevada Pale Ale and the bitter San Francisco-brewed Anchor Steam Beer, are sold throughout the state, while Red Tail Ale and Lagunitas IPA are found throughout

Northern California. Expect to pay $6–8 for a pint of draught beer, about the same for a bottle of imported beer.

A decent glass of **wine** in a bar or restaurant costs $6–9, a bottle $20–30 (often more in LA and San Francisco). Buying from a supermarket is better still – a decent bottle of wine can be purchased for as little as $7–8.

Cocktails are extremely popular, especially during **happy hour** (usually any time between 5pm and 7pm), when drinks have a couple of dollars knocked off and there may be some finger food thrown in too. Varieties are innumerable, sometimes specific to a single bar or cocktail lounge, and they cost $6–15, though typically are around $7–9.

Increasingly an alternative to drinking dens, **coffee shops** play a vibrant part in California's social scene and are havens of high-quality coffee far removed from the stuff served in diners and convenience stores. In larger towns and cities, cafés will boast of the quality of the roast and offer a full array of espressos, cappuccinos, lattes and the like, served straight, iced, organic or flavoured with syrups. Herbal teas and light snacks are often also on the menu.

The media

Like the rest of the country, California has a welter of media for an English- and Spanish-speaking public. The quality and level of parochialism does vary but you'll never be short of a paper to read, radio channel to tune in to, or TV station to watch.

Newspapers

Every major urban centre in California has its own **newspaper**, from the politically obsessed *Sacramento Bee* via the respected *San Francisco Chronicle* to the Hollywood hype of the *Los Angeles Times*. You'll also be able to pick up *USA Today*, the moderate if rather toothless national daily, while such East Coast stalwarts as the *New York Times*, the *Washington Post* and the *Wall Street Journal* should be available in most towns and upscale hotels, with a slight price premium.

As in any North American town, the best place to turn for **entertainment listings** – not to mention an irreverent take on local government and politics – is one of the many freesheets

---

WINERY TOURS

California is justly known around the country and indeed the world as a wine-producing powerhouse. You can learn a lot about California wine by taking a **winery tour** at any number of the state's boutique vintners or calling in for a tasting; many places offer these free or for $5–10, but some charge as much as $50 for rare vintages. Particular winery recommendations are given in the relevant sections of the Guide.

available on most street corners – *LA Weekly*, *SF Weekly*, etc. Since clubs and bars open and close so frequently, they're the best source of up-to-date listings available. We've noted local titles in relevant towns throughout the Guide; many have online editions too.

Radio

Owned by faceless multimedia conglomerates, the majority of California's radio stations won't tell you anything particularly useful or insightful about the state – unless you're a fan of zealous political ranting, round-the-clock sports coverage or, more helpfully, traffic reports. It's best to skip most speciality stations on the AM frequency – although AM chat shows, with their often angry callers and hosts can be hilarious and illuminating, if not in the intended sense. On FM, you'll find the usual mix of rock, pop, Latin, country and hip-hop, peppered by ads. Many stations have astonishingly limited playlists – songs will often be played half a dozen times a day. You could also tune in to satellite radio, which comes with most rental cars and typically includes fewer ads.

If you're struggling to find satisfying local news, a safe harbour is **National Public Radio (NPR)**, the listener-funded talk station with a refreshingly sober take on news and chat (FM frequencies vary). To check for local frequencies for the World Service log on to the BBC (W bbc.co.uk/worldservice), Radio Canada (W rcinet.ca) or the Voice of America (W voanews.com).

Television

In California, you'll have access to all the usual stations: from major networks like ABC, CBS and NBC, to smaller ones like CW and MyNetwork. Expect talk shows in the morning, soaps in the afternoon, big-name comedies and dramas during primetime, rounded off by comedian-led chat shows after the 11pm news. If it's all too commercial-heavy, there's always PBS, the rather earnest, ad-free alternative, which fills its schedule with news, documentaries and imported period dramas. The precise channel numbers vary from area to area.

There's a wider choice of channels on **cable**, including CNN and MTV, as well as the Discovery and History channels, plus **premium channels** like HBO and Showtime, which are often available on hotel TV systems, showing original series and blockbuster movies.

Festivals and public holidays

Someone is always celebrating something in California, although apart from national holidays, few festivities are shared throughout the entire state. Instead, there is a multitude of local events: art and craft shows, county fairs, ethnic celebrations, music festivals, rodeos, sandcastle-building competitions, and many others of every kind.

Among California's major annual events are the **LGBT freedom** parades held in June in LA (see p.61) and, particularly, San Francisco (see p.483); the **Academy Awards** in LA in early March (see p.80); and the world-class **Monterey Jazz Festival** in September (see p.407). In addition, the tourist board can provide full lists, or you can just phone the visitor centre in a particular region ahead of your arrival and ask what's coming up.

The biggest and most all-American of the national festivals and holidays is **Independence Day** on the fourth of July, when Americans commemorate the signing of the Declaration of Independence in 1776 by getting drunk, saluting the flag, and blowing things up with fireworks. **Halloween** (October 31) lacks any such patriotic overtones and is not a public holiday despite being one of the most popular yearly flings. Traditionally, kids run around the streets banging on doors and collecting sweets, but in bigger cities Halloween has grown into a massive LGBT celebration: in West Hollywood in LA and San Francisco's Castro district, the night is marked by mass cross-dressing, huge block parties and general debauchery. More sedate is **Thanksgiving**, on the fourth Thursday in November, which is essentially a domestic affair, when relatives return to the familial nest to stuff themselves with roast turkey, and (supposedly) fondly recall the first harvest of Pilgrims

---

TOP 5 FESTIVALS
Chinese New Year San Francisco (see p.423)
International Surf Festival Los Angeles (see p.108)
Mendocino Whale Festival Mendocino (see p.619)
Palm Springs International Film Festival Palm Springs (see p.218)
Pumpkin Festival Half Moon Bay (see p.520)

and Native Americans in Massachusetts. **Christmas** is another family occasion and is celebrated much as it is in other countries – preceded, of course, by a commercial onslaught.

Local festivals are detailed throughout the Guide. LA has a particularly packed calendar of events (see p.61), as does San Francisco (see p.423).

Public holidays

On national **public holidays** (see box above), banks, government offices and many museums are likely to be closed all day. Small stores, as well as some restaurants and clubs, are usually closed as well, but shopping malls, supermarkets and department and chain stores increasingly remain open, regardless of the holiday. Most parks, beaches and cemeteries stay open during holidays, too.

Sports and outdoor pursuits

Nowhere in the country do competitive sports have a higher profile than in California. The big cities generally have at least one team in each of the major professional sports – football, baseball and basketball – and support teams in soccer, volleyball, ice hockey, wrestling and even roller derby. And in California, where being physically fit and adventurous often appears to be a condition of state citizenship, the locals are passionate about outdoor pursuits; the most popular include hiking, surfing, cycling and skiing.

California's landscape is another enormously compelling reason to visit, with some of the most fabulous **backcountry and wilderness areas** in the US coated with dense forests and capped by great mountains. While there are huge areas that are only reachable on foot, the excellent road system makes much of it easily accessible, aided by spacious and beautiful campgrounds right where you need them. Unfortunately, it isn't all as wild as it once was, and the more popular areas can get pretty crowded.

Spectator sports

For foreign visitors, American sports can appear something of a mystery; one unusual feature is that in all the major sports the divisions are fixed, apart from the occasional expansion, so there is no fear of relegation to lower leagues. Another puzzle is the passion for **intercollegiate sports** – college and university teams, competing against one another in the Pacific-10 Conference, usually with an enthusiasm fuelled by local rivalries. In Los Angeles, USC and UCLA have an intense and high-powered sporting enmity, with fans on each side as vociferous as any European soccer crowd, and in the San Francisco Bay Area, the rivalry between UC Berkeley and Stanford is akin to that of Britain's Oxford and Cambridge.

Football

Professional football (American football) in the US attracts the most obsessive and devoted fans of any sport, during its short season from September until the **Super Bowl** at the end of January.

The game lasts for four fifteen-minute quarters, with a fifteen-minute break at half-time. But since time is only counted when play is in progress, matches can take at least three hours to complete, mainly due to interruptions for TV advertising.

All major teams play in the National Football League (**NFL**; Ⓦ nfl.com), the sport's governing body, which divides the teams into two conferences of equal stature, the National Football Conference (**NFC**) and the American Football Conference (**AFC**). In turn, each conference is split into four divisions, North, East, South and West. For the end-of-season play-offs, the best team in each of the eight divisions, plus two wildcards from each conference, fight it out for the title.

The California teams are the **Oakland Raiders**, who have not appeared in the Super Bowl since 2003; the **San Diego Chargers**, who have only once made it to the big game, in 1995; and the **San Francisco 49ers**, who have five Super Bowl wins and lost the showpiece finale in 2013.

Tickets usually cost at least $70 for professional games and can be very hard to come by, while college games can be as low as $10 and are more readily available – check at the respective campuses detailed in the Guide.

FOOTBALL TICKETS

Oakland Raiders ☎ 800 724 3377, 🖫 raiders.com.
San Diego Chargers ☎ 877 242 7437, 🖫 chargers.com.
San Francisco 49ers ☎ 800 746 0764, 🖫 49ers.com.

Baseball

Baseball is often called "America's pastime", though various scandals have somewhat tarnished its old-time image. Despite this, the sport's stars continue to earn a lot of publicity, not to mention money.

Games are played – 162 each in the regular season – almost every day from April to September, with the division and league championship play-offs, followed by the **World Series** (the best-of-seven match-up between the American and National League champions), lasting through October.

All major-league (🖫 mlb.mlb.com) baseball teams play in either the **National League** or the **American League**, each of equal stature and split into three divisions: East, Central and West. For the end-of-season play-offs and the World Series, the best team in each of the six divisions plus a second-place wildcard from each league fight it out for the title. In 2010 the unfancied San Francisco Giants finally lifted the curse that had been hanging over them since they relocated from New York by winning the World Series and have since repeated the feat in 2012 and 2014.

California's other major-league clubs are the **Oakland Athletics (A's)**, **Los Angeles Dodgers** and **San Diego Padres**. There are also numerous minor-league clubs, known as "farm teams" because they supply the top clubs with talent. **Tickets** cost $10–80, and are generally available on the day of the game.

BASEBALL TICKETS

Los Angeles Angels of Annaheim ☎ 888 796 4256,
🖫 losangeles.angels.mlb.com.
Los Angeles Dodgers ☎ 866 363 4377, 🖫 losangeles.dodgers
.mlb.com.
Oakland Athletics ☎ 877 493 2255, 🖫 oakland.athletics.mlb
.com.
San Diego Padres ☎ 877 374 2784, 🖫 sandiego.padres.mlb.com.
San Francisco Giants ☎ 877 483 4849, 🖫 sanfrancisco.giants
.mlb.com.

Basketball

Basketball is one of the few professional sports that is also actually played by many ordinary Americans, since all you need is a ball and a hoop. The men's professional game is governed by the National Basketball Association (**NBA**; 🖫 nba.com), which oversees a season running from November until the play-offs in June. Games last for an exhausting 48 minutes of actual playing time, around two hours total.

California's professional men's basketball teams consist of the **Los Angeles Lakers**, the **Golden State Warriors** (who play in Oakland), the **Sacramento Kings** and the **Los Angeles Clippers**. The Lakers are historically the most successful team and have won five of the championships since the millennium, the most recent in 2010, while the resurgent Warriors won in 2015 and lost the 2016 final. LA's **UCLA** once dominated the college game, especially in the 1960s, while **USC**, **UC Berkeley** and **Stanford** also field perpetually competitive intercollegiate teams, the last being the predominant force in the Pac-10 athletic conference in recent years.

The women's professional game is run by the **WNBA** (🖫 wnba.com); the season runs from May till September. The only Californian team in the league are the **Los Angeles Sparks**; **tickets** start around $10, which is much more reasonable than the $50-plus for a decent seat at the men's game.

BASKETBALL TICKETS

NBA

Golden State Warriors ☎ 888 479 4667, 🖫 nba.com/warriors.
Los Angeles Clippers ☎ 888 895 8662, 🖫 nba.com/clippers.
Los Angeles Lakers ☎ 800 462 2849, 🖫 nba.com/lakers.
Sacramento Kings ☎ 916 928 3650, 🖫 nba.com/kings.

WNBA

Los Angeles Sparks ☎ 310 330 2434, 🖫 sparks.wnba.com.
Sacramento Monarchs ☎ 916 419 9622, 🖫 wnba.com/
monarchs.

Ice hockey

Despite California's sun-and-sand reputation, **ice hockey** enjoys considerable popularity in the state, although most of the players are imported from more traditionally hockey-centric regions in Canada, Eastern Europe and Scandinavia. The domestic title is the **Stanley Cup**, contested by the play-off winners of the two **NHL** (National Hockey League; 🖫 nhl.com) conferences (Eastern and Western).

The season runs from October to the play-offs in May and June – amazingly for such a fast and physical sport, each team plays several times a week.

California boasts three NHL teams that manage to draw considerable crowds. The **San Jose Sharks** sell out nearly every game and regularly reach the play-offs, while the **Anaheim Mighty Ducks** last lifted the Stanley Cup in 2007. The **Los Angeles Kings** complete the trio and won the title in 2012 and 2014. **Tickets** start at about $30.

ICE HOCKEY TICKETS

Anaheim Mighty Ducks ☎ 877 945 3946, Ⓦ nhl.com/ducks.
Los Angeles Kings ☎ 888 546 4752, Ⓦ nhl.com/kings/.
San Jose Sharks ☎ 800 755 5050, Ⓦ nhl.com/sharks/.

Soccer

In the main, the traditional American sports rule, but **soccer** has been gaining ground, especially as a participation sport for youngsters of both sexes. At the professional level, **Major League Soccer** (MLS; Ⓦ mlssoccer.com) was established in 1996 on the back of the US hosting the World Cup two years earlier. The game continues to get injections of exposure, usually with the signing of high-profile old pros from Europe such as David Beckham or Thierry Henry in recent years.

The **Los Angeles Galaxy**, **San Jose Earthquakes** and Carson-based **Chivas USA** all play in the Western Conference of the MLS. The Galaxy have had plenty of success, winning the MLS Cup five times between 2002 and 2014.

The season runs from March to October and tickets cost $15–50.

SOCCER TICKETS

Chivas USA ☎ 877 244 8271, Ⓦ mlssoccer.com/meta/club/chivas-usa/.
Los Angeles Galaxy ☎ 877 342 5299, Ⓦ lagalaxy.com.
San Jose Earthquakes ☎ 877 782 5301, Ⓦ sjearthquakes.com.

Outdoor pursuits

When and where to enjoy the most popular outdoor activities is detailed in the relevant chapters, along with listings of guides and facilities. As well as the activities below, other options include both fresh-water and salt-water **fishing** – it's usually easier if you have your own gear but it can be rented in some places – and **horseriding**. Prices for horseriding vary more widely than for other activities, ranging from $50 to $100 for rides that might not differ all that much in length, so it's a good idea to seek out the best deals.

STATE AND NATIONAL PARKS

The US's protected backcountry areas fall into a number of potentially confusing categories. Most numerous are California's **state parks** (Ⓦ www.parks.ca.gov), which include beaches, historic parks and recreational areas, not necessarily in rural areas. Typically you pay for parking rather than entry, with daily fees usually $8–12; you are unlikely to save money by buying the **Annual Day-Use Pass** ($125) available online and at most parks.

National parks – such as Yosemite, Death Valley and Joshua Tree – generally charge entry fees of $15–20 per car (valid seven days). These are supplemented by the smaller **national monuments** (generally $5), like Devils Postpile, that have just one major feature. If you plan on visiting a few of these, invest in the **America the Beautiful Annual Pass** ($80 from any national park entrance or online), which grants both driver and passengers (or if cycling or hiking, the holder's immediate family) twelve months' access to all the federally run parks and monuments, historic sites, recreation areas and wildlife refuges across the country.

California's eighteen **national forests** cover twenty percent of the state's surface area. Most of them border the national parks and are less tightly regulated. The federal government also operates **national recreation areas**, often huge hydro dams where you can jet-ski or windsurf free of the necessarily restrictive laws of the national parks. Campgrounds and equipment rental outlets are always abundant. Excellent, free **ranger programmes** – guided walks, video presentations and campfire talks – are held throughout the year.

All the above forms of protected land can contain **wilderness areas**, which aim to protect natural resources in their most native state. In practice, this means there's no commercial activity at all; buildings, motorized vehicles and bicycles are not permitted, nor are firearms or pets. Overnight camping is allowed, but **wilderness permits** (usually free) must be obtained from the land management agency responsible. In California, Lava Beds, Lassen, Death Valley, Sequoia and Kings Canyon, Joshua Tree, Pinnacles, Point Reyes and Yosemite all have large wilderness areas – 94 percent of Yosemite, for example – with only the regions near roads, visitor centres and buildings designated as less stringently regulated "front country".

Hiking

California offers virtually unlimited **hiking** opportunities, from coastal trails through dense forest paths to some stunning mountain ranges that are bound to test your stamina. All you need, of course, is stout footwear and to be prepared for the possibility of some drastic changes in the weather.

No special permits are required for **day-hikes**. Simply arrive at the trailhead of your choice with the appropriate gear – map, raincoat, comfortable boots, etc – and head off into the wilderness. **Overnight trips** usually require **wilderness permits** (see box opposite), which operate on a quota system in popular areas in peak periods. If there's a specific hike you want to take, obtain your permit well ahead of time (at least two weeks, or more for popular hikes). Before completing the form for your permit, be sure to ask a park ranger for weather conditions and general information about the hike you're undertaking.

In California, the San Francisco-based grassroots environmental organization the **Sierra Club** (❶415 977 5500, ❿sierraclub.org) offers a range of backcountry hikes into otherwise barely accessible parts of the High Sierra wilderness, with food and a guide provided. The tours are mostly in the summer, and are heavily subscribed, making it essential to book at least three months in advance: check the website for availability and to make reservations. You can expect to pay around $700 for seven days and will also have to pay $39 to join the club.

Hikes covered in the Guide are given with length and estimated walking time for a healthy, but not especially fit, adult. State parks have graded trails designed for people who drive to the corner store, so anyone used to walking and with a moderate degree of fitness will find their ratings conservative.

Backcountry camping

When **camping rough**, check that fires are permitted before you start one; in times of high fire danger, campfire permits (available free from park rangers) may be necessary even for cooking stoves. Stoves are preferable to using local materials, since in some places firewood is scarce, although you may be allowed to use deadwood. No open fires are allowed in wilderness areas, where you should also try to camp on previously used sites. Where there are no toilets, **bury human waste** at least four inches into the ground and a hundred feet from the nearest water supply and camp. Always **take out what you take in** (or more if you come across some inconsiderate soul's litter), and avoid the old advice to burn rubbish; wildfires have been

TOP 5 OUTDOOR ACTIVITIES

Hiking Half Dome Yosemite National Park (see p.338)

Ocean kayaking Mendocino (see p.618)

Rafting the Kern River Kernville (see p.303)

Riding the Giant Dipper rollercoaster Santa Cruz (see p.409)

Skiing and boarding on Squaw Valley Lake Tahoe (see p.572)

started in this way. **Water** should be boiled for at least five minutes, or treated with an iodine-based purifier (such as Potable Aqua) or a giardia-rated filter, available from camping and sports shops.

Finally, don't use **soaps or detergents** (even special ecological or biodegradable soaps) anywhere near lakes and streams; people using water purifiers or filters downstream won't thank you at all. Instead carry water at least a hundred feet (preferably two hundred) from the water's edge before washing.

Equipment

Choose your tent wisely. Many Sierra sites are on rock with only a thin covering of soil, so driving pegs in can be a problem; freestanding dome-style tents are therefore preferable. Go for one with a large area of mosquito netting and a removable flysheet: tents designed for harsh European winters can get horribly sweaty once the California sun rises. In fact, travelling in summer you may seldom use a flysheet, as it rarely rains and little dew settles in the night.

Most developed campgrounds are equipped with fire rings with some form of grill for cooking, but many people prefer a **Coleman stove**, powered by white gas (a kind of super-clean gasoline). Both stoves and white gas (also used for MSR backcountry stoves) are widely available in camping stores. Other camping stoves are less common. Equipment using butane and propane – Camping Gaz and, to a lesser extent, EPI gas, Scorpion and Optimus – is often unavailable outside of major camping areas: stock up when you can. If you need methylated spirits for your Trangia, go to a hardware store and ask for denatured alcohol.

Airlines often have a complete ban on transporting fuel and gas canisters, and are extremely reluctant to transport stoves. Liquid fuel bottles and fuel pumps for MSR and similar stoves (even if empty, washed out and virtually odourless) are routinely confiscated at check-in, so fly-in visitors are better off bringing a gas burner and buying canisters once they arrive.

OUTDOOR DANGERS AND WILDLIFE

You'll probably meet many kinds of **wildlife** (see p.683) and come upon unexpected **hazards** on your travels through non-urban California, but only a few are likely to cause problems.

ACUTE MOUNTAIN SICKNESS

With much of the High Sierra above ten thousand feet, altitude sickness is always a possibility. Only those planning to bag one of the 14,000ft peaks are likely to suffer much more than a slight headache, but it pays to **acclimatize** slowly. Limit your exertions for the first day, drink plenty of fluids, eat little and often, and note any nausea, headaches or double vision.

BEARS

Bear encounters are rare, and virtually unknown outside national parks and forests. If you do meet one, it will be a black bear – the last California grizzly was shot in 1922. To reduce the likelihood of an unwanted encounter, make some noise as you walk. If you see a bear before it detects you (they've got fairly poor eyesight but an acute sense of smell), give it a wide berth; but if a bear visits your camp, scare it off by yelling and banging pots and pans. The bear isn't interested in you but in your food, and you should do everything you safely can to prevent them from getting it – bears who successfully raid campgrounds can become dependent on human food and will be shot. Campgrounds in areas where bears are common come equipped with steel **bear lockers** for storing food when not preparing or eating it. In the backcountry, you are increasingly required to store food within a hard plastic **bear-resistant food canister**. These can be purchased ($50–80) or rented (usually $5/trip) from camp stores in Yosemite and Sequoia and Kings Canyon national parks. Hanging or counterbalancing food in a tree is a disaster, as Sierra bears either chew through the supporting rope or even send a cub along a branch. And finding a suitable tree after a long day's hike is tricky. Finally, never feed a bear or get between a mother and her cubs. Cubs are cute; irate mothers are not.

CACTI

Keep an eye out for the 8ft **cholla** (pronounced "choy-uh"), or "jumping cholla", because of the way segments seem to jump off and attach themselves to you if you brush past. Don't use your hands to get them off – you'll just spear all your fingers. Instead, use a stick or comb to flick off the largest piece and remove the remaining spines with tweezers. The large pancake pads of prickly pear cactus are also worth avoiding: in addition to the larger spines, they have thousands of tiny, hair-like stickers that are almost impossible to remove. You should expect a day of painful irritation before they begin to wear away.

CAMPGROUND CRITTERS

Ground squirrels, chipmunks, skunks and raccoons are usually just a nuisance, though they carry diseases and you should avoid contact. Only the **alpine marmot** is a real pest, as it likes to chew through radiator hoses and car electrics to reach a warm engine on a cold night. Before setting off in the morning from high-country trailheads, check under the hood for gnawed components; boots and rucksacks can also fall prey to marmot scrutiny.

DROWNING

Fast-flowing meltwater **rivers** are the single biggest cause of death in Kings Canyon and are a danger elsewhere in the Sierra Nevada. The riverbanks are strewn with large, slippery boulders – keep well clear unless you are specifically there for river activities.

Watersports

Surfing is probably the best-known California pastime, immortalized in the songs of the Beach Boys. The California coast up to a little north of San Francisco, especially the southern half, is dotted with excellent surfing beaches. Some of the finest places to catch a wave, with or without a board, are at Tourmaline Beach near San Diego, Huntington Beach and Malibu in Los Angeles, along the coast north of Santa Barbara and at Santa Cruz – where there's a small but worthy surfing museum. **Windsurfing** is more commonly practised on lakes and protected inland lagoons, as the ocean is usually too rough, and again there are plenty of places to rent a board or get lessons.

California also has some of the world's best **rafting** rivers, most of which cascade off the

GIARDIA

This waterborne protozoan causes an **intestinal disease**, symptoms of which are chronic diarrhoea, abdominal cramps, fatigue and loss of weight. To avoid catching it, never drink directly from rivers and streams, no matter how clear and inviting they may look (you never know what unspeakable acts people – or animals – further upstream have performed in them).

MOSQUITOES

Common around water, these insects are more pesky than dangerous. Cover up around dusk and carry insect **repellent** or candles scented with citronella to keep them at bay.

MOUNTAIN LIONS

Count yourself lucky if you see one of these magnificent beasts (also known as cougars, panthers and pumas), as they are being hard hit by urban expansion into former habitats (from deserts to coastal and subalpine forests). Avoid walking by yourself, especially after dark, when lions tend to hunt. Make some noise as you walk, wield a stick, and keep children close to you. If you encounter one, **don't run**. Instead, face the lion and make yourself appear larger by raising your arms or holding your coat above you, and it will probably back away. If not, throw rocks and sticks in its vicinity. If it attacks, fight back. Its normal prey doesn't do this and it will probably flee.

POISON OAK

Recognized by its shiny configuration of three dark-green-veined leaves (turning red or yellow in the fall) that secrete an oily juice, this twiggy shrub or climbing vine is found in open woods or along stream banks throughout much of California. It's highly **allergenic**, so avoid touching it. If you do, washing with strong soap usually helps, though you are better off applying an oil-removal product such as Tecnu as soon after contact as possible. In extreme cases, see a doctor.

RATTLESNAKES

In the desert areas and drier foothills up to around 6000ft you may come across rattlesnakes, which seldom attack unless provoked: do not tease or try to handle them. When it's hot, snakes lurk in shaded areas under bushes and around wood debris, old mining shafts and piles of rocks. When it's cooler, they sun themselves out in the open, but they won't be expecting you and, if disturbed, may attack. When hiking, you'll be far better served by **strong boots** and long trousers than sandals and shorts. Not only do they offer some protection in case of attack, but firm footfalls send vibrations through the ground, giving ample warning of your approach. Walk heavily and you're unlikely to see anything you don't want to.

Rattlesnake **bites** are rarely fatal, but you might suffer severe tissue damage. If bitten, try to remain calm and still, keep the bitten limb below the heart and send someone for medical help. Do not tourniquet, cut or suck the bitten area.

SCORPIONS

Scorpions are generally non-aggressive, but they are extremely **venomous** and easily disturbed.

TICKS

When hiking in the foothills you should periodically check your clothes for ticks – pesky, bloodsucking, burrowing insects that are known to carry **Lyme disease**. If you have been bitten, and especially if you get flu-like symptoms, get advice from a park ranger.

western side of the Sierra Nevada. The majority are highly seasonal, normally rafted from mid-April to the end of June. Rivers and rapids are classed according to a grading system, ranging from a Class I, which is designed to be easy, to a Class VI, which is dicing with death. Trips can be as short as a couple of hours, taking in the best a river has to offer (or just the most accessible section), or extend up to several days, allowing more time to hike up side canyons, swim or just laze about on the bank. You might expect to pay around $100 for a four- to six-hour trip, up to $180–200 a day for longer outings, including food and camping equipment rental. **Kayaking** is another popular water-based activity, both on the many rivers and, increasingly, in the ocean. Equipment rental starts at around $20 per hour, and can exceed $70 for longer, guided day-trips.

Cycling

Cycling is an extremely popular outdoor activity, as well as being a means of local transport (see p.33). California is home to some highly competitive, world-class road races, particularly around the Wine Country. The heavy-duty, all-terrain **mountain bike** was invented in Marin County, designed to tackle the slopes of Mount Tamalpais, and there are now countless trails that weave throughout California's beautiful backcountry. Special mountain-bike parks, most operating in summer only, exploit the groomed, snow-free runs of the Sierra ski bowls of Lake Tahoe and Mammoth. In such places, and throughout California, you can rent bikes for $25–50 a day.

Winter sports

Skiing and **snowboarding** are wildly popular, with downhill resorts all over eastern California – where it snows heavily most winters. In fact, the Sierra Nevada Mountains offer some of the best skiing in the US, particularly around Lake Tahoe (see p.572), where the 1960 Winter Olympics were held. You can rent equipment for about $30–70 a day, plus another $60–80 a day for lift tickets. A cheaper option is **cross-country skiing**, or ski-touring. A number of backcountry ski lodges in the Sierra Nevada offer a range of rustic accommodation, equipment rental and lessons, from as little as $25 a day for skis, boots and poles, up to about $200 for an all-inclusive weekend tour.

Mountaineering

During the summer months, when the snows have melted and laid bare the crags of California's peaks, there is a thriving **mountaineering** community, especially around Mount Shasta in the far north and in parts of the High Sierras. If you are not very experienced and do not have your own equipment, you can rent just about anything you might possibly need and get expert advice, lessons or a guided expedition.

Shopping

Not surprisingly, the richest state in the land of rampant consumerism is something of a shopper's paradise and, especially in the two major metropolises, you'll be able to find just about anything your heart may desire. Apart from redwood carvings on the far north coast, California cannot really boast a wealth of intrinsically Californian souvenirs to take home, beyond the obvious mini Golden Gate Bridges and ironic LA snow globes found in the tackier tourist shops. Details of specific shopping locations are given in the relevant chapters.

Remember that a **sales tax** is added to virtually everything you buy except for groceries and prescription drugs; it is seldom included in the quoted price. The base rate starts around 8 percent but can escalate to 10 percent, especially in Southern California.

Malls

Visitors to California, especially on their first visit to the US, cannot fail to be impressed by the ubiquitousness of the ultimate American shopping venue, the mall. Whether these are of the "**strip mall**" variety, strung out along major arteries on the edges of most towns, or showpiece complexes in desirable neighbourhoods, they unabashedly glorify commercialism and consist mostly of well-known multinational chains. The summit of consumer excess is Rodeo Drive in Beverly Hills, where the Hollywood stars go to shop. Many chic designers have flagship boutiques on the strip, and appointment-only menswear merchant Bijan, at no. 420, claims to be the most expensive shop in the world, with the average suit costing $50,000.

Arts and crafts

California is home to many **artists**, and their paintings, sculptures and other creations can easily be found, both in big-city galleries and in smaller communities with a reputation for creativity, such as Mendocino. Being original artworks, these will set you back a fair amount, maybe even thousands of dollars, depending on how established the artist is. Quaint gift shops selling attractive items from all over the world also abound and are a good source of souvenirs and presents, even if they are not specifically local. Some places, such as the Gold Country towns and Redwood Country, do offer more indigenous goods, as do the few Native American reservations.

Books and music

There is a strong intellectual tradition in the state, which shows in its manifold quality **bookshops**. The most famous browsing territory is around UC Berkeley but all the large cities and quite a few small towns offer lots of reading material. Likewise, the state that spawned psychedelia and other musical trends is rich in **music shops**, both for listening material and quality instruments. The three branches of Amoeba Records in Berkeley, San Francisco and LA are among the biggest and best in the world. Areas strong on books and music also tend to inspire related alternative shopping possibilities, with anti-establishment and political T-shirts, posters and so on readily available.

Food and drink

One fine tradition that has survived since more rustic times is the **farmers' market**, examples of which pop up regularly in the metropolitan areas, as well as in the state's smaller towns. It can come as a pleasant surprise to stumble on a street full of stalls selling fresh country produce in the middle of downtown Oakland, for example. Most concentrate solely on consumable goods but the larger ones may have a few gift stalls as well.

California's famous **wineries** are not only great for tastings (see p.38) – you can also take away a couple of bottles for a special occasion or even get a case shipped interstate or abroad, though complicated laws mean not all companies are allowed to do so. Meanwhile, other seasonal and **speciality produce** proliferates in certain locales, such as olives in Corning and artichokes in Moss Landing.

Travel essentials

Costs

California is one of the pricier US states in which to travel. While car rental, gas, clothes and consumer goods are usually cheaper than in Western Europe and Australasia, the benefit is often less than it seems once you've factored in the additional **sales and hotel tax** or added the cost of rental-car insurance. Eating and drinking seem a bargain (and fast-food joints are), but in more upscale establishments you'll be adding close to 25 percent to your expected total to cover taxes and **tips** (see p.48).

For museums and similar attractions, the prices we quote in the Guide are generally for adults; you can assume that **children** (typically aged from 5 to 12 or 14) get in for half or up to three-quarters of the adult fee. Generally youth and **student cards** are of little benefit; take it if you have one, but don't make any special effort to get one.

Daily costs vary enormously, and the following estimates are per person for two people travelling together. If you are on a tight budget, using public transport, camping or staying in hostels, and cooking most of your own meals, you could scrape by on little over $50 a day. A couple renting a car, staying in budget motels, and eating out a fair bit are looking at more like $100 per person. Go a step up from this – stay in comfortable B&Bs, eat at nicer restaurants and add in a few whale-watching trips and shows – and you can easily find yourself spending $250 a day.

Crime and personal safety

Though California isn't trouble-free, you're unlikely to have any run-ins if you stick to the tourist-friendly confines of the major cities, or most rural areas. The lawless reputation of Los Angeles is far in excess of the truth; at night, though, a few areas – notably Compton, Inglewood and East LA – are off-limits. San Francisco, too, has its pockets of crime and decay, especially the Tenderloin. But by being careful, planning ahead and taking care of your possessions, you should be able to avoid any problems.

Foreign visitors should carry some form of **photo ID** – preferably a passport – at all times. For US residents, other photo ID such as a driver's licence will suffice.

Mugging and theft

If you're unlucky enough to get mugged, just hand over your money; resistance is generally not a good idea. After the crime occurs, report it immediately to the police at ☎911 so you can later attempt to recover your loss from an insurance provider – unlikely, but worth a try. One prime spot to be mugged is at an ATM outside the tourist areas, where you may be told to make the maximum withdrawal and hand it over. Needless to say, you should treat ATM use with the strictest caution and not worry about looking paranoid.

If your **passport** is stolen (or if you lose it), call your country's consulate (see p.30) and pick up or have an application form sent to you, which you must submit with a copy of any available ID and a reissuing fee. While you are away, it's smart to keep a photocopy of your passport in a separate place in case of such a misfortune.

Though crimes committed against tourists driving **rental cars** are rare, you should still exercise common sense. Keep doors locked and hide valuables out of sight, either in the boot (trunk) or the glove compartment, and leave any valuables you don't need for your journey back in your hotel safe.

Breaking the law

Aside from speeding or parking violations, one of the most common ways visitors accidentally break the law is through **jaywalking**, or crossing the road against red lights or away from intersections. Fines can be stiff, and the police will definitely not take pity on you if you mumble that you "didn't think it was illegal".

Alcohol laws provide another source of irritation to visitors, particularly as the law prohibits drinking spirits, wine or beer in most public spaces like parks and beaches, and, most frustrating of all to European tourists, alcohol is officially off-limits to anyone under 21. Some try to get around this with a phoney driver's licence, even though getting caught with a **fake ID** will put you in jeopardy, particularly if you're from out of the country. **Drink driving** is aggressively punished throughout the state, with loss of licence, fines and potential jail time for those caught failing the Breathalyzer test. The current limit is a blood-alcohol level of .08, or three drinks within a single hour for a 150-pound person.

In November 2016 the recreational use of marijuana was legalized in California. At the time of writing the full regulations had not been announced but it is likely you will be able to buy up to an ounce (28.5 grams). Shops licensed to sell the weed are unlikely to appear before 2018. Punishment for being caught with any other drugs will be even stiffer.

Other infringements include **insulting a police officer** (ie arguing with one) and **riding a bicycle at night** without proper lights and reflectors.

Culture and etiquette

One point of eternal discussion is **tipping**. Many workers in service industries get paid very little and rely on tips to bolster their income. Unless you've had abominable service (in which case you should tell the management), you really shouldn't leave a bar or restaurant without leaving a tip of at least **fifteen percent**, and about the same should be added to taxi fares. A hotel porter deserves roughly $1 for each bag carried to your room; a coat-check clerk should receive the same per coat. When paying by credit card you're expected to add the tip to the total bill before filling in the amount and signing.

Smoking is a much frowned upon activity in California, which has banned it in all indoor public places, including bars and restaurants, and some cities have even banned it on beaches and in outdoor spaces. In fact, you can spend weeks in the state barely ever smelling cigarette smoke. Never-

theless, cigarettes are sold in virtually any food shop, drugstore and bar, and also from the occasional vending machine.

Electricity

The US operates on 110V at 60Hz and uses two-pronged plugs with the flat prongs parallel. Foreign devices will need both a plug adapter and a transformer, though laptops and phone chargers automatically detect and cope with the different voltage and frequency.

Health

Foreign travellers should be comforted to know that in California, emergency services will get to you sooner and charge you later. For an **ambulance**, dial ☏911 toll-free from any phone. If you need urgent medical attention but are able to get to the hospital without an ambulance, head for the hospital's walk-in emergency room. For your nearest hospital or dental office, check with your hotel or dial information at ☏411. A good resource is the California Department of Public Health (☏916 558 1784, ⊛cdph.ca.gov).

Should you need to see a **doctor**, lists can be found in the *Yellow Pages* or online under "Clinics" or "Physicians and Surgeons". Be aware that even consultations are costly, usually around $100 each visit, payable in advance. Keep receipts for any part of your medical treatment, including prescriptions, so that you can claim against your insurance once you're home.

For minor ailments, stop by a local **pharmacy**. Foreign visitors should note that many medicines available over the counter at home – codeine-based painkillers, for one – are **prescription-only** in the US. Bring additional supplies if you're particularly brand-loyal.

By far the most common tourist illness in California is **sunburn**: south of Santa Barbara and in the state's interior, the summer sun can be fierce, so plenty of protective sunscreen (at least SPF 30) is a must. Surfers and swimmers should also watch for strong currents and **undertows** at some beaches: we've noted in the Guide where the water can be especially treacherous. Note that despite the media's frenzied circling around stories of **sharks**, these are extremely rare.

Insurance

The US has no national healthcare system, despite some improvements made by the Obama administration, and no reciprocal treatment arrangements with other countries. All foreign visitors, therefore, would do well to take out an **insurance** policy before travelling to cover against theft, loss and illness or injury. Before paying for a new policy, however, it's worth checking whether you are already covered – some all-risks home insurance policies may cover your possessions when overseas, and many private medical schemes include coverage abroad.

After exhausting the possibilities above, you might want to contact a **specialist travel insurance** company. A typical travel insurance policy usually provides cover for the loss of baggage, tickets, and – up to a certain limit – cash or cheques, as well as cancellation or curtailment of your journey. Most of them exclude so-called dangerous sports unless an extra premium is paid: in America, this can mean scuba diving, whitewater rafting and windsurfing. Many policies can be changed to exclude coverage you don't need – for example, sickness and accident benefits can often be excluded or included at will. If you do take medical coverage, ascertain whether benefits will be paid as treatment proceeds or only after return home, and if there is a 24-hour medical emergency number. When securing **baggage coverage**, make sure that the per-article limit – typically under £500 – will cover your most valuable possession. If you need to make a claim, you should keep receipts for medicines and medical treatment, and in the event you have anything stolen, you must obtain an official theft report from the police.

Internet

The spread of **wireless hotspots** all over the state means anyone travelling with a laptop or PDA enabled for wi-fi should have no trouble getting connected, often at fast speeds. At some locations you'll need to use your credit card to sign up for a service, though most accommodation, cafés and

some restaurants have unsecured access or will give customers the password for free. Many libraries have free wi-fi and internet terminals but the advent of wireless means that the former **internet cafés** (with a dozen or more machines usually charged at around $3–5 an hour) have largely been superseded.

Since most accommodation and places to eat in California offer free wi-fi, reviews in the Guide only highlight places where there is no wi-fi, where you have to pay for it, or where it is limited to a certain part of an establishment.

Laundry

The larger hotels provide a laundry service at a price. Cheaper motels and hostels may have self-service laundry facilities, but in general you'll be doing your laundry at a **laundromat**. A typical wash and dry costs $5–6.

LGBT travellers

California's easy-going attitude is evident in its vibrant LGBT scene. The heart of gay California (and perhaps of gay America) is **San Francisco**, which has been almost synonymous with gay life since World War II, when suspected homosexuals, purged by the military at their point of embarkation, stayed put rather than going home to face stigma and shame. This, and the advent of gay liberation in the early 1970s, nurtured a community with powerful political and social connections.

San Francisco's LGBT scene is easy to find (see p.482), but there are also strong communities in **Los Angeles**, centred in **West Hollywood** (see p.146), **Palm Springs** (see p.210) and **Santa Cruz** (see p.415). Be aware, though, that outside major urban centres and particularly in the deserts of interior California, attitudes may be more conservative and openness about your sexuality may provoke hostility in locals.

Mail

Post offices are usually open Monday to Friday from 9am to 5pm (with larger branches also open Saturday from 9am–1pm), and there are blue **mailboxes** on many street corners. **Ordinary mail** within the US costs 47¢ for letters weighing up to an ounce; addresses must include the **zip code**, which can be found at Ⓦusps.com. The return address should be written in the upper left corner of the envelope. Stamps to anywhere else in the world cost $1.15.

Rules on sending **parcels** are very rigid: packages must be sealed according to the instructions given at Ⓦusps.com. To send anything out of the country, you'll need a green **customs declaration form**, available from the post office. Postal rates for airmailing a parcel weighing up to 1lb to Europe, Australia and New Zealand are $15–18.

Maps

Rand McNally produces good low-cost foldout maps of the state, and its *Road Atlas* covers the whole country plus Mexico and Canada, and is a worthwhile investment if you're travelling further afield. For **driving or cycling** through rural areas, the *California Atlas & Gazetteer* (published by DeLorme) and *Benchmark California Road and Recreation Atlas* are valuable companions, with detailed city plans, marked campgrounds, and national park and forest information.

The **American Automobile Association** (Ⓦaaa .com) has offices in most large cities and provides excellent free maps and travel assistance to both its members and members of affiliated organizations elsewhere.

Hikers should visit ranger stations in parks and wilderness areas, which sell good-quality local topographic maps for around $6–10. Camping stores generally have a good selection, too. The *National Geographic/Trails Illustrated* topographic maps are particularly good and cover a range of destinations including Sequoia and Kings Canyon, Yosemite, Death Valley and Joshua Tree national parks, and Santa Monica Mountains National Recreation Area.

Money

US banknotes ($1, $5, $10, $20, $50 and $100) are all the same size so be sure to check what you are handing over. The dollar is made up of 100 cents with coins of 1 cent (known as a penny, and regarded as worthless), 5 cents (a nickel), 10 cents (a dime) and 25 cents (a quarter). Quarters are very useful for buses, vending machines, parking meters and telephones, so always carry plenty. For current **exchange rates**, see Ⓦxe.com.

A **credit card** is more or less de rigueur anywhere in the US. For many services, it's simply taken for granted that you'll be paying with plastic. When renting a car (or even a bike) or checking into a hotel, you are usually asked to show a credit card to establish your credit-worthiness – even if you intend to settle the bill in cash. **Visa** and **MasterCard** are the most widely used, **Diners Club**, **American Express** and **Discover** are less so. When paying with a credit card, you'll occasionally be required to show supporting photo ID, so be sure to carry your driver's licence or passport.

You may never need to visit **banks** but they are generally open from 9am until 5pm Monday to Thursday and 9am to 6pm on Friday, and sometimes on Saturday morning. Some banks in large towns will change major **foreign currency**, but it is far better to buy US dollars before you arrive. Credit card **cash advances** and debit card withdrawals are easy at abundant **ATMs**, though there is usually a transaction fee of $2–4.

Opening hours

Public holidays (see p.40) may shut down certain businesses altogether and otherwise throw a wrench into your well-laid travel plans. Beyond this, regular opening hours are more predictable, and though listed for each attraction in the Guide, most operate according to the same general schedule.

As a general rule, most **museums** are open Tuesday to Saturday (occasionally Sunday, too) from 10am until 5 or 6pm, with somewhat shorter hours at weekends. Many museums will also stay open late one evening a week – usually Thursday or Friday, when ticket prices are sometimes reduced. Government **offices**, including post offices, are open during regular business hours, typically 8 or 9am until 5pm, Monday to Friday (though some post offices are open on Saturday morning). Most **shops** are open daily from 10am until 5 or 6pm, while speciality stores can be more erratic, usually opening and closing later in the day, from noon to 2pm until 8 or 9pm, and remaining shuttered for two days of the week. **Malls** tend to be open from 10am until 7 or 8pm daily, though individual stores may close before the mall does. For visitor centre opening hours, see "Tourist information" (see p.52); for banks, see "Money" (see opposite).

While some diners stay open 24 hours, the more typical **restaurants** open daily around 11am or noon for lunch and close at 9 to 10pm. Places that serve breakfast usually open early, between 6 and 8am, serve lunch later, and close in the early or mid-afternoon. Dance and live music **clubs** often won't open until 9 or 10pm, and many will serve alcohol until 2am and then either close for the night or stay open until dawn without serving booze. **Bars** that close at 2am may reopen as early as 6am to grab bleary-eyed regulars in need of a liquid breakfast.

Some tourist attractions, visitor centres, motels and campgrounds are only open during the traditional **tourist season**, from Memorial Day (the last Monday in May) to Labor Day (the first Monday in September), though California's benign weather extends that considerably, and the desert areas have their peak season through the winter.

Phones

Mobile phone reception is excellent in all but the remotest areas. Ask your provider to confirm that your phone will work on US frequencies (most do these days) and get it set up for international use. **Roaming** rates can be pretty high and if you're planning to make a lot of calls it will work out cheaper to **buy a SIM card or phone** in California, though the lower cost is counterbalanced by the need to tell all your friends your new phone number. Basic, new phones can be picked up for as little as $30; it is probably most convenient to go for a prepay service, which you can top up as you go.

Public phones are less plentiful than they used to be. Local calls mostly cost 50¢, and any number

prefixed by 1800, 1888, 1877 or 1866 is free (if called from landlines; mobile phones will incur normal charges; note we do not include the initial 1 throughout the Guide). Some numbers covered by the same area code are considered so far apart that calls between them count as non-local ("zone calls") and cost much more. Pricier still are long-distance calls (ie to a different area code and preceded by a 1), for which you'll need plenty of change. Rates are much cheaper using **phone cards** – typically in denominations of $5, $10 and $20 – bought from general stores and some hostels. There are many brands, some quoting long-distance rates as low as 5¢ a minute, but beware of hidden costs such as a 50¢ connection fee, only mentioned in the fine print. Making telephone calls from **hotel rooms** is usually more expensive than from a payphone ($1–2/call), though many hotels offer free local calls from rooms – ask when you check in.

One of the most convenient ways of phoning home from California is via a **telephone charge card** from your phone company back home. Calls made from most hotel, public and private phones will be charged to your account. Since most major charge cards are free to obtain, it's certainly worth getting one at least for emergencies; but bear in mind that rates aren't necessarily cheaper than calling from a public phone.

Photography

With fabulous scenery and great light much of the time, California is a photographer's paradise. Bring plenty of digital memory or be prepared to periodically visit photo shops and burn your images onto CD. As ever, try to shoot in the early morning and late afternoon when the lower-angled light casts deeper shadows and gives greater depth to your shots. Wildlife is also more active at these times.

It is never a good idea to take photos of **military installations** and the like, and with the current heightened security, airports, ports and harbours, and some government buildings, may be considered sensitive.

Senior travellers

Establishments vary in their definition of **seniors**: in some places it's over-55s, in others over-65s. Seniors can regularly find **discounts** of anywhere from ten to fifty percent at cinemas, museums, hotels, restaurants, performing arts venues and the occasional shop. On Amtrak, seniors can get a fifteen percent discount on most regular fares. On Greyhound the discount is around five to ten percent. If heading to a national park, don't miss the Senior Pass, which, when bought at a park for a mere $10, provides a lifetime of free entry to federally operated recreation sites, as well as half-price discounts on concessions such as boat launches and camping. California's senior residents can apply for a Golden Bear Pass ($5; Ⓦparks.ca.gov), which allows complimentary parking at all state-operated facilities, though it doesn't cover boating fees, camping and the like.

Time

California runs on Pacific Standard Time (PST), which is eight hours behind GMT, and jumps forward an hour in summer (the second Sunday in March to the first Sunday in November). During most of this eight-month daylight saving period, when it is noon on Monday in California it is 3pm in New York, 8pm in London, 5am on Tuesday in Sydney, and 7am on Tuesday in Auckland.

Tourist information

The **California office of tourism** website (Ⓦ visit california.com) is a reasonable starting point for information. Much of the same material is available in its free tourism information packet, which can be ordered online or by calling ☎877 225 4367.

Visitor centres go under a variety of names, but they all provide detailed information about the local area. Typically they're open Monday to Friday 9am to 5pm and Saturday 9am to 1pm, except in summer, when they may be open seven days a week from 8am or 9am until 6pm or later. In the US, visitor centres are often known as the "Convention and Visitors Bureaus" (CVB), while in small towns many operate under the auspices of the **Chamber of Commerce**, which promotes local business interests. You'll also find small visitor centres in airports, where there's usually a free phone system connecting to leading hotels.

Park visitor centres should be your first destination in any national or state park. Staff are usually outdoors experts, and can offer invaluable advice on trails, current conditions, and the full range of outfitting or adventure specialists. These are also the places to go to obtain national park permits and, where applicable, permits for fishing or backcountry camping.

Travelling with children

There's plenty to occupy kids in California, from theme parks to miles of beachfront. **Hotels** and motels will usually allow kids under a certain age (often 12) to stay for free in the same room as their parents; most places will add extra cots at nominal charges.

Restaurants often try hard to lure parents in with their kids. Most of the national chains offer high chairs and a special menu, packed with huge, cheap (if not necessarily healthy) meals like miniburgers and macaroni cheese. Most large cities have natural history museums or aquariums, and quite a few have hands-on children's **museums**. Virtually all museums and tourist attractions offer reduced rates for kids. Contact the California Office of Tourism for excellent, free brochures that can answer most questions.

Getting around

Under-2s travel for free on domestic **flights**, and usually for ten percent of the adult fare on international flights – though that doesn't necessarily mean they get their own seat. Kids aged from 2 to 12 may be entitled to cut-price tickets, though recent airline-industry economic troubles have reduced perks like these to a large degree.

Most families choose to travel **by car**, but if you're hoping to enjoy a driving holiday with your kids, it's essential to plan ahead. Don't set unrealistic targets, pack plenty of sensible snacks and drinks, plan to stop every couple of hours, arrive at your destination well before sunset, and avoid travelling through big cities during rush hour. Note that when **renting a car** the company is legally obliged to provide free car seats for kids.

Travelling **by bus** (see p.33) may be the cheapest way to go, but it's also the most uncomfortable for kids. Babies and toddlers can travel (on your lap) for free, whereas children aged 2 to 12 get a 25 percent discount off the standard fare.

Even if you discount the romance of the rails, **train travel** is the best option for long journeys – not only does everyone get to enjoy the scenery, but you can get up and walk around, relieving pent-up energy. Most cross-country trains have sleeping compartments, which may be quite expensive but are a great adventure. Children's discounts are slightly better than on buses or planes, with babies and toddlers riding free and kids from 2 to 12 half-price.

Travellers with disabilities

Under the Americans with Disabilities Act (ADA), all public buildings have to be **wheelchair accessible** and provide suitable toilet facilities; almost all street corners have dropped kerbs; public telephones are specially equipped for hearing-aid users; and most public transport has accessibility aids such as subway stations with lifts and buses that "kneel" to let riders board. Even cinemas are now required to allow people in wheelchairs to have a reasonable, unimpeded view of the screen. Most hotel and motel chains offer accessible **accommodation**, with new standards of access that meet or, in some cases, exceed the requirements of the ADA, by building new facilities, retrofitting older hotels, and providing special training to all employees. However, the situation may be more problematic at B&Bs that were built a century ago and where a narrow stairway may be the only option.

Information

The **California Office of Tourism** (see opposite) has lists of facilities for disabled visitors at accommodation and attractions. **National organizations** facilitating travel for people with disabilities include SATH, the Society for the Advancement of Travelers with Handicaps (☎ 212 447 7284, ⓦ sath.org), a nonprofit travel-industry grouping made up of travel agents, tour operators, and hotel and airline management; contact them in advance so they can notify the appropriate members. **Mobility International USA** (☎ 541 343 1284, ⓦ miusa.org) answers transport queries and operates an exchange programme for people with disabilities. **Access-Able** (☎ 303 232 2979, ⓦ access-able.com) is an information service that assists travellers with disabilities by putting them in contact with people with similar conditions.

Getting around

Major car-rental firms can provide vehicles with hand controls for drivers with leg or spinal disabilities, though these are typically available only on the pricier models. Parking regulations for disabled motorists are now uniform: licence plates for the disabled must carry a three-inch-square international access symbol, and a placard bearing this symbol must be hung from the car's rear-view mirror.

American **airlines** must by law accommodate customers with disabilities, and some even allow attendants of those with serious conditions to accompany them for a reduced fare. Almost every **Amtrak train** includes one or more cars with accommodation for disabled passengers, along with wheelchair assistance at train platforms, adapted on-board seating, free travel for guide dogs, and discounts on fares, all with 24 hours' advance notice. Passengers with hearing impairment can get information by calling ☎ 800 523 6590 (TDD) or checking out ⓦ amtrak.com.

By contrast, travelling by **Greyhound** and **Amtrak Thruway** bus connections is often problematic. Buses are not equipped with platforms for wheelchairs, though there is intercity assistance with boarding, and disabled passengers may be able to get priority seating. Call Greyhound's ADA customer assistance line for more information (☎ 800 752 4841, ⓦ greyhound.com).

The great outdoors

Disabled citizens or permanent residents of the US can obtain the **America the Beautiful Access Pass**, a free lifetime entrance pass to federally operated parks, monuments, historic sites, recreation areas and wildlife refuges. It also provides a fifty percent discount on fees charged for facilities such as camping, boat launching and parking. The pass is available from the National Park Service (ⓦ nps.gov) and must be picked up in person from the areas described. The **Disabled Discount Pass** ($3.50; ⓦ parks.ca.gov) offers half-price concessions on parking and camping at state-run parks, beaches and historic sites.

Los Angeles

VIEW OVER DOWNTOWN LA

1

Los Angeles

Thanks to Hollywood, most people on the planet have at least an idea of what Los Angeles is like, though this usually involves lots of palm trees, movie stars and glamour. The City of Angels, Tinseltown or just "La-La Land" is the home of the world's movie and entertainment industry, the palaces of Beverly Hills, Sunset Strip, the original Disneyland, the Dodgers and the Lakers and a beach culture that inspired California's modern surfing boom in the 1950s, the Beach Boys, the Doors and the Red Hot Chili Peppers. Yet first-time visitors should expect some surprises, beginning with the vast size of the place, hard to absorb until you actually get here. LA is only America's second biggest city in terms of population, but it's stitched together by an intricate network of freeways crossing a thousand square miles of widely varying architecture, social strata and cultures.

Beyond the skyscrapers, Downtown LA actually has an historic Spanish-Mexican heart and is a traffic-clogged sixteen miles from the hip ocean enclaves of Santa Monica and Venice Beach – and thanks to high crime and gangster rap, South Central LA and Compton have become bywords for violence and gangs such as the Crips and the Bloods.

Bordered by snowcapped mountains and the Pacific Ocean, Los Angeles spreads across a great desert basin. The entertainment industry has been hyping the place ever since film-makers arrived a century ago, attracted by a climate that allowed them to

Highlights

❶ The Broad This futuristic shrine to Basquiat, Hirst, Johns, Koons and Warhol is a work of art in itself. **See p.67**

❷ Hollywood Boulevard The vaunted main strip in Hollywood is packed with gorgeous Art Deco theatres, tacky but fun museums, the Walk of Fame and the home of the Oscars. **See p.78**

❸ Golden Triangle/Rodeo Drive For high-end consumers (and avid window-shoppers), this compact section of Downtown Beverly Hills, featuring jewellery, fashion and beauty boutiques, is the main reason to visit Los Angeles. **See p.95**

❹ The Getty Center A colossal, Modernist arts centre, the Getty is stuffed with treasures of the Old World and is set on a hillside providing a great view of the metropolis. **See p.100**

❺ Venice Beach Trawling the promenade between Santa Monica and Venice is an LA tradition, taking in the surfers, sand, musclemen, skaters and assorted eccentrics. **See p.105**

❻ Magic Mountain Kids might prefer Disneyland, but thrill-seekers should skip Mickey Mouse and make for the mother of all rollercoaster parks. **See p.120**

❼ Musso & Frank Grill This classically dark and moody watering hole has long been a favourite hangout for movie stars of the Golden Age and today's brattier celebrities. **See p.139**

HIGHLIGHTS ARE MARKED ON THE MAP ON PP.58–59

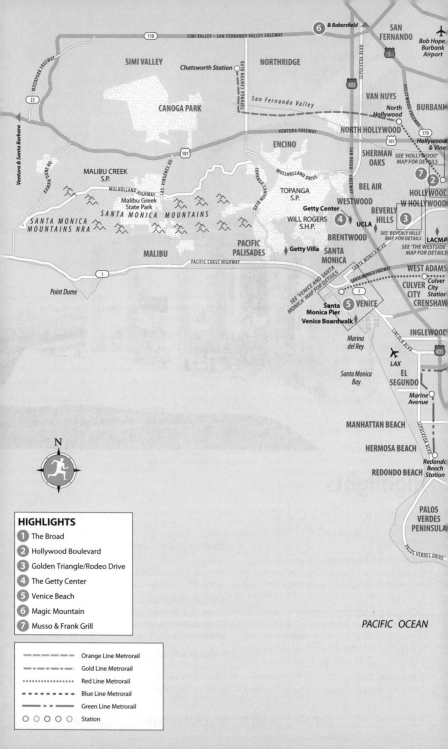

118 SIMI VALLEY - SAN FERNANDO VALLEY FREEWAY

6 & Bakersfield

SAN FERNANDO

Bob Hope Burbank Airport

SIMI VALLEY

Chatsworth Station

NORTHRIDGE

Moorpark Freeway

23

CANOGA PARK

San Fernando Valley

VAN NUYS

North Hollywood

BURBANK

Ventura & Santa Barbara

ENCINO

Ventura Freeway

NORTH HOLLYWOOD

Hollywood & Vine

MALIBU CREEK S.P.

MULHOLLAND DRIVE

SHERMAN OAKS

SEE 'HOLLYWOOD' MAP FOR DETAILS

7

2

MULHOLLAND HIGHWAY

Malibu Greek State Park

SANTA MONICA MOUNTAINS

TOPANGA S.P.

BEL AIR

HOLLYWOOD

W HOLLYWOOD

SANTA MONICA MOUNTAINS NRA

WESTWOOD

Getty Center

4

UCLA

BEVERLY HILLS

3

SEE 'BEVERLY HILLS MAP FOR DETAILS

MALIBU

WILL ROGERS S.H.P.

BRENTWOOD

LACMA

SEE 'THE WESTSIDE MAP FOR DETAILS

PACIFIC PALISADES

Getty Villa

SANTA MONICA

PACIFIC COAST HIGHWAY

SANTA MONICA BLVD

WEST ADAMS

1

SANTA MONICA FREEWAY

Point Dume

SEE 'VENICE AND SANTA MONICA MAP FOR DETAILS

1

CULVER CITY

Culver City Station

CRENSHAW

Santa Monica Pier

5

VENICE

Venice Boardwalk

INGLEWOOD

LINCOLN BLVD

405

Marina del Rey

LAX

Santa Monica Bay

EL SEGUNDO

Marine Avenue

MANHATTAN BEACH

HERMOSA BEACH

SEPULVEDA BLVD

REDONDO BEACH

Redondo Beach Station

N

HIGHLIGHTS

1 The Broad

2 Hollywood Boulevard

3 Golden Triangle/Rodeo Drive

4 The Getty Center

5 Venice Beach

6 Magic Mountain

7 Musso & Frank Grill

PALOS VERDES PENINSULA

PALOS VERDES DRIVE

PACIFIC OCEAN

------ Orange Line Metrorail

-- - -- - Gold Line Metrorail

············· Red Line Metrorail

- - - - - Blue Line Metrorail

— · — · — Green Line Metrorail

○ ○ ○ ○ ○ Station

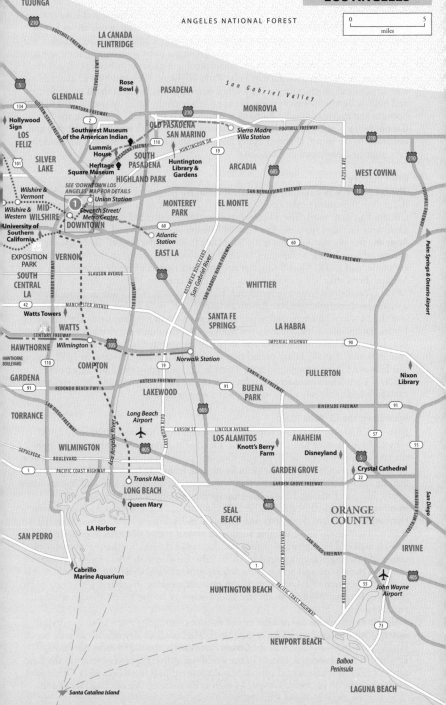

film outdoors year-round. Since then, the money and glitz of Hollywood have enticed countless thousands of would-be actors, models and other budding celebrities to cast their lot in this hard-edged glamour town, their triumphs and failures becoming intrinsic to the city's towering myths. Today LA seems to be re-inventing itself again, as indie musicians, writers and designers (many fleeing high rents in San Francisco) are colonizing neighbourhoods such as Echo Park, Highland Park and Silver Lake, adding a bohemian and artistic vibe to a city often stereotyped as being in thrall to celebrity and beauty. Beyond the city proper lies the San Fernando Valley or simply "**the Valley**", home to the movie studios of **Burbank** and **Universal City**, while to the east, the **San Gabriel Valley** is anchored by historic **Pasadena** and the lavish **Huntington Library and Gardens**. To the south, **Orange County** features a strip of affluent beach towns and the ever-popular **Disneyland** in Anaheim.

Brief history

The LA region was settled by **Chumash** and **Tongva** peoples thousands of years before the arrival of Spanish settlers on September 4, 1781 (a date commemorated by the LA County Fair each year). The 44 colonists from Mexico decided to locate their settlement six miles from the San Gabriel Mission (see p.117), and named it **Los Angeles** after the Spanish phrase for "**Our Lady Queen of the Angels**" (ie Mary, the mother of Jesus). Due to flooding, in 1818 the town was moved to the present site of **El Pueblo**, and in 1821 a still tiny Los Angeles became part of newly independent Mexico. Even after being swallowed up by the US after the Mexican–American War in 1846, LA remained largely insignificant. Indeed, up to the Civil War in 1861, LA was a small town comprising white American immigrants, poor Chinese labourers and wealthy Mexican ranchers, with a population of less than five thousand. The remaining Native Americans, displaced from the San Gabriel Mission, were virtually enslaved by the growing number of settlers (a real slave market operated in LA); they were often paid in booze, if at all, a dark period that is rarely acknowledged today. In 1871, a gang war between Chinese *tongs* (secret societies) in LA resulted in the death of a police officer – a notorious **massacre** of at least nineteen Chinese immigrants by a vigilante mob followed (only one of the victims was a *tong* gangster).

Boomtown: the 1870s to 1920s

Between 1870 and 1900 LA's population exploded from just over 5000 to 102,500 – by 1920 it was over half a million. The arrival of the **transcontinental railroad** gave the city a massive boost in 1876, with thousands coming to live in what was billed as a Mediterranean-style paradise for clean living and, ironically from today's viewpoint, healthy air. Ranches were broken up into innumerable suburban lots, and scores of new towns, like San Pedro and Santa Monica, sprang up, largely thanks to **Collis P. Huntington**, president of the Southern Pacific Railroad Company, and his son **Henry Huntington**, who laid down over one thousand miles of tram tracks throughout the region in seemingly uninhabitable areas with no real centre (the tram lines were later entirely replaced by highways). Land speculators did the rest, marketing an enduring image of Los Angeles, epitomized by the family-size suburban house (with a swimming pool and two-car garage) set amid the orange groves in a glorious land of sunshine. Yet in the 1890s much of LA was pitted with **oil wells**, peaking in around 1901 with 1150 pumping for over 200 companies (the boom was over by the 1920s, though some oil remains today).

All this development drained the city of the one commodity essential to its survival: **water**. With the Los Angeles River exhausted, Machiavellian city officials secretly began buying land and water rights in the **Owens River Valley**, about 250 miles northeast of LA; by 1913 the longest aqueduct in the world was delivering Owens water to the hose pipes of LA (the whole sordid episode was dramatized in Roman Polanski's *Chinatown*). Meanwhile, by 1912, movie companies such as Paramount, Warner Bros, RKO and

1

LA'S FESTIVALS

JANUARY–MARCH

Tournament of Roses See p.114.

Chinese New Year Early to mid-Feb ☎213 617 0396, ⓦlachinesechamber.org. Three days of dragon-float street parades, tasty food and cultural programmes, based in Chinatown, Monterey Park and Alhambra.

Mardi Gras Mid-Feb. Floats, parades, costumes, and lots of singing and dancing at this Latin fun-fest, with traditional ceremonies on Olvera St, downtown (☎213 625 7074), and campy antics in West Hollywood (☎310 289 2525).

The Academy Awards See p.80.

St Patrick's Day March 17 ☎213 689 8822. Parade along Colorado Blvd in Old Town Pasadena, or in Hermosa Beach. No parade but freely flowing green beer in the "Irish" bars along Fairfax Ave.

APRIL AND MAY

Long Beach Grand Prix Mid-April ☎562 981 2600, ⓦgplb.com. Some of auto-racing's best drivers and souped-up vehicles zoom around Shoreline Drive south of downtown in the city's biggest annual event.

Cinco de Mayo May 5 ☎213 628 1274. Spirited parade along Olvera St with Latino music taking over several downtown blocks. There are also celebrations in most LA parks.

JUNE–AUGUST

LA Pride Mid-June ☎323 969 8302, ⓦlapride.org. Parade on Santa Monica Blvd in West Hollywood. Carnival atmosphere, hundreds of vendors, and an all-male drag football cheerleading team.

Playboy Jazz Festival Mid-June ☎213 450 1173, ⓦhollywoodbowl.com/playboyjazz. Renowned event held at the Hollywood Bowl, with a line-up of traditional and non-traditional musicians.

Lotus Festival First weekend after July 4 ☎213 413 1622. An Echo Park celebration featuring pan-Pacific food, music and, of course, the resplendent lotus blooms around the lake.

International Surf Festival Early Aug ☎310 802 5413, ⓦsurffestival.org. Tournament and celebration in the South Bay that provides an exciting three-day spectacle, which also includes volleyball matches, lifeguard races, sand soccer and sandcastle design.

Long Beach Jazz Festival Mid-Aug ☎562 424 0013, ⓦlongbeachjazzfestival.com. At the Rainbow Lagoon Park in Downtown Long Beach, relax and enjoy famous and local performers.

SEPTEMBER–DECEMBER

Long Beach Blues Festival Early Sept ☎562 985 7000, ⓦnewbluesfestival.com. Hear top blues performers at this annual event at Cal State University at Long Beach.

Watts Towers Day of the Drum/Jazz Festival Late Sept ☎213 4874646, ⓦwattstowers.org. Two days of free music – a wealth of African, Asian, Cuban and Brazilian drumming. Taking place the same weekend, at the same place, the Jazz Festival is the most long-standing such event in LA.

Halloween Oct 31. A wild parade in West Hollywood, with all manner of bizarre outfits and characters on display (☎310 289 2525). Or you can opt for the Halloween-themed events on the *Queen Mary* (☎562 435 3511).

Dia de los Muertos Nov 2 ☎213 625 5045. The "Day of the Dead", celebrated authentically throughout East LA and more blandly for tourists on Olvera St. Mexican traditions, such as picnicking on the family burial spot and making skeleton puppets, are faithfully upheld.

Hollywood Christmas Parade End Nov ☎323 469 2337, ⓦthehollywoodchristmasparade .com. The first and best of the many Yuletide events, with a cavalcade of mind-boggling floats, marching bands and famous and quasi-famous names from film and TV.

Holiday Boat Parade Early Dec ☎310 670 7130, ⓦmdrboatparade.org. Marina del Rey is the site for this ocean-going display of brightly lit watercraft, supposedly the largest boat parade in the West.

1

Columbia were setting up production near LA, and the 1920s saw **Hollywood** entering its golden age. Los Angeles hosted the **1932 Summer Olympics**, confirming its arrival on the world stage.

Post World War II

More **boom years** followed World War II, when along with heavy manufacturing, the entertainment and real-estate sectors drew ever-increasing numbers of people from around the country, and LA's population exploded again, eventually eclipsing Chicago as the nation's second-largest metropolis in 1980. Ethnic tensions exploded, too: in 1965, the **Watts Riots** lasted six days and left 32 dead, a reaction by the African American community to discrimination and a long record of police brutality by the LAPD. LA also started to develop distinctive pop cultures of its own, beginning with **surfing** in the 1950s and the music of the **Beach Boys** and **the Doors** in alternative Venice Beach in the 1960s, to the skateboarders of 1970s **Dogtown** and eventually the **West Coast hip-hop** scene which blew up in LA in the 1980s. LA once again hosted the **Olympics** in 1984, marred somewhat by the boycott of the Soviet Union and its allies.

Tough times and recovery

After the Cold War ended in the 1990s, Southern California was hit hard by cutbacks in defence spending, particularly in the aeronautics industry. The **riots of 1992** (see p.680) exacerbated tensions, which were only increased by two earthquakes and various floods and fires in Southern California during the same period.

Following the **economic turmoil** that began in the US in 2008, Los Angeles saw local unemployment climb to around twelve percent, the bottom drop out of the local real estate market, and government services cut back dramatically. Since then the economy has recovered somewhat (unemployment was around seven percent in 2016), especially in entertainment, light manufacturing and shipping – the port of LA and Long Beach handles more than sixty percent of the ocean-going cargo coming to the West Coast. LA is the third-largest economic metropolitan area in the world, after Tokyo and New York, and immigration from Asia and Mexico continues to boost the population (LA is now over fifty percent Latino). Democrat **Antonio Villaraigosa** became the city's first elected Latino mayor in 2005 (current mayor and fellow Democrat **Eric Garcetti** was elected in 2013, becoming the city's first Jewish leader). And though it remains the "Gang Capital of America", crime has dropped dramatically from its 1990s highs, reaching a fifty-year low in 2013 – the city is safer than it's been in decades, making this a great time to visit.

Downtown LA

Since the opening of the **Staples Center** in 1999, **DOWNTOWN LA** has been experiencing something of a renaissance, with many of its graceful old banks and hotels turned into apartments and the enormous **LA Live** complex opening in 2008. It remains a diverse neighbourhood, however, with, in the space of a few blocks, adobe buildings and Mexican market stalls, **skid row** (one of the highest concentrations of homeless people in the US), Japanese shopping plazas and avant-garde art galleries, high-rise corporate towers and antique movie palaces.

Downtown can easily be seen in a day on foot, but if your feet get tired you can hop aboard the **DASH buses** that run every five to ten minutes through key areas, costing only 50¢. Parking lots can be expensive; street parking is a good alternative, except on Bunker Hill, where the meters cost at least $2 per hour. Downtown is the hub of the MTA networks and easily accessible by public transport, especially around the grand colossus of Union Station.

El Pueblo de Los Angeles

Paseo de la Plaza, and N Main St **Visitor Center** E 10 Olvera St • Free • ☎ 213 628 1274, ⓦ elpueblo.lacity.org • **Tours** Tues–Sat
10am–12.30pm on request; 50min • Free • ⓦ lasangelitas.org • Metro Gold, Purple, Red Line to Union Station

LA was born at **El Pueblo de Los Angeles**, an historic district centred on the old plaza just
across Alameda Street from **Union Station**. The site of the original Spanish settlement of
1818, its few remaining early buildings evoke a strong sense of LA's Hispanic origins
– the rest is filled in with period replicas and a few modern buildings with Spanish
Colonial-style façades. The shady, Mexican-style Los Angeles Plaza Park (or just "the
Plaza", laid out in the 1820s) lies at the heart of the district, and the old church on the
western side, Nuestra Señora Reina de los Angeles or simply **La Placita**, 535 N Main St
(daily 6.30am–8pm; ☎213 629 3101) to locals, is the city's oldest (1823).

On the south side of the plaza, the **Old Plaza Firehouse Museum** (Tues–Sun 10am–
3pm; free) dates back to 1884 and contains a small but intriguing roomful of

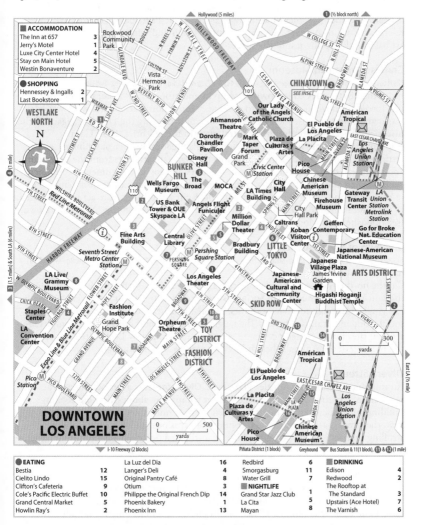

EATING				DRINKING	
Bestia	12	La Luz del Dia	16	Redbird	6
Cielito Lindo	15	Langer's Deli	4	Smorgasburg	11
Clifton's Cafeteria	9	Original Pantry Café	8	Water Grill	7
Cole's Pacific Electric Buffet	10	Otium	3	NIGHTLIFE	
Grand Central Market	5	Philippe the Original French Dip	14	Grand Star Jazz Club	1
Howlin Ray's	2	Phoenix Bakery	1	La Cita	5
		Phoenix Inn	13	Mayan	8

DRINKING	
Edison	4
Redwood	2
The Rooftop at The Standard	3
Upstairs (Ace Hotel)	7
The Varnish	6

1 firefighting gear. Next door, stately **Pico House** was a grand Italianate-style hotel completed in 1870 by Pío Pico, the last governor of California under Mexican rule (the ground floor is occasionally used for exhibits and events).

La Plaza de Cultura y Artes

501 N Main St • Mon & Wed–Sun noon–7pm • Free • ☎ 213 542 6200, ⓦ lapca.org • Metro Gold, Purple, Red Line to Union Station

The best place to get an understanding of the history of El Pueblo, and the long history of Mexican-Americans, is the enlightening **La Plaza de Cultura y Artes**, at the southwest corner of Los Angeles Plaza Park. The centre occupies two stately properties: the 1888 Brunswig Building and the 1883 Plaza House. The main exhibition charts Mexican-American history beginning with the founding of LA in 1781, and a no-holds-barred review of atrocities committed by the Spanish against the indigenous Tongva. The career of **Pío Pico** is covered, as is the Mexican–American War and local *bandidos*, such as **Tiburcio Vasquez** (his Carte de Visite is displayed). The modern **Chicano** movement has its own gallery, Calle Principal is an evocative re-creation of Los Angeles Main Street in the 1920s and temporary exhibits (mostly art based) take up the rest of the space.

Chinese American Museum

425 N Los Angeles St • Tues–Sun 10am–3pm • Free • ☎ 213 485 8567, ⓦ camla.org • Metro Gold, Purple, Red Line to Union Station

From the 1870s, LA's Chinatown grew up in and around El Pueblo; the community was forced to move in the 1930s to make way for Union Station, and what was left was demolished in subsequent years in favour of preserving the Hispanic legacy of the historic district. Just south of the central plaza in the red-brick 1890 Garnier Building, the **Chinese American Museum** details the local history of Chinese settlement, society and culture in this area through rare artefacts from the nineteenth and twentieth centuries, such as revealing letters, photos and documents. Permanent exhibits chart the rise of Chinese communities in LA, immigration from China and re-create the Sun Wing Wo Chinese herb shop circa 1900 (the store actually operated in the building from 1891 to 1948). There are also displays on the "New Chinatown" (see opposite) and Monterey Park.

Museum of Social Justice

115 Paseo De La Plaza • Thurs–Sat 10am–3pm, Sun 10am–1pm • Free • ☎ 213 613 1096, ⓦ museumofsocialjustice.org • Metro Gold, Purple, Red Line to Union Station

On the northern edge of the plaza (inside La Plaza United Methodist Church), the thought-provoking **Museum of Social Justice** showcases the history of social change in Los Angeles through revolving exhibits, especially focusing on the local Methodists' social work and ethnic outreach. The neighbouring **Biscailuz Building** was completed in 1926 as the church conference centre, and features a mural by Leo Politi that depicts the Blessing of the Animals (held here every year on Easter Sunday).

Olvera Street

Running north from Los Angeles Plaza Park, **Olvera Street** is a curious attempt at restoration, a pseudo-Mexican village market comprising about thirty old-looking buildings that opened back in 1930. Taken over for numerous festivals throughout the year, the street is at its best on such communal occasions, and regularly features strolling mariachi bands, Aztec- and Mexican-themed processions, and various dancers and artisans.

Avila Adobe

10 Olvera St • Daily 9am–4pm • Free • ☎ 213 628 1274, ⓦ elpueblo.lacity.org • Metro Gold, Purple, Red Line to Union Station

The **Avila Adobe** is touted as the oldest structure in Los Angeles (built by ex-*alcalde* Don Francisco Avila around 1818), although it was almost entirely rebuilt out of

reinforced concrete following the 1971 Sylmar earthquake. The house is furnished
as it might have appeared in the late 1840s, and the courtyard outside contains
exhibits on the history of LA's water supply and aspects of *Californio* history
(including a free video shown throughout the day), plus a display on Christine
Sterling, whose efforts transformed El Pueblo from slum to tourist attraction in
the 1920s.

Sepulveda House Museum
12 W Olvera St • Tues–Sun 10am–3pm • Free • Metro Gold, Purple, Red Line to Union Station

Built in 1887 for formidable businesswoman Señora Eloisa Martinez de Sepúlveda, the
quaint Eastlake Victorian-style **Sepulveda House Museum** once served as a boarding
house, private home and commercial space. Today the back of the house features a
replica of the boarding house kitchen of the 1890s, plus Señora Sepulveda's bedroom,
while the front is occupied by the América Tropical Interpretive Center.

América Tropical Interpretive Center
Sepulveda House, 125 Paseo de La Plaza (enter from Olvera St) • Tues–Sun 10am–3pm • Free • ☎ 213 485 6855, ⊛ theamericatropical.org • Metro Gold, Purple, Red Line to Union Station

David Siqueiros (1896–1974), one of the greatest Mexican artists of the twentieth
century, painted the epic 80-by-18ft *América Tropical* on the exterior of Italian Hall in
El Pueblo in 1932. The mural depicts a Mexican Indian, crucified on a double cross
beneath an American eagle – controversial to say the least, it was painted over within a
decade. After a mammoth restoration project, what's left of the mural (mostly a ghostly
outline) can be seen from a rooftop viewing platform, accessible from the **América
Tropical Interpretive Center**. The centre provides context about the life, work and legacy
of Siqueiros, with exhibits that examine the mural as a political statement, and its
influence on mural artists based in Los Angeles.

Italian American Museum of Los Angeles
103 Main St • Tues–Sun 10am–3pm • Free • ☎ 213 485 8432, ⊛ italianhall.org • Metro Gold, Purple, Red Line to Union Station

Opened in 2016 in Italian Hall (built in 1908 as an Italian community centre), the
Italian American Museum of Los Angeles showcases the contribution of Italian
Americans to LA, with absorbing exhibits and videos highlighting the everyday life of
immigrant families in the nineteenth century – including the bemused Italian reaction
to Prohibition in 1919. Little Italy was located in the blocks north of Los Angeles Plaza
Park in the early twentieth century, now Chinatown (see below).

Chinatown

What is now **Chinatown** was formally established in 1938 along North Broadway
and North Spring Street after the original Chinatown was demolished to build
Union Station. It's not the bustling affair you'll find in a number of other US cities,
unless it's Chinese New Year, when there's a parade of dragons and firework
celebrations. Apart from the good restaurants here (see p.131), official attractions
comprise a handful of small shopping malls such as pedestrianized **Old Chinatown
Central Plaza** at 943 N Broadway, where you can pick up an assortment of lanterns,
teapots and jade jewellery – aimed more at tourists than residents. Start exploring at
the traditional **East Gate** on the edge of Central Plaza, where there's a statue of
revered Chinese leader Sun Yat-sen. From here Gin Ling Way cuts through the mall
to the **West Gate** on Hill Street, passing the iconic **Hop Louie Restaurant pagoda** (on
Mei Ling Way), built in 1941 to house the *Golden Pagoda Restaurant*. It's a half-mile
south to **Thien Hau Temple** at 750 Yale St, one of the district's most traditional
Taoist shrines, dedicated to Mazu, the goddess of the sea – it was actually built for
Chinese-Vietnamese refugees in 2005.

1

Bunker Hill and the Financial District

Developed in the late 1860s, **Bunker Hill** was once LA's most elegant neighbourhood, its elaborate Victorian mansions and houses connected by funicular railroad to the growing business district down below on Spring Street. These structures were all wiped out by 1960s urban renewal and replaced with a forest of glossy high-rises that form LA's central **Financial District** today.

Wells Fargo History Museum

333 S Grand Ave • Mon–Fri 9am–5pm • Free • ☎ 213 253 7166, ⓦ wellsfargohistory.com • Metro Purple/Red Line to Pershing Square

At the base of the towering Wells Fargo Center sits the **Wells Fargo History Museum**, charting the history of Wells Fargo & Co, the current banking colossus that was founded in New York in 1852 to service the huge amounts of cash pouring out of Gold Rush California. Exhibits include rare photographs, the 26-ounce Challenge Nugget (of gold), a re-created assay office from the nineteenth century and an original Concord stagecoach.

OUE Skyspace LA

633 W 5th St • Daily 9am–11pm • $19 • ☎ 213 894 9000, ⓦ skyspace-la.com

Two blocks south of Wells Fargo Center, the **US Bank Tower** (1018ft), completed in 1989, was the tallest building on the West Coast until 2016, when 1100ft **Wilshire Grand Center** took the title (see below). You can shoot up to the US Bank Tower's spectacular observation deck, dubbed **OUE Skyspace LA**, and for an extra $8 you can slip down a death-defying transparent glass slide attached to the outside of the building between the 70th and 69th floors. The cylindrical tower features Lawrence Halprin's huge **Bunker Hill Steps** at its base, supposedly modelled after the Spanish Steps in Rome.

Los Angeles Public Library

630 W 5th St • Mon–Thurs 10am–8pm, Fri & Sat 9.30am–5.30pm, Sun 1–5pm • ☎ 213 228 7000, ⓦ lapl.org

Completed in 1926, **Los Angeles Public Library** (just below US Bank Tower) is topped with a distinctive tiled mosaic pyramid, but it's the interior that deserves most attention. The main attraction is the stunning *History of California*, a four-part mural completed in 1933 by illustrator Dean Cornwell.

The Museum of Contemporary Art

250 S Grand Ave • Mon, Wed & Fri 11am–6pm, Thurs 11am–8pm, Sat & Sun 11am–5pm • $12, includes admission to the Geffen Contemporary at MOCA; free Thurs 5–8pm • ☎ 213 626 6222, ⓦ moca.org • Metro Purple/Red Line to Civic Center

Based at the California Plaza, a billion-dollar complex of offices and luxury condos, the **Museum of Contemporary Art (MOCA)**, was designed by showman architect Arata Isozaki, its silhouette offering an array of geometric red shapes recognizable from TV advertisements filmed here.

Much of the gallery is used for temporary exhibitions but there are usually some spaces dedicated to the **permanent collection**, mostly mid-twentieth-century American art, particularly from the abstract expressionist period, including top work by usual suspects Franz Kline, Jackson Pollock and Mark Rothko. You'll also find plenty of pop art, in

---

LA'S TALLEST TOWER

Topping out at 1100ft in 2016, the **Wilshire Grand Center** at Figueroa Street and Wilshire Boulevard is now the tallest building west of the Mississippi, a massive project funded predominantly by Korean Air. The stylish steel-and-glass skyscraper got exemption from a city ordinance that requires all tall buildings to have helipads on the roof (for safety reasons), and instead its 18ft steel spire glows with LED lights. The tower contains a spectacular InterContinental hotel and an **observation deck** that should be open to the public sometime in 2017 (see ⓦ wilshiregrandcenter.com).

1

ANGELS FLIGHT

Linking South Hill Street (near Grand Central Market) with California Plaza Watercourt at 350 S Grand Ave in the Financial District, a journey of just 298ft, the **Angels Flight** funicular once promoted itself as "the shortest railway in the world". The original opened in 1901, a block north of the current location, but was dismantled in 1969; it reopened here in 1996, but was suspended indefinitely in 2013 due to safety concerns. The tracks (and cars) are still there, but though the campaign to reopen it has made some progress, there was no re-start date in sight at the time of research – see ⓦ angelsflight.org for the latest (the railway needs to raise $50,000 in annual insurance premiums just to maintain the site, even with the trams not working).

Robert Rauschenberg's junk collages, Claes Oldenburg's papier-mâché hamburgers and Andy Warhol's print-ad black telephone. The museum is also strong on **photography**, exhibiting Diane Arbus, Larry Clark, Robert Frank, Lee Friedlander and Cindy Sherman.

The Broad

221 S Grand Ave • Tues & Wed 11am–5pm, Thurs & Fri 11am–8pm, Sat 10am–8pm, Sun 10am–6pm • Free (special exhibitions from $12) • ☏ 213 232 6200, ⓦ thebroad.org

Just across the street from MOCA, **The Broad** opened in 2015 to house the fabulous contemporary art collection established by philanthropists Eli and Edythe Broad. It's already one of LA's most popular sights, with its distinctive, metallic, perforated exterior (by Diller Scofidio + Renfro) part of the attraction; the first- and third-floor galleries are connected by a 105ft escalator and cylindrical lift that zip through the central storage vaults at the heart of the complex. The first floor features temporary shows (tickets required), and you'll also need a separate ticket to view the glimmering, otherworldly lights of Yayoi Kusama's **Infinity Mirrored Room** (first floor), which allows for one person at a time to take a look for just one minute (check ahead to see if this is still on display). Note that the museum gets very busy at peak times (weekends in summer and holidays), when it's worth making **advance reservations** for special exhibitions (which generally cost $12–15) – your ticket will also allow timed entry to the permanent galleries.

The third floor

The **permanent collection** (which rotates) resides on the bright, futuristic **third floor**, with the main hall dominated by the massive cartoonish canvases of **Takashi Murakami** and **Jeff Koon**'s exuberant *Tulips* installation. Koons is featured in his own gallery behind here, containing his huge blue-metallic *Balloon Dog* and memorable gold-hued sculpture of *Michael Jackson and Bubbles* (the chimp). Robert Therrien's *Under the Table*, a giant table and chairs installation, fills a whole gallery, while **Jean-Michel Basquiat** and **Keith Haring** also get their own space (Haring's striking *Red Room* is usually on display).

Damien Hirst's typically cynical box of animal skeletons (*Something Solid Beneath the Surface of All Creatures Great and Small*) should be on display somewhere, as should **Jasper Johns**'s *Flag 1967* and giant canvases by **Cy Twombly**. **Andy Warhol** is represented by *Twenty Jackies*, *Single Elvis* and many others, while the museum also holds the largest collection of **Cindy Sherman**'s photographic works. Look out also for **Kara Walker**'s harrowing *African't*, a series of life-size cut-outs that seem innocent enough at first glance, but which are in fact engaged in degrading acts of sex and violence representing antebellum America.

Walt Disney Concert Hall

111 Grand Ave • Self-guided audio tours most days 10am–2pm; tour days vary: noon & 1pm • Free • ☏ 213 972 4399, ⓦ musiccenter.org • Metro Purple, Red Line to Civic Center

LA's finest jewel of modern architecture is **Walt Disney Concert Hall**, a Frank Gehry-designed, 2300-seat acoustic showpiece whose titanium exterior resembles something akin to colossal broken eggshells. Part of the **Music Center** stable of

1

WALT DISNEY'S SECRET GARDEN

When visiting Walt Disney Concert Hall, don't miss the grandly titled **Walt Disney Concert Hall Community Park** (public entrances at 2nd St and Grand Ave, and 1st St and Hope St; daily sunrise–sunset; free), actually a small garden and hidden gem that curves around the back of the concert hall 30ft above the street. Gehry's stunning **Lillian Disney Memorial Fountain** is shaped like a giant lily and covered by broken pieces of Royal Delft porcelain vases.

---

venues, the **LA Philharmonic** (see p.143) is based here, and with the hall's rich, warm acoustics and features such as a colossal, intricate pipe organ, it may be the best place to hear music in the city, perhaps in all of California. Self-guided **audio tours** (1hr; narrated by actor John Lithgow) are the easiest way to explore the hall; days vary for the free one-hour **guided tours** – visit the website for the latest schedule. Note that no tours include the actual auditorium – for that you'll have to see a show.

Cathedral of Our Lady of the Angels

555 W Temple St • Mon–Fri 6.30am–6pm, Sat 9am–6pm, Sun 7am–6pm • Free tours Mon–Fri 1pm (Wed 1.15pm) • ☎ 213 680 5200, ⓦ olacathedral.org • Metro Purple/Red Line to Civic Center

The $200-million **Cathedral of Our Lady of the Angels** is one of LA's Modernist colossuses, completed by 2002 to a design by lauded Spanish architect José Rafael Moneo. The centrepiece of the local Catholic archdiocese is a truly massive structure – eleven concrete storeys tall and capable of holding three thousand people. The interior is the highlight, featuring tapestries of saints, giant bronze doors, ultra-thin alabaster screens for diffusing light, a grand marble altar, and $30 million worth of art and furnishings (including the Retablo Ezcaray, an ornate wood altarpiece from 1687 Spain). Actor Gregory Peck is buried in the crypt, along with the relics of Roman Saint Vibiana (a third-century virgin martyr and patroness of the cathedral).

The Civic Center and City Hall

Separated from El Pueblo by the Santa Ana Freeway (US-101), most of the **Civic Center** is a collection of plodding bureaucratic office buildings. Built in 1928 at 200 N Spring St (public entrance at 201 Main St), stands LA's famous Art Deco **City Hall**, known to the world through LAPD badges seen in TV shows ever since *Dragnet*, and until 1960 the city's tallest structure (at 454ft); it still houses the mayor's office and the Los Angeles City Council. Go up to the 27th-storey **observation deck** for spectacular views across Downtown (Mon–Fri 9am–5pm; free; ☎ 213 978 1059, ⓦ lacity.org). You'll have to go through a security check and take three sets of elevators (take the first up to the 22nd floor and follow the signs).

Little Tokyo

A significant Japanese community has existed in Los Angeles since 1903, and today the colourful shopping and restaurant district of **Little Tokyo** is centred on **Historic First Street**, between San Pedro and Central, where the **Koban Visitor Center** (307 E 1st St; Mon–Sat 10am–6pm; ☎ 213 613 1911, ⓦ littletokyola.org) provides maps and information. You'll also find the **Japanese Village Plaza** (most stores daily 9am–6pm; ⓦ japanesevillageplaza.net) here, a touristy outdoor mall, marked with a traditional tori gate and lined with sushi bars and shops in faux Japanese style. More authentic experiences can be found at the district's traditional Japanese shrines; **Koyasan Buddhist Temple** (founded in 1912) is accessed via a narrow lane next to the *Miyako Hotel* at 342 E 1st St (usually open Sundays only, but go to the office on the right to ask about visiting), while grander **Higashi Honganji Buddhist Temple** (daily 10am–5pm) at 505 E 3rd St was founded in 1904 with the current incarnation completed here in 1976.

Japanese American National Museum

100 N Central Ave • Tues, Wed & Fri–Sun 11am–5pm, Thurs noon–8pm • $10 • ☎ 213 625 0414, ⓦ janm.org

Across the road from Japanese Village Plaza, the lavish modern premises of the **Japanese American National Museum** house exhibits on everything from origami to traditional furniture, and folk craftwork to the internment of Japanese Americans during World War II. Opposite, the **Go For Broke National Education Center** (355 E 1st St; Tues, Wed & Fri 11am–6pm, Thurs noon–8pm, Sat 10am–6pm, Sun 11am–6pm; $10, $15 combined with museum; ⓦ goforbroke.org) contains the "Defining Courage Experience", with hands-on exhibits charting the challenging experiences of Japanese Americans in World War II.

The Geffen Contemporary at MOCA

152 N Central Ave • Mon, Wed & Fri 11am–6pm, Thurs 11am–8pm, Sat & Sun 11am–5pm • $12; free Thurs 5–8pm; includes admission to Museum of Contemporary Art • ☎ 213 626 6222, ⓦ moca.org • Metro Gold Line to Little Tokyo/Arts District Station

Built in 1947 for Union Hardware and later used as a police garage, the **Geffen Contemporary at MOCA** was artfully renovated by Frank Gehry in the 1980s, and is now the alternative exhibition space to its more mainstream sibling, the Museum of Contemporary Art (see p.157). It's a massive, luminous hall where the Geffen presents huge installation pieces, architecture retrospectives and other big shows with a voracious need for space.

Japanese American Cultural & Community Center

244 S San Pedro St • **Doizaki Gallery** Tues–Fri noon–5pm, Sat & Sun 11am–4pm • Free • ☎ 213 628 2725, ⓦ jaccc.org

The relatively modest **Japanese American Cultural & Community Center** runs various visual and cultural art programmes at the **Aratani Theatre** throughout the year, while its **Doizaki Gallery** shows traditional and contemporary Japanese drawing and calligraphy, along with costumes, sculptures and other associated art forms. Behind the cultural centre, serene **James Irvine Japanese Garden** (Tues–Fri 10am–5pm; free), with a stream running along its sloping hillside, was carved out of a flat lot to become the "garden of the clear stream", and makes the site seem a world away from LA's expanse of asphalt and concrete.

The Arts District

Downtown's burgeoning **Arts District**, just east of Little Tokyo (between Alameda St and the Los Angeles River), is a once gritty neighbourhood being gradually converted by warehouse galleries and boutiques, in part sparked by the **Southern California Institute of Architecture**'s conversion of the old Santa Fe Freight Depot in 2000. There's been an artist presence here since the 1970s, but it's only in recent years that loft conversions and major galleries have arrived, with **Hauser Wirth & Schimmel** (Wed & Fri–Sun 11am–6pm, Thurs 11am–8pm; ☎ 213 943 1620, ⓦ hauserwirth.com) at 901 E 3rd St one of the most high profile. **Art Share LA** at 801 E 4th Place provides subsidized work lofts for artists and runs its own gallery (Wed–Sun 1–6pm; ⓦ artsharela.org), while **Project Space** (ⓦ alldayeveryday.com) at 2028 E 7th St contains galleries, pop-up retail and a bar. Budding architects will enjoy the **A+D Architecture & Design Museum** (Tues–Fri 11am–5pm, Sat & Sun noon–6pm; $7; ☎ 213 346 9734, ⓦ aplusd.org), 900 E 4th St, which moved here in 2015, and puts on rotating exhibits of the latest trends in art, photography and especially progressive architecture and design, with an emphasis on LA. The **Institute of Contemporary Art, Los Angeles** (formerly the Santa Monica Museum of Art; ⓦ theicala.org) is also expected to open here in 2017. A spate of massive mixed-use developments (including a Herzog & de Meuron-designed skyscraper complex) and shopping mall construction looks set to transform the neighbourhood utterly over the next few years.

1

Broadway Theater District

Down the hill from the Financial District lies the still down-at-heel but rapidly developing **Broadway Theater District** (aka "Historic Downtown"). Stretching for six blocks from Third to Ninth along South Broadway, it constitutes one of the last remaining urban pockets of classic cinema architecture in the country – though none of the twelve movie palaces here shows movies regularly. **Broadway** itself once formed the core of Los Angeles's most fashionable shopping and entertainment district, brimming with cinemas and department stores. Today it's a bustling, slightly run-down Hispanic community, whose vendors operate out of hundred-year-old buildings, the salsa music and street culture making for one of the city's most electric environments.

The 1893 **Bradbury Building** at 304 S Broadway (lobby Mon–Sat 9am–5pm; free), features a magnificent sunlit atrium surrounded by wrought-iron balconies and open-cage elevators; scenes from both *Blade Runner* and *Citizen Kane* were filmed here. Opposite at 307 S Broadway, the opulent 1918 **Million Dollar Theater** was built by theatre magnate Sid Grauman, who went on to build the Egyptian and Chinese theatres in Hollywood. Further along at 615 S Broadway, the **Los Angeles Theater** completed in 1931, features a lavish French Baroque lobby behind a triumphal arch façade, lined by marble columns supporting an intricate mosaic ceiling; the 2000-seat auditorium is enveloped by trompe l'oeil murals and lighting effects. Both these venues are open only for private events.

Grand Central Market

317 S Broadway, between 3rd and 4th • Daily 8am–10pm • ☎213 624 2378, ⓦgrandcentralmarket.com • Metro Purple, Red Line to Pershing Square

Established in 1917, the indoor **Grand Central Market** provides a good taste of modern Broadway – everything from apples and oranges to *carne asada* and pickled pig's feet. It's also a great place to eat, from cheap burritos and overstuffed *pupusas* to Cuban sandwiches and old-fashioned American-Chinese food.

The Fashion District

The southern edge of Downtown LA harbours the welter of commercial activity in the **Fashion District**, where wholesale buyers, retail shoppers, designers, fashion students and Hollywood stylists can pick up decent fabric for as little as $2 per yard.

Highlights include the **California Market Center**, at 110 E 9th St and Main (typically Mon–Fri 9am–5pm; ☎213 630 3600, ⓦcaliforniamarketcenter.com), which fills three million square feet and seemingly has just as many visitors; the **Flower Market**, 754 Wall St, between 7th and 8th (Mon & Wed 8am–noon, Tues & Thurs 6am–11pm, Fri 8am–2pm, Sat 6am–2pm; entry $2, Sat $1; ☎213 627 3696, ⓦoriginallaflowermarket .com), which has a voluminous selection of blooms that you can buy for a fraction of the prices charged elsewhere; and **Santee Alley** (between Maple Ave and Santee St, running from Olympic Blvd to Twelfth St; most stores daily 9.30am–6pm; ⓦ thesanteealley.com), a chaotic market thick with hundreds of vendor shops and stalls selling everything from the cheapest sunglasses to smart suits.

FIDM Museum and Galleries

919 S Grand Ave • Tues–Sat 10am–5pm • Free • ☎ 213 623 5821, ⓦ fashionmuseum.org • Metro Blue, Expo, Purple, Red lines 7th St/Metro Center

Near Grand Hope Park, to the west of the downtown area, the **FIDM Museum and Galleries** features items drawn from the Fashion Institute of Design & Merchandising's precious collection of ten thousand pieces of costume and apparel – French gowns, Russian jewels, quirky shoes and so on. The main draw is the "**Art of Motion Picture Costume Design**" show that runs from February to April – roughly Oscar time – displaying colourful outfits from Oscar-nominated films that year, but might include anything from Liz Taylor's *Cleopatra* garb to the spacey get-ups from *Star Wars*.

LA Live and the Grammy Museum

800 W Olympic Blvd **LA Live** ☎ 213 763 6030, ⓦ lalive.com • **Grammy Museum** Mon–Fri 10.30am–6.30pm, Sat & Sun 10am–6.30pm • $12.95 • ☎ 213 765 6800, ⓦ grammymuseum.org • Metro Blue, Expo lines to Pico

Just north of the Staples Center arena is retail behemoth **LA Live**, a $2.5-billion shopping and entertainment complex that features cinemas, sports facilities and broadcast studios, upper-end hotels, a central plaza, a bowling alley and numerous arcades, restaurants and clubs. It also contains the entertaining **Grammy Museum**, not just devoted to all things Grammy Awards (usually held in the on-site **Microsoft Theater** in February), but recorded music in general, with interactive displays over four floors including the Songwriters Hall of Fame, stage outfits and exhibits on Ray Charles and Sam Cooke, personal artefacts from Elvis Presley, Miles Davis and Neil Diamond, and a real recording studio.

Northeast LA

Connoisseurs of historic architecture and Native American art may consider an excursion into **Northeast Los Angeles**, home of a handful of attractions linked to LA's Victorian heyday, all of which lie close to the Arroyo Seco in the **Montecito Heights** and relatively affluent **Mount Washington** neighbourhoods, some four miles from Downtown. For contemporary chic, head to **York Boulevard** in **Highland Park**, lined with trendy boutiques, retro shops and art galleries.

Heritage Square Museum

3800 Homer St, Montecito Heights • Fri–Sun 11.30am–4.30pm • $10 • ☎ 323 225 2700, ⓦ heritagesquare.org • Metro Gold Line to Heritage Square/Arroyo Station

Since 1969, nine of the most striking Victorian houses from around Los Angeles have been brought together to form the fascinating **Heritage Square Museum** in Montecito Heights (though the museum's freeway-adjacent home is less than ideal). This fenced-off ten-acre park includes the 1875 Palms Depot railway station, the 1893 Longfellow-Hastings Octagon House and the 1898 Lincoln Avenue Methodist Church.

Lummis Home

200 E Ave 43, Mount Washington • Sat & Sun 10am–3pm • Free • ☎ 323 661 9465 • Metro Gold Line to Heritage Square/Arroyo Station

The intriguing **Lummis Home** is the well-preserved legacy of **Charles F. Lummis**, a publicist who was at the heart of LA's nineteenth-century boom. An early champion of

1

civil rights for Native Americans, Lummis built his home as a cultural centre where the literati of the day would meet. He built it between 1897 and 1910 in an ad hoc mixture of Mission and medieval styles, constructing the thick walls out of rounded granite boulders taken from the nearby riverbed and the beams over the living room from old telephone poles. The plaster-and-tile interior features rustic, hand-cut timber ceilings and home-made furniture, all a fitting reflection of its rugged owner, one of the few individuals to reach LA by walking – from Cincinnati.

East LA

Of the many Hispanic neighbourhoods all over LA, one of the longest standing is **East LA**, beginning two miles east of Downtown, a buzzing district of markets, shops and street-corner music (it's officially 97 percent Hispanic today). There are few specific "sights" in East LA. The best plan is just to turn up on a Saturday afternoon – the liveliest part of the week – and stroll along **Whittier Boulevard**, the commercial heart of the community. Head eastward from Burger Avenue (just beyond I-710, 5 miles east of Downtown) and check out the taco trucks, Mexican-style hot dogs (wrapped in bacon and known as an "East LA Ditch Dog"), street vendors and **botánica shops**, where you can browse amid the shark's teeth, dried devilfish and plastic statuettes of Catholic saints, and buy magical herbs, ointments or candles after consulting the shopkeeper and explaining (in Spanish) what ails you. The **Latino Walk of Fame** features sun-shaped plaques honouring Latino heroes such as Cesar Chavez, scattered along Whittier between Burger and Clela avenues.

El Mercado de Los Angeles

3425 E 1st St, Boyle Heights • Daily 10am–8pm • ☎ 323 268 3451 • Metro Gold Line to Indiana

Only slightly less exotic fare than on Whittier Boulevard can be found in **El Mercado de Los Angeles** (aka "El Mercadito"), an indoor market somewhat similar to Olvera Street (see p.64) but much more authentic. An indoor warren of vendor stalls sell *botanicas*, clothing, Latin American food and arts-and-crafts pieces; on the top floor, where the restaurants are located, mariachi bands play until well after midnight every day.

Central LA

Central LA is united by little more than freeways and large distances separating the major points of interest, though there's quite a bit worth seeing. Immediately northwest of Downtown, **Echo Park** was where the upper crust of LA society lived luxuriously in the late nineteenth and early twentieth centuries in stylish Victorian houses (now either preserved or decrepit), while **Silver Lake** is one of the hippest neighbourhoods in the city. Further west, **Wilshire Center** and **Koreatown** carry more exotic allure, mainly in the form of excellent Korean restaurants.

Echo Park

To the northwest of Downtown LA is **Echo Park**, a small oasis of palm trees and lotus blossoms set around **Echo Park Lake** and one of the city's coolest neighbourhoods. In the hulking white **Angelus Temple** (ⓦangelustemple.org) on the northern side of the lake, the evangelist **Aimee Semple McPherson** used to preach sermons to five thousand people in the 1920s, with thousands more listening in on the radio (it's still home to the Foursquare Church that she founded). You can **rent paddleboats** (typically $10/hr; Mon–Fri 9am–7pm, Sat & Sun 9am–dusk) or grab a drink from *Square One* in the

1

FILIPINOTOWN

Historic Filipinotown (or "Hi-Fi") covers the southwest portion of Echo Park (roughly bounded by Hoover St, Glendale Blvd, Temple St and Beverly Blvd). As the name suggests this was one of the main areas Filipinos first settled during the early twentieth century, and though the area is now much more diverse, an estimated 10,000 Filipino Americans still live here. Highlights include the modest **Filipino Christian Church** at 301 N Union Ave, the giant **Gintong Kasaysayan, Gintong Pamana mural** ("Filipino Americans: a glorious history, a golden legacy") in Unidad Park and plenty of authentic Filipino restaurants. The **Annual Historic Filipinotown Festival** is held every first Saturday and Sunday of August. See ⓦ historicfilipinotown.com.

historic **boathouse** on the eastern edge of the lake, where you'll also see the beloved Art Deco statue "**Lady of the Lake**", completed by LA artist Ada Mae Sharpless in 1935. Otherwise the neighbourhood primarily appeals for its funky, **bohemian atmosphere**, with countless affordable (for LA) bungalows and apartments around the park housing the city's next generation of artists, musicians and film-makers; painter Jackson Pollock, and actors Leonardo DiCaprio and Shia LaBeouf grew up here when it was a lot grungier.

Silver Lake

Just northwest of Echo Park, **Silver Lake** is a fashionable district that was once home to some of Hollywood's first movie studios, since converted into restaurants and galleries, or at least warehouses and storage units. Walt Disney opened his second studio in 1926 at 2719 Hyperion Ave (now demolished), and the Keystone Kops were dreamed up in Mack Sennett's studio at 1712 Glendale Blvd (now a storage facility).

The district is also known for its LGBT bars, quirky dance clubs and leftist bookstores attracting plenty of hipsters and celebrities – singers Katy Perry, Beck and Tom Waits have all been residents. French writer **Anaïs Nin** (and husband Rupert Pole) lived at 2335 Hidalgo Ave from 1962 until 1977; the house was designed by Eric Lloyd Wright (grandson of Frank), but it's not open to the public. Other than soaking up the scene on **Sunset Boulevard**, students of architecture should check out some of the area's other Modernist treasures (see box below).

Wilshire Center and Koreatown

Wilshire Boulevard leaves Downtown between Sixth and Seventh as the main route across seventeen miles of Los Angeles to Santa Monica's beachside Palisades Park – for many this is the **main street of Los Angeles**. Three miles west of Downtown, beyond Hoover Street, lies the **Wilshire Center** district, which blends into the ever expanding **Koreatown** south of Eighth Street. The first local landmark you'll pass is the elegant **Bullocks Wilshire** department store at 3050 Wilshire Blvd, built in 1929 and the most complete and unaltered example of Zigzag Art Deco architecture in the city. The store closed in 1993 and the building is now the law library of adjacent **Southwestern University**. Further along is **Wilshire Christian Church** (3435 Wilshire Blvd, at Normandie), completed in 1927 with

SILVER LAKE MODERNISM

Silver Lake harbours an intriguing collection of Modernist houses nestled in the hills, designed by the likes of Richard Neutra and R.M. Schindler and highlighted by John Lautner's **Silvertop**, completed in 1963 (2138 Micheltorena St; best viewed from 2100 Redcliff Drive), with its projecting roofs and balconies, wraparound glass windows and sweeping concrete curves. Architecture buffs can take an in-depth look with Architecture Tours LA (daily 9.30am & 1.30pm; $75–80 per person; ☏ 323 464 7868, ⓦ architecturetoursla.com).

1

an unusual Romanesque Revival style and 200ft tower, now owned by the Oasis Church (🔊 oasisla.org), and **Wilshire Boulevard Temple**, 3663 Wilshire Blvd (tours by appointment only; ☎ 213 835 2195, 🔊 wbtla.org), home of the Jewish Congregation B'nai B'rith; its vast 135ft-tall Byzantine dome was completed in 1929.

Koreatown

Two blocks south of Wilshire Boulevard, between Vermont and Western, **Koreatown** is home to the largest concentration of Koreans outside Korea and five times bigger than Chinatown and Little Tokyo combined. In reality, the comparison is unfair, for Koreatown is an active residential and commercial district, not just a tourist sight, and boasts as many bars, theatres, community groups, banks and shopping complexes as it does restaurants. For a taster, wander along **Olympic Boulevard**, the main drag, taking in the traditional Korean gazebo at Irolo, the **Thal Mah Sah Buddhist Temple** at 3505 W Olympic Blvd and the **Koreatown Galleria** (Mon–Sat 10am–9pm, Sun 11am–9pm; 🔊 koreatowngalleria.com) at 3250 W Olympic Blvd, a shrine to modern Korean culture. The annual **Korean Festival & Parade** takes place in October.

Korean Cultural Center

5505 Wilshire Blvd • Mon–Fri 10am–5pm, Sat 10am–1pm • Free • ☎ 323 936 7141, 🔊 kccla.org • Bus #720

To get a better understanding of Koreatown's art and culture visit the **Korean Cultural Center**, which has a museum displaying photographs, antiques and craftwork from Korea and the local immigrant community, and rotating exhibitions of fine art, folk work and applied crafts, plus theatrical performances. A more comprehensive **Korean American National Museum** (🔊 kanmuseum.org) should be opening in spanking-new premises at 605 S Vermont Ave (at 6th St) in 2018.

South LA

Lacking the scenic splendour of the coast, the glamour of West LA or the history of Downtown, **SOUTH LA** comprises such notable neighbourhoods as **Watts**, **Compton** and **Inglewood**, but beyond the **USC campus** and **Exposition Park** it hardly ranks on the tourist circuit – especially since it burst onto the world's TV screens as the focal point of the April 1992 **riots**. Better known as **South Central**, LA City Council voted to change the name in 2003 in the hopes of disassociating the area with long-term connotations of gang violence and economic depression, captured in the work of local rappers NWA, Ice-T and Long Beach's Snoop Dogg, and hard-hitting movies such as *Colors*, *Boyz N the Hood* and *Straight Outta Compton*.

Most LA visitors go out of their way to avoid the area, but there are a handful of sights worth considering during daylight hours, notably the USC campus, Exposition Park and the revived **West Adams** district just south of, and paralleling, the I-10 freeway. Beyond here, the vast urban bleakness of South LA has a few isolated spots of interest; it's generally a place to visit with caution or with someone who knows the area, though it's safe enough in daytime around the main drags.

University of Southern California

850 W 37th St **Walking tours** 4 daily Mon–Fri; 45min (reservations required) • Free • ☎ 213 740 6605, 🔊 visit.usc.edu/tours • **Doheny Memorial Library** 3550 Trousdale Pkwy • Hours vary, often Mon–Thurs 9am–8pm, Fri & Sat 9am–5pm, Sun noon–5pm • ☎ 213 740 2924 • Metro Expo Line to Expo Park/USC

The 226-acre University Park campus of **University of Southern California** (USC), a few miles south of Downtown along Figueroa Street, is a beautiful enclave of wealth in one of the city's poorer neighbourhoods. USC (somewhat unkindly dubbed the "University of Spoiled Children" by cynics) is one of the most expensive universities in the country, carefully walled off from the rough neighbourhood that surrounds it. Although sizeable, the architecturally rich campus is reasonably easy to get around, though you'll learn more on free **walking tours**. Without a guide, a good place to start is in the **Doheny Memorial Library**, an inviting 1932 Romanesque Revival structure where you can pick up a campus map and browse a large stock of overseas newspapers and magazines.

Fisher Museum of Art
823 Exposition Blvd • Sept–May Tues–Fri noon–5pm, Sat noon–4pm • Free • ☎ 213 740 4561, ⓦ fisher.usc.edu • Metro Expo Line to Expo Park/USC

USC's art collection is housed in the **Fisher Museum of Art**, founded in 1939 by oil heiress and collector Elizabeth Holmes Fisher. Exhibitions change, and the gallery is closed for university holidays and during summer months, so check ahead. At least one exhibition a year features art from the permanent collection, with gems such as *A Stream in the Rockies* by Albert Bierstadt, *Venus Wounded by a Thorn* by Rubens and *Tax Collector* by Brueghel the Younger, eighteenth-century British portraiture, nineteenth-century French Barbizon paintings as well as a vast ensemble of modern and contemporary work.

Exposition Park
700 Exposition Park Drive • Free (parking $12/day) • Metro Expo Line to Expo Park/USC

Across Exposition Boulevard from the USC campus, the 160-acre **Exposition Park** served as an agricultural fairground from 1872 to 1913, and now incorporates lush landscaped gardens and a number of enticing museums.

California Science Center
700 Exposition Park Drive • Daily 10am–5pm • Free (parking $12/day) • ☎ 323 724 3623, ⓦ californiasciencecenter.org

One of the highlights of Exposition Park is the **California Science Center**, which has scores of quirky displays aimed at making the world of science more fun for youngsters. In 2012 it also became the final home of the **Space Shuttle Endeavour** and an excellent accompanying exhibition (timed tickets required at weekends and holidays; free). Other displays include a real A-12 Blackbird spy plane, a walk-in periscope, an imitation earthquake and a demonstration wind tunnel. The centre's **IMAX Theater** plays a range of kid-oriented documentaries on a gigantic curved screen (adults $8.50, kids [4–12] $5.25). Note also there are extra charges for the Ecology Cliff Climb ($3.50), High Wire Bicycle ($2) and the Motion-Based Simulator ($5), though passes that include all three cost just $7.50.

THE USC TROJANS

South of USC and Exposition Park, the **Los Angeles Memorial Coliseum** was the site of the 1932 and 1984 Olympic Games, but now hosts home games for the dominant USC football team, one of the top squads in the country having won eleven national championships. Known as the **Trojans**, the team's rivalry with Notre Dame (Indiana) is one of the greatest in US college sports – the two fight it out for the "Jeweled Shillelagh" every November. The rivalry with UCLA is just as fierce, the two schools competing annually for the "Victory Bell". The **USC Ticket Office** is located in the Student Union Building, 3601 Trousdale Pkwy (Mon–Fri 9am–5pm; tickets from $75; ☎ 213 740 4672, ⓦ usctrojans.com; see also ⓦ ticketmaster.com). If you can't make a game, the imposing grand arch on the Art Moderne façade and muscular, headless commemorative statues at the Coliseum, completed in 1923, still create enough interest to make the place worth a look – **Los Angeles Coliseum Historic Tours** (1hr 30min; $25; ☎ 213 741 0410) usually run Wed–Sun 10am–1.30pm (self-guided visits till 4pm; $10), and include the USC Recruit Lounge, Coliseum Boardroom, press box, locker rooms and Players' Tunnel (self-guided tours are limited to the Peristyle arches and Court of Honor). Tickets can be purchased through Ticketmaster or at the Coliseum Box Office located at Gate 28A, 3911 S Figueroa St.

1

California African American Museum

600 State Drive • Tues–Sat 10am–5pm, Sun 11am–5pm • Free (parking $12/day) • ☎ 213 744 7432, ⓦ caamuseum.org

The absorbing **California African American Museum** lies on the east side of Exposition Park, next to the Science Center, with diverse temporary exhibitions on the history and culture of African Americans (with special emphasis on California), as well as a good range of painting and sculpture from African American and African artists.

Natural History Museum

900 Exposition Blvd • Daily 9.30am–5pm • $12, kids (3–12) $5; parking $12/day • ☎ 213 763 3466, ⓦ nhm.org

At the northwest corner of Exposition Park, the **Natural History Museum** is an explosion of Spanish Revival architecture, with echoing domes, travertine columns and a marble floor constructed in 1913. Foremost among the exhibits is the **Dinosaur Hall** containing a tremendous stock of dinosaur bones and fossils, with twenty individually imposing skeletons including a range of Tyrannosaurus Rex specimens, and the astonishing frame of a Diatryma – a huge prehistoric bird incapable of flight. More contemporary (relatively speaking) bones of Ice Age-era ground sloths, mammoths, lions and the like are also on view – many of them dug out of the muck of the La Brea Tar Pits, where the Page Museum is a satellite of this one (see p.93). In the fascinating **California History Hall** the creation and development of LA is charted with a series of dioramas from the 1930s and Walt Disney's animation stand from 1923. Topping the whole place off is the **Hall of Gems and Minerals**, several astonishing roomfuls of crystals, and an enticing display of three hundred pounds of gold, safely protected from prying fingers. The seasonal **Butterfly Pavilion** (mid-April to early Oct) and **Spider Pavilion** (mid-Sept to early Nov) require timed tickets (both an extra $5 for adults and $3 for kids).

The Watts Towers

1765 E 107th St • Tours (30min) every 30min Thurs–Sat 10.30am–3pm, Sun 12.30–3pm • $7 • ☎ 213 847 4646, ⓦ wattstowers.org • Metro Blue Line to 103rd St/Watts Towers

The district of **Watts**, on the eastern side of South LA and nine miles south of Downtown, achieved notoriety as the scene of the six-day **Watts Riots** of August 1965. Today it remains an edgy part of the city with a persistent gang problem despite falling crime rates and attempts to revitalize the area. There is one good reason to come here: to see the internationally famous, Gaudí-esque **Watts Towers**, one of Southern California's most iconic visual landmarks. Constructed from iron, stainless steel, old bedsteads and cement, and decorated with fragments of bottles and around 70,000 crushed seashells, these seventeen striking pieces of street art were built by Italian immigrant Simon Rodia, who had no artistic training but laboured over the towers' construction from 1921 to 1954, refusing offers of help and unable to explain either their meaning or why he was building them. Once finished, he left the area, refused to talk about the towers, and faded into obscurity, dying in 1965. Entry is by **guided tour** only, but you can still see the towers through the fence if you visit when it's closed.

The campus includes the **Watts Towers Arts Center** (free), which organizes the Saturday **Day of the Drums Festival** and Sunday **Watts Towers Jazz Festival** on the last weekend in September.

Compton

Despite its fame as the home of many of LA's rappers – NWA, for example, sang venomously of its ills on their album *Straight Outta Compton* – not to mention tennis legends Serena and Venus Williams, **Compton** is not a place where strangers should attempt to sniff out the local music or sports scenes. History buffs, however, might enjoy a stop for the free guided tours at the **Dominguez Rancho Adobe Museum** at 18127 S Alameda St (Wed, Sat & Sun 1pm, 2pm & 3pm; also first Thurs & Fri of each month; ☎310 603 0088, ⓦdominguezrancho.org; best visited by car), a restored Spanish hacienda that chronicles the social ascent of its founder, Juan José Dominguez – one of the soldiers who left Mexico with Padre Junípero Serra's expedition to found the California missions. His long military service was acknowledged in 1784 by the granting of 75,000 acres of land here (long since subdivided into tiny modern parcels). The six main rooms of the 1826 adobe (built by Juan José's descendant Manuel Dominguez) are on display with their original furnishings, or at least replicas of them, and are well worth a look for anyone intrigued by the pre-American period in California.

West Adams

The charming **West Adams** neighbourhood, running along Adams Boulevard from Crenshaw Boulevard to Hoover Street, was one of LA's few racially mixed neighbourhoods in the early part of the twentieth century, and still boasts some terrific architecture from that era. Known in the Twenties and Thirties as **"Sugar Hill"**, it was one of the spots where silent-screen movie stars tended to live, and became a favourite among black celebrities in the 1940s and 1950s; Joe Louis, Little Richard and Ray Charles were all residents, with Charles' studio located at 2107 Washington Blvd. Today the area is remaking itself yet again, this time as the centre of LA's black LGBT community, though Latinos make up half the population.

William Andrews Clark Memorial Library

2520 Cimarron St, at W Adams Blvd • Guided tours by appointment only • Free • ☎ 323 731 8529, ⓦ clarklibrary.ucla.edu • Bus #14, #37

The finest building in West Adams is the French Renaissance **William Andrews Clark Memorial Library**, with its elegant symmetry, yellow-brick walls, formal gardens and grand entrance hall completed in 1926. As millionaire heir to a copper fortune, founder of the LA Philharmonic, and a US Senator from Montana, Clark amassed this great book collection before donating it to UCLA, which continues to oversee it as a non-circulating library. Besides rare volumes by Pope, Fielding, Dryden, Swift and Milton, plus a huge set of letters and manuscripts by Oscar Wilde, the library includes four Shakespeare folios, a group of works by Chaucer, and copies of key documents in American history, such as ones pertaining to the Louisiana Purchase.

WEST ADAMS ARCHITECTURE

West Adams boasts one of the largest collections of historic homes west of the Mississippi, with most built between 1880 and 1925 in diverse architectural styles. Busby Berkeley's old estate, the 1913 **Guasti Villa**, 3500 W Adams Blvd, is a graceful Beaux Arts/Italian Renaissance creation that might fit in nicely in Italy but is now home to a New Age spiritual institute, the Peace Awareness Labyrinth & Gardens (grounds Tues–Fri noon–4pm; free). Nearby, the **Lindsay House**, no. 3424, a terracotta curiosity completed around 1910 with a heavy stone façade and unique tile work, has become the Our Lady of Bright Mount, a Polish Catholic church. Elsewhere, the **South Seas House**, 2301 W 24th St (Mon–Wed 8am–7pm, Thurs 8am–6pm, Fri 9am–6pm, Sat 10am–2pm; free; ☎323 373 9483), is a city-run community centre that you can visit to sample the place's odd 1902 blend of Victorian and Polynesian architecture, while the **Britt House**, 2141 W Adams, is a 1910 Neoclassical gem with grand white columns and adjoining gardens. It's now home to the sports foundation LA84, whose library boasts a large selection of books on athletics (by appointment only; Mon–Fri 8.30am–5pm; free; ⓦla84.org). Finally, **Stimson House** is an iconic Richardsonian Romanesque castle at 2421 S Figueroa St, north of West Adams, built in 1891 for millionaire lumberman Thomas Stimson and now the home of a Sisters of St Joseph of Carondelet convent.

1

Hollywood

Ever since movies and their stars became international symbols of the good life, **HOLLYWOOD** has been a magnet to millions of tourists on celebrity-seeking pilgrimages and an equal number of hopefuls drawn by the prospect of riches and glory. In reality, this is a densely populated, mostly immigrant, low-income residential neighbourhood, and movie stars actually spent little time here – leaving as soon as they could afford to for the privacy of the hills or coast. Even as early as the 1930s Hollywood had developed into a gritty district rife with prostitution and petty thievery, and subsequent decades only accelerated the decline. Although the area continues to be a secondary centre for the film business, with abundant technical service companies such as prop shops and equipment suppliers, all the big film companies (other than Paramount) relocated long ago to places like Burbank. Things have brightened up in the past few years, however, with the construction of new tourist plazas and shopping malls along the legendary stretch of **Hollywood Boulevard.** The contrasting qualities of freshly polished nostalgia, corporate hype and deep-set seediness also make Hollywood one of LA's most diverse areas – and one of its best spots for bar-hopping and clubbing, with a range of affordable options (see p.139).

Hollywood Boulevard

The few short blocks of **Hollywood Boulevard** in downtown Hollywood contain the densest concentration of celebrity glamour and film mythology in the world. The decline that blighted the area from the early 1960s is slowly receding in the face of prolonged efforts by local authorities, from increasing police patrols to inviting all manner of new malls to take root here. Nevertheless the place still gets edgy after dark away from the main tourist zones, when petty thieves go hunting for the odd purse or wallet.

Hollywood and Vine

Today the junction of **Hollywood and Vine** is the nexus for an especially heavy dose of redevelopment, led by the opening of the mammoth **W Hollywood Hotel**. Other Hollywood icons can be found nearby: at 1750 N Vine St the **Capitol Records Building** resembles a stack of 45rpm records and served as the music company's headquarters from 1956 (it was sold to a developer in 2006, but Capitol continues to use the building as its West Coast office); while the 1930 **Pantages Theater**, 6233 Hollywood Blvd (☎323 468 1770, ⊚hollywoodpantages.com), has one of the city's greatest interiors, a melange of Baroque and Art Deco styling that sees mainly touring stage productions.

Hollywood Walk of Fame

Hollywood Blvd (1.3 miles from N Gower St to N La Brea Ave); and Vine St (from Yucca St to Sunset Blvd) • Metro Red Line Hollywood/Highland

Comprising over 2500 pink terrazzo and brass stars embedded in the pavements along fifteen blocks of Hollywood Boulevard and three blocks of Vine, the **Hollywood Walk of Fame** is one of the area's biggest tourist attractions. Started in 1960 by the local chamber of commerce, the Walk honours the big names in radio, television, movies, music and theatre, though selected stars have to attend the unveiling and part with $30,000 (as of 2017) for the privilege of being included: among them are Marlon Brando (1717 Vine St),

---

HOLLYWOOD FARMERS' MARKET

Lining Ivar Avenue and Selma Avenue, between Sunset and Hollywood boulevards, the popular **Hollywood Farmers' Market** (Sun 8am–1pm; ⊚hollywoodfarmersmarket.net; Metro Red Line to Hollywood/Vine Station) features over a hundred vendors selling a variety of produce, from local citrus fruits and avocados to more exotic specimens like cherimoyas.

HOLLYWOOD

1

● SHOPPING	
Amoeba Music	3
Larry Edmunds	
Book Shop	1
Samuel French Theatre	
& Film Bookshop	2

N

● EATING		Roscoe's House of Chicken		Dragonfly	19	■ DRINKING	
25 Degrees	1	and Waffles	7	El Floridita	17	Boardner's	8
Cactus Taqueria	10	Sanamluang Café	5	Fonda Theatre	14	Burgundy Room	11
Fred 62	3	Yuca's	4	Hotel Café	9	Dresden Room	12
Jitlada	8			Sound Nightclub	7	Frolic Room	5
Miceli's	2	■ NIGHTLIFE		Three Clubs	18	Good Luck Bar	16
Moun of Tunis	6	Avalon	1	The Virgil	13	Musso & Frank Grill	3
Off Vine	9	Bar Sinister	6			Stout Burgers & Beer	15
Osteria Mozza	12	Catalina Bar & Grill	2				
Pink's Hot Dogs	11	Couture Los Angeles	10				
Providence	13	Dirty Laundry	4				

■ ACCOMMODATION	
Banana Bungalow	8
Hollywood Bed & Breakfast	7
Hollywood Celebrity	2
Magic Castle Hotel	6
Orange Drive Hostel	1
Orchid Suites	3
The Redbury	4
USA Hostels – Hollywood	5

Marlene Dietrich (6400 Hollywood Blvd), Michael Jackson (6927 Hollywood Blvd), Elvis Presley (6777 Hollywood Blvd) and Ronald Reagan (6374 Hollywood Blvd). Notable by their absence, Julia Roberts, Robert Redford and Dustin Hoffman are just three of the A-listers that (as yet) have refused to turn up. Look out for the unique moon-shaped monuments to the Apollo 11 mission, at the corners of Hollywood and Vine.

Egyptian Theatre

6712 Hollywood Blvd • Tours, one a month, Sat 10.30am • Tours $9; films $11 • ☎ 323 466 3456, ⓦ americancinemathequecalendar.com • Metro Red Line Hollywood/Highland

The venerable **Egyptian Theatre** was the site of the very first Hollywood premiere (*Robin Hood*, an epic swashbuckler starring Douglas Fairbanks Sr) in 1922. Financed by impresario **Sid Grauman**, the Egyptian was a glorious fantasy in its heyday, modestly seeking to re-create the Temple of Thebes, with usherettes dressed as Cleopatra. It has since been lovingly restored by the American Cinematheque film foundation and now plays an assortment of classics, documentaries, avant-garde flicks and foreign films to small but appreciative crowds. Excellent one-hour **guided tours** (one per month, see the website for dates) take in the projection room and cover the painstaking restoration of the building.

1

Ripley's Believe It or Not! and around

6780 Hollywood Blvd • Daily 10am–midnight • $20, kids (5–12) $10; combo tickets with Wax Museum and Guinness Museum $29.99, kids $17.99 • ☎ 323 466 6335, ⓦ ripleys.com/Hollywood • Metro Red Line Hollywood/Highland

Unless you have very bored kids in attendance, the three cheesy attractions at the eastern corners of the Hollywood and Highland intersection shouldn't detain you, though of the three, the Hollywood branch of the ubiquitous **Ripley's Believe It or Not!** is the most fun. This outpost contains two floors of more than three hundred wacky exhibits, ranging from shrunken heads and two-headed goats, to an actual Autobot Transformer model from the Transformer movies and an ancient Egyptian mummified foot.

The **Hollywood Wax Museum** (Mon–Thurs & Sun 9am–midnight, Fri & Sat 9am–1am; $20, kids (5–12) $10; ⓦ hollywoodwaxmuseum.com) opposite at 6767 Hollywood Blvd is crammed full of life-sized re-creations of movie stars, though Madame Tussauds is more realistic (see below). The **Guinness World Record Museum** (same details as Wax Museum; ⓦ guinnessmuseumhollywood.com) next door at 6764 Hollywood Blvd is housed in the historic **Hollywood Theatre**, opened in 1913 and given a gorgeous Art Deco makeover in 1938. The exhibits inside will appeal to fans of world record factoids, but could do with an update.

Hollywood & Highland Center and Dolby Theatre

6801 Hollywood Blvd **Hollywood & Highland Center** Mon–Sat 10am–10pm, Sun 10am–7pm • Free (parking $2/2hr) • ⓦ hollywoodandhighland.com • **Dolby Theatre** Tours (30min) every 30min daily 10.30am–4pm • $22 • ☎ 323 308 6300, ⓦ dolbytheatre.com • Metro Red Line Hollywood/Highland

The modern **Hollywood & Highland Center**, on the northwest side of the eponymous intersection, was the spur to much recent development in the area, its chain retailers, restaurants and clubs making central Hollywood safe again for corporate America; its specially designed **Dolby Theatre** is the annual location of **the Oscars** (the fun **guided tours** take in the posh Dolby Lounge and the chance to see a real statuette). Still, despite its eye-catching Pop architecture – a replica of the Babylonian set from the 1916 D.W. Griffith spectacular *Intolerance*, with super-sized columns, elephant statues and colossal archway – it's not much different inside to your average suburban mall. The **Hollywood Visitor Information Center** is also here (see p.128).

Madame Tussauds Hollywood

6801 Hollywood Blvd • Daily 10am–7pm (extended hours seasonally, see website) • $29.95 (discounts online) • ☎ 323 798 1670, ⓦ madametussauds.com/Hollywood • Metro Red Line Hollywood/Highland

Like Ripley's Believe it or Not!, Hard Rock Café and Irish-theme pubs, every major city seems to have a **Madame Tussauds** waxworks museum, and Hollywood is no exception, this branch tucked in to the western side of the Hollywood & Highland Center. To be fair, it is quite a spectacle, with a vast array of scarily life-like wax models representing the gamut of Hollywood movies, from Westerns to *Star Trek*, with US sports heroes thrown in.

TCL Chinese Theatre

6925 Hollywood Blvd • Tours (20min) daily 10am–8.30pm (every 15–30min) • Tours $15 • ☎ 323 464 8111, ⓦ tclchinesetheatres.com • Metro Red Line Hollywood/Highland

One site that the Hollywood & Highland Complex has nearly swallowed up is the **TCL Chinese Theatre**, which opened in 1927 and has now expanded into a multiplex,

---

THE OSCARS

The **Academy Awards** (☎ 310 247 3000, ⓦ oscars.org) are usually presented in March at a star-studded ceremony in the Dolby Theatre in the Hollywood & Highland Center (see p.147) on Hollywood Boulevard. Bleacher seats (free) are available to watch the stars arrive on the red carpet, but you have to apply at the Oscars website months in advance (Sept usually).

HOLLYWOOD IMPRESSIONS AT THE CHINESE THEATRE

Opened in 1927 as a lavish setting for premieres of swanky new productions, the **TCL Chinese Theatre** (see opposite) was for many decades *the* spot for movie first nights, and the public crowded behind the rope barriers in the thousands to watch the movie aristocrats arriving for the screenings. The main draw, of course, has always been the assortment of **cement handprints and footprints** embedded in the theatre's forecourt. The idea came about when actress Norma Talmadge accidentally – though some say it was a deliberate publicity stunt – trod in wet cement while visiting the construction site with owner Sid Grauman, who had established a reputation for creating garish movie palaces based on exotic themes. The first formally to leave their marks were Mary Pickford and Douglas Fairbanks Sr, who ceremoniously dipped their digits when arriving for the opening of **King of Kings**, and the practice continues today. It's certainly fun to work out the actual dimensions of your favourite film stars, and to discover if your hands are smaller than Julie Andrews' or your feet bigger than Rock Hudson's.

its main auditorium restored to its gloriously kitschy origins. This was another of Sid Grauman's showpieces from the early days of the movie biz, an odd version of a classical Asian temple, replete with dubious Chinese motifs and upturned dragon-tail flanks, and the lobby's Art Deco splendour and the grand chinoiserie of the auditorium certainly make for fascinating viewing. **Guided tours** of the theatre include a look at VIP seating and balconies for the glitterati who attend premieres of big-budget spectaculars. Afterwards, linger in the theatre's forecourt to see the **handprints** and **footprints** left in cement by Hollywood's big names (see box above). You'll probably encounter hundreds of other sightseers, as well as celebrity impersonators – Elvis, Marilyn and *Star Wars* characters among them – low-rent magicians, smiling hawkers and assorted oddballs vying for your amusement and money.

El Capitan Theatre

6838 Hollywood Blvd • ☎ 866 546 6984, ⓦ elcapitantheatre.com • Metro Red Line Hollywood/Highland

The **El Capitan Theatre** is a colourful 1926 movie palace, with a Spanish Baroque and Moorish façade and a wild South Seas-themed interior of sculpted angels and garlands, plus grotesque sculptures of strange faces and creatures. Twice restored in recent years, the theatre also has one of LA's great signs, a multicoloured profusion of flashing bulbs and neon tubes, and today it hosts Disney premieres (Disney owns it). The old Masonic Temple next door hosts the TV talk show of comedian **Jimmy Kimmel** (which tapes at 4pm Mon–Thurs; for free tickets visit ⓦ 1iota.com or call ☎ 866 546 69849), while on the other side of the theatre kids will go gaga for the **Disney Studio Store and Ghirardelli Soda Fountain** (Mon–Thurs & Sun 10.30am–10pm, Fri & Sat 10.30am–11pm).

Hollywood Museum

1660 N Highland Blvd, at Hollywood • Wed–Sun 10am–5pm • $15 • ☎ 323 464 7776, ⓦ thehollywoodmuseum.com • Metro Red Line Hollywood/Highland

Just south of Hollywood Boulevard, the **Hollywood Museum** exhibits the fashion, art design, props and special effects taken from a broad swath of movie history, including franchises such as the Harry Potter series. Given that this is the old Max Factor Building (1935), there's also a reproduction of Max Factor's movie make-up rooms, where Marilyn Monroe turned into a blonde (she was naturally a brunette). The permanent Monroe collection includes her million-dollar honeymoon dress, make-up bag and Springolator high heels, while various changing exhibits display a hodgepodge of items, from Elvis' bathrobe to Rocky's boxing gloves. The creepy basement contains Hannibal Lecter's entire prison cell from *Silence of the Lambs*.

1

THE ROCK WALK

Around one mile southwest of the Hollywood & Highland Complex lies the celebrated **Guitar Center Hollywood** at 7425 Sunset Blvd (Mon–Fri 10am–9pm, Sat 10am–8pm, Sun 11am–8pm; ☎ 323 874 1060, ⓦ stores.guitarcenter.com/Hollywood). This vast musical-instrument store features the **Rock Walk**, with handprints of over four hundred guitar gods embedded in the manner of the movie stars' at the Chinese Theatre, in this case with performers from AC/DC and ZZ Top to The Cure and Les Paul.

Hollywood Forever Cemetery

6000 Santa Monica Blvd **Grounds** Mon–Fri 8.30am–5pm, Sat & Sun 8.30am–5.30pm (Cathedral Mausoleum daily 10am–2pm) • Free • ☎ 323 469 1181, ⓦ hollywoodforever.com • **Tours** Sat 10am (2hr) • $15 • ☎ 818 517 5988, ⓦ cemeterytour.com • Bus #4 from Vermont/ Santa Monica metro station (Red Line)

Given its location a few blocks south of Sunset Boulevard, it's fitting that the **Hollywood Forever Cemetery** is the final resting place to more of Hollywood's stars than anywhere else. Founded in 1899 and overlooked by the famous water tower of neighbouring Paramount Studios, the cemetery displays myriad tombs of dead celebrities, most notably in its southeastern corner, where the **Cathedral Mausoleum** includes, at no. 1205, the resting place of **Rudolph Valentino**. In 1926, ten thousand people packed the cemetery when the celebrated screen lover died aged just 31, and to this day on each anniversary of his passing (August 23), at least one "**Lady in Black**" will likely be found mourning – a tradition that started as a publicity stunt in 1931 and has continued ever since. Appropriately enough, one of said ladies, historian Karie Bible, serves as a cemetery guide, and her weekly **tours** are great opportunities to find out more about the famous and forgotten names buried here. If you visit in the summer don't miss **Cinespia** (May–Sept Sat 7.30pm; tickets $12–18; ⓦ cinespia.org), when thousands come with beach chairs, blankets, beer, wine (no spirits allowed) and food to sit on the Fairbanks Lawn and watch classic movies projected onto the wall of the mausoleum.

Paramount Studios

Melrose Gate Visitor Entrance, 5555 Melrose Ave, at Windsor Blvd • Tours (2hr) daily 9am–4pm, every 15–30min • $55 • ☎ 323 956 1777, ⓦ paramountstudiotour.com • Bus #10, #48

One of the few true movie-making attractions remaining in Hollywood, the **Paramount Studios** were built in 1917 as the Peralta Studios and purchased by their current owner in 1926. The original iconic arched entrance – which Gloria Swanson rode through in *Sunset Boulevard* – is now inside the complex opposite Bronson Avenue (you can just about see it from Melrose Ave), but the only way to get inside the 65-acre lot is on a **guided tour**. The tours are not quite the standard of Universal's theme-park madness or

TOMBS OF HOLLYWOOD

The most pompous tomb in the **Hollywood Forever Cemetery** (see above) belongs to **Douglas Fairbanks Sr**, who, with his wife Mary Pickford (herself buried at Forest Lawn Glendale), did much to introduce nouveau riche snobbery to Hollywood. Even in death Fairbanks keeps a snooty distance from the pack, his ostentatious memorial (complete with pond) only reachable by a shrub-lined path from the mausoleum. More visually appealing, on the south side of Fairbanks' memorial lake, stands the appropriately black bust of **Johnny Ramone**, showing the punk pioneer rocking out with dark, mop-top intensity (band mate Dee Dee Ramone is also buried here). Further west, **Mel Blanc**, "the man of a thousand voices" – among them Bugs Bunny, Porky Pig, Tweety Bird and Sylvester – has an epitaph that simply reads "That's All, Folks". Other more modest graves to look out for are those of legendary director Cecil B. DeMille, George Harrison (of the Beatles), director John Huston, actor Tyrone Power, Benjamin "Bugsy" Siegel, Terry the dog (Toto in the Wizard of Oz) and cenotaphs to actresses Hattie McDaniel and Jayne Mansfield.

1

Warner Bros' close-up journey, but if you want to poke around sound stages and classic backlots like the New York street (and have plenty of cash), it's definitely worth it.

East Hollywood

East Hollywood lies across Hwy-101 from its tourist-friendly neighbour, a densely populated neighbourhood best known for **Los Angeles City College** and **Barnsdall Art Park** (daily 6am–10pm). The latter has been developed as a cultural hub, comprising the Barnsdall Gallery Theatre, Junior Arts Center and the **Los Angles Municipal Art Gallery** (Thurs–Sun noon–5pm; free; ☎323 644 6269, ⊕lamag.org), which offers a changing programme of contemporary art exhibitions, mainly from Californian artists. The park is also the home of the first LA house designed by **Frank Lloyd Wright**.

Hollyhock House

4800 Hollywood Blvd (Barnsdall Art Park) • Thurs–Sun 11am–4pm • $7 • ☎ 323 913 4030, ⊕ barnsdall.org • Metro Red Line Vermont/Sunset

Set handsomely on a small hill in Barnsdall Art Park, the **Hollyhock House** was architect Frank Lloyd Wright's first contribution to LA. Covered with Maya motifs and geometric renderings of the hollyhock flower, the house, completed in 1921 for oil heiress Aline Barnsdall, is an intriguingly obsessive dwelling, whose original furniture (now replaced by detailed reconstructions) continued the conceptual flow. Visits are self-guided, with docent-led tours (45min) offered Tuesdays and Wednesdays for $70 (reservations required).

Los Feliz

Northeast of East Hollywood, **Los Feliz** is an affluent, hillside district crammed with expensive mansions and celebrity inhabitants – Ryan Reynolds, Scarlett Johansson, Kristen Stewart and Olivia Wilde are all recent residents. It's also the home of several more houses designed by Frank Lloyd Wright and his son. You'll find most of the restaurants and shops on **Hillhurst Avenue,** between Los Feliz Boulevard and Prospect Avenue.

Ennis House

2655 Glendower Ave • ⊕ ennishouse.com • Bus #180/181 from Hollywood/Western metro station (Red Line)

Ennis House, a Lloyd Wright gem completed in 1924, looms over Los Feliz like a Maya temple. One of four of his local structures to feature "textile" concrete blocks, its pre-Columbian appearance has added atmosphere to dozens of film and TV productions, from Vincent Price's *The House on Haunted Hill* to Ridley Scott's *Blade Runner*. The house was sold for around $4.5 million in 2011, but with the stipulation it be open to the public twelve days a year (you can also get a very close look as Glendower Avenue winds around it). Because of ongoing renovation it hasn't opened since the sale – check the website or tour operators (⊕architecturetoursla.com) for the latest.

Lovell House

4616 Dundee Drive • Closed to the public

Deep into the hills of Los Feliz, Richard Neutra's **Lovell House** is a set of sleek, white rectangles and broad window bands that looks quite contemporary for a 1929 building,

---

EAST HOLLYWOOD'S ETHNIC ENCLAVES

East Hollywood is home to two intriguing ethnic enclaves. **Little Armenia** (⊕littlearmenia.com), roughly bounded south of Hollywood Boulevard by US-101, Vermont Avenue and Santa Monica Boulevard, has been home to a sizeable Armenian-American community since the 1970s; highlights include the **St Garabed Armenian Apostolic Church** on Alexandria Avenue. **Thai Town**, just to the north (Hollywood Blvd between Normandie and Western), is crammed with Thai restaurants, markets, shops and massage spas.

1

A HISTORY OF HOLLYWOOD

Strangely enough, Hollywood started life in the 1880s as a **temperance colony**, created to be a sober, God-fearing alternative to raunchy Downtown LA, eight miles away by rough country road. In 1911 residents were forced, in return for a regular water supply, to become an LA suburb. The film industry, then gathering momentum on the East Coast, needed a place with cheap labour, low taxes, compliant government, guaranteed sunshine and a diverse assortment of natural backdrops to stand in for any worldwide location, and most importantly, a distant spot to dodge Thomas Edison's patent trust, which tried to restrict film-making nationwide. Southern California was the perfect spot. A few offices affiliated with Eastern film companies appeared in downtown in 1906 and the first true studios opened in nearby Silver Lake, but independent hopefuls soon discovered the cheaper rents on offer in Hollywood. The first **Hollywood studio** opened in 1911 (the long-vanished Nestor Studio, at the corner of Sunset and Gower), and within three years the place was packed with film-makers – many of them, like **Cecil B. DeMille**, who from 1913 until the early 1920s shared his barn-converted office space with a horse, destined to be the big names of the future.

RICHES AND FAME

The industry expanded fast, bringing riches and fame – with momentum provided by the overnight success of DeMille's *The Squaw Man* (1914), filmed inside the former barn itself, which is now the **Hollywood Heritage Museum** (2100 N Highland Blvd; Sat & Sun noon–4pm; $7; ☎ 323 874 2276, ⓦ hollywoodheritage.org), exhibiting interesting antiques and treasures from the silent era. English vaudeville entertainer **Charlie Chaplin** arrived at Keystone Studios in 1913 (which was still based in Echo Park) – his first movie *Making a Living* was released the following year (the "Little Tramp" character debuted in *Kid Auto Races at Venice* a few months later). Yet movie-making was far from being a financially secure business, and it wasn't until the release of D.W. Griffith's **The Birth of a Nation** in 1914 that the power of film was demonstrated. The film's racist account of the Civil War and Reconstruction caused riots outside cinemas and months of critical debate in the newspapers, and for the first time drew the middle classes to moviehouses – despite the exorbitant $2 ticket price. It also perfected the narrative style and production techniques that gradually became standard in classic Hollywood cinema. Griffith and Chaplin went on to co-found **United Artists** in 1919 with actors Mary Pickford and Douglas Fairbanks, Sr.

ENDURING SUCCESS

Modern Hollywood took shape from the 1920s on, when film production grew more specialized, the "**star system**" was perfected, and many small companies either went bust or were incorporated into one of the handful of bigger studios that came to dominate film-making. The **Golden Age** of the studio system peaked from the 1930s to the late 1940s, when a Supreme Court ruling put an end to studio monopolies owning their own exhibitors and theatres. Despite lean years from the later 1950s until the 1970s, and the onslaught of competition from television and other sources, Hollywood slowly rebounded. These days, the studios have become profitable adjuncts to global media empires; despite releasing a small but steady stream of artsy, thoughtful movies each year, critics point out that the industry relies on $200-million spectacles aimed at teenage boys to keep its accounts balanced, and the creative spark has mostly migrated to cable television. Whatever the structure or quality of the business, though, the film industry's enduring success is in making slick, big spectacle flicks that sell – from Rhett Butler romancing Scarlett O'Hara to the blue aliens of **Avatar**, a movie that made over US$2 billion.

making it one of LA's landmarks of early Modernism. The house is privately owned and rarely opens to the public.

Sowden House

5121 Franklin Ave • Not open for tours • ⓦ sowdenhouse.com

The **Sowden House** is a pink box with concrete jaws designed by Frank Lloyd Wright's son Lloyd in 1926. Though not open for tours (the house is rented for special events), it and other homes in the area can be viewed (at least from the outside) on a trip sponsored by Architecture Tours LA (see box, p.73).

Griffith Park

4730 Crystal Springs Drive • Daily 5am–10.30pm, mountain roads close at dusk • Free • ☎ 323 913 4688, ⓦ laparks.org/griffithpark

Built on land donated by Gilded Age mining millionaire Griffith J. Griffith, vast **GRIFFITH PARK**, between Los Feliz and the San Fernando Valley, offers gentle greenery and rugged mountain slopes, a welcome respite from the chaos of LA. Above the landscaped flat sections, the hillsides are rough and wild, marked only by foot and bridle paths, leading into desolate but unspoiled terrain that gives great views over the LA basin and out towards the ocean. The only thing marring the landscape is the occasional **wildfire**, the most recent of which, in May 2007, burned out well-loved spots like Dante's View. So be alert if you arrive at the height of summer.

There are two **main entrances**. Western Canyon Road, north of Los Feliz Boulevard, enters the park through the **Ferndell** – as the name suggests, a lush glade of ferns, from which numerous trails run deeper into the park – and continues up to the **Griffith Observatory**. The **northern end** of the park, over the hills in the San Fernando Valley, is best reached directly by car from the Golden State Freeway, although you can take the park roads (or explore the labyrinth of hiking trails) that climb the park's hilly core past some of its wildlife lurking in the brush.

Griffith Observatory

2800 E Observatory Rd **Observatory** Tues–Fri noon–10pm, Sat & Sun 10am–10pm • Free • **Planetarium** Tues–Fri 12.45–8.45pm, Sat & Sun 11.45am–8.45pm • $7 • ☎ 213 473 0800, ⓦ griffithobservatory.org

Completed as a WPA (Works Progress Administration) project in 1935, the **Griffith Observatory** is familiar from its use as a backdrop in *Rebel Without a Cause*, *Transformers* and numerous low-budget sci-fi flicks. This astronomical icon now presents an array of high-tech exhibits for young and old alike – highlighted by the twelve-inch Zeiss refracting telescope, the trio of solar telescopes for viewing sunspots and solar storms, and other assorted, smaller telescopes set up on selected evenings for inspecting the firmament at your own pace. A full range of modern exhibits covers the history of astronomy and human observation, including a camera obscura and a 150ft timeline of the universe. The attached **Samuel Oschin Planetarium** shows four different movies on various aspects of the Universe.

Los Angeles Zoo and Botanical Gardens

5333 Zoo Drive • Daily 10am–5pm • $20, kids (2–12) $15 • ☎ 323 644 4200, ⓦ lazoo.org • Bus #96

Kids might enjoy the **Los Angeles Zoo and Botanical Gardens**, one of the biggest zoos in the country and home to a thousand creatures. The biggest draws tend to be Camp

---

ACTIVITIES IN GRIFFITH PARK

The steeper parts of Griffith Park, which blend into the foothills of the Santa Monica Mountains, offer a variety of **hiking trails**, with some 55 miles in the park overall, but there are plenty of other ways to navigate your way over the hillsides. The highest point in the area – the summit of Mount Hollywood (1640ft) – is a good hike for those in shape, but there are plenty of lesser jaunts too. You can get maps at the **Ranger Station**, 4730 Crystal Springs Drive (open daily during daylight hours; ☎ 323 913 4688).

MOUNTAIN BIKING
Spokes 'N Stuff 4730 Crystal Springs Ave ☎ 323 662 6573, ⓦ spokes-n-stuff.com. Rent bikes from this shop near the ranger station, good for touring the upper trails and canyons as well as the easier lower slopes; $8/hr, $25/day, cash only. Summer only Mon–Fri 2pm–dusk, Sat & Sun 10.30am–dusk.

HORSERIDING
Sunset Ranch 3400 N Beachwood Drive ☎ 323 469 5450, ⓦ sunsetranchhollywood.com. Provides guided rides through the area; $40/1hr; $60/2hr. Daily 9am–4pm.

SWIMMING
The Plunge 3401 Riverside Drive and Los Feliz Blvd ☎ 323 644 6878. Griffith Park's historic public swimming pool (built in 1927) is located outdoors (unheated); $3.50, kids (17 and under) $1. Late June to late Aug Mon–Fri 11am–2pm & 3–6pm, Sat & Sun 1–5pm.

Gorilla, its troupe of sixteen chimpanzees, the elephants, rare snow leopards and "Reggie the alligator" (illegally dumped by his former owners).

Travel Town Museum

5200 Zoo Drive • Mon–Fri 10am–4pm, Sat & Sun 10am–6pm • Free; miniature train $2.75 • ☎ 323 662 5874, ⓦ traveltown.org • Bus #96

Close to the LA Zoo, the **Travel Town Museum** maintains a lot full of creaky locomotives and antique trucks from all over Southern California, plus a miniature train that circles the perimeter to keep the little ones occupied.

Forest Lawn Hollywood Hills

6300 Forest Lawn Drive • Daily 8am–5pm • Free • ☎ 323 254 7251, ⓦ forestlawn.com • Bus #222 from Hollywood/Vine metro station (Red Line)

Bounding Griffith Park's northwest rim, **Forest Lawn Hollywood Hills** is a cemetery of the stars that, while not quite as florid as its Glendale counterpart, offers poignant memorials to such figures as Gene Autry, Lucille Ball, Albert "Cubby" Broccoli, David Carradine, Bette Davis, Marvin Gaye, Buster Keaton, Charles Laughton, Stan Laurel, Liberace and Jack Webb. The site also features a replica of Boston's Old North Church, a Liberty Bell and *Birth of Liberty*, a giant mosaic.

The Autry Museum of the American West

4700 Western Heritage Way • Tues–Fri 10am–4pm, Sat & Sun 10am–5pm • $10 • ☎ 323 667 2000, ⓦ theautry.org • Bus #96

The **Autry Museum of the American West**, near the junction of the Ventura and Golden State freeways, was founded in 1988 by **Gene Autry** (1907–98), the "singing cowboy" who cut more than six hundred discs beginning in 1929, starred in blockbuster Hollywood Westerns during the 1930s and 1940s, and became even more of a household name through his TV show in the 1950s. His permanent collection of Americana – from tribal clothing and religious figurines to Albert Bierstadt paintings and Frederic Remington's romantic sculptures of early twentieth-century Western life – offers an insight into the many cultures that have shaped the West.

The Hollywood Hills

Just to the west of Griffith Park, and rising to the north of downtown Hollywood, the **HOLLYWOOD HILLS** feature the most opulent selection of properties to be found in California. Around these canyons and slopes, which run from Hollywood itself into Benedict Canyon above Beverly Hills, mansions are so commonplace that only the half-dozen full-blown castles really stand out (see box below). Beginning at US-101,

---

HOLLYWOOD HILLS' ARCHITECTURAL WONDERS

The architectural highlights of Hollywood Hills include the **Chemosphere**, 776 Torreyson Drive, a giant UFO house hovering above the canyon on a long pedestal, designed by quirky architect John Lautner in 1960 and now home to irreverent publisher Benedikt Taschen; and **Case Study House #21 (or Bailey House)**, 9038 Wonderland Park Ave, Pierre Koenig's 1959 hillside glass-and-steel box, part of the influential Case Study Program that tried to bring Modernism to the middle class in the Forties and Fifties. Koenig's other notable home, **Case Study House #22 (1959)**, also known as the **Stahl House**, 1635 Woods Drive, has an even more spectacular layout, famously perched above a cliff, and including a swimming pool. Best of all, the house is on view for occasional one-hour tours ($60 for one person, or $35 each for two or more; ☎ 208 331 1414, ⓦ stahlhouse.com). Unfortunately, most of the area's other houses are hidden away, and there's no real way to explore in depth without your own car, a copy of the latest *Thomas Guide* map and, if possible, a detailed guide to LA architecture.

1

THE HOLLYWOOD SIGN

The famed **Hollywood sign** began life on the slopes of Mount Lee in 1923 as a billboard for the **Hollywoodland** real estate development and originally contained its full name; however, in 1949 when a storm knocked down the "H" and damaged the rest of the sign, the "land" part was removed and the rest became the familiar symbol of the area and of the entertainment industry. Unfortunately, the current incarnation has literally lost its radiance: it once featured 4000 light bulbs that beamed the district's name as far away as LA Harbor, but a lack of maintenance and an abundance of thievery put an end to that practice.

RESTRICTED ACCESS

The sign has also gained a reputation as a suicide spot, ever since would-be movie star Peg Entwistle terminated her career and life here in 1932, aged 24 – no mean feat, with the sign being as difficult to reach then as it is now. Less fatal mischief has been practised by students of nearby Caltech, who on one occasion renamed the sign for their school, while other defacers have included USC, UCLA, the US Navy and Fox Television. Because of this sullied history, there's no public road to the sign (Beachwood Drive comes nearest, but ends at a closed gate) and you'll incur minor cuts and bruises while scrambling to get anywhere near. In any case, a razor wire fence, infrared cameras and radar-activated zoom lenses have been installed to catch graffiti writers, and innocent tourists who can't resist a closer peek are also liable for a steep fine. The **best views** can be had from the Griffith Observatory (see p.85), and, more distantly, from the junction of Hollywood Blvd and North Highland Ave. For a much easier glimpse, see Ⓦ hollywoodsign.org.

Mulholland Drive, named after LA's most renowned hydro-engineer, runs west along the crest, providing magnificent vistas of the Los Angeles basin and the San Fernando Valley at night, when both spread out like sparkling grids for many miles below.

The Hollywood Bowl

2301 N Highland Ave • Los Angeles Philharmonic concerts July–Sept • ☎ 323 850 2000, Ⓦ hollywoodbowl.com • Bus #237 from Hollywood/Highland metro station (Red Line)

Near the Hollywood Freeway, the **Hollywood Bowl** is a natural amphitheatre that's better known for its bandshell, which is an open-air auditorium that opened in 1921 and has since become something of an icon for outdoor stages. The Beatles played here in the mid-1960s, but the Bowl's principal function is as the occasional summer home of the Los Angeles Philharmonic. The **Hollywood Heritage Museum** (see box, p.84) is located in parking lot D.

Hollywood Bowl Museum

2301 N Highland Ave • Late June to late Sept Tues–Sat 10am–showtime, Sun 4pm–showtime • Late Sept to late June Tues–Fri 10am–5pm • Free • ☎ 323 850 2058, Ⓦ hollywoodbowl.com

An overview of the Bowl's history can be gleaned from the video inside the **Hollywood Bowl Museum** near the entrance. The auditorium has gone through many incarnations and composition materials, from concrete and fibreglass to steel and even cardboard (for acoustics). With a collection of musical instruments from around the world, the museum also features recordings of notable symphonic moments in the Bowl's history and architectural drawings by Lloyd Wright, Frank's son, who contributed a design for one of the many shells.

West LA

What is loosely called the **Westside** of Los Angeles begins immediately beyond Hollywood in **WEST LA** – which contains some of the city's most expensive neighbourhoods. Bordered by the Santa Monica Mountains to the north and the Santa

1

Monica Freeway to the south, and Hollywood and the beach cities to the respective east and west, this swath of the city best embodies the stylish images that Los Angeles projects to the outside world.

Highlights include the impressive collection of the **LA County Museum of Art (LACMA)**, the restaurants and boutiques of **West Hollywood**, **Beverly Hills** and the **UCLA campus** in **Westwood**, though you should also make time for the outstanding **Getty Center**, positioned high above the LA basin.

Fairfax District

The heart of Los Angeles's Jewish community from the 1950s to the 1970s, the **Fairfax District** lies to the east of **Fairfax Avenue**, and is still laced with temples, yeshivas, kosher butcher shops and delis.

Farmers' Market

6333 W 3rd St, at Fairfax Ave • Mon–Fri 9am–9pm, Sat 9am–8pm, Sun 10am–7pm • Free • ☎ 323 933 9211, ⊕ farmersmarketla.com • Bus #16, #17, #316

The most enticing attraction in Fairfax District is the long-standing **Farmers' Market**, a rabbit warren of restaurants, bakeries and produce stands. Started in 1934 as a little agricultural co-op, the market has since expanded to the point where it's a social phenomenon in its own right, always buzzing with tourists and locals who come to meet and eat and, increasingly, to shop.

The Grove

189 The Grove Drive, off 3rd St • Mon–Thurs 10am–9pm, Fri & Sat 10am–10pm, Sun 10am–8pm • Free • ☎ 323 900 8080, ⊕ thegrovela .com • Bus #16, #17, #316

Next door to the Farmer's Market, **The Grove** is a three-level, $100-million mall that offers branches of all the major chain stores, a fourteen-screen cinema, dancing fountain (on the hour), the "Spirit of Los Angeles" bronze statue and a free trolley (Mon–Thurs & Sun noon–7.45pm, Fri & Sat 1–8.45pm) that trundles the three-quarters of a mile to the market.

CBS Television City

7800 Beverly Blvd, at Fairfax Ave • Apply for free CBS tickets at ☎ 323 570 0059, ⊕ cbstelevisioncity.com • Bus #14, #37

The **CBS Television City** studio complex is a sprawling black cube built in 1952 – and something of an architectural eyesore – but a worthwhile destination if you fancy sitting in an audience for long-running game show *The Price Is Right*, the network's *Late Late Show with James Corden* (Mon–Thurs 3pm; standby tickets sometimes available at 3pm) or HBO late-night series *Real Time with Bill Maher* (Fri 5.30pm; apply for free tickets at ⊕ real-time-with-bill-maher-blog.com or ☎ 323 575 4321).

Los Angeles Museum of the Holocaust

100 S The Grove Drive (Pan Pacific Park) • Mon–Thurs, Sat & Sun 10am–5pm, Fri 10am–2pm • Free • ☎ 323 651 3704, ⊕ lamoth.org • Bus #14, #37

Leafy **Pan Pacific Park** contains the thought-provoking **Museum of the Holocaust**, charting the terrible history of the Nazi era 1933 to 1945 using interactive technology and multimedia exhibits. The experience is quite chilling: lights dim as you enter the lower galleries, and you end up at the harrowing "Concentration Camps" exhibit. You exit the museum at the astounding Tree of Testimony, a seventy-screen video sculpture wall, and the similarly poignant **Los Angeles Holocaust Monument**, featuring six 18ft black-granite columns (each representing a million Jews killed by the Nazis) inscribed with the events of that horrific period.

The Miracle Mile

1

To the south of the Fairfax District, **Miracle Mile** is the 1.5-mile section of Wilshire Boulevard between Fairfax and Highland avenues (also known as **Mid-Wilshire**), the premier property development strip of the 1930s and still lined with faded Art Deco monuments – none better than the **El Rey Theatre**, 5515 Wilshire Blvd, a thriving concert venue (see p.142) with a flashy neon sign. Today the strip is best known for its museums, giving it another nickname, "**Museum Row**".

Los Angeles County Museum of Art

5905 Wilshire Blvd • Mon, Tues & Thurs 11am–5pm, Fri 11am–8pm, Sat & Sun 10am–7pm • $15 • ☎ 323 857 6000, ⓦ lacma.org • Bus #720 from Wilshire/Western metro station (Purple Line)

The **Los Angeles County Museum of Art** (LACMA) is one of the largest museums west of the Mississippi, a seven-building complex containing around 100,000 objects dating from ancient times to the present. Critics argue that the complex is architecturally muddled and that it lacks major showstoppers, but aficionados will still find plenty of gems here, especially in the **Pavilion for Japanese Art**.

The Ahmanson Building – Levels 1 and 2

From the main entrance, turning right (east) takes you to the four-floor **Ahmanson Building**, which opens with some rare Polynesian artefacts in the **Art of the Pacific** galleries (Level 1), though most visitors make for the **modern art** galleries on Level 2, which are especially rich in the work of **Picasso**. His classic Blue Period *Portrait of Sebastia Juñer Vidal* is on show in gallery 225, while his anguished *Weeping Woman with Handkerchief* usually resides in gallery 234 (along with Magritte's distinctive *Ceci n'est pas une pipe*). Gallery 211 is also packed with Picasso's work, including the startling *Women of Algiers, after Delacroix*. Other highlights on this level are a compelling collection of **German Expressionism** and **Abstract** art from the likes of Kandinsky and Klee (210), and Dix and Beckmann (207), plus giant canvases from Warhol, Clyfford Still, de Kooning (*Montauk Highway*), Pollock and Rothko (galleries 217–219). Don't miss *La Gerbe* in the entrance lobby, a huge ceramic installation by Matisse commissioned for an LA couple in the 1950s and later transported here.

The Ahmanson Building – Levels 3 and 4

Level 3 of the Ahmanson provides an overview of **European art** from medieval religious imagery to a rather unfashionable collection of Renaissance, Mannerist and French Neoclassical works. There's plenty of good stuff here, however, including El Greco's *The Apostle Saint Andrew*, an uncommonly reserved portrait (308); Paolo Veronese's twin paintings *Allegories of Navigation*, vivid Mannerist figures filling the frame from an imposing low angle; and Titian's *Portrait of Giacomo Dolfin*, a carefully tinted study by the great colourist (all in gallery 315). Gallery 309 contains some decent Impressionist work from the usual suspects, with Renoir's *Two Girls Reading*, a couple of rustic images from Gauguin and Monet's energetic portrait of Le Havre port the standouts. Northern European paintings include Hans Holbein's tiny but resplendent *Portrait of a Young Woman with White Coif* (along with giant canvases by Rubens and Frans Snyders in gallery 320), a number of Frans Hals pictures of cheerful burghers (324), and Rembrandt's probing *Portrait of Marten Looten* and *Raising of Lazarus* (324). Level 4 contains a moderately interesting sample of **Islamic Art** and sculptures and artefacts from **South and Southeast Asia**.

The Hammer Building

The second floor of the **Hammer Building** (connected to the Ahmanson on the third floor) is crammed with **Chinese and Korean artworks** such as ancient lacquerware trays, hanging scrolls, bronze drinking vessels, glazed stone bowls and jade figurines. Level 3

1

THE WESTSIDE

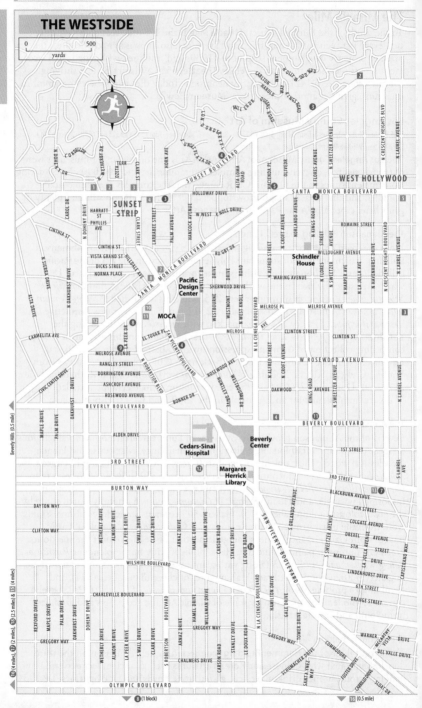

0 — 500
yards

N

WEST HOLLYWOOD

SUNSET STRIP

SUNSET STRIP

SANTA MONICA BOULEVARD

SUNSET BOULEVARD

HOLLOWAY DRIVE

Schindler House

Pacific Design Center

MOCA

MELROSE AVENUE

BEVERLY BOULEVARD

Cedars-Sinai Hospital

Beverly Center

Margaret Herrick Library

BURTON WAY

WILSHIRE BOULEVARD

3RD STREET

OLYMPIC BOULEVARD

Beverly Hills (0.5 mile)

15 (4 miles), 17 (2 miles), 18 (2.5 miles) & 13 (4 miles)

8 (1 block)

16 (0.5 mile)

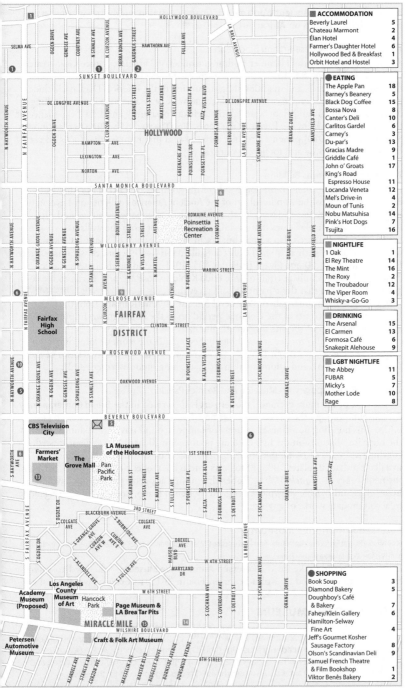

ACCOMMODATION

Beverly Laurel	5
Chateau Marmont	2
Élan Hotel	4
Farmer's Daughter Hotel	6
Hollywood Bed & Breakfast	1
Orbit Hotel and Hostel	3

EATING

The Apple Pan	18
Barney's Beanery	5
Black Dog Coffee	15
Bossa Nova	8
Canter's Deli	10
Carlitos Gardel	6
Carney's	3
Du-par's	13
Gracias Madre	9
Griddle Café	1
John o' Groats	17
King's Road Espresso House	11
Locanda Veneta	12
Mel's Drive-in	4
Moun of Tunis	2
Nobu Matsuhisa	14
Pink's Hot Dogs	7
Tsujita	16

NIGHTLIFE

1 Oak	1
El Rey Theatre	14
The Mint	16
The Roxy	2
The Troubadour	12
The Viper Room	4
Whisky-a-Go-Go	3

DRINKING

The Arsenal	15
El Carmen	13
Formosa Café	6
Snakepit Alehouse	9

LGBT NIGHTLIFE

The Abbey	11
FUBAR	5
Micky's	7
Mother Lode	10
Rage	8

SHOPPING

Book Soup	3
Diamond Bakery	5
Doughboy's Café & Bakery	7
Fahey/Klein Gallery	6
Hamilton-Selway Fine Art	4
Jeff's Gourmet Kosher Sausage Factory	8
Olson's Scandinavian Deli	9
Samuel French Theatre & Film Bookshop	1
Viktor Benês Bakery	2

houses the **Art of the Ancient World** gallery (mainly Assyrian and Egyptian artefacts), plus revolving exhibits on **African Art**.

The Pavilion for Japanese Art and Bing Center

At the eastern end of the Hammer Building, iconoclastic architect Bruce Goff created the exquisite **Pavilion for Japanese Art** to re-create the effects of traditional shoji screens, filtering varying levels and qualities of light through to the interior. Displays include painted screens and scrolls, ceramics and lacquerware, viewable on a ramp spiralling down to a small, ground-floor waterfall that trickles pleasantly amid the near-silence of the gallery. Across from the Pavilion, the **Leo S. Bing Theater** in the **Bing Center** (movies $15; ☎323 857 6010) presents a regular series of film programmes that focus on classic Hollywood, art-house and foreign favourites.

The Art of the Americas Building

Next to the Bing Center on the south side of the complex, the **Art of the Americas Building** is home to the wonderful **Art of the Ancient Americas** galleries on Level 4; Jorge Pardo's controversial design for this section is a cross between a cave and hip lounge bar, with display cases that undulate and swell out from the walls in a vivid tangerine colour. There's also a small but fascinating collection of Spanish Colonial art by Mexican artists such as Miguel Cabrera (galleries 408–409), and classic images from Rufino Tamayo and **Diego Rivera** (galleries 405–406), including the latter's iconic *Flower Day* and his only portrait of wife **Frida Kahlo** (whose *Weeping Coconuts* is also in gallery 406). Note that these paintings often revolve.

The more conventional galleries on Level 3 focus on **American art**, from the landscapes and portraits of the Colonial period up to the home-grown Impressionism and Social Realism of the late nineteenth and early twentieth centuries. Although the collection here is also rotated, typical highlights include the work of John Singleton Copley (the regal *Portrait of a Lady*; 313), Winslow Homer (the dusty realism of the *Cotton Pickers*; 313), and Thomas Eakins (the writhing, nude *Wrestlers*; 312).

The Broad Contemporary Art Museum and Resnick Pavilion

To the west of the main entrance, **modern art** is showcased in the **Broad Contemporary Art Museum**, though the key collection is now housed in the Broad downtown (see p.67). This building now houses an array of temporary and travelling exhibits, though the huge installations on the first floor are permanent; Richard Serra's giant, rusted, curving steel walls of *Band*; the brilliant *Metropolis II* by Chris Burden (a kinetic installation that circulates 100,000 toy cars through a model city every Fri & Sat); and the neon tubes of *Miracle Mile* by Robert Irwin. Just adjacent, the **Resnick Pavilion**, a huge, glass-and-marble showpiece designed by Renzo Piano, houses temporary galleries to accommodate works of any size.

Petersen Automotive Museum

6060 Wilshire Blvd, at Fairfax Ave • Daily 10am–6pm • $15 (parking $12 after first 30min) • ☎ 323 930 2277, Ⓦ petersen.org • Bus #720 from Wilshire/Western metro station (Purple Line)

Car lovers should make for the **Petersen Automotive Museum** – the hard-to-miss building was renovated by Kohn Pedersen Fox in 2015, its exterior wrapped in a

---

THE ACADEMY MUSEUM

Los Angeles and Hollywood have been crying out for a decent museum dedicated to the movies and the Oscars for years, and it finally looks like happening; sometime in 2018 the spanking new, Renzo Piano-designed **Academy Museum** should be open next door to LACMA (see p.89) on Wilshire Boulevard. LACMA has donated the 1939 May Company department store building at the corner of Wilshire and Fairfax to the museum. Visit Ⓦ oscars.org/museum for the latest.

mesh of stainless-steel ribbons, lit by glowing red LED lights. Inside are three floors loaded with all kinds of vehicles, with periodic exhibits on topics like the golden age of custom cars in the 1950s and 1960s and "million-dollar" vehicles such as the 1919 Bentley and 1961 Ferrari. Visits begin on the third "**History**" floor, which takes you on a journey through California's vehicular past, including a gallery dedicated to Hollywood (think Batmobile and the Pontiac Aztek from *Breaking Bad*). "**Industry**" is the theme of the second floor, with the Customization Gallery featuring hot rods and custom cars. The **Forza Motorsports Racing Experience**, a racing car simulator, is also on this floor. The first floor is dedicated to "**Artistry**", featuring the BMW Art Car collection, with cars adorned by the likes of Alexander Calder, David Hockney and Robin Rhode.

La Brea Tar Pits and Museum

5801 Wilshire Blvd **Tar Pits** Daily 6am–10pm • Free • **Page Museum** Daily 9.30am–5pm • $12 (parking $12) • ☎ 323 934 7243, ⊚ tarpits.org • Bus #720 from Wilshire/Western metro station (Purple Line)

The **La Brea Tar Pits**, comprising the larger Lake Pit and scores of smaller pools of smelly, viscous asphalt (it's not technically tar) in **Hancock Park**, are one of LA's most famous natural formations. Tens of thousands of years ago during the last Ice Age, primeval creatures from tapirs to mammoths tried to drink from the thin layer of water covering the petroleum in the pits, only to become stuck fast and preserved for modern science. Millions of bones belonging to the animals (and one set of human bones) have been found here since 1913 (the site was previously developed as an oil field), with some of them displayed in the **Page Museum**, where you can spot the skeletons of your favourite extinct creatures, from giant ground sloths to menacing sabre-toothed tigers. Films in the **3-D Theater** (extra $4) bring the site to life, and **Excavator Tours** (included) take you around the whole park and into the **Observation Pit** and **Project 23** dig site on the west side (otherwise off-limits). The park itself is free to wander, with **Pit 91** the best place to get a sense of what an archeological dig in a tar pit looks like.

Craft and Folk Art Museum

5814 Wilshire Blvd • Tues–Fri 11am–5pm, Sat & Sun 11am–6pm • $7 • ☎ 323 937 4230, ⊚ cafam.org • Bus #720 from Wilshire/Western metro station (Purple Line)

The **Craft and Folk Art Museum** has a small selection of handmade objects from all over the world – rugs, pottery, clothing and so on – with rotating exhibitions featuring the likes of handmade tarot cards, ceramic folk art and highly detailed Asian textiles.

West Hollywood

Between Fairfax Avenue and Beverly Hills, **West Hollywood** is synonymous with social tolerance and upmarket trendiness, and has a sizeable LGBT contingent. **Santa Monica Boulevard** is the district's main drag, where you'll find flashy dance clubs and bars, with the hub of social activity around the intersection with **San Vicente Boulevard**. The **West Hollywood Design District** (loosely centred between San Vicente, Melrose Ave and Robertson and Beverly blvds; ⊚ westhollywooddesigndistrict.com), features galleries, furniture designers and fashion boutiques. Check out the celebrated **Phyllis Morris** furniture showroom at 655 N Robertson Blvd (Mon–Fri 10am–5pm).

Melrose Avenue

Four blocks south of Santa Monica Boulevard is **Melrose Avenue**, which between Fairfax Avenue and Doheny Drive is LA's trendiest shopping street, in its heyday an eccentric world of its own, thick with underground art galleries, palm readers and head shops. Since the 1990s, though, a crush of designer shops, salons and restaurants has been gaining ground at the expense of the quirkier tenants, though there are still enough curiosities and eye-popping boutiques to make for an interesting stroll.

1

LITTLE ETHIOPIA

For a tiny taste of East Africa visit the **Little Ethiopia** district, the stretch of Fairfax Ave between Olympic Blvd and Whitworth Drive in West LA, home to numerous Ethiopian restaurants, stores and businesses.

Pacific Design Center

8687 Melrose Ave • Mon–Fri 9am–5pm • ☎ 310 657 0800, ⓦ pacificdesigncenter.com • Bus #704

The west end of Melrose, near San Vicente Boulevard, is dominated by the hulking, bright-blue glassy pile of the **Pacific Design Center**, a marketplace for more than a hundred art galleries and stores designed by César Pelli in 1975. It's known as the "Blue Whale" for the way it dwarfs its low-rise neighbours, along with its counterparts, the geometric Green Building (1988) and Red Building (2012) superblocks.

MOCA Pacific Design Center

8687 Melrose Ave • Tues–Fri 11am–5pm, Sat & Sun 11am–6pm • Free • ☎ 310 289 5223, ⓦ moca.org • Bus #704

Overshadowed by the giant Red and Green buildings behind it, the modest **MOCA Pacific Design Center** focuses on architecture and design with a sleek, modern bent, often participating in exhibitions with MOCA (see p.66) and Geffen Contemporary (see p.69).

MAK Center for Art and Architecture

835 N Kings Rd • Wed–Sun 11am–6pm • $7; free Fri 4–6pm • ☎ 323 651 1510, ⓦ makcenter.org • Metro Red Line to Vermont Beverly (then take northbound #10 or #11 bus)

Two blocks north of Melrose, the **MAK Center for Art and Architecture** plays host to a range of avant-garde music, art, film and design exhibitions. The centre occupies the 1922 **Schindler House**, for years the blueprint of California Modernist architecture, designed by Austrian émigré architect R.M. Schindler with sliding canvas panels meant to be removed in summer, exposed roof rafters and open-plan rooms facing onto outdoor terraces.

Sunset Strip

Above West Hollywood, the roughly two-mile-long conglomeration of restaurants, plush hotels and nightclubs on Sunset Boulevard has long been known as the **Sunset Strip**. Many tourists come to the strip to see the renowned *Whisky-a-Go-Go* club (see box below), while others come just to check out the enormous **billboards**: fantastic

THE SUNSET STRIP MUSIC SCENE

Sunset Strip came to national fame in the 1960s when a scene developed around the landmark **Whisky-a-Go-Go** club, 8901 Sunset Blvd, which featured seminal rock bands such as Love and Buffalo Springfield, as well as the manic theatrics of Jim Morrison and the Doors. In the 1970s and 1980s it became a haven for heavy and glam rockers, notably Van Halen and Guns N' Roses. More recently, LA bands Jane's Addiction, Rage Against The Machine, Red Hot Chili Peppers and Linkin Park have started careers on the Strip. Although no longer rock central for genuine indie bands – look for that around Echo Park and Silver Lake – there are still enough clubs to keep music tourists occupied for a night or two.

The rock scene is focused on the west side of the strip (see p.142) around *Whisky-a-Go-Go* and *Roxy*, no. 9009, both of which still offer shows from some of the loudest and angriest rock and punk bands, with *Viper Room*, no. 8852, also providing a thrill for indie rock and DJ sets in the same area. Times are a-changin' though – the annual **Sunset Strip Music Festival** held its last event in 2014, and posh hotels and boutiques are now more prevalent than grungy clubs and bars.

commercial murals animated with eye-catching gimmicks, movie ads with names of celebrities in gargantuan letters, and half-naked models hawking the trendiest brands of perfume, jewellery, clothing and spirits.

Beverly Hills

Probably the most famous neighbourhood in the world, **Beverly Hills** has, through its relentless PR machine, made itself internationally synonymous with free-spending wealth and untrammelled luxury, if not necessarily good taste. The town divides into two distinct halves, separated by Santa Monica Boulevard. To the south is the flashy **Golden Triangle** business district, which fills the wedge between Santa Monica and Wilshire boulevards, ground zero for window-shopping and gawking at major and minor celebrities. **Rodeo Drive** cuts through the triangle in a two-block-long, concentrated showcase of the most expensive names in international fashion. It's a dauntingly stylish area, each boutique trying to outshine the rest, crowned by the tourist trap of **Two Rodeo** at Wilshire, a faux-European shopping alley that is the height of pretentious kitsch, its phoney cobblestone street hiding a parking lot below.

1

Paley Center for Media
465 N Beverly Drive • Wed–Sun noon–5pm • Free, suggested donation $10 (parking free) • ☎ 310 786 1000, Ⓦ paleycenter.org • Bus #720 (Beverly and Wilshire)

The entertaining **Paley Center for Media** features a collection of more than 140,000 television and radio programmes and presents rotating exhibits on famous TV characters from the twentieth century, and the best of radio and TV sitcoms, dramas and thrillers.

Beverly Hills Hotel
9641 Sunset Blvd, at Rodeo Drive • ☎ 310 276 2251 • Bus #2, #302

Above Santa Monica Boulevard is the posh part of residential Beverly Hills, its gently curving drives converging on the highly iconic florid pink-plaster **Beverly Hills Hotel** (see p.129). Built in 1913 to attract wealthy settlers to what was then a town of just five hundred people, the hotel's social cachet makes its *Polo Lounge* a prime spot for movie execs to power lunch.

Virginia Robinson Gardens
1008 Elden Way • Tours Tues 10.30am & 1.30pm, Sat 2pm, by appointment only (check website for current schedule) • $11 • ☎ 310 550 2087, Ⓦ robinsongardens.org • Bus #2, #302

In the verdant canyons and foothills above Sunset, a number of palatial estates lie hidden away behind landscaped security gates. One of the few open to the public is the wooded **Virginia Robinson Gardens**, which holds six acres of over a thousand plant varieties, including some impressive Australian king palm trees, around a Beaux Arts-style mansion and iconic Renaissance Revival pool pavilion. Built in 1911 for retail tycoons Virginia and Harry Robinson, the mansion was one of the first in the area; tours include a walk through the antique-laden house, but mostly focus on the gardens.

Greystone Mansion and Park
905 Loma Vista Drive • Park daily 10am–5pm • Free • ☎ 310 285 6830, Ⓦ greystonemansion.org • Bus #2, #302

The biggest house in Beverly Hills, 50,000-square-foot Tudor-style **Greystone Mansion**, was built in 1928 by oil titan Edward Doheny (his son, Ned, was shot to death here one year later). It's a favourite movie location, appearing in *There Will Be Blood* (2007), *The Big Lebowski* (1998) and even *Star Trek Into Darkness* (2013) amongst many others. Though rarely open, the mansion does host Friends of Greystone events throughout the year (check the website), and the **Music in the Mansion** chamber music programme (monthly Sundays Jan–June, 2pm; $20; ☎310 285 6850). The grounds are now maintained as a public park by the city as **Greystone Park**, so you can admire the mansion's limestone façade and intricately designed chimneys for free, then stroll through the sixteen-acre gardens, where you'll find koi-filled ponds and expansive views of the LA sprawl.

Century City and around
The bland high-rise boxes of **Century City**, just west of Beverly Hills, were erected during the 1960s on what was the backlot of the 20th Century-Fox film studio. The district's main focus, as is so often the case in LA, is a large shopping mall, **Westfield**

BEVERLY HILLS TROLLEY

For a complete overview of the shopping scene, including Rodeo Drive and beyond, take a forty-minute trip on the **Beverly Hills Trolley**, which offers tourists a glimpse of the town's highlights. The trolley departs hourly from the corner of Rodeo Drive and Dayton Way (Jan–June & Sept–Nov Sat & Sun 11am–4pm; also July, Aug & Dec Tues–Sun same hours; $5; ☎ 310 285 112).

1

MANOR, MADNESS AND MURDER AT GREYSTONE

If you visit Beverly Hills in the winter be sure to attend one of Theatre 40's special performances of **The Manor** by Katherine Bates; the audience follows the actors through the first floor of Greystone Mansion (see opposite) as the tragedy unfolds. Performances run throughout January and February, and occasionally in the summer (tickets $60; ☎ 310 364 0535, ⓦ theatre40.org).

Century City (Mon–Sat 10am–9pm, Sun 11am–7pm), 10250 Santa Monica Blvd, which is loaded with upscale boutiques and department stores and one of the better moviehouses for current films. To the southwest, the still-functional **20th Century-Fox** studios are strictly off-limits and don't offer tours.

Annenberg Space for Photography

2000 Ave of the Stars • Wed–Sun 11am–6pm • Free • ☎ 213 403 3000, ⓦ annenbergspaceforphotography.org • Bus #28

The top cultural attraction in Century City is the **Annenberg Space for Photography**, a series of fabulous galleries exhibiting both digital and print photography – the circular digital gallery is especially eye-popping. Exhibits change every six months.

Museum of Tolerance

9786 W Pico Blvd, at Roxbury Drive • Mon–Fri & Sun 10am–5pm; Nov–March closes at 3.30pm on Fri • $15.50 • **Anne** Mon–Wed & Sun 10am–6.30pm, Thurs 10am–9.30pm, Fri 10am–5pm; Nov–March closes at 3.30pm on Fri • $15.50 • ☎ 310 553 8403, ⓦ museumoftolerance.com • Bus #28

In the eastern section of Century City below Beverly Hills, the poignant **Museum of Tolerance** is an extraordinary interactive experience established by the Simon Wiesenthal Center to chart the story of Fascism and the genocide of Jews and other atrocities in contemporary world history. Among other exhibits, it leads the visitor through multimedia re-enactments outlining the rise of Nazism to a harrowing conclusion in a replica gas chamber. The newest exhibit (with separate admission), simply entitled "**Anne**", focuses on the life and legacy of **Anne Frank** through rare artefacts, photographs and a copy of her original diary.

Westwood and UCLA

Just west of Beverly Hills, on the north side of Wilshire Boulevard, **WESTWOOD** is one of LA's more user-friendly neighbourhoods, a grouping of low-slung Spanish Revival buildings that went up in the late 1920s under the name **Westwood Village**. It's based around **Broxton Avenue**, along with the nearby campus of the nascent **University of California, Los Angeles (UCLA)**, which had moved from East Hollywood. Because of its ease for pedestrians, the neighbourhood has limited and expensive street parking; for minimum frustration, find a cheap parking lot and dump your vehicle there for a few hours while you explore.

Hammer Museum

10899 Wilshire Blvd, at Westwood • Tues–Fri 11am–8pm, Sat & Sun 11am–5pm • $10; free Thurs • ☎ 310 443 7000, ⓦ hammer.ucla.edu • Bus #720

Art lovers should not miss UCLA's **Hammer Museum**, home of the largest collection of works by French satirist **Honoré Daumier** outside of Paris, as well as a cache of minor works by Titian, Rembrandt and Rubens. The museum was founded by businessman **Armand Hammer** (1899–1990), former Chairman of Occidental Petroleum, and still houses his personal collection of **nineteenth-century French art**, including works by Edgar Degas, Paul Cézanne, Paul Gauguin, Vincent van Gogh, and Camille Pissarro. Be sure to also seek out his impressive trove of American paintings by Gilbert Stuart, Thomas Eakins and John Singer Sargent. The museum also features rotating exhibits from the university's Grunwald Center holdings of more than 45,000 prints, drawings

1

and photographs – recent acquisitions include a collection of drawings and works on paper by Jackson Pollock, Willem de Kooning, Andy Warhol and Ed Ruscha.

Westwood Village Memorial Park

1218 Glendon Ave (just south of Wilshire Blvd) • Daily 8am–5pm • Free • ☎ 310 474 1579, ⓦ dignitymemorial.com • Bus #720

Oil magnate Armand Hammer (see p.97), was buried in 1990 in a speckled marble tomb sharing the tiny cemetery of **Westwood Village Memorial Park** with the likes of movie stars Jack Lemmon, Farrah Fawcett, Natalie Wood, Burt Lancaster and Dean Martin, authors Truman Capote and Ray Bradbury, jazz drummer Buddy Rich, and, to the left of the entrance in the far northeast corner, **Marilyn Monroe**, who rests under a lipstick-covered plaque (Playboy Hugh Hefner paid $75,000 for the crypt next to her).

The UCLA campus

405 Hilgard Ave • ☎ 310 825 4321, ⓦ ucla.edu • Parking available on campus: $1/20min–$20/day from self-service pay stations; $12 day-pass available from parking booths • Bus #720

On the northern side of Westwood, the **UCLA campus** comprises a group of lovely Romanesque Revival structures and more angular modern buildings spread across well-landscaped grounds. It's worth a wander if you've time to kill, particularly for a couple of good exhibition spaces. Before embarking on your exploration, pick up a **map** from various information kiosks scattered around campus.

Mildred E. Mathias Botanical Garden

777 Tiverton Drive • Mon–Fri 8am–5pm, Sat & Sun 8am–4pm • Free • ☎ 310 825 1260, ⓦ botgard.ucla.edu

A good place to start in the UCLA campus is the **Mildred E. Mathias Botanical Garden**, a bucolic glade containing almost four thousand rare and native species on the east side of the university, where you can pick your way along sloping paths through the redwoods and fern groves, past small waterfalls splashing into lily-covered ponds.

Powell Library

10740 Dickson Plaza • Hours vary; during main semesters Mon–Fri 7.30am–11pm, Sat 9am–5pm, Sun 1–10pm • Free • ☎ 310 825 1938, ⓦ library.ucla.edu

UCLA's **Powell Library** is a Romanesque Revival beauty completed in 1929, with a spellbinding interior of graceful arches, columns and stairwell, and an array of medieval ornament to complement its ecclesiastical feel. The highlight is the dome above the **reading room**, where Renaissance printers' marks are inscribed, among them icons representing such pioneers as Johann Fust and William Caxton.

Murphy Sculpture Garden

Charles E Young Drive • Daily 24hr • Free

Tucked away in the northeastern corner of the UCLA campus, the large **Murphy Sculpture Garden** has seventy works by such major names as Jean Arp, Henry Moore, Henri Matisse and Jacques Lipchitz. Highlights include Henry Moore's *Two-Piece Reclining Figure, No. 3* (1961), Jacques Lipchitz's *Baigneuse* (Bather; 1923–25), and Rodin's *Walking Man* (1877–78), his famous nude composed of only a torso and legs. Look out also for Gaston Lachaise's *Amazonian Standing Woman*, a proud, voluptuous 1933 bronze sculpture, and George Tsutakawa's *OBOS-69* (1969), a bizarre silicon bronze creation in a fountain resembling a pile of TV sets.

The Fowler Museum at UCLA

308 Charles E Young Drive • Wed noon–8pm, Thurs–Sun noon–5pm • Free • ☎ 310 825 4361, ⓦ fowler.ucla.edu

A worthy diversion while on the UCLA campus is the **Fowler Museum at UCLA**, which displays objects representing the ancient, traditional, and contemporary cultures of

FROM TOP VENICE BEACH (P.105); SURFERS ON MALIBU BEACH (P.106) >

1

Africa, Native and Latin America, Asia and the Pacific Ocean – everything from the complex batik textiles of Indonesia and the vivid papier-mâché sculptures of Mexico, to Yoruba beaded arts of Nigeria, and pre-Columbian ceramic vessels of Peru.

Bel Air

One of the most famous, affluent communities in America, **Bel Air** blankets the hillsides north of Westwood, boasting one of the most exquisite hotels in the LA region, *Hotel Bel Air* (owned by the Sultan of Brunei), and the most exclusive club, the Bel-Air Country Club. The exquisite **Hannah Carter Japanese Garden** has been closed since 2011, but was sold to real estate developer Mark Gabay for $12.5 million in 2016 – the new owner may open it again to the public (check ⓦ hannahcarterjapanesegarden .com). Incidentally, though Will Smith's breakthrough TV sitcom *The Fresh Prince of Bel Air* was set here in the early 1990s, the exterior shots were filmed in nearby Brentwood (and the show was filmed entirely in studios).

The Getty Center

1200 Getty Center Drive (main entrance on N Sepulveda Blvd) • Tues–Fri & Sun 10am–5.30pm, Sat 10am–9pm • Free (parking $15) • ☎ 310 440 7300, ⓦ getty.edu • Bus #234/734 from Expo/Sepulveda metro station, or #720 from Santa Monica

In the otherwise undistinguished Brentwood district, Getty Center Drive leads up to the monumental **Getty Center**, a gleaming 110-acre complex that towers over the city as oil baron J. Paul Getty (1892–1976) once towered over his competitors. Getty started building this massive collection in the 1930s, storing much of it in his house, now the **Getty Villa** (see p.106), until the Getty Museum opened in 1974 on a bluff overlooking the Pacific Ocean. Designed by arch-Modernist **Richard Meier**, the Center was built in classical travertine for about $1 billion and was a decade in the making. Although the Getty Foundation shelled out a ten-figure sum for the Center, it still has billions in reserve and must, by law, spend hundreds of millions each year from its endowment. Thus, it plays an elephantine role on the international art scene and can freely outbid its competitors for anything it wants.

North Pavilion

The galleries in the **North Pavilion** are arranged according to period and theme, beginning with **Renaissance Art in Italy and Northern Europe 1450–1600** on the **upper level**. Highlights here include the deft *Hunting on the Lagoon* by Vittore Carpaccio and Correggio's *Head of Christ* in gallery 204, Andrea Mantegna's stoic but affecting *Adoration of the Magi* (203) and Titian's *Venus and Adonis* (205), depicting in muted colours the last moments between the lovers before the latter is gored by a wild boar. Also in gallery 205 is El Greco's *Christ on the Cross* and Titian's *Portrait of Alfonso d'Avalos*, rumoured to have been purchased for an astounding $70 million in 2003.

On the lower level, **Collecting in Northern Europe 1450–1600** contains a variety of curios and objects such as an extraordinary display cabinet from Augsburg, Germany, while **Sacred Art 1150–1600** is designed to resemble a medieval cathedral treasury replete with religious art and stained-glass panels. **European Glass and Ceramics 1400–1700** showcases the Getty's extensive collection of glass and maiolica.

East Pavilion

The **East Pavilion** features primarily **seventeenth-century Baroque art**, including Dutch, French, Flemish and Spanish paintings on the upper level, as well as sculpture and **Italian decorative arts** dating from 1600 to 1800 on the lower level. Among the highlights are Rubens' *Entombment* (202) a pictorial essay supporting the Catholic doctrine of transubstantiation (De la Tour's wonderful

Musician's Brawl is also in 202), and several Rembrandts in gallery 205: *Daniel and Cyrus*, in which the Persian king tries foolishly to feed the bronze statue he worships; *An Old Man in Military Costume*, the exhausted, uncertain face of an old soldier; and the great portrait of *Saint Bartholomew*, which JP purchased in 1962 for a mere $532,000. The art world had changed by 1995 when the Getty had to cough up $36 million for Rembrandt's masterful *Abduction of Europa*. Don't miss Ter Brugghen's *Bacchante with Ape* in gallery 203, a striking but slightly disturbing vision of drunkenness.

South Pavilion

The **South Pavilion** houses **eighteenth-century paintings** on the **upper level** and the majority of the museum's **European decorative arts** collection on the **lower level**, complete with elaborately furnished panelled rooms, dating up to 1800. As the main collection is, not surprisingly, determined by the enthusiasms of Getty himself, there's a formidable array of ornate furniture, clocks, chandeliers, tapestries and gilt-edged commodes, designed for the French nobility from the reign of Louis XIV, filling several overwhelmingly opulent rooms. The Getty's collection of **pastels** on the upper level (usually in dimmed gallery 206) is also magnificent; many critics believe the eighteenth-century portrait of *Gabriel Bernard de Rieux* by Maurice-Quentin de la Tour to be the best pastel ever created (it's not always on show). There are massive Gainsborough portraits in 202, and work from Tiepolo and Canaletto in 205.

West Pavilion

The **West Pavilion** features sculpture and Italian decorative arts of the 1700s through 1900, as well as nineteenth-century paintings on the **upper level**. Most of the Getty's major crowd-pleasers are in **gallery 204**: *Irises* by Van Gogh (the Getty Trust snatching up the vivid floral icon for an unknown but undoubtedly mind-blowing price in 1990); the strikingly austere *Milliners* by Degas; the inevitable Monet haystacks plus his gorgeous *Still Life with Flowers and Fruit*; a sprightly portrait of *Albert Cahen d'Anvers* by Renoir; *The Rue Mosnier with Flags* and *Spring* by Manet; and *Still Life with Apples* by Cézanne. *The Ransom* by John Everett Millais is displayed in gallery 201, while *Bullfight* by Goya, in which the bull stares triumphantly at a group of unsuccessful matadors, and J.M.W. Turner's *Modern Rome-Campo Vaccino*, which the Getty acquired in 2011 for $44.9 million, are both in gallery 201.

Key acquisitions on the **lower level** include Pietro Cipriani's *Medici Venus* and Jean-Désiré Ringel d'Illzach's 9ft-high vase covered with life casts of spiders, juniper branches and scraps of lace (gallery 103).

Photographs, drawings and modern sculpture

The museum also boasts an extensive and highly absorbing collection of **photographs** by Man Ray, Laszlo Moholy-Nagy and other notables; these light-sensitive artworks cannot be on permanent display and tend to feature only in changing exhibitions in the West Pavilion's 7000-square-foot **Center for Photographs**. Similarly, the Getty's precious collection of **drawings** is only displayed in temporary exhibitions, usually in the West Pavilion. Among the best are Albrecht Dürer's meticulous *Study of the Good Thief*, a portrait of the crucified criminal who was converted on the cross; Giovanni Piranesi's dramatic image of a ruined, but still monumental, *Ancient Port*; and William Blake's bizarre watercolour of *Satan Exalting over Eve*, an expressionless devil hovering over his prone captive. Some 28 examples of contemporary and modern **sculpture** are featured throughout the centre grounds, including *Gandydancer's Dream* by Mark di Suvero and Martin Puryear's *That Profile*, commissioned by the Getty in 1999.

1

Santa Monica and around

For many Angelenos, **SANTA MONICA** represents the impossible dream – a low-key, tolerant beachside town with a relaxed air and easy access to the rest of the city. Set along a white-sand beach and home to some of LA's finest stores, restaurants and galleries, this small community has little of the smog or searing heat that can make the rest of the metropolis unbearable. Friendly and liberal, Santa Monica is a great spot to visit, a compact, accessible bastion of oceanside charm that, incidentally, has traditionally attracted a large contingent of British expats (though many have recently left "Little Britain", as it's called, in search of cheaper rents).

Lying across Centinela Avenue from West LA, Santa Monica reaches nearly three miles inland, but most of its attractions lie within a few blocks of the beach and Palisades Park, the famous, cypress-tree-lined strip that runs along the top of the bluffs and makes for striking views of the surf below.

Santa Monica splits into three distinct portions. **Downtown**, holding a fair chunk of Santa Monica's history and its day-to-day business, is mostly inland but is more interesting closer to the coastal bluffs. Just to the west there's the famous **pier** and **beach**, while **Main Street**, running south from downtown towards Venice, is a style-conscious quarter, with designer restaurants and fancy shops.

Bergamot Station

2525 Michigan Ave • Galleries mostly Tues–Fri 10am–6pm, Sat 11am–5.30pm • Free • ☎ 310 453 7535, ⓦ bergamotstation.com • Metro Expo line to 26th St/Bergamot Station

Santa Monica has a number of fine **galleries** selling works by emerging local and international artists. Near the intersection of I-10 and Cloverfield Boulevard, **Bergamot Station**, the city's aesthetic hub, is a collection of former tramcar sheds housing around thirty small art galleries. Many of LA's latest generation of artists have shown here. If you want to check out more art, continue on to the **18th Street Arts Center**, back towards the beach at 1639 18th St (Mon–Fri 11am–6pm; ☎310 453 3711, ⓦ18thstreet.org), a hip and modern centre for various types of art, much of it experimental.

Third Street Promenade

3rd St, between Wilshire Blvd and Broadway • Metro Expo line to Downtown Santa Monica

The **Third Street Promenade** is a three-block pedestrian stretch of Santa Monica that's one of LA's most densely touristed, especially during summer weekends. It's fun to hang out in the cafés, bars and clubs, and the promenade can be really busy at night, when huge numbers of tourists and locals jostle for space with pavement poets and swinging jazz bands under the watchful eyes of water-spewing, ivy-draped **dinosaur sculptures**. The mall is anchored at its southern end by **Santa Monica Place**, a lively outdoor retail complex with access to the Promenade.

Santa Monica Pier and around

Ocean and Colorado aves • Daily 24hr • Free • **Pier Shop & Visitor Center** Mon–Thurs 11am–5pm, Fri–Sun 11am–7pm • ☎ 310 458 8901, ⓦ santamonicapier.org • Metro Expo line to Downtown Santa Monica

Jutting out into the bay at the foot of Colorado Avenue, **Santa Monica Pier** is an iconic example of an old-fashioned, festive beach-town hub, dating back to 1909 and featuring in numerous movies with its giant rollercoaster, Ferris wheel and a restored 1922 wooden **carousel** (Mon & Thurs 11am–5pm, Fri–Sun 11am–7pm; July & Aug also open Tues 3–7pm; $2 a ride, kids under 13 $1; ☎310 394 8042).

Other family-friendly attractions include the **Oatman Rock Shop** (Mon–Thurs 11am–5pm, Fri–Sun 11am–7pm), **Trapeze School** (daily 8.30am–10pm;

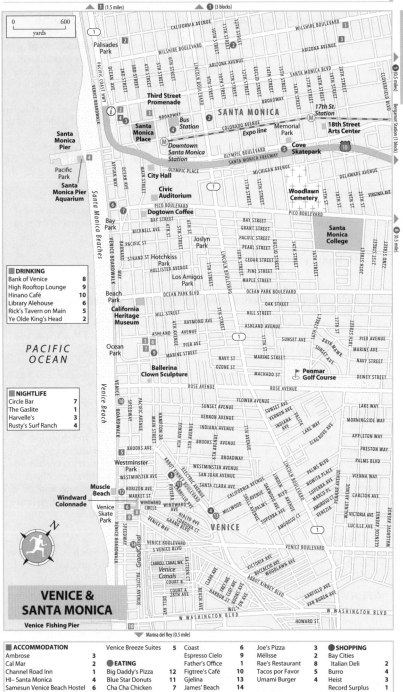

VENICE & SANTA MONICA

Venice Fishing Pier

DRINKING

Bank of Venice	8
High Rooftop Lounge	9
Hinano Café	10
Library Alehouse	6
Rick's Tavern on Main	5
Ye Olde King's Head	2

NIGHTLIFE

Circle Bar	7
The Gaslite	1
Harvelle's	3
Rusty's Surf Ranch	4

ACCOMMODATION		Venice Breeze Suites	5	Coast	6	Joe's Pizza	3	SHOPPING	
Ambrose	3			Espresso Cielo	9	Mélisse	2	Bay Cities	
Cal Mar	2	EATING		Father's Office	1	Rae's Restaurant	8	Italian Deli	2
Channel Road Inn	1	Big Daddy's Pizza	12	Figtree's Café	10	Tacos por Favor	5	Burro	4
HI– Santa Monica	4	Blue Star Donuts	11	Gjelina	13	Umami Burger	4	Heist	3
Samesun Venice Beach Hostel	6	Cha Cha Chicken	7	James' Beach	14			Record Surplus	1

1

ⓦtrapezeschool.com), **Playland Arcade** (Mon–Thurs 10am–10pm, Fri & Sat 10am–1am, Sun 10am–midnight) and the thrill rides of **Pacific Park** (hours vary, often summer daily 11am–11pm, Sat & Sun closes 12.30am; unlimited rides $29.95 or $5–8/ride; ⓦpacpark.com). The **Santa Monica Pier Aquarium**, below the pier at 1600 Ocean Front Walk (Tues–Fri 2–5pm, Sat & Sun 12.30–5pm; $5, kids under 13 free; ⓦhealthebay.org/smpa), is where you can find out about marine biology and touch sea anemones and starfish.

Just south of the pier, Santa Monica has its own miniature version of Venice's **Muscle Beach** (this was the original, established in 1934); a workout area loaded with rings, bars and other athletic equipment for would-be bodybuilders and fitness fans. The adjacent **International Chess Park** is a fancy name for a serviceable collection of chessboards that attracts a range of players from rank amateurs to slumming pros.

Main Street

Five minutes' walk from Santa Monica Pier, **Main Street** is an enticing collection of boutiques, bars and restaurants that forms one of the most popular shopping strips on the Westside.

California Heritage Museum

2612 Main St • Wed–Sun 11am–4pm • $8 • ☎ 310 392 8537, ⓦ californiaheritagemuseum.org • Metro Expo line to Downtown Santa Monica

One of the few sights on Main Street in Santa Monica, the **California Heritage Museum** hosts temporary displays on California cultural topics, from old fruit-box labels to modern skateboards, and has permanent exhibits on regional pottery, furniture, quilts and decorative arts. The building itself is as interesting as the exhibits, a Queen Anne-style gem built in 1894 by lauded architect Sumner P. Hunt for Roy Jones, son of the founder of Santa Monica.

Venice

Immediately south of Santa Monica, **VENICE** is the eccentric, loopy version of Los Angeles, home to outlandish skaters, brazen bodybuilders, panhandlers, streetballers, buskers and street-side comedians. It's been this way since the 1950s and 1960s, when the Beats and then bands like the Doors bummed around the beach, and though gentrification has definitely had an impact in recent years, Venice retains an edgy feel in parts, with a gang culture that has never really been eradicated. It wasn't always like this. Venice was laid out in the marshlands of Ballona Creek in 1905 by developer **Abbot Kinney** as a romantic replica of the northern Italian city. His twenty-mile network of canals and waterfront homes never really caught on, although a later remodelling into a low-grade version of Coney Island postponed its demise for a few decades.

Inland Venice

Windward Avenue is the Venice's main artery, running from the beach into what was the Grand Circle of the canal system – now paved over – and the original

---

GEHRY'S HOUSE

Fans of big-name architect **Frank Gehry** will no doubt want to check out one of the first structures that made his reputation, the artist's own **Gehry Residence**, 1002 22nd St at Washington Ave in Santa Monica, a deconstructivist fantasy with assorted structural ideas thrown together and bundled up with concrete walls and metal fencing. The Gehrys bought the place in 1977 (the original bungalow was built in 1920), but have since added to it many times, with the last major transformation in 1991. Though it's not open to the public you can get close enough for a decent look.

1

LORDS OF DOGTOWN

In the 1970s the district around the ruined Pacific Ocean Park on the south side of Santa Monica was known as **Dogtown** (the "POP" was a pier theme park that closed in 1968, and was demolished in 1975). It was here in the early 1970s that a group of surfers and skateboarders known as the **Z-boys** revolutionized skateboarding; newly developed polyurethane wheels allowed them to move the skateboards in ways similar to surfboards on water, and in 1977 member Tony Alva "invented" the first aerial. Though the Z-boys soon split up, their story was fictionalized in the 2005 movie **Lords of Dogtown** and the location of their Zephyr surf shop (long since closed) at 2003 Main St (at Bay St) is protected as a City Landmark; it's now occupied by **Dogtown Coffee** (Mon–Fri 5.30am–5pm, Sat & Sun 6.30am–5pm). Today the **Venice Breakwater** remains a celebrated local surf spot, while the **Cove** is a 20,000-square-foot skatepark at 14th and Olympic.

Romanesque arcade, around the intersection with Pacific Avenue, is alive with health-food shops, trinket stores and rollerblade rental stands. Here and there colourful giant **murals** depict everything from a shirtless Jim Morrison (1811 Ocean Front Walk) to Botticelli's *Venus* on rollerskates (Windward at Speedway Ave). The remaining **canals** are just a few blocks south, accessed on Dell Avenue between Washington and Venice boulevards, where the original quaint little bridges survive. A short distance inland, much of **Abbot Kinney Boulevard** is a fine stretch for hanging out, sipping a latte, deciphering modern art and having a bite in a smart restaurant.

Venice Beach

Most people are drawn to **Venice Beach**; nowhere else does LA parade itself quite so openly, colourfully and aggressively as it does along the **Venice Boardwalk**, a wide pathway also known as Ocean Front Walk. Year-round at weekends and every day in summer it's packed with jugglers, fire-eaters, Hare Krishnas, rasta guitar players and, of course, teeming masses of tourists. West of Windward is **Muscle Beach**, a legendary weightlifting centre where serious hunks of muscle pump serious iron, and high-flying gymnasts swing on the adjacent rings and bars. Rollerbladers, skateboarders, volleyball players and cyclists are ubiquitous throughout the area, and there are **rental shacks** along the beach for picking up skates, surfboards or bikes.

It's an easy two-mile stroll between Santa Monica Pier and Venice Beach, but you can also catch numerous buses between the two on Main Street (bus #1). Be warned that Venice Beach at night can still be a dangerous place, and walking on the beach after dark is illegal in many stretches.

Will Rogers State Historic Park

1501 Will Rogers Park Rd (off W Sunset Blvd), Pacific Palisades • Park daily: summer 8am–dusk; rest of year 8am–6pm; visitor centre Thurs–Sun 10.30am–5.30pm; free hourly tours of museum Thurs & Fri 11am–3pm, Sat & Sun 10am–4pm • Free; parking $12 • ☎ 310 454 8212, ⓦ parks.ca.gov/willrogers

North of Santa Monica in the Pacific Palisades neighbourhood lies **Will Rogers State Historic Park**, the home and ranch of the Depression-era cowboy movie-star, philosopher and journalist **Will Rogers**. At the time he was one of America's most popular figures, renowned for saying that he "never met a man he didn't like". The ranch-style house was built in 1928 and serves as an informal **museum** (guided tours only) filled with cowboy gear and Native American art. The surrounding 200-acre park has miles of foot- and bridle paths, the most appealing being the three-mile trek up to **Inspiration Point**, where you can enjoy magnificent vistas of the Pacific and the sweeping curve of Santa Monica Bay.

1

The Getty Villa

17985 Pacific Coast Hwy (Hwy-1), Pacific Palisades • Mon & Wed–Sun 10am–5pm • Free, by advance, timed-entry ticket only; parking $15 •
☏ 310 440 7300, ⓦ getty.edu • Bus #534

Five miles northwest along the coast from Santa Monica, the **Getty Villa** was built by oil tycoon J. Paul Getty in 1974 adjacent to his home in Pacific Palisades, serving as the original Getty Museum until the current centre was completed (see p.100). It now serves as the Getty Foundation's spectacular showcase for its wide array of **Greek**, **Etruscan** and **Roman antiquities**. Modelled after the Villa dei Papiri, a Roman country house buried by Mount Vesuvius in 79 AD, the museum is built around its own fetching gardens, peppered with black, faintly menacing replicas of stern-looking Roman heads.

The rooms in the Getty Villa are grouped in themes ranging from religious and mythic to theatrical to martial. Highlights include the *Getty Kouros*, a rigidly posed figure of a boy that conservators openly admit could be a later forgery, as well as Athenian vases, many of them the red-ground variety, ancient kylikes, or drinking vessels, and ceremonial amphorae, or vases given as prizes in athletic contests. Not to be missed is a wondrous Roman-era skyphos, a fragile-looking blue vase decorated with white cameos of Bacchus and his friends, properly preparing for a bacchanalia.

Malibu and around

Everyone has heard of **MALIBU**; it's been immortalized in surfing movies since the 1960s, Courtney Love sung about it and it serves as the fictional home of *Two and Half Men* and *Iron Man*. While its pop, Hollywood image is not so very far from the truth, you might not think so on arrival. The succession of ramshackle surf shops and fast-food stands scattered along both sides of Pacific Coast Highway (PCH) around the graceful **Malibu Pier** don't exactly reek of money, but the secluded estates just inland are as valuable as any in the entire country: Halle Berry, Jeff Bridges, Mel Gibson, John McEnroe, Steven Spielberg and Barbra Streisand are among numerous stars that have homes here.

Malibu beaches

A major surfing nexus, **Malibu Lagoon State Beach** includes celebrated **Surfrider Beach**, which first gained recognition when the sport was brought over from Hawaii and mastered by Southern California pioneers. The waves are best in late summer, when storms off Mexico cause them to reach upwards of 8ft – not huge for serious pros, but big enough for amateurs. Located near the **Malibu Pier**, the beach remains one of the most surfed spots in California.

Five miles up the coast from the pier, **Zuma Beach** is the largest of the LA County beaches, easily connected to the San Fernando Valley by Kanan Dume Road. Adjacent

---

MALIBU AND MODERN SURFING

Though Polynesians and especially Hawaiians have been surfing for hundreds of years (legendary surfer Duke Kahanamoku popularizing the sport in California in the 1920s), modern surf culture really went mainstream on LA beaches and especially Malibu in the late 1950s. Movies such as *Gidget* (1959), filmed on Malibu's Surfrider Beach and Leo Carrillo State Park (see p.131), sparked a flood of interest and instigated the genre known as beach party films (1963's *Beach Party* was also filmed in Malibu), as well as the surf music of Dick Dale, the **Beach Boys** (formed in nearby Hawthorne, LA, in 1961) and others. It wasn't all fun though; environmentalism has always been a key aspect of surf culture, and the **Surfrider Foundation** (ⓦ surfrider.org) was formed in Malibu in 1984 by surfers to protest threats to their local breaks – it's now a global activist movement.

1

Point Dume State Beach, below the bluffs, is more relaxed, and the rocks here are also a good place to look out for seals and migrating grey whales in winter, as the point above – best accessed by car or a longish path – juts out into the Pacific at the northern lip of Santa Monica Bay. **El Matador State Beach**, about 25 miles up the coast from Santa Monica, is about as close as you can get to the private-beach seclusion enjoyed by the stars, thanks to its northern location and an easily missable turn off Pacific Coast Highway. Another five miles along the highway, where Mulholland Drive reaches the ocean, **Leo Carrillo** ("ca-REE-oh") **State Park** marks the northwestern border of LA County. The mile-long sandy beach is divided by Sequit Point, a small bluff that has underwater caves and a tunnel you can pass through at low tide, and is also one of LA's best campgrounds (see box, p.131).

Adamson House and Malibu Lagoon Museum

23200 Pacific Coast Hwy • Both Fri & Sat 11am–3pm (house by tour, last one at 2pm) • $7 joint ticket • ☎ 310 456 8432, ⓦ adamsonhouse.org • Bus #534 from Santa Monica

The **Adamson House** is a stunning, historic Spanish Revival-style home built in 1929 behind Malibu Lagoon State Beach, featuring opulent decor and colourful "Malibu Potteries" tile work (guided hour-long tours are the only way inside). The adjoining **Malibu Lagoon Museum**, formerly the Adamsons' five-car garage, chronicles the history of the area from the days of the Chumash people to the "gentlemen" ranchers and the birth of modern surfing.

Malibu Creek State Park

1925 Las Virgenes Rd, at Mulholland Hwy, Calabasas • Daily dawn–dusk; visitor centre Sat & Sun noon–4pm • Free; parking $12/day • ☎ 818 880 0367, ⓦ malibucreekstatepark.org

Much of **Malibu Creek State Park** belonged to 20th Century-Fox studios between 1946 and 1974, which filmed many Tarzan pictures here and used the chaparral-covered hillsides to simulate South Korea for the TV show *M*A*S*H*. Remnants of the *M*A*S*H* set are still on display, along with a re-creation of the iconic signpost and information panels. The 8000-acre park otherwise includes dramatic canyon vistas, oak woodlands, rolling hills of tallgrass, a large volcanic swimming hole, Century Lake and nearly fifteen miles of hiking trails, making it crowded on summer weekends but fairly accessible and pleasant the rest of the time, and it's possible to camp here (see box, p.131).

The South Bay

South of Venice, the charmless high-rise condos of Marina del Rey and the faded resort town of Playa del Rey offer little to interest visitors. Head south of LAX, however, and you'll come to an eight-mile strip of enticing beach towns – **Manhattan Beach**, **Hermosa Beach** and **Redondo Beach**, part of the region known as the **SOUTH BAY** – which are quieter, smaller and more insular than the Westside beach communities. Visible all along this stretch of the coast and loosely considered part of South Bay, the large green peninsula of **Palos Verdes** is a high-end residential area, while the rough-hewn working town of **San Pedro** is sited on LA Harbor, which with its municipal LA and Long Beach sections is the busiest cargo port in the country.

Manhattan Beach

Beach Cities Transit bus #109 from LAX

The most northerly city of South Bay, **Manhattan Beach** is a likeable place with a healthy, well-to-do air, home mainly to white-collar workers whose multimillion-dollar

1

THE SOUTH BAY STRAND

The South Bay cities share an inviting beachside path, officially the **Marvin Braude Bike Trail** but still known locally as **The Strand** (the trail actually runs for 22 miles from Will Rogers State Beach all the way to Torrance). Here the joggers, dog walkers and roller skaters are more likely to be locals than tourists. Each city has at least one municipal pier and a beckoning strip of white sand lining the path, with most oceanside locations equipped for surfing and beach volleyball. The **International Surf Festival** across all three beach towns takes place in early August (🌐 surffestival.org), a good time to see California leisure life at its finest.

stucco homes tumble towards the beach. These days, **Manhattan Beach Pier**, built in the 1920s, is used mainly for strolling, but is also the site of the accurately named Roundhouse, sitting at the end. This encloses the fine **Roundhouse Aquarium** (summer Mon–Fri 2–8pm, Sat & Sun 9am–8pm; rest of year Mon–Fri 2–5pm, Sat & Sun 10am–dusk; free, suggested donation $2; 🌐 roundhouseaquarium.org), a mildly interesting spot where you can look at crabs, eels, lobsters, squid and – in their own touch tank – tide-pool creatures like anemones and sea stars.

Hermosa Beach

Bus #130 from Harbor Gateway Transit Center metro station (Silver Line); Beach Cities Transit bus #109 from LAX

To the south of Manhattan Beach, **Hermosa Beach** has a lingering bohemian feel of the Sixties and Seventies in certain spots, despite being just as pricey as its neighbours, and features a lively beachside strip, most energetic near the foot of the pier on Twelfth Street. Packed with restaurants and clubs – the **Lighthouse Café** has been a seminal jazz nightclub here since 1949 (see p.143) – the area has long been a major hangout for hedonists of all stripes. A good time to come is during the **Fiesta Hermosa** (🌐 fiestahermosa.net), a three-day event held on Memorial Day (late May) and again over Labor Day weekend (early Sept) that's good for fun music (including surf rock), tasty food and displays of regional arts and crafts.

Redondo Beach

Torrance bus #3 from Carson metro station (Silver Line); Beach Cities Transit bus #109 from LAX

Despite some decent strips of sand and fine views of Palos Verdes' stunning greenery, **Redondo Beach**, south of Hermosa, is much less inviting than its relaxed neighbours. Condos and hotels line the beachfront, and the yacht-lined King's Harbor is off-limits to curious visitors. The unusual horseshoe-shaped **Redondo Beach Pier** (🌐 redondopier.com) at the end of Torrance Boulevard was comprehensively rebuilt in 1995, and features bars, shops, venerable diners such as *Tony's On The Pier* (opened 1952 and serving over fifteen million mai tais in souvenir glasses since then) and live music most nights.

Palos Verdes

A great green hump marking LA's southwest corner, **Palos Verdes** is a rich enclave holding a number of affluent, gated communities, but can be enjoyable for the bluffs and coves along its protected coastline.

Wayfarers Chapel

5755 Palos Verdes Drive S • Daily: 9am–5pm; Visitor Center 10am–5pm • ☎ 310 377 1650, 🌐 wayfarerschapel.org • Bus #344 from Harbor Gateway Transit Center metro station (Silver Line)

Don't miss **Wayfarers Chapel** on the south coast of Palos Verdes, designed by Frank Lloyd Wright's son in 1951 and now LA's ultimate spot for weddings, the redwood grove around the chapel symbolically growing and weaving itself into the stunning,

1

glass-framed structure. Inside the adjacent **Visitor Center** you'll find displays about the life of Emanuel Swedenborg (whose Swedenborgian Church now operates the chapel), and Lloyd Wright's design.

Point Fermin Park

807 W Paseo Del Mar **Park** daily sunrise–sunset • Free • ☎ 310 548 7705 • **Lighthouse** Tues–Sun 1–4pm (guided tours 1pm, 2pm & 3pm) • Free, donation requested • ☎ 310 241 0684, ⓦ pointferminlighthouse.org • Bus #246 from Pacific Ave/21st St metro station (Silver Line)

Southeast along the coast of Palos Verdes, **Point Fermin Park** is a small tip of land poking into the ocean at LA's southernmost point. The squat redwood **Point Fermin Lighthouse** here is an 1874 Eastlake structure with a striking cupola that looks more like a house, though it's been deactivated since 1941.

Cabrillo Marine Aquarium

3720 Stephen White Drive • Tues–Fri noon–5pm, Sat & Sun 10am–5pm • Suggested donation $5, parking $1/hr • ☎ 310 548 7562, ⓦ cabrillomarineaquarium.org • Bus #246 from Pacific Ave/21st St metro station (Silver Line)

Cabrillo Beach Coastal Park contains the excellent **Cabrillo Marine Aquarium**, displaying a diverse collection of marine life that has been imaginatively and instructively assembled: everything from predator snails, octopuses and jellyfish to larger displays on otters, seals and whales. The main building was designed by Frank Gehry in 1981.

San Pedro

Roughly considered part of South Bay, the scruffy harbour district of **SAN PEDRO** was a small fishing community until the late nineteenth century, when the construction of the Port of Los Angeles nearby brought a huge influx of foreign labour. Many of these immigrants, and their descendants, never left the place, lending a discernible ethnic mix to the town. Irascible author **Charles Bukowski** lived at 1148 W Santa Cruz St from 1978 until his death in 1994 (he's buried at Green Hills Memorial Park in nearby Rancho Palos Verdes), and his house may eventually become a museum.

LA Maritime Museum

Berth 84, at the western edge of 6th St • Tues–Sun 10am–5pm • Suggested donation $5 • ☎ 310 548 7618, ⓦ lamaritimemuseum.org • Metro Silver Line to Harbor Blvd/1st St

A good chunk of San Pedro's nautical history is revealed in the **LA Maritime Museum** on the harbour's edge, housed in the former Municipal Ferry Building that was in use from 1941 to 1963. It now holds art and artefacts from the glory days of San Pedro's fishing and whaling industries, among other collections, with displays on everything from old-fashioned clipper-ship voyages to contemporary diving expeditions.

USS Iowa

Berth 87, 250 S Harbor Blvd • Daily 10am–5pm (last ticket sold 4pm) • $19.95 (parking first hour free, then $2/hr) • ☎ 877 446 9261, ⓦ pacificbattleship.com • Metro Silver Line to Harbor Blvd/1st St

Built in 1939, the giant battleship **USS Iowa** served throughout World War II and the Korean War, finally being decommissioned in 1990. In 2012 she was berthed just north of the Maritime Museum and has been comprehensively restored, with the interior loaded with displays and exhibits about life and war at sea.

SS Lane Victory

Berth 49, at 3600 Miner St • Daily except Thurs 9am–4pm • $7 • ☎ 310 519 9545, ⓦ lanevictory.org • Metro Silver Line to Harbor Beacon Park & Ride

Two miles south of the Maritime Museum along San Pedro harbour, the **SS Lane Victory** is a huge, ten-thousand-tonne cargo ship that was built in the shipyard in 1945 and operated in Korea and Vietnam. Tours take you through its many cramped spaces, including the engine and radio rooms, crew quarters, galley and bridge.

1

SAN PEDRO DOWNTOWN TROLLEY

A collection of three classic 1908 Pacific Electric Red Cars (two replica trolleybuses, one restored), the free **San Pedro Downtown Trolley** links most of the city's major attractions (usually early May to early Sept Sat noon–6pm, Sun noon–8pm; ⓦ sptrolley.com). The buses run alongside Harbor Boulevard making a loop from Ports O'Call Village, passing the Maritime Museum, USS *Iowa*, the historic downtown area, and trundling all the way down to Cabrillo Marine Aquarium.

Warner Grand Theatre

478 W 6th St • ☎ 310 548 7466, ⓦ grandvision.org • Metro Silver Line to Pacific Ave/7th St

Old downtown San Pedro is focused on the restored, opulent **Warner Grand Theatre**, a terrific 1931 Zigzag Moderne (Art Deco) moviehouse and performing arts centre with dark geometric details, grand columns and sunburst motifs, a style that almost looks pre-Columbian.

Wilmington

Between San Pedro and Long Beach soar two tall road bridges, giving aerial views of huge facilities thick with oil wells and docks. Just inland lies the predominantly Latino community of **Wilmington**.

Banning Museum

401 E Main St • Entry by guided tour only: Tues–Thurs 12.30pm, 1.30pm & 2.30pm; Sat & Sun hourly 12.30–3.30pm • $5 • ☎ 310 548 7777, ⓦ banningmuseum.org • Bus #246 from Harbor Gateway Transit Center metro station (Silver Line)

Wilmington is home to the **Banning Museum**, the opulent Greek Revival-style home of Phineas Banning (1830–85), the "Father of Los Angeles Harbour". Banning arrived in California in 1851 and soon established his own stagecoach and shipping company, but he's best remembered today for spurring the creation of what would become the port of Los Angeles in the 1860s and 1870s. Built in 1864, his 23-room house remains an engaging spot to visit; it's crammed with elegant Victorian touches (chandeliers, place settings and the like), while there are several restored carriages and stagecoaches kept in an outside barn.

Drum Barracks Museum

1052 Banning Blvd • Tours Tues–Thurs 10am & 11.30am, Sat & Sun 11.30am & 1pm • $5 • ☎ 310 548 7509, ⓦ drumbarracks.org • Bus #232 from Pacific Coast Hwy/Figueroa Place metro station (Silver Line)

Well worth a visit in Wilmington is the **Drum Barracks Museum**, the Civil War-era federal staging-point for attacks in the Southwest against Confederates and, later, Native Americans. The sole remaining building – the 1862 Junior Officers' Quarters – houses a collection of military antiques and memorabilia, such as a 34-star US flag and assorted guns, muskets and weaponry, including an early prototype of a machine gun.

Long Beach and Santa Catalina Island

One of the largest ports in the world, **Long Beach** is best known as the resting place of the *Queen Mary* – even though it's also the region's second-largest city, with nearly half a million people. **Downtown Long Beach**, 25 miles south of Downtown LA, is quite flashy, with office buildings, a conference centre, hotels, a shopping mall, and some of the best preserved early twentieth-century buildings on the coast.

Inland, running from Ocean Boulevard to Third Street, the three-block strip known as **The Promenade** is lined with touristy restaurants and stores that can get busy at weekend nights. To the south, **Shoreline Village** (daily 10am–9pm; ☎562 435 2668, ⓦshorelinevillage.com) is a waterfront entertainment belt that used to feature carnival rides and a carousel until the 1940s, but is now mostly a ragtag collection of shops, funfair arcades and restaurants. Perhaps the most intriguing destination in the area is **Santa Catalina Island**, twenty miles offshore and easily reached by ferry.

Aquarium of the Pacific

100 Aquarium Way · Daily 9am–6pm · $29.95, kids (3–11) $17.95 · ☎562 590 3100, ⓦ aquariumofpacific.org · Metro Blue Line to Downtown Long Beach

The most popular family attraction in Long Beach is the entertaining **Aquarium of the Pacific**, which exhibits more than eleven thousand marine species from the Pacific region, from the familiar sea lions and otters, tide-pool creatures and assorted ocean flora, to the more exotic leopard sharks and giant Japanese spider crabs. The aquarium's interactive **Shark Lagoon** is especially fun (kids can touch the gentle bamboo and epaulette sharks), while visitors can also feed the tropical Australian parrots in **Lorikeet Forest**. The equally popular **Behind the Scenes Tour** (extra $19) takes you into the "wet side" of the aquarium, and includes feeding some of the fish.

Long Beach Museum of Art

2300 E Ocean Blvd · Thurs 11am–8pm, Fri–Sun 11am–5pm · $7 · ☎562 439 2119, ⓦ lbma.org · Long Beach bus #21 from Downtown Long Beach metro station (Blue Line)

Set in a magnificent clifftop home built in 1912, overlooking Long Beach Harbor, the **Long Beach Museum of Art** displays changing exhibitions in a variety of mediums, some from its eclectic permanent collection of everything from English Staffordshire figurative ceramics to California Modernism and contemporary art of California.

Museum of Latin American Art

628 Alamitos Ave · Wed, Thurs, Sat & Sun 11am–5pm, Fri 11am–9pm · $10 (free Sun) · ☎562 437 1689, ⓦ molaa.com · Long Beach bus #111 from Downtown Long Beach metro station (Blue Line)

Several blocks north of the ocean in the **East Village Arts District**, the **Museum of Latin American Art** is LA's only major museum devoted solely to Latino art. Showcasing artists from Mexico to South America, the collection includes big names like Mexican muralist José Orozco, as well as newcomers working within contexts that range from social criticism to magical realism.

Pacific Island Ethnic Art Museum

695 Alamitos Ave · Wed–Sun 11am–5pm · $5 · ☎562 216 4170, ⓦ pieam.org · Long Beach bus #111 from Downtown Long Beach metro station (Blue Line)

Opposite the Museum of Latin American Art lies the much smaller **Pacific Island Ethnic Art Museum**, opened in 2010 with a focus on the art of the Pacific islands but especially the culture of Micronesia. Exhibitions rotate, but the permanent collection is an impressive ensemble of ornate masks, textiles, body ornaments and musical instruments.

LONG BEACH WHALE-WATCHING TRIPS

Between November and March, more than fifteen thousand grey and fin whales (and large numbers of blue whales) cruise the "**Whale Freeway**" past Long Beach on their annual migration to and from winter breeding and birthing grounds in Baja California. **Harbor Breeze Cruises**, at 100 Aquarium Way, next to the Aquarium of the Pacific ($45, kids [3–11] $25; ☎562 983 6880, ⓦlongbeachcruises.com), operates good two-hour whale-watching trips.

1

The Queen Mary

1126 Queens Hwy • Mon–Thurs 10am–6pm, Fri–Sun 10am–7pm • $29 self-guided tours, kids (4–11) $19.50 (parking $18) • ☎ 562 499 1050, ⓦ queenmary.com • Metro Blue Line to Downtown Long Beach

Long Beach's most famous attraction is, of course, the mighty **Queen Mary**, the 1936 Art Deco ocean liner purchased by the city of Long Beach in 1967. Now a luxury hotel, the ship is also open for exhibits that include extravagantly furnished lounges and luxurious first-class cabins, and a wealth of gorgeous Art Deco details in its glasswork, geometric decor and chic streamlining; there are also shops and restaurants and even a wedding chapel. Various add-ons can increase the price of admission: Diana: Legacy of a Princess, A Royal Exhibition ($32) and the themed Paranormal Ship Walk ($44).

Santa Catalina Island

The enticing island of **SANTA CATALINA**, 22 miles long and twenty miles offshore from Long Beach, is mostly preserved wilderness grazed by a herd of 150 **bison** (said to be descendants of buffalo brought over for a movie shoot in 1924). It does have substantial charm, however, and provides a stark contrast to the metropolis, with unspoiled biking, hiking and diving on offer. Indeed, with cars largely forbidden, the four thousand islanders walk, ride bikes or drive golf carts.

Avalon

The island's one town, **AVALON**, can be fully explored on foot in an hour. Begin at the sumptuous Art Deco **Catalina Casino** (tours daily 11.45am & 2.30pm; $13; ☎310 510 0179), 1 Casino Way, a circular structure completed in 1929 (built as a theatre, not an actual casino), that still shows movies nightly at 7.30pm, and features mermaid murals, gold-leaf ceiling motifs and an Art Deco ballroom. Just beyond the casino on St Catherine Way, the **Descanso Beach Club** (☎310 510 7410) offers snorkelling, kayaking, a 32ft climbing wall, snuba and a 3700ft zip line, as well as beach parties every Saturday afternoon (summer only 2–5pm; free).

The absorbing **Catalina Island Museum** (daily 10am–5pm; $7.50; ☎310 510 2414, ⓦcatalinamuseum.org) at 217 Metropole Ave (a 10min walk from the Catalina Express Terminal), displays Native American artefacts from Catalina's past and explains Hollywood's use of the island as a film location.

Wrigley Memorial and Botanical Garden

1400 Avalon Canyon Rd • Daily 8am–5pm • $7 • ☎ 310 510 2897, ⓦ catalinaconservancy.org

Roughly three miles southwest of Avalon, the **Wrigley Memorial and Botanical Garden** displays all manner of endemic flora and fauna over forty acres. Completed in 1934, the stately Wrigley Memorial honours chewing gum magnate William Wrigley Jr, who bought the controlling stake in Catalina Island in 1919 and was responsible for much subsequent development.

Two Harbors

The other settlement on Santa Catalina is the village of **Two Harbors** on the narrow isthmus at the north end of the island, eighteen miles from Avalon (by trail it's over 25 miles, a two-day hike). Known for its **hiking** and **watersports**, it's also infamous for being near the spot where actress **Natalie Wood** drowned in mysterious circumstances in 1981.

ARRIVAL AND INFORMATION   **SANTA CATALINA ISLAND**

By ferry Fast ferries run from Long Beach Downtown Landing (1hr), San Pedro (1hr 15min) and Dana Point (1hr 30min) to Avalon with Catalina Express at least four times daily ($72 return, $74 from Dana Point; ☎800 481 3470, ⓦ catalinaexpress.com); Catalina Flyer runs once daily from Newport Beach (1hr 15min; $70 return; limited service Dec–Feb; ☎800 834 7744, ⓦ catalinainfo.com). Service to and from Two Harbors (1hr 15min) is available from the San

Pedro Terminal with Catalina Express ($36 one-way).

Information Visitor Center at the foot of the Green Pier in Avalon; issues maps (daily 9am–5pm; ☎310 510 1520, ⓦcatalinachamber.com). The Santa Catalina Island Company manages most of the island's facilities (ⓦvisitcatalinaisland.com), while most of the island is administered by the Catalina Island Conservancy (ⓦcatalinaconservancy.org).

GETTING AROUND AND TOURS

By bus The Safari Bus (☎310 510 4205) links Avalon with Two Harbors (2hr; $57 one-way), including stops at Little Harbor ($32), Airport in the Sky ($16), and the trailhead for Black Jack Junction ($16). Buses run daily, departing Avalon at 10am, and leaving Two Harbors for the return journey at 4.30pm. Avalon Transit (ⓦcityofavalon.com/transit) operates two electric bus routes; the Garibaldi Downtown runs through Avalon from the Catalina Express Terminal (Cabrillo Mole) to the Via Casino Archway; the Garibaldi Wrigley Botanic shuttles between Tremont St in Avalon and the Wrigley Memorial and Botanical Garden. Buses run every 20min daily (see website for current schedule). Fares are $1 (no change given).

By taxi Taxis are available at the Catalina Express Terminal (☎310 510 0025). Flat rates are $220.25 to Two Harbors

(1hr 20min), $180.50 to Little Harbor (45min) and $111.25 to the airport (30min); local rides are on the meter.

By bike Plenty of outlets rent bikes in Avalon (see Brown's Bikes; $8–18/hr; ⓦcatalinabiking.com); you can bike around town without a permit, but to explore further inland you must buy a one-year membership ($35) from the Catalina Island Conservancy.

Tours Santa Catalina Island Co offers various tours, including the 3hr Inland Expedition ($90), sundown cruises ($75) and glass-bottom-boat rides ($19), while Catalina Adventure Tours provides a similarly priced roster (☎310 510 2888, ⓦcatalinaadventuretours.com).

Diving The island is a popular place to dive and snorkel, with areas such as the Avalon Underwater Dive Park rich in schools of flying fish and the bright orange Garibaldi (guided dives $115; ⓦcatalinadiverssupply.com).

The San Gabriel and San Fernando valleys

Running north of central LA, beyond the crest of the hills, lie two long, expansive valleys that start close to one another a few miles north of Downtown and span outwards in opposite directions. To the east, the **SAN GABRIEL VALLEY** was settled by farmers and cattle ranchers as foothill communities, which grew into prime resort towns, luring many here in the early twentieth century. **Pasadena**, the largest of the modest cities, holds many elegant period houses, as well as the fine **Norton Simon Museum** and the **Old Pasadena** outdoor shopping mall. South of Pasadena lies the **Huntington Library and Gardens**, a stash of art and literature ringed by botanical gardens that in itself is worth a trip to the valley.

North of Downtown LA and spreading west, the **SAN FERNANDO VALLEY** is, to most Angelenos, simply "**the Valley**": a sprawl of tract homes, mini-malls, fast-food drive-ins, and car-parts shops that has more of a middle-American feel than anywhere else in LA. For most people, the main reason to come out here is to tour the movie studios in **Burbank** and **Universal City**. Elsewhere, **Forest Lawn Cemetery** is a prime example of graveyard kitsch that's hard to imagine anywhere except in LA, and thrilling **Magic Mountain** easily outdoes Disneyland for death-defying rides.

Pasadena

In the 1880s, wealthy East Coast tourists who came to California looking for the good life found it in **PASADENA**, ten miles north of Downtown LA. A century later the downtown area underwent a major renovation, with modern shopping centres slipped in behind 1920s façades, but the historic parts of town have not been forgotten. Indeed, though the city is best known for its annual **Rose Bowl Game** and **Tournament of Roses Parade** (see box, p.114) it is also home to a smattering of intriguing museums and galleries. Pasadena is also the location of the **California Institute of Technology** (**Caltech**; ⓦcaltech.edu), the world-famous research university, with former students

1

including Gordon Moore, co-founder of Intel, and Sabeer Bhatia, founder of Hotmail. For monthly architectural tours of Caltech visit ⓦcats.caltech.edu.

Old Pasadena

Between Fair Oaks and Euclid avenues along Colorado Boulevard, the historic shopping precinct of **Old Pasadena** draws visitors for its fine restaurants, galleries and theatres, and is accessible by light-rail connection on the **Metro Gold Line** (see p.127). Pasadena Heritage offers an excellent overview of Old Pasadena (walking tours first Sat of the month 9am; $15; ☎626 441 6333, ⓦpasadenaheritage.org).

USC Pacific Asia Museum

46 N Los Robles Ave • Wed–Sun 10am–6pm • $10 • ☎ 626 449 2742, ⓦ pacificasiamuseum.org • Metro Gold line to Memorial Park

The absorbing **USC Pacific Asia Museum** occupies the former home and art galleries of anthropologist Grace Nicholson, who had this Chinese-style palace built between 1924 and 1929 with a sloping tiled roof topped with ceramic-dog decorations, inset balconies and dragon-emblazoned front gates. The museum includes thousands of historical treasures and everyday objects from Asia and the Pacific islands, including decorative jade and porcelain, various swords and spears, a large cache of rare Japanese paintings and 150 pieces of finely crafted Chinese jade (including a pair of earrings thought to have been owned by China's last Dowager Empress).

Pasadena Museum of California Art

490 E Union St • Wed–Sun noon–5pm • $7 • ☎ 626 568 3665, ⓦ pmcaonline.org • Metro Gold line to Memorial Park

The three-storey **Pasadena Museum of California Art** specializes in Californian art since the state became part of the Union in 1850, in all kinds of media from painting to digital. Exhibitions usually change every six months.

Norton Simon Museum

411 W Colorado Blvd • Mon, Wed & Thurs noon–5pm, Fri & Sat 11am–8pm, Sun 11am–5pm • $12 • ☎ 626 449 6840, ⓦ nortonsimon.org • Metro Gold line to Memorial Park

The excellent **Norton Simon Museum** merits at least an afternoon to wander through its spacious galleries, containing the finest collection of **Western European paintings** in the state (many donated by industrialist Norton Simon, who funded the museum in the 1970s). Highlights include Dutch paintings such as Frans Hals' quietly aggressive *Portrait of a Young Man* and Rembrandt's vivacious *Portrait of a Boy*, and Italian Renaissance masterpieces from Botticelli, Raphael, Giorgione, Bellini and others. Jacopo Bassano's *Flight into Egypt* features one of the most expressive angels ever painted.

There's also a good sprinkling of French Impressionists and post-Impressionists: Monet's *Mouth of the Seine at Honfleur*, Manet's *Ragpicker* and a Degas capturing the extended yawn of a washerwoman in *The Ironers*, plus works by Cézanne, Gauguin and Van Gogh. Also don't miss Goya's *Saint Jerome*, as raw and ferocious as any of his great works, and

---

TOURNAMENT OF ROSES

Pasadena's most notable festival, the New Year's Day **Tournament of Roses Parade**, began in 1890 to celebrate and publicize the mild Southern California winters, and now attracts more than a million visitors every year to watch its marching bands and elaborate flower-emblazoned floats along a five-mile stretch of Colorado Boulevard, Pasadena (Jan 1; ☎626 795 9311, ⓦtournamentofroses.com). It coincides with the annual **Rose Bowl** football game.

Also fascinating is the official headquarters of the Pasadena Tournament of Roses Association, **Tournament House**, 391 S Orange Grove Blvd (tours Feb–Aug Thurs 2 & 3pm; free; ☎626 449 4100), a pink 1906 Italian Renaissance-style mansion (once owned by William Wrigley Jr, the chewing gum magnate), that's well worth a look for its grand interior and the surrounding Wrigley Gardens, which contain up to 1500 types of rose.

EARTHQUAKE CENTRAL: THE SAN FERNANDO VALLEY   1

The devastating 6.7-magnitude **earthquake** that shook LA on the morning of January 17, 1994, was one of the biggest disasters in US history. Fifty-five people were killed, two hundred more suffered critical injuries, and the economic cost was estimated at $8 billion. One can only guess how much higher these totals would have been had the quake hit during the day, when the many collapsed stores would have been crowded with shoppers and the freeways full of commuters. The quake, with its epicentre in the San Fernando Valley community of **Northridge**, eclipsed LA's previous worst earthquake in modern times, the 6.6-magnitude tremor of February 1971, which had its epicentre in Sylmar – also in the Valley.

In the unlikely event that a sizeable earthquake strikes when you're in LA, protect yourself under something sturdy, such as a heavy table or a doorframe, and well away from windows or anything made of glass. In theory, all the city's new buildings are "quake-safe", though as the 1994 quake recedes in memory, the retrofitting of older buildings seems to diminish in perceived importance. So when the inevitable "Big One" – a quake in the 8-plus-range – arrives, no one knows exactly what will be left standing.

Henri Rousseau's *Exotic Landscape*. The Norton Simon also boasts a solid collection of Modernist greats, from Georges Braque and Pablo Picasso to Roy Lichtenstein and Andy Warhol, and a fine collection of **Asian art**, including many Buddhist and Hindu figures.

Pasadena Museum of History

470 W Walnut St, at Orange Grove Blvd • Wed–Sun noon–5pm • $7 • Tours of the Fenyes Mansion Fri–Sun 12.15pm • $15 (includes museum entry) • ☎ 626 577 1660, ⓦ pasadenahistory.org • Metro Gold line to Memorial Park

From Old Pasadena, Orange Grove Boulevard takes you to the **Pasadena Museum of History**, which has fine displays on Pasadena's history and tasteful gardens, but is most interesting for the on-site **Fenyes Mansion**. Decorated with its original 1906 furnishings and paintings, this elegant Beaux Arts mansion served as the Finnish Consulate from 1948 to 1964; tours include entry to the adjacent **Finnish Folk Art Museum**, once the consulate sauna and now furnished in the style of a nineteenth-century Finnish farmhouse.

Gamble House

4 Westmoreland Place • 1hr tours every 20–30min Thurs–Sun noon–3pm; 20min tours Tues 12.15pm & 12.45pm • $15 (1hr); $8 (20min) • ☎ 626 793 3334, ⓦ gamblehouse.org • Metro Gold line to Memorial Park

The **Gamble House** is one of the highlights of Pasadena, a 1908 Arts and Crafts-style masterpiece combining elements from Swiss chalets and Japanese temples in a romantic, sprawling shingled house (entry is by guided tour only). The area around the Gamble House holds at least eleven other houses attributed to the two brothers (the firm of Greene & Greene) who designed it, including Charles Greene's own house at 368 Arroyo Terrace (closed to the public).

Mount Wilson Observatory

Mount Wilson Red Box Rd (5 miles off Hwy-2) • Daily 10am–5pm (weather permitting) • Free ($5 pass required to park in Skyline Lot) • ☎ 626 440 9016, ⓦ mtwilson.edu

From Hwy-210 at La Cañada, the winding Angeles Crest Highway (Hwy-2) heads up

THE ROSE BOWL

Incongruously sited just to the north of Gamble House, the 104,000-seat **Rose Bowl** (ⓦ rosebowlstadium.com), built in 1922, is the home of the UCLA Bruins (American) football team (ⓦ uclabruins.com) and the site of the annual **Rose Bowl game**, held on New Year's Day, one of the most famous and most-watched college games of the year. Every second Sunday of each month, the **Rose Bowl Flea Market** (9am–4.30pm; $9; early entry 5–9am $15–20; ⓦ rgcshows.com) takes place in the parking lots around the stadium.

1

into the mountains above Pasadena towards the **Mount Wilson Observatory**, which at 5715ft, is visible from much of the Los Angeles area (smog allowing). The observatory was founded in 1904, and today you can view the historic Hooker 100-inch telescope (completed 1917) from the Visitors' Gallery inside the dome, peruse the small Astronomical Museum and grab a sandwich at the *Cosmic Café* (Sat & Sun 10am–4pm). Guided tours (April–Nov only; $15), which get you into some restricted areas, run Saturdays and Sundays at 1pm.

The Huntington Library

1151 Oxford Rd, off Huntington Drive, San Marino • Mon & Wed–Sun 10.30am–4.30pm • $23 Mon–Fri, $25 Sat & Sun • ☎ 626 405 2100, ⊕ huntington.org • Bus #78, #79, #378

Three miles southeast of Old Pasadena, the fantastic **Huntington Library** contains the art collections of Henry Huntington, owner of the Pacific Electric Railway Company and the largest landowner in the state. In 1910 he moved to this estate and devoted himself full-time to buying rare books and manuscripts. In addition to his library, which opened to the public in 1928, the **Huntington Art Gallery** contains the finest collection of British portraits outside of the UK, while the Huntington's **botanical gardens** cover the surrounding 120 acres.

The Library

Completed in 1920, the **Library** has a two-storey exhibition hall containing rare manuscripts and books, among them a Gutenberg Bible on vellum, a 1623 folio edition of Shakespeare's plays and the **Ellesmere Chaucer**, a circa-1410 illuminated manuscript of *The Canterbury Tales*. Displays around the walls trace the history of printing and of the English language from medieval manuscripts to a King James Bible, from Milton's *Paradise Lost* and Blake's *Songs of Innocence and Experience* to first editions of Swift, Dickens, Woolf and Joyce.

Huntington Art Gallery

The original Huntington residence, a grand Beaux Arts mansion completed in 1911 and done out in Louis XIV carpets and later French tapestries, is now the **Huntington Art Gallery**, home to an exceptional collection of European and especially British paintings. The stars of the collection are Gainsborough's masterful *Blue Boy,* Reynolds' *Mrs Siddons as the Tragic Muse*, *Pinkie* by Thomas Lawrence and John Constable's *View on the Stour near Dedham*. Just as striking are Turner's *Grand Canal, Venice*, awash in hazy sunlight and gondolas, and William Blake's *Satan Comes to the Gates of Hell*, which is quite the portrait of Old Nick, in this case battling Death with spears.

Virginia Steele Scott Galleries of American Art

The **Virginia Steele Scott Galleries of American Art** display American paintings from the 1690s to the 1950s, with highlights including *The Long Leg* by Edward Hopper, Warhol's *Small Crushed Campbell's Soup Can*, and *Global Loft (Spread)* by Robert Rauschenberg. Don't miss also the incredibly expressive *Breakfast in Bed* by Mary Cassatt, Frederic Edwin Church's monumental *Chimborazo* and Harriet Hosmer's remarkable marble sculpture, *Zenobia in Chains*, acquired by the Huntington in 2007. The Dorothy Collins Brown Wing is devoted to the work of early twentieth-century Pasadena architects Charles and Henry Greene, designers of Gamble House (see p.115), while the nearby **MaryLou and George Boone Gallery**, once Henry Huntington's garage, hosts changing exhibitions.

Botanical Gardens

The 120 acres of beautiful themed **Botanical Gardens** surrounding the buildings include a Desert Garden with the world's largest collection of desert plants, including

1

twelve acres of cacti; lush rose, palm and subtropical gardens; a sculpture garden full of Baroque statues; a Chinese Garden and the Japanese Garden dotted with koi ponds, cherry trees and "moon bridges". While strolling through these assorted wonders, you might also call in on Huntington and his wife, buried in a neo-Palladian marble **Mausoleum** at the northwest corner of the estate.

Mission San Gabriel Arcángel

428 S Mission Drive, San Gabriel (entrance at 427 S Junipero Serra Drive) **Old Mission church** Daily 6.30am–8pm • Free • **Museum and gardens** Mon–Sat 9am–4.30pm, Sun 10am–4pm • $6 • ☎ 626 457 3035, ⓦ sangabrielmissionchurch.org • Bus #487, #489

Just 2.5 miles south of the Huntington Library in small **San Gabriel** stands the valley's original Spanish settlement, the church and grounds of **Mission San Gabriel Arcángel**, established here in 1771 by Franciscan priest Junípero Serra to minister to the local Tongva people (who subsequently were virtually wiped out by disease – some six thousand are buried here). The current church dates from around 1805. Despite decades of damage by earthquakes and the elements, the church and grounds have been repaired and reopened, their old winery, cistern, kitchens, gardens and small adobe museum giving some sense of mission-era life.

Glendale

Lying at the eastern end of the San Fernando Valley, **GLENDALE** is best known for its branch of **Forest Lawn Cemetery**, its pompous landscaping and pious artworks attracting celebrities by the dozen. Though born in Iowa, actor John Wayne actually grew up here in the 1920s, when LA was dubbed "the west coast of Iowa" for attracting waves of Midwest émigrés. The city is otherwise home to the largest **Armenian** community in the US, the Dreamworks Animation studios, Nestlé's US headquarters and **Americana at Brand** (Mon–Thurs 10am–9pm, Fri & Sat 10am–10pm, Sun 11am–8pm; ⓦ americanaatbrand.com), 889 Americana Way, a posh outdoor mall and entertainment complex with a popular musical fountain.

Museum of Neon Art

216 S Brand Blvd • Thurs–Sat noon–7pm, Sun noon–5pm • $10 (parking $1/hr) • ☎ 818 696 2149, ⓦ neonmona.org • Metrolink to Glendale Transportation Center

Glendale's **Museum of Neon Art** is dedicated to all things neon, but particularly the historic illuminated signs that once dotted so much of California; gems include the 1930s *Brown Derby* sign from Hollywood, Oakland's elaborate 1950s *Hofbrau* and Glendale's slick *Zinke's Shoe Repairs* sign.

Forest Lawn Cemetery

1712 S Glendale Ave • Daily 8am–5pm • Free • ☎ 323 254 3131, ⓦ forestlawn.com • Museum Tues–Sun 10am–5pm • Free • ☎ 323 340 4921 • Metrolink to Glendale Transportation Center

It's best to climb the hill and see the **Forest Lawn Cemetery** in reverse from the **Forest Lawn Museum**, whose hodgepodge of historical bric-a-brac includes coins from ancient Rome, Viking relics, medieval armour, Bouguereau's romantic painting *Song of the Angels* and a mysterious sculpted Easter Island moai figure.

THE ELECTRIC DUSK DRIVE-IN

Glendale is home to that classic American experience, the drive-in movie. The **Electric Dusk Drive-In** runs two to three times a month (on Sat evenings at around 6.30pm) at 2930 Fletcher Drive at San Fernando Rd (off I-5). You can also lounge on Astroturf mats at the front of the screen. Tickets are $10–14 per person if you buy in advance online; on the gate, they are $13–16 (cash only). See ⓦ electricduskdrivein.com for dates.

1

Hall of the Crucifixion-Resurrection

Tues–Sun 10am, 11am, noon, 2pm, 3pm & 4pm • Free

Next door to the Forest Lawn Museum, the **Hall of the Crucifixion-Resurrection** houses the biggest piece of Western religious art in the world: *The Crucifixion* by Jan Styka – an oil painting nearly 200ft tall and 45ft wide – though you're only allowed to see it during the special unveilings on the hour (25min).

Freedom and Great mausoleums

From the museum, the terraced gardens lead down past sculpted replicas of the greats of classical European art, and on to the **Freedom Mausoleum**, home to a handful of the cemetery's better-known graves. Just outside the mausoleum's doors, Errol Flynn lies in an unspectacular plot, allegedly buried with six bottles of whisky at his side, while nearby is the grave of Walt Disney, who wasn't frozen, as urban myth would have it. Inside the mausoleum itself you'll find Nat King Cole, Jeanette MacDonald and Alan Ladd, all close to each other on the first floor. To the left, heading back down the hill, the **Great Mausoleum** is notable for the tombs of Clark Gable, Jean Harlow and Michael Jackson.

The Burbank studios

In the heart of the "Valley", the otherwise dull city of **BURBANK** is the place where many movie and TV studios relocated from Hollywood in the 1950s through to the 1970s; today it's still home to media giants such as the Walt Disney Company, Warner Bros Entertainment, Warner Music Group and Nickelodeon. NBC, however, moved from its old studios (now known as the **Burbank Studios**; ⓦtheburbankstudios.com), to Universal City (see opposite), while its long-running *Tonight Show* (with Jimmy Fallon) relocated to New York in 2014 after a 42-year stint in Burbank.

Warner Bros Studios

3400 W Riverside Drive • Tours (2hr 15min) daily 8.30am–3pm • $62; parking (3400 Warner Blvd) $10 • ☎ 877 492 8687, ⓦ wbstudiotour.com • Metrolink to downtown Burbank, then bus #155

Although you can't get into Disney, **Warner Bros Studios** does offer worthwhile **tours** (via carts) of its sizeable facilities and active backlot, where *ER* and *Friends* were filmed in the 1990s. Current TV shows you might see being filmed (you must apply for tickets to attend the shows separately) include *The Big Bang Theory*, *Conan* (Conan

---

LA STUDIOS AND TAPINGS: THE BEST OF THE REST

In LA you can attend live recordings of many primetime US TV shows: Jimmy Kimmel (see p.81); Bill Maher and James Corden (see p.88); or visit Paramount Studios (see p.82). Note that Fox Studios in Century City is not open for tours. Visit ⓦ on-camera-audiences.com or ⓦ 1iota. com to learn about the waiting-list process for live tapings of *American Idol*, *So You Think You Can Dance* and *Dancing With the Stars* (all taped at CBS Television City), and *The Voice* (various studios in LA).

Sony Pictures Studios 10202 W Washington Blvd, Culver City ☎ 310 244 8687, ⓦ sonypicturesstudiostours .com. This is the original MGM Studios where classics like *Wizard of Oz* and *Gone With the Wind* were filmed. Tours run Mon–Fri 9.30am, 10.30am, 1.30pm & 2.30pm ($40; free parking).

Ellen DeGeneres Show Warner Bros Studios. Free tickets at ⓦ ellentv.com/tickets. Usually Mon–Thurs 4pm.

The Talk CBS Studio Center, 4024 Radford Ave, Studio City. Free tickets at ⓦ cbs.com/shows/the_ talk. *The Talk* films live Mon–Thurs 11am & Thurs 1pm (it's the only way you can visit the historic CBS lot).

Talking Dead CBS Television City, Fairfax District. Free tickets at ⓦ 1iota.com/Show/212/Talking-Dead. Sun 4pm.

1

GREAT WALL OF LOS ANGELES

Designed by local artist Judith Baca and completed between 1976 and 1983, the **Great Wall of Los Angeles** is the world's longest mural at 2754ft, painted along the walls of the Tujunga Wash Flood Control Channel (LA River) in Valley Glen, seven miles west of Burbank. It's quite a spectacle, covering aspects of California history from Native Americans to the 1950s in a series of vibrant pop art-like images. See ⓦ sparcmurals.org for a taster. The mural runs along Coldwater Canyon Avenue, between Burbank Boulevard and Oxnard Street near the Valley College Campus; if driving take Hwy-101, exit on Coldwater Avenue and head north (park along the street). The closest Metro station is Valley College on the Orange Line.

O'Brien records his TBS talk show from historic Stage 15; ⓦ teamcoco.com/tickets), the *Ellen DeGeneres Show* (see box opposite), *Shameless* and *2 Broke Girls*.

Universal Studios Hollywood

100 Universal City Plaza, Universal City • Daily: usually summer 8am–10pm; rest of year 10am–6pm • Day-pass $105 (2 days $119), kids (3–9) $99; parking $10–18 • ⓣ 818 508 9600, ⓦ universalstudioshollywood.com • Metro Red Line to Universal City

The largest of the Burbank backlots belongs to **Universal Studios** in Universal City, three miles southwest of Warner Bros, though the section you get to visit is essentially a theme park (most NBC shows have now moved here, but you won't get anywhere near filming). Admission includes the **studio tour** (every 5–10min; 45min) with the first half featuring a tram ride through a make-believe set where you can see the house from *Psycho* and the shark from *Jaws*, have a close encounter with King Kong (a 3-D experience created by Peter Jackson) and get to experience a high-speed car chase in *Fast & Furious – Supercharged!* You'll also see the Wisteria Lane set from hit series *Desperate Housewives*. Other park theme rides are based on the studio's TV and film franchises: the immensely popular **Wizarding World of Harry Potter**, **Despicable Me Minion Mayhem** and **The Simpsons Ride**, a wacky trip into the Krustyland theme-park-within-a-theme-park; eat at Krusty Burger, buy souvenirs at the Kwik-E-Mart or grab a beer at Moe's Tavern. The **Walking Dead Attraction** comes replete with zombies and other post-apocalyptic fun. **Universal CityWalk**, a three-block entertainment, dining and shopping promenade (ⓦ citywalkhollywood .com), is just next door.

Nethercutt Museum and Collection

Nethercutt Collection 15200 Bledsoe St, Sylmar • Guided tour only Thurs–Sat 10am & 1.30pm • Free • **Nethercutt Museum** 15151 Bledsoe St, Sylmar • Tues–Sat 9am–4.30pm • Free • ⓣ 818 364 6464, ⓦ nethercuttcollection.org

Located in the sleepy town of Sylmar, the wonderful **Nethercutt Collection** is a storehouse for all kinds of Wurlitzer organs, old-time player-pianos, cosmetic paraphernalia, Tiffany stained glass and classic French furniture; there are also two dozen antique cars on view from the 1920s and 1930s. The adjoining **Nethercutt Museum** is a stunning showroom filled with more than 130 collectors' vintage automobiles such as Packards, Mercedes, Bugattis and especially the Duesenbergs, splendid machines driven by movie stars in the Jazz Age.

William S. Hart Ranch and Museum

24151 Newhall Ave, Newhall • Mid-June to Aug Wed–Sun 11am–4pm; Sept to mid-June Wed–Fri noon–3pm, Sat & Sun 11am–4pm • Free • ⓣ 661 254 4584, ⓦ hartmuseum.org

Located in **Santa Clarita**, twenty miles north of Burbank, the **William S. Hart Ranch and Museum** contains a fine collection of Western art, featuring native artworks, Remington sculptures, displays of spurs, guns and lassoes, Tinseltown costumes and authentic

1

cowhand clothing, all housed in a Spanish Colonial mansion on a 265-acre ranch built by the silent-era cowboy actor in 1927. Entrance to the museum is by guided tour only, every thirty minutes. The 1910 **Ranch House** (same hours as museum), located next to the picnic area in William S. Hart Park is open for self-guided visits; inside are Hart's tack and saddle collection, personal furnishings and additional Hollywood mementoes.

Six Flags Magic Mountain

26101 Magic Mountain Pkwy, Valencia • Hours vary, often summer daily 10.30am–9pm; rest of year Sat & Sun 10.30am–6pm • $79.99, kids (under 48"/1.2m) $54.99 (discounts on website); parking $20; Six Flags Hurricane Harbor $41.99, kids $33.99 • ☎ 661 255 4100, ⓦ sixflags.com/magicmountain

Some 25 miles north of Burbank, **Six Flags Magic Mountain** boasts some of the wildest rollercoasters and rides in the world – highlights include the Viper, a huge orange monster with seven loops; the Goliath, full of harrowing 85mph dips; Tatsu, which sends you through the requisite loops while strapped in face-down at a 90-degree angle; and Full Throttle, which speeds through a record-breaking 160ft loop – it's the tallest and fastest looping rollercoaster in the world. Finally, don't let the slow speed of "X2" fool you – it's one of the newest "fifth dimension coasters", with fog, flames, and sound effects, and where your seat pivots and pitches independently of the direction of the track, and is utterly terrifying. Of the other rides, "Lex Luthor: Drop of Doom" stands out for its 400ft freefall, the tallest drop tower ride in the world, the **New Revolution** is a virtual reality coaster and **Justice League Battle for Metropolis**, opened in 2017, is a spectacular "dark" video-game ride featuring the Joker, wind, fire, fog and other special affects. The adjacent water park, **Six Flags Hurricane Harbor**, provides aquatic fun for kids who need to cool off.

Ronald Reagan Library and Museum

40 Presidential Drive, Simi Valley • Daily 10am–5pm • $16 • ☎ 805 577 4000, ⓦ reaganfoundation.org

Some 35 miles west of Burbank and 28 miles north of Malibu, the community of Simi Valley contains the **Ronald Reagan Library and Museum**, a tribute to the life and times of the 40th US president, a man who is still accorded saint-like reverence within the US Conservative movement and Republican Party. The museum is crammed with interactive exhibits, videos and even games that explore Reagan's life and career from movie star to president, including a full-size replica of the White House Oval Office (in which, Reagan proudly maintained, he never took off his suit jacket) and there's a special hangar housing the **Air Force One** Boeing 707 used by presidents between 1973 and 2001. Rather bizarrely, the hangar also contains the actual "**Ronald Reagan Pub**" from Ballyporeen, Ireland, that Reagan visited in 1984 – it closed in 2004, and its signage and fittings were transported here the following year. The pub was originally *O'Farrell's*, but the proud owners renamed it after the president's visit. Alas, alcohol is no longer served – it's a snack and coffee bar.

Orange County

Although **ORANGE COUNTY**, a densely populated region that merges into the southeast of Los Angeles, has long been emblematic of conservative white suburbia, the reality is now a bit different. Certain sections of the county have a tolerant, even progressive, bent, especially in the inland part of the region, and Hispanics and Asians increasingly populate cities like Anaheim, Garden Grove, Santa Ana and Westminster. For most visitors, however, Orange County means **Disneyland**; even though it only exists on roughly one square mile of land, it continues to dominate the **Anaheim** area. Elsewhere, the thrill rides at **Knott's Berry Farm** provide a cheaper alternative; the **Crystal Cathedral** is an imposing reminder of the potency of the US evangelical

1

movement; and the **Richard Nixon Library and Birthplace** is a good spot to find out about the infamous life and career of Tricky Dicky. On the coast, a string of towns from Long Beach to the borders of San Diego County 35 miles south, swanky condos line the sands and the ambience is easy-going and affluent. As the names of the main towns suggest – **Huntington Beach**, **Newport Beach** and **Laguna Beach** – there are few reasons beyond sea and sand to come here. The other place that merits a stop is just inland at **San Juan Capistrano**, site of the best kept of all the California missions.

Disneyland

1313 Harbor Blvd, Anaheim • Hours vary, usually June–Aug daily 8am–midnight; Sept–May Mon–Fri 10am–6pm, Sat 9am–midnight, Sun 9am–10pm • $105, kids (3–9) $99; Disney California Adventure Park $95, day-pass for both $160; parking $18 • ☎ 714 781 4565, ⓦ disneyland.com • From Downtown LA it takes about 45min by car on the Santa Ana Freeway (I-5); 30min by train to Fullerton, from where OCTD buses will drop you at Disneyland; or bus MTA #460 takes about 90min, and Greyhound takes 45min to Anaheim, from where it's an easy walk to the park

In the early 1950s, illustrator and film-maker **Walt Disney** conceived a theme park where his internationally famous cartoon characters – Mickey Mouse, Donald Duck, Goofy and the rest – would come to life, animated quite literally, and his fabulously successful company would rake in even more money. Opening way back in 1955, **DISNEYLAND** is still world-renowned as one of the defining hallmarks of American culture, a theme-park phenomenon with the emphasis strongly on family fun.

Not including the newer **California Adventure Park** annexe (see p.122), the Disneyland admission price includes all the rides, although during peak periods you might have to wait in line for hours – queues are shortest when the park opens, so choose a few top rides and get to them very early. Most people try to visit just for the day, but there are suitably Disney-themed **hotels** (see p.130). If the **fast food** available in the park doesn't appeal, you could head to Anaheim and Fullerton (see p.138).

The main park

From the front gates, **Main Street** leads through a scaled-down, camped-up replica of a bucolic Midwestern town, filled with souvenir shops and diners, toward **Sleeping Beauty's Castle**, a pseudo-Rhineland palace recently reopened to fascinating effect, with narrow corridors and stairs leading to brightly coloured, three-dimensional scenes from the classic Disney cartoon. **New Orleans Square**, nearby, contains the two best rides in the park: **the Pirates of the Caribbean**, a boat trip through underground caverns, singing along with drunken pirates, and the **Haunted Mansion**, a riotous "doom buggy" tour in the company of the house spooks. In **Adventureland**, the antiquated **Jungle Cruise** (an original from 1955), has "tour guides" making crude puns about the fake animatronic beasts creaking amid the scenery, and **Indiana Jones Adventure**, a giddy journey down skull-encrusted corridors in which you face fireballs, burning rubble, venomous snakes and, inevitably, a rolling-boulder finale.

Less fun are the neighbouring areas of **Critter Country** and **Frontierland**, where the main attraction, **Big Thunder Mountain Railroad**, is a drab, slow-moving coaster. **Splash Mountain** at least has the added thrill of getting drenched by a log-flume ride, and **Pirate's Lair on Tom Sawyer Island** has been themed around Disney's movie franchise *Pirates of the Caribbean*: you can poke around the spooky Dead Man's Grotto for hidden treasure, and explore the skeletons littered through a shipwreck at Smuggler's Cove.

Continue counterclockwise around the park to reach **Fantasyland**, which shows off the cleverest, but also the most sentimental, aspects of the Disney imagination: **Peter Pan's Flight**, a fairy-tale flight over London, and **It's a Small World**, a tour of the world's continents in which animated dolls warble the same cloying song over and over. For tots who just can't get enough saccharine, there's **Toontown**, thick with slow-moving bumper cars and other kiddie amusements. Fantasyland mercifully gives way to

1

Tomorrowland, Disney's vision of the future, where the **Space Mountain** rollercoaster zips through the pitch-blackness of outer space; and the **Finding Nemo Submarine Voyage** picks up where its predecessor, 20,000 Leagues Under the Sea, left off, giving you a quick underwater tour of notable aquatic scenes from the hit movie.

Disney California Adventure Park

The **Disney California Adventure Park** is technically a separate park but is connected to the main one in architecture and style – although it's much less popular. Aside from its slightly more exciting rollercoasters and better food, the California Adventure is really just another "land" to visit, albeit a much more expensive one.

There's a handful of highlights. Grizzly River Run is a fun giant-inner-tube ride, splashing through plunges and "caverns"; Soarin' Around the World is an exciting trip on a mock-experimental aircraft that buzzes through hairpin turns and steep dives; and the **Paradise Pier** zone has a slew of old-fashioned carnival rides – from California Screamin', a sizeable rollercoaster, to the Ferris-like Mickey's Fun Wheel – that only faintly recall the wilder, harder-edged sideshows of California's past. There's also a rather tame zone devoted to Tinseltown, **Hollywoodland**, which, aside from a few theatres and special-effects displays, features the Twilight Zone Tower of Terror, a shock-drop ride in a haunted hotel.

Knott's Berry Farm

8039 Beach Blvd (off the Santa Ana Freeway), Buena Park • Hours vary, usually June–Aug Mon–Thurs & Sun 10am–11pm, Fri & Sat 10am–midnight; rest of year Mon–Fri 10am–6pm, Sat 10am–10pm, Sun 10am–7pm • $72, kids (3–11) $42; parking $18 • ☎ 714 220 5200, ⓦ knotts.com

If you're a bit fazed by the excesses of Disneyland, you might prefer the more down-to-earth **Knott's Berry Farm**, whose rollercoasters are far more exciting than anything at its rival. Although there are ostensibly six themed lands here, you should spend most or all of your time in just half of them: **Fiesta Village**, home to the Jaguar, a high-flying coaster that spins you around the park concourse; **Ghost Town**, with fun wooden coasters and log flumes; and the **Boardwalk**, which is all about heart-thumping thrill rides. Knott's also has its own adjacent water park, **Knott's Soak City Waterpark** (June–Sept only, hours vary but generally daily 10am–5pm or 7pm; $43, kids $26; ⓦ soakcityoc.com), which offers fourteen drenching rides of various heights and speeds.

Christ Cathedral (Crystal Cathedral)

13280 Chapman Ave, Garden Grove • Cathedral Cultural Center Mon–Fri 10am–3pm, Sat 9am–4pm • Tours every 30min, Mon–Sat 10am–3pm • Free • ☎ 714 971 4000, ⓦ christcathedralcalifornia.org

In the otherwise average Orange County small town of Garden Grove (six miles south of Anaheim), the giant **Crystal Cathedral** is a glittering Philip Johnson design of tubular space-frames and plate-glass walls that formed part of the vision of evangelist Robert Schuller of Crystal Cathedral Ministries. The cathedral was completed in 1981, but the Ministries filed for bankruptcy in 2010, selling the building two years later to the Catholic Church – it is now formally known as **Christ Cathedral**. Regardless of ownership it's a fascinating building, with the sparkling **Prayer Spire** an especially bold piece of architecture, and the organ inside one of the world's biggest. Tours begin at the **Cathedral Cultural Center** with the "Becoming Christ Cathedral: Faith and Transformation" exhibit.

Nixon Presidential Library and Museum

18001 Yorba Linda Blvd, Yorba Linda • Mon–Sat 10am–5pm, Sun 11am–5pm • $16 • ☎ 714 983 9120, ⓦ nixonlibrary.gov

In freeway-caged **Yorba Linda**, about nine miles northeast of Anaheim, the **Nixon Presidential Library and Museum** stand as tribute to the controversial and generally vilified 37th President, who will be forever associated with the Watergate scandal and his subsequent resignation in 1974. Though the special **Watergate exhibit** that opened in 2011 certainly pulls no punches, it's not surprising that the rest of the site offers a relatively rosy overview of Nixon's life, beginning with his humble **birthplace** behind the museum, restored to appear as it was in 1913 (the house was moved from its original location in Yorba Linda). The museum itself charts Nixon's career from vice president under Eisenhower from 1953 to 1961 to president in 1969 with items such as the presidential limousine, snippets of TV coverage and heaps of campaign relics. Also on view is the **World Leaders Gallery** of Nixon's heyday, with Mao, Brezhnev and de Gaulle among them, cast in bronze and arranged in rigid poses. You can also get up close to the **helicopter** he used as president – and when he was whisked away from the White House after resigning in disgrace. Nixon's grave is also on site.

Huntington Beach

HUNTINGTON BEACH is a compact town of engaging single-storey cafés and beach stores grouped around the 1850ft **Huntington Beach Pier** (daily 5am–midnight), off the Pacific Coast Highway (PCH) at Main Street – also the place where the **Surfers Walk of Fame** commemorates the sport's towering figures. One block south, the sleek **Pacific City** retail hub contains shops, restaurants and the **LOT 579** (p.138) food market. Otherwise the **beach** is the primary focus, with some of the best surf breaks in the US. The four main beaches are Sunset Beach and three-mile Bolsa Chica State Beach (northwest; $15/vehicle), Dog Beach (west), the 3.5-mile **Huntington City Beach** either side of the pier ($15 parking), and Huntington State Beach (south; $15/vehicle).

International Surfing Museum

411 Olive Ave • Tues–Sun noon–5pm • $2 • ☎ 714 960 3483, ⓦ surfingmuseum.org

Surf history is chronicled at the **International Surfing Museum**, two blocks inland from the city pier, which features exhibits on surfing legends, historic posters from surfing contests, and an array of traditional, contemporary and far-out boards (including the world's largest).

Bolsa Chica State Ecological Reserve

3842 Warner Ave (off PCH) • **Reserve** daily sunrise–sunset; **Interpretive Center** daily 9am–4pm • Free • ☎ 714 846 1114, ⓦ bolsachica.org

Four miles north of downtown Huntington Beach and the pier, nature lovers won't want to miss the **Bolsa Chica State Ecological Reserve**, a sizeable wetland preserve.

SURF CITY USA

Huntington Beach is proud of its official designation "**Surf City USA**", with a surf pedigree that goes back to a demonstration by pioneer surfer George Freeth in 1914 and Duke Kahanamoku's visit in 1925. The first West Coast Surfing Championship was held at Huntington in 1959 and local surfer Robert August starred in seminal movie **Endless Summer** in the 1960s. Veterans such as Corky Carroll (the first real professional surfer) and Peter Townend (first world champion) still live in Huntington, and it remains the location of the annual **US Open of Surfing**. Today local surfers still flock to the south side of the pier (especially in winter), where the pilings provide a unique sandbar and current rotation. Rent boards ($10/hr; $40/day) at **Huntington Surf & Sport** near the pier at 300 Pacific Coast Hwy (Mon–Thurs & Sun 8am–9pm, Fri & Sat 8am–10pm; ⓦ hsssurf.com) or **Dwight's Beach Concession** at 201 Pacific Coast Hwy (daily 9am–5pm; ⓦ dwightsbeachconcession .com). **Corky Carroll's Surf School** (ⓦ surfschool.net) at Bolsa Chica State Beach (perfect for beginners) is one of many outfits offering lessons (private lesson $90–130/2hr). Be sure to grab a post-surf treat at *Sugar Shack* (p.138), a local tradition, or a drink at *Duke's* (p.138). See also ⓦ surfcityusa.com.

1

Exploring the five miles of trails will get you acquainted with some of the current avian residents of this salt marsh, including a fair number of herons, egrets and grebes, and even a few peregrine falcons and endangered snowy plovers. The **Interpretive Center** adds context with three salt-water tanks containing native marine life (sea cucumbers, crabs and starfish), and exhibits highlighting the ecological and human history of the area. On the other side of the PCH lies **Boca Chica State Beach**, a popular surf break.

Newport Beach

Ten miles south of Huntington Beach, **NEWPORT BEACH**, with its bevy of yachts and yacht clubs, is posh even by Orange County standards. Although there are hardly any conventional "sights" in town, the place to hang out is on the thin **Balboa Peninsula**, along which runs the three-mile-long strand. The most youthful and boisterous section is about halfway along, around **Newport Pier** at the end of 20th Street. North of here, beachfront homes restrict access, but to the south, around the **Balboa Pier**, is a tourist-friendly area with a marina from which you can escape to Santa Catalina Island (see p.112).

Orange County Museum of Art
850 San Clemente Drive • Wed–Sun 11am–5pm, Fri until 8pm • $10, free Fri • ☎ 949 759 1122, ⓦ ocma.net

Newport Beach is home to the **Orange County Museum of Art**, one of the county's few modern art institutions on a par with its LA rivals. Its collection focuses on contemporary work from California artists like Lari Pittman, Ed Ruscha and Ed Kienholz, and there are periodical retrospectives of great twentieth-century figures as well as up-and-coming southern Californian artists.

Laguna Beach

Eleven miles southeast of Newport Beach, nestled among the crags around a small sandy strip is **LAGUNA BEACH**, which has a relaxed and tolerant feel among its inhabitants, who range from millionaires to middle-class gays and lesbians, and offers a flourishing arts scene in the many streetside galleries. The PCH passes right through the centre of town, a few steps from **Main Beach** at Broadway Street.

Laguna Art Museum
307 Cliff Drive • Mon, Tues, Fri–Sun 11am–5pm, Thurs 11am–9pm • $7 • ☎ 949 494 8971, ⓦ lagunaartmuseum.org

One of the few conventional attractions in Laguna Beach is the excellent **Laguna Art Museum**, which holds fine exhibitions drawn from its stock of solely California art from the nineteenth century to the present. Painter **Norman St Clair** was drawn here in 1903, and the museum evolved from the development of an art colony in subsequent years. The city is still famed for its annual **arts festivals**, including the Pageant of the Masters in July (ⓦ foapom.com) and Plein Air Painting Invitational in October (ⓦ lagunapleinair.org). Celebrated muralist **Wyland** lives in Laguna Beach, with his **Wyland Galleries** (daily 9am–9pm; ⓦ wyland.com) half a mile south of the museum at 509 S Coast Hwy.

THE STARS OF NEWPORT BEACH

Movie stars often preferred the healthy sea breezes of Newport Beach to Beverly Hills. **John Wayne** famously spent his last, increasingly controversial, years in the town, moving into a large waterfront home in 1966 (now torn down); he was buried in the Pacific View Memorial Park cemetery in nearby Corona del Mar in 1979. His boat *Wild Goose* is now part of the Hornblower Cruises fleet (ⓦ hornblower.com), but usually rented for private charters (you'll see it in the harbour). Other celebs that once lived here include Nicolas Cage, Shirley Temple, James Cagney and George Burns. Learn all about them on a Fun Zone Boat Company (harbour tour 45min; daily noon, 2pm, 4pm & 6pm; $14; ☎ 949 673 0240, ⓦ funzoneboats.com).

Pacific Marine Mammal Center
20612 Laguna Canyon Rd • Daily 10am–4pm • Free • ☎ 949 494 3050, ⊛ pacificmmc.org

About two and a half miles inland from downtown Laguna Beach is a sight not to be missed by lovers of sea life: the **Pacific Marine Mammal Center**, a rehabilitation centre that lets you watch as underweight, injured or otherwise threatened seals and sea lions are nursed back to health.

Crystal Cove State Park
8471 N Coast Hwy, Laguna Beach • Daily sunrise–sunset • Free, parking $15/day • ☎ 949 494 3539, ⊛ crystalcovestatepark.org

Some 2.5 miles northwest of downtown Laguna Beach lies an unspoiled three-mile-long coastline, protected as **Crystal Cove State Park**, which also holds two thousand acres of rugged inland terrain good for hiking, horseriding and biking, on trails that cross hilly peaks and ravines – it's perfect to explore on foot, far from the crowds, and offers good beachside accommodation (see p.130).

San Juan Capistrano

Most of the small town of **SAN JUAN CAPISTRANO** is built in a Spanish Colonial style derived from **Mission San Juan Capistrano**, 26801 Ortega Hwy at Camino Capistrano in the centre of town (daily 9am–5pm; $9; ☎ 949 234 1300, ⊛ missionsjc.com), a short walk from the Amtrak stop. The seventh of California's missions, it was founded by Junípero Serra in 1776; soon after, the **Great Stone Church** was erected, the ruins of which are the first thing you see as you walk in – it was destroyed by an earthquake soon after its 1812 completion. Today the **Serra Chapel**, which dates back to the 1780s, is the small and narrow spiritual centre of the mission, set off by a sixteenth-century altar from Barcelona. In a side room, the tiny chapel of **St Peregrine** (the patron saint of cancer sufferers) is kept warm by the heat from the dozens of candles lit by miracle-seeking pilgrims who arrive here from all over the US and Mexico. Other restored buildings include the kitchen, smelter and workshops used for dyeing, weaving and candle making. The mission is most celebrated locally for its annual migration of **cliff swallows**; the birds begin to arrive in March from their winter home in Argentina, building nests in the mission eaves and departing in October.

ARRIVAL AND DEPARTURE   LOS ANGELES

BY PLANE
LOS ANGELES INTERNATIONAL AIRPORT (LAX)
Los Angeles International Airport (LAX) lies 16 miles southwest of Downtown LA (☎ 310 646 5252, ⊛ lawa.org).

Buses Take the free "C" shuttle to the Metro Bus Center, to connect with regular city buses. Alternatively, the LAX Flyaway bus service (☎ 866 435 9529) links LAX with Downtown's Union Station ($9 one-way), the UCLA campus in Westwood (at parking structure 32 on Kinross Ave) and Hollywood ($8 one-way). Buses run every 30min, 24hr, except at Westwood, which runs 6am–11pm ($10 one-way). You can also pick up the Santa Monica Big Blue Bus (see p.128) from Metro Bus Center.

Shuttle bus (shared van) SuperShuttle (☎ 800 258 3826, ⊛ supershuttle.com) and Prime Time Shuttle (☎ 800 733 8267, ⊛ primetimeshuttle.com) run all over town around the clock and take 30–60min depending on your destination; fares are around $17 to Downtown and the Westside, up to $40 for more outlying areas. Shuttles run from outside the baggage reclaim areas, and you should

never have to wait more than about 15min.

Taxis Taxis (on the meter) will cost around $50 from LAX to West LA, $55 to Hollywood, $40 to Santa Monica, around $100 to Disneyland, and a flat $46.50 to downtown from LAX; a $4 surcharge applies for all trips starting from LAX (⊛ taxicabsla.org for more information).

Metro Free shuttle bus service G runs to the Aviation/LAX Station on the Metro Green Line (see p.127), which runs between Norwalk and Redondo Beach; getting to Downtown Los Angeles (or anywhere else of interest other than Redondo Beach) involves at least one time-consuming transfer (tough with luggage), but it's a cheap option ($1.75).

REGIONAL AIRPORTS
If you're arriving from elsewhere in the US or from Mexico, you may also land at one of the regional airports in the LA area.

Hollywood Burbank Airport Burbank ☎ 818 840 8840, ⊛ bobhopeairport.com. Convenient for the Valley and Hollywood. The Airport Train Station is a short walk or free shuttle ride from the terminal, with Metrolink (p.127) and

1

Amtrak providing regular service into LA.

Long Beach Airport ☏562 570 2619, ⊚lgb.org. Good for the South Bay. Taxis charge around $60 to Downtown LA and $45 to Disneyland and San Pedro. Long Beach Transit buses also serve the airport ($1.25; ⊚lbtransit.com).

John Wayne Airport ☏949 252 5200, ⊚ocair.com. The fastest way to get to Orange County and Disneyland (connected by the Disneyland Resort Express bus). The airport is served by OCTA (⊚octa.net) buses #76, #212 and the i-Shuttle Route A to the closest Metrolink station.

Ontario International Airport ☏909 937 2700, ⊚lawa.org. Only useful for the eastern suburbs (it's 38 miles east of Downtown LA), and served by Omnitrans bus #61 to Pomona and #81 to Chino (⊚omnitrans.org).

BY TRAIN

Amtrak's Union Station lies on the north side of Downtown at 800 N Alameda St (☏213 624 0171), from which you can reach Metrorail and Metrolink lines and also access the nearby Patsaouras Transit Plaza, which offers connections to bus lines. To get to San Francisco (10hr 30min) you'll need to change trains in San Luis Obispo or switch to a bus in Santa Barbara.

Destinations (Amtrak) Fullerton (for Disneyland; 11 daily; 31min); Portland, OR (1 daily; 31hr 22min); Sacramento (1 daily; 13hr 49min); San Diego (11 daily; 2hr 45min–2hr 55min); Santa Barbara (6 daily; 2hr 35min–2hr 44min); Tucson (2 daily; 9hr 30min).

BY BUS

The main Greyhound bus terminal, at 1716 E 7th St (☏213 629 8401), is in a seedy section of Downtown, though access is restricted to ticket holders and it's safe enough inside. Take a taxi: on the meter Downtown locations should be $10–15, while Santa Monica will be around $55. Mega Bus and Bolt Bus (both with frequent service to Las Vegas, Oakland and San Francisco) use Patsaouras Transit Plaza, at Union Station.

Destinations Bakersfield (11 daily; 2hr 10min–2hr 35min); Las Vegas (10 daily; 5hr–7hr 55min); Palm Springs (3 daily; 2hr 30min–3hr 30min); Phoenix (8 daily; 6hr 50min–8hr 35min); Sacramento (8 daily; 7hr 15min–9hr 45min); San Diego (19 daily; 2hr 10min– 2hr 55min); San Francisco (10 daily; 7hr 25min–12hr 5min); Santa Barbara (4 daily; 2hr 10min–2hr 40min).

GETTING AROUND

DRIVING

Traditionally the most popular way to get around LA is to drive. However, traffic is bumper-to-bumper much of the day (it's often described as "stop-and-start" by local media), and improvements in public transport mean that driving is no longer the fastest way to get around the core city areas. Travelling by car can be more convenient if you are aiming to see sights in Greater LA (the Valley, Malibu, Orange County etc), given how spread out things are, and rentals are easy to pick up at LAX (see p.125). Note that LA rush-hour traffic runs (on the freeways at least) from 5am to 9am Monday to Friday; it picks up again at 3pm and runs until 7pm – avoid freeways and the Pacific Coast Highway

(PCH) at these times if you can (KNX AM News Radio 1070 has the most traffic reports; also on FM at 97.1). Sunday afternoons can also be a nightmare coming into the city, especially during the summer months; similarly, if the Dodgers or Lakers are playing, getting in and out of Downtown Los Angeles takes hours. The California Department of Transportation (CalTrans; ☏800 427 7623, ⊚dot.ca.gov/cgi-bin/roads.cgi) gives up-to-the-minute details of road conditions throughout the state.

PUBLIC TRANSPORT

The bulk of LA's public transport is operated by the LA County Metropolitan Transit Authority (MTA or "Metro"). Its massive

---

LA WITHOUT A CAR?

In *LA Story* (1991), Steve Martin's character responds to a request to walk six blocks with amused disbelief: "Walk? A walk in LA?" Even today Angelenos will happily get in their cars to drive to a shop just at the end of the block. LA has always been a city of freeways and cars, and while it really is just too big to explore entirely on foot, public transport has definitely improved in the last 25 years, with Metro lines and buses now providing a surprisingly efficient method of zipping around the city without your own wheels. The **Metro** (see opposite) is the way to go; starting at Union Square in Downtown LA, the **Gold Line** connects to a host of attractions on the way to Pasadena (see p.113), while the major sight-seeing stops of Hollywood/Vine, Hollywood/Highland and Universal City lie on the **Red Line**; get a taster of Koreatown on the **Purple Line**, Exposition Park/ USC, Westwood and Santa Monica on the **Expo Line** and even Long Beach and Redondo Beach via the **Blue Line** and **Green Line**. Disneyland is also well served by buses and trains (see opposite). Almost everywhere else is covered by LA's buses, now run entirely on CNG gas, making them the cleanest in the US. Scrolling red LED displays at major bus stops tell you when the next bus is coming (usually every 10min on main routes) and express buses are just as fast as cars.

1

GUIDED TOURS OF LA

An enlightening way to see LA is on a **guided tour**, especially if it's based around a special theme. One type of trek to avoid are the uninspired bus tours that focus on the homes of the stars (ie their ivy-covered security gates), and advertise their overpriced services around central Hollywood.

★ **Bikes And Hikes** 8250 Santa Monica Blvd, West Hollywood ☎ 323 796 8555, ⓦ bikesandhikesla .com. Exercising while on holiday seems especially apt in health-conscious LA, and these informative tours involve calorie-burning bike rides (including the amazing "LA in a day" a 6–7hr odyssey; $162; 3hr in Hollywood is $76) and hikes (Hollywood Hills; $52).

LA Conservancy ☎ 213 623 2489, ⓦ laconservancy .org. Offer walking tours ($15) for various sections and buildings in Downtown LA, which concentrate on the city's architecture, history and culture.

Melting Pot Food Tours 8484 Wilshire Blvd, Beverly Hills ☎ 424 247 9666, ⓦ meltingpottours .com. Foodies will get a kick out of these specially tailored culinary tours, taking in the Farmers' Market in Fairfax District ($59), Old Pasadena ($75), Thai Town (by celebrity chef Jet Tila; $175) and East LA ($75). Food samples included.

Union Station, on Chavez Ave at Vignes St in Downtown LA, serves many thousands of commuters travelling by Metrorail, Metrolink and Amtrak. On the east side of the station is the Patsaouras Transit Plaza, where you can hop on a bus.

METRORAIL

LA's Metrorail (ⓦ metro.net) subway and light-rail system encompasses six major lines, though extensions are planned in coming years. Trains run daily from 5am to midnight (2am Fri & Sat), about every 5min during peak hours and every 10–15min at other times. The system connects with the Metro Liner bus rapid transit system (the Orange Line for the San Fernando Valley and Silver Line for San Gabriel Valley). On Metro Rail and the Metro Orange Line, fares ($1.75 one-way; day-passes $7; seven days $25) must be loaded on a TAP stored-value card ($1); purchase your fare before you board at self-service TAP vending machines; Silver Line single fares are $2.45. The new Crenshaw/LAX Line should be up and running in 2019, linking the Expo and Green lines.

Expo Line Light rail connecting Santa Monica with Downtown LA (7th St/Metro Center).

Red Line Subway connecting Union Station in Downtown LA with North Hollywood, via 7th Street/Metro Center, Hollywood/Vine and Universal City.

Purple Line Subway connecting Union Station in Downtown LA with Wilshire/Western (following the same route as the Red Line to Wilshire/Vermont); extension planned to Westwood (earliest 2023).

Green Line Light-rail line between Redondo Beach and Norwalk, via Long Beach and LAX.

Blue Line Light-rail line running a north–south route between Long Beach and Downtown LA (7th Street/Metro Center) via South LA, Watts and Compton.

Gold Line Light rail from Pasadena and Azusa (APU/Citrus College) to East LA (Atlantic) via Downtown LA (Union Station), Little Tokyo, Chinatown, Heritage Square, Southwest Museum and Mission.

Silver Line (Metro Liner bus) Runs west from the El Monte Station in the San Gabriel Valley to Downtown LA (Union Station), then south to the Harbor Gateway Transit Center in South LA.

Orange Line (Metro Liner bus) Runs from Chatsworth in the San Fernando Valley and the Warner Center in Woodland Hills, to the North Hollywood Red Line Metro Station.

METROLINK

Metrolink commuter trains (☎ 800 371 5465, ⓦ metrolinktrains.com) ply primarily suburban-to-downtown routes on weekdays, which can be useful if you find yourself in any such far-flung districts, among them places in Orange, Ventura, Riverside and San Bernardino counties. The system reaches as far as Oceanside in San Diego County, where you can connect to that region's Coaster and Sprinter commuter rail (see p.176). Metrolink one-way fares range from $3.50–16.75. San Juan Capistrano station at 26701 Verdugo St is served by regular Amtrak and Metrolink connections to Los Angeles (1hr 20min) and San Diego (1hr 30min).

MTA BUSES

Although initially bewildering, the MTA bus network is really quite simple: the main routes run east–west (eg between Downtown and the coast) and north–south (eg between Downtown and the South Bay). With a bit of planning you should have few real problems – though always allow plenty of time. Information on bus routes is available at ⓦ metro.net. Buses on the major arteries between Downtown and the coast run roughly every 15–25min, 5am–2am; other routes, and the all-night services along the major thoroughfares, are less frequent, sometimes only hourly. At night, be careful not to get stranded Downtown waiting for connecting buses. On buses, you can pay for a single ride with cash using exact change or a TAP stored-value card (see above). Standard

1

one-way fare is $1.75, but express buses (a limited commuter service) and any others using a freeway are usually $2.50. A seven-day pass is $25, also valued on the Metro.

OTHER BUSES

DASH buses operate through the LA Department of Transportation, or LADOT (☎ 213 808 2273, ⓦ ladottransit .com), with a flat fare of 50¢ (or just 35¢ using a TAP card) for broad coverage throughout Downtown and very limited routes elsewhere in the city. LADOT also operates quick, limited-stop routes called commuter express ($1.50–4.25 depending on distance). Other local bus services include those for Orange County (OCTD; ☎ 714 636 7433, ⓦ octa .net), Long Beach (LBTD; ☎ 562 591 2301, ⓦ lbtransit.org), Culver City (☎ 310 253 6500, ⓦ culvercity.org/bus) and Santa Monica (☎ 310 451 5444, ⓦ bigbluebus.com).

BUSES TO ORANGE COUNTY BEACHES

OCTA bus (ⓦ octa.net) #1 runs hourly from Long Beach (where you can connect with LA Metro) along the coast to Huntington Beach (Pacific Coast Hwy at Balboa; 30min), then on to Newport Beach (15min), Laguna Beach (30min) and San Clemente for connections to San Diego.

TAXIS

You can find taxis at most terminals and major hotels. Fares start at $2.85, plus $2.70 for each mile (or 30¢ per 37 seconds of waiting time), with a $4 surcharge if you're picked up at LAX. The driver won't know every street in LA but will know the major ones; ask for the nearest junction and give directions from there. If you encounter problems visit ⓦ taxicabsla.org. Assuming you have a smartphone, Uber is widely available in LA.

Among the more reliable taxi companies are

Independent Cab ☎ 323 666 0050, ⓦ taxi4u.com
LA Checker Cab ☎ 800 300 5007, ⓦ ineedtaxi.com
Yellow Cab ☎ 424 222 2222, ⓦ layellowcab.com
United Independent Taxi ☎ 213 483 7669, ⓦ unitedtaxi .com

CYCLING

Cycling in LA may sound crazy, but in some areas it can be one of the better ways of getting around, especially along the coast or in Griffith Park. For maps and information, contact the LA Department of Transportation, 100 S Main St, 9th Floor (☎ 213 972 4962, ⓦ bike.lacity.org).

Bike share The city's first bike-share scheme launched in Downtown LA in 2016 (ⓦ bikeshare.metro.net), with rates of $3.50/30min; Santa Monica has its own system (ⓦ santamonicabikeshare.com).

INFORMATION

Downtown and Hollywood The LA Tourism & Convention Board (ⓦ discoverlosangeles.com) operates two visitor centres: at the North Entrance ticket booth of the Natural History Museum, 900 Exposition Blvd in Downtown LA (daily 9.30am–5pm, ☎ 213 763 3466); and at the Hollywood & Highland center, 6801 Hollywood Blvd in Hollywood (Mon–Sat 10am–10pm, Sun 10am–7pm; ☎ 323 467 6412).

Beverly Hills Visitor Center 9400 S Santa Monica Blvd (Mon–Fri 9am–5pm, Sat & Sun 10am–5pm; ☎ 310 248 1015, ⓦ lovebeverlyhills.com).

Huntington Beach Visitor Center 301 Main St (Mon–Fri 9am–5pm; ☎ 714 969 3492, ⓦ surfcityusa.com); also a kiosk at the pier (summer Mon–Fri 10.30am–7pm, Sat & Sun 10am–7pm; rest of year Mon–Fri noon–5pm, Sat &

Sun 11am–5pm).

Laguna Beach Visitor Center 381 Forest Ave (daily 10am–5pm; ☎ 800 877 1115, ⓦ visitlagunabeach.com).

Newport Beach Helpful kiosk at Fashion Island inside the Atrium Court (L/2), 401 Newport Center Drive (Mon–Fri 10am–9pm, Sat 10am–7pm, Sun 11am–6pm ☎ 855 5 639 7678, ⓦ visitnewportbeach.com).

Santa Monica Visitor Center 1920 Main St, Suite B, between Pico Blvd and Bay St; (Mon–Fri 9am–5.30pm and Sat & Sun 9am–5pm; ☎ 310 393 7593). There's also a Visitor Information Kiosk at 1400 Ocean Ave (daily: late May to Aug 9.30am–5.30pm; Sept to late May 9.45am–4.30pm; ☎ 310 393 0410, ⓦ santamonica.com), just south of Santa Monica Blvd in Palisades Park.

ACCOMMODATION

LA has plenty of accommodation from budget motels to world-class resorts. A handful of **hostels** are dotted all over the city, many in good locations, though at some stays are limited to a few nights and at others a nonstop party atmosphere prevails. Surprisingly, there are a few **campgrounds** on the edge of the metropolitan area (see box, p.131), but you'll need a car to get to them. There are plenty of **motels** near LAX, with the cheapest generally around $90, but even these have complimentary transportation to and from the terminals.

DOWNTOWN AND AROUND

The Inn at 657 657 & 663 W 23rd St ☎ 213 741 2200, ⓦ patsysinn657.com; map p.63. Excellent B&B, halfway between downtown and Exposition Park (just off I-110), with

four smart, modern rooms in an elegant 1900 building. $169

★**Jerry's Motel** 285 Lucas Ave ☎ 213 481 8181, ⓦ jerrysmotel.com; map p.63. Hip, remodelled motel with neat, stylish rooms, free parking, large flat-screen TVs

1

WHERE TO STAY?

LA is so big that the area in which you stay will have a big impact on your travel plans. **Downtown**, the historic heart of the city, has both chic hotels and basic dives, but getting to the coast from here can be a hassle; **Hollywood**, **West LA** and **West Hollywood** are safe, relatively central options for seeing the whole city, while **Santa Monica** and **Venice** are predominantly mid-to-upper-range territory, perfect for soaking up the beach culture but a long way from the cultural attractions inland. It's only worth staying in **Orange County** (p.120), thirty miles southeast of Downtown, if you're aiming for Disneyland or are travelling along the coast.

and loads of satellite channels; just outside Downtown, this is a bargain. **$89**

Luxe City Center Hotel 1020 S Figueroa St ☎ 213 748 1291, ⊚ luxecitycenter.com; map p.63. Chic, Downtown chain that offers sleek, contemporary decor, soothing tones and a host of amenities, including free use of local Gold's gym. **$240**

Westin Bonaventure 404 S Figueroa St ☎ 213 624 1000, ⊚ thebonaventure.com; map p.63. Modernist luxury hotel with five glass towers that resemble cocktail shakers, a six-storey atrium with a "lake", and elegant cone-shaped rooms. A breathtaking exterior elevator ride ascends to a rotating cocktail lounge. **$269**

HOLLYWOOD

★**Hollywood Bed & Breakfast** 1701 N Orange Grove Ave ☎ 323 874 8017, ⊚ hollywoodbandb.com; map p.79. Fun, convenient place to stay, a quirky B&B in a 1912 home that looks a little like something out of *Dr Seuss,* close to all the action, with four cosy rooms and a small pool. **$150**

Hollywood Celebrity 1775 Orchid Ave ☎ 323 850 6464, ⊚ hotelcelebrity.com; map p.79. A good choice on the affordable boutique scene, with a great location in central Hollywood and rooms with charming furnishings. **$169**

★**Magic Castle Hotel** 7025 Franklin Ave ☎ 323 851 0800, ⊚ magiccastlehotel.com; map p.79. Justly popular hotel boasting single rooms (with queen beds) and spacious one- and two-bedroom suites in a neat, modern style, with a heated pool. As well as the breakfast, there's free soda, candy, chocolate, crackers, nuts, granola bars and cookies 24 hours a day. **$199**

Orchid Suites 1753 Orchid Ave ☎ 800 537 3052, ⊚ orchidsuites.com; map p.79. Roomy, if spartan, suites with cable TV, kitchenette, laundry room and heated pool. Very close to the most popular parts of Hollywood and adjacent to the massive Hollywood & Highland mall. **$169**

The Redbury 1717 Vine St ☎ 323 962 1717, ⊚ theredbury.com; map p.79. Hollywood's most stylish boutique hotel; the theme is "bohemian counterculture" but with a sort of nineteenth-century, European elegance (more Byron than Beats) – they even call their luxurious suites "flats"; with full kitchens and washer-dryers. **$247**

WEST HOLLYWOOD

Chateau Marmont 8221 Sunset Blvd ☎ 323 656 1010, ⊚ chateaumarmont.com; map pp.90–91. Iconic hotel opened in 1929, modelled loosely on the Château d'Amboise in France's Loire Valley, which has hosted all manner of celebrities from Greta Garbo to Robert De Niro (in 1982 John Belushi was found dead of a drug overdose in bungalow #3). A bit worn these days, though, despite the glamour/infamy. Come for the history, but don't expect any kind of deal. **$575**

Élan Hotel 8435 Beverly Blvd ☎ 323 658 6663, ⊚ elanhotel.com; map pp.90–91. Good-value boutique hotel with an elegant, contemporary theme located in a busy shopping zone just north of the Beverly Center mall. As well as the free breakfast, there's a free wine and cheese reception in the late afternoon. Also with fitness centre and spa. **$250**

BEVERLY HILLS

Beverly Hills Hotel 9641 Sunset Blvd ☎ 310 276 2251, ⊚ dorchestercollection.com; map p.95. The classic Hollywood resort (the "Pink Palace" was built in 1912), with a bold colour scheme and Mission-style design, and surrounded by its own exotic gardens. Features marbled bathrooms, DVD players, jacuzzis and other such luxuries, as well as the famed *Polo Lounge* restaurant. **$765**

Beverly Hilton 9876 Wilshire Blvd ☎ 310 274 7777, ⊚ beverlyhilton.com; map p.95. This prominent, geometric white hotel at the corner of Wilshire and Santa Monica has a pool and gym, plus in-room plasma TVs, boutique decor and balconies. Whitney Houston died here in 2012; on a lighter note it is the scene of the annual Golden Globes awards and boasts one of the few remaining *Trader Vic's* bars. **$299**

Maison 140 140 S Lasky Drive ☎ 310 281 4000, ⊚ maison140.com; map p.95. High-profile place for hipsters, boasting rooms with contemporary French design, CD and DVD players and internet access, plus salon, bar and fitness room. **$195**

WEST LA

Beverly Laurel 8018 Beverly Blvd ☎ 323 651 2441; map pp.90–91. The coffee shop, *Swingers,* attracts the most attention here; the motel has nice retro 1960s

1

touches, though the rooms are plain. Good location, not far from the Fairfax District and Beverly Hills. **$180**

★ **Farmer's Daughter Hotel** 115 S Fairfax Ave ☎ 323 937 3930, ⊛ farmersdaughterhotel.com; map pp.90–91. Conveniently located across from (naturally) the Farmers' Market, this is a handsome boutique property with internet access, DVD players, flat-screen TVs and elements of "country styled" Midwestern kitsch. **$237**

SANTA MONICA AND VENICE

★ **Ambrose** 1255 20th St, Santa Monica ☎ 310 315 1555, ⊛ ambrosehotel.com; map p.101. The best choice for inland Santa Monica, with Arts and Crafts-styled decor and boutique rooms. **$349**

Cal Mar 220 California St, Santa Monica ☎ 310 395 5555, ⊛ calmarhotel.com; map p.101. Good for its central location, and the garden suites have CD/DVD players and dining rooms, kitchens and balconies. There's a heated pool, fitness room and airport shuttle too. **199**

Channel Road Inn 219 W Channel Rd, Pacific Palisades ☎ 310 459 1920, ⊛ channelroadinn.com; map p.101. B&B rooms in a romantic getaway nestled in lower Santa Monica Canyon (northwest of the city of Santa Monica), with ocean views, a hot tub and free bike rental. Enjoy complimentary grapes and champagne in the sumptuous rooms, each priced according to its view. **$345**

★ **Venice Breeze Suites** 2 Breeze Ave, Venice ☎ 310 566 2222, ⊛ venicebreezesuites.com; map p.101. Excellent location right on the boardwalk with sensational roof deck and serviced apartments equipped with full kitchens (some with ocean views). **$218**

LONG BEACH AND SANTA CATALINA ISLAND

Atwater Hotel 120 Sumner Ave, Avalon, Santa Catalina Island ☎ 310 510 2500, ⊛ visitcatalinaisland .com. This 1920s hotel offers reasonable rates right in the heart of Avalon, with simple but clean and sleek rooms, and free continental breakfast at nearby Ben's Bakery. **$119**

Mt Ada 398 Wrigley Rd, Avalon, Santa Catalina Island ☎ 310 510 2030, ⊛ visitcatalinaisland.com. For those with plenty of cash, this is the final word in Santa Catalina luxury: a gorgeous property on a hall overlooking Avalon built by tycoon William Wrigley Jr in 1921, with breakfast, lunch, evening wine and hors d'oeuvre and just six cosy period rooms with views over the ocean. **$480**

★ **Varden** 335 Pacific Ave, Long Beach ☎ 562 432 8950, ⊛ thevardenhotel.com. A 1920s building modernized with sleek white contemporary decor and cosy rooms with flat-screen TVs and boutique touches. The location a block from Pine Ave also makes this a great choice. **$139**

DISNEYLAND AND AROUND

Courtyard Anaheim Buena Park 7621 Beach Blvd, Buena Park ☎ 714 670 6600, ⊛ marriott.com. The best bet for visiting Knott's Berry Farm, with in-room fridges plus free parking, pool, spa, bar and restaurant. **$169**

Disneyland Hotel 1150 W Cerritos Ave, Anaheim ☎ 714 956 6400, ⊛ disneyland.disney.go.com. A thousand identical rooms in a huge, monolithic pile – but still, an irresistible stop for many. Also with pools, faux beach and interior shopping. The Disneyland monorail stops outside, though park admission is separate. The most fun of three similarly priced Disney hotels. **$329**

Park Place Inn 1544 S Harbor Blvd, Anaheim ☎ 714 776 4800, ⊛ parkplaceinnandminisuites.com. Best Western chain hotel across from Disneyland, with some mini-suites with fridges and microwaves, plus pool, sauna and jacuzzi. **$152**

Pavilions 1176 W Katella Ave, Anaheim ☎ 714 776 0140, ⊛ pavilionshotel.com. Convenient Best Western hotel offering basic rooms with fridges and microwaves, as well as a pool, spa, sauna, and shuttle to Disneyland. **$143**

ORANGE COUNTY COAST

Hilton Waterfront Beach Resort 21100 Pacific Coast Hwy ☎ 714 845 8000, ⊛ hilton.com. A towering high-rise with beautifully furnished rooms and the added attractions of private balconies, serpentine pool, spa, and rentals of everything from surfboards to rollerblades; rooms have views of gardens or ocean; big savings can be found in low season. **$255**

Huntington Surf Inn 720 Pacific Coast Hwy ☎ 714 536 2444, ⊛ huntingtonsurfinn.com. Right on the beach and close to the pier, with nine simple but super-cool rooms featuring a pop art theme based on Southern California beach and surfing culture – and lots of pro surfers really do stay here. **$149**

Laguna Beach House 475 N Coast Hwy ☎ 949 497 6645, ⊛ thelagunabeachhouse.com. Stylish boho hotel (with a 1950s surfer theme) right on the coast with contemporary rooms, pool and a host of extras (use of boogie boards, free wine and cookies every evening). **$199**

HOSTELS

Banana Bungalow 5920 Hollywood Blvd ☎ 877 977 5077, ⊛ bananabungalow.com; map p.79. Large, popular hostel, just east of the heart of Hollywood, with airport shuttles, internet, tours to Venice Beach and theme parks, and in-room kitchens and many other amenities. There's a similarly priced branch in West Hollywood at 603 N Fairfax Ave (☎ 323 655 2002). Dorms **$38**, doubles **$100**

HI–Santa Monica 1436 2nd St, at Broadway, Santa Monica ☎ 310 393 9913, ⊛ hilosangeles.org; map p.101. A few blocks from the beach and pier, the building was LA's Town Hall from 1887 to 1889, and retains its

1

CAMPING LA

Camping in the LA area is possible, notably in Malibu. Reserve America (☎800 444 7275, ⓦreserveamerica.com) processes reservations at many of the **campgrounds** listed below and can look for an alternative if your chosen site is full.

CAMPGROUNDS

Bolsa Chica Campground 17851 Pacific Coast Hwy (1.5 miles south of Warner Ave) ☎714 846 3460, ⓦreserveamerica.com. Facing the ocean in Huntington Beach, also near a thousand-acre wildlife sanctuary and birders' paradise, with fishing opportunities as well. Campers with a self-contained vehicle only; no tent camping. From $55

★**Crystal Cove State Park** 8471 Pacific Coast Hwy, north of Laguna Beach ☎949 494 3539, ⓦcrystalcovestatepark.com. Two thousand acres of woods and nearly four miles of coastline (rich with tide pools) make this tent-camping park (*Moro Campground*) a good choice for all manner of activities. Note there is no beach camping; *Moro* is on the bluffs overlooking the ocean, and the park's primitive campgrounds are a three- to four-mile hike inland

from the parking lot. Pitches from $55

Leo Carrillo State Park 35000 W Pacific Coast Hwy, Malibu ☎800 444 7275. Campgrounds in sight of the ocean, 25 miles northwest of Santa Monica on the Pacific Coast Hwy. Pitches from $45

Malibu Creek State Park 1925 Las Virgenes Rd, Calabasas ☎818 880 0367. A rustic campground in a park that can become crowded at times. Sixty sites in the shade of huge oak trees, almost all with fire pits, solar-heated showers, and flush toilets. Pitches from $45

Point Mugu State Park 9000 W Pacific Coast Hwy, Malibu ☎310 457 8143. On the northwestern edge of the Santa Monica Mountains, this park has five miles of shoreline, with sand dunes and canyons, and the waters are good for surfing and fishing. Primitive sites $10, developed $45

historic charm, with a pleasant inner courtyard, movie room – and 260 beds. Reservations essential in summer. Dorm $49

Orange Drive Hostel 1764 N Orange Drive, Hollywood ☎323 850 0350, ⓦorangedrivehostel.com; map p.79. Centrally located hostel (right behind the Chinese Theatre), offering tours to film studios, theme parks and homes of the stars. Dorms $40, doubles $98

Orbit Hotel and Hostel 603 N Fairfax Ave, West Hollywood ☎323 655 1510, ⓦorbithotel.com; map pp.90–91. Retro 1960s hotel and hostel with sleek Day-Glo furnishings and modern decor, offering a movie screening room, patio, café, private baths in all rooms, and shuttle tours. Dorms $37, doubles $99

★**Samesun Venice Beach Hostel** 25 Windward Ave, Venice ☎310 399 7649, ⓦsamesun.com; map p.101.

Just off the Venice boardwalk (some rooms get ocean views), with dorms and simple but stylish double rooms with shared or private bathrooms. Great kitchen and laundry facilties, too. Dorms $45, doubles $130

Stay on Main Hotel 636 S Main St, Downtown ☎213 213 7829, ⓦstayonmain.com; map p.63. Lodging near a gritty section of Downtown, offering clean, simple but stylish accommodation, with shared bunk rooms and private rooms with and without private bath. Dorms $55, doubles $105

★**USA Hostels – Hollywood** 1624 Schrader Ave ☎323 462 3777, ⓦusahostels.com; map p.79. A block south of the centre of Hollywood Blvd, near major attractions, and with a games room, private baths, bar and garden patio, as well as airport and train shuttles. Dorms $49, doubles $140

EATING

Given its glamorous associations, it's no surprise that LA is one of America's culinary hotspots when it comes to gourmet dining, though on a street level it's true that **Mexican food** is the closest thing to an indigenous LA cuisine with a taqueria on every other block, while purveyors of **East Asian food** and gourmet **street carts** have also boomed in recent years. Many of the city's **higher-end restaurants** serve **California cuisine**, the signature style of top-notch LA eating, blending French-styled food with fresh local ingredients in an eclectic, harmonious brew.

DOWNTOWN AND AROUND

★**Bestia** 2121 7th Place ☎213 514 5724, ⓦbestiala .com; map p.63. Creative, multi-regional Italian restaurant, with menus based on over sixty different house-cured meats and charcuterie, and Napolitana pizzas baked in wood-fired ovens (mains $15–19). Mon–Thurs &

Sun 5–11pm, Fri & Sat 5pm–midnight.

★**Cielito Lindo** 23 Olvera St ☎213 687 4391, ⓦcielito lindo.org; map p.63. Celebrated Mexican joint at the north end of Olvera since 1934; expect long lines for their tasty fried taquitos with shredded beef and avocado sauce ($1.75). Mon–Thurs & Sun 9am–11pm, Fri & Sat 9am–midnight.

1

LA FOOD TRUCKS TO TRACK DOWN

LA's food truck scene is worth sampling, but check websites or Twitter for the latest locations and times.

Bollywood Bites ⓦthebollywoodbites.com. Sumptuous Indian cuisine – bowls ($8.75) of chicken curry, chana masala and so on, usually in Westwood.

Guerrilla Tacos ⓦguerrillatacos.com. Small menu of near-perfect tacos ($4–12) filled with sweet potato and feta, crab or rib-eye steak (see website for locations). Mon–Sat 10am–2pm, Sun 10am–5pm.

Lobsta Truck ⓦlobstatruck.com. Mouthwatering lobster rolls ($13) and crab rolls ($12) in various locations (the bricks-and-mortar *Lobsta Shack* is open daily at 701 W Cesar Chavez Ave in Downtown LA). Wed–Sun.

Ricky's Fish Tacos ⓦtwitter.com/RickysFishTacos. Highly sought after Ensenada-style catfish and shrimp tacos ($3.50–4) from Ricky Piña. Usually open Wed–Sun 11.30am–4pm, but you'll have to check his Twitter feed for locations.

Clifton's Cafeteria 648 S Broadway, ☎213 627 1673, ⓦcliftonsla.com; map p.63. Classic 1935 cafeteria with bizarre decor: giant faux redwood tree, waterfall and stuffed grizzly. The food was revamped in 2015, with plays on traditional American snacks: jell-o in little jam cups, on top of cheesecake, plus corned beef and cabbage and the like. Look for Ray Bradbury's favourite booth, decorated with memorabilia. Tues–Thurs 11am–9pm, Fri 11am–10pm, Sat 10am–10pm, Sun 10am–9pm.

Cole's Pacific Electric Buffet 118 E 6th St ☎213 622 4090; map p.63. In the same seedy spot since 1908, this is LA's oldest restaurant. The decor and food haven't changed much, and the rich, hearty French-dip sandwiches are still loaded with steak, pastrami or brisket – a dish supposedly invented at this very spot, a claim challenged by *Philippe's* (see opposite). Mon–Wed & Sun 11am–midnight, Thurs–Sat 11am–2am.

★**Grand Central Market** 317 S Broadway, between 3rd and 4th sts ☎213 624 2378, ⓦgrandcentralmarket .com. Venerable food market crammed with office workers chowing down during the week, with tempting options including the *China Café* (9am–10pm), breakfast specialist *Eggslut* (8am–4pm), *Horse Thief BBQ* (11am–10pm) and *Sarita's Pupuseria* (9am–6pm) for Salvadorean *pupusas* (stuffed tortillas). Market daily 8am–10pm.

★**Howlin Ray's** 727 N Broadway Ave (Far East Plaza) ☎213 935 8399, ⓦhowlinrays.com. Nashville's signature spicy hot fried chicken sandwich ($11) arrived in LA in 2016 and instantly became a cult hit – expect long lines at this counter-only Chinatown mall diner. Wed–Sun 11am–4pm.

La Luz del Dia 1 Olvera St ☎213 628 7495, ⓦluzdeldia .com; map p.63. Mexican place that's been here since 1959, worth seeking out for its authentic Michoacán food, fiery tacos ($2.15), tostadas ($4.40) and combo plates ($6.50–8.80), served in portions sizeable enough to make you sweat with a smile. Mon 11am–3.30pm, Tues–Thurs 10am–8pm, Fri & Sat 10am–9pm, Sun 8.30am–9pm.

Original Pantry Café 877 S Figueroa St ☎213 972 9279, ⓦpantrycafe.com; map p.63. Hearty portions of meaty American cooking – chops and steaks, mostly – since 1924, in this diner owned by former mayor Dick Riordan. The breakfast is the best option (available all day); plates from $5.50 (cash only). Daily 24hr.

Otium 222 S Hope St ☎213 935 8500, ⓦotiumla.com; map p.63. Trendy new restaurant from chef Tim Hollingsworth, featuring a terrace opposite the Broad lined with olive trees and contemporary American dishes such as foie-gras funnel cake with strawberries ($27) and big fin squid ($19). Tues–Thurs 11.30am–2.30pm & 5.30–10pm, Fri 11.30am–2.30pm & 5.30–11pm, Sat 10.30am–2.30pm & 5.30–11pm, Sun 10.30am–2.30pm & 5.30–10pm.

★**Philippe the Original French Dip** 1001 N Alameda St ☎213 628 3781, ⓦphilippes.com; map p.63. This 1908 sawdust café that serves up the eponymous sandwich with turkey, ham, lamb, pork or beef dipped in roasting pan juices – an amazingly good and filling treat for $7.50. Cash only. Daily 6am–10pm.

★**Phoenix Bakery** 969 N Broadway, Chinatown ☎213 628 4642, ⓦphoenixbakeryinc.com; map p.63. Chinatown's largest and oldest bakery has been knocking out its famous strawberry whipped-cream cake since 1938 (from $9.95), among numerous other sweet treats. Daily 9am–7.30pm.

Phoenix Inn 301 Ord St, Chinatown ☎213 629 2812, ⓦphoenixinn.us; map p.63. Chinatown restaurant open since 1965 that offers an array of tasty noodle soups, hot pots, fried noodles and tofu items. The seafood, duck and sliced prime rib are also worth a try (most mains from $9–14). Daily 11am–1am.

Redbird 114 E 2nd St ☎213 788 1191, ⓦredbird.la; map p.63. Chef Neal Fraser's innovative, contemporary American cuisine served in the beautifully converted 1885 rectory of the old Cathedral of Saint Vibiana. Dishes might include chicken pot pie ($16), the sensational barbecue smoked tofu ($25) and rainbow curried carrots ($13), as well as plenty of fresh fish. Mon–Thurs 5–10pm, Fri 11.30am–2pm & 5–11pm, Sat 10am–2pm & 5–11pm, Sun 10am–2pm & 5–10pm.

★**Smorgasburg** Alameda Produce Market, 785 Bay St ☎ 718 928 6603 ⓦ la.smorgasburg.com. The hip weekly Williamsburg (New York) food market now has a branch in LA, with around a hundred delectable stalls such as Black Sugar Ribs Co, Burritos La Palma, Donut Friend, Sticky Rice on Wheels and TJ's Tacos. Go hungry. Sun 10am–5pm.

Water Grill 544 S Grand Ave ☎ 213 891 0900, ⓦ watergrill.com; map p.63. One of the top-priced, top-notch spots for munching on California cuisine, with the focus on seafood, prepared in all manner of colourful ways – such as mint bass ceviche, or big-eye tuna with pomegranate couscous (mains $26–58). Mon–Thurs 11.30am–10pm, Fri 11.30am–11pm, Sat 5–11pm, Sun 4–10pm.

CENTRAL LA

★**Dong Il Jang** 3455 W 8th St, Koreatown ☎ 213 383 5757. Cosy little Korean restaurant – one of K-Town's oldest – where the meat is cooked at your table and the food is consistently good, especially the grilled chicken, kimchi fried rice and roasted *gui* prime rib. Tempura dishes and a sushi bar are an added draw. Tues–Sun 11.30am–10pm.

Intelligentsia 3922 W Sunset Blvd, Silver Lake ☎ 323 663 6173, ⓦ intelligentsiacoffee.com. Coffee connoisseurs should make the trip to the king of LA's café scene, where top blends are fresh-roasted daily in vintage German roasters. Mon–Wed & Sun 6am–8pm, Thurs–Sat 6am–10pm.

★**Langer's Deli** 704 S Alvarado St, Westlake (MacArthur Park) ☎ 213 483 8050, ⓦ langersdeli.com; map p.63. Offers more than twenty ways of eating what is easily LA's best pastrami sandwich since 1947. Located in a dicey spot west of Downtown; kerbside pick-up available (hot pastrami sandwich $14.95). Mon–Sat 8am–4pm.

★**Original Tommy's Hamburgers** 2575 Beverly Blvd, Westlake ☎ 213 389 9060, ⓦ originaltommys.com. One of the prime LA spots for big, greasy, tasty burgers, home-made chilli and scrumptious fries – and, many would say, the best. Located right off the 101 freeway in a somewhat grim section of Westlake. Daily 24hr.

Taylor's Steak House 3361 W 8th St, Koreatown ☎ 213 382 8449, ⓦ taylorssteakhouse.com. Old-school steakhouse marooned in Koreatown but still serving the best slabs of meat in the city for the price; prime top sirloin is $26.95 (14-ounce) and the French onion soup ($4.95) is magnificent. Mon–Thurs 11.30am–9.30pm, Fri 11.30am–10.30pm, Sat 4–10.30pm, Sun 4–9.30pm.

HOLLYWOOD AND AROUND

25 Degrees 7000 Hollywood Blvd (Hollywood Roosevelt Hotel) ☎ 323 785 7244, ⓦ 25degrees restaurant.com; map p.79. The top gourmet burger joint in town, where you can pack your home-made burger

(from $15) with fried eggs, avocado, prosciutto, pesto, even artisan cheeses, along with more traditional toppings. Daily 24hr.

Cactus Taqueria 950 Vine St ☎ 323 464 5865; map p.79. This tiny shack on the corner is a good spot to keep the evening going while you're club-hopping, with delicious quesadillas and burritos ($4.75) – and the best fish tacos in Hollywood ($2.25). Cash only. Mon–Thurs & Sun 8am–3am, Fri & Sat 8am–4am.

Fred 62 1854 N Vermont Ave, Los Feliz ☎ 323 667 0062, ⓦ fred62.com; map p.79. Designed like something out of the 1950s and on the way to Griffith Park, this diner offers stylish, affordable California-cuisine twists on familiar staples like salads, burgers ($9) and fries, and a tempting array of pancakes and omelettes ($7–12). Daily 24hr.

Jitlada 5233 Sunset Blvd (Thai Town) ☎ 323 667 9809; map p.79. In a dreary mini-mall, but a cult favourite; the spicy chicken, squid, oxtail curry, papaya salad, and fishball and other seafood curries more than make up for the setting. Affordable prices, too (combo specials $12.95). Tues–Sun 11am–3pm & 5–10.30pm.

Miceli's 1646 N Las Palmas Ave ☎ 323 466 3438, ⓦ micelis.restaurant; map p.79. Generous, old-style pizzas ($15–26) have been served by *Miceli's* since 1949, laden with gooey cheese and plenty of tomato sauce. It's hardly nouvelle cuisine, but you'll be too busy scarfing it down to notice. Daily 11.30am–10pm.

Moun of Tunis 7445 Sunset Blvd ☎ 323 874 3333, ⓦ mounoftunis.la; map p.79. Mouthwatering Tunisian and Moroccan food presented in huge, multi-course meals, heavy on the spices and rich on the exotic flavours – plus regular belly dancing. Set menus range from $18 (vegetarian) to $30 per person. Daily 5–11pm.

Off Vine 6263 Leland Way ☎ 323 962 1900, ⓦ offvine .com; map p.79. Dine on eclectic California cuisine – Cornish game hen with cornbread, turkey breast with jalapeño relish – in a renovated but still funky Craftsman bungalow (mains $20–39). Daily 11.30am–10.30pm.

★**Osteria Mozza** 6602 Melrose Ave ☎ 323 297 0100, ⓦ osteriamozza.com; map p.79. Italian fine dining culinary star (from the Mario Batali stable) with an amazing mozzarella bar showcasing handcrafted varieties from cream-filled burrata to spongy bufala ($17–26). Mon–Fri 5.30–11pm, Sat 5–11pm, Sun 5–10pm.

★**Pink's Hot Dogs** 709 N La Brea Ave ☎ 323 931 7594, ⓦ pinkshollywood.com; map p.79. Depending on your taste, these monster hot dogs – topped with anything from bacon and chilli cheese to pastrami and Swiss cheese – are lifesavers or gut bombs, served here since 1939 (from $4.40). Mon–Thurs & Sun 9.30am–2am, Fri & Sat 9.30am–3am.

★**Providence** 5955 Melrose Ave ☎ 323 460 4170, ⓦ providencela.com; map p.79. Near the top of the LA pricey-restaurant scale (dinner *prix fixe* menu $120–185; lunch $95), and for good reason: the place is swarming with

1

foodies, who come for the black sea bass, foie-gras ravioli, lump blue crab and plenty of other tremendous choices crafted by chef Michael Cimarusti. Mon–Thurs 6–10pm, Fri noon–2pm & 6–10pm, Sat 5.30–10pm, Sun 5.30–9pm.

Roscoe's House of Chicken and Waffles 1514 N Gower St ☎323 466 7453, ⊛roscoeschickenandwaffles .com; map p.79. This diner – a soul food restaurant chain founded in 1975 by Herb Hudson, a Harlem native – attracts all sorts for its fried chicken, greens and thick waffles ($9–16). Mon–Thurs 8.30am–midnight, Fri & Sat 8am–4am, Sun 8am–midnight.

Sanamluang Café 5176 Hollywood Blvd (Thai Town) ☎323 660 8006; map p.79. You can't beat the cheap, excellent and plentiful noodles, or the squid salad and spicy shrimp soup, at this nearly-all-night Thai place (classic tom *kha kai* $6.95; pad thai $6.25). Daily 11am–3.30am.

★**Yuca's** 2056 N Hillhurst Ave, Los Feliz ☎323 662 1214, ⊛yucasla.com; map p.79. A hidden jewel serving considerable burritos (from $5.85), Yucatan-style pork, and beef tacos ($3.50–4), and which despite its small size has garnered a national following. Mon–Sat 11am–6pm.

WEST HOLLYWOOD

Barney's Beanery 8447 Santa Monica Blvd ☎323 654 2287, ⊛barneysbeanery.com; map pp.90–91. Hundreds of bottled beers and hot dogs, hamburgers (from $9.50) and classic bowls of chilli ($5.50), served in a hip, grungy environment since 1927. Angelenos can be divided up by those who love or hate the place – everyone knows it. Mon–Fri 11am–2pm, Sat & Sun 9am–2am.

Bossa Nova 685 N Robertson Blvd ☎310 657 5070, ⊛bossanovafood.com; map pp.90–91. Enticing Brazilian restaurant with a menu that includes South American staples (shrimp croquettes, fried yucca, etc) and more unexpected items such as chicken skewers, filet mignon and pasta (mains $12.50–24). Mon–Thurs 11am–11.30pm, Fri & Sat 11am–3.30am, Sun 11am–midnight.

Canter's Deli 419 N Fairfax Ave ☎323 651 2030, ⊛cantersdeli.com; map pp.90–91. Huge pastrami sandwiches ($14.50) and excellent kosher matzo balls and chicken soups served by waitresses in pink uniforms and running shoes. Live music nightly in *Canter's* adjoining "Kibbitz Room" till 1.40am. Open since 1931. Daily 24hr.

Carlitos Gardel 7963 Melrose Ave ☎323 655 0891, ⊛carlitosgardel.com; map pp.90–91. Seriously rich and tasty Argentine cuisine – heavy on the beef and spices, with sausages and garlic adding to the kick (steaks $29–52). Mon–Thurs & Sat 6–11pm, Fri 11.30am–2.30pm & 6–11pm, Sun 5–10pm.

Carney's 8351 Sunset Blvd ☎323 654 8300, ⊛carneytrain.com; map pp.90–91. This renovated train carriage has become something of an LA icon (featuring in TV show *Entourage*) – though the food is standard diner

fare (with especially good burgers and hot dogs) the novelty of eating in an old Pacific Railroad train makes a trip worthwhile. Mon–Thurs & Sun 11am–midnight, Fri & Sat 11am–3am.

Du-par's 6333 W 3rd St ☎323 933 8446, ⊛dupars.net; map pp.90–91. A long-standing LA institution (since 1938), located in the Farmers' Market, which draws a whole host of old-timers for its gut-busting comfort food, from chicken pot pie to cheeseburgers to the beloved buttermilk hot cakes (most dishes $10–15). Daily 24hr.

Gracias Madre 8905 Melrose Ave ☎323 978 2170, ⊛graciasmadreweho.com; map pp.90–91. "Thank you mother" specializes in organic, plant-based (vegan) Mexican-inspired food, with tasty mains ranging from black bean burgers and enchiladas stuffed with zucchini, cashews and avocado, to coconut ceviche tostada and grilled corn cakes (mains $13–20). Mon–Fri 11am–11pm, Sat & Sun 10am–11pm.

★**Griddle Café** 7916 Sunset Blvd ☎323 874 0377, ⊛thegriddlecafe.com; map pp.90–91. The postmodern Hollywood version of a diner, where the pancakes, chilli and omelettes come with various outlandish toppings (Oreos, breakfast cereal, etc), and the cheesecake French toast will make you cheer (mains $8–15). Mon–Fri 7am–4pm, Sat & Sun 8am–4pm.

King's Road Espresso House 8361 Beverly Blvd ☎323 655 9044, ⊛kingsroadcafe.com; map pp.90–91. Pavement café in the centre of a busy shopping strip, with good breakfasts and lunches and some of the best coffee in the city. Popular with the hipster crowd as well as a few tourist interlopers. Breakfast plates $8.75–15.50. Mon–Fri 6am–5pm, Sat & Sun 7am–4pm.

★**Locanda Veneta** 8638 W 3rd St ☎310 274 1893, ⊛locandaveneta.net; map pp.90–91. Scrumptious ravioli, risotto, veal and carpaccio with a Venetian slant – it's pricey, but you can't go wrong at one of LA's culinary hotspots (dinner mains $27.95–39.95, pasta $14.95–27.95). Mon–Fri 11am–10pm, Sat 5–10.30pm, Sun 5–9.30pm.

★**Mel's Drive-in** 8585 Sunset Blvd ☎310 854 7201, ⊛melsdrive-in.com; map pp.90–91. This classic Googie diner with the iconic sign is loads of fun (once home to *Ben Franks*, it's now part of a mini-chain), offering all the usual staples (burgers, breakfasts, shakes) plus jukebox selector on every table. Daily 24hr.

BEVERLY HILLS

Cut 9500 Wilshire Blvd (Beverly Wilshire) ☎310 276 8500, ⊛wolfgangpuck.com; map p.79. This hotel steakhouse, with chef Wolfgang Puck at the helm, was designed by Richard Meier and looks like the Getty Center cafeteria. If you fancy a splurge on exquisite steaks that cost up to $100, Kobe short ribs, and Maine lobster, this is the place. Mon–Thurs 6–10pm, Fri 6–11pm, Sat 5.30–11pm.

Nate 'n Al 414 N Beverly Drive ☎310 274 0101, ⓦnatenal.com; map p.79. The best-known Jewish deli in Beverly Hills, here since 1945, famed for its smoked fish (especially wild smoked salmon), corned beef, beef hot dogs and potato pancakes. Get there early to grab a booth. Breakfast plates $9–13. Daily 7am–9pm.

★**Nobu Matsuhisa** 129 N La Cienega Blvd ☎310 659 9639, ⓦnobumatsuhisa.com; map pp.90–91. The biggest name in town for sushi, charging the highest prices. Essential if you're a raw-fish aficionado with a wad of cash; combo lunches $22–30, or fixed-price meals $70–200. Mon–Fri 11.45am–2.15pm & 5.45–10.15pm, Sat & Sun 5.45–10.15pm.

Spago 176 N Cañon Drive ☎310 385 0880, ⓦwolfgangpuck.com; map p.79. Flagship restaurant that helped nationalize Cal cuisine (in a different location), and still good for supping on Wolfgang Puck's latest concoctions, among them slow-roasted turbot and brioche-stuffed quail (six-course tasting menu $95). Mon 6–10pm, Tues–Fri noon–2.30pm & 6–10pm, Sat noon–2.30pm & 5.30–10.30pm, Sun 5.30–10pm.

WEST LA

★**The Apple Pan** 10801 W Pico Blvd, West LA ☎310 475 3585; map pp.90–91. Grab a spot at the U-shaped counter and enjoy freshly baked apple pie with vanilla ice cream and nicely greasy hamburgers (from $7–8). An old-time joint that opened in 1947, and was supposedly the inspiration for the Johnny Rockets chain. Daily 11am–midnight.

Black Dog Coffee 5657 Wilshire Blvd, Mid-Wilshire ☎323 933 1976, ⓦblackdogcoffee.com; map pp.90–91. Great choice on Miracle Mile, serving excellent espresso from roasters Groundwork Coffee, sandwiches, salads, authentic Chicago hot dogs ($6) and plenty of vegan options. Mon–Fri 7am–6pm, Sat & Sun 8am–4pm.

★ **Diddy Riese Cookies** 926 Broxton Ave, Westwood ☎310 208 0448, ⓦdiddyriese.com. This Westwood staple has a cult following among UCLA students for cookies (especially the peanut butter flavour; 50¢ each, dozen for $4.50) and ice-cream sandwiches ($2), made with cookies. Mon–Thurs 11am–midnight, Fri 11am–1am, Sat noon–1am, Sun noon–midnight.

John o' Groats 10516 W Pico Blvd, Rancho Park ☎310 204 0692, ⓦogroatsrestaurant.com; map pp.90–91. Excellent breakfasts and lunches (mostly staples like bacon and eggs, oatmeal, and waffles), but come outside of the morning rush hour. A full breakfast will set you back $15–20. Daily 7am–3pm.

★**Tsujita** 2057 Sawtelle Blvd, West LA ☎310 231 7373, ⓦtsujita-la.com; map pp.90–91. One of the hottest ramen noodle shops in the city, with mouthwatering *tsukemen*, dipping noodles with an incredible pork broth ($9.95), served at lunch only. Daily 11am–2am.

SANTA MONICA

Cha Cha Chicken 1906 Ocean Ave ☎310 581 1684, ⓦchachachicken.com; map p.101. This no-frills Caribbean beach shack south of the pier is old-school Santa Monica, with excellent jerk chicken (half-chicken $13.95), cubano sandwiches ($9.75) and fresh fruit juices ($3). Mon–Fri 11am–10pm, Sat & Sun 10am–10pm.

Coast 1 Pico Blvd (Shutters on the Beach) ☎310 587 1707, ⓦshuttersonthebeach.com; map p.101. This classy hotel restaurant is right on the beach, the perfect place to eat breakfast or just check out the boardwalk scene with a chilled wine and guacamole dip. Mains $19–31. Daily 7am–10pm.

★**Espresso Cielo** 3101 Main St ☎310 314 9999, ⓦsm.espressocielo.com; map p.101. Beautifully crafted coffees from Vancouver's lauded 49th Parallel roasters, in a sunny setting near the beach. Also serves a good range of teas and excellent locally made pastries. Daily 7am–7pm.

★**Father's Office** 1018 Montana Ave ☎310 736 2224, ⓦfathersoffice.com; map p.101. If you're as interested in celebrity-spotting as in dinner, check out this chic gastropub, which opened back in 1953, where the craft beers and the chef Sang Yoon's "Office Burger" ($12.50) have garnered a loyal following. Mon–Thurs 5pm–1am, Fri 4pm–2am, Sat noon–2am, Sun noon–midnight.

Joe's Pizza 111 Broadway ☎310 395 9222, ⓦjoespizza .com; map p.101. New Yorkers like to complain about LA pizza (with some justification), though this branch of the famous West Village, New York takeaway features the requisite crispy, thin pizza prepared with aplomb (slices $2.75–4). Mon–Thurs & Sun 10am–midnight, Fri & Sat 10am–3am.

Mélisse 1104 Wilshire Blvd ☎310 395 0881, ⓦmelisse .com; map p.101. Top of the line in some people's minds for LA dining (it does have two Michelin stars), Josiah Citrin's California-French restaurant offers a fixed-price $145 four-course menu that may include duck breast with cherries, Sonoma sausage or seafood. Tues–Thurs 6–9.30pm, Fri 6–10pm, Sat 5.45–10pm.

24-HOUR EATS

25 Degrees Hollywood. See p.133
Bob's Big Boy, Burbank. See p.138
Canter's Deli West Hollywood. See p.134
Fred 62 Los Feliz. See p.133
Mel's Drive-in West Hollywood. See p.134
Original Pantry Café Downtown. See p.132
Original Tommy's Hamburgers Central LA. See p.133
Randy's Donuts Inglewood. See p.136

1

★**Rae's Restaurant** 2901 Pico Blvd ☎310 828 7937; map p.101. Classic diner dating from 1958, which serves heavy, tasty comfort food. Its turquoise-blue façade and interior have been seen in many films, notably *True Romance*, Steve Martin's *Bowfinger* and the remake of *Starsky and Hutch*. Eat for under $10, cash only. Daily 5.30am–9pm.

Tacos por Favor 1408 Olympic Blvd ☎310 392 5768, ⓦtacosporfavor.net; map p.101. Uninspiring from the outside, but this humble spot has some of the city's best chow, including great tacos (from $2.75) and tortas, and hefty burritos ($4.85–9.50) that are easy on your wallet – but not your waistline. Daily 8am–8pm.

★**Umami Burger** 525 Broadway ☎310 451 1300, ⓦumami.com; map p.101. Home of the truffle burger ($13.50), manly chick burger ($12), maple bacon fries ($6.50) and several other artful creations (including ahi tuna burger), this mini chain has become a major coast-to-coast fad. Mon–Thurs 11am–11pm, Fri 11am–midnight, Sat 10.30am–midnight, Sun 10.30am–11pm.

VENICE

Big Daddy's Pizza 1425 Ocean Front Walk ☎310 806 8486, ⓦbigdaddyspizzavenice.com; map p.101. Classic hole-in-the-wall on the Boardwalk that's been an institution with local surfers and kids for years; grab one of the huge slices of pizza ($6), lobster roll for $16 (or fried Oreo on a stick; $6) and munch on the beach. Daily 10am–9.30pm.

★**Blue Star Donuts** 1142 Abbot Kinney Blvd ☎310 450 5630, ⓦbluestardonuts.com; map p.101. Fabulous gourmet doughnuts at an outpost of the lauded Portland outfit, offering chic flavours such as lemon, poppy and buttermilk and blueberry, bourbon and basil. Daily 7am until they run out.

Figtree's Café 429 Ocean Front Walk ☎310 392 4937, ⓦfigtreescafe.com; map p.101. Tasty veggie food and grilled fresh fish on a sunny patio just off the Boardwalk. Health-conscious fans come in droves for breakfast (mains from $9.95). Daily 8am–9pm.

★**Gjelina** 1429 Abbot Kinney Blvd ☎310 450 1429, ⓦgjelina.com; map p.101. Cool American bistro serving great small plates like grilled octopus ($20) and grilled king oyster mushrooms ($10), pizzas ($13–17) and various charcuterie ($7–20). Daily 8am–midnight.

James' Beach 60 N Venice Blvd ☎310 823 5396, ⓦjamesbeach.com; map p.101. Another Venice institution, known locally for its fresh mahi-mahi tacos ($24); with its casual beach vibe not far from the boardwalk, it makes it a fun place for food, wine or cocktails. Mon & Tues 6pm–1.30am, Wed–Sun 11.30am–1.30am.

MALIBU

★**Nobu Malibu** 22706 Pacific Coast Hwy ☎310 317 9140, ⓦnoburestaurants.com. This is what you expect in Malibu: amazing ocean views, romantic setting and celeb chef's top-notch seafood (black cod miso, yellowtail sashimi) overlooking Surfrider beach and the Malibu Pier. Dishes (simply divided into "hot" and "cold") ranges $12–56. Mon–Thurs noon–10pm, Fri & Sat 9am–11pm, Sun 9am–10pm.

LAX AND THE SOUTH BAY

★**Pann's** 6710 La Tijera Blvd, Inglewood ☎323 776 3770, ⓦpanns.com. One of the all-time great Googie diners since 1958 – with a pitched roof, big neon sign, exotic plants and wealth of primary colours – where you can't go wrong with the classic burgers or biscuits and gravy (mains $10–15). Mon & Tues 7am–3pm, Wed & Sun 7am–9pm, Thurs–Sat 7am–10pm.

Polly's on the Pier 233 N Harbor Drive, Redondo Beach ☎310 318 3736. Great place to start the day or have lunch, right on Redondo Beach Pier, with buttermilk pancakes (from $6.20) and breakfast plates ($8–12) to burgers and sandwiches ($8–11). Daily 5am–2pm.

★**Randy's Donuts** 805 W Manchester Ave, Inglewood ☎310 645 4707, ⓦrandysdonuts.com. Built in 1953, this pop art fixture is hard to miss, thanks to the colossal doughnut sitting on the roof (memorably featured in *Iron Man 2*). Excellent for its piping-hot treats ($0.95–1.35), which you can pick up at the drive-through on your way to or from LAX. Daily 24hr.

Uncle Bill's Pancake House 1305 Highland Ave, Manhattan Beach ☎310 318 1556, ⓦunclebills.net. Popular local diner (opened by "Uncle Bill" McElroy in 1961), just up from the beach (often long lines for breakfast), with stellar ocean views and excellent diner classics (fish and chips, burgers, pancakes). Mon–Fri 6am–3pm, Sat & Sun 7am–3pm.

LONG BEACH

Alegria Cocina Latina 115 Pine Ave ☎562 436 3388, ⓦalegriacocinalatina.com. Tapas, gazpacho and a variety of *platos principales* served with sangria on the patio, and to the beat of live flamenco at weekends. Good location near the harbour in downtown Long Beach (mains $14–23). Mon–Thurs 5–10pm, Fri & Sat 5pm–2am, Sun 11.30am–10pm.

Johnny Reb's 4663 N Long Beach Blvd ☎562 423 7327, ⓦjohnnyrebs.com. The waft of barbecue ribs, catfish and hush puppies alone may draw you to this prime Southern spot, where the portions are large and the prices reasonable (lunch mains $12–27). Mon–Thurs & Sun 7am–9pm, Fri & Sat 7am–10pm.

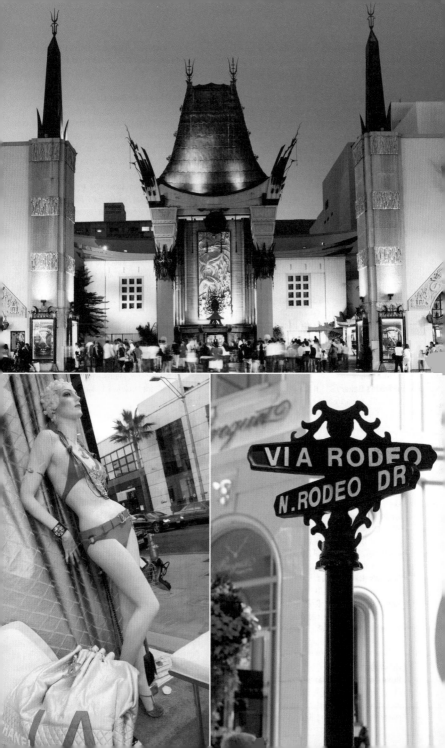

1

THE SAN GABRIEL AND SAN FERNANDO VALLEYS

Bob's Big Boy 4211 W Riverside Drive, Burbank ☎818 843 9334, ⓦbigboy.com. The classic chain diner, fronted by the plump burger lad, and a veritable pop-architecture classic (1949), saved from demolition through the efforts of preservationists. Burgers from $9.79. Daily 24hr.

Don Cuco 218 E Orange Grove Ave, Burbank ☎818 955 8895, ⓦdoncuco.com. Top-notch quesadillas, spicy soups, burritos and potent margaritas are the prime draws at this small Mexican restaurant, open since 1969. Mains $9–22. Mon–Thurs 11am–10pm, Fri–Sun 11am–11pm.

★**Dr Hogly Wogly's Tyler Texas BBQ** 8136 Sepulveda Blvd, Van Nuys ☎818 780 6701, ⓦhoglywogly.com. You could be in for a long wait for some of the best chicken, sausages, ribs and beans in LA since 1969, despite the long drive to the middle of nowhere. Three-meat combos from around $26. Mon–Thurs & Sun 11am–9pm, Fri & Sat 11am–10pm.

Fair Oaks Pharmacy & Soda Fountain 1526 Mission St, South Pasadena ☎626 799 1414, ⓦfairoaks pharmacy.net. Restored soda fountain with many old-time drinks such as lime rickeys, root beer floats, milk shakes and egg creams – a historic 1915 highlight along the former Route 66. Mon–Sat 9am–9pm, Sun 10am–7pm.

★**Porto's Bakery** 315 N Brand Blvd, Glendale ☎818 956 5996, ⓦportosbakery.com. Top-notch café serving Cuban flaky pastries ($0.90) and sandwiches, rum-soaked cheesecakes, muffins, Danishes, croissants, tarts and cappuccino. Mon–Sat 6.30am–8pm, Sun 7am–6pm.

ORANGE COUNTY

ANAHEIM

★**Anaheim Packing House** 440 S Anaheim Blvd ☎714 533 7225, ⓦanaheimpackingdistrict.com. Symbol of Anaheim's revitalized downtown, housed in a 1919 orange packing warehouse, this hip food hall features more than twenty artisanal stalls, from *Rolling Boil* hot pots and curries at *Adya*, to soul food at *Georgia's* and posh fish and chips at *The Chippy*. Daily 9am–midnight.

Angelo's Hamburgers 511 S State College Blvd, Anaheim ☎714 533 1401, ⓦangeloshamburgers.com. Straight out of *Happy Days*, a drive-in complete with rollerskating car-hops, neon signs, vintage cars and, incidentally, good cheeseburgers for just $3.75. Mon–Wed & Sun 8am–11pm, Thurs–Sat 8am–1am.

HUNTINGTON BEACH

Duke's & Barefoot Bar 317 Pacific Coast Hwy (Pier Plaza) ☎714 374 6446, ⓦdukeshuntington.com. Local institution right on the pier, with a Hawaiian theme and plenty of surf tributes. Full meals served in the dining room

(hula pie, poke tacos, seven spice ahi tuna; mains $10.50–17), with cocktails and burgers/sandwiches in the bar. Mon 3.30–9pm, Tues–Fri 11.30am–9.30pm, Sat 11am–9.30pm, Sun 10am–9pm.

Huntington Beach Beer Co 201 Main St ☎714 960 5343, ⓦhbbeerco.com. One of several brewpubs here, serving decent food and a range of seasonal craft beers on tap from the refreshing Huntington Beach Blonde ale to the punchy Surf Rye'ot IPA. Daily 11am–midnight.

LOT 579 21010 Pacific Coast Hwy (Pacific City mall) ☎949 675 7829, ⓦgopacificcity.com/lot-579. Artisanal food hall containing some real gems: freshly caught seafood at *Bear Flag Fish Co*, *Hans' Homemade Ice Cream*, Aussie meat pies at *Pie-Not* and *Popbar* (gelato on a stick). Sun & Mon 11am–8pm, Tues–Sat 11am–9pm.

★**Sugar Shack Cafe** 213 Main St, Huntington Beach ☎714 536 0355, ⓦhbsugarshack.com. Local surfer hangout since 1967, knocking out excellent breakfast plates ($8–11), burgers and sandwiches. Mon, Tues, Thurs & Fri 6am–2pm, Wed 6am–8pm, Sat & Sun 6am–3pm.

NEWPORT BEACH

Ruby's 1 Balboa Pier, Newport Beach ☎949 675 7829, ⓦrubys.com. The first and finest of the retro-streamline 1940s diners in this chain – in a great location at the end of Balboa's popular pier. Mostly offers the standard fare of burgers and fries. Mon–Fri 8am–8pm, Sat & Sun 7am–8pm.

LAGUNA BEACH

Nick's Laguna Beach 440 S Coast Hwy ☎949 376 8595, ⓦnicksrestaurants.com. A popular weekend breakfast spot and American bistro offering finely crafted menus with plenty of seafood such as ahi salad and shrimp taquitos, as well as wicked asparagus fries and classics such as rib-eye sandwich. Breakfast plates $8–16. Mon–Wed 11am–10pm, Thurs & Fri 11am–11pm, Sat 7.30am–11pm, Sun 7.30am–10pm.

★**Rasta Taco** 170 Beach St ☎949 715 1510, ⓦrastataco.com. This celebrated food truck's first brick-and-mortar location, with a takeaway window and patio where you can munch on delicious tilapia, jerk chicken and *carne asada* tacos (from $7). Mon–Fri 11am–8pm, Sat & Sun 10am–8pm.

★**Rooftop Lounge** La Casa Del Camino, 1289 S Coast Hwy ☎855 990 0282, ⓦrooftoplagunabeach.com. Enjoy sensational views and sunsets atop *La Casa del Camino* hotel while sipping mojitos ($13) or dining on ceviche ($15) or tuna sandwiches ($17). Mon–Thurs 11.30am–9pm, Fri & Sat 11.30am–10pm, Sun 10.30am–9pm.

Urth Caffè 308 N Coast Hwy ☎949 376 8888, ⓦurthcaffe.com. Serving organic tea-and-java

1

concotions, plus items such as Urth bread pudding, salads, sandwiches and vegan dishes. Located inside a 1917 home. Mon–Thurs & Sun 6am–11pm, Fri & Sat 6am–midnight.

DRINKING

As you'd expect, LA's **bars** reflect their locality: a clash of artists, grizzled old-timers, and financial whiz kids Downtown; tourists but also serious hedonists and leather-clad rockers in Hollywood; movie-star wannabes and self-proclaimed producers in West LA; a mix of tourists, locals and British expats in Santa Monica; and a more oddball selection in Venice. A few hard-bitten bars are open the legal maximum hours (from 6am until 2am daily), though the busiest hours are between 9pm and midnight. During **happy hour**, usually from 5 to 7pm or 4 to 6pm, drinks are cheap and sometimes half-price.

DOWNTOWN AND AROUND

★**Edison** 108 W 2nd St ☎213 613 0000, ⓦedison downtown.com; map p.63. One of LA's best uber-chic bars, with stunning antique industrial decor (it's located in Downtown's first power plant, dating from 1910), retro lounge music, upmarket food, a nice (though pricey) range of cocktails and a smart dress code. Wed–Fri 5pm–2am, Sat 7pm–2am.

HMS Bounty 3357 Wilshire Blvd, Koreatown ☎213 385 7275. An authentic dive experience, this grungy bar, advertising "Food and Grog", is a hotspot for hipsters and grizzled old-timers – they come for the dark ambience, cheap and potent drinks, and kitschy nautical motifs. Mon–Thurs & Sun 11am–1am, Fri & Sat 11am–2am.

Redwood 316 W 2nd St ☎213 680 2600, ⓦtheredwoodbar.com; map p.63. Solid choice for serious drinking and cheap all-American grub since 1943, now remade into a "pirate bar" featuring skull-and-crossbones decor and live rock and rockabilly music most nights (sometimes $10 cover). Daily 11am–2am.

The Rooftop at The Standard 550 S Flower St ☎213 892 8080; map p.63. The poseur pinnacle in Downtown LA, this is an alcohol-fuelled playpen where the silk-shirted-black-leather-trousers crowd goes to hang in red metallic "pods" with waterbeds and sprawl out on a rooftop Astroturf lawn, with modern corporate towers looming overhead. Daily noon–10pm.

Upstairs (Ace Hotel) 929 S Broadway ☎213 623 3233; map p.63. Another fabulous rooftop hotel bar, with shady trees, loungers, a pool and events every night – DJs, live bands, book release parties and pop-up shops. Daily 11am–2am.

The Varnish 118 E 6th St ☎213 265 7089, ⓦthebonaventure.com; map p.63. Cocktail specialist, housed inside a refurbished storage room at *Cole's* (p.132). Daily 7pm–2am.

HOLLYWOOD

Boardner's 1652 N Cherokee Ave ☎323 462 9621, ⓦboardners.com; map p.79. Former historic dive bar from 1942 now remodelled into sleek, yuppie-friendly confines for tasteful drinking (and a decent happy hour), with an impressively dark and luminous design. Also offers regular electronica, indie rock and burlesque shows. Daily 4pm–2am.

Burgundy Room 1621 Cahuenga Blvd ☎323 465 7530; map p.79. A classic place to get down and dirty with the old Hollywood dive-bar vibe, with a cramped interior, gloomy lighting, stiff drinks, a growling crowd of regulars, decent DJs and a rocking jukebox. Daily 8pm–2am.

★**Dresden Room** 1760 N Vermont Ave ☎323 665 4294, ⓦthedresden.com; map p.79. One of the neighbourhood's classic bars and restaurants, perhaps best known for its "Blood and Sand" whisky cocktails and evening show (Tues–Sat 9pm–1.15am), in which the husband-and-wife lounge act of Marty and Elayne take requests from the crowd of old-timers and hipsters. Mon–Sat 4.30pm–2am, Sun 4.30pm–midnight.

Formosa Café 7156 Santa Monica Blvd ☎323 850 9050, ⓦtheformosacafe.com; map pp.90–91. Started in 1925 as a watering hole for Charlie Chaplin's adjacent United Artists studios, this creaky old spot is still alive with the ghosts of Bogie and Marilyn. Drink the potent spirits, but stay away from the insipid Chinese food. Mon–Sat 4pm–2am, Sun 10am–2am.

Frolic Room 6245 Hollywood Blvd ☎323 462 5890; map p.79. This classic LA bar (opened in 1930 inside the Pantages Theatre), decorated with Hirschfeld cartoons of celebrities, offers affordable drinks and a dark, authentic old-time ambience. Daily 11am–2am.

Good Luck Bar 1514 Hillhurst Ave ☎323 666 3524, ⓦgoodluckbarla.com; map p.79. A hip Los Feliz retro-dive, this hangout is popular for its cheesy Chinese decor and cocktails ($11) straight from the heyday of *Trader Vic's*. Located near the intersection of Sunset and Hollywood boulevards. Mon–Fri 7pm–2am, Sat & Sun 8pm–2am.

★**Musso & Frank Grill** 6667 Hollywood Blvd ☎323 467 7788, ⓦmussoandfrank.com; map p.79. If you haven't had a drink in this landmark bar, open since 1919 (located in the centre of the district), you haven't been to Hollywood. It also serves pricey diner food. Tues–Sat 11am–11pm, Sun 4–9pm.

Stout Burgers & Beer 1544 N Cahuenga Blvd ☎323 469 3801, ⓦstoutburgersandbeers.com; map p.79. A truly stout brick cube of a place that's known for its inventive burgers and microbrewed beer, both quite good, and its thirty brews on tap and 4am closing time provide its true watering-hole bona fides. Daily 11.30am–4am.

1

WEST LA

The Arsenal 12012 W Pico Blvd ☎310 575 5511, ⓦarsenalbar.com; map pp.90–91. Lively place that offers fine pub food (notably the salt-and-pepper calamari), a dancefloor with pop and hip-hop sounds, and tasty cocktails, mostly under $10. Nothing to do with the London football club. Mon & Tues 5pm–midnight, Wed–Sat 5pm–2am, Sun 10am–midnight.

★El Carmen 8138 W 3rd St ☎323 852 1552, ⓦelcarmenla.com; map pp.90–91. Faux dive-bar with a south-of-the-border theme pushed to the extreme, with black-velvet pictures of Mexican wrestlers, steer horns, stuffed snakes and much tongue-in-cheek grunge, as well as signature margaritas and a good range of tequilas. Daily 5pm–2am.

Snakepit Alehouse 7529 Melrose Ave ☎323 653 2011, ⓦsnakepitalehouse.com; map pp.90–91. One of the better bars along the Melrose shopping strip, small and not too showy, with a mix of jaded locals and tourists who come to slurp down tropical concoctions. Mon 5pm–2am, Tues–Thurs 1pm–2am, Fri–Sun noon–2am.

SANTA MONICA AND VENICE

Bank of Venice 80 Windward Ave, Venice ☎310 450 5222, ⓦbankofvenicepublichouse.com. Gastropub in a historic 1906 building (one block off the beach), best known for its local microbrews, Californian wines by the glass, live sports events on TVs and fun atmosphere. Mon–Thurs 11am–midnight, Fri 11am–2am, Sat 10am–2am, Sun 10am–midnight.

★High Rooftop Lounge Hotel Erwin, 1697 Pacific Ave, Venice ☎800 786 7789, ⓦhighvenice.com; map p.101. This stylish rooftop bar offers spectacular sunset views just steps from the beach, with innovative cocktails (think blood orange julep) and great snack food. Mon–Thurs 3–11pm, Fri 1pm–midnight, Sat noon–midnight, Sun noon–11pm.

★Hinano Café 15 W Washington Blvd, Venice ☎310 822 3902; map p.101. Chilled beach shack – an untouristy place for a drink, with pool tables, good and cheap burgers, shambling decor and a mostly local crowd. Open since 1962, this was Jim Morrison's local, allegedly. Cash only. Daily 8am–2am.

Library Alehouse 2911 Main St, Santa Monica ☎310 314 4855, ⓦlibraryalehouse.com; map p.101. Presenting the choicest brews from West Coast microbreweries and beyond, this is a good spot to select from a range of well-known and obscure labels while munching on a decent selection of food. Daily 11.30am–midnight.

Rick's Tavern on Main 2907 Main St, Santa Monica ☎310 392 2772, ⓦrtavern.com; map p.101. Dark and rowdy neighbourhood joint off the Main St shopping strip, with sports on TV and boisterous regulars on the bar stools. Mon–Thurs 4pm–2am, Fri 3pm–2am, Sat & Sun noon–2am.

Ye Olde King's Head 116 Santa Monica Blvd, Santa Monica ☎310 451 1402, ⓦyeoldekingshead.com; map p.101. British-heavy joint with jukebox, dartboards and signed photos of all your favourite rock dinosaurs; don't miss the steak-and-kidney pie, afternoon tea, or fish and chips. Daily 10am–2am.

NIGHTLIFE

Nightlife in LA can be among the best in the country, with many options for serious partying and debauchery. Weekend nights are the busiest, but during the week things are often cheaper. Where they exist, **cover charges** range widely, depending on the night and the establishment (often $5–20). Except at all-ages, alcohol-free clubs, the minimum age is 21, and it's normal for ID to be checked, so bring photo ID. LA also has an overwhelming choice of **live music** venues, offering everything from punk to salsa.

CLUBS

The clubs of LA range from posey hangouts to industrial noise cellars. Some of the hottest club nights are usually the most transient, especially those catering to the house, ambient, techno or hip-hop scenes; see *A Club Called Rhonda* (ⓦtwitter.com/rhondaintl), the Wednesday-night *Low End Theory* (ⓦlowendtheoryclub.com) and *Lights Down Low* (ⓦlightsdownlow.net). Always check *LA Weekly* (ⓦlaweekly.com) or *Time Out* (ⓦtimeout.com/los-angeles) before setting out. Check also LA's live venues (see opposite): *The Echo* (see p.142) hosts legendary club nights Dub Club (Wed), Funky Sole (Sat) and Part Time Punks (Sun).

Most of the top clubs are either in Hollywood or West Hollywood, while Downtown is home to a handful of itinerant clubs operating above and below board. LA also has an established LGBT scene (see p.146).

DOWNTOWN AND CENTRAL LA

★La Cita 336 Hill St ☎213 687 7111, ⓦlacitabar.com; map p.63. Classic Latino bar and dance club with outdoor patio (from 4pm) that attracts hordes of hipsters for its Punky Reggae Party on Fridays (free before 10pm, then $5) and its Rockabilly Thursdays happy hour (4–9pm). Mon–Fri 11am–2am, Sat & Sun 10am–2am.

Mayan 1038 S Hill St ☎213 746 4287, ⓦclubmayan .com; map p.63. Formerly a groovy pre-Columbian-style movie palace, now hosting Electric Mass Fridays (Top 40, pop and hip-hop on the main floor, Latin rhythms on the mezzanine; $12 after 10.30pm) and nonstop disco, salsa

1

and house tunes on Saturdays ($10–20). Fri & Sat 9pm–2.30am.

HOLLYWOOD AND WEST HOLLYWOOD
1 Oak 9039 Sunset Blvd ☏310 274 2326, ⊛1oakla .com; map pp.90–91. A-listers favour this stylish West Hollywood club (outpost of the Las Vegas and New York originals), with plush lounge and exorbitant bottle-service, but dress like a Kardashian and you should get in. Tues, Thurs & Sat 10pm–2am.

★**Avalon** 1735 N Vine St ☏323 462 8900, ⊛avalon hollywood.com; map p.79. Major dance club spinning old-school favourites, along with the usual techno and house, with the occasional big-name DJ dropping in. Prices are among the most expensive in town. Cover $15–25. Fri 9.30pm–5am, Sat 9.30pm–7am.

Bar Sinister 1652 N Cherokee ☏323 462 1934, ⊛barsinister.net; map p.79. Best known for its memorably spooky Goth music and anaemic-looking vampire types on Saturdays ($10–15), with an S&M area upstairs. Drinks $14–15. Connected to *Boardner's* bar (see p.139). Cover $10–15. Sat 10pm–3am.

Couture Los Angeles 1640 N Cahuenga Blvd ☏323 464 2065, ⊛couturehollywood.com. Fashion-inspired lounge/club, where bottles start at $450 and you'll see plenty of celebs (or at least models) swanning around. It's not all posers, though; Outspoken (Fri) and Clinic (Wed) are popular underground-leaning house and techno parties. Cover from $20. Mon, Wed, Fri & Sat 10pm–2am.

★**Dirty Laundry** 1725 N Hudson Ave ☏323 462 6531, ⊛dirtylaundrybarla.com; map p.79. Fun bar and club (allegedly in Rudolph Valentino's former speakeasy) known for its Super Soul Monday (live soul and jazz), inventive cocktails (bacon Manhattan slushy or almond old-fashioned, anyone?) and "hidden" entrance along an alley; ring the correct buzzer to get in (check on Twitter (@dirtylaundrybar). Tues–Sat 10pm–2am.

Dragonfly 6510 Santa Monica Blvd ☏323 466 6111, ⊛thedragonfly.com; map p.79. Unusual decor, two large dance rooms and a mix of house and disco club nights and live music. Cover $10–20. Thurs–Sat 10pm–3am.

Sound Nightclub 1642 Las Palmas Ave ☏323 962 9000, ⊛soundnightclub.com; map p.79. A solid Hollywood bet for big, sweaty dance parties, especially those hosted by the Framework stable. Cover $10–20. Mon & Thurs–Sat 10pm–3.30am.

Three Clubs 1123 N Vine St ☏323 462 6441, ⊛threeclubs.com; map p.79. Dark, perennially trendy bar and club where the usual crowd of hipsters drops in for retro, rock and funk music, and gets pleasingly plastered. Colourless exterior and lack of good signage makes the joint even hipper. Daily 5pm–2am.

The Virgil 4519 Santa Monica Blvd ☏310 660 4540, ⊛thevirgil.com; map p.79. This stylish bar and comedy

club in East Hollywood transforms into a DJ showcase every Thursday (10pm–2am) for Funkmosphere, LA's longest-running party for 1980s-inspired funk, boogie and electro ($5 after 10.30pm), plus a mash up of hits, hip-hop and house every Friday and Saturday. Daily 7pm–2am.

SANTA MONICA
Circle Bar 2926 Main St ☏310 450 0508, ⊛circle-bar .com; map p.101. Old-fashioned dive (based on the original 1949 oval-shaped bar) that mainly draws a crowd of high-fiving party dudes who get plastered on the pricey but potent drinks and struggle to keep the beat on the dancefloor. No cover. Daily 9pm–2am.

The Gaslite 2030 Wilshire Blvd ☏310 829 2382, ⊛thegaslite.com; map p.101. Though it features a small dancefloor, the real appeal of this hip, kitschily decorated club is its karaoke. Santa Monicans rush here at weekends – so come early if you want to take to the mike. Daily 4pm–2am.

LIVE MUSIC VENUES
Since the nihilistic punk bands of thirty years ago distanced the city from its spaced-out cocaine-cowboy image, LA's rock and pop scene has been second to none. The home of Guns N' Roses, Metallica, Red Hot Chili Peppers, Green Day and Linkin Park (named after Lincoln Park in Santa Monica) has been revitalized by artists and bands such as Banks, Best Coast, Haim, Hollywood Undead, Local Natives and Shlohmo. As the cradle of West Coast gangsta rap, hip-hop is also prevalent, whether mixed in dance music by Westside DJs or in its more authentic form in the inner city (best avoided by out-of-towners).

Most venues open at 8 or 9pm; headline bands are usually onstage between 11pm and 1am. Cover (or ticket) prices range widely from $5 to $75. You'll need to be 21 and will likely be asked for ID. As ever, *LA Weekly* is the best source of listings.

MAJOR VENUES
Dolby Theatre 6801 Hollywood Blvd, Hollywood ☏323 308 6300, ⊛dolbytheatre.com. Part of the colossal Hollywood & Highland mall, a media-ready theatre partly designed to host the Oscars, as well as major and minor pop acts and special events.

Greek Theatre 2700 N Vermont Ave, Griffith Park ☏323 665 1927, ⊛lagreektheatre.com. Outdoor, summer-only venue (May–Oct) hosting mainstream rock and pop acts and seating for five thousand. Parking can be a mess, so come early.

Hollywood Palladium 6215 Sunset Blvd, Hollywood ☏323 962 7600, ⊛livenation.com. Once a big-band dance hall, with an authentic 1940s interior, now home to all manner of hard rock, punk and rap outfits.

Microsoft Theater 777 Chick Hearn Court ☏714 763 6030, ⊛microsofttheater.com. Grand auditorium that's

1

part of the colossal LA Live complex (see p.62), best known for hosting award shows (Grammies, MTV Music Awards, American Music Awards) and lighter pop and rock concerts.

Staples Center 865 S Figueroa St, Downtown ☎213 742 7340, ⓦstaplescenter.com. Big, glassy sports arena (home to the LA Lakers and Clippers) that's also a good showcase for major Top 40 rock and pop acts.

The Wiltern 3790 Wilshire Blvd, Mid-Wilshire ☎213 388 1400, ⓦwiltern.com. A striking, blue Zigzag Art Deco movie palace, renovated and converted into a top performing space for standard pop acts as well as edgy alternative groups.

ROCK AND POP

The Echo 1822 Sunset Blvd, Echo Park ☎213 413 8200, ⓦtheecho.com. An Echo Park club with scrappy indie-rock bands playing in a dark, intense little hole for a crowd of serious hipsters. A good place to catch what's bubbling up on the underground music scene; morphs into hip dance club Friday and Saturday nights. See also sister venue *Echoplex*, through the alley at 1154 Glendale Blvd. Open daily, see website for times and cover.

El Rey Theatre 5515 Wilshire Blvd, Mid-Wilshire ☎323 936 4790, ⓦtheelrey.com; map pp.90–91. Although not as famous as its Sunset Strip counterparts, this rock and alternative venue is possibly the best spot to see explosive new bands and still-engaging oldsters.

Fonda Theatre 6126 Hollywood Blvd, Hollywood ☎323 464 6269, ⓦfondatheatre.com; map p.79. A charming, renovated old theatre that began life in 1926 and still hosts theatrical productions, but more typically alternative rock and dance acts.

★**Hotel Café** 1623 N Cahuenga Blvd, Hollywood ☎323 461 2040, ⓦhotelcafe.com; map p.79. Comfortable spot for acoustic acts and singer-songsmiths, as well as indie bands. Usually has the best line-up in town

for this sort of thing, with two stages. Daily, shows usually from 7pm.

The Roxy 9009 W Sunset Blvd, West LA ☎310 276 2222, ⓦtheroxy.com; map pp.90–91. Among the top showcases for the music industry's new signings, intimate and with a great sound system, on the western – but still frenetic – end of the strip. Punk and hip-hop dominate. Hours vary, see website for upcoming shows.

The Troubadour 9081 Santa Monica Blvd, West Hollywood ☎310 276 6168, ⓦtroubadour.com; map pp.90–91. An old 1957 mainstay that's been through a lot of incarnations in its fifty years. Used to be known for folk and country rock, then metal, now for various flavours of indie rock. Tickets $12–35. Hours vary, see website for upcoming shows.

The Viper Room 8852 Sunset Blvd, West Hollywood ☎310 358 1881, ⓦviperroom.com; map pp.90–91. Great live acts nightly – expect almost any musician to show up on stage. Partly owned by Johnny Depp until 2004, and the place where River Phoenix died of a drug overdose in 1993. Daily 8pm–2am.

★**Whisky-a-Go-Go** 8901 Sunset Blvd, West Hollywood ☎310 652 4202, ⓦwhiskyagogo.com; map pp.90–91. Legendary spot since 1964, and still important for LA's rising music stars. Mainly hard rock and metal, though you might catch an alternative act now and then. Daily 10am–2am.

COUNTRY AND FOLK

Cody's Viva Cantina 900 Riverside Drive, Burbank ☎818 845 2425, ⓦvivacantina.com. A Mexican restaurant on the far side of Griffith Park, where you can hear some of LA's most engaging country, bluegrass and honky-tonk artists performing nightly. Mon–Wed & Sun 11am–10pm, Thurs–Sat 11am–midnight.

PRO SPORTS IN LA

Baseball The LA Dodgers (☎323 224 1500, ⓦlosangeles.dodgers.mlb.com) play at Dodger Stadium, 1000 Elysian Park Ave, near Downtown; the LA Angels of Anaheim (☎714 940 2000, ⓦlosangeles.angels.mlb.com) at Angel Stadium, 2000 Gene Autry Way, Anaheim in Orange County; seats for both $15–150.

Basketball The Lakers (tickets $25–260; ☎213 480 3232, ⓦnba.com/lakers), Clippers ($20–250; ☎213 742 7430, ⓦnba.com/clippers), and women's Sparks ($10–55; ☎213 742 7340, ⓦsparks .wnba.com) all play at the Staples Center, 1111 S Figueroa St in Downtown LA.

Football LA was without pro franchise between 1994 (when the Raiders moved back to Oakland) and 2016, when the Los Angeles Rams (ⓦtherams.com) arrived from St Louis – temporarily based at the Los Angeles Memorial Coliseum, they plan to move into the brand-new Los Angeles Entertainment Center in Inglewood in 2019.

Hockey The Kings are based at the Staples Center ($25–135; ☎213 742 7100, ⓦkings.nhl.com), and Orange County's Anaheim Ducks play at Honda Center, 2695 E Katella Ave, Anaheim ($20–175; ☎714 704 2500, ⓦanaheimducks.com).

Soccer The Galaxy ($20–125; ☎310 630 2200, ⓦlagalaxy.com) play at the StubHub Center, 18400 Avalon Blvd, in the South Bay city of Carson.

1

Cowboy Palace Saloon 21635 Devonshire St, Chatsworth ☎ 818 341 0166, ⊛ thecowboypalace saloon.com. Worth a trip to this distant corner of the San Fernando Valley for down-home helpings of tub-thumping country-and-western concerts and Sunday barbecues. Daily 2pm–2am.

Kulak's Woodshed 5230 Laurel Canyon Blvd, North Hollywood ☎ 818 766 9913, ⊛ kulakswoodshed.com. Nightly shows in a cramped but colourful space, ranging from country, folk and spoken-word to performance art and poetry. Most shows $10 (no food or alcohol).

Rusty's Surf Ranch 256 Santa Monica Pier ☎ 310 393 7437, ⊛ rustyssurfranch.com; map p.101. Offers not only surf music – and displays of old-time longboards – but also rock, pop, folk and even karaoke. Always a popular spot for tourists, near the end of the pier. Daily 11.30am–2am.

JAZZ AND BLUES

The Baked Potato 3787 Cahuenga Blvd W, Studio City ☎ 818 980 1615, ⊛ thebakedpotato.com. A small but near-legendary contemporary jazz spot since 1970, where many reputations have been forged. Daily 7pm–2am.

Catalina Bar & Grill 6725 Hollywood Blvd, Hollywood ☎ 323 466 2210, ⊛ catalinajazzclub.com; map p.79. A jazz institution with plenty of style and atmosphere, filling meals and potent drinks. It can get pricey, though. Tues–Sun 6.30pm–midnight.

Grand Star Jazz Club 943 Sun Mun Way, Downtown ☎ 213 626 2285, ⊛ grandstarjazzclub.com; map p.63. Solid Chinatown haunt for live jazz and blues since 1946, plus some hip-hop and funk thrown in as well. Also features DJs spinning breakbeats and other dance tunes. Wed–Sun 5pm–2am.

Harvelle's 1432 4th St, Santa Monica ☎ 310 395 1676, ⊛ harvelles.com; map p.101. A stellar blues joint near the Third Street Promenade, open since 1931 and offering different performers nightly plus a little funk, R&B and burlesque. Tickets from $5. Daily 8pm–2am.

The Lighthouse Café 30 Pier Ave, Hermosa Beach ☎ 310 376 9833, ⊛ thelighthousecafe.net. Adjacent to the beach, this old-time favourite since 1949 offers salsa, country, jazz and reggae as well as karaoke and occasional comedy. Mon–Fri 5pm–2am, Sat & Sun 11am–2am.

The Mint 6010 W Pico Blvd, south of Mid-Wilshire ☎ 323 954 9400, ⊛ themintla.com; map pp.90–91. A small, intense spot that's off the beaten path but worth the ramble to hear the latest in the city's avant-garde jazz sounds, as well as singer-songwriters. Daily 7pm–2am.

SALSA

★ **El Floridita** 1253 N Vine St, Hollywood ☎ 323 871 8612, ⊛ elfloridita.com; map p.79. Decent Mexican and Cuban food complements a fine line-up of Cuban and salsa artists, who play on weekends and jam on other nights. Salsa nights: Mon, Wed, Fri 8pm–1am, Sat 9.30pm–2am.

PERFORMING ARTS AND FILM

LA's range of **performing arts** is increasingly broad and impressive, with national-calibre groups and performers appealing to audiences well beyond Southern California. LA boasts a world-class conductor and orchestra for **classical music**, and **comedy** is an especially big draw. Not surprisingly, though, it's **film** that is still the chief cultural staple of the region.

CLASSICAL MUSIC, OPERA AND DANCE

The Los Angeles Philharmonic and LA Opera are the major names for classical music and opera in the city, and perform regularly. Contemporary dance and ballet is also well represented, though the Los Angeles Ballet has struggled financially in recent years.

MAJOR VENUES

Center for the Art of Performance at UCLA, Westwood Blvd, Westwood (Central Ticket Office in James West Alumni Center, just east of Pauley Pavilion) ☎ 310 825 2101, ⊛ cap.ucla.edu. Coordinates a wide range of companies in music, theatre and dance (Sept–June), and runs a fine dance series, often with an experimental bent. Box office Mon–Fri 10am–4pm.

Disney Hall 1st St, at Grand Ave, Downtown ☎ 323 850 2000, ⊛ laphil.com. LA's most renowned cultural attraction (along with the Getty Center), which hosts the LA Philharmonic in a striking Frank Gehry-designed building.

The Dorothy Chandler Pavilion Music Centre, 135 N Grand Ave, Downtown ☎ 213 972 7211, ⊛ musiccenter .org. Long-standing warhorse of the arts community, used by LA Opera and other top names.

The Hollywood Bowl 2301 N Highland Ave, Hollywood ☎ 323 850 2000, ⊛ hollywoodbowl.org. A famed bandshell (see p.87) that hosts the LA Philharmonic and summer open-air concerts, usually of the pops variety.

The Shrine Auditorium 665 W Jefferson, South LA ☎ 213 748 5116, ⊛ shrineauditorium.com. Huge, 1926 Moorish curiosity that hosts touring pop acts, choral gospel groups and countless award shows.

Zipper Concert Hall 200 S Grand Ave, Downtown ☎ 213 621 2200, ⊛ colburnschool.edu. Part of the esteemed performing-arts Colburn School across from Disney Hall, this warm and modern facility hosts a broad range of troupes, from dance to classical, and chamber music.

1

GROUPS AND INSTITUTIONS

★ **Da Camera Society** Mount St Mary's University, 10 Chester Place ☎ 213 477 2929, ⓦ dacamera.org. This organization's "Chamber Music in Historic Sites" provides a great opportunity to hear chamber works in stunning settings, from grand churches to private homes, including Doheny Mansion near USC. Ticket prices vary.

LA Opera Dorothy Chandler Pavilion, Music Center, 135 N Grand Ave ☎ 213 972 8001, ⓦ laopera.com. Stages productions between Sept and June, from epic *opera seria* to lighter operettas. The mainstream-heavyweight in town; Plácido Domingo is the general director.

Long Beach Opera 507 Pacific Ave, Long Beach (venues rotate) ☎ 562 432 5934, ⓦ longbeachopera .org. Despite being eight years older than the LA Opera, this alternative company presents the freshest and edgiest work in town, from lesser-known pieces by old masters to craggy newer works by local composers and librettists.

Los Angeles Ballet 11755 Exposition Blvd, West LA (venues rotate) ☎ 310 998 7782, ⓦ losangelesballet .org. Features a Nov–May programme with standards like the *Nutcracker* and a good number of new and modern works.

Los Angeles Chamber Orchestra 350 S Figueroa St (venues rotate) ☎ 213 622 7001, ⓦ laco.org. Presents a range of chamber works, not all canonical, from different eras. Prices vary widely.

Los Angeles Master Chorale Disney Hall, 111 S Grand Ave, Downtown ☎ 213 972 2782, ⓦ lamc.org. Classic canonical works, along with newer commissions and experimental pieces, are showcased by this choral institution.

Los Angeles Philharmonic Disney Hall, 111 S Grand Ave, Downtown ☎ 323 850 2000, ⓦ laphil.org. The big name in the city performs throughout the year, and conductor Gustavo Dudamel always provides a rousing programme, from powerful Romantic works to modern pieces, with an accent on Latin American works.

COMEDY

LA has a wide range of comedy clubs. While rising stars and beginners can be spotted on the "underground" open-mike scene, most of the famous comics, both stand-up and improv, appear at the more established clubs in Hollywood, West LA or the valleys. These venues usually have a bar (and a two-drink minimum) and put on two shows per evening, generally starting at 8pm and 10.30pm – the later one being more popular.

Comedy & Magic Club 1018 Hermosa Ave, Hermosa Beach ☎ 310 372 1193, ⓦ comedyandmagicclub.info. Notable South Bay comedy space where Jay Leno sometimes tests material. Tickets can run up to $30, depending on the performer. Tues–Sun 8pm–midnight.

The Comedy Store 8433 W Sunset Blvd, West LA ☎ 323 656 6228, ⓦ thecomedystore.com. LA's premier comedy

showcase and popular enough to be spread over three rooms – which means there's usually space, even at weekends. Two drink minimum. Daily 7pm–2.30am.

★ **Groundlings** 7307 Melrose Ave, West LA ☎ 323 934 4747, ⓦ groundlings.com. Pioneering venue where only the gifted survive (Melissa McCarthy and Kristen Wiig among them), with furious improv events and high-wire comedy acts that can inspire greatness or groans. No alcohol. Shows usually start Mon–Sat 8pm and Sun 7.30pm.

The Improv 8162 Melrose Ave, West LA ☎ 323 651 2583, ⓦ improv.com. Long-standing brick-walled joint that spawned a national chain. Still known for hosting some of the best acts working in both stand-up and improv. One of LA's top comedy spots – so make reservations in advance. Daily 6pm–2am.

The Laugh Factory 8001 Sunset Blvd, West Hollywood ☎ 323 656 1336, ⓦ laughfactory.com. Stand-ups of varying reputations, with the odd big name and regular ensemble shows. Daily 7pm–2am.

Second City Studio Theater 6560 Hollywood Blvd, Hollywood ☎ 323 464 8542, ⓦ secondcity.com. Groundbreaking comedy troupe with numerous branches in LA, hosting nightly improv and sketch comedy sometimes built around lengthy routines and theme performances. Shows usually Mon–Fri 8pm, Sat 3.30pm, Sun 1.30pm.

THEATRE

While the bigger venues host a predictable array of musicals and classics with an all-star cast of celebrities, more than a hundred small theatres with fewer than a hundred seats can be found around Los Angeles. Tickets are less expensive than you might expect: a big show will set you back at least $50, or up to $100–150 for some blockbusters (matinees are cheaper), with smaller shows around $10 to $20.

MAJOR THEATRES

★ **The Actors' Gang** 9070 Venice Blvd, Culver City ☎ 310 838 4264, ⓦ theactorsgang.com. A cross between a major and an alternative theatre; having fewer than a hundred seats keeps it cosy, though it does host the odd spectacular production that features semi-famous names from film or TV. Tim Robbins is artistic director.

Ahmanson Theatre Music Center, 135 N Grand Ave, Downtown ☎ 213 628 2772, ⓦ centertheatregroup .org. A two-thousand-seat theatre hosting colossal travelling shows from Broadway. If you've seen a major production advertised on TV and on the sides of buses, it's probably playing here.

Geffen Playhouse 10886 Le Conte Ave, Westwood ☎ 310 208 5454, ⓦ geffenplayhouse.com. A five-hundred-seat, quaint Spanish Revival building that often hosts one-person shows. There's a decidedly Hollywood connection, evident in the crowd-pleasing nature of many of the productions.

Mark Taper Forum 135 N Grand Ave, Downtown ☎ 213 628 2772, ⓦ centertheatregroup.org. Mainstream theatre in the three-quarter round, with a mix of classic and contemporary works. Located in the Music Center.

Pantages Theater 6233 Hollywood Blvd, Hollywood ☎ 323 468 1770, ⓦ hollywoodpantages.com. Quite the stunner: an exquisite, atmospheric Art Deco theatre in the heart of historic Hollywood, hosting major touring Broadway productions.

FRINGE THEATRES

★ **The Complex** 6476 Santa Monica Blvd, Hollywood ☎ 323 465 0383, ⓦ complexhollywood.com. A group of alternative companies revolving around five small theatres, where you're likely to see any number of dynamic productions.

Highways Performance Space 1651 18th St, Santa Monica ☎ 310 315 1459, ⓦ highwaysperformance.org. Located in the 18th St Arts Center, an adventurous theatre that offers a range of topical drama and politically charged productions, with a strong bent towards the subversive.

Hudson Theatres 6539 Santa Monica Blvd, Hollywood ☎ 323 856 4252, ⓦ hudsontheatre.com. Socially conscious "message" plays alternate with more satirical, comedic works at this venue for upcoming actors. The complex consists of three stages, plus a café and art gallery.

Open Fist Theatre 6209 Santa Monica Blvd, Hollywood ☎ 323 882 6912, ⓦ openfist.org. As you might expect from the name, biting and edgy works are often the focus at this small theatre company that employs a limited cast of spirited unknowns.

Steve Allen Theater 4773 Hollywood Blvd ☎ 323 666 4268, ⓦ trepanyhouse.org. An intriguing East Hollywood showcase for the independent productions of Trepany House, an outlet for new-talent theatre, music and film founded by artistic director Amit Itelman in 2012.

Theatre West 3333 Cahuenga Blvd West, Hollywood ☎ 323 851 7977, ⓦ theatrewest.org. A classic venue that's always a good spot to see inventive, sometimes odd, productions with a troupe of excellent young up-and-comers.

Theatricum Botanicum 1419 N Topanga Canyon Blvd, Topanga ☎ 310 455 3723, ⓦ theatricum.com. Terrific spot in the Santa Monica Mountains showing a range of classic (often Shakespearean) and modern plays in an idyllic outdoor setting.

CINEMA

Major feature films are often released in LA months (or years) before they play anywhere else, and a huge number of cinemas show both the new releases and the classics – with fewer screens showing independent and foreign movies. Tickets at the premier cinemas usually cost $8 (before noon) then $12–18 ($21 for IMAX/3-D).

MAINSTREAM CINEMAS

AMC Century City 15 10250 Santa Monica Blvd, Westfield Century City ☎ 310 277 2262, ⓦ amctheatres .com. One of the best places to see new films in LA. The theatres are somewhat boxy, but if you're after crisp projection, booming sound and comfy seating, there are few better choices.

Arclight 6360 Sunset Blvd, Hollywood ☎ 323 464 1478, ⓦ arclightcinemas.com. All-reserved seats in fourteen theatres, top-of-the-line projection, good sightlines, wide seats and – best of all – the iconic Cinerama Dome, a white hemisphere that has the biggest screen in California.

Bruin 948 Broxton Ave, Westwood ☎ 310 208 8998, ⓦ regencymovies.com. Dashing 1937 moviehouse that's a city landmark for its wraparound marquee and sleek Moderne styling.

Regal 14 at LA Live 800 W Olympic Blvd, Downtown ☎ 877 835 5734, ⓦ lalive.com. Between parking and a movie ticket ($15–16), it'll cost you $25 just to see a Hollywood flick here, but if you want huge screens, booming Dolby sound and plenty of 3-D/special effects wizardry, there are few better spots in the city.

Village Theatre 961 Broxton Ave, Westwood ☎ 310 248 6266, ⓦ regencymovies.com. One of the best places to watch a movie in LA, with a giant screen, fine seats and good balcony views, and a frequent spot for Hollywood premieres. The marvellous 1931 exterior features a white spire.

ART-HOUSE AND REVIVAL

Aero 1328 Montana Ave, Santa Monica ☎ 310 466 3456, ⓦ americancinemathequecalendar.com. American Cinematheque presents an eclectic programme of classic and art-house movies in this fine old venue from 1940 (tickets $11).

Cinefamily at the Silent Movie Theatre 611 N Fairfax Ave, south of West Hollywood ☎ 323 655 2510, ⓦ cinefamily.org. Boasting some of the most inspired movie-buff showings in town, this 1942 theatre presents silent films (with live accompaniment), and cult, foreign, avant-garde and long-forgotten flicks, along with more familiar classics and indie films (tickets $12–14).

The Landmark 10850 W Pico Blvd, West LA ☎ 310 470 0492, ⓦ landmarktheatres.com. Huge, twelve-screen multiplex with comfortable furnishings including couches, excellent sound and projection. One of the top venues for un-Hollywood fare in LA. Tickets $10.50–13.50.

New Beverly Cinema 7165 Beverly Blvd, Mid-Wilshire ☎ 323 938 4038, ⓦ newbevcinema.com. Worthwhile for

1

its excellent art films and revival screenings, with some imaginative double bills – the 1929 building originally served as a candy store, with current owner Quentin Tarantino. Tickets from $8.

Nuart 11272 Santa Monica Blvd, West LA ☎ 310 281 8223, ⓦ landmarktheatres.com. Another historic theatre (1929) that shows rarely seen classics, documentaries and edgy foreign-language films, and is the main option for

independent film-makers testing their work. Sometimes offers brief December previews of Oscar contenders. Tickets $9–11.

★**Warner Grand Theatre** 478 W 6th St, San Pedro ☎ 310 548 7672, ⓦ grandvision.org. Restored 1931 Zigzag Moderne masterpiece (see p.110). Now a repertory cinema and performance hall; San Pedro Film Festival based here in Oct. Tickets vary

LGBT LA

Although nowhere near as big as that of San Francisco, LA's **LGBT scene** is almost as well established. The best-known area is **West Hollywood** ("WeHo") which is synonymous with the (affluent, white) gay lifestyle, centred on where Santa Monica Blvd meets San Vicente Blvd. **Silver Lake**, especially along Hyperion and Sunset, has much more of a vibrant ethnic and working-class mix. Gay couples will find themselves accepted at most LA **hotels**, but the most well-known gay establishment is the *Ramada Plaza* (ⓦ ramadaweho.com). See also useful websites such as ⓦ frontiersla.com and Los Angeles LGBT Center's ⓦ lalgbtcenter.org.

BARS AND CLUBS

The Abbey 692 N Robertson Blvd, West Hollywood ☎ 310 289 8410, ⓦ theabbeyweho.com; map pp.90–91. West Hollywood party central: a crazy, busy club scene in the heart of gay WeHo that offers great people watching, go-go dancers and buzzing atmosphere. Daily 11am–2am.

Akbar 4356 Sunset Blvd, Silver Lake ☎ 323 665 6810, ⓦ akbarsilverlake.com. A curious blend of patrons – manual labourers and bohemians, old-timers and newbies – frequent this cosy, unpretentious watering hole. Also presents occasional dance events such as "Bears in Space". Daily 4pm–2am.

FUBAR 7994 Santa Monica Blvd, West Hollywood ☎ 323 654 0396, ⓦ fubarla.com; map pp.90–91. If you recognize the acronym, you'll know what you're in for at this high-energy club, a popular scene that offers regular dance events, plus Friday-night drag shows. Daily 4pm–2am.

Micky's 8857 Santa Monica Blvd, West Hollywood ☎ 310 657 1176, ⓦ mickys.com; map pp.90–91. Lively, pulsating scene with a full range of club nights, including the usual Seventies and Eighties dance-pop, thundering house and hip-hop beats, and drag shows. Mon & Tues 5pm–2am, Wed & Thurs 9pm–2am, Fri & Sat 9pm–4am, Sun 3pm–2am.

Mother Lode 8944 Santa Monica Blvd, West Hollywood ☎ 310 659 9700; map pp.90–91. Strong drinks and wild dancing to house and garage music make this one of the more colourful and frenetic of WeHo's clubs. Mon–Sat 3pm–2am, Sun 3pm–midnight.

Rage 8911 Santa Monica Blvd, West Hollywood ☎ 310 652 7055, ⓦ theragenightclub.com; map pp.90–91. Very flashy gay men's club and neighbourhood favourite, playing the latest house and Latin pop to a long-established crowd. Mon 5pm–1am, Tues 8pm–2am, Wed–Sun 9pm–2am.

SHOPPING

Shopping in LA is an art – besides the run-of-the-mill chain retailers you'll find anywhere, there are big **department stores** and mega-sized **malls** where most of the hardcore shopping goes on, and, of course **Rodeo Drive**, two blocks of the world's most exclusive shopping. Trendy boutiques line **Melrose Ave** in Hollywood, and **Third St in Santa Monica** (p.102) and **La Brea Ave** in West LA. The few blocks above Prospect on Vermont Ave in **Los Feliz** are home to some of the underground's groovier shops, while the **Fashion District** is good for both browsing wholesalers and for retail (see p.70) and includes the **Santee Alley flea market** (ⓦ thesanteealley.com). Venice boasts the hipster cool strip of **Abbot Kenny Blvd**, featuring fashionable stores such as Burro (ⓦ burrogoods.com) and Heist (ⓦ shopheist.com).

THE PIÑATA DISTRICT

Downtown LA is laced with wholesale shopping districts, from flowers and toys to fabrics and sewing machines, but the most intriguing to explore is the **Piñata District** at Olympic Boulevard and Central Avenue (extending between 8th and 10th), where, surprise, surprise, the main product is multicoloured Mexican piñatas in all shapes and sizes – stores here also carry all the kitschy toys and treats to put in your piñata, too. There are boxes of spicy Mexican sweets, dried chillies and, at weekends, street vendors selling all manner of tasty snacks.

DEPARTMENT STORES AND MALLS

Each of LA's neighbourhoods has a collection of ordinary stores and mini-malls. A step up from these in price and quality are department stores, which are often included within massive malls and resemble self-contained city suburbs, around which Angelenos do the bulk of their serious buying.

Beverly Center 8500 Beverly Blvd, West Hollywood ☎ 310 854 0070, ⓦ beverlycenter.com. Seven acres of boutiques, Macy's and Bloomingdale's, all in one complex that is receiving a glossy $500 million makeover by Studio Fuksas of Rome, designers of Ferrari's headquarters. Work should be completed by 2018, but the centre will remain open throughout. Mon–Fri 10am–9pm, Sat 10am–8pm, Sun 11am–6pm.

Del Amo Fashion Center 3525 W Carson St, Torrance ☎ 310 542 8525, ⓦ simon.com/mall/del-amo-fashion-center. The South Bay's own super-mall, one of the country's largest, with Sears, Macy's and JCPenney, and a wealth of mid-level retailers. Mon–Fri 10am–9pm, Sat 10am–8pm, Sun 11am–7pm.

The Grove 189 The Grove Drive, Mid-Wilshire ☎ 323 900 8080, ⓦ thegrovela.com. A giant, open-air mega-structure by the Farmers' Market; has all the usual chain retailers, restaurants and movie theatres, and a more stylish design than the typical "dumb-box" construction found elsewhere. Mon–Thurs 10am–9pm, Fri & Sat 10am–10pm, Sun 10am–8pm.

Hollywood & Highland Center 6801 Hollywood Blvd, Hollywood ☎ 323 817 0200, ⓦ hollywoodandhighland.com. Colossal mega-mall with a design inspired by an ancient film set, but offering the same old corporate boutiques and trendy shops, and a cineplex connected to the Chinese Theatre. Mon–Sat 10am–10pm, Sun 10am–7pm.

Santa Monica Place Broadway, at 2nd St, Santa Monica ☎ 310 260 8333, ⓦ santamonicaplace.com. Old Frank Gehry-designed mall that was radically reconfigured into an open-air design in 2010. Sits at the south end of the Third Street Promenade, and is anchored by Bloomingdale's and Nordstrom. Mon–Sat 10am–9pm, Sun 11am–8pm.

Westfield Century City 10250 Santa Monica Blvd, Century City ☎ 310 277 3898, ⓦ westfield.com/centurycity. An outdoor mall with one hundred upscale shops and one of the better food courts around. The place to come to see stars do their shopping, and a spot to catch a first-run movie in excellent surroundings at the AMC Century 15 Theaters. Mon–Sat 10am–9pm, Sun 11am–7pm.

Westside Pavilion 10800 Pico Blvd, at Westwood, West LA ☎ 310 470 8752, ⓦ westsidepavilion.com. Postmodern shopping complex centre with Nordstrom and Macy's; the former western side of the mall has been converted into The Landmark theatres. Mon–Fri 10am–9pm, Sat 10am–8pm, Sun 11am–6pm.

FOOD AND DRINK

Many LA delis are open round the clock; some supermarkets are open 24hr, or at least until 10pm; and there are also ethnic groceries and more expensive gourmet markets.

BAKERIES

Bouchon Bakery 235 N Canon Drive (1/F lobby), Beverly Hills ☎ 310 271 9910, ⓦ thomaskeller.com; map pp.90–91. Outpost of Thomas Keller's famed culinary empire selling his signature macarons, croissants and a whole host of breads, cakes and pastries. Daily 7am–9pm.

Diamond Bakery 335 N Fairfax Ave, West LA ☎ 323 655 0534; map pp.90–91. In the heart of the Fairfax District since the 1960s, this classic Jewish bakery provides a number of traditional favourites, including *babka*, *challah*, *mandelbrot* and *rugelach*, and a legendary pumpernickel bread. Daily 7am–6pm.

Doughboy's Café & Bakery 8136 W 3rd St, Mid-Wilshire ☎ 323 852 1020, ⓦ doughboysbakeryla.com; map pp.90–91. Tasty pizzas, pancakes, scones and sandwiches are available for midday meals, but the real highlight of this Westside bakery is the bread: rich, hearty loaves with interesting ingredients like walnuts, olives and various cheeses. Mon–Thurs & Sun 7am–9pm, Fri & Sat 7am–10pm.

Gourmet Cobbler Factory 33 N Catalina Ave, Pasadena ☎ 626 795 1005. Bakery selling a range of yummy, fruity cobblers, from blackberry to apple and peach, pecan and sweet potato. Occupies a prime spot near Old Pasadena. Tues–Sat 11am–8pm, Sun noon–5pm.

Viktor Benês Bakery 8330 W Santa Monica Blvd, West Hollywood, ☎ 323 654 5543, ⓦ viktorbenes.com; map pp.90–91. This is the place to go for freshly baked bread, coffee cakes, Danish pastries, various chocolate-oriented treats and the signature "Alligator" (pecan coffee cake). Daily 7am–10pm.

DELIS AND GROCERY STORES

Bay Cities Italian Deli 1517 Lincoln Blvd, Santa Monica ☎ 310 395 8279, ⓦ baycitiesitaliandeli.com; map p.101. An excellent, centrally located deli and retailer with an Italian focus. Offers piles of fresh pasta, meat, home-made pasta, spices and sauces, along with many imports, desserts, espresso and terrific lunchtime sandwiches. Tues–Sun 9am–6pm.

★ **The Cheese Store of Beverly Hills** 419 N Beverly Drive, Beverly Hills ☎ 310 278 2855, ⓦ cheesestorebh.com; map p.95. More than four hundred types of cheese from all over the world, including every kind produced in the US, with many of them suspended invitingly over your head. Typically high prices to match. Mon–Sat 10am–6pm, Sun noon–5pm.

Jeff's Gourmet Kosher Sausage Factory 8930 W Pico Blvd, West LA ☎ 310 858 8590, ⓦ jeffsgourmet.com;

1

map pp.90–91. A top-notch vendor of well-crafted sausages, from merguez to jalapeño to Polish to veal bratwurst and Cajun chicken. Mon–Thurs & Sun 11am–11pm, Fri 9.30am–2pm.

Olson's Scandinavian Deli 5560 W Pico Blvd, Mid-Wilshire ☎323 938 0742, ⊛olsonsdeli.com; map pp.90–91. Herring, meatballs and assorted sausages at this Swedish grocer, one of the few Scandinavian food retailers in LA and definitely worth a try. Tues–Fri 10am–6pm, Sat & Sun 10am–5pm.

Say Cheese 2800 Hyperion Ave, Silver Lake ☎323 665 0545, ⊛saycheeselosangeles.com. A distinctive array of French and other international cheeses, priced moderately to steeply. The delicious sandwiches may be your best bet. Mon–Fri 10am–7pm, Sat 8.30am–7pm, Sun 10.30am–5pm.

GALLERIES

Fahey/Klein Gallery 148 N La Brea Ave, West LA ☎323 934 2250, ⊛faheykleingallery.com; map pp.90–91. Major dealers in rare, twentieth-century and contemporary art photography, from Edward Weston and Berenice Abbott to Man Ray, Henri Cartier-Bresson and Herb Ritts. Tues–Sat 10am–6pm.

★ **Hamilton-Selway Fine Art** 8678 Melrose Ave, West Hollywood ☎310 657 1711, ⊛hamiltonselway.com; map pp.90–91. Home to the largest collection of Andy Warhol prints and paintings on the West Coast, this commercial gallery also deals in the work of Jean-Michel Basquiat, Jasper Johns, Robert Rauschenberg, Roy Lichtenstein, Keith Haring and other pop art icons. Mon–Fri 9am–5pm, Sat 10am–5pm.

La Luz de Jesus Gallery 4633 Hollywood Blvd, Los Feliz ☎323 666 7667, ⊛laluzdejesus.com; map pp.90–91. Incredibly influential gallery since the 1980s (especially in the Lowbrow Art Movement and Pop Surrealism genres). Shares space with Wacko (see below). Tues–Sat 10am–6pm.

BOOKS

★ **Book Soup** 8818 W Sunset Blvd, West Hollywood ☎310 659 3110, ⊛booksoup.com; map pp.90–91. Great selection of books, right on Sunset Strip. Narrow, winding aisles stuffed pell-mell with books, strong in entertainment, travel and photography. Mon–Sat 9am–10pm, Sun 9am–7pm.

Distant Lands 20 S Raymond Ave, Pasadena ☎626 449 3220, ⊛distantlands.com. Well-stocked travel bookstore in Old Pasadena, with some fairly hard-to-find titles, as well as maps and travel gear. Also hosts the occasional public speaker and globe-trotting slide show. Mon–Thurs 10.30am–8pm, Fri & Sat 10.30am–9pm, Sun 11am–6pm.

Hennessey & Ingalls 300 S Santa Fe Ave, Downtown ☎310 458 9074, ⊛hennesseyingalls.com; map p.63. An impressive range of art and architecture books makes this bookstore the best in LA in its field, though many of the volumes are quite expensive. Daily 10am–8pm.

Iliad Bookshop 5400 Cahuenga Blvd, North Hollywood ☎818 509 2665, ⊛iliadbooks.com. Easily one of LA's best used booksellers, and meriting a trip out to North Hollywood. Features a broad selection of affordable titles, including some you probably won't find anywhere else. Mon–Sat 10am–10pm, Sun noon–6pm.

Larry Edmunds Book Shop 6644 Hollywood Blvd ☎323 463 3273, ⊛larryedmunds.com; map p.79. Many stacks of books, a large number of them out of print, are offered on every aspect of film and theatre, with movie stills and posters. Located at the centre of tourist-oriented Hollywood. Mon–Fri 10am–5.30pm, Sat 10am–6pm, Sun noon–5.30pm.

★ **Last Bookstore** 453 S Spring St (entrance on 5th St), Downtown ☎213 488 0599, ⊛lastbookstorela .com; map p.63. The largest independent bookstore in California with thousands of secondhand books – all of them costing just $1 each – as well as a pricier selection, a vinyl record store and puffy sofas to sit on. The Spring Arts Collective gallery is upstairs. Mon–Thurs 10am–10pm, Fri & Sat 10am–11pm, Sun 10am–6pm.

Samuel French Theatre & Film Bookshop 7623 Sunset Blvd, West Hollywood ☎866 598 8449, ⊛samuelfrench.com; map p.79. LA's broadest selection of theatre books is found in this local institution, along with a good collection of movie- and media-related titles. Mon–Sat 10am–6pm, Sun 10am–5pm.

Taschen 354 N Beverly Drive, Beverly Hills ☎310 274 4300, ⊛taschen.com; map p.95. Fun, edifying and weird titles that focus on everything from Renaissance art to Americana kitsch to fetish photography. Cheap volumes on both familiar and obscure subjects. Mon–Sat 10am–7pm, Sun noon–5pm.

Vroman's 695 E Colorado Blvd, Pasadena ☎626 449 5320, ⊛vromansbookstore.com. One of the San Gabriel Valley's major retailers, offering a good selection with a café. Although there are no real bargains, other, smaller used book-stores can be found within a few blocks. Mon–Thurs 9am–9pm, Fri & Sat 9am–10pm, Sun 10am–8pm.

Wacko 4633 Hollywood Blvd, Los Feliz ☎323 663 0122, ⊛soapplant.com. Although also great for its eclectic gift selection, this Los Feliz favourite stocks an excellent array of titles leaning toward the alternative: art and architecture, bizarre fetishes, alternative history, music guides, and conspiracy theories and assorted rants. Mon–Wed 11am–7pm, Thurs–Sat 11am–9pm, Sun noon–7pm.

MUSIC

★ **Amoeba Music** 6400 W Sunset Blvd, Hollywood ☎323 245 6400, ⊛amoeba.com; map p.79. A vast selection of titles – supposedly numbering around half a million – on CD, tape and vinyl, which you can listen to at booths throughout the store. Also presents occasional in-store live music. Mon–Sat 10.30am–11pm, Sun 11am–10pm.

Fingerprints 420 E 4th St, Long Beach ☎562 433 4996. Fine indie outfit in the South Bay, offering alternative-leaning CD and vinyl, plus in-store performances from local rockers. Mon–Thurs & Sun 10am–9pm, Fri & Sat 10am–10pm.

Freakbeat Records 13616 Ventura Blvd, Sherman Oaks ☎818 995 7603, ⓦfreakbeatrecords.com. One of the Valley's biggest dealers in CDs and vinyl, the store has plenty to browse over (and listen to), from vintage 1960s surf pioneers to latter-day punk nihilists, with cheap prices, too. Mon–Sat 11am–8pm, Sun noon–6pm.

★**Record Surplus** 12436 Santa Monica Blvd, Santa Monica ☎310 979 4577, ⓦrecordsurplusla.com; map p.101. Massive LP collection of surf music, ancient rock'n'roll, Sixties soundtracks, and unintentionally hilarious spoken-word recordings. Prices are excellent, with many CDs offered for low prices. Mon–Sat 11am–10pm, Sun 11am–7pm.

Rockaway Records 2395 Glendale Blvd, Silver Lake ☎323 664 3232, ⓦrockaway.com. Great place to come for both used CDs and LPs, as well as DVDs. Also offers old magazines, posters and memorabilia. Just east of the Silver Lake reservoir. Daily 11am–7pm.

DIRECTORY

Currency exchange Outside of banking hours, exchange offices are scattered inconveniently throughout town. Most reliable are those at LAX; hours vary by terminal (often daily until 11pm; ☎310 649 2801).

Directory inquiries ☎411.

Emergencies ☎911 for fire, police and medical emergencies. For less urgent needs: LAPD ☎877 275 5273, ⓦlapdonline.org.

Hospitals The following have 24hr emergency departments: Cedars-Sinai Medical Center, 8700 Beverly Blvd, Beverly Hills (☎310 423 3277, ⓦcedars-sinai.edu); Good Samaritan Hospital, 1225 Wilshire Blvd, Downtown (☎213 977 2121, ⓦgoodsam.org); UCLA Medical Center, 10833 Le Conte Ave, Westwood (☎800 825 631, ⓦuclahealth.org).

Mexican Tourist Office and Consulate 2401 W 6th St, 5th floor, Downtown (☎800 446 3942, ⓦvisitmexico .com).

Pharmacies Late hours at Horton & Converse, 11600 Wilshire Blvd, West LA (Mon–Fri 9am–9pm, Sat & Sun 9am–6pm; ☎310 478 0801), while Walgreens at 3201 W 6th St in Wilshire Center (☎213 251 0179) and 8770 W Pico Blvd (☎310 275 2117) in West LA are both open 24hr.

Post office The main Downtown post office is at 900 N Alameda St (Mon–Fri 8am–5.30pm, Sat 8am–4pm; ☎213 617 4404), north of Union Station. Zip Code is 90012.

Taxes LA sales tax is nine percent (when combined with the 7.5 percent state tax); Santa Monica sales tax is 9.5 percent. Hotel taxes are variable, generally fourteen percent.

San Diego and around

MARINA AND SAN DIEGO SKYLINE

San Diego and around

Southern California (or just SoCal) is the California of popular imagination, a land of affluent beach communities, serious surfers and seemingly perfect, year-round weather. With Tijuana just across the border, there is a visible Mexican influence, though the concentration of military bases and industry here attracts Americans from all over the country, and it has a reputation for being the most conservative part of the state. Nevertheless, San Diego is a lot more laidback and visitor-friendly than Los Angeles, with its gracefully curving bay, clutch of fine museums in Balboa Park and the large-scale tourist attractions of San Diego Zoo and SeaWorld.

Outside San Diego County's urban centre, you can find a host of compelling destinations, beginning with the beaches of **Coronado**, just across the bay. The **North County** includes small, enticing coastal communities from the northern edge of San Diego itself to Oceanside, as well as the vineyards and avocado groves that reach east into wilder mountain country. Beyond the beach towns, you can explore the forest-smothered hills and state parks via hiking trails and obscure backroads.

San Diego

Basking in the sun, but tempered by ocean breezes, **SAN DIEGO** is a big city that feels more like a family holiday resort, with most tourists coming for its fun beaches, major showstoppers like the **San Diego Zoo** and **SeaWorld**, and a mind-bending array of museums in **Balboa Park**. It has history too, notably in the **Gaslamp Quarter** and **Old Town** districts, whose building styles range from true historic preservation to pseudo-historic kitsch.

The traditional image of San Diegans as conformist, affluent and Republican is true to a certain extent – San Diego County (which includes the city) has as much in common with Salt Lake City or Phoenix as it does with Los Angeles or San Francisco (noted Republican Congressman Darrell Issa represents the district). However, the city itself is far more Democratic, with a vibrant gay scene in **Hillcrest** and increasing numbers of liberal students and professionals. The presence of three **college campuses** – SDSU, UCSD and USD – has also helped the city lose some of its rigid character. Though its hedonism is on display at the beaches, elsewhere there's a persistently conservative, anti-reformist air. A series of economic and political scandals have rocked the city, including the huge pension-fund scandal of 2003, and in 2013 San Diego mayor Bob Filner resigned after being accused by at least eight women of sexual

CASA DE BALBOA

Highlights

❶ Balboa Park The museum centrepiece of San Diego, a 1400-acre green space loaded with history, science and art, and crowned with the city's popular zoo. **See p.161**

❷ Mission Beach The most free-spirited of the city's surfing beaches, with acres of bronzed flesh and bikini babes, chaotic bars and even carnival rides. **See p.171**

❸ San Diego food trucks The city's lauded food-truck scene offers everything from gourmet lobster and salmon tacos, to hickory-smoked barbecue and Korean street food. **See p.179**

❹ Cruisin' Grand Americana at its finest, a free evening car show, food festival and freak show rolled into one. **See p.196**

❺ Peterson's Donut Corner This legendary shop in Escondido knocks out mouthwatering doughnuts in a variety of flavours, all huge, sticky and delicious. **See p.198**

❻ Julian A charming Western town offering breezy mountain scenery, gold-mine relics, antiques and galleries, and sumptuous apple pies. **See p.199**

HIGHLIGHTS ARE MARKED ON THE MAP ON P.154

harassment. San Diego also shares with LA many of the same extremes of rich and poor, oceanside and inland, respectively, with most of the prime-time tourist draws on or within a few miles of the water.

Travellers barely notice this darker side – long white beaches, sunny weather and bronzed bodies give rise to the city's nickname, "Sandy Ego".

Brief history

Historically home to the **Kumeyaay** people (who still live in the region on thirteen reservations), the first European to land on California soil, Portuguese adventurer and Spanish agent Juan Rodríguez Cabrillo, put ashore at Point Loma, ten miles from today's Downtown San Diego, in 1542. European settlement didn't begin until two centuries later, however, with the building in 1769 of the **Mission San Diego de Alcalá** – the first of Junípero Serra's Catholic missions in modern-day California – and a Spanish military garrison or *presidio* on a site overlooking San Diego Bay. This original

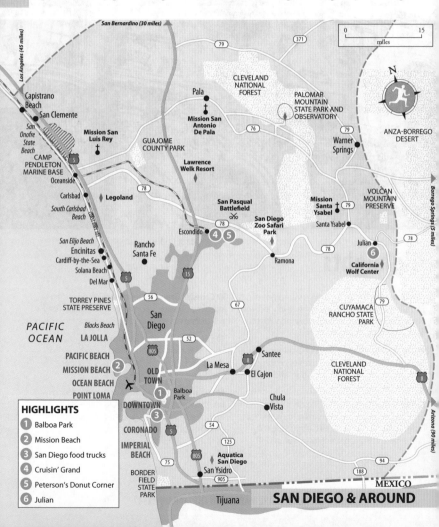

HIGHLIGHTS

1. Balboa Park
2. Mission Beach
3. San Diego food trucks
4. Cruisin' Grand
5. Peterson's Donut Corner
6. Julian

SAN DIEGO & AROUND

LA FRONTERA

Just fifteen miles south of San Diego lies the heavily fortified US–Mexican border and the iconic booze-soaked border city of **Tijuana**, gradually recovering some of the day-trip trade it lost in 2009 (as a result of Mexico's drug war). Its laidback bars and restaurants make quite a contrast to those north of the border and as long as you stick to the main, heavily policed tourist areas, it's now pretty safe, at least during the day.

To visit Tijuana take the **San Diego Trolley** (see p.176) 45min to San Ysidro and simply walk across the border: there are usually no controls at all passing into Mexico, and if you are just going to Tijuana, no forms to fill in. Stop at the tourist office before leaving the immigration zone for a map, then take the left-hand exit for taxis, or the right-hand exit if you prefer the twenty-minute walk to **Avenida Revolución**, the main tourist drag; it's a fairly well-signed route via the footbridge and along Calle 1a.

Heading back into the US it's a very different story. Canadians and even US citizens now require a passport to enter and everyone can expect a meticulous immigration and customs check. Foreigners that entered the US via the ESTA programme (see p.29) should show the immigration officers the US arrival stamp in their passports; assuming the date on it has not expired you should have no problem re-entering (if you have the I-94 or I-94W form, don't surrender this on entering Mexico, and show these when going back to the US). If you are entering the US from Mexico for the first time (assuming you are a citizen of a country that participates in the Visa Waiver Programme), there's no need to apply for ESTA: you'll need to fill in an I-94W form instead.

Note that the border crossing back into the US can be crazily busy at peak times (weekends and work rush hours), with long lines and waits of up to two to three hours: countless Mexicans stream in and out of Southern California every day. Taking a car over the border is even more hassle and not worth it for short trips.

settlement, known today as **Old Town**, remained small and largely insignificant long after California was absorbed by the US in 1848, and it wasn't until the late 1860s that real estate developer **Alonzo Horton** began to promote his "New Town", closer to the bay and shipping, which ultimately became today's Downtown San Diego. The city missed out on the new mail route to the West and was plagued by a series of droughts through the 1860s, causing many bankruptcies and economic problems. Although the transcontinental Santa Fe Railroad link was short-lived – repeated flooding forced the terminus to be moved north to Los Angeles, depriving San Diego of direct rail service to the East – its establishment in 1878 resulted in an economic boom through the 1880s. In 1915 came the first of two international expositions in Balboa Park (the Panama-California Exposition, and the California Pacific International Exposition in 1935), which were to establish San Diego's nationwide reputation.

In part because of its lack of direct railway access to the East Coast, the city has long been overshadowed by Los Angeles in trade and economic significance, though it has used its strategic seaside location to become a martial stronghold. During **World War II**, the US Navy took advantage of the city's sheltered bays, and much of San Diego's economy came to be dominated by the military – the population more than doubled between 1930 and 1950. After the Cold War the military sector reduced dramatically; San Diego has since become a biotech industry hub and is home to telecommunications giant Qualcomm, founded here in 1985. However, with a formidable population of over 1.3 million people, making it the eighth-largest city in the US, it is San Diego's reputation as an ocean-oriented "resort city" that provides much of its current appeal.

Downtown San Diego

Loosely bordered by the arc of San Diego Bay and the I-5 freeway, **DOWNTOWN** is, for those not headed straight to the beach, the nexus of San Diego and the best place to start a tour of the city. Kick-started in the late 1970s, various preservation and

2

restoration projects have improved many of the area's older buildings, resulting in pockets of stylishly renovated turn-of-the-twentieth-century architecture, while there are numerous postmodern corporate towers left over from the boomtown Eighties and Nineties – giving the skyline a mildly dated look. **Broadway** slices through the centre of downtown and is most lively between Fourth and Fifth, where the pedestrian traffic is a mix of shoppers, sailors, yuppies, homeless people and tourists. Although this is far from the free-spirited, somewhat chaotic strip of LA's Broadway (much less New York's), there are still a few points of interest here and there.

Although downtown is largely safe by day, at night it can be unwelcoming and deserted in spots. Unless you're with a local or someone who knows their way around, after-dark activities are best confined to the popular and well-policed Gaslamp Quarter.

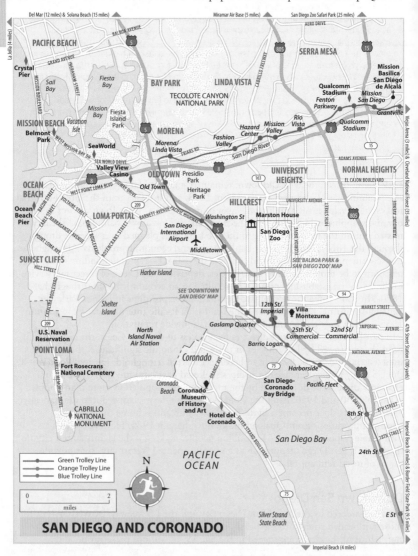

JESSOP'S CLOCK

Since 1985 the 22ft-tall **Jessop's Clock** has been the one inescapable historic highlight of indoor shopping mall **Horton Plaza**. An intriguing antique from the California State Fair of 1907 (commissioned by city jeweller, Joseph Jessop), the outdoor pendulum clock was moved to the then-new plaza with the Jessop & Sons jewellery store. In 2012 Horton Plaza terminated its rental agreement with the Jessop family (who still own the clock): at the time of writing a proposal to move the clock to San Diego Zoo seemed to have fallen through, and for the moment the clock remains in place.

2

The Museum of Contemporary Art

1001 & 1100 Kettner Blvd, between Broadway and B St • Thurs–Tues 11am–5pm • $10 • ☎ 858 454 3541, ⓦ mcasd.org

Just north of Broadway, next to the 1915 Santa Fe Depot (Amtrak station), the **Museum of Contemporary Art** (MCA San Diego) is the essential first stop for art in Southern California outside of LA. Its permanent collection focuses on American works, pop art and the indigenous art of Mexico, and also offers the usual mainline retrospectives of Abstract Expressionism, Minimalism, Conceptual Art and various other totems of modern art. But its temporary shows are the real draw, often involving irreverent imagery drawn from the intersection of pop-culture surrealism, ethnic subcultures and socioeconomic issues. The complex comprises two adjoining buildings: the depot's old halls, preserved (if slightly altered) as the **Jacobs Building** – now showcasing various installation and multimedia pieces that would be too huge to display elsewhere – and the much newer metal, concrete and glass box of the **Copley Building**, which presents rotating exhibitions. The museum also has a La Jolla branch (see p.173).

Horton Plaza

324 Horton Plaza • Mon–Sat 10am–8pm, Sun 11am–6pm • ☎ 619 239 8180, ⓦ westfield.com/hortonplaza

A half-mile east of the Museum of Contemporary Art along Broadway, many visitors linger around the newly renovated fountains (and **ArtsTix** booth) in Horton Plaza Park outside **Horton Plaza**, a giant mall of more than a hundred stores and San Diego's de facto city centre. Planned in 1977 and completed in 1985, Horton Plaza's quick success caused local real estate prices to soar and condo development to surge, and gave shopping-mall developer **Jon Jerde** the green light to stamp his neon-bedecked, pop-art-flavoured design on malls across the country. The complex's whimsical style is inevitably a colossal tourist draw, though there's nothing on the shopping front you won't find in every other American mall – and with anchor tenant Nordstrom closing in 2016, the mall's future seems uncertain.

The Gaslamp Quarter

Just south of Broadway and Horton Plaza, the **GASLAMP QUARTER** occupies a sixteen-block area of handsome, historic buildings running south to K Street, bordered by Fourth and Seventh. The core of San Diego when it was still a frontier town, the district – known then as **Stingaree** after a stingray found in San Diego Bay – was rife with prostitution, opium dens and street violence, a chaotic scene that played out beneath the wrought-iron balconies and Victorian gingerbread of the nineteenth-century piles lining the street. The area predictably decayed until its revitalization in the late 1970s under an intensive urban-renewal campaign, after which it started to mutate into the heavily tourist-oriented zone it is today, and the target for many visitors for after-hours drinking and debauchery.

What remaining flophouses and dive bars there are make a dramatic contrast with the new cafés, antique stores and art galleries – all under the glow of ersatz "gas lamps" powered by electricity. There are a couple of intriguing museums and any number of worthwhile restaurants, bars and clubs here to keep you occupied and well lubricated, and the district's relatively high police profile is designed to keep the area clean and safe.

2

Gaslamp Museum at the Davis-Horton House

410 Island Ave • Tues–Sat 10am–5pm, Sun noon–4pm • $10 • ☎ 619 233 4692, ⓦ gaslampquarter.org

The square where the Gaslamp Quarter walking tour starts (see box opposite) is within the grounds of the **Gaslamp Museum at the Davis-Horton House**. The house is in part named for William Heath Davis, who had several New England saltbox-style homes (wooden frame houses with a long, pitched roofs that slope down to the back), including this one, designed in modules in 1850 and shipped here via Cape Horn. Davis believed that a waterfront location would stimulate growth – the fledgling city had previously been located a few miles inland and to the north, the site of today's Old Town San Diego (see p.166), and although he was initially wrong and eventually died penniless, the more influential **Alonzo Horton** (namesake of the city's signature mall) did manage to fulfil Davis's goals for waterfront growth in the late 1860s. Horton is thought to have lived briefly in this remaining saltbox structure. Replete with photographs, each room of the house commemorates a

DOWNTOWN
SAN DIEGO

DRINKING
Altitude Sky Lounge	15
Cat Eye Club	13
Craft & Commerce/	
False Idol	3
Dublin Square	10
Mission Brewery	14
Waterfront	1

NIGHTLIFE
Café Sevilla	9
Casbah	2
Chee-Chee Club	5
Fluxx	11
House of Blues	4
Omnia	12
Onyx Room	8
Parq	7
Spreckels Theatre	6

TOURING THE GASLAMP QUARTER

The Gaslamp Quarter is fascinating to explore, not least for the scores of late nineteenth-century buildings – rich with period detail and styles from Eastlake to Queen Anne, with some Spanish Colonial and Baroque Revival touches as well – in various stages of renovation. Few are better than the grandiose **Louis Bank of Commerce**, 835 Fifth Ave, an eye-popping Victorian confection from 1888 replete with carved wooden-and-terracotta bay windows, a sheet-metal frieze across the front, and a pair of squat, colourful little towers on top. In its early years it was variously home to an ice-cream parlour, a brothel and an oyster bar favoured by Wyatt Earp. The Gaslamp Quarter Historical Foundation organize walking tours of the area each Saturday (see p.177).

2

different period with its decor, from its use as a pre-Civil War military officers' barracks, to a county hospital, to a private residence.

Horton Grand Hotel

311 Island Ave • ☏ 619 544 1886, ⓦ hortongrand.com

Opposite the Gaslamp Museum lies the **Horton Grand Hotel** (see p.177), created by cobbling together two hotels dating from 1886, the **Grand Horton** and the **Brooklyn Kahle Saddlery Hotel** – where Wyatt Earp lived for most of the seven years he spent in San Diego from the late 1880s. The Grand Horton section is an elegant, ornate structure built as a replica of the Innsbruck Inn in Vienna, while the *Saddlery Hotel* sports a more familiar Victorian/Western style (the name comes from a saddle shop that opened here in 1912). Go inside to admire the one-hundred-year-old oak Grand Staircase, and the life-size papier-mâché horse (dubbed "Sunshine") in the front lobby.

Chinese Historical Museum

404 3rd Ave • Tues–Sat 10.30am–4pm, Sun noon–4pm • $5 • ☏ 619 338 9888, ⓦ sdchm.org

Two blocks southwest of the *Horton Grand Hotel*, the small **Chinese Historical Museum** occupies the Chinese Mission building, built in 1927 and serving as a place of worship and a social centre for San Diego's Chinese community for over thirty years. The museum contains art and artefacts from household items to paintings and calligraphy (in the Dr. Sun Yat-Sen Memorial Extension across the street), which give some sense of life in the early Chinatown here. The museum also hosts monthly **walking tours** of Asian American history in the district, covering eight blocks.

Petco Park and the Padres

100 Park Blvd • Baseball tickets from $15.50 • ☏ 619 795 5005, ⓦ petcoparkevents.com • Tours daily 10.30am, 12.30pm & 3pm • $15, call ☏ 619 795 5011

The flow of visitors to the Gaslamp Quarter increases whenever there's a game at **Petco Park** stadium a few blocks to the southeast. The stadium has done much to revitalize this part of downtown; it has an attractive open-air layout and draws hordes of **Padres** baseball fans (ⓦ sandiego.padres.mlb.com). The Padres are a Major League Baseball team with a mediocre record though they have won the National League twice (1984 and 1998), losing in the World Series both times. Still, the team is fanatically supported and seeing a game is a fun way to spend an evening or afternoon. Alternatively you can also take a **guided tour** of the stadium, a one-hour-twenty-minute spin around the press box, bullpen, dugout, old Western Metal Supply Co building and VIP areas.

Marina District

The streets south of the Gaslamp Quarter are now occupied by expensive condos and the **San Diego Convention Center**, a $165-million complex with a sail-like roof resembling the yachts in the nearby **Marina**. Continuing north along San Diego's appealing, curved **bayfront**, the pathway of the **Embarcadero** runs a mile or so along

2

CHICANO PARK MURALS

Around one mile southeast of Petco Park lies one of San Diego's most tantalizing sights, the mural-smothered walls of **Chicano Park**. The "park" is actually around seven acres of public land beneath the San Diego–Coronado Bay Bridge, where Hwy-75 intersects with I-5, in Barrio Logan (Logan Ave and National Ave). The area has been a major Mexican-American (Chicano) community since World War II, and the murals started to appear in the early 1970s as a protest against indiscriminate construction in the neighbourhood. The murals (around forty large-scale ones) are painted on concrete pillars and abutments, depicting images of pre-Columbian gods, animals and Mexican revolutionary and cultural heroes. The murals have been restored several times, most recently in 2012–2013. See ⓦchicano-park.com for more details.

the bay, curling around to the western end of downtown; along this stretch, the expansive green lawn of **Embarcadero Marina Park South** provides some summertime amusement in its summer pops series (ⓦsandiegosymphony.com). Although the route is favoured by strollers, joggers and kite-flyers, some tourists get no further than **Seaport Village** at 849 W Harbor Drive (daily 10am–10pm; ☏619 235 4014, ⓦseaportvillage.com), a predictable array of trinket shops, mid-range boutiques and diners. Film buffs should visit **Kansas City Barbecue** at 600 W Harbor Drive (daily 11am–2am; ☏619 231 9680, ⓦkcbbq.net), which shamelessly milks the fact that the bar scenes from the popular 1986 movie *Top Gun* were filmed here.

USS Midway Museum
910 N Harbor Drive • Daily 10am–5pm, last admission 4pm • $20 • ☏619 544 9600, ⓦmidway.org

Just north of Seaport Village lies the grey bulk of giant aircraft carrier **USS Midway**, now a museum permanently docked here to show off its formidable collection of naval hardware and weapons to the public. For those with a taste for naval history from World War II to the first Gulf War (the life cycle of the ship), touring the innards of the old-time carrier is a memorable experience, enhanced by the presence of flight simulators and 29 restored planes parked at the site (from Dauntless dive bombers to F-4 Phantoms).

Maritime Museum
1492 N Harbor Drive • Daily: summer 9am–9pm; rest of year 9am–8pm • $16 • ☏619 234 9153, ⓦsdmaritime.org

Half a mile north of the USS *Midway*, the **Maritime Museum** offers an enlightening look at shipping of past eras, highlighted by a collection of nine boats such as the 1863 *Star of India*, the world's oldest active iron sailing ship, which began its career in the Isle of Man and then hauled working-class British emigrants to New Zealand. Other vessels include the *Californian*, a modern replica of an 1847 revenue cutter that patrolled the Pacific Coast during the Gold Rush; the HMS *Surprise*, a replica of an eighteenth-century, 24-gun frigate, which served in the film *Master and Commander*; and a creaky Soviet diesel submarine, the *B-39*, which was only decommissioned in the 1990s, well into the nuclear-sub era. On the *Pilot*, a 1914 commercial pilot boat, you can take a 45-minute cruise on the bay (5 daily) for an extra $5 on top of museum admission; an excursion on board the *Californian* starts at $60 (3hr). Since most of these craft are seaworthy, some may be cruising around elsewhere when you come to visit; call ahead to make sure that the boat you're interested in will be on view.

Little Italy
At the northern end of downtown, **Little Italy** (ⓦlittleitalysd.com) is one of the city's historic international neighbourhoods, today mostly worth visiting for its **restaurants** and occasional festivals. Opening in 2017, the **Piazza della Famiglia** is set to become the heart of the district, comprising a pedestrianized block of Date Street between

India and Columbia. The late-May **Sicilian Festival** (ⓦsicilianfesta.com) and mid-October **Little Italy Festa** are among the festive highlights, both featuring authentic, delicious Italian food, traditional and modern Italian music, arts and crafts. Don't miss the neighbourhood's farmers' market, the **Little Italy Mercato**, held every Saturday from 8am to 2pm on West Cedar Street from Kettner Boulevard to Front Street, which features fresh produce, snacks and local artwork.

Firehouse Museum

1572 Columbia St • Thurs & Fri 10am–2pm, Sat & Sun 10am–4pm • $3 • ☎ 619 232 3473, ⓦ sandiegofirehousemuseum.com

One of the few sights in Little Italy not associated with eating is the **Firehouse Museum**, situated in San Diego's oldest firehouse (the "6 House" dates from 1915). Displays include firefighting equipment, paraphernalia and uniforms, as well as archaic hand-pumps, cranks and sirens, and photographs recalling some of San Diego's most destructive fires and the horses and firefighters who had to battle them.

Balboa Park and San Diego Zoo

1549 El Prado • Buses #3, #7 and #120 from downtown; Balboa Park tram trolley (daily: June–Oct 9am–8pm; Nov–May 9am–6pm; every 8–40min; free) runs between the main museums and the Inspiration Point parking lot on Park Blvd (also free) • ⓦ balboapark.org

Less than two miles northeast of downtown, the 1400 sumptuous acres of **BALBOA PARK** feature one of the largest collections of museums in the US, marked by a verdant landscape of trees, gardens, promenades and Spanish Colonial buildings – and of course, the ever-popular **San Diego Zoo**. A desolate stretch of cacti and scrubland until 1898, the park began to take shape when one Kate Sessions began cultivating nurseries and planting trees in lieu of rent. The first buildings were erected for the 1915 Panama-California International Exposition, held to celebrate the opening of the Panama Canal, and memories of its success lingered well into the Depression, until in 1935 another building programme was organized for the California Pacific International Exposition. Five years later the park was in such sparkling condition that Orson Welles decided to use it to film insert shots of Charles Foster Kane's monumental Xanadu enclave for *Citizen Kane*; today the park is an essential stop on any trip to Southern California.

Most of the major museums flank **El Prado**, the park's pedestrian-oriented east–west axis, which encompasses the charming **Plaza de Panama** at the heart of the park, and is best explored from the west via Laurel Street and the Cabrillo Bridge.

The Museum of Man

1350 El Prado • Daily 10am–5pm • $13 • ☎ 619 239 2001, ⓦ museumofman.org

This handsome Neo-Baroque folly is an anthropological showcase which, among other things, offers demonstrations of Mexican loom-weaving, replicas of huge Maya monuments, Egyptian mummies, and interesting Native American artefacts including

BALBOA PARK TICKETS AND TOURS

If you're planning on spending a lot of time in Balboa Park, the cheapest way to see the museums is to buy the $55 **Multi-Day Explorer**, a week-long pass that allows one-time admission to all fourteen of the park's museums and its Japanese garden (plus the San Diego Zoo, for an extra $39). This pass, along with the **One-Day Explorer** that covers any five museums ($45), is available at all the museums and at the **visitor centre** (see p.177), located in the **House of Hospitality** at 1549 El Prado. This is the best place to find information about each individual museum, and to buy the useful **Balboa Park** map and guide. If you're interested in a basic hour-long **tour** of the park, drop by the House on Saturdays at 10am, or for a more architecture-oriented journey, come by on the first Wednesday of the month at 9.30am; for a history and garden tour, visit at 11am on Sundays and Tuesdays. All walks are free.

bowls, toys, garments and other items from the Kumeyaay people native to the region. The museum is housed in the **California Building**, constructed for the 1915 Panama-California Exposition, a lavish structure that almost overshadows the collection. Just to the north, theatre buffs will want to drop in on **The Old Globe** complex (see p.186), which was built in 1935 for the exposition and now features a trio of theatre companies putting on plays by Shakespeare and other playwrights.

California Tower

1350 El Prado • Daily tours 10.20am–4.20pm (every 40min) • $22.50, includes Museum of Man admission • ☎ 619 239 2001, Ⓦ museumofman.org

After being closed to the public for 80 years, the iconic 198ft **California Tower** at the Museum of Man opened again in 2015. The ornate pinnacle blends several Spanish styles from Plateresque to Churrigueresque, soaring into the blue sky like a Sevilla cathedral. Getting to the top involves climbing a narrow staircase up seven floors (accessed from the second floor of the museum) in small, guided groups, but the reward is a wonderful view of the city. Entry is by timed tickets (arrive 15min before your start time), purchased at the museum or online.

San Diego Art Institute

1439 El Prado • Tues–Sat 10am–5pm, Sun noon–5pm • $5 • ☎ 619 236 0011, ⓦ sandiego-art.org

The **San Diego Art Institute** is a sporadically interesting venue for the works of its members, showcasing everything from pedestrian pieces by artists-in-training to unexpectedly fascinating mixed-media and curious installation art. New shows for regional artists open monthly.

Mingei International Museum

1439 El Prado • Tues–Sun 10am–5pm • $10 • ☎ 619 239 0003, ⓦ mingei.org

The **Mingei International Museum** displays rotating exhibits of folk art, featuring everything from jewellery from China to Mexico, to golden Kazakh artefacts, to functional pop sculpture in the form of vases, mugs and plates.

The San Diego Museum of Art

1450 El Prado • Mon, Tues, Thurs & Sat 10am–5pm, Fri 10am–8pm, Sun noon–5pm • $15; Sculpture Court and Garden is free • ☎ 619 232 7931, ⓦ sdmart.org

Adorned with fountains, the tranquil **Plaza de Panama** fronts the **San Diego Museum of Art**, its heavily ornamented Plateresque façade modelled on Spain's University of Salamanca and completed in 1926. It's the main venue for any big shows that come through town – collections from Egypt, China and Russia (to name a few). In the permanent collection, there's a solid stock of European paintings from the Renaissance to the nineteenth century, among them some lesser works by Giorgione, Veronese and Van Dyck; the highlights are some agreeable works by Rembrandt and Hals, and El Greco's charismatic *Penitent St Peter*. The biggest surprises are found amid the exquisitely crafted pieces in the Asian section, mainly from China and Japan but with smaller works from India and Korea. The **Sculpture Court and Garden** offers free exploration at any time; it has a number of important works by artists that include Henry Moore, Louise Nevelson, David Smith and Alexander Calder. Take a break at the *Panama 66* microbrewery and restaurant (see p.181).

The Timken Museum of Art

1500 El Prado • Tues–Sat 10am–4.30pm, Sun noon–4.30pm • Free • ☎ 619 239 5548, ⓦ timkenmuseum.org

On the east side of Plaza de Panama, the squat, Modernist 1960s **Timken Museum of Art** is the only museum in the park that has free admission. Though it only shows around fifty of its artworks – from the early Renaissance to the Impressionist era – at one time, aficionados should look out for some real gems. Portraits by Hals, David, Van Dyck and Rubens stand out, as does Rembrandt's moving incarnation of *St Bartholomew*, while Veronese's *Madonna and Child with St Elizabeth* is the highlight of the small Italian collection. Pieter Brueghel's *Parable of the Sower* is magnificent, but just as appealing for many will be the museum's stirring collection of Russian religious icons, showcasing the imposing wood-panelled *Last Judgment*, arranged in a strict, five-storey hierarchy like a business office for the afterlife.

Botanical Building

1549 El Prado • Fri–Wed 10am–4pm • Free

North of the Timken Museum, facing the photogenic Lily Pond, the distinctive wood-ribbed domes of the **Botanical Building** date back to the 1915 Exposition and features more than two thousand regional and tropical plants – making for a refreshing break from all the museums.

Casa de Balboa

1649 El Prado • **Museum of Photographic Arts** Tues–Sun 10am–5pm; summer Thurs until 8pm • Pay what you wish (suggested $8) • ☎ 619 238 7559, ⓦ mopa.org **San Diego History Center** Daily 10am–5pm • $10 • ☎ 619 232 6203, ⓦ sandiegohistory.org **Model Railroad Museum** Tues–Fri 10am–4pm, Sat & Sun 11am–5pm • $10.75 • ☎ 619 696 0199, ⓦ sdmrm.org

Another architectural beauty constructed for the 1915 Panama-California Exposition, the **Casa de Balboa** is now home to three museums that are mainly of interest to aficionados. The **Museum of Photographic Arts** offers a fine permanent collection dating back to the daguerreotype process and includes the work of Mathew Brady, Alfred Stieglitz, Paul Strand and other big names; rotating exhibits typically showcase the work of local and historical artists, with a bent towards popular culture.

The **San Diego History Center** holds galleries that chart the booms that have elevated San Diego from scrubland into the eighth largest city in the US within 150 years, and the architectural and historical background of Balboa Park.

The **Model Railroad Museum** displays tiny, elaborate replicas of cityscapes, deserts and mountains, as well as the little trains that chug through them (at 27,000 square feet, it's one of the largest indoor model railway displays in the world).

Reuben H. Fleet Science Center

1875 El Prado • Daily 10am–6pm • $19.95, kids (3–12) $16.95; includes IMAX films • ☎ 619 238 1233, ⓦ rhfleet.org

At the far eastern end of El Prado, near Park Boulevard, the **Reuben H. Fleet Science Center** presents an assortment of child-oriented exhibits of varying interest, loaded with flashing buttons, high-tech gizmos, wacky sounds and goofy effects, and focusing on the glitzier, more rudimentary aspects of contemporary science, as well as the IMAX theatre and motion simulator.

Natural History Museum

1788 El Prado • Daily 10am–5pm • $19 • ☎ 619 232 3821, ⓦ sdnhm.org

The impressive **Natural History Museum**, on the north side of El Prado at its eastern end, features a great collection of fossils, a curious array of stuffed creatures, hands-on displays of minerals, and entertaining exhibits on dinosaurs and crocodiles. The more scholarly topics – such as the controversial links between birds and late-period, chicken-sized dinos – are interspersed with crowd-pleasing exhibits on menacing T-Rexes and other kid-friendly topics.

Spanish Village Art Center

1770 Village Place • Daily 11am–4pm • Free • ☎ 619 233 9050, ⓦ spanishvillageart.com

A short walk behind the Natural History Museum, the **Spanish Village Art Center** dates from the California Pacific 1935 Expo (it really does mimic a medieval Spanish village), and features the work of some three hundred craftspeople in three dozen different studios and galleries, where you can watch them practise their skills in painting, sculpture, photography, pottery and glass-working. If you continue north from here you'll find yourself at the gates of the San Diego Zoo (see opposite).

Pan American Plaza and around

El Prado holds most of Balboa Park's highlights, and only if you have a significant amount of time (or are a car, aeroplane or sports enthusiast) should you venture further south, in the direction of **Pan American Plaza**. The shady, lush **Palm Canyon** (daily 24hr; free), two acres holding some 450 palms, and the **Japanese Friendship Garden** (daily 10am–7pm, last entry 6pm; $8, $13 with special exhibitions; ☎ 619 232 2721, ⓦ niwa.org), with the familiar bonsai, koi, and meditative Zen garden, make for refreshingly tranquil escapes.

Spreckels Organ Pavilion

1549 El Prado, Suite 10 • Concerts Sun 2–3pm (also summer Mon 7.30–9.30pm); International Summer Organ Festival mid-June to Aug Mon 7.30pm • Free • ☎ 619 7028138, ⓦ spreckelsorgan.org

The world's largest outdoor pipe organ, with no fewer than 5,017 pipes, was donated to San Diego in 1914 for the Panama-California Exposition and is now preserved in the **Spreckels Organ Pavilion**, an elaborate vaulted structure with highly ornate gables. Weekly Sunday concerts have been performed here by the Civic Organist since 1917; British-born Carol Williams is the current maestro and the first woman to have the job. During the annual **International Summer Organ Festival** internationally renowned organists get their turn to play at Spreckels every Monday evening.

Marie Hitchcock Puppet Theater

2130 Pan American Rd • Summer Wed–Sun 11am, 1pm & 2.30pm; rest of year Wed, Thurs & Fri 10am & 11.30am, Sat & Sun 11am, 1pm & 2.30pm • $5, under 2 free ☎ 619 544 9203, ⓦ balboaparkpuppets.com

2

One of the most compelling family attractions near Pan American Plaza is the **Marie Hitchcock Puppet Theater** in the Palisades Building (erected for the 1935 exposition), with lively puppet productions involving fairy tales and ventriloquists.

Automotive Museum

2080 Pan American Plaza • Daily 10am–5pm • $9 (free Tues) • ☎ 619 231 2886, ⓦ sdautomuseum.org

Halfway along Pan American Plaza, the **Automotive Museum** will delight vintage car enthusiasts with its host of old Model Ts and fancy Rolls Royces as well as more obscure models like the 1912 Flying Merkle cycle and the 1948 Tucker Torpedo – one of only fifty left. Frank Sinatra's 1967 Austin Petrol is also on display.

Air & Space Museum

2001 Pan American Plaza • Daily: summer 10am–5pm; rest of year 10am–4.30pm • $19.50 • ☎ 619 234 8291, ⓦ sandiegoairandspace.org

At the southern end of Pan American Plaza, the cylindrical **Air & Space Museum** showcases the history of aviation with seventy planes like the Spitfire, Hellcat, and the sleek spy plane Blackbird; there's a MiG-17 and F-4 Phantom locked in a dogfight, Apollo and Gemini reproductions in the space age gallery, and special galleries on World War I and II.

San Diego Zoo

2920 Zoo Drive • Daily: mid-June to early Sept 9am–9pm; early Sept to mid-June 9am–5pm • Day ticket including bus tours and Skyfari $50, kids (3–11) $40; combined ticket including Safari Park $90, kids (3–11) $70 • ☎ 619 231 1515, ⓦ sandiegozoo.org

Easily one of the city's biggest and best-known attractions, **San Diego Zoo** lies immediately north of the main museums in Balboa Park and is generally regarded as the premier zoo in the country. As zoos go, it undoubtedly deserves its reputation, with more than four thousand animals from eight hundred different species, as well as some pioneering techniques for keeping them in captivity: animals are restrained in open spaces with moats or ridges rather than bars. It's an enormous place, and you can easily spend a full day or more here, checking out major sections devoted to the likes of chimps and gorillas, sun and polar bears, lizards and lions, flamingoes and pelicans, and habitats such as the rainforest. There's also a **children's zoo** in the park, with walk-through birdcages and an animal nursery, and **Conrad Prebys Australian Outback** highlighting Australian animals such as wombats, wallabies and koalas. Take a **guided bus tour** early on to get an idea of the layout, or survey the scene on the vertiginous **Skyfari**, an overhead tramway. Bear in mind, though, that many of the creatures get sleepy in the midday heat and retire behind bushes to take a nap. Moreover, the zoo's beloved giant **pandas** Bai Yun, Gao Gao and their offspring spend a lot of time sleeping

---

BALBOA PARK MINIATURE RAILROAD

Kids and fans of miniature railways will enjoy the pint-sized Balboa Park Miniature Railroad (☎ 619 239 4748) at 1800 Zoo Place (just outside San Diego Zoo), which takes a three-minute, half-mile spin through a leafy section of the park. It usually operates Sat & Sun 11am–4.30pm year-round, and daily 11am–6.30pm in summer. Train tickets are $3 for ages 1 and older.

or being prodded by biologists in the park's Giant Panda Research Station. If you have access to a car you might want to consider visiting the associated **San Diego Zoo Safari Park** at Escondido, 35 miles north (see p.197) – combo tickets are available.

Hillcrest

Buses #3, #83, #120 from downtown

Two miles north of downtown and on the northwest edge of Balboa Park, **Hillcrest** is a lively and arty area, thanks to the wealthy liberals who've moved into the district in recent decades and the general sprucing-up of the place. As a result the neighbourhood is littered with locally owned businesses, interesting cafés and restaurants (see p.181) and an appealing collection of Victorian homes. It's also known as being the centre of the city's **LGBT community** (see p.187), with a handful of gay-oriented hotels and some colourful street life around University and Fifth, where the district's signature sign, dating back to 1940, is prominently displayed. The **Hillcrest Block Party** kicks off San Diego Pride weekend in July (Ⓦsdpride.org), and in 2012 a giant rainbow flag was raised at the corner of University and Normal.

Marston House Museum & Gardens

3525 7th Ave • Fri–Mon 10am–5pm; 40–45min tours every 30min • $15 • ☏ 619 297 9327, Ⓦ sohosandiego.org

The only conventional attraction in Hillcrest is the **Marston House Museum & Gardens**, a 1905 charmer whose rustic Arts and Crafts design little resembles the later Modernist work of its co-architect Irving Gill. This house has a warmly elegant late-Victorian feel, and is well worth a look for anyone with an interest in houses of the era; tours provide a glimpse into the lifestyle of one of San Diego's most prominent and progressive families (George W. Marston and his wife, Anna Gunn Marston). It's surrounded by five acres of rolling lawns and manicured formal gardens.

Old Town

Bus #30 from downtown; Green Line to Old Town station • Ⓦ oldtownsandiegoguide.com

Some four miles north of downtown, **OLD TOWN** is where the city of San Diego began in 1769, when the Spanish established their *presidio* and mission here. By the 1870s, current Downtown San Diego had largely replaced Old Town and its buildings gradually crumbled. Preservation of the area began in 1968, much of it within the **Old Town State Historic Park**, and it's still the best place to get a sense of the city's Hispanic roots away from its modern high-rises.

Old Town State Historic Park

4002 Wallace St • Daily: May–Sept 10am–5pm; Oct–April 10am–4pm (tours daily 11am & 2pm) • Free • ☏ 619 220 5422, Ⓦ parks.ca.gov • Site is opposite the Old Town Transit Center, with Coaster, Trolley and MTS Bus service to downtown; by car, take I-5 and exit on Old Town Ave (exit 19), following the signs; or from I-8 turn-off onto Taylor St and left onto Juan St

Much of Old Town is now preserved within **Old Town State Historic Park**, an illuminating (and free) living museum that commemorates San Diego in the Mexican and early American periods of 1821 to 1872. Featuring 25 structures, some of them original **adobes** displaying many of their original furnishings, there's a working blacksmith shop, friendly *burros* (small donkeys) and several small museums.

Though rife with tacky gift shops in places, the park is especially enjoyable on a Sunday afternoon, when there is occasional free Latin music and folk dancing. As for **food**, several stalls serve fresh tortillas, and there are various Mexican restaurants that are well worth a try (see p.181).

FROM TOP OLD POINT LOMA LIGHTHOUSE (P.171); MISSION BEACH (P.171) >

Casa de Estudillo

4000 Mason St

One of the more significant structures in the state park is the **Casa de Estudillo**, completed by the Mexican commander of the *presidio*, José Maria de Estudillo, in 1829, and inherited by his son, later the city treasurer and tax assessor under American rule. For many years, the building was known as "Ramona's Marriage Place" from Helen Hunt Jackson's influential romantic novel about early California, *Ramona* (1884); the house was actually remodelled to match descriptions in the novel, and reopened in 1910 as an unashamed *Ramona* tourist attraction (despite the novel being entirely fictional). Today the house has been redesigned to more accurately tell the story of the Estudillo family, who lived here until 1887.

Casa de Bandini (The Cosmopolitan)

2660 Calhoun St • Restaurant: Mon–Fri 11am–9pm, Sat & Sun 10am–9pm • ☏ 619 297 1874, ⓦ oldtowncosmopolitan.com

Completed in 1829, **Casa de Bandini** was the adobe home of the Peruvian-born politician and writer Juan Bandini and became the de facto social centre of San Diego during the mid-nineteenth century. In 1869 American stagecoach operator Albert Seeley transformed the building into the **Cosmopolitan Hotel**, considered among the finest in the state; its many elegant period appointments are still visible in the dining room. The site later became a grocery, pickle cannery and is now a popular hotel and restaurant, named once again *The Cosmopolitan*.

San Diego Union Museum

2602 San Diego Ave

The wood-frame **San Diego Union Museum** was actually fabricated in Maine in 1851, and shipped around Cape Horn to become the first office of the *San Diego Union* newspaper; the building is restored as it was when the first edition was printed in 1868. Visitors can view the original printroom with an original Washington press and the editor's office.

Seeley Stable Museum

2630 Calhoun St

The **Seeley Stable Museum** is a reconstruction of Albert Seeley's original stable and barns, used for his San Diego to LA stage line in the 1880s, and now crammed with a fine collection of horse-drawn buggies, wagons, carriages and other Old West memorabilia.

Wells Fargo History Museum

2733 San Diego Ave • Daily 10am–5pm • Free • ☏ 619 238 3929, ⓦ wellsfargohistory.com

The **Wells Fargo History Museum**, one in the bank's national chain of Wild West museums, showcases some old telegraphs, an overland Concord coach from 1867, and assorted coins, maps and assay supplies – housed in the Colorado House, a replica of an 1851 hotel and saloon.

Whaley House Museum and Old Adobe Chapel

Whaley House Museum 2476 San Diego Ave • Summer daily 10am–9.30pm; rest of year Sun–Tues 10am–4.30pm, Thurs–Sat 10am–9.30pm • $8; $13 after 5pm • **Old Adobe Chapel** 3963 Conde St • Sat & Sun 11am–5pm by appointment • Free • ☏ 619 297 7511, ⓦ whaleyhouse.org

Just beyond the Old Town State Historic Park gates, the independently run **Whaley House Museum** was the first brick building in California (1857) and the home of Thomas Whaley, a New York entrepreneur drawn by the Gold Rush. It displays furniture and photos from his general store, as well as a reconstruction of a courtroom from 1869, when the building housed the county courthouse. What really gets most visitors excited, however, is the site's reputation as being **haunted** by the ghost of

KOBEY'S SWAP MEET

The huge Kobey's Swap Meet, essentially an open-air flea market offering everything from tacky souvenirs and Mexican arts and crafts to finer handmade jewellery and antiques, takes place close to Old Town in the parking lots around the Valley View Casino Center (San Diego Sports Arena), 3500 Sports Arena Blvd (Fri–Sun 7am–3pm; $1 admission Fri, $2 weekends; ☏ 619 226 0650, ⓦ kobeyswap.com).

2

"Yankee Jim" Robinson, hanged in 1852 by a kangaroo court for stealing a rowing boat; the grounds upon which the house stands were used for public hangings before Whaley's arrival (some believe that the spirit of one Violet Whaley, who committed suicide here in 1885, also haunts the house). Note, though, that the museum website, in all seriousness, makes it clear that it cannot guarantee ghost sightings, though "occasionally visitors do report supernatural encounters within the museum's walls". Just down the street from the Whaley House, you can peer into the atmospheric, sculpture-filled interior of the **Old Adobe Chapel**, built as a home in 1850 and converted to a chapel by Don José Aguirre in 1858. It was used as a place of worship until it was bulldozed in 1917, and rebuilt twenty years later.

Sheriff's Museum

2384 San Diego Ave • Wed–Sun: April–Sept 11am–6pm; Oct–March 11am–5pm • Free • ☏ 619 260 1850, ⓦ sheriffsmuseum.org

The mildly entertaining **Sheriff's Museum** in Old Town chronicles the history of the San Diego County Sheriff's Department, from its inception in 1850 to the present day. Inside you'll find vintage police cars, motorcycles and jail cells from various eras, and plenty of hands-on exhibits; kids can sit on the bikes and play with handcuffs, bulletproof vests and the old police siren (you've been warned).

Heritage Park

2454 Heritage Park Row • Senlis Cottage & Temple Beth Israel daily 9am–5pm • Free • ☏ 858 565 3600, ⓦ sdparks.org

The county-managed **Heritage Park** is a small ensemble of preserved Victorian buildings from the 1880s and 1890s, gathered from around the city. They include San Diego's first synagogue, the 1889 **Temple Beth Israel** (it now hosts weddings, receptions and bar mitzvahs) and six cottages that were once home to the town sheriff, the doctor and a cousin of General Sherman. All are closed to the public apart from the 1896 **Senlis Cottage**, a typically modest working-class home of the period. The view of the harbour from the park is worth the climb alone.

Presidio Park and around

Junípero Serra Museum 2727 Presidio Drive • Summer Fri–Sun 10am–5pm; rest of year Sat & Sun 10am–4pm • $6 • ☏ 619 232 6203, ⓦ sandiegohistory.org **Mormon Battalion Historic Site** 2510 Juan St • Daily 9am–9pm (last tour 8pm) • Free • ☏ 619 298 3317

The Spanish Revival building that now sits atop **Presidio Park** in Old Town is only a 1929 approximation of the original 1769 Mission San Diego de Alcalá – which was relocated in 1774 – but contains the illuminating **Junípero Serra Museum**, which displays Spanish furniture dating back to the sixteenth century, along with weapons, diaries and documents pertaining to the leading Catholic missionary of California. Hoping to convert the local Kumeyaay people, Serra was a Franciscan friar who founded nine Spanish missions in California, beginning with San Diego (though the local Kumeyaay reduced the mission to ashes in 1775). The museum also lionizes the yeoman struggles of a few devoted historians to preserve the area's Spanish past in the face of dollar-hungry developers. The **Mormon Battalion Memorial Visitor Center**, just outside the park, presents artefacts, paintings and multimedia about the 500-troop, 2000-mile saga of the Mormon Battalion March during the Mexican–American War – the longest US military infantry march in history, slogging more than halfway across the continent from Council Bluffs, Iowa, to San Diego, in 1846 to 1847.

Mission Basilica San Diego de Alcalá

10818 San Diego Mission Rd · Daily 7am–7pm; Museum 9am–4.45pm · Free · ☎ 619 283 7319, ⓦ missionsandiego.com · Green Line to Mission San Diego Station

Seven miles northeast of Presidio Park and Old Town, the all-white Spanish-style **Mission Basilica San Diego de Alcalá** was relocated here in 1774 to be closer to a water source and to be further away from conflict with the local Kumeyaay people – which still didn't prevent Padre Luis Jayme, California's first Christian martyr, from being clubbed to death a year later. Long abandoned, the mission was fully reconstructed in 1931 to resemble the fourth church that stood here in 1813, and still hosts a working parish, offering confession, weddings, baptisms and daily masses. Walk through the dark and echoey church – the fourteenth-century stalls and altar were imported from Spain – to the **garden**, where two small crosses mark the graves of Native American neophytes, making this California's oldest cemetery. A small **museum** holds a collection of Native American crafts and articles from the mission, including the crucifix said to have been held by Mission founder Junípero Serra at his death in 1784 – he's actually buried in Carmel (see p.404).

Ocean Beach

Bus #923 from downtown

Ruled by the Hell's Angels in the 1960s, **OCEAN BEACH**, seven miles northwest of downtown (and four miles west of Old Town), is now a relaxed beach community that big-moneyed interests have been trying to develop for decades, with limited success. While the single-storey adobe dwellings that were home to several generations of Portuguese fishing families as recently as the 1980s have virtually disappeared, overdevelopment has otherwise been kept at bay, at least near the shore, where a 30ft building height limit does much to keep things under control. Indeed, the quaint, old-time streets and shops near the coast have preserved some of their ramshackle appeal and funky character. The two big hangouts include the main drag of **Newport Street**, where backpackers populate the snack bars, surf and skate rental shops, and other San Diegans come for the myriad antique malls, and **Voltaire Street**, which, true to its name, has a good range of independent-minded local businesses. There is often good surf, and the beach itself can be quite fun – especially at weekends, when the local party scene cranks up. Ocean Beach has one of the state's longest **piers**, at 2000ft, meant mainly for fishing and strolling. Where Voltaire Street meets the waves, you can visit Ocean Beach's other major attraction, **Dog Beach**, the only sand strip in the area where pooches are allowed to frolic without leashes – great for canines, if not necessarily for small children. South of the pier rise the dramatic **Sunset Cliffs**, a prime spot for twilight vistas, though notoriously unstable – more than a few people have tumbled over the edge following an afternoon of excess on the beach.

Point Loma and Cabrillo National Monument

Cabrillo National Monument 1800 Cabrillo Memorial Drive · Daily 9am–5pm, last entry 4.30pm · Seven-day pass $10/vehicle, $5/pedestrian or cyclist · ☎ 619 557 5450, ⓦ nps.gov/cabr · To get here from downtown, take bus #923 and switch to #28, then #84

South of Ocean Beach, the hilly green peninsula of **POINT LOMA** is mostly owned by the US Navy, which keeps it attractive, unspoiled and largely inaccessible. After a six-mile ride to the point's southern extremity, you reach **Cabrillo National Monument**, the spot where captain Juan Rodríguez Cabrillo and his crew became the first Europeans to land in California in 1542, though they quickly reboarded their vessel and sailed away. In the American era, the site was recognized for its military value, and various abandoned gun emplacements and fortifications now dot the landscape, left over from the first half of the twentieth century.

EXPLORING LIBERTY STATION

Located on the eastern side of Point Loma (on the waterfront just west of the airport), **Liberty Station** (ⓦ libertystation.com) is the ambitious re-development of the former Naval Training Center San Diego, which closed in 1997. Today the district features shops, hotels, restaurants and museums centred on converted base buildings along Historic Decatur Rd. The Arts District at the northern end features several high-end galleries, plus the **Liberty Public Market**, 2820 Historic Decatur Rd (daily 11am–7pm; ⓦ libertypublicmarket.com), an artisan food court, and the **New Americans Museum** at 2825 Dewey Rd (Wed–Sun 10am–4pm, Sat & Sun 11am–4pm; free; ☏ 619 756 7707, ⓦ newamericansmuseum.org), which explores the politically charged topic of American immigration. The **Women's Museum of the California** at 2730 Historic Decatur Rd (Wed–Sun noon–4pm; $5; ☏ 619 233 7963, ⓦ womensmuseumca.org) holds fascinating exhibitions on women's history, while the **Visions Art Museum**, 2825 Dewey Rd (Tues–Sat 10am–4pm; $7; ☏ 619 546-4872, ⓦ visionsartmuseum.org) is a repository of contemporary quilts and brightly patterned textiles. The only public transport is bus#28 from Old Town.

The monument's startling vistas, across to downtown and along the coast to Mexico, easily repay the journey here. After enjoying the view, you can explore the marine life in the many tide pools around the shoreline, reached on a clearly marked **nature walk** beginning near the monument. The **visitor centre** has information on the history and wildlife of the point, and the nearby 1855 **Old Point Loma Lighthouse** (within the national monument), whose interior contains replica Victoriana and equipment from the 1880s. The structure's main purpose was ultimately unfulfilled: soon after it was built, it was discovered that its beacon would be obscured by fog, and another lighthouse was erected at a lower elevation.

On the southwest-facing cliffs of the lighthouse, a sheltered viewing station with telescopes makes it easy to see the November to March **whale migration**, when scores of grey whales pass by on their journey between the Arctic Ocean and their breeding waters off Baja California.

Mission Beach

Bus #8 from Old Town

Built on a sandbar between the Pacific Ocean and Mission Bay, the community of **MISSION BEACH** spans nearly two miles of oceanfront some eight miles northwest of downtown. Today it's one of the most popular and entertaining of San Diego's city beaches, with throngs of sun-seekers enjoying surfing, cycling and rollerblading down Ocean Front Walk, the concrete boardwalk running the length of the beach (the fastest way to travel when summer traffic is bumper-to-bumper on Mission Blvd), and Frisbee tossing on the sands. Old-fashioned fun can be had at one of the lively bars here, or at the historic amusements of **Belmont Park**, but it's **SeaWorld**, across the mud flats and lagoons of Mission Bay, that draws the most visitors.

Belmont Park

3146 Mission Blvd • June–Aug: Mon–Thurs & Sun 11am–11pm, Fri & Sat 11am–midnight; March–May & Sept & Oct: Mon–Thurs & Sun 11am–8pm, Fri & Sat 11am–10pm; Nov & Dec: Mon, Thurs & Sun 11am–6pm, Fri & Sat 11am–10pm; Jan & Feb: Fri & Sat 11am–10pm, Sun 11am–8pm • Most rides $3–6; unlimited park pass $28.95/day • ☏ 858 228 9283, ⓦ belmontpark.com • Bus #8 from Old Town

The ageing amusements at **Belmont Park** are loads of fun for adults and kids alike, with the two main attractions both dating from 1925: the **Giant Dipper** rollercoaster (with a 73ft drop; $6), one of the few of its era still around, and the heated **Plunge Pool** ($7/day), once the setting for famous celluloid swimmers Johnny Weissmuller and Esther Williams. Of the newer draws, **FlowRider** ($20/hr) is a simulated-wave pool that allows you to get a vague sense of what surfing and wakeboarding are like without having to venture into the ocean, while the more intense **FlowBarrel** ($40/hr) is a 10ft-high wave, for people who have a little more familiarity with actual surf. Beyond the main attractions, the park offers an assortment of lesser carnival thrills, trinket stores, mini-golf and countless seaside snack joints.

SeaWorld San Diego

500 Sea World Drive • Daily: hours vary seasonally (at least 11am–5pm); mid-June to Aug 9am–9pm • $89 (ages 3 and above, website discounts available); parking extra $17 • ☎ 800 257 4268, ⓦ seaworldparks.com • Bus #8 from Old Town

The giant amusement park of **SeaWorld**, the San Diego branch of an entertainment colossus that stretches from California to Texas to Florida, remains one of the city's most popular attractions for its amusement park rides, shows, marine life exhibits and especially its ensemble of eleven **killer whales**. Despite this, there has been a decrease in visitor numbers at all SeaWorld branches following the negative publicity in the wake of the 2013 documentary *Blackfish* – a film produced after a SeaWorld Orlando trainers was killed by one of the park's killer whales. SeaWorld has since announced that it will **end its killer whale breeding programme**, and refocus its signature killer whale shows on natural whale behaviour from 2017, when a whole raft of new shows will be launched in San Diego aimed to stem the decline in visitor numbers.

Elsewhere there are various seal and dolphin shows, "Wild Arctic" has walruses, beluga whales and polar bears; "Shark Encounter" features sharks circling menacingly around visitors walking through a submerged viewing tunnel; and there are assorted aquariums, tide pools and sites devoted to penguins, flamingoes and catfish. Some of the park's other attractions, however, have devolved into standard theme-park fare that includes the likes of giant-inner-tube rides ("Shipwreck Rapids"), motion simulators ("Riptide Rescue") and the Manta rollercoaster.

Pacific Beach

North of the spirited amusements of Mission Beach lies the more sedate **PACIFIC BEACH**, where expensive oceanside homes with tidy lawns suggest haute bourgeoisie refinement, though there's still plenty to enjoy and the district is the best of the San Diego beach towns to stay (see p.178). The beach around **Crystal Pier** is a decent spot to laze in the sun, while **Garnet Avenue**, running inland from the pier, is lined by hip eating joints, bars and clubs. For many, though, Pacific Beach is synonymous with **surfing**, and is one of the prime strips of coastline in the area specifically set up for it.

La Jolla and around

"A nice place – for old people and their parents", wrote Raymond Chandler of **LA JOLLA** (pronounced "la hoya") in the 1950s, though that didn't stop him from moving here (his former house is at 6005 Camino de la Costa) and setting much of his final novel *Playback* in the town, renaming it "Esmeralda". Indeed, it's long been a place that has attracted the rich and famous: actor Gregory Peck was born here in 1916, Raquel Welch attended La Jolla High School in the 1950s, and presidential candidates John McCain and Mitt Romney have homes near the beach. Pop-guru Deepak Chopra even ran his Center for Well Being in La Jolla until 2002.

AQUATICA SAN DIEGO – SEAWORLD'S WATER PARK

SeaWorld's largest theme-park spin-off is **Aquatica San Diego**, a massive water park crammed with several thrilling waterslides, huge wave pool and shallow pools for little ones. The park is at 2052 Entertainment Circle in Chula Vista, 16 miles southeast of downtown (nowhere near SeaWorld), and best accessed by car. The park is open daily through summer, 10am–5pm, with tickets $44 for adults and $33 for kids (3–9). If you intend to also visit SeaWorld, check the website for combo tickets (☎ 612 226 3901, ⓦ aquaticabyseaworld.com/en/sandiego).

SAN DIEGO SURF HOTSPOTS & SURF SCHOOLS

You can rent surfboards (around $30/day) at La Jolla Surf Systems, 2132 Avenida De la Playa in La Jolla (☎858 456 2777, ⊛lajollasurfsystems.com), and at Iron Cross Surfboards, 2107 San Elijo Ave in Cardiff-by-the-Sea (☎760 436 1900, ⊛ironcrosssurfboards.com).

Black's Beach 12600 N Torrey Pines Rd, La Jolla. This is the region's premier, though unofficial, clothing-optional beach and one of the top surfing beaches in Southern California (advanced surfers only).

Cardiff Reef Hwy-101 (Cardiff State Beach), Cardiff-by-the-Sea. Home to celebrated local surfer Rob Machado, and the infamous "Cardiff Kook" surfer statue. Cardiff Reef and nearby Pipes are known for their smooth and consistent wave shapes (for pros and novices).

Tourmaline Surfing Park A mile north of the Pacific Beach pier, La Jolla Blvd at Tourmaline St (☎619 221 8900). "Turmo" is regularly pounded by heavy waves and is reserved exclusively for surfing, as well as for windsurfing – no swimmers are allowed.

Windansea Beach 6800 Neptune Place, La Jolla. If you don't have a board, this is a good alternative a few miles north of Pacific Beach, a favourite surfing hotspot that's also fine for swimming and hiking alongside the oceanside rocks and reefs.

SURF SCHOOLS

San Diego Surf School 4850 Cass St, North Pacific Beach ☎858 205 7683, ⊛sandiegosurfingschool.com. Well-established school with lessons held at North Pacific Beach or Ocean Beach, with private sessions $75/hr and group lessons $55 for 1hr 30min. Board rentals from $30/day.

Surf Diva 2160 Avenida de la Playa, La Jolla ☎858 454 8273, ⊛surfdiva.com. The first all-girls surf school still offers women-only surf camps as well as highly rated lessons open to all ($85/hr, or group lessons for $65/1hr 30min).

These days La Jolla, thirteen miles northwest of Downtown San Diego, is rolling in new money, and its opulence is far less stuffy and more welcoming. The main section, around **Prospect Street** and **Girard Avenue**, has spotless pavements flanked by crisply trimmed grass, and the many upscale art galleries sit alongside chic cafés and swanky boutiques.

Although it's fairly expensive, La Jolla is worth a visit at least once to savour the elegance of the place – don't miss the ornate pink *La Valencia Hotel*, frequented by Hollywood's elite in the 1930s and 1940s (see p.179).

Museum of Contemporary Art

700 Prospect St • Mon, Tues & Thurs–Sun 11am–5pm • $10 • ☎858 454 3541, ⊛mcasd.org

The La Jolla branch of San Diego's **Museum of Contemporary Art** (see p.173) has a huge, rotating stock of works from 1955 onwards. Minimalism, pop art and California Art are in evidence, bolstered by strong temporary shows involving installations, sculpture and multimedia – ultimately a collection of work no less daring or fascinating than that presented by the museum's downtown counterpart. There is also an outdoor **sculpture garden**, with fabulous views of the Pacific surf crashing against the rocks below the building's huge windows.

The museum building was once the 1915 residence of **Ellen Scripps**, a local philanthropist who injected her seemingly endless wealth into La Jolla through the first half of the twentieth century. She commissioned early Modernist architect Irving Gill to design her house, and today the Scripps name is still almost everywhere, notably in the tasteful **Ellen Browning Scripps Park**, north of the museum along Coast Boulevard, where the fine views and grassy layout ensure its popularity as a wedding location.

La Jolla Cove

Coast Blvd • Daily 9am–dusk • Free

The northern edge of Ellen Browning Scripps Park overlooks **La Jolla Cove**, a craggy and beautiful expanse marked off as an ecological reserve, whose clear waters make it

2

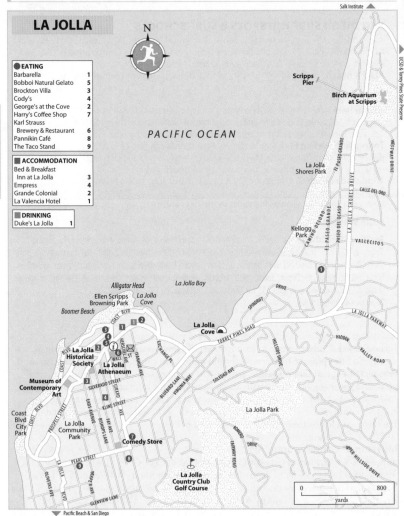

LA JOLLA

N

Salk Institute

● EATING
Barbarella	1
Bobboi Natural Gelato	5
Brockton Villa	3
Cody's	4
George's at the Cove	2
Harry's Coffee Shop	7
Karl Strauss Brewery & Restaurant	6
Pannikin Café	8
The Taco Stand	9

■ ACCOMMODATION
Bed & Breakfast Inn at La Jolla	3
Empress	4
Grande Colonial	2
La Valencia Hotel	1

■ DRINKING
Duke's La Jolla	1

PACIFIC OCEAN

Scripps Pier
Birch Aquarium at Scripps
UCSD & Torrey Pines State Preserve

La Jolla Shores Park
WESTWAY DRIVE
EL PASEO GRANDE
LA JOLLA SHORES DRIVE
CALLE DEL ORO

Kellogg Park
CAMINO DEL ORO
PASEO DEL OCASO
EL PASEO GRANDE
VALLECITOS

Alligator Head
La Jolla Bay
DRIVE
La Jolla Cove
Ellen Scripps Browning Park
La Jolla Cove
Boomer Beach
COAST BLVD
SPINDRIFT
LA JOLLA PARKWAY

La Jolla Cove
TORREY PINES ROAD
HIDDEN VALLEY ROAD
HILLSIDE DRIVE

La Jolla Historical Society
HERSCHEL AVE
IVANHOE AVE
EXCHANGE PL
La Jolla Athenaeum
WALL ST
COAST BLVD
SOLEDAD AVE

Museum of Contemporary Art
SILVERADO STREET
PROSPECT STREET
EADS AVENUE
BLUEBIRD LANE
VIRGINIA WAY

Coast Blvd City Park
KLINE STREET
FAY AVE
BISHOPS LANE
La Jolla Park

La Jolla Community Park
Comedy Store
ROMERO DRIVE
FAIRWAY ROAD

PEARL STREET
GRAPE AVE
LA JOLLA BLVD
OLIVETAS AVE
UPPER HILLSIDE DRIVE

La Jolla Country Club Golf Course
GLENVIEW LANE

0   800
yards

▼ Pacific Beach & San Diego

perfect for snorkelling or scuba diving. However, **surfing is banned**, and you should keep your hands off the officially protected aquatic flora and fauna, no matter how enticing it looks. One problem, however, is access, with street parking spaces (free) very limited in high season; aim for the paid Coast Walk public parking (daily 11am–10pm; $1.75/30min) on Coast Boulevard, just off Prospect Street.

Birch Aquarium at Scripps

2300 Expedition Way (off N Torrey Pines Rd) • Daily 9am–5pm • $18.50, kids (3–17) $14; parking free for 3hr • ☏ 858 534 3474, ⓦ aquarium.ucsd.edu

On a bluff overlooking the Pacific, lies the **Birch Aquarium at Scripps**, part of the Scripps Institute of Oceanography, providing entertaining views of captive marine life and informative displays on ecology. The highlights include the Hall of Fishes, a huge, 70,000-gallon tank with a thick kelp forest that's home to countless sea creatures, and the smaller but revamped "ElasmoBeach" tank, displaying a range of fearsome leopard sharks and rays. Feeding shows throughout the day provide the most colour, while the newer display of seahorse species provides a less frenzied spectacle.

University of California, San Diego (UCSD)

Gilman Entrance Information Center 9500 Gilman Drive • Mon–Fri 7am–7pm, Sat & Sun 7am–5pm • ☎ 858 534 2230, ⓦ ucsd.edu • **Geisel Library** Hours vary, usually Mon–Thurs 8am–9.45pm, Fri 8am–5.45pm, Sat 10am–5.45pm, Sun noon–7.45pm; free tours Sun 2pm (2hr) • ⓦ libraries.ucsd.edu • Bus #30 from downtown terminates at the University Town Centre transport hub

On a hillside setting above the Birch Aquarium and also reached from Torrey Pines Road, the **University of California, San Diego (UCSD)** campus has two highlights. The first, the weird concrete-buttress spectacle of the **Geisel Library**, was named after the creator of Dr Seuss, and looks it – resembling something like a ziggurat crossed with a UFO (Theodor Geisel was a longtime resident of La Jolla, and died here in 1991). Then there's the **Stuart Collection** (☎ 858 534 2117, ⓦ stuartcollection.ucsd.edu), specially commissioned outdoor sculptures located throughout the campus and including works by Bruce Nauman, Robert Irwin, John Baldessari, Nam June Paik and Jenny Holzer. The first acquisition, from 1983, is still among the best: Niki de Saint Phalle's **Sun God**, a chunky, colourful bird on a concrete arch, whose outstretched wings welcome visitors to the parking lot opposite Peterson Hall, and which acts as the university's unofficial icon, routinely decorated in garish outfits during key events or holidays. Get maps of the campus at the **Gilman Entrance Information Center** (which is the starting point for the Sunday tours).

Torrey Pines State Natural Reserve

12600 N Torrey Pines Rd • Daily 7.15am–sunset (5–8pm) • Free (parking $10–15) • **Visitor centre** Daily: May–Sept 9am–6pm; Oct–April 10am–4pm; guided nature walk (free) Sat & Sun 10am, noon & 2pm • ☎ 858 755 2063, ⓦ torreypine.org

Some five miles north of the UCSD campus, Torrey Pines Road provides the only access (via a steep path) to **Torrey Pines State Beach**, part of the **Torrey Pines State Natural Reserve**. This slice of protected wilderness harbours the country's rarest species of pine, the Torrey Pine – one of two surviving stands. Thanks to salty conditions and stiff ocean breezes, the pines contort their ten-foot frames into a variety of tortured, twisted shapes that can be viewed at close quarters from the **Guy Fleming Trail**, a loop two-thirds of a mile long that starts near the beachside parking lot. The **visitor centre** will tell you all about the pines, especially if your visit coincides with a guided nature tour. A three-quarter-mile **beach trail** leads from the centre down to Flat Rock and a popular beach, great for sunbathing and picnics, though no picnicking is allowed on the cliffs above the beach. Continuing beyond the reserve will lead you into the North County town of Del Mar (see p.190).

ARRIVAL AND DEPARTURE   SAN DIEGO

By plane San Diego International Airport (ⓦ san.org) is just three miles northwest of downtown. Metropolitan Transit System's Bus #992 (daily 5am–11.30pm; every 15min Mon–Fri, every 30min Sat & Sun; $2.25) connects with downtown and the Trolley, Coaster and Amtrak stations. Taxis are always available (around $18 to downtown), and all major car rental desks are represented at the terminals. Alternatively, shared shuttle services such as SuperShuttle (☎ 800 258 3826, ⓦ supershuttle.com) can take you downtown for $14 one-way.

KAYAK THE SEVEN CAVES

The **La Jolla Caves** are an enchanting set of seven caves tucked in between La Jolla Cove and La Jolla Shores – only one is accessible by land (**Sunny Jim's Cave**), making the other six prime targets for kayakers: Arch Cave, Clam's Cave, Little Sister, Sea Surprize, Shopping Cart and White Lady. You can only enter the caves with a licensed guide – recommended operators include La Jolla Kayak (☎ 858 459 1114, ⓦ lajollakayak.com) and Bike and Kayak Tours (☎ 858 454 1010, ⓦ bikeandkayaktours.com), with two-hour tours usually $40–45 per person.

2

By train Amtrak trains use the Santa Fe Railroad Depot, close to the western end of Broadway at 1050 Kettner Blvd (☎ 800 872 7245).

Destinations Anaheim (11 daily; 1hr 58min–2hr 15min); Los Angeles Downtown (11 daily; 2hr 45min–3hr); Oceanside (11 daily; 50min–1hr 4min); San Juan Capistrano (11 daily; 1hr 24min–1hr 39min); Santa Barbara (4 daily; 5hr 35min–5hr 45min); Solana Beach (11 daily; 35–40min).

By bus The Greyhound bus terminal is at 1313 National Ave (☎ 619 515 1100), just east of Petco Park and conveniently located next to the 12th & Imperial Transit

Center (for tram trolley and bus connections). Note that all journeys to San Francisco (12–14hr) and Las Vegas (8–9hr) require a change in Los Angeles or San Bernardino.

Destinations Escondido (2 daily; 40min); Los Angeles Downtown (16 daily; 2hr 10min–3hr 15min); Oceanside (6 daily; 50min); Phoenix, AZ (2 daily; 8hr 20min–8hr 30min); San Bernardino (2 daily; 2hr 40min); Tijuana, Mexico (18 daily; 1hr 10min).

By ferry Ferries ($4.25; 15min) cross the bay to Coronado (see p.187) from Broadway Pier in Downtown San Diego and also the Convention Center on the hour, Sun–Thurs 9am–9pm & 9am–10pm Fri & Sat.

GETTING AROUND

Despite its size, **getting around** San Diego without a car is slow but not too difficult, whether you use buses, the light-rail-like San Diego Trolley, or a rented bike. Travelling can be harder at night, with most public transport routes closing down around 11pm or midnight. **Taxis** are also an affordable option: meters start at $2.80 and the average fare is from $6 for a jaunt around downtown to $20–25 to get up to the more northerly beaches (Ocean, Mission or Pacific).

BY BUS

The Metropolitan Transit System (MTS; ☎ 619 595 4555, ⓦ sdmts.com) is the most convenient and accessible means of public transport in the region. One-way fares are $2.25–2.50, and $5–10 for the most lengthy journeys into rural terrain; the exact fare is required when boarding (dollar bills are accepted). Service is reliable and frequent, particularly downtown. If you're headed anywhere in the North County, you'll take Breeze Buses from the Amtrak station at Santa Fe depot (fares $1.75, day-pass $5; ☎ 800 266 6883, ⓦ gonctd.com).

Passes The stored value Compass Card ($2), allows you to buy various bus passes for unlimited rides on most bus and trolley routes for one- to four-day visits ($5, $9, $12 and $15 respectively), available from the Transit Store (see below). Transfers to premium express, rural, access and special services will require the price of the higher fare.

Transit Store 12th & Imperial Transit Center, 1255 Imperial Ave (Mon–Fri 9am–5pm; ☎ 619 234 1060); local bus timetables, free regional transport guides and travel passes.

Destinations (from downtown) Balboa Park #3, #7, #120; Coronado, Silver Strand and Imperial Beach #901, #904; Hillcrest #3, #83, #120; La Jolla #30; Pacific Beach #30; Ocean Beach #923; Old Town #30.

Destinations (from Old Town) Ocean Beach #35; Mission Beach and Pacific Beach #8, #9, #27, #30.

BY TROLLEY

Complementing county bus lines is the San Diego Trolley, often called the "Tijuana Trolley" because it travels to the US–Mexico border in San Ysidro (see box, p.155). One-way tickets are $2.50 and should be bought from the machines at trolley stops, which also offer return tickets. Of the three routes, the Blue Line is the more visitor-oriented, starting

with Old Town and heading south to Little Italy and Downtown San Diego, then on to the Mexican border. From the transfer station at Imperial and 12th, the trolley's Orange Line usefully loops around downtown, but offers little else of interest to visitors, darting out towards the eastern suburbs. The newer Green Line also reaches these suburbs, starting at Old Town, but is really only useful for visitors headed to Mission San Diego or Qualcomm Stadium. Trolleys leave every fifteen minutes during the day (starting around 5am); the last service back from San Ysidro leaves at 1am, so an evening of south-of-the-border revelry and a return to San Diego the same night is quite possible.

BY TRAIN

The Coaster (☎ 800 262 7837, ⓦ gonctd.com/coaster) is a commuter light-rail system that links downtown to the North San Diego County coast. On weekdays, eleven trains run southbound from Oceanside to downtown (Santa Fe Depot), with the same number returning northbound (and an extra two trains on Friday night), while six trains make the trip on Saturdays and just four on Sundays and holidays. The Coaster also provides a cheap, alternative way of reaching Los Angeles, with transfers at Oceanside onto the Metrolink commuter rail system (see p.127), linking San Diego County all the way to Downtown LA and even up to Oxnard in Ventura County.

Destinations (from downtown) Carlsbad Village (57min); Encinitas (41min); Oceanside (1hr 2min); Old Town (6min); Solana Beach (36min); Sorrento Valley (27min).

Fares (from downtown): $4 to Old Town; $5 to Sorrento Valley; $5.50 to all other stations ($2 to $2.75 for seniors); $12 for a day-pass. Includes free transfer to Sprinter or Breeze services within two hours of purchase.

The Sprinter (☎ 800 262 7837, ⓦ gonctd.com/sprinter) light-rail system operates along Hwy-78 over

OLD TOWN TROLLEY TOUR

Not to be confused with the San Diego Trolley, the **Old Town Trolley Tour** (☎ 619 298 8687, ⓦ trolleytours.com/san-diego) is a two-hour narrated trip around San Diego's most popular sites, including downtown, Balboa Park, the San Diego Zoo, Old Town and Coronado, aboard an open-sided motor-driven carriage. If you're short of time, the tour is a simple way to cover a lot of ground quickly. You can buy tickets ($39, kids 4–12 $19) on the bus and hop on and off all day (daily: late June to mid-Aug 8.50am–7pm; March to late June & mid-Aug to Oct 8.50am–6pm; Nov–Feb 8.50am–5pm; every 30min) at any of the stops. Leaflets detailing the various routes are found in hotel lobbies and at visitor centres.

2

fifteen North County stations for 22 miles between Oceanside and Escondido. It runs every 30 minutes from 4am to 9pm on weekdays (later Fri nights), with more sporadic service on weekends; tickets are $2 one-way and $5 for a day-pass.

Destinations (from Oceanside) Escondido (53min); San Marcos (40min); Vista (23min).

BY BICYCLE

San Diego is a fine city for cycling, with many miles of bike paths. You can carry bikes on the San Diego Bay ferry and certain city bus routes for no charge. Board at any bus stop displaying a bike sign and fasten your bike securely to the rack on the front of the bus (outside) with the retaining bar (let the driver know before you start) – the rack can only take two bikes. See ⓦ sdmba.com and ⓦ sdbikecoalition .org for an introduction to the scene.

Bike share DecoBike San Diego, the city's bike-share scheme (ⓦ decobikesandiego.com), offers bikes all over the city for $5/30min or $35/1 week.

Bike rental Bicycle Discovery, 742 Felspar St, Pacific Beach (Mon–Sat 10am–7.30pm, Sun 10am–5.30pm; $7/ hr, $25/day; ☎ 858 272 1274, ⓦ bicycle-discovery.com); Cheap Rentals, 3689 Mission Blvd, Mission Beach (daily 9am–7pm; $5/hr, $12/day; ☎ 858 488 9070, ⓦ cheap-rentals.com).

INFORMATION AND TOURS

Visitor information centres San Diego: 996 N Harbor Drive (daily: June–Sept 9am–5pm; Oct–May 9am–4pm; ☎ 619 737 2999, ⓦ sandiego.org); Balboa Park: 1549 El Prado (daily 9.30am–4.30pm; ☎ 619 239 0512, ⓦ balboapark.org); La Jolla: 1162 Prospect St (daily: late May to early Sept 10am–6pm; early Sept to late May 10am–5pm; ☎ 858 454 5718, ⓦ lajollabythesea.com).

Boat tours Flagship Cruises, 990 N Harbor Drive (☎ 619 234 4111, ⓦ sdhe.com) offers many boat trips including one- to two-hour harbour cruises ($25–30) and whale-watching expeditions (Dec–April $40–55).

Walking tours The Gaslamp Quarter Historical Foundation runs a 1hr 30min walking tour (Sat 11am & Thurs 1pm; $20; ☎ 619 233 4692, ⓦ gaslampfoundation .org/book-a-tour) that begins at the small cobbled square at 4th and Island. Aside from exploring architectural gems including the Louis Bank of Commerce (see box, p.159), you'll hear about the exploits of gunslingers like Wyatt Earp, the more colourful of the town's Victorian-era prostitutes, and other assorted miscreants who made Stingaree the dynamic town it once was.

ACCOMMODATION

Downtown offers the best base if you're without a car, featuring two **hostels** and a batch of affordable **hotels** in renovated classic buildings – along with a few chic **boutique hotels**. Prices are more expensive at beachside **motels** and hotels – and can be stratospheric at the bigger-name golf-and-tennis resorts – though Ocean Beach and Pacific Beach have **hostels**, too. Another group of motels can be found around Old Town, and some of the cheapest motels line the interstate highways into the city. If you're arriving in summer, it's wise to **book in advance**.

HOTELS

DOWNTOWN

★ **Bristol** 1055 1st Ave ☎ 619 232 6141, ⓦ thebristol sandiego.com; map p.158. Excellent value at this friendly, centrally located boutique hotel with stylish modern decor and posh amenities, plus iPod docks and flat-screen TVs. $143

Courtyard by Marriott San Diego Downtown 530 Broadway ☎ 619 446 3000, ⓦ marriott.com; map p.158.

Stunning historic renovation of a 1920s Renaissance Revival bank, now home to swanky rooms and suites, and loaded with beautiful period detail in the lobby and even a conference room in a one-time bank vault. $260

Horton Grand Hotel 311 Island Ave, at 3rd ☎ 800 542 1886, ⓦ hortongrand.com; map p.158. This classy amalgam of two century-old hotels (see p.159) has fireplaces in most of the rooms and balconies in some, plus a restaurant and piano bar. Somewhat minimal

2

amenities for such a historic spot, though. $185

★**Indigo** 509 9th Ave ☎619 727 4000, ⓦhotelindsd.com; map p.158. Smart boutique digs in the Gaslamp Quarter that offers the usual business-class amenities (including a gym), plus special touches such as local art on the walls and rooftop terrace bar with a fire pit. $180

Kimpton Solamar 435 6th Ave ☎619 819 9500, ⓦhotelsolamar.com; map p.158. Modern boutique hotel central to the Gaslamp Quarter, whose rooms have flat-screen TVs and CD and DVD players, and which also offers spa and gym. Suites with jacuzzis add to the hip appeal. Doubles $250, suites $310

La Pensione 606 W Date St, at India ☎619 236 8000, ⓦlapensionehotel.com; map p.158. Good-value hotel within walking distance of the city centre in Little Italy. Minimalist-Modernist rooms are small but equipped with microwaves, fridges and cable TV, and there's an on-site laundry. $160

The US Grant 326 Broadway ☎800 237 5029, ⓦusgrant.net; map p.158. Across from Horton Plaza, this has been downtown's poshest address since 1910, with grand Neoclassical design, chandeliers, marble floors, plus cosy but comfortable rooms. The elegant ballrooms and swanky conference rooms are also worth a peek. $230

Westgate Hotel 1055 2nd Ave ☎800 522 1564, ⓦwestgatehotel.com; map p.158. Centrally sited hotel near Horton Plaza with a florid lobby (almost to the point of kitsch), elegant rooms furnished with balconies and antiques, and CD and DVD players. Also with spa and gym. $210

OLD TOWN, HILLCREST AND BALBOA PARK

Best Western Plus Hacienda Hotel 4041 Harney St, Old Town ☎800 888 1991, ⓦhaciendahotel-oldtown.com. Most decent hotels around Old Town are of the chain variety, and this is among the best, featuring mock Spanish Colonial design, pool, jacuzzi, gym and clean, modern rooms – plus free airport shuttle. $140

Britt Scripps Inn 406 Maple St, near Balboa Park ☎888 881 1991, ⓦbrittscripps-inn.com. Fetching Victorian inn located in a marvellously restored 1887 Queen Anne mansion, with nine plush rooms offering antiques, flat-screen TV and some modern boutique touches, too. $133

Inn at the Park 525 Spruce St, near Balboa Park ☎619 291 0999, ⓦshellhospitality.com. This renovated apartment complex dates from 1926 and is now a stately hotel with spacious suites featuring kitchens and pleasant, large sitting areas. $189

Sommerset Suites Hotel 606 Washington St, Hillcrest ☎800 962 9665, ⓦsommersetsuites.com. Well-equipped suites offering balconies or patios, with kitchens, pool and spa. One of the better deals in the area. $177

OCEAN BEACH AND POINT LOMA

Dolphin Motel 2912 Garrison St ☎866 353 7897, ⓦdolphin-motel.com. The epitome of the roadside motel, in this case offering small, clean rooms with queen beds and a good location roughly between Ocean Beach and Point Loma, within easy reach of the airport. Offseason rates can drop as low as $55. $90

Inn at Sunset Cliffs 1370 Sunset Cliffs Blvd, Point Loma ☎866 786 2543, ⓦinnatsunsetcliffs.com. Perched on a precipice above the ocean, this property has a range of rooms, from entry-level suites with poolside access or kitchens to more elaborate digs with jacuzzis, luxury decor and stunning oceanside views. $175

MISSION BEACH AND PACIFIC BEACH

Bahia Resort 998 W Mission Bay Drive, Mission Beach ☎800 576 4229, ⓦbahiahotel.com. Prime beachside accommodation with expansive ocean views, watersport rentals, pool and jacuzzi. Rooms vary, from cosy and pleasant options in a palm-garden setting to pricier bayside suites. All have fridges. $299

Beach Cottages 4255 Ocean Blvd, Mission Beach ☎858 483 7440, ⓦbeachcottages.com. Right on the beach, three blocks south of the pier, this relaxing spot offers a wide range of accommodation, from simple and rather frayed motel units to more elaborate cottages. Most have kitchenettes; all have fridges. Motel rooms $160, studios $250, cottages and apartments $305

★**Crystal Pier Hotel** 4500 Ocean Blvd, Pacific Beach ☎800 748 5894, ⓦcrystalpier.com. Beautiful deluxe cottages built in 1930 and situated right on Crystal Pier. All rooms are suites with private decks, and most have kitchenettes. It can get pricey (up to $525/night); you stay literally on the water. Most rooms are booked many months in advance (3-night minimum in summer). $325

Ocean Park Inn 710 Grand Ave, Pacific Beach ☎858 483 5858, ⓦoceanparkinn.com. Another solid beachfront choice, with microwaves and fridges, plus a pool and spa. Nothing too flashy, but the central location on the boardwalk is a very good draw. $179

Red Roof Inn 4545 Mission Bay Drive ☎858 483 4222, ⓦinnatpacificbeach.com. If you're headed to SeaWorld (three miles away), you'll need to save your money for the sky-high tickets – and with that in mind, this is a relatively cheap choice whose basic motel rooms have fridges and microwaves, plus access to a heated pool. $129

★**Tower23** 4551 Ocean Blvd, Pacific Beach ☎866 869 3723, ⓦt23hotel.com. Named after a lifeguard tower, this is among the most chic of San Diego's boutique hotels, offering rooms with flat-screen TVs and designer furnishings, and even more stylish suites that come with balconies, poolside *cabanas* for privacy and whirlpool tubs. Doubles $419, suites $520

LA JOLLA

★ **Bed & Breakfast Inn at La Jolla** 7753 Draper Ave ☎ 800 582 2466, ⓦ innlajolla.com; map p.174. Designed in 1913 by early Modernist Irving Gill, this is a collection of fifteen themed rooms – topped by the $478-a-night Irving Gill Penthouse, inexplicably decorated in Victoriana – with tranquil gardens and great service. It's close to the beach and art museum, too. **$239**

Empress 7766 Fay Ave ☎ 858 454 3001, ⓦ empress -hotel.com; map p.174. A good range of rooms and suites at this centrally located property, where the larger units also have jacuzzis and there's internet access, continental breakfast, gym, spa and sauna. **$209**

Grande Colonial 910 Prospect St ☎ 888 530 5766, ⓦ thegrandecolonial.com; map p.174. A 1913 landmark in the heart of La Jolla and a short walk from the cove. The cosy but elegant rooms have boutique furnishings and there are excellent package deals. **$280**

La Valencia Hotel 1132 Prospect St ☎ 800 451 0772, ⓦ lavalencia.com; map p.174. Opened in 1926, this radiant-pink favourite of early Hollywood celebs is a slightly less glamorous spot today, but no less plush, with capacious rooms and suites and elaborate villas. All boast beautiful decor, nice amenities and good sea or garden views, plus there's an on-site pool, spa and fitness centre. **$299**

HOSTELS

HI-San Diego Downtown Hostel 521 Market St, between 5th and 6th, downtown ☎ 619 525 1531, ⓦ sandiegohostels.org; map p.158. Centrally located, especially good for the Gaslamp Quarter and Horton Plaza.

Free breakfast, plus a library, kitchen, and various organized trips to Tijuana and other places. Dorms **$39**, doubles **$98**

HI-San Diego Point Loma Hostel 3790 Udall St, Ocean Beach ☎ 619 223 4778, ⓦ sandiegohostels.org. Well run and friendly, located a few miles from the beach and six miles from downtown. The hostel features a large kitchen, free breakfast, a patio and weekly bonfires. Dorms **$27**, doubles **$68**

★ **ITH Zoo Hostel** 3751 6th Ave, Hillcrest ☎ 619 955 7723, ⓦ ithhostels.com. ITH Hostels & Eco Lodging's ultra-hip backpacker and eco-friendly ethos – free breakfast and dinner (pizza), communal trips, night-time social activities, trips to Tijuana and generally cool staff – has been a big hit in their home town of San Diego, so book ahead if you intend to join in the fun. Bright, comfy dorms, free towels, laundry, pool table, TV lounge and library. The owners runs several hostels in the area, if this one is full. Dorms **$31**

USA Hostels – Ocean Beach 4961 Newport Ave, Ocean Beach ☎ 619 223 7873, ⓦ usahostels.com/locations/ san-diego-ocean-beach. Multicoloured and lively spot a block from the beach, offering barbecues, bike and surfboard rentals, free shuttle to the zoo, airport and downtown, plus nightly movies. Free sheets, showers and continental breakfast. Dorms **$42**, doubles **$125**

USA Hostels – San Diego 726 5th Ave, between F and G, downtown ☎ 619 232 3100, ⓦ usahostels.com/ locations/san-diego; map p.158. This well-placed hostel on the edge of the Gaslamp District is a converted 1890s building, with six to eight beds per room. Sheets and breakfast included, plus organized tours to Tijuana; this is one of the city's best hostels. Dorms **$35**, doubles **$85**

EATING

Although the range isn't quite as wide as LA's, you'll find everything from old-time coffee shops and food trucks (see box below), to stylish restaurants and international eateries in San Diego. The city's close links with Mexico are highlighted by the plethora of excellent taco joints, and the emerging "**Cali-Baja**" cuisine movement (a blend of the Baja Mediterranean food pioneered in Tijuana with local seafood and Californian seasonal produce).

SAN DIEGO'S GOURMET FOOD TRUCKS

Don't leave San Diego without sampling the city's dynamic **food truck** scene; enthusiastic, innovative chefs, fresh produce and gourmet menus mean these ain't your average kebab vans. Always check Twitter feeds (listed on the websites below) for the latest locations, times and menus (see also ⓦ sdfoodtrucks.com).

Devilicious ⓦ deviliciousfoodtruck.com. A San Diego institution, with their signature butter-poached lobster grilled cheese sandwich a real treat.

Mangia Mangia ⓦ mangiamangiamobile.com. Italian food truck with delights such as the pizza burger, eggplant parmigiana sandwich and spaghetti with meatballs.

Super Q Food Truck ⓦ superqfoodtruck.com. Hickory-smoked barbecue comes to San Diego;

magnificent brisket, pulled pork and crispy sweet potato fries.

Tabe BBQ ⓦ tabebbq.com. Some of the best Asian-fusion street food in the whole country: think chargrilled pork or beef marinated in a traditional, spicy Korean sauce.

Two for the Road ⓦ twofortheroadsd.com. Classic American food with zip – think New England lobster rolls, kicked-up corn dogs, crabcakes, burgers and genuine whoppie pies flown in from Maine.

RESTAURANTS

The Gaslamp Quarter has the greatest concentration of tourist-friendly restaurants and bars, which are especially crazy on weekend nights and heavy on all-American food like ribs and burgers. Little Italy, on the northern fringes of downtown, appeals for its handful of decent restaurants, and more bohemian Hillcrest has a number of spots to hang out and chow down. The beach towns, best known for seafood, get more expensive the further north you go.

DOWNTOWN

Blind Burro 639 J St ☎619 795 7880, ⒲theblind burro.com; map p.158. Sample the city's burgeoning Cali-Baja food scene at this popular restaurant serving seafood and more traditional Mexican dishes from *carne asada* tortas ($15) to coffee-rubbed salmon tacos ($15). Mon–Thurs 11am–11pm, Fri & Sat 11am–1.30am, Sun 10am–10pm.

★**Cafè 222** 222 Island Ave, at 2nd ☎619 236 9902, ⒲cafe222.com; map p.158. Hip café serving some of the city's best breakfasts and lunches, with excellent pancakes, French toast, and pumpkin-and-peanut-butter waffles, and inventive twists on traditional sandwiches and burgers (including vegetarian), at reasonable prices (most mains $9–13). Daily 7am–1.45pm.

Dobson's 956 Broadway Circle ☎619 231 6771, ⒲dobsonsrestaurant.com; map p.158. This elegant restaurant in an old two-tier building is a San Diego institution, loaded with business types in power ties. The cuisine leans towards continental, from crab hash and oyster salad to flatiron steak and rack of lamb (mains $16–42). Owner Paul Dobson is actually a professional bullfighter (fights are still held in Tijuana). Mon–Fri 11.30am–10pm, Sat 5–10pm.

The Kebab Shop 630 9th Ave ☎619 525 0055, ⒲thekebabshop.com; map p.158. Cheap Turkish (or "California Mediterranean") mini-chain that's a great place to get your fill of lamb, chicken and falafel kebabs (from $7.99), or enjoy a shawarma sandwich or some tasty rotisserie meat. Mon–Sat 10.30am–10pm, Sun 10.30am–9pm.

★**Nobu** 207 5th Ave (Hard Rock Hotel) ☎619 814 4124, ⒲noburestaurants.com/san-diego; map p.158. Chef Nobu Matsuhisa launched his San Diego venture in 2007, and it's been almost as successful as his New York original, serving the same high-quality sushi and classic dishes such as black cod with miso ($35) and yellowtail sashimi with jalapeno ($25). Mon–Thurs & Sun 5.30–10pm, Fri & Sat 5.30–10.30pm.

La Puerta 560 4th Ave ☎619 696 3466, ⒲lapuertasd .com; map p.158. Cheap beers and good tequila provide the right refreshment for knocking back some of the city's best tacos, burritos and tortas, with a mean guacamole to boot. Inexpensive prices (mains $8–12) and a convivial

atmosphere. Mon–Fri 11am–2am, Sat & Sun 10am–2am.

Rei Do Gado 939 4th Ave ☎619 702 8464, ⒲reidogado .net; map p.158. Brazilian-style barbecue (*churrasco*), delivered via a grand buffet (lunch $24.95–32.95; dinner $54.45) of forty different salads, side dishes and meat selections. You pick what you want from an array of meat skewers – piping hot and ready to devour. Mon–Thurs & Sun 11am–10pm, Fri & Sat 11am–11pm.

Taka 555 5th Ave ☎619 338 0555, ⒲takasushi.com; map p.158. Excellent sushi (from $5/piece) and hot and cold starters – as well as sashimi, teriyaki and fried rice – in a modern atmosphere with a fair mix of hipsters and families (mains $16–25). Mon–Thurs & Sun 5–9.30pm, Fri & Sat 5–10.30pm.

LITTLE ITALY

Ballast Point Tasting Room & Kitchen 2215 India St ☎619 255 7213, ⒲ballastpoint.com; map p.158. This lauded microbrewery is just as popular for its food as its beers (like Black Marlin porter and Wahoo White Belgian ale), such as its tasty burger ($13), spicy guava shrimp tacos ($14) and crispy fish and chips ($12). Daily 11am–11pm.

★**Bracero Cocina de Raíz** 1490 Kettner Blvd ☎619 756 7864, ⒲bracerococina.com; map p.158. Javier Plascencia, one of Tijuana's most celebrated chefs, serves his innovate Cali-Baja cuisine in a rustic-chic dining room; Tijuana's original Caesar's salad ($12.50), small plates such as wood-grilled octopus ($16.95) and shrimp and bone marrow *sopes* ($14.95), plus larger dishes such as crispy brisket and short-rib ($26). Mon 11.30am–9pm, Tues–Thurs 11.30am–10pm, Fri & Sat 11.30am–11pm, Sun 11.30am–9.30pm.

The Crack Shack 2266 Kettner Blvd ☎619 795 3299, ⒲crack-shack.com; map p.158. This laidback outdoor dining space from *Juniper & Ivy's* Richard Blais offers perfectly fried chicken ($15–28) and breakfast sandwiches ($9–13) served all day from a walk-up counter – there's even a bocce court. Mon–Thurs & Sun 9am–10pm, Fri & Sat 9am–11pm.

Filippi's Pizza Grotto 1747 India St ☎619 232 5094, ⒲realcheesepizza.com; map p.158. A good spot for affordable favourites like thick, chewy pizzas (from $12.50) and pasta dishes (from $7.95), including a fine lasagne (mains $12–16). Meals are served in a small room at the back of an Italian deli, open since 1950. Sun & Mon 11am–10pm, Tues–Thurs 11am–10.30pm, Fri & Sat 11am–11.30pm.

★**Herb & Wood** 2210 Kettner Blvd ☎619 955 8495, ⒲herbandwood.com; map p.158. Rustic, wood-fired pizzas ($18–19) from celebrity chef Brian Malarkey, served in a stylish, contemporary space, as well as tempting small plates such as grilled king trumpet mushrooms ($9) and roasted baby turnips ($8). Tues–Thurs & Sun 5.30–10pm, Fri & Sat 5.30–11pm.

Indigo Grill 1536 India St ☎619 234 6802, ⓦcohn restaurants.com/indigogrill; map p.158. Among the most feted of Little Italy's restaurants, this one appeals for its experimental modern Latin American cuisine, like Indian corn pudding with squash and plantains, blueberry-glazed rack of lamb, jalapeno pappardelle and meringue "fire cake" – though main courses can be a little pricey ($24–32). Mon–Thurs & Sun 5–9pm, Fri & Sat 5–10pm.

★**Ironside Fish & Oyster** 1654 India St ☎619 269 3033, ⓦironsidefishandoyster.com; map p.158. Fresh seafood served in a converted 1920s warehouse decked out with a wall of piranha skulls, golden mermaid statues, a 14-foot copper bar and live fish tanks. Sample the exceptional raw bar, 1lb lobster rolls ($22), fish and chips ($16) and killer cocktails. Mon–Thurs 11.30am–midnight, Fri 11.30am–2am, Sat 11am–2am, Sun 11am–midnight.

Juniper & Ivy 2228 Kettner Blvd ☎619 269 9036, ⓦjuniperandivy.com; map p.158. Innovative American food ("left coast cuisine") from *Top Chef* alum Richard Blais, featuring all sorts of molecular gastronomy, foie-gras cookies, corn carbonara, barbecue carrots, squab pot pie and more. Mon–Thurs & Sun 5–10pm, Fri & Sat 5–11pm.

Prepkitchen 1660 India St ☎619 398 8383, ⓦprepkitchenlittleitaly.com; map p.158. Part of another local mini-chain specializing in creative small plates, from bacon-wrapped dates ($13.95) to local mussels and fries ($17.75). Mon–Thurs 11.30am–3pm & 5–9pm, Fri 11.30am–3pm & 5–10.30pm, Sat 10am–3pm & 5–10.30pm, Sun 10am–3pm & 5–9pm.

HILLCREST

Crest Café 425 Robinson Ave ☎619 295 2510, ⓦcrestcafe.net. If you're in the mood for cheap diner-style fare, this is the spot – with satisfying salads, burgers, pancakes and desserts. The salmon scramble, meatloaf and flatiron chimichurri steak are also worth a try (mains from $11). The butter burger ($12.50) now has a cult following after featuring on TV show *Diners, Drive-Ins & Dives*. Daily 7am–midnight.

El Cuervo 110 W Washington St ☎619 295 9713. Long-standing cheap and tasty Mexican joint that can hit the spot after a day at Balboa Park – featuring Tijuana-style tacos ($2.75–4.60), good *carne asada*, burritos and shrimp, as well as more exotic offerings like beef-tongue tacos. Mon–Sat 7am–10pm, Sun 7am–9pm.

★**Lucha Libre Taco Shop** 1810 W Washington St ☎619 296 8226, ⓦtacosmackdown.com. Mexican wrestling-themed taco house that's known for its fat burritos (from $7.50), stuffed with marinated shrimp, steak and avocado, chipotle steak and fries ($9.75), and

bacon-wrapped hot dogs ($1.50). Mon–Thurs & Sun 8am–11pm, Fri & Sat 8am–2.30am.

Marketplace Deli 2601 5th Ave ☎619 239 8361, ⓦthemarketplacesd.com. Just south of Hillcrest near the entrance to Balboa Park, this is a winner for its prime pizzas and sandwiches, and especially "the Reuben": pastrami, sauerkraut and cheese on rye bread. Also offers good tuna melts and pasta salads, at easy-to-swallow prices (lunch specials from $5). Mon–Fri 7am–7pm, Sat 8am–7pm, Sun 8am–4pm.

Panama 66 San Diego Museum of Art, 1450 El Prado, Balboa Park ☎619 696 1966, ⓦpanama66.blogspot.com. Great location in the middle of Balboa Park (elegantly set inside the Museum of Art's May S. Marcy Sculpture Court), featuring sandwiches, light meals and all-local craft beers on tap. Mon 11am–5pm, Tues, Thurs & Fri 11am–10pm, Wed 11am–11.30pm, Sat & Sun 10am–10pm.

OLD TOWN

Berta's 3928 Twiggs St ☎619 295 2343, ⓦbertas inoldtown.com. Solid south-of-the-border restaurant, offering well-priced, authentic cooking from all over Latin America. The affordable and tasty dishes include empanadas, seafood soups and paella (mains $18–22). Tues–Sun 11am–10pm.

Jack and Giulio's 2391 San Diego Ave ☎619 294 2074, ⓦjackandgiulios.com. Old-time Northern Italian food since 1961, this comfy, affordable spot serves decent lasagne and gnocchi (pastas $15–19), as well as top-notch scampi, steak and veal (mains $18–27). Mon–Thurs & Sun 4.30–9pm, Fri & Sat 4.30–9.30pm.

Old Town Mexican Café 2489 San Diego Ave ☎619 297 4330, ⓦoldtownmexcafe.com. Among the better Mexican diners in Old Town, where the crowds queue up for the likes of *pozole* soup and *carne asada* tacos; apart from at breakfast, you'll probably have to wait for a table. Mains $12–20, tacos $4.50. Mon–Thurs & Sun 7am–11pm, Fri & Sat 7am–2am.

OCEAN BEACH AND POINT LOMA

★**Hodad's** 5010 Newport Ave, Ocean Beach ☎619 224 4623, ⓦhodadies.com. In business in one spot or another since 1969, this is one place in town you can get a damn fine burger, whether it comes straight up (from $5.75) or includes cheese ($6), tuna or veggies (both $6.50). Fries and rings complete a meal at this cheap, justly popular spot. Daily 11am–10pm.

Ortiz's Taco Shop 3704 Voltaire St ☎619 222 4476. Among the best tortas, burritos, enchiladas and tacos ($2.50–3.50) in the city, with cheap prices, authentic recipes and enough oomph to get you revved up for a day on the waves. Note that the location is inland, halfway between Ocean Beach and Old Town. Daily 8am–11.30pm.

2

★**Point Loma Seafoods** 2805 Emerson St ☎619 223 1109, ⓦpointlomaseafoods.com. Mid-priced counter serving up San Diego's freshest fish in a basket, with good platters and seafood cocktails, along with mean crabcake ($13) and scallop sandwiches ($14.80). With views across the bay to downtown, this popular joint is packed at weekends; don't even try to find an adjacent parking spot. Mon–Sat 9am–8pm, Sun 10am–8pm.

South Beach Bar & Grille 5059 Newport Ave, Ocean Beach ☎619 226 4577, ⓦsouthbeachob.com. A relaxed and friendly place known for its excellent fish tacos (from $3.50), including versions with mahi-mahi, lobster, shark and oysters, plus seafood tostadas, steamed mussels and other marine dishes. Daily 11am–2am.

PACIFIC BEACH

Enoteca Adriano 4864 Cass St ☎858 490 0085, ⓦenotecaadriano.com. Italian wine bar that, aside from its primo vino, happens to have terrific pasta as well, including gnocchi and pappardelle, and a redoubtable chicken saltimbocca (pasta $15–24; mains $24–26). Daily 5–10pm.

The Fishery 5040 Cass St ☎858 272 9985, ⓦthefishery .com. Wide range of seafood for varying prices at this straightforward fish house, where you can get your fill of oysters, jumbo lump crabcake and ceviche tostadas, as well as shrimp or swordfish tacos (mains $16–38). Daily 11am–10pm.

★**Kono's Surf Club Café** 704 Garnet Ave ☎858 483 1669, ⓦkonoscafe.com. A great choice for breakfast burritos or lunch on the boardwalk, with hefty portions of eggs, potatoes, toast and sandwiches, and especially plump burgers and burritos – all at affordable prices (most plates $6–9). Adjacent to Crystal Pier. Mon–Fri 7am–3pm, Sat & Sun 7am–4pm.

★**Sushi Ota** 4529 Mission Bay Drive ☎858 270 5670, ⓦsushiota.com. San Diego's best sushi restaurant lies just off I-5, 2.5 miles inland from the beach, worth the trip for its sumptuous cuts of locally sourced snow crab, tuna, yellowtail and salmon (5 pieces from $12), as well as teriyaki and tempura dishes ($16–28). Mon 5.30–10.30pm, Tues–Fri 11.30am–2pm & 5.30–10.30pm, Sat & Sun 5–10.30pm.

World Famous 711 Pacific Beach Drive ☎858 272 3100, ⓦworldfamouspb.com. Beachfront restaurant serving lobster tacos, prime rib hash, crab and shrimp enchiladas and bread-pudding French toast for lunch (mains $11–15); it also boasts solid breakfasts and decent pasta and steak dinners. Daily 7am–midnight.

LA JOLLA

Barbarella 2171 Avenida de la Playa ☎858 454 7373, ⓦbarbarellarestaurant.com; map p.174. Eclectic eatery that serves up a hearty menu of omelettes and frittatas,

pizza and pasta, risotto and seafood, and even burgers and fries (mains $7.95–15.95). Mon–Thurs 9.30am–9pm, Fri 9.30am–10pm, Sat 8.30am–10pm, Sun 8.30am–9pm.

Brockton Villa 1235 Coast Blvd ☎858 454 7393, ⓦbrocktonvilla.com; map p.174. Mid-priced California cuisine, featuring glittering views of the ocean from a classic 1894 beach cottage, and a seasonal menu, typically including seafood, rack of lamb, steak and pasta. Also features inventive choices for breakfast ($10–14), like *carne asada* eggs Benedict. Daily 8am–9pm.

★**Cody's** 8030 Girard Ave ☎858 459 0040, ⓦcodyslj .com; map p.174. You can sit on the patio and catch a glimpse of La Jolla Cove at this innovative California cuisine spot that does tasty buttermilk pancakes, sage sausage, eggplant sandwiches and scrumptious burgers (mains $13–21). Daily 8am–3pm.

George's at the Cove 1250 Prospect St ☎858 454 4244, ⓦgeorgesatthecove.com; map p.174. Longtime local favourite split into three sections – the chic *Ocean Terrace* (daily 11am–10pm) with sea views and mid-range salmon, steak, pasta and seafood dishes (mains $16–40); *Level2* with sandwiches, skinny cocktails and house-infused vodkas (daily 11.30am–midnight); and the pricey *California Modern*, with creative tasting menus (four courses $75) featuring lobster stew, halibut ceviche and duck breast with foie gras (Mon–Thurs 6–10pm, Fri–Sun 5–10pm).

Harry's Coffee Shop 7545 Girard Ave ☎858 454 7381, ⓦharryscoffeeshop.com; map p.174. This old gem was opened by New York transplant Harry Rudolph in 1960, inspired by the diners of his native Brooklyn, with breakfast served all day – plates of bacon pancakes, French toast, Reuben sandwiches, tuna melts and burgers ($8–13). Daily 6am–3pm.

Karl Strauss Brewery & Restaurant 1044 Wall St ☎858 551 2739, ⓦkarlstrauss.com; map p.174. La Jolla's neighbourhood brewpub knocks out excellent craft beers to wash down perfectly grilled burgers ($12.95) and beer-brined chops ($21.95). Mon–Thurs & Sun 11am–9pm, Fri & Sat 11am–10pm.

★**The Taco Stand** 621 Pearl St ☎858 551 6666, ⓦletstaco.com; map p.174. Crazy popular taco joint (be prepared to wait in line), inspired by the taco stands of Tijuana, selling burritos, quesadillas and the signature tacos (from handmade corn tortillas), stuffed with rotisserie-marinated pork, battered fish, spicy shrimp Angus steak and more, plus Mexican Coca-Cola in the fridge. Mon–Thurs & Sun 9am–9pm, Fri & Sat 9am–10pm.

CAFÉS AND ICE CREAM

DOWNTOWN AND LITTLE ITALY

Bird Rock Coffee Roasters 2295 Kettner Blvd, Little Italy ☎619 272 0203, ⓦbirdrockcoffee.com; map p.158. Stylish contemporary coffee chain based in San Diego, offering organic and Fair Trade certified coffees with specials such as nitrogen-infused cold coffee in addition to the usual brews. Mon–Fri 6am–6pm, Sat & Sun 7am–7pm.

Caffè Italia 1704 India St, Little Italy ☎ 619 234 6767, ⓦ caffeitalialittleitaly.com; map p.158. Sandwiches, salads and great coffee, espresso and desserts, including good gelato, served in a sleek modern interior or outside. Cash only. Mon–Thurs 7am–10pm, Fri 7am–11pm, Sat 8am–11pm, Sun 8am–10pm.

Extraordinary Desserts 1430 Union St, Little Italy ☎ 619 294 7001, ⓦ extraordinarydesserts.com; map p.158. Beloved dessert specialist founded by local pastry chef Karen Krasne, with favourites such as the passion fruit ricotta cake supplemented by delicious panini, salads and artisan cheese, as well as over fifty types of tea, gourmet coffee and organic wines. Mon–Thurs 8.30am–11pm, Fri 8.30am–midnight, Sat 10am–midnight, Sun 10am–11pm.

Upstart Crow 835 W Harbor Drive, downtown ☎ 619 232 4855, ⓦ upstartcrowtrading.com; map p.158. This coffee bar fused with a bookshop offers a lively cross-section of customers, great coffee, well-chosen reading material and free Saturday-night jazz performances. Daily 9am–9pm.

OLD TOWN, HILLCREST AND BALBOA PARK

★ Caffè Calabria 3933 30th St, Hillcrest ☎ 619 291 1759, ⓦ caffecalabria.com. Serious coffee for serious coffee drinkers, with some fine espresso and French and Italian roasts from their own roasted beans, which you can also buy to take home. Also offers good pastries, pizza and panini. Mon & Tues 6am–3pm, Wed–Fri 6am–11pm, Sat & Sun 7am–11pm.

Gelato Vero Caffè 3753 India St, at the western end of Hillcrest ☎ 619 295 9269, ⓦ gelatoverocaffe.com. San Diego isn't known for its ice cream, but you can get it here

– from stracciatella to tiramisu to a bevy of fruit flavours – along with Indian chai tea and good espresso from *Caffè Calabria*. Mon–Thurs 6am–midnight, Fri 6am–1am, Sat 7am–1am, Sun 7am–midnight.

OCEAN BEACH

Jungle Java 5047 Newport Ave ☎ 619 224 0249. If sipping espresso and munching on pastries while shopping for plants sounds like a good idea, this is the place for you – another of this city's quirky shops, with a good range of teas and coffees to go with your ferns and creepers. Cash only. Daily 7am–7pm.

MISSION BEACH

Swell Coffee Co 3833 Mission Blvd ☎ 858 539 0039, ⓦ swellcoffeeco.com. A rare coffee joint that, along with delicious espressos and the rest, has excellent food including great sandwiches ($13) and salads ($12) and breakfasts. Daily 7am–4pm.

LA JOLLA

★ Bobboi Natural Gelato 8008 Girard Ave ☎ 858 999 1362, ⓦ bobboi.com; map p.174. Best ice cream in southern California, with amazing flavours that range from blends of fresh and organic cantaloupe, passion fruit and lemon, to charcoal vanilla (with activated carbon) and black mission fig and ricotta cheese. Mon–Thurs 11.30am–9.30pm, Fri 11.30am–10.30pm, Sat & Sun 11am–10.30pm.

Pannikin Café 7467 Girard Ave ☎ 858 454 5453, ⓦ pannikincoffeeandtea.com; map p.174. Modest spot that feels warm and lived-in (it's been here since 1968), where you can knock back a java, read the paper and enjoy a sandwich, with none of the attitude you might find elsewhere. Daily 6am–6pm.

DRINKING

San Diego has a respectable range of **bars** throughout much of the city, with the Gaslamp Quarter being a good place to get dressed up for cocktails or for pure sports-bar swilling, while the beach communities offer a more rowdy atmosphere, abetted by plenty of beer and loud music. Since the 1990s the city and surrounding area has also developed a reputation for **microbreweries** (or "craft beer" as it's known in the US), an astounding 120 at last count. And don't forget San Diego's burgeoning **tiki bar** scene – one of the world's best mai tai cocktails is served here.

DOWNTOWN AND LITTLE ITALY

★ Altitude Sky Lounge 660 K St, at Marriott Gaslamp Hotel, downtown ☎ 619 446 6086; map p.158. With great views of downtown, Petco Park and the bay, this rooftop bar is also good for knocking back colourful cocktails and lounging on the plush furniture with other out-of-towners. Sun–Thurs 5pm–1.30am, Fri & Sat 5pm–2am.

Cat Eye Club 370 7th Ave, downtown ☎ 619 330 9509, ⓦ cateyeclubsd.com; map p.158. This cocktail lounge has tapped into San Diego's developing tiki bar scene, with retro 1950s decor, fake palm trees and huge cocktails ($11

– ginger mojitos, caramelized pineapple margaritas, pain killers and the like – stuffed with tropical fruit and served in kitsch tiki god cups. Thurs 6pm–1am, Fri & Sat 6pm–2am.

★ Craft & Commerce/False Idol 675 W Beech St, Little Italy ☎ 619 269 2202, ⓦ falseidoltiki.com; map p.158. Two bars in one, fronted by a fashionable gastropub, offering craft cocktails in a library-themed space (adorned with vintage taxidermy), and the *False Idol* tiki bar tucked away behind a door just beyond the main entrance, with iconic *Trader Vic's* mai tais served in custom-made tiki mugs (daily 6pm–2am, reservations recommended). Daily 5pm–2am.

2

Dublin Square 554 4th Ave, downtown ☎619 239 5818, ⓦdublinsquareirishpub.com; map p.158. Get your fill of leek soup, shepherd's pie and grilled potato "boxty" as you quaff Irish beer and spirits here. Even the breakfast steak is marinated in Guinness, and the chocolate cake is given a whisky boost. Mon–Thurs 10.30am–2am, Fri & Sat 8am–2am.

★**Mission Brewery** 1441 L St, downtown ☎619 544 0555, ⓦmissionbrewery.com; map p.158. One of the most centrally located microbreweries in the city, housed in the 1894 Wonder Bread Building. Core beers include the Kolsch-style Mission Blonde, Mission IPA and the Dark Seas Russian imperial stout. Tours available Fri–Sun 2pm, 4pm & 6pm. Mon–Thurs & Sun noon–10pm, Fri & Sat noon–midnight.

Waterfront 2044 Kettner Blvd, Little Italy ☎619 232 9656, ⓦwaterfrontbarandgrill.com; map p.158. A mixed bag of working-class boozers and slumming hipsters are drawn to this old-time Little Italy joint for burgers, fish'n'chips and bar food, and a convivial atmosphere. An essential stop to see the real drinker's San Diego. Daily 6am–2am.

OCEAN BEACH AND MISSION BEACH

Bali Hai Restaurant 2230 Shelter Island Drive, Shelter Island ☎619 222 1181, ⓦbalihairestaurant.com. This retro Polynesian-themed restaurant, open since 1955, serves mediocre food but is an essential San Diego experience for the harbour views and its "World Famous Bali Hai Mai Tai" ($9.25), the iconic rum cocktail invented by the *Trader Vic's* founder in the 1940s. Also serves Zombie, Goof Punch and Mr Bali Hai ($22) in their signature Bali Hai keeper tiki mug.

Mon–Thurs 11.30am–10pm, Fri & Sat 11.30am–11pm, Sun 9.30am–10pm.

Cannonball 3105 Ocean Front Walk, Mission Beach ☎858 228 9304, ⓦcannonballsd.com. This rooftop bar and sushi spot is the perfect place to end the day on Mission Beach, serving craft cocktails in a pool-like setting. Daily 11.30am–9pm.

The Holding Co 5046 Newport Ave, Ocean Beach ☎619 341 5898, ⓦthcob.com. The former *Gallagher's* spot has been transformed into a cleaner, friendlier bar, still featuring great live bands and DJs every night and happy hour (Mon–Fri 4–7pm, beers $4), but with the added draw of peanut butter Jameson shots ($5). Mon–Fri 4pm–2am, Sat & Sun noon–2am.

Sunshine Company 5028 Newport Blvd, Ocean Beach ☎619 222 0722, ⓦsunshinecompanyoceanbeach .com. A friendly neighbourhood joint since 1974 within easy reach of the water that's good for sampling the spirit(s) of Ocean Beach, loading up on beer and bar food, and mixing with the surfer dudes and hipsters. Mon–Fri 11am–2am, Sat & Sun 10am–2am.

LA JOLLA

Duke's La Jolla 216 Prospect St ☎858 454 5888, ⓦdukeslajolla.com; map p.174. Overlooking La Jolla Cove, this another Polynesian-themed spot, serving decent food (try the Hula pie, made with macadamia nut ice cream), but great for the signature mai tais ($11), coconut mojito ($12) and gin fizz ($13), especially during aloha hour (daily 3–6pm, half-price drinks). Daily 8am–9.30pm.

NIGHTLIFE

San Diego's **club scene** has been evolving in recent years – Hillcrest is notable for its gay-oriented spots (see p.187), while more chichi spots can be found in the Gaslamp Quarter. When it comes to **live music**, though largely overshadowed by LA, San Diego has a number of good choices downtown (the **Stone Temple Pilots** were formed here in the 1980s, and singer-songwriter **Jason Mraz** emerged from the local coffee-house scene in 2000). For listings, pick up the free *San Diego Reader* (ⓦsandiegoreader.com), buy the *San Diego Union-Tribune* (ⓦsandiegouniontribune.com) or seek out the youth-oriented *San Diego CityBeat* (ⓦsdcitybeat.com) at some of the live music venues listed below.

CLUBS

Café Sevilla 353 5th Ave, Gaslamp Quarter ☎619 233 5979, ⓦcafesevilla.com; map p.158. Traditional Spanish cuisine and tapas upstairs, hip Latin American-style club downstairs, with salsa and Spanish dance grooves to dance to, and flamenco performances to keep you entertained. Mon 11.30am–1am, Tues–Fri 11.30am–1.30am, Sat & Sun 10am–1.30am.

Club Sabbat 3811 Park Blvd, Numbers Night Club (1 mile east of Hillcrest) ☎619 795 8578, ⓦclubsabbat .net. This thrice-monthly club night sees a lively black-clad crowd moving to classic and modern dark beats – goth, industrial, darkwave and anything else that makes you want to crawl back to the thirteenth century ($7 cover).

2nd, 4th and 5th Saturdays 9pm–2am.

Fluxx 500 4th Ave, Gaslamp Quarter ☎619 232 8100, ⓦfluxxsd.com; map p.158. Posh, bottle-service dance club featuring house, hip-hop, celebrity performances, cool design (check the 15ft rope chandelier), contemporary art and an actual robot that delivers champagne to tables. Dress code is strictly enforced. Fri & Sat 9pm–2am.

Omnia 454 6th Ave, Gaslamp Quarter ☎619 544 9500, ⓦomnianightclub.com; map p.158. Luxury club in a historic warehouse (the less crazy sister of the famous club in Las Vegas), with top-notch visiting DJs and a rooftop area. To party with the likes of the Kardashians you'll need to glam up and pay up ($15 for drinks). Fri & Sat cover $20–30. Thurs–Sat 9pm–2am.

Onyx Room 852 5th Ave, Gaslamp Quarter ☎619 235 6699, ⓦonyxroom.com; map p.158. Groovy bar with lush decor, where you can knock back a few cocktails, then hit the back room for live jazz and dance tunes. The chic lounge upstairs has pricier drinks and bigger attitudes. It's another place where you need to dress up. Tues, Fri & Sat 9pm–2am.

Parq 615 Broadway, downtown ☎619 727 6789, ⓦparqsd.com; map p.158. One of the city's newest and most happening clubs, with high-quality sound system, over-the-top decor and excellent DJs. Fri & Sat 10pm–2am.

Thrusters Lounge 4633 Mission Blvd, Pacific Beach ☎858 483 6334, ⓦthrusterslounge.com. Cosy bar and club where the hip-hop and dance beats come hard and heavy, and jazz and rock make occasional appearances as well. Cheapish drinks and the infamous "shlong island iced tea". Mon–Fri 5pm–2am, Sat & Sun 11am–2am.

ROCK AND PUNK VENUES

Brick by Brick 1130 Buenos Ave, Mission Bay (six miles north of downtown) ☎619 675 5483, ⓦbrickbybrick .com. Cool lounge that's one of the better-known indie spots around town, attracting a broad mix of local indie rock, metal, hip-hop and burlesque acts. Most shows $10–35. Daily 7pm–2am.

★**Casbah** 2501 Kettner Blvd, downtown ☎619 232 4355, ⓦcasbahmusic.com; map p.158. If you're up for a night of hipstering, this is a good spot to begin – a grungy joint that nevertheless hosts a solid, varying roster of blues, funk, reggae, rock and indie bands. Despite the cramped interior, it's popular with locals. Most shows $10–20. Daily 8.30pm–2am.

House of Blues 1055 5th Ave, downtown ☎619 299 2583, ⓦhouseofblues.com; map p.158. The heavyweight on the local concert scene, drawing big-name rock and pop acts. The environment's a little too well scrubbed – as are the bands – but you can sometimes see a good show here. Don't miss the Bead Wall, an entire wall covered in Mardi Gras beads from New Orleans. Daily 4–11pm.

Soda Bar 3615 El Cajon Blvd (three miles northeast of Hillcrest) ☎619 255 7224, ⓦsodabarmusic.com. Sited in a dicey neighbourhood, but this modest lounge provides a sense of what's bubbling under the SD music scene, with all kinds of rock, punk, metal and oddball acts on view, plus

karaoke. Most tickets $8–20. Daily 5pm–2am.

Winston's Beach Club 1921 Bacon St, Ocean Beach ☎619 222 6822, ⓦwinstonsob.com. A former bowling alley turned semi-dive bar, this local club has rock bands most nights, with occasional reggae and comedy acts as well. Daily 1pm–2am.

POP, FOLK AND ECLECTIC

Bar Pink 3829 30th St (two miles east of Hillcrest) ☎619 564 7194, ⓦbarpink.com. Loaded with pink elephant decor to the point of nausea, this lounge has nightly music ranging from hip-hop-spinning DJs and various local rockers and thrashers, to oddball art-music hybrids that make more sense once you've had a few cocktails. Daily noon–2am.

Lestat's Coffee House 3433 Adams Ave (three miles northeast of Hillcrest) ☎619 282 0437, ⓦlestats.com. Part of a 24hr coffee shop, this performance venue presents nightly entertainment, from open-mikes and comedy showcases to indie rock, singer-songwriters and even belly-dancing. A must for fans of the eclectic. Daily 24hr (most live shows 9pm).

Queen Bee's 3925 Ohio St, North Park (two miles east of Hillcrest) ☎619 255 5147, ⓦqueenbeessd.com. The definition of eclectic, this all-ages venue hosts various rock and indie bands, but also offers tango and salsa classes (Sun; $10), open-mike and rap nights, poetry and spoken-word shows, and arty performances that don't fit into a single category. Daily noon–midnight.

Spreckels Theatre 121 Broadway, downtown ☎619 234 8397, ⓦspreckels.net; map p.158. Former 1912 moviehouse, now converted into an elegant venue for pop and soft-rock acts, as well as comedy, world beat, jazz, and speakers on popular topics. Box office Mon–Fri noon–6pm.

JAZZ

Dizzy's 4275 Mission Bay Drive, Pacific Beach ☎858 270 7467, ⓦdizzysjazz.com. As the name suggests, this joint is devoted to straight-up jazz and little else – literally, because gigs are held in the San Diego Jet Ski Rentals showroom, forcing you to focus on the music instead of chatting over dinner and cocktails. Cover $15–20 (cash only). See website for showtimes.

ENTERTAINMENT

The performing arts in San Diego are represented by both provincial and national-quality venues, depending on the medium, especially when it comes to theatre, classical music and opera. San Diego also has a handful of charming venues for classic, revival and art films, though first-run multiplexes are thicker on the ground, usually devoted to the latest Tinseltown product; tickets are around $11.50.

CONCERT VENUES

Humphrey's by the Bay 2421 Shelter Island Drive, Point Loma ☎619 220 8497, ⓦhumphreysconcerts

.com. Also including a restaurant, this mainstream concert venue draws a range of mellow, agreeable pop, blues, jazz, country, folk and soft-rock acts, often of national calibre

2

SAN DIEGO TICKETS

Depending on availability, **half-price tickets** bought on the day for theatre and classical music events are available from the ArtsTix Ticket Center in Horton Plaza Park, at the South Pavilion next to the Balboa Theatre (28 Horton Plaza; usually Tues–Thurs 10am–4pm, Fri & Sat 10am–6pm, Sun 10am–2pm; ☎858 381 5595, ⓦsdartstix.com). Full-price advance sales are also available, and on Saturday, half-price tickets are issued for Sunday performances. Otherwise, tickets for major shows can be purchased from the venue directly or through operators such as Ticketmaster (☎619 220 8497, ⓦticketmaster.com); check the local papers for times and venues.

(times vary according to show).

Sleep Train Amphitheatre 2050 Entertainment Circle, Chula Vista ☎619 671 3500, ⓦlivenation .com. Huge venue that can seat 20,000, featuring big-name concert tours throughout the spring, summer and fall.

Valley View Casino Center 3500 Sports Arena Blvd, Mission Bay ☎619 224 4171, ⓦvalleyviewcasinocenter .com. San Diego's premier indoor concert venue, featuring everything from pop concerts, circus acts and ice shows to various sports events.

Viejas Arena San Diego State University campus, 5500 Canyon Crest Drive ☎619 594 6947, ⓦas.sdsu.edu/ viejas_arena. Multipurpose arena at San Diego State University, home of the San Diego State Aztecs men's basketball and women's basketball teams, but also a major rock and pop venue.

CLASSICAL MUSIC AND OPERA

Athenaeum Music & Arts Library 1008 Wall St, La Jolla ☎858 454 5872, ⓦljathenaeum.org. A delightful, esteemed music and arts library built in an elegant Spanish Renaissance style in 1921, which has regular performances of music (mainly jazz and classical), as well as a pleasant art gallery.

Copley Symphony Hall 750 B St, downtown ☎619 235 0804, ⓦsandiegosymphony.org. Opened in 1929 as the Gothic Revival Fox Theatre (for movies), this venerable hall is now the home of the San Diego Symphony orchestra.

Mandeville Center Mandeville Lane off Gilman Ave, UCSD campus, north of La Jolla ☎858 534 3230, ⓦmandeville.ucsd.edu. Offers jazz, classical and world music throughout the year, as well as dance performances and choral groups.

San Diego Opera Civic Theatre, 1200 3rd Ave, downtown ☎619 533 7000, ⓦsdopera.com. Puts on four annual productions of familiar music (Mozart, Puccini, Verdi, etc) and frequently boasts top international guest performers during its Jan–May season.

THEATRE

There's a thriving theatre scene in San Diego, with several mid-sized venues and many smaller fringe venues putting on quality shows. Tickets are usually over $50 for a major production, or $10–25 for a night on the fringe. The *San Diego Reader* (ⓦsandiegoreader.com) carries full listings.

Balboa Theatre 868 4th Ave, at E, downtown ☎619 570 1100, ⓦsandiegotheatres.org. Grandly restored Spanish Revival moviehouse from 1924 that has a range of classical, operetta, musicals, film, dance and more.

Civic Theatre 1100 3rd Ave, at B, downtown ☎619 570 1100, ⓦsandiegotheatres.org. Three-thousand seater opened in 1965, geared towards mainstream entertainment, mainly off-Broadway touring shows and musical revivals.

Cygnet Theatre 4040 Twiggs St, Old Town ☎619 337 1525, ⓦcygnettheatre.com. Though few venture to Old Town for theatre, this smallish venue provides a good reason; it hosts a range of twentieth-century classics and more contemporary productions in an intimate showcase for some of the area's better dramatic and comedic talent.

La Jolla Playhouse UCSD campus, 2910 La Jolla Village Drive ☎858 550 1010, ⓦlajollaplayhouse.org. Splashy modern complex that hosts a range of productions, typically a mix of off-Broadway favourites and contemporary dramatic and musical shows.

The Old Globe 1363 Old Globe Way, Balboa Park ☎619 234 5623, ⓦtheoldglobe.org. As you'd expect from the name, a fine showcase for the works of the Bard, but also featuring more current entertainment, including off-Broadway favourites, revivals and children's plays.

San Diego Repertory Theatre Lyceum Theatre, 79 Horton Plaza, downtown ☎619 544 1000, ⓦsdrep .org. A key San Diego theatre that presents consciousness-raising productions of the political and cultural variety, along with a mix of classics and travelling musicals.

FILM

Landmark Cinemas ⓦlandmarktheatres.com. For more adventurous programmes – foreign-language films, monochrome classics or cult favourites – try this cinema chain: The Ken, 4061 Adams Ave (☎619 283 5909), or the Hillcrest Cinemas, 3965 5th Ave (☎619 819 0236).

LGBT SAN DIEGO

Although central San Diego is generally welcoming to visitors of all orientations, several hotels and bed and breakfasts are noted for their friendliness toward **gay and lesbian** travellers: **Inn at the Park** (see p.178) is a good choice. **Hillcrest** is the heart of San Diego's gay scene, with the focus on University Ave, while the primary source of gay and lesbian news and events is online *San Diego Gay & Lesbian News* (w sdgln.com). The **San Diego LGBT Visitors Center**, 502 University Ave, Hillcrest (Wed–Sun 10am–4pm; t 619 432 5428, w fabsandiego.tumblr.com) is a wonderful resource for LGBT tourists (offering advice on hotels and nightlife), while the **San Diego LGBT Community Center**, 3909 Centre St, Hillcrest (Mon–Fri 9am–10pm, Sat 9am–7pm; t 619 692 2077, w thecentersd.org), has served the community for decades.

GAY BARS AND CLUBS

Baja Betty's 1421 University Ave, Hillcrest t 619 269 8510, w bajabettyssd.com. Convivial joint that draws the crowds for its decent Mexican food, spectacular margaritas and themed dance nights. Mon–Fri 11am–1am, Sat & Sun 10am–1am.

Chee-Chee Club 929 Broadway, downtown t 619 234 4404; map p.158. Rumpled dive bar with a casual atmosphere and mixed crowd of grizzled regulars, and a bit less attitude than at some of the Hillcrest clubs. Daily noon–2am.

Flicks 1017 University Ave, Hillcrest t 619 297 2056, w sdflicks.com. Popular drinking joint that plays music videos on large screens and offers pinball, pool and occasional comedy as well. Mon, Wed & Thurs 4pm–2am, Tues & Fri 2pm–2am, Sat & Sun noon–2am.

Hillcrest Brewing Co 1458 University Ave, Hillcrest t 619 269 4323, w hillcrestbrewingcompany.com. Only in California: the world's first LGBT microbrewery, located next to the iconic Hillcrest Pride Flag, serving handcrafted beer and stone-fired pizzas. Mon–Fri 3pm–1.30am, Sat noon–1.30am, Sun 9am–11pm.

Lips 3036 El Cajon Blvd, northeast of Hillcrest t 619 295 7900, w lipssd.com. Drag Central in San Diego, with regular performances from smart-alec queens and chic divas alike. Signature events include drag karaoke and bingo, and a curious Sunday Gospel Brunch as well. $5 cover Tues–Thurs & Sun, $10 cover Fri & Sat (plus daily $15 food minimum per person). Tues–Sat 6.45pm–midnight, Sun 11am–midnight.

The Rail 3796 5th Ave, Hillcrest t 619 298 2233, w thebrassrailsd.com. High-energy dancing every night at this long-standing neighbourhood hangout (open since the 1950s), with a mixed gay and straight crowd, and disco, house and Eighties music pumping from the speakers. Mon & Thurs 9pm–2am, Fri & Sat 2pm–2am, Sun 2–6pm.

Rich's 1051 University Ave, Hillcrest t 619 295 2195, w richssandiego.com. Primarily a gay club, *Rich's* now attracts numerous straights for the heavy dance grooves at weekends and the frenzied environment. Cover charge most nights. Wed–Sun 10pm–2am.

Urban Mo's 308 University Ave, Hillcrest t 619 491 0400, w urbanmos.com. Epicentre for drinking in the area, this is a restaurant and bar that features assorted drink specials and dance parties, plus regular drag events. Daily 9am–1.30am.

DIRECTORY

Beach and surf conditions t 619 221 8824, w surfingsandiego.com.

Disabled assistance Accessible San Diego (t 858 279 0704, w access-sandiego.org); Access to Independence of San Diego, 8885 Rio San Diego Drive (t 619 293 3500, w accesstoindependence.org).

Emergencies t 911.

Hospitals For non-urgent treatment, the cheapest place is the Beach Area Family Health Center, 3705 Mission Blvd, Mission Beach (Mon–Wed & Fri 8.30am–5.30pm, Thurs 9am–6pm; t 619 515 2444, w fhcsd.org).

Left luggage At the Greyhound terminal (see p.176) and, for ticketed train and trolley travellers, at the Santa Fe Depot.

Library The Central Library (Mon–Thurs 9.30am–7pm, Fri & Sat 9.30am–6pm, Sun noon–6pm), 330 Park Blvd, at 11th Ave, near Petco Park, has free internet access.

Pharmacy There's plenty downtown open from 9am, but for a 24-hour pharmacy, go to Walgreens, 3005 Midway Drive, north of the airport (t 619 221 0834), and 3222 University Ave, east of Hillcrest (t 619 528 1793).

Post office 51 Horton Plaza, downtown (Mon–Fri 9.30am–5pm, Sat 10am–4pm t 800 275 8777); in La Jolla at 1140 Wall St (Mon–Fri 8.30am–5pm, Sat 9am–1pm).

Taxes Sales tax is 8 percent; hotel tax is 10.5 percent, or 12.5 percent for hotels with more than 70 rooms.

Coronado and around

Just across San Diego Bay from Downtown San Diego (but an independent city), the bulbous isthmus of **CORONADO** is a well-scrubbed resort community with the **North Island Naval Air Station** at its western end, which encompasses a group of eight US military facilities – one of the reasons you're apt to see so many sailors and soldiers in town. Although Coronado has an appealing, vaguely New England air, with an assortment of cosy "saltbox" houses, the town is of limited interest, save for its historic hotel and the long, thin **beach** – a natural breakwater for the bay – that runs south. Just beyond, and much less upscale, **Imperial Beach**'s chief draw is simply the peace of its sands, and, if you have an equestrian bent, its nearby horseriding trails. A few miles to the south, across the **Mexican border**, lies the party-town of **Tijuana** (see box, p.155).

Hotel del Coronado

1500 Orange Ave • Guided tours Mon, Wed & Fri 10.30am–noon; Sun & Sat 2–3.30pm • $20 • Tour reservations through the Coronado Visitor Center (see opposite) ☎ 619 437 8788, ⓦ hoteldel.com

The town of Coronado grew up around the **Hotel del Coronado**, a Victorian whirl of red turrets and towers erected as a health resort in 1888. Using Chinese labourers who worked round-the-clock shifts, the hotel was built to appeal to well-heeled enthusiasts of healthy living, as well as rich hypochondriacs. Reached through the lobby and courtyard, a small basement **museum** details the history of the "Del", including its most notable moment, when Edward VIII (then Prince of Wales) met Coronado housewife Wallis Warfield Simpson here in 1920, which eventually led to their marriage and his abdication of the British throne. Also not to be missed is the tablecloth signed by Marilyn Monroe and the rest of the cast who filmed Billy Wilder's *Some Like It Hot* here in 1958, when it doubled as a ritzy Miami Beach resort. Outside are the sands upon which Monroe memorably flirted with Tony Curtis as he pretended to be a yachting playboy with a Cary Grant accent. A guided historical **tour** takes in many of these highlights as it wends its way around the hotel, beginning in the lobby.

Coronado Museum of History and Art

1100 Orange Ave • Mon–Fri 9am–5pm, Sat & Sun 10am–5pm • Free, suggested donation $5 • ☎ 619 435 7242, ⓦ coronadohistory.org

On the same site as the local visitor centre, the **Coronado Museum of History and Art** contains displays chronicling the town's early pioneers and first naval aviators, as well as its history of yachting, architecture and ferries. For a look at the historical and architectural importance of the buildings in town, the museum offers the hour-long **Coronado Heritage Walk** (Wed 10.30am; $15, includes museum admission; reservations required ☎ 619 437 8788).

Silver Strand State Beach

5000 Silver Strand Blvd (Hwy-75) • Daily 8am–dusk • Free, parking $10/day • ☎ 619 435 5184, ⓦ parks.ca.gov • Bus #901 from Downtown San Diego via *Hotel del Coronado* ($2.25)

Some of the seven-mile-long sandy isthmus of the **Silver Strand** south of Coronado is given over to military training facilities, at least until you come to **Silver Strand State Beach** (five miles south of *Hotel del Coronado*), where there are facilities for RVs. This is a pleasant spot to rollerblade or bike, or get into the local spirit by surfing or jet-skiing. The park encompasses 2.5 miles of Pacific Ocean beach and a half-mile by the bay, with fabulous views of Downtown San Diego (the water on the bay side is usually warmer and calmer, perfect for swimming).

Imperial Beach

The small city of **IMPERIAL BEACH** is eight miles south of Coronado, just nine miles north of Tijuana at the far southwest corner of the US. It offers excellent conditions for surfing, and until 2011 was the site of the **US Open Sandcastle Competition**, one of the

EVENINGS AT THE DRIVE-IN

If you're driving and fancy a little 1950s nostalgia check out the **South Bay Drive-In**, 2170 Coronado Ave, near Imperial Beach (☎619 423 2727, ⊛southbaydrivein.com), one of the few movie venues of its kind left in Southern California, offering three outdoor screens showing mainstream flicks for $9 per person, cash only (daily, evenings only).

nation's largest such events – after fundraising problems, a smaller version was revived in 2013 as the one-day **Sun & Sea Festival** (late June; ⊛sunandseafestival.com). Also worth a look is the beachside **farmers' market** near the pier, 10 Evergreen St (Fri 2–7pm; ⊛imperialbeachfarmersmarket.org), which has a good array of produce and children's activities on offer.

2

Border Field State Park

1500 Monument Rd • Daily: Summer 9.30am–7pm; early Sept–Oct & mid-March to late May 9am–6pm; Nov to mid-March 9am–5pm • Free, parking $5/vehicle • ☎619 575 3613, ⊛parks.ca.gov

Around 7 miles south of Imperial Beach, **Border Field State Park** was named for the place where surveyors from the US and Mexico agreed on an international boundary after their war in 1848. Today the park is an important wildlife habitat, its sand dunes and salt marshes providing refuge to endangered birds such as the Western Snowy Plover, the California Least Tern and the Light-footed Clapper Rail. The actual memorial and monumental column that marks the international boundary – the romantically named **Border Monument #258** – can only be viewed from Monument Mesa, because it now lies behind two intimidating border fences. Note also that due to budget cuts the park will be **closed to vehicles** Monday to Friday (though open to cyclists and pedestrians) for the foreseeable future (you can park at the gate and walk in).

ARRIVAL AND INFORMATION

CORONADO

By boat The simplest way to get here from Downtown San Diego is on the San Diego Bay ferry (Sun–Thurs 9am–9pm; Fri & Sat 9am–10pm; $4.25 each way; 15min), leaves Broadway Pier on the hour, returning on the half-hour. Tickets are available on the pier at Flagship Cruises, 990 N Harbor Drive (☎619 234 4111, ⊛sdhe.com).

By bus From the Coronado Ferry Landing on 1st St, shuttle bus #904 runs the mile up Coronado's main street,

Orange Ave, to the *Hotel del Coronado*; alternatively, use bus #901 from downtown San Diego, which runs to Coronado and on to Imperial Beach. To return to San Diego from Imperial Beach, take bus #933 or #934 to the nearest Blue Line trolley station.

Coronado Visitor Center 1100 Orange Ave (Mon–Fri 9am–5pm, Sat & Sun 10am–5pm; ☎619 437 8788, ⊛coronadovisitorcenter.com).

ACCOMMODATION AND EATING

★**1906 Lodge** 1060 Adella Ave ☎619 437 1900, ⊛1906lodge.com. Beautifully restored Mission-style property two blocks from the beach (built in 1906 by Will Sterling Hebbard and Irving Gill), featuring elegant, contemporary rooms, sumptuous breakfast buffet and free cookies at 3pm. **$239**

Burger Lounge 922 Orange Ave ☎619 435 6835, ⊛burgerlounge.com. Continuing the Southern California trend of nouveau burger joints, this mini-chain offers juicy grass-fed beef patties (from $7.95) and the usual shakes, fries and rings to go with them. Mon–Thurs & Sun 10.30am–9pm, Fri & Sat 10.30am–10pm.

Coronado Brewing Co 170 Orange Ave ☎619 437 4452, ⊛coronadobrewingcompany.com. A solid

choice if you crave handcrafted brews with names like Seacoast Pilsner, Mermaid's Red Ale and Idiot IPA, served alongside standard pasta, seafood and burgers ($12–15). There's also a branch in Imperial Beach (875 Seacoast Drive). Mon–Thurs & Sun 10.30am–9pm, Fri & Sat 10.30am–10pm.

★**Hotel del Coronado** 1500 Orange Ave ☎800 468 3533, ⊛hoteldel.com. The luxurious spot that put Coronado on the map is still the area's major tourist sight (see opposite) – millions have been poured into the complex in renovations, and the striking rooms and suites, expansive bay views and old-fashioned Victorian charm from 1888 still give the place plenty of appeal. **$339**

Peohe's 1201 1st St ☎619 437 4474, ⊛peohes.com.

Polynesian-themed restaurant whose supreme bayside views of downtown San Diego are matched only by its pricey but delicious bourbon pork chops, lobster tail, truffle risotto, Pacific fire shrimp and assorted steaks (mains $25–45). Mon–Thurs 11.30am–2.30pm & 5–9.30pm, Fri & Sat 11.30am–2.30pm & 5–10pm, Sun 10am–2.30pm & 4.30–9.30pm.

El Rancho 370 Orange Ave ☎619 435 2251, ⓦelrancho-coronado.com. One of the cheapest deals on this side of the water (rates as low as $79 in offseason): a small, clean motel with ten units offering basic decor, but equipped with microwaves and fridges. **$140**

The North County coast

The small seaside towns of the **North County coast** are mostly conservative, moneyed communities attracting a mix of tight-lipped business commuters, beach-bumming surfer dudes and crewcut-sporting tough guys attached to Marine Corps Base Camp Pendleton. The main attraction, of course, is the ocean itself – miles of gorgeous beaches with great opportunities for swimming and surfing – but some fabulous places to eat, a smattering of historic sights and family-friendly big-hitters such as Legoland California make for an enticing stopover on the route north to LA.

Del Mar

On the northern edge of the city of San Diego, the tall bluff that contains Torrey Pines State Preserve (see p.175) marks the southern boundary of **DEL MAR**, a wealthy seaside town of just over four thousand, famed for its horse races and inviting, sandy beaches. Del Mar's other main event is the **San Diego County Fair** (Tues–Thurs 11am–10pm, Fri 11am–11pm, Sat 10am–11pm, Sun 10am–10pm; $16; ☎858 755 1161, ⓦsdfair .com), held throughout June until July 4 at the Del Mar Fairgrounds (2260 Jimmy Durante Blvd, next to the racetrack). It's an old-fashioned fair with barbecues, kiddie games and livestock shows, though it's mixed with contemporary events, including film screenings, and low-key concerts by pop acts and soft-rockers. Since 2015, the three-day **Kaaboo Music Festival** (one-day passes from $120; ⓦkaaboodelmar.com) has been held here every September, attracting DJs and bands from Lenny Kravitz and Aerosmith to Ludacris and Flo Rida.

Del Mar Racetrack

2260 Jimmy Durante Blvd • General admission on race days from $6, parking $10/vehicle • ☎858 755 1141, ⓦdmtc.com

Del Mar is best known for the **Del Mar Racetrack**, which has been going strong since 1937, originally founded by investors including Bing Crosby and Gary Cooper. It's still one of the most revered and popular tracks in the country, staging horse races between late July and early September (and since 2014, November to mid-December). On race days, free shuttles run between the track and the Amtrak/Coaster station at Solana Beach.

The beach

Del Mar Lifeguards ☎858 755 1556

Del Mar offers a wonderful two-mile stretch of sandy **beach**, with the area known as **Main Beach** running from Powerhouse Park and the 15th Street surf break to 29th Street, and **North Beach** running from 29th Street to the Solana Beach border. North Beach is also known as "Dog Beach", and is open to pet dogs year-round.

ARRIVAL AND DEPARTURE   **DEL MAR**

By bus North County Transit bus #101 (daily 5am–10pm, every 20–30min; $1.75) runs between La Jolla's Gilman Transit Center (25min) and Del Mar (Camino Del Mar and 15th St), and goes on to Encinitas (27min) and Oceanside (1hr 12min).

ACCOMMODATION AND EATING

Best Western Premier Hotel Del Mar 720 Camino del Mar ☎858 755 9765, ⓦbestwestern.com. If the *L'Auberge* room rate seems a little steep, this hotel is a good alternative, with clean and simple rooms, pool and continental breakfast. $165

Jake's Del Mar 1660 Coast Blvd ☎858 755 1002, ⓦjakesdelmar.com. Right on the ocean with some lovely sea views, excellent for seafood and chowders, as well as steaks, burgers and Asian dishes such as wasabi ahi tuna and sashimi. Mains $24–44. Mon 5–9pm, Tues–Thurs 11.30am–2.30pm & 5–9pm, Fri 11.30am–2.30pm & 5–9.30pm, Sat 11.30am–2.30pm & 4.30–9.30pm, Sun 10am–2pm & 4.30–9pm.

L'Auberge Del Mar 1540 Camino del Mar ☎858 259 1515, ⓦlaubergedelmar.com. If you want to hit the track or the fair overnight, you can stay in style at this place loaded with chic restaurants, tennis courts and swanky rooms and cabanas by the pool, and offering top-notch spa and massage services, too. $339

Solana Beach

Just over two miles north along the coast from Del Mar, **SOLANA BEACH** is another affluent place of over 12,000 people, and in 2003 became the first US city to ban smoking from its coastline. The oceanside views are best appreciated from **Solana Beach County Park** (also known as "Pillbox" or "Fletcher Cove"), which also offers good diving and surfing opportunities. The town itself makes a reasonable place for an overnight stop, with around eighty art galleries, antiques stores, boutiques and cafés in the **Design District** (ⓦshopcedros.com) along Cedros Avenue (south of Lomas Santa Fe Drive). Also here is the **Solana Beach Farmers' Market** (Sun noon–5pm; ⓦsolanabeachfarmersmarket.com), at Cedros and Rosa, and the excellent **Carruth Cellars Winery**, 118 S Cedros Ave (daily 11am–10pm; tastings $15 for six wines; ⓦcarruthcellars.com).

Rancho Santa Fe

If you're driving, take a quick, four-mile detour inland along Hwy-8, passing the town of **RANCHO SANTA FE**, a small ultra-posh community with a distinctive flavour of 1920s and 1930s Spain, whose architecture is enforced by an all-powerful "Art Jury" that rigidly disallows any deviation from the prevailing quaintness. Notable residents include Microsoft founder Bill Gates, who bought weight-loss guru Jenny Craig's horse ranch here for $18 million in 2014.

ARRIVAL AND DEPARTURE   SOLANA BEACH

By train Amtrak and Coaster (see p.176) trains arrive at 105 N Cedros Ave (Solana Beach Transit Center), two blocks from the beach.
Destinations Los Angeles (11 daily; 2hr 7min–2hr 21min); Oceanside (11 daily; 15–26min); San Diego (11 daily; 37–51min).

By bus North County Transit bus #101 (daily 5am–10pm, every 20–30min; $1.75) runs between La Jolla's Gilman Transit Center (35min) and Solana Beach Transit Center via Del Mar, and goes on to Encinitas (15min) and Oceanside (55min). Bus #308 (daily 6.15am–8.30pm, hourly; $1.75) shuttles back and forth to Escondido Transit Center, also via Del Mar.

ACCOMMODATION, EATING AND DRINKING

Courtyard San Diego Solana Beach 717 S Hwy-101 ☎858 792 8200, ⓦmarriott.com. An affordable option not far from the waterside, with pool, gym, hot tub and high-speed internet. $160

Culture Brewing Co 111 S Cedros Ave, ☎858 345 1144, ⓦculturebrewingco.com. Local brewpub that serves drinks only (though there's a rotating selection of local vendors selling pizzas and the like through the week on site), in smaller "taster" sizes as well as full pours; top picks include the Peppermint Stout, Coffee IPA and the refreshing La Cerveza. Daily noon–9pm.

Naked Café 106 S Sierra Ave ☎858 259 7866, ⓦthenakedcafe.com. Fabulous breakfast spot with fresh, tasty food (many gluten-free and vegetarian options) and awesome views of Fletcher Cove (mains $8–12). Daily 7.30am–2.30pm.

ENTERTAINMENT

Belly Up Tavern 143 S Cedros Ave ☎858 481 9022, ⓦbellyup.com. Mid-sized hall that plays host nightly to an eclectic range of live music – anything from grizzled rockers to salsa spectaculars and tub-thumping DJs (most

2

tickets $18–20). Daily 9pm–1am.
North Coast Repertory Theatre 987 Lomas Sante Fe Drive ☎858 481 1055, ⓦnorthcoastrep.org. Merits a

break from the beach, with raucous comedies and affecting dramas, and many local and world premiere productions.

Encinitas and around

The major flower-growing centre of **ENCINITAS**, three miles north of Solana Beach, is at its best during the spring, when its blooms of floral colour are most radiant. It's no surprise that revered Indian guru Paramahansa Yogananda, founder of the **Self-Realization Fellowship** in 1920, came here to meditate and write his *Autobiography of a Yogi* in 1936; named in the guru's honour, **Swami's Beach** is one of the best spots for surfing along this part of the coast. One mile north, **Moonlight Beach** is the most enticing stretch for swimming and lounging on the sand.

Self-Realization Fellowship

215 W K St • Hermitage Sun 2–4pm; Meditation Gardens Tues–Sat 9am–5pm, Sun 11am–5pm • ☎760 753 1811, ⓦyogananda-srf.org

Advocating an ecumenical philosophy with spiritual themes, the Self-Realization Fellowship now extends to several properties in town, with the serene **Hermitage** (where the rooms used by Paramahansa Yogananda are preserved as a shrine) and **Meditation Gardens** open to the public. The adjacent **SRF Encinitas Retreat** offers daily programmes for those "desiring spiritual renewal" (Ravi Shankar gave his first US concert here in 1957, and ex-Beatle George Harrison was a regular visitor). Sunday services and weekly meditation classes (open to the public) are held at the **Encinitas Temple** (ⓦencinitastemple.org), built in 1977 two blocks away at 939 Second St, while the three **Golden Lotus Towers** nearby on Hwy-101 were designed and dedicated by Yogananda in 1948.

San Diego Botanic Garden

230 Quail Gardens Drive • Daily 9am–5pm • $14 (parking $2) • ☎760 436 3036, ⓦsdbgarden.org

Established on ranch land donated in 1957, the tranquil **San Diego Botanic Garden** hosts thirty different natural environments, ranging from vast groves of bamboo (the largest in the US) and California endemics, to palms and selections of foliage from each continent.

San Elijo Lagoon Ecological Reserve

2710 Manchester Ave, Cardiff-by-the-Sea • Daily sunrise–sunset; Nature Center daily 9am–5pm • Free • ☎760 634 3026, ⓦsanelijo.org • No public transport

Two miles south of Encinitas, in neighbouring Cardiff-by-the-Sea, lies the wetlands of the **San Elijo Lagoon Ecological Reserve**, a thousand acres rich with endemic plants, fish and birds – and based around marshes, scrubland and chaparral – which you can explore on seven miles of hiking trails. The **Nature Center** contains interactive exhibits about the history and ecology of the lagoon.

ARRIVAL AND DEPARTURE

ENCINITAS AND AROUND

By train Encinitas station (25 E D St) is connected to San Diego and Oceanside via the Coaster service every 30–40min (see p.176); Amtrak trains from San Diego to Los Angeles (2hr 7min–2hr 16min) also stop here three times a day in each direction.
Destinations (Coaster) Oceanside (16min); San Diego

Downtown (45min); Solana Beach (6min).
By bus North County Transit bus #101 (daily 5am–10pm, every 20–30min; $1.75) runs between La Jolla's Gilman Transit Center (50min) and Encinitas via Solana Beach (15min), then on to Oceanside (40min).

ACCOMMODATION

Inn at Moonlight Beach 105 N Vulcan Ave ☎760 561 1755, ⓦinnatmoonlightbeach.com. Tranquil B&B with four elegant rooms and suites with tasteful decor and

wholesome breakfast – the beach is two blocks away. **$129**
Moonlight Beach Motel 233 2nd St ☎760 753 0623,

ⓦmoonlightbeachmotel.com. The bargain rooms at this friendly, old-fashioned beach motel have kitchenettes (with microwave), private decks, cable TV and fridges, just two blocks from the beach. $80

San Elijo State Beach Campground 2050 S Coast Hwy-101, Cardiff-by-the-Sea ⓣ800 444 7275 ⓦreserveamerica.com. For a serene alternative to the hotels in town, try the campground at this beachside state park just south of Encinitas, which offers fishing, hiking and swimming. Pitches from $35

EATING

Lotus Cafe & Juice Bar 765 S Coast Hwy-101 ⓣ760 479 1977, ⓦlotuscafeandjuicebar.com. Fresh, natural and healthy food, in keeping with the yogi traditions of the town, with such dishes as black bean enchiladas ($9.95) and swami's lasagna (veggie; $9.95). Daily 8am–9pm.

Q'ero 564 S Coast Hwy-101 ⓣ760 753 9050, ⓦqerorestaurant.com. A fabulous place whose Peruvian and Latin American cuisine leans heavily towards seafood, steak and lamb, with prime grilled prawns, quinoa salad and empanadas (mains $18–21). Tues & Wed 11am–3pm, Thurs–Sat 11am–9pm.

★**Seaside Market** 2087 San Elijo Ave, Cardiff-by-the-Sea ⓣ760 753 5445, ⓦseasidemarket.com. Locally celebrated for its Burgundy pepper tri-tip steak (aka "Cardiff crack"), sold vacuum-packed or in sandwiches ($7.99), along with salads, breakfast plates, burritos and home-made soups. Daily 7am–10pm.

★**V G Donuts & Bakery** 106 Aberdeen Drive, Cardiff-by-the-Sea ⓣ760 753 2400, ⓦvgbakery.com. Join the lines of eager locals at the crack of dawn (doughnuts are baked twice daily at 4am and 4pm) for the sumptuous pastries and doughnuts (from $0.90) at this old-fashioned bakery, a tradition since 1969. Mon–Sat 5am–9pm, Sun 5am–7pm.

Carlsbad

Some ten miles along the coast from Encinitas lies the affluent beach town of **CARLSBAD**, whose twee, pseudo-Teutonic architecture derives from the early 1880s belief that water from a local spring had the same invigorating qualities as the waters of Karlsbad, a spa town in Bohemia (now Karlovy Vary in the Czech Republic). "Carlsbad" thus became a health resort, promoted by pioneer-turned-entrepreneur John Frazier, whose bronze image overlooks the (now dry) original springs near Carlsbad Boulevard and Carlsbad Village Drive.

Surfers are the main visitors to **South Carlsbad State Beach** at 7201 Carlsbad Blvd, which offers a busy clifftop campground (see p.194), swimming, fishing and scuba diving. One of several local lagoons that are good for birdwatching (grebes, terns, coots and pelicans), the **Buena Vista Lagoon** is a nature reserve of over two hundred acres, which also offers plenty of opportunities for strolling on the paths around it. The local Audubon Society has more information at its **nature centre**, 2202 S Coast Hwy-101 (Tues–Sat 10am–4pm; Sun 1–4pm; ⓣ760 439 2473, ⓦbvaudubon.org), and hosts regular guided walks.

Legoland California

1 Legoland Drive (I-5 Cannon Rd E exit) • **Legoland** School holidays daily 10am–8pm, otherwise Thurs–Mon 10am–5pm • $95, kids (3–12) $89; parking $12 • ⓣ760 918 5346, ⓦlegoland.com/california • **Water Park** June–Aug daily 10am–7pm (Sept, Oct, April, May Sat & Sun noon–5pm) • $101, kids (3–12) $95, includes Legoland (no separate admission) • **Sea Life Aquarium** Daily: June–Aug 9am–8pm; Sept–May 9am–5pm • $22 (adults & kids); $98, kids (3–12) $92 with Legoland • Major discounts are available online • ⓦvisitsealife.com

By far the most popular attraction in Carlsbad is the family-friendly theme park of **Legoland California**, where kids (ages 2–12 is the target range) are encouraged to climb on larger-than-life Lego bricks, make their way through colourful mazes, ride the Coastersaurus rollercoaster and other pint-sized thrill rides, spray water cannons from boats in Splash Battles, operate miniature cars and ships, and view assorted places built on a minuscule scale – among them New Orleans, Las Vegas, Washington DC and the coastline of Southern California. The resort complex also includes **Legoland Water Park**, with Lego-themed rides and slides, and **Sea Life Aquarium**, home to two hundred species of sea creatures, from a range of sharks and rays to moon jellyfish and seahorses.

2

By train Carlsbad Village Station at 2775 State St is connected to Downtown San Diego and Oceanside by the regular Coaster train service (see p.176).
Destinations Downtown San Diego (57min); Encinitas (16min); Oceanside (5min); San Diego Old Town (50min).
By bus North County Transit bus #101 (daily 5am–10pm, every 20–30min; $1.75) runs between La Jolla's Gilman

Transit Center (1hr 15min) and Carlsbad Village Station via Solana Beach (45min) and Encinitas (25min), and goes on to Oceanside (10min).
Carlsbad Visitor Center 400 Carlsbad Village Drive, in the Old Santa Fe Depot (Mon–Fri 9am–5pm, Sat 10am–4pm, Sun 10am–3pm; ☎760 434 6093, ⓦvisitcarlsbad.com).

ACCOMMODATION

Carlsbad Inn Beach Resort 3075 Carlsbad Blvd ☎760 434 7020, ⓦcarlsbadinn.com. One of the less expensive hotels in the area, whose rooms come with DVD players, kitchenettes, spas and fireplaces – there are more expensive suites and condos available with wide views of the Pacific. Doubles $189, suites $250
Pelican Cove Inn 320 Walnut Ave ☎760 434 5995, ⓦpelican-cove.com. Wonderful B&B, close to the beach

and Carlsbad centre, with comfy rooms with gas fireplaces, friendly owners Kris and Nancy Nayudu, home-made cookies and excellent French toast breakfast. $110
South Carlsbad State Beach Campground 7201 Carlsbad Blvd ☎800 444 7275, ⓦreserveamerica .com. This beach park has a campground, but for RVs only; the inland sites are a bit cheaper than those on the beachfront ($50). Inland sites from $35

EATING

Carlsbad Chocolate Bar 2998 State St ☎760 434 4479, ⓦcarlsbadchocolatebar.com. Great little café where chocolate and coffee are the main attractions (lots of chocolate to take away also); save room for the pastries, muffins and cupcakes here after dinner. Mon–Thurs 9am–8pm, Fri & Sat 9am–9pm, Sun 8am–7pm.
★**Tip Top Meats** 6118 Paseo del Norte ☎760 438 2620, ⓦtiptopmeats.com. Old-fashioned butcher's and deli here since 1967, whose hefty fare features the likes of German bratwurst, stuffed cabbage and smoked Polish

sausages; you can also get great sandwiches and breakfasts here (mains under $10). Daily 6am–8pm.
Vigilucci's Cucina Italiana 2943 State St ☎760 434 2500, ⓦvigiluccis.com. One of the best Italian restaurants in southern California (now part of a mini-chain); friendly, fun staff, freshly made, delicious food and a connoisseurs selection of Italian wines (pastas $17–32; mains $21–42). Mon–Thurs 11.30am–9.30pm, Fri & Sat 11.30am–10pm, Sun 11am–9.30pm.

Oceanside

The most northerly city on the coast of San Diego County, **OCEANSIDE**, five miles north of Carlsbad, is dominated by the huge **Marine Corps Base Camp Pendleton**, though its downtown is charming and its beaches are beautiful, embellished by the fetching **Oceanside Pier**, that extends nearly two thousand feet into the waves. First built in 1888, it's one of the longest wooden piers in the US. Just inland from the pier (centred on the corner of Pier View Way and S Tremont St), the **Sunset Market** (Thurs 5–9pm) combines gourmet food stalls with live entertainment. The city's surf credentials include the **Supergirl Pro** (ⓦsupergirlpro.com) held every July, the world's premier women's surf event, and an excellent surf museum.

California Surf Museum

312 Pier View Way • Daily 10am–4pm, Thurs until 8pm • $5 • ☎760 721 6876, ⓦsurfmuseum.org

One of Oceanside's prime attractions is the **California Surf Museum**, which has permanent displays on the history of surfboards, from the earliest Polynesian wooden planks, as well as information about professional surfer Bethany Hamilton, who lost her left arm in a shark attack on the island of Kauai in 2003. Temporary exhibits focus on other aspects of California's quintessential watersport.

Oceanside Museum of Art

704 Pier View Way • Tues–Sat 10am–4pm, Sun 1–4pm • $8 • ☎760 435 3720, ⓦoma-online.org

The **Oceanside Museum of Art**, partially housed in a spartan but elegant Irving Gill design from 1934 (the striking modern structure by Fredrick Fisher is a 2008 addition), contains a fine range of contemporary art from glassworks to photography to multimedia, typically shown in rotating exhibitions.

Old Mission San Luis Rey de Francia

4050 Mission Ave (4 miles inland from Oceanside via Hwy-76) • **Chapel** daily 7am–5pm • Free • **Museum** daily 10am–5pm Mon–Fri 9.30am–5pm, Sat & Sun 10am–5pm • $7 • ☎ 760 757 3651, ⓦ sanluisrey.org • From Oceanside station take bus #303

The **Old Mission San Luis Rey de Francia**, founded in 1798 by Padre Fermín Lasuén (Junípero Serra's successor), was the largest of the Spanish California missions and once the centre for three thousand Native American converts (known as "Luiseños", but Payómkawichum in their own language). Franciscan monks still inhabit the mission (restored in the 1890s), and there's a **museum** and a serene, candlelit **chapel** with a handsome, all-white Spanish Colonial façade. Even if you don't go inside, look around the foundations of the guards' barracks immediately outside the main building and, across the road, the remains of the mission's ornate **sunken gardens**, once **lavanderías** where the inhabitants did their washing.

Guajome Regional Park

Park 3000 Guajome Lake Rd (off Hwy-76) • Day-use 9.30am–sunset • Parking $3 • ☎ 760 724 4489, ⓦ sdparks.org **Rancho Guajome** 2210 N Santa Fe Ave • Wed–Sun 9.30am–4pm; tours Wed–Fri noon, Sat & Sun noon & 2pm • Free • ☎ 760 724 4082

Eight miles northeast of downtown Oceanside, **Guajome Regional Park** has five miles of trails and picnic tables and playgrounds, but its centrepiece is the **Rancho Guajome Adobe**, an arcaded Spanish Colonial gem that's popular for weddings. The structure was completed in 1853 for newlyweds Cave Couts and Ysidora Bandini, socialites who later entertained celebrities like Helen Hunt Jackson – who, according to legend, based the title character of *Ramona*, her sentimental tale of Native American life in the mission era, on Ysidora's maid. After Couts' death in 1874, his son and Ysidora tried to maintain the place but over the years it became dilapidated, until it was finally bought by the county in 1973 and restored in the 1990s.

ARRIVAL AND INFORMATION   OCEANSIDE

By train The Amtrak station is at 235 S Tremont St, part of the Oceanside Transit Center (also used by Metrolink, Sprinter and Coaster trains), and a short walk from the seafront.

Destinations Amtrak: Los Angeles (11 daily; 1hr 49min–2hr); San Diego 11 daily (51min–1hr 7min); Santa Barbara (4 daily; 4hr 39min–4hr 48min); Solana Beach (11 daily; 14–22min); Coaster (every 30–40min): Carlsbad (5min), Encinitas (17min), San Diego (1hr), Solana Beach (23min); Sprinter (every 30min): Escondido (53min); Metrolink (6 daily): Anaheim (1hr 11min); Irvine (49min); Orange (1hr 7min); San Juan Capistrano (34min).

By bus The Greyhound station (☎ 760 722 1587) is at 215 S Tremont St, next to the train station. North County Transit bus #101 (daily 5am–10pm, every 20–30min; $1.75) runs between La Jolla's Gilman Transit Center (1hr 25min) and Oceanside Transit Center via all major communities along the coast.

Destinations (Greyhound) Anaheim (3 daily; 1hr 25min); Los Angeles (6 daily; 1hr 50min–2hr 35min); San Diego (5 daily; 50min).

California Welcome Center 928 North Coast Hwy-101 (daily 9am–5pm; ☎ 760 721 1101, ⓦ visitoceanside.org).

ACCOMMODATION AND EATING

Bagby Beer Co 601 S Coast Hwy-101 ☎ 760 512 3372, ⓦ bagbybeer.com. Oceanside's excellent microbrewery offers open-air seating and a variety of craft beers, from Bohemian-style Pils to Imperial IPA, as well as tacos ($12–13), burgers ($12) and pizzas (from $13). Mon–Thurs & Sun 11am–10pm, Fri & Sat 11am–11pm.

Beach Break Café 1802 S Coast Hwy-101 ☎ 760 439 6355, ⓦ beachbreakcafe.net. Laidback surf café, knocking out huge breakfast portions ($7.50–13), burgers

($8.75) and sandwiches ($8–11). Daily 7am–2pm.

Southern California Beach Club 121 S Pacific St ☎ 877 477 7368, ⓦ southerncalifbeachclub.com. There are plenty of motel chains in Oceanside, but for more luxury opt for this beachside alternative, offering a variety of properties for rent, from one-bedroom studios to two-bedroom condos, with kitchens, balconies and DVD players typically included. **$230**

San Onofre State Beach

5200 S Pacific Coast Hwy (I-5 Exit Basilone Rd) • Daily dawn–dusk • Free, parking $15/vehicle • ☎ 949 492 4872, Ⓦ parks.ca.gov

Twenty miles north of Oceanside, just before I-5 crosses into Orange County (see p.120), uncluttered **San Onofre State Beach** is best known for the collection of world-class surfing spots known as **Trestles**. The beach is host to all manner of professional surfers and international competitions during the year; however, it's only accessible by a 1.5-mile hiking trail.

2

ACCOMMODATION   SAN ONOFRE STATE BEACH

San Onofre State Beach, Bluffs Campground I-5 (Exit Basilone Rd) ☎ 800 444 7275, Ⓦ reserveamerica .com. Camping is offered at the park near the sandstone

bluffs; no hookups, but showers and toilets. Mid-May to Sept only. Inland, the park's *San Mateo Campground* offers similar facilities. **$35**

Inland North County

Unlike the coast, **inland North County** has no sizeable towns and is mostly given over to farming, with a terrain of dense forests, deep valleys and mile-high mountain ranges. Besides a few reminders of ancient indigenous cultures, remnants from the mission era, and a few settlements, it's best to make for the area's state parks and enjoy some leisurely countryside walks, or venture further east to the dramatic Anza-Borrego Desert (see p.237).

Escondido and around

Founded in 1888 and now boasting a population of around 145,000, **ESCONDIDO** is one of the region's fastest-growing cities, where retirees and ex-urbanites mix with hip younger folk, well away from most of San Diego County's tourist traffic. Though it remains one of America's bastions of conservatism, the annual spectacle of **Cruisin' Grand** (April–Sept Fri 5–9pm; Ⓦ cruisingrand.com) sees over five hundred hot rods and pre-1973 historic cars on show along the main drag, Grand Avenue, accompanied by DJs and live bands – locals like to walk their dogs, sample the snack stalls and take in the colourful characters on parade. One block off Grand Avenue lies **Grape Day Park** (Ⓦ grapedaypark.org), home to the civic centre and a couple of decent museums but otherwise notable for "Vinehenge", its vineyard-themed playground, where children can frolic on oversized leaves and vines and slide through a tunnel of giant grapes.

Escondido History Center

321 N Broadway (Grape Day Park) • Tues–Sat 1–4pm • Free (donation requested) • ☎ 760 743 8207, Ⓦ escondidohistory.org

The **Escondido History Center** features several Victorian-era buildings relocated to Grape Day Park in the 1970s, including the city's original 1888 Santa Fe train depot (where you'll find docents and exhibits), an 1890 Victorian country home, an old-fashioned blacksmith's and the first city library (1895).

California Center for the Arts

340 N Escondido Blvd • Thurs–Sat 10am–5pm, Sun 1–5pm • $8 • ☎ 760 839 4120, Ⓦ artcenter.org

The **California Center for the Arts** has a surprisingly good contemporary art museum, showcasing a range of traditional media as well as avant-garde, installation, multimedia and video-art exhibitions, and two theatres that present comedy, musicals and dance performances along with live jazz, classical and world music.

Queen Califia's Magical Circle

Iris Sankey Arboretum, Kit Carson Park, Bear Valley Pkwy at Mary Lane • Free • Summer Tues–Sun 8.30am–3.30pm; rest of year Tues–Fri 9am–noon (also second Sat of the month 9am–noon) • Free • Ⓦ queencalifia.org

No trip to Escondido would be complete without a stop at the eye-opening **Queen Califia's Magical Circle**, Niki de Saint Phalle's bizarre, strangely delightful art garden completed in 2003 and based around nine of her more fanciful mosaic sculptures, including such oddments as hissing snake heads and gilded humans riding multicoloured birds.

Orfila Winery

13455 San Pasqua Valley Rd · Daily 11am–7pm, tours at noon · Free; tastings $12 (for 6 wines) · ☎ 760 738 6500 ext 24, ⓦ orfila.com

Five miles south of Escondido amid stunning scenery, the **Orfila Winery** offers tastings of local Rhône-style wine produced by a former Napa Valley vintner, as well as tours of the handsome facility, which is surrounded by seventy acres of hillside vineyards.

Welk Resorts San Diego

8860 Lawrence Welk Drive · ☎ 760 749 3000, ⓦ welkresorts.com/san-diego

Eight miles north of Downtown Escondido, off I-15, is the one of the area's biggest attractions, **Welk Resorts San Diego**, a thousand-acre holiday complex of golf courses, spas, eight swimming pools, villas and the **Welk Dinner Theater**, where you can enjoy anything from forgotten Broadway stars to a Beatles tribute band (show $49; with buffet $68).

Rising from accordion-playing unknown to musical juggernaut, TV bandleader **Lawrence Welk** (1903–1992) was the inventor of "champagne music" in the 1930s – basically waltzes and polkas with a touch of sanitized swing – during the playing of which bubbles would float through the air around his band. Displayed around the theatre lobby, the Welk hagiography follows the peculiar career of the thick-accented, native North Dakotan who most people assumed was an immigrant fresh from Central Europe. In 1964 Welk went for a drive north of San Diego, planning to invest in a grove of orange trees; instead he bought a motel and a golf course, a venture that has since blossomed into a multi-location chain of resorts.

San Diego Zoo Safari Park

15500 San Pasqual Valley Rd · Hours vary, usually daily 9am–5pm, summer until 8pm · $50, kids $40, joint ticket with San Diego Zoo $90, kids $70; parking $12 · ☎ 619 718 3000, ⓦ sdzsafaripark.org

Ten miles east of Escondido on Hwy-78, the **San Diego Zoo Safari Park** is the major tourist attraction in the area, the sister location to San Diego Zoo (see p.165). It's an 1800-acre enclosure featuring a sizeable tropical-bird aviary, mock African bush and Kilimanjaro hiking trail, elephant rides, and various films and exhibitions. With lions, tigers, cheetahs, deer and monkeys roaming about, it's a great stop for kids, and merits the cost of the pricey joint ticket with the main zoo.

San Pasqual Battlefield State Historic Park

15808 San Pasqual Valley Rd (Hwy-78) · Sat & Sun 10am–5pm (Nov–March 10am–4pm) · Free · ☎ 760 737 2201, ⓦ parks.ca.gov

Just one mile further along Hwy-78 from the safari park, the visitor centre at **San Pasqual Battlefield State Historic Park** details the small but bloody 1846 battle in the Mexican–American War, which is re-created every year (on the Sunday closest to December 6). The victor is still debated; the Americans ultimately held the field, but suffered more casualties. The short **Battlefield Monument Trail** loops around the battle site itself and offers information on the region's ecosystem and native cultures predating the arrival of white colonists.

Mission San Antonio de Pala Asistencia

3015 Pala Mission Rd, Pala · Church daily 7am–6pm; Museum daily 10am–5pm · Free, donation requested · ☎ 760 742 3317, ⓦ missionsanantonio.org

Hwy-S6 leads fifteen miles north from Escondido to **Mission San Antonio de Pala Asistencia**, near the junction of Hwy-76, inside the Pala Indian Reservation. Built as an outpost or *asistencia* of Mission San Luis Rey by Padre Antonio Peyrí in 1816, it lay in ruins until the local Luiseño began rebuilding it in the late 1890s. When the indigenous Cupeños were ousted from their tribal home at the turn of the twentieth century they joined the Luiseño here, and the mission served as their church; today the local tribe is known as the Pala Band of Mission Indians. Although the current buildings are just replicas of the originals – including the distinctive freestanding bell tower – they do offer an eerie atmosphere, with an evocative cemetery, lovely gardens and a **museum** which contains artefacts created by the native Pala people and dating back to the days of the original mission.

ARRIVAL AND INFORMATION

ESCONDIDO AND AROUND

By train Escondido is about 40 miles north of San Diego on I-15 and is the terminus of the Sprinter rail service (one-way $2, day-pass $5; ☎ 800 262 7837, ⓦ gonctd.com/sprinter), which links to Oceanside (every 30min; 53min), from where you can access the entire coast of the state on public transport. The station is part of Escondido Transit Center, 796 W Valley Pkwy, in downtown.

By bus The Greyhound bus station is next to the transit centre at 700 W Valley Pkwy.
Destinations San Bernardino (change for Los Angeles; 2 daily; 2hr); San Diego (2 daily; 40min).
Escondido Visitor Center 235 E Grand Ave (Tues–Fri 10am–4pm; ☎ 760 839 4777, ⓦ visitescondido.com).

ACCOMMODATION AND EATING

Unless you've come to partake in the glories of Lawrence Welk, Escondido is not really a good place to **stay**, with only a few reasonable options of the chain-motel variety.

★ **Peterson's Donut Corner** 903 S Escondido Blvd ☎ 760 745 777. This place doles out fabulous doughnuts at all hours ($0.85 each), a popular local fixture since 1981; try the old-fashioned style with nuts ($1). Daily 24hr.
Stone Brewing World Bistro & Gardens 1999 Citracado Pkwy ☎ 760 294 7866, ⓦ stonebrewing .com. Nationally renowned microbrewery, with such tasty offerings as Arrogant Bastard Ale and Stone Ruination IPA to wash down a decent pub menu (stinky cheese plate $18; jamon Serrano-wrapped trout $22). See website for tours of the brewery. Mon–Thurs & Sun 11am–10pm, Fri & Sat 11am–11pm.

★ **Vincent's** 113 W Grand Ave ☎ 760 745 3835, ⓦ vincentsongrand.com. This place is worth seeking out for its tremendous (if pricey) French cuisine, of which the tournedos Merlot, rack of lamb and duck à l'orange are particular highlights (mains $18–38). Tues–Sat 5–9.30pm.
Welk Resorts San Diego 8860 Lawrence Welk Drive ☎ 800 932 9355, ⓦ welkresorts.com/san-diego. Range of comfy rooms and condos at this massive resort, but you really come here for the activities and shows (see p.197); eight pools with waterslides, spa golf, tennis and various other sports. Good deals and big discounts available online. **$200**

Cleveland National Forest

Headquarters 10845 Rancho Bernardo Rd, Suite 200, San Diego • ☎ 858 673 6180, ⓦ fs.usda.gov/cleveland • Descanso is accessible from San Diego via I-8, while Palomar is best reached from Escondido on Hwy-78

Much of the hilly country east of San Diego is encompassed by the half-million-acre **Cleveland National Forest**, which stretches south almost to the Mexican border. Highlights include the **Laguna Mountain Recreation Area** (40min from Downtown San Diego) and the scenic **Ortega Highway**, which connects San Juan Capistrano and Temecula Valley Highway. There are plenty of trails to explore in the main **Palomar**, **Trabuco** and **Descanso** ranger districts of the forest, most of them running from one to ten miles, with the exception of the daunting **Pacific Crest Trail**, which covers a hundred miles here – a fraction of its full 2650-mile length as it heads from Mexico to Canada. Otherwise, there's a full range of activities available, from fishing to scenic drives, but be careful during the summer or excessively hot and dry periods – Cleveland National Forest is known for its significant potential for **wildfires**.

Palomar Mountain State Park

19952 State Park Rd (Hwy-S7) • Daily sunrise–sunset • $8/day per vehicle, cash only • ⓣ 760 742 3462, ⓦ palomarsp.org

A tranquil enclave within Cleveland Forest, the 1900-acre **Palomar Mountain State Park** (35 miles northeast of Escondido), harbours groves of pine, fir and cedar trees and a cool, high altitude, with relatively easy hiking trails.

Palomar Observatory

35899 Canfield Rd, Palomar Mountain (via Hwy-S6) • Daily 9am–4pm, until 3pm in winter • Free • Guided tours April–Oct Sat & Sun 11am & 1.30pm, $5 • ⓣ 760 742 2119, ⓦ astro.caltech.edu/palomar

Eight miles east of the Palomar Mountain State Park on winding Hwy-S6, at 5500ft, sits the two-hundred-inch Hale telescope of CalTech's **Palomar Observatory**, capable of seeing a billion light years into the cosmos. Although visitors aren't able to view the distant galaxies directly, the telescope apparatus inside the **Visitors Gallery** is impressive in itself and the **A.W. Greenway Jr. Visitor Center** has exhibits on the history of the Observatory, major scientific discoveries made with Palomar's telescope and a striking collection of deep-space photographs taken with the powerful lens.

INFORMATION

CLEVELAND NATIONAL FOREST

Descanso District Ranger Station 3348 Alpine Blvd, Alpine (Mon–Fri 8.30am–4pm; ⓣ 619 445 6235). Around 31 miles east from San Diego, off I-8 exit 33.

Palomar District Ranger Station 1634 Black Canyon Rd, Ramona (Mon–Fri 8.30am–4pm; ⓣ 760 788 0250). Around 18 miles east from Escondido, off Hwy-78.

Trabuco District Ranger Station 1147 E 6th St, Corona (Mon–Fri 8.30am–4pm; ⓣ 951 736 1811). Around 25 miles east of Anaheim (p.120), off I-15, exit 96.

CAMPGROUND

Palomar Mountain State Park 9952 State Park Rd (Hwy-S7) ⓣ 800 444 7275, ⓦ reserveamerica.com. In the park you can camp at *Doane Valley* campground (or *Cedar Grove* with groups; $90); first come, first served Dec–March, rest of year by reservation. Pitches from $30

Julian and around

Some forty miles east of Escondido (and 60 miles northeast of San Diego), **JULIAN** is a tiny crossroads community enlivened by a series of rustic bakeries, boasting formidable cider and apple pies that can draw a fair crowd of weekend visitors. On the eastern border of Cleveland National Forest the village was, amazingly, once the second biggest town in the San Diego area, thanks to an 1869 gold discovery here. Its population declined after that, and it faded into small-town obscurity. Today there are plenty of antiques shops and Western-themed boutiques here, and access to worthwhile park sites, wineries, horserides and scenic drives. At an elevation of 4000ft, the town also provides a temperate base from which to make forays into the Anza-Borrego Desert (see p.237), fewer than ten miles to the east.

To get a sense of the full scope of history and activities, drop by the visitor centre (see p.200), which has information and photos, and offers a **walking tour** of the local highlights. With its quaint buildings and rustic charm, Julian's appeal centres on its **Main Street**, where the **Julian Cider Mill** at no. 2103 (Mon–Thurs 9.30am–5pm, Fri–Sun 9.30am–5.30pm; ⓦ juliancidermillinc.com) sells a huge range of apple-related produce and merchandise.

Julian Pioneer Museum

2811 Washington St • April–Nov Thurs–Sun 10am–4pm • Free • ⓣ 760 765 0227, ⓦ julianpioneermuseum.org

An array of Gold Rush-era mining equipment is on display at the **Julian Pioneer Museum**, also featuring antiques and cast-offs from the late Victorian era, among them pianos, an old-time buggy, lace craftworks and historic apparel, stuffed animals and Native American relics – all housed in a former blacksmith shop built in 1888.

Julian Mining Company

4444 Hwy-78 (3 miles west of Julian) • Sat 10am–5pm, Sun noon–5pm • Gold panning $9 • ☎ 951 313 0166,
ⓦ julianminingcompany.com

You can try your hand at mining at **Julian Mining Company**, where you can pan for gold or tag on to larger groups learning about Native Americans, local farm life, the Revolutionary War or the Civil War – it's oriented more towards families and school groups.

Volcan Mountain Wilderness Preserve

1209 Farmer Rd/Wynola Rd • Daily 8am–sunset; summit April–Nov Sat & Sun 9am–5pm only • Guided treks April–Oct usually once a month, Sat or Sun • Free • ☎ 760 765 4098, ⓦ volcanmt.org

Rising above Julian off Farmer Road, the 5000ft-high **Volcan Mountain Wilderness Preserve** makes for an intriguing day out. Whether self- or fully guided, the main trek is a five-mile round-trip to the summit, from where you can get a scintillating overview of the region; shorter trails pass through orchards, oak groves and mixed conifer forest.

California Wolf Center

Kenis/Christiansen Private Rd, off KQ Ranch Rd • Tours: Sat & Sun 10am & 2pm • $20 • Wolf Pack tours Mon 10am, Fri 2pm • $30 •
Reservations required • ☎ 760 765 0030, ⓦ californiawolfcenter.org

For a natural experience of a very different kind, visit the **California Wolf Center**, four miles south of Julian on Hwy-79, whose programmes provide a look at the steely-eyed North American grey wolves in their packs and discuss the need to reintroduce them to the wild. Visits are by reservation only.

Mission Santa Ysabel Asistencia

23013 Hwy-79 (1.5 miles north of Santa Ysabel) • Daily: late May to early Sept 8am–5.30pm; early Sept to late May 8am–4pm • Free

The small **Mission Santa Ysabel Asistencia** is a 1924 reconstruction of an 1818 original structure that served as an outpost of the San Diego mission (p.170). Sitting in moody isolation, the mission has a small modern chapel and a one-room **museum** detailing the history of the site (including the story of the "lost bells"). Outside is a Native American burial ground, and the church continues to serve the local Kumeyaay people on the Santa Ysabel Reservation.

ARRIVAL AND INFORMATION

JULIAN AND AROUND

By car Julian lies at the junction of Hwy-79 from Escondido and Hwy-78 from the Salton Sea (p.235) – there is no public transport.

Chamber of Commerce The visitor centre is housed in the century-old Julian Town Hall at 2129 Main St (daily 10am–5pm; ☎ 760 765 1857, ⓦ visitjulian.com).

ACCOMMODATION

Julian Gold Rush Hotel 2032 Main St ☎ 800 734 5854, ⓦ julianhotel.com. The oldest functioning hotel in the state, opened in 1897 by a freed slave; the pair of rooms, plus a cottage and small house, are decorated in period style, and rates include afternoon tea and a full breakfast. **$135**

Julian Lodge 2720 C St ☎ 800 542 1420, ⓦ julianlodge .com. Only a replica of the historic 1885 Washington Hotel, but with a rustic atmosphere and many rooms at cheap

prices, also offering a buffet-style continental breakfast. **$85**

Shadow Mountain Ranch 2771 Frisius Rd ☎ 760 765 0323, ⓦ shadowmountainranch.net. Old cattle ranch with the most distinctive digs in town; it has a conventional Victorian room and two cottages, as well as a more unusual "Grandma's Attic" done up in lace and satin, a storybook cottage and modern treehouse, and a "Gnome Home" that's even kitscher than it sounds. **$109**

EATING

Dudley's Bakery 30218 Hwy-78, Santa Ysabel (just before the junction with Hwy-79) ☎ 760 765 0488, ⓦ dudleysbakery.com. Justly famous since 1963 for its home-baked breads and pastries – among them black olive and basil, and garlic sourdough – at giveaway prices.

Mon 9am–1pm, Thurs–Sun 8am–5pm.

Julian Grille 2224 Main St ☎ 760 765 0173, ⓦ juliangrille.com. One of the best options for a sit-down meal in town, from sumptuous stuffed filet mignon ($32) and sweet walnut salad ($9.50) to skillet trout ($17.95), set

in a cosy cottage dating from the 1920s. Ask for the "locals menu", which features special deals. Mon 11am–2.30pm, Tues–Sun 11am–2.30pm & 4.30–10pm.
★ **Julian Pie Company** 2225 Main St ☎ 760 765 2449, ⓦ julianpie.com. Julian is celebrated for its old-fashioned apple pie and this venerable store offers three kinds, as well as wonderful fruit-pie combinations using cherries, raspberries, peaches and boysenberries. Grab a bag of "Apple Memories" for the road, pieces of pie crust cut into apple shapes. Daily 9am–5pm.

Cuyamaca Rancho State Park

13652 Hwy-79 (9 miles south of Julian) • Daily sunrise–sunset • $8/day per vehicle • ☎ 760 765 0755, ⓦ crspia.org

The oaks, willows, sycamores and pines of **Cuyamaca Rancho State Park** are set in landscapes ranging from lush subalpine meadows to stark mountain peaks. However, most of the park's 25,000 acres, including its wilderness area, campgrounds and hiking trails, were damaged in wildfires in 2003. In the years since, an army of volunteers has rebuilt the park's facilities and reconstructed its trails, and life has very gradually returned – the park is a marvel of adaptability and revival in the face of natural, cyclical catastrophe. Most of the trails, together stretching some one hundred miles, have now been reopened, as have the **campgrounds**. Much of the park remains noticeably denuded of trees, years after the fire: post-fire vegetation is dominated by herbs, shrubs and re-sprouting oak species, and without active reforestation, the conversion of much of the park to shade-intolerant brush and exotic annuals could become permanent.

If you're a birdwatcher, check out the excellent **museum** (Sat & Sun 10am–4pm; free) in the same building as the visitor centre that gives a rundown of the native wrens, hawks, bluebirds and woodpeckers.

INFORMATION AND CAMPGROUNDS | CUYAMACA RANCHO STATE PARK

Park Visitor Center Pick up information and maps at 12551 Hwy-79 (Sat & Sun 10am–4pm), sixteen miles south of Julian in the heart of the park.
Campgrounds ☎ 800 444 7275, ⓦ reserveamerica .com (reservations required April to Oct weekends). You can pitch a tent at any of the park's campgrounds – *Green Valley* and *Paso Picacho* are the most popular sites, with showers and toilets. Pitches from $30

The deserts

JOSHUA TREE NATIONAL PARK

The deserts

Contrary to the monotonous landscape you might expect, the deserts of Southern California are a kaleidoscope of light, colour and texture, dotted with everything from ramshackle settlements to swanky resorts such as Palm Springs. The one thing you can rely on is that, for a large part of the year, they will be uniformly hot and dry. In fact, during the blazing summer months you'd be well advised to give them a miss altogether. And don't count on rain to cool things off – rainfall in this landscape is highly irregular and a whole year's average of three or four inches may fall in a single storm.

3

Most of the 39,000 square miles that make up the Californian deserts are protected in state and national parks, but not all are entirely empty. The US government uses vast areas as military bases for training and weapons testing, but in spite of this, most of the region remains an unspoiled wilderness, and could easily be the highlight of your trip to California.

The **Colorado Desert** (or **Low Desert**) in the south stretches down to the Mexican border and east into Arizona. Most visitors to the region head straight for **Palm Springs**, a few square miles overrun with the famous, the starstruck, the aspirational and, above all, the ageing. It is said, not completely in jest, that the average age and average temperature of Palm Springs are about the same – a steady 88. It's the sort of town that fines homeowners who don't maintain their property to a suitable standard. It's the first stopping point east from LA on I-10 and is the hub of the **Coachella Valley**, whose farming communities have the distinction of forming part of the most productive irrigated agricultural centre in the world, growing dates, oranges, lemons and grapefruit in vast quantities, though sadly they're steadily giving way to the region's ever-expanding condos and golf courses.

To see the desert at its natural best, head for **Joshua Tree**, one of the most bewitching of California's national parks and just three hours from LA. A day-trip from Palm Springs would give you a taste, but you really need a couple of days to fully appreciate Joshua Tree's haunting silent landscape, hiking among the weird craggy trees, experiencing the crimson sunsets, then camping out amid the enigmatic boulder stacks and the cries of coyotes. Further south, only the highly saline **Salton Sea** and the bizarre **Salvation Mountain** break the arid monotony before you reach

Highlights

❶ Palm Springs Modernism Soak up Palm Springs' mid-twentieth-century Modern architecture. Take the guided tour, attend Modernism Week, stay in a Modernist resort or just buy the map and drive around the gems in the residential districts. **See p.215**

❷ Living Desert Marvel at the desert's unique flora, fauna and culture at this combined zoo, botanic garden and museum in swanky Palm Desert. **See p.223**

❸ Joshua Tree National Park Unique freaky trees, gorgeous granite boulders and coyotes that howl in the warm night air make this an essential stop, especially if you have a tent. See p.228

❹ Salvation Mountain Surviving on little more than religious devotion, one man produced his personal monument to God, a bizarrely colourful synthesis of found objects, straw bales and paint. **See p.236**

❺ Borrego Palm Canyon An hour's stroll across the Anza-Borrego Desert brings you to one of the largest natural oases left in the United States, a dense cluster of over a thousand mop-headed fan palms beside a crisp stream. **See p.240**

❻ Historic Route 66 Trace a short stretch of the renowned Mother Road in search of classic Americana, such as *Roy's Motel & Café* in Amboy. **See p.247**

HIGHLIGHTS ARE MARKED ON THE MAP ON PP.206–207

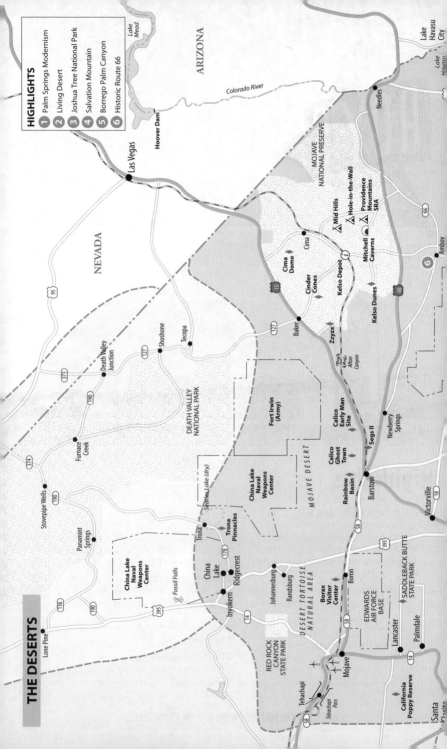

THE DESERTS

ARIZONA

NEVADA

Lake Mead

Hoover Dam

Las Vegas

Colorado River

Lake Havasu City

Lake Havasu

Needles

MOJAVE NATIONAL PRESERVE

Hole-in-the-Wall

Mid Hills

Providence Mountains SRA

Mitchell Caverns

Cima

Cima Dome

Cinder Cones

Kelso Depot

Kelso Dunes

Amboy

Baker

Zzyzx

Mojave Rd Afton Canyon

Shoshone

Tecopa

Death Valley Junction

DEATH VALLEY NATIONAL PARK

Furnace Creek

Stovepipe Wells

Panamint Springs

Searles Lake (dry)

Fossil Falls

Lone Pine

Fort Irwin (Army)

Calico Early Man Site

Calico Ghost Town

Segs II

Newberry Springs

Rainbow Basin

Barstow

Victorville

China Lake Naval Weapons Center

Trona

Trona Pinnacles

China Lake

Ridgecrest

Inyokern

Johannesburg

Randsburg

MOJAVE DESERT

Borax Visitor Center

Boron

EDWARDS AIR FORCE BASE

SADDLEBACK BUTTE STATE PARK

Lancaster

Palmdale

DESERT TORTOISE NATURAL AREA

RED ROCK CANYON STATE PARK

Mojave

Tehachapi

Tehachapi Pass

CALIFORNIA POPPY RESERVE

Santa

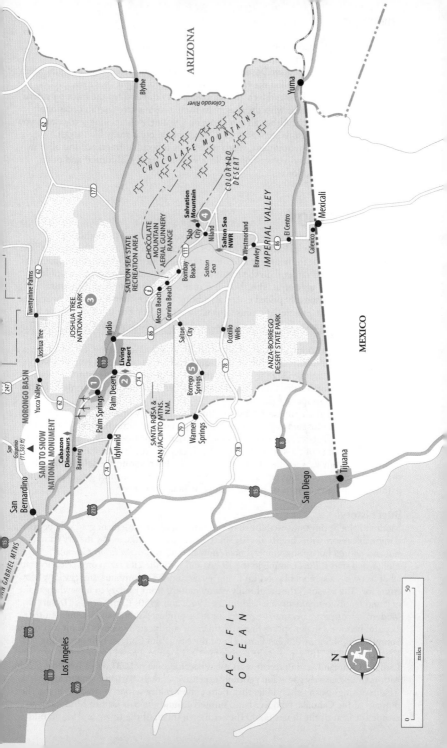

the **Anza-Borrego Desert**, whose starkly beautiful vistas are punctuated by several oases and unusual vegetation.

Virtually lifeless, the **Mojave Desert**, mythic badland of the West, has no equal when it comes to desolation. Called the **High Desert** because its height above sea level averages around two thousand feet, the Mojave is very dry and for the most part dead flat, dotted here and there with the shaggy form of a Joshua tree and an occasional abandoned miner's shed. Although it is short on genuinely compelling attractions, you should linger a little just to see – and smell – what a desert is really like: a vast, impersonal, extreme environment, sharp with its own peculiar fragrance and alive in spring with acres of fiery-orange poppies (the state flower of California) and other brightly coloured wildflowers.

Palm Springs

3

With its manicured golf courses, condominium complexes and thousands of millionaires in residence, **PALM SPRINGS** does not conform to any typical image of the desert. Purpose-built for luxury and leisure, it tends to attract conspicuous consumers and comfort seekers rather than the scruffier desert rats and low-rent retirees of less geographically desirable areas. But though it may seem harder to find the natural attractions and reasonably priced essentials among the glitz, they do exist; trawling the boutique shops, art galleries and museums while soaking up the sunshine can be fun, and there are few places in the US so associated with the intriguing "**Desert Modern**" style of the 1950s.

Downtown Palm Springs stretches for about half a mile along Palm Canyon Drive, a wide, bright and modern strip full of boutiques and restaurants that's engulfed the town's original Spanish-village-style structures. The **Uptown Design District** section, running along North Palm Canyon Drive from about Hermosa Place to Alejo Road is lined with stylish shops (see p.218).

Palm Springs isn't all rampant consumerism, though. It's worth spending time in the **Palm Springs Art Museum** and admiring the architecture of **Little Tuscany** (also known as the Heritage District and "the tennis club district"), just west of North Palm Canyon Drive, where some of the finest small hotels congregate. You'll soon want to stray further, best done by spending half a day riding the **Palm Springs Aerial Tramway** into the San Jacinto Mountains and strolling the easy trails, then returning to explore the palm-filled **Indian Canyons** or rugged beauty of **Tahquitz Canyon**.

Brief history

Modern Palm Springs was established in the 1880s, and the settlement gradually became a fashionable resort with "health tourists" in the early 1900s, attracted by the dry climate, sun and natural hot-springs mineral pool (now the site of the *Spa Resort Casino*). Hollywood stars started coming in the 1920s, and since then it's taken on a celebrity status all of its own – a symbol of good LA living away from the amorphous, smoggy city. Most come for "**The Season**", the delightfully balmy months from January to May when all the golf and tennis tournaments are held. In the 1940s and 1950s Palm Springs' "**Desert Modern**" architecture became the model for mass-produced suburban housing, but the city also became a major Spring Break destination; continued rowdiness meant that mayor **Sonny Bono** (of Sonny & Cher fame) closed the city's Palm Canyon Drive to Spring Breakers in 1990. The city was the setting for 1991's seminal novel *Generation X* by Douglas Coupland, and in recent years it has become a major **LGBT** resort (see box, p.210), with many exclusively gay – and generally expensive – hotels, bars and restaurants.

Palm Springs wasn't always like this. Before the wealthy settlers moved in, it was the domain of the **Cahuilla**, who lived and hunted around the San Jacinto Mountains to escape the heat of the desert floor. They still own much of the town, and via an odd

DESERT SURVIVAL

The desert is rarely conquered by pioneering spirit alone, and every year people die here from heat exhaustion and dehydration. Yet even in summer, lots of visitors do come to the deserts, when daytime temperatures frequently exceed 120°F (49°C). You'll appreciate travelling here more if you visit during the **cooler months**, from October to May, when daytime temperatures range from the mid-sixties to the low nineties, though night-time temperatures, particularly at high elevations, can drop to below freezing.

Loose, full-length clothing and a wide-brimmed hat will not only help shield you from the sun, but may also prevent bites, stings and scratches from desert flora and fauna (see pp.44–45). That said, many people travel the deserts in shorts, T-shirt and sunglasses, and get by quite happily.

Bear in mind too that while the desert may be a danger to man, man is also a danger to the desert. Smog from Los Angeles drifts quickly eastward and you may notice patches of it obscuring vistas here. To reduce your own impact, exercise common sense: remove nothing from the land except your rubbish and leave only footprints behind.

DRIVING THROUGH

If you're sticking to the main highways, filling your water containers and gas tank should be all the preparation you need. On steep gradients, there is a chance of getting an **overheated engine**. If your car's temperature gauge rises alarmingly, turn the air-conditioning off and the heater on full-blast to cool the engine quickly. If this fails and the engine blows, stop with the car facing into the wind and the engine running, pour water over the radiator grille, and top up the water reservoir. Also consider taking along a windshield reflector to keep the car cool when parked.

On less well-travelled routes it could be a long time before anyone comes along. Be sure you have plenty of food and drink and consider carrying an **emergency pack** with flares, a first-aid kit, matches and a compass, a shovel, extra gasoline and even a tyre pump. In an emergency, never leave the car: you'll be harder to find wandering around alone.

HIKING AND CAMPING

While heading off on a short walk doesn't require much preparation, **longer hikes** are limited by your inability to carry enough water. The following pointers should help you get back safely.
Register your plans If you get lost, find some shade and wait. So long as you've registered your itinerary, the rangers will eventually come and fetch you. In areas where registration is not required, tell somebody where you are going and your expected time of return.
Take a map and compass And know how to use them.
Hike when it's cool Avoid hiking when the mercury goes over 90°F (32°C). Early morning and late afternoon are the best times, though you could even go at night, especially when moonlit.
Take enough water The body can lose around 3–4 litres of water each day; even when you're not thirsty, you're continually dehydrating and you should keep drinking. As a rule, for a full-day hike take at least 4 litres, and don't save it for the walk back (assuming you have water waiting at the end of your hike). Waiting for thirst, dizziness, nausea or other signs of dehydration before doing anything can be dangerous. If you notice any of these symptoms, or feel weak and have stopped sweating, it's time to get to a doctor.
Take enough food Eat well, packing in the carbohydrates.
Camp safely Never camp in a wash (a dry creek or stream bed). Flash floods can appear from nowhere: an innocent-looking dark cloud can turn a dry wash into a raging river. And don't attempt to cross flooded areas until the water has receded.

chequerboard system of land allotment, every other square mile of Palm Springs is theirs and forms part of the **Agua Caliente Indian Reservation** – a Spanish name which means "hot water", referring to the ancient mineral springs on which the town rests. The land was allocated to the tribe in 1896, but exact zoning was never settled until the 1940s, by which time the development of hotels and leisure complexes was well under way. The Cahuilla, finding their land built upon, were left with no option but to charge rent, a system that has made them one of the richest of the native tribes in America – and the money continues to pour in, thanks in part to revenue from a new **spa** and the **casinos** of Coachella Valley.

3

LGBT PALM SPRINGS

Palm Springs now claims to have overtaken Key West as America's largest **gay resort**, with dozens of exclusively gay-clothing-optional inns and hotels flying the rainbow flag. With great weather almost all year round, it is hard to resist working on your tan by the pool all day while regaining your strength for dinner or a night around the clubs and bars.

The local press estimate that the LGBT community accounts for around forty to sixty percent of the town's residents; **Arenas Road**, near South Indian Canyon Drive, has become something of a gay village. Elsewhere businesses catering to a broader clientele are often gay-run and there's a general sense that the gay and straight communities coexist happily.

That said, in 2003 conservative city officials tried to shut down the event of the gay men's calendar, the White Party (see box, p.218), but the election of an openly gay mayor, Ron Oden, in November of that year brought a considerably warmer welcome for the revellers (Oden's successor and mayor until 2015, Steve Pougnet, is also gay, as is current mayor, Rob Moon). Lesbians get their turn a couple of weeks earlier during what's known as the Dinah Shore Weekend (see box, p.218), while later in the year the town hosts the Palm Springs Pride weekend (see box, p.218).

For information on other LGBT events, the local tourist machine puts out the free *Palm Springs Official Gay Visitors Guide* (🌐 visitgaypalmsprings.com).

PRACTICALITIES

Such is the power of the pink dollar in Palm Springs that virtually all hotels here are gay-friendly, though the Warm Sands district, half a mile southwest of downtown, contains around thirty exclusively **gay hotels**, most of them hedonistic fun palaces. More resorts populate the Deepwell neighbourhood to the south along San Lorenzo Rd and the Las Palmas area on North Palm Canyon Drive.

Hotel hosts are a mine of information about the trendiest restaurants and bars and will happily point you towards the sort of thing you're after, but restaurants with a strong gay following include *Shame on the Moon,* (see p.223) *Jake's* (see p.217) and *Johannes* (see p.217). For predominantly gay bars and clubs try *Hunter's* (see p.217) and *Toucans Tiki Lounge* (see p.217).

Village Green Heritage Center

221 S Palm Canyon Drive **Heritage Center** • Mid-Oct to May Wed & Sun noon–3pm, Thurs–Sat 10am–4pm • $2 • ☎ 760 323 8297, 🌐 palmsprings.com/history **Agua Caliente Cultural Museum** • June–Aug Fri–Sun 10am–5pm; Sept–May Wed–Sun 10am–5pm • Free • ☎ 760 778 1079, 🌐 accmuseum.org

The early history of Palm Springs is preserved at the **Village Green Heritage Center**, a small brick plaza around a fountain surrounded by two historic properties. The **McCallum Adobe**, the oldest building in Palm Springs, was built in 1884 for John McCallum, the first white settler, and is filled with old photos, paintings, clothing, tools and Native American artefacts. Next door is **Miss Cornelia's Little House**, built in 1893 from railroad ties and purchased by sisters Cornelia and Florilla White in 1913; it's now furnished with antiques from the pioneer era. Also on the plaza, the **Agua Caliente Cultural Museum** charts the history and culture of the local Agua Caliente Band of Cahuilla Indians, with a small but absorbing collection of basketry and pottery.

Palm Springs Art Museum

101 Museum Drive, at W Tahquitz Canyon Way • Tues, Wed & Fri–Sun 10am–5pm, Thurs noon–8pm • $12.50; free Thurs 4–8pm • ☎ 760 322 4800, 🌐 psmuseum.org

Don't miss the **Palm Springs Art Museum**, where the obvious wealth of its benefactors has been put to superb use in a striking Brutalist building complete with cactus-filled sculpture gardens. The focus is on both older and contemporary art, principally from California, though with wider-ranging Native American and Southwestern art too. Galleries with diverting exhibits surround a large central space, dotted with works by major sculptors such as Henry Moore, Barbara Hepworth and Alexander Calder. The mezzanine is usually devoted to Mesoamerican artworks often contrasting Classic-period figurines with more modern works, perhaps by twentieth-century Mexican muralists, Rivera, Orozco and Siqueiros. Spend a few minutes admiring the excellent contemporary **studio glass** collection with marvellous cast works such as Clifford Rainey's *Fragmented Shadow of Time* and Karen LaMonte's *Pianist's Dress Impression*. Look out, too, for Duane Hanson's unnervingly realistic *Old Couple on a Bench* – their watches even tell the time if the staff remember to change the batteries.

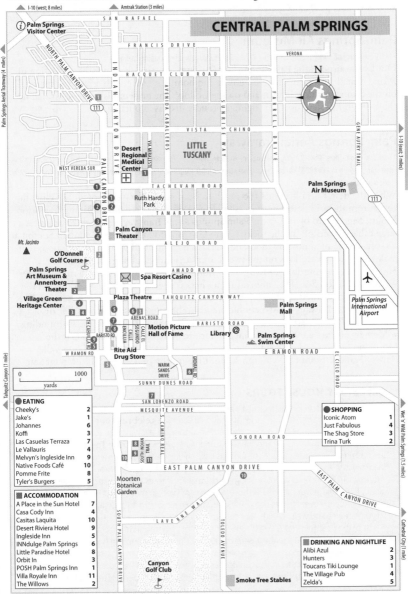

CENTRAL PALM SPRINGS

EATING
Cheeky's	2
Jake's	1
Johannes	6
Koffi	3
Las Casuelas Terraza	7
Le Vallauris	4
Melvyn's Ingleside Inn	9
Native Foods Café	10
Pomme Frite	8
Tyler's Burgers	5

ACCOMMODATION
A Place in the Sun Hotel	7
Casa Cody Inn	4
Casitas Laquita	10
Desert Riviera Hotel	9
Ingleside Inn	5
INNdulge Palm Springs	6
Little Paradise Hotel	8
Orbit In	3
POSH Palm Springs Inn	1
Villa Royale Inn	11
The Willows	2

SHOPPING
Iconic Atom	1
Just Fabulous	4
The Shag Store	3
Trina Turk	2

DRINKING AND NIGHTLIFE
Alibi Azul	2
Hunters	3
Toucans Tiki Lounge	1
The Village Pub	4
Zelda's	5

Moorten Botanical Garden & Cactarium

1701 S Palm Canyon Drive • Late Sept to late June Mon, Tues & Thurs–Sun 10am–4pm; late June to late Sept Mon, Tues & Thurs–Sun 9am–1pm • $5 • ☎ 760 327 6555, ⓦ moortenbotanicalgarden.com

Once you've cooled off indoors, check out Downtown Palm Springs' most anarchic piece of landscape gardening at **Moorten Botanical Garden & Cactarium**. Founded in 1938, this bizarre and somewhat shambolic cornucopia of just about every desert plant – cacti, succulents, dwarf trees etc – is interesting only for those who won't be venturing beyond town to see them in their natural habitat.

Palm Springs Air Museum

745 N Gene Autry Trail • Daily 10am–5pm • $16 • ☎ 760 778 6262, ⓦ palmspringsairmuseum.org

Out by the airport, the **Palm Springs Air Museum** contains an impressive collection of World War II European and US fighters and bombers, along with associated material on the campaigns they flew in and on their pilots. The museum is easily identified by the F-14 and F-16 "Top Gun" fighters proudly displayed outside.

Palm Springs Aerial Tramway

1 Tram Way • Mon–Thurs 10am–9.45pm, Fri–Sun 8am–10.30pm; closed Sept for maintenance • $25.95; $36 with dinner at *Pines Café* (after 4pm); parking $5 • ☎ 888 515 8726, ⓦ pstramway.com • 4 miles southwest of Hwy-111 on Tram Way (6 miles from downtown); no public transport, taxis around $30

When the desert heat becomes too much to bear, you can travel through five climatic zones from the arid desert floor to (sometimes) snow-covered alpine hiking trails atop Mount San Jacinto by riding the **Palm Springs Aerial Tramway**. Every thirty minutes a large cable car sets off up the rocky Chino Canyon, bound for the Mountain Station at 8516ft – a rise of almost six thousand feet. Each car is fitted with a rotating floor that makes two full revolutions on the twelve-minute journey, giving breathtaking 360-degree views outdone only by those from the top, which stretch 75 miles all the way to the Salton Sea. The temperature up here is a welcome 30°F cooler than in the valley, so bring something to keep warm, or hide indoors where you can watch a decent video on the tramway's construction or relax in the cafeteria-style *Pines Café*, or fine-dining *Peaks Restaurant* (☎760 325 4537). To stray further into the surrounding wilderness of the 14,000-acre **Mount San Jacinto State Park** (see p.219), exit the Mountain Station and descend a concrete pathway less than a mile to Long Valley Ranger Station. From here you can summit the nearby peak of 10,834ft **Mount San**

CELEBRITY HOUSE TOURS

Knowing that they're in the thick of a megastar hideaway, few can resist the opportunity to see the homes and country clubs of the international elite on a **celebrity tour** of Palm Springs. As tacky as they are, these tours have some voyeuristic appeal, allowing you to spy on places like Bob Hope's enormous house and the star-studded area known as **Little Tuscany** – Palm Springs' prettiest quarter, where the famous keep their weekend homes (crooner Barry Manilow is still spotted around town). The tours only view the houses through the minibus window, but in the end it's not the homes that make the tours worthwhile but rather the fascinating trivia about the lives of those who live (or lived) in them. Most of the big names had their heyday over fifty years ago (Kirk Douglas, Frank Sinatra and Liz Taylor among them) so you'll need to be well up with your classic movies to really appreciate the fine detail.

Best of the Best Tours (☎760 320 1365, ⓦ thebestofthebesttours.com) conduct entertaining jaunts around Palm Springs (daily; $40; 1hr 30min), driving past enough homes to satiate most people's celebrity craving.

Of course, if you've got a car, you can do it yourself with a *Map of the Stars' Homes* from the visitor centre (see p.214), but you'll miss the sharp anecdotal commentary that makes it such fun.

MOVIE MEMORIES IN PALM SPRINGS?

An upcoming attraction in Palm Springs will have more in common with Hollywood than the desert. Assuming funds are raised, the **Motion Picture Hall of Fame** (ⓦmotionpicturehall offame.info), 296 S Palm Canyon Drive, should be open by 2017 or 2018, featuring a large exhibition hall of movie memorabilia and regular Hall of Fame induction ceremonies.

Jacinto (5.5 miles one-way), or explore a number of other shorter forest trails; the three-quarter-mile Discovery Trail loop and the mile-and-a-half Desert View Trail, with views down onto the Coachella Valley below (note that free wilderness permits are required from the Ranger Station for trails beyond the valley). In winter, if there's been enough snow, you can rent ski and snowshoe equipment from the **Adventure Center**, a short distance from the bottom of the concrete pathway (see p.214).

Indian Canyons

3

38500 S Palm Canyon Drive • Oct–June daily 8am–5pm; July–Sept Fri–Sun 8am–5pm • $9 • ☎ 760 323 6018, ⓦ indian-canyons.com • Drive along S Palm Canyon Drive for about 3 miles south to the clearly signposted entrance, from where paved roads run to the entrances of each of the canyons

The best known and most accessible of the Palm Springs canyons are Palm Canyon, Andreas Canyon and Murray Canyon, known collectively as **Indian Canyons**, on part of the Agua Caliente Indian Reservation that lies to the south of downtown. Centuries ago, ancestors of the Cahuilla tribe settled in the canyons and developed extensive communities, made possible by the good water supply and animal stock. They grew crops of melons, squash, beans and corn, hunted animals, and gathered plants and seeds for food and medicines. Evidence of this remains, and mountain sheep still roam the remoter areas despite the near extinction of some breeds.

The most popular target is fifteen-mile-long **Palm Canyon**, which comes choked with palms – some three thousand over seven miles – beside a seasonal stream along which runs the easy 1.5-mile Palm Canyon Trail. A one-mile loop visits the best of **Andreas Canyon**, noted for its rock formations and more popular than **Murray Canyon**, which is difficult to reach but offers a twelve-foot waterfall as a reward for those prepared to hike two miles. A tiny trading post at Palm Canyon sells hiking maps, refreshments and assorted native crafts, but to indulge in real Wild West fantasy you should see things on **horseback** (see p.214) – well worth it, especially if you go in the early morning to escape the midday heat.

Tahquitz Canyon

500 W Mesquite Ave • Oct–June daily 7.30am–5pm; July–Sept Fri–Sun 8am–5pm • $12.50 • Free guided tours (8am, 10am, noon and 2pm) • ☎ 760 416 7044, ⓦ tahquitzcanyon.com

After years of hippie colonization and subsequent abandonment, the Agua Caliente Cahuilla Indians now manage the **Tahquitz Canyon**, where the visitor centre contains a small artefact-filled museum and a theatre showing a video on the canyon's shamanic legend. Either take a self-guided hike in the palmless canyon itself, or join one of the free guided tours, which spend around two and a half hours hiking through entrancing desert country and past a sixty-foot waterfall.

ARRIVAL AND DEPARTURE   PALM SPRINGS

By car Palm Springs lies 110 miles east of Los Angeles along Hwy-111. Arriving by car, off I-10 exit 120, you'll reach the town on N Palm Canyon Drive, the main thoroughfare.

By train Amtrak trains arrive at a desolate platform three miles north of Palm Springs on Palm Springs Station Rd (at

N Indian Canyon Drive), half a mile south of I-10. A taxi to downtown will cost around $17–20, but you'll need to reserve one in advance (see p.214).

Destinations Los Angeles (3 weekly; 3hr 33min), New Orleans (3 weekly; 43hr 4min), San Antonio (3 weekly; 26hr 14min), Tucson (3 weekly; 6hr 52min).

DINOSAURS AND WINDMILLS

After trawling through the dull eastern suburbs of Los Angeles, I-10 throws you a couple of surprises at the San Gorgonio Pass. First up, seventeen miles before Palm Springs, are the **Cabazon Dinosaurs** (☎951 922 8700, ⓦcabazondinosaurs.com), two massive fibreglass beasts (claimed to be the world's biggest) flanking the highway. Kids might persuade you to part with $10 ($9 children) to enter the World's Biggest Dinosaurs Museum (Mon–Fri 9.30am–7.30pm, Sat & Sun 9am–8pm), 50770 Seminole Drive, Cabazon, or you could just visit the gift shop in the belly of the 150-foot-long apatosaurus that's full of creationist nonsense about the "intelligent design" of dinosaurs.

A mile on, you'll see over three thousand **wind turbines** dotting the valley ahead, their glinting steel arms sending shimmering patterns across the desert floor. Along with Tehachapi Pass (see p.244), this is one of the largest concentrations of windmills in the country, generating enough electricity to service a small city, and the conditions are perfect. The sun beating down on the desert creates a low-pressure zone that sucks air up from the cooler coastal valleys, funnelling it through the San Gorgonio Pass, the only break between two 10,000-foot-plus ranges of mountains. Strong winds often howl for days in spring and early summer, reaching an average speed of between fourteen and twenty miles per hour.

Palm Springs Windmill Tours (☎442 333 7188, ⓦwindmilltours.com) run 1hr 45min tours (Wed, Sat & Sun 9am; $49) making a circuit of the bases of the towers and plying you with facts. Casual observers will be happy just driving by or stopping for a few snaps.

By bus Greyhound buses now stop at the SunLine Transit bus station, 72-480 Varner Rd in Thousand Palms, an inconvenient 9 miles east of Downtown Palm Springs. Take a taxi (around $40) or SunLine bus #32. For all major destinations in the Coachella Valley (between Palm Springs and Coachella and Mecca, on the Salton Sea), SunLine Transit (☎800 347 8628, ⓦsunline.org) operates daily from 6am to 8pm (until 11pm on some routes) and charge $1/ride, plus an extra 25¢ for transfers (unlimited within two hours of purchase); a day-pass costs $3.

Destinations by Greyhound Calexico (Mexican border; 3 daily; 2hr 50min–3hr 5min); Indio (3 daily; 35min); Los Angeles (3 daily; 2hr 30min–3hr 30min).

By plane Several airlines serve Palm Springs International Airport, 3400 E Tahquitz Canyon Way (☎760 318 3800), where you can take a taxi (it's just two miles to Palm Canyon Drive, around $9–10) or catch bus #24 then transfer to the #111 into town. Tickets are often expensive, and if you're flying to California it is usually cheaper to fly into Los Angeles and rent a car from there.

INFORMATION AND ACTIVITIES

Palm Springs Visitor Center On the approach to town from I-10, 2901 N Palm Canyon Drive (daily 9am–5pm; ☎800 347 7746, ⓦvisitpalmsprings.com). You can't miss the visitor centre installed in a revamped, former gas station designed by Mid-Century Modern leading light Albert Frey.

Horseriding Smoke Tree Stables, 2500 Toledo Ave (☎760 327 1372, ⓦsmoketreestables.com), offers scheduled one-hour ($50) and two-hour ($100) riding tours of the Indian Canyons. Tours start at 8am daily; closed late June to early Sept. Longer rides are available by advance arrangement.

Skiing and snowshoeing From Nov 15 until April 15, snow conditions permitting, the Adventure Center (Thurs, Fri & Mon 10am–4pm, Sat & Sun 9am–4pm) in Long Valley – reached via the aerial tramway – offers cross-country skiing ($21/day) and snowshoeing ($18/day).

GETTING AROUND

By bus Downtown Palm Springs is only a few blocks long and a couple of blocks wide and is manageable on foot. SunLine Transit (see above) operates local buses for longer trips. While the system is extensive and services fairly frequent, it is never a quick way to get about and you may prefer a taxi (see below).

By taxi Call American Cab (☎760 322 4444). Meters start at $3, plus $3.12/mile. Uber's base fare is $1, with $1.15/mile plus $0.15/minute and a minimum of $5.50.

By car To get the absolute best out of Palm Springs and the surrounding towns you should think about car rental. All the major companies are at the airport; Enterprise at 4041 Airport Center Drive (Mon–Fri 8am–6pm, Sat 9am–noon; ☎760 327 2699) often rents cars from $35–45/day.

By bike If you're not planning to stray too far, rent a bike or tandem from Bike Palm Springs, 194 S Indian Canyon Drive (☎760 832 8912, ⓦbikepsrentals.com; closed June–Aug), from $23/half day.

ACCOMMODATION

Palm Springs was designed for the rich, and big luxury **resorts** and country clubs are everywhere. Comfort and style also come in large doses at smaller and very tasteful hotels. Don't fight it: even if such places are outside your normal budget this is a place to splurge. You may find them surprisingly affordable if you **visit in summer** (May–Sept) when temperatures rise and prices drop dramatically (the rates listed below are for the cheapest doubles in winter). If you couldn't care less about cachet, **low-priced motel chains** are liberally represented. Regardless of where you stay, no Palm Springs lodging is without a **pool**.

If you're travelling in a group, it may work out cheaper to rent an **apartment/condo**: check with agencies such as Vacation Palm Springs (☎0800 590 3110, ⓦvacationpalmsprings.com), Palm Springs Rental Agency (☎0800 875 0885, ⓦpalmspringsrentals.com) and ⓦairbnb.com. One-bedroom places start around $110 a night or $450 a week.

HOTELS

A Place in the Sun Hotel 754 San Lorenzo Rd ☎760 325 0254, ⓦaplaceinthesunhotel.com; map p.211. Built in the early 1950s as a retreat for the production crew of the film *A Place in the Sun*, starring Elizabeth Taylor, this is a popular (pet-friendly) option set around a palm-fringed salt-water pool, with comfy studios and bungalows featuring rattan furniture and bright, snappy colours. **$119**

Casa Cody Inn 175 S Cahuilla Rd ☎760 320 9346, ⓦcasacody.com; map p.211. Built in the 1920s by glamorous Hollywood pioneer Harriet Cody (Buffalo Bill's cousin), this historic B&B offers tastefully furnished Southwestern-style rooms, a shady garden, great pool and tasty buffet breakfasts in a good location two blocks from downtown. All options but the "rooms" have a kitchen.

Families and small groups should go for the gorgeous two-bedroom adobe cottage ($429). **$99**

Desert Riviera Hotel 610 E Palm Canyon Drive ☎760 327 5314, ⓦdesertrivierahotel.com; map p.211. Palm Springs most popular hotel for good reason, a 1951 gem with lush gardens, mountain views, heated pool, jacuzzi and simple, but cosy rooms with a host of nice little extras (like a welcome basket of tasty treats). **$229**

Ingleside Inn 200 W Ramon Rd ☎1800 772 6655, ⓦinglesideinn.com; map p.211. Set in a serene enclave a couple of blocks from downtown, this loosely Spanish-style inn is the last of Palm Springs' original hotels, dating from 1935. It once drew the likes of Garbo, Dalí and Brando and still has enough real class to lure the glitterati. Each room is different, but all have a restrained elegance, often with

PALM SPRINGS' DESERT MODERN ARCHITECTURE

Palm Springs' popularity among the rich and famous during the Forties, Fifties and Sixties saw a massive building boom. The more discerning newcomers employed young, Modernist architects such as Richard Neutra, who was "governed by the goal of building environmental harmony, functional efficiency, and human enhancement into the experience of everyday living". His work, and that of contemporaries Albert Frey and R.M. Schindler, became known as **Mid-Century Modern**, with its expression in these parts often dubbed Desert Modern or even Palm Springs Modern. After several decades in the architectural wilderness, Palm Springs has seen a surge of interest in its soaring rooflines, glass walls, unity of form and sympathy for the desert setting. The town's renewed cachet means long-ignored houses by the movement's luminaries are now highly sought after. Many can be viewed from the road by driving the route on the *Palm Springs Modern map* ($5) from the visitor centre; don't miss the 1959 Bank of America at 588 S Palm Canyon Drive (still a bank), Palm Springs City Hall, constructed between 1952 and 1957 (3200 E Tahquitz Canyon Way), and Palm Springs Post Office, built in 1970 at 330 W Amado Rd. You'll see a lot more (and learn fascinating details about the architects and their clients) by joining Palm Springs Modern Tours (☎760 318 6118, ⓦpalmspringsmoderntours.com). Their three-hour minivan tours ($85) visit the exteriors of assorted residential, commercial and civic buildings, including Richard Neutra's 1946 Kaufmann House (designed for Edgar Kaufmann, who commissioned Frank Lloyd Wright's Fallingwater in Pennsylvania); the 1968 Elrod Residence, with its spectacular living room used for scenes in the Bond flick *Diamonds are Forever*; and the 1962 House of Tomorrow, which later became Elvis and Priscilla's "Honeymoon Hideaway". Tours run all year on demand, but less frequently in summer.

If you're really keen, plan your visit around **Modernism Week** (ⓦmodernismweek.com), in mid- to late February, when there are double-decker bus tours, talks, movie showings and cocktail parties in fabulous houses. Book events and accommodation months in advance.

3

PALM SPRINGS POOLS & SPAS

Agua Caliente Casino Resort Spa 32-250 Bob Hope Drive, Rancho Mirage ☎ 760 202 2121, ⓦ hotwatercasino.com. For a wonderfully relaxing experience, visit the luxurious day-spa at the Agua Caliente Casino in nearby Rancho Mirage (see p.223). Here, $30 gives you a sauna, spa pool, steam and eucalyptus rooms, and as much time in the fitness centre as you desire. You're encouraged, of course, to spend a lot more on massages (from $89) and assorted skin and body care treatments (from $130), and at the on-site casino. Spa daily 9am–7pm.

Palm Springs Swim Center 405 S Pavilion Way (in Sunrise Plaza) ☎ 760 323 8278, ⓦ palmsprings-ca .gov. If your hotel facilities aren't large enough, make straight for this Olympic-sized pool managed by the city ($5, kids 4–12 $3). Mon–Fri 5.30–8.30am & 11am–7pm, Sat & Sun 7am–5pm.

Wet 'n Wild 1500 Gene Autry Trail ☎ 760 327 0499, ⓦ wetnwildpalmsprings.com. Cool off at this 16-acre water park, where you can surf on a one-acre wave pool and mess around on numerous waterslides. Buy tickets online for discounts ($38.99, kids 3–11 $27.99; parking $10). March to mid-Oct daily 10am–6pm (check website for monthly variations).

antiques. Of course there are private patios and a lovely pool, and the excellent *Melvyn's Restaurant* is on site (see opposite). **$143**

★ **Orbit In** 562 W Arenas Rd ☎ 877 996 7248, ⓦ orbitin .com; map p.211. Modernist nirvana with two nearly adjacent locations: the super-stylish nine-room *Orbit In* itself, built in 1957, with its boomerang bar beside a chilled pool (where complimentary Orbitinis are served); and the more secluded 1940s "Hideaway", with lawns, a fire pit and guest kitchen/lounge. Cruise town on the free bikes or relax in rooms equipped with DVD and CD player. It's adults-only and a two-night stay is required. Orbit In **$169**, Hideway **$179**

★ **POSH Palm Springs Inn** 530 E Mel Ave ☎ 760 992 5410, ⓦ poshpalmsprings.com; map p.211. Cosy B&B downtown, with friendly owners Tony and Santo, superb breakfasts and happy hour (4–5pm) featuring the celebrated POSH martinis. The 1930s-inspired rooms are arranged around a pool patio, with two featuring kitchens. **$225**

Villa Royale Inn 1620 S Indian Trail ☎ 1800 245 2314, ⓦ villaroyale.com; map p.211. Beautiful inn with individually designed and exquisitely furnished rooms and suites, most with jacuzzi, situated around a pool. In the winter season meals and drinks are served from the romantic, bougainvillea-draped *Europa* restaurant. **$245**

The Willows 412 W Tahquitz Canyon ☎ 1800 966 9597, ⓦ thewillowspalmsprings.com; map p.211. Built in 1925, this was once the estate of legendary New York attorney Samuel Untermyer, whose friends – among them Clark Gable, Carole Lombard and Albert Einstein – holed up here during the 1930s. Opulently decorated rooms, gorgeous lush grounds, a stunning Mount San Jacinto backdrop, sumptuous breakfasts and an ideal downtown location make this well worth the splurge. **$385**

GAY ACCOMMODATION

Casitas Laquita 450 E Palm Canyon Drive ☎ 760 416 9999, ⓦ casitaslaquita.com; map p.211. A private women's resort in a rustic Southwestern-styled compound decorated with Native American crafts and motifs. All rooms have kitchen, private bathroom, and TV and CD players; some come with a fireplace. Breakfast ingredients are delivered to your room. **$165**

INNdulge Palm Springs 601 Grenfall Rd ☎ 760 327 1408, ⓦ inndulge.com; map p.211. Award-winning clothing-optional gay men's resort in the heart of Warm Sands, one of the most popular gay areas of Palm Springs, with stylish rooms equipped with DVD players – and full kitchens in all suites. Doubles **$109**, suites **$159**

Little Paradise Hotel 435 Avenida Olancha ☎ 855 855 3130, ⓦ littleparadisehotel.com; map p.211. The former *Queen of Hearts* is no longer a strictly lesbian resort, but remains very LGBT friendly, with just nine rooms around a great heated pool, private mist-cooled patio, free bikes and gorgeous views of the Santa Rosa Mountains. **$195**

CAMPGROUNDS

Whitewater Preserve 9160 Whitewater Canyon Rd, 17 miles north of Palm Springs and 5 miles north of I-10 ☎ 760 325 7222; map p.220. Basic tent camping (water and toilets but no showers) beside a year-round stream on a former trout farm now run as a nonprofit wildlife preserve. Open all year. Permits required (phone or in person; free), but camping is free (max 3 days). **Free**

EATING

Palm Springs **restaurants** run the gamut from moneyed elegance to fast food, with some good international options in between. Several of the best places shut up shop entirely in July and August, while those that stay open often offer substantial discounts – a good time to indulge. Only at the finest restaurants need you book in summer, but in winter places fill up quickly and **reservations** are essential.

RESTAURANTS

Cheeky's 622 N Palm Canyon Drive ☎760 327 7595, ⓦcheekysps.com; map p.211. *The* place for breakfast, using seasonal, local and organic ingredients for the likes of fresh peach sourdough french toast ($11), or one of their half-dozen types of bacon – or even a bacon flight ($5). Also inventive lunches. Wed–Mon 8am–2pm (closed Wed June–Sept).

Jake's 664 N Palm Canyon Drive ☎760 327 4400, ⓦjakespalmsprings.com; map p.211. Dine on the lovely mist-cooled patio or in the main restaurant on beautifully constructed lunchtime sandwiches and salads (around $12–15), and dinners that might include pork chop in blackberry gastrique (caramelized sugar) and garlic mashed potatoes ($24). Tues–Thurs 11am–2.45pm & 5–8.45pm, Fri 11am–2.45pm & 5.30–9.45pm, Sat 10am–2.45pm & 5.30–9.45pm, Sun 10am–2.45pm (closed June–Sept).

★**Johannes** 196 S Indian Canyon Drive ☎760 778 0017, ⓦjohannesrestaurants.com; map p.211. The best of the modern, downtown restaurants, this unpretentious place offers superb-quality Asian and Austrian dishes – schnitzel is a speciality ($22). Mains might include crispy roasted half duck ($32) or even organic chicken curry ($22). Tues–Sun 5–10pm.

Las Casuelas Terraza 222 S Palm Canyon Drive ☎760 325 2794, ⓦlascasuelas.com; map p.211. *Las Casuelas* opened its original establishment in 1958, but you can't beat this Spanish-Colonial-style sister restaurant for its bustling atmosphere, stacks of mist-cooled outdoor seating centred on a palm-roofed bar, and usually some live entertainment. The food suffers from north-of-the-border blanding but is still tasty, and with combination plates for $14 and $5.75 margaritas it's not too expensive. Mon–Fri 11am–10pm, Sat & Sun 8am–10pm.

Le Vallauris 385 W Tahquitz Canyon Way ☎760 325 5059, ⓦlevallauris.com; map p.211. Landmark French-Mediterranean restaurant with famed patio lined with giant ficus trees and pianist at the bar. Decor includes Flemish tapestries and Louis XV furniture but there's nothing stuffy

about the impeccable service or superb food. Main courses are $19–34 at lunch, $36–48 at dinner, plus there's a *prix fixe* menu ($59) and Sunday brunch ($49.50). Daily 11.30am–2.30pm & 5–10.30pm (closed July & Aug).

Melvyn's Ingleside Inn 200 W Ramon Rd ☎760 325 2323, ⓦinglesideinn.com; map p.211. This classical continental restaurant is old-fashioned in the best possible way – elegant, understated and serving beautifully prepared dishes such as their signature veal with avocado and mousseline sauce. Most dinner mains run $23–35. Book in advance and leave time for a cocktail or two in the intimate bar beforehand. Piano accompaniment, dancing and celebrity-spotting are de rigueur. Mon–Fri 11.30am–3pm & 6pm–2am, Sat & Sun 9am–3pm & 6pm–2am.

Pomme Frite 256 S Palm Canyon Drive ☎760 778 3727, ⓦpomme-frite.com; map p.211. Semi-casual French-Belgian joint that lends an air of Europe to Downtown Palm Springs. Kick off with steamed artichoke ($9.95), perhaps followed by a pot of steamed mussels ($19.99) or Belgian beef stew ($19.95). Daily 5–10.30pm.

★**Tyler's Burgers** 149 S Indian Canyon Drive ☎760 325 2990, ⓦtylersburgers.com; map p.211. Awesome old-fashioned burgers (from $7.50), fries and classic home-made coleslaw ($3.50) at modest prices either inside or on the patio. Cash only. Mon–Sat 11am–4pm (closed Aug).

CAFÉS

Koffi 515 N Palm Canyon Drive ☎760 416 2244, ⓦkofficoffee.com; map p.211. The best espresso around (served in real cups if you wish), plus nice garden seating out back. Daily 6am–6pm.

Native Foods Café 1775 E Palm Canyon Drive (Smoke Tree Village Mall) ☎760 416 0070, ⓦnativefoods.com; map p.211. This totally vegan chain café puts a creative twist on traditional vegetarian fare. An eclectic menu, including tacos, pizzas, salads and a variety of veggie burgers, and modest prices (average $10–11) make it a worthwhile spot. Daily 11am–9pm.

DRINKING AND NIGHTLIFE

Palm Springs' main drag is particularly crowded on Thursday evenings, when the surprisingly lively **VillageFest** street fair (Oct–May 6–10pm; June–Sept 7–10pm; ⓦpalmspringsvillagefest.com) draws equal numbers of tourists and young locals. Traffic is temporarily barred from half a dozen blocks of N Palm Canyon Drive, which sprouts a kids' play-zone and booths selling everything from fresh-baked bread to tacky souvenirs and local crafts. Visit ⓦwww.palmspringslife .com for news on the current events and nightlife situation.

Alibi Azul 369 N Palm Canyon Drive ☎760 325 5533, ⓦalibiazul.com; map p.211. The perfect spot for watching the action along Palm Canyon Drive is the patio here (at the 1934 General Telephone building), where the whole table-and-seats ensemble gently swings. Go easy on the cocktails as you tuck into their tapas-style small plates. Daily 11am–midnight.

Hunters 302 E Arenas Drive ☎760 323 0700, ⓦhunterspalmsprings.com; map p.211. Large and lively gay bar and dance club that's the mainstay of the LGBT scene with everything from trivia quizzes, pool table and all-day happy hour (until 7pm) to raunchy catwalk shows. Daily 10am–2am.

Toucans Tiki Lounge 2100 N Palm Canyon Drive

3

☎760 416 7584, ⓦtoucanstikilounge.com; map p.211. The best gay dance-bar in town with a lively scene most nights – DJs, drag shows, 80s nights, etc – particularly on Fridays and Saturdays when go-go boys and girls heat things up. Mon, Tues, Thurs & Fri 2pm–2am, Wed 2–8pm, Sat & Sun noon–2am.

The Village Pub 266 S Palm Canyon Drive ☎760 323 3265, ⓦpalmspringsvillagepub.com; map p.211. Worthwhile as a restaurant, with lots of salads, pizzas and burgers at reasonable prices, but best for a few drinks (13

brews on tap) and a little dancing at the upstairs Loft (Thurs–Sat). Live music nightly and no cover. Daily 10am–2am.

Zelda's 611 S Palm Canyon Drive ☎760 325 2375, ⓦzeldasnightclub.com; map p.211. There's not much of a cutting edge at Palm Springs' main nightclub, but the venue is pretty flash and there's always a fun atmosphere with a broad-spectrum crowd dancing to Top 40, hip-hop, retro and whatever guest DJs put together. Dress up. Tues & Thurs–Sat 9pm–2am.

ENTERTAINMENT

Annenberg Theater 101 Museum Drive ☎760 325 4490, ⓦpsmuseum.org; map p.211. Situated inside Palm Springs Art Museum (see p.223), this theatre has a seasonal programme of shows, films and classical concerts. Box office Wed–Fri 10am–4pm.

Palm Canyon Theatre 538 N Palm Canyon Drive ☎760

323 5123, ⓦpalmcanyontheatre.org; map p.211. The city's premier venue for live theatre and touring musicals – 2017's line-up included *Evita*, *Rock of Ages* and *In the Heights*. Nov–May most days at 1.30pm & 7pm. Box office Tues–Sat 10am–4pm.

SHOPPING

Iconic Atom 1103 N Palm Canyon Drive ☎760 322 0777, ⓦtrinaturk.com. This vintage store has a cult following, with an artfully curated selection of clothes, jewellery, art and knick-knacks from the 1950s to the 1970s. Fri–Sun 10am–6pm.

Just Fabulous 515 N Palm Canyon Drive ☎760 864 1300. A bookshop, gift shop and home decor store which is also particularly strong on Palm Springs architecture. Mon–Fri 9am–5pm, Sat & Sun 9am–6pm.

The Shag Store 725 N Palm Canyon Drive ☎760 322 3400, ⓦshagthestore.com. Store and gallery dedicated

to 1950s pop art-inspired artist Shag (aka Josh Agle), selling prints, original art, books and other merchandise from cocktail napkins to cigarette lighters (think *Pink Panther* cartoon). Mon–Thurs 10am–5pm, Fri–Sun 10am–8pm.

Trina Turk 891 N Palm Canyon Drive ☎760 416 2856, ⓦtrinaturk.com. Local designer Trina Turk's flagship store is crammed with her "California chic" fashion (for men and women), housed in the 1960s low-slung, glass-walled Albert Frey building. Mon–Fri 10am–5pm, Sat 10am–6pm, Sun 11am–5pm.

PALM SPRINGS FESTIVALS AND EVENTS

If you're around in mid-January, don't miss out on the **Palm Springs International Film Festival** (ⓦpsfilmfest.org), which brings more nightlife to the city than the rest of the year combined, while the sister **International Festival of Short Films** runs in September. The town's gay community drives some of the bigger annual events: the **White Party** (ⓦjeffreysanker.com) in April or May is the single biggest event of the gay year, when over fifteen thousand men flock to Palm Springs for four days of hedonism centred on the *Renaissance Hotel*. It's been going since 1989 and has grown to the point where there are A-list celebrity shows and nonstop parties throughout the four days (often in and around hotel pools). The biggest event, an all-nighter of epic proportions (9pm–7am), is held on the Saturday at the Palm Springs Convention Center (from $160). A three-day weekend pass giving access to the four major events goes for around $375 and up. **Palm Springs Pride** (☎760 416 8711, ⓦpspride.org) takes place on the first weekend in November, drawing gay crowds for three days of entertainment, a street parade and more partying. The **Dinah Shore Weekend** (or just "the Dinah"; ⓦthedinah.com; weekend passes from $250 for 7 parties) in late March or early April is a major five-day lesbian fiesta that traditionally coincides with the ANA Inspiration Championship golf tournament held at Mission Hills Country Club (in Rancho Mirage) on the Dinah Shore Tournament Course, named for her contribution to the game. The tournament ranks second only to the US Women's Open on the LPGA Tour, but golf often plays second fiddle to the numerous hotel pool parties throughout Palm Springs and the Coachella Valley, at what has become the world's biggest lesbian vacation event. The major music festival, **Coachella**, is held in April (see p.222).

GETTING AROUND THE DESERT

Public transport in the desert is poor. Los Angeles connects easily with the major points – Palm Springs, Barstow, Las Vegas – but without your own vehicle you're stuck upon arrival. If you have a car, it will need to be in good working order. While the $500 banger you picked up in LA might be fine for the freeways, don't expect it to cope with the worst of the desert. Three major interstate **highways** cross the desert from west to east. I-15 cuts directly northeast through the middle of the Mojave on its way from Los Angeles to Las Vegas, passing through Barstow where I-40 heads eastwards to the Grand Canyon. I-10 takes you from LA through the Palm Springs and Joshua Tree area, heading into southern Arizona. Some fast, empty secondary roads can get you safely to all but the most remote areas of the desert, but be wary of using the lower-grade roads in between, which are likely to be unmaintained and are often only passable with four-wheel drive.

Other than in the Palm Springs area, basic **motels** in the California deserts are cheap, and you can generally budget for $50–75/night. However, even if cost is no object, you'll get a greatly heightened sense of the desert experience by spending some time **camping** out.

3

DIRECTORY

Hospital Desert Regional Medical Center, 1150 N Indian Canyon Drive ☎ 760 323 6511, ⓦ desertregional.com.
Library Palm Springs Public Library, 300 S Sunrise Way (Mon & Thurs 10am–6pm, Tues & Wed 10am–8pm, Fri & Sat 10am–5pm; ☎ 760 322 7323, ⓦ palmspringsca.gov).

Offers free internet access.
Pharmacy Rite Aid Drug Store, 366 S Palm Canyon Drive; open 24hr.
Post office 333 E Amado Rd (Mon–Fri 8am–5pm, Sat 9am–3pm).

Around Palm Springs

As the largest desert community by far, Palm Springs makes an obvious base for exploring the surrounding regions, particularly the towns of the **Coachella Valley** and Idyllwild, a small mountain resort set among the pines high above Palm Springs that's also ideal for weekend retreats from LA.

Idyllwild

Five thousand feet up the slopes of Mount San Jacinto, **IDYLLWILD** is the perfect antidote to the in-your-face success of Palm Springs, fifty road-miles away. Pine-fresh, cool and snow-covered in winter, this small alpine town of about two thousand inhabitants has only a few chalet-style restaurants and hotels, but has developed a reputation as an arts hub in recent years. The **Idyllwild International Festival of Cinema** (ⓦ idyllwildcinemafest.com) is an indie movie festival held every January, while the **Stratford Players** (ⓦ stratfordplayers.com) have been performing live theatre at a variety of venues here since 2013.

Mount San Jacinto State Park & San Bernardino National Forest

State Park Headquarters 25905 Hwy-243 • Staffed intermittently Mon–Fri 8am–4pm • ☎ 951 659 2607, ⓦ parks.ca.gov **Idyllwild Ranger Station** (National Forest) 54270 Pine Crest Ave, at Hwy-243 • Fri–Tues 8am–noon & 1–4pm • ☎ 909 382 2921, ⓦ fs.usda.gov/sbnf

The main activity in Idyllwild is to set out on the magnificent trails of **Mount San Jacinto State Park** or the surrounding wilderness of the **San Bernardino National Forest**. Note that in recent years this section of the forest has been badly impacted by **forest fires** – check the latest in Palm Springs.

The Forest Service's **Idyllwild Ranger Station** has stacks of information about hiking and camping in the area. Free day-use hiking passes for the state park or national forest hiking trails are available here, at trailheads or the state park headquarters. If you plan to hike deeper into the San Bernardino National Forest, check if you also need an **Adventure Pass** ($5/day), which also allows you to park at the trailheads.

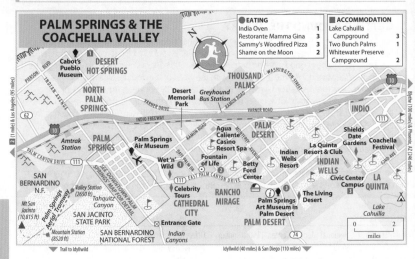

PALM SPRINGS & THE COACHELLA VALLEY

● EATING		■ ACCOMMODATION	
India Oven	1	Lake Cahuilla	
Restorante Mamma Gina	3	Campground	3
Sammy's Woodfired Pizza	3	Two Bunch Palms	1
Shame on the Moon	2	Whitewater Preserve	
		Campground	2

Hikes to consider include the **Deer Springs Trail** in the state park (six miles round-trip; 3–4hr; 1700ft ascent), which leads up to Suicide Rock, one of two distinctive peaks rising a couple of thousand feet above the town. To get to the top of the Aerial Tramway (see p.212), follow the **Devil's Slide Trail** in the national forest (sixteen miles round-trip; 7–9hr; 2300ft ascent); permits are limited, and often run out at weekends.

ARRIVAL AND DEPARTURE IDYLLWILD

By car From Palm Springs head twenty miles west along I-10 to Banning, then take the exit for Hwy-243, which sweeps you up the mountain on a good but sharply curving road. There is no public transportation to Idyllwild.

ACCOMMODATION

Places to stay are scattered along the roads that fan out from Idyllwild's central shopping area. You can set up **camp** anywhere over two hundred feet away from trails and streams, or in designated Yellow Post Sites (Adventure Pass needed), which have fire rings but no water. There are also drive-in campgrounds run by the Forest Service (☎ 1800 444 6777, ⓦ recreation.gov) and one at Idyllwild Park, on the edge of the town (☎ 1800 234 7275, ⓦ rivcoparks.org) at a cost of $25/night (year-round; reservations April–Oct only).

Idyllwild RV Campground 24400 Canyon Trail ☎ 951 659 4097, ⓦ thousandtrails.com. Woodsy campground and RV park on the edge of town with spacious tent sites, RV hookups and a nature trail. Cabin rentals are also available. Pitches $33, hookups $44, cabins $119

Quiet Creek Inn 26345 Delano Drive ☎ 800 450 6110, ⓦ quietcreekinn.com. Beautifully appointed forest cabins set up for maximum relaxation. Most have a deck overlooking a creek and a fireplace with wood provided. Follow Tollgate Rd off Hwy-243, a mile east of the centre. $187

★**Strawberry Creek Bunkhouse** 25525 Hwy-243 (half a mile north of the ranger station) ☎ 951 659 2201, ⓦ strawberrycreekbunkhouse.com. About the best value around these parts, featuring wood-panelled rooms and catering to hikers, climbers and fishing folk. All have forest-view balconies and kitchenettes, and there's a range of pricier luxury cabins with spa tub and fireplace. A continental breakfast basket is included. $99

Strawberry Creek Inn 26370 Hwy-243 ☎ 951 659 3202, ⓦ strawberrycreekinn.com. Pampered luxury in B&B style a few hundred yards south of the centre of town. Rooms are comfortable and well appointed, but vary in theme – Santa Fe, fall, etc – so ask to see a few. $129

EATING

Café Aroma 54750 N Circle Drive ☎ 951 659 5212, ⓦ cafearoma.org. This upscale restaurant-cum-art gallery does everything from fresh espresso and scones early on, to dinners such as scampi ravioli or osso buco (veal shank). Mains $14–30. Most nights there is some form of live music. Mon, Wed & Thurs 11am–9pm, Fri 11am–10pm,

Sat 7am–10pm, Sun 7am–9pm.

Higher Grounds 54245 N Circle Drive ☎ 951 659 1379, ⓦ highergroundscoffee.com. You can get your organic java fix at this centrally located spot. Sun–Thurs 7am–7pm, Fri & Sat 7am–9pm.

Red Kettle 54220 N Circle Drive ☎ 951 659 4063, ⓦ redkettleinc.com. For straightforward diner food, this is a locals' favourite serving fine all-day breakfasts ($8–9), burgers and sandwiches. Daily 7am–2pm.

DIRECTORY

Library 54401 Village Center Drive (Mon & Wed 10am–6pm, Tues noon–8pm, Thurs & Fri noon–5pm, Sat 10am–4pm; ☎ 951 659 2300). Offers free internet access.

Coachella Valley

Palm Springs may have the prestige, but it is the towns of the **Coachella Valley** – Cathedral City, Desert Hot Springs, Rancho Mirage, Palm Desert, Indio, Indian Wells and La Quinta – that have the bulk of the swanky resorts, big-name shops and elegant restaurants these days. On initial acquaintance, it is hard to tell one town from another as they form an amorphous twenty-mile sprawl of gated communities, country clubs and golf courses. Not all the boundaries between them are clearly marked, and on their main drags they tend to share faceless low-slung architecture – but differences become evident to those who have time to explore. The valley extends for some 45 miles south of Palm Springs to the Salton Sea (see box, p.236), connected for most of its length by Hwy-111, though if you've got a specific destination in mind and want to avoid endless stop lights, consider the faster I-10 which runs parallel about four miles to the north.

Desert Hot Springs

Isolated on the north side of I-10, twelve miles north of Palm Springs, the growing city of **DESERT HOT SPRINGS** was honoured in a 1999 competition for having the best-tasting water in the country. The underground wells for which the town is named supply water for the multitude of swimming pools as well as for drinking. A good jumping-off point for visiting Joshua Tree National Park (see p.228), it's also home to the curious **Cabot's Pueblo Museum**.

Cabot's Pueblo Museum

67616 E Desert View Ave • June–Sept Wed–Sat 9am–1pm (tours 9.30am, 10.30am & 11.30am); Oct–May Tues–Sun 9am–4pm (tours 9.30am, 10.30am & 11.30am, 1.30pm & 2.30pm) • $13 • ☎ 760 329 7610, ⓦ cabotsmuseum.org

---

GOLF IN THE COACHELLA VALLEY

Look on Google Earth and the Coachella Valley seems to be all golf courses –125 of them. They smother Rancho Mirage, Palm Desert, Indian Wells and La Quinta where a home beside the fairway proclaims your arrival among the Coachella Valley elite. The top courses are among the finest anywhere, the barren mountains all around in spectacular contrast to the lush, green fairways and placid water traps. Of course, watering all those fairways is completely unsustainable, but no one seems too concerned about the gradually draining aquifer that underlies most of the valley, as long as places like Palm Desert's Bighorn and Indian Wells' Vintage Club Mountain Course continue to grace the pages of golfing magazines.

Many of the courses are **private**, with annual membership running up to $25,000 on top of a $350,000 initial joining fee. Semi-private and **public courses** are more accessible, though green fees can still be steep in winter: for bargains go in summer and play in the less fashionable afternoon or evening. One of the best public courses is the 36-hole Desert Willow Golf Resort, 38995 Desert Willow Drive, Palm Desert (☎ 760 346 7060, ⓦ desertwillow.com), where morning green fees run over $150 in the popular winter season but drop as low as $65 in summer ($52 in the afternoon). Golf club rentals range from $65–75. Alternatively, try one of the reservation agents such as Golf a la Carte (☎ 760 397 7670, ⓦ palmspringsgolf.com), who book **tee times** at a range of courses up to two months in advance.

The "father of Desert Hot Springs", one Cabot Yerxa, built the whimsical four-storey Hopi-style structure that is now **Cabot's Pueblo Museum** over a twenty-year period. After a peripatetic adulthood in Alaska, Cuba and all over California, Cabot became Desert Hot Springs' first resident in 1913, then laboriously hand-dug the first well. He returned in his mid-50s in 1939 and began constructing what he intended to be both his house and a monument to the Native American people he had grown to love. Without formal plans and using home-made adobe bricks and any secondhand bits of wood he could get his hands on, he fashioned a wonderful, rambling, asymmetrical structure – adhering to the belief that symmetry retains evil spirits. Cabot died in 1965 having completed 35 rooms, several of which can now be visited on an entertaining 45-minute guided tour.

ACCOMMODATION

DESERT HOT SPRINGS

Two Bunch Palms 67425 Two Bunch Palms Trail ☎ 800 472 4334, ⓦ twobunchpalms.com; map p.220. Adults-only luxury resort nestled in between the trailer parks, a favourite of celebrities from Los Angeles thanks to its secluded chalets, suites and gorgeous rooms. Day-spa visitors (10am–6pm) are also welcome, but only if they take a package including one treatment (from $165); spending your days soaking in the hot-springs pool with a book and a cocktail, with intermittent breaks for mud baths and massages, is not a bad way to pass the time. **$279**

Cathedral City

About five miles east of Palm Springs along Hwy-111, **CATHEDRAL CITY** ("Cat City") has no cathedral, but takes its name from the now-hidden Cathedral Canyon, which reminded early explorers of some medieval minster. The town boomed during Prohibition when the absence of a police force encouraged bawdy establishments to set up shop. You may well come here to drink or dine, or to tap into the **gay scene** that's second only to the one in

COACHELLA AND STAGECOACH

Since 1999 the **Coachella Valley Music and Arts Festival** (commonly known simply as "Coachella"), has been held across several stages at the Empire Polo Club south of Downtown Indio at 81-800 Ave 51 (two miles west of Coachella itself). The massive three-day rock and alternative music festival is packed with big-name artists and is wildly popular, despite the high cost of attending: tickets sell out in hours and since 2013 events now span two three-day-long weekends in April. Coachella 2016 artists featured A$AP Rocky, Chvrches, Ellie Goulding, Grimes, Ice Cube, Sia and The Damned.

PRACTICALITIES

First you need to purchase a **festival pass** (from $399 per person online); passes are only good for the dates of the weekend you choose (you must buy two passes to attend both weekends), and there are no one-day passes. **Advance sales** typically take place a year before the festival, so make sure you check the website (ⓦ coachella.com) for updates.

Thousands of festival-goers **camp** on the polo field adjacent to the venue grounds, which features a recycling facility, general store, showers, mobile phone charging stations and an internet café with free wi-fi. **Parking** is free (no RVs), but camping is $99 per car/pitch (in addition to the festival pass). Posher camping in safari tents and around Lake Eldorado is also available, from $3196 for four people.

Plenty of nearby **resorts** offer packages, which include festival shuttle buses, but these can start at over $2500 (see ⓦ valleymusictravel.com). If you want to stay somewhere cheaper but don't want the hassle of driving every day, you can still take one of the festival shuttle buses for $60 (for three days).

STAGECOACH FESTIVAL

The **Stagecoach Festival** (ⓦ stagecoachfestival.com) is the outdoor country music festival "cousin" of Coachella, typically taking place one week later at the same venue, the Empire Polo Club. All the big names have attended in the past – Kenny Chesney, Toby Keith, Miranda Lambert, Blake Shelton, Taylor Swift and Carrie Underwood – and tickets start at $269 for three days. Camping, transportation and accommodation arrangements and costs are similar to Coachella.

Palm Springs, but during the day there's not a lot to see except for Jennifer Johnson's fabulous *Fountain of Life* sculpture (Town Square Park, Buddy Rogers Ave, just off Hwy-111), complete with mosaic bighorn sheep, lizards and tortoises. Fans of **Frank Sinatra** make the pilgrimage to **Desert Memorial Park**, 37-705 Da Vall Drive, where the crooner's modest gravestone is often covered in flowers (Sonny Bono is also buried here).

EATING   CATHEDRAL CITY

★ **India Oven** 35875 Date Palm Drive ☎ 760 770 3918, ⓦ india-oven.com; map p.220. The area's best curry restaurant is a modest affair, but the flavours are excellent. Drop in for a vegetarian or meaty lunchtime curry special ($7.49), or something off the menu such as shrimp masala ($12.99) washed down with a mint lassi ($3.50). Sun–Thurs 5–9pm, Fri & Sat 5–9.30pm (closed Mon July & Aug).

Rancho Mirage

Some 4.5 miles east along the valley from Cathedral City, the generally staid **RANCHO MIRAGE** tends to attract dignitaries – and high-profile substance abusers. This so-called "Playground of the Presidents" was home to former President Gerald Ford until his death in 2006, and is also host to the upscale rehab clinic founded by his wife in 1982, the **Betty Ford Center**. Frank Sinatra was the first of the stars to move to Rancho Mirage in 1956, and others soon followed. The city now recognizes its more illustrious associations in its street names: Frank, Gerald, Bob Hope and Dinah Shore all have drives named after them. The city's newest high-profile project is the construction of a family-friendly **Observatory** next to the Rancho Mirage Library on Hwy-111, which should be open by the end of 2017.

EATING   RANCHO MIRAGE

★ **Shame on the Moon** 69950 Frank Sinatra Drive, at Hwy-111 ☎ 760 324 5515, ⓦ shameonthemoon.com; map p.220. A loyal band of wealthy greyhairs frequent this dark, intimate restaurant/bar that's been here since the mid-1980s but feels very Sinatra 1960s; there's no cocktail menu, but the team will whip up something fabulous to order. Dinner is along the likes of sesame-crusted seared ahi tuna steak ($24.95) and in summer there are often three-course specials around $25. Reservations a must in winter. Daily 5–10pm.

Palm Desert

Three miles east of Rancho Mirage along Hwy-111, **PALM DESERT** is the safest place to witness the wildlife that flourishes in this inhospitable climate thanks to the **Living Desert** (see p.223), but on nearby **El Paseo**, sometimes called the "Rodeo Drive of the Desert", you can glimpse a different species of local creature. The wealthy and the wishful thinkers flock to this mile-long strip of fashionable stores and galleries (think Gucci, Kate Spade and Louis Vuitton), which loops south off Hwy-111 and is one of the very few places in the whole Coachella Valley where you might leave your car and stroll. Come late October or early November, the increasingly prevalent species *Homo golfus* turns out en masse for the nation's only **golf-cart parade** (☎ 760 346 6111, ⓦ golfcartparade.com), with decorated buggies proceeding along El Paseo. For more cultured pursuits, you'll find the **Palm Springs Art Museum in Palm Desert** (Sept–May Tues, Wed, Fri–Sun 10am–5pm, Thurs noon–8pm; June–Aug Fri–Sun 10am–5pm; free; ☎ 760 322 4800, ⓦ psmuseum.org) where El Paseo meets Hwy-111 (western end); this outpost of the original (see p.210) opened in 2012 to showcase rotating exhibitions of contemporary sculpture, painting, photography and new media. The **Santa Rosa & San Jacinto Mountains National Monument Visitor Center** (daily: May–Sept 8am–3pm; Oct–April 9am–4pm; free; ☎ 760 862 9984), at 51500 Hwy-74 just south of town, contains exhibits about desert wildlife, history and a short nature trail.

Living Desert

47900 Portola Ave • Daily: June–Sept 8am–1.30pm; Oct–May 9am–5pm • $19.95, kids (3–12) $9.95 • ☎ 760 346 5694, ⓦ livingdesert.org

Encompassing over 1200 acres of irrigated and manicured sections of land, the **Living Desert** is a modern zoo and botanical garden, its various sections each representing a different desert region from around the world. Stroll among the cacti of the Mojave or the Chihuahua gardens, through an area specially designed to attract butterflies, or into a palm oasis. North American desert animals – coyotes, foxes, bighorn sheep, snakes and mountain lions – are supplemented by sections devoted to African species, such as wild dogs, gazelles, zebras, giraffes (feed them for $5), cheetahs and warthogs. There are shady *palapas* and cooling "mist stations" everywhere, but it is still best to arrive as the gates open for cool and fragrant morning air, particularly if you fancy the wilderness trail system, which penetrates the hill country behind the zoo. If you can't stand to walk around in the heat, hop on the shuttle ($6 all day), which makes frequent circuits of the park.

INFORMATION	PALM DESERT

Palm Desert Visitor Center 73-510 Fred Waring Drive (Mon–Fri 8am–5pm; ☎760 568 1441, ⓦpalm-desert .org). Information on regional events and sights.

3	EATING

Restorante Mamma Gina 73-705 El Paseo ☎760 568 9898, ⓦmammagina.com; map p.220. Long-standing Palm Desert favourite combining the freshest ingredients in original Tuscan recipes such as *scaloppini piccata* or lobster meat and black-ink ravioli. Dinner mains $27–45, pastas $22–28. Mon–Thurs & Sun 4–9pm, Fri & Sat 4–9.30pm. **Sammy's Woodfired Pizza** 73-595 El Paseo (The Gardens Mall) ☎760 836 0500, ⓦsammyspizza.com; map p.220. Local outlet of this California chain pizzeria, which does a great job offering whole-wheat and gluten-free crusts on concoctions such as prosciutto, arugula and pear, along with Neopolitan classics (pizzas $12.25–13.75). Mon–Thurs & Sun 11am–9pm, Fri & Sat 11am–9.30pm.

Indian Wells

Two miles east of Palm Desert on Hwy-111, the adjoining city of **INDIAN WELLS** has one of the highest per-capita incomes in the US, as well as the largest concentration of the Coachella Valley's grand **resorts**. It's known for its four-day New Year **Jazz Festival**, its high-profile **tennis tournament** (the BNP Paribas Open; ⓦbnpparibasopen.com) in March and its prestigious **Desert Town Hall Lecture Series** (ⓦdeserttownhall.org), held mid-February to mid-April in the *Renaissance Indian Wells Resort & Spa* at 44400 Indian Wells Lane (off Hwy-111); four talks by high-profile speakers such as George W. Bush, Tony Blair, Pervez Musharraf and Desmond Tutu. You must buy tickets to all four events ($400–550).

La Quinta

A few miles east from Indian Wells lies **LA QUINTA**, named for the Valley's first exclusive resort – Rancho La Quinta – which was built in 1927 and thrived during the Depression, when Hollywood's escapist popularity rose as the country suffered. Director Frank Capra wrote the script for multiple-Oscar-winner *It Happened One Night* at the resort in 1934 and considered the place so lucky he kept coming back, bringing stars such as Greta Garbo in his wake. Today **La Quinta Resort & Club** (ⓦlaquintaresort.com), 49-499 Eisenhower Drive, is still so posh that it's not marked on the main road (take Washington St south to Eisenhower to find it). The Santa Rosa Mountain backdrop is stunning, and the rich no longer get very dressed up, so you won't feel out of place if you come for a drink or meal at *Morgan's in the Desert*, its premier bar and restaurant. If you visit in early March, make time for **La Quinta Arts Festival** (ⓦlqaf.com), which serves up fine art and entertainment, usually held in Civic Center Campus, 78495 Calle Tampico (south of Hwy-111 via Washington St).

ACCOMMODATION	LA QUINTA

Lake Cahuilla 58075 Jefferson St ☎760 564 4712, ⓦrivcoparks.org; map p.220. Large campground for tents and RVs by a 135-acre lake roughly fifteen miles east of Palm Springs. There are showers, a dump station for RVs, a summer-only swimming pool and a wi-fi station. Pitches $15, hookups $22

Indio
In stark contrast to its neighbours, **INDIO** is a low-key town whose agricultural roots show in its many date and citrus outlets; approaching along 50th Avenue, you'll pass so many date groves you'll think you're in Saudi Arabia. Other than desert fruits, Indio is best known for hosting the annual **Coachella Festival** (see box, p.222).

Shields Date Garden Store & Café
80–225 Hwy-111 • Daily 9am–5pm; café Sun & Mon 7am–2.30pm, Tues–Sat 7am–2.30pm & 5–9.30pm • Free • ☎ 760 347 7768, ⓦ shieldsdategarden.com

Just outside Indio, stop in at the **Shields Date Garden Store & Café**, built in 1924 but renovated in the 1950s, for date pancakes ($13), signature date salad ($10), date shakes ($4.75) or date burgers ($14.80). Wander out to see the date palms (all with ladders attached for harvesting), and don't miss the free 15-minute film, *The Romance and Sex Life of the Date*; its cheesy commentary was partly recorded in the 1950s by Floyd Shields, who set up the town's huge February **Date Festival** which draws people from as far as LA to its wonderfully goofy camel and ostrich races.

Morongo Basin

Driving from Palm Springs (or Los Angeles) to Joshua Tree National Park, the easiest access is through the vast tract of high desert known as the **MORONGO BASIN**, almost a thousand square miles of which is taken up by the massive Marine Corps Air Ground Combat Center (MCAGCC), just north of Twentynine Palms. Set aside a little time to visit the wildlife haven of the **Big Morongo Canyon Preserve**, the oddball **Desert Christ Park** and the Western charms of **Pioneertown**. Much of the San Bernardino Mountain range that surrounds the basin has been incorporated within the **Sand to Snow National Monument** (ⓦ fs.fed.us/visit/sand-to-snow-national-monument), created in 2016 and set to offer an increasing amount of outdoor activities in the coming years. To the west lies **San Gorgonio Mountain** (11,503ft), the highest peak in Southern California.

Big Morongo Canyon Preserve
11055 E Drive (signposted off Hwy-62) • Daily 7.30am–sunset • Free, donation suggested • ☎ 760 363 7190, ⓦ bigmorongo.org

Heading north from I-10 along Twentynine Palms Highway (Hwy-62), spend an hour or two at the **Big Morongo Canyon Preserve**, a wildlife refuge tucked away on the edge of the Little San Bernardino Mountains about 1.5 miles southeast of the town of Morongo Valley. Trails and boardwalks snake through the cottonwoods and willows of a vast oasis that's one of the largest bodies of marshy surface water for miles around. It's a big hit with wildlife; birdwatchers come hoping to spot vermilion and brown-crested flycatchers, Bell's vireo, summer tanager and a whole lot more.

Yucca Valley and Pioneertown
The Morongo Basin's largest settlement is **YUCCA VALLEY**, an ugly string of highway-side malls ten miles northeast of Big Morongo Canyon Preserve. The main attraction here is the **Desert Christ Park** (daily 7am–dusk; free; ⓦ desertchristpark .org), 56200 Sunnyslope Drive, a fittingly bizarre addition to the region; over forty of local sculptor Frank Antone Martin's massive, fifteen-foot-tall white concrete figures were erected here in the 1950s and depict tales from the Bible. To get here, take Pioneertown Drive north off Hwy-62 and, after half a mile, turn right onto Sunnyslope Drive and continue half a mile. Return to Pioneertown Drive and continue 3.5 miles north to **Pioneertown**, an Old West movie set created in 1946 for films and TV series (Roy Rogers and Gene Autry were investors) – a nice bit of

3

synthetic cowboy country in case there isn't enough of the real thing around for you. Several re-enactment groups perform shoot-em-up skits on Mane Street most Saturdays and Sundays (2.30–3.30pm; free).

ACCOMMODATION   PIONEERTOWN

Pioneertown Motel 5040 Curtis Rd ☎760 365 7001, ⓦpioneertown-motel.com. Definitely the most entertaining place to stay in the region, with clean but ageing rooms made more appealing by a full kitchen and a variety of decor: cowboy, pioneer, seascape, etc. **$99**

EATING AND DRINKING

Pappy & Harriet's 53688 Pioneertown Rd ☎760 365 5956, ⓦpappyandharriets.com. Tap into good food and a great atmosphere at this Tex-Mex and mesquite barbecue specialist (ribs $19), in premises that served as the film set's original "cantina" in the 1940s. There's live music pretty much every night of the week (local favourites the Shadow Mountain Band play Sat at 5pm). Mon 5pm–2am, Thurs–Sun 11am–2am.

Joshua Tree

Six miles east of Yucca Valley, the Mojave Desert town of **JOSHUA TREE** straddles the intersection of Twentynine Palms Highway (Hwy-62) and Park Boulevard, which runs five miles south to Joshua Tree National Park's West Entrance (see p.233). There's not much to the town itself, though it does attract a mixed bunch of artists who have opened some small, offbeat galleries, and musicians who run the excellent **Joshua Tree Music Festival** in mid-May and in mid-October (ⓦjoshuatreemusicfestival.com).

ACCOMMODATION AND EATING   JOSHUA TREE

★**Crossroads Café** 61715 Twentynine Palms Hwy (Hwy-62) ☎760 366 5414, ⓦcrossroadscafejtree.com. Great place for breakfasts ($8–12), burgers ($9.50), real espresso ($2.50), smoothies ($5.25) and even microbrews ($4). Mon–Sat 7am–9pm, Sun 7am–8pm.

High Desert Motel 61310 Twentynine Palms Hwy (Hwy-62) ☎760 366 1978, ⓦhighdesertmotel.com. The cheapest place to stay in town offers basic but clean rooms with all the necessary (including microwaves), and a small outdoor pool. **$54**

★**Joshua Tree Coffee Co** 61738 Twentynine Palms Hwy (Hwy-62) ☎760 799 8210, ⓦjtcoffeeco.com. This no-frills coffee shop is worth braving long queues for its high-quality drinks, served in cramped, steampunk quarters from locally roasted beans. The nitro iced coffee is an addictive treat. Daily 7am–6pm.

Joshua Tree Inn 61259 Twentynine Palms Hwy (Hwy-62) ☎760 366 1188, ⓦjoshuatreeinn.com. This slightly run-down 1950s motel has comfortable rooms and suites with kitchens set around a pool, but is mainly of interest to fans of Donovan (his favourite, Room 11, is named after the singer; $164) and Gram Parsons (see box, p.233) who died in Room 8 ($114). You can inscribe your thoughts in a little book known as the Sacred Heart Journal and add your guitar pick to the collection. **$94**

Sacred Sands 63155 Quail Springs Rd ☎760 424 6407, ⓦsacredsands.com. For top-end luxury, book one of the two rooms at this gorgeous straw-bale B&B just off the road into the national park; sumptuous fittings include outdoor baths and even a sleeping platform under the stars (two-night minimum). **$329**

★**Spin and Margie's Desert Hideaway** 64491 Twentynine Palms Hwy (Hwy-62) ☎760 366 9124, ⓦdeserthideaway.com. With cool, tiled rooms vibrantly decorated in a Western style, some with full kitchen, you'll want to stay longer here than the two-night minimum, relaxing in the cactus garden or playing petanque. **$145**

SHOPPING

Coyote Corner 6535 Park Blvd ☎760 366 9683, ⓦjtcoyotecorner.com. Wooden cabin selling books, guides, souvenirs (T-shirts, mugs and the like) – you can also fill up water containers and bottles (free) before heading into the park, or have a shower ($4 for 7.5min, 20min limit). Mon–Fri 9am–6pm, Sat & Sun 9am–7pm.

Nomad Ventures 61795 Twentynine Palms Hwy ☎760 366 4684, ⓦnomadventures.com. Climbers and hikers needing to buy or rent gear should stop by this adventure sports shop, across the street from Coyote Corner. Daily 9am–7pm.

DIRECTORY

Library 6465 Park Blvd and Hwy-62 (Mon–Wed 11am–7pm, Thurs 10am–6pm, Sat 9am–5pm; ☎760 366 8615). Offers free internet access.

Twentynine Palms

Fifteen miles east of the town of Joshua Tree and just two minutes' drive from Joshua Tree National Park's North Entrance, the small highway-side desert town of **TWENTYNINE PALMS** (locally known as "two-nine") is a pleasant enough place despite the occasional artillery booms from the nearby marine base. The town runs for almost five miles along the highway and is divided into two sections separated by a small hill. The only sights to speak of are the national park's **Oasis Visitor Center** (see p.233) on the eastern edge of town and the nearby **Old Schoolhouse Museum** at 6760 National Park Drive (June–Aug Sat & Sun 1–4pm; Sept–May Wed–Sun 1–4pm; free; ☎760 367 2366, ⊛29palmshistorical.com), whose partly restored schoolroom from 1927 has displays on the local mining industry, the military presence and desert wildlife.

INFORMATION   **TWENTYNINE PALMS**

Chamber of Commerce 73484 Twentynine Palms Hwy (Mon–Fri 9am–5pm, Sat & Sun 10am–4pm; ☎760 367 6197, ⊛29chamber.org).

Library 6078 Adobe Rd (Mon–Wed 11am–7pm, Thurs 10am–6pm, Sat 9am–5pm; ☎760 367 9519). Offers free internet access.

ACCOMMODATION

★**29 Palms Inn** 73950 Inn Ave (off National Park Drive) ☎760 367 3505, ⊛29palmsinn.com. This is the best place in town to stay, where an array of cosy adobe bungalows and wood-framed cabins are set around attractively arid grounds and gardens, and a central pool area contains a restaurant and bar. The inn was built in 1928 on the Oasis of Mara (see box, p.234). It's worth upgrading to a bungalow or even the lovely 1930s "Irene's

Historic Adobe", which sleeps four. Cabins $70, bungalows $85, Irene's $220
Harmony Motel 71161 Twentynine Palms Hwy (Hwy-62) ☎760 367 3351, ⊛harmonymotel.com. Quirky, old-fashioned motel from 1952, on a hilltop overlooking town, with ageing but large, clean and comfy rooms (some with full kitchens), plus tranquil pool area. U2 stayed here whilst working on *The Joshua Tree* album. $82

EATING

29 Palms Inn 73950 Inn Ave (off National Park Drive) ☎760 367 3505, ⊛29palmsinn.com. With its excellent sautéed mushrooms ($9) and dinners (steaks from $22),

and many of the ingredients grown in the oasis gardens, this is one of the best places to eat in town. Mon–Sat 11am–2pm & 5–9pm, Sun 9am–2pm.

Joshua Tree National Park

Covering a vast area where the high Mojave meets the lower Colorado Desert, **JOSHUA TREE NATIONAL PARK** is one of the most magical and intriguing of California's national parks. Almost 1250 square miles have been set aside for the park's ragged and gnarled namesakes, which flourish in an otherwise sparsely vegetated landscape.

Joshua trees (see box, p.230) are only found in the northwestern quarter of the park, where they form a perfect counterpoint to surreal clusters of monzogranite boulders, great rock piles pushed up from the earth by the movements of the Pinto Mountain Fault running directly below. Often as tall as a hundred feet, the rock edges are rounded and smooth from thousands of years of flash floods and winds, but there are enough nodules, fissures and irregularities to make this superb **rockclimbing** territory.

Visiting the park

Joshua Tree is a mystical, even unearthly, landscape best appreciated at sunrise or sunset when the whole desert floor is bathed in red light. At noon it can feel like an alien and

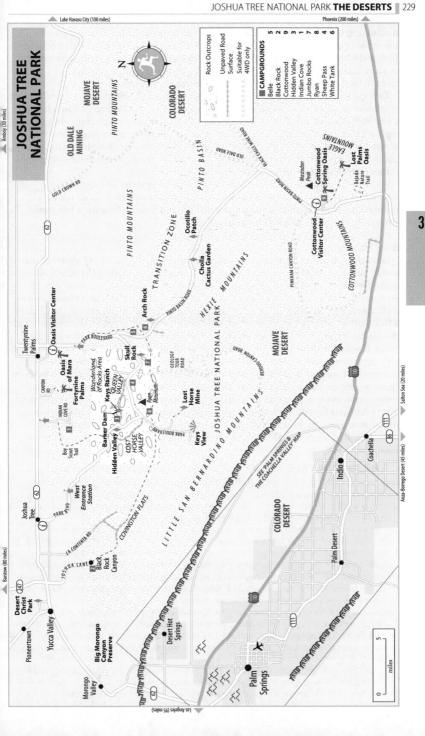

JOSHUA TREE NATIONAL PARK

Lake Havasu City (100 miles)

Amboy (30 miles)

Phoenix (200 miles)

Rock Outcrops

Unpaved Road
Surface
Suitable for
4WD only

CAMPGROUNDS
Belle	5
Black Rock	2
Cottonwood	9
Hidden Valley	3
Indian Cove	7
Jumbo Rocks	1
Ryan	8
Sheep Pass	4
White Tank	6

N

MOJAVE DESERT

COLORADO DESERT

PINTO MOUNTAINS

OLD DALE MINING

GOLD CROWN RD

PINTO MOUNTAINS

TRANSITION ZONE

PINTO BASIN

OLD DALE ROAD

BLACK EAGLE MINE ROAD

PINTO BASIN ROAD

Mastodon Peak

Cottonwood Spring Oasis

Lost Palms Oasis

EAGLE MOUNTAINS

Cottonwood Visitor Center

Bajada Nature Trail

COTTONWOOD MOUNTAINS

PINKHAM CANYON ROAD

Ocotillo Patch

Cholla Cactus Garden

HEXIE MOUNTAINS

Arch Rock

PINTO BASIN ROAD

Oasis Visitor Center

Twentynine Palms

Oasis of Mara

Fortynine Palms

PARK BOULEVARD

CANYON RD

INDIAN COVE RD

Skull Rock

Wonderland of Rocks Area

QUEEN VALLEY

Keys Ranch

Ryan Mountain

GEOLOGY TOUR ROAD

BERDOO CANYON ROAD

MOJAVE DESERT

Lost Horse Mine

Keys View

Barker Dam

Hidden Valley

Boy Scout Trail

LOST HORSE VALLEY

PARK BOULEVARD

COVINGTON FLATS

West Entrance Station

PARK BLVD

Joshua Tree

62

LA CONTENTA RD

JOSHUA LANE

Black Rock Canyon

Barstow (80 miles)

247

Desert Christ Park

Pioneertown

Yucca Valley

Morongo Valley

62

Big Morongo Canyon Preserve

Desert Hot Springs

LITTLE SAN BERNARDINO MOUNTAINS

JOSHUA TREE NATIONAL PARK

COLORADO DESERT

SEE 'PALM SPRINGS & THE COACHELLA VALLEY MAP'

10

111

86

Coachella

Indio

Palm Desert

Salton Sea (20 miles)

Anza-Borrego Desert (45 miles)

10

111

Palm Springs

Los Angeles (95 miles)

0   5
miles

3

threatening furnace, with temperatures often reaching 125°F (52°C) in summer, though dropping to a more bearable 70°F (21°C) in winter. If you're visiting between May and October, you must stick to the higher elevations to enjoy Joshua Tree with any semblance of comfort. In the Low Desert part of the park, the Joshua trees thin out and the temperature rises as you descend below three thousand feet.

The best way to enjoy the park is to be selective, especially in the hotter months when you'll find an ambitious schedule impossible. Day-trips could include a leisurely drive along **Park Boulevard** and **Pinto Basin Road** – the paved roads which run right through the park – perhaps joining a tour of Keys Ranch and driving up to Keys View. For desert-lovers a couple of nights camping out is a highlight that shouldn't be missed, and experienced hikers may want to take advantage of the park's excellent if strenuous trails and backcountry opportunities (see box, p.234).

Many of the park side roads are unmarked, hard to negotiate and restricted to four-wheel-drive use. If a road is marked as such, don't even think about taking a normal car – you'll soon come to a grinding halt, and it could be quite a few panic-stricken hours before anybody finds you.

Brief history

"Joshua Tree" may be a familiar name today, thanks in part to U2's 1987 album of that name, but previously it was almost unknown. Unlike the vast bulk of the state, nobody, save a few Native Americans, prospectors and cowboys, had penetrated these remote environs. The first native group known to inhabit the area was the **Pinto Culture** (four to eight thousand years ago), followed by the **Serrano** (who were living around the Oasis of Mara until the early twentieth century), the **Chemehuevi** (who began to intermingle with the Serrano from 1867) and the **Cahuilla** (in the western and southern sections of the park). Despite receiving only around four inches of annual rainfall, the area is surprisingly lush, and it was grass that attracted the first significant pioneers. Forty-niners hurrying through on their way to the Sierra Nevada goldfields told tales of good pastures and early cattlemen were quick to follow in the 1850s, while rustlers discovered that the natural rocky corrals made perfect sites for branding their illegitimate herds before moving them out to the coast for sale. Ambushes and gunfights drove the rustlers to seek refuge in the mountains, where they discovered small traces of gold and sparked vigorous mining operations that continued until the 1940s. In recognition of the uniqueness of the area

---

THE JOSHUA TREE

Unique to the Mojave Desert, the **Joshua tree** (*Yucca brevifolia*) is one of its oldest residents, with large examples probably over three hundred years old: the lack of growth rings makes their age difficult to determine. The Joshua tree isn't, in fact, a tree at all, but a type of yucca, itself a type of agave and therefore a giant member of the lily family.

Awkward-looking and ungainly, it got its unusual name from Mormons who travelled through the region in the 1850s and imagined the craggy branches to be the arms of Joshua leading them to the Promised Land. Of course, Native Americans had been familiar with Joshua trees for millennia, weaving the tough leaves into baskets and sandals, and eating the roasted seeds and flower buds. The trees became equally useful for homesteaders who arrived in the wake of the Mormons – the lack of better wood forced them to press the trunks of Joshua trees into use for fences and building material.

Joshua trees only grow at altitudes over **two thousand feet** and prefer extreme aridity and a bed of coarse sand and fine silt. By storing water in their spongy trunks, they can grow up to three inches a year, ultimately reaching heights of forty feet or more. To conserve energy, they only bloom when conditions are right, waiting for a crisp winter freeze, timely rains and the pollinating attentions of the yucca moth before erupting in a springtime display of creamy white-green flowers, which cluster on long stalks at the tips of the branches. Successful young saplings start life as a single shoot, but eventually a terminal bud dies or is injured and the plant splits to form two branches, which in turn divide over time, producing the Joshua trees' distinctive shapes.

BIKING AND ROCK CLIMBING IN JOSHUA TREE

While driving through Joshua Tree lessens your contact with the desert, and the need to carry all your water limits the scope for hiking, **biking** strikes a nice balance. With cyclists restricted to roads open to motor vehicles, you shouldn't come expecting genuine off-road action, but there's an increasing number of bikeable and challenging dirt roads. Armed with your own set of wheels (there is no bike rental anywhere near the park), consider heading out on popular fifteen- to twenty-mile routes like the Geology Tour Road, Covington Flats Road and Pinkham Canyon Road. These and more are listed in the *Joshua Tree Guide* (see p.233).

Since the 1970s, the fractured lumps of golden rock that pepper the northwestern corner of the park have become fabulously popular and world renowned for **rock climbing** and **bouldering**. Climbers keen to find a springtime training ground while the Sierra crags were still under snow began putting up routes which now see sticky-rubber traffic from October to May – the summer months are generally way too hot. In spring and fall, rock climbers sometimes base themselves here for weeks, usually at the *Hidden Valley* campground. Climbers should read the climbing ethics section of the park website and may want to call at the climbing shops in the township of Joshua Tree to obtain guidebooks; Coyote Corner (see p.226) lends guidebooks short term, but you'll probably want to buy one. The most comprehensive book is Randy Vogel's *Rock Climbing: Joshua Tree*, though his condensed and much cheaper *Joshua Tree National Park: Classic Rock Climbs* may suit short-term visitors. Beginners, or those after instruction and guiding, should contact one of the climbing schools that operate here. Both Joshua Tree Rock Climbing School (☎ 760 366 4745, ⊚ joshuatreerockclimbing.com) and Uprising (☎ 1888 254 6266, ⊚ joshuatreeuprising.com) offer a range of one-day courses for around $175 and improvers' weekends for around $350. Check the websites for course dates, or go for private guiding which costs around $385 a day for one person or $275 each for two (Uprising is usually a little cheaper).

3

and the need for its preservation, the national park system took the land under its jurisdiction as a national monument in 1936 and has vigilantly maintained its beauty ever since. The park lost some of the original area to mining interests in the 1950s, but that was more than compensated for in 1994, when it was promoted to a **national park**, with the addition of 365 square miles.

Hidden Valley and around

Approaching from the township of Joshua Tree on Park Boulevard, you enter the park at the **West Entrance**. Some five miles along the road a well-signposted one-mile nature trail loops into **Hidden Valley**, a near-complete natural circle of rock mounds where cattle rustlers used to hide out. To the north, a side road leads past the entrance to Keys Ranch (see below) to the rain-fed **Barker Dam**, Joshua Tree's crucial water supply, built around the turn of the twentieth century by cattlemen (and rustlers) to prevent their poor beasts from expiring halfway across the park. The route back from the dam passes a number of petroglyphs and looks over the **Wonderland of Rocks** area, which comprises giant, rounded granite boulders that draw **rock climbers** from all over the world.

Keys Ranch

Guided walking tour Oct–May daily 10am & 1pm, June–Sept Sat 6pm • $10 • Reservations required, first-come, first-served on the day of the tour, at Oasis Visitor Center ☎ 760 367 5522

Just northeast of the Hidden Valley campground sits the **Keys Ranch**, only accessible by joining the informative and entertaining ranger-led **guided walking tour**, which begins at the entrance to the ranch and takes around one hour and thirty minutes. The ranch was once home to tough desert rat and indefatigable miner Bill Keys, a Russian by birth who lived here with his family from 1910 until his death (at age 89) in 1969 – long after less hardy men had abandoned the arid wasteland. He was briefly famous in 1943, when he was locked away for shooting one of his neighbours over a right-of-way argument, only to be bailed out by a friend, the mystery writer Erle Stanley Gardner. Keys and family made a spartan but surprisingly comfortable living from growing vegetables, mining, ranching and working as a farrier and general trader for just about everything a desert dweller could desire. The tour visits their ramshackle home, orchard site, workshop and even a schoolhouse that operated for seven years from 1935.

Keys View
Perched on the crest of the Little San Bernardino Mountains, **Keys View** lies at the end of a paved side road (Keys View Rd) eight miles south of Park Boulevard, a 5185ft-high vista offering the best views in the whole park. On a good day, you can see as far as the Salton Sea and the snow-covered peak of San Gorgonio Mountain – a brilliant desert panorama of badlands and mountains. The trouble is, "good" days are rare since LA smog is funnelled between the mountains straight to Joshua Tree National Park, with the result that **air pollution** is a significant issue.

3

Skull Rock and Arch Rock
Park Boulevard runs southeast through the park, past the start of the Ryan Mountain hike (see box, p.234) and the turn-off for **Geology Tour Road**, which leads down through the best of Joshua Tree's rock formations. A little further on, the *Jumbo Rocks* campground is the start of a hiking loop (1.7 miles) through boulders and desert washes to **Skull Rock**, which can also be easily seen from the road immediately east of the campground; the name alludes to the two hollows in the granite, eroded by rainwater to look like giant eye sockets.

Continuing southeast through the park, now on Pinto Basin Road, you'll pass *White Tank* campground (see p.235), which is worth a short stop for its trail through huge granite domes to photogenic **Arch Rock**; the trail starts by site 9.

Cholla Cactus Garden
Five miles southeast of *White Tank* campground, almost at the transition zone between the Colorado and Mojave deserts and on the fringes of the Pinto Basin, the **Cholla Cactus Garden** is a quarter-mile loop through an astonishing concentration of the "jumping" **cholla** cactus (see box, p.234), as well as creosote bushes, jojoba and several other cactus species. It's a beautiful spot at any time, but come at dusk or dawn for the best chance of seeing the mainly nocturnal desert wood rat. Nearby, the almost barren desert at **Ocotillo Patch** comes stuffed with spindly ocotillo plants, most attractive in spring for their scarlet blooms.

Cottonwood Spring
Seven miles from the southern entrance to the park, **Cottonwood Spring** was used for centuries by the Cahuilla Indians, and later became an important water stop for prospectors and miners. Ruins of abandoned gold mills can still be seen nearby. The springs are a great place to hike: the Mastodon Peak and Lost Palms Oasis trails start here (see box, p.234), and a short, easy walk down Cottonwood Wash leads to a dry falls, then through palo verde and desert willow trees to the remains of Moorten's Mill.

ARRIVAL AND GETTING AROUND   **JOSHUA TREE NATIONAL PARK**

Besides camping (see opposite), there is neither lodging nor anywhere to eat or buy supplies within the park, so the Morongo Basin towns of Yucca Valley, Joshua Tree and Twentynine Palms are the main bases from which to explore.

By public transport Visiting the park without your own transport is not really an option: at best, you're looking at a ten-mile desert walk from Joshua Tree or Twentynine to get

to anything of interest; MBTA buses (⑩ mbtabus.com; $2.50) link Palm Springs with both places via a change in Yucca Valley (buses #12 & #13 to Yucca Valley, then bus #1),

SAFE AT HOME: GRAM PARSONS IN JOSHUA TREE

A relatively minor star in his lifetime, **Gram Parsons**, the wild country outlaw of early Seventies rock, has since become one of the era's icons. His musical influence spreads wide, from ageing rockers such as his old friend Keith Richards to Evan Dando, Beck and the current breed of alt-country misfits, but his fame owes as much to his drug- and booze-fuelled life and the bizarre circumstances surrounding his death at the age of 27. It is a story embellished over the years by myth, fabrication and gossip. Joshua Tree was Gram's escape from the LA music pressure-cooker, and photos show him hanging out with Richards in pharmaceutically altered states, communing with nature, and scanning the night sky for UFOs. On his final visit, Gram and three friends spent September 18, 1973, consuming as much heroin, morphine, marijuana and Jack Daniels as possible, with Gram finally OD'ing that night in Room 8 at the *Joshua Tree Inn*.

Parsons' stepfather stood to benefit from Gram's estate if he could get the body back to Louisiana for burial. However, Gram and his friend and tour manager, Phil Kaufman, had already agreed that "the survivor would take the other guy's body out to Joshua Tree, have a few drinks and burn it". Three days after Gram's death, Kaufman persuaded an airline employee to release Gram's casket, drove out to Joshua Tree, doused his body in gasoline and executed the wishes of his deceased friend. The body wasn't completely consumed, however, and Grams' remains now lie in a New Orleans cemetery. Kaufman was only charged with theft of a coffin and had to pay a $300 fine plus $708 for the coffin.

Fans come to stay at the *Joshua Tree Inn* (see p.226) and to visit a **makeshift shrine** near where his body was cremated. From the Cap Rock parking lot at the start of Keys View Rd, follow a well-defined but unmarked trail around the west side of the rock to a point close to the road intersection. Here, a rock alcove is usually plastered with dedications, though the rangers consider it to be graffiti and periodically clean it off. For many years the spot was marked by a small concrete plinth daubed with "Gram – Safe at Home".

3

but services are limited (bike racks available).
By car Less than an hour's drive northeast from Palm Springs (or 2hr from Los Angeles), Joshua Tree National Park is best approached through the Morongo Basin (see p.225) along Hwy-62, which branches off I-10; you can enter the park via the West Entrance at the town of Joshua Tree (see p.226), or the North Entrance at Twentynine Palms (see p.228), both with visitor centres.

INFORMATION

It's worth stopping at one of the visitor centres to collect the **free national park map** and *Joshua Tree Guide*, which are fine for most purposes, though hikers will want a more detailed map, the best being the National Geographic Trails Illustrated *Joshua Tree National Park* ($11.95). Park staff run free, campground-based **ranger programmes** (generally mid-Feb to May and mid-Oct to mid-Dec, but also summer weekends), which might include campfire talks, discovery walks and geology hikes: check at the visitor centres for the current schedule or contact ☎ 760 367 5500, ⓦ nps.gov/jotr.

Entrance fee $20/vehicle for 7 days, $10/cyclist or hiker.
Cottonwood Visitor Center (8 miles north of I-10 and the South Entrance at Cottonwood Spring): daily 8.30am–4pm. Exhibits here cover the park's natural history and desert ecology. Rangers can provide advice and maps, there's a bookshop, and videos are shown on demand.
Joshua Tree Visitor Center (West Entrance) 6554 Park Blvd, Joshua Tree (1 block south of Hwy-62): daily 8am–5pm. Busiest visitor centre, but the rangers do their best to field questions. Exhibits cover park geology, but also the human history of the region, plus sections on rock climbing and hiking. Café and bookshop on site, videos shown on demand.
Oasis Visitor Center (North Entrance) 74485 National Park Drive, Twentynine Palms (at the junction of Utah Trail): daily 8.30am–5pm. The main visitor centre has displays on the natural formation of the park, and especially its two types of desert environment. Park videos shown on request between 11am–3pm.

CAMPGROUNDS

Joshua Tree National Park has nine **campgrounds**, all concentrated in the northwest except for one at Cottonwood by the southern entrance. All have tables, fire rings (bring your own wood) and vault toilets, but only two (*Black Rock* and *Cottonwood*) have water supplies and flush toilets. The lack of showers and electrical and sewage hookups at any of the sites keeps the majority of RVs at bay, but in the popular winter months the sites fill up quickly, especially at weekends. All pitches are good for up to six people and two vehicles and are first-come, first-served, though *Black Rock* and *Indian Cove* can be reserved from October to May. **Winter** nights can be very cold, and campers here between November and March should come with warm jackets and sleeping bags or head for the lower (and warmer) *Cottonwood* campground.

Over eighty percent of the park is designated wilderness where **backcountry camping** is permitted, provided you register before you head out. Twelve backcountry boards are dotted through the park at the start of most trails. Here you can self-register, leave your vehicle and study the regulations that include prohibition of camping within a mile of a road and five hundred feet of a trail. These campgrounds are listed from northwest to southeast through the park.

Black Rock (100 sites; 4000ft). A large campground only accessible from outside the park. Reserve by calling ☎ 877 444 6777, ⊛ recreation.gov. Water available. $20

Indian Cove (101 sites; 3200ft). Another large campground only accessible from outside the park. It's set among granite boulders and a trail from the eastern

NATURE TRAILS AND HIKES IN JOSHUA TREE

To get a real feel for the majesty of the desert, you'll need to leave the main roads behind and hike, or at least follow one of the short (and mostly wheelchair-accessible) **nature trails** which have been set up throughout the park to help interpret something of desert ecology and plant life.

The more strenuous **hikes** outlined below are generally safe, but be sure to **stick to the trails**: Joshua Tree is full of abandoned gold mines, not all of them adequately fenced. Most of the listed trails are in the slightly cooler and higher Mojave Desert, but even on the easier trails allow around an hour per mile: there's very little shade and in summer you'll tire quickly. If you're experienced, well equipped and fancy heading out on anything more ambitious than the hikes described here (perhaps into the Pinto Basin), be sure to discuss your plans with a ranger; and anyone planning to stay out overnight in the wilderness must **register** at one of the trailhead backcountry boards. Finally, remember never to venture anywhere without a detailed map.

NATURE TRAILS

These are listed northwest to southeast through the park.
Oasis of Mara (800-yard loop). A series of explanatory panels around a significant fan-palm oasis right by the Oasis Visitor Center.
Cholla Cactus Garden (400-yard loop). A beautiful stroll among these superbly photogenic cacti, 20 miles north of Cottonwood Visitor Center.
Bajada (400-yard loop). Investigate the flora of a naturally sloping drainage half a mile north of the South Entrance.

RECOMMENDED HIKES

These are listed northwest to southeast through the park.
49 Palms Oasis (3 miles; 2hr) Moderately strenuous (300ft elevation gain, twice), this leaves the badly signposted Canyon Rd six miles west of the visitor centre at Twentynine Palms. A barren, rocky trail leads to this densely clustered and partly fire-blackened oasis, which continues to flourish on the seepage down the canyon. There's not enough water to swim in, nor are you allowed to camp (the oasis is officially closed 8pm–7am), but a late afternoon or evening visit presents the best wildlife rewards.
Lost Horse Mine (4 miles; 3hr) Starting a mile east of Keys View Rd, this moderately difficult trail climbs 450ft to the mine, which produced around five million dollars' worth of gold and silver between 1894 and 1931 (in today's money). The hike takes you through abandoned mining sites, with building foundations and equipment still intact, to the top of Lost Horse Mountain (5278ft).
Ryan Mountain (3 miles; 2hr) Some of the best views in the park are from the top of Ryan Mountain (5461ft), seven hundred strenuous feet above the desert floor. Start at the parking area near the *Sheep Pass* campground and follow the trail past the Indian Cave, which contains bedrock mortars once used by the Cahuilla and Serrano.
Mastodon Peak (3 miles; 2hr) Another peak climb, less strenuous than Ryan Mountain but with great views, especially south to the Salton Sea. Start from the *Cottonwood* campground.
Lost Palms Oasis (7.2 miles; 5hr) This moderate trail, starting from the *Cottonwood* campground or nearby trailhead, leads across desert washes and past palo verde, cottonwood and ironwood trees to the largest stand of palms in the park. The trail offers a possible scrambling side-trip to Victory Palms. There's little surface water, but often enough to lure bighorn sheep.

section of the campground road leads to Rattlesnake Canyon – its streams and waterfalls (depending on rainfall) breaking an otherwise eerie silence among the monoliths. Reservations on ☎877 444 6777, ⓦrecreation.gov. Water available at the Indian Cove Ranger Station. $20

Hidden Valley (44 sites; 4200ft). Popular campground that is almost entirely occupied by rock climbers in spring and fall. No water. $15

Ryan (31 sites; 4300ft) Medium-sized campground amid some lovely rocks and trees. No water. $15

Sheep Pass (6 group sites; 4500ft). This site is reserved for group camping. $25

Jumbo Rocks (124 sites; 4400ft). The highest and largest site in the park, often busy and with regular ranger programmes including a free one on Sat evenings (spring–fall). No water. $15

Belle (18 sites; 3800ft). Small, quiet site amid some lovely rocks. No water. $15

White Tank (15 sites; 3800ft) Relatively small and quiet site with a short nature trail to Arch Rock. No water. $15

Cottonwood (62 sites; 3000ft). At a lower elevation, this is the pick for the cooler winter months. Water available. $20

The Imperial Valley and the Salton Sea

The patch of the Colorado Desert **south** of Joshua Tree and Palm Springs is one of the harshest of all the California desert regions and its foreboding aspect discourages exploration. Sandwiched between Hwy-111 and Hwy-86, which branch off I-10 soon after Palm Springs and the Coachella Valley, the area from the **Salton Sea** (see box, p.236) down to the migrant-worker towns of the agricultural **Imperial Valley** lies in the two-thousand-square-mile Salton Basin: the largest area of dry land below sea level in the western hemisphere. Frankly, there's little reason to head out this way unless you're heading for **Anza-Borrego Desert State Park** (see p.237) or the Mexican border, though **Salvation Mountain** is one of California's quirkier gems.

Salton Sea State Recreation Area

100–225 State Park Rd, Mecca (30 miles south of Indio on Hwy-111) • Park open 24hr daily; visitor centre June–Sept Fri–Sun 10am–4pm, Oct–May daily 10am–4pm • $5 • ☎760 393 3810, ⓦparks.ca.gov/saltonsea

If you're curious about the Salton Sea, make for the **SALTON SEA STATE RECREATION AREA**, a protected reserve covering 14 miles of the northeastern lakeshore. It's a popular site for campers, boaters and anglers, though increasing salinity has limited the number of types of fish in the lake (most fish currently caught are tilapia). Start at the visitor centre close to the northern entrance, where exhibits provide context and the latest information on the lake, and rangers offer guided tours in the park's interpretive boat to view migrating birds (Oct–May only). The centre overlooks **Varner Harbor**, the main base for boating and waterskiing. From here you can explore the shoreline on the **Ironwood Nature Trail** (nature trail brochures available at the visitor centre), which runs south through groves of salt cedars and smoke trees to sandy **Mecca Beach** (2 miles round-trip), a popular swimming area. Showers are available to wash off the salt and algae. From here you can continue for another mile to undeveloped **Corvina Beach** (4.5 miles round-trip), a strip of largely deserted white sand.

Birdwatching is best from November through to February, while fishing is better between June and September (though this is the hottest time of year). The park has five **campgrounds**, with developed sites at Headquarters (Varner Harbor) and Mecca Beach ($20–30), and three primitive sites ($10) at Corvina (which does have flush toilets, water and cold showers), Salt Creek (toilets), and Bombay Beach, though the latter is **closed** for the foreseeable future due to budget constraints.

Bombay Beach

At the southern end of the recreation area, 16 miles from the visitor centre, **BOMBAY BEACH** is a fascinating community that looks like something out of a post-apocalyptic movie, with half the town flooded by the lake or half-buried in mud and salt, and the stench of rotting fish wafting in from the beach. A dyke protects the remaining structures – mostly mobile homes – though many of these look equally abandoned. With no gas station for miles around, most of the three hundred or so locals – a mix of white retirees and younger African Americans – rely on electric golf carts to get around. Bombay Beach was founded in 1929 as a resort for weekenders and retirees, but was devastated by floods in 1976 and 1977.

Sonny Bono Salton Sea National Wildlife Refuge

906 W Sinclair Rd (at Gentry Rd), Calipatria · Daily dawn–dusk; visitor centre March–Oct Mon–Fri 7am–3.15pm; Nov–Feb Mon–Fri 7am–3.15pm, Sat & Sun 8am–4.15pm · Free · ☎ 760 393 5278, ⓦ fws.gov/refuge/sonny_bono_salton_sea

Despite its long history of environmental challenges, the Salton Sea remains an important wintering area for shorebirds and waterfowl. Brown pelicans come by in summer, and terns and cormorants also nest here. The best place to see them is the **Sonny Bono Salton Sea National Wildlife Refuge** at the lake's southern tip. There's a viewing platform by the informative **visitor centre**, or you can take the Rock Hill Trail for a closer look, a twenty-minute walk to the water's edge. To get to the refuge, take Sinclair Road, off Hwy-111 four miles south of **Niland**, or follow the signs off Hwy-86 at **Westmorland**; both routes run past fields of alfalfa, cantaloupe, tomatoes and other crops, proof that just about anything will grow in this fertile land provided it is suitably irrigated.

Salvation Mountain and Slab City

Beal Rd, Niland · Daily 24hr · Free · ☎ 760 332 8016, ⓦ salvationmountaininc.org · Turn east off Hwy-111 along Niland's Main St and drive three miles

Even if you not an ornithologist, it's worth the journey around the Salton Sea to visit **Salvation Mountain**, a fantastical work of large-scale religious folk art that appeared in the 2007 movie *Into the Wild*. The mountain was worked on continuously, starting in 1985, by friendly eccentric Leonard Knight. He devoted his later life to this wildly coloured mass of straw and adobe, liberally painted with extracts from the Bible and exhortations to "Repent" – there's even an abandoned motorboat used to represent Noah's Ark. Though Leonard passed away in 2014, his fans and supporters hope to

THE RISE AND FALL OF THE ACCIDENTAL SEA

At 35 miles long by 15 miles wide, the **Salton Sea** is California's largest lake, but one which only came into existence a century ago. Over the millennia, the shallow Salton Basin has repeatedly filled with floodwaters that spilled over from the Colorado River some fifty miles to the east, but each time the lake has dried up. When European Americans started pushing into the West, they recognized that the fertile Salton Basin and the surrounding Imperial Valley could be made super-productive by channelling water from the Colorado. In 1901, a development company did just that, but river silt soon blocked the channel and in 1905 almost the entire flow from the Colorado River was pouring into the Salton Basin. The deluge wasn't stanched for almost two years, by which time it had formed the Salton Sea – a huge fresh-water lake up to fifty feet deep (only the Hoover Dam, completed in 1935 upstream in Nevada, finally ended flooding in the Imperial Valley). After World War II the sea's shores became extremely fashionable among the wealthy, attracting Frank Sinatra, Dean Martin and others to its yacht clubs; in its 1950s heyday, the lake was actually a bigger tourist draw than Yosemite National Park. A series of mid-1970s storms caused the lake to rise and swallow shoreline developments, but pollution was already having a detrimental impact on tourism. Nestled 235ft below sea level, the Salton Sea has no natural outlet and has been plagued over the years by agricultural run-off and toxic wastes carried in by two rivers from Mexico (the New and the Alamo), making it excessively saline. Despite several plans to restore the sea in the last ten years, progress has been snail-paced; see ⓦ water.ca.gov/saltonsea for the latest. Ironically, virtually abandoned resort towns such as **Bombay Beach** on the east side of the lake are starting to attract more visitors these days, drawn by the photogenic ruined section of town half-buried in mud and salt.

maintain the mountain with donations (through Salvation Mountain Inc, a public charity), though the desert is gradually taking it back, with plants poking through and the paint cracking and peeling (graffiti is now also a problem).

A short drive further along the road lies **Slab City**. The remnants of abandoned 1940s Camp Dunlap Marine Training Facility now attracts squatters and seasonal snowbirds (retirees escaping colder climates), who live "off the grid" in RVs and trailers among the remaining cement foundations (no mains electricity, no water, no sewers). In recent years the state has considered selling the land (which it officially owns), a move vociferously resisted by the residents. While here, check out **East Jesus** (ⓦeastjesus.org), a sort of steampunk garden made out of trash, an experimental, habitable, art installation in progress begun by the late Charles Stephen Russell in 2006 and run on solar power (at the time of research the collective was trying to raise funds to buy the East Jesus site land from the state). Overnight campers are asked for a $10 donation.

Anza-Borrego Desert State Park

3

Covering over 900 square miles, the **ANZA-BORREGO DESERT STATE PARK** (daily sunrise–sunset, excluding the campground; day-use fee $5; ☎760 767 5311, ⓦparks .ca.gov), southwest of the Salton Sea, is the largest state park in the country outside Alaska and comes with a legend-strewn history spanning Native American tribes, the first white trailfinders and Gold Rush times. It boasts multifarious varieties of vegetation and geological quirks that can, with a little effort, be as rewarding as those of the better known deserts to the north.

The park takes its double-barrelled name from Juan Bautista de Anza, a Spanish explorer who crossed the region in 1774, and the Spanish for the native bighorn sheep, *borrego cimarron*, which eats the brittlebush and agave found here. Some of Anza-Borrego can be covered by car (confidence on gravel roads is handy), although you'll need four-wheel drive for the more obscure – and most interesting – routes, and there are over five hundred miles of hiking trails and dirt roads.

During the fiercely hot summer months, the place is best left to the lizards, although most campgrounds and many hotels stay open all year. The most popular time to visit is the desert **blooming season** (typically a couple of weeks between late February and early April), though there's a fifty percent chance in any given year that the wildflowers won't bloom at all. If you strike it lucky you'll be rewarded with scarlet ocotillo, orange poppies, white lilies, purple verbena and other intensely colourful – and fragrant – wildflowers. For the latest information call the 24-hour Wildflower Hotline (☎760 767 4684). Take the usual desert precautions (see box, p.209) and beware, this is mountain lion territory (see box, p.45). People also visit to look at the amazing, clear **starry skies** – Borrego Springs was designated as the country's second Dark Sky community, after Flagstaff, Arizona.

Though accessible from the Salton Sea along Hwy-178 or Hwy-S22, the Anza-Borrego is usually approached from San Diego, through Julian (see p.199). This way you'll hit the park at Scissors Crossing, with most of the developed facilities to the north and much of the more interesting historical debris to the south.

Borrego Springs

Human activity in Anza-Borrego revolves around **Borrego Springs**, a tiny, peaceful town in the heart of the park that remains self-contained and remarkably uncommercialized. Base yourself here or camp at *Borrego Palm Canyon* campground, just outside of town, where there's an abundance of ranger-led hikes and campfire talks: check with the visitor centre (see p.239) for the latest details. If you're camping out, it's the place to gather (expensive) supplies – but don't expect any big supermarket chains here.

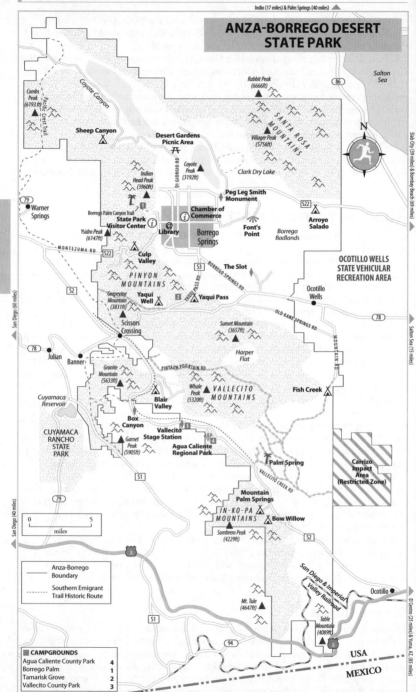

ANZA-BORREGO DESERT STATE PARK

Indio (17 miles) & Palm Springs (40 miles)

Slab City (39 miles) & Bombay Beach (69 miles)

N

Salton Sea

86

Combs Peak (6193ft) ▲

Coyote Canyon

Rabbit Peak (6666ft) ▲

SANTA ROSA MOUNTAINS

Villager Peak (5756ft) ▲

Pacific Crest Trail

Sheep Canyon ⚔

Desert Gardens Picnic Area ⛺

Clark Dry Lake

Indian Head Peak (3960ft) ▲

BORREGO-SALTON 1 RD

Coyote Peak (3192ft) ▲

Peg Leg Smith Monument

S22 ⚔ Arroyo Salado

79 ● Warner Springs

Borrego Palm Canyon Trail

State Park Visitor Center ⓘ

1

@ Library ⓘ

Chamber of Commerce

Borrego Springs

Font's Point

Borrego Badlands

Ysidro Peak (6147ft) ▲

MONTEZUMA RD S22

Culp Valley ⚔

S3

BORREGO-SPRINGS RD

The Slot

Ocotillo Wells

OCOTILLO WELLS STATE VEHICULAR RECREATION AREA

52

PINYON MOUNTAINS

Grapevine Mountain (3831ft) ▲

Yaqui Well ⚔

YAQUI PASS RD

2 Yaqui Pass

OLD KANE SPRINGS RD

78

Salton Sea (15 miles)

Scissors Crossing

Sunset Mountain (3657ft) ▲

Harper Flat

78 Julian ● Banner ●

PINYON MOUNTAIN RD

Granite Mountain (5633ft) ▲

Blair Valley ⚔

Whale Peak (5320ft) ▲

VALLECITO MOUNTAINS

Fish Creek ⚔

Cuyamaca Reservoir

Box Canyon ⚔

Garnet Peak (5905ft) ▲

Vallecito Stage Station

3

Agua Caliente Regional Park

4

CUYAMACA RANCHO STATE PARK

Palm Spring

VALLECITO CREEK RD

Carrizo Impact Area (Restricted Zone)

S1

San Diego (40 miles)

79

Mountain Palm Springs

IN-KO-PA MOUNTAINS

Bow Willow ⚔

0   5
miles

Sombrero Peak (4229ft) ▲

S2

San Diego & Imperial Valley Railroad

El Centro (25 miles) & Yuma, AZ (85 miles)

——— Anza-Borrego Boundary

- - - - Southern Emigrant Trail Historic Route

8

Mt. Tule (4647ft) ▲

Ocotillo ●

Table Mountain (4089ft) ▲

8

S1

94

USA
MEXICO

■ **CAMPGROUNDS**
Agua Caliente County Park   4
Borrego Palm   1
Tamarisk Grove   2
Vallecito County Park   3

INFORMATION

BORREGO SPRINGS

Chamber of Commerce 786 Palm Canyon Drive (Mon–Sat 9am–4pm, slightly shorter hours in summer; ☎ 800 559 5524, ⓦ borregospringschamber.com). Local information.

Library 587 Palm Canyon Drive, by the Mall (Tues & Thurs 9am–6pm, Wed noon–8pm, Fri & Sat 9am–5pm; ☎ 760 767 5761). Offers free internet access.

State Park Visitor Center (see below).

ACCOMMODATION

There are some delightful primitive campgrounds in the park (see box, p.240), plus a couple of developed campgrounds closer to town and a handful of lovely places to stay. In high season, even the basic motels seem quite expensive, though rates drop dramatically in summer.

HOTELS

★**Borrego Valley Inn** 405 Palm Canyon Drive ☎ 760 767 0311, ⓦ highwaywestvacations.com. Elegant adobe-styled 14-room B&B set in a cactus garden with two heated pools (one clothing-optional) and hot tubs. Terracotta-tiled a/c rooms come with fireplace and kitchenette, a hearty continental breakfast and, in the winter season, there are afternoon snacks. There's a two-night minimum stay at winter weekends and from mid-Feb to the end of April, and multi-night summer discounts. $\overline{215}$

Palm Canyon Hotel & RV Resort 221 Palm Canyon Drive ☎ 760 767 5341, ⓦ highwaywestvacations.com. Modern hotel a mile west of town done in ersatz Old West style, with comfortable rooms, vintage airstream trailer rentals and full-hookup RV sites ($55–125). $\overline{165}$

The Palms Hotel 2220 Hoberg Rd ☎ 760 767 7788, ⓦ thepalmsatindianhead.com. Stylish 1950s Modernist hotel – once the domain of Monroe, Brando and other celebrities – with a great pool, all very tastefully done. There are no phones or alarm clocks in rooms; the emphasis is very much on relaxation. $\overline{189}$

★**Stanlunds Resort Inn & Suites** 2771 Borrego Springs Rd ☎ 760 767 5501, ⓦ stanlunds.com. This 1960s-era motel offers the cheapest rooms around (some with kitchenettes), located three-quarters of a mile south of town along Borrego Springs Road. There's a nice pool and continental breakfast is provided on winter weekends. $\overline{75}$

CAMPGROUNDS

Campgrounds can be reserved through ⓦ reserveamerica .com or at ☎ 800 444 7275 (essential for holidays and weekends, and in the March–April blooming season; no reservations/first-come, first-served, May–Sept). Other than the two developed campgrounds reviewed below, there are nine designated primitive campgrounds in the park (see box, p.240).

Borrego Palm 200 Palm Canyon Drive ☎ 760 767 5311; map opposite. The largest campground and the only one with RV hookups (tents cannot use these), one mile from the visitor centre. Drinkable water, restrooms and hot, coin-operated showers are available. Reservations Oct–April, discount June–September. Pitches $\overline{25}$, RV hookups $\overline{35}$

Tamarisk Grove 13 miles south of Borrego Springs on Hwy-S3; map opposite. Refurbished in 2013, with toilets. Water is available but not potable, so bring drinking water or boil it. The coin-operated showers are much better since the renovation. Closed June–Sept. Pitches $\overline{25}$

EATING

The bulk of Borrego Springs' restaurants and shops are either in The Center or The Mall, opposite each other on Palm Drive. The best places to eat often close in summer, but there is always somewhere open.

Coyote Steakhouse The Palms Hotel, 2220 Hoberg Rd ☎ 760 767 7788, ⓦ thepalmsatindianhead.com. Hotel restaurant with a patio overlooking the pool, perfect for enjoying desert sunsets. The varied dinner menu offers everything from sashimi to rack of lamb (*prix fixe* menu $19–24). Wed–Sun 5–9pm (June–Sept Fri & Sat only).

Los Jilberto's 655 Palm Canyon Drive ☎ 760 767 1008. The locals' favourite: a cheap but good Mexican taco shop (especially good fish tacos) – eat in or take away, but remember to add the home-made salsa (especially the pickled carrots). Daily 7am–10pm.

Red Ocotillo 721 Avenida Sureste, off Christmas Circle ☎ 760 767 7400. Sit inside or on the shaded patio to enjoy breakfast delights such as eggs benedict with home-made Hollandaise sauce, a Reuben sandwich for lunch, or fish and chips for dinner (most mains $7–15). Daily 7am–8.30pm (check hours June–Sept).

State Park Visitor Center

200 Palm Canyon Drive • Mid-May to mid-Oct Sat & Sun 9am–5pm; mid-Oct to mid-May daily 9am–5pm • ☎ 760 767 4205, ⓦ parks.ca.gov

Your first stop in Anza-Borrego Desert State Park, two miles west of Borrego Springs,

3

BACKCOUNTRY CAMPING IN ANZA-BORREGO

Anza-Borrego Desert State Park manages two developed campgrounds (see p.239) and nine primitive campgrounds, but this is one of the few parks that allows **open camping**, giving you the freedom to pitch a tent pretty much anywhere without a permit – although it's advisable to let someone know your plans. The few provisos are that you don't drive off-road, don't camp near water holes, do camp away from developed campgrounds, light fires only in fire rings or metal containers, collect no firewood and leave the place as you found it, or cleaner.

Primitive campgrounds fill on a first-come, first-served basis; those in the backcountry always have space. Primitive campgrounds have no showers and usually no tables, and only have (non-flushing) vault toilets (Yaqui Pass has no toilets at all). All are accessible by road vehicles and are free (but you still need to pay the day-use fee if you have a car), except for *Sheep Canyon* ($10) and *Bow Willow* ($15), which are the only ones with tables and fire rings (they are sometimes described as "developed" but *Bow Willow* is very isolated, 55 miles south of the visitor centre). Most sites are below 1800ft, which is fine in winter, but in the hotter months you might try *Culp Valley*, eight miles southwest of Borrego Springs, at a blissfully balmy 3400ft. The campgrounds are:

- *Arroyo Salado* (880ft) – 19 miles east of Borrego Springs (Hwy-S22)
- *Blair Valley* (2500ft) –32 miles south of Borrego Springs (Hwy-S2)
- *Bow Willow* (950ft) – 55 miles south of Borrego Springs (off Hwy-S2)
- *Culp Valley* (3400ft) –10 miles west of Borrego Springs (Montezuma Valley Rd, Hwy-S22)
- *Fish Creek* (280ft) – 30 miles southeast of Borrego Springs (off Split Mountain Rd)
- *Mountain Palm Springs* (760ft) – 54 miles south of Borrego Springs (off Hwy-S2)
- *Sheep Canyon* (1500ft) – 14 miles northwest of Borrego Springs (end of DiGiorgio Rd, four-wheel drive only)
- *Yaqui Pass* (1730ft) – 12 miles south of Borrego Springs (Yaqui Pass Rd, Hwy-S3)
- *Yaqui Well* (1400ft) – 13 miles south of Borrego Springs (off Hwy-78).

---

should be the excellent **State Park Visitor Center**, which is so well landscaped into the desert floor that you barely notice it as you approach. Here you can also pick up an informative free newspaper, which contains a detailed map of the park along with numerous suggestions for hikes. Outside, the quarter-mile **All-Access Nature Trail** allows you to weave across the desert and identify the flora.

Borrego Palm Canyon Trail

A mile to the north of the park visitor centre, the main *Borrego Palm Canyon* campground marks the start of the **Borrego Palm Canyon Trail** (three-mile round-trip; 600ft elevation). It follows a detailed nature trail to one of the largest oases left in the US, with a quarter-mile of stream densely flanked by around a thousand mop-topped California fan palms (sometimes known as Washingtonia palms from their Latin name, *Washingtonia filifera*) – the only palms native to the western United States.

Peg Leg Smith and Font's Point

Six miles east of Borrego Springs along Hwy-S22, there's a memorial marker to **Thomas "Peg Leg" Smith** (1801–1866), an infamous mountain man and local spinner of yarns from the Gold Rush days who is further celebrated by a festival of tall tales – the **Peg Leg Liars Contest** – which takes place at this spot on the first Saturday in April. Anybody can get up before the judges and fib their hearts out for five minutes, with the most outrageous stories earning a modest prize. Roughly four miles further on, a fairly tough dirt road (check with the State Park visitor centre for conditions) leads to **Font's Point** and a view over the **Borrego Badlands** – a long, sweeping plain devoid of vegetation, whose strange, stark charms are oddly inspiring. Sunset and sunrise are the best times to fully appreciate the layered alluvial banding.

The Slot

If you want to be outside but shaded from the sun's fierce rays, make for **The Slot**, a narrow fifty-foot-deep canyon carved from the soft rock by infrequent flooding – though frequent enough that you definitely shouldn't venture here if there's any sign of rain in the vicinity. You can walk down into the canyon and follow it downstream for five minutes to a quarter-mile-long section where it's just wide enough for one person to squeeze through. To get here, travel 1.5 miles east from the junction of Borrego Springs Road and Hwy-78, then follow the very sandy Buttes Pass Road for 1.8 miles, keeping left at the only junction. The road is usually passable for ordinary cars but if you have any doubts about your or your vehicle's abilities, turn back.

Anza-Borrego south: Hwy-S2

At Scissors Crossing, Hwy-78 from Julian intersects Hwy-S2, which heads towards the park's southeast corner. It follows the line of the old **Butterfield Stage Route**, which began service in 1857 and was the first regular line of communication between the eastern states and the newly settled West. Along the way you pass through **Blair Valley**, with its primitive campground, to **Box Canyon**, where the Mormon Battalion of 1847, following what is now known as the **Southern Emigrant Trail Historic Route**, forced a passage along the desert wash. It isn't especially spectacular, but makes for some safe desert walking, never more than a couple of hundred yards from the road. Five miles further on, the **Vallecito Stage Station** (Sept–May Mon–Fri 9.30am–5pm, Sat & Sun 9.30am–sunset; June–Aug closed; day-use fee $3; ☎760 765 1188) is a reconstruction of the old Butterfield Stage Station and gives a good indication of the comforts – or lack of them – of early desert travel. The building is in the grounds of **Vallecito County Park campground** (see below).

A further three miles south, the **Agua Caliente Regional Park** (Sept–May daily 9.30am–sunset; $3/vehicle; ☎760 765 1188) contains a couple of naturally fed spring pools: one large outdoor affair kept at its natural 96°F and one smaller indoor pool at a more modest temperature, fitted with water jets. Most visitors stay at the **campground** (see below), which surrounds the pools and gives you longer access for evening soaking.

South of here lies the least-visited portion of Anza-Borrego, good for isolated exploration and undisturbed views around Imperial Valley, where there's a vivid and spectacular clash as grey rock rises from the edges of the red desert floor, and a primitive **campground** close to the small oasis at *Mountain Palm Springs*.

CAMPGROUNDS

Agua Caliente Regional Park 39555 Great Southern Overland Stage Rte of 1849 (Hwy-S2) ☎760 765 1188 (reservations ☎877 565 3600); map p.238. Large, developed campground with full hookups (electricity, water, sewer), bathrooms and access to the pools (above). Avoid holiday weekends and it's largely deserted. Open Sept–May. Pitches $24, hookups $33

Vallecito County Park 37349 Great Southern Overland

ANZA-BORREGO HIKING AND BIKING

Recreational opportunities in the park are strictly controlled to preserve the fragile ecosystem. **Hiking** is perhaps the most obvious pursuit, with the Borrego Palm Canyon Trail (see opposite) being the most popular. If you'd prefer to have the desert to yourself, consider one of the other hikes listed in the park's free annual newspaper: the **Peña Spring Trail** (0.6 miles round-trip) is good for spotting birds and wildlife, or try the tougher **Hellhole Canyon/Maidenhair Falls Trail** (6 miles round-trip), which involves some rock scrambling and ends at a canyon oasis. Both trails are a few miles southwest of the visitor centre.

Mountain bikers are not allowed on hiking trails, but you've free rein on almost 500 miles of dirt roads that cross the desert and mountains. For rentals try Bike Borrego, 583-D Palm Canyon Drive, Borrego Springs ($35/day; ☎760 767 4255, ⓦbikeborrego.com). It usually closes late May through to Sept.

Stage Rte of 1849 (Hwy-S2) ☎760 765 1188; map p.238. Offers 44 primitive sites (no hookups), including 22 spaces just for tents. There are tables, fire rings, barbecue grills, water taps, toilets, showers and a large covered picnic area. Open Sept–May. $22

The Western Mojave

The **western expanse** of the **Mojave Desert** spreads out on the north side of the San Gabriel Mountains, fifty miles from Los Angeles via Hwy-14. It's a barren plain that drivers have to cross in order to reach the alpine peaks of the eastern Sierra Nevada Mountains or Death Valley, at the Mojave's northern edge. The few towns that have taken root in this stretch of desert over the past few decades are populated by two sorts of people: retired couples who value the dry, clean air, and **aerospace** workers. The region's economy is wholly based on designing, building and testing aeroplanes, from B-1 bombers for the military to the *Voyager*, which made the first nonstop flight around the globe in 1987. The post-World War II establishment of **Edwards Air Force Base**, on the desert and dry lakebeds east of the town of Mojave, has made the region the aerospace capital of the world, as well as one of the fastest-growing regions in California.

Lancaster, south of Edwards Air Force Base, is the largest town and one of the few places to pick up supplies; **Mojave**, thirty miles north, is a desert crossroads that caters mainly to drive-by tourists. **Tehachapi**, twenty miles west and a few thousand feet higher, offers a cool retreat. Hwy-14 joins up with US-395 another forty miles north, just west of the huge naval air base at **China Lake** and the faceless town of **Ridgecrest**, useful mainly as a jumping-off point for more interesting attractions.

Palmdale

About the only thing of interest in **PALMDALE**, a small city some 62 miles north of Los Angeles, is the **Blackbird Airpark** (Fri–Sun 11am–4pm; free; ☎661 274 0884), three miles east of Hwy-14 at 2503 Avenue P (at E 25th St). The two sinister-looking black planes standing by the roadside here are the fastest and highest-flying planes ever created. The Lockheed A-12 was designed in the 1950s as a prototype for the 1964 Lockheed SR-71 – the *Blackbird* – a reconnaissance plane that could reach 2100 miles per hour at 85,000ft. Also on display is the once ultra-secret D-21 drone and the only remaining U-2 "D" model spy plane in the world. Unless you strike one of the infrequent "open cockpit" days, all you can do is admire their sleek lines and astonishing statistics. If you visit when the park's closed, you still get to see the key planes from outside the fence, though you won't get access to the small on-site exhibit. The adjacent **Joe Davies Heritage Airpark** (Fri–Sun 11am–4pm; free; ☎661 267 5611) displays over 21 aircraft designed or produced at the city's United States Air Force Plant 42 (such as the F-104 Starfighter and the giant B-52 Stratofortress), a major US air force manufacturing centre.

Lancaster and around

Nine miles north of Palmdale along the Antelope Valley, **LANCASTER** was founded in 1876 when the Southern Pacific Railroad arrived and is now the largest city in the region with a population of around 168,000. In recent years a relatively strong economy has meant a revitalized downtown and dramatically renovated **Lancaster Boulevard**, while in 2014 Lancaster became the first city in the US to require solar panels on all new homes. Other than wandering the pleasant boutiques and restaurants downtown, there's little in the way of sights, with the deserts to the west holding most interest.

Antelope Valley California Poppy Reserve

15101 Lancaster Rd • Daily sunrise–sunset • $10/vehicle • ☎ 661 724 1180, ⓦ parks.ca.gov

Turn west in Lancaster from Hwy-14 along Avenue I (which becomes Lancaster Rd) and follow it fourteen miles to reach the **Antelope Valley California Poppy Reserve**, blanketed in the bright orange of California's state flower, the Golden Poppy, each spring. You can stroll the easy desert trails at any time of year, but the main reason to come is to see the flowers; it is a temperamental and unpredictable plant, but given enough rain it usually blooms (perhaps two or three years in every five) between mid-March and late May; for updates, call the Wildflower Hotline (☎ 661 724 1180). During the blooming season you can also visit the excellent **Jane S Pinheiro Interpretive Center** (mid-March to mid-May daily 9am–5pm), which is neatly embedded in the hillside and has displays of desert flora and fauna.

Saddleback Butte State Park and Hi Vista

170th St E, between E Ave J and E Ave K • Daily sunrise–sunset • $6/vehicle • ☎ 661 946 6092, ⓦ parks.ca.gov

Seventeen miles east of Lancaster, **Saddleback Butte State Park** centres on a smallish granite butte (3651ft), whose slopes are home to a splendid collection of Joshua trees. It's also a likely spot to catch a glimpse of the endangered desert tortoise, for whom the park provides a refuge from the motorcyclists and ATV enthusiasts who tear around the region. There's a half-mile nature trail and a simple **campground** (pitch $20), which is mostly underused but is popular for stargazing at summer weekends. Just six miles north of the park (head east on East Ave K, then north on 200th St East), the desert community of **HI VISTA** is the home of the iconic **Calvary Baptist Church**, one of the key locations for Quentin Tarantino's *Kill Bill* films (East Ave G, at 198th St East).

Antelope Valley Indian Museum

15701 E Ave M, between E 150th & E 170th • Sat & Sun 11am–4pm • $3 • ☎ 661 946 3055, ⓦ avim.parks.ca.gov

Five miles southwest of Saddleback Butte, the **Antelope Valley Indian Museum**, housed in a mock Swiss chalet painted with Native American motifs, contains an extensive collection of more than 3000 artworks and ethnographic artefacts from all over the state. The museum has its roots in the folk art collection of one H. Arden Edwards, a self-taught artist who built the house here in 1928.

EATING AND DRINKING
LANCASTER

Crazy Otto's Diner 43528 20th St W ☎ 661 948 6502, ⓦ crazyottosdiners.com. The home of "the biggest omelette in the world" in 2002 (regular omelettes are $10.50–12.50) is a classic Western diner chain with sassy waitresses and excellent comfort food. Daily 6am–2pm.

★ **Kinetic Brewing Company** 735 W Lancaster Blvd ☎ 661 942 2337, ⓦ kineticbrewing.com. Great little brewpub, with a vast range of beers on tap ($5–6) and great pub food (burgers, ploughman's and the like $8–14). Mon–Wed 11.30am–10pm, Thurs 11.30am–11pm, Fri & Sat 11.30am–midnight, Sun 11.30am–9pm.

Mojave

Strung out along Hwy-14 thirty miles north of Lancaster, **MOJAVE** is a major junction on the interstate rail network, though it's used solely by freight trains. The town itself – essentially a mile-long highway strip of gas stations, $50-a-night motels, and franchised 24-hour fast-food restaurants – is a good place to fill up on essentials before continuing north into Owens Valley or Death Valley.

Mojave hit the headlines in 2004 as the launch and landing site of **SpaceShipOne**, which became the first privately funded spaceship to achieve suborbital flight (around 62 miles above the earth) twice within fourteen days, thereby claiming the $10 million reward from the X Prize Foundation.

The same clear, dry conditions that favour space launching make the **Mojave Air & Space Port** (ⓦ mojaveairport.com), a mile east of town on Airport Boulevard, the perfect parking lot for mothballed aeroplanes. Surplus commercial airliners are pastured here, often for years, and you can see the rows of Airbus and 747 tailplanes still decked out in the livery of their owners. Flight fans should aim to visit during the once-monthly "Plane Crazy" Saturdays (when you can wander around the site; see website), or set up base camp at the *Voyager Airport Restaurant* (see below) – the facility is otherwise closed to the public.

EATING   **MOJAVE**

Voyager Airport Restaurant Mojave Air & Space Port, Airport Blvd ☎ 661 824 2048, ⓦ mojaveairport.com. Housed in the old airport terminal building, spy on the activity of this working airport, listen in to the tower through radios at each table and access free wi-fi whilst enjoying ham and eggs. Mon–Fri 7am–3pm, Sat 8am–3pm, Sun 8am–2pm.

The Desert Tortoise Natural Area

Randsburg–Mojave Rd, California City • Daily 8am–sunset • Free • ☎ 951 683 3872, ⓦ tortoise-tracks.org

Some 23 miles northeast of Mojave, you might fancy taking a detour to see California's state reptile at the **Desert Tortoise Natural Area**, a forty-square-mile area of protected habitat amid desert torn up by off-roaders. To get there, drive through California City before turning north onto the unsurfaced Randsburg–Mojave Road, which runs four miles to the site. Here you'll find panels explaining the area's significance, and a network of easy desert trails which spur off the quarter-mile Main Loop Trail. Free leaflets provide guidance.

Red Rock Canyon State Park

Hwy-14, Cantil • Daily 24hr; visitor centre spring & fall Fri noon–7pm, Sat 9am–7pm, Sun 9am–3pm • $6/vehicle • ☎ 661 946 6092, ⓦ parks.ca.gov

Beyond Mojave the desert is virtually uninhabited, the landscape marked only by the bald ridges of the foothills of the Sierra Nevada Mountains that rise to the west. Some 24 miles north of Mojave, Hwy-14 passes through **Red Rock Canyon State Park**, a brilliantly coloured, rocky badland of wonderfully eroded formations.

The highway passes right through the centre of the most impressive section, though if you walk just a hundred yards from the road you're more likely to see an eagle or coyote. Better still, call at the state park **visitor centre**, which can point you to a number of short trails. It also runs a weekend ranger programme of nature walks and campfire talks, ranging from guest lectures by Native Americans to discussions on moviemaking in the area. Heading further north along US-395 brings you to the **Owens Valley** (see p.270) and the western entrance to **Death Valley** (see p.258).

Tehachapi

About twenty miles west from Mojave, Hwy-58 rises to **TEHACHAPI**, a small city and pretty apple-growing centre at 4000ft that offers respite from the Mojave's heat as well as a couple of minor sights. Some 4500 wind generators – built here since the early 1980s – make the **Tehachapi Pass Wind Farm**, ranked along Cameron Ridge to the east, one of the world's most productive renewable-energy stations. They're very visible from Hwy-58, but there are few places to stop so you may prefer to follow Tehachapi Willow Springs Road, a minor route between Tehachapi and Mojave running just south of Hwy-58.

Train enthusiasts cross states to see groaning diesels hauling their mile-long string of boxcars around the **Tehachapi Loop**, eight miles northwest of town. Built in 1876 as the only means of scaling the steep slopes of the region, the tracks double back on themselves to make a complete 360-degree loop. It's an impressive sight to watch a train over 85 boxcars long twisting around a mountain, its front end 77ft above its tail. For the best view, follow the signs three miles from the Keene exit to a roadside plaque commemorating the loop's engineers.

¡SI, SE PUEDE!

Just two miles north of the Tehachapi Loop in Keene, the **César E. Chávez National Monument** (daily 10am–4pm; free; ☎ 661 823 6134, ⓦ nps.gov/cech), 29700 Woodford-Tehachapi Rd, honours one of the most influential Latino leaders in US history. **César E. Chávez** (1927–1993) helped farm workers – mostly poor Mexican-Americans – to create the country's first permanent agricultural union in 1962, bringing attention to the plight of US farm workers and eventually securing higher wages and safer working conditions. Exhibits and videos tell the story, while the Memorial Garden contains the Chávez gravesite. The monument forms part of the Nuestra Señora Reina de la Paz complex, the home and workplace of the Chávez family and his organizations. See also the National Chavez Center website (ⓦ chavezfoundation.org).

INFORMATION   TEHACHAPI

Chamber of Commerce 209 E Tehachapi Blvd (Mon–Fri 10am–1pm & 2–5pm; ☎ 661 822 4180, ⓦ tehachapi .com). Located right by the train tracks in the older section of town; provides information on pick-your-own-fruit orchards, antiques shops and ostrich farms.

ACCOMMODATION AND EATING

Best Western Plus Country Park Hotel 420 W Tehachapi Blvd ☎ 661 823 1800, ⓦ bestwestern.com. The town's most comfortable lodgings is also the most popular, so make reservations in advance. The modern *BW* chain rooms come with all the standard extras and there's a heated outdoor pool. $128
The Shed 333 E Tehachapi Blvd ☎ 661 823 8333. Next to the visitor centre, this former agricultural shed from the 1930s is good for country-style breakfasts, apple-pie breaks and espresso (mains $9–21). Thurs & Sun 7am–4pm, Fri & Sat 7am–9pm.
Tehachapi Mountain Park Campground Water Canyon Rd (off Highline Rd) ☎ 661 868 7000. Eight miles southwest of town, there's camping among the pines at a refreshing 6000ft, with toilets and water but no other facilities; it's sometimes snowbound in winter. $18

Boron

Busy Hwy-58 runs east from Mojave, skirting the northern side of Edwards Air Force Base for thirty miles to **BORON**, a one-street town of just over 2000 people. The town is dominated by the **Rio Tinto Boron Mine**, the largest borax mine in the world, opened in 1927 and converted to an open-pit operation in the 1950s.

Borax Visitor Center

Borax Rd • Daily 9am–5pm • Free • ☎ 760 762 7588, ⓦ borax.com/about-borax/visitor-center

Learning about borax might sound as exciting as watching cement dry, but the **Borax Visitor Center**, accessed via the Borax Road exit off Hwy-58, is certainly illuminating and the mine itself is mind-numbingly big. The centre is a modern complex on a hill overlooking a processing plant and the vast open-cast borax mine itself; borax is sodium borate, a crystalline mineral which was originally used as a flux to improve the working properties of gold and silver, but more recently has found applications in everything from washing detergents to flat-screen TVs and fibreglass. The centre is primarily a promotional tool for the Borax division of the Rio Tinto Group, which owns the site, but call in if only to see the ten-minute video (complete with a 1960s snip of Ronald Reagan advertising hand cleaner), which finishes with curtains opening on a great view into the mile-wide, 650ft-deep pit.

Twenty Mule Team Museum

26962 Twenty Mule Team Rd, at Boron Ave • Daily 10am–4pm • Free • ☎ 760 762 5810

Learn more about the tortured history of borax extraction and the role of the "twenty-mule teams", which hauled ten-tonne wagons of the mineral out of Death Valley and elsewhere in the 1880s, at the **Twenty Mule Team Museum** in Downtown Boron. The museum also commemorates movies filmed around here – parts of *Erin Brockovich*, for one – and has a display on the **Solar Energy Generating Station** (SEGS), whose shiny mirrors spread six miles across the desert around the junction of Hwy-58 and US-395.

Randsburg

The near ghost town of **RANDSBURG**, thirty miles north of Boron along US-395, retains a certain Wild West charm with its 200-yard-long main street, two bars and a dozen shops. The **Rand Desert Museum**, 161 Butte Ave (Sat & Sun 10am–4pm; free; ☎760 371 0965, ⊚randdesertmuseum.com), chronicles the glory days of the 1890s, when upwards of three thousand people lived in the town, mining gold, silver and tungsten out of the arid, rocky hills. Scruffy-looking shacks surrounded by the detritus of ancient mines line the streets, which are very quiet midweek but pick up a little at weekends when off-roaders descend on the place and a couple of antique-cum-knick-knack shops open up.

ACCOMMODATION, EATING AND DRINKING   RANDSBURG

★**General Store** 35 Butte Ave ☎760 374 2143, ⊚randsburggeneralstore.com. Fascinating slice of history: there's an embossed tin ceiling, 1904 soda fountain (the super-thick chocolate shakes and "Black Bart" banana splits are locally celebrated), and a small restaurant (sandwiches, breakfasts, hot dogs) surrounded by shelves of groceries and mining supplies. Mon 10am–4pm, Thurs–Sun 10am–5pm.

Goat's Sky Ranch 130 Butte Ave ☎760 374 2285, ⊚goatsskyranch.com. Excellent B&B with roots in 1903 (the wood floors are original) and six period B&B rooms

plus five self-sufficient cabins ($125) surrounded by cactus gardens, random antiques and a wooden deck for lounging. Operated by professional motocross rider and local legend Goat Breker. **$85**

White House Saloon 168 Butte Ave ☎760 374 2464. Bar that looks like something straight out of a Western (it allegedly dates back to the 1890s), with lots of bikers, cold beers (Mojave Red on tap), decent chilli and burgers and fries (around $9), but come here for the atmosphere, not the food. Cash only. Fri–Sun 11am–5pm.

Ridgecrest

Twenty miles north of Randsburg, Hwy-178 branches east off Hwy-395 towards Death Valley, passing through the small city of **RIDGECREST**, essentially a long string of malls along China Lake Boulevard. It's dominated by the huge Naval Air Weapons Station China Lake just to the north, with jet fighters screaming past overhead, taking target practice on land that's chock-full of ancient **petroglyphs** – the largest grouping in the western hemisphere, but with strictly controlled access.

Maturango Museum

100 E Las Flores Ave, at China Lake Blvd • Daily 10am–5pm • $5 (store and local information area is free) • ☎760 375 6900, ⊚maturango.org

You can get some idea of the native culture of the Mojave Desert by visiting the **Maturango Museum**, which has exhibits on both the natural and cultural history of the region, including examples of the rock-art figures pecked into dark basalt rocks. To get out and see the figures and designs in their natural surroundings, join a seasonal, full-day, volunteer-led **tour of the Coso petroglyphs** in Little Petroglyph Canyon (mid-Feb to mid-June & mid-Sept to mid-Dec most Sat and Sun; $55). However, since these petroglyphs are on the Navy base, foreigners are banned and US citizens must fill in the online application form and Navy SECNAV form in advance (but you must submit the form in person, by fax, or by US mail only), and bring proof of US citizenship, valid vehicle registration and insurance (your vehicle will be inspected).

ACCOMMODATION AND EATING   RIDGECREST

If you end up spending the night in Ridgecrest, your best bet is the cluster of motel chains along central China Lake Blvd.

Casey's Steaks & Barbeque 1337 N China Lake Blvd ☎760 446 8000, ⊚caseyssteaksbbq.com. No-frills diner,

serving a combination of American classics from burgers ($9.50) to barbecue dinners (from $10.50) and Tex-Mex food (3 tacos from $8.50). Their Original BBQ Sauce is so popular it's now sold in bottles. Mon–Thurs 11am–9.30pm, Fri & Sat 11am–10pm, Sun 11am–9pm. ★**Mon Reve** 126 Balsam St ☎760 375 3212. This authentic French restaurant (seriously: the owner is from Normandy) has developed quite a cult following, with all the classics done simply and beautifully; French onion soup, escargot, filet mignon and crème brûlée, among many others. Tues–Fri 11am–1.30pm & 5.30–8.30pm, Sat 5.30–8.30pm.

Trona Pinnacles and Searles Valley

Hwy-178 runs northeast from Randsburg past the burro corrals and out into the dry and desolate **Searles Valley** bound for Death Valley National Park. Some sixteen miles northeast of Randsburg, a five-mile dirt road (passable except after rain) leads to the **Trona Pinnacles National Natural Landmark** (unrestricted access; free), where over five hundred tufa (calcium carbonate) spires and ridges stretch up to 140ft. Mostly conical and grouped in clusters, these soft rock pinnacles were considered sufficiently extra-terrestrial-looking to form a backdrop for parts of *Star Trek V* and *Planet of the Apes*, and are best viewed on the half-mile nature trail. There's free **camping** with a vault toilet but no water supply. You can find basic supplies six miles north on Hwy-178 at the industrial and substantially run-down borax-processing town of **Trona**.

Old Route 66

The long desert drive from LA to Las Vegas takes you along I-15, part of which follows the original line of **Route 66**, the most celebrated of American highways, built to link LA with Chicago in the 1920s but since largely overlaid by the interstate system (see box, p.248). In California you'll see little of the old road – or anything else of great interest – from the freeway, so you should take time out to explore a few minor attractions. **Victorville** warrants a brief detour to view the highway-side Americana in the Route 66 Museum, but **Barstow** is better for what lies nearby, particularly the coloured rocks of Rainbow Basin and the faux ghost town of Calico. Further east there are early human remains at the **Calico Dig**, and the etymological curiosity that is **Zzyzx**, a small desert hamlet 12 miles south of **Baker**.

Victorville

The first town of any size on I-15 is **VICTORVILLE**, some eighty miles northeast of LA. It has all the motels, fast-food joints and gas stations you could ask for along the freeway, but it's worth ducking off into the old town centre for a quick look at the small **California Route 66 Museum**, 16825 D St, at 5th (Mon & Thurs–Sat 10am–4pm, Sun 11am–3pm; free; ☎760 951 0436, ⊛califrt66museum.org). Inside are devotional displays relating to the westernmost strip of the "Mother Road". Relics from an old roadside attraction called "Hulaville" are the museum's most interesting feature, but there are also various old-time videos and a stack of nostalgic merchandise.

EATING **VICTORVILLE**

Emma Jean's Holland Burger Café 17143 D St ☎760 243 9938, ⊛hollandburger.com. Soak up the Mother Road Americana two miles north of Downtown Victorville at this classic cinder blocks diner that's been serving straightforward breakfasts and burgers since 1947. Mon–Fri 5am–2.45pm, Sat 6am–12.30pm.

Barstow and around

Almost thirty desert miles northeast of Victorville, **BARSTOW** is the crossroads of the Mojave and provides a welcome opportunity to stretch your legs, though for many months of the year, the relentless sun keeps people in their air-conditioned homes for a good part of the day. It's a small town, consisting of just one main road – part of the original **Route 66** (see box below) – which is lined with a selection of motels and restaurants that make a budget overnight stop possible. Historical interest focuses on the grand **Harvey House** (W barstowharveyhouse.com) on North First Avenue, also known as the Casa del Desierto (the "house of the desert"), built as a train station in 1911 (trains still stop here) and now home to the local Chamber of Commerce and a couple of mildly interesting museums. Incidentally, **Hinkley**, just 14 miles northwest of Barstow, which became infamous after its groundwater contamination case was the subject of the Julia Roberts movie *Erin Brockovich* in 2000, is now a virtual ghost town. Much of the movie was filmed in and around Barstow, and Boron (see p.245).

Harvey House museums

681 N First Ave **Western American Railroad Museum** Fri–Sun 11am–4pm · Free · ☎ 760 256 9276, W barstowrailmuseum.org **Route 66 "Mother Road" Museum** Fri–Sun 11am–4pm · Free · ☎ 760 255 1890, W route66museum.org

Harvey House contains the **Western American Railroad Museum,** dedicated to preserving the history of Southwest railroading with outdoor displays of rolling stock and locomotives, and also the **Route 66 "Mother Road" Museum**, full of highway Americana and some classic photos of yesteryear Barstow.

Mojave River Valley Museum

270 E Virginia Way · Daily 11am–4pm · Free · ☎ 760 256 5452, W mojaverivervalleymuseum.org

For an overview of the social and natural history of the area, visit the **Mojave River Valley Museum**, which contains a sizeable archeological collection including material from the Calico Dig (see p.247).

ROUTE 66 IN CALIFORNIA

The advent of the interstates in the 1950s was the death knell for what John Steinbeck called **The Mother Road**. The umbilical cord between Chicago and Los Angeles, Route 66 was conceived in the 1920s when existing roads were stitched together to form a single 2400-mile route across eight states. It was just one of many such migration routes, but is the one that most captured the public imagination – not least through Nat King Cole's 1946 hit (*Get your kicks on*) *Route 66* – and became America's most famous highway. As freeways obliterated the old road and franchise hotels and restaurants populated their flanks, the old diners and mom-and-pop motels gradually disappeared, further enhancing its iconic status.

Large sections of the old route vanished long ago, but it was the realization that some of the last vestiges were about to disappear that kick-started a revival. Sections of the original route have since sprouted Route 66 signs, though these were promptly liberated by fans and you now tend to see "Historic Route 66" shields painted onto the asphalt. After considerable lobbying by Route 66 associations, Bill Clinton passed a National Preservation Bill benefiting the Route 66 Corridor in 1999, and the tourist machine now promotes the old road vigorously. Some 320 miles of the original route ran through California, and Kingman, Barstow and San Bernardino all get name-checked in the famous song, but the best-preserved section is in the Mojave Desert east of Barstow.

Fans will want to visit the small **museums** in Victorville (see p.247) and Barstow (see p.247), or even try to track down San Bernardino's classic 1949 *Wigwam Motel*, at 2728 W Foothill Blvd (☎ 909 875 3005, W wigwammotel.com; $85), but for most it's enough to drive the desert section that loops south off I-40 from Ludlow to Essex. One essential stop is **Amboy**, a place that seems instantly familiar from dozens of road-trip movies and car commercials principally because of the Googie "retro-future" sign for *Roy's Motel & Café*, a 1938 landmark (W rt66roys .com). The whole minuscule town – including post office, abandoned church and dirt airstrip – was bought in 2005 by fast-food chicken magnate Albert Okura, who has reopened the gas station (expensive, and only on-demand) and sells snacks, though the café and motel seem unlikely to reopen anytime soon.

To delve deeper, check out websites such as W national66.org and W historic66.com.

FIELDS OF MIRRORS

Eight miles east of Barstow on I-40 is the hundred-acre field of mirrors, aka the **SEGS II (Daggett) Solar Power Plant**, completed in 1985 and a surreal example of how California is putting its deserts to use. Anyone who has seen the film *Bagdad Café* (see p.693) will remember the light reflections the mirrors give off for miles around.

Rainbow Basin

Around eight miles north of Downtown Barstow via Irwin Road then Fossil Bed Road, **Rainbow Basin** (unrestricted access), comprises rock formations cast in myriad shades, from vivid greens to deep reds, by thirty million years of wind erosion. The winding four-mile loop road around the canyon is best tackled around dawn or dusk. Camping is also available.

ARRIVAL AND INFORMATION

BARSTOW AND AROUND

By bus Greyhound buses stop at 1611 E Main St (☎760 256 8757), where it crosses I-15, a mile east of downtown. Destinations Las Vegas (8 daily; 2hr 35min–2hr 45min); Los Angeles (5 daily; 2hr 15min–4hr 30min); Victorville (3 daily; 35min).

By train The unstaffed Amtrak station is in Harvey House (see opposite) on 1st St.
Destinations Albuquerque (1 daily; 12hr 51min); Chicago (1 daily; 39hr 24min); Flagstaff (1 daily; 6hr 40min); Los Angeles (1 daily; 4hr 31min); Victorville (1 daily; 39min).

California Welcome Centre Four miles west of Barstow in the Tanger Outlet Mall off I-15 at the Lenwood Rd exit (Mon–Fri 11am–6pm; ☎760 253 4782, ⓦvisitcalifornia .com). Has a good selection of maps of the surrounding area, lodging and restaurant guides, and various flyers on local attractions.

Chamber of Commerce Harvey House (Mon–Fri 8.30am–5pm and Sat 10am–2pm; ⓦbarstowchamber .com).

ACCOMMODATION

Ayres Hotel Barstow 2812 Lenwood Rd ☎760 307 3121, ⓦayreshotels.com. Best of several motel chains that surround Barstow (which offer good value overall), friendly, super-clean and well equipped with all the usual extras and a heated pool. **$119**

Route 66 Motel 195 W Main St ☎760 256 7866, ⓦroute66motelbarstow.com. A genuine Route 66 motel since 1922, its yard dotted with hulks of 1940s and 1950s cars and decorated with old gas station signs. Rooms are old and a bit crummy, but some have round double beds (all have flat-screens, fridges and microwaves). **$50**

EATING AND DRINKING

Bagdad Café 46548 National Trails Hwy, Newberry Springs (23 miles southeast of Barstow) ☎760 257 3101. Throwback, shabby diner that's become an iconic stop along Route 66 on the back of the 1988 German film of the same name. Browse the scrapbook, sip a coffee and take a look at the old Airstream trailer from the movie, which rots outside; to be frank the food here isn't great, but come for the ambience. Take the first Newberry Springs exit off I-40 and continue 3 miles east. Daily 7am–7pm.

DiNapoli's Firehouse 1358 E Main St ☎760 256 1094, ⓦdinapolisfirehouse.com. Rustic, regional Italian joint decorated with firefighting memorabilia and selling tasty hand-tossed pizza (from $15.95), hearty pasta dishes (from $12.95) and seductive desserts. Mon–Sat 11am–9pm.

Idle Spurs Steakhouse 690 Old Hwy-58 ☎760 256 8888, ⓦthespurs.us. This Barstow institution just north of town has been serving the best steaks around, washed down with microbrews or something from their extensive wine list, since the 1950s. Try the top sirloin ($20) or perhaps a sirloin and lobster tail combo ($45). Tues–Fri 11am–9pm, Sat & Sun 4–9pm.

Rosita's Restaurant 540 W Main St ☎760 256 1058, ⓦrositasrestaurant.net. Freshly made tortilla chips and excellent salsa set the tone for this cavernous and authentic Mexican place, opened in 1954. There's a massive range of combination dishes ($15) plus lunch and early dinner specials ($9–10). Tues–Sat 11am–9pm, Sun 10.30am–8pm.

Slash X Ranch Café 28040 Barstow Rd (Hwy-247) ☎760 252 1197, ⓦslashxoffroad.com. Lively bar and café ten miles south of town on Hwy-247. A Barstow favourite since 1954 (and popular with dirt bikers, who tear up the desert nearby), it's great for burgers or just a few cold beers. Another place associated with the *Erin Brockovich* movie (bar scene). Fri 10am–4pm, Sat 8am–6pm, Sun 8am–5pm.

3

Calico Ghost Town

36600 Ghost Town Rd, Yermo • Daily 9am–5pm • $8, admission free with camping ($30) • ☎ 760 254 2047, ⓦ cms.sbcounty.gov

Attractively set in the colour-streaked Calico Hills seven miles northeast of Barstow along I-15, then three miles north, the contrived **Calico Ghost Town** once produced millions of dollars of silver and borax and supported a population of almost four thousand. Founded in 1881, the town was quickly deserted when the silver ran out and has now been rather insensitively restored, with souvenir shops, hot-dog stands and a main thoroughfare lined with ersatz saloons, an old schoolhouse, a vaudeville playhouse and shops kitted out in period styles. However, should you so desire, there are miles of mining shafts and tunnels open to crawl around in.

Calico Early Man Site

Minneola Rd exit off I-15 • Sat 9am–4pm (Fri noon–Sun noon first weekend of every month, Oct–May) • $5, digs included • ⓦ calicoarchaeology.com

The **Calico Early Man Site**, six miles northeast of the I-15 Calico exit, then 2.5 miles north has become one of the most important archeological sites in North America since Louis Leakey excavated it in 1964. Some of the old tools found here have been dated at around 20,000 years old, controversially establishing mankind's presence here several thousand years earlier than was previously thought – and the debate rages on. The self-guided tour of the dig isn't very instructive, so try to visit on one of the "dig weekends" (first full weekend each month, Oct–May), which makes it all come alive.

Afton Canyon

AFTON CANYON, 37 miles northeast of Barstow, is only a couple of hundred feet deep but is striking nevertheless, with multicoloured strata formed by erosion from an extinct lake. This is one of the three places where the **Mojave River** flows above ground throughout the year, making this a marshy hub for almost two hundred types of desert creatures, including rare bird species such as the vermilion flycatcher and summer tanager.

Baker

A couple of motels and restaurants and some fairly expensive gas stations just about sums up **BAKER**, twenty miles northeast of Afton Canyon on I-15. Death Valley lies immediately north, and it's in honour of the town's proximity to the country's hottest place that Baker has the world's tallest functioning **thermometer**, rising 134ft to commemorate the highest temperature ever recorded in the US – 134°F (56.6°C) in 1913. Baker is also a springboard for the Mojave National Preserve (see opposite). Look out also for the *UFO Hotel* (ⓦ ufohotel.com) a goofy inn designed to look like an alien spacecraft (there have been several UFO sightings in the area) – opening is pending the raising of funds, but you can visit **Alien Fresh Jerky** store at 72242 Baker Blvd, for the latest (daily 8am–7pm; ⓦ alienfreshjerky.com).

EATING   BAKER

Mad Greek Cafe 72112 Baker Blvd ☎ 760 733 4354. Standing out from the franchise joints, this touristy diner serves an eclectic and good-value range of choices, among them gyros, kebabs, burgers, Mexican dishes, espresso, pastries and delicious fresh strawberry shakes – more a sundae than a drink. Most dishes cost $8–11. Daily 24hr.

Mojave National Preserve

In 1994, 2500 square miles of undeveloped country wedged between I-15 and I-40 were set aside as the **MOJAVE NATIONAL PRESERVE**, a perfect spot to take a break from the freeway and maybe camp out a night or two to prepare for the excesses of Las Vegas, seventy miles ahead. It's a little higher than much of the desert hereabouts, making it a bit cooler in summer but also subject to winter snows.

The preserve's main roads all lead to the graceful Mission Revival-style **Kelso Depot**, 35 miles southeast of Baker, built in 1924 for workers on the Union Pacific Railroad and now the main visitor centre (see below). There's no roofed accommodation in the park but there are several **campgrounds** (see below).

Kelso Dunes

Approaching Kelso from Baker, Kelbaker Road shoots past a series of dramatic black-and-red **cinder cones**, created ten thousand years ago. Visible to the south of the Kelso Depot, are the spectacular **Kelso Dunes**, a golden five-mile stretch of sand reaching seven hundred feet high. A sandy trail off Kelso Dunes Road wanders up to the dunes, where in half an hour you can be scrambling around and listening out for a faint booming sound caused by dry sand cascading down the steep upper slopes: apparently a rare phenomenon. There are free primitive camping spots nearby.

Cima and around

Twenty miles northeast of Kelso, the small town of **CIMA** (there's a little store here, but no gas station) heralds **Cima Dome**, a perfectly formed batholith rising some 1500ft above the desert floor and cloaked in dense stands of Joshua trees. These are best explored on the **Teutonia Peak Trail** (four miles round-trip).

Southeast of Cima, Mojave Road and Black Canyon Road provide access to the *Mid Hills* campground, from where the moderately difficult **Mid Hills to Hole-in-the-Wall Trail** (eight miles each way; 1200ft ascent) winds through Wild Horse Canyon and ends up at the *Hole-in-the-Wall* campground. You can also drive to *Hole-in-the-Wall* campground, where there's a **visitor centre** (May–Sept Fri–Sun 9am–4pm; Oct–April daily 9am–4pm) and another great hike along the **Rings Trail** (half-mile round-trip), which involves a little scrambling and a descent into Banshee Canyon using metal rings anchored to the rock wall.

INFORMATION   MOJAVE NATIONAL PRESERVE

Mojave is a big preserve (larger than Yosemite) so be sure to **go prepared**: fill up and buy supplies before entering, as there's no gas station, just one tiny shop at Cima, and only camping for accommodation. Entrance to the preserve is free, with open access 24hr daily.

Kelso Depot Visitor Center In the heart of the preserve (Thurs–Mon 10am–5pm; ☏760 252 6108, ⓦnps.gov/ moja), with excellent displays that focus on the region's geology, flora, fauna and social history.

ACCOMMODATION

The authorities allow limited, primitive, roadside camping at designated spots. Consult the park newspaper for full details, or head straight for Kelso Dunes Rd, where there are numerous spots a mile beyond the hiking trailhead.

Mojave National Preserve campgrounds There are two formal campgrounds at Mojave National Preserve; both are first-come, first-served and open year-round, and offer fire rings, tables, toilets and water: the cool (sometimes snowy in winter) *Mid Hills* campground which is beautifully sited at 5600ft; and the 4400ft *Hole-in-the-Wall* campground, situated among striking volcanic rock formations and so named by Bob Hollimon, a member of the Butch Cassidy gang, because it reminded him of his former hideout in Wyoming. Both campgrounds charge per pitch $12

Death Valley, Owens Valley and the Eastern Sierra

ANCIENT BRISTLECONE PINE FOREST

Death Valley, Owens Valley and the Eastern Sierra

The far eastern edge of California, rising up from the Mojave Desert and cleaving to the border with Nevada, is a long narrow strip as scenically dramatic as anywhere else in the state, veering from blistering desert to ski country in the lee of the mighty Sierra Nevada mountains. It's a region devoid of interstates, scarcely populated and, but for the scant reminders of gold-hungry pioneers, developed in only the most tentative way.

At the region's base, technically forming the Mojave's northern reach, is **Death Valley National Park**. With the highest average summer temperatures on earth, and so remote that it's almost a region unto itself, this vast reserve is a distillation of the classic desert landscape: an arid, otherworldly terrain of brilliantly coloured, bizarrely eroded rocks, mountains and sand dunes.

North of Death Valley, the towering **eastern** peaks of the **Sierra Nevada** are perfectly described by their Spanish name, which literally translates as "snowcapped saw". Virtually the entire alpine reaches of the range are preserved as wilderness, and hikers and mountaineers can get to higher altitudes quicker here than almost anywhere else in California: well-maintained roads lead to trailheads at over 8000ft, providing swift access to spires, glaciers and clear mountain lakes. **Mount Whitney**, the tallest peak in the contiguous US, is located near the southernmost point of the chain, which continues north for an uninterrupted 150 miles to the backcountry of Yosemite National Park, and well beyond.

At the foot of Mount Whitney, 5-mile-wide **Owens Valley** starts, hemmed in to the east by the **White Mountains**, nearly as high but far drier and less hospitable than the Sierra Nevada, and home to ancient, gnarled **bristlecone pines**. In between the two mountain ranges, US-395 runs the length of the valley, which has few signs of settlement at all beyond sporadic roadside towns and the larger town of **Bishop**. An hour's drive further north, **Mammoth Lakes** is the Eastern Sierra's busiest resort, thick with skiers in winter and fishing and cycling enthusiasts in summer. Finally, at the point where many turn west for Yosemite, bizarre rock formations rise from the placid blue waters of primordial **Mono Lake**, set in a dramatic desert basin of volcanoes and steaming hot pools. Beyond, and far enough out of the way to deter crowds, lies the wonderful ghost town of **Bodie**, which preserves a palpable sense of Gold Rush town life eight thousand feet up in a parched, windswept valley.

Highlights

❶ Dante's View Marvel at the multicoloured mountains and blinding saltpans of Death Valley from this spectacular viewpoint. **See p.262**

❷ Rhyolite Assorted Gold Rush ruins, a house made from bottles and a weird collection of fibreglass sculptures make this an essential stop on the fringe of Death Valley. **See p.264**

❸ Mount Whitney The highest point in the US outside of Alaska possesses iconic appeal; its epic summit views are best appreciated as part of an overnight camping trip. **See p.270**

❹ Ancient Bristlecone Pine Forest Visit the alpine forest in the lofty, weathered White Mountains to see the gnarled and wizened forms of the world's most ancient living things – some nearly five millennia old. **See p.276**

❺ Mono Lake Paddle among the lakeside tufa towers on canoe or kayak trips through this otherworldly, highly photogenic landscape. **See p.288**

❻ Bodie Bring a picnic and your camera and leave half a day to explore the best-preserved ghost town in the West. **See p.291**

HIGHLIGHTS ARE MARKED ON THE MAP ON P.256

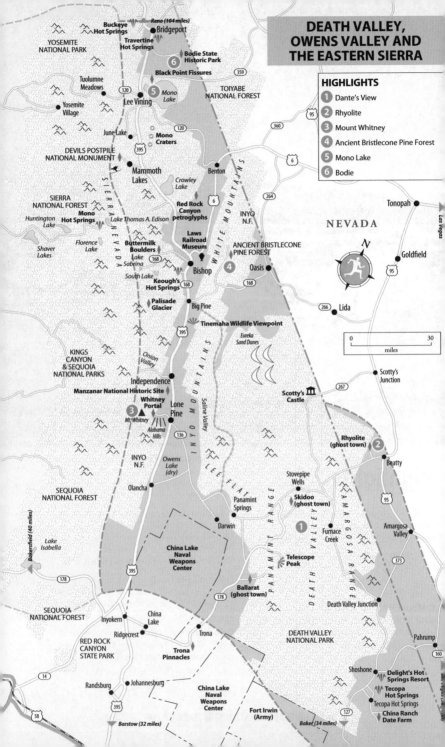

DEATH VALLEY, OWENS VALLEY AND THE EASTERN SIERRA

HIGHLIGHTS

1 Dante's View
2 Rhyolite
3 Mount Whitney
4 Ancient Bristlecone Pine Forest
5 Mono Lake
6 Bodie

NEVADA

Reno (104 miles)

Buckeye Hot Springs
Bridgeport
Travertine Hot Springs
6 Bodie State Historic Park
Black Point Fissures
YOSEMITE NATIONAL PARK
TOIYABE NATIONAL FOREST
359

Tuolumne Meadows
120
5 Mono Lake
Yosemite Village
Lee Vining
360
95

June Lake
120
Mono Craters
395

DEVILS POSTPILE NATIONAL MONUMENT
Mammoth Lakes
6
Tonopah

Crowley Lake
Benton
264
Goldfield
95

SIERRA NATIONAL FOREST
Mono Hot Springs
Lake Thomas A. Edison
6
INYO N.F.

Huntington Lake
Red Rock Canyon petroglyphs
Buttermilk Boulders
Lake Sabrina
168
Laws Railroad Museum
ANCIENT BRISTLECONE PINE FOREST
4

Shaver Lakes
Florence Lake
South Lake
Bishop
Oasis
Lida
266

Keough's Hot Springs
168
168

Palisade Glacier
Big Pine

Tinemaha Wildlife Viewpoint
395

KINGS CANYON & SEQUOIA NATIONAL PARKS
Eureka Sand Dunes
Scotty's Junction
267

Onion Valley
Independence
Saline Valley
Scotty's Castle

Manzanar National Historic Site
Whitney Portal
3 ▲ Mt. Whitney
Lone Pine
Alabama Hills
136
Rhyolite (ghost town) 2
Beatty

INYO N.F.
Owens Lake (dry)
95

SEQUOIA NATIONAL FOREST
Olancha
Stovepipe Wells
Amargosa Valley

Panamint Springs
Skidoo (ghost town)
1
Furnace Creek
373

Darwin

Bakersfield (40 miles)
Lake Isabella
178
CHINA LAKE NAVAL WEAPONS CENTER
Telescope Peak
PANAMINT RANGE

SEQUOIA NATIONAL FOREST
Ballarat (ghost town)
178
Death Valley Junction

Inyokern
China Lake
Trona
DEATH VALLEY NATIONAL PARK
Pahrump

RED ROCK CANYON STATE PARK
Ridgecrest
Trona Pinnacles
127
160

14
Randsburg
Johannesburg
395
China Lake Naval Weapons Center
Shoshone
Delight's Hot Springs Resort
Tecopa Hot Springs
Tecopa Hot Springs
China Ranch Date Farm

58
Barstow (32 miles)
Fort Irwin (Army)
Baker (34 miles)

0 — 30 miles
N

SIERRA NEVADA
WHITE MOUNTAINS
INYO MOUNTAINS
LEE FLAT
DEATH VALLEY
AMARGOSA RANGE

GETTING AROUND   **DEATH VALLEY, OWENS VALLEY AND THE EASTERN SIERRA**

By car Getting around the region is best done by car, primarily using US-395 – the lifeline of the Owens Valley and pretty much the only access to the area from within California. Once north of Freeman Junction, where Hwy-178 branches west toward San Joaquin Valley, no road crosses the Sierra Nevada until Hwy-120 lunges over 10,000ft Tioga Pass into Yosemite. Hwy-190, heading east from Hwy-395 just south of Mount Whitney, cuts through the Panamint Range into Death Valley.

By bus Neither Amtrak nor Greyhound run any services in the region, and the only long-distance public transport is the bus service by Eastern Sierra Transit (☎ 760 872 1901, ⓦ estransit .com), which travels along Owens Valley linking Lancaster in the south (see p.242) and Reno, Nevada, in the north (see p.579). Both cities have onward connections, and buses generally have racks or space on board to accommodate bikes.

By taxi A couple of small companies operate what are effectively taxi services that run up to mountain trailheads: visitor centres and outdoor gear shops are the best source for information.

Hwy-127: The southern approach to Death Valley

Hwy-127 branches off I-15 at Baker (see p.250) and cuts across desolate Mojave Desert landscape into Amargosa Valley before reaching any civilization. The highway heads north, skirting Tecopa Hot Springs after fifty-odd miles before heading through Shoshone, which has a gas station and decent motel, and Death Valley Junction; from here, it's an easy 30-mile drive to the heart of Death Valley National Park, **Furnace Creek**, passing Zabriskie Point and the junction for Dante's View (see p.262) along the way.

4

Tecopa Hot Springs and around

Tecopa Hot Springs Resort 860 Tecopa Hot Springs Rd (2 miles off Hwy-127) • Call for hours • Day-use $8 • ☎ 760 852 4420, ⓦ tecopahotsprings.org • **Delight's** 368 Tecopa Hot Springs Rd • Mon–Fri 10am–5pm, Sat & Sun 10am–10pm • weekdays $15; weekends $20 • ☎ 760 852 4343, ⓦ delightshotspringsresort.com

Fifty miles north of Baker (and just 80 miles west of Las Vegas), the tiny village of **TECOPA** has become a popular winter retreat, thanks to the natural **Tecopa Hot Springs**, which can be experienced in separate men's and women's clothing-free concrete bathhouses at the *Tecopa Hot Springs Resort*. For a more intimate experience, head for nearby **Delight's Hot Springs Resort**, where you can soak in private mineral pools.

China Ranch Date Farm

China Ranch Rd (off Furnace Creek Rd) • Daily 9am–5pm • Free • ☎ 760 852 4415, ⓦ chinaranch.com

Even if you're not staying in or around Tecopa, it's worth making a detour to **China Ranch Date Farm** (7 miles southeast of *Tecopa Hot Springs Resort*), where you're free to wander among the mostly young groves, follow a shady streamside nature path, explore more widely along the Old Spanish Trail (a pack route between old mission stations), or retire to the cactus garden to enjoy a refreshing date shake and, of course, buy some dates. At cooler times of year, ask about the mile-long desert **trail** to a section of the Amargosa River, which though tiny, supports abundant birdlife and assorted invertebrates. There's even a small waterfall.

ACCOMMODATION   **TECOPA HOT SPRINGS AND AROUND**

★**Cynthia's** 2001 Old Spanish Trail Hwy ☎ 760 852 4580, ⓦ discovercynthias.com. Three miles south of Tecopa, this resort offers a wide range of accommodation, including a thirteen-bed hostel fashioned from an old trailer home with full kitchen. Additional ageing trailer homes house private en-suite rooms and have a real desert feel. For a prettier and more peaceful setting beside groves of date palms, go for *Cynthia's* three romantic tipis located 4 miles north at China Ranch Date Farm. Tipis come with comfy beds, fresh linen, rugs on the ground, a fire grate for winter use, but there's no longer use of a kitchen. Dorms $25, doubles $98, tipis $165

Delight's Hot Springs Resort 368 Tecopa Hot Springs Rd ☎ 760 852 4343, ⓦ delightshotspringsresort.com.

Dated but well-kept cabins and motel rooms feature kitchenettes; there's also an RV-only campground. Guests enjoy 24hr access to on-site hot pools and clubhouse. RV hookup $39, cabins and motel $100
Tecopa Hot Springs Resort 860 Tecopa Hot Springs Rd

☎ 760 852 4420, ⓦ tecopahotsprings.org. Choose between serviceable motel rooms, cabins (some with kitchenette), and camping; all options include 24hr access to hot springs. Pitches $25, RV hookup $35, cabins and motels $105

EATING AND DRINKING

★ Death Valley Brewing 102 Old Spanish Trail Hwy ☎ 760 852 4273, ⓦ deathvalleybrewing.com. Even this remote corner of California has its own microbrewery, though it does close for the summer. Literally a shack in the desert, the beers sold here are unpasteurized and unfiltered

– think basil beer, honey date ale and the popular "Nowhere" series of Belgian ales. Food includes burgers ($5-6, including a veggie option) and pulled pork sandwiches. Cash only. Mid-Oct to April Fri–Sun noon–6pm.

Amargosa Opera House and Death Valley Junction

Hwy-127 and State Line Rd • Tours $5 • ☎ 760 852 4441, ⓦ amargosa-opera-house.com

Some forty miles north of Tecopa on Hwy-127, you reach the tiny and virtually abandoned settlement of **DEATH VALLEY JUNCTION**, a former Pacific Coast Borax Company town. It offers no fuel or supplies, but it does boast the **Amargosa Opera House**, the creation of Marta Becket, a New York dancer and artist who settled here in 1967. Becket painted the theatre's interior balconies with sixteenth-century Spanish nobles and revellers, apparently a confidence-building gesture for whenever audiences dwindled in her early days in the desert. For many years, Becket took on almost all the roles in her ballet-pantomimes, but she is now well into her 90s and performed her last show in 2012; the non-air-conditioned venue now books random shows between November and May (tickets around $20–25). **Tours** of the Opera House are generally available year-round by stopping off at the adjacent *Amargosa Hotel* (see below) between 8am and 5pm.

ACCOMMODATION AND EATING   DEATH VALLEY JUNCTION

Amargosa Hotel Hwy-127 and State Line Rd ☎ 760 852 4441, ⓦ amargosa-opera-house.com/hotel.htm. Part of the Amargosa Opera House, the *Amargosa Hotel* is a pleasantly run-down adobe structure built by the Pacific Coast Borax Company in 1924. Its eighteen rooms have neither TVs nor phones, but many have been hand-painted

by Marta Becket. Ask to see a few before choosing – there's a trompe l'oeil wardrobe in the Jezebel room and cherubs in the Baroque. In the same building, the *Amargosa Café* (open Fri & Sun 8am–3pm, Sat 8am–3pm & 6.30–9pm) does excellent diner food ($8–12) and great pies. $75

Death Valley National Park

Initially, **Death Valley** seems like an inhuman environment: burning hot, apparently lifeless and almost entirely without shade, much less water. If you drive through in just half a day, it can appear barren and monotonous, but longer visits reveal multiple layers of interest. Death Valley itself is just the central portion (but very much the focal point) of much bigger **Death Valley National Park**, which is the largest US national park outside of Alaska. Grand vistas sweep down from the subalpine slopes of 11,000ft **Telescope Peak** to **Badwater**, the lowest point in the western hemisphere at 282ft below sea level; sharply silhouetted hills are eroded into deeply shadowed crevices, their exotic mineral content turning million-year-old mud flats into rainbows of sunlit phosphorescence; and stark hills harbour the bleached ruins of mining enterprises that briefly flourished against all odds.

It seems impossible that such a dry landscape could support any kind of life, yet it is home to a great variety of creatures, from snakes and giant eagles to tiny fish and bighorn sheep.

Throughout the park, roads and services are sparse, mostly concentrated in the central north/south-trending valley for which the park is named. Hwy-190 runs part of the length of the valley, linking **Furnace Creek** and **Stovepipe Wells**, the park's two main outposts for provisions and accommodation. Forays from these bases give access to extensive **sand dunes**, intriguing **ghost towns** and cool high-country camping in the **Panamint Range** far above the valley floor.

While you could quite easily see many of Death Valley's essential sights in a day, you should aim to spend at least one night here if you have the time – preferably camped out somewhere far from the main centres of activity. Be sure to spend some time on

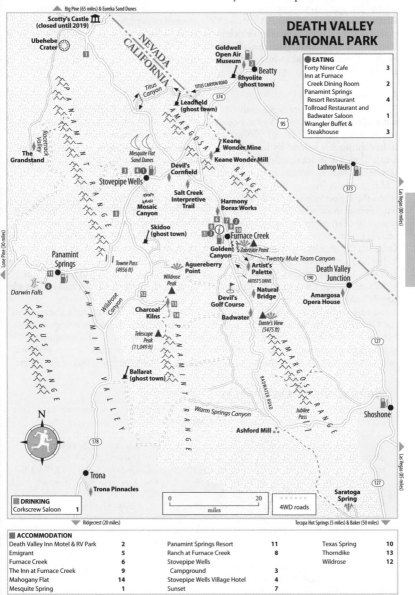

DEATH VALLEY NATIONAL PARK

EATING

Forty Niner Cafe	3
Inn at Furnace Creek Dining Room	2
Panamint Springs Resort Restaurant	4
Tollroad Restaurant and Badwater Saloon	1
Wrangler Buffet & Steakhouse	3

DRINKING

Corkscrew Saloon 1

ACCOMMODATION

Death Valley Inn Motel & RV Park	2	Panamint Springs Resort	11	Texas Spring	10
Emigrant	5	Ranch at Furnace Creek	8	Thorndike	13
Furnace Creek	6	Stovepipe Wells Campground	3	Wildrose	12
The Inn at Furnace Creek	9	Stovepipe Wells Village Hotel	4		
Mahogany Flat	14	Sunset	7		
Mesquite Spring	1				

foot to best experience the park's gargantuan spaces and unique landforms. Sunrise and sunset are the best times to witness the vibrant colours that are usually bleached out by the midday sun, and they're also the most likely times for spotting **wildlife** – mostly lizards, snakes and small rodents, which tend to hide out through the heat of the day.

Many of the park's top sights lie south of Furnace Creek along **Badwater Road**, where colourful rocks line Artist's Drive and a small pond marks the lowest point in the western hemisphere at Badwater itself. The mountains to the immediate east offer a pair of extraordinary viewpoints – **Dante's View** and **Zabriskie Point**. With **Scotty's Castle closed** until at least 2019, make time instead to explore **Ubehebe Crater** and (if you're driving a high-clearance vehicle) **Racetrack Valley** while you're up in the remoter northern section of the park. Finally, on Death Valley's western flank rises **Telescope Peak** and **Wildrose Peak**, which are much cooler places to hike in the scorching summer months.

Brief history

The sculpted rock layers exposed in Death Valley, tinted by oxidized traces of various **mineral deposits**, comprise a nearly complete record of the earth's past. Relatively young **fossils** lie at the feet of 500-million-year-old mountains and the valley floors hold deposits left behind by Ice Age lakes, which covered most of the park's low-lying areas. There's also dramatic evidence of volcanic activity, particularly at the massive **Ubehebe Crater** in the northern reaches of the park.

Humans have lived in and around Death Valley for ten thousand years, since a time when the region was still filled by a massive lake, the climate was quite mild and wildlife was more abundant. Later, wandering tribes of desert **Shoshone** wintered near perennial fresh-water springs in the warm valley, spending the long, hot summers at cooler, higher elevations in the surrounding mountains. Some of their descendants, the **Timbisha Shoshone**, still live on a forty-acre patch of land at Furnace Creek, the Death Valley Indian Community reservation (population around fifty, year-round). Displaced and then virtually ignored for decades, the tribe finally gained federal recognition in 1982, and in 2001 was granted 7500 acres of park and nearby land; the band of people largely keep to themselves.

The first non-natives passed through Death Valley in 1849, looking for a short cut to the Gold Rush towns on the other side of the Sierra Nevada; despite running out of food and water, most managed to survive, though the death of one of their number encouraged a survivor of these "**Lost '49ers**" to dub the place Death Valley on their way out. For the next 75 years, the only people willing to brave the hardships of the desert

---

WHEN TO VISIT DEATH VALLEY

Unsurprisingly most people choose to visit Death Valley – the hottest place on earth based on a year-round average (see box, p.263) – in the **winter**. In these cooler months, daytime temperatures average around 70–80°F (21–27°C) making visiting the sights quite manageable and meaning even lowland hiking is a pleasure. But the park is really known for its **summer air temperatures**, which average 112°F (44°C) and in July 1913 peaked at 134°F (56.7°C), a mark now acknowledged as the highest temperature ever recorded worldwide (a 136°F mark recorded in Libya in 1922 was discredited by a team of weather experts in 2012). There are frequent periods when the temperature tops 120°F (49°C) daily, and this is when many European visitors arrive, joining the car manufacturers who have been bringing their latest models out here for extreme testing ever since Dodge paved the way in 1913.

The best time to visit is **spring**, especially March and early April, when wildflowers may be in bloom (though many years they refuse to play ball), daytime temperatures average a manageable 83°F (28°C), and nights are pleasantly cool. At any time between October and May, Death Valley is generally mild, with occasional rainfall on the surrounding mountains causing flash floods through otherwise bone-dry gullies and washes.

DESERT SAFETY

Be mindful of **desert safety** (see box, p.209) when visiting Death Valley (staying hydrated really is a matter of life or death here), and always remain aware of dangers associated with the region's flora and fauna (see box, p.44). It pays to note, however, that more people die in Death Valley in car accidents than by any other means.

were miners, who searched for – and found – deposits of gold, silver and copper. The most successful mining endeavours, though, were centred on **borates**, a harsh alkaline used in detergent soaps (and, eventually, in a variety of industries – everything from cosmetics to nuclear reactors). In the late nineteenth century, borate miners developed twenty-mule-team wagons to haul the borate ore across the deserts to the railroad line at Mojave.

In the 1920s, the first tourist facilities were developed, and in 1927 the *Inn at Furnace Creek* was built on the site of the former Furnace Creek mining camp. Six years later, the US government purchased two million acres of Death Valley and its environs to preserve the land as a national monument. In 1994, Congress accorded it national park status and added a further 1.3 million acres to its total area, making Death Valley larger than Yellowstone National Park.

Furnace Creek

Furnace Creek is the hub of Death Valley, essentially an extended resort with the park's only significant **visitor centre** (see p.267), three campgrounds, hotels *Inn at Furnace Creek* (see p.268) and *Ranch at Furnace Creek* (see p.268), several restaurants, a couple of bars, a general store, a post office and a **gas station** (expensive gas available 24hr with a credit card). The *Ranch at Furnace Creek* is the only place in the national park to offer organized **outdoor activities** and also features a large **swimming pool** (see p.268).

Borax Museum

Ranch at Furnace Creek grounds • Daily: May–Sept 9am–9pm; Oct–April 11am–7pm • Free • ☎ 760 786 2345

Furnace Creek is home to the small **Borax Museum**, located in an 1883 wooden building, the valley's oldest structure, that once served as a miners' bunkhouse. The story of the mineral and its excavation in Death Valley is rather plodding, but the museum's intriguing collection of Native American arrowheads, some dating back two thousand years, is worth seeking out. Outside, heavy-wheeled borax wagons and an old steam locomotive are arranged around an 1880s *arrastre* used for grinding up gold ore. Armed with a little background knowledge, head two miles north to the adobe ruins of the **Harmony Borax Works** (unrestricted entry), where a quarter-mile interpretive trail tells of the mine and borax processing plant that operated here between 1883 to 1888 – this was essentially the birthplace of the celebrated "Twenty Mule Teams".

Along Badwater Road

A good first stop while driving south along **Badwater Road** from Furnace Creek is **Golden Canyon**, where periodic rainstorms over the centuries have washed a fifty-foot-deep, slot-shaped gully through the clay and silt, revealing golden-hued walls that are particularly vibrant in early evening. A three-quarter-mile-long interpretive trail winds into the U-shaped upper canyon, from where a circular hike (see box, p.264) continues. Five miles further on, signs point to **Artist's Drive**, a twisting one-way loop road. It's perhaps best left until the drive back, especially if this means catching the afternoon sun on the **Artist's Palette**, an evocatively eroded hillside covered in an intense mosaic of reds, golds, blacks and greens.

Devil's Golf Course

A couple of miles south of Artist's Drive, a dirt road heads a mile or so west to **Devil's Golf Course**, where instead of three-irons and putters, you'll find a peculiar field of salt pinnacles and hummocks protruding up a few feet from the desert floor. Capillary action draws saline solutions from below the surface, where alternating layers of salt and alluvial deposits from ancient lakes have been laid down over the millennia. As the (very) occasional rainfall evaporates, the salt accretes to form a landscape as little like a golf course as you could imagine: small golf-hole-sized apertures in the mounds apparently give the place its name.

Badwater

From Devil's Golf Course, it's five miles south to **Badwater**, an unpalatable but non-poisonous thirty-foot-wide pool of water, loaded with chloride and sulphates and the only home of the endangered, soft-shelled Badwater snail. Notice how much hotter it feels in the humid air beside the water; also be sure to take a look up on the hill across the road, where a lofted sign marks sea level some 280ft above. From the pool, two rather uninteresting hikes, both around four miles long, lead across the hot, flat valley floor to the two **lowest points in the western hemisphere**, both at 282ft below sea level. Neither are marked and there's little satisfaction in being just two feet lower than you were at the roadside, though it's certainly worth wandering a half-mile out to where the salt deposits form polygonal shapes on the valley floor.

4 Zabriskie Point

The badlands around **Zabriskie Point**, four miles south of Furnace Creek off Hwy-190 and overlooking Badwater and Artist's Palette, were the inspiration for Michaelangelo Antonioni's eponymous 1970 film. Proximity to Furnace Creek makes this a popular sunrise destination, as photographers try to capture the early rays catching **Manly Beacon**, an eminence rising above the badlands below.

Dante's View

Twenty miles south of Zabriskie Point and at the terminus of a steeply inclined road, **Dante's View** stands almost 6000ft above the blinding white saltpan of Badwater, and from this outstanding vista, the valley floor far below indeed looks infernal. The view is best appreciated in early morning, when the pink-and-gold Panamint Range across the valley is highlighted by the rising sun; it's well worth the drive any time of day, however.

BADWATER ULTRAMARATHON

Driving through Death Valley in mid-July can seem like madness even in an air-conditioned vehicle, but an international field of almost a hundred masochists choose this time of year to run the gruelling **Badwater Ultramarathon** (🌐 badwater.com). Billed as "The World's Toughest Foot Race", it is undoubtedly one of the most demanding, extreme and prestigious in the world. Searing heat and draining dehydration are constant threats along the 135-mile route, which kicks off 282ft below sea level at Badwater and, after a total elevation gain of around 14,000ft, finishes at 8371ft **Whitney Portal**, the primary trailhead for ascents of Mount Whitney. Around four-fifths of the field typically finish, the slowest finishers taking around two days.

Al Arnold was the first to run the course in 1977, but the race didn't actually get under way until 1987; it has been run every year since. The current men's record, set in 2007 by Brazilian Valmir Nunes, is 22 hours 51 minutes (though American Pete Kostelnick logged a time of just 21 hours 56 minutes after a night start in 2016), while the best female result is by American Jamie Donaldson, whose 2010 time was 26hr 16min (American Alyson Venti clocked 25hr 53min in 2016, again with a night start).

WHAT MAKES DEATH VALLEY SO HOT AND DRY?

It's no surprise that **Death Valley** is **hot and dry** – it's part of the northern Mojave Desert, after all – but certain factors combine to make this patch of land hotter than anywhere else on the planet, based on a year-round average of 77.15°F (25°C).

Perhaps the biggest contributor to the region's unforgiving heat is its location: Death Valley sits at sea level in the **rain shadow** of four mountain ranges, so it receives an average precipitation of only an inch and a half each year. Moisture in wind off the Pacific Ocean is lost as rainfall in the Coast Range of the western part of California, then as snowfall when the air struggles over the 14,000ft crest of the Sierra Nevada. Very little moisture is left by the time the air gets east of the Sierra, and the last of it is squeezed out as it climbs over the Argus Range and the 11,000ft Panamint Range.

As this very dry air descends from these heights, it compresses, causing it to heat up until it finds itself trapped in a narrow basin where the beating sun, a lack of shade-giving plants and the low altitude all allow the air temperature to reach almost unbearable levels. Even overnight the air doesn't get much chance to cool, as the surrounding mountains trap it to create strong, hot winds; at times it can feel like you're standing in front of a massive hairdryer.

Keane Wonder Mine and Mill

Twenty miles north of Furnace Creek, **Keane Wonder Mine and Mill** were certainly quite wonderful during their heyday. Between 1904, when Jack Keane discovered the mine, and 1916, gold and silver worth then $1.1 million was extracted here. The ore was then carried to the mill on the floor of Death Valley using a three-quarter-mile-long aerial tramway, which remains more or less intact. Note that access to the mine and mill, from the junction of Keane Wonder Road and Beatty Cut-off Road, has been **closed** for several years due to **safety hazards** – check at the visitor centre before setting out.

Salt Creek Interpretive Trail

Just off Hwy-190, fourteen miles north of Furnace Creek, the **Salt Creek Interpretive Trail** is a half-mile boardwalk loop leading through a spring-fed wash. As usual, dawn and dusk offer your best chances of spotting the likes of bobcats, foxes, coyotes and great blue herons that come here to drink. Also keep a keen eye on the water for the rare Salt Creek pupfish, a species unique to Death Valley and a living remnant of the area's lake-filled past.

Mesquite Flat Sand Dunes and Devil's Cornfield

Just after Hwy-190 bends west towards the northern reaches of the valley floor, the most extensive of Death Valley's sand dunes spread out: **Mesquite Flat Sand Dunes** comprise fifteen rippled and contoured square miles of ever-changing sand formations, some over one hundred feet high. Most people are happy to photograph them from the road (best in early morning and late afternoon), but while there are no formal trails, it's easy enough to choose a route to the nearest of the dunes (about a half-mile away), or even to the top of the highest dune (3–4 miles round-trip). Across Hwy-190 from the dunes stands **Devil's Cornfield**, an expanse of tufted arrowweed grasses perched on mounds that make them look like alien shocks of corn.

Stovepipe Wells

A couple of miles on from the Mesquite Flat Sand Dunes, **Stovepipe Wells** is a good place to take a break with views of the dunes; it's also handy for trips to **Mosaic Canyon** (see box, p.264). The area includes a ranger station, grocery store, campground (see p.268), gas station and motel (see p.268), with associated family **restaurant** (see p.269) and bar.

Rhyolite and around

Northeast of Stovepipe Wells and across the Nevada border, a side road heads just outside the park boundary to the intriguing ghost town of **Rhyolite**, a former gold town whose mines were prematurely closed in 1912 after just six boom years. Mismanagement and a lack of technological know-how were largely to blame, and the working Bullfrog Mine nearby attests to the area's continuing mineral wealth. By the time of its demise, Rhyolite had spread over the hillside (made of the town's namesake mineral) and even had its own train station. The station is still the dominant structure, but the remains of other buildings, including a jail, schoolhouse and bank, also still stand, as does Tom Kelly's **bottle house**, built of some thirty thousand beer and spirit bottles in 1906.

Goldwell Open Air Museum

Just under 1 mile south of Rhyolite • Museum: daily 24hr; Visitor centre: Mon–Sat 10am–4pm; 10am–2pm in summer • Free • ☎ 702 870 9946, ⓦ goldwellmuseum.org

Near Rhyolite, the roadside **Goldwell Open Air Museum** is a distinctly oddball sculpture garden that was the brainchild of Belgian artist Albert Szukalski, who passed away in

---

HIKING AND BIKING AROUND DEATH VALLEY

In June, July and August, you should restrict your Death Valley **hiking** ambitions to the cooler trails around Telescope Peak and Wildrose Peak in the Panamint Range. You'll need to carry all your **water** with you and will want a wide-brimmed **hat**. In the cooler months, lowland hikes become an appealing proposition.

Mountain biking along hiking trails is prohibited within the national park, but that still leaves a great network of asphalt and dirt roads to explore; bike rentals are available in Furnace Creek (see p.267). The map provided with your entry ticket shows the major four-wheel-drive routes: Echo Canyon into the Funeral Mountains and the Inyo Mine, Cottonwood Canyon from Stovepipe Wells, and the Warm Springs Canyon/Butte Valley road in the south of the park are all worthwhile.

Whatever you do, always register your intended route at the visitor centre in Furnace Creek (see p.267) or any ranger station, and for anything a little more adventurous than the walks listed here, be sure to procure a **topographic map** from the visitor centre.

TOP HIKES

Golden Canyon to Zabriskie Point (5 mile round-trip; 3hr; 500ft ascent). An unmaintained, moderately strenuous trail along ridges and through badlands to Zabriskie Point. Done in reverse, it's all downhill.

Gower Gulch Loop (4 mile round-trip; 2–3hr; 200ft ascent). Loop walk starting at Golden Canyon and following the interpretive trail to marker #10. From there, follow a trail down Gower Gulch back to the start, including an easy scramble down a couple of dry falls. A leaflet on the hike is available from the Furnace Creek visitor centre.

Mosaic Canyon (2 mile round-trip; 1hr; 100ft ascent). A rough three-mile access road just west of Stovepipe Wells leads to the trailhead for a relatively easy hike through this narrow canyon, full of water-polished marble and mosaic-patterned walls. Beyond this most heavily trafficked section, the canyon carries on for another mile, with some scrambling at the upper end.

Telescope Peak (14 mile round-trip; 8hr; 3000ft ascent). This easy-to-follow but strenuous trail climbs from the trailhead by *Mahogany Flat* campground. It skirts a pair of 10,000ft peaks and continues through bristlecone pines to the summit and its grand panorama of Death Valley, Mount Whitney and the eastern face of the Sierra Nevada. Sign the summit register while you admire the view. There's no water en route except for snowmelt (which can persist into June following heavy winters); be sure to purify it before drinking. Crampons and ice axes may be required in harsh winters, and at all times you should self-register in the book a short way along the trail.

Wildrose Peak (8 mile round-trip; 5hr; 2300ft ascent). If winter conditions or your own level of fitness rule out Telescope Peak, this hike makes a perfect, easier alternative – although by no means is it easy. Start by the Charcoal Kilns on Wildrose Canyon Road and wind up through piñon pines and juniper to a stunning summit panorama.

4

2000 after getting other artists to contribute. Goldwell is filled with structures built from car parts and an arresting series of white fibreglass figures arranged in imitation of *The Last Supper*, and you can't help but notice the huge sheet-metal miner and similarly proportioned penguin that greet you as you enter.

Beatty

Chamber of Commerce 119 E Main St • Tues–Sat 9am–3pm • ☎ 775 553 2424, ⓦ beattynevada.org • **Beatty Museum** 417 Main St • Daily 10am–3pm • Free • ☎ 775 553 2303, ⓦ beattymuseum.org

Less than ten miles from the national park's eastern boundary, you'll find **BEATTY**, Nevada, home to a gas station, a casino, a small **Chamber of Commerce**, and the folksy **Beatty Museum**, its distinctive olive-green building the best place in the area to learn about the local Bullfrog Mining District's glory days of the early 1900s.

Titus Canyon Road

From Rhyolite and Beatty, you can coast back down into the national park on NV-374, watching Death Valley unfold from above. A short distance west of the Rhyolite turn-off, begin exploring one-way **Titus Canyon Road** (high-clearance vehicles recommended), an epic 26-mile route that winds past a handful of rusty corrugated-iron shacks – all that's left of **Leadfield**, a circa-1926 mining town that never quite boomed. The highlight of the route is **Titus Canyon** itself, a narrow defile where the road is forced to follow a dry riverbed between steep walls only thirty feet apart. Parts of the canyon may be viewed from a parking area three miles east of Scotty's Castle Road.

Scotty's Castle

Closed until 2019 due to flood damage

On the northern edge of the park, fifty-plus miles from Furnace Creek, stands **Scotty's Castle**. Executed in extravagant Spanish Revival style, this grand mansion was built during the 1920s – at a cost of $2 million – as the desert retreat of wealthy Chicago insurance broker Albert Johnson, and has essentially been left as it was when Johnson died in 1948. Traditionally one of the park's biggest attractions, the whole site was devastated by flash flooding in October 2015 – the park is aiming to reopen Scotty's Castle in 2019.

Ubehebe Crater

Eight miles southwest of Scotty's Castle – though it may as well be five hundred miles for all the people who venture here – gapes the half-mile-wide, 500ft-deep **Ubehebe Crater**, the rust-coloured result of a massive volcanic explosion some three thousand years ago. Half a mile south sits its thousand-year-old younger brother, **Little Hebe**; beyond the pair of craters, Racetrack Road (high-clearance vehicles recommended) continues twenty dusty miles south to **Teakettle Junction**, where visitors hang teakettles, many of them elaborately decorated, on a signpost.

Racetrack Valley

From Teakettle Junction, it's seven miles to **Racetrack Valley**, a 2.5-mile-long mud flat punctuated by the **Grandstand**, a bizarre black-rock intrusion that breaks up the place's symmetry. Park two miles south of the Grandstand, then walk a half-mile southeast for the best view of the **Racetrack**, where small boulders seem slowly to be racing, leaving faint trails in their wake. Scientists believe that the rocks are pushed along the sometimes icy surface by very high winds, though no one has ever seen them move. Two miles further on, there's a very primitive, waterless **campground**.

Eureka Sand Dunes

A high-clearance vehicle is recommended (see box below) to visit **Eureka Sand Dunes**, which are located forty miles northwest of Scotty's Castle along the mostly unpaved Big Pine Road. Looming taller than the Mesquite Flat Sand Dunes near Stovepipe Wells (see p.263), these piles stand up to seven hundred feet high, making them the highest dunes in California and a dramatic place to witness sunrise or sunset. While here, keep your eyes open for the Eureka Dunes grass and evening primrose, both indigenous to the area and federally protected.

Western Death Valley

West of Stovepipe Wells, Hwy-190 climbs steeply and features a sprinkling of minor sights along the way. Emigrant Canyon Road branches south from here, providing an opportunity to escape the heat of the desert floor and climb into the mountainous, pine-clad backcountry on the western slopes of the **Panamint Range**, where you'll find the coolest temperatures in the park.

Aguereberry Point

Ten miles along Emigrant Canyon Road, a nine-mile dirt track turns off to the very meagre remains of **Skidoo**, a 1915 gold-mining camp of seven hundred people that was watered by snowmelt from Telescope Peak, 23 miles away, and kept informed by telegraph from Rhyolite. There's very little to see, so a better side-trip is to **Aguereberry Point**, a wonderful viewpoint from which you can gaze six thousand feet down into Death Valley; it's reached along a six-mile dirt road off Emigrant Canyon Road.

Charcoal Kilns and Telescope Peak

Deep in the Panamint Range, the *Wildrose* campground (see p.269) marks the start of a sometimes steep, five-mile road up Wildrose Canyon to the **Charcoal Kilns**. This series of ten massive, beehive-shaped stone kilns, each some 25ft tall, were completed in 1877 to make charcoal from piñon and juniper logs for use in the smelters of the local Modock silver mines, and the sight of their symmetry here is striking, to say the least. Beyond the kilns, the road deteriorates (high-clearance vehicles recommended) and climbs through juniper and pine forests past a pair of free campgrounds (see map, p.259) and the trailhead for the demanding hike up 11,049ft **Telescope Peak** (see box, p.264).

Panamint Springs

Near the national park's western boundary along Hwy-190, you pass **Panamint Springs**, twenty miles southwest of Stovepipe Wells. Here there's just a motel (see p.268), campground (see p.268) and the associated restaurant (see p.269). A mile west, a

---

EXPLORING DEATH VALLEY'S BACKCOUNTRY

Paved roads visit just a small fraction of what Death Valley National Park has to offer, and minor dirt roads (many not shown on the map the park provides on entry) thread into a **backcountry** full of abandoned mines and dramatic (if bone-dry) scenery.

Going backcountry, however, involves increased **risk**. Even if you're only visiting established sights such as Racetrack Valley or driving Titus Canyon Road, the threat of sharp rocks causing flat tyres is greatly increased. While high-clearance vehicles with heavy-duty tyres are recommended for these roads, ordinary cars can sometimes get by with care. That said, one flat is an inconvenience; two can mean a towing fee well into the hundreds (if not thousands) of dollars.

If you're keen to do some real exploring, talk to the rangers at the visitor centre, who will furnish you with the free *Death Valley Backcountry Roads* map, which shows all backroads and ranks them in five levels of difficulty. Most really do need a **high-clearance four-wheel-drive** vehicle; if you're renting, be sure to check that your insurance will cover you.

2.5-mile dirt road brings you to the start of a mile-long creekside trail leading to spring-fed **Darwin Falls**, a series of small cascades. The main lower and upper falls are a combined 80ft high – it's hardly dramatic, but the 20ft lower falls does feed a welcome and shady cottonwood oasis and comes as a quirky find in the desert. Because it's a working water source for Panamint Springs, swimming is not allowed.

Owens Lake

From Panamint Springs, most visitors continue west towards Lone Pine (see p.270), passing the dry bed of what, until 1926, was **Owens Lake**, which for part of the nineteenth century carried steamships loaded with gold bullion. The Owens River that flowed into the lake was diverted to Los Angeles in 1913, via the aqueduct that parallels US-395, leaving a pan of toxic alkali dust. Though some of the river flow has been restored (thanks to a shallow flooding programme initiated by the Los Angeles Department of Water and Power, in cooperation with Audubon California), and the lake now contains some water, it remains a massive source of dust pollution (the dust contains cadmium, nickel and arsenic). Incredibly, a chain of wetlands on the old borders of the lake, fed by springs and artesian wells, provides a thriving habitat for snowy plovers, gulls, avocets, grebes and sandpipers. The new improvements include beautifully landscaped public access areas and trails that opened in 2016. See ⓦowenslakeproject.com for the latest on conservation efforts.

Lee Flat and Saline Valley

Adventurous drivers with sturdy, high-clearance vehicles might fancy exploring the northwestern corner of the national park. Joshua trees may come as a surprise sight in Death Valley, but **Lee Flat**, about twenty miles northwest of Panamint Springs along paved but rough Saline Valley Road, off Hwy-190, boasts a forest of them on its higher slopes. From here, you can continue on a very rough 50-mile trek out to **Saline Valley** – get the *Death Valley Backcountry Roads* map (free from the visitor centre) and ask about the latest road conditions. The area's highlights are the generally clothing-free **hot springs** at Saline Warm Springs and the adjacent Palm Hot Springs, both easily identified by palm trees. Other than hot water, vault toilets and a free, primitive campground, there are no facilities, so be sure to tote along everything you'll need. From here, it's possible to continue north past Saline Valley Dunes to eventually connect with US-395 at Big Pine.

ARRIVAL AND INFORMATION

DEATH VALLEY NATIONAL PARK

By car Death Valley is a long way from anywhere, with Las Vegas being the nearest city, over 130 miles away. There's no scheduled public transport into the park. Be sure to top up your tank before you head in, as gas is notoriously expensive in the park.

Operating hours and entrance fee Death Valley National Park is open daily 24hr, year-round. Entrance to the park (good for seven days) is $25 per vehicle, $20 per person on motorcycles and $12 per person for those mad enough to walk or bicycle (see box opposite). There are no staffed entrance booths, so pay at one of the self-serve machines near park entrances, or at one of the ranger stations or visitor centres. At the latter you'll get an excellent map, the park newspaper with up-to-date details on campgrounds and visitor services, and a glossy booklet

on the national park.

Furnace Creek Visitor Center ☏ 760 786 3200, ⓦnps .gov/deva. The primary park visitor centre is right in the heart of the valley on Hwy-190, 30 miles from Death Valley Junction. A 20min park film is shown throughout the day. Daily 8am–5pm.

Stovepipe Wells Ranger Station ☏ 760 786 2342. The only other significant source of information within the park is this small ranger station at Stovepipe Wells Village, 24 miles from Furnace Creek on Hwy-190. Daily 8am–5pm.

Facilities There are no banks in the park, but Furnace Creek and Stovepipe Wells both have ATMs. The park's only mobile phone coverage is around Furnace Creek (all major networks). The nearest supermarket can be found in Pahrump, Nevada.

ACTIVITIES AND TOURS

Bike rental ☏ 760 786 3371. The *Ranch at Furnace Creek* offers bike rental (Sept to early May only: $15/hr; $49/24hr) and a range of suggested rides on asphalt or dirt roads.

Golf ☏ 760 786 2345. Palms and tamarisk trees line the fairways of the *Ranch at Furnace Creek's* eighteen-hole public golf course (early Oct to early May $73.50, early May

4

to Aug $30, Sept to early Oct $52.50, including cart) – the world's lowest grass course, at 214ft below sea level.

Horseriding Furnace Creek Stables ☎760 614 1018, ⓦfurnacecreekstables.net. To check out the scenery and get a sense of how pioneers might have experienced Death Valley, join one of the walking-pace horseriding tours (mid-Oct to mid-May daily 8am, 10.30am & 1pm; $60/1hr, $80/2hr). Sunset rides ($75; 1hr 10min), carriage rides

($40) and monthly moonlight rides ($95; 1hr) are also available. Mid-Oct to early May only.

Swimming Pool ☎760 786 2345. The *Ranch at Furnace Creek* features a large swimming pool (guests free, others $5 for 7am–1pm or 5–11pm; buy passes at the front desk), which is constantly fed by hot mineral water and kept at 82°F – it's a little warm for real swimming, but great for wallowing.

ACCOMMODATION

While the main sights of Death Valley can be seen in a day, you really should try to spend the night. To get the full impact of a desert visit, **camping** is the most rewarding way to stay. If camping isn't an option, you're limited to fairly expensive **hotels** and **motels** inside the park, or lower-cost choices in towns on the park's fringes such as Tecopa (see p.257) and Beatty (see p.265).

HOTELS AND MOTELS

Within the park, only the *Inn at Furnace Creek* is worthy of special praise; otherwise, you have a choice of fairly overpriced motel-style accommodation at Furnace Creek, Stovepipe Wells and Panamint Springs. Beyond the park boundaries, the range of options expands and prices come down, though you lose the chance to wake up with Death Valley all around you. Be sure to make reservations as early as possible, especially during peak winter holiday periods.

★**Inn at Furnace Creek** Hwy-190, Furnace Creek ☎760 786 2345, ⓦfurnacecreekresort.com. This beautiful Mission-style adobe hotel, built in 1927 amid date palms and tended lawns, is *the* place to stay in the park. Rooms are modern but tastefully done (a major renovation should be complete by late 2017), many with great views across the valley to the Panamint Range. Laze by the pool, which has bar service and is fed by naturally heated mineral springs. The on-site restaurant (see opposite) is the best around. Open year-round beginning Oct 2017; it's especially busy mid-Feb to mid-April. **$399**

Panamint Springs Resort 40440 Hwy-190, Panamint Springs ☎775 482 7680, ⓦpanamintsprings.com. Ageing and pretty basic motel rooms (and no pool) 35 miles west of Stovepipe Wells, made more appealing by its restaurant and bar (see opposite). There's an adjacent campground (see below). **$99**

Ranch at Furnace Creek Hwy-190, Furnace Creek ☎760 786 2345, ⓦfurnacecreekresort.com. Functional, family-oriented and cheaper than the *Inn at Furnace Creek*, the *Ranch* lacks much of its atmosphere. Features comfortable motel rooms and rather austere 1930s cabins, but at least you get free access to the chlorine-free mineral swimming pool. Cabins **$114**, doubles **$159**

Stovepipe Wells Village Hotel 51880 Hwy-190, Stovepipe Wells ☎760 786 2387, ⓦdeathvalleyhotels .com. The cheapest option that's close to most of the park's main attractions offers comfortable rooms, a mineral-water pool, a restaurant (see opposite) and a bar. Free wi-fi in lobby only. **$130**

CAMPGROUNDS AND RV PARKS

Almost all the campgrounds in Death Valley National Park are operated by the National Park Service and cost anywhere from nothing to $18 a night. The majority of National Park sites cannot be reserved (all are first come, first served except *Furnace Creek*, which takes reservations from mid-October through mid-April), and stays are limited to thirty days (so people don't move in for the winter). Take note of the altitude listed for each, as this gives an idea of what temperature to expect. RV drivers will only find hookups inside the park at Stovepipe Wells and Panamint Springs, though most surrounding towns have RV facilities. Free backcountry camping is allowed in most areas of the park, provided you keep 2 miles away from any roads (paved or otherwise) and two hundred yards from water sources. No permits are required, but voluntary backcountry registration is strongly recommended and you'll likely need to carry in your own water.

IN THE LOWLANDS

Emigrant 2100ft; map p.259. Eight miles west of Stovepipe Wells, this is the only free lowland campground, and it's tents-only. Fires are not allowed, but there are flush toilets and water. Open all year. **Free**

Furnace Creek −196ft ☎877 444 6777, ⓦrecreation .gov. Though one of the largest campgrounds in the park, it still fills up very early at winter weekends. Comes equipped with water, flush toilets and a dump station. Reserve up to six months in advance during winter (mid-Oct to mid-April). Open all year. Pitches **$22**, RV hookup **$36**

Mesquite Spring 1800ft. Fairly small, pleasant and relatively shady site near Scotty's Castle on the north side of the park. Has water, flush toilets and a dump station. Open all year. Pitches **$14**

Panamint Springs Resort 1950ft 40440 Hwy-190, Panamint Springs ☎775 482 7680, ⓦpanamintsprings .com. Commercial campground with tent sites, water and electric hookups, plus complimentary showers for guests. Open all year. Pitches **$10**, RV hookup **$35**

Stovepipe Wells Campground Sea level. Large campground close to the Stovepipe Wells restaurant and pool. Comes with water, flush toilets and some fire pits. Open mid-Oct to mid-May. Pitches $\overline{\$14}$

Sunset −196ft. This enormous site, right in Furnace Creek, is virtually an RV parking lot. Fires are not allowed but there's water, flush toilets and a dump station. Open mid-Oct to mid-April. Pitches $\overline{\$14}$

Texas Spring Sea level. Furnace Creek's quietest site with water, flush toilets and fires permitted. First-come, first-served. Open mid-Oct to mid-May. Pitches $\overline{\$16}$

IN THE HILLS

Mahogany Flat 8200ft. The remotest and coolest campground in the park; virtually identical to *Thorndike* (see below). Open March–Nov. $\overline{\text{Free}}$

Thorndike 7400ft. This small campground in the pines is usually only accessible via high-clearance or four-wheel-drive vehicles. There are pit toilets, but bring your own water. Open March–Nov. $\overline{\text{Free}}$

Wildrose 4100ft. Expect moderate temperatures at this site on the way to the Charcoal Kilns. There are pit toilets and drinking water. Open all year. $\overline{\text{Free}}$

BEATTY

Death Valley Inn Motel & RV Park 651 US-95 ☎ 775 553 9400 (motel), ☎ 775 553 9702 (RV park), ⊕ death valleyinnmotel.com. The best accommodation option outside the national park boundary has clean and spacious rooms, RV hookups, a pool and a hot tub. RV hookup $\overline{\$38}$, doubles $\overline{\$77}$

EATING

Within the park, the best selection of **eating and drinking** places is at Furnace Creek, though there are restaurants at Stovepipe Wells and Panamint Springs. Expensive **grocery stores** with limited supplies are in Furnace Creek and Stovepipe Wells.

Forty Niner Cafe Ranch at Furnace Creek, Hwy-190, Furnace Creek ☎ 760 786 2345, ⊕ furnacecreekresort .com. Diner-style family restaurant with respectable sandwiches and burgers ($12–15), pasta ($16), and steak and fish mains ($18–28). Mid-Oct to mid-May daily 7am–9pm; mid-May to mid-Oct call ahead to check hours.

★**Inn at Furnace Creek Dining Room** Hwy-190, Furnace Creek ☎ 760 786 3385, ⊕ furnacecreekresort .com. Come here for gourmet dining in a beautiful room that's almost unchanged since the 1920s. Soups, salads, sandwiches and pizza are available for lunch (when dress is casual); at dinner (call ahead for reservations), expect the likes of chilled crab gazpacho and mesquite-grilled quail, followed by tortilla-crusted barramundi (mains $26–38), and be prepared to dress up a bit, as shorts and T-shirts aren't allowed. It's also a great spot for afternoon tea or an evening cocktail; breakfast is also available. Daily 7–9.30am, noon–2.30pm & 5–8.30pm.

Panamint Springs Resort Restaurant 40440 Hwy-190, Panamint Springs. Expect solid breakfasts (from $10) in the morning and good salads ($7–18), burgers

(from $10) and pizzas ($15–36) at lunch and dinner. Eat either inside or out on the shady terrace, which is sometimes cool enough for summer dining or sipping a beer in the night air. Daily 7am–9pm.

Tollroad Restaurant and Badwater Saloon Stovepipe Wells Village Hotel 51880 Hwy-190, Stovepipe Wells ☎ 760 786 2387, ⊕ deathvalleyhotels.com. Operated concurrently and decorated in predictably Western motifs, these neighbouring establishments complement one another with pricey breakfasts and dinners available at the former (mains $15–27), and slightly more affordable lunches (mains $8–18), beers and bar snacks on offer at the latter (saloon open daily 11.30am–9pm). Daily 7–10am & 5.30–9pm.

Wrangler Buffet & Steakhouse Ranch at Furnace Creek, Hwy-190, Furnace Creek ☎ 760 786 2345, ⊕ furnacecreekresort.com. The *Ranch*'s main, ageing, restaurant offers buffets at breakfast ($13) and lunch ($16), while dinner options include chicken breast and assorted steaks (mains $28–50) with sides. Breakfast Oct–May daily 6–9am; May–Oct daily 6–10am; lunch year-round daily 10.30am–2pm; dinner year-round daily 5–9pm.

DRINKING

Corkscrew Saloon Ranch at Furnace Creek, Hwy-190, Furnace Creek ☎ 760 786 2345, ⊕ furnacecreekresort .com. After a day in the sun, enjoy this basic bar with locally brewed Badwater Ale, jukebox, draught beer, espresso – there's a limited selection of light meals (11am–9pm) and

pizza to go (11am–9.30pm), but you are better off sticking with drinks here. Note that a major renovation of the *Ranch* will include a new bar replacing the *Corkscrew* by late 2017. Daily 11am–midnight.

DIRECTORY

Farabee Jeep rentals Inn at Furnace Creek ☎ 760 786 9872, ⊕ farabeejeeps.com. A great way to spend a few days exploring less visited locales such as the Racetrack and Saline Valley is to rent a jeep (Sept–May only; $175–195/24hr). You must be over 25 and should carefully check

rental insurance beforehand.

Internet The only access in the park is through wi-fi at the hotels or via a couple of computers in the *Ranch*'s general store – both charge about $5 an hour.

4

Owens Valley

Rising out of the northern reaches of the Mojave Desert, the Sierra Nevada mountains announce themselves with a bang. Two hundred miles north of Los Angeles, **Mount Whitney** is the highest point on a silver-grey knife-like ridge of pinnacles that forms an 11,000ft rampart of granite. It provides a wonderful backdrop to **OWENS VALLEY**, a hot, dry and numinously thrilling stretch of desolate, semi-desert landscape, running north from **Lone Pine** to beyond **Bishop**.

The small towns along Owens Valley's length don't really amount to much, and if you're intent on visiting California's more cultural sights, you could easily drive through here in half a day. However, for scenic beauty and access to a range of outdoor activities, this region is hard to beat. Twisting mountain roads rise quickly from the hot valley floor to cool, 10,000ft trailheads that are ideal for **hiking** among Sierra lakes and forests or setting out for the summit of Mount Whitney and its neighbouring peaks.

Owens Valley is billed as the deepest valley in the US, and with its floor averaging 4000ft of elevation and the mountains on either side topping out above 14,000ft, this claim seems completely believable. Its eastern wall is formed by the contiguous **Inyo Mountains** and **White Mountains**; rounded and weathered (and less dramatic) in comparison with the Sierra, they possess their own beauty, especially around the wonderful **Ancient Bristlecone Pine Forest**, which contains the world's oldest trees.

US-395 runs the length of Owens Valley, a vital lifeline through a region that's sparsely populated outside of a handful of small towns, though a few solitary souls live in old sheds and caravans off the many dirt roads and tracks that cross the valley floor. Naturally a semi-desert that receives only around five inches of rain a year, the region relies on Sierra snowmelt, which once made it a prime spot for growing apples and pears. Since 1913, though, its plentiful natural water supply has been drained away to slake the massive thirst of Los Angeles (see box, p.299).

Lone Pine, Mount Whitney and around

Little more than a single-street rural town strung with motels, gas stations and restaurants, **LONE PINE** is lent a more vibrant air by being at the crossroads of desert and mountains. Any night of the week, there'll be desert dwellers mixing with Mount Whitney wilderness hikers, and tourists recovering from the rigours of Death Valley. It also makes a good base and supply post for exploring the area, particularly if you're not prepared to camp out.

Part of what makes Lone Pine special is the unparalleled access it provides to the 14,497ft summit of **MOUNT WHITNEY** – the highest point in the US outside Alaska. The view of the sharply pointed High Sierra peaks dominating the skyline to the west of town – captured by photographer Ansel Adams in a much-reproduced shot of the full moon suspended above stark cliffs – is fantastic.

SIERRA PASS AND TRAILHEAD CLOSURES

After coming through the Mojave Desert or Death Valley, it seems hard to imagine that many of the passes across the Sierra Nevada can remain closed due to snow well into May. The authorities try to open **Tioga Pass** (Hwy-120 from Mono Lake into Yosemite) by Memorial Day weekend (at the end of May), but particularly harsh winters sometimes leave it closed until June. Passes north of Yosemite, **Sonora Pass** (Hwy-108) and **Ebbetts Pass** (Hwy-4), tend to open a couple of weeks earlier, in mid-May. All three close again with the first heavy snowfall, usually by November (if not earlier). **Carson Pass** (Hwy-88), yet further north, stays open all year. For information on the state of the highways, contact Caltrans (☎ 1 800 427 7623, ⓦ dot.ca.gov).

Eastern Sierra **trailheads** are equally affected by snow, with most only accessible from May until early November. Even in June and early July, many of the higher trails can be impassable without an ice axe and crampons.

Museum of Western Film History

701 S Main St (US-395) • April–Oct Mon–Wed 10am–6pm, Thurs–Sat 10am–7pm, Sun 10am–4pm; Nov–March Mon–Sat 10am–5pm, Sun 10am–4pm • $5 • ☎ 760 876 9909, ⓦ museumofwesternfilmhistory.org

Lone Pine and the nearby Alabama Hills have been the locations for hundreds of films, commercials and television shows since *The Roundup* (1920), and the place to key into the scene is the Museum of Western Film History at the southern end of town. Watch the twelve-minute film, then browse the impressive collection of old movie posters, the 1937 Plymouth driven by Humphrey Bogart through the nearby Alabama Hills in *High Sierra*, and some fabulous suits by Nudie, the rodeo tailor. (You also can't miss his fabulous white 1975 Cadillac Eldorado convertible with its five-foot-wide bullhorns, silver dollar upholstery and mounted revolvers with mother-of-pearl grips.) There is also the **Lone Pine Film Festival** (ⓦ lonepinefilmfestival.org), usually held over the second weekend in October, which focuses on Westerns.

Alabama Hills

Between Lone Pine and the Sierra Nevada stand the **Alabama Hills**, a rugged expanse of brown, tan, orange and black granite and some metamorphic rock that's been sculpted into bizarre shapes over 160 million years. Some of the oddest formations are linked by **Picture Rocks Circle**, a paved road that loops around from Whitney Portal Road, passing rocks apparently shaped like bullfrogs, walruses and baboons; it takes a degree of imagination and precise positioning to pick them all out, but it's an attractive drive nonetheless, especially at sunset. A map (free from the visitor centres) details the best spots and marks the sites used as backdrops for many early Westerns, as well as the 1939 epic *Gunga Din* and, more recently, the Arabian desert in *Iron Man* (2008).

There's also plenty of scope for hiking and scrambling among the rocks. A couple of fairly unspectacular but photogenic natural **rock arches** act as a focus for your wanderings; dusk is particularly pleasant, with the scent of sagebrush in the air. The best of the arches is off Movie Road, just west of Lone Pine, where a ten-minute walk should find you at an eight-foot span.

Whitney Portal

Ten miles west of – and far above – Lone Pine (via Whitney Portal Rd) lies **Whitney Portal** (usually accessible May to early Nov), the trailhead for hiking up Mount Whitney. Even if a full-on slog to the summit is furthest from your mind, you might appreciate a refreshing break from the valley frazzle in the cool shade of the pines and hemlocks. What's more, there's a small fast-food counter and general store for when you need fortifying between strolls around the trout-stocked pond, along the cascading Lone Pine Creek or up the lovely, moderately strenuous Mount Whitney Trail to **Lone Pine Lake** (5 miles round-trip; no permit required).

Manzanar National Historic Site

5001 US-395 • Site: dawn–dusk; Interpretive Center daily: June–Sept 9am–5.30pm; Oct–March 9am–4.30pm • Free • ☎ 760 878 2194, ⓦ nps.gov/manz

Eleven miles north of Lone Pine on US-395, on the former site of the most productive of Owens Valley's apple and pear orchards, stand the concrete foundations of **Manzanar National Historic Site**, where more than ten thousand Americans of Japanese descent were corralled during World War II. Considering them a threat to national security, the US government uprooted entire families, confiscated all their property and brought them here until the end of the war. Claims for compensation were only settled in 1988 when President Reagan finally offered the sixty thousand survivors of the state's internment camps an official apology and agreed to pay millions of dollars in damages.

Ringed by barbed wire, the camp was filled with row upon row of wooden barracks; however, everything was razed when the camp closed after the war. Now only a couple of pagoda-like sentry posts, an auditorium and a small cemetery remain among the sagebrush and scraggy cottonwoods. As the bronze plaque on the guardhouse says: "May the injustices and humiliation suffered here as a result of hysteria, racism and economic exploitation never emerge again."

Former internees return each year on the last Saturday in April, leaving mementoes on a kind of cenotaph in the cemetery, which is inscribed with Japanese characters meaning "soul-consoling tower". The National Park Service has turned the auditorium into an excellent **Interpretive Center**, where the moving 22-minute film *Remembering Manzanar* runs every half-hour. Pick up a leaflet for the three-mile **auto tour** past 27 points of interest around the camp, including remaining examples of Japanese gardens. Also check the website for details of free, guided **walking tours** (30min–1hr 30min).

ARRIVAL AND INFORMATION

LONE PINE, MOUNT WHITNEY AND AROUND

BY BUS
Eastern Sierra Transit buses stop outside *McDonald's* at 601 S Main St. In addition to the services below, the Lone Pine Express runs between Lone Pine, Big Pine and Bishop (Mon–Fri 6.15am, 8.30am & 5pm).

Destinations Big Pine (4–7 weekly; 45min); Bishop (4–7 weekly; 1hr 15min); Lancaster (3 weekly; 3hr); Mammoth Lakes (4–7 weekly; 2hr 10min); Reno (4 weekly; 6hr).

TOURIST INFORMATION
Much of the region is protected within the massive Inyo National Forest and covered by the very helpful *Inyo National Forest* map ($10), which details everything

between Mount Whitney and Yosemite National Park, including many hiking routes and all campgrounds.

Eastern Sierra Interagency Visitor Center For details on hiking and camping throughout eastern California, visit this excellent centre (daily: May–Oct 8am–5pm; Nov–April 9am–5pm; ☎760 876 6222, ⓦwww.fs.usda.gov/inyo), which is located 2 miles south of town on US-395 at the junction of Hwy-136.

Lone Pine Chamber of Commerce 120 S Main St (May–Sept Mon–Sat 8.30am–5pm; Nov–April Mon–Fri 8.30am–4.30pm; ☎760 876 4444, ⓦlonepinechamber .org). A good resource for local information.

ACCOMMODATION

Accommodation is limited to a few motel-style places in town and plenty of **campgrounds**, all off Whitney Portal Rd, which heads west from Lone Pine.

MOTELS AND HOSTEL
★**De La Cour Ranch** 5000 Horseshoe Meadow Rd ☎760 264 3213, ⓦdelacour-ranch.com. Located 9 miles west of (and 2000ft higher than) Lone Pine on a lavender and horse ranch, this delightful spot has three cabins set in a fold in the hills with long views. All come with comfortable beds, but lack electricity. The two tent cabins have portable lanterns and share an external bathroom, while the main cabin has an indoor toilet and shower, a kitchen, propane wall lights and sleeps four relatively comfortably. It's a great getaway, so bring your own food and you won't need to leave for a couple of days. Tent cabins $60, main cabin $100
Dow Villa Motel 310 S Main St (US-395) ☎760 876 5521, ⓦdowvillamotel.com. The *Dow Villa* is a sizeable complex featuring an older section built in 1923 to house movie-industry visitors, although John Wayne always requested Room 20 in the newer motel section. There's an impressive range of accommodation here, from basic rooms without bathrooms, to plush motel units – some with big TV, DVD players and whirlpool tubs. $89
Lone Pine Budget Inn 138 W Willow St ☎760 876 5655, ⓦlonepinebudgetinn.com. This simple motel features tidy rooms outfitted with mini-fridges, microwaves and a/c; the motel is located in the centre of

town just off US-395. $140
Whitney Portal Hostel 238 S Main St (US-395) ☎760 876 0030, ⓦwhitneyportalstore.com. Though it lacks a backpacker hostel feel, this friendly option (bang in the centre of Lone Pine) has dorms containing three to five beds (each with en-suite bathroom), plus private en-suite rooms. There's a communal fridge and microwave; non-guests can shower for $7 (towel and soap provided). Dorms $27 (only available mid-March to mid-Nov); doubles $98

CAMPGROUNDS
Portagee Joe Campground 3800ft; Tuttle Creek Rd ⓦinyocountycamping.com. A county-operated campground that's handily sited just three-quarters of a mile outside Lone Pine, with vault toilets, potable water and some shade (but no showers). Follow Whitney Portal Rd for half a mile, then turn left onto Tuttle Creek Rd. Open all year. Pitches $14
Tuttle Creek Campground 5120ft. Basic waterless campground (with vault toilets) 3 miles outside of Lone Pine on Horseshoe Meadow Rd. No reservations. Open all year. Pitches $5
Whitney Portal Family Campground 8100ft; 13 miles west of Lone Pine on Whitney Portal Rd ☎877

HIKING MOUNT WHITNEY

Hiking up to the **14,497ft summit** of Mount Whitney is a real challenge: it's a very strenuous, 22-mile round-trip, made especially difficult by the lack of oxygen atop the highest point in the 48 contiguous United States. Vigorous hikers starting before dawn from the 8360ft trailhead can be up and down the mountain in one very long, arduous day, but a couple of days spent acclimatizing is advisable (see box, p.44), and the whole experience is greatly enhanced by camping out at least one night (if not two) along the route. The trail gains well over a mile in elevation, cutting up past alpine lakes to boulder-strewn, 13,600ft Trail Crest Pass; from here it ascends along the clifftops to finally reach the rounded, rocky hump of the summit itself, which doubles as the southern terminus of the 211-mile John Muir Trail leading south from Yosemite National Park. Water is available along the first half of the route, but must be filtered or purified before drinking.

Ambitious hikers with experience in scrambling or technical rock climbing will enjoy the **"Mountaineers' Route"**, which follows the North Fork of Lone Pine Creek, taking a more direct and much steeper (though no quicker) route to the summit past the bases of the numerous rock climbs on the mountain's east face. Ropes aren't generally needed, but you'll need a head for heights and wearing a helmet is advised. Ask for directions and current conditions at the ranger station and the Whitney Portal store.

The **Inyo National Forest**, which manages Mount Whitney, also controls permits for various other sections of the 78,000-acre wilderness area detailed in this chapter. Except for the Mount Whitney Trail and the North Fork of Lone Pine Creek (the aforementioned Mountaineers' Route), day-use permits are not required, but a permit (free; reservations $5/person) is needed if you want to spend the night; enquire at the Eastern Sierra Interagency Visitor Center (see opposite) just outside Lone Pine. Sixty percent of permits can be reserved ahead of time. Out of season (Nov–April), self-issued permits are available at local ranger stations and the Eastern Sierra Interagency Visitor Center.

OBTAINING PERMITS

Such is the popularity of Mount Whitney that from May to October, **overnight and day-hikers** must obtain a permit ($6 transaction fee, plus $15 reservation fee if successful) through the Whitney Zone **lottery**, which takes place in February. Dates in July, August and September (the only time the trail is generally free of snow) fill up fast, so May (when you may need an ice axe), June, and October (when there may be early snow on the ground) are better bets; in any case, the more flexible you can be with your dates, the greater likelihood you'll land a permit. The permit quota used for day-hikers is less competitive, though you should seriously consider your ability and fitness before setting out.

Enter the lottery online at Ⓦ recreation.gov (usually closes on March 15 at midnight Eastern time) for an overnight (for camping on the way up or down) or day-use (if you intend to climb in one day) wilderness permit. If you're not that organized (or miss out, as around half the applicants seem to), your best shot is to check the website for availability. Starting in mid-May, you can apply for any spaces at least two days before your planned ascent. Free **last-minute permits** can be obtained from the Eastern Sierra Interagency Visitor Center a day in advance of your planned ascent after 11am; try to avoid weekends, when demand is highest.

There are no toilets along the Mount Whitney Trail, so all hikers are required to carry out all solid waste: special "wag bags" are issued with all wilderness permits. Overnight hikers are also required to pack their food in a **bear-resistant food canister**, which can be rented from the ranger station ($2.50/day; min $5), the Whitney Portal Store (rent $2/day or buy for $50) and local sporting-goods stores. Once armed with a permit, drive to Whitney Portal, where you can park for the duration of your hike; alternately, Lone Pine Chamber of Commerce can put you in touch with a shuttle service up to the trailhead, or you can hitch a ride. Day-hikers will want to **camp** at the small, first-come, first-served *Whitney Trailhead Campground* ($13; one-night maximum stay) and be ready for an early start. Overnight hikers have more leisure and can plan to hike to one of two designated campgrounds (both first-come, first-served and free): shaded *Outpost Camp* at 3.8 miles and the far more austere *Trail Camp* at 6.2 miles.

4

444 6777, ⓦ recreation.gov. This 43-site campground is at the base of the Mount Whitney trail (8100ft), with potable water and vault toilets. Open late May to late Oct. Pitches $22

Whitney Trailhead Campground 8300ft; 13 miles west of Lone Pine on Whitney Portal Rd. Hiker-oriented spot with several stream-side sites that are the perfect place to crash the night before a Whitney ascent; maximum one-night stay (vault toilets and potable water). No reservations. Open mid-May to late Oct. Pitches $13

EATING

Lone Pine offers an adequate range of **restaurants** for the few nights you're likely to spend here, from rustic, very informal breakfast joints to more sophisticated options such as *Seasons Restaurant*.

Alabama Hills Cafe & Bakery 111 W Post St ☎ 760 876 4675. Stop in for some of the finest pancakes ($6.50 and up) around, then be sure to take away some own-baked goods for later. Daily 6am–2pm.

Mt. Whitney Restaurant 227 S Main St ☎ 760 876 5751. Reliable diner offering several types of patties in the Mt Whitney Burger – buffalo, elk, ostrich and venison among them – that backs up its claim to serve "the best burgers in town" ($14). Daily 6am–9pm.

Seasons Restaurant 206 S Main St ☎ 760 876 8927, ⓦ seasonslonepine.com. Lone Pine's fanciest restaurant serves excellent home-made pasta dishes ($18–23) and marvellous steaks ($26–30) – there's also elk, lamb and duck on the menu. April–Oct daily 5–9pm; Nov–March Tues–Sun 5–9pm.

Independence and around

The sleepy town of **INDEPENDENCE**, six miles north of Manzanar, was founded on July 4, 1862, a fact celebrated annually with a parade down Edwards Street (US-395); the event is followed by a popular barbecue and fireworks show in **Dehy Park** along tree-shaded Independence Creek on the north side of town. The park is marked by a large steam locomotive, which once ran from here to Nevada along narrow-gauge tracks.

Eastern California Museum

155 N Grant St • Daily 10am–5pm • Free, but donations appreciated • ☎ 760 878 0258, ⓦ inyocounty.us/ecmsite

The main reason to stop in Independence is to visit the **Eastern California Museum**, three blocks west of the porticoed Inyo County Courthouse, which contains an evocative and affecting exhibit detailing the experiences of many of the young children held at Manzanar in the 1940s (see p.271). The museum has reconstructed part of a family-sized barrack unit, and also holds an extensive collection of photos of camp life (not always on show) taken by Toyo Miyatake, who was interned at Manzanar and managed to smuggle in a camera and film.

The museum also has displays on native Paiute basketry and the natural environment of Owens Valley, including exhibits on the **California bighorn sheep**, a protected species which inhabits the Sierra Nevada due west of Independence. These nimble rockclimbers with massive curling horns now number around five hundred throughout the region, though efforts to establish new populations have often been thwarted by appreciative mountain lions, which promptly prey upon them.

Onion Valley

West from Independence, minor Onion Valley Road twists up the eastern escarpment of the Sierra Nevada to the pine-shrouded trailhead at **Onion Valley**, fifteen miles away. *Onion Valley* campground (see opposite) marks the start of **hiking** trails across the mountain range into Kings Canyon National Park, a twenty-mile journey over Kearsarge Pass to Cedar Grove (see p.320). This is the shortest, least arduous foot route across the Sierra; a wilderness permit is required.

ARRIVAL AND DEPARTURE

INDEPENDENCE AND AROUND

By bus Eastern Sierra Transit buses stop on US-395 in front of the Courthouse (168 Edwards St), near the intersection with Market St.

Destinations Big Pine (4–7 weekly; 30min); Bishop (4–7

weekly; 1hr); Lancaster (3 weekly; 3hr 15min); Mammoth   Lakes (4–7 weekly; 1hr 50min); Reno (4 weekly; 5hr 45min).

ACCOMMODATION

MOTELS

Winnedumah Hotel 211 N Edwards St (US-395) ☎ 760 878 2040, ⓦ winnedumah.com. The circa-1927 *Winnedumah Hotel* was once a film-star haven that has retained its atmosphere – especially in the comfy lounge, which comes decorated with local paintings and native crafts. The hearty breakfasts are a highlight. **$125**

CAMPGROUNDS

Independence Creek Campground 3800ft; 0.5 miles west of Independence on Onion Valley Road. Situated

next to burbling Independence Creek, this 25-site county-operated campground is a warmer option than the far higher *Onion Valley* campground (see below). Potable water and vault toilets available. Open all year. Pitches **$14**

Onion Valley Campground 9200ft; 15 miles west of Independence on Onion Valley Rd ☎ 877 444 6777, ⓦ recreation.gov. There are 29 choice sites available at this high altitude campground that's well placed for forays into the High Sierra. Potable water and vault toilets available. Open May–Nov, reservations advised. Pitches **$19**

EATING

Still Life Cafe 135 S Edwards St (US-395) ☎ 760 878 2555. The top pick among Independence's admittedly slim restaurant pickings, this wonderfully eccentric restaurant serves burgers and sandwiches for lunch and excels with its evening French menu, which might extend to entrecôtes of

pork with caramelized onions or a delicious tuna-packed pasta puttanesca (mains $17–32). Be prepared to be patient – you can wait for an hour per course – and bring an appetite for French wines. Thurs–Mon noon–1.30pm & 4–9pm (call to confirm).

Big Pine and around

4

There's not a great deal to the small town of **BIG PINE**, 26 miles north of Independence, but it does act as a gateway to three of the most impressive natural phenomena in California: the **Palisade Glacier**, in the Sierra Nevada to the west of town; the **Ancient Bristlecone Pine Forest**, in the barren White Mountains to the east; and the northern reaches of Death Valley – in particular Eureka Sand Dunes (see p.266) and Saline Valley (see p.267).

Tinemaha Wildlife Viewpoint

Tinemaha Wildlife Viewpoint, just east of US-395 and nine miles south of Big Pine, warrants a brief pause for spotting members of the five-hundred-strong herd of **tule elk**, a protected California species that was nearly wiped out by the end of the nineteenth century. A few dozen were relocated here from San Joaquin Valley in 1914 and have thrived in the century since.

Keough's Hot Springs

800 Keough Hot Springs Rd · Mon & Wed–Thurs 11am–7pm, Fri 11am–8pm, Sat 9am–8pm, Sun 9am–7pm · $12 · ☎ 76 0 872 4670, ⓦ keoughshotsprings.com

Just off US-395 about eight miles north of Big Pine, you can make a worthwhile diversion to **Keough's Hot Springs**, a mineral-water-fed swimming pool and hot soaking pool that became the social centre of the region after it opened here in 1919. The large pool features a cascading spray from above that's a true delight to stand beneath.

A couple of hundred yards before the entrance to Keough's Hot Springs, a dirt road cuts north to some **natural hot springs**, where locals have created a couple of clothing-optional bathing pools, their idyllic setting slightly marred by the overhead power wires and indiscriminate littering.

ARRIVAL AND DEPARTURE   BIG PINE AND AROUND

By bus Eastern Sierra Transit buses stop along US-395 (Main St bus shelter) near its intersection with Dewey St. Destinations Bishop (4–7 weekly; 30min); Lancaster (3

weekly; 3hr 10min); Lone Pine (4–7 weekly; 50min); Mammoth Lakes (4–7 weekly; 1hr 20min); Reno (4 weekly; 5hr 15min).

ACCOMMODATION AND EATING

Glacier View Campground 4000ft; 0.5 miles north of Big Pine at the junction of US-395 and Hwy-168 ☎ 760 872 6911. Conveniently placed camping spot on the floor of the valley (with showers and hookups available), although its location makes it baking hot in high summer. Open April–Oct. Pitches $\underline{\$20}$

Jeff's Country Kitchen 181 S Main St (US-395) ☎ 760 938 2402. Specializing in home-style breakfasts ($8–12) and gut-busting sandwiches (from $9.75), this diner is a smart stop when trundling through Owens Valley. Daily 7am–7.30pm.

Keough's Hot Springs Keough's Hot Springs Rd ☎ 760 872 4670, ⓦ keoughshotsprings.com. The area's prime hot springs resort has a variety of accommodation options on hand, from tent cabins without bathrooms and a so-called modular retreat (a two-bedroom mobile home) to RV and tent sites. Pool fees ($12) are included in all roofed accommodation rates. Open year-round. Pitches $\underline{\$28}$, RVs $\underline{\$33}$, tent cabins $\underline{\$90}$, modular retreat $\underline{\$140}$

Starlight Motel 511 S Main St (US-395) ☎ 760 938 2011. Tidy lodging in the heart of town, with simple but adequate rooms and few frills, other than cable TV and a shady barbecue deck. $\underline{\$110}$

The White Mountains

Rising to the east of Big Pine, the intimidating **WHITE MOUNTAINS** are effectively an alpine desert: bald, dry and little-visited, yet almost as high as the Sierra Nevada across Owens Valley. The range is made up of some of the oldest, most fossil-filled rock in California, and geologically has more in common with the Great Basin to the east than the spiky Sierra, which came into being several hundred million years later. It looks like it, too: the scrubby, undulating high country appears more Scottish than Californian. The mountains are accessible via Hwy-168; if you go, be sure to fill up on **gas** and **drinking water**, both of which are unavailable east of US-395.

Ancient Bristlecone Pine Forest

White Mountain Rd • Visitor centre: May & Oct to mid-Nov Fri–Mon 10am–4pm; June–Sept daily 10am–4pm • Schulman Grove $3 per person or $6 per car • ☎ 760 873 2500, ⓦ www.fs.usda.gov/inyo

Harbouring the oldest known living things on earth (see box opposite), the fascinating **Ancient Bristlecone Pine Forest** is rendered off-limits by snow for all but three or four months of the year. **Schulman Grove** is the most accessible concentration of trees, some 23 miles from Big Pine along White Mountain Road that twists north from Hwy-168. The grove is split up into three self-guided nature trails, all at 10,000ft and therefore more taxing than their relatively short lengths would indicate; each sets out from the stylish, eco-friendly **visitor centre**. Best is the four-mile **Methuselah Trail**, which loops around past the oldest tree, the 4700-year-old Methuselah, though you'll have to guess which of the trees it is since it's unmarked due to fears of vandalism. This route links to the Bristlecone Cabin Trail (2 miles), which winds past cabins from an old Mexican mining venture.

Back at the visitor centre, you can learn about the crucial research undertaken by the grove's namesake, Dr Edmund Schulman. An early practitioner of dendrochronology, Schulman revealed the extreme age of these trees in the mid-1950s and applied the knowledge gained from core samples to correct a puzzling error in early carbon-dating techniques. Free ranger talks are scheduled frequently throughout July and August.

Patriarch Grove

Patriarch Grove, twelve miles on from Schulman Grove along a dusty dirt road that gives spectacular views of the Sierra Nevada to the west and the Great Basin to the east, contains the Patriarch Tree, the largest of the bristlecone pines. Four miles beyond here, a research station (closed to the public) studies the physiology of high-altitude plant and animal life, which is in many ways similar to that of the arctic regions. From here, you can hike to the summit of **White Mountain Peak** (14 miles round-trip; 6–8hr; 2500ft ascent), the highest point in its namesake range and, at 14,246ft, the third highest in California. If you venture up, be forewarned that you'll need to carry all your drinking water with you through the peak's desolate moonscape.

BRISTLECONE PINES

Great Basin **bristlecone pines** (*Pinus longaeva*) are the oldest known living things on earth – some have been alive for over 4700 years (1500 years more than any sequoia). The oldest examples cling to thin alkaline soils between 10,000 and 11,000ft, where low precipitation keeps the growing season to only 45 days a year. But such conditions, which limit the trees' girth expansion to an inch every hundred years, promotes the dense, resin-rich and rot-resistant wood that lasts for millennia. Battered by the harsh environment into bizarrely beautiful shapes and forms, they look like nothing so much as twenty-foot lumps of driftwood. The most photogenic examples comprise mostly **dead wood**, the live section often sustained by a thin ribbon of bark. Even when dead, the wind-scoured trunks and twisted limbs hang on without decaying for upwards of another thousand years, slowly being eroded by wind-driven ice and sand.

Bristlecones thrive at lower altitudes and in richer soils than those in the White Mountains, growing tall and wide. But they seldom live as long as specimens subjected to the harsher conditions and, in fact, they're hardly recognizable as bristlecone pines – only the five-needle bundles and egg-shaped, barbed cone which lends the tree its name give away its true identity.

For more information, consult the Inyo Forest website at ⓦ www.fs.usda.gov/inyo or, better still, the excellent ⓦ sonic.net/bristlecone.

ACCOMMODATION   THE WHITE MOUNTAINS

Bishop's ranger station has information on backcountry camping in the area and which springs and small creeks are flowing.

Grandview Campground 8600ft; White Mountain Rd (16 miles from Big Pine). This waterless campground (with vault toilets) is 5 miles south of Schulman Grove, and while its views are indeed grand over Owens Valley far below, be prepared for strong wind gusts at times. No reservations. Open May–Oct. Pitches $5

Palisade Glacier

Palisade Glacier is the southernmost glacier in the US and the largest in the Sierra Nevada. It sits at the foot of the impressive Palisade Crest, centre of one of the greatest concentrations of enjoyable alpine **climbing** in the Eastern Sierra: Norman Clyde Peak in the south is named after California's most prolific early mountaineer; the immense bulk of Temple Crag offers a range of routes unparalleled outside of Yosemite Valley; and, to the north, Thunderbolt Peak and Mount Agassiz are highlights of the Inconsolable Range. Palisade Glacier itself is an excellent introduction to snow and ice climbing, though like most glaciers throughout the world, it is gradually shrinking.

Hikers not suitably equipped for technical climbing can still get a sense of this wondrous area by hiking from the trailhead at Big Pine Canyon, ten miles west of Big Pine at the end of Glacier Lodge Road – to reach the trailhead, simply follow Crocker Avenue out of Big Pine (this becomes Glacier Lodge Rd). July, August and September are generally snow-free and best for hiking along the **Big Pine Creek North Fork Trail** to **First Lake** (9 mile round-trip; 5–7hr; 2300ft ascent). From here, a network of shorter trails diverges to six more lakes and the base of Palisade Glacier (18 mile round-trip from the parking lot; 10–12hr; 4600ft ascent). Backcountry campers must obtain a **permit** (see box, p.273).

ACCOMMODATION   PALISADE GLACIER

Big Pine Canyon Trailhead Campgrounds Glacier Lodge Rd ☎ 760 873 2500. Near the Big Pine Creek North Fork trailhead, you'll find three campgrounds – *Sage Flat*, *Upper Sage* and *Big Pine Creek* – all above 7000ft and with water and vault toilets. Open May–Oct. Pitches $23
First Falls Campground 8300ft. This walk-in site with five pitches (all with fire rings) is set beyond the Big Pine Canyon trailhead and is reached by walking about one mile along the Big Pine Creek North Fork Trail. Open May–Oct. Free

Glacier Lodge 100 Glacier Lodge Rd ☎ 760 938 2837, ⓦ glacierlodge395.com. Right at the end of Glacier Lodge Rd, this slightly more luxurious option offers seven rustic cabins (with basic kitchens and showers), RV and tent camping, overnight parking for hikers ($5/night), a limited general store (offering breakfast, lunch and dinner) and showers (10am–4pm only; $4, $5 with towel). Open April–Nov. Pitches $25, RV $35, cabins $159

Bishop

Fifteen miles north of Big Pine, the laidback town of **BISHOP** rivals Mammoth Lakes as the **outdoor pursuits** capital of the Eastern Sierra – with a population of nearly 4000, it's the largest settlement in Owens Valley. It doesn't have downhill skiing on its doorstep, but its proximity to the wilderness makes it an excellent base from which to explore the surrounding mountains; if you want to try cross-country skiing, fly-fishing and especially rock climbing (see below) on the High Sierra peaks around Rock Creek, about twenty miles north of Bishop, there's no better place to be, with some of the world's best mountaineers offering their services through lessons and guided trips.

Mountain Light Gallery

106 S Main St (US-395) at Line St • Mon–Sat 10am–5pm, Sun 11am–4pm • Free • ☎ 760 873 7700, Ⓦ mountainlight.com

Specific sights in Bishop are few, though anyone interested in gorgeous images of the Sierra and beyond should visit the brilliant **Mountain Light Gallery**, which is lined with photographs by Galen Rowell, one of the world's foremost landscape photojournalists until his untimely death in a plane crash in 2002. Also a talented rock climber and mountaineer, Rowell photographed the region for over thirty years and extended his oeuvre to Patagonia, the Himalayas, northern Canada, Alaska, Antarctica and other wild places. You'll have to part with well over $500 to own one of his framed, large-scale photos, but at the very least, the gallery is well worth a half-hour's browsing.

Owens Valley Paiute-Shoshone Cultural Center

2300 W Line St (Hwy-168) • Tues–Sat 10am–5pm • Free • ☎ 760 873 8844, Ⓦ bishoppaiutetribe.com

The Owens Valley is still home to members of the Nuumu (Paiute) and Newe (Shoshone) people, and their legacy is preserved at the **Owens Valley Paiute-Shoshone Cultural Center**, containing a small museum with cultural displays on both tribes.

ARRIVAL AND INFORMATION   BISHOP

By bus Eastern Sierra Transit buses stop at Vons/Kmart, 1200 N Main St (US-395).

Destinations Big Pine (4–7 weekly; 30min); Lancaster (3 weekly; 4hr); Lee Vining (4 weekly; 1hr 20min); Lone Pine (4–7 weekly; 1hr 10min); Mammoth Lakes (4–7 weekly; 50min); Reno (4 weekly; 4hr 45min).

Bishop Area Chamber of Commerce & Visitors Bureau is located at 690 N Main St (Mon–Fri 10am–5pm, Sat 10am–4pm; ☎ 760 873 8405, Ⓦ bishopvisitor.com) and is a terrific source for local information. For specific questions on hiking and camping in the area, and for permission to visit the local petroglyphs, contact or visit the White Mountain Public Lands Information Center, 798 N Main St (May–Oct daily 8am–noon & 1–5pm; Nov–April Mon–Fri 9am–noon & 1–5pm; ☎ 760 873 2500), which also issues wilderness permits.

ACTIVITIES

Fishing Bishop attracts brigades of fishing enthusiasts seeking rainbow trout stocked in local streams and lakes by the state government. The main trout season runs from late April to late October, heralded by the Blake Jones Trout Derby in mid-March at Pleasant Valley Reservoir, 6 miles north along US-395. There's also a huge assembly of fisherfolk on the last Saturday in April around Crowley Lake, an artificial reservoir built 30 miles north of town to hold water diverted from Mono Lake.

Rock climbing For expert instruction on guided rock climbing, alpine climbing and ski mountaineering, contact Sierra Mountain Center, 200 S Main St (☎ 760 873 8526, Ⓦ sierramountaincenter.com), or Sierra Mountaineering International, 236 N Main St (☎ 760 872 4929, Ⓦ sierramountaineering.com). Wilson's Eastside Sports, 224 N Main St (daily: May to mid-Oct 9am–9pm, reduced hours mid-Oct to April; ☎ 760 873 7520, Ⓦ eastsidesports .com), is an excellent mountaineering and sporting-goods supply shop with gear rental, details on the nearby Buttermilk Boulders, a climbers' notice board and current information on trailhead shuttles.

ACCOMMODATION

There's a reasonable range of **accommodation** in Bishop, for which advance booking is advised on summer weekends (especially during **festivals**; see box opposite). Apart from *Brown's Town Campground* (see opposite), you'll find plenty of Inyo National Forest campgrounds in the area, with space almost always available.

BISHOP FESTIVALS

Bishop comes alive over the last weekend in May for **Mule Days** (☎760 872 4263, ⓦmuledays .org), with a huge parade, mule-drawn chariot racing, country hoedown, arts-and-crafts fair and much more. At the end of summer, the first weekend in September sees the **Tri-County Fair** (☎760 873 3588, ⓦtricountyfair.com), which includes a rodeo.

Creekside Inn 725 N Main St ☎760 872 3044, ⓦbishopcreeksideinn.com. A modern, upscale hotel in the centre of town, *Creekside Inn* offers large rooms (some with kitchenette for $10–20 extra) and an outdoor pool. $140

Brown's Town Campground Schober Lane, off US-395, a mile south of town ☎760 873 8522, ⓦbrownscampgrounds.com. This sizeable, Old West–themed RV and tent campground boasts a great deal of shade, as well as a kids' play area and other facilities. Open March–Nov. Pitches $25, RV hookups $30

★**Joseph House Inn** 376 W Yaney St ☎760 872 3389, ⓦjosephhouseinn.com. Bishop's most upscale B&B includes three acres of gardens, beautifully decorated rooms, outdoor hot tub, wine and cheese on arrival, and a full gourmet breakfast served either inside or on the terrace. $165

Trees Motel 796 W Line St ☎760 873 6391, ⓦbishopmotels.net/trees-motel. This fairly basic, family-owned motel has low rates, comfy rooms (with microwaves and cable TV) and is in a quiet location off Main St. $90

EATING AND DRINKING

Black Sheep Coffee Roasters 232 N Main St (US-395) ☎760 872 4142, ⓦblacksheepcoffeeroasters.com. If you take your coffee seriously, you'll feel right at home here, where baristas brew up all manner of intriguing, aromatic roasts. Light meals and smoothies are all available as well. Mon–Thurs 6.30am–6pm, Fri & Sat 6.30am–7pm, Sun 7am–6pm.

★**Erick Schat's Bakkerÿ** 736 N Main St (US-395) ☎760 873 7156. This huge, bustling pseudo-Dutch bakery has been baking its celebrated "Original Sheepherder Bread" for decades ($3.95). There are dozens of other varieties on offer, as well as outdoor tables for tucking into good sandwiches ($8–10). Don't leave without some banana walnut bread ($5) or apple strudel ($10). Daily 6am–6pm.

Jack's Restaurant & Bakery 437 N Main St (US-395) ☎760 872 7971. Well-regarded diner that bakes its own bread for its range of burgers and sandwiches (around $9).

Leave space for a plate of Jack's locally famous waffles or a slice of fruit pie. Daily 6am–9pm.

Mahogany Smoked Meats 2345 N Sierra Hwy (US-395) ☎760 872 3685, ⓦsmokedmeats.com. Located almost 2 miles north of town, this basic takeaway (with a few tables) dates back to 1922, and still makes the best sandwhiches in town, many based around its mahogany-smoked bacon (from $7.50). Daily 5.30am–5pm.

Whiskey Creek 524 N Main St (US-395) ☎760 873 7777, ⓦwhiskeycrk.com. Among Bishop's more upscale restaurants, *Whisky Creek* was reopened by the son of Erick Schat in 2016 after a two-year hiatus. The focus is traditional American food, from freshly baked breads and home-made soups, to juicy steaks, slow-roasted prime rib and authentic Western barbecue (mains $16–30). Daily 11am–10pm.

DIRECTORY

Cinema Bishop Twin Theatre, 237 N Main St (☎760 873 3575), shows the latest Hollywood offerings.

Hospital Northern Inyo Hospital, 150 Pioneer Lane (☎760 873 5811, ⓦnih.org), has 24hr emergency and intensive care.

Internet The library at 210 Academy St (Wed & Fri 10am–6pm, Tues & Thurs noon–8pm, Sat 10am–4pm; ☎760 873 5115) has speedy internet access.

Showers and laundry Wash Tub, 236 N Warren St (daily 7am–10pm; ☎760 873 6627) offers showers for $5, as well as coin-operated washers and dryers.

Around Bishop

You may well stay and eat in Bishop, but the main attractions lie outside town, mostly along **South Lake Road** (Hwy-168), which climbs some fifteen miles west through aspens and cottonwoods to a cluster of alpine lakes and 10,000ft trailheads. Roughly seven miles southwest of central Bishop, narrow, unpaved Buttermilk Road leads northwest off Hwy-168 into an arid land of lumpy hills and large, golden-granite rocks known as the **Buttermilk Boulders**. Year-round, rock climbers pit themselves against an almost limitless selection of low-lying boulder problems in this beautiful setting.

South Lake and Lake Sabrina

Seven miles beyond the Buttermilk Road junction, Hwy-168 forks: to the left, South Lake Road heads another seven miles up to **South Lake**, while the state highway to the right ends about four miles on at **Lake Sabrina**. A number of **hiking routes** set off into the High Sierra from trailheads at this pair of lakes, and between May and September you'll also find numerous **campgrounds** at elevations between 7500 and 9000ft (see below).

The trail from South Lake over Bishop Pass heads into Dusy Basin, where you can see the effects of centuries of glaciation in the bowl-like cirques and giant "erratic" boulders left by receding masses of ice. Another path follows the northern fork of Bishop Creek under the rust-coloured cliffs of the Paiute Crags before climbing over Paiute Pass into the Desolation Lakes area of John Muir Wilderness.

Laws Railroad Museum

395 Silver Canyon Rd • Daily: summer 9.30am–4pm, rest of year 10am–4pm • Donation • ☎ 760 873 5950, ⊕ lawsmuseum.org

On the northern fringe of Bishop, US-6 splits off from US-395 and runs toward the California–Nevada border. Four miles along from this junction is the worthwhile **Laws Railroad Museum**, a handful of relocated old buildings and a slender black train known as the "Slim Princess", all arranged in the restored old town of **Laws**. From 1883 to 1959, this was an important waystation on the narrow-gauge line between Carson City and Owens Lake, just south of Lone Pine.

Red Rock Canyon petroglyphs

Northwest of Bishop, a stark desert plateau harbours the **Red Rock Canyon petroglyphs** (not be confused with Red Rock Canyon in Nevada, or Red Rock Canyon State Park near Mojave, see p.244), where ancient native peoples carved a number of mysterious and beautiful designs – spirals, geometric forms, even spacey figures – onto rocks. There are no permits, fees or gates to open, but before visiting you must sign in at the White Mountain Ranger District Visitor Center in Bishop (see p.278), where you'll get a map pinpointing three petroglyph concentrations – the most interesting being at Chidago Canyon (turn off US-6, 20 miles north of Bishop) and Red Rock Canyon itself.

ACCOMMODATION   AROUND BISHOP

★**Inn at Benton Hot Springs** 55137 Hwy-120, Benton (35 miles north of Bishop on US-6) ☎ 760 933 2287, ⊕ bentonhotsprings.org. Few places are better for enjoying the desert skies at night than this remote destination located 4 miles west of US-6's junction with Hwy-120. A wide range of lodging options includes 1940s inn rooms, a bungalow, 1870s Conway House and RV/tent camping (no hookups); all but the inn rooms have private outdoor soaking tubs. Inn accommodation includes a gourmet breakfast and shared tubs. Pitches **$50**, doubles **$119**, Conway House/Bungalow doubles **$179**

Parchers Resort 5001 South Lake Rd ☎ 760 873 4177, ⊕ parchersresort.net. With a general store, fishing shop, horseriding, kayak rentals, and cabins of varying degrees of luxury (deluxe options cost around $155), *Parchers* is a full-service getaway on the edge of the wilderness. Rustic cabins **$140**

Sabrina Campground 9000ft; Hwy-168 (Lake Sabrina Rd). Eighteen miles from Bishop (3 miles from Lake Sabrina) and set very close to burbling Bishop Creek, this popular campground features eighteen sites (with potable water and vault toilets), half of which are in the shade. Open May–Sept. Pitches **$24**

Mammoth Lakes and around

By the time you've travelled forty miles north of Bishop on US-395, you've climbed up to around 6500ft and into **Mono Basin**, heralded by the pine-shrouded town of **MAMMOTH LAKES** three miles west of the highway. Together with the associated skiing, snowboarding and mountain-biking hotspot of **Mammoth Mountain**, this is the Eastern Sierra's biggest resort, and one that's challenged in California only by those around Lake Tahoe. Popular

BODIE GHOST TOWN (P.291) >

with Southern Californians who speed up here for the weekend, it's rapidly joining the ranks of the winter-sports mega-resorts such as Vail in Colorado, Whistler in British Columbia and Big Sky in Montana. A single company now owns the ski operation, large chunks of Mammoth real estate and the **Village at Mammoth** development, complete with pricey hotels, swanky stores and direct access to the mountain via the Village Gondola; the tiny nearby airport even has scheduled flights from the Bay Area, Denver, San Diego and Los Angeles during ski season. Although skiing and summer fishing are Mammoth's traditional attractions, the town is increasingly hyped for its accessible mountain-biking terrain and a number of on- and off-road bike races.

Residents are torn between enthusiasm for the town's major-destination profile and nostalgia for simpler times. For the moment, however, Mammoth remains unbeatable for outdoor activities and is as scenically dramatic as just about anywhere in the Sierra Nevada. You may find the resort trappings oppressive and the town overpriced, but it's easy to escape to higher reaches during the day and return each evening to good food, lively bars and even movie theatres. Mammoth is all about getting **outdoors**, so aside from eating, drinking and mooching around the sports shops and factory clothing outlets, you'll find little reason to spend much time in town.

Mammoth Museum

5489 Sherwin Creek Rd, Mammoth Lakes • June–Sept daily 10am–6pm • Free, $5 suggested donation • ☎ 760 934 6918, ⓦ mammothmuseum.org

You can learn about Mammoth's gold-mining and timber-milling origins at the small **Mammoth Museum**, located in the Hayden Cabin. This hand-built log structure was constructed between 1927 and 1937 on the banks of Mammoth Creek by Margaret and Emmett Hayden, as a hunting and fishing lodge – it was painstakingly restored as a museum in the 1990s. The modest but enlightening displays – mostly old photos, information boards and a few historic artefacts – also cover the history of the native Paiute people.

Mammoth Mountain

10001 Minaret Rd, Mammoth Lakes • Gondola (Main Lodge): mid-Nov to Sept daily 9am–4.30pm • $29 return • ⓦ mammothmountain.com

There's more fun to be had four miles west of Mammoth Lakes' centre at **Mammoth Mountain Ski Resort**, centred on the slopes of the dormant volcano known as **Mammoth Mountain** (11,053ft) – the Panorama Gondola will whisk you to the top in under ten minutes. At the summit, the **Eleven53 Interpretive Center** (free with gondola ticket) features interactive exhibits on the region and allows you to enjoy the fine mountain views through telescopes.

If you'd rather work up a sweat, there are a number of ways to do just that: **hiking** (see box, p.284) and **biking** are chief among them, and there's no shortage of people willing to get you **rock climbing** (see p.278).

Mammoth Mountain Bike Park

10001 Minaret Rd, Mammoth Lakes • June–Sept daily 9am–4.30pm • $17 plus bike rental • ☎ 760 934 0706, ⓦ mammothmountain.com

Though Mammoth Mountain is best known for winter sports (see p.286), in summer its slopes transform into the 3500-acre **Mammoth Mountain Bike Park**, with over eighty miles of groomed single-track trails. Chairlifts quickly give you and your bike an altitude boost, allowing you to hurtle down the twisting, sandy trails, brushing pines and negotiating small jumps and tree roots along the way. Beginners often take the **Downtown** run into Mammoth Lakes (from where a bike shuttle bus returns you to the bike park), while those with a little more skill or ambition might opt for the **Beach Cruiser**, which carves its way down the western side of the mountain from near the summit. Experts – and those with a death wish – can tackle the **Kamikaze**, scene of the ultimate downhill race that's

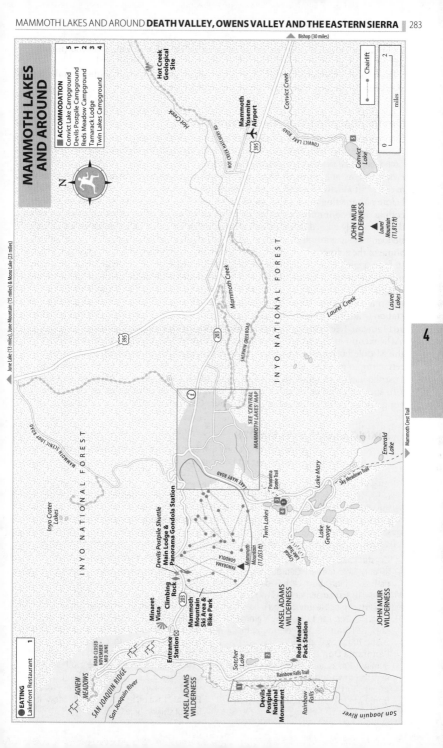

MAMMOTH LAKES AND AROUND

ACCOMMODATION
Convict Lake Campground	5
Devils Postpile Campground	1
Reds Meadow Campground	2
Tamarack Lodge	3
Twin Lakes Campground	4

● EATING
Lakefront Restaurant	1

N

Bishop (30 miles)

June Lake (13 miles), June Mountain (15 miles) & Mono Lake (23 miles)

Hot Creek Geological Site

Mammoth Yosemite Airport

395

Hot Creek

Convict Creek

Convict Lake

CONVICT LAKE ROAD

HOT CREEK HATCHERY RD

JOHN MUIR WILDERNESS

Laurel Mountain (11,812 ft)

Laurel Lakes

Laurel Creek

Mammoth Creek

SHERWIN CREEK ROAD

203

395

INYO NATIONAL FOREST

INYO NATIONAL FOREST

Inyo Crater Lakes

MAMMOTH SCENIC LOOP ROAD

SEE CENTRAL MAMMOTH LAKES MAP

LAKE MARY ROAD

Panorama Dome Trail

Lake Mary

Lake George

Emerald Lake

Sky Meadows Trail

Mammoth Crest Trail

Twin Lakes

Crystal Lake Trail

Devils Postpile Shuttle
Main Lodge & Panorama Gondola Station

Minaret Vista

Climbing Rock

203

Mammoth Mountain Ski Area & Bike Park

PANORAMA GONDOLA

Mammoth Mountain (11,053 ft)

AGNEW MEADOWS

ROAD CLOSED NOVEMBER - MID JUNE

SAN JOAQUIN RIDGE

San Joaquin River

Entrance Station

ANSEL ADAMS WILDERNESS

ANSEL ADAMS WILDERNESS

Sotcher Lake

Reds Meadow Pack Station

Devils Postpile National Monument

Rainbow Falls Trail

Rainbow Falls

San Joaquin River

JOHN MUIR WILDERNESS

Chairlift

0   1   2
miles

4

traditionally formed the centrepiece of the annual World Cup racing weekend (usually around late September), when competitors hit speeds of sixty miles per hour.

The basic "pedal-only" fee ($17) gives you access to the trails; in addition, bike rentals are available for four hours ($36) and full days (from $44).

Devils Postpile National Monument

Devils Postpile Access Rd, Mammoth Lakes • Late June to early Oct daily 24hr; shuttle bus: late June–early Sept daily 7.30am–7pm (last bus leaves Devils Postpile 7.45pm), every 20min–45min from the Mammoth Mountain Adventure Center, Minaret Rd • Entrance free; shuttle bus day-pass $7 per person • ☏ 760 934 2289, ⓦ nps.gov/depo

From the base of Mammoth Mountain Ski Resort, Hwy-203 (Minaret Rd) winds its way over 9175ft **Minaret Summit** (typically open June to mid-Oct) on the San Joaquin Ridge before plummeting toward the headwaters of the Middle Fork of the San Joaquin River, ending some eight miles beyond at Reds Meadow Resort. This is the only road access into the evocatively named **Devils Postpile National Monument**, which centres on a collection of slender, blue-grey basalt columns ranged like hundreds of massive pencils stood on end. Some of the columns are as tall as sixty feet, while others are twisted, warped and broken to form a talus slope of shattered rubble. Devils Postpile was formed as lava from a vent near Mammoth Mountain cooled and fractured into multi-sided forms, a phenomenon best appreciated by skirting round to the top of the columns. The Postpile itself is a half-mile stroll from *Devils Postpile Campground* (see p.287) and a small adjacent **ranger station** (mid-June to mid-Oct daily 9am–5pm), where you can join daily, ranger-led walks at 11am and free evening campfire programmes (twice weekly at 8pm).

The second highlight of Devils Postpile National Monument is **Rainbow Falls**, where the Middle Fork of the San Joaquin River plunges 101ft into a deep pool, the spray refracting to give the falls its name, especially at midday. It's two miles from Devils Postpile itself through Reds Meadow, reached via a very pleasant hike (see box below).

In summer, Minaret Road is closed to private vehicles during the day to prevent congestion, so you **must use the shuttle bus**. Campers are allowed vehicular access at all

---

HIKING AROUND MAMMOTH

Interwoven among the bike trails on Mammoth Mountain are a couple of **hiking paths** which top out at the summit. The views are stupendous, but as with many volcanoes, the hiking isn't the best and you're better off simply riding the gondola (see p.282) and saving your legs for hikes elsewhere.

Below are the best of the numerous **short hikes** around Mammoth Lakes. No permits are required for these, though you'll need to obtain a free **wilderness permit** if you plan to camp in the adjacent Ansel Adams or John Muir wilderness areas. The number of overnight hikers allowed to set off from each trailhead is limited during the **quota season** from May to October. Visit ⓦ www.fs.usda.gov/inyo to reserve a permit ($5 reservation fee) between two days to six months in advance, or turn up at the visitor centre after 11am on the day before you plan to hit the trail.

Crystal Lake (3.5 miles round-trip; 2hr; 650ft ascent). From the Lake George trailhead, the path skirts high above Lake George, revealing increasingly dramatic views as you climb towards Crystal Lake, hunkered below Crystal Crag. Fit hikers can tack on the Mammoth Crest Trail (a further 2.5 miles round-trip; 2–3hr; 1000ft ascent).

Panorama Dome Trail (1 mile round-trip; 30min; 100ft ascent). Tremendous views over the town and beyond reward hikers of this short sylvan trail, which sets out from Twin Lakes on Lake Mary Road (see map, p.283).

Rainbow Falls Trail (5 miles; 2hr; 300ft ascent). This moderate hike combines the two key features of Devils Postpile National Monument, just over the crest from Mammoth. Start from the Rainbow Falls trailhead and stroll south for eye-popping close-up views of Rainbow Falls before cutting around to Devils Postpile itself.

Sky Meadows Trail (4 miles; 1hr 30min–2hr; 1200ft ascent). Starting at the southern end of Lake Mary, this delightful hike along wildflower-flanked Coldwater Creek passes Emerald Lake on its way to Sky Meadow at the foot of striking Blue Crag.

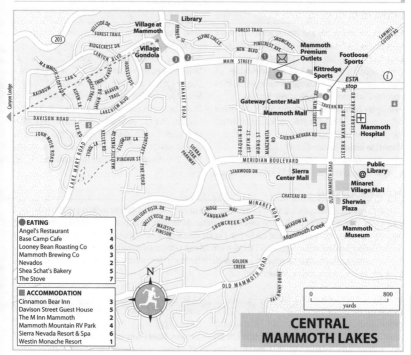

EATING

Angel's Restaurant	1
Base Camp Cafe	4
Looney Bean Roasting Co	6
Mammoth Brewing Co	3
Nevados	2
Shea Schat's Bakery	5
The Stove	7

ACCOMMODATION

Cinnamon Bear Inn	3
Davison Street Guest House	5
The M Inn Mammoth	2
Mammoth Mountain RV Park	4
Sierra Nevada Resort & Spa	6
Westin Monache Resort	1

CENTRAL MAMMOTH LAKES

times, and, outside shuttle hours, others can drive along Minaret Road; if you drive in before 7am, you can leave whenever you wish.

During the day, the furthest you can drive without taking the shuttle bus is **Minaret Vista**, a parking lot high on San Joaquin Ridge with a jaw-dropping view of the **Minarets**, a spiky volcanic ridge just south of pointed Mount Ritter – one of the Sierra Nevada's most enticing peaks.

ARRIVAL AND DEPARTURE
MAMMOTH LAKES AND AROUND

By plane Mammoth Yosemite Airport lies 7 miles east of Mammoth Lakes on US-395. There's car rental here and Mammoth Taxi offers shared rides into town for $17 per person (⊕mammoth-taxi.com).

By car Hwy-203 runs 3 miles west from US-395 into the town of Mammoth Lakes, from where it continues 6 miles to Mammoth Mountain's Main Lodge, ascends San Joaquin Ridge then descends into Devils Postpile National Monument.

By bus Year-round Eastern Sierra Transit buses run from Mammoth Lakes *McDonald's* (1 Sierra Park Rd). There's also

a seasonal YARTS service to Tuolumne Meadows ($9) and Yosemite Valley ($18; July & Aug 3/day daily; June & Sept 3 daily Sat & Sun; ⊕yarts.com), which departs from *Mammoth Mountain Inn* (opposite the Main Lodge), and the Village at Mammoth complex (6201 Minaret Rd), and stops at June Lake and Lee Vining en route.

Destinations (Eastern Sierra Transit) Big Pine (4–7 weekly; 1hr 15min–1hr 35min); Bishop (4–7 weekly; 55min–1hr 15min); Lancaster (3 weekly; 4hr 55min); Lee Vining (4 weekly; 20min); Lone Pine (4–7 weekly; 2hr 10min–2hr 25min); Reno (4 weekly; 3hr 55min).

GETTING AROUND AND INFORMATION

By bus Pick up a free town map detailing the half-dozen free bus routes. The most useful buses are the Town Trolley (summer daily 9am–10pm; every 20–30min) and the Lakes Basin Trolley, which connect the town (The Village at Mammoth, 6201 Minaret Rd) with the Twin Lakes and Lake

Mary (summer daily 9am–6pm, every 30min).

Mammoth Lakes Welcome Center 2510 Main St (Hwy-203), daily 8am–5pm (⊕760 924 5500, ⊕visitmammoth.com), on the main road into town, a half-mile east of the town centre.

ACTIVITIES

Fishing Rent gear, get fly and spinner advice and gather the latest news at Kittredge Sports, 3218 Main St (Mon–Fri 8am–7pm, Sat & Sun 7am–7pm; ☎760 934 7566, ⓦkittredgesports.com). Mary Lake and Crowley Lake are popular – and sometimes crowded – fishing spots, as is the trout-filled San Joaquin River near Devils Postpile.

Helicopter tours Take a spectacular ride with SkyTime Helicopter Tours (☎321 247 8687, ⓦskytime.com) from Mammoth Yosemite Airport, starting at $88 per person.

Mountain biking Footloose Sports, 3043 Main St (daily 8am–7pm; ☎760 934 2400, ⓦfootloosesports.com), rents full-suspension bikes ($18/hr; $54/day) plus current demo models ($33/hr; $99/day), and also organizes weekly group rides.

Rock and alpine climbing Mammoth Mountain runs family-oriented sessions on a 32ft artificial climbing rock (late June to Sept daily 10am–5pm; single climb $17, or $39 for an Adventure Pass covering all activities) in front of the *Mammoth Mountain Inn*. To get out on the real stuff, contact Southern Yosemite Mountain Guides (☎559 642 2817, ⓦsymg.com), which offers all manner of rock and alpine guiding services. The many Bishop-based guide services (see p.278) also operate trips in the Mammoth area.

ACCOMMODATION

Every other building in Mammoth is seemingly a condo, but there are numerous other **accommodation** options (including a hostel), so beds are at a premium only during ski-season weekends. Winter prices are highest, summer rates (quoted here) are still fairly high and some relative bargains can be found in the months between. If you fancy staying in a **condo**, contact Mammoth Mountain Reservations (☎800 223 3032, ⓦmammothreservations.com) or seach the listings on ⓦairbnb.com.

Some twenty **campgrounds** lie within a ten-mile radius of the town of Mammoth Lakes, the two main concentrations being around Twin Lakes and along Minaret Road.

MOTELS, B&BS AND CONDOS

Cinnamon Bear Inn 113 Center St ☎800 845 2873, ⓦcinnamonbearinn.com; map p.285. A reasonably priced, 22-room B&B inn done in New England Colonial style, with comfortable rooms, all with TV and phone (and some with DVD player), plus use of hot tub and wine-and-nibbles happy hour on arrival. Some rooms have kitchenettes and one has a four-poster bed, while four economy rooms sleep two (but ideally suit singles). Doubles $119

Davison Street Guest House 19 Davison St ☎858 755 8648, ⓦmammoth-guest.com; map p.285. Mammoth's premier backpacker hostel is in a wooden A-frame chalet with mountain views from its deck.

SKIING AT MAMMOTH

With one of the longest ski seasons in California extending from early November often into June, as well as 28 lifts, 150 trails and more than its fair share of deep, dreamy powder, **Mammoth Mountain Ski Resort** (daily 8.30am–4pm; ☎800 626 6684, ⓦmammothmountain.com) ranks as one of California's premier ski mountains. It's well balanced, too, with roughly equal areas of beginner, intermediate and expert terrain, plus seven snow parks and three halfpipes. Add to that a cat's cradle of intersecting gondolas and chairlifts, bundles of snowmaking equipment and a whole resort of bars and restaurants designed with après-ski in mind, and you're presented with a staggering number of winter activity options.

Pick up **lift tickets** (from $105) from the Main Lodge on Minaret Road, where you can also rent **equipment** (from $40 for basic skis, boots and poles, or snowboard and boots), and reserve a one-day beginner package with a lesson, gear rental and lift ticket.

Off the mountain, you'll find heaps of **cross-country skiing** trails; *Tamarack Lodge* (see opposite) offers ski packages, including instruction, tours and rentals, and charges $28 a day for access to its network of trails.

If you prefer a motorized approach to the white stuff, you can rent gear and clothing from DJ's Snowmobile Adventures (☎760 935 4480, ⓦsnowmobilemammoth.com), which has rentals for one hour (single $75, double $95) or longer.

JUNE MOUNTAIN

Mammoth Mountain is also the owner of the **June Mountain** ski area, 3819 Hwy-158 (☎888 586 3686, ⓦjunemountain.com) in the small town of June Lake, twenty miles northwest of Mammoth Lakes, with a similar range of activities but fewer crowds (Mammoth lift tickets are valid at June Mountain). It's worth visiting the June Meadows Chalet, located at the top of Chairlift 1, for the sensational views from the *Antler Bar* alone.

FESTIVALS IN MAMMOTH LAKES

During the **Mammoth Lakes Jazz Jubilee**, a four-day festival held around the second weekend in July (Ⓦmammothjazz.org), local bars, restaurants and impromptu venues book a wide range of jazz combos. Blues fans, meanwhile, should turn up for the **Festival of Beers & Bluesapalooza** (Ⓦmammothbluesbrewsfest.com), which happens over the first weekend in August.

There's a spacious lounge and good cooking facilities; bunks are set in fairly compact dorms, with bunk bed/ double rooms with shared bathroom (for 3–4 people; from $83) and one en-suite double room also on offer. Dorms **$37.72**, double **$96.50**

The M Inn Mammoth 75 Joaquin Rd ☎760 934 2710, Ⓦthemammothinn.com; map p.285. This clean and functional small hotel features minimalist styling in its ten rooms, all with private baths (and some with jacuzzis); there are also a couple of cheaper rooms with shared bath. Breakfast is a simple self-service affair. **$145**

★ **Sierra Nevada Resort & Spa** 164 Old Mammoth Rd ☎760 934 2515, Ⓦthesierranevadaresort.com; map p.285. With a terrific lobby with a massive open fire surrounded by comfy benches, this renovated hotel has comfortable, great-value rooms, some of which come with a working fireplace for an extra $30. Rates include access to a pool, a hot tub and even a mini-golf course. There are also several fully self-contained three-bedroom chalets that are great for groups. Doubles **$129**, chalet **$499**

Tamarack Lodge 163 Twin Lakes Rd ☎760 934 2442, Ⓦtamaracklodge.com; map p.285. Away from town in a wooded setting right by Twin Lakes, on the edge of a cross-country ski area, this rustic, yet luxurious lodge offers rooms in the main building (some with shared bathroom), plus fully self-contained cabins (some with wood-burning stoves). Doubles **$89**, cabins **$239**

Westin Monache Resort 50 Hillside Drive ☎760 934 0400, Ⓦwestinmammoth.com; map p.285. This plush destination is set right in the heart of the Village at Mammoth, with beautifully decorated public areas, 230 lovely rooms, an outdoor pool, hot tub and gym. It's smartly located with easy access to loads of restaurants and bars. **$290**

CAMPGROUNDS AND RV PARKS

Convict Lake Campground 7600ft; Convict Lake Rd ☎760 924 5500; map p.283. This wooded, lakeside national forest campground is situated just west of US-395, about 4 miles south of the Mammoth turn-off, and it boasts the longest open season in the area. Showers are available at nearby *Convict Lake Resort* (☎760 934 3800, Ⓦconvictlake .com; $3 for three minutes). Late April–Oct. Pitches **$23**

Devils Postpile Campground 7500ft; map p.283. National Park Service campground along Minaret Road (with potable water and flush toilets, but no showers), half a mile from the Postpile itself and a good base for hikes to Rainbow Falls or along the John Muir Trail. Late June–Oct. Pitches **$20**

Mammoth Mountain RV Park 2667 Main St ☎760 934 3822, Ⓦmammothrv.com; map p.285. A year-round, all-mod-cons RV park right in town opposite the visitor centre, with a shady pool, hot tub, kids' play areas, tent sites and a range of partial and full hookup sites. Pitches **$31**, RV hookup **$52**

Reds Meadow Campground 7600ft; Minaret Rd (off Hwy-203); map p.283. This popular national forest campground (with potable water and flush toilets) is within easy hiking distance of Devils Postpile, Rainbow Falls and a nice nature trail around Sotcher Lake. It also comes with a natural hot-spring bathhouse open to all. Mid-June to mid-Oct. Pitches **$22**

Twin Lakes Campground 8700ft; Lake Mary Rd ☎760 934 5795, Ⓦrecreation.gov; map p.283. With a pleasant lakeside setting among the pines and plenty of hiking trails nearby, this is the longest open of five near-identical sites in this area of glacially scooped lake beds, about 3 miles southwest of Mammoth Lakes. Late May to Oct. Pitches **$22**

4

EATING

Mammoth Lakes easily has the best and broadest selection of **restaurants**, **cafés** and **bars** (some with **live music**) on this side of the Sierra, many of them ranged around the central plaza at the Village at Mammoth. Pick up groceries at Vons (daily, 24hr), 481 Old Mammoth Rd, and healthy items at Sierra Sundance Whole Foods, 26 Old Mammoth Rd (Mon–Sat 9am–7pm, Sun 9am–5pm).

Angel's Restaurant 3516 Main St, at Sierra Blvd ☎760 934 7427, Ⓦangelsdining.com; map p.285. The menu has a Southwestern kick at this broadly appealing, family-friendly restaurant. The smoked chicken wings ($15) are very good, and there's a selection of burgers ($16) and mains ($12–22), such as pesto pizza, pistachio pasta and smoked brisket. Mon–Thurs & Sun 5–9pm, Fri & Sat 5–10pm.

Base Camp Cafe 3325 Main St ☎760 934 3900, Ⓦbasecampcafe.com; map p.285. A great, low-cost spot that's often bustling with large numbers of customers who come here for hearty breakfasts (mostly $10–12), tasty wraps and sandwiches, and bargain daily specials, as well as organic espresso coffees and microbrews. Daily 6am–5pm.

Lakefront Restaurant Tamarack Lodge 163 Twin Lakes Rd ☎760 934 2442, ⓦtamaracklodge.com; map p.283. Superb lake views accompany outstanding dishes from a French-Californian influenced menu that might include Alaskan halibut ($48), roasted baby beets ($13) and a sumptuous selection of desserts and ports. Daily 5.30–9.30pm.

★**Looney Bean Roasting Co** Mammoth Mall (26 Old Mammoth Rd) ☎760 934 1345, ⓦlooneybean.com; map p.285. This is the most vibrant of Mammoth's coffee bars, with good java, muffins and more, served to dedicated regulars either inside (where there's a stack of magazines) or alfresco. Daily 5.45am–7pm.

★**Mammoth Brewing Co** 18 Lake Mary Rd ☎760 934 7141, ⓦmammothbrewingco.com; map p.285. The region's premier microbrewery serves excellent beers, from Golden Trout Pilsner to IPA 395, plus tasty pub food such as chilli-dusted pork rinds, bison burgers and flatbread pizzas (mains $9–18). Mon–Thurs & Sun 10am–9.30pm, Fri &

Sat 10am–10.30pm.
Nevados 6042 Minaret Rd ☎760 934 4466, ⓦnevadosrestaurant.com; map p.285. Nevados' eclectic fine dining menu features anything from roasted Brussels sprout linguini with shrimp ($29) to pistachio-crusted venison medallions ($38). Daily 5.30–9pm.

Shea Schat's Bakery 3305 Main St ☎760 934 6055; map p.285. The best range of baked goods in town, either to take away or to eat in with a coffee. Known for its Sheepherder bread, but the crisp Danishes, pullaway breads, baklava and handmade chocolates are all a delight, while the deli sandwiches are fine in their own right (from $7.50). Daily 6.30am–6pm.

The Stove 644 Old Mammoth Rd ☎760 934 2821, ⓦthestoverestaurantmammoth.com; map p.285. A long-standing Mammoth favourite for its traditional country cooking, *The Stove* serves egg, waffle and pancake breakfasts (around $11–12) and sandwiches ($11–13) – all in large portions. Daily 6.30am–2pm.

DIRECTORY

Bookshop Booky Joint at 437 Old Mammoth Rd (daily 9am–8pm; ☎760 934 5023, ⓦbookyjoint.com) has Mammoth Lakes' best all-round book and magazine selection.
Hospital Mammoth Hospital, 85 Sierra Park Rd (☎760 934 3311, ⓦmammothhospital.org). Modern hospital with 24hr emergency care.
Internet Mammoth Lakes Library, 400 Sierra Park Rd

(Mon–Fri 10am–7pm, Sat 10am–5.30pm; ☎760 934 4777), has free internet access and wi-fi; there's also free wi-fi (with purchase) at *Looney Bean Roasting Co* (see above).
Laundry Aloha Sudz (daily 7am–9pm), Mammoth Mall at 26 Old Mammoth Rd (next to *Looney Bean*).
Showers Mammoth Lakes: Mammoth Mountain RV Park (daily 10am–5pm; $5).

Mono Lake and around

The blue expanse of bizarre **Mono Lake** (pronounced MOH-no) sits in the middle of volcanic desert tableland, its sixty square miles reflecting the statuesque, snowcapped mass of the mountains that loom overhead to the immediate west. At over a million years old, it's an ancient lake with two large volcanic islands – light-coloured **Paoha** and black **Negit** – surrounded by extremely salty, alkaline water. It all resembles a science-fiction landscape, with great towers and spires formed by mineral deposits ringing the shores; hot springs surround the lake, and all around the basin are signs of lava flows and volcanic activity, especially in the cones of Mono Craters, just to the south. **Mark Twain**, who visited in the 1860s, called it the "Dead Sea of California" in *Roughing It*, "one of the strangest freaks of nature found in any land", "an unpretending expanse of greyish water" with alkali so rich he could wash his clothes by simply dipping them in. Today the lake's most distinctive feature, its strange, sandcastle-like **tufa** formations, were increasingly exposed from the early 1940s to the mid-1990s as the City of Los Angeles diverted water that had historically flowed into the lake (see box, p.290). The towers of tufa were formed underwater, where calcium-bearing fresh-water springs well up through the carbonate-rich lake water; the calcium and carbonate combine as limestone, slowly growing into the weird formations seen today.

The lake is accessible from tiny **Lee Vining**, thirty miles north of Mammoth Lakes, and the peaceful town of **Bridgeport**, 25 miles further north along US-395. In the late nineteenth century, however, the place to be was **Bodie**, today a fascinating ghost town.

Lee Vining

Just above the southwest shore of Mono Lake, **LEE VINING** is the only settlement anywhere nearby; it offers a basic range of visitor services but not a great deal more. Before striking out for a close look at the lake and its tufa, call in at both of the excellent visitor centres close at hand: the **Mono Lake Committee Information Center & Bookstore** on US-395 near Third Street (daily: summer 8am–9pm, rest of year 9am–5pm; ☎760 647 6595, ⓦmonolake.org) in the heart of Lee Vining, and the **Mono Basin National Forest Scenic Area Visitor Center** (June–Aug daily 8am–5pm; Sept, Oct, April, May Thurs–Mon 9am–4.30pm; ☎760 647 3044, ⓦwww.fs.usda.gov/inyo), one mile north of town along US-395. The former is partly a showcase venue for the committee's ongoing battle for Mono Lake's restoration, and its fine video presentations, knowledgeable staff and well-curated selection of books concentrating on the environment and the Eastern Sierra make it a smart first stop in the area. The latter centre is perched on a lovely viewpoint well above the lake and features lake-related exhibits, presentations by rangers and a few engaging short films, as well as information on the surrounding Inyo National Forest lands.

ARRIVAL AND DEPARTURE

LEE VINING

By bus Eastern Sierra Transit buses stop along US-395: at the Chevron gas station (heading south) and in front of the Caltrans yard (across from the Chevron gas station) heading north.

Destinations Big Pine (4 weekly; 2hr 25min); Bishop (4 weekly; 2hr 5min); Bridgeport (4 weekly; 30min); Lone Pine (4 weekly; 3hr 15min); Mammoth Lakes (4 weekly; 20min); Reno (4 weekly; 3hr 25min).

TOURS AND ACTIVITIES

Tours and guided walks To add an educational component to your explorations, attend a free Patio Talk at the Mono Basin National Forest Scenic Area Visitor Center (daily in summer 11.15am & 2.15pm) or take the free South Tufa Tour (meet at the South Tufa kiosk, see p.291) daily in summer 10am, 1pm & 6pm.

Canoe trips You can also sign up for one of the Mono Lake Committee's hour-long canoe trips (late June to early Sept Sat & Sun 8am, 9.30am & 11am; $25; reservations recommended ☎760 647 6595), on which you'll paddle

around the tufa towers, learn about their formation and hear details of migrating birdlife and the brine shrimp and alkali flies on which they feed.

Kayak tours Mammoth Lakes-based Caldera Kayaks runs 3hr natural history paddling tours on Mono Lake (late June to early Oct; $110 each for two, $75 each for groups of three or more; reservations on ☎760 934 1691, ⓦcalderakayak .com); tours after August 1 often visit the lake's volcanic islands. Tours depart from the south shore of Mono Lake.

ACCOMMODATION

While indoor **accommodation** is concentrated in Lee Vining, there are a number of $16–21 Forest Service **campgrounds** set along Lee Vining Creek off Tioga Pass Road (Hwy-120).

El Mono Motel US-395 at 3rd St ☎760 647 6310, ⓦelmonomotel.com. This seasonal motel (it generally opens with Tioga Pass; see p.270), is the cheapest in town and has rooms that are small (no TVs or phones), but are well kept and cheerfully decorated. **$72**

Lundy Canyon Campground 7660 ft Lundy Lake Rd ☎760 932 5440. Eight miles from Lee Vining (3 miles west of US-395), featuring 36 pitches, all with tables and

fire rings. Groves of aspen trees line the campground along the banks of picturesque Mill Creek. Bring your own water. Open mid-April to mid-Nov. Pitches **$16**

Mono Vista RV Park 57 Beavers Lane ☎760 647 6401, ⓦmonovistarvpark.net. Catering to RVs and tents, this central spot also offers wi-fi ($3/day, $14/ week), as well as 24hr showers. Open April–Oct. Pitches **$24.64**, RV **$39.20**

YOSEMITE-BOUND?

Although Lee Vining is more than two hours by car from Yosemite Valley, it makes an affordable base for exploring the eastern reaches of **Yosemite National Park** (see p.329), particularly the Tuolumne Meadows area, only 21 miles to the west over Tioga Pass.

Murphey's Motel 51493 US-395 near 2nd St ☎ 760 647 6316, ⓦ www.murpheysyosemite.com. A central, well-presented motel where rooms include cable TV, a/c, and bathrooms with both shower and tub. Some units have a kitchen at no extra cost. Open year-round. **$118**

EATING

Bodie Mike's US-395 (in between 3rd and 4th sts) ☎ 760 647 6316. This indoor-outdoor spot is a good place to enjoy rib-sticking barbecue (ribs, burgers, etc) on a summer evening. Count on spending $15–20 per person. May–Oct daily 1.30–10pm.

Latte Da Coffee Café US-395 at 3rd St ☎ 760 647 6310. Operated as part of the *El Mono Motel* (see p.289), rustic *Latte Da* brews organic espresso and has pleasant outdoor seating. Mid-May to Oct daily 7am–8pm.

Nicely's US-395 at 4th St ☎ 760 647 6477. This circa-1950s vinyl-seated place serves reliable American fare to visitors and dedicated locals alike. All your diner favourites are here, including three-egg omelettes, jumbo burgers and fries, and fried chicken, plus an obligatory slice of one of *Nicely*'s many fruit pies (mains $10–15). April–Oct daily 7am–9pm; Nov–March Mon & Thurs–Sun 7am–9pm.

THE BATTLE FOR MONO LAKE

Mono Lake is one of North America's oldest lakes and has survived several ice ages – not to mention all the volcanic activity the area could throw at it. The **lake's biggest threat**, however, has been the City of Los Angeles, which owns the riparian rights to Mono Lake's catchment.

From 1892 to 1904, the fledgling city of Los Angeles experienced a severe drought and began looking to the Owens River as a reliable source of water that could be channelled south to the city. Under the auspices of Los Angeles's Department of Water and Power, the city steadily bought up almost the entirety of Owens Valley (a story element dramatized in the 1974 film *Chinatown*), then diverted the river and its tributaries into a 223-mile, gravity-driven **aqueduct** to ship this water to Los Angeles. Farms and orchards in once-productive Owens Valley were rendered useless without water, and Owens Lake near Lone Pine was left to dry up entirely.

The aqueduct was completed in 1913, but the growing city demanded ever more water. Consequently, in 1941, Los Angeles diverted four of Mono Lake's five feeder streams through an 11-mile tunnel into its Los Angeles Aqueduct, sparking a legal battle surrounding the depletion of the lake itself that soon turned into one of California's greatest **environmental controversies**.

Over the next fifty years, Mono Lake's **water level** dropped over 45ft, a disaster not only because of the lake's unique beauty, but also because the lake is the primary nesting ground for **California gulls**, as well as a critical resting point for hundreds of thousands of migratory **eared grebes** and **phalaropes**. As the lake's water level continued to drop ever more precipitously, the islands in its centre (where the gulls historically lay their eggs) became peninsulas, and these colonies fell prey to coyotes and other mainland predators. Furthermore, as less and less freshwater reached the lake, its content became increasingly saline, a development that threatened its unique ecosystem, as pretty much all that will thrive amid Mono Lake's harsh conditions are brine shrimp and alkali flies, both essential food sources for the birdlife. Humans, too, have been affected by all the environmental changes throughout the decades: winds that blow across saltpans left behind by the receding water create alkaline clouds containing selenium and arsenic – both contributors to lung disease.

Seemingly oblivious to the plight of the lake, the City of Los Angeles built a **second aqueduct** in 1970, and the water level dropped even faster, sometimes falling eighteen inches in a single year. Prompted by scientific reports of an impending ecological disaster, a small group of activists launched the **Mono Lake Committee** (ⓦ monolake.org) in 1978, fighting for the ecosystem's preservation through the courts and publicity campaigns – "Save Mono Lake" bumper stickers have been de rigueur for concerned California citizens for decades. Though the California Supreme Court declared in 1983 that Mono Lake must be restored, it wasn't until 1994 that emergency action was taken. A target water height of 6377ft above sea level (later raised to 6392ft) was grudgingly agreed upon to make **Negit Island** safe for nesting birds. Streams dry for decades are now flowing again, and warm springs formerly located by lakeside trails are submerged. Still, Mono Lake's height of 6378ft in 2016 (following several very dry winters) is well under its target and still 39ft below its pre-diversion level in 1941 – a figure Mono Lake Committee estimates is still some 20 years off. If it is not achieved by 2020, the Water Board will hold a hearing to decide if further revisions are needed.

★**Whoa Nellie Deli** Hwy-120 at US-395 ☎ 760 647 1088, ⓦ whoanelliedeli.com. The best fast food for miles around is served inside the unlikely setting of Tioga Gas Mart, although in summer you can sit at an outside table. There's always a lively atmosphere as the kitchen dishes out great tortilla soup, wild buffalo meatloaf ($18.95), fish tacos ($12.50), pizza slices, burgers and steaks, along with espresso, microbrews and margaritas. May–Oct daily 6.30am–8.30pm.

South Tufa and Navy Beach

The most appropriate first stop at Mono Lake is **South Tufa** ($3 entry), five miles east of US-395 via Hwy-120, which is the single best place to admire the lake's bizarre tufa spires. Boardwalks and trails wind among these twenty-foot-high limestone towers and along the lakeshore, where photo ops turn up around every corner. Less than one mile to the east, you'll find **Navy Beach** (free), where you can float in water at least twice as buoyant and saline as – and a hundred times more alkaline than – sea water. Note that even towards the end of summer, the lake's water is chilly, and some find that the salt stings. Also keep a look out for the small, but wonderfully intricate **sand tufas** nearby.

Panum Crater

Adjacent to the south shore of the lake, but back a couple of miles toward Hwy-120, stands **Panum Crater**, a 700-year-old volcano riddled with deep fissures and 50ft towers of lava; it's accessed by the short and fairly easy **Plug Trail** and **Rim Trail**. This is the most recent of the **Mono Craters**, a series of volcanic cones that stretches twelve miles south from here. The craters constitute the youngest mountain range in North America, formed entirely over the last forty thousand years.

Mono County Park and Black Point Fissures

Along the northwest shore of Mono Lake and a few miles east of US-395, a side road leads to **Mono County Park**, where a boardwalk trail heads near the edge of the lake and its finest examples of mushroom-shaped tufa towers; look for the signs along the boardwalk as it descends to the lake denoting past water levels by year. A further five miles along this (mostly washboard gravel) side road is the trailhead for **Black Point Fissures**, the result of a massive underwater eruption of molten lava some thirteen thousand years ago. As the lava cooled and contracted, cracks and fissures formed on the top, some only a few feet wide but as deep as fifty feet. Pick up a directions leaflet from the visitor centre, be prepared for hot, dry and sandy conditions, and give yourself at least a couple of hours to explore.

Bodie State Historic Park

Bodie Rd (Hwy-270), 13 miles east of US-395 • Daily: mid-March to Oct 9am–6pm; Nov to mid-March 9am–4pm • $8 • ☎ 760 647 6445, ⓦ www.parks.ca.gov/bodie

In the 1880s, the gold-mining town of **Bodie**, eighteen miles north of Lee Vining and then thirteen miles (the final three of them dirt) east of US-395 along Hwy-270, boasted three breweries, some sixty saloons and dance halls, and a population of nearly ten thousand. It also had a reputation as the raunchiest and most lawless mining camp in the West. Contemporary accounts describe a town that ended each day with a shootout on Main Street, while the firehouse bell, rung once for every year of a murdered man's life, seemed to never stop tolling. The town hit the headlines in 1877, when a rather unproductive mine collapsed and exposed an enormously rich vein. Within four years, Bodie was the second largest town in the state after San Francisco, even supporting its own Chinatown. By 1885, millions of tons of **gold and silver** had been extracted, but a drop in the gold price made mining largely unprofitable. The town dwindled and then was virtually destroyed by two disastrous fires, the second in 1932. The school finally closed in 1942, but a few hardly souls stuck it out until the early 1960s, when the site was taken over by the State of California.

A good self-guided tour booklet (available at entry, $2) leads you around many of the 150-odd wooden buildings – about six percent of the original town – surviving in a state of arrested decay around the intact town centre. Some buildings have been re-roofed and others supported in some way, but the town by and large presents a faithful preservation: even the dirty dishes look much as they did, little damaged by decades of weathering.

What remains has been turned into **Bodie State Historic Park**, where the lack of theme-park tampering gives the place an authentically eerie atmosphere absent from other US ghost towns. Bodie is almost 8400ft above sea level and, although the park is open year-round, snow often prevents vehicular access between December and April; call ahead for road conditions. If you can get in during that time, wrap up: Bodie is often cited on the national weather report as having the lowest temperature in the US. Whenever you go, bring everything you need, as there are no services at the site.

Bodie buildings and tours

The **Miner's Union Building** on Main Street was the centre of Bodie's social life; founded in 1877, the union was the first in California, organized by workers at the Standard and Midnight mines. The building now houses a small **museum** (daily: June–Aug 9am–6pm; May & Sept 9am–5pm; free) that paints a graphic picture of mining-town life. Various **tours** depart from here in summer, though schedules are flexible and you should call ahead if you have specific interests. One such tour visits the **Standard Consolidated Stamp Mill** (generally summer daily, 11am, 1pm & 3pm; 50min duration; $6), which is otherwise off-limits. Other town highlights include the **Methodist church** with its intact pipe organ, the **general store** with its beautiful pressed-steel ceiling, the **saloon**, the **morgue** – complete with (empty) caskets – and the **cemetery** on the hill, where lie the remains of Bill Bodey, after whom the town was (sort of) named.

Bridgeport and around

Some 25 miles north of Lee Vining on US-395 is tiny **BRIDGEPORT**, an isolated village in the middle of a mountain-girt plain that provided the new start in life for fugitive Robert Mitchum in the 1947 film-noir masterpiece *Out of the Past*. The gas station he owned in the film is long gone from Bridgeport's time-warped Main Street, but the place is otherwise little changed from a pretty, high-country ranching community typically full of fishing enthusiasts.

From Bridgeport, US-395 continues north into Nevada, passing east of Lake Tahoe (see p.568) and through the state's capital city, Carson City (see p.583), before continuing on to the gambling hotspot of Reno (see p.579).

Travertine Hot Springs and Buckeye Hot Springs

If you're looking to wind down after a few days of wrestling trout around Bridgeport, be sure to pay a visit to one of a pair of joint-relaxing (and free) natural hot springs in the area. **Travertine Hot Springs** is just south of Bridgeport – follow US-395 a half-mile south of town, turn left into Jack Sawyer Road, fork left at the first junction and keep right for a mile (avoid summer weekends when it tends to get overcrowded). Many locals, however, prefer the stream-side setting of lovely **Buckeye Hot Springs**, reached by following US-395 four miles north of Bridgeport, turning left for *Buckeye Campground* and continuing 4.6 miles to where a short, but steep path leads from a dirt parking area to three small pools beside chilly Buckeye Creek.

VULCANISM AND HOT SPRINGS IN THE EASTERN SIERRA

One of the pleasures of any extended visit to Owens Valley is soaking your bones in one of the region's numerous **hot springs**. Few (if any) are well signposted and most are primarily used by locals, who are welcoming enough if you're respectful. Springs tend to be tucked away down rutted dirt roads and often comprise little more than a ring of rocks or a hollowed-out tub into which people have diverted hot-spring water to create pools of differing temperatures. Most are **clothing-optional**, and you stand a good chance of standing out as a tourist if you don't strip off at certain springs. We've mentioned several springs in the text – those in Saline Valley (see p.267), Keough's Hot Springs (see p.275), Travertine Hot Springs and Buckeye Hot Springs (see p.292) – but the best idea is simply to ask around.

All the springs are the result of groundwater being heated by magma, which rises close to the surface in these parts. In fact, Mammoth Mountain stands on the edge of a geologically volatile region known as the **Long Valley Caldera**. A vast oval some eighteen by twelve miles, the Caldera was formed 760,000 years ago when a massive eruption spread ash as far as Nebraska. Vulcanism continued with the creation of Mammoth Mountain around 50,000 years ago, the Mono Craters and, most recently, **Paoha Island** in Mono Lake, only about 300 years back.

To get a brief taster, visit **Hot Creek Geological Site** (daily dawn–dusk; free) three miles east of US-395 on unpaved Hot Creek Hatchery Road, three miles south of the exit for Mammoth Lakes. Jets of boiling water mix with chilly snowmelt water to form pools ranging from tepid to scalding. This was once a popular bathing spot, but after a geyser erupted in the pool in 2006, the US Forest Service banned swimming. It's still worth a quick detour, however.

United States Geological Survey scientists monitor ground-temperature changes, land deformation, and frequency and amplitude of quakes. An **eruption** is unlikely in the near future, but you can keep up to date at USGS' California Volcano Observatory site at ⓦ volcanoes.usgs.gov/observatories/calvo.

4

ARRIVAL AND ACTIVITIES

By bus Eastern Sierra Transit buses stop along US-395, at 121 Emigrant St (by the park).
Destinations Big Pine (4 weekly; 2hr 55min); Bishop (4 weekly; 2hr 35min); Lee Vining (4 weekly; 30min); Lone Pine (4 weekly; 3hr 45min); Mammoth Lakes (4 weekly; 1hr 20min); Reno (4 weekly; 2hr 55min).

BRIDGEPORT AND AROUND

Fishing Ken's Sporting Goods at 258 Main St (late April to Sept Mon–Thurs 7am–7pm, Fri & Sat 7am–8pm, Sun 7am–6pm; reduced hours Oct to late April; ☏ 760 932 7707, ⓦ kenssport.com) is home to local fishing information and all the tackle you'll need.

ACCOMMODATION

Bodie Hotel 281 Main St (US-395) ☏ 760 616 1977, ⓦ bodievictorianhotel.com. This whitewashed hotel occupies an 1880s building which, like several in Bridgeport, is said to have been transported from Bodie. Floors are far from level, but rooms all have bathrooms and are in bordello-chic style. Open April–Nov. **$125**

The Cain House 340 Main St (US-395) ☏ 760 932 7383, ⓦ silvermapleinn.com. Managed concurrently with the *Silver Maple Inn* right next door, *Cain House* is a delightfully furnished 1890s B&B with beautifully appointed rooms and one two-room cottage. Open May–Oct. Doubles **$130**, cottage **$200**

EATING

High Sierra Bakery 172 Main St (US-395) ☏ 760 914 4002, ⓦ highsierrabakery.com. Town institution, run by the Nugent family since 1952, with decent coffee and a tempting selection of criossants, chocolate eclairs, crumbcakes, doughnuts and other pastries, plus salads and sandwiches made on fresh baked breads (sandwiches from $8). Summer daily 6am–4.30pm.

Rhino's Bar & Grille 226 Main St (US-395) ☏ 760 932 7345. Reasonably priced chicken wings ($10 for twenty wings) and huge sandwiches ($11.75) are served amid

classic American bar-and-grill decor, complete with licence plates on the rafters. March–Dec daily 11am–10pm.

Virginia Creek Settlement US-395 ☏ 760 932 7780, ⓦ virginiacrksettlement.com. For driving a mere 5 miles south of Bridgeport along US-395, you're rewarded with home-style Italian and American cuisine at *Virginia Creek Settlement*, renowned in the region for its tasty steaks (from $25.95), pasta dishes (from $15.95) and pizzas (large from $19.45). Daily: mid-April to Oct 6.30am–4pm & 5–9pm; Nov to mid-April 5–8pm.

San Joaquin Valley and the Western Sierra

YOSEMITE NATIONAL PARK

5

San Joaquin Valley and the Western Sierra

The vast interior of California – stretching three hundred miles from the edges of the Mojave Desert in the south right up to the Gold Country and Northern California in the north – is covered by the wide floor of agricultural San Joaquin Valley, flanked on the east by the massive Sierra Nevada mountains. It's the latter region that attracts most attention, for good reason; Yosemite National Park is one of America's most spectacular tracts of natural wilderness, a mesmerizing blend of snowcapped peaks, dense pine forests and shimmering waterfalls.

The San Joaquin Valley is radically different from the rest of California – flat as a pancake, the valley now almost totally comprises farmland. And the area is much more conservative and Midwestern in feel compared to the rest of the state; between the settlements, the drab hundred-mile vistas of almond groves and vineyards can be sheer torture. Little seems to have changed since the 1960s, when Joan Didion dismissed valley towns that "seem so flat, so impoverished, as to drain the imagination" and that "hint at evenings spent hanging around gas stations, and suicide pacts sealed in drive-ins". The weather, too, can be a challenge; summers in the San Joaquin are frequently scorching and winters bring the cold and thick tule fog, so aim to visit in spring or fall; March, when the fruit trees are in full bloom, is particularly appealing.

Indeed, Coastal Californians primarily pass through the valley to reach the **Sierra Nevada**, which contain the glistening summits of some of the highest mountains in the US. Here a trio of **national parks** cover the mountains' foothills and upper reaches. **Yosemite** – one of the absolute must-sees in California, if not the world – is accompanied by **Sequoia**, where the last few stands of giant sequoia trees form the centrepiece of a rich natural landscape. Sharing a common border with Sequoia is **Kings Canyon** – together they make up one huge park –which presents a similar, slightly wilder array of Sierra wonders and giant trees.

GETTING AROUND   **SAN JOAQUIN VALLEY AND THE WESTERN SIERRA**

Trains and frequent Greyhound buses run through the valley, stopping in the larger cities and towns along Hwy-99 – Merced being the most useful with its bus connections to Yosemite. Otherwise, getting to the mountains is all but impossible without your own vehicle, though with a bit of advance planning, you can join one of the many camping trips organized by the Sierra Club, the California-based environmentalist group (see box, p.332).

Highlights

❶ Basque cuisine Sample one of Bakersfield's Basque restaurants, notably the *Noriega Hotel*, where groaning dishes and jugs of wine are served at long, communal tables. **See p.302**

❷ Kern River Experience some of California's finest and most accessible whitewater rafting on the Kern, which spills off the lofty slopes of Mount Whitney. **See p.303**

❸ Forestiere Underground Gardens Delve below baked San Joaquin Valley hardpan and into a labyrinth of rooms where an Italian subway-tunneller carved out his home and fruit orchard. **See p.308**

❹ Giant Forest The densest collection of the world's largest trees, the mighty sequoias, looms in this section of Sequoia National Park, accessible by a panoply of trails. **See p.315**

❺ Hike Half Dome Follow the incomparable Mist Trail to the summit of Yosemite's most famous peak, which forms the sheerest cliff in North America. **See p.338**

HIGHLIGHTS ARE MARKED ON THE MAP ON P.298

5

By train Amtrak's San Joaquin service runs five times daily between Bakersfield and Oakland; Amtrak Thruway buses continue into San Francisco from Emeryville, one stop before Oakland, or you can connect via BART in Richmond, further north. In the south, Amtrak Thruway bus connections from San Diego, Orange County and Los Angeles link with the train at Bakersfield.

By bus San Joaquin Valley bus routes are primarily operated by Greyhound, other than a pair of lines run by Orange Belt Stages (☎ 800 266 7433, ⓦ orangebelt.com), which connects the valley with both Las Vegas and the Central Coast.

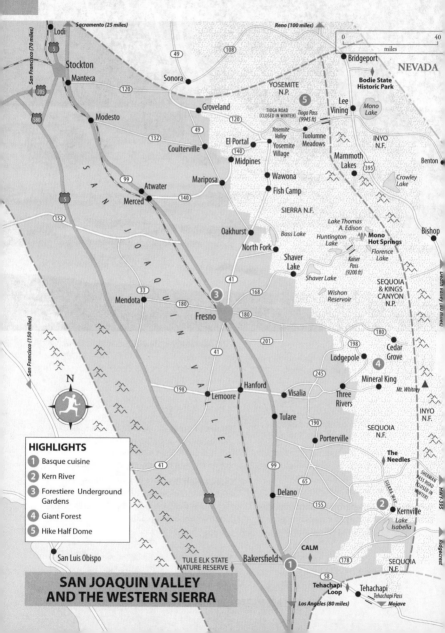

HIGHLIGHTS

1. Basque cuisine
2. Kern River
3. Forestiere Underground Gardens
4. Giant Forest
5. Hike Half Dome

SAN JOAQUIN VALLEY AND THE WESTERN SIERRA

San Joaquin Valley

5

The **SAN JOAQUIN VALLEY** grows more fruit and vegetables than any other agricultural region of its size in the world – a fact that touches the lives, in one way or another, of every one of its inhabitants. It wasn't always like this. In the 1860s, the Geological Survey of California described the valley as "bone dry, parched, and baked and crisped". Over the ensuing decades a vast system of levees, aqueducts and reservoirs transformed the valley into the nation's garden, and the abundance of low-paying agricultural jobs has encouraged decades of immigration from south of the border. This is where **Cesar Chavez** and Dolores Huerta formed the National Farm Workers Association in the 1960s, and there are now towns in San Joaquin Valley where Spanish is the first language and **taquerias** outnumber burger joints.

However, there's more to San Joaquin Valley than farming. **Bakersfield**, just across the rocky peaks north of Los Angeles, offers its own **country music** scene and famed **Basque cuisine**, while the state's finest **whitewater rafting** is on offer on the nearby Kern River. **Fresno** boasts the bizarre labyrinth of **Forestiere Underground Gardens**, while boisterous **Modesto** was the inspiration for the movie *American Graffiti*.

Bakersfield and around

A city of some 370,000, **BAKERSFIELD**'s flat and featureless look does nothing to suggest that this is California's liveliest **country-music** community, with a number of venues where locally and nationally rated musicians perform. It also has the country's largest community of Basque descent, making it *the* place to taste **Basque cuisine**, at its best in one of the specialist restaurants run by descendants of sheepherders who migrated to the San Joaquin Valley in the early twentieth century. Its increasingly vibrant **downtown** includes the burgeoning **Arts Alive District** of galleries and shops, while **Old Town Kern** in East Bakersfield (primarily around Baker St) is also known as Basque Block. Separating the two areas is **Mill Creek**, a series of landscaped parks along the old Kern Island Canal that features a 1.5-mile towpath walk and a covered bridge.

The city has its roots in a farm and stagecoach rest stop owned by Ohio-born Colonel Thomas Baker, which he built on the swampy banks of the Kern River in 1863 – the city was incorporated ten years later. **Oil** was discovered in the region in 1899 and Bakersfield has since cemented its hold on the state's production – incredibly, the surrounding Kern County produces ten percent of all US output. Low oil prices since 2015 have hit the local economy hard, however, with widespread layoffs. The agricultural sector remains strong, with the city home to Bolthouse Farms (known in the US for its carrot juice) and huge groves of oranges, pistachios and almonds.

Kern County Museum

3801 Chester Ave • Tues–Sat 10am–4pm, Sun noon–5pm • $10 • ☎ 661 437 3330, ⓦ kernpioneer.org

The **Kern County Museum**, a mile north of downtown, documents the city's petrochemical roots through "Black Gold: The Oil Experience", a modern science, technology and history exhibit complete with 1922 pump jacks, a moderately enlightening eighteen-minute movie, and Bakersfield Sound memorabilia. Leave time

---

BAKERSFIELD'S BIG SHOE

Just south of downtown, at 931 Chester Ave, lies one of Bakersfield's quirkiest sights. Built in 1947, this **giant shoe** (30ft long and 20ft high), built of plaster on a wood frame with a 50ft long "shoelace", was originally Deschwanden's Shoe Repair Shop. It still operates today as **The Big Shoe Shoe Repair** (Mon–Fri 9am–6pm, Sat 10am–5pm; ☎661 864 1002). The city's other famous icon is the **Bakersfield Sign**, a neon arch that has spanned Sillect Ave (at Buck Owens Blvd) since 1949.

to browse the fifty-plus (mostly) restored rail wagons and assorted buildings of the **Pioneer Village** outside, many dating from the late nineteenth or early twentieth century. Visitors needing to get kids out of the heat will want to check out the hands-on science exhibits in the site's **Lori Brock Children's Discovery Center**.

Bakersfield Museum of Art

1930 R St • Mon–Wed & Fri 10am–4pm, Thurs 10am–8pm, Sat & Sun noon–4pm • $10 • ☎ 661 323 7219, ⊛ bmoa.org

Bakersfield is a country town, but for something a little more highbrow visit the **Bakersfield Museum of Art**, which usually has interesting touring exhibits, along with its own collection with works by Georgia O'Keeffe and Diego Rivera.

California Living Museum

10500 Alfred Harrell Hwy • Daily 9am–4pm • $9 • ☎ 661 872 2256, ⊛ calmzoo.org

Wildlife fans will have to stray out of the city, where the greatest interest is at the **California Living Museum (CALM)**, some twelve miles east of town off the road to Kernville (Hwy-178). It's effectively a small zoo, but one focusing solely on California's native species and only those animals that have been injured and cannot be returned to the wild. Stroll around the landscaped grounds past the golden and bald eagles, pause to admire the black bears and "Cats of California" (mountain lions and bobcats), then head to the reptile house with its array of snakes and lizards. The animals tend to hide from the heat of the day, so come early.

ARRIVAL AND DEPARTURE

BAKERSFIELD AND AROUND

By bus The Greyhound bus station is downtown at 1820 18th St (☎ 661 327 5617).

Destinations Hanford (1 daily, 3hr 10min); Los Angeles (12 daily; 2hr 10min–2hr 40min); Merced (5 daily; 3hr 20min–

4hr 25min); San Francisco (2 daily; 7hr).

By train The Amtrak station is located downtown at 601 Truxtun Ave, the southern terminus of Amtrak's San Joaquin route from Sacramento and Oakland (onward connections to LA via Thruway bus).

Destinations Fresno (6 daily; 2hr); Hanford (6 daily; 1hr 20min); Merced (6 daily; 3hr); Oakland (4 daily; 6hr 10min); Sacramento (2 daily; 5hr 15min).

INFORMATION

The Convention and Visitors Bureau This tourist information centre is located at 515 Truxtun Ave (Mon–Fri 8am–5pm; ☎ 661 852 7282, ⓦ visitbakersfield.com) right by the downtown Amtrak station.

Internet Free internet access at the Beale Memorial Library, 710 Truxtun Ave (Mon–Thurs 11am–7pm, Fri & Sat 10am–6pm; ☎ 661 868 0701).

ACCOMMODATION

Bakersfield Marriott at the Convention Center 801 Truxtun Ave ☎ 661 323 1900, ⓦ marriott.com. Business hotel with standard rooms, but the only decent choice downtown (along with the *Padre*), connected to the Rabobank Arena– the free parking and complimentary cheese and wine every afternoon make this a reasonable deal. **$189**

EZ-8 2604 Buck Owens Blvd (entrance on Riverside Drive) ☎ 661 322 1901, ⓦ ez8motels.com. One of Bakersfield's cheapest motels; it's old and it can be noisy, but it has wi-fi access ($4.99/24hr), cable TV and it's just a short stagger from *Buck Owens' Crystal Palace*. **$47**

Kern River Campground Lake Ming Rd (15 miles east of downtown) ☎ 661 868 7000, ⓦ co.kern.ca.us. On the shores of Lake Ming are Bakersfield's nearest tent sites, grassy and reasonably shaded, with toilets and showers but with no hookups. Half-price mid-Oct to mid-March. Pitches **$24**

★Padre Hotel 1702 18th St ☎ 661 427 4900, ⓦ thepadrehotel.com. Wonderful conversion of a classic hotel from 1928, now given the boutique treatment with large flat-screen TVs, teak furnishings and super-stylish bathrooms. Icons of Bakersfield life are referenced in bespoke wallpaper featuring oil derricks and steer skulls. There are also iPod docking stations. Also home to some of the best places to eat and drink in town (see p.302). **$209**

EATING

★24th Street Cafe 1415 24th St ☎ 661 323 8801, ⓦ 24thstreetcafe.com. Bakersfield's best breakfast spot is decked out like a classic old-school diner (the building opened as a coffee shop in 1950), with huge plates of pumpkin pancakes, chicken-fried steak and eggs and burgers for under $12. Daily 6am–2.30pm.

Dewar's Candy Shop 1120 Eye St ☎ 661 322 0933, ⓦ dewarscandy.com. This old-fashioned sweet shop (selling taffy/rock, chocolates and the like), open since 1909, features an authentic soda fountain, sundaes ($6.65), ice cream by the scoop ($2.60) and shakes and malts ($7.35) in flavours ranging from peanut butter to pumpkin. Daily 10am–9pm.

Mama Roomba 1814 Eye St ☎ 661 322 6262, ⓦ mamaroomba.com. Caribbean and Mexican touches add interest to this small tapas-style restaurant, where you might sample garlic octopus, corn-and-cheese empanadas or a larger dish such as Havana-style pork chops with fried onions (mains $10–17). Wash it down with a jug of sangria. Mon–Fri 11am–10pm, Sat 5–10pm.

COUNTRY MUSIC IN BAKERSFIELD

The main reason to dally for more than a few hours in Bakersfield is to hear **country music**. The roots of Bakersfield's scene are with the Dust Bowl Okies who arrived in the San Joaquin Valley during the Depression, bringing their instruments and campfire songs with them. This rustic entertainment quickly broadened into more contemporary styles, developed in the bars and clubs where future legends such as local boys Merle Haggard and Buck Owens cut their teeth. During the late 1950s and 1960s the city become known for its distinctive "**Bakersfield Sound**", a far less slick and commercial affair than its Nashville, Tennessee counterpart: check out the 1988 hit *Streets of Bakersfield*, a duet by the late Buck Owens and Dwight Yoakam. Other major country artists linked to Bakersfield include Wynn Stewart (who died in 1985), Susan Raye (most popular in the 1970s and 1980s) and Freddie Hart, born in 1926 and still performing into his eighties.

Orient yourself at the **Crystal Palace & Buck Owens' Museum** (Tues–Sat 11am–4pm; $5, but visible for free during any show), which contains a collection of knick-knacks Buck picked up over the years – promo photos, bolo tie clasps, platinum records, red-white-and-blue guitars and a glittering display of rhinestone jackets.

5

★**Noriega Hotel** 525 Sumner St ☎661 322 8419, ⓦnoriegahotel.com. The most authentic Basque restaurant in town is this 1893 place where louvred shutters and ceiling fans cool diners at long, communal tables. They serve an all-you-can-eat set menu of soup, salad, beans, pasta, a meat dish, and cheese to finish, along with jug wine to keep you going. There are three sittings ($11 breakfast; $18 lunch; $24 dinner), and reservations are recommended for dinner, which often include the Basque speciality of pickled tongue. Tues–Sun 7–9am, noon–2.30pm & 7–9.30pm.

Wool Growers 620 E 19th St ☎661 327 9584, ⓦwoolgrowers.net. Another top Basque restaurant choice, with meals served family-style on communal tables. The set lunch is a bargain $14 (including amazing beans and soups), while dinner mains include breaded veal ($19), roast tri-tip ($20), and oxtail stew ($26). Mon–Sat 11.30am–2pm & 6–9pm.

Woolworth's Diner Five & Dime Antique Mall, 1400 19th St ☎661 321 006. Step back in time at this classic luncheonette, set in an old Art Moderne Woolworth's store designed in 1939; burgers, hot dogs and fabulous shakes (from $7.50). Mon–Sat 11am–4pm, Sat noon–4pm.

DRINKING AND NIGHTLIFE

★**Buck Owens' Crystal Palace** 2800 Buck Owens Blvd ☎661 328 7560, ⓦbuckowens.com. Very much a showpiece for Buck Owens' music and memorabilia, though the master himself died in 2006. It's a cabaret-style setup (Tues–Thurs free, Fri & Sat $5) with burgers and grills available while local and touring bands perform on Wednesday and Thursday; Tuesday is karaoke night; Sunday is just brunch, no live music, no cover. Buck's old band, The Buckeroos (sometimes fronted by his son Buddy), usually perform on Friday and Saturday nights. Tues–Thurs 11am–10pm, Fri & Sat 11am–midnight, Sun 9.30am–2pm.

Guthrie's Alley Cat 1525 Wall St ☎661 324 6328. In an alley parallel to 19th St, this dim dive bar with pool table and cheap drinks has been a long-standing favourite since 1940, and is packed at the weekends. Check out the Al Hirschfeld mural inside, one of only six in existence. Mon–Fri 9am–2am, Sat 10am–2am.

Lengthwise Brewing Co 7700 District Blvd ☎661 836 2537, ⓦlengthwise.com. This local microbrewery, located southwest of downtown, is known for its delicious beers – Lengthwiser Golden Ale, Harvest Moon Wheat Ale, Double ZZ Razzberry Ale among them – plus sandwiches and "beer bathed" fish 'n' chips. Mon–Thurs 11am–9pm, Fri & Sat 11am–10pm, Sun 11am–5pm.

Padre Hotel 1702 18th St ☎661 427 4900, ⓦthepadrehotel.com. This hotel (see p.301) lies at the heart of the downtown scene: there's *Brimstone*, the sports and cocktail bar with great pub food; and *Prairie Fire*, a lounge, rooftop deck with smooth sounds, fire pit, a light menu and occasional live music, especially on Sangria Sundays. There's also the classy *Belvedere Room* with its 20ft ceiling, fresh seasonal cooking (mains $25–30) and a wine list with plenty by the glass (mostly Californian with French and New World wines plugging the gaps). Brimstone Mon–Thurs & Sun 8am–11.30pm, Fri & Sat 8am–1.30am; Prairie Fire Tues–Thurs & Sun 6–10pm, Fri & Sat 5pm–midnight; Belvedere Room Mon–Thurs & Sun 5–9pm, Fri & Sat 5–10pm.

★**Trout's** 805 N Chester Ave ☎661 399 6700, ⓦtherockwellopry.webs.com. One country venue not to be missed – and the last of the genuine old honky-tonks – this slightly seedy country-music bar, a couple of miles north of downtown, has been in business since 1931. There's live music nightly on a couple of dancefloors and you can get up to speed with free evening line-dance lessons (Tues–Thurs 6.30–9pm). There's a small cover charge for live sets (around $5). Mon–Thurs 6–10pm, Fri 6pm–2am, Sat 11am–2am, Sun 11am–6pm.

ENTERTAINMENT

★**Gaslight Melodrama Theatre & Music Hall** 12748 Jomani Drive, off Allen Rd ☎661 587 3377, ⓦwww .themelodrama.com. This old time vaudeville theatre is great fun, with over-the-top productions from traditional Westerns to modern adaptations and spoofs – the audience is encouraged to boo, hiss and cheer. Tickets $25. Shows Fri & Sat 7pm, Sun 2pm; box office Mon, Tues, Thurs & Fri 11am–6pm, Sat 1–6pm, Sun 11am–4.30pm.

Rabobank Arena 1001 Truxtun Ave ☎661 852 7300, ⓦrabobankarena.com. This stadium, theatre and convention centre is Bakersfield's major event venue (it's also home of the Bakersfield Condors ice hockey team), hosting major pop concerts, family shows like Disney on Ice, musicals and the Bakersfield Symphony Orchestra (ⓦbsonow.org).

Kernville and the Kern River

Some fifty miles northeast of Bakersfield lies the small town of **KERNVILLE** on the banks of the **Kern River**, which churns down from the slopes of Mount Whitney and spills into Lake Isabella, just downstream. It's a peaceful, retiree-dominated place, but at summer weekends, or anytime in July and August, it's full of adrenalin junkies mountain biking along the local trails or negotiating the rapids in all manner of aquatic paraphernalia.

5

KERN RIVER ADVENTURES

Three main sections of the Kern River are regularly **rafted**: the **Lower Kern**, downstream of Lake Isabella (Class III–IV; generally June–Aug); the **Upper Kern**, immediately upstream of Kernville (Class III–IV; early May to June); and **The Forks**, fifteen miles upstream of Kernville (Class V; early May to June), which drops an impressive 60ft per mile. As you'd expect, kayaking is also big here, and Sierra South (see below) supplement their rafting operation with one of Southern California's top kayaking schools.

By far the most popular section of the river is the Upper Kern, the site for the **Lickety-Split** rafting trip – one for families and first-timers, with some long, bouncy rapids. This one-hour excursion (including the bus ride to the departure point) costs around $35–40, and with over half a dozen operators running trips throughout the day, there is little need to reserve ahead. Other trips run less frequently and you should reserve in advance, though you've got a better chance midweek when crowds are thinner and prices a few dollars lower. The pick of these are the day-trips on the Upper Kern, which run close to the $160 mark ($185 at weekends), the two-day Lower Kern trip (weekdays $334; weekends $410) and the two- or three-day backcountry trips on The Forks, which range around $710–900. Wetsuits (essential early in the season and for the longer trips) usually cost extra. Within this basic framework there are any number of permutations, some involving inflatable kayaks.

Permits, available free from the Kernville Ranger Station and any of the area's other Forest Service offices, are necessary even if you have your own equipment for private rafting or kayaking expeditions.

RAFTING AND KAYAKING

Mountain & River Adventures 11113 Kernville Rd ☎760 376 6553, ⓦ mtnriver.com. Kern River rafting trips from $40 (1hr), as well as rock climbing up to intermediate grades and their own outdoor climbing wall ($25.75/2hr).

Sierra South 11300 Kernville Rd ☎760 376 3745, ⓦ sierrasouth.com. Tube, raft or kayak down the Kern, with the Lickety-Split raft trip (Class II–III)

$35–39, and guided multiday kayak trips generally costing around $305 for two days. They also offer full-day beginner's rockclimbing trips ($125/day) on the nearby Kernville Slab.

Whitewater Voyages 11006 Kernville Rd ☎760 376 1500, ⓦ whitewatervoyages.com. Long-running operator, offering rafting on the Kern and numerous other rivers from April to July for $110 (half-day).

Most people come to ride the Kern, which ranks as one of the steepest "navigable" rivers in the United States, dropping over 12,000ft in 150 miles and producing some truly exhilarating **whitewater** opportunities, especially along the forty-mile section around Kernville. The tougher stuff is generally left to the experts, but during the season, which usually runs from May until early August (longer after heavy winters), commercial rafting operators vie for custom (see box above). Hwy-178 (Kern Canyon Rd) runs between Bakersfield and Kernville, traversing narrow, steep and dry **Kern River Canyon**, studded with occasional foothill pines, buckeye, oaks and grasses. Known as the Lower Kern, the waterflow of river here is regulated by the Lake Isabella dams, providing an extended season for whitewater rafting from below the dam to Democrat Beach.

Kern Valley Museum

49 Big Blue Rd, Kernville • Thurs–Sun 10am–4pm • Free • ☎760 376 6683, ⓦ kernvalleymuseum.org

If you've got time to kill, delve into the native, gold mining and lumbering history in the **Kern Valley Museum**, or take a look at their film room of movies shot in the area, mostly Westerns: John Wayne features prominently.

INFORMATION

Chamber of Commerce 11447 Kernville Rd (Jan–April & Sept–Dec Mon–Fri 9am–3pm; May–Aug Mon–Fri 9am–3pm & Sat 10am–2pm; ☎760 376 2629, ⓦ gotokernville .com). Contact this central office for general information.

KERNVILLE AND THE KERN RIVER

Kernville Ranger Station 105 Whitney Rd (daily 8am–4.30pm; ☎760 376 3781, ⓦ www.fs.usda.gov/ sequoia). For details on the wooded country to the north, call in at the ranger station next to the Kern Valley Museum.

5

ACCOMMODATION

Kernville is big enough to have a bank, ATM, post office and supermarket, but there isn't a very wide range of **accommodation**. A handful of motels on Lake Isabella start at around $90 in summer and various RV parks around town have sites for **camping**, but you are better off in the string of riverside campgrounds to the north in the Sequoia National Forest (see below).

Kernville Inn 11042 Kernville Rd ☎877 393 7900, ⓦ kernvilleinn.com. The best-value motel, right in the centre and with a pool and comfortable rooms, including some pricier ones with kitchens. Rates increase by $20 at weekends. **$99**
Sequoia Lodge 16123 Sierra Way ☎760 376 2535, ⓦ sequoialodge.net. Right on the Kern River, located

three miles from Kernville, this place has fourteen rustic but comfy rooms, which come with kitchenettes. **$99**
Whispering Pines Lodge 13745 Sierra Way (1 mile north of town) ☎760 376 3733. Relaxed spot with luxurious cottages, many with balconies overlooking the river, plus a nice pool and a delicious breakfast served on the terrace. **$180**

EATING AND DRINKING

Cracked Egg Café 15 Big Blue Rd ☎760 376 2185. This rustic diner is the best breakfast and lunch option in town; the chicken-fried steak and eggs plate will keep you going all day. Daily 7am–2pm.
Kern River Brewing Co 13415 Sierra Way ☎760 376 2337, ⓦ kernriverbrewing.com. Lively restaurant and bar serving burgers, salads and great fish and chips ($9.75), plus four toothsome microbrews on tap ($4). It's all eased down with occasional live music (particularly on summer weekends). April–Sept Mon–Thurs & Sun 11am–10pm,

Fri & Sat 11am–11pm; Oct–March Mon–Thurs & Sun 11.30am–9.30pm, Fri & Sat 11.30am–11pm.
McNally's 7300 Kern River Hwy (Hwy-99), Fairview (15 miles north of Kernville) ☎760 376 2430. Great, cut-to-order steaks in an unpretentious family-dining setting, right on the Kern River. Best known for its giant, 40-ounce porterhouse, aka "the logger" (steaks from $26). April to late Nov Mon–Thurs & Sun 4–8pm, Fri & Sat 4–9pm; mid-Feb to March Fri–Sun 4–8pm (closed late Nov to mid-Feb).

Sequoia National Forest

Wedged between Kernville and Sequoia National Park lies **SEQUOIA NATIONAL FOREST**, a vast canopy of pine trees punctuated by massive, glacier-polished domes and gleaming granite spires. Much of it is untouched wilderness that's barely less stunning than the national parks to the north; in recognition of this, and as one of Bill Clinton's final gestures before leaving office, a large section was re-designated the **Giant Sequoia National Monument** (unrestricted access). True to its name, it's packed with giant sequoias (in 38 small groves) and, as the forest is far less visited than the national parks, it's perfect for those seeking total solitude; hiking trails run virtually everywhere. Camping only requires a free permit for your stove or fire, available from the ranger stations dotted around the perimeter of the forest, which also have details of the scores of drive-in campgrounds – some free, others up to $27 a pitch.

Sierra Way

From Kernville, **Sierra Way** (aka Hwy-99) follows the Upper Kern River north past numerous basic camping sites (free) and half a dozen shaded, waterside campgrounds (mostly $22; reserve for summer weekends on ☎877 444 6777), eventually reaching Johnsondale Bridge, twenty miles north of Kernville. From the bridge, hikers can follow the **River Trail** upstream, passing the numerous rapids of The Forks section of the Kern, great for spotting rafters and kayakers on weekend afternoons and even for camping at one of several free walk-in sites along the river; the first campground is about a ten-minute hike along the trail from the bridge.

Beyond Johnsondale Bridge, Sierra Way climbs another four miles to tiny **Johnsondale** – just a seasonal store and restaurant – where narrow and winding paved Forest Road 22S82 (Lloyds Meadow Rd) cuts twenty miles north to the Jerkey Meadow trailhead.

The Western Divide Highway

Continuing along Sierra Way from Johnsondale, it's five miles to a road junction where you join the twisting and narrow **Western Divide Highway** which, after a couple of miles, passes the **Trail of a Hundred Giants** (parking $5/day), an easy, one-mile paved interpretive trail around a stand of huge sequoias. Further north, you catch glimpses of magnificent Sierra vistas as the road climbs above the 7000ft mark, but for the best views it's worth pressing on five miles to the 7200ft exfoliated scalp of **Dome Rock**, just half a mile off the highway, or **The Needles**, a further three miles on. This series of tall pinnacles – the Magician, the Wizard and the Warlock, among others – presents some of America's most demanding crack climbs, and can be visited on the moderate, undulating hiking and biking **Needles Lookout Trail** (5 miles round-trip; 2hr on foot), which starts three miles off the highway up a dirt road. The final switchback leads to a fire-lookout station (generally open to visitors Wed–Sun 9am–6pm during the June–Oct fire season), precariously perched atop the Magician and with supreme views over the Kern Valley and across to Mount Whitney.

From here onwards, the Western Divide Highway becomes Hwy-190, executing endless twists and turns forty miles down to the valley town of **Porterville**, where you can turn right for Sequoia and Kings Canyon national parks or continue another sixteen miles to rejoin Hwy-99 and head north to Visalia.

ARRIVAL AND DEPARTURE
SEQUOIA NATIONAL FOREST

By car There's no public transport to the forest, but the roads are in good shape, though subject to snow closure in winter (mid-Nov to mid-May). To find out about conditions and closures, visit ⊚ dot.ca.gov/cgi-bin/roads.cgi or call ☎ 800 427 7623.

ACCOMMODATION

Brewer's Ponderosa Lodge 56692 Aspen Drive, Ponderosa ☎ 559 542 2579, ⊚ brewersponderosalodge .com. Down the road from *Mountain Top*, with two large, pleasant motel-type rooms, a restaurant, bar, grocery store and expensive gas. **$92**

Lower Peppermint Campground Lloyd Meadow Rd (Forest Rd 22S82), 10 miles north of Johnsondale ☎ 559 539 2607, ⊚ www.fs.usda.gov/sequoia. Tranquil site at 5300ft, with seventeen pitches, toilets and water, just off Peppermint Creek. Lots of trails nearby, through giant sequoia groves, up mountains, and alongside wild rivers. Note that this is black bear country. Pitches from **$20**

Mountain Top B&B 56816 Aspen Drive, Ponderosa (off Hwy-190, 27 miles east of Springville) ☎ 559 542 2639. Tranquil getaway surrounded by pine trees, with two cosy en-suite rooms and a large, shared living room with large-screen satellite TV. **$140**

Visalia

Seventy miles north of Bakersfield, the agricultural town of **VISALIA** makes a comfortable base for exploring Sequoia and Kings Canyon national parks, an hour's drive east along Hwy-198. It also has the only **bus service** into the parks.

The oak forests which initially lured San Joaquin's first settlers in 1852 (led by one Nathaniel Vise) have long gone, but Visalia remains a pretty place with a compact and leafy town centre that invites strolls in the relative cool of the evening.

ARRIVAL AND DEPARTURE
VISALIA

By bus Greyhound/Orange Belt Stage Lines, along with KART buses from Hanford (see p.306) and the shuttle to Sequoia and Kings Canyon national parks (see p.312), arrive at the downtown transit centre at 425 E Oak St (☎ 559 734 3507).

Destinations Bakersfield (5 daily; 1hr 15min–2hr 10min); Fresno (5 daily; 45min–1hr); Hanford (2 daily; 30–40min); Los Angeles (4 daily; 3hr 40min–4hr 25min).

ACCOMMODATION

Lamp Liter Inn 3300 W Mineral King Ave ☎ 559 732 4511, ⊚ lampliter.net. Pleasant hotel with spacious rooms (with cable TV), surrounded by lawns and featuring a very nice pool, sports bar and grill. **$88**

★ **The Spalding House** 631 N Encina ☎ 559 739 7877, ⊚ thespaldinghouse.com. Local lumberman W.R. Spalding built this fine Colonial Revival home in 1901, now a beautifully appointed B&B. Suites all have separate bathrooms and sitting rooms. **$95**

EATING AND DRINKING

Brewbakers Brewing Co 219 E Main St ☎ 559 627 2739, ⓦ brewbakersbrewingco.com. Dine among the polished steel and brass tanks of this lively brewpub, which serves tempting burgers, salads and thick, chewy pizza, mostly for under $15. There's often live music to encourage you to sample their half-dozen brews. Daily 11.30am–11.30pm.

Café 225 225 W Main St ☎ 559 733 2967, ⓦ cafe225 .com. A modern bistro and tapas bar with an eclectic menu that features artichoke fritters ($7.50), steak frites ($20)

and goat cheese and roast lamb pizza ($12). Mon–Sat 11am–10pm.

★ **The Vintage Press** 216 N Willis St ☎ 559 733 3033, ⓦ thevintagepress.com. Serving California continental cuisine, this fine restaurant ranks as one of the best in the region. Succumb to wild mushrooms in puff pastry with cognac, followed by red snapper with toasted almonds and capers and finally a dessert and coffee (mains $24–45). Mon–Sat 11.30am–2pm & 5.30–10pm, Sun 10am–2pm & 5–10pm.

Hanford

Restful, small-town **HANFORD**, twenty miles west of Visalia on Hwy-198, was named after James Hanford in 1877, a paymaster on the Southern Pacific Railroad who became popular with his employees when he took to paying them in gold.

Courthouse Square

Today Hanford has a population of around 56,000, centred on **Courthouse Square**, the core of local life at the beginning of the twentieth century. The honey-coloured **Kings County Courthouse** retains many of its Neoclassical features from 1896, including a magnificent staircase; it served as a courthouse till 1976, and today houses offices, small shops and restaurants.

China Alley and the Taoist Temple

Taoist Temple: 12 China Alley • First Sat of the month noon–6pm • Free • ☎ 559 582 4508, ⓦ chinaalley.com

Much less ostentatious than Courthouse Square are the rows of two-storey porched dwellings, four blocks east on **China Alley** (entrance on Green St, just north of 7th St), marking the district that was home to most of the eight hundred or so **Chinese** families who came to Hanford to work on the railroad in the 1870s. At the centre of the community was the **Taoist Temple**. Built in 1893, the temple served both a spiritual and a social function, providing free lodging to work-seeking Chinese immigrants, and was used as a Chinese school during the early 1920s. Everything inside is original, from the teak burl figurines to the marble chairs, and it's a shame that entry is so restricted.

Hanford Carnegie Museum

109 E 8th St • Tues–Sat 10m–5pm • $3 • ☎ 559 584 1367, ⓦ hanfordcarnegiemuseum.org

Housed in the old Carnegie Library, completed in a typical Romanesque style in 1905, the **Hanford Carnegie Museum** chronicles the history of the Hanford area with displays of antique furniture, black and white photos and assorted bric-a-brac, doubling as the local tourist information centre. Pioneer aviator Amelia Earhart's friendship with Hanford resident Mary Packwood is documented, as is the **Mussel Slough Tragedy**, an 1880 land dispute that resulted in seven deaths.

ARRIVAL AND DEPARTURE   HANFORD

By bus KART buses (☎ 559 584 0101, ⓦ mykartbus.com) arrive on 7th St near the town's visitor centre. Greyhound runs a limited service to the town from 310 N Brown St, just off 7th.

Destinations (Greyhound) Bakersfield (1 daily; 3hr 10min); Visalia (2 daily; 30–40min); (KART) Fresno (2 daily

Mon–Fri; 1hr); Visalia (3 daily Mon–Fri; 20min–1hr).

By train The Amtrak station is at 200 Santa Fe Ave.

Destinations Bakersfield (7 daily; 1hr 35min); Fresno (7 daily; 35min); Merced (7 daily 1hr 40min); Sacramento (3 daily; 2hr 45min–4hr).

ACCOMMODATION AND EATING

Sequoia Inn 1655 Mall Drive ☎559 582 0338, ⓦthesequoiainn.com. If you need to stay in Hanford you'll find there are some decent chain motels, but this one is independently owned by the Tachi-Yokut tribe, and offers spacious, sleek, business-style rooms, an outdoor pool and continental breakfast. $95

Star Restaurant 325 N Douty St ☎559 582 0481. Take a trip back in time at this old-school diner (it's actually been around since 1901), with no-frills cooking – hamburger and fries, pancake specials and pork chops all under $10. Mon–Fri 6am–2.20pm.

Superior Dairy 325 N Douty St ☎559 582 0481. Sample the rich creaminess of the made-on-the-premises ice cream at Hanford's classic 1929 sweet emporium ($4.25 for a giant scoop). Daily 11am–9.30pm.

Fresno

With a population of over half a million, **FRESNO** is the largest city between LA and San Francisco and an increasingly Hispanic one (officially around fifty percent of the inhabitants). In some ways it feels little more than an overgrown farming town but it's very much the hub of business in the San Joaquin Valley and is experiencing ongoing urban renewal. Witness such stridently modern buildings as the delta-winged, steel-and-glass **Fresno City Hall**, close to the Amtrak station and the downtown **Chukchansi Park** stadium for Fresno's Minor League baseball team, the Grizzlies. Still, there's an odd mix of civic pride and urban decay, the latter fuelling Fresno's status as one of the US's crime hotspots.

Nevertheless, consider spending a night here in order to visit the fascinating **Forestiere Underground Gardens**, a one-of-a-kind warren of rooms hewn out of the hardpan to protect one man and his crops from the heat, and to sample the dining and nightlife in the vibrant **Tower District**, three miles north of downtown. Once something of a hippie hangout due to its proximity to the City College campus, today the district has a well-scrubbed liberal feel, plus several blocks of antiques shops, bookstores and eating places.

5

Forestiere Underground Gardens

5021 W Shaw Ave • 1hr tours on the hour: March & Nov Sat & Sun 11am–3pm; April, May, Sept & Oct Wed–Fri 11am–3pm, Sat & Sun 10am–3pm; June–Aug Wed–Sun 10am–4pm • $15 • ☎ 559 271 0734, ⊕ undergroundgardens.com

The one place that turns Fresno into a destination in its own right is **Forestiere Underground Gardens**, seven miles northwest of the centre, a block east of the Shaw Avenue exit off Hwy-99. A subterranean labyrinth of over fifty rooms, the gardens were constructed by Sicilian émigré and former Boston and New York subway tunneller Baldassare Forestiere, who came to Fresno in 1905. In a fanatical attempt to stay cool and protect his crops, Forestiere put his digging know-how to work, building underground living quarters and skylit orchards with just a shovel and wheelbarrow using chunks of hardpan to create supporting arches. He gradually improved techniques for maximizing his yield but wasn't above playful twists like a glass-bottomed underground aquarium and a subterranean bathtub fed by water heated in the midday sun. He died in 1946, his forty years of work producing a vast earth honeycomb, part of which was destroyed by the construction of Hwy-99 next door, while another section awaits restoration. Wandering around the remainder of what he achieved is a fascinating way to pass an hour out of the heat of the day, enlivened by the tour guide's anecdotes.

Meux Home Museum

1007 R St, at Tulare • Guided tours Fri–Sun noon–3pm • $5 • ☎ 559 233 8007, ⊕ meux.mus.ca.us

The **Meux Home Museum** is Fresno's only surviving late nineteenth-century house, completed in 1889 for what was then the staggering sum of $12,000. This was the home of a doctor (and ex-Confederate soldier) who arrived from the Deep South, bringing with him the novelty of a two-storey house and a plethora of trendy Victorian features – all quite out of sync with the Fresno that has sprawled up around it. The ten rooms have been furnished to represent its 1890s glory.

Fresno Art Museum

2233 N 1st St, in Radio Park • Thurs–Sun 11am–5pm • $10 • ☎ 559 441 4221, ⊕ fresnoartmuseum.org

A couple of miles north of downtown is the **Fresno Art Museum**, which has a changing roster of high-quality modern art in addition to an attractive sculpture garden and rooms devoted to pre-Columbian Mexican art spanning Mesoamerican styles from 2500 years ago until the arrival of the Spanish. There's also a relatively minor but beautiful 1926 Diego Rivera canvas, *El Dia de las Flores, Xochimilco*, along with an explanation of how it came to be here.

Kearney Mansion Museum

7160 W Kearney Blvd • Sat & Sun tours at 1pm, 2pm & 3pm • $5 per person entry to mansion; additional $5 per vehicle entry to Kearney Park • ☎ 559 441 0862, ⊕ valleyhistory.org

If you have time to spare, head seven miles west from downtown Fresno along Kearney Boulevard, a long, straight, palm-lined avenue that was once the private driveway through the huge Kearney Park to the **Kearney Mansion Museum**. It was built between 1900 and 1903 for M. Theo Kearney, an English-born agricultural pioneer and raisin mogul, who maintained it in the opulent French Renaissance style to which he seemed addicted. He had even grander plans to grace Fresno with a French château, the mind-boggling designs for which are displayed here.

FRESNO COUNTY BLOSSOM TRAIL

During the spring blooming season, allow an hour or two to follow at least part of the 62-mile **Blossom Trail**, southeast of Fresno, which weaves among fruit orchards, nut trees, citrus groves and the vineyards that make the city the world's raisin capital. Late February to early March is best (see ⊕ gofresnocounty.com/blossomtrail).

ARRIVAL AND DEPARTURE
FRESNO

5

By plane Fresno Yosemite International Airport (ⓦ flyfresno.com) is five miles east of downtown Fresno. There are car rental companies here and YARTS buses system (see p.340) runs to Yosemite National Park.
By bus The Greyhound terminal is downtown at 2660 Tulare St (ⓣ 559 268 1829).

Destinations Los Angeles (11 daily; 4hr 20min–5hr 20min); Merced (5 daily; 1hr 10min); Modesto (6 daily; 1hr 45min–2hr 10min); San Francisco (2 daily; 4hr 30min–4hr 50min).
By train The Amtrak terminal is downtown at 2650 Tulare St.
Destinations Bakersfield (7 daily; 2hr 5min); Merced (7 daily; 1hr); Sacramento (3 daily; 2hr 11min–3hr 25min).

ACCOMMODATION

There is little accommodation beyond **motels**, many clustered near the junction of Olive Ave (the Tower District's main drag) and Hwy-99: avoid the marginal places charging rock-bottom rates.

Homewood Suites by Hilton Fresno 6820 N Fresno St ⓣ 559 440 0801, ⓦ homewoodsuites3.hilton.com. Justly popular business hotel offering good value; spacious studios, and more expensive one- and two-bedroom suites with fully equipped kitchens, plus billiards rooms and outdoor pool. **$219**
La Quinta Inn Fresno Yosemite 2926 Tulare St ⓣ 559 442 1110, ⓦ lq.com. Decent chain motel option

close to downtown, with comfy, well-appointed rooms, flat-screen TVs, a gym and staff that really care about the place. **$84**
TownePlace Suites Fresno 7127 N Fresno St ⓣ 559 435 4600, ⓦ marriott.com. This Marriott-owned place, just slightly north of downtown Fresno, offers an elegant studios and pricier one- and two-bedroom suites. There's a gym but no pool. **$160**

EATING

★**Ampersand Ice Cream** 1940 N Echo Ave ⓣ 559 264 8000, ⓦ ampersandicecream.com. The region's best ice cream, featuring local produce (strawberries, berries, nectarines and the like) and flavours such as whisky caramel, and salt and coffee – eat at tables topped with wood from recycled bowling alleys. Tues–Sun 11am–11pm.
Grandmarie's Chicken Pie Shop 861 E Olive Ave ⓣ 559 237 5042. For iconic Valley diner food visit this old-fashioned restaurant, locally famed for its chicken pot pie (and excellent fruit pies) at bargain prices since 1956 (mains from $8). Mon–Fri 7am–7pm, Sat & Sun 8am–8pm.
Roger Rocka's Dinner Theater 1226 N Wishon Ave

ⓣ 559 266 9494, ⓦ rogerrockas.com. For dinner with entertainment thrown in, attend a Broadway-style show in this 250-seat theatre preceded either by a sumptuous buffet (Thurs & Sun; $55 all up) or a table-service meal (Fri–Sun; $59). Show only $32. Thurs–Sat 5.30–10pm, Sun 11am–4pm & 5.30–10pm.
Veni Vidi Vici 1116 N Fulton St ⓣ 559 266 5510, ⓦ venividivicirestaurant.com. For a quality evening meal check out this dim-lit, moody restaurant (with a patio for outdoor dining) boasting an eclectic range of dishes such as Vietnamese baby spinach salad ($12) and juniper-berry pork chop ($28). After 10pm it becomes a lively bar. Daily 5.30pm–2am.

DRINKING

Sequoia Brewing Co 777 E Olive Ave ⓣ 559 264 5521, ⓦ sequoiabrewing.com. Step up to the local brewpub, where eleven excellent tap beers are supplemented by live music (Wed, Fri & Sat; no cover) and good-value meals

that extend to brick-oven pizzas, pasta dishes and salads. Mon–Thurs 11am–10pm, Fri & Sat 11am–midnight, Sun 11am–9pm.

Northern San Joaquin Valley

Times are rough for the cities of the northern San Joaquin Valley, which often feel worlds away from California's sun and surf stereotypes. Founded on agriculture, towns here had the hearts ripped out of them by suburban sprawl in the latter half of the twentieth century. In recent years, large amounts were spent to smarten up downtowns but this led to a wave of city bankruptcies after the 2008/2009 financial crisis – in 2012 **Stockton** became the largest US city to ever file for bankruptcy protection (Detroit took the title in 2013), and ranked as one of the most dangerous cities in America.

The region offers little in the way of attractions, though you may want to spend the night in **Merced**, especially if you are Yosemite-bound, while **Modesto** offers a couple of interesting sites and vestiges of the 1950s tied to seminal movie *American Graffiti*.

5

Merced and around

The best thing about sluggish **MERCED**, a city of around 82,000 some forty-five miles north of Fresno, is its proximity to Yosemite National Park (see p.329); the "Gateway to Yosemite" is less than two hours away by car. In the town itself, the courthouse is a gem of a building in the main square that's maintained as the **Merced County Courthouse Museum**.

Merced County Courthouse Museum

N St, at W 21st • Wed–Sun 1–4pm • Free • ☎ 209 723 2401, ⓦ mercedmuseum.org

This striking Italian Renaissance-style structure with columns, elaborately sculptured window frames and a cupola topped by a statue of the Goddess of Justice (minus her customary blindfold), was raised in 1875 when it completely dominated the few dozen shacks that comprised the town. Impressively restored in period style, **Merced County Courthouse Museum** now contains local memorabilia – the most exotic item being an 1870s Taoist shrine, found by chance in a makeshift temple above a Chinese restaurant.

Castle Air Museum

5050 Santa Fe Drive, Atwater • Daily: April–Sept 9am–5pm; Oct–March 10am–4pm • $12 • ☎ 209 723 2182, ⓦ castleairmuseum.org • #W1 bus (ⓦ mercedthebus.com), runs out here from Merced about every 90min; $1.50 each way

Six miles north of Merced, close to the commuter town of **Atwater** – and signposted off Hwy-99 – lies the **Castle Air Museum**, home to fifty-odd military aircraft that date from World War II to the Vietnam War, mostly bulky bombers with a few fighters thrown in, including the world's fastest plane, the SR-71 Blackbird (over 2350 mph).

ARRIVAL AND INFORMATION   MERCED AND AROUND

By bus Greyhound buses stop downtown at 710 W 16th St, at N (☎ 209 722 2121), where you'll find the information centre. Four to five daily YARTS buses (☎ 877 989 2787, ⓦ yarts.com) depart here to Yosemite Valley (2hr 50min to the visitor centre).
Destinations Bakersfield (5 daily; 3hr 20min–4hr 15min); Fresno (5 daily; 1hr 10min); Los Angeles (5 daily; 6–7hr 5min); Modesto (5 daily; 55min); Sacramento (4 daily; 2hr 45min–3hr); San Francisco (1 daily; 3hr 35min).
By train The Amtrak station is somewhat isolated at 324 W 24th St and K St, about six blocks northeast of the Courthouse. Note that passenger trains do not travel further south than Bakersfield (Amtrak will arrange an

onwards bus for Los Angeles; for San Francisco you normally switch to a bus at Emeryville or Stockton).
Destinations Bakersfield (7 daily; 3hr–3hr 14min); Fresno (7 daily; 1hr); Modesto (7 daily; 35min); Sacramento (2 daily; 2hr 20min).
By car If you're looking to rent a car to head up to Yosemite, try Enterprise, 1334 W Main St (Tues–Fri 7.30am–6pm, Sat 9am–noon; ☎ 209 722 1600).
California Welcome Center The tourist information centre is located at the bus station at 710 W 16th St (Mon–Sat 8.30am–5pm, Sun 10am–4pm; ☎ 209 724 8104, ⓦ visitmerced.travel).

ACCOMMODATION

Bear Creek Inn 575 W North Bear Creek Drive ☎ 209 723 3991, ⓦ bearcreekinnmerced.com. B&B in a lovely 1930s Colonial-style house with five rooms furnished with polished floors, plain painted walls and an understated smattering of antique furnishings. It's all tastefully done and breakfast is served in a grand dining room. $159
HI-Merced Home Hostel ☎ 209 725 0407, ⓔ merced @hiusa.org. Reservations-only six-bed hostel that has limited check-in and access hours (7–9am & 5–10pm) and no wi-fi (and no showers in the morning), but this is a small price to pay for a ride to and from the bus and train stations,

an enthusiastic welcome from the retired couple owners and as much information as you can handle. Discounts for HI members. Address supplied on booking. Dorms $25, doubles $60
Slumber Motel 1315 W 16th St ☎ 209 722 5783, ⓦ slumbermotel.com. Plenty of decent chain motels line Hwy-99 near the Merced exits, but this is the pick of basic, budget motels half a mile west of the Transpo Center (left as you step out of the door), with ageing but adequate rooms, a small pool and cable TV. $55

EATING AND DRINKING

Branding Iron Restaurant 640 W 16th St ☎ 209 722 1822, ⓦ thebrandingiron-merced.com. Venerable

steakhouse open since 1952, celebrating California's ranching culture with cowboy decor and quality steaks (from $19).

Mon–Thurs 11.30am–2pm & 5–9pm, Fri 11.30am–2pm & 5–9.30pm, Sat 5–9.30pm, Sun 5–9pm.
Cinema Café 661 W Main St ☎ 209 722 2811. The retro salt and pepper shakers behind the open kitchen match the lime-green counter stools in this decent breakfast and lunch diner. They serve up the the usual range of burgers and sandwiches plus Mexican specials (most dishes under

$10). Daily 6am–2pm.
H&W Family Drive-In 121 W 16th St (just off Hwy-99) ☎ 209 722 8595. Old-fashioned diner with "car-hop" service, serving cheap but mouthwatering burgers (bacon double cheeseburger for $3.99), though the real attraction is the home-made root beer. Eat in the car or sit outside at covered tables. Daily 10.30am–9pm.

Modesto

Forty miles north of Merced along Hwy-99 you reach the city of **MODESTO**, which got its unusual name after prominent San Francisco banker William Ralston was too modest to accept the new town being named after him in 1870. Today it's a city of some 205,000 and surrounded by rich farmland (especially almonds and grapes – the largest winery in the world, E&J Gallo, is here), though the region remains plagued by foreclosures, crime and high unemployment. Modesto also ranks among the top car theft cities in the US – don't leave anything valuable in your vehicle. If that doesn't put you off, come for the **McHenry Mansion**, a rare Victorian gem, and fans of *American Graffiti* will want to cruise the city that inspired the movie.

McHenry Mansion

906 15th St, at 1st • Mon–Fri & Sun 12.30–4pm (tours every 30min; 45–50min) • Free • ☎ 209 549 0428, ⓦ mchenrymansion.org
Built in 1883, the grand Italianate **McHenry Mansion** is jam-packed with fixtures, fittings and the personal effects of a family whose fate was linked with Modesto for years. Robert McHenry was a successful wheat rancher in the mid-nineteenth century who did much to bring about a general uplift in the agricultural wellbeing of the area. **Tours** led by volunteers, the only way to visit the interior, enhance appreciation of the house, its history and its restoration after having been rented out as apartments until the early 1970s.

McHenry Museum

1402 I St, at 14th • Tues–Sun noon–4pm • Free • ☎ 209 577 5235, ⓦ mchenrymuseum.org
A block from the McHenry Mansion, a fine Victorian building originally financed by the McHenry family as the fledgling city's library in 1912 now operates as the **McHenry Museum**, which sports mock-ups of a blacksmith's shop, dentist's surgery and gathering of cattle brands, revealing something of bygone days, although lacking the period atmosphere of the mansion.

ARRIVAL AND INFORMATION   MODESTO

By bus Greyhound buses stop downtown at the Modesto Transport Center, 1001 9th St at J (☎ 209 526 4314).

Destinations Fresno (6 daily; 1hr 45min–2hr 10min); Los Angeles (6 daily; 6hr 20min–8hr 5min); Merced (5 daily;

AMERICAN GRAFFITI

Modesto was the childhood home of movie director George Lucas of **Star Wars** fame, and became the inspiration (though not the location) for his movie *American Graffiti* (1973), the classic portrayal of growing up in small-town America during the late 1950s. The movie contains a number of references to local people, particularly the teachers who rubbed Lucas up the wrong way in his formative years. Sadly, after an especially unruly "Graffiti Night" in 1993 (traditionally the first big weekend after school ended for the summer in June), local ordinances put an end to the fine art of **cruising**, though in recent years the American Graffiti Classic Car Show (middle weekend in June) has stepped in with hundreds of classic cars from all over the state and beyond, dusted off and cruised through the city. Despite the cruising ban, you'll still see the better-kept rigs parked here on Friday and Saturday nights (until 10pm), when Elvis and Marilyn impersonators are often in evidence. Lucas himself is honoured with a bronze statue at Five Points (the intersections of McHenry Ave, J St, 17th St, Downey and Needham).

5

45–55min); San Francisco (2 daily; 2hr 30min).

By train The Amtrak station is inconveniently located 4 miles northeast of downtown at 1700 Held Drive.

Destinations Bakersfield (7 daily; 3hr 50min); Fresno (7 daily; 1hr 45min); Merced (7 daily; 34–43min); Sacramento

(2 daily; 1hr 40min).

Modesto Convention & Visitors Bureau 1150 9th St at L St (Mon–Fri 8am–5pm; ☎888 640 8467, ⓦvisit modesto.com).

ACCOMMODATION AND EATING

★**A&W Root Beer Drive-In** 1404 G St ☎209 522 7700. This Californian fast-food chain celebrates the *American Graffiti* era with rollerskating "car-hop" waitresses serving root-beer floats ordered from illuminated car-side menus, and the sounds of the 1950s ring through the speakers. Mon–Sat 10am–8.30pm, Sun 11am–8pm.

Dewz Restaurant 1505 J St ☎209 549 1101, ⓦdineatdewz.com. Local favourite, specializing in fresh, California cuisine with Asian and French influences, from roast organic chicken to lobster bisque and roasted pumpkin ravioli (dinner mains $24–34). Mon–Thurs

11am–3pm & 4.30–9.30pm, Fri 11am–3pm & 4.30–10.30pm, Sat 4.30–10.30pm.

Doubletree by Hilton Hotel 1150 9th St ☎209 526 6000, ⓦdoubletree3.hilton.com. The usual motel chains surround Modesto, but this is the best choice in the heart of downtown, with comfy business-style rooms, pool, free cookies, sauna and exercise room (parking $12/day). **$126**

★**Queen Bean Coffee House** 1126 14th St at K St ☎209 521 8000. Serves breakfast, espresso, cakes and great sandwiches in a converted house, and often has bands playing at weekends. Mon–Thurs 7.30am–8pm, Fri–Sun 7.30am–10pm.

Sequoia and Kings Canyon national parks

Jointly administered and sharing a long common border, **SEQUOIA AND KINGS CANYON NATIONAL PARKS** contain an immense variety of geology, flora and fauna. **Sequoia National Park**, as you might expect from its name, boasts the thickest concentration – and the biggest individual specimens – of giant sequoia trees found anywhere in the world. These ancient trees tend to outshine (and certainly outgrow) the other features of the park – an assortment of meadows, peaks, canyons and caves swathed in pine and fir. **Kings Canyon National Park** doesn't have as many big trees, but compensates with a gaping canyon gored out of the rock by the Kings River, which cascades in torrents down from the High Sierra during the spring snowmelt period. There's less of a packaged tourism feel here than in Yosemite: the few established sights (principally the big trees) are near the main roads and tend to concentrate the crowds, leaving the vast majority of the landscape untrammelled and unspoiled, but well within reach for willing hikers. Linking the parks is the **Generals Highway**, actually a fairly slow and winding paved road which connects two of the biggest sequoias hereabouts, the General Sherman Tree in Sequoia and the General Grant Tree in Kings Canyon.

Approaching from the south, you twist your way up from Three Rivers to **Giant Forest** in Sequoia, site of the parks' best museum, right in the heart of a grove of enormous trees. From here, **Crescent Meadow Road** spurs off southeast past dramatic **Moro Rock** and under the **Tunnel Log** to **Crescent Meadow** and **Tharp's Cabin**, fashioned from a fallen sequoia. The Generals Highway continues northeast to **Lodgepole**, a base for excellent trails leading through deep forests, with longer treks rising above the tree line to reveal the barren peaks and superb vistas of the High Sierra. Further north, **Grant Grove** in Kings Canyon offers accommodation and dining, making this the main base for visiting sights such as the **General Grant Tree** and assorted sequoia graveyards – fields of massive severed stumps. Some twenty-five miles to the north and then east, **Cedar Grove** huddles in the bottom of Kings Canyon at the start of most of the marked hikes. Access is along Hwy-180, which spectacularly skirts, and then dives into, the colossal canyon. The **best time to visit** the parks is in late summer and fall when the days are still warm. At high altitude the nights are quite chilly, but the roads remain free of snow and most visitors have left. Bear in mind that although most roads are kept open throughout the winter, Hwy-180 into Kings Canyon is usually closed mid-November to mid-April due to

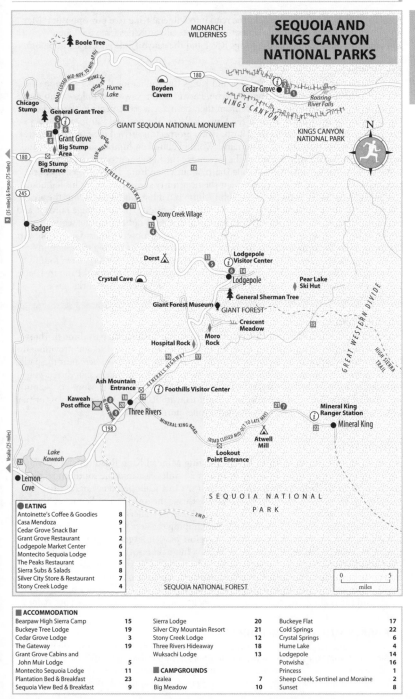

SEQUOIA AND KINGS CANYON NATIONAL PARKS

● EATING

Antoinette's Coffee & Goodies	8
Casa Mendoza	9
Cedar Grove Snack Bar	1
Grant Grove Restaurant	2
Lodgepole Market Center	6
Montecito Sequoia Lodge	3
The Peaks Restaurant	5
Sierra Subs & Salads	8
Silver City Store & Restaurant	7
Stony Creek Lodge	4

■ ACCOMMODATION

Bearpaw High Sierra Camp	15	Sierra Lodge	20	Buckeye Flat	17
Buckeye Tree Lodge	19	Silver City Mountain Resort	21	Cold Springs	22
Cedar Grove Lodge	3	Stony Creek Lodge	12	Crystal Springs	6
The Gateway	19	Three Rivers Hideaway	18	Hume Lake	4
Grant Grove Cabins and		Wuksachi Lodge	13	Lodgepole	14
John Muir Lodge	5			Potwisha	16
Montecito Sequoia Lodge	11	**■ CAMPGROUNDS**		Princess	1
Plantation Bed & Breakfast	23	Azalea	7	Sheep Creek, Sentinel and Moraine	2
Sequoia View Bed & Breakfast	9	Big Meadow	10	Sunset	8

5

rockfall hazards, while snow blocks the road into Mineral King (see box opposite). May and June can also be opportune times to visit, especially in Kings Canyon, where snowmelt dramatically swells the Kings River and the canyon-side yuccas are in bloom.

Brief history

The land now encompassed by Sequoia and Kings Canyon national parks was once the domain of **Yokuts sub-tribes** – the Monache, Potwisha and Kaweah peoples – who made summer forays into the high country from their permanent settlements in the lowlands, especially along the Middle Fork of the Kaweah River. The first real European contact came with the 1849 **California Gold Rush**, when prospectors arrived in search of pastures and a direct route through the mountains. Word of abundant lumber soon got out, and loggers came to stake their claims in the lowlands. The high country was widely ignored until 1858, when local natives led **Hale Tharp**, a cattleman from Three Rivers, up to the sequoias around Moro Rock. Tharp spent the next thirty summers here in his log home (see p.316); legendary conservationist John Muir visited him and wrote about the area, bringing it to the attention of the general public. Before long, narrow-gauge railways and log flumes littered the area, mainly for clearing fir and pine rather than the sequoias, which tended to shatter when felled. Nonetheless, Visalia conservationist George Stewart campaigned in Washington for some degree of **preservation** for the big trees, and in 1890, Sequoia was created as the country's **second national park**. Six days later, four square miles around Grant Grove was protected as Grant Grove National Park; in 1940, this area was incorporated into newly formed Kings Canyon National Park.

Three Rivers

Approaching Sequoia National Park from the south and Visalia, you pass through **Three Rivers**, a foothill community strung out for seven miles along Hwy-198 and providing the greatest concentration of accommodation and restaurant options anywhere near the parks. As you approach the centre of town, six miles from the park entrance, a sign directs you three miles north to the **Kaweah Post Office** (43795 North Fork Drive; Mon–Fri 1–2pm), the smallest post office still operating in California, with its original brass-and-glass private boxes here since 1910 (it originally opened 4 miles north in 1890).

Mineral King

A couple of miles north of Three Rivers, twisting Mineral King Road (open late May to Oct) dates from the early 1880s and branches 23 miles east into the southern section of Sequoia National Park to **Mineral King**, which sits in a scalloped bowl at 7800ft surrounded by snowy peaks and glacial lakes. This is the only part of Sequoia's high country that is accessible by car (but not RVs, buses or trailers) and makes a superb hiking base. Eager prospectors built the road hoping the area would yield silver. It didn't, the mines were abandoned and the region was left largely in peace until the mid-1960s, when Disney threatened to build a huge ski resort here. Thankfully, the plan was defeated and the area was protectively absorbed by the national park in 1978. Today there are just a few small stands of sequoias, a couple of basic campgrounds, one small resort and near-complete tranquillity. Having negotiated the seven-hundred-odd twists and turns along the road, you can relax by the Kaweah River's East Fork before

---

PARK, MONUMENT OR FOREST?

With two **national parks** and the **Giant Sequoia National Monument**, all surrounded by **Sierra National Forest** and **Sequoia National Forest**, the Sequoia and Kings Canyon region is a patchwork of federally administered areas. For the most part, it won't matter which section you're in, though regulations (particularly for hunting and camping) are more relaxed in the national forests.

WINTER IN SEQUOIA AND KINGS CANYON

Usually between November and May, the high country of both parks is covered in a blanket of **snow**, and while this limits a great deal of sightseeing and walking, it also opens up opportunities for some superb winter activities. With tyre chains, **access** is seldom much of a problem. Both main roads (Hwy-198 and Hwy-180) into the parks are kept open all year. The Generals Highway is also ploughed after snowfall, but sometimes takes a few days to clear. Kings Canyon's Cedar Grove is off-limits to cars from about mid-November to mid-April, but Grant Grove remains open all year. Facilities are restricted, however, and camping is only available at snow-free sites in the lowlands.

The parks' major winter activities are **cross-country skiing** and **snowshoeing**. Hwy-180 provides access to two places at the hub of miles of marked trails: Grant Grove Market at Grant Grove Village offers ski and snowshoe rentals (Nov–April; ☎ 559 335 5500), and you'll also find guided naturalist snowshoe walks available on winter Saturdays, as well as restaurants and accommodation; *Montecito Sequoia Lodge* (see p.322), with its own groomed trails threading Sequoia National Forest, is also open to day-visitors for $25 and offers rental packages for $25–30 per day. Nearby, the mile-long Big Meadows Nordic Ski Trail is perfect beginner's terrain. To the south, *Wuksachi Lodge* (see p.322) has groomed trails and plenty of scope in the backcountry: skis ($20/day) and snowshoes ($18/day) can both be rented at on-site Alta Market. Unless you're staying at *Wuksachi Lodge* or are a super-hardy camper, you'll need to return to Three Rivers for somewhere to stay.

hiking up over steep Sawtooth Pass and into the alpine bowls of the glaciated basins beyond. There's also a gentler introduction to the flora and fauna of Mineral King by way of a short **nature trail** from *Cold Springs Campground*.

Pick up wilderness permits (see box, p.319) for overnight hikes at the **Mineral King ranger station** (see p.321), opposite *Cold Springs Campground*. From late May to mid-July, you'll want to protect any vehicles left overnight against **marmot** attack: chicken wire can be rented or bought from *Silver City Mountain Resort* (see p.322), which, unless you're committed to camping, is the only place to stay (or dine, for that matter) in the Mineral King area.

Giant Forest

Continuing into Sequoia National Park on Hwy-198 from Three Rivers, you almost immediately encounter the cramped **Foothills Visitor Center** (see p.321) before coming upon **Hospital Rock** further on. It's impressively decorated with rock drawings from an ancient Monache settlement, whose evolution and culture is explained in the adjacent exhibit. **Generals Highway** then twists tortuously uphill into **GIANT FOREST**, the world's greatest accessible concentration of giant sequoias.

Giant Forest Museum

Generals Hwy · Daily: mid- to late May & Sept to mid-Oct 9am–4.30pm; late May to Aug 9am–6pm · Free · ☎ 559 565 4480, ⓦ nps.gov/seki

The excellent **Giant Forest Museum** is the best place to begin your Sequoia visit in earnest. Inside, there's compelling film footage of sequoia-felling and early tourism, while outside, the fire-damaged Sentinel Tree is cordoned off to allow seedlings a chance to establish themselves. Various short hikes fan out from here through the big trees, including the **Beetle Rock Trail** (5min round-trip), which affords a view down to San Joaquin Valley, and the **Big Trees Trail** (0.6-mile loop; 30min–1hr), which follows a well-formed boardwalk along the perimeter of Round Meadow.

Along Crescent Meadow Road

The park's densest concentration of sights is along **Crescent Meadow Road**, which spurs off the main highway just before the Giant Forest Museum. The first photo op is the **Auto Log**, a fallen trunk originally chiselled flat enough for motorists to nose up onto it, though rot has now put an end to this practice. Beyond here, a side loop leads to

5

Moro Rock, a granite monolith streaking wildly upwards from the green hillside. On a rare air-pollution-free day, views from its remarkably level top can stretch 150 miles across San Joaquin Valley; it's far more likely you'll be able to enjoy a clear vista of the towering Sierra in the other direction. Thanks to well-constructed stairs, it's a relatively efficient climb to the summit, although at nearly 7000ft above sea level, the nearly four hundred steps may be a strain for some.

Back on Crescent Meadow Road, you pass under the **Tunnel Log**: a tree that fell across the road in 1937 and has since had a vehicle-sized hole cut through its lower half. Further on, **Crescent Meadow** is, like other grassy fields in the area, more accurately a marsh, and too wet for the sequoias that form an impressive ring around its perimeter. Looking across the meadow gives the best opportunity to appreciate the changing shape of the ageing sequoia. The trail circling its perimeter (1.5 miles; 1hr; mainly flat) leads to **Log Meadow**, to which farmer Hale Tharp, searching for a summer grazing ground for his sheep, was led by local Native Americans in 1856. He became one of the first white men to see the giant sequoias, and the first to actually live in one – a hollowed-out specimen which still exists, remembered as **Tharp's Log**, an easy fifteen-minute walk from the parking area. Peer inside to appreciate the hewn-out shelves.

General Sherman Tree

North of Crescent Meadow Road, Generals Highway enters the thickest section of Giant Forest and passes the biggest sequoia of them all: the **General Sherman Tree**, reachable on foot by various connecting trails, is estimated to be 2300–2700 years old, is 275ft high and has a base diameter of 36.5ft. While it's certainly a thrill to be face-to-bark with what is widely held to be the largest living thing on earth, its extraordinary dimensions are hard to grasp in the midst of all the other monstrous sequoias in its midst – not to mention the other tremendous batch that can be seen along the **Congress Trail** (2 miles; 1–2hr; negligible ascent), which starts from the General Sherman Tree itself. A **free shuttle bus** runs from Giant Forest to the General Sherman Tree's parking area, itself about a half-mile from the great tree.

THE LIFE OF THE GIANT SEQUOIA

Call it what you will – the sierra redwood, *Sequoiadendron giganteum*, or just "big tree" – but the **giant sequoia** is the earth's most massive living thing. Some of these arboreal monsters weigh in at a whopping one thousand tonnes, courtesy of a thick trunk that barely tapers from base to crown. Many are two thousand (or even three thousand) years of age.

Sequoias are only found in around 75 isolated groves on the western slopes of California's **Sierra Nevada**, and grow naturally between elevations of 5000ft and 8500ft from just south of Sequoia National Park to just north of Yosemite National Park. Specimens planted all over the world during the nineteenth century seem to thrive, but haven't yet reached the enormous dimensions seen here.

The cinnamon-coloured bark of young sequoias is easily confused with that of the incense cedar, but as they age, there's no mistaking the thick spongy outer layer that protects the sapwood from the fires that periodically sweep through the forests. **Fire** is, in fact, a critical element in the propagation of sequoias; the hen-egg-sized female cones pack hundreds of seeds, but require intense heat to open them. Few seeds ever sprout as they need perfect conditions, usually where an old tree has fallen and left a hole in the canopy, allowing plenty of light to fall on rich mineral soil.

Young trees are conical, but as they mature, lower branches drop off to leave a top-heavy crown. A **shallow, wide root system** keeps them upright, but eventually heavy snowfall or high winds topple ageing trees. With its tannin-rich timber, a giant sequoia may lie where it fell for hundreds of years: John Muir discovered one still largely intact with a 380-year-old silver fir growing out of the depression it had created.

5

Crystal Cave

Cave Rd • Family Tours (50min) daily mid-May to Nov, check website for schedule • Family Tour $16; Discovery Tour $18; Wild Cave Tour $135 • ⓦ explorecrystalcave.com

When you've had your fill of the magnificent sequoia trees, consider a trip nine miles northwest from Giant Forest to **Crystal Cave**, which holds a fairly diverting batch of stalagmites and stalactites. The early morning Family Tours are not usually full, and whatever time you go, remember to take a jacket as the cave is at a constant 50°F (10°C); you'll also want to be prepared for a half-mile walk to the cave's entrance. Those with a deeper interest in the cave's origins and features should join the **Discovery Tour** (90min) or even the **Wild Cave Tour** (4–6hr).

Tickets for cave tours cannot be bought at the caves themselves; rather, you'll need to purchase them online at ⓦ recreation.gov, March to mid-October only (up to thirty days in advance), or less reliably at the Lodgepole or Foothills visitor centres (see p.321) at least a couple of hours beforehand – in July and August tours are always sold out days in advance. From mid-October to November tickets must be purchased at the Foothills visitor centre or Giant Forest Museum (see p.315).

Lodgepole, Wuksachi and Stony Creek Village

Whatever your plans, make sure you stop at **LODGEPOLE**, three miles north of the General Sherman Tree, where the **visitor centre** (see p.321) shows a short film, *Saving Sequoias*, detailing the restoration of the Giant Forest area in the late 1990s. With its grocery store, showers, laundry and campground, Lodgepole is very much at the centre of Sequoia's visitor activities, and its situation at one end of Tokopah Valley, a glacially formed canyon (not unlike far larger Yosemite Valley), makes it an ideal starting point to explore a number of hiking trails (see box opposite).

Beyond Lodgepole, Generals Highway turns west and runs four miles to **Wuksachi**, a modern lodge built at the same time that Giant Forest received its makeover, and where you'll find the fancy *Wuksachi Lodge Dining Room* (see p.322). The road soon swings north again and passes into Giant Sequoia National Monument, where facilities and accommodation are available at **STONY CREEK VILLAGE** (see p.318).

Grant Grove

A good base for exploring the northern sections of the parks, Kings Canyon's **Grant Grove** is set amid concentrated stands of sequoias, sugar pines, incense cedar, black oak and mountain dogwoods. You'll find accommodation and a place to eat at *Grant Grove Cabins* (see p.323) and *John Muir Lodge* (see p.323), along with a post office and a small supermarket.

Grant Grove's handy **visitor centre** (see p.321) can supply all the background information you'll need, and contains a small **museum** (free) with old-time photos, a cross-section of a tree and a kids' Discovery Room where you can examine tree seeds under a microscope.

Grant Grove is home to a couple of trees that rival the General Sherman for bulk: the **Robert E. Lee Tree** and the **General Grant Tree**. The General Grant is the world's second largest tree and was proclaimed the "Nation's Christmas Tree" by President Coolidge in 1926. A half-mile trail calls at the **Fallen Monarch**, which you can walk through, and the **Gamlin Cabin**, the first permanent home in Kings Canyon, and where Israel and Thomas Gamlin lived while exploiting their timber claim until 1878. The massive stump of one of the trees' scalps remains after a slice was shipped to the 1876 Centennial Exhibition in Philadelphia – an attempt to convince cynical easterners that such enormous trees really existed out west.

EXPLORING THE SEQUOIA AND KINGS CANYON BACKCOUNTRY

5

The **trails** in Sequoia and Kings Canyon national parks see far less traffic than those in Yosemite, but can still get busy in high summer. Almost all those leaving from Mineral King and Kings Canyon climb very steeply, so if you're looking for easy and moderate hikes, try the Little Baldy or Tokopah Falls trails.

There are **no restrictions** on day-hikes, but a quota system (late May to late Sept) applies if you plan to camp in the backcountry. A quarter of the spaces are offered on a first-come, first-served basis, so provided you are fairly flexible, you should be able to land something by turning up at the ranger station nearest to your proposed trailhead from 1pm on the day before you wish to start. Details for advance **wilderness permits** are given at ⊕ nps.gov/seki/planyourvisit/wilderness_permits.htm. Late May to late September there is a $10 per permit, plus a $5 per person wilderness permit fee, which entitles you to camp in the backcountry, preferably at an already impacted site. Applications for reservations are only accepted by fax or by US mail, starting on March 1 and at least two weeks before your start date (download the application on the website); outside the quota period, permits can be self-issued at most visitor centres and are free. Park visitor centres sell an excellent 1:80,000 scale Trails Illustrated **topographical map** of the parks (#205; $12).

Remember that this is **bear country** (see box, p.332). Bear canisters can be rented ($5 for 3 nights) at Mineral King, Foothills, Lodgepole, Grant Grove and Cedar Grove, or purchased (about $70) at the Lodgepole store and most visitor centres.

TRAILS FROM MINERAL KING

Eagle Lake Trail (7 miles round-trip; 4–6hr; 2200ft ascent). Starting from the parking area one mile beyond the ranger station, this trail begins gently but grows steeper towards lovely Eagle Lake. Highlights include Eagle Sink Hole (where the river vanishes) and some fantastic views.

Paradise Peak via Paradise Ridge Trail (9 miles round-trip; 9hr; 2800ft ascent). A superb walk that begins opposite *Atwell Mill Campground* and climbs steeply to Paradise Ridge, which affords views of Moro Rock. From here, it's a fairly flat stroll to Paradise Peak (9300ft).

TRAILS FROM GIANT FOREST, WOLVERTON AND LODGEPOLE

Alta Peak and Alta Meadows Trail (14 miles round-trip; 8–10hr; 4000ft ascent). Starting at the Wolverton Trailhead, this strenuous but rewarding hike initially follows the Lakes Trail (see below) before eventually taking on a daunting ascent to stunning Alta Peak.

Little Baldy Trail (3.5 miles round-trip; 2–3hr; 700ft ascent). Setting out from Little Baldy Saddle, six miles north of Lodgepole, this loop trail leads to a rocky summit with spectacular views.

Tokopah Falls Trail (3 miles round-trip; 2–3hr; 500ft ascent). This fairly easy valley walk begins beside the Marble Fork of the Kaweah River and leads to impressive granite cliffs and Tokopah Falls, which cascade into a cool pool that's perfect for a bracing dip. Start at the eastern end of *Lodgepole Campground*.

The Watchtower and Lakes Trail (13 miles round-trip; 6–8hr; 2300ft ascent). A popular, if fatiguing, trail that leads up from the Wolverton Trailhead to the Watchtower (3–5hr round-trip), an exposed tower of granite overlooking Tokapah Falls far below. From here, the path leads past three lakes set in increasingly gorgeous and stark glacial cirques. The two furthest lakes, Emerald Lake (9200ft) and Pear Lake (9500ft), are home to primitive campgrounds that, for the adventurous and experienced, make good starting points for self-guided trekking into the High Sierra.

TRAILS FROM KINGS CANYON

Cedar Grove Overlook Trail (5 miles round-trip; 3–4hr; 1200ft ascent). Starting half a mile north of Cedar Grove Village on Pack Station Rd, this excellent trail switchbacks steadily and steeply through forest and chaparral to a marvellous viewpoint overlooking Kings Canyon.

Mist Falls Trail (9 miles round-trip; 3–5hr; 600ft ascent). This easy, sandy trail starts from Road's End, eventually climbing steeply past numerous thundering cataracts to Mist Falls, one of the tallest waterfalls in the two parks.

Rae Lakes Loop (46 miles; 4–5 days round-trip). One of the best multiday hikes, this trek follows the Kings River up past Mist Falls and beyond, through Paradise Valley and Castle Domes Meadow to Woods Creek Crossing, where you meet the John Muir Trail. It follows this popular route for eight miles, passing Rae Lakes before returning to Kings Canyon along Bubbs Creek and the South Fork of the Kings River.

5

Big Stump Area

Two miles south of Grant Grove, the **Big Stump Area** gets its name, unsurprisingly, from the gargantuan stumps that litter the place – remnants of logging of sequoias carried out between 1892 and 1918. An easy trail (one to two miles, depending on how many sad stumps you can bear to see) leads through this scene of devastation to the **Mark Twain Stump**, the headstone of another monster killed to impress; a 1350-year-old sequoia that was felled in 1891 after a team of two men allegedly spent thirteen days sawing it (there's no evidence Mark Twain had anything to do with it).

Boole Tree

Consider a side-trip past the sequoia graveyard of Big Stump to a trailhead for the **Boole Tree**, the world's fattest sequoia (the world's sixth largest tree) and one that towers above the forest where all other sequoias were felled – the loggers apparently appreciated its girth (it's named after Franklin A. Boole, supervisor of the logging operation who spared it in the 1890s). It's seldom visited, perhaps on account of its position on a two-mile loop trail: take the gentler left-hand trail and you'll arrive in about a half-hour.

Hume Lake

About eight miles north of Grant Grove, a minor road spurs off three miles to **Hume Lake**, actually a reservoir built in 1908 to provide water for logging flumes. Well placed for local hiking trails, it's also a delightful spot to swim or launch your canoe, and makes a good place to spend a night beside the lake at the comparatively large *Hume Lake Campground* (see box, p.322). At the head of the lake, *Hume Lake Christian Camps* provides expensive gas, groceries, an ATM and a coffee shop.

Hwy-180 into Kings Canyon

From Grant Grove, Hwy-180 descends into **Kings Canyon**, which by some measurements is the deepest canyon in the US at about 7900ft; the canyon's walls of granite and gleaming blue marble, and the white pockmarks of spectacularly blooming yucca plants (particularly in May and early June), make for a visually stunning spectacle. A vast area of the wilderness beyond is drained by the South Fork of the Kings River, a raging torrent during springtime's spate of snowmelt, and perilous for wading at any time: people have been swept away even when paddling close to the bank in a seemingly placid section. Note that **Boyden Cavern** (near the foot of Kings Canyon), usually open mid-May to November, was closed after forest fire damage in August 2015, but should reopen for tours by the end of 2017 – check the website for the latest (ⓦcaverntours.com/boyden-cavern).

Cedar Grove

Past Boyden Cavern, Kings Canyon sheds its V-shape and gains a floor. Among incense cedars at an altitude of 4600ft is the area's only settlement, **Cedar Grove**, comprising a lodge and casual restaurant (see p.324), several campgrounds (see box, p.322), a **visitor centre** (see opposite) and a food store.

Three miles east is **Roaring River Falls**, which, when in full rush, undoubtedly merits its name. Apart from the obvious appeal of the mountain scenery, the main things to see in this area are the birdlife and flowers – leopard lilies, shooting stars, violets, Indian paintbrush, lupine and others – best seen on the **nature trail** around the edge of **Zumwalt Meadow** (1.5 miles; 1–2hr; flat). The meadow boasts a collection of big-leaf maple, cat's-tails and creek dogwood, and there's often a chance for an eyeful of animal life as well.

Just a mile further on, the highway terminates at **Roads End**, from where a network of hiking trails penetrates the multitude of canyons and peaks that constitute the

5

Kings River Sierra; almost all these routes are best enjoyed with a tent and backcountry provisions. To obtain **wilderness permits** in this area, call at **Roads End Wilderness Permit Station** (late May to late Sept daily 7.30am–3.30pm) at the end of Hwy-180. The less ambitious only need to venture about one hundred yards riverward to **Muir Rock** to see where John Muir (see box, p.330) conducted early meetings of the Sierra Club.

ARRIVAL AND DEPARTURE   SEQUOIA AND KINGS CANYON NATIONAL PARKS

By public transport Both national parks are accessible by public transport from late May to September via the Sequoia Shuttle ($15 return, including park entrance fee; ☎ 877 404 6473, ⓦ sequoiashuttle.com), which runs daily from Visalia hotels (6–10am hourly, returning 2.30–6.30pm hourly) to Giant Forest Museum (2hr 30min). The Big Trees Shuttle ($15 return, including park entrance fee; ⓦ bigtreestransit.com) runs from Fresno to Grant Grove (daily at 7am & 9am; returning 3.30pm & 5.30pm; 2hr 30min).

By car The parks are easy to reach by car. The fastest approach is along Hwy-180 from Fresno via the Big Stump Entrance, though it's slightly shorter to take Hwy-198 from Visalia, a 55-mile drive that nonetheless includes a tortuous 15-mile ascent after the Ash Mountain Entrance. Consider looping in one entrance and out the other, and make sure you stock up in advance on cash and gas, though some of both is available in or near the parks.

GETTING AROUND AND INFORMATION

The parks are always open: entry costs $30 per car or $15 per hiker or biker, and is valid for seven days in both parks. Fees are collected at the entrance stations.

PARK TRANSPORT

Park shuttle buses Once in the park, the Sequoia Shuttle (late May to early Sept daily 8am–6.30pm, every 15–30min) offers free rides: Route 1 (Green Route) plies Generals Highway between Giant Forest, the General Sherman Tree and Lodgepole; Route 2 (Grey Route) links Giant Forest with Crescent Meadow via Moro Rock; Route 3 (Purple Route) connects Lodgepole and Wuksachi with *Dorst Creek Campground*.

TOURIST INFORMATION

Cedar Grove Visitor Center Hwy-180, 32 miles beyond Big Stump Entrance Station (late May to early Sept Tues–Sun 9am–5pm; ☎ 559 565 3793).
Foothills Visitor Center Generals Hwy, 1 mile beyond

Ash Mountain Entrance Station (daily 8am–4.30pm; ☎ 559 565 4212, ⓦ nps.gov/seki); also serves as the headquarters of the parks.
Kings Canyon (Grant Grove) Visitor Center Three miles beyond Big Stump Entrance Station on Hwy-180 (daily: summer 8am–5pm; rest of year 9am–4.30pm; ☎ 559 565 4307).
Lodgepole Visitor Center Generals Hwy, 21 miles beyond Ash Mountain Entrance Station (daily: mid- to late May 8am–4.30pm; late May to Sept 7am–5pm; Sept to mid-May 9am–4.30pm; ☎ 559 565 4436).
Mineral King Ranger Station Mineral King Rd, 27 miles beyond Three Rivers (daily: June to late Sept 8am–3.45pm; ☎ 559 565 3768).

ACTIVITIES

Cycling Bikes are not permitted on trails within the parks, thus limiting you to park roads – many of which are very steep and have limited space for passing. A better bet is the network of trails in the adjacent national forests.
Horseriding To enjoy the scenery from horseback, visit one of two locations: Grant Grove Stables (June–Sept; ☎ 559 335 9292), near the General Grant Tree in Grant Grove, and Cedar Grove Pack Station (May to mid-Oct;

☎ 559 565 3464), just outside Cedar Grove Village. Both offer one-hour ($40) and two-hour ($70) rides.
Rafting From April to June, Three Rivers-based Kaweah Whitewater Adventures (☎ 559 740 8251, ⓦ kaweah -whitewater.com) runs a series of rafting trips on the Kaweah River between Three Rivers and Lake Kaweah. Trips range from a relatively gentle Class III 2hr jaunt ($50) to a Class IV full-day trip ($100–120).

ACCOMMODATION

Inside and between the parks, much of the **accommodation** is managed by Delaware North (☎ 877 436 9615, ⓦ visitsequoia.com). Space is at a premium in summer, when making reservations a couple of months in advance is advisable. Price and availability force many to stay just **outside the parks**: there's limited choice along Hwy-180, but Three Rivers, on Hwy-198, has a good selection. Except during public holidays, there's always plenty of **camping** space in the parks and adjacent national forests.

5

CAMPING IN AND AROUND SEQUOIA AND KINGS CANYON NATIONAL PARKS

Except during public holidays, there's always plenty of **camping** space in the parks and adjacent national forests. All campgrounds listed below are first-come, first-served except for *Buckeye Flat*, *Lodgepole*, *Potwisha*, *Princess*, *Sunset* and *Hume* (reserve up to six months ahead on ☎877 444 6777, ⓦrecreation.gov). RV drivers won't find any hookups, but there are summer-only dump stations at *Potwisha*, *Lodgepole* and *Princess*. Collecting "dead and down" firewood is permitted in both the national parks and national forests, but for cooking, you'll really want to bring a portable stove. There are public **showers** at several locations (see p.324). For those wanting to camp in the wilderness, **backcountry** camping (see box, p.319) is permitted.

CAMPGROUNDS

The altitude of each campground indicates the expected temperatures – the higher you go, the cooler it gets overnight. Fees are sometimes reduced (or waived entirely) outside summer and when piped water is disconnected, especially in winter. Campgrounds are listed south to north.

Cold Springs 7500ft; Mineral King. Excellent shaded riverside site 25 miles east of Hwy-198, with some very quiet walk-in sites. Drinking water available. Late May to mid-Oct. **$12**

Potwisha 2100ft. Smallish, RV-dominated spot close to Hwy-198, 4 miles northeast of the park's Ash Mountain entrance and beside the Marble Fork of the Kaweah River. Water and flush toilets. Year-round. **$22**

Buckeye Flat 2800ft. Peaceful, trailer-free campground a short distance east of Hwy-198, very close to Hospital Rock and beside the Middle Fork of the Kaweah River. Water and flush toilets. Mid-March to late Sept. **$22**

Lodgepole 6700ft, 4 miles north of Giant Forest. The largest and busiest of all the national park campgrounds, close to all Lodgepole facilities (market, snack stand, laundry, showers). Reservations are essential between late May and late September, when pay showers, a camp store, water and flush toilets are all made available. Late April to Nov. **$22**

Big Meadow 7600ft 3 miles east of Generals Hwy, midway between Lodgepole and Grant Grove Village. Sprawling, under-utilized national forest campground. No water, vault toilets. Open from snowmelt to first snowfall. **Free**

Azalea, Crystal Springs and Sunset 6500ft. Comparable large campgrounds all within a few hundred yards of the Kings Canyon Visitor Center at Grant Grove. *Azalea* open year-round; *Crystal Springs* late May to late Sept, *Sunset* late May to late Sept. *Azalea* and *Crystal Springs* **$18**, *Sunset* **$22**

Princess 5900ft. National forest campground with water and vault toilets, handily sited along the highway into Kings Canyon. Early May to late Sept. **$25**

Hume Lake 5300ft. Another national forest campground fitted with water, toilets and, for the brave, chilly lake swimming. Early May to late Sept. **$22**

Sheep Creek, Sentinel and Moraine 4600ft; Cedar Grove Village ☎800 444 6777, ⓦrecreation.gov. National Park Service-operated campgrounds set very near one another and the Cedar Grove visitor centre. All have flush toilets. *Sheep Creek* is open late May to late Sept, *Sentinel* late April to mid-Nov and *Moraine* late May to early Sept. **$18**

SEQUOIA NATIONAL PARK

Bearpaw High Sierra Camp 11.3-mile walk east of Crescent Meadow (High Sierra Trail) ☎ 559 565 4070. Soft beds, fluffy towels, hot showers and hearty meals served up in magnificent wilderness are the draws for this cluster of six wooden-floored permanent tents set at 7800ft. There's no electricity, everything is helicoptered in for the season, and breakfast and dinner are included in the price. Most weekends and holidays are taken immediately after booking opens on January 2, though you've got a reasonable chance of snagging an on-spec place on weeknights in June and September. Mid-June to mid-Sept. **$350**

★**Silver City Mountain Resort** 51490 Mineral King Rd (24 miles east of Three Rivers) ☎559 561 3223, ⓦsilvercityresort.com. A bucolic retreat in the woods since the 1930s, with delightful rustic cabins featuring potbelly stoves, kitchens and propane lighting, and some have their own bathroom; the more modern chalets boast full bathrooms and electric lighting (generators run 10hr a day). Sheets, towels, washcloths and pillowcases are provided for $45, or you're welcome to bring your own; note that there's a two-night minimum stay. Bring food for self-catering, though there's a store with limited supplies, and the resort has a restaurant attached (see p.324). Late May to early Oct. **$100**

Wuksachi Lodge 64740 Wuksachi Way (off Generals Hwy, 23 miles beyond Ash Mountain Entrance Station). Directly competing with the *John Muir Lodge* for the best rooms in the parks, the *Wuksachi* is a lot newer (it opened in 1999), comprising several blocks of rooms scattered in the woods around an elegant central lounge and restaurant. Year-round. **$255**

GIANT SEQUOIA NATIONAL MONUMENT

Montecito Sequoia Lodge 63410 Generals Hwy (10

miles east of Big Stump Entrance Station) ☎ 559 565 3388, ⓦ mslodge.com. A large camp often full of families and large groups, tastefully set next to an artificial lake, with all manner of activities on offer: canoeing, swimming, horseriding, wakeboarding and volleyball in summer; snowshoeing, skating and cross-country skiing in winter. It's booked in six-night blocks from mid-June to early September (though you can book Saturday night separately), but at other times you can almost always stay in rustic cabins or lodge rooms with private bathroom. Rates include all meals (which are pretty good) and many of the activities. You may or may not feel compelled to participate in one of the camp's morning powwows, when traditional call-and-response chants are led by university-age counsellors. Year-round. Cabins $99, doubles $149

Stony Creek Lodge 65569 Generals Hwy (13 miles east of Big Stump Entrance Station) ☎ 559 335 5500, ⓦ sequoia-kingscanyon.com. Set just outside Sequoia National Park's northern boundary, these plain and comfortable motel-style rooms include TVs and showers and are set very near a good restaurant and grocery store. Early May to early Oct. $189

KINGS CANYON NATIONAL PARK

Cedar Grove Lodge 86724 Hwy-180 (32 miles beyond Big Stump Entrance Station). Cosy lodge right by the Kings River. The 21 rooms have private bathrooms and a/c. May to mid-Oct. $140

Grant Grove Cabins and John Muir Lodge 86728 Hwy-180 (3 miles beyond Big Stump Entrance Station). The parks' widest selection of ways to sleep under a roof: canvas-roofed tent cabins (late May to early Sept); ageing, rustic cabins (May–Oct; $104); modernized bath cabins (late April to late Oct; $129); or the swanky, modern and year-round *John Muir Lodge*, with very comfortable hotel rooms ($201). Tent cabins $67

THREE RIVERS AND LEMON COVE

Buckeye Tree Lodge 46000 Hwy-198, Three Rivers (just southwest of Sequoia's Ash Mountain Entrance) ☎ 559 561 5900, ⓦ buckeyetree.com. Small, careworn

but comfortable modern rooms with TV, private bathrooms and verandas overlooking the foaming Kaweah River. Comes equipped with a nice pool. $110

The Gateway 45978 Hwy-198, Three Rivers (just southwest of Sequoia's Ash Mountain Entrance) ☎ 559 561 4133, ⓦ gateway-sequoia.com. Old, but clean and perfectly functional motel-style rooms with TV; there's also a honeymoon cabin with dry sauna and patio, as well as a two-bedroom house sleeping eight with self-catering facilities. It's located right beside the Kaweah River – the better rooms have a deck overlooking the water. Doubles $150, cabin $199, house $365

Plantation Bed & Breakfast 33038 Hwy-198, Lemon Cove (17 miles southwest of Sequoia's Ash Mountain Entrance) ☎ 559 597 2555, ⓦ theplantation.net. Luxurious – yet shockingly affordable – *Gone with the Wind*-themed B&B with comfortable en-suite rooms and truly delicious breakfasts. The Belle Watling room comes bordello-hued with a claw-foot tub. Outside there's a heated pool, hot tub and lawns dotted with palm trees. $119

Sierra Lodge 43175 Hwy-198, Three Rivers (4 miles southwest of Sequoia's Ash Mountain Entrance) ☎ 559 561 3681, ⓦ sierra-lodge.com. Usually the best of Three Rivers' inexpensive motels – an old but spacious and clean lodge with pool and modernized en-suite rooms, many with decks and some featuring wood-burning fireplaces. Certain suites even have cooking facilities. It's right next to the highway, but traffic noise is minimal overnight. $119

Three Rivers Hideaway 43365 Hwy-198, Three Rivers (4 miles southwest of Sequoia's Ash Mountain Entrance) ☎ 559 561 4413, ⓦ threerivershideaway.com. This small RV and tent site also has renovated cabins at some of the lowest prices around. Pitches $30, RV $30, cabins $99

ALONG HWY-180

Sequoia View Bed & Breakfast 1384 S Frankwood Ave, Sanger (35 miles west of Kings Canyon's Big Stump Entrance) ☎ 559 787 9412, ⓦ svbnb.com. Located 20 miles east of Fresno, this small winery has three large and tastefully furnished luxury suites, two with king-sized sleigh beds and one with a balcony above the tasting room. $139

EATING

Assuming you're not camping or self-catering, you'll most likely **eat** close to where you're staying. There are **food markets** and fairly basic summer-only **cafeterias** at Lodgepole (the most extensive), Stony Creek and Cedar Grove, though none of them are spectacular and prices will be higher than places outside the park. Much the same applies to **restaurants**, with Three Rivers offering the best local selection at reasonable prices. In the restaurants inside the parks, diner food prevails, with the exception of the classy restaurant at *Wuksachi Lodge*.

SEQUOIA NATIONAL PARK

Lodgepole Market Center 63204 Lodgepole Rd (21 miles beyond Ash Mountain Entrance Station) ☎ 559 565 3301. Likely the best of the parks' budget eating places, with ready-made sandwiches and salads in the

Watchtower Deli section and plenty for picnics in the grocery store. May–Oct daily 11am–6pm.

The Peaks Restaurant Wuksachi Lodge (23 miles beyond Ash Mountain Entrance Station) ☎ 559 565 4070. The finest restaurant in the parks, with burgers

5

and the like ($13.50) at lunch and more formal dinners such as pan-seared rainbow trout ($25.75) and steaks ($29) served in a baronial-style room. Daily 7–10am, 11.30am–3pm & 5–9.30pm (bar open until 11pm).

Silver City Store & Restaurant 51490 Mineral King Rd (24 miles east of Three Rivers) ☎ 559 561 3223. Five miles before the end of the road to Mineral King, this off-the-grid resort boasts a small, low-cost restaurant and food store. It's perhaps best known for its delectable fruit pies (available Tues and Wed only). Late May to early Oct: store Mon & Thurs–Sun 8am–8pm, Tues & Wed 9am–5pm; restaurant Mon & Thurs–Sun 8–10am, noon–2.30pm & 5–10pm.

SEQUOIA NATIONAL FOREST

Montecito Sequoia Lodge 63410 Generals Hwy (10 miles east of Big Stump Entrance Station) ☎ 559 565 3388. This family-style restaurant serves hearty buffet breakfasts ($9.95), lunches ($9.95) and dinners ($19.95) at long tables in an enormous room. Daily 7.30–9am, noon–1pm & 5.30–7pm.

Stony Creek Lodge 65569 Generals Hwy (13 miles east of Big Stump Entrance Station) ☎ 559 335 5500. If you're looking for reasonably priced pizza, calzone and self-serve salad after a day of trekking, this diner-restaurant is a solid choice (mains from $9). Early May to early Oct Mon–Thurs & Sun 11am–7.30pm, Fri & Sat 11am–8.30pm.

KINGS CANYON NATIONAL PARK

Cedar Grove Snack Bar 86724 Hwy-180 (32 miles beyond Big Stump Entrance Station). A casual snack bar that serves barely adequate egg and pancake breakfasts,

burgers and sandwiches for $8–12, plus a handful of steak and chicken dinners ($15–20); eat on the balcony overlooking the river. Early May to late Oct daily 7.30–10.30am, 11.30am–2.30pm & 5–8pm.

Grant Grove Restaurant 86728 Hwy-180 (3 miles beyond Big Stump Entrance Station). Reopened in 2017 after renovation, and now offering some of the best menus in the parks, from basic but tasty burgers, sandwiches and standard American breakfasts to fish, chicken and steak dinners. Daily 7am–9pm.

THREE RIVERS

Antoinette's Coffee & Goodies 41727 Hwy-198 (6 miles southwest of Sequoia's Ash Mountain Entrance) ☎ 559 561 2253. This delightful café serves fresh coffee (from Maverick's Roasting Company of Visalia) and delectable pastries such as the "Morning Glory muffin" and the pumpkin chocolate chip muffin. Mon, Wed, Thurs & Fri 6.30am–1pm, Sat 7am–3pm, Sun 7am–1pm.

Casa Mendoza 40869 Hwy-198 (6 miles southwest of Sequoia's Ash Mountain Entrance) ☎ 559 561 7283. This popular spot dishes up authentic but no-frills Mexican mains (most well under $10), best eaten outside and accompanied by a cool cerveza on a balmy summer evening. Daily 10am–8pm.

Sierra Subs & Salads 41717 Hwy-198 (6 miles southwest of Sequoia's Ash Mountain Entrance) ☎ 559 561 4810, ⓦ sierrasubsandsalads.com. Justly popular snack stop next to the gas station, selling delicious and wholesome wraps, salads (from $7) and panini (from $5.55), from tuna melts to burgers ($6). Tues–Sat 10.30am–6pm, Sun 10.30am–5pm.

DIRECTORY

Banks There are no banks in either park, but credit cards are widely accepted. Lodgepole, Stony Creek Resort, Grant Grove and Cedar Grove have ATMs.

Internet access Three Rivers Library, 42052 Eggers Drive (Tues & Thurs noon–5pm & 6–8pm, Wed & Fri 10am–1pm & 2–6pm), 5 miles southwest of Sequoia's Ash Mountain Entrance, offers free wi-fi.

Laundry Lodgepole, Cedar Grove and Stony Creek Resort each have coin-operated laundries open daily (8am–8pm) throughout summer.

Gas There's no gas available in the parks, so you'll want to top up your tank in Visalia or Fresno – or, although it's pricier, in Three Rivers and Dunlap (20 miles west of Grant

Grove). In desperation, you can get expensive gas at Stony Creek (summer only, 24hr with credit card) or Hume Lake (year-round 24hr with credit card).

Phones Mobile-phone coverage is patchy at best in the parks, but public phones exist at most of the visitor centres.

Post offices Lodgepole (Mon–Fri 8am–1pm & 2–4pm); Grant Grove (Mon–Fri 9am–3.30pm).

Showers Lodgepole Market (summer daily 8am–1pm & 3–7.45pm; coin-op, 12 quarters for 10min), Stony Creek Resort (mid-May to Sept daily 9am–6pm; $4 token for 10min), Grant Grove (summer daily 10am–1pm & 3–7.45pm; 4 quarters for 3min) and Cedar Grove (summer daily 8am–1pm & 3–8pm; $3.50 for 10min).

Sierra National Forest

If you fancy exploring gorgeous granite and cedar country without the clamour of the national parks to the north and south, head for **SIERRA NATIONAL FOREST**, a gaping tract of land between Kings Canyon and Yosemite. It's far less well known than

Yosemite, Sequoia or Kings Canyon and lacks the environmental protection bestowed upon the parks – many of the rivers have been **dammed** as part of the Big Creek Hydroelectric Project that helped make San Joaquin Valley the agricultural heart of California in the twentieth century. With only modest hyperbole, the Sierra meltwater in these parts is touted as "the hardest-working water in the world".

Portions of Sierra National Forest have been developed into resort areas that are better for fishing and boating than hiking, and hordes of residents of San Joaquin Valley stream up here throughout the summer for weekend getaways. However, around **Kaiser Pass**, you'll find isolated alpine landscapes served by decent campgrounds, a couple of minor resorts and even some relaxing **hot springs**. Further remote corners to explore include the rugged, unspoilt terrain of vast **John Muir Wilderness** and neighbouring **Ansel Adams Wilderness**, both of which contain some of the starkest peaks and lushest alpine meadows of the High Sierra. If you want to hike and camp in near-isolation, these are the places to

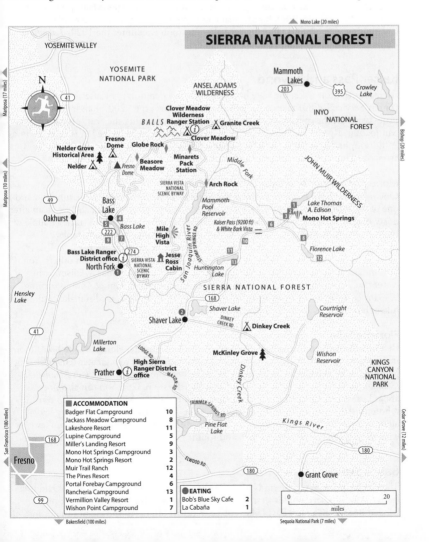

SIERRA NATIONAL FOREST

Mono Lake (20 miles)

YOSEMITE VALLEY

YOSEMITE NATIONAL PARK

Mammoth Lakes

203

Crowley Lake

395

ANSEL ADAMS WILDERNESS

INYO NATIONAL FOREST

41

N

Mariposa (17 miles)

Mariposa (10 miles)

Bishop (20 miles)

Clover Meadow Wilderness Ranger Station

B A L L S

Granite Creek

Clover Meadow

Fresno Dome

Globe Rock

Nelder Grove Historical Area

Nelder

Beasore Meadow

Fresno Dome

Minarets Pack Station

Middle Fork

JOHN MUIR WILDERNESS

SIERRA VISTA NATIONAL SCENIC BYWAY

Arch Rock

49

Bass Lake

Oakhurst

Bass Lake

222

5

9

7

4

Mile High Vista

Mammoth Pool Reservoir

Kaiser Pass (9200 ft) & White Bark Vista

1

2 3

6

Lake Thomas A. Edison

Mono Hot Springs

8

Florence Lake

12

Bass Lake Ranger District office

North Fork

274

SIERRA VISTA NATIONAL SCENIC BYWAY

Jesse Ross Cabin

Huntington Lake

San Joaquin River

KAISER PASS RD

10

11

13

Hensley Lake

41

SIERRA NATIONAL FOREST

168

Shaver Lake

Shaver Lake

DINKEY CREEK RD

Dinkey Creek

Courtright Reservoir

Millerton Lake

LODGE RD

High Sierra Ranger District office

Prather

McKinley Grove

Dinkey Creek

Wishon Reservoir

KINGS CANYON NATIONAL PARK

MAXON RD

San Francisco (180 miles)

168

Fresno

TRIMMER SPRINGS RD

Pine Flat Lake

Kings River

ELWOOD RD

180

Grant Grove

Cedar Grove (12 miles)

99

ACCOMMODATION	
Badger Flat Campground	10
Jackass Meadow Campground	8
Lakeshore Resort	11
Lupine Campground	5
Miller's Landing Resort	9
Mono Hot Springs Campground	3
Mono Hot Springs Resort	2
Muir Trail Ranch	12
The Pines Resort	4
Portal Forebay Campground	6
Rancheria Campground	13
Vermillion Valley Resort	1
Wishon Point Campground	7

EATING	
Bob's Blue Sky Cafe	2
La Cabaña	1

0   20

miles

Bakersfield (100 miles)

Sequoia National Park (7 miles)

5

do it, though you'll need a vehicle: public transport is virtually nonexistent. Further north, **Bass Lake** is an immensely popular destination for Californians from as far as the Bay Area, while the **Sierra Vista National Scenic Byway** follows a gorgeous, if slow-going path through a little-seen area of the Sierra Nevada's western flanks.

Visit **ranger stations** (see p.328) in the area for suggestions on dozens of hikes, to pick up free camping permits (usually necessary for overnight hikes) and purchase maps.

Shaver Lake and Huntington Lake

From the ranger station in Prather, Hwy-168 climbs rapidly over eighteen miles to **SHAVER LAKE**, an artificial lake and mile-high, pine-girt community full of fisherfolk and jet-skiers in summer (ⓦshaverlake.com). From here it's another twenty or so miles northeast to **Huntington Lake**, a reservoir (at 6955ft), which feels more isolated. A side road leads one mile east off the highway to the mile-long **Rancheria Falls Trail** (350ft ascent), which winds through broadleaf woods to its 150ft-tall namesake falls. Continuing west around Huntington Lake, you soon encounter the 1920s *Lakeshore Resort* and numerous campgrounds (see p.329).

Kaiser Pass and beyond

After Huntington Lake, the state highway ends and deteriorated Kaiser Pass Road (Forest Service Rd 80) takes over, plodding its way over the 9200ft **Kaiser Pass** (open June–Oct), on the other side of which is a vast basin draining the South Fork of the San Joaquin River. The lumpy road eventually reaches a fork: to the left is Lake Thomas A. Edison, its approach marred by a huge earthen dam, while to the right is more attractive Florence Lake, another reservoir.

Mono Hot Springs and Lake Thomas A. Edison

One reason to head left here is **Mono Hot Springs**, two miles north of the junction and one of the best things about the region; it's an excellent place to relax and clean up after dusty hikes through the adjacent wilderness. Across the river, follow a track a couple of hundred yards downstream to a pair of five-foot-deep concrete **bathing tanks** (unrestricted access) that are perfect for soaking your bones while stargazing. This is just one of many pools on this side of the river; ask around for details on others. You can find accommodation (see p.328) here or at nearby **Lake Thomas A. Edison**, where a **water taxi** (June–Sept; usually departs *Vermilion Valley Resort* 9am & 4pm, returning 9.45am & 4.45pm; $12 one-way, $21 return; ☎559 259 4000, ⓦedisonlake.com/hikers/ferry) ferries wilderness hikers across the lake.

Florence Lake

Reached through an unearthly landscape of wrinkled granite, **Florence Lake** holds more immediate appeal than Lake Thomas A. Edison, mainly due to a greater sense of being hemmed in by the mountains. There's a small store here, as well as *Jackass Meadow Campground* (see p.328) and the Muir Trail Ranch (see p.329). You can also hop aboard the Sierra Queen **ferry** (June to late Sept; five daily; $13 one-way, $25 return; ⓦflorence-lake.com), which skips across the lake and helps open up multiday hikes along the John Muir and Pacific Crest trails connecting this area of the Sierra Nevada with the national parks to the north and south.

Bass Lake

The northern reaches of Sierra National Forest are most easily reached from Oakhurst (see p.340), just seven miles west of the biggest tourist attraction in the area: pine-fringed **BASS LAKE**. Tiny Bass Lake Village traces its origins to the establishment in

1895 of the first hydroelectric generating project in Central California, while the four-mile-long Bass Lake Reservoir itself was created in 1910. A stomping ground of Hell's Angels in the 1960s – the leather and licentiousness memorably described in Hunter S. Thompson's *Hell's Angels* – Bass Lake is nowadays a family resort, crowded with boaters and anglers in summer. *Miller's Landing Resort* (see p.329), on the southwestern tip of the lake, is the best place in the area to rent aquatic equipment, including speed boats ($110/hr) and patio boats ($350/day) equipped with gas barbecues, as well as jet-skis ($100/hr), paddleboards ($20/hr, $75/day), fishing boats ($25/hr, $115/day), canoes and kayaks. For detailed campground and hiking information, consult the Bass Lake Ranger District office (see p.328).

Sierra Mono Museum

33103 Rd 228, North Fork • Tues–Sat 10am–3pm • $7 • ☎ 559 877 2115, ⊛ sierramonomuseum.org

In tiny **NORTH FORK**, about ten miles south of Bass Lake village, the **Sierra Mono Museum** is home to several fine examples of local Native American basketry and beadwork (mostly from the local Mono people), as well as a great deal of animal taxidermy. The museum also hosts an annual Mono powwow, usually over the first weekend in August. The **Northfork Rancheria of Mono Indians of California**, a federally recognized tribe, is headquartered in North Fork, and it's also the starting point of the Sierra Vista National Scenic Byway.

Sierra Vista National Scenic Byway

If you find Bass Lake too commercial and overcrowded, the antidote starts in North Fork. The peaceful **SIERRA VISTA NATIONAL SCENIC BYWAY** makes a ninety-mile circuit east of Hwy-41 and provides access to trailheads that lead into the magnificent High Sierra. Generally snow-free between July and October (sometimes earlier), the route requires at least five hours of driving time, and can be especially slow-going on the rough dirt roads along its north side. Stock up on supplies before you start – there are a couple of shops and gas stations dotted along the way, but they're not cheap and selection is quite limited. Accommodation on the circuit is largely limited to campgrounds, some of them free but lacking water and flush toilets.

The south side

Assuming you tackle the Byway counter-clockwise (the easiest direction for route-finding), begin on **Forest Road 81** (aka **Minarets Rd**), 4.5 miles south of North Fork off Road-225, and continue north, loosely following the San Joaquin River. The first point of interest is the **Jessie Ross Cabin**, fifteen miles along. It's an interesting hewn-log structure dating from the 1860s that's been restored, brought to this site and left open for visitors to poke around inside.

Ten miles later, **Mile High Vista** (at 5300ft) reveals endless views of muscle-bound mountain ranges and bursting granite domes stretching all the way to Mammoth Mountain (see p.282). Further on, an eight-mile side road cuts south to **Mammoth Pool**, a dammed catchment of the San Joaquin River that's popular with anglers.

Back on the Byway, you'll pass the rather disappointing **Arch Rock** (at 6200ft), where the earth under a slab of granite has been undermined to leave a kind of bridge. Continue climbing from here to **Minarets Pack Station** (June–Sept; ☎ 559 868 3405, ⊛ highsierrapackers.org/min.htm) at 7000ft, where a humble general store has a smattering of snacks and cold drinks for sale; **horseriding trips** are also available from $120. This area is a good base for wilderness trips, many of which start by the **Clover Meadow Wilderness Ranger Station** (June–Sept daily 9am–5pm), a couple of miles up a spur road; stop in to pick up a wilderness permit. Nearby are two wonderful free **campgrounds**, *Clover Meadow* and *Granite Creek*, both open June through to September and set at 7000ft; the former has potable water.

5

The north side

Minarets Pack Station marks the end of the asphalt; for the next eight miles on Forest Road 7 (aka Beasore Rd), you're on rough dirt, generally navigable in ordinary passenger vehicles when clear of snow, but still requiring careful driving. The hulking form of **Globe Rock** (a large granite sphere perched precariously on the hillside at 7152ft) heralds the welcome return to a paved surface, which runs down to **Beasore Meadow** (6800ft) where **Jones' Store** (June–Oct) has supplied groceries, gas and basic meals (daily 8am–8pm) since the early 1900s, and offers showers to hikers. A short distance further on is **Cold Springs Summit**, the highest point on the Byway at 7308ft and the junction with unpaved **Sky Ranch Road** (follow it right to continue the Byway). A few miles on a 1.7-mile spur leads to excellent *Fresno Dome Campground* (6400ft; no water; $23.62, plus $7/vehicle), a great base for a moderately strenuous walk to the top of its exfoliated granite namesake (7540ft).

The Byway then passes several $23–26 campgrounds, most without running water, en route to the **Nelder Grove** (unrestricted entry), a couple of miles north of Sky Ranch Road along another dirt road. Over one hundred giant sequoias are scattered throughout the forest here (at around 5300ft), though the overall impression is of devastation, something in sad evidence given the number of enormous stumps among the second-growth sugar pine, white fir and cedar. The mile-long "Shadow of the Giants" interpretive walk explains the logging activities that took place here in the 1880s and early 1890s, and, with its low visitor count, it offers a more serene communion with these majestic trees than in nearby Sequoia or Yosemite. A second interpretive trail leads to the 246ft-tall **Bull Buck Tree**, which, with its base circumference of 99ft, was once a serious contender for the world's largest tree; though slimmer in the base, Sequoia National Park's General Sherman Tree is taller and broader at the top, and so takes the prize. From here, it's seven twisting miles back to Hwy-41, reached at a point around four miles north of Oakhurst and Bass Lake.

INFORMATION

SIERRA NATIONAL FOREST

High Sierra Ranger District Office One of the best sources of information on the Sierra National Forest, this office (daily 8am–4.30pm; ☎ 559 855 5355) is located along Hwy-168 (29688 Auberry Rd) in Prather en route to Shaver Lake.

Bass Lake Ranger District Office Another good source of information on the national forest, this office (Mon–Fri 8am–4.30pm; ☎ 559 877 2218) is at 57003 Rd 225, in North Fork. It also has plenty of details on the Sierra Vista National Scenic Byway.

ACCOMMODATION

Campgrounds are first-come, first-served unless otherwise noted.

SHAVER LAKE AND HUNTINGTON LAKE

Lakeshore Resort 61953 Huntington Lake Rd, Huntington Lake ☎ 559 893 3193. True to its name, this waterside destination features rustic, knotty-pine cabins built between 1922 and 1940, most of which sleep four or five, and some of which have kitchens. There's a good restaurant (daily 8am–9pm in summer; irregular hours rest of year), lively log-built saloon, gas station, post office and general store all a short stroll from the lake (no cellphone service, but free wi-fi in lodge). Year-round. RV $40, cabins $105

Rancheria Campground 7000ft; 63001 Huntington Lake Rd (off Hwy-168); reserve on ☎ 877 444 6777 or ⓦ recreation.gov. Popular campground set along the shores of Huntington Lake. Water and flush toilets. June to late Oct. Pitches $30

KAISER PASS AND BEYOND

Badger Flat Campground 8000ft; Kaiser Pass Rd (5.1 miles off Hwy-168). Located about 5 miles on from Huntington Lake at a sandy spot near Rancheria Creek. No water, pit toilets. June–Oct. Pitches $22

Jackass Meadow Campground 7200ft; Kaiser Pass Rd (21 miles off Hwy-168). Located, unnervingly, just below Florence Lake dam, sites here are shaded and set near the South Fork of the San Joaquin River. No water, vault toilets. June–Oct. Pitches $26

Mono Hot Springs Campground 6700ft; Edison Lake Rd (1.6 miles off Kaiser Pass Rd) reserve on ☎ 877 444 6777 or ⓦ recreation.gov. Fairly well-used campground flanking Mono Hot Springs Resort with some shaded sites. No water, vault toilets. June–Oct. Pitches $26

★**Mono Hot Springs Resort** 70,000 Edison Lake Rd

☎ 559 325 1710, ⓦ monohotsprings.com. On the banks of the San Joaquin River, this resort is a modest affair with individual mineral baths, showers and massages ($70/hr). Accommodation ranges from simple cabins through to more commodious en-suite options with kitchen. There's typically a three-night minimum. The resort also has a small lunch-and-dinner restaurant, a limited general store and a post office. Prices include complimentary use of the therapeutic mineral pools and on-site spa. Mid-May to Oct. Pitches __$119__

Muir Trail Ranch Lakeshore (4 miles beyond Florence Lake via hiking trail) ☎ 209 966 3195, ⓦ muirtrailranch .com. This remote cabin and tent retreat with hot springs is located amid magical scenery. When not taken over by groups, it's open for short stays (usually at the start and end of the season). Access is by the cross-lake ferry (see p.326); you then either hike to the ranch or arrange to be met with a horse. June–Sept. Rate includes tent cabin, breakfast, packed lunch and dinner. Tent cabins __$330__, log cabins __$370__

Portal Forebay Campground 7200ft; Kaiser Pass Rd (13.6 miles off Hwy-168). Beautiful campground about 14 miles beyond Huntington Lake, on Portal Forebay Lake. No water, vault toilets. June–Oct. Pitches __$22__

Vermillion Valley Resort Edison Lake Rd ☎ 559 259 4000, ⓦ edisonlake.com. Located at Lake Thomas A. Edison and just 1 mile off the Pacific Crest and John Muir hiking trails, this friendly place also caters to boaters and anglers. It's a full-service resort with motel lodging and a small range of cabins to choose from; there's also a restaurant (daily 7am–8pm) and small store. May–Oct. Tent cabin __$67.50__, doubles __$97__, yurt cabin __$107__

BASS LAKE

Lupine Campground 3400ft; Bass Lake turn-off (Rd 222), 6.25 miles off Hwy-41; reserve on ☎ 877 444 6777 or ⓦ recreation.gov. Reserve your site at this lakeside campground in advance, as this is one of the most popular – but best – places in the area for tent-camping. Year-round. Pitches __$30__

Miller's Landing Resort 37976 Rd 222 ☎ 559 642 3633, ⓦ millerslanding.com. Down by the southwestern tip of the lake, *Miller's Landing* offers a dozen deluxe cabins in the lake-adjacent forest that sleep six or more. You'll also find public showers ($3) and laundry facilities. Pitches __$220__

The Pines Resort 54432 Rd 432 ☎ 559 642 3121, ⓦ basslake.com. Situated on the north side of the lake, this swanky destination consists of luxurious two-storey chalets with kitchens and even more palatial lakeside suites. Pitches __$179__

Wishon Point Campground 3400ft; Forest Rd 222 (S Shore Rd); reserve on ☎ 877 444 6777 or ⓦ recreation.gov. Should *Lupine Campground* be packed solid, try less-used but still lakeside and shaded *Wishon* as an alternative (has drinking water and flush toilets). April–Sept. Pitches __$30__

EATING

SHAVER LAKE AND HUNTINGTON LAKE

Bob's Blue Sky Cafe 41781 Hwy-168 (Tollhouse Rd), Shaver Lake ☎ 559 841 7106. With affordable, locally beloved breakfasts and veggie sandwiches on the menu, this spot is a smart stop if you're on your way to Huntington Lake and beyond (mains $6–12). Mon–Thurs 7am–2pm, Fri–Sun 7am–5pm.

NORTH FORK

La Cabaña 32762 Rd 222 ☎ 559 877 3311, ⓦ lacabana mexicanrestaurant.com. The top Mexican restaurant in the region is informal, the place to enjoy excellent plates of enchiladas and the like for around $8. Tues noon–3pm & 4.30–7.30pm, Wed–Sat 10.30am–3pm & 4.30–7.30pm.

Yosemite National Park

No temple made with hands can compare with the Yosemite. Every rock in its walls seems to glow with life. Some lean back in majestic repose; others, absolutely sheer or nearly so for thousands of feet, advance beyond their companions in thoughtful attitudes, giving welcome to storms and calms alike, seemingly aware, yet heedless, of everything going on about them.
                                                                                    John Muir, *The Yosemite*

More gushing adjectives have been thrown at **YOSEMITE NATIONAL PARK** than anywhere else in California. But however excessive the hyperbole may seem, once you enter the park and turn the corner that reveals Yosemite Valley – only a small part of the park, but the one at which most of the verbiage is aimed – you realize it's actually an understatement. For many, **Yosemite Valley** represents the single most dramatic piece of geology in the world. Just seven miles long and one mile across at its widest point, it's walled by nearly vertical, three-thousand-foot cliffs whose sides are streaked by cascading waterfalls and whose tops, a variety of domes and pinnacles, form a jagged silhouette against the sky. Sights at ground level are just as staggeringly impressive: grassy meadows

5

are framed by oak, cedar, maple and fir trees, with a variety of wildflowers on hand as well, to say nothing of scores of deer and black bears. As if all that weren't enough, in the southern reaches of the park near **Wawona**, sequoias grow almost as densely – and to dimensions as vast – as those in Sequoia National Park to the south.

Understandably, you're not the first to appreciate Yosemite's appeal. Each year Yosemite has to cope with almost four million visitors, and if you're looking for some semblance of peace, it's advisable to avoid Yosemite Valley and Wawona at weekends and holidays (there's maximum of 21,000 visitors a day allowed into the valley at peak periods, with cars turned away once the cap is reached). That said, the whole park is diverse and massive enough to endure the crowds: if you visit at any time of year out of high summer (including winter, when waterfalls turn to ice and trails are blocked by snow), Yosemite Valley manages to resist becoming too thronged. Further-flung reaches of the park, especially around the crisp alpine landscapes of **Tuolumne Meadows** (pronounced "too-WALL-um-nee") and the wild backcountry beyond, are much less busy all year round, providing just about the most placid, elemental setting you could imagine.

Brief history

Yosemite Valley was created over thousands of years by glaciers gouging through and enlarging the canyon of the Merced River; the ice scraped away much of the softer portions of granite, but only scarred the harder sections, which became the present cliffs. As the glaciers melted, a lake formed and filled the valley, but it eventually silted up to create the present valley floor. The **Awahneechee** people occupied the area quite peaceably for some four thousand years until the mid-nineteenth century, when the increasingly threatening presence of white Gold Rush settlers in San Joaquin Valley provoked the tribes to raid the nearest encampments. In 1851, Major James Savage led the **Mariposa Battalion** in pursuit of the Native Americans, trailing them beyond the foothills and becoming the first white men to set foot in Yosemite Valley. It wasn't long before the two groups clashed

---

JOHN MUIR AND THE SIERRA CLUB

John Muir was one of nature's most eloquent advocates, a champion of all things wild who spent ten years living in Yosemite Valley in the 1870s, and the rest of his life campaigning for its preservation. Born in Scotland in 1838, he grew up in Wisconsin, became a mechanical inventor and endured the near-loss of one of his eyes before embarking on his first journey at the age of 27, noting in his diary, "All drawbacks overcome … joyful and free … I chose to become a tramp." After walking a thousand miles to Florida with little more than a volume of Keats' poems and a plant press for company, he ended up in California in 1868, where he famously asked for directions to "anywhere that is wild". Working in Yosemite Valley as a sheepherder, mill worker and hotel clerk, he spent every waking moment exploring the mountains and waterfalls, travelling light and usually going to sleep hungry under the stars.

He dubbed the Sierra Nevada the "**Range of Light**", and spent years developing his theory of how glaciers shaped the range. His articles gradually won him academic acceptance, and the general public was soon devouring his journal-based books, such as *My First Summer in the Sierra* and *The Yosemite*, both of which became classics.

Muir was desperate to protect his beloved landscape from the depredations of sheep grazing, timber cutting and homesteading, and through magazine articles and influential contacts he goaded Congress into creating Yosemite National Park in 1890. Two years later, he founded the **Sierra Club**, an organization whose motto "Take only photographs; leave only footprints" has become a model for like-minded groups around the world. Despite his successes, Muir failed to save Yosemite's Hetch Hetchy Valley (see p.336) from being dammed, a blow that undoubtedly hastened his death in 1914.

The publicity Muir generated aided the formation of the present **National Park Service** in 1916, which promised, and has since provided, greater protection for Yosemite. This inspirational man is honoured in place names throughout California, not least in the 211-mile John Muir Trail, which twists through his favourite scenery from Yosemite Valley south to Mount Whitney.

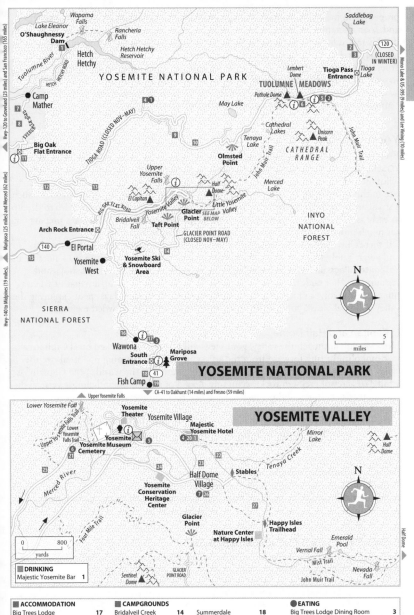

YOSEMITE NATIONAL PARK

YOSEMITE VALLEY

DRINKING
Majestic Yosemite Bar 1

ACCOMMODATION		CAMPGROUNDS				EATING	
Big Trees Lodge	17	Bridalveil Creek	14	Summerdale	18	Big Trees Lodge Dining Room	3
Evergreen Lodge	7	Camp 4	25	Tamarack Flat	13	Half Dome Village Pavilion	7
Half Dome Village	26	Crane Flat	12	Tioga Lake	3	Degnan's Deli	5
Housekeeping Camp	24	Dimond O	8	Tuolumne Meadows	6	Majestic Yosemite Dining Room	4
Majestic Yosemite Hotel	20	Hetch Hetchy	1	Upper Pines	27	Pizza Deck and Village Bar	7
Tuolumne Meadows Lodge	5	Hodgdon Meadow	11	Wawona	16	Tuolumne Meadows	
White Chief Mountain Lodge	19	Lower Pines	23	White Wolf	4	Lodge Dining Room	2
White Wolf Lodge	4	North Pines	22	Yosemite Creek	9	White Wolf Lodge Dining Room	1
Yosemite Cedar Lodge	15	Porcupine Flat	10			Yosemite Valley Lodge Food Court	6
Yosemite Valley Lodge	21	Sawmill	2				

5

properly, and the original population was moved out to make way for farmers, foresters and, soon after, tourists (the first group of sightseers arrived in 1855). Appreciative visitors quickly rallied forward-thinking lawmakers to conserve the natural beauty of the area, and in 1864, President Abraham Lincoln signed into law the Yosemite Grant, which set aside Yosemite Valley and the Mariposa Grove for public use and preservation – a landmark move that predated the creation of Yellowstone National Park by eight years. In 1890, Yosemite became the third national park in the US, thanks in great part to the campaigning work of Scottish naturalist **John Muir** (see box, p.330).

Yosemite Valley

Even the most evocative photography can only hint at the pleasure of simply gazing at **YOSEMITE VALLEY**. From three-thousand-foot granite cliffs to the subtle colourings of wildflowers, the variations in the valley can be both enormous and discreet. Nowhere else in the world is there such an array of rock faces and waterfalls concentrated in such a small area – though a relatively dry winter can cause many of these cascades to dry up as early as July. Easy walks around the lush meadows to waterfalls and lakes prepare you for much more taxing treks into the backcountry (see box, p.338).

If there's any drawback to Yosemite Valley, it's that it is the busiest part of the park, and you're rarely far from other visitors or the park's commercial trappings – notably in **Yosemite Village** and **Half Dome Village**, the two main concentrations of shops and restaurants. That said, most crowds can be left behind by following any path that's unpaved or involves much of a slope; in any event, a couple of days spent exploring the valley will likely leave you ready to press on to the park's less crowded regions.

El Capitan and Half Dome

However you approach the valley, your view will be partially blocked by **El Capitan**, a vast monolith jutting forward from the adjacent cliffs and looming 3593ft above the valley floor. One of the largest pieces of exposed granite in the world, "The Captain" is a full 320 acres of grey-tan rock, seemingly devoid of vegetation and almost vertical. Its enormous size and nearly sheer face have drawn rock climbers from all over the world for decades (see p.342).

The grandeur of El Capitan is matched only by stunning 8842ft **Half Dome**, which rises almost 5000ft from the valley floor. Its 2000ft northwest face is only seven degrees away from being perfectly vertical, making it the sheerest cliff in North America. Though stunning from the valley, the best views of Half Dome are from Glacier Point (see p.337), especially around sunset.

Ambitious day-hikers can reach the dome's thirteen-acre summit over the course of a highly demanding all-day trek (see box, p.338), tackling the final section by way of a harrowing steel-cable staircase brilliantly hooked onto the rock's curving back.

SMARTER THAN THE AVERAGE BEAR

Given Yosemite's high visitor numbers, the park's **bears** have acquired a familiarity with humans that can make these wily omnivores quite determined to get a free meal. They're perfectly undeterred by tent walls or car doors, and safe **food storage** is now mandatory in the park. As is often said, "A fed bear is a dead bear", so do them and yourself a favour by keeping all food and odorous items – including deodorant, sunscreen and toothpaste – either inside your room or in metal lockers at campgrounds, parking lots and trailheads. If you don't, you stand to be fined up to $5000.

In the backcountry, campers must use portable plastic **bear canisters** to store food. Sows have taught their cubs to climb along slender branches, so the old method of hanging food in trees is no longer a viable option.

You are encouraged to **report bear-related problems** and sightings on ☎ 209 372 0322.

WINTER IN YOSEMITE

From December to April, those prepared to cope with blocked roads – Tioga Pass is invariably closed through winter – and below-freezing temperatures are amply rewarded at Yosemite, for it's at this time that thick snow, frozen waterfalls and far fewer people make for almost unimaginable beauty and silence. **Accommodation** is not only cheaper in winter (check ⓦyosemitepark.com for special deals), but much easier to obtain, though certain weekends can still fill up. Many low-country **campgrounds** remain open and restrictions on backcountry camping are eased – though you'll certainly want to tote a four-season sleeping bag and tent.

Much of Yosemite is fabulous **cross-country skiing** territory. Lessons, equipment rental, tows, downhill skiing and snowboarding, and twenty-five miles of groomed cross-country trails are available at **Yosemite Ski & Snowboard Area** (formerly Badger Pass Ski Area; generally open mid-Dec to April; all-day lift ticket $48, ski rentals $37/day; ☎209 372 1000, ⓦtravelyosemite.com/winter/yosemite-ski-snowboard-area), which is accessible via free shuttle bus from Yosemite Valley. The overnight cross-country ski trips to Glacier Point (see p.337) are excellent ($350/person for one night, $550 for two nights). **Ice skating** is another popular winter pastime at the open-air Half Dome Village rink in Yosemite Valley ($11, plus $4.50 skate rental).

If you plan to drive into the park, be aware that **tyre chains** are recommended from November to April and can be rented in the gateway towns. Inside the park, chains are only available for sale – and expensively at that.

The major waterfalls

At 2425ft, **Yosemite Falls** is widely claimed to be the fifth-highest waterfall in the world, and the highest in North America. It's a somewhat spurious assertion, since it's actually two falls separated by 675ft of churning rapids and chutes known as **Middle Cascade**. Nonetheless, 1430ft **Upper Yosemite Fall** and 320ft **Lower Yosemite Fall** are magnificent, especially in May and early June when run-off from melting snow turns them into foaming torrents; flow typically dries up by mid-August. A quarter-mile asphalt trail (from shuttle bus stop 6) leads towards the falls along a route of incense cedars and ponderosa pines, creating a perfect photo op.

Perhaps the most sensual waterfall in the park is 620ft **Bridalveil Fall**, a slender ribbon at the valley's western end, which in Ahwahneechee goes by the name of *Pohono* ("spirit of the puffing wind"). Winds often blow the cascade outward up to twenty feet away from its base, drawing the spray into a delicate lacy veil, particularly between April and June. The quarter-mile trail from the parking lot is four miles west of Yosemite Village and not accessible by shuttle bus.

Two of the park's most striking falls are guaranteed to remain active year-round, but are sequestered away from the valley up the Merced River canyon beyond Happy Isles (see p.335). It's a relatively easy walk to get a distant glimpse of 317ft **Vernal Fall**, a curtain of water about eighty feet wide that casts bright rainbows as you walk along the wonderful Mist Trail (see box, p.338). It requires much more commitment to reach the waterfall itself – as well as a steep climb further upstream to 594ft **Nevada Fall**, a sweeping cascade that free-falls for half its height, then fans out onto a granite apron below.

Yosemite Village

Very much the heart of the valley, **Yosemite Village** is not really a cohesive "village" at all, but a scattered settlement of low buildings where mule deer wander freely. You'll find yourself returning time and again to visit shops, restaurants, banking facilities, internet access points, the post office and the **Yosemite Valley Visitor Center** (see p.341), where you can watch the 23-minute film *Spirit of Yosemite*, with its strikingly beautiful footage of the park throughout the seasons. For more iconic images, walk a few steps east to the **Ansel Adams Gallery** (daily: summer 9am–6pm; rest of year 10am–5pm) and its collection of fine-art prints, posters and postcards by the famed photographer.

5

Yosemite Museum

9037 Village Drive • May–Oct daily 10am–4pm • Free

Immediately west of the visitor centre, the **Yosemite Museum** is home to a selection of artefacts focusing on the area's Native American heritage, specifically the local Ahwahneechee (who were a blend of Northern Paiute and Southern Sierra Miwok peoples at the time of European contact) and neighbouring Mono Lake Paiute (with whom the Ahwahneechee traded and intermarried). One of the few crafts to flourish after contact with whites was **basketwork**: fine examples on display include a superbly detailed 1930s Mono Lake Paiute basket which is almost three feet in diameter, and its even larger Miwok/Paiute equivalent, painstakingly created by famed basket-maker Lucy Telles. Basket-making demonstrations are given by Ahwahneechee practitioners throughout the day. A couple of **feather-trimmed dance capes** warrant a look, as does the buckskin dress worn by natives in the 1920s and 1930s during tourist demonstrations of basket-weaving and dance. Though completely alien to the Miwok tradition, the Plains-style buckskin clothing and feather headdresses fulfilled the expectations of the whites who came to watch. Outside, a self-guided trail weaves around the **Indian Village of the Ahwahnee**, with its reconstructed traditional bark-covered buildings, roundhouse and Miwok cabin.

Fifty yards west of the museum is the **Yosemite Cemetery** (always open; free), which holds the graves of early white settlers, including those of early orchardist **James Lamon** and park guardian **Galen Clark**.

Majestic Yosemite Hotel

1 Ahwahnee Drive (0.5 miles east of Yosemite Village) • Shuttle stop 3

One essential stop, even if you don't intend to stay or eat, is the **Majestic Yosemite Hotel** (formerly *The Ahwahnee*; see p.342). It was built in grand style in 1927 from local rock and is decorated with Native American motifs and some wonderful oriental rugs and carpets. Originally intended to blend into its surroundings and attract wealthier tourists, it still does both fairly effortlessly. At the very least, pop in for a few minutes to sink into a deep chair or sofa and view the collection of paintings of Yosemite's early days.

Half Dome Village and the eastern valley

At some point, almost everyone finds themselves at the eastern end of Yosemite Valley, home to all the main campgrounds along with the permanent cabins of *Housekeeping Camp* and the tent cabin complex of **Half Dome Village**. This is a direct descendant of Camp Curry, founded in 1899 by David and Jeannie Curry, who were keen to share their adopted home in the valley and charged just $12 a week for a "good bed, and a clean napkin at every meal". It's now a rambling area of tent cabins and wooden chalets centred on a small complex of restaurants, shops, pay showers and an outdoor amphitheatre hosting ranger programmes and evening shows. There's also an outdoor ice rink (in winter), bike rental and a kiosk that rents rafts for use on the nearby Merced River.

Yosemite Conservation Heritage Center

9006 South Side Drive • May–Sept Wed–Sun 10am–4pm • Free • Shuttle stop 12

The western end of Half Dome Village is marked by the park's original visitor centre, now the **Yosemite Conservation Heritage Center** (formerly the LeConte Memorial Lodge). A small, rough-hewn granite-block structure, it's where the **Sierra Club** maintains displays on its own history, runs a conservation library and has a fascinating relief map of the valley dating back to the 1880s. The Lodge itself was built by the Sierra Club between 1903 and 1904 to commemorate eminent geologist (and early supporter of John Muir) **Joseph LeConte** (1823–1901), and as the Sierra Club's Yosemite headquarters, it was managed for a couple of summers in the early 1920s by **Ansel Adams** (see box opposite). Evening programmes here (usually Fri–Sun; free) are a little more highbrow than those elsewhere in the park and might include a slide show or talk by some luminary; check the *Yosemite Guide* for details (see p.340).

ANSEL ADAMS

5

Few photographers have stamped their vision on a place as unforgettably as **Ansel Adams** did with Yosemite Valley. While he worked all over the American West, Yosemite was Adams' home and the subject of his most celebrated works, icons of American landscape photography such as 1940's *Jeffrey Pine – Sentinel Dome, Clearing Winter Storm* from 1944 and *Moon and Half Dome* from 1960.

Born in 1902 into a moderately wealthy San Francisco family, Adams was given a Box Brownie camera when he was 14, on his first trip to Yosemite. He claimed that he knew his "destiny" on that first visit and soon turned his attentions to the mountains.

He first made a mark in 1927 with *Monolith, The Face of Half Dome*, his first successful **visualization**: Adams believed that, before pressing the shutter, the photographer should have a clear idea of the final image and think through the entire photographic process, considering how lenses, filters, exposure, development and printing need to be used to achieve that visualization. This approach may seem obvious today, but compared to the hit-and-miss methods of the time, it was little short of revolutionary.

In the 1940s, there was still very little money in photography, and Adams took on commercial assignments, including shooting menu photos for *The Ahwahnee* (now the *Majestic Yosemite Hotel*). While still demanding the highest standard of reproduction, the artist had tempered his perfectionism by the 1950s and allowed his work to appear on postcards, calendars and posters. By now he was virtually a household name, and for the first time in his life he began making money to match his status as the grand old man of Western photography. His final triumph came in 1979, when New York's MoMA hosted the huge "Yosemite and the Range of Light" exhibition. That same year, he was asked to make an official portrait of President Jimmy Carter – the first time a photographer had been assigned an official presidential portrait – and was subsequently awarded the nation's highest civilian honour, the Medal of Freedom.

Throughout his life, Adams was equally passionate about **conservation**. He had a direct hand in the 1940 creation of Kings Canyon National Park, and two years later he became a director of the **Sierra Club**, overseeing several successful environmental campaigns until 1971. He never quit campaigning for conservation.

Adams died on April 22, 1984, aged 82, and posthumously lent his name to Yosemite's Mount Ansel Adams, as well as to a huge chunk of the High Sierra immediately southeast of the park now known as Ansel Adams Wilderness.

Nature Center at Happy Isles

May to early Sept daily 9.30am–5pm • Free • Shuttle stop 16

One mile southeast of Half Dome Village, the **Nature Center at Happy Isles** contains a family-friendly set of displays on flora and fauna, a hands-on exhibit allowing you to feel how hunks of rough granite get weathered down to sand, and a display on a year in the life of a bear. Also don't miss the terrific rockfall presentation at the rear of the centre, where a number of explanatory panels highlight the pulverized rock and flattened trees resulting from a massive rockfall that cascaded down here from Glacier Point in 1996.

Mirror Lake

One of the most rewarding of the easy trails near Half Dome Village leads from shuttle stop 17 and around the edge of the valley floor to **Mirror Lake** (2 miles; 1hr; 100ft ascent). This calm lake (often dry by late summer) reflects the great bulk of Half Dome far above; it's best seen in early morning when it's quieter. Most visitors to Mirror Lake follow the traffic-free paved road from the shuttle stop, but several smaller parallel paths (found to the left of the main track) will steer you clear of the asphalt and crowds.

Northern Yosemite

From Yosemite Valley, Big Oak Flat Road climbs rapidly to Crane Flat, where there's a store and the closest gas station to the valley. From here, Hwy-120 runs west to the park's Big Oak Flat Entrance and **Hetch Hetchy**, once a scenic rival for Yosemite Valley.

5

East of Crane Flat, **Tioga Road** climbs through dense forests into the Yosemite high country around Tenaya Lake, Tuolumne Meadows and Tioga Pass – open grasslands pocked by polished granite domes and with a southern horizon delineated by the sawtooth crest of the **Cathedral Range**.

Hetch Hetchy

John Muir's passion for Yosemite Valley was matched by his desire to preserve the beauty of **Hetch Hetchy**, eighteen miles north of the valley along Evergreen and Hetch Hetchy roads via Crane Flat. Once a near replica of Yosemite Valley, with grassy, oak-filled meadows and soaring granite walls, it's now largely under the dammed waters of slender Hetch Hetchy Reservoir. When it came under threat from San Francisco power- and water-supply interests in 1901, Muir battled for twelve years, instigating the first-ever environmental letter-writing campaign to Congress. Eventually, in 1913, the cause was lost, and now only the view of granite domes and waterfalls from the path crossing O'Shaughnessy Dam (completed in 1923) gives some sense of what it must have been like. Proposals to restore Hetch Hetchy Valley have been floated since the late 1980s, but influential figures such as Senator Dianne Feinstein oppose this, and in 2012, San Francisco voters rejected funding for just a study of what restoration would mean. Today what remains is best seen on a short and mostly flat hike which initially crosses the dam, passes through a short tunnel and follows the north bank of the reservoir to **Wapama Falls** (5 miles round-trip) and on to **Rancheria Falls** (a further 8 miles round-trip). Both falls are at their best in May and June, and are dry by August.

Tioga Road and Tuolumne Meadows

East from Crane Flat, **Tioga Road** almost immediately passes a parking lot from where you can follow a mile-long walking trail to the **Tuolumne Grove** of giant sequoias. Although it's nowhere near as spectacular as the Mariposa Grove (see p.337), it's easier to reach – and it's always humbling to stroll among these giants. Tioga Road then climbs steadily through deep pine forests past *White Wolf* and *Porcupine* campgrounds, rising above 8000ft just before **Olmsted Point** – right up there with Glacier Point as one of Yosemite's most jaw-dropping roadside views – which gallantly looks down Tenaya Creek towards Half Dome.

The alpine area around **Tuolumne Meadows** ("meadow in the sky") has an atmosphere quite different from Yosemite Valley, fifty-five miles away (about a 1hr30min drive). The landscape here, at 8600ft, is far more wide open and the air always possesses a fresh, crisp bite. That said, there can still be a fair amount of human activity at peak times in the vicinity of the *Tuolumne Meadows* campground (see p.345) and *Tuolumne Meadows Lodge* (see p.343) – together constituting the only accommodation base in the area.

Being almost five thousand feet higher than Yosemite Valley makes Tuolumne Meadows a better starting point for **hiking** (see box, p.339) into the surrounding High Sierra wilderness. The meadows are the largest in the entire Sierra: twelve miles long, between one quarter and one half-mile wide, and threaded by the Tuolumne River. Snow usually stays until the end of June, forcing **wildflowers** to contend with a short growing season. They respond with a burst of colour in July, a wonderful time to visit.

The distinctively glaciated granite form of **Lembert Dome** squats at the eastern end of the meadows, gazing across the grasslands towards its western twin, **Pothole Dome**, a great sunset destination. The mountain scenery is particularly striking to the south, where the **Cathedral Range** offers a horizon of slender spires and knife-blade ridges. Look for the appropriately named **Unicorn Peak** and **Cathedral Peak**, the latter a textbook example of a glaciated "Matterhorn", where glaciers have carved away the rock on all sides and left a sharp, pointed summit. Some of the best views are from the naturally carbonated **Soda Springs**, described in 1863 as "pungent and delightful to the taste" – and so it is, though the National Park Service discourages drinking from it.

The "Getting Around" section (see p.341) has information on buses to Tuolumne Meadows from Yosemite Valley, as well as seasonal shuttles operating in the area.

Southern Yosemite

The southern end of the park contains a broad swathe of sharply peaked mountains that extend twenty miles from the foothills in the west to the High Sierra's crest in the east. In summer, visitors congregate at **Wawona**, where the hotel and campground provide most services, or at nearby **Mariposa Grove**, the most impressive of the park's stands of giant sequoias. Roughly midway between Yosemite Valley and Wawona, Glacier Point Road carves its way to the park's most famous vista at **Glacier Point**, which epically clings to the rim of Yosemite Valley.

Glacier Point, Sentinel Dome and Taft Point

The most spectacular views of Yosemite Valley are from **Glacier Point**, the top of an almost sheer, 3200ft cliff, thirty-two miles by road (usually open May–Oct) from Yosemite Valley. The valley floor lies directly below the viewing point, with tremendous views almost straight across to Half Dome and, further beyond, the snowcapped summits of the High Sierra. It's possible to get here on foot along the very steep Four Mile Trail (see box, p.338), though you may prefer to let the **Glacier Point Tour and Hikers Bus** (see p.341) do the climbing for you before you embark on the toe-jamming descent back into the valley.

Along Glacier Point Road you'll pass **Yosemite Ski & Snowboard Area** (see box, p.333) and you'll also find a number of signposted trailheads from which you can launch all manner of hikes. One of the best is to the 8122ft summit of **Sentinel Dome** (2 miles round-trip), a granite scalp topped by the rotting remains of a Jeffrey pine made famous by Ansel Adams' photos from the 1940s. From Sentinel Dome's parking area, a second dusty trail leads west to **Taft Point** (2 miles round-trip), where El Capitan and Yosemite Falls can be seen from a vertiginous viewpoint. Nearby, the granite edges of the valley rim have been deeply incised to form what are known as the **Taft Point Fissures**.

Wawona

There's a relaxed pace at **Wawona**, twenty-seven miles (about a 1hr drive) south of Yosemite Village along Wawona Road. Most people spend their time here strolling the grounds of the landmark *Big Trees Lodge* (see p.342), while close by is the **Pioneer Yosemite History Center**, a collection of buildings culled from the early times of white settlers' habitation that can be visited on a self-guided walking tour (open-access; free). The jail, homesteads and covered bridge are good for a scoot around, and through the summer months (particularly weekends) the buildings are open and interpreted by attendant rangers. Away from the main road, the area makes a quiet spot for a picnic.

Mariposa Grove

The **Mariposa Grove**, three miles east of Wawona Road (Hwy-41) on a small road that cuts off just inside the park's **South Entrance**, is the biggest – and best – of Yosemite's groves of giant sequoia trees. The Grove was closed between 2015 and 2017 to restore much of the area to its natural beauty – check the park website for the latest developments. A new consolidated parking area and information station has been constructed at the South Entrance, and many of the roads have been converted into hiking trails; tram tours and the old gift shop have gone. The Wawona–Mariposa Grove shuttle has been replaced with a free shuttle between the South Entrance and the Grove.

Trails around the sequoia groves call first at the **Fallen Monarch**, familiar from the 1899 photo, widely reproduced on postcards, in which cavalry officers and their horses stand atop the prostrate tree. The most renowned of the stand of trees, well marked along the route, is the **Grizzly Giant**, thought to be 2700 years old and with a lower branch thicker than the trunk of any non-sequoia in the grove. Other highlights include the **Wawona Tunnel Tree**, through which people drove their cars until it fell in 1969, the similarly broad **California Tunnel Tree**, which you can walk through, and all manner of trees which have grown together, split apart, been struck by lightning or are simply staggeringly large. It's also worth dropping into the **Mariposa Grove Museum** (May–Sept daily 10am–4.30pm;

5

HIKING IN YOSEMITE

Given that 96 percent of Yosemite National Park is designated wilderness, it's clear that the best way to absorb the park's singular beauty is on foot and off-pavement. There are no restrictions on **day-hiking** in Yosemite, so for each of the following hikes, you need only equip yourself properly – map, sunscreen, extra clothing, water, food, etc – get to the trailhead and set off. Unless otherwise noted, the following distances and times are for round-trip hikes.

DAY-HIKES FROM YOSEMITE VALLEY

Four Mile Trail to Glacier Point (10 miles; 5–6hr; 3200ft ascent). Magnificent views of Yosemite Valley and Sentinel Rock from a steep asphalt path that's one of the valley's more popular day-hikes. Generally open May–Oct.

Half Dome (16 miles; 10–12hr; 4800ft ascent). This is one of the valley's finest and most arduous walks, initially following the Mist Trail (see below) and continuing around the back of Half Dome. The final 900ft ascend over the huge, smooth, humped back, aided by a pair of steel cables (in place late May to early Oct) and wooden steps. Once atop the summit, anyone concerned about the validity of their outdoor credibility will want to edge out to the very lip of the abyss and peer down the sheer, 2000ft northwest face. Note that if you plan a one-day assault, you'll need to start at the crack of dawn; alternately, you may wish to backpack in and camp near Half Dome's rear base for a far shorter (and more enjoyable) ascent. After years of hinting at doing so, the National Park Service finally instituted a permit reservation system in 2010 for day-hike ascents, so you'll need to apply for a permit (distributed by lottery via ⓦrecreation.gov; $8, plus application fee of $4.50) if you want to day-hike to the rounded summit during the high season (May–Oct); plan to start at dawn, if not before. Visit ⓦnps.gov/yose/planyourvisit/halfdome.htm for all the latest details, including an explanatory video.

Mist Trail to the top of Vernal Fall (3 miles; 2–3hr; 1100ft ascent). If you only do one hike in Yosemite, this should be it – especially during spring's snowmelt when Vernal Fall is often framed by a rainbow and you're likely to get drenched in spray (bring an extra water-resistant layer). Start at shuttle stop 16 and head uphill, crossing a footbridge with great views of Vernal Fall. From here, follow the Mist Trail along a narrow path which, though hardly dangerous, demands sure footing and a head for heights. At the top of Vernal Fall, either retrace your steps to the trailhead or return via the somewhat rocky John Muir Trail.

Upper Yosemite Fall (7.2 miles; 6–8hr; 2700ft ascent). This popular yet energy-sapping hike climbs steeply to the north rim of the valley, offering staggering views of Upper Yosemite Fall and the opportunity to sit virtually right next to it, allowing you to gaze down at the Lilliputian activity in Yosemite Village far below. Its northern aspect keeps the trail open longer than most

free), towards the top end of the trail, where you'll find modest displays and photos of the mighty trees (see box, p.316).

Yosemite gateway towns

The heavy demand for accommodation within the park drives many visitors to consider staying in one of the small, mostly former gold-mining towns along the main access roads leading into Yosemite. These communities gear themselves to park-bound travellers and do a reasonable job of offering both lodging and food, though the inconveniences presented by their distance from most park sights may be too much of a deterrent for some.

Groveland

Your best bets for bases outside the park itself are towns to the west, particularly tiny **GROVELAND**, forty-five miles from Yosemite Valley on Hwy-120. Its main drag boasts sidewalks with verandas and has several good places to stay (see p.343) and eat (see p.346).

Mariposa

South of the park, Hwy-140 runs through the bustling Gold Rush town of **MARIPOSA**, about forty miles from the valley, which boasts the oldest law-enforcement establishment

(April–Dec) but it's best done during the spring snowmelt: start before 7am to avoid the worst of the midday heat. The trailhead is adjacent to *Camp 4* (shuttle stop 7).

DAY-HIKES FROM TUOLUMNE MEADOWS

Lembert Dome (4-mile loop; 3–4hr; 850ft ascent). Great views from the top of Tuolumne Meadows' most prominent feature, plus examples of glacially polished rock and erratic boulders left behind by retreating glaciers. Start at the parking lot at Lembert Dome's base and follow signs for Dog Lake, then head right to ascend via the bare rock of the dome's northeast corner. Descend, then turn right to complete a loop around the dome.

Cathedral Lakes (8 miles; 4–6hr; 1000ft ascent). A strong candidate for the best Tuolumne day-hike, this route follows the John Muir Trail as far as a pair of gorgeous tarns in open alpine country, where you'll enjoy long views up towards a serrated skyline. Begin from the trailhead just west of Tuolumne Meadows Visitor Center, from which the views of the twin spires of Cathedral Peak become steadily more impressive the further you hike. Near the peak's base are Upper Cathedral Lake (with excellent camping) and Lower Cathedral Lake, a divine spot lodged in a cirque now partly filled with lush meadows; the latter lake is split by a ridge of hard rock polished smooth by ancient glaciers.

MULTIDAY HIKES

Camping out overnight opens up the majority of Yosemite's more than eight hundred miles of backcountry trails. Choosing from the enormous range of paths is almost impossible, though some of the most popular are those running between Yosemite Valley and Tuolumne Meadows, a two-day hike for anyone with reasonable fitness.

For any overnight trips, you'll need a **wilderness permit**, available free from any national park ranger station – locations include Wawona, Big Oak Flat, Hetch Hetchy and Tuolumne – or the Wilderness Center in Yosemite Village. Numbers are limited by a quota system; sixty percent can be reserved ahead of time while the remaining forty percent is available on a first-come, first-served basis no earlier than 11am the day before your hike begins. Large groups, people with tight schedules and anyone hiking at busy times should definitely make **reservations** (details at ⓦ nps.gov/yose/planyourvisit/wildpermits.htm; $5/confirmed reservation plus $5/person), available up to 24 weeks in advance. Reservations aren't needed from November to April.

When obtaining your permit, you'll be instructed in **backcountry etiquette** (see p.43), especially water purification, waste disposal and proper use of the required **bear-resistant food canister**, which you can rent for $5 per week (plus $95 deposit) from the Wilderness Center (summer) or Valley Visitor Center (rest of year). **Camping gear** (though not tents) can be rented quite reasonably from Yosemite Mountaineering School (see p.341).

west of the Mississippi still in continuous use: the **Mariposa County Courthouse**, at 5088 Bullion St near Eighth Street. Built without nails in 1854, its lumber material was rough-cut from a nearby stand of white pine, and you can still spot the saw marks on the hand-planed spectator benches. During opening hours (Mon–Fri 8am–4pm; ⓦ mariposa court.org), you can sit in on proceedings. The convicted were often sent down the street to the **Historic 1858 Jail**, 5012 Bullion St at Fifth Street, which remained in use until 1963. The town's heritage is further celebrated at the **Mariposa Museum and History Center**, 5119 Jessie St, at Twelfth Street (daily 10am–4pm; $5; ☎ 209 966 2924, ⓦ mariposamuseum .com), mildly diverting for its mock-up of a Gold Rush-era store and the large-scale mining paraphernalia scattered about outside. Check here for tours of the Historic 1858 Jail.

California State Mining and Mineral Museum

Mariposa County Fairgrounds, Hwy-49 • Thurs–Sun: May–Sept 10am–5pm; Oct–April 10am–4pm • $4 • ☎ 209 742 7625, ⓦ www.parks.ca.gov

Possibly of more interest than Mariposa's historic offerings, the **California State Mining and Mineral Museum**, two miles south of Mariposa on Hwy-49, revels in this region's glory days of the mid-nineteenth century with realistic reconstructions of a mine and stamp mill. There's also a vault where, among assorted other treasures, lies the largest existing crystalline gold nugget in California, a fourteen-pound chunk uncovered in 1864 and valued at over $275,000 in 2016.

5

Midpines and El Portal

North of Mariposa along Hwy-140, which winds appealingly along the Merced River en route to Yosemite, lies the very tiny towns of **MIDPINES** (7 miles north of Mariposa) and **EL PORTAL** (another 22 miles on), which also offer affordable lodging (see p.343) closer to the park; the latter is home mostly to National Park Service housing and facilities, fifteen miles from Yosemite Valley.

Oakhurst

Yosemite visitors arriving via Fresno and southern points beyond will come through **OAKHURST**, fifteen miles outside the park's South Entrance at the junction of Hwy-41 and Hwy-49; the mostly charmless town is a growing sprawl of strip malls and sky-high signs for chain hotels and fast-food restaurants. Despite its lack of atmosphere, it makes a handy base for the southern section of the park and day-trips into Yosemite Valley, forty-five miles distant.

Fish Camp

The tiny huddle of hotels which makes up **FISH CAMP** sits about a dozen miles north of Oakhurst along Hwy-41, handy for Wawona and the Mariposa Grove and also good for keeping kids occupied with the **Yosemite Mountain Sugar Pine Railroad**, 56001 Hwy-41 (March–Oct daily; $24; ☎559 683 7273, ⓦymsprr.com), a two-mile track into the forest plied by an oil-burning steam locomotive that once carted hewn timber. In the height of summer, several train trips run each day, giving you the option of picnicking in the woods at the far end.

Lee Vining

From late May or early June until October or November (depending on snowfall), you can approach Yosemite from the east over the beautiful but harrowingly steep 10,000ft Tioga Pass via US-395 and the small town of **LEE VINING** (see p.289). You're almost two hours' drive from the Yosemite Valley heartland, but this area provides fine access to Tuolumne Meadows (see p.336).

ARRIVAL AND INFORMATION   YOSEMITE NATIONAL PARK

BY CAR

Getting to Yosemite by car is straightforward, although parking can be a problem on summer weekends. Three roads from San Joaquin Valley converge near Yosemite Valley, roughly in the centre of the park's 1200 square miles and home to its most dramatic scenery: Hwy-120 from Manteca (the best approach from the San Francisco Bay Area); Hwy-140 from Merced; and Hwy-41 from Fresno, which passes the Mariposa Grove and Wawona, from where it's under 25 miles to Yosemite Valley. All these roads are generally kept open throughout the year, though Hwy-120 is the first to close under the duress of extreme winter weather. The only road into the eastern side of the park is Hwy-120, which branches off from US-395 close to Lee Vining and ascends 10,000ft Tioga Pass, though this route is usually closed from October or November to May or June, or whenever rough weather strikes.

BY BUS

Greyhound provides bus service to Merced, where the efficient YARTS bus system (☎877 989 2787, ⓦyarts.com) runs May–Sept along Hwy-140 to Yosemite Valley (4 daily; $13 one-way; 3–4hr); it also runs a service to/from Fresno

Yosemite International Airport (ⓦflyfresno.com) and Fresno Amtrak/Greyhound station (6 daily; $15; 4hr 30min), and also Mammoth Lakes (see p.280). Tickets can be bought on board or online, and all fares include the park entrance fee.

PARK ENTRY

Yosemite National Park (general information ☎209 372 0200, ⓦnps.gov/yose) is always open. Park entry is $30 per vehicle including passengers ($25 Nov–March), or $15 for each cyclist and hiker, and is valid for seven days. Pay at the ranger stations when you enter or leave, or if they're closed, at the visitor centre in Yosemite Valley. To encourage use of public transport, YARTS bus passengers pay no entry fees.

TOURIST INFORMATION

On arrival at any park entrance, you'll be given an excellent map of the park, the glossy annual *Yosemite* booklet and the current *Yosemite Guide* newspaper, which is updated regularly to cover events and the extensive range of (mostly free) ranger programmes.

Big Oak Flat Information Station 400ft beyond Big Oak Flat Entrance (May–Oct daily 8am–5pm; ☎209 379

1899). Less robust than the visitor centres at Yosemite Valley and Tuolumne Meadows, but definitely worth a short stop if you're driving into the park from the west.

Mariposa County Visitor Center 5158 Hwy-140, Mariposa (daily: mid-May to mid-Oct 9am–7pm; mid-Oct to mid-May 8am–5pm; ☏ 209 966 7081, ⓦ mariposachamber .org). Duck into this helpful centre southwest of the park to pick through a sizeable bundle of brochures and maps.

Tuolumne Meadows Visitor Center Eight miles beyond Tioga Pass Entrance (late May to late Sept daily 9am–5pm; ☏ 209 372 0263). Geared towards visitors seeking information on Tuolumne Meadows and the park's wild northern reaches.

Tuolumne Meadows Wilderness Center Six miles beyond Tioga Pass Entrance (late May to mid-Oct daily 8am–5pm; ☏ 209 372 0745). Hikers about to delve into Yosemite's northern and eastern backcountry will want to stop here for permits and other pre-trek planning.

Wawona Information Station Five miles beyond South Entrance (May–Oct daily 8.30am–5pm; ☏ 209 375 9531). Convenient for visitors entering the park via Fresno and Oakhurst.

Yosemite Sierra Visitors Bureau 40343 Hwy-41, Oakhurst (Mon–Sat 8.30am–5pm, Sun 9am–1pm; ☏ 559 683 4636, ⓦ yosemitethisyear.com). Armloads of information on the Yosemite region is available at this well-staffed centre on the northern edge of Oakhurst.

Yosemite Valley Visitor Center Yosemite Village (daily 10am–6pm; ☏ 209 372 0299). The park's main information outpost is best for its interpretive displays and *Spirit of Yosemite* film.

Yosemite Valley Wilderness Center Yosemite Village (May–Oct daily 8am–5pm; ☏ 209 372 0745). Visit for hiking permits and all the route-planning assistance you could ever hope to get.

GETTING AROUND

Valley Visitor Shuttle If you're driving in just for the day, leave your vehicle in one of the day-use parking lots at Yosemite and Half Dome villages, then use the free and frequent Valley Visitor Shuttle that passes close to all the main points of interest, as well as trailheads and accommodation areas. In high season, the service runs roughly every 10–20min (7am–10pm) to most sections of the valley, with slightly reduced hours at other times.

Tuolumne Meadows Shuttle This free bus service runs along Tioga Rd, linking Tuolumne Meadows with Olmsted Point, just west of Tenaya Lake (June to mid-Sept daily 7am–6pm).

By bike Although bicycles are not allowed off paved surfaces in Yosemite, cycling around the 12 miles of dedicated bike paths is an excellent way to get around the valley. Bike stands at *Yosemite Valley Lodge* and *Half Dome Village* (April–Nov only, 9am–6pm; ⓦ travelyosemite .com) both rent city bikes for about $12/hr or $34/day.

By bus and guided tours Of the many bus tours on offer, the most engaging is the 4hr Glacier Point Tour (May–Nov daily; $41, or $25 one-way; ☏ 209 372 4386, ⓦ travelyosemite.com), from *Yosemite Valley Lodge* – one-way tickets allow the option of hiking back down. All are reserveable at accommodation reception areas or by phone. Other options are particularly popular with hikers, including the service that stops at roadside trailheads on the way to Tuolumne Meadows: the Tuolumne Meadows Hikers' Bus (mid-June to early Sept; $14.50 one-way, $23 return) makes a 2hr 30min run, leaving *Half Dome Village* at 8am and departing *Tuolumne Meadows Lodge* at 2.05pm, leaving you with a few hours to enjoy Tuolumne Meadows.

ACTIVITIES

Horseriding and muleriding ☏ 209 375 6502. Saddle trips accommodating riders of all levels operate out of Big Trees Lodge Stable, 8308 Wawona Rd, usually open late May to early Sept daily 7am to 5pm: rides cost $61 for 2hr. Reservations essential.

Mountaineering The Yosemite Mountaineering School and Guide Service (☏ 209 372 8344, ⓦ travelyosemite .com/things-to-do/rockclimbing) runs daily courses between April and October ranging from one-day beginners' classes (from $143) through to intermediate courses and private full-day guided climbs (from $167).

Photography The Ansel Adams Gallery in Yosemite Village (ⓦ anseladams.com; see p.333) runs assorted free photography walks (check *Yosemite Guide* for times) and more specialized courses.

Rafting Inside the park, *Yosemite Valley Lodge*, *Majestic Yosemite Hotel* and the Tour and Activities Kiosks (daily 7.30am–3.30pm) at Yosemite and Half Dome villages rent six-berth rafts ($29.50/person; late May to late July only), allowing you to float gently along a placid 3-mile section of the Merced River; the cost includes a return bus ride. Outside the park (April to June), far more rugged (Class III–IV) one-day trips are run in the traditional guided fashion by nonprofit ARTA River Trips (☏ 209 962 7873, ⓦ arta.org), Whitewater Voyages (☏ 800 400 7238, ⓦ whitewatervoyages.com) and Zephyr Whitewater Expeditions (☏ 800 431 3636, ⓦ zrafting .com), all charging around $109–115 per person for a half day, and $155–175 for a full day.

Swimming There are swimming pools in the valley at *Yosemite Valley Lodge* and *Half Dome Village* (both free to hotel guests; $5 for others), while the *Big Trees Lodge* and the *Majestic Yosemite* both have pools for the exclusive use of guests. There are also numerous small river beaches throughout the Yosemite Valley and at Wawona.

5

ACCOMMODATION

For **accommodation** it the park itself, it's essential to book well in advance, and anything other than camping can be quite expensive. All accommodation in the national park – the majority of it right in Yosemite Valley – is operated by Aramark's Yosemite Hospitality (☎ 888 413 8869, ⊚ travelyosemite.com). A somewhat inconvenient option is to stay in one of the gateway towns outside the park and commute in for your daily visits; El Portal and Midpines along Hwy-140 and Groveland along Hwy-120 are your best bets.

HOTELS, MOTELS AND CABINS
YOSEMITE VALLEY

Half Dome Village 9010 Half Dome Village Drive (1 mile from Yosemite Village); map p.331. A large family-oriented area dotted mostly with canvas tent cabins fitted with beds on a wooden plinth (some heated; no electricity, shared bathroom). There are also cramped solid-walled cabins with their own bathroom (electricity, but no TVs or phones) and a few spacious motel-style rooms. Open daily mid-March to Nov. Tent cabins $\underline{126}$, cabins $\underline{199}$, doubles $\underline{235}$

Housekeeping Camp 9005 Southside Drive (0.5 miles from Yosemite Village at shuttle stop 12); map p.331. Ranks of simple, concrete-walled and plastic-roofed cabins with beds on sleeping platforms and the use of a fire grate and picnic table. April to mid-Oct. $\underline{99}$

★ **Majestic Yosemite Hotel** (formerly The Ahwahnee) 1 Ahwahnee Drive (near Yosemite Village, at shuttle stop 3); map p.331. The finest place to stay in Yosemite since 1927, with rooms decorated in the hotel's Native American motif. Despite astronomical rates, it's usually booked solid quite far in advance, but it's still worth visiting to view the wonderfully grand public areas. Open year-round. $\underline{448}$

Yosemite Valley Lodge 9006 Yosemite Lodge Drive (0.5 mile west of Yosemite Village at shuttle stop 8); map p.331. A sprawling choice that's popular with tour groups for its proximity to restaurants, grocery stores and a pool, making it perhaps the most convenient choice in the valley. Rooms are motel-style and come with a private bathroom, TV and phone, but no a/c. Year-round. $\underline{235}$

OUTSIDE YOSEMITE VALLEY

★ **Big Trees Lodge** 8308 Wawona Rd, Wawona; map p.331. An elegant New England-style hotel, parts of which date from 1879, with attractive public areas, wooden verandas and grounds that include a pool, tennis courts and a golf course. Rooms all lack phones, TVs and a/c, but have been restored with old-style furniture, Victorian patterned wallpaper and ceiling fans – though those in the main lodge are fairly small and lack bathrooms (en-suite rooms from $190). Open late March to late Nov. $\underline{130}$

ROCK CLIMBING IN YOSEMITE

Rock climbers around the world flock to Yosemite, drawn by the challenge of inching up 3000ft walls of sheer granite that soar towards the California sun. Acres of superb, clean rock, easily accessible world-class routes and reliably clear summer weather draw a vibrant climbing community bubbling over with campfire tales.

The best place to marvel at climbers' antics is from the roadside next to **El Capitan Meadows**, always dotted with tourists training binoculars on the park's most hulking slab of granite, **El Capitan**. The apparently featureless face hides hairline crack systems a thousand feet long and seemingly insurmountable overhangs whose scale is made apparent only by the flea-like figures of climbers.

The world's most famous climb, **The Nose**, traces a line up the prow of El Capitan. Climbers typically spend three to five nights on the route, but speed attempts have brought the record down to an astounding 2 hours, 23 minutes and 46 seconds. The **North American Wall** route lies to the right, passing directly through a massive stain on the rock that looks remarkably like a map of North America.

BRIEF HISTORY

Technical rock climbing kicked off in Yosemite Valley in 1933, when four Bay Area climbers reached what is now known as the lunch ledge, 1000ft up Washington Column – the tower opposite Half Dome. After World War II, Swiss-born blacksmith **John Salathé** pushed standards to new levels by climbing **Lost Arrow Spire**, which rises to the right of Yosemite Falls and casts an afternoon shadow on the wall nearby.

For the next twenty years, Salathé's mantle was assumed by classical purist **Royal Robbins** and brash **Warren Harding**. Little love was lost between the two men, but when Robbins' team first scaled the face of **Half Dome** in 1957, Harding was on the summit to congratulate them. The climb ranked as the toughest in North America, and Yosemite became an

Tuolumne Meadows Lodge Tuolumne Meadows Lodge Rd (off Hwy-120); map p.331. Seventy canvas tent cabins, each with four beds and a wood-burning stove but no electricity, located at nearly 9000ft and perfect for the first or last night of a long hiking trip. Meals and showers available. Mid-June to mid-Sept. $125

★ **White Wolf Lodge** White Wolf Rd (off Hwy-120, 30 miles from Yosemite Valley); map p.331. Spacious four-berth canvas-tent cabins each fitted with wood-burning stove and candles (no electricity). Four motel-style cabins are available (with propane heaters and electricity). Open July & Aug. Tent cabins $120, motel-style cabins $160

HWY-120 TOWARDS GROVELAND
Entries are listed by increasing distance from Yosemite.
Evergreen Lodge 33160 Evergreen Rd (7 miles north of Hwy-120 and Big Oak Flat Entrance) ☎209 379 2606, ⓦevergreenlodge.com; map p.331. Scattered amid pines, this resort comprises 88 modernized cabins around the main lodge and recreation building. So-called custom camping means being provided with tent, mattress and sleeping bag. There's a general store with an espresso bar, good restaurant, bar (the only places you'll find TV) and nightly entertainment. You can rent bikes and join a number of tours and activities. Custom camping $130, cabin $230
Yosemite Westgate Lodge 7633 Hwy-120 (13 miles from Big Oak Flat Entrance) ☎209 962 5281, ⓦyosemite

westgate.com. The closest standard motel to the park that you'll find along Hwy-120, with the comforts of satellite TV, pool and hot tub. There's a decent restaurant next door. $170
Hotel Charlotte 18736 Hwy-120, Groveland, 24 miles from Big Oak Flat Entrance ☎209 962 6455, ⓦhotelcharlotte.com. This charming ten-room hotel, dating back to 1921, has been lovingly updated. Most rooms are small, but all have beautiful old-fashioned bathrooms, a/c units and satellite TV. $149
★**Groveland Hotel** 18767 Hwy-120, Groveland (24 miles from Big Oak Flat Entrance) ☎209 962 4000, ⓦgroveland.com. Gorgeous mining-era hotel with luxurious and antique-filled rooms, most with deep baths and all individually styled. Suites feature spa tubs and real fires. $179

HWY-140: TOWARDS EL PORTAL, MIDPINES AND MARIPOSA
Entries are listed by increasing distance from Yosemite.
Yosemite Cedar Lodge 9966 Hwy-140, El Portal (8 miles west of Arch Rock Entrance) ☎209 379 2612, ⓦstayyosemitecedarlodge.com. Large hotel complex with indoor and outdoor pools, an on-site restaurant and two hundred rooms and suites. There's a fair chance of finding availability here when everywhere else is full. $159
Bear Creek Cabins 6993 Hwy-140, Midpines (22 miles west of Arch Rock Entrance) ☎888 303 6993, ⓦyosemitecabins.com. Choose between four large,

international forcing ground for aid climbing.

By this point, even seemingly unclimbable El Capitan felt within reach. Following a lengthy period of unsuccessful summit attempts – during which Harding used four massive pitons fashioned from stove legs scavenged from Berkeley's city dump and drove them into what are still known as the Stoveleg Cracks – the legendary climber and two colleagues finally topped out in 1958 after a single thirteen-day push, the culmination of 47 days' work on The Nose.

The 1960s became the **Golden Age** of climbing, when Yosemite Valley drew a motley collection of dropouts and misfits, many ranking among the world's finest climbers. Purists at the top of their sport became disenchanted with the artificiality of aid ascents and began to "free" pitches: not hauling up on all the hardware, but using it only for protection in case of a fall. The culmination of years of cutting-edge climbing and months of route-specific training was Lynn Hill's groundbreaking free ascent of The Nose in 1993, praised and admired by all – if ruefully by some in Yosemite's traditionally male-dominated climbing community.

Climbers employ death-defying **pendulums**, during which they repeatedly sweep across the rock face to gain momentum until they can lunge out at a tiny flake of granite or fingertip hold. They are forced to spend nights slung in a kind of lightweight camp bed known as a **portaledge** and haul food, gallons of water, sleeping bags, warm clothing and wet-weather gear. As veteran Yosemite climber John long writes: "Climbing a wall can be a monumental pain in the ass. No one could pay you enough to do it. A thousand dollars would be too little by far. But you wouldn't sell the least of the memories for ten times that sum."

PRACTICALITIES
The **best months** for climbing in Yosemite Valley are April, May, September and October. In summer, climbs on the domes around Tuolumne Meadows are cooler and usually considered a better bet. In the valley, everyone stays at bohemian *Camp 4* (see p.344), where there's a great sense of camaraderie and a much-used **notice board** for teaming up with climbing partners, selling gear, organizing a ride or just meeting friends.

5

well-maintained log cabins: two sleep four and come with kitchenette, while two very spacious (more expensive) suites come with a separate living room, gas fireplace and a full kitchen. All have satellite TV and access to a deck and barbecue area. Cabin $109

★Yosemite Bug Rustic Mountain Resort 6979 Hwy-140, Midpines (22 miles west of Arch Rock Entrance) ☎ 209 966 6666, ⓦ www.yosemitebug.com. Sprawling across twenty acres of woodland, this hostel and lodge is the handiest budget accommodation near Yosemite. Basic self-catering facilities exist for those staying in the HI-affiliated dorms, but there's also the excellent, licensed *June Bug Cafe* (see p.346). There's also tent cabins, shared-bath private rooms and very cosy and distinctively decorated en-suite rooms with decks (but no phone or TV). There's a lounge with books and games, access to a good summer swimming hole, hot tub, sauna, massage and yoga classes, and a YARTS bus stop at the head of the resort's long entry road. Dorms $34 ($31 for HI members) tent cabin $75, doubles $135

River Rock Inn 4993 7th St, Mariposa (32 miles from Arch Rock Entrance) ☎ 209 966 5793. This peaceful and welcoming seven-room budget motel just off Mariposa's main drag features stylishly decorated, if smallish rooms (plus a couple of larger suites) equipped with a/c and fridge. Doubles $139, suites $179

Comfort Inn Yosemite Valley Gateway 4994 Bullion St, Mariposa (32 miles from Arch Rock Entrance) ☎ 209 966 4344, ⓦ choicehotels.com. A modern mid-range motel with a/c in all rooms; there's also access to an outdoor pool and hot tub. $150

★**Highland House Inn** 3125 Wild Dove Lane, Mariposa (36 miles from Arch Rock Entrance) ☎ 559 696 3341, ⓦ highlandhouseinn.com. It's worth the effort to reach this tranquil B&B, tucked away amid ponderosa pines and incense cedars about 12 miles northeast of Mariposa. The three attractively furnished rooms all have private bathroom with baths and showers, with the largest boasting a four-poster bed, fireplace and DVD player. Breakfasts are substantial, there's a full kitchen for guests' use and the common area even has a pool table. $139

HWY-41: TOWARDS FISH CAMP, OAKHURST AND AHWAHNEE

Entries are listed by increasing distance from Yosemite.

White Chief Mountain Lodge 7776 White Chief Mountain Rd, Fish Camp (2 miles south of South Entrance) ☎ 559 683 5444. Sequestered in a peaceful setting just off Hwy-41, *White Chief*'s ageing, but clean and well-equipped motel rooms are one of the better-value options in the region. April–Oct. $116

Narrow Gauge Inn 48571 Hwy-41, Fish Camp (4 miles south of South Entrance) ☎ 559 683 7720, ⓦ narrowgaugeinn.com. Attractive lodge with a wide selection of rooms, many with a balcony and views over the forest;

there's also a good restaurant on site (see p.347). The inn has a pool and spa. $185

Hounds Tooth Inn 42071 Hwy-41, Oakhurst (13 miles south of South Entrance) ☎ 559 642 6600, ⓦ houndstoothinn.com. Luxurious B&B with a dozen individually decorated rooms, most with either a fireplace or spa bath (or both) and all with a/c. The affable hosts provide complimentary wine each evening. $140

★**Homestead Cottages** 41110 Rd 600, Ahwahnee (23 miles south of South Entrance) ☎ 559 683 0495, ⓦ homesteadcottages.com. Seven miles west of Oakhurst, you'll find this handful of beautiful adobe cottages, all fitted with a/c, television and gas grill; the complex features full self-catering facilities, as well as a comfortable lounge area and lovely deck. It's pricier than other accommodation options in the area, but well worth the splurge. $259

CAMPGROUNDS

Unless otherwise noted, all listed campgrounds have running tap water, and they all have toilets (*Tamarack Flat*, *Yosemite Creek* and *Porcupine Flat* have non-flushing vault toilets). None have showers or laundry facilities (see p.347).

YOSEMITE VALLEY

Camp 4 4000ft; map p.331. First-come, first-served walk-in campground that's popular with rock climbers and located west of – and well away from – the valley's other campgrounds. It's a fairly bohemian (some would say squalid) place, with six-person sites just a few yards from a dusty parking lot. It's often full by 9am, especially in spring and summer, so join the queue early. Year-round. Price is per person. $6

North Pines, **Lower Pines and Upper Pines** 4000ft. The three main campgrounds in the valley are largely indistinguishable and exceptionally crowded, but also pine-shrouded and well-developed; they're quite popular with RV users. Reservations essential. *North Pines* April to early Nov, *Lower Pines* March–Oct, *Upper Pines* year-round. Pitches $26

OUTSIDE YOSEMITE VALLEY

Bridalveil Creek 7200ft; map p.331. First-come, first-served campground in the high country off Glacier Point Rd. Good access to wilderness trails. July to late Sept. Pitches $18

Crane Flat 6200ft; map p.331. Sizeable campground (166 sites) northwest of the valley near the Merced Grove of sequoias. Reservations required. Mid-July to mid-Oct. Pitches $26

Hodgdon Meadow 4900ft; map p.331. Relatively quiet campground just inside the park's western boundary and a short distance from Hwy-120. Reservations required mid-April to mid-Oct; first-come, first-served at other times. Year-round. Discount mid-Oct to mid-April. Pitches $26

Porcupine Flat 8100ft; map p.331. Attractive, relatively small (52 sites) first-come, first-served campground along Tioga Rd, almost 40 miles from Yosemite Valley. Bring water in

case the adjacent stream is dry. July to mid-Oct. Pitches $12
Tamarack Flat 6300ft; map p.331. Somewhat remote, first-come, first-served campground 2 miles south of Tioga Rd, 23 miles from the valley and with limited RV access. Bring water in case the adjacent creek is dry. Late May to mid-Oct. Pitches $12
Tuolumne Meadows 8600ft; map p.331. Very large (over three hundred sites) and popular stream-side campground set beside a subalpine meadow. Half its sites are available by advance reservation, the other half by same-day reservation. Late June to late Sept. Pitches $26
Wawona 4000ft; map p.331. The only developed campground in the park's southern reaches is approximately a mile north of the *Big Trees Lodge*. Some walk-in sites are reserved for car-free campers. Reservations required mid-April to mid-Oct; first-come, first-served the rest of year. Discount mid-Oct to mid-April. Open year-round. Pitches $26
White Wolf 8000ft; map p.331. First-come, first-served tent and RV campground 1 mile north of Tioga Rd, midway between Yosemite Valley and Tuolumne Meadows. Wood and charcoal fires are permitted, and each campground contains a fire ring, picnic table and food locker. Early July to late Sept. Pitches $18
Yosemite Creek 7600ft; map p.331. First-come, first-served tent-only spot that's ideal for escaping Yosemite Valley's crowds, though it can fill up very quickly in the summer. It's inconveniently sited 5 miles off Tioga Rd along an unpaved track, almost equidistant between the valley and Tuolumne Meadows. Bring water in case the adjacent creek is dry. Mid-July to early Sept. Pitches $12

OUTSIDE YOSEMITE NATIONAL PARK

Dimond O 4400ft; Evergreen Rd (1 mile west of Big Oak Flat Entrance); reserve on ☎877 444 6777 or Ⓦ recreation.gov; map p.331. Lovely campground just outside the national park in neighbouring Stanislaus National Forest boasting tent and RV sites, vault toilets and a fine riverside setting. May–Sept. Pitches $21
Sawmill 9800ft; Saddlebag Lake Rd (4 miles north of Tioga Pass Entrance); map p.331. Primitive walk-in campground around 400yd from its parking lot, sited amid jagged peaks (in Inyo National Forest), that feel a world away from the glaciated domes around Tuolumne Meadows only 12 miles to the southwest. No water. June–Sept. Pitches $16
Summerdale 5000ft; Hwy-41 (1.5 miles south of South Entrance); reserve on ☎877 444 6777 or Ⓦ recreation .gov; map p.331. Sierra National Forest campground near the park's South Entrance, and handy for visits to both Wawona and the Mariposa Grove. No water. June–Oct. Pitches $30
Tioga Lake 9700ft; Hwy-120, 1 mile north of Tioga Pass Entrance; map p.331. One of the highest-elevation places in or around Yosemite that you can drive to, inside the Inyo National Forest right on the lake. Pitch a tent beside one of the picnic tables. June–Sept. Pitches $21

CAMPING IN YOSEMITE NATIONAL PARK

As is the case when visiting any national park, **camping** is the best way to really feel part of your natural surroundings, though this is less true in Yosemite Valley's crowded campgrounds. Between June and September it's almost essential to reserve beforehand (☎877 444 6777, Ⓦ recreation .gov); seven of the campgrounds (both in Yosemite Valley and outside of the valley; see opposite) are on the reservation system, but even the remaining first-come, first-served campgrounds usually fill by noon. Availability opens in one-month chunks, five months in advance, so to make reservations for the month beginning July 15, you should try to reserve on February 15 (from 7am Pacific time). Otherwise, you'll need to show up at the Half Dome Village Reservations Office (see p.334) very early in the morning and hope for cancellations. Between May and mid-September, you're only allowed to camp for one week in Yosemite Valley or Wawona and a total of two weeks in the entire park; outside this summer season you can move in for up to a month. Camping outside recognized sites in the valley is strictly forbidden. **RV** campers can use all the main campgrounds: there are no hookups, but you'll find dump stations at Upper Pines (year-round) and near Wawona and Tuolumne Meadows (summer only) campgrounds.

In addition to the main campgrounds, there are **backpackers' campgrounds** in Yosemite Valley (April to mid-Oct), Tuolumne Meadows (July to late Sept), White Wolf (July to mid-Sept) and Hetch Hetchy (year-round), designed for hikers about to start (or just finishing) a wilderness trip. Sites cost $6 per night (no reservations required; pay using envelopes at the campground) and you must have a valid a **wilderness permit** (see box, p.339).

Finally, with enough time, you'll want to get to one of the **primitive backcountry campgrounds**, which are designed for hikers and have fire rings and some source of water (which must always be treated). To enjoy these sites or camp anywhere else in the backcountry, you must get a wilderness permit and pitch your tent at least one mile from any road, four miles from a populated area and at least one hundred yards from water sources and trails. Camping on the summit of Half Dome is not permitted.

5

EATING

Generally, **eating** in Yosemite is more a function than a pleasure. Food, whether in restaurants or in the stores around Yosemite Village (where there's a supermarket), Half Dome Village, Wawona and Tuolumne Meadows, is more expensive than outside the park. **Outside the park**, the dining options are broader, especially in Groveland and Mariposa.

YOSEMITE VALLEY

Degnan's Deli Yosemite Village; map p.331. Some of the best takeaway food in the valley: Peet's coffee, bowls of soup and chilli ($5–6), as well as massive, freshly made sandwiches and salads ($7–8). Daily 7am–6pm.

Half Dome Village Pavilion Half Dome Village; map p.331. Come here for basic breakfasts ($3.50–10.50) featuring eggs, bacon, pancakes and the like. Dinner runs to a salad bar ($5), and simple steak and pasta dishes (main $10–15). Bring beer or wine from the adjacent *Village Bar* (see below). Daily 7–10am & 5.30–8.30pm.

★**Majestic Yosemite Dining Room** Majestic Yosemite Hotel ☎209 372 1489; map p.331. One of the most beautiful restaurants in the US, built in a baronial style with iron chandeliers, floor-to-ceiling windows and 34ft-high ceilings with beams. The best (and priciest) food in Yosemite: eggs benedict ($16.50), spinach salad with bacon ($11.25) and grilled swordfish ($30.75); the Sunday brunch buffet ($49) is marvellous. There's casual dress during the day, but in the evening men need long trousers, collared shirt and closed shoes; women should be similarly smartly attired. Mon–Sat 7–10am, 11.30am–3pm & 5.30–9pm, Sun 7am–3pm.

★**Pizza Deck and Village Bar** Half Dome Village; map p.331. Very much the place to head to on a balmy evening after a day on the trail. Jostle for an outdoor table while you wait for a decent, build-your-own pizza (large from $25) and enjoy an elegant 23oz schooner of draught beer, or even a daiquiri or margarita. Jan–Nov daily 11am–10pm.

Yosemite Valley Lodge Food Court Yosemite Valley Lodge; map p.331. A bright self-serve cafeteria with a full range of cold and cooked breakfasts ($6–12), muffins, pastries and coffee. Simple lunch and dinner options range from pizzas ($8–9) or sandwiches ($6.50) to cobb salad ($10) and turkey with mashed potatoes and stuffing ($15). Daily 6.30am–10pm.

OUTSIDE YOSEMITE VALLEY

Big Trees Lodge Dining Room Big Trees Lodge; map p.331 . Enjoy a casual lunch of barbecue mountain burger ($15.25) or chicken sandwich ($13.25), then dress smartly for dinner to enjoy seared mountain trout ($22.50) or pot roast ($18.50). There's a Saturday barbecue (June–Sept 5–7pm; from $22). Daily 7–10am, 11am–3pm & 5–9.30pm.

Tuolumne Meadows Lodge Dining Room Tuolumne Meadows ☎209 372 8413; map p.331. Family-style breakfasts ($6–12) and burgers, steak, chicken and fish dinners ($15–30) served in a dining tent beside the Tuolumne River. Box lunches are also available. Reserve for dinner. July to mid-Sept daily 7–9am & 5.30–8pm.

White Wolf Lodge Dining Room White Wolf Rd (off Hwy-120, 30 miles from Yosemite Valley) ☎209 252 4848; map p.331. Standard breakfasts, boxed lunches (noon–2pm) and in the evening, portions of American cuisine (over $20). July to late Sept daily 7.30–10am & dinner seatings at 6pm, 6.30pm, 7.15pm & 7.45pm.

GROVELAND

The Cellar Door Groveland Hotel, 18767 Main St (Hwy-120) ☎209 962 4000. The classiest restaurant in town features a seasonally changing menu and nightly chef's specials – perhaps crabcakes with coriander and caper sauce, or honey-glazed baby back pork ribs. Expect to pay at least $50 for three courses, including a glass or two from the sprawling wine list. Daily: June–Sept 7.30–10am & 5.30–9pm; Oct–May 5.30–9pm.

Cocina Michoacana 18370 Main St (Hwy-120) ☎209 962 6651. Mexican spot where $10–12 will get you either a brunch of scrambled eggs with strips of *carne asada* or one of the daily lunch specials. Later, the kitchen serves a full range of Cal-Mex favourites, including terrific fajitas for two ($25) and breaded shrimps. Daily 10am–10pm.

Fork & Love Restaurant (Hotel Charlotte) 18736 Main St (Hwy-120) ☎209 962 6455, ⌨forkandlove.com. With a menu largely focused on small plates, this hotel restaurant is the place to go west of the park for potato gnocchi ($15), tomato curry ($15) and steaks ($24), served in a rustic and spacious dining room. Wed–Sun 6–10pm.

Mountain Sage Coffee 18653 Main St (Hwy-120) ☎209 962 4686. The smartest stop for coffee, espresso and pastries in Groveland, with a lush garden for relaxed sipping. Mon & Wed–Sun 7am–3pm.

MARIPOSA AND MIDPINES

Happy Burger Diner 5120 Hwy-140, Mariposa ☎209 966 2719, ⌨happyburgerdiner.com. An enormous array of good, cheap diner food – breakfast burrito ($6), tuna melt ($10), teriyaki chicken salad ($10), burgers galore ($8–12) – to take away or eat in at Formica booths. There's a fun jukebox and the entire place is decorated with tragic album covers from the 1970s. Daily 6am–9pm.

High Country Health Foods & Cafe 5186 Hwy-49, Mariposa ☎209 966 5111, ⌨highcountryhealthfoods .com. Daytime café with sandwiches, salads, burritos and fruit smoothies – all under $11. There's also a health-food store next door (open 1hr later) offering bread, organic fruit and goodies in bulk containers for making your own trail mix. Mon–Sat 8am–6pm, Sun 9am–4pm.

★**June Bug Cafe** Yosemite Bug Rustic Mountain

Resort, 6979 Hwy-140, Midpines ☏ 209 966 6666. Licensed restaurant with quality food at very reasonable prices: wholesome breakfasts ($7–10), lunches to eat in ($7–14) or take away ($7–8) and dinner platters such as spice rubbed trout ($19). There are several good craft beers on tap as well, plus excellent fruit pies, and patio seating. Daily 6.30am–4pm & 6–11pm.

★**Savoury's** 5034 Hwy-140, Mariposa ☏ 209 966 7677, ⓦsavouryrestaurant.com. The pick of Mariposa's restaurants offers a relaxed atmosphere with a touch of class. Modern decor of concrete floors and painted block walls (hung with striking Yosemite prints) sets the tone for delectable dishes such as chipotle chicken ($19), shrimp skewers ($19) and Parmesan polenta ($17); desserts and the wine list are impressive. June–Sept daily 5–9.30pm; Oct–May Mon, Tues & Thurs–Sun 5–9.30pm.

Sugar Pine Cafe 5038 Hwy-140, Mariposa ☏ 209 742 7793, ⓦsugarpinecafe.com. Red leatherette booths and diamond-tiled floors lend a retro feel to this 1940s quality diner where everything is made from scratch, including all the excellent baked goods – apple turnovers, scones, blackberry pie and German chocolate cake. There's a short menu of breakfasts (most under $10) and sandwiches ($8–14), as well as a handful of dinner mains ($13–21). Mon & Sun 7am–3pm Tues–Sat 7am–8.30pm.

FISH CAMP

★**Narrow Gauge Inn Dining Hall & Buffalo Bar** 48571 Hwy-41 ☏ 559 683 6446, ⓦnarrowgaugeinn .com. Fine dining in a cosy mountain setting, where smartly presented mains such as Colorado loin of lamb ($26) and butternut squash pasta ($18) complement the candlelit mood. Be sure to drop into the adjacent *Buffalo Bar* for a cocktail beforehand. April–Oct Wed–Sun 5–9pm.

DRINKING AND ENTERTAINMENT

Evening entertainment includes ranger-led campfire talks at many park campgrounds, occasional stargazing sessions, natural history slide shows and music performances. The *Yosemite Guide* covers events and the theatre programme.

YOSEMITE VALLEY

Majestic Yosemite Bar Majestic Yosemite Hotel ☏ 209 372 1489; map p.331. A great spot to enjoy a cocktail ($14.25), glass of wine ($11.50 and up) or an antipasti plate for two ($24). The outdoor area is a wonderful place to sit and gaze up at the surrounding cliffs. Daily 11am–10pm.

Yosemite Theater Yosemite Village ⓦyosemite conservancy.org/yosemite-theater. Behind the Yosemite Valley Visitor Center, this venue hosts 1hr 30min one-man evening shows (April–Sept Wed & Thurs; $10) by Lee Stetson, who has been impersonating John Muir since 1983.

GROVELAND

★**Iron Door Saloon** 18761 Hwy-120 ☏ 209 962 8904. This wonderfully atmospheric bar reliably claims to be the oldest saloon in California, open, allegedly, since 1896, though the building dates back to 1852 (and it really does have iron doors, transported from England as fire doors in 1937). There's a pool table and all manner of paraphernalia on the walls (with dollar bills on the ceiling), plus live music most weekends and a decent restaurant next door. Daily 7am–1am.

DIRECTORY

Banks There are no banks in Yosemite, though there are several 24hr ATMs located around the park at Yosemite Village, *Yosemite Valley Lodge*, Half Dome Village, Wawona and Tuolumne Meadows.

Books The Yosemite Bookstore (daily 9am–5pm), near the Yosemite Valley Visitor Center, has a good selection of park-related books and maps; the Ansel Adams Gallery (see p.333) specializes in photography and nature publications; the Mountain Shop (daily 8am–8pm) at Half Dome Village stocks climbing guides.

Internet One first-come, first-served 30min session per week is allowed at the Yosemite Village public library (see below), plus free wi-fi.

Laundry *Housekeeping Camp* 0.5 miles from Yosemite Village (coin-op; 8am–10pm).

Library The Yosemite Village public library (Tues & Wed 10am–3pm, Thurs 1.30–6pm; ☏ 209 372 4552) is located just west of the Yosemite Museum in a building signed "Girls Club".

Medical assistance Yosemite Medical Clinic (☏ 209 372 4637), 9000 Ahwahnee Drive, between Yosemite Village and *Majestic Yosemite Hotel*, has 24hr emergency care as well as drop-in and urgent care, and accepts appointments. Dental treatment is also available. Summer daily 9am–7pm; rest of year Mon–Fri 9am–5pm.

Gas Unavailable in Yosemite Valley, but is sold at Crane Flat (summer 8am–8pm, rest of year 8am–5pm or 24hr with credit or debit card) and Wawona (Big Trees Lodge Service Station year-round 8am–5pm or 24hr with credit or debit card); expect to pay well above what you would outside the park.

Post Office Yosemite Village (Mon–Fri 8.30am–5pm, Sat 10am–noon); Yosemite Valley Lodge (Mon–Fri 12.30–2.45pm); Wawona Post Office (Mon–Fri 9am–5pm, Sat 9am–noon); Tuolumne Meadows (Mon–Fri 9am–5pm, Sat 9am–1pm).

Showers Half Dome Village (open 24hr; $5); *Housekeeping Camp* (daily 7am–10pm; $5).

The Central Coast

MISSION SAN ANTONIO DE PADUA

The Central Coast

The hundreds of miles of California's central coast between Los Angeles and San Francisco cover one of the most beautiful oceanside stretches anywhere in the world, a blend of sandy beaches and jagged cliffs, rural charm and urban energy. Indeed, first-time visitors may be surprised to find just how much of the area survives in its natural state, despite nestling snugly between two of the largest and richest metropolitan regions in the US. All along the coast, sea otters and seals play in the waves, and endangered grey whales pass close by on their annual migration from Alaska to Central America. The region also offers a unique insight into California's Spanish heritage, with colonial architecture, elegant missions and a Mexican influence that is reflected in everything from taco joints to it's large Latino population. Wine is also a growing draw, with Santa Barbara, Carmel and Paso Robles vineyards offering an increasingly sophisticated alternative to the more established Napa/Sonoma further north.

At **Big Sur**, the brooding Santa Lucia Mountains of the Coast Range rise steeply from the thundering Pacific surf, while **Point Lobos**, at the area's northern tip, is a fine place to experience this barely touched environment at its most dramatic. Nature aside, though, the Central Coast also marks the gradual transition from Southern to Northern California. The two largest towns here are **Santa Barbara**, a conservative, wealthy resort city less than one hundred miles northwest of Los Angeles, and **Santa Cruz**, about 75 miles south of San Francisco, where tie-dyed hippies, punks and university students blend with yuppie refugees from the Bay Area. What the two towns have in common is miles of broad, clean **beaches**, with chilly waters but excellent surf, and branches of the University of California energizing local nightlife. In between, smaller **San Luis Obispo** provides a feasible base for the Central Coast's biggest tourist attraction, **Hearst Castle** – an opulent hilltop palace that was once the estate of publishing tycoon William Randolph Hearst. **Monterey**, 120 miles south of San Francisco, was the capital of California under Spain, and later Mexico, and today retains more of its early nineteenth-century architecture than any other city in the state. It's also a good base for visiting one of the most beautiful of all the Spanish missions, which stands three miles south in the upper-crust seaside resort of **Carmel**.

BIXBY CREEK BRIDGE, BIG SUR

Highlights

❶ Channel Islands National Park This beguiling chain of desert islands off the coast northwest of Los Angeles offers spectacular hiking and the chance to spot migrating whales. **See p.357**

❷ Hearst Castle One of the most intriguing sights in California: a palatial monument to the life and ego of publishing magnate William Randolph Hearst. **See p.380**

❸ Mission San Antonio de Padua The best preserved of all the state's missions is an evocative place to imagine the colonial California of a few centuries ago. **See p.384**

❹ Big Sur Boasting a strikingly rugged coastline and some of the state's most stunning waterfalls, this sparsely populated region continues to retain its wild character. **See p.388**

❺ Monterey Bay Aquarium The superb, enormous Outer Bay tank and ever-charming sea otters help make this sea-life museum a world-class destination. **See p.399**

❻ Santa Cruz Beach Boardwalk A classic California seaside promenade where carnival food, amusement arcades and a rickety old wooden rollercoaster all make for irresistible fun. **See p.409**

HIGHLIGHTS ARE MARKED ON THE MAP ON P.352

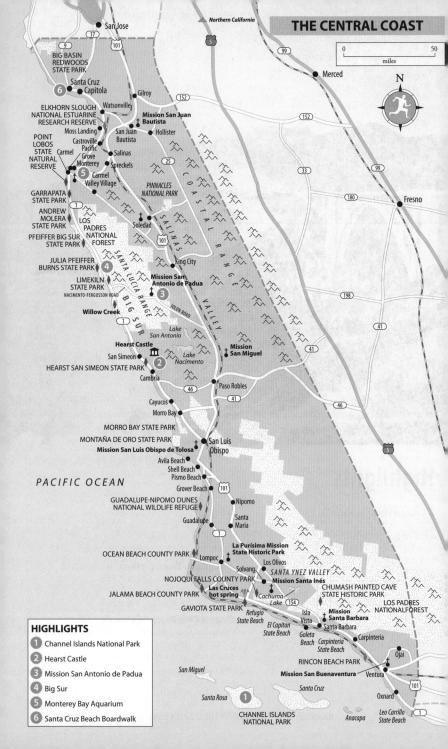

THE CENTRAL COAST

Northern California

0   50
miles

N

San Jose

BIG BASIN
REDWOODS
STATE PARK

Santa Cruz
Capitola

Merced

Gilroy

Watsonville

ELKHORN SLOUGH
NATIONAL ESTUARINE
RESEARCH RESERVE

**Mission San Juan
Bautista**

Moss Landing

POINT
LOBOS
STATE
NATURAL
RESERVE

Castroville
Pacific
Carmel

Monterey
Grove

San Juan
Bautista

Hollister

Salinas

Spreckels

Carmel
Valley Village

Fresno

GARRAPATA
STATE PARK

ANDREW
MOLERA
STATE PARK

LOS
PADRES
NATIONAL
FOREST

**PINNACLES
NATIONAL PARK**

PFEIFFER BIG SUR
STATE PARK

Soledad

JULIA PFEIFFER
BURNS STATE PARK

King City

LIMEKILN
STATE PARK

**Mission San
Antonio de Padua**

NACIMIENTO-FERGUSSON ROAD

Willow Creek

*Lake
San Antonio*

Hearst Castle

San Simeon

*Lake
Nacimiento*

**† Mission
San Miguel**

HEARST SAN SIMEON STATE PARK

Cambria

Paso Robles

Cayucos

Morro Bay

MORRO BAY STATE PARK

MONTAÑA DE ORO STATE PARK

Mission San Luis Obispo de Tolosa

San Luis
Obispo

Avila Beach

Shell Beach

Pismo Beach

Grover Beach

GUADALUPE-NIPOMO DUNES
NATIONAL WILDLIFE REFUGE

Nipomo

Guadalupe

Santa
Maria

**La Purísima Mission
State Historic Park**

OCEAN BEACH COUNTY PARK

Lompoc

Los Olivos

Solvang

SANTA YNEZ VALLEY

NOJOQUI FALLS COUNTY PARK

Mission Santa Inés

**Las Cruces
hot spring**

JALAMA BEACH COUNTY PARK

*Cachuma
Lake*

CHUMASH PAINTED CAVE
STATE HISTORIC PARK

LOS PADRES
NATIONALFOREST

GAVIOTA STATE PARK

*Refugio
State Beach*

Isla
Vista

*El Capitan
State Beach*

Goleta
Beach

**† Mission
Santa Barbara**

Santa Barbara

*Carpinteria
State Beach*

Carpinteria

RINCON BEACH PARK

Ojai

San Miguel

Mission San Buenaventura

Ventura

*Santa
Cruz*

Oxnard

Santa Rosa

1

Anacapa

*Leo Carrillo
State Beach*

CHANNEL ISLANDS
NATIONAL PARK

PACIFIC OCEAN

HIGHLIGHTS

1 Channel Islands National Park

2 Hearst Castle

3 Mission San Antonio de Padua

4 Big Sur

5 Monterey Bay Aquarium

6 Santa Cruz Beach Boardwalk

GETTING AROUND   **THE CENTRAL COAST**

By train Traveling around the Central Coast is easy enough: some of the best views in the state can be had from Amtrak's daily Coast Starlight train, which runs right along the coast up to San Luis Obispo before cutting inland north to San Francisco. The Pacific Surfliner, by contrast, is a shorter jaunt along the southern coastal section, linking San Luis Obispo to Los Angeles and San Diego with a daily service.

By car and bus Greyhound buses stop at most of the towns, particularly those along the main highway, US-101 – though the best route, if you've got a car, is seaside Hwy-1, which hugs the coast all the way but takes perhaps twice as long.

6

Ventura and around

Some forty miles beyond the western fringes of Los Angeles, the small city of **VENTURA** offers the first worthwhile stop on coastal US-101. It's the main ferry port for the Channel Islands (see p.357) but also features a charming downtown and a scattering of relics from the Spanish, Mexican and early American past. The town grew up around Mission San Buenaventura, but it wasn't until oil was discovered nearby in the 1920s that Ventura really took off and it's now considered a rapidly expanding part of the LA metro area. Development straggles along US-101 for several miles, but the historic **downtown** lies at the western (and far more tranquil) end of Main Street (take the **California Street exit** from US-101).

Downtown Ventura

The core of **Downtown Ventura** lies along **Main Street** between Fir Street and Ventura Avenue, an elegant strip lined with Spanish Revival and converted nineteenth-century buildings. Highlights include the gorgeous **Watermark** at 598 E Main St, originally constructed as the Ventura Guaranty Building & Loan in 1928, and now a hip rooftop lounge and restaurant (see p.355). The exquisite interior features three large murals by Californian artist Norman Kennedy, while the red-brick façade combines Moorish and zigzag modern elements. The **Bank of Italy Building** at 394 E Main St, a Beaux-Arts gem built in 1924, has also been converted into shops and restaurants. See also the Neoclassical **City Hall** at 501 Poli St (two blocks north of Main St), built in 1912 as the county courthouse (it became City Hall in 1972) with a distinctive copper-sheathed dome.

Mission San Buenaventura

211 E Main St • Mon–Fri 10am–5pm, Sat 9am–5pm, Sun 10am–4pm • $4 • ☎ 805 643 4318, ⓦ sanbuenaventuramission.org

The last Spanish Franciscan mission to be established by Junípero Serra (see p.672) himself and one of the most tranquil, the **Mission San Buenaventura** was founded in 1782 near a **Chumash** village, though what remains today dates primarily from the early nineteenth century. The peak years for the mission were 1802 to 1821; it was secularized by the Mexican government in 1836 and largely abandoned thereafter, but today it's a thriving Catholic community once again. Enter via the adjacent gift shop on Main Street, where there's a one-room **museum** of ancient religious artefacts (vestments from the Philippines and two crumbling wooden bells from the 1700s), plus an informative video on Serra himself, before entering the tranquil garden. Here there are several statues, shrines and a Spanish-tile fountain, while the church itself retains its elegant bell tower and antique-looking interior, lined with paintings depicting the Stations of the Cross.

Ortega Adobe

215 W Main St • Daily 9am–4pm • Free • ☎ 805 658 4726, ⓦ cityofventura.net/ortegaadobe

The modest **Ortega Adobe** is a whitewashed, Spanish-style dwelling from 1857 that's best known as the birthplace of "Ortega Famous Green Chiles" (a major B&G Foods brand in the US). Interpretive panels inside provide the history of the adobe and its residents – Emilio Ortega started roasting and canning green chillies in his mother's kitchen in 1897.

Albinger Archaeological Museum

113 E Main St • Early June to early Sept Sat & Sun 11am–4pm • Free • ☎ 805 648 5823, ⓦ cityofventura.net/albinger

The summer-only **Albinger Archaeological Museum** has displays of historical artefacts recovered from a single dig site next to Mission San Buenaventura. Relics include ancient Chumash bowls, shell beads and bone whistles, along with remnants of the Spanish era, including parts of the nearby mission's original foundation and crumbling water filtration building dating from the 1780s.

6

The beachfront

Ventura's regenerated beachfront is anchored by the wooden **Ventura Pier**, located where California Street ends, an historic gem dating back to 1872, making it one of California's oldest. It now features interpretive display panels, a snack bar, seafood restaurant and spectacular views of the Channel Islands, coastline and mountains. For surfing, walk half a mile west along the **Ventura Promenade** to **Surfer's Point**, a thin strip of sand that's a prime spot to take a board out onto the undulating water. Just southeast from the pier, **San Buenaventura State Beach** offers another decent stretch of sand, while 2.5 miles southeast, **Ventura Harbor** is lined with shops and restaurants, as well as the Ventura Harbor Village mall. The **Channel Islands National Park visitor centre** is also located here (p.358).

Olivas Adobe Historical Park

4200 Olivas Park Drive • Grounds daily 11am–4pm, house tours Sat & Sun 11am–4pm • $5 • ☎ 805 658 4728, ⓦ cityofventura.net/olivasadobe

A glimpse of early life in California can be found at **Olivas Adobe Historical Park**, about five miles southeast of downtown (one mile east of Ventura Harbor), where the titular adobe was once the centrepiece of land baron Raymundo Olivas's estate in the 1840s, before the Mexican–American War permanently altered the balance of power in the region. Still, Olivas, his wife and their 21 children lived out the century here, and today it's still decorated in the rustic, yet elegant "California Rancho" style appropriate for a major landowner of the mid-nineteenth century, with antique tools and furnishings and a family chapel on display, as well as rose and herb gardens.

ARRIVAL AND DEPARTURE   VENTURA

By train Amtrak trains (Pacific Surfliner only) pull in at Harbor Blvd and Figueroa St, a short walk from downtown's Main St or the beach. Around ten trains (from and to San Luis Obispo, Los Angeles and San Diego) serve the station daily (LA is around 1hr 35min).

By bus The nearest Greyhound bus station is the transit centre in Oxnard at 201 E 4th St (10 miles from Downtown Ventura); take the local transport service, Gold Coast Transit ($1.50; ☎ 805 487 4222, ⓦ goldcoasttransit.org), to continue on to Ventura, Ojai and other towns in Ventura County. Greyhound serves Los Angeles (4 daily; 1hr 20min–2hr 15min) and all major stops to San Francisco (2 daily; 9hr 25min–9hr 55min) from Oxnard.

INFORMATION AND ACTIVITES

Visitor Center 101 S California St (Mon–Sat 9am–5pm, Sun 10am–4pm; ☎ 805 648 2075, ⓦ visitventuraca.com).
Surfing You can rent boards at Ventura Surf Shop, 88 E Thompson Blvd (daily 9am–6pm; ☎ 805 643 1062), two blocks inland near the train station. Rental rates range $15–30/2–24hr); wetsuits go for around $15/24hr, and you should expect to put down a refundable deposit on any rented items.

ACCOMMODATION AND EATING

Allison's Country Cafe 3429 Telegraph Rd ☎ 805 650 1766, ⓦ allisonscountrycafe.com. Ventura's top spot for breakfast, *Allison's* specializes in affordably priced pancakes, waffles, hash browns and biscuits and gravy – all served in hearty portions. Daily 7am–2pm.

★**Beacon Coffee** 5777 Olivas Park Drive, at Bunsen Drive ☎ 805 644 9072, ⓦ beaconcoffee.com. This hip So-cal espresso joint offers high-quality Colombian and Guatemalan coffee and delicious gelato in summer. Mon–Fri 7am–2pm, Sat & Sun 8am–2pm.

Victorian Rose 896 E Main St ☎805 641 1888, ⓦvictorianroseventura.com. Old-fashioned and a bit tatty in places, this B&B is nevertheless one of the most enticing places to stay on the coast. An old church, steeple and all, built in 1880 and converted in 1999, it oozes character, with five rooms crammed with antiques. **$99**

Watermark on Main 598 E Main St ☎805 643 6800, ⓦwatermarkonmain.com. Set in a beautiful old bank building, this complex features a plush first-floor restaurant serving locally inspired seafood and steaks (mains $18–37), and the *W20 Rooftop Lounge*, open Fri–Sat 5pm–1am and Sun 2–6pm, with cocktails and live music. Tues–Thurs 5.30–10pm, Fri & Sat 5–10pm, Sun 10am–2pm.

6

Ojai

Nestling in arid hills fifteen miles north of Downtown Ventura via Hwy-33, **OJAI** (pronounced "O-hi"), is a wealthy resort community frequented by weekend jet-setters and celebrities from Los Angeles. The main focus is the Spanish Revival centre along **West Ojai Avenue** (Hwy-150) between Signal and Fox, created by Ohio glassworks magnate **Edward Libbey** and featuring the post office's iconic **bell tower** (said to be modelled on churches in Havana, Cuba), the adjoining, curvaceous **pergola** along the edge of Libbey Park (though this was rebuilt in 1999) and the Spanish Colonial-style **shopping arcade** on the opposite side of the street, crammed with galleries, wine-tasting shops and ice-cream parlours. Libbey fell in love with the town and essentially rebuilt it after a devastating fire in 1917 – his efforts are commemorated each year on **Ojai Day** (see box below). Today chain stores (other than a few gas stations) are prohibited by city ordinance, the outdoor bookshop **Bart's Books**, 302 W Matilija St (daily 9.30am–6pm), has been here since 1964, and the **Farmers' Market** (Sun 9am–1pm) at 300 E Matilija St is well known (even by Californian standards) for its local organic produce. Producer Jerry Bruckheimer has a home here, as does comedian Ellen DeGeneres and a host of other movie starlets.

Ojai Valley Museum

130 W Ojai Ave • Tues–Sat 10am–4pm, Sun noon–4pm • $5 • ☎805 640 1390, ⓦojaivalleymuseum.org

Get to grips with the history of Ojai at the **Ojai Valley Museum**, set inside the former St Thomas Aquinas Catholic Church. Exhibits cover Chumash culture, the Mexican ranchero period and Edward Libbey's conversion of the town in 1917 (its original name was Nordhoff). A large art gallery contains work by local artists.

Ojai Olive Oil Company

1811 Ladera Rd (off Hermitage Rd) • Tasting Room: Mon, Tues, Thurs & Fri 9am–1pm, Wed 9am–4pm, Sat 10am–4pm • Free • ☎805 646 5964, ⓦojaioliveoil.com

Olives are a major Californian crop, and the best place to learn about them is the enlightening **Ojai Olive Oil Company**, where fascinating tours (given by the French owner Wed & Sat on demand; 25–45min) show how olive oil is produced and the tasting room offers samples of oils and vinegars.

NAMASTE OJAI

Numerous festivals and events – celebrating everything from film and music to wine and spirituality – take place in and around Ojai throughout the year (ⓦojaifestivals.com). The highlight is **Ojai Day** (mid-October; ⓦojaiday.com), a street fair founded to honour Edward Libbey (he was too modest to allow his name to feature) that includes local food, music and crafts, as well as belly dancing, aromatherapy and poetry readings. The annual celebration culminates with the painting of a giant mandala. The **Ojai Music Festival** (founded in 1947), held on the first weekend after Memorial Day (usually early June), features performances by some of the world's top musicians and composers of contemporary classical music (ⓦojaifestival.org). Ojai is also home to the annual **Ojai Playwrights Conference** (ⓦojaiplays .org) held every August – professional writers and actors attend a ten-day workshop, followed by a public theatre festival.

Krishnamurti Visitor Center and Library

1098 McAndrew Rd • Fri 1–5pm, Sat & Sun 10am–5pm • Free • ☎ 805 646 2390, ⊛ kfa.org

Given Ojai's standing as a New Age hub, it's no surprise that it's home to the headquarters of the Krishnamurti Society. The organization honours the Indian Theosophist who, from the 1920s, lived and lectured in Ojai Valley, which he considered "a vessel of comprehension, intelligence and truth". Pine Cottage, the house where **Jiddu Krishnamurti** lived between 1922 and his death in 1986, is now the **Krishnamurti Visitor Center and Library**, four miles northeast of town, which details the philosopher's progressive ideas on spirituality through books, DVDs and other media.

ARRIVAL AND INFORMATION   OJAI

By bus You can reach Ojai from Ventura or Oxnard via Gold Coast Transit ($1.50; ☎ 805 487 4222, ⊛ goldcoast transit.org).

Visitors Bureau 109 N Blanche St, Suite 103 (Mon–Fri 8am–5pm; ☎ 888 652 4669, ⊛ ojaivisitors.com).

ACCOMMODATION AND EATING

★ **Emerald Iguana Inn** 108 Pauline St ☎ 805 646 5277, ⊛ emeraldiguana.com. Romantic boutique hotel in a whimsical property offering gorgeous rooms and tranquil gardens (with pool and jacuzzi). Also has larger cottages with full kitchens (from $229). Two-night minimum. **$169**

Lavender Inn 210 E Matilija St ☎ 805 646 6635, ⊛ lavenderinn.com. Along with its flowery rooms and one large cottage (from $295), this tasteful B&B, built in 1874, also has lovely gardens and a day spa; it even offers cooking classes. **$145**

Ojai Café Emporium 108 S Montgomery St ☎ 805 646 6723, ⊛ ojaicafeemporium.com. The best affordable option in town, where visitors routinely dig into breakfasts of waffles and omelettes, and lunches of burgers, sandwiches and salads – all of which hover between $9–18. Daily 7am–3pm.

Pepper Tree Retreat 1130 McAndrew Rd ☎ 805 646 4773, ⊛ peppertreeretreat.com. Set in a 1910 ranch house very near the Krishnamurti Visitor Center and Library (see above), offering eight modern rooms in which you can further pursue the holistic spirit. It's here that Krishnamurti once hosted Aldous Huxley, Igor Stravinsky and the Beatles – so fittingly, you can stay in the Lennon Room, Huxley Room or Stravinsky Suite. **$155**

Suzanne's Cuisine 502 W Ojai Ave ☎ 805 640 1961, ⊛ suzannescuisine.com. Ojai's top restaurant offers an eclectic lunchtime menu that includes grilled cheese sandwiches ($11.75) and salmon pasta salad ($13.25). Come evening, items become pricier ($18–36) but more robust, with rack of lamb, Cornish game hen, and several seafood and savoury pasta mains on offer. Wed–Sun & Mon 11.30am–2.30pm & 5.30–9pm.

Rincon Beach Park

US-101 Exit 83 (Bates Rd) • Daily 8am–dusk • Free

The area's best surfers head to **Rincon Beach Park**, about fifteen miles northwest of Downtown Ventura along US-101, a legendary point where many Los Angeles surf gods have ventured to get away from the Malibu crowds. It's best surfed in the winter at low tide to take advantage of its killer reef-break.

Carpinteria

Three miles northwest of Rincon Beach Park, **CARPINTERIA** is a seaside hamlet known for its laidback Southern California beach vibe. The town boasts a small, but high-quality **farmers' market** at 800 Linden Ave (Thurs: most of year 4–7pm; winter 3–6pm; ☎ 805 962 5354), as well as celebrated **Chocolats du CaliBressan**, the luxurious chocolate shop founded by Frenchman Jean-Michel Carre at 4193 Carpinteria Ave (Mon–Fri 10am–6.30pm, Sun 10am–5.30pm; ☎ 805 684 6900, ⊛ chococalibressan .com). There's also the **California Avocado Festival** (early October; ⊛ avofest.com), which presents the subtropical fruit in all its native glory. Several long, uncluttered and uncrowded **beaches** line the town to the south, with regular closures along part of the shoreline every winter and spring to allow for bird and seal activity.

INFORMATION   **CARPINTERIA**

Chamber of Commerce 1056-B Eugenia Place (Mon–Fri 8am–5pm; ☎ 805 684 5479, ⓦ carpinteriachamber.org).

ACCOMMODATION, EATING AND DRINKING

Carpinteria State Beach Campground 205 Palm Ave ☎ 800 444 7275, ⓦ reserveamerica.com. A campground on one of the better stretches of sand in these parts, with tide pools and regular winter sightings of whales and sea lions. $45

★ **Island Brewing Co** 5049 6th St ☎ 805 745 8272, ⓦ islandbrewingcompany.com. One of the coast's most popular microbreweries offers craft beers such as Island Blonde Ale and Avocado Honey Ale (from $7), with views of the ocean and a kids' playroom. You are allowed to bring in snacks from adjacent food trucks or popular burger joint *Spot* across the street. Mon–Thurs noon–9pm, Fri noon–10pm, Sat 11am–10pm, Sun 11am–9pm.

6

Channel Islands National Park

Stretching north from Santa Catalina Island off the coast of Los Angeles, a chain of fascinating desert islands is preserved as the **CHANNEL ISLANDS NATIONAL PARK**, offering excellent hiking trails, splendid views of marine life and fishing, as well as scuba diving through the many caves, coves and shipwrecks in the Pacific. Five of the eight islands are accessible as part of the park, though the closest, Anacapa, some fourteen miles south of Ventura, sees the most visitor traffic. The best time to visit is between February and April, when you can engage in **whale watching**.

Before launching an expedition, visit the main **Channel Islands National Park visitor center** (see p.358), where exhibits cover the geology and plant and animal life of these beautiful islands, including seals, sea lions, pelicans and giant kelp forests. You'll also find current information on procuring any necessary hiking and diving **permits**, plus an **observation tower** from which on clear days you can view the islands.

Anacapa Island

Covering a mere one square mile, **Anacapa** (Chumash for "mirage") **Island** actually comprises two islets. **West Anacapa** is largely a refuge for nesting brown pelicans, with most of it off-limits except **Frenchy's Cove**, a pristine beach and good base for scuba or snorkelling expeditions. Most boat trips visit **East Anacapa**, which has a 1.5-mile nature trail, and is known for its signature **Arch Rock** – a thin, rocky bridge that stretches over the ocean's waves. There are no beaches here, but swimming in the cove where the boats dock is allowed.

Santa Cruz Island

West of Anacapa, **Santa Cruz Island** is the largest of the Channel Islands, and is the destination for kayak trips from Ventura and Santa Barbara (see p.359). Boats go to either **Scorpion Anchorage** (a small visitor centre is located in the historic Scorpion ranch house) or **Prisoners Harbor**. **Scorpion Beach** offers swimming, diving, snorkelling and kayaking. The island is also rich in its fauna – including bald eagles, scrub jays and native foxes – and boasts diverse landscapes that range from forbidding canyons to lovely green valleys. Its western three-quarters is owned by the Nature Conservancy and is off-limits to hiking and camping; **Mount Diablo** (2450ft) is the Channel Islands' highest point.

Santa Rosa Island

Almost as big as Santa Cruz, **Santa Rosa Island** has many grasslands, canyons and steep ravines, but overall contains gentler terrain – though it's still compelling for its hiking and kayaking opportunities. The best beach, **Water Canyon Beach**, is just over a mile from the pier in Bechers Bay and just down the canyon from the campground. Especially interesting are the island's archeological sites, some of which date back 11,000 years and are still being investigated for their Chumash relics (a Chumash village survived here until 1820).

San Miguel Island

The most distant of the Channel islands at fifty miles offshore, windswept **San Miguel Island** is alive with elephant seals and sea lions, and is thought to be the burial place of sixteenth-century Spanish explorer Juan Cabrillo. No grave has been found, but a monument has been erected at **Cuyler Harbor** on the island's eastern end. Seasoned hikers may also wish to make the rugged cross-island trip to Point Bennett to spy on the plentiful wildlife. However, the island is only for the most gung-ho nature explorers: it's frequently foggy and windy, and its surrounding rocks make for a white-knuckle sailing trip (park-approved boat tours only). A free permit (including liability waiver) is required to visit San Miguel, provided by tour operators; the island was a former bombing range and there are possible unexploded ordnance (visitors must be accompanied by a ranger beyond the ranger station).

Santa Barbara Island

South of the main islands lies the smallest of the Channel group, **Santa Barbara Island**, named by Sebastian Vizcaíno, who dropped by on St Barbara's Day, December 4, 1602. The island's main attraction these days is its remarkable wildlife – sea lions, kestrels, larks and meadowlarks – which can be seen on land gradually recovering its native flora after years of destruction by now-extinct rabbits.

INFORMATION AND TOURS   CHANNEL ISLANDS NATIONAL PARK

Though the park is open 24 hours a day (and is free), the only way to visit the islands is by air or by boat through operators that run from Ventura Harbor. Note that there are no services (or food stores) on the islands, so bring what you need.

Channel Islands National Park visitor center 1901 Spinnaker Drive (daily 8.30am–5pm; ☎ 805 658 5730, ⓦ nps .gov/chis). The best information source for trip-planning is on the mainland, next to the ferry landing in Ventura Harbor.

Large boat tours Island Packers, 1691 Spinnaker Drive (reservations 8.30am–5pm on ☎ 805 642 1393, ⓦ island packers.com) is the official park boat concessionaire. Boats to Anacapa (1hr) run 3–7 days/week (docking involves climbing up a steel-rung ladder, then climbing 157 stairs to the top of the island); boats to Santa Cruz (1hr) run 5–7 days/week, while trips to Santa Rosa (3hr) run April through to early November, 2–4 days/week. Boat trips to San Miguel (4hr) run April through early November, just 4–8 days per month. Trips to Santa Barbara Island (3hr) usually run spring to the fall, just 2–4 days/month, though service was suspended in 2016 (indefinitely) due to pier damage.

Fares Day fares include 2–5hr on the given island: Anacapa

and Santa Cruz ($59), Santa Rosa and Santa Barbara ($82), San Miguel ($105). Camper/overnight fares are $79 for Anacapa and Santa Cruz, $114 for Santa Rosa and Santa Barbara and $147 for San Miguel. Whale-watching trips that last about 3hr start at $38.

Small boat tours Truth Aquatics, 301 W Cabrillo Blvd, Santa Barbara (☎ 805 962 1127, ⓦ truthaquatics.com), has alternative itineraries to all the islands on smaller vessels (and at higher prices), including two-day hiking, diving and kayaking excursions, April to September.

By plane You can also reach Santa Rosa (25min) and San Miguel (40min) islands on expensive charter flights operated by Channel Islands Aviation (from nearby Camarillo Airport year-round, on demand; ☎ 805 987 1301, ⓦ flycia.com). Half-day (3hr on island) and full-day (4.5hr) trips start at $1100 for the whole plane, which seats eight (they will also drop off and pick up overnight campers).

ACCOMMODATION

Campgrounds ☎ 877 444 6777, ⓦ recreation.gov. Camping opportunities abound on the islands, with one campground on each island (pit toilets only) and limited backcountry sites (on Santa Cruz and Santa Rosa Islands only) available for those who wish to rough it. Potable

water is only available at the *Scorpion Ranch* campground on Santa Cruz and the *Water Canyon* campground on Santa Rosa. To rent camping gear, contact Channel Islands Outfitters, 117 Harbor Way, Santa Barbara (Mon–Fri 9am–5pm; ☎ 805 899 4925, ⓦ channelislandso.com). **$15**

Santa Barbara and around

Founded by the Spanish in 1782, **SANTA BARBARA** is an affluent seaside city beautifully situated on the gently sloping hills above the Pacific Ocean. The town's low-rise Spanish Colonial Revival buildings feature red-tiled roofs and white stucco walls, an evocative backdrop to the palm-lined **beaches** that wind along the gently curving bay. A weekend escape for much of the nation's old money since the late 1870s, Santa Barbara was devastated by a major **earthquake** in 1925. In the aftermath local authorities decided to rebuild virtually the entire city as an ersatz mission-era Spanish town – even the lavish **El Paseo** shopping mall (on State St) has a whitewashed adobe façade. This decision was surprisingly successful, and the "Santa Barbara Style" – a blend of Spanish Colonial Revival and other Mediterranean architectural schools – is now synonymous throughout California and beyond with genteel oceanside living in antique splendour. There's plenty to see here if the region's history interests you and **downtown**, squeezed between the south-facing **beaches** and the foothills of the Santa Ynez Mountains, has one of the region's liveliest street scenes. The city's main drag, **State Street**, is home to an assortment of diners, wineries, bookshops, coffee bars and nightclubs catering as much to the wants and needs of locals – among them over twenty thousand **UC Santa Barbara** students – as those of visitors.

El Presidio de Santa Bárbara State Historic Park

123 E Canon Perdido St • Daily 10.30am–4.30pm • $5 • ☎ 805 965 0093, ⓦ sbthp.org/presidio.htm

The historic centre of Santa Barbara lies mostly along State Street a few blocks inland from US-101, where the town's few genuine mission-era structures are preserved as **El Presidio de Santa Bárbara State Historic Park**. Here you'll find a collection of whitewashed adobe buildings built around the fourth (and last) of the Spanish military garrisons in the region, though most of what you see today, including the visitor centre, was reconstructed in the 1990s (the fort was abandoned in the 1840s). There's an enlightening exhibition on the city's early **Japanese community**, and various buildings re-create the padre's quarters, kitchens, artfully decorated chapel and workshops. The site also includes the modest **El Cuartel**, the second-oldest building in California, a genuine Spanish relic dating from 1788, and now housing historical exhibits and a scale model of the small Spanish colony.

Casa de la Guerra

15 E de la Guerra St • Fri–Sun noon–4pm • $5 (free with El Presidio admission) • ☎ 805 965 0093, ⓦ sbthp.org

The humble **Casa de la Guerra** preserves what was, in the 1830s, one of the more upscale residences in town (though still built in the spartan Spanish Colonial style). Constructed between 1818 and 1828 by José de la Guerra, the fifth *comandante* of the presidio, these days it holds antique spurs, saddles, toys and weapons, plus exhibits on the de la Guerra family, who occupied the house until 1943.

Santa Barbara Historical Museum

136 E de la Guerra St • Tues–Sat 10am–5pm, Sun noon–5pm • Free • ☎ 805 966 1601, ⓦ santabarbaramuseum.com

To get an overview of the city's history, visit the **Santa Barbara Historical Museum**, built in the 1960s to look like a Spanish Colonial mission (though the Covarrubias Adobe at the museum's core dates from 1817). An illuminating permanent exhibition chronicles the story of Santa Barbara, beginning with ancient **Chumash** artefacts and early Spanish items (a seventeenth-century walnut chest, and the leather chair of Mexican **General Vallejo** included), plus portraits of city notables, the pawned jewellery of **Pío Pico**, the last governor of Alta California, and an intact nineteenth-century Chinese shrine. High-quality temporary exhibitions cover aspects of Spanish- and Mexican-era life.

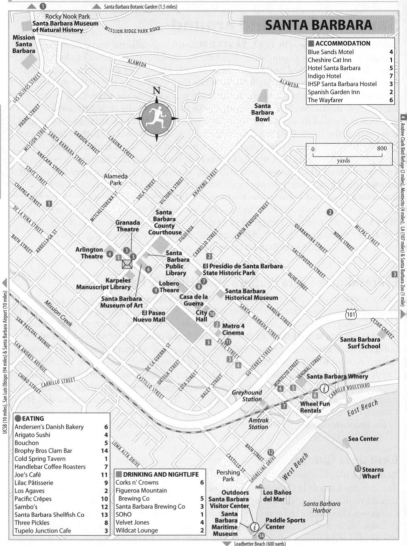

SANTA BARBARA

■ ACCOMMODATION

Blue Sands Motel	4
Cheshire Cat Inn	1
Hotel Santa Barbara	5
Indigo Hotel	7
IHSP Santa Barbara Hostel	3
Spanish Garden Inn	2
The Wayfarer	6

● EATING

Andersen's Danish Bakery	6
Arigato Sushi	4
Bouchon	5
Brophy Bros Clam Bar	14
Cold Spring Tavern	1
Handlebar Coffee Roasters	7
Joe's Café	11
Lilac Pâtisserie	9
Los Agaves	2
Pacific Crêpes	10
Sambo's	12
Santa Barbara Shellfish Co	13
Three Pickles	8
Tupelo Junction Cafe	3

■ DRINKING AND NIGHTLIFE

Corks n' Crowns	6
Figueroa Mountain Brewing Co	5
Santa Barbara Brewing Co	3
SOhO	1
Velvet Jones	4
Wildcat Lounge	2

Santa Barbara Museum of Art

1130 State St • Tues, Wed & Fri–Sun 11am–5pm, Thurs 11am–8pm • $10, free Thurs 5–8pm • ☎ 805 963 4364, ⓦ sbmuseart.org

Set in the heart of downtown, the fine **Santa Barbara Museum of Art** features European and American paintings, classical Greek and Egyptian statuary and a decent Asian collection that comprises some exquisite Chinese pieces (including the enigmatic *Seated Luohan* statue from the thirteenth century). Highlights from the painting collection include a gorgeous **Degas**, *Three Dancers in Yellow*, and a smattering of Impressionists from Monet's *Waterloo Bridge* series to Renoir's *Villas in Bordighera*. Look out also for **Aristide Maillol**'s sensual sculpture *Bather Putting Up Her Hair*, and *Pont Saint-Michel* by Matisse. **Van Gogh** is represented by the bleak *Outskirts of Paris*, and there are a couple of vibrant works by **Chagall**, including *Blue Angel*. American painters include realists such as George Bellows (look for his dramatic *Steaming Streets*) and postwar Californian Modernists such as Richard Diebenkorn (*Woman and Checkerboard*).

Santa Barbara County Courthouse

1100 Anacapa St • Grounds and clock tower Mon–Fri 8am–5pm, Sat & Sun 10am–4.30pm; tours Mon–Fri 10.30am & 2pm, Sat & Sun 2pm; tours of the clock gallery Wed, Fri, Sat 1–2pm • Free • ☎ 805 962 6464, Ⓦ santabarbaracourthouse.org

Completed in 1927, the spectacular **Santa Barbara County Courthouse** is a Spanish Revival gem – a monumental variation on the mission theme that, with its striking murals, tilework and Spirit of the Ocean fountain, is widely regarded as one of the finest public buildings in the US. Enjoy a free tour (Ⓦsbcourthouse.org) of the four-building complex, or take a break in the sunken gardens, explore the quirky staircases or take the elevator up to the 70ft "El Mirador" **clock tower** for a sensational view of the city. The **clock gallery** contains the elaborate workings of the clockface mechanism and a small exhibit.

6

Karpeles Manuscript Library

21 W Anapamu St • Wed–Sun noon–4pm • Free • ☎ 805 962 5322, Ⓦ rain.org/~karpeles/sb.html

One of several such museums located around the US, Santa Barbara's beautifully decorated **Karpeles Manuscript Library** is home to a diverse array of original documents on display in temporary exhibitions. At any given time, the collection may include such notable items as the Constitution of the Confederate States of America, Napoleon's battle plans for his Russian invasion, handwritten orchestral scores and the manuscripts of famous figures such as Mark Twain, Thomas Edison, John Locke and Jorge Luis Borges.

The Waterfront

Half a mile down State Street from downtown, Cabrillo Boulevard runs along the south-facing Waterfront – a long, clean strip stretching from the yacht and fishing harbour beyond palm-lined **West Beach** to the volleyball courts and golden sands of **East Beach**.

Stearns Wharf and Sea Center

Sea Center 211 Stearns Wharf • Daily 10am–5pm • $8.50; teens (13–17) $7.50; kids (2–12) $6 • ☎ 805 962 2526, Ⓦ sbnature.org

At the foot of State Street, take a stroll among the pelicans along **Stearns Wharf**, built in 1872 and the oldest wooden pier in California. The wharf is lined with knick-knack shops, seafood restaurants, ice-cream stands and Santa Barbara Museum of Natural History's **Sea Center**, offering a tot-friendly selection of touch tanks, interactive exhibits, whale bones and tide pools.

Santa Barbara Maritime Museum

113 Harbor Way • Late May to early Sept Thurs–Tues 10am–6pm; early Sept to late May Thurs–Tues 10am–5pm • $8 • ☎ 805 962 8404, Ⓦ sbmm.org

Overlooking the marina, the **Santa Barbara Maritime Museum** occupies the site of the 1943 Naval Reserve Center and showcases an eclectic collection of artefacts relating to every aspect of the region's maritime history. The first floor begins with Chumash relics (including a redwood plank canoe), plus a section on **Richard Henry Dana**, author of *Two Years Before the Mast* (1840), which includes one of the earliest descriptions of Santa Barbara. Here also is a massive **Fresnel lens** created in France for the Point Conception Lighthouse in 1854, a display of old diving helmets, and scale models of ships created by Dwight Brooks. Upstairs the Munger Theater shows a series of excellent videos through the day, and there are displays on environmental issues (including the deadly oil spill of 1969), the mysterious Golenta Cannons, the history of local surfing, sailors' tattoos and scrimshaw (engraved whale bone and teeth).

6

Mission Santa Barbara

2201 Laguna St • Daily 9am–4.30pm • $5 • ☎ 805 682 4713, ⓦ sbmission.org • Take SBMTD bus #22 (daily 6.30am–5.30pm) from the
County Courthouse along Anapamu St, or walk or drive from State St up Mission St and Mission Canyon

The mission from which the city takes its name, **Mission Santa Barbara**, is located on the
slopes about a mile and a half northwest of downtown. Known as the "Queen of the
Missions", its imposing twin-towered façade – facing out over a perfectly manicured
garden towards the sea – combines Romanesque and mission-era styles, giving it a
formidable character lacking in some of the prettier outposts in California's chain of
missions. As a consequence it's by far the most popular, attracting tour buses and
thousands of visitors, despite remaining an active place of worship. The present structure,
built to replace a series of three adobe churches that had been destroyed by earthquakes,
was finished and dedicated in 1820 by Franciscan friars; the huge 1925 earthquake also
badly damaged the structure, and the ensuing restoration cost nearly $400,000.

Today, you enter via the lush **Sacred Garden** and wander through the **Cemetery**
containing the remains of some four thousand Native Americans, many of whom
helped build the original complex, before entering the much restored main **church**
itself. The **museum** – the best of all the Californian missions – includes an absorbing
Chumash section (the rarely remembered 1824 Chumash Revolt is covered), and an
exhibit on the crafts and trades practised at the mission. Take time to study the
incredible black and white photographs on display, which include a Chumash chief in
ceremonial dress (from 1878) and a group of Franciscan fathers in the 1880s.

Santa Barbara Museum of Natural History

2559 Puesta del Sol Rd • Daily 10am–5pm • $12 • ☎ 805 682 4711, ⓦ sbnature.org

Half a mile beyond Mission Santa Barabara, the **Santa Barbara Museum of Natural
History** showcases intriguing items of yore from Chumash culture, plus various
dioramas of mammals, birds, reptiles and insects. There's also a planetarium and actual
skeletons of such extinct creatures as the pygmy mammoth, taken from Santa Rosa
Island off the Santa Barbara coast in Channel Islands National Park (see p.357).

Santa Barbara Botanic Garden

1212 Mission Canyon Rd • Daily: March–Oct 9am–6pm; Nov–Feb 9am–5pm • $10 • ☎ 805 682 4726, ⓦ sbbg.org

For a lovely stroll amid nature, head further into the hills beyond Mission Santa
Barbara until you come to the splendid **Santa Barbara Botanic Garden**, which feature
pleasant hiking trails that wind amid endemic cacti, manzanita, trees and wildflowers
– a relaxing respite among hillside meadows and glades.

ARRIVAL AND DEPARTURE
SANTA BARBARA

By plane 8 miles west of town, Santa Barbara Airport
(☎ 805 967 7111), has a limited and often expensive
scheduled service to other cities in the Western US, with
American, United and Alaska airlines. Public buses ($1.75)
run into town from Moffett Rd across from the terminal.
By bus Greyhound stop near the Amtrak station at 224
Chapala St.

Destinations Los Angeles (4 daily; 3–4hr); San Francisco (2
daily; 8hr 25min–8hr 55min).
By train Amtrak trains stop at 209 State St, one block
south of US-101.
Destinations Los Angeles (2 daily; 2hr 45min); San Luis
Obispo (3 daily; 2hr 40min); Salinas (1 daily; 5hr 50min);
San Jose (1 daily; 7hr 30min); Oakland (1 daily; 8hr 45min).

SANTA BARBARA'S MOXI

Santa Barbara's newest and perhaps most ambitious tourism project is the **Wolf Museum of
Exploration + Innovation**, aka **MOXI**, a massive, family-friendly science museum that will
also feature a third-floor Sky Garden. The complex will hopefully be open sometime in 2017, in
newly built premises at 125 State St. See ⓦ moxi.org for the latest.

INFORMATION AND GETTING AROUND

Visitor Center 1 Garden St (Feb–Oct Mon–Sat 9am–5pm, Sun 10am–5pm; Nov–Jan Mon–Sat 9am–4pm, Sun 10am–4pm; ☎805 965 3021, ⓦsantabarbaraca.com).

Outdoors Santa Barbara Visitor Center 113 Harbor Way (daily 11am–5pm; ☎805 884 1475, ⓦoutdoorsb .noaa.gov), will prove especially helpful should you wish to visit the Channel Islands off Santa Barbara's coast.

Local buses Santa Barbara mainly involves walking and short drives, though there's a 50¢ shuttle that loops between downtown and the beach, and from the harbour to the zoo. Other areas are covered by Santa Barbara Metropolitan Transit District (SBMTD) buses (fares $1.75; ☎805 963 3366, ⓦsbmtd.gov).

Water taxi Lil' Toot, Santa Barbara's water taxi, provides 15min narrated boat rides (daily noon–6pm, every 30min; $5; ⓦcelebrationsantabarbara.com) between Santa Barbara Harbor and Stearns Wharf. Sunset cruises are $40.

ACTIVITIES

Surfing Santa Barbara Surf School (daily 9am–5pm; ☎805 708 9878, ⓦsantabarbarasurfschool.com), 1 N Calle Cesar Chavez, Suite 11, offers lessons ($65–85 for 1hr 30min) and board/wetsuit rentals ($45/day).

Paddle Boarding To get out on the water, contact Paddle Sports Center, 117 Harbor Way (☎805 617 3425, ⓦpaddlesportsca.com), where a paddleboard costs $20/hr.

Kayaking Kayaks are also available from Paddle Sports Center (see above), starting at $12–15/hr.

Bicycling Try Wheel Fun Rentals at 23 E Cabrillo Blvd (Daily: March–Oct 8am–8pm; Nov–Feb 8am–6pm; ☎805 966 2282, ⓦwheelfunrentals.com), with basic bikes going for $36/day; surreys are also available ($29/hr), along with maps of Santa Barbara's extensive system of cycling paths.

Hiking Get good hiking information from Santa Barbara Hikes (ⓦsantabarbarahikes.com); the longest and most enjoyable trail leads west twelve miles along the bluffs to Isla Vista and UC Santa Barbara, passing a mile or so back from rarely crowded Arroyo Burro Beach (locally known as "Hendry's"), four miles west of the wharf at the end of Las Positas Rd.

Swimming Just west of Stearns Wharf, aquatic athletes keep in shape in the heated, 50m Los Baños del Mar swimming pool (a 1939 Art Deco gem), 401 Shoreline Drive (Mon–Fri 7–8am, noon–2pm, 7.15–8.15pm, Sat & Sun noon–2pm; $6; ☎805 966 6110, ⓦfriendsoflosbanos .org), an open-air, year-round facility.

ACCOMMODATION

Home to some of the West Coast's most deluxe resorts, Santa Barbara is among California's priciest places to **stay**, with many properties charging $250–300 a night (and often more at summer weekends). The less expensive places are usually booked throughout summer, but if you get stuck, try airbnb or enlist the assistance of Hot Spots, a local hotel-reservation site that offers discounted rates on lodging (☎800 793 7666, ⓦhotspotsusa.com).

★**Blue Sands Motel** 421 S Milpas St ☎805 965 1624, ⓦbluesandsmotel.com. It may look like your average roadside motel at first, but the *Blue Sands* is actually the city's best deal for accommodation: clean rooms with gas fireplaces, kitchenettes and flat-screen TVs – along with a heated pool. **$185**

Cheshire Cat Inn 36 W Valerio St ☎805 569 1610, ⓦcheshirecat.com. Loaded with twee Victorian decor, this B&B has twelve rooms, four Craftsmen-style cottages and a coach house, and features a hot tub, baths for guests' use and an *Alice in Wonderland* theme – certain rooms have names such as Tweedle Dee and Mad Hatter. Afternoon wine hour included. Doubles **$199**, cottages **$319**

Hotel Santa Barbara 533 State St ☎805 957 9300, ⓦhotelsantabarbara.com. Considering its prime downtown location, this historic hotel (dating back to 1926) offers good value for its comfortable rooms and complimentary breakfast. Parking $15/day. **$189**

Indigo Hotel 121 State St ☎805 966 6586, ⓦindigo santabarbara.com. Trendy boutique hotel a couple of blocks from the beach and the Funk Zone, with small but cosy rooms decorated with bright, contemporary artwork and rooftop lounge. Parking $30/night. **$155**

IHSP Santa Barbara Hostel 111 N Milpas St ☎805 705 9195, ⓦihspsantabarbara.com. Santa Barbara's top hostel is pricey, but offers friendly staff, free parking and clean, comfy accommodation (dorms and private rooms with shared bathrooms). Full kitchen and do-it-yourself pancake breakfast included. Dorms **$45**, doubles **$100**

★**Spanish Garden Inn** 915 Garden St ☎805 564 4700, ⓦspanishgardeninn.com. Likely the finest boutique lodging you'll find in Santa Barbara, offering elegant rooms with designer furnishings and fireplaces, with access to an on-site fitness centre. **$429**

★**The Wayfarer** 12 E Montecito St ☎805 845 1000, ⓦwayfarersb.com. Santa Barbara's chic-hipster boutique hotel offers small but stylish rooms and also pricey shared dorms (with bunk beds), as well as continental style complimentary breakfast. Dorms **$99**, doubles **$199**

EATING

Andersen's Danish Bakery 1106 State St ☎ 805 962 5085, ⓦ andersenssantabarbara.com The place to be seen on the main strip, with a large outdoor patio, tempting breakfast menu (from waffles to eggs benedict, $11–17) and superb Danish pastries – it was founded by Danish baker Alfred Andersen in 1976. Daily 8am–9pm.

Arigato Sushi 1225 State St ☎ 805 965 6074, ⓦ arigatosb.com. The main draw for excellent sushi in town is this boutique Japanese spot, with the requisite Modernist chic and hipster diners. Mon–Thurs 5.30–10pm, Fri–Sun 5.30–10.30pm.

★ **Bouchon** 9 W Victoria St ☎ 805 730 1160, ⓦ bouchonsantabarbara.com. Among the town's top choices for elite dining, this California cuisine favourite presents such rotating items as rack of lamb, venison, maple-glazed duck breast and a full selection of fresh seafood ($26–42), all served amid bright and cheery environs. Mon–Thurs & Sun 5–9pm, Fri & Sat 5–10pm.

Brophy Bros Clam Bar 119 Harbor Way ☎ 805 966 4418, ⓦ brophybros.com. Marina restaurant overlooking the fishing boats known for its fun, often raucous atmosphere and fresh seafood – think excellent oysters/raw bar, crabcakes ($23.95), swordfish ($24) and seafood pasta ($19.95). Daily 11am–10pm.

★ **Handlebar Coffee Roasters** 128 E Canon Perdido St ☎ 719 201 3931, ⓦ handlebarcoffee.com. Hip coffee shop serving the best espresso in town (with beans sourced from Colombia), bagels, Danish pastries and croissants – expect long queues in the mornings. Daily 7am–5pm.

Joe's Café 536 State St ☎ 805 966 4638, ⓦ joescafesb .com. This long-established bar (open since 1928) and grill is a smart place to stop off for a burger, steak sandwich, pork chop or chowder, all $15 or under. It's more or less midway between the beach and downtown's sights and museums. Daily 7.30am–10pm.

Lilac Pâtisserie 1017 State St ☎ 805 845 7400, ⓦ lilacpatisserie.com. This gluten-free bakery and café is the place to indulge in high-quality cakes; think delicious chocolate sea salt caramel cake, decadent lemon raspberry cake and the luscious coconut cream cake (slices $8). Tues–Thurs 8am–7pm, Fri–Sun 8am–8pm.

Los Agaves 600 N Milpas St ☎ 805 564 2626, ⓦ los-agaves.com. Expect terrific *mole* dishes, quesadillas, *chile poblano* and sautéed shrimp – not to mention belt-busting burritos – at this inexpensive Mexican haunt (most mains $10–17). Mon–Fri 11am–9pm, Sat & Sun 9am–9pm.

Pacific Crêpes 705 Anacapa St ☎ 805 882 1123, ⓦ pacificcrepe.com. Doling out what are likely the best crêpes you'll find between Los Angeles and San Francisco, the French chefs here do an especially good job on the dessert varieties. Most options run $11–17. Thurs–Sat 5.15–10pm (ish) it becomes the *5 and ¼ Wine Bar*. Mon–10am–3pm, Tues–Sun 9am–3pm.

Sambo's 216 W Cabrillo Blvd ☎ 805 965 3269, ⓦ firstsince57.com. Popular brunch spot with tables overlooking the beach, great pancakes and complimentary mini muffins. Established by Sam Battistone in 1957 (with partner Newell Bohnett, thus "Sam-Bo"), this was once part of a massive chain – today it's the only one left, in part because of the racist connotations of the name (it became associated with *The Story of Little Black Sambo*). Dodgy history aside, the food is pretty good. Daily 6.30am–3pm.

Santa Barbara Shellfish Co 230 Stearns Wharf ☎ 805 966 6676, ⓦ shellfishco.com. This no-frills seafood shack is lightly better than the other restaurants on the wharf, with a few outdoor tables and cramped interior knocking out fresh lobster tacos ($18.95), clam chowder ($7.95), steamed crab (from the Channel Islands; $16.95) and calamari sandwiches ($11.95). Daily 11am–10pm.

Three Pickles 126 E Canon Perdido St ☎ 805 965 1015, ⓦ threepickles.com. Great-value, huge sandwiches, from tuna and hot pastrami to roast beef and turkey ($7.99). They also do salads and soups, plus bags of dill pickles. Reverts to *Lovejoy's Pickle Room* cocktail bar from 4.30pm. Mon–Sat 11am–3.30pm.

★ **Tupelo Junction Cafe** 1218 State St ☎ 805 899 3100, ⓦ tupelojunction.com. A top place for breakfast, featuring Southern-style cooking: mushroom-and-truffle

---

COLD SPRING TAVERN

Tucked away in the hills above Santa Barbara (14 miles northwest from downtown on Hwy-154, near the spectacular San Marcos Pass), the **Cold Spring Tavern** (5995 Stagecoach Rd ☎ 805 967 0066, ⓦ coldspringtavern.com) is an essential California experience, offering fresh regional game in a rustic, lodge-like setting. The restaurant dates all the way back to 1865, when it was established as a stagecoach stop known as the Cold Spring Relay Station. Try to visit at the weekend, when there's live music and tri-tip steak sandwiches cooked on outdoor barbecues (just get there early, as it gets very busy; reservations recommended). Other favourites include venison sausage stuffed mushrooms ($9.50), Cold Spring chilli ($7), venison steak sandwiches ($13.50), barbecue pork ribs ($25) and sautéed duck breast ($27.50). Wash them down with a selection of California microbrews or Santa Ynez Valley wines. The tavern is open Mon–Fri 11am–3pm & 5–9pm, Sat & Sun 8am–3pm & 5–9pm.

SANTA BARBARA'S WINE TRAIL

Around 29 wineries make up the **Santa Barbara Urban Wine Trail** (ⓦurbanwinetrailsb.com), with tasting rooms from local vineyards accessible by foot in the Funk Zone between the beach and US-101. Fees range from $5–15 and typically include tasters of 5–8 wines. Top picks include the Area 5.1 Winery, 137B Anacapa St (Mon–Thurs noon–7pm, Fri–Sun noon–8pm), with its retro Cold War theme and its innovative Syrah/Malbec/Cab blends; Lafond Winery, 111 E Yanonali St (Sun–Thurs 10am–6pm, Fri & Sat 10am–7pm), renowned for its Pinot Noir and Chardonnay; and the Santa Barbara Winery, 202 Anacapa St (Sun–Thurs 10am–6pm, Fri & Sat 10am–7pm), the oldest in the county.

6

scrambles ($15), crabcake and potato hash ($18) and vanilla French toast ($14). Equally fine lunches and dinners are also on offer. Mon 8am–3pm, Tues–Sun 8am–3pm & 5–8pm.

DRINKING AND NIGHTLIFE

There are quite a few bars and clubs along State St, especially downtown, while the **Funk Zone** (the blocks between US-101 and the ocean, east of State St) is sprinkled with raucous bars, cutting-edge galleries and wineries (see box above). For the most up-to-date listings, grab a copy of the free weekly *Santa Barbara Independent* (ⓦindependent.com), which is widely available around town every Thursday.

★**Corks n' Crowns** 32 Anacapa St ❷805 845 8600, ⓦcorksandcrowns.com. Justly popular tasting room in the Funk Zone, where you can sample flights of three wines ($8–20), arranged by theme, plus beer flights (4 craft beers in each) – everything changes monthly. Daily 11am–7pm.

★**Figueroa Mountain Brewing Co** 137 Anacapa St ❷805 694 2252, ⓦfigmtnbrew.com. An enjoyable Funk Zone brewpub where you'll find around 22 rotating speciality and cask beers – usually including the Hoppy Poppy IPA, Stearns Irish Stout and Paradise Road Pilsner – served at indoor and outdoor seating. Mon–Thurs & Sun 11am–11pm, Fri & Sat 11am–midnight.

Santa Barbara Brewing Co 501 State St ❷805 730 1040, ⓦsbbrewco.com. Serviceable American pub grub – burgers, sandwiches, seafood – accompanies solid handcrafted beers at this popular watering hole. The Rincon Red Ale and State Street Stout are both worth a swig. Mon–Wed 11.30am–11.30pm, Thurs & Fri 11.30am–midnight, Sat 11am–1am, Sun 11am–11.30pm.

SOhO 1221 State St (upstairs in Victoria Court) ❷805 962 7776, ⓦsohosb.com. The best place for eclectic live shows, with blues, funk, rock or reggae bands performing on any given night (tickets $8–25); the occasional big jazz name even comes through from time to time. Also a restaurant serving Californian cuisine. Mon–Thurs & Sun 6.30–11pm, Fri 5pm–2am, Sat 6.30pm–2am.

Velvet Jones 423 State St ❷805 965 8676, ⓦvelvet-jones.com. This veteran local venue is a good place to catch an indie show; reggae and hip-hop acts also appear regularly. Most shows $5–22. Wed–Sat 8pm–2am.

Wildcat Lounge 15 W Ortega St ❷805 962 7970, ⓦwildcatlounge.com. Santa Barbara's main hotspot for dancing, as well as catching electronica DJs and various bands. The chic atmosphere brings in a mix of locals, students and out-of-towners. The *Wildcat* is apparently referenced in a Katy Perry song ("This Is How We Do") – Perry grew up in Santa Barbara and used to hang out here. Cover $5–10. Daily 4pm–2am.

ENTERTAINMENT

Arlington Theatre 1317 State St ❷805 963 4408, ⓦthearlingtontheatre.com. This landmark 1931 theatre is an intact and functional movie palace and performance venue, with a trompe l'oeil interior modelled after an atmospheric Spanish village plaza.

Granada Theatre 1214 State St ❷805 899 2222, ⓦgranadasb.org. The home of the modest, but respected Santa Barbara Symphony (Oct–May; tickets $35–80;

❷805 898 9386, ⓦthesymphony.org), this circa-1924 Moorish-flavoured venue has been gloriously renovated to serve as the town's primary performing arts centre.

Santa Barbara Bowl 1122 N Milpas St ❷805 962 7411, ⓦsbbowl.com. This 4562-seat amphitheatre is the city's premier venue for outdoor concerts (April–Oct), built in a picturesque canyon 1.5 miles northwest of State St in 1936, as a WPA project.

DIRECTORY

Santa Barbara Public Library Internet access at 40 E Anapamu St (Mon–Thurs 10am–7pm, Fri & Sat 10am–5.30pm, Sun 1–5pm; ❷805 962 7653).

Post office 1221 State St, inside Victoria Court (Mon–Fri 10am–5pm).

6

SANTA BARBARA FESTIVALS

Santa Barbara's biggest annual party, the week-long **Old Spanish Days Fiesta** (held every August) was actually started as a tourist attraction in 1924. Today it features parades, traditional Spanish dancing and musical performances, a horse show and rodeo (𝕨oldspanishdays-fiesta .org). It's not the city's only major festival. Santa Barbara's annual **Summer Solstice Celebration** (held over three days around June 21) features a colourful parade that draws up to 100,000 people (𝕨solsticeparade.com), while the **Santa Barbara International Film Festival** (sbiff.org) is held over eleven days (usually February) in the historic Riviera Theatre, 2044 Alameda Padre Serra.

Coastal Santa Barbara

Heading further along the Central Coast from the city of Santa Barbara and into **western Santa Barbara County**, you can either cut inland on Hwy-154 through Santa Ynez Valley (see below) or continue along US-101's **coastal route**, where several prime beaches beckon during the first 25 miles. First is **Goleta Beach** – popular with families – near the grubby town of **Isla Vista**, which itself borders the **University of California, Santa Barbara** campus. Isla Vista Beach has some good tide pools and, at its west end, a popular surfing area at **Coal Oil Point** ("Devereux Beach" to locals), named after natural tar deposits that seep through its sand.

Almost twenty miles outside Santa Barbara, **El Capitán State Beach** ($10/vehicle; ☏805 968 1033, 𝕨parks.ca.gov) is a popular surfing spot, with some tide pools as well. **Refugio State Beach** ($10/vehicle; ☏805 968 1033, 𝕨parks.ca.gov), another three miles along US-101, is one of the prettiest in California – palm trees dotting the sands next to a small creek lend it a tropical feel. Windswept **Gaviota State Park**'s beach ($10/ vehicle; ☏805 968 1033, 𝕨parks.ca.gov) isn't as pretty as that at Refugio thirteen miles east, but there's a fishing pier and a large wooden railway viaduct that bridges the mouth of the canyon. Also in the park is tiny **Las Cruces hot spring** (aka Gaviota Hot Springs), a pool of 100°F mineral water set in a shady, peaceful ravine. To get there, take the exit for Hwy-1 (Lompoc/Vandenberg AFB) off US-101, but turn immediately right off the ramp onto a small road, continuing a quarter of a mile to the parking area at the end. Walk about three-quarters of a mile up the trail (signposted) and look for the murky pools – the soothing water feels far better than it looks.

Santa Ynez Valley

An alternative to US-101's coastal route out of Santa Barbara is Hwy-154, which climbs steeply over **San Marcos Pass** and drops into **Santa Ynez Valley**. It's a pleasant route through an increasingly respected **wine-growing region** (see box, p.368) – popularized by 2004 movie *Sideways* – that culminates in the Danish town of **Solvang**.

Chumash Painted Cave State Historic Park

Painted Caves Rd • Open access • Free • ☏ 805 733 3713, 𝕨 parks.ca.gov

Over one thousand years ago, Native American artists adorned the walls of **Chumash Painted Cave State Historic Park** with vivid ochre and red pictographs. You can't actually enter the sandstone cave – it's been closed off to protect against vandalism – but peering in will still give you a good look, offering a perspective of the natives' view of supernatural forces and the afterlife. The cave is awkward to get to: it lies around three miles along the windy, single-lane Painted Caves Road off Hwy-154 ("Painted Caves Rd" is signposted, but the cave is not). The route up offers sensational views along the coast, but there's only a small sign when you reach the cave – and very little space to park your car by the side of the road.

Solvang

Although anyone that has actually been to Denmark will be bewildered by the faux windmills and kitsch stores that fill **SOLVANG** ("sunny fields" in Danish), people come by the busload to visit the community, which was at least established in 1911 by genuine Danish teachers from the Midwest looking for a place to found a Danish folk school. In 1947 the town was "discovered" by the US media and today, about three miles east of US-101 on Hwy-246, it exists as a sort of Scandinavian fantasyland, though the restaurants and especially its five historic **bakeries** (still operated by Danish-Americans) knock out tasty treats. Wandering its colourful streets can be a welcome break from all things Spanish Revival (though there is also a mission here). Hwy-246 becomes **Mission Drive** in town, with **Copenhagen Drive** running parallel to the south lined with shops and restaurants and plenty of parking (free).

6

Copenhagen House, 1660 Copenhagen Drive (Mon–Fri 10am–5pm, Sat & Sun 10am–6pm; ⓦthecopenhagenhouse.com) serves as a designer showroom for Danish brands, and contains the free Amber Museum and whimsical Great Hall of the Danes Viking exhibit. The **Hans Christian Andersen Museum**, upstairs at 1680 Mission Drive (daily 10am–5pm; free; ☎805 688 2052, ⓦsolvangca.com/museum/h1.htm) can be fun for kids, with displays on the Danish writer's life and works such as *Thumbelina* and *The Ugly Duckling*.

Elverhøj Museum of History & Art

1624 Elverhoy Way • Wed–Sun 11am–4pm • Suggested donation $5 • ☎805 686 1211, ⓦ elverhoj.org

One of the town's more serious museums, the **Elverhøj Museum of History & Art** features displays on Danish culture and the Danish-American experience, including the obligatory Viking galleries but also a room dedicated to the history of Solvang. The museum occupies the former home of artists Viggo Brandt-Erichsen and his wife, Martha Mott, built in the style of an eighteenth-century Danish farmhouse.

Mission Santa Inés

1760 Mission Drive (Hwy-246) • Daily 9am–4.30pm • $5 • ☎805 688 4815, ⓦ missionsantaines.org

On the eastern edge of Solvang, humble **Mission Santa Inés** was established in 1804, and though the structure has undergone numerous restorations, the key adobe buildings are original – the trompe l'oeil green-marble trim on the church's interior walls is one of the best surviving examples of mission-era folk art. Generally far less busy than Santa Barbara's mission, the dimly lit, atmospheric interior with its simple wood ceiling seems far older; look out for two rare eighteenth-century paintings believed to be from Mexico. You enter the mission through the gift shop and a slightly old-fashioned museum of religious art and vestments, and can also tour the beautifully maintained gardens and cemetery. This is another active place of worship, with the church barred to visitors during services.

INFORMATION   SOLVANG

Visitors Bureau 1639 Copenhagen Drive (☎805 688 6144, ⓦ solvangusa.com).

ACCOMMODATION

Note that the "windmill" motel featured in the movie *Sideways* is now the *Sideways Inn*, just off US-101, 3.5 miles west of Solvang (it really looks like a windmill). Paul Giamatti staggers down to the *Hitching Post II* on Hwy-246 to sample the wine, where Maya (Virginia Madsen) waits tables.

King Frederik Inn 1617 Copenhagen Drive, ☎800 549 9955, ⓦ kingfrederikinn.com. Offering some of Solvang's most affordable accommodation, this is a clunky, ultra-basic "Old World" property with standard motel units, pool, hot tub and continental breakfast. **$149**

The Landsby 1576 Mission Drive ☎805 688 3121, ⓦ thelandsby.com. Rooms at this elegant boutique feature a clean, contemporary Scandinavian design (think upscale Ikea), with blonde woods and brushed brass accents enhanced with local artwork. **$169**

6

WINERIES OF THE SANTA YNEZ VALLEY

Wine aficionados shouldn't miss a visit to Santa Barbara County's plenteous vineyards, many of which are situated in **Santa Ynez Valley**, northwest of the city of Santa Barbara. Although it's not exactly Bordeaux (or even Napa Valley), the area does offer plenty of wineries with the requisite tastings and merchandise for sale. Get more information by contacting the **Santa Barbara County Vintners' Association** (☎ 805 688 0881, ⓦ sbcountywines.com) or by visiting WineCountry.com (ⓦ santabarbara.winecountry.com).

Cloud Climbers By reservation only on ☎ 805 646 3200, ⓦ ccjeeps.com. True oenophiles may enjoy a more extensive trip courtesy of this local tour company, which for $139 will take you on a six-hour jeep tour of local wineries, with lunch and tasting fees for four included.

EATING AND DRINKING

★**Bacon & Brine** 1618 Copenhagen Drive ☎ 805 688 8809, ⓦ baconandbrine.com. Flagship for celebrity chef Pink (aka Crystal DeLongpre) and her wife, Courtney Rae, featuring local organic and artisanal sandwiches for lunch (from $11.25), plus a refined dinner menu that might include rabbit confit ($26), hand-rolled pasta with mother hen sauce ($19) and whisky bread pudding ($8). Mon–Thurs & Sun 11am–3pm & 5–9pm, Fri & Sat 11am–3pm & 5–10pm.

Paula's Pancake House 1531 Mission Drive ☎ 805 688 2867, ⓦ paulaspancakehouse.com. Reliable and affordable breakfast choice for its Danish apple pancakes ($8–9); other winners on the menu include omelettes and Belgian-style waffles. Daily 6am–3pm.

Pea Soup Andersen's Restaurant 376 Avenue of the Flags, Hwy-246, Buellton (3.5 miles from Solvang) ☎ 805 688 5581. It may be inundated with travellers – its billboards are plastered along US-101 for miles – but this long-popular roadside inn and diner remains a solid, inexpensive choice for garden salads, fried ham and cheese Monte Cristo sandwiches and the namesake vegetarian soup. Daily 7am–10pm.

Solvang Bakery 438 Alisal Rd ☎ 805 688 4939, ⓦ solvangbakery.com. Traditional Danish bakery run by the Halme family, best known for their magnificent gingerbread houses, though the usual array of tasty Danish pastries, butter cookies and cupcakes is also on offer. Mon–Thurs & Sun 7am–6.30pm, Fri & Sat 7am–8pm.

Solvang Brewing Co 1547 Mission Drive ☎ 805 688 2337, ⓦ solvangbrewing.com. Even Solvang has its own microbrewery (this is California after all), though the food menu is Danish-inspired. Try the Great Dane Pale Ale or Odin's Stout. Party central, especially at the weekends. Daily 11am–2am.

Solvang Restaurant 1672 Copenhagen Drive ☎ 805 688 4645, ⓦ solvangrestaurant.com. Another *Sideways* location famed for Arne's "famous" *aebleskiver*, traditional pancake balls drizzled with powdered sugar and raspberry sauce. Have a seat in a hand-carved wooden booth, or order a few from the takeaway window ($3.85 for three). Mon–Fri 6am–3pm (4pm summer), Sat & Sun 6am–5pm.

La Purísima Mission State Historic Park

2295 Purísima Rd • Daily 9am–5pm; visitor centre Mon 11am–3pm, Tues–Sun 10am–4pm • $6/vehicle • ☎ 805 733 3713, ⓦ lapurisimamission.org

Some eighteen miles northwest of Solvang and signposted off Hwy-246, **La Purísima Mission State Historic Park** is the most complete and authentic reconstruction of any of the 21 Spanish missions in California, and one of the best places to get an idea of what life was like in these early settlements. La Misión la Purísima Concepción de Maria Santísima was founded in 1787 on a site three miles north of here, and by 1804 had converted around 1500 Chumash, one-third of whom died in a smallpox epidemic over the next two years. In 1812, an earthquake destroyed all the buildings (the site is preserved today as **Mission Vieja**), and the Franciscan fathers decided to move to the present site. The new design was the only mission in the chain to be built in a linear fashion rather than a defensive quadrangle, normally used to both confine Native Americans and keep others out – an especially important detail as the number of able-bodied residents had been slashed by the epidemic. The complex did not last long, however, after the missions were secularized in 1834; like all the rest, it was soon abandoned and gradually fell into disrepair. The buildings that stand here today were rebuilt on the ruins of the mission as part of a Depression-era work project between 1933 and 1940.

The heart of the mission is a narrow church, decorated as it would have been in the 1820s. On display in the nearby old wagon-house are small but engaging presentations of documents and artefacts from the mission era, as well as photographs of the mission's reconstruction; the **visitor centre** also contains a host of intriguing exhibits.

Pismo Beach and around

Roughly twenty miles up US-101 from the humdrum commercial centre of Santa Maria, you enter the domain of the so-called Five Cities, of which **PISMO BEACH** is by far the most desirable for visitors. It's here in the self-proclaimed "Clam Capital of the World" that Hwy-1 reconnects with US-101 for a dozen miles on its inland approach to San Luis Obispo (see p.371). As you continue northbound from Pismo Beach, you can follow the Avila Road exit to the area's last outpost of Southern California-style beach life, **Avila Beach**, where the party atmosphere continues all summer long despite the looming presence of the nuclear Diablo Canyon Power Plant straddling an earthquake fault a mere six miles up the coast.

Downtown and Pismo State Beach

Most of Pismo Beach's commercial activity churns near where Pomeroy Avenue crosses Hwy-1 (Cabrillo Hwy). If you have no interest in pursuing any watersports during your visit, you can still walk out on the 1200-foot **Pismo Beach Pier** for overhead views of surfers riding the waves. The sandy city beach stretches north and south from here, merging into the more pristine **Pismo State Beach** ($10/vehicle; ☎805 473 7220, ⓦparks.ca.gov) three miles south next to the town of **Oceano**. This is a good place to see the black-and-orange **monarch butterflies** that spend the winter (Nov–Feb) here in eucalyptus trees within their own designated grove; for more information, visit ⓦmonarchbutterfly.org. However, the once-plentiful **Pismo clam** that gave the town its name (from the Chumash word *pismu*, or "blobs of tar" that the shells resemble) have been so depleted that any you might dig up nowadays are probably under the 4.5-inch legal minimum size.

The lower end of the beach, south of Grand Avenue, is open to off-road vehicle enthusiasts, who tear over the sandpiles at **Oceano Dunes State Vehicular Recreation Area** (daily 6am–11pm; $5/vehicle; ☎805 473 7220) in dune buggies and four-wheel drives, motoring along the beach to reach them. This is California's only **drive-on beach**, with another portion of the dunes protected as the **Pismo Dunes Natural Preserve**.

Guadalupe-Nipomo Dunes National Wildlife Refuge

Guadalupe-Nipomo Dunes National Wildlife Refuge Oct–Feb dawn–dusk • Free • ☎ 805 343 9151, ⓦ fws.gov **Guadalupe-Nipomo Dunes Center** 1065 Guadalupe St, Guadalupe • Wed–Sun 10am–4pm • $5 • ☎ 805 343 2455, ⓦ dunescenter.org

A few miles south of Pismo State Beach, the continuing piles of sand dunes are protected within the **Guadalupe-Nipomo Dunes National Wildlife Refuge**, where you can look for whales out at sea, or climb 550-foot peaks. The tallest found along the California coast, these dunes are adjacent to wetlands that act as habitat for endangered sea birds. You can access the dunes at two places; hiking in from the Oceano Dunes SVRA (accessed along Oso Flaco Lake Rd, three miles off Hwy-1), a 4.5 mile round-trip hike; or from the **Rancho Guadalupe Dunes Preserve** parking lot, at the end of Main Street (Hwy-166, 2.8 miles off Hwy-1). A donation is asked for at the gate, from which it's another two miles west to the parking lot, and four-mile round-trip hike to the wildlife refuge (across the Santa Maria River). Access to the refuge is closed during plover breeding season (March–Sept).

Bizarrely, buried within these dunes is much of the movie set for Cecil B. DeMille's original 1924 silent epic, *The Ten Commandments* (later remade with Charlton Heston), when the sands stood in for ancient Egypt in the director's monumental re-creation of "The City of Pharaoh". Disinterred relics from the set, which was buried instead of taken apart to save money, are on view in the **Dunes Center** in the nearby small town of **Guadalupe** (15 miles south of Pismo Beach on Hwy-1), where Spanish signs and advertisements far outnumber those in English, and ramshackle saloons, cafés and vegetable stalls line the dusty streets.

Dinosaur Caves Park

2701 Price St (off US-101) • Dawn–dusk • Free • ☎ 805 773 4657, ⓦ pismobeach.org

Around two miles north of Pismo Beach you'll come to the redoubtable **Dinosaur Caves Park**, where craggy sea stacks dot the landscape and poke out in the waves, their various caves, coves, arches and passages making for a geologist's and kayaker's delight. All kinds of rock, from mica to serpentine, are mashed together in this dramatic, mottled seascape, with the best views available by paddling out into the protected inlet. Don't get your hopes up for seeing extinct reptiles, however – the place was named for a short-lived tourist attraction that took the form of a concrete dinosaur.

INFORMATION   PISMO BEACH

Visitor Information Center 581 Dolliver St (Hwy-1) at Hinds Ave (Mon–Fri 9am–5pm, Sat 11am–4pm, Sun 10am–2pm; ☎ 805 773 7034, ⓦ classiccalifornia.com).

Alternatively, visit the kiosk on Pismo Beach Pier (summer daily 10am–5pm; rest of year Fri–Sun 10am–5pm).

ACTIVITIES

Bicycling Head downtown to Beach Cycle Rentals, 519 Cypress St (☎ 805 773 5518, ⓦ piersidesurfco.com), for reasonably priced rentals of a range of bikes by the hour (from $8) or longer.

Clamming Before you set out on your mollusc-digging adventure, you'll need to familiarize yourself with current regulations and also procure a state fishing licence from the California Department of Fish and Game (☎ 916 928 6882, ⓦ dfg.ca.gov); a one-day licence costs $15.12.

Dune-riding To experience the thrill of careening over the

sandpiles at Oceano Dunes, go to Sun Buggy & ATV, 328 Pier Ave in Oceano (☎ 866 728 4443, ⓦ sunbuggy.com/pismo), which rents all manner of dune buggies and all-terrain vehicles. A two-seat dune buggy goes for $225/2hr; a four-seater, $348, but there are cheaper ATVs available (from $45/2hr).

Kayaking To best explore nearby Dinosaur Caves Park, rent a kayak from Central Coast Kayaks, 1879 Shell Beach Rd (☎ 805 773 3500, ⓦ centralcoastkayaks.com). Solo kayaks cost $20/hr; tandems are $25/hr.

ACCOMMODATION

Kon Tiki Inn 1621 Price St ☎ 805 773 4833, ⓦ kontikiinn.com. Right on the beach, featuring a health club, decent restaurant and pool to go with its comfy, motel-style rooms, many featuring balconies and sea views. $185

North Beach and Oceano campgrounds ☎ 800 444 7275, ⓦ reserveamerica.com. This pair of beach-adjacent campgrounds, both located at Pismo State Beach, are often

booked solid throughout summer, but can be fairly mellow during other seasons. $35

Sea Gypsy 1020 Cypress St ☎ 805 773 1801, ⓦ seagypsymotel.com. All standard rooms, studios and two-room/two-bath suites at the beachfront here are decked out in clean, modern decor. Many units feature a full kitchen, while some come with balcony – sea views are more expensive ($115–308). Doubles $98, suites $308

EATING

★**Cracked Crab** 751 Price St ☎ 805 773 2722, ⓦ crackedcrab.com. People have driven great distances for the clam chowder here (bowls $9), but this popular restaurant also serves excellent shrimp and fish meals. Expect a one-pound crab dinner (served with vegetables, basmati rice and warm sourdough rolls) to cost $38–54.

Mon–Thurs & Sun 11am–9pm, Fri & Sat 11am–10pm.

Rosa's 491 Price St ☎ 805 773 0551, ⓦ rosasrestaurant.com. Cheery and bright, family-operated Italian diner that serves up hearty pasta ($13.45–16.95), pizza ($13.45) and seafood dishes ($17–18.50). Mon–Fri 11.30am–2pm & 4–9.30pm, Sat & Sun 4–9.30pm.

SANTA MARIA-STYLE BARBECUE

One of the largest cities on the coast, **Santa Maria** is a fairly uninspiring commercial centre of endless strip malls and highways, twenty miles southeast of Pismo Beach on US-101, but it does have one, fairly major, redeeming quality. The **barbecue style** here has garnered praise from culinary critics and Hollywood starlets alike (Zac Efron among them), thanks to local methods (cooked over local red oak), quality **"Tri-Tip" beef** (a triangular cut below the sirloin), special seasoning (salt, pepper and garlic salt) and the garnish of local pinquito beans. The style has its roots in the no-frills Spanish ranchero cookouts of the nineteenth century, though today it's fashionable to pair meats with local wines and fresh strawberries. Local hotspots include the *Garden Room Restaurant* at the *Santa Maria Inn* (801 S Broadway), and *Shaw's Steak House* (714 S Broadway); visit ⓦsantamariavalleyBBQ.com or ⓦsantamariavisitor.com for more tips.

6

Avila Beach

North of Pismo Beach, the coastline becomes more rugged, with caves and tide pools lurking below ever-eroding bluffs, and sea lions frolicking (or simply lazing) in the many coves. The three-mile-long strand in front of the summer resort town of **AVILA BEACH** is finally recovering from a devastating ecological disaster caused by a 1990s spill from a nearby oil refinery. The ambitious clean-up and reconstruction project that began soon after the spill has helped restore much of the area to its original state, including the 1,685ft-long **Avila Beach Pier** (where you can spot grey and humpback whales).

ACCOMMODATION   AVILA BEACH

Avila Lighthouse Suites 550 Front St ☎805 627 1900, ⓦavilalighthousesuites.com. This swanky property right on the coast has ocean-view apartments that variously come equipped with fireplaces and kitchens. **$299**

Inn at Avila Beach 256 Front St ☎805 595 2300, ⓦavilabeachca.com. This charming inn wears its faded beachfront style well, and its nightly rates are among the best you'll find in the area in high season. **$169**

EATING AND DRINKING

Olde Port Inn 3993 Avila Beach Drive (Harford Pier) ☎805 595 2515, ⓦoldeportinn.com. Dramatically perched at the end of Harford Pier in Port San Luis, this is Avila Beach's choice (if priciest) spot to eat. Naturally, the menu primarily consists of seafood, so try the fish tacos (two for $18) for lunch or the spicy *cioppino* stew ($35) for dinner. Summer daily 11.30am–9pm; rest of year Mon–Fri 5–9pm, Sat & Sun 11.30am–9pm.

San Luis Obispo

The inviting community of **SAN LUIS OBISPO** (locally, "SLO") is an underappreciated gem – part agricultural, part collegiate and a pleasant place to dawdle and browse. The town boasts well-preserved architecture, from turreted Victorian residences along Buchon Street, south of the town centre, to the Art Deco **Fremont Theater** on Monterey Street, with its distinctive "fin". There are a number of good places to eat, some decent pubs and clubs, and – summer weekends notwithstanding – affordable accommodation, all set amid a vibrant community energized by **Cal Poly** San Luis Obispo's twenty thousand students.

Mission San Luis Obispo de Tolosa

751 Palm St • Daily: early March to early Nov 9am–5pm; early Nov to early March 9am–4pm • Free • ☎805 543 6850, ⓦmissionsanluisobispo.org

San Luis Obispo's eminently walkable core is built around the **Mission San Luis Obispo de Tolosa**, founded in 1772 by Father Serra himself. A fairly plain but large, L-shaped church, it was the fifth structure in California's mission trail and the prototype for the now-ubiquitous red-tiled roof – developed as a replacement for the original, flammable thatch, which caught fire here in 1776 during an attack by Native Americans. The current structure dates back to 1793, though it's been renovated many times and the murals inside are mostly a 2002 addition. The mission **museum**, located in the padre's adobe living quarters, contains an exceptional collection of Chumash artefacts, ranging from arrowheads to stone tools and necklaces, plus fascinating old photos, an ornate Visalia saddle and even a few objects left by nineteenth-century Chinese migrants. Wander through the garden to find a native Chumash oven and grapevines of the sort used in the production of some of California's earliest wines.

Mission Plaza

From Mission San Luis Obispo de Tolosa, **Mission Plaza**'s terraces step down along **San Luis Obispo Creek** – a leafy, restful spot adorned with endemic California trees and plants, crisscrossed by footpaths and bridges. The plaza is overlooked by a number of stores and outdoor restaurants on the south bank, and makes for a delightful place to dawdle.

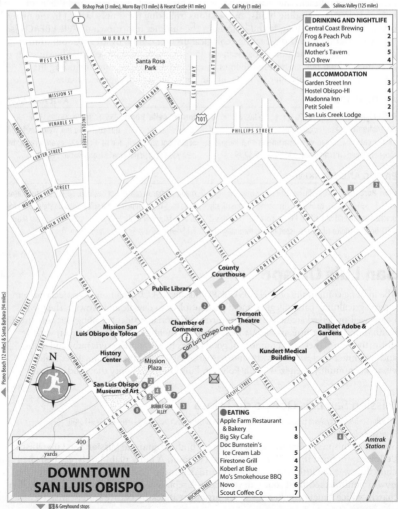

DOWNTOWN
SAN LUIS OBISPO

Bishop Peak (3 miles), Morro Bay (13 miles) & Hearst Castle (41 miles) — Cal Poly (1 mile) — Salinas Valley (125 miles)

Pismo Beach (12 miles) & Santa Barbara (94 miles)

& Greyhound stops

DRINKING AND NIGHTLIFE

Central Coast Brewing	1
Frog & Peach Pub	2
Linnaea's	3
Mother's Tavern	5
SLO Brew	4

ACCOMMODATION

Garden Street Inn	3
Hostel Obispo-HI	4
Madonna Inn	5
Petit Soleil	2
San Luis Creek Lodge	1

EATING

Apple Farm Restaurant & Bakery	1
Big Sky Cafe	8
Doc Burnstein's Ice Cream Lab	5
Firestone Grill	4
Koberl at Blue	2
Mo's Smokehouse BBQ	3
Novo	6
Scout Coffee Co	7

THE WORLD'S FIRST MOTEL

The Milestone Mo-Tel opened in San Luis Obispo in 1925 at 2223 Monterey St, was designed to take advantage of growing car ownership among Americans. Initially, enthusiastic Model T drivers had used automobile "campgrounds" for overnight stays, pitching tents alongside their cars, and since San Luis Obispo is about halfway between San Francisco and Los Angeles, it became an especially popular choice for overnight stops. Savvy architect **Arthur Heineman** recognized the potential of adapting the bungalow concept for the travel industry, combining the convenience of a campground with the comfort and respectability (not to mention higher prices) of a hotel – a "motor hotel" which, because those words couldn't fit onto the sign, became a "mo-tel".

Heineman and his brother Alfred opened the first motel in the auto nexus of San Luis Obispo, but envisioned a chain stretching from San Diego to Seattle, each one-day's journey from the next. Unfortunately, only one motel was built, and Heineman didn't even manage to copyright the word he'd coined. It entered the dictionary in 1950, long after hundreds of copycats had sprung up across America.

The *Milestone*, later the *Motel Inn*, closed in 1991 and it's been almost completely demolished – the original "Motel Inn" sign remains, for now, as does the old mission-style lobby building; the site is being developed into a **new 55-room hotel and RV park** that should be open by 2017.

Higuera Street

San Luis Obispo's main drag, **Higuera Street** (pronounced "hee-GEHR-ah"), a block south of Mission Plaza, springs to life for the town's weekly **Farmers' Market** (Thurs 5–9pm; free), when it's closed to cars and filled with food booths and musicians. Less appetizing – but just as interesting to some – is **Bubble Gum Alley**, a narrow passage off Higuera Street near its intersection with Broad Street, where the walls are slathered in chewed pieces of the alley's namesake elastic candy, some well over fifty years old.

San Luis Obispo Museum of Art

1010 Broad St • Mon & Wed–Sun 11am–5pm • Free • ☎ 805 543 8562, ⓦ sloma.org

The small but thoughtfully curated **San Luis Obispo Museum of Art** focuses on contemporary, living California artists, with mostly rotating exhibits that feature painting, sculpture, printmaking and photography; artists such as Lisa Occhipinti and Carol Goldmark have been showcased here.

Dallidet Adobe & Gardens

1185 Pacific St • March–Oct Fri 10am–4pm, Sun 1–4pm • Donation requested • ☎ 805 543 0638

At the end of Pacific Street stands the **Dallidet Adobe & Gardens**, one of San Luis Obispo County's oldest buildings. Constructed in 1856 by a disillusioned French forty-niner who, eluded by fortune in the Mother Lode, ended up living in town, it's set among manicured grounds with two redwoods over 125ft tall.

Bishop Peak

If you fancy a hike, you can head up 1546ft **Bishop Peak**, which looms over San Luis Obispo to the northwest and is the tallest point among a chain of peaks known as the Morros. Two paths, Bishop Peak Trail (4 miles; 1200ft ascent) and Felsman Loop (3 miles; 700ft ascent), wind through grassland and oak woodland up and around the mountain's rocky slopes, and are accessible via both Patricia Drive Trailhead and Highland Drive Trailhead. Visit ⓦ santalucia.sierraclub.org for trailhead directions and further details.

ARRIVAL AND DEPARTURE   **SAN LUIS OBISPO**

By train Amtrak trains stop several times each day at 1011 Railroad Ave, at the end of Santa Rosa St, one-half mile south of the town centre. This is the northern terminus of the *Pacific Surfliner* route, from which you can transfer to

6

LLOYD WRIGHT IN SAN LUIS

You might not expect to find work by celebrated architect **Frank Lloyd Wright** in this quiet corner of California, but the **Kundert Medical Building**, 1106 Pacific St, was constructed here in 1956, right at the end Wright's long and productive career. It's still a doctor's surgery (no admittance except for patients), at the intersection of Santa Rosa and Pacific, but you can get a good look from the outside; it resembles a truncated chunk of Wright's much earlier Robie House in Chicago, with oddball window cut-outs set amid the red-brick design.

Coast Starlight trains covering the entire coast.
Destinations Los Angeles (3 daily; 5hr 20min–5hr 40min); Oakland (1 daily; 5hr 50min) and connecting to San Francisco via shuttle bus; San Jose (1 daily; 4hr 35min); Santa Barbara (3 daily; 2hr 35min).

INFORMATION AND GETTING AROUND

Visitor Center Collect a free walking-tour map highlighting much of San Luis Obispo's best architecture from the visitor centre at 895 Monterey St (Mon–Wed & Sun 10am–5pm, Thurs–Sat 10am–7pm; ☎805 781 2777, ⓦ visitslo.com).
Listings To find out what's on and where, pick up the free weekly *New Times* (ⓦ newtimesslo.com) or the entertainment section of the daily *San Luis Obispo Tribune* (ⓦ sanluisobispo.com).
By bus You can get around town for $1.25 on the local transit system, SLO Transit (☎805 541 2877, ⓦ slocity.org), or the wider-ranging Regional Transit Authority ($1.50–3; ☎805 781 4472, ⓦ slorta.org), which links to Morro Bay and Pismo Beach, among other nearby destinations.

ACCOMMODATION

Garden Street Inn 1212 Garden St ☎805 545 9802, ⓦ gardenstreetinn.com. This very central B&B is in a restored c.1887 Victorian home and features comfortable, mildly themed rooms and suites (Emerald Isle, Walden, etc). There's complimentary wine on arrival and gourmet cooked breakfasts. **$169**
Hostel Obispo-HI 1617 Santa Rosa St ☎805 544 4678, ⓦ hostelobispo.com. A tidy, comfortable hostel set about one block from the train station. There's a lounge and patio, as well as bike rentals and pancake breakfasts. Dorms **$34**, doubles **$65**
Madonna Inn 100 Madonna Rd ☎805 543 3000, ⓦ madonnainn.com. The raft of standard "theme" rooms, cottages and suites – from fairy-tale cute to Stone Age caveman – at this kitsch monstrosity can come as a disappointment to some, and its imposingly shocking-pink, chalet-style lobby may be enough to satiate your curiosity. Still, it's an essential landmark for many visitors. **$205**
★**Petit Soleil** 1473 Monterey St ☎805 549 0321, ⓦ petitsoleilslo.com. This very stylish French-themed B&B offers modern decor in each uniquely designed room; there's also an even more elegant "Joie de Vivre" suite, and exceptionally tasty continental breakfasts. **$179**
San Luis Creek Lodge 1941 Monterey St ☎800 593 0333, ⓦ sanluiscreeklodge.com. With 25 pleasant rooms spread across three buildings – each in a vaguely Greek Revival, Tudor or Craftsman style – this centrally located inn is a smart option. Some units have fireplaces, jacuzzis or balconies, and breakfast is included. **$189**

EATING

Apple Farm Restaurant & Bakery 2015 Monterey St ☎805 544 6100, ⓦ applefarm.com/dining. Set inside the *Apple Farm Inn* on the edge of town, this casual, family-style restaurant serves traditional American dishes, straight-up breakfasts of pancakes ($9–10) and French toast ($10.50), plus pies galore (including the classic apple; slices from $6). Daily 7am–9pm.
★**Big Sky Cafe** 1121 Broad St ☎805 545 5401, ⓦ bigskycafe.com. This airy, modern spot cooks with an emphasis on both vegetarian fare and seafood. It's popular for items such as *pozole* stew ($11.25) and ginger noodles ($8.25), as well as carnivore-friendly choices such as braised lamb shank ($19.25) and reuben sandwiches ($14.95). Mon–Thurs 7am–9pm, Fri 7am–10pm, Sat 8am–10pm, Sun 8am–9pm.
★**Doc Burnstein's Ice Cream Lab** 860 Higuera St ☎805 548 1986, ⓦ docburnsteins.com. Mini-chain offering just about every kind of ice-cream flavour you can imagine, from key lime pie and mint fudge oreo to merlot raspberry truffle and vanilla chai. Summer Mon–Wed & Sun 11am–10pm, Thurs–Sat 11am–11pm; rest of year Mon–Wed & Sun noon–9pm, Thurs–Sat noon–10pm
Firestone Grill 1001 Higuera St ☎805 783 1001, ⓦ firestonegrill.com. Family-oriented restaurant, also popular with Cal Poly students, for its fun outdoor patio, sports TVs and food, especially its famous tri-tip sandwich ($9.25) and other barbecue items (rack of ribs $21.99). Mon–Wed & Sun 11am–10pm, Thurs–Sat 11am–11pm.

Koberl at Blue 998 Monterey St ☏ 805 783 1135, ⓦ epkoberl.com. Swanky destination in an 1890s landmark with bare brick walls, dark wood fixtures and a dressier crowd than most spots in town. Graze on snacks in the lounge or, in the restaurant, opt for dinner portions of coriander scallops ($30), strip steak ($36) or rack of lamb ($39). Daily 4–10pm (bar open until midnight Mon–Wed & Sun, 2am Thurs–Sat).

Mo's Smokehouse BBQ 1005 Monterey St ☏ 805 544 6193, ⓦ mosbbq.com. Go for the tender pulled pork or ribs ($22.95) at this moderately priced joint, and pair your wonderfully roasted meat with a side of beans, slaw or fried green tomatoes. Mon–Wed 11am–9pm, Thurs–Sat 11am–10pm.

Novo 726 Higuera St ☏ 805 543 3986, ⓦ novo restaurant.com. With a rear dining patio that backs up onto San Luis Creek, *Novo* specializes in affordable fusion dining that is incredibly popular (make reservations in advance): international dishes, from grilled lamb kefta ($17) to Thai red vegetable curry ($18), are mixed and matched with aplomb. Mon–Sat 11am–9.30pm, Sun 10am–2pm & 5–9.30pm.

★ **Scout Coffee Co** 1130 Garden St ☏ 805 439 2175, ⓦ scoutcoffeeco.com. Small family-owned joint selling exceptional espresso and other coffee drinks (sourced from sister company HoneyCo Coffee Roasters) in modern, stylish premises, plus pastries and light snacks. Daily 6.30am–8.30pm.

6

DRINKING AND NIGHTLIFE

★ **Central Coast Brewing** 1422 Monterey St ☏ 805 783 2739, ⓦ centralcoastbrewing.com. One of the region's most popular microbreweries is an essential pit stop for craft beer lovers; try the Cervantez amber lager, or the tasty Facilitator IPA. Mon–Fri noon–9pm, Sat & Sun 11am–9pm.

Frog & Peach Pub 728 Higuera St ☏ 805 595 3764, ⓦ frogandpeachpub.com. This popular tavern is great for cheap drinks and a lively atmosphere, and there's live music nightly across a broad range of genres. Occasional door charge on the weekends ($5–10). Daily noon–2am.

Linnaea's 1110 Garden St ☏ 805 541 5888, ⓦ linnaeas .com. San Luis Obispo's original coffee bar serves good espresso and regularly offers live music – from indie rock to

folk to piano blues – on its small stage. Free, but donations to performers appreciated. Mon–Wed 6.30am–10pm, Thurs & Fri 6.30am–11pm, Sat 7am–11pm, Sun 7am–10pm.

Mother's Tavern 725 Higuera St ☏ 805 541 8733, ⓦ motherstavern.com. One of the most popular bars in town, offering drink specials and regular performances by DJs and local karaoke wizards. No cover usually. Daily 11am–2am.

SLO Brew 736 Higuera St ☏ 805 543 1843, ⓦ slobrew .com. This brewpub serves great burgers and is a major music venue on the local scene; shows featuring local and touring bands are booked several times weekly. Tickets $8–30. Sun & Mon 11am–midnight, Tues–Sat 11.30am–2am.

Morro Bay to Cambria

In San Luis Obispo, US-101 and Hwy-1 diverge once again, with the former speeding up through Paso Robles and Salinas Valley (see p.383) while the latter follows a spectacular coastal route to Hearst Castle (see p.380) and Big Sur beyond, passing first through the coastal communities of **Morro Bay** and genteel **Cambria**.

Morro Bay

Set thirteen miles up Hwy-1 from San Luis Obispo, in the considerable shadow of massive **Morro Rock**, the easy-paced coastal town of **MORRO BAY** makes for a mellow stopover en route to thronged Hearst Castle. Not only is it situated near a collection of wetlands and mud flats (as well as a seawater inlet), but local fishing boats routinely unload their catches to sell in the many fish markets along the waterfront. The bayfront **Embarcadero** is the main focus of the town, lined by a mix of seafood restaurants and touristy shops, though it's generally a low-key and fun place to trawl up and down. There are plenty of activities on offer here (kayak and boat rentals), despite the vistas of harbour seals, pelicans and the giant rock itself being marred somewhat by the chimneys of Morro Bay Power Plant.

Morro Rock

Most impressive from a distance, particularly from Cerro Alto (see p.376), **Morro Rock** (581ft) dominates the fine harbour of Morro Bay itself. The eighth in the area's chain

6

of nine extinct volcanoes, it soars up from the sea close to the coast; the northernmost plug is buried further from shore under the Pacific Ocean's churning waters. According to local lore, Morro Rock was named by sixteenth-century explorer Juan Cabrillo, who thought it looked like Moorish turbans worn in what's now southern Spain; centuries later, road-builders thought it looked more like a quarry for gathering stone and altered its look for the worse. Quarrying ended in 1969 and today the rock is connected to the mainland via a causeway; you can drive up to its base and park in its shadow (or at the small beach on the southern side), but can go no further. Though Chumash and Salinan tribe members can climb Morro Rock for annual ceremonies, it's off-limits to the general public as the Morro Rock State Preserve, in order to protect the nesting areas of the endangered peregrine falcon.

Morro Bay State Park

Morro Bay State Park 1 State Park Rd • $8/vehicle • ☎ 805 772 2560, ⓦ parks.ca.gov **Museum of Natural History** Daily 10am–5pm • Adults $2, kids 16 and under free • ☎ 805 772 2694

Around 1.5 miles south of the Embarcadero, **Morro Bay State Park** boasts a pretty lagoon and fine marina, as well as opportunities for hiking, fishing and camping (see opposite). Its **Museum of Natural History** is an excellent interactive ecology museum aimed squarely at curious kids, where the best display offers visitors the chance to build their own sand dune; the museum's setting also provides a fine vista from a point above the bay. Just north of here but still within the park, you may wish to paddle a kayak (see below) in order to see the **Blue Heron Rookery Natural Preserve**, where eucalyptus trees attract great sea birds, egrets and cormorants, though you're not allowed to land here since it's a protected reserve.

El Moro Elfin Forest

Dawn–dusk • Free • ⓦ elfin-forest.org

On the southeast side of Morro Bay and accessed via the small community of Los Osos is intriguing **El Moro Elfin Forest**, a pristine preserve of pygmy oak trees that offers delightful strolling over walkways and paths amid extensive sand dunes; a boardwalk loops through the centre with extensions to two bay overlooks (Bush Lupine Point and Sienna's View), with another extension to the end of 16th Street in Los Osos, where there is limited parking.

Montaña de Oro State Park

Daily dawn–dusk • Free • ☎ 805 772 7434, ⓦ parks.ca.gov

Southwest from El Moro Elfin Forest down Los Osos Valley Road (which turns into Pecho Valley Rd), **Montaña de Oro State Park** is much less developed than Morro Bay State Park and contains excellent tide pools, as well as a good beach at Spooner's Cove. The windswept promontory stands solidly against the crashing sea, offering rugged hiking along the shore and through the sagebrush and eucalyptus trees of the upland hillsides, which in spring are covered in golden poppies and gave rise to the park's name, Spanish for "gold mountain". Primitive camping is available (see opposite).

Cerro Alto

One of the best views of Morro Rock – and indeed, much of the surrounding coastline – is from atop **Cerro Alto**, a 2624ft volcanic cone reached via Hwy-41 nine miles east of Morro Bay. The trailhead (parking $10/vehicle) is at the *Cerro Alto Campground* (see opposite), with the shortest route a steep 1.95-mile ascent and a much easier 2.75-mile trail.

INFORMATION AND ACTIVITIES   **MORRO BAY**

Tourism office 695 Harbor St, just inland from the Embarcadero (Mon–Fri 8am–4.30pm; ☎ 805 225 1570, ⓦ morrobay.org).

Kayaking To access Blue Heron Rookery and other nearby offshore sights, rent a vessel from Kayak Horizons, 551 Embarcadero (daily 9am–5pm; ☎ 805 772 6444, ⓦ kayakhorizons.com). Rates are $14/hr and $35/half-day for a kayak.

ACCOMMODATION

Cerro Alto Campground Hwy-41, midway between Atascadero and Morro Bay ☎800 444 7275, ⓦreserveamerica.com. This Los Padres National Forest campground is in the mountains east of Morro Bay and boasts hiking opportunities in the immediate vicinity. Drinking water available. $20

Masterpiece Hotel 1206 Main St ☎805 772 5633, ⓦmasterpiecehotel.com. An enjoyable lodging choice in town, featuring Spanish-Moorish architecture,

well-appointed rooms containing microwaves, fridges and various classical artworks on the walls (hence the name of the place). Some rooms are even fitted with balconies and fireplaces. $110

Montaña de Oro State Park (Islay Creek) Campground 3550 Pecho Valley Rd, Los Osos ☎800 444 7275, ⓦreserveamerica.com. Just inland from Spooner's Cove beach and open throughout the year, this slightly remote park's campground is a bit wilder than

6

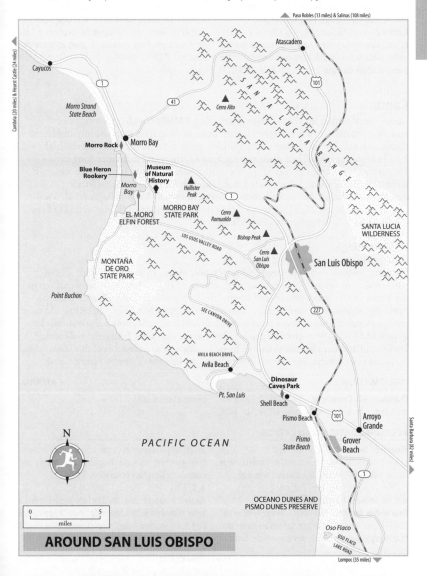

AROUND SAN LUIS OBISPO

others in the region, so you're more likely to find solitude here. $25

Morro Bay State Park Campground 1 State Park Rd ☎800 444 7275, ⓦreserveamerica.com. Large,

year-round campground located in the heart of the state park. It features a full complement of options, from drive-in and walk-in sites to larger pitches designed for groups and RV campers. $35

EATING

★ **Giovanni's Fish Market** Embarcadero (1001 Front St) ☎805 772 2123, ⓦgiovannisfishmarket.com. Best of the no-nonsense fish restaurants that line the northern end of the Embarcadero, with amazing clam chowder and very fresh seafood, everything from fish and chips to smoked fish, ceviche, oysters and scallops. Daily 11am–6pm.

Hofbrau 901 Embarcadero ☎805 772 2411, ⓦhofbraumorrobay.com. People come from all over the region to eat at this no-frills roast-beef specialist on the bayfront, where the dipped beef sandwiches ($9.95) are

the main events but the fish and chips ($7.75) are also quite good. Order at the counter first. Daily 11am–9pm.

★ **Libertine Brewing Co** 801 Embarcadero ☎805 772 0700, ⓦlibertinepub.com. Excellent brewpub with a mind-bending 48 taps of not just their own beers – Edna Table Saison, Pacific Ocean Blue Gose – but also craft beers from across the region. Food options include tasty cod tacos ($13), chowder ($7) and addictive pub nachos ($12). Mon–Sat 11am–11pm, Sun 10am–11pm.

Cambria

About twenty miles up Hwy-1 from Morro Bay, **CAMBRIA** is glutted with pricey amenities, thanks in part to everything it's done to cash in on its proximity to Hearst Castle, ten miles or so further north. Hidden away in a wooded valley off the highway, Cambria was an established town serving local ranchers and fishermen long before Hearst Castle became the region's prime tourist attraction, and it maintains a certain allure since its residents have enacted ordinances that make any view-blocking development illegal. The older section of town, known as Main Village, is half a mile east of Hwy-1 along Main Street, while the newer part of town (home to most of the cheaper hotels) is referred to as East Village.

Nitt Witt Ridge

881 Hillcrest Drive • Free (tours by appointment) • ☎805 927 2690

Cambria holds one acknowledged oddity: **Nitt Witt Ridge**. This patently weird slice of whimsy was the brainchild of one Art Beal, who came to Cambria from San Francisco in the 1920s and bought a plot of land where, over a fifty-year period, he built a Baroque castle out of trash, thus earning him the moniker "Captain Nitt Witt". Recycling old toilet seats as picture frames or water pipes as handrails, this eccentric misfit's glorious folly lay abandoned for ten years after his death in 1992 at the age of 96. Today, the California Historical Landmark has been restored by new owners, who offer tours of this labyrinthine house that's an offbeat, low-rent counterpoint to the luxuries of nearby Hearst Castle.

INFORMATION   CAMBRIA

Chamber of Commerce 767 Main St (Mon–Fri 9am–5pm, Sat & Sun noon–4pm; ☎805 927 3624, ⓦvisitcambriaca.com).

ACCOMMODATION AND EATING

Bluebird Inn 1880 Main St ☎805 927 4634, ⓦbluebirdinncambria.com. Situated in Cambria's Main Village, this no-frills motel offers standard units with basic decor and amenities, plus more elaborate creek-side rooms with balconies and fireplaces. $109

FogCatcher Inn 6400 Moonstone Beach Drive ☎805 927 1400, ⓦfogcatcherinn.com. Set just across the road from lovely Moonstone Beach, this is one of the better (if

pricier) lodging options in Cambria. Smart, modern rooms come complete with gas fireplaces, mini-fridges and microwaves; some have ocean views. $165

★ **Robin's** 4095 Burton Drive ☎805 927 5007, ⓦrobinsrestaurant.com. You'll be hard-pressed to find a better restaurant in this area of San Luis Obispo County than indoor-outdoor *Robin's*, where brilliant main courses such as shellfish paella and a variety of curries (Indian, Thai,

FROM TOP MONTEREY BAY AQUARIUM (P.399); HEARST CASTLE (P.380) >

Malaysian) fill out a diverse menu. Dinner mains range from $20–30. Sun–Thurs 11am–9pm, Fri & Sat 11am–9.30pm.

The Sow's Ear Cafe 2248 Main St ☏ 805 927 4865,

⊚ thesowsear.com. This local favourite is known for its range of mid-priced cuisine, including unique items like lobster pot pie ($23.95) and honey-pecan-crusted catfish ($21.95). Daily 5–9pm.

Hearst Castle and around

Forty-plus miles northwest of San Luis Obispo, **HEARST CASTLE** sits on a hilltop overlooking rolling ranchlands and the Pacific Ocean. Far and away the biggest attraction for miles, the former holiday getaway of **William Randolph Hearst** is one of the most opulent and extravagant homes in the world. Its interior combines walls, floors and ceilings torn from European churches and castles with Gothic fireplaces and Moorish tiles. Nearly every room is bursting with Greek vases and medieval tapestries, and even the many pools are lined with works of art. Though the castle was once a weekend retreat for the most famous politicians and movie stars of the 1920s and 1930s – Hearst's highly selective range of guests included Winston Churchill, Walt Disney and Charles Lindbergh, while the most frequent weekenders were Cary Grant and Charlie Chaplin – it now brings in more than one million visitors a year as a state-operated entity.

Hearst San Simeon State Historical Monument

The property Hearst himself referred to as simply "the ranch" – its official name is **Hearst San Simeon State Historical Monument** – is the extravagant palace one would expect from the man whose grandstanding character and domination of the national media inspired Orson Welles's classic film *Citizen Kane*. The structure is actually more a complex of buildings than a "castle"; three guesthouses circle the hundred-room main Casa Grande, in which Hearst himself held court. What may come as a surprise is the harmony with which the many diverse art treasures he collected were brought together by his mother's favourite architect, **Julia Morgan** – herself a pioneer in the use of Spanish mission elements in California architecture. Here, Morgan received only $80,000 for her efforts, a paltry sum that nonetheless didn't keep her from acting as Hearst's personal architect for several more decades.

The ranchland had been in the family since 1865, bought by Hearst's father, mining magnate and senator George Hearst; following the 1919 death of Hearst's mother, Phoebe, construction began in earnest on his fantasies. This began on the southern edge of the 390-square-mile ranch, which became Hearst's own private, free-roaming zoo full of lions, tigers, zebras and bears. Though it continued for another three decades, the work was never truly completed, since rooms would often be torn out as soon as they were finished in order to accommodate more acquired treasure. It's no wonder that the castle looks more like a church than a mansion: the main façade is a twin-towered copy of a Mudejar cathedral in Ronda, Spain, while the main door was pilfered from a convent there.

Casa Grande

The main house, **Casa Grande** stands at the top of steps that curve up from an expansive **Neptune Pool** (one of the most photographed in the world), which is filled with pure spring water and lined by a Greek colonnade and marble statues. Indoors, the **Roman Pool** is lined with blue Venetian glass and gold tiles, its soft lights reflecting in the water's steamy surface.

Highlights inside the castle include the **Refectory**, a stunning dining chamber lined with choir stalls removed from Spanish and Italian churches and bedecked pompously with heraldic flags; the **Library**, stuffed with thousands of rare and musty volumes; and

WILLIAM RANDOLPH HEARST: THE REAL CITIZEN KANE

Born in 1863, **William Randolph Hearst** was the only son of a multimillionaire mining engineer. Throughout his life, he remained avidly devoted to his mother, Phoebe Apperson Hearst, one of California's most sincere and generous philanthropists – a founder of both the University of California and the Traveler's Aid Society. Hearst learned his trade in New York working for the inventor of inflammatory **"yellow journalism"**, Joseph Pulitzer, who had four rules for how to sell newspapers: emphasize the sensational, elaborate the facts, manufacture the news and use games and contests. When he published his own newspaper, Hearst took this advice to heart, his *Morning Journal* fanning the flames of American imperialism to help ignite the **Spanish–American War** of 1898. As he told his correspondents in Cuba: "You provide the pictures, and I'll provide the war." Hearst eventually controlled an empire that, at its peak during the 1930s, sold 25 percent of the newspapers in the entire country, including three New York papers, the *Washington Times* and the *Detroit News* – as well as *Cosmopolitan* and *Good Housekeeping* magazines. In California, Hearst's power was even more pronounced, with his San Francisco and Los Angeles papers controlling over sixty percent of the total market. Besides his many newspapers, Hearst also owned eleven radio stations and two movie studios.

It was through his movie-studio proprietorship that he made his mistress **Marion Davies** a star. Davies' relationship with Hearst endured despite constant accusations of gold-digging and rumours swirling around a mysterious death on board Hearst's boat (allegedly, Hearst murdered film-studio pioneer Thomas Ince and covered it up). When the Depression hit, Hearst was forced to sell off most of his holdings but remained a wealthy man; he continued to exert power and influence until his death, aged 88, at Davies' ranch in 1951. She stuck by him until the end, despite the private sniggers of his upper-crust cohorts; in explanation, Davies is said to have shrugged, "My mother raised me to be a gold-digger, but I fell in love".

the **Gothic Suite**, where Hearst conducted his daily business in medieval splendour, and whose grand, gloomy fireplace may have served as the inspiration for Kane's more colossal, jaw-like hearth. The **private cinema** is also not to be missed, where Hearst saw first cuts of Hollywood films before they were released to the general public. The one disappointing element of the interior is its art collection: there are plenty of cherry-cheeked Madonnas and minor Old Masters, but not a single standout work – Hearst's taste was clearly more decorative than artistic.

The grounds

Outside the castle proper, the seventeen **Neptune Pool dressing rooms** are still hung with period swimwear and sports equipment. Also of note are the elaborate **guesthouses**, the highlight of which is the Eastern-themed **Casa del Mar** – which Marion Davies claimed was Hearst's favourite spot on the whole estate – and **Casa del Monte**, a smaller guesthouse loaded with tapestries and overlooking the Santa Lucia Mountains. The estate's extensive Italian- and Spanish-influenced gardens, terraces and walkways merit a full tour in themselves as they feature hundreds of rare and imported species of flowers and trees.

INFORMATION   HEARST CASTLE

Visitor Center It's well signed off Hwy-1, eight miles north of Cambria at 750 Hearst Castle Rd. If you arrive early for your scheduled tour, you can pass time in its mildly diverting museum (daily 9am–5pm; free).

TOURS

To properly absorb Hearst Castle, it's recommended you take one of the daily **guided tours** ($25–36; ☎ 800 444 4445, ⊕ hearstcastle.com), all of which depart from the visitor centre. For each of the following daytime tours, allow at least **one hour**, including the trundling bus ride from the visitor centre to the hilltop. It's highly recommended you **reserve** as far ahead as possible – you can do so up to 56 days in advance. All tours leave from the same depot at the rear of the visitor centre, through the double doors past the ticket office. Make sure you collect your tickets before queuing up for the tour. Wheelchair-accessible tours are also available.

Grand Rooms Tour (year-round; $25; 1hr) Most appropriate if you're visiting Hearst Castle for the first time, this tour takes in essential spaces such as the Refectory and Billiard Room, as well as the Neptune and Roman Pools and the gardens. Crucially, it also includes a showing of the short documentary film *Building the Dream*.

Upstairs Suites Tour (year-round; $25; 1hr) Docent narratives on this tour are highly informative as you poke around the Gothic Suite, containing Hearst's library and office, and the Doge's Suite, his Venetian-flavoured bedroom. This tour offers more personal insight into Hearst than merely gawping at the staterooms on the Grand Rooms Tour's circuit. Pool visits and film showing included.

Cottages & Kitchen Tour (year-round; $25; 1hr) This tertiary tour is more geared toward serious Hearst aficionados, concentrating as it does on Casa del Monte and Case del Mar guesthouses, as well as the property's kitchen. Pool visits and film showing included.

Evening Tour (March–May & Oct–Dec most Fri & Sat; $36; 1hr 40min) The most unusual of all the tours finds docents decked out in period garb as they escort visitors through the castle on a twilight circuit combining elements of the first three tours – all while eerily speaking of Hearst in the present tense. The visit ends at the lamplit Neptune Pool with stories of the legendary figures who once frolicked there after dark. No film showing.

San Simeon

The old fishing pier at **San Simeon**, the remains of a harbour town along the coast just north of Hearst Castle, is where Hearst's considerable treasures were unloaded, along with the many tonnes of concrete and steel that went into the building of his palatial estate. Before the Hearsts bought up the adjacent land, San Simeon was a whaling and shipping port, of which all that remains is a one-room schoolhouse and the circa-1852 **Sebastian's General Store & Cafe**, 442 SLO San Simeon Rd (Tues–Sun 11.30am–4.30pm; ☎805 927 3307), a combination post office, café, history museum and souvenir shop. It's also the home of the **Hearst Ranch Winery tasting room** (daily 11am–5pm; $10 tastings; ☎805 927 4100). The peaceful and lovely **beach** flanking the pier is protected by San Simeon Point, which hooks out into the Pacific and makes the large cove relatively safe for swimming.

Coastal Discovery Center

SLO San Simeon Rd • Sat & Sun 11am–5pm • Free • ☎ 805 927 6575, ⓦ montereybay.noaa.gov

Inside the entrance to William Hearst Memorial State Beach, just across from the turning to Hearst Castle on Hwy-1, the **Coastal Discovery Center** contains interactive exhibits highlighting the cultural and natural history of San Simeon and the offshore **Monterey Bay National Marine Sanctuary** (stretching from Marin to Cambria).

Piedras Blancas elephant seal rookery

Just a 4.5 miles miles north of San Simeon on Hwy-1, the **Piedras Blancas elephant seal rookery** (part of Hearst San Simeon State Park), makes for an astounding spectacle, with huge elephant seals lazing in the sand, their distinctive rubbery noses and deep bellows echoing across the beach. A boardwalk follows the beach (its strictly prohibited to go on the sand itself) and volunteers are on hand to answer questions in the summer (ⓦelephantseal.org). Some 23,000 northern elephant seals call in here annually, though they spend eight to ten months a year in the open ocean – the best time to see them on the beach is during birthing and breeding season (Dec–March), and also April–May and July–Sept, when they come in to moult (younger seals return one last time Oct–Nov).

Beyond here, the highway seems to drop off in mid-air, marking the southern edge of Big Sur (see p.388), one of the most dramatic stretches of coastline in North America.

ACCOMMODATION   SAN SIMEON

San Simeon Lodge 9520 Castillo Drive ☎805 927 4601, ⓦ sansimeonlodge.net. The most reliably clean of the roadside motels located three miles south of San Simeon proper, this inn has an outdoor heated pool, gym and compact but comfy rooms. **$80**

Paso Robles and the Salinas Valley

From San Luis Obispo, US-101 cuts north through **Paso Robles** and the **Salinas Valley** and takes no more than four hours to cover the 230 miles to San Francisco, compared to the full day it takes to drive scenic Hwy-1 through Big Sur. The highway runs through farmland that's so fertile, it's earned the nickname the "Salad Bowl of the World", thanks to the millions of lettuce heads (known as "green gold") it produces, picked largely by Mexican immigrants who populate the small towns dotting the valley.

6

Paso Robles

The small city of **PASO ROBLES** ("ROBE-ulls") is thirty miles north of San Luis Obispo and surrounded by horse ranches, nut farms and **wineries** (see box below), its primary appeal to visitors. Despite a 6.5 magnitude earthquake in 2003 that caused a nineteenth-century clock tower to collapse downtown, the town has rebounded quickly and there's little evidence of destruction.

Devotees of the films *East of Eden* and *Rebel without a Cause* will want to drive about thirty miles east of Paso Robles on Hwy-46, past the junction of Hwy-41 near Cholame; it's here that many come to pay their respects at the stainless-steel monument near the site where **James Dean** fatally crashed in a silver Porsche 550 Spyder on September 30, 1955.

INFORMATION   PASO ROBLES

Chamber of Commerce A smart first stop for brochures and maps of the area is here, at 1225 Park St (Mon–Fri 8.30am–4.30pm, Sat 10am–2pm; ☎ 805 238 0506, ⓦ pasorobleschamber.com).

ACCOMMODATION

Ann & George's Bed and Breakfast 1965 Niderer Rd ☎ 805 423 2760, ⓦ voladoresvineyard.com. Out among the vines five miles southwest of Paso Robles, offering bucolic and comfortable – if expensive – lodging (just 2 rooms), amid Voladores Vineyard. Discounts are offered for multiple-night stays. **$260**

Melody Ranch Motel 939 Spring St ☎ 805 238 3911, ⓦ melodyranchmotel.com. Austere, but clean and well placed for exploring Downtown Paso Robles on foot, this is an affordable alternative to the city's increasingly upper-crust accommodation scene. **$90**

Paso Robles Inn 1103 Spring St ☎ 805 238 2660, ⓦ pasoroblesinn.com. Centrally located right on the town square, this inn has comfortable rooms, some of which include two-person balcony tubs fed by local hot springs water. **$139**

PASO ROBLES WINERIES (AND BREWERY)

The Paso Robles area of San Luis Obispo County has become one of California's most celebrated **wine** regions, a development that's helped turn Paso Robles itself into an increasingly popular weekend getaway destination for visitors from both the Bay Area and Southern California. The local visitor centre stocks a free map of the area's 150-odd wineries; visit ⓦ pasowine.com for more information.

Firestone Walker Brewing Company 1400 Ramada Drive; ☎ 805 225 5911, ⓦ firestonebeer .com. If you prefer beer to wine, this local powerhouse brewery is well worth a stop for lunch, a pint and even a tour (30–45min; $3). Daily 10am–5pm; tours daily 11.30am–2.30pm.

Tablas Creek Vineyard 9339 Adelaida Rd ☎ 805 237 1231, ⓦ tablascreek.com. Founded by the Perrin family of Châteauneuf-du-Pape fame, TablasCreek is perhaps best known for its Rhône-style wines (and especially the the limited-run Panoplie varietal, which combines Mourvèdre, Grenache and Syrah grapes). Tastings from $15, tours daily 10.30am & 2pm. Daily 10am–5pm.

Turley Wine Cellars 2900 Vineyard Drive ☎ 805 434 1030, ⓦ turleywinecellars.com. One of the most highly regarded wine producers hereabouts, whose superb Ueberroth Vineyard Zinfandel is made from grapes grown in a vineyard that dates back to 1885. Tastings $10. Daily 10am–5pm.

EATING

Buona Tavola 943 Spring St ☎ 805 237 0600, ⓦ btslo .com/paso-robles. If you're craving Italian food during your Paso Robles visit there are plenty of options downtown, but this one of the best, offering tasty Northern Italian pastas ($15–27) and mains such as chicken marinated with garlic and herbs ($28.75). Mon–Thurs 11.30am–2pm & 5.30–9.30pm, Fri 11.30am–2pm &

5.30–10pm, Sat 5.30–10pm, Sun 5.30–9.30pm.
Red Scooter Deli 1102 Pine St ☎ 805 237 1780, ⓦ redscooterdeli.com. Tiny breakfast and sandwich place, offering artfully made delights such as eggs benedict (served over a croissant; $6.50) and hot French dip sandwiches ($10). Mon–Fri 8am–5pm, Sat & Sun 9am–4pm.

Mission San Miguel

775 Mission St, San Miguel • Daily 10am–4.30pm • Museum $3, church free • ☎ 805 467 3256, ⓦ missionsanmiguel.org

Less than ten miles north of Paso Robles, be sure to pull off US-101 at tiny **San Miguel** for a peek at one of the most intact and authentic of California's Spanish missions, **Mission San Miguel**. Founded in 1797 as the sixteenth mission in the chain, the current church building dates from around 1818 and is the only one not to have undergone heavy-handed restoration – its colourful frescoes, naïf altar and pulpit are all originals, created in the early 1820s by Don Esteban Munras (from Monterey) and local Salinas artists under his direction.

The enlightening **museum** occupies the surrounding adobe structures, notable for their rough imprecision, with irregularly arched openings and unplastered walls forming a courtyard around a cactus garden. There's a room dedicated to the indigenous **Salinan** people – still awaiting official federal recognition as a tribe – as well as kitchens, an original open-style wine vat and sleeping quarters with period furnishings. The 2249 Salinan people buried in the cemetery at the back are commemorated with a simple wood cross.

Mission San Antonio de Padua

End of Mission Rd, Jolon • Tues–Sun 10am–4pm • Grounds and church free, museum $5 • ☎ 831 385 4478, ⓦ missionsanantonio.net

For a trip well off the region's main highway, venture fifty miles northwest of Paso Robles to fascinating **Mission San Antonio de Padua**, the most remote link along California's chain of Franciscan mission outposts. To reach it, drive north on US-101 to Bradley, then follow Jolon Rd (County Rd G18), then Mission Road twenty miles to the entrance of Fort Hunter Liggett Army base. After inspecting your driver's licence/passport and vehicle registration, uniformed guards will grant passage five miles into the base, where the mission sits.

This undervisited complex (mostly reconstructed by 1952) is less sanitized than most other missions, and offers a clear glimpse into how life might have been for the missionaries and their converts. Founded in 1771 as the third mission in California, San Antonio de Padua was among the most prosperous. Around the extensive grounds in a wide valley of oak trees and tall grasses, there's a monastic peace, especially around the inner courtyard and dim **church** with its flickering candles, this incarnation dating back to 1813.

Pinnacles National Park

5000 Hwy-146 • Open 24hr • $15/vehicle, valid 7 days • ☎ 831 389 4485, ⓦ nps.gov/pinn

Some 73 miles north of Paso Robles, US-101 skirts **Soledad**, a quiet, predominantly Mexican farming town (Steinbeck set *Of Mice and Men* around here), principally of interest for its proximity to **Pinnacles National Park**'s western entrance, as well as its panaderías offering cakes and fresh tortillas.

The inland region's major natural attraction – and California's newest national park, thanks to Congressional legislation passed in 2012 – Pinnacles National Park is studded with startling volcanic spires, cool caves and brilliant reds and golds, all set against blue sky. It's best visited in spring (especially March and April), when the air is still cool and the chaparral hillsides are lushly green and sprinkled with wildflowers. Also watch for legions of bees, as this park boasts the highest known bee diversity in the world – some four hundred species in all.

Although Pinnacles has east and west entrances, no road transects its steep spires; several paths allow you to explore its wonders from either entrance, however, and for most, Pinnacles' main allure is a day or two spent **hiking** some of the park's 35 miles of lovely, well-maintained trails. Pinnacles is compact enough that it's quite possible to hike from one side to the other and back in one long day, as only three miles separate the dead ends of its east and west roads. Note that shade is rare here, however, so avoid hiking in the middle of the day in summer and remember to carry plenty of water. Backcountry camping is not permitted.

One of the best hikes is the **Balconies Trail** (two-mile loop; 100ft ascent), most easily accessed from the west, which skirts the multicoloured, 600ft face of the Balconies outcrop, then returns via a series of talus **caves** (be sure to pack a flashlight or headlamp) formed by huge boulders now wedged between the walls of the narrow canyons. An excellent **park loop** (10 miles; 1600ft ascent) can be undertaken from either entrance, a trek that, by combining several trails (including the Balconies), takes in the best of the park's high and low country.

ARRIVAL AND INFORMATION

PINNACLES NATIONAL PARK

Eastern entrance Somewhat surprisingly, most of the park's facilities are centred around the more remote eastern entrance (open 24hr; leave US-101 at King City (exit 281), take County Road G13 northeast to Bitterwater, then travel northwest on Hwy-25), including the Pinnacles Visitor Center (daily 9.30am–5pm; ☏ 831 389 4485, ⓦ nps.gov/pinn) and Bear Gulch Nature Center (daily June–Oct 10am–4pm; Nov–May Sat & Sun

10am–4pm; ☏ 831 389 4486).

Western entrance Amenities at Pinnacles' western entrance (gates open 7.30am–8pm) consist of little more than a ranger station (Sat & Sun 9am–4.30pm; ☏ 831 389 4427) and toilets, with overnight stays not allowed. Still, its accessibility off US-101 from Soledad, from where Hwy-146 runs eleven winding miles to the park, makes it the better option for day-visits.

ACCOMMODATION

PINNACLES NATIONAL PARK

Inn at the Pinnacles 32025 Stonewall Canyon Rd ☏ 831 678 2400, ⓦ innatthepinnacles.com. For the most upscale lodging in the area, head to this swanky inn on Hwy-146 just short of the park's western entrance, where a welcome swimming pool, in-room fireplaces and private patios are part of every accommodation package. **$235**

Pinnacles Campground ☏ 831 389 4455, ⓦ recreation .gov. Within Pinnacles National Park (accessed only from the

east side), this swimming-pool-equipped campground is a routinely popular place to pitch a tent, making reservations virtually essential March–Sept. **$23**

SOLEDAD

Soledad Motel 8 1013 S Front St, Soledad ☏ 831 678 3814, ⓦ soledadmotel8.com. Dull but serviceable, this motel makes for a budget-friendly overnight stop along US-101 in Salinas Valley. **$72**

EATING

La Fuente 101 Oak St, Soledad ☏ 831 678 3130. Among the handful of Mexican restaurants in Soledad, *La Fuente* stands out for its excellent main courses such as chicken

enchiladas and beef tacos, all around $10–12. Mon–Sat 11am–8pm, Sun 10am–8pm.

Salinas

The seat of Monterey County, **SALINAS**, sits less than thirty miles north of Soledad on US-101 and is a sprawling, agricultural-based city of 150,000 inhabitants. Although it's perhaps best known these days for the **California Rodeo** (daily tickets $10–25; ☏ 831 775 3100, ⓦ carodeo.com) – held during the third week in July and the biggest such event in the state – it's also the 1902 birthplace of Nobel Prize-winning writer **John Steinbeck** (see box, p.386); in fact, Salinas and its namesake agricultural valley to the south are often bracketed as Steinbeck Country. Despite leaving in his mid-20s to live in Monterey and, later, New York, the region heavily nurtured his imagination, and many of his naturalistic stories and novels, including the epic *East of Eden*, were set in and around the valley.

It was also in Salinas that the United Farm Workers union had great success in organizing and demanding better pay and working conditions for Salinas Valley's almost exclusively Latino agricultural workforce. The galvanizing leadership of **César Chávez** and **Dolores Huerta** in the 1960s and early 1970s masterminded an extremely effective boycott of the valley's main product, lettuce.

In downtown Salinas, be sure to stroll tree-lined Main Street and take in its done-up Victorian buildings, clothing boutiques and craft stores (including the **Halltree Antique Mall** Mon–Fri 10am–5.30pm, Sat & Sun 10.30am–5pm), as well as the 1921 Art Deco **Fox Theater** at no. 241.

National Steinbeck Center

1 Main St • Daily 10am–5pm • $12.95 ($10.95 from 4pm) • ☎ 831 775 4721, ⓦ steinbeck.org

The best introduction to both the man and the region is the large, modern **National Steinbeck Center**, which takes you on an engaging, interactive journey through the author's life and work. Two 12-minute biographical films (shown on loop) offer an informative and lively approach to Steinbeck and set the tone for the rest of the museum, throughout which snippets of films and material from sound archives play prominent roles. Loosely organized around his major works, from *East of Eden* and *Of Mice and Men* (with replicas of migrant shacks) to *The Pearl* and *Travels with Charley* (Steinbeck's actual camper van is on display), it's all inspiring enough that you may well find yourself purchasing a novel or two from the excellent on-site shop.

Steinbeck House

132 Central Ave • Tues–Sat 11.30am–2pm • Tours summer Sun noon, 1pm & 2pm; $10 • ☎ 831 424 2735, ⓦ steinbeckhouse.com

The author's childhood home, the **Steinbeck House**, two blocks west of the museum, has been turned into an English-style tearoom (high tea served second Sat of the month noon–2pm, $25). The handsome Queen Anne-style Victorian building was built in 1889 and purchased by Steinbeck's father in 1900. There's a **gift shop** in the cellar (Tues–Sat 11am–3pm), while monthly **tours** ($10) run between May and September (check the website for dates).

THE NOVELS OF JOHN STEINBECK

John Steinbeck's novels and short stories are as remarkable for their historical content as for their narratives; Steinbeck had a newspaperman's eye for the hardships of working-class life. *The Grapes of Wrath* (1939), his best-known work, was made into a film starring Henry Fonda while the book was still at the top of the bestseller lists, having captured the popular imagination for its portrayal of the Depression-era miseries of the Joad family on their migration to California from Oklahoma's dust bowl. *Cannery Row* followed in 1945, a nostalgic portrait of Monterey fisheries, which, ironically, went into steep decline the year the book was published. Steinbeck spent the next four years writing *East of Eden* (1952), an allegorical retelling of the biblical story of Cain and Abel against the landscape of the Salinas Valley; in this book, which he saw as his masterpiece, Steinbeck expresses many of the values that underlie the rest of his works.

Much of Steinbeck's writing is concerned with the dignity of labour, as well as the inequalities of an economic system that "allows children to go hungry in the midst of rotting plenty". Although he was circumspect about his own political stance, there was a violent backlash against Steinbeck in Salinas for what were seen as his Communist sympathies once *The Grapes of Wrath* became a bestseller. Later, he was so wounded at the outcry over his worthiness for the Nobel Prize for Literature in 1962 that he never wrote another word. He died in New York City in 1968; his ashes are buried in the family plot at the **Garden of Memories Cemetery**, 768 Abbott St, in Salinas.

ARRIVAL AND DEPARTURE

SALINAS

By bus Greyhound buses trundling between Los Angeles and San Francisco stop outside the Amtrak station at 3 Station Place, a short walk from Main St.
Destinations Los Angeles (3 daily; 7hr 5min–8hr 15min); San Francisco (3 daily; 3hr 40min–4hr 20min).

By train Amtrak Coast Starlight trains leave once a day in each direction, from 11 Station Place.
Destinations Los Angeles (1 daily; 9hr 12min); Santa Barbara (1 daily; 6hr 7min); San Luis Obispo (1 daily; 3hr 19min); San Jose (1 daily; 1hr 43min); Oakland (1 daily; 2hr 56min).

INFORMATION AND GETTING AROUND

California Welcome Center If you're driving, this is a useful stopoff just off US-101 at 1213 N Davis Rd (daily 9am–5pm; ☏ 831 757 8687).
Visitor Center The small information centre is at 222 Main St, near the Steinbeck Center (Mon–Fri 8am–5pm;

☏ 831 435 4636, ⓦ destinationsalinas.com).
By bus Monterey–Salinas Transit bus #20 ($2.50; ⓦ mst.org) makes the 55min trip to Monterey several times daily from the Transit Center at 110 Salinas St.

6

ACCOMMODATION AND EATING

★**First Awakenings** 171 Main St ☏ 831 784 1125, ⓦ firstawakenings.net. Locally renowned breakfast and lunch spot, with sensational wheatgerm and blueberry pancakes ($9.19), excellent salads ($11–14) and hefty sandwiches and burgers ($11–13). Daily 7am–2pm.
Laurel Inn Motel 801 W Laurel Drive ☏ 831 449 2474, ⓦ laurelinnmotel.com. Among the horde of franchise

motel signs visible from US-101, this is a dependable option, with comfy rooms and a pool. $89
Rosita's Armory Cafe 231 Salinas St ☏ 831 424 7039. Salinas' oldest Mexican restaurant, boasting big green booths and delicious mains such as cheese-stuffed enchiladas and *chile colorado* – all for about $12 a platter. Mon–Sat 10am–8.30pm, Sun 10am–4pm.

San Juan Bautista

Some twenty miles northeast of Salinas on US-101, tiny **SAN JUAN BAUTISTA** is an old town that, but for a modest smattering of shops selling collectibles, has hardly changed since it was bypassed by the railroad in 1876. The community's commercial centre, a block south of the plaza, lines Third Street in a row of evocatively decaying façades.

Mission San Juan Bautista

406 2nd St • Daily 9.30am–4.30pm • $4 • ☏ 831 623 4528, ⓦ oldmissionsjb.org

Founded in 1797, the **Mission San Juan Bautista**, the largest of the California missions – and still the parish church of San Juan Bautista – stands on the north side of the town's central plaza, where its original bells still ring out. The arcaded monastery wing that stretches to the left of the church contains relics and historical exhibits, including a vast collection of ceremonial robes. If it all looks a bit familiar, you may have seen it before – the climactic stairway chase scene in Alfred Hitchcock's *Vertigo* was filmed here.

San Juan Bautista State Historic Park

2nd St, between Washington and Mariposa • Daily 10am–4.30pm • $3 • ☏ 831 623 4881, ⓦ parks.ca.gov

The town that grew up around Mission San Juan Bautista was once the largest in central California and has been preserved as **San Juan Bautista State Historic Park**, with exhibits around the spacious central square interpreting all the restored buildings. On the west side of the plaza is the two-storey, balconied adobe **Plaza Hotel**, which was a popular stop on the stagecoach route between San Francisco and Los Angeles in the 1860s. Next door, the 1840 **Castro-Breen Adobe**, once the administrative headquarters of Mexican California, eventually belonged to the Breen family – survivors of the ill-fated Donner Party (see box, p.579) who made a small fortune in the Gold Rush.

Plaza Hall-Zanetta House

Across from Mission San Juan Bautista, large **Plaza Hall-Zanetta House** was built to serve as the seat of the emergent county government, but when the county seat was awarded instead to Hollister – a small community eight miles east, and the scene of a motorcycle gang's rampage that inspired the movie *The Wild One* – the building was turned into a dance hall and saloon. The adjacent **Plaza Stables** and Blacksmith Shop, a perfectly preserved blacksmith shop plus a display of a range of old stagecoaches and wagons; here you can also learn how to decipher an array of cattle brands, from "lazy H" to "rockin' double B".

ACCOMMODATION AND EATING SAN JUAN BAUTISTA

Hacienda de Léal 410 The Alameda ☎ 831 623 4380, ⊛ haciendadeleal.com. One of San Juan Bautista's only places to bed down for the night is this charming lodge, where you'll have simple but elegant rooms with Mexican-inspired decor and access to the outdoor, heated swimming pool. $115

Jardines de San Juan 115 3rd St ☎ 831 623 4466, ⊛ jardinesrestaurant.com. The top Mexican restaurant in town boasts filling and reasonably priced mains ($10–15), excellent margaritas and shaded seating under an attractive arbour. Mon–Thurs & Sun 11.30am–9pm, Fri & Sat 11.30am–10pm.

Big Sur

While not an official geographical designation, **BIG SUR** is the de facto regional name for the spectacular ninety miles of rocky cliffs and crashing seas along the California coast between San Simeon and the Monterey Peninsula. Driving north on Hwy-1, you'll know you've reached it when the estuaries and beaches of the Central Coast give way to a jagged-edged coastline and dense tangles of redwoods, the southernmost groves in the trees' long coastal chain.

Before the region's highway was completed in 1937, the few inhabitants of Big Sur had to be almost entirely self-sufficient by farming, raising cattle and trapping sea otters for their furs. The only connections with the rest of the world were via the infrequently used steamship line to Monterey, or a nearly impassable trail over the mountains to Salinas Valley. Despite improved transport links, fewer people live here today (about one thousand) than in 1900, and much of the land not in the hands of the federal and state governments is still owned by a handful of families, many of whom are descendants of Big Sur's original pioneers. Locals have banded together to protect the land from obtrusive development, while also fighting government plans to allow offshore oil drilling; to their credit, their ornery determination has paid off.

Big Sur's coast is also the protected habitat of the **sea otter**, and **grey whales** pass by close to the shore on their annual winter migration. A visit in April or May will reveal vibrant **wildflowers** and lilac-coloured ceanothus bushes under increasingly foggy skies, though the sun generally shines unhindered during the fall months. Summer weekends see the roads and campgrounds packed to overflowing – and the wildness of the area dampened – by eager visitors.

Resist the temptation to bust through Big Sur in a single day; the best way to enjoy its isolation and beauty is slowly. Leave the car behind as often as you can and wander through its numerous parks, where a mere ten-minute walk can completely remove you from any hint of the built environment.

The central section of Big Sur around CA-1 is the most developed and interesting for first-time visitors, with the region's three main inhabited areas all near **Pfeiffer Big Sur State Park** (see p.391): around the post office, two miles south of the park (aka **Loma Vista**); at **Fernwood**, a mile north past the park's main entrance; and at an area called the **Big Sur Village**, a further mile and a half north. Pfeiffer Big Sur is a great base for Big Sur exploration, where you can swim among giant boulders, hike up redwood canyons to a waterfall or sunbathe on a beautiful, sandy beach. Conveniently, its day-use fee ($10) is also valid at **Julia Pfeiffer Burns** and **Andrew Molera state parks** to the south and north, respectively.

Willow Creek and Jade Cove

The southern coastline of Big Sur is the region at its most gentle, with sandy beaches nestled below eroding yellow-ochre cliffs. Thirty miles north of Piedras Blancas elephant seal rookery (see p.382), the cliffs become steeper and the road more tortuous around the vista point at **Willow Creek**, where you can watch surfers and sea otters playing in the waves (albeit not together). **Jade Cove**, one mile north, takes its name from the translucent stones sometimes found here, mainly by scuba divers offshore; crashing waves at this rocky cove reinforce the awesome power of the sea. To reach it, follow a brambly trail ten minutes from the highway, marked by a wooden stile in the cattle fence.

6

Sand Dollar Beach

Daily 10am–6pm (no camping) • $10/vehicle • ☎ 805 434 1996, ⓦ campone.com

Half a mile north of Jade Cove is **Sand Dollar Beach**, the longest stretch of sand along the Big Sur coast and a good place to enjoy the surf or watch the **hang-gliders** that launch from sites in the mountains off Plaskett Ridge Road. This steep, one-lane route, which ends at Nacimiento–Fergusson Road several winding miles north, is great fun on a mountain bike and leads to a few isolated campgrounds along the ridge.

Kirk Creek and Limekiln State Park

Limekiln State Park $10/vehicle • ☎ 831 434 1996, ⓦ parks.ca.gov

The coastal campground (see p.393) at **Kirk Creek** sits at the foot of Nacimiento–Fergusson Road, which twists over the Santa Lucia Mountains to Salinas Valley via Mission San Antonio de Padua (see p.384). Just across the highway from the campground is the Vicente Flat Trailhead, from which an excellent, if taxing, **hike** leads deep into Los Padres National Forest.

Small **Limekiln State Park**, two miles north of Kirk Creek, is named after the hundred-year-old kilns that survive in good condition along the creek behind the park campground (see p.393). In the 1880s, local limestone was burned in these kilns to extract lime powder for use as cement, then carried on a complex aerial tramway to be loaded onto ships down at Rockland Landing; the ships that carried the lime powder to Monterey in turn brought supplies to isolated Big Sur. An easy two-mile **hike** at Limekiln leads to the park's namesake waterfall – a moss-laden vertical cascade that's well worth an hour, or more if you wish to linger along the lush trail.

Esalen Hot Springs

55000 Hwy-1 • Hot springs daily 1–3am • $30 (reservations essential) • ☎ 831 667 3047, ⓦ esalen.org

Twelve miles north of Limekiln State Park, the **Esalen Institute** (ESS-uhlun), is named for the Esselen band of local Native Americans who once frequented the healing waters of the natural **Esalen Hot Springs** here, located at the top of a cliff two hundred feet above the raging Pacific surf. Since the 1960s, when all sorts of people came to Big Sur to smoke dope and get back to nature, the springs have been owned and operated by the Esalen Institute – the devotees of which tend to arrive in luxury vehicles for overnight stays, massage treatments, yoga workshops and seminars on "potentialities and values of human existence". Esalen's hot springs, however, are available to non-guests, albeit only in the very wee hours.

Julia Pfeiffer Burns State Park

Mile 35.8 Hwy-1 • Open 30min before sunrise to 30min after sunset • $10/vehicle (day-use) • ☎ 831 667 2315, ⓦ parks.ca.gov

Named after one of the region's early pioneers, **Julia Pfeiffer Burns State Park**, three miles north of Esalen along McWay Creek, has some of the best day-hikes in Big Sur.

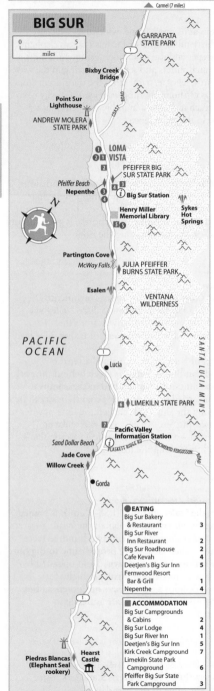

The most popular walk here is an easy, ten-minute jaunt that begins at the parking area, then heads through a tunnel under the highway, along the edge of a cliff and, finally, to a viewpoint over the spectacular **McWay Falls**, which crashes colourfully onto a beach below Saddle Rock. A less-travelled path leads down from Hwy-1 two miles north of the waterfall (at milepost 37.85) through a 200ft-long tunnel to the wave-washed remains of a small wharf at **Partington Cove**, one of the few places in southern Big Sur where you can actually reach the seashore itself.

Henry Miller Memorial Library

48603 Hwy-1 • Daily 11am–6pm (Jan–March 10am–5pm) • Free • ☎ 831 667 2574, ⓦ henrymiller.org

About eight miles north of Julia Pfeiffer Burns State Park, stop in at the **Henry Miller Memorial Library**, where the secluded front lawn is a pleasant place to grab a coffee or use the free wi-fi. There's little Millerabilia on display, but employees will happily show you plenty if you ask. Miller's own home, back near Partington Cove, is now a private residence; the house at this location was owned by Miller's old compatriot Emil White and now stands as a ramshackle arts centre, bookstore and performance venue-cum-monument to the author of *Tropic of Cancer* (see box, p.698).

Nepenthe and Pfeiffer Beach

Nepenthe 48510 Hwy-1 • ⓦ nepenthbigsur.com • **Pfeiffer Beach** Daily 9am–8pm • $10/vehicle • ☎ 805 434 1996, ⓦ campone.com

Sited dramatically high above the coast, around a quarter mile north of the Henry Miller library, the **Nepenthe** complex comprises a restaurant (see p.393) and cheaper *Café Kevah* – as well as the Phoenix gift shop and bookstore (daily 10.30am–7pm) full of novels by Kerouac, Henry Miller and Robert Louis Stevenson.

Nearby, unmarked Sycamore Canyon Road leads a mile west to Big Sur's

---

BIG SUR

0 — 5
miles

Carmel (7 miles)

GARRAPATA STATE PARK

Bixby Creek Bridge

COAST ROAD

Point Sur Lighthouse

ANDREW MOLERA STATE PARK

❶ LOMA ❷❶ VISTA
❷ PFEIFFER BIG SUR STATE PARK
Pfeiffer Beach ❸
Nepenthe ❸
❹ ❹ ⓘ Big Sur Station
❹

Henry Miller Memorial Library
❺❺

Sykes Hot Springs

Partington Cove
McWay Falls JULIA PFEIFFER BURNS STATE PARK

Esalen

VENTANA WILDERNESS

PACIFIC OCEAN

SANTA LUCIA MTNS

Lucia

❻ LIMEKILN STATE PARK

Pacific Valley Information Station
ⓘ
PLASKETT RIDGE RD
Sand Dollar Beach
Jade Cove
Willow Creek
❼

NACIMIENTO-FERGUSSON ROAD

Gorda

● EATING	
Big Sur Bakery & Restaurant	3
Big Sur River Inn Restaurant	2
Big Sur Roadhouse	2
Cafe Kevah	4
Deetjen's Big Sur Inn	5
Fernwood Resort Bar & Grill	1
Nepenthe	4

■ ACCOMMODATION	
Big Sur Campgrounds & Cabins	2
Big Sur Lodge	4
Big Sur River Inn	1
Deetjen's Big Sur Inn	5
Kirk Creek Campground	7
Limekiln State Park Campground	6
Pfeiffer Big Sur State Park Campground	3

Piedras Blancas (Elephant Seal rookery)
Hearst Castle

San Luis Obispo (41 miles)

THE BEATS IN BIG SUR

In 1960, **Jack Kerouac** spent several weeks in Big Sur, meditating and drinking in a small cabin owned by poet (and owner of City Lights) Lawrence Ferlinghetti in **Bixby Creek Canyon**, (which Kerouac refers to as "Raton Canyon"). He wrote about his experiences in *Big Sur* (1962), one of Kerouac's darkest and brutally honest novels (though it starts out happily enough with his exploration of the valley), as he descends into spirals of self-doubt, madness and alcoholism. Today you can stop at **Bixby Creek Bridge** (see p.392), but the beach below is virtually inaccessible, the valley itself a patchwork of private plots and cabins. Kerouac also visited **Nepenthe** (see p.393) with the gang – poet Michael McClure, Neal Cassady, Ferlinghetti, poet Lew Welch, painter Victor Wong and poet Philip Whalen – where they ate Heavenburgers and got smashed on Manhattans, after bathing at **Esalen Hot Springs** (see p.389). The Beats followed in the footsteps of irascible author **Henry Miller**, who lived here between 1944 and 1963 (he recorded his life along the coast in *Big Sur and the Oranges of Hieronymus Bosch*, published in 1957). Miller's former home is also private, but you can visit the **Henry Miller Memorial Library** (see opposite) – despite a history of mutual admiration (and sometimes criticism), Kerouac and Miller never got to meet.

6

finest strand, **Pfeiffer Beach**, a white-sand, sometimes windy stretch dominated by a charismatic hump of rock whose colour varies from brown to red to orange in the changing light. Park where you can at the end of the road and walk through an archway of cypress trees along the lagoon down to the sand.

Just over one mile north, you'll find the region's post office, as well as an absurdly expensive **gas station** in the area known as Loma Vista.

Sykes Hot Springs

One mile north of Loma Vista along Hwy-1, the road drops behind a coastal ridge into the inland valley of the Big Sur River, where most accommodation and dining options are located. A popular hike leads steeply up from the Pine Ridge Trailhead behind Big Sur Station (see p.393) and ten miles into the mountains to **Sykes Hot Springs** (unrestricted entry, but overnight camping permit required), just downstream from a set of free, primitive campsites along the river in Ventana Wilderness. This extraordinary – and popular – amble is an overnight expedition and requires several hours of hiking each way.

Pfeiffer Big Sur State Park

47225 Hwy-1 (mile 47.2) • Open 30min before sunrise to 30min after sunset • $10/vehicle (day-use) • ☎ 831 667 2315, ⦿ parks.ca.gov

Plumb in the middle of the Big Sur River's valley, **Pfeiffer Big Sur State Park** is one of the most beautiful and enjoyable parks in all of California, with miles of hiking trails and excellent river swimming. In late spring and summer, the Big Sur's crystal-clear waters run highest, creating deep swimming holes among the large boulders plunked along the bottom of its narrow, steep-walled gorge. Nude sunbathing is tolerated (other than at weekends and holidays, when the park tends to be overrun with swarms of children) and, since the park is sheltered a few miles inland, the weather is warmer and sunnier than elsewhere in Big Sur. The park is also home to the largest **campground** (see p.393) in the region.

The most popular hiking trail in the park leads to sixty-foot **Pfeiffer Falls** (Valley View Trail, 2 miles round-trip), up a narrow canyon shaded by redwood trees. The bridges over the river here possess an understated grace, as does the nearby amphitheatre – built by the Civilian Conservation Corps during the Depression – where rangers offer excellent campfire talks and slide shows during summer months. The park is named for early pioneer John Pfeiffer whose **Homestead Cabin** is on view near the campground (Julia Pfeiffer was his sister).

Andrew Molera State Park

Mile 51.2 Hwy-1 • Open 30min before sunrise to 30min after sunset • $10/vehicle (day-use) • ☎ 831 667 2315, ⓦ parks.ca.gov

Andrew Molera State Park, five miles north of Pfeiffer Big Sur State Park, is the largest park in Big Sur, its two-plus miles of rocky oceanfront easily reached by a mile-long trail; you'll also find a walk-in campground here. The park occupies the site of what was once the El Sur Ranch, one of the earliest and most successful Big Sur cattle ranches, initially run in the early nineteenth century by Juan Bautista Alvarado, who became California governor in 1836; it was later overseen by English sea captain Roger Cooper, whose **cabin** is preserved here. Although Cooper's cabin isn't open to the public, you can reach the site via the park's fifteen miles of hiking trails, which are also used by Molera Horseback Tours for a variety of guided **horseriding treks** (1hr 30min–2hr 30min; $58–114; ☎ 831 625 5486, ⓦ molerahorsebacktours.com).

Point Sur Lighthouse

Hwy-1 (19 miles south of Carmel) • April–Sept Sat & Wed 10am & 2pm, Sun 10am (also Thurs 10am July & Aug); Oct–March Sat & Sun 10am, Wed 1pm; check website for moonlight tour schedule • Regular tour $12, moonlight tour $20 • ☎ 831 625 4419, ⓦ pointsur.org

Three miles north of Andrew Molera State Park along Hwy-1, **Point Sur Lighthouse** occupies a magical location, perched 360ft above the surf on a tall volcanic outcrop that juts into the sea from an overgrown sandbank. The only way to visit is by taking a walking **tour** offered once or twice monthly (first-come, first-served, no reservations, maximum of 40 people); set aside three hours to tour the lighthouse, built in 1889, and its ancillary buildings. Families manned the lighthouse until 1974 (it's now automated).

Bixby Creek Bridge

Six miles north of Point Sur Lighthouse, **Bixby Creek Bridge** was ranked as the longest single-span concrete bridge in the world when its construction was completed in 1932. It's the most impressive (and photogenic) engineering feat of the entire Coast Road project, a local construction programme sponsored by the Works Progress Administration during the Depression and indelibly connected with *Big Sur* by Jack Kerouac (p.697). A few miles north, **Rocky Creek Bridge** is another scenic spot to pull over.

Garrapata State Park

Hwy-1 (7 miles south of Carmel) • Free • ☎ 831 624 4909, ⓦ parks.ca.gov

The northernmost stop along Big Sur's coast, and about seven miles before Hwy-1 begins to drop into Carmel, is wildflower-rich **Garrapata State Park**. A mile-long trail leads from the highway out to the tip of **Soberanes Point**, a beautiful spot from which you can look for sea otters and grey whales; a couple of very rugged hiking trails head inland from the main trailhead along the highway as well.

ARRIVAL AND DEPARTURE
BIG SUR

By car Most visitors will need a car to follow Hwy-1's dramatic path through Big Sur. However, the exhilarating route, which winds through bedrock cliffs several hundred feet above the Pacific Ocean, is also, despite its narrow width, a perennial favourite with cyclists.

By bus The only public transport through Big Sur is Monterey–Salinas Transit (MST) bus #22 ($3.50), which departs from Monterey Transit Plaza and runs as far south as Nepenthe. Its schedule varies throughout the year – call ☎ 888 678 2871 or check ⓦ mst.org.

INFORMATION

Gas stations and grocery stores are scattered and surprisingly scarce throughout Big Sur, so you should expect those you do find to be premium-priced; it's best to fill your tank and go shopping before your visit. Note as well that mobile-phone coverage around Big Sur is patchy at best, while wi-fi is available at certain lodgings.

Big Sur Station Pfeiffer Big Sur State Park (daily 9am–4pm; ☎ 831 667 2315). Be sure to stop here at the Pine Ridge Trailhead, where helpful personnel distribute backcountry camping and campfire permits for Ventana Wilderness in the adjacent Santa Lucia Mountains, and are otherwise the region's finest repository of park information.

Big Sur Chamber of Commerce Big Sur Village (☎ 831 667 2100, ⓦ bigsurcalifornia.org). Limited hours.

ACCOMMODATION

In keeping with Big Sur's backwoods qualities, most **accommodation** is in rustic lodges, at varying levels of affordability. Note that the relatively few places on offer are full most nights throughout summer (especially on weekends), so book well in advance. **Campgrounds** are dotted all along the Big Sur coast and remain popular year-round, while a few less developed ones exist in the Santa Lucia Mountains above.

Note that the following listings are ordered from south to north. Rather than indicate each location's street address along Hwy-1, distances from the nearest state park are instead used as a guide.

Kirk Creek Campground Hwy-1, 2 miles south of Limekiln State Park ☎ 805 434 1996, ⓦ campone.com. Set on an exposed bluff in Big Sur's southern reaches, this is the only campground in the area that is both right on the coast and contains walk-in sites. No potable water. Walk-in **\$5**, drive-in **\$25**

Limekiln State Park Campground ☎ 800 444 7275, ⓦ reserveamerica.com. Small campground with showers and easy access to trails leading to limekilns (see p.389), redwoods and a waterfall. **\$35**

★ **Deetjen's Big Sur Inn** Hwy-1, 7 miles north of Julia Pfeiffer Burns State Park ☎ 831 667 2377, ⓦ deetjens .com. Built by a Norwegian immigrant from the 1930s to the 1960s, this laidback compound (with great restaurant and bar) spread across several buildings offers comfortably rustic lodging. Ski-lodge-style log cabins feature fireplaces, rocking chairs, old-fashioned leaded windows and lots of wood panelling. **\$105**

Big Sur Lodge In Pfeiffer Big Sur State Park ☎ 805 667 3100, ⓦ bigsurlodge.com. This plush lodge features well-furnished rooms, each with a porch and enormous, sit-down shower. Some rooms have fireplaces, while all have

access to a nice outdoor pool and restaurant. Rates include entrance fee to area state parks. **\$239**

Pfeiffer Big Sur State Park Campground ☎ 800 444 7275, ⓦ reserveamerica.com. Big Sur's biggest and most popular campground has spacious and well-shaded sites, many situated among the redwoods. Showers, a well-stocked store and even a launderette are all available. Walk-in **\$5**, drive-in **\$35**

Big Sur Campgrounds & Cabins Hwy-1, 1 mile north of Pfeiffer Big Sur State Park ☎ 831 667 2322, ⓦ bigsurcamp.com. This inviting riverside campground has the area's best cabins: wooden "camping cabins" that sleep up to three, as well as fancier units fitted with private bathrooms. Pitches **\$63**, camping cabins **\$175**, cabins **\$240**

Big Sur River Inn Hwy-1, 2.5 miles north of Pfeiffer Big Sur State Park ☎ 831 667 2700, ⓦ bigsurriverinn .com. A woodland lodge with a handful of fine riverside suites, complete with down quilts and verandas; less expensive, but still delightful motel-style rooms are situated across the highway. There's a handy grocery store and charming restaurant (see p.394) on site as well. **\$245**

EATING

A number of places to **eat** in Big Sur are attached to the inns listed above. Many are fairly basic burger-and-beer joints, but there are a few special ones worth searching out – some for their good food, others for their views of the Pacific. Due to Big Sur's isolation, prices here can be considerably higher than what you'd expect to pay in a proper town. The following listings are ordered from south to north, with approximate distances from the region's state parks used as a guide.

Deetjen's Big Sur Inn Hwy-1, 7 miles north of Julia Pfeiffer Burns State Park ☎ 831 667 2378, ⓦ deetjens .com. Excellent, unhurried breakfasts (around \$9.50–16) and a variety of top-quality fish and vegetarian dinners (mains \$24–42) are served in a snug, redwood-panelled room. Mon–Fri 8am–noon & 6–9pm, Sat & Sun 8am–12.30pm & 6–9pm.

★ **Nepenthe** Hwy-1, 3 miles south of Pfeiffer Big Sur State Park ☎ 831 667 2345, ⓦ nepenthebigsur.com. Definitely not for the thrifty, this high-profile steak-and-seafood restaurant boasts a warm amber mood, unforgettable views (sunset whale watching is possible in season) and an

après-ski-like atmosphere. Mains run \$29–44.50. *Café Kevah* below offers cheaper snacks and light meals. Daily 11.30am–4.30pm & 5–10pm (10.30pm in July & Aug).

Fernwood Resort Bar & Grill Hwy-1, half a mile north of Pfeiffer Big Sur State Park ☎ 831 667 2129. This hotel diner (with atmospheric tavern) serves good salads and sandwiches for \$11–17, while pizzas (\$19–28) are available at dinner. Daily 11am–10pm (tavern open till 1am Fri & Sat).

Big Sur Bakery & Restaurant Hwy-1, 1.5 miles south of Pfeiffer Big Sur State Park ☎ 831 667 0520. Far from simply churning out delectable cakes and pastries, this moderately priced café has an on-site rotisserie in which it

6

cooks all its meats. The lunch menu features terrific wood-fired pizzas and sandwiches, while the dinner menu features meat, seafood (roasted sea bass) and vegetarian mains ($18–32). Mon 8am–3.30pm, Tues–Sun 8am–9pm.

Big Sur River Inn Restaurant Hwy-1, 2.5 miles north of Pfeiffer Big Sur State Park ☎831 667 2700, ⓦbigsurriverinn.com. Open since 1934, this classy restaurant presents a creative range of seafood and meat dishes ($14.25–38.75) at dinner in a spacious, redwood-log dining room, complete with toasty fireplace. Breakfast

($11.25–16.75) is served, while there's also a deli-style burrito bar at lunch, as well as a sizeable patio where bands perform on certain Sundays. Daily 8–11am, 11.30am–4.30pm & 5–9pm.

Big Sur Roadhouse (Glen Oaks) Hwy-1, 2.5 miles north of Pfeiffer Big Sur State Park ☎831 667 2370, ⓦglenoaksbigsur.com/big-sur-roadhouse. Offers seasonal Californian cuisine for breakfast and lunch, with excellent sandwiches and salads ($8–12), in a cosy cottage featuring designer Steve Justrich's "homegrown modernism". Daily 8am–2.30pm.

Monterey Peninsula

Immediately north of Big Sur, the rocky promontory and gnarled cypress trees of the **MONTEREY PENINSULA** amplify the collision between cliffs and thundering sea. Though the manicured towns here now thrive thanks to a regular flow of tourists, each manages to retain its individual character. Secluded **Carmel** is by far the poshest, although its star-struck election of Clint Eastwood as mayor in 1986 somewhat dispelled its sniffy reputation for a time. Around the peninsula and to the northwest, the resolutely upscale village of **Pebble Beach** is primarily known for its golf courses (it last hosted the US Open in 2010, and will for a sixth time in 2019), while **Pacific Grove** stands at the peninsula's tip with spectacular views over the sea – a pleasant, if rather sleepy, place best known for butterflies and Victorian architecture. The largest town, and the most convenient and practical base from which to explore the peninsula, is **Monterey** itself; it was the capital of California under both the Spanish and the Mexicans, and today it retains many old adobe houses and places of genuine historic appeal.

Monterey

The city of **MONTEREY** rests in a quiet niche along the bay formed by the forested Monterey Peninsula; it proudly proclaims itself the most historic city in California – a boast that, for once, may be true. Its compact centre features some of the best vernacular **buildings** of California's Spanish and Mexican colonial past, most of which stand unassumingly within a few blocks of the tourist-thronged waterfront. The single best stop – and one of the unmissable highlights of the entire Central Coast – is the **Monterey Bay Aquarium**, a mile west of downtown along **Cannery Row**.

Brief history

Monterey was named by Spanish merchant and explorer **Sebastian Vizcaíno**, who landed here in 1602 to find an abundant supply of freshwater and wild game. Despite his enthusiasm for the site, the area was not colonized until 1770, when the second mission in the California chain – the headquarters of the whole operation – was established in Monterey before being moved to its permanent site in Carmel (the presidio remained in Monterey). During the era of Spanish rule, Monterey was also the military headquarters for the whole of Alta California, and thereafter continued to be the capital of a truly enormous, albeit sparsely populated, territory that extended east to the Rocky Mountains and north to Canada. In 1818, Argentinian privateer (but French-born) **Hipólito Bouchard** sacked the city (the newly independent Argentines tasked him with harassing the Spanish colonies), the only time the US West Coast has been attacked successfully.

When the Mexican–American War began in earnest in 1846, the United States in the form of **Commodore Sloat** took possession of Monterey without resistance. The town hosted California's first **constitutional convention** in 1849, but the discovery of gold in the Sierra Nevada foothills soon focused attention upon San Francisco, and Monterey became something of a backwater, barely affected by the waves of immigration that soon flowed into California. By the 1950s, even the local fishery had collapsed and tourism is now Monterey's main livelihood.

Fisherman's Wharf

1 Old Fisherman's Wharf (end of Olivier St); parking at 245 Washington St ($1/30min, $15 daily maximum) • Ⓦ montereywharf.com

Monterey's downtown extends half a mile inland from the waterfront, though most visitors focus on **Fisherman's Wharf**, where the catch of the day is more likely to be families from San Jose than the formerly abundant sardines. Though the pier dates back to 1870, most of the commercial fishermen moved out long ago (the last active wholesale fish market closed in the 1960s), leaving the pier shacks as relics of a once-prosperous industry. Scores of chubby **sea lions** have persevered, however, and continue to float by under the piers, along with the odd sea otter, gulls, pelicans and cormorants. Though the shops and seafood restaurants on the wharf (all selling variations on chowder, fish and chips and shellfish) are rather tacky, the colourful, rickety wood buildings are very photogenic (viewed from the shore) and at least most of the businesses here remain locally owned, in contrast to Cannery Row (see p.399). This is also the place to take **whale-watching** trips (see p.405).

6

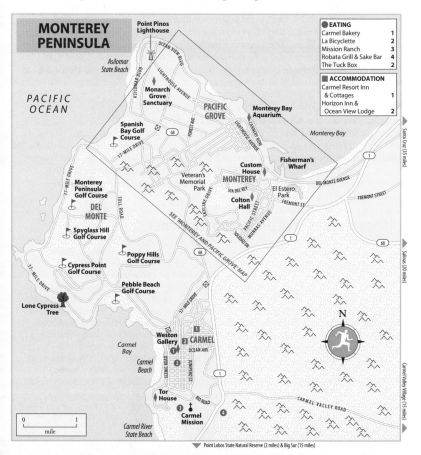

6

Dali17

5 Custom House Plaza • Mon–Thurs & Sun 10am–5pm, Fri & Sat 10am–7pm • $20 • ☎ 831 372 2608, ⓦ dali17.com

The most prominent attraction on Custom House Plaza, the square that acts as a gateway to Fisherman's Wharf, opened in the former Museum of Monterey space in 2016 as **Dali17**. Inside is an intriguing collection of 577 works by Surrealist artist **Salvador Dalí**, who was an early member of the Carmel Art Association, and spent summers at the *Hotel Del Monte* in Monterey in the 1940s (he'd fled Europe because of World War II). It's important to note, however, almost everything here is either an original lithograph, sketch or print, many associated with books illustrated by Dalí, rather than his celebrated oil paintings – no melting clocks here (no originals, at least). Though that might make the $20 admission seem a bit steep, the collection still offers a deep and nuanced interpretation of Dalí's oeuvre, from illustrations of Dante's *Divine Comedy* and the twisted writings of Marquis de Sade to his *Biblia Sacra* series. Don't miss Dalí's wonderful enhancement of Goya's acerbic *Los Caprichos*, a set of 80 prints originally published in 1799. Movies on Dalí and his connection to the region show daily from 11am.

Monterey State Historic Park

Custom House Plaza • Walking tours Tues–Sun 10.30am, 12.30pm & 2pm (1hr) • $5 • ☎ 831 649 7118

Scattered around Downtown Monterey are the buildings that make up **Monterey State Historic Park**, an artfully maintained collection of centuries-old structures that tell the story of early California better than anywhere else in the state. Begin at **Pacific House**, on Custom House Plaza, where you can get **tour** tickets (many buildings can only be viewed on a guided tour) and information about the other properties. Note that due to budget cuts listed opening times may not be accurate – check at Pacific House first to see what's open.

Pacific House Museum

Custom House Plaza • Daily 10am–4pm • Free • ☎ 831 649 7118, ⓦ parks.ca.gov

Constructed by David Wright (Scottish-born builder of the Old Whaling Station) in 1847 and serving various functions over the years, the fine adobe premises of the **Pacific House Museum** chronicles the history of Monterey when it was the capital of Spanish and Mexican California. The **Monterey Museum of the American Indian** upstairs displays traditional weaved baskets, pottery and other Native American artefacts, especially from the local **Rumsien** people.

ROBERT LOUIS STEVENSON AND MONTEREY

California's Gold Rush in 1849 bypassed Monterey for San Francisco, leaving the community as little more than a somnolent Mexican fishing village – which was pretty much how the town looked in the fall of 1879, when a feverishly ill 29-year-old Scotsman arrived by stagecoach, flat broke and desperately in love with a married woman. **Robert Louis Stevenson** came to Monterey for fresh air and to see **Fanny Osbourne**, whom he had met while travelling in France two years before. He stayed here three months, writing occasional articles for the local newspaper and telling stories in exchange for his meals at a saloon-restaurant run by Frenchman Jules Simoneau. It's said that Stevenson started writing *Treasure Island* here and used Point Lobos (see p.404) as his inspiration for Spyglass Hill. Stevenson witnessed Monterey – no longer politically crucial, but not yet a tourism hotspot – in transition, something he addressed in his essay *The Old and New Pacific Capitals*. He foresaw that the lifestyle that had endured since the Mexican era was no match for the "Yankee craft" of the "millionaire vulgarians of the Big Bonanza" – **Charles Crocker**, for one. One of San Francisco's "Big Four" railroad barons (see box, p.543), Crocker made Stevenson sound positively prescient by opening his lavish Hotel Del Monte in 1880, which helped turn the sleepy town into a seaside resort practically overnight. Stevenson moved on to San Francisco (see p.437) and eventually married Fanny in May 1880. His lodgings in Monterey are preserved as the **Robert Louis Stevenson House** (see opposite).

Custom House

Custom House Plaza • Daily 10am–4pm • Free • ☎ 831 649 7118, ⓦ parks.ca.gov

One of the more impressive colonial buildings here, the handsome, two-storey **Custom House** once acted as California's main port of entry. The current building dates from an extensive 1841 renovation of an earlier edifice, erected perhaps in the early 1820s (it's not known for sure), though it's likely that a structure has stood here since the early days of Spanish occupation. The balconied building now displays 150-year-old crates of coffee and liquor inside, as well as exhibits on the Mexican-era "hide and tallow" trade.

Old Whaling Station

99 Pacific St (entrance on Seeno St, inside Heritage Harbor business complex) • Tues–Fri 10am–2pm • Free • ☎ 831 649 7118, ⓦ jlmontereycounty.org

Just around the corner from Custom House Plaza, the **Old Whaling Station** was built in 1847 by Scottish adventurer David Wright – supposedly modelled after his home in Scotland and surrounded by flowery gardens, it's one of the prettiest adobe homes in town. Wright sold it just two years later to seek his fortune in the goldfields and by the 1850s it was being used by Portuguese whalers (their great iron pots used to render blubber are still on site). The house has been restored by the Junior League of Monterey County and contains period antiques and furnishings.

First Brick House

Seeno St, inside Heritage Harbor business complex • Fri–Sun 10am–4pm • Free • ☎ 831 649 7118, ⓦ parks.ca.gov

American newcomer Gallant Dickinson built the **First Brick House** in 1847, and it still stands out among the nearby wooden and adobe-style homes. The ground floor contains exhibits on Monterey history, while the kitchen has been restored as it looked when the house was used in later years as a restaurant.

Casa de Oro

210 Olivier St • Thurs–Sun 11am–3pm • Free • ☎ 831 649 3364, ⓦ historicgardenleague.org

The two-story limestone rock and adobe **Casa de Oro** was built by Thomas Larkin (see p.674) in about 1845, but it was leased around 1850 to one Joseph Boston as one of the first general merchandise stores in the area. Today it's operated by the Historic Garden League of Monterey as the **Jos Boston & Co store**, offering themed 1850s merchandise, local crafts and antiques, along with their **Picket Fence garden shop** next door (same hours).

Robert Louis Stevenson House

530 Houston St • Sat & Sun 10am–4pm • Free • ☎ 831 649 7118, ⓦ parks.ca.gov

This two-storey sturdy 1830s building gained its current title of **Robert Louis Stevenson House** after the then unknown Scottish author stayed here in the fall of 1879. At that time it was the French Hotel, and the ailing Stevenson resided here while courting his future wife, Fanny Osbourne. Today the house contains many of his personal effects.

Larkin House

464 Calle Principal • Tours by appointment only, starting at $75 for up to 12 people • ☎ 831 649 7172

The adobe-brick **Larkin House**, half a mile south of Custom House Plaza, is the former home of successful entrepreneur **Thomas Larkin**, the first and only American Consul to California. The New England-born Larkin, the wealthy owner of a general store and redwood lumber business, was one of the most important and influential figures in early California, actively involved in efforts to attract American settlers here and lobbying Californians to turn towards the increasingly powerful United States (and away from the erratic government of Mexico). Through his designs for his own house and the Custom House, Larkin is credited with developing the now-familiar Monterey style of architecture, which combines local adobe walls and the balconies of Southern plantation homes with a puritan Yankee's taste. Larkin House, the first two-storey adobe in

California, is filled with many millions of dollars of antiques and is surrounded by lush **gardens** (these are always open, even if the house is not), dating from 1927.

Colton Hall and Old Monterey Jail

570 Pacific St • Daily 10am–4pm • Free • ☎ 831 646 5640, ⓦ monterey.org/museum

The watershed **California constitutional convention** of 1849 was held in the then newly completed town hall, a grand white stone building known today as **Colton Hall**. It was commissioned by **Reverend William Colton**, the first American *alcalde* (mayor-judge) of Monterey (1846–49). Still owned by the city of Monterey (it's not part of the state historic park), its re-created meeting room is furnished as it was in the mid-nineteenth century with plank floors, quill pens on the tables and an early map of the West Coast, all used to draw up the boundaries of the nascent Golden State. A small one-room museum chronicles its later history as a public school.

Next door, the granite cells of tiny **Old Monterey Jail** (daily 10am–4pm; free; ☎ 831 646 5640), built in 1854 and used – shockingly – until 1956, contain a few exhibits and quotes from novels that reference the cramped prison.

Monterey Museum of Art

559 Pacific St • Mon & Thurs–Sun 11am–5pm • $10 • ☎ 831 372 5477, ⓦ montereyart.org

Aficionados will appreciate the **Monterey Museum of Art**, with a small but wonderfully focused collection of paintings by locally based artists, many associated with the art colony and **Monterey School** that developed here after World War I. Impressionist **M. Evelyn McCormick** (1862–1948), *en plein air* adherent **Armin Hansen** (1886–1957) and Irish-born **John O'Shea** (1876–1956) are well represented, but the museum also features work by Modern and Contemporary artists such as **William Theophilus Brown** (1919–2012), a member of the Bay Area Figurative Movement, and abstract painter **Joan Savo** (1918–1992). Perhaps the most impressive department here is **photography**, with prints by masters such as Dorothea Lange and Ansel Adams always on display.

Royal Presidio Chapel (San Carlos Cathedral)

500 Church St • **Royal Presidio Chapel** Daily 10am–6pm • **Heritage Center** Wed 10am–noon, Fri 10am–3pm, Sat 10am–2pm, Sun 1–3pm (every 2nd and 4th Mon 10am–noon & 1.15–3.15pm) • Free • ☎ 831 373 2628, ⓦ sancarloscathedral.org

Junípero Serra's original mission church wasn't completely abandoned when he moved to Carmel, and a more permanent church, now known as the **Royal Presidio Chapel** (aka San Carlos Cathedral), was completed in 1795 to serve the presidio (Spanish garrison) in Monterey. The handsome, pale yellow façade, is evocative of Mexican colonial architecture, though the interior (still a well-used place of worship) is of less interest. The chapel a is short walk from downtown (it's on the Monterey State Historic Park trail map). The **Heritage Center** is located in the Parish Offices Building next to the church – displays inside include a remnant of the **Vizcaíno-Serra Oak** (the tree where the 1602 Vizcaíno expedition took shelter, and where Serra held the first Mass in 1770), items found during recent archeological digs and pieces of the whale-bone pavement that once led to the church.

Presidio Museum

570 Pacific St • Daily 10am–4pm • Free • ☎ 831 646 5640, ⓦ monterey.org/museum

Looming over Downtown Monterey and Fisherman's Wharf, the **Presidio of Monterey** is a massive US army base (containing the Defense Language Institute) that remains largely off-limits save for the **Lower Presidio**, which has been leased to the city and contains the small but illuminating **Presidio Museum**. The site of the original Spanish fortress known as El Castillo (now long gone) was nearby, and the museum chronicles the history of the military base, which was redeveloped and expanded by the Americans in the 1840s as Fort Mervine (it was renamed in 1904 in respect of its Spanish heritage). The museum building was built in 1906 as a munitions store, just below the grand **Sloat Monument** on the hill above (honouring the naval commander who raised the US flag here in 1846).

Look out also for the tiny **Bouchard Memorial**, commemorating the six days in 1818 when Monterey was Argentine territory (ask a docent). A classic B-movie, *Sergeant Murphy*, starring former president Ronald Reagan, was filmed here in 1938.

Cannery Row
ⓦ canneryrow.com

The pleasantly landscaped Monterey Coastal Trail (for bikes and pedestrians) runs west along the seafront from Fisherman's Wharf to **Cannery Row** (under a mile), a waterfront street once known as Ocean View Avenue and renamed after John Steinbeck's evocative 1945 portrait of the rough-and-ready men and women who worked in and around the thirty-odd fish canneries here. The first, slightly more genteel section of posh hotels and restaurants runs from Reeside Avenue to Drake Avenue, while the main segment (parallel to Wave St) lies between Hoffman and David, a heavily commercialized strip of chain restaurants and stores (think *Bubba Gump Shrimp* and *Sunglasses Hut*), and even a Steinbeck-themed Wax Museum about a million miles from the author's description of the Row as a "poem, a stink, a grating noise, a quality of light, a tone, a habit, a nostalgia, a dream". Statues of the author (and the **Cannery Row Monument**, a 15ft rock-and-bronze sculpture commemorating Ed Ricketts and other colourful Row characters), plus the old cannery buildings themselves (the **Monterey Canning Co** is the most famous example), are all that remain as a reminder of the street's former role.

During World War II, Monterey was the sardine capital of the western world, catching and canning some 200,000 tonnes each year. However, overfishing ensured that by the time Steinbeck's celebrated novel was published, the sardines were more or less all gone; the canneries were subsequently abandoned and fell into disrepair (the last closed in 1973).

Pacific Biological Laboratories
800 Cannery Row • Free 1hr tours monthly April–Nov, check website • ☎ 831 646 5640, ⓦ monterey.org/museums • Reservations required

One of the few historic sights on Cannery Row, **Pacific Biological Laboratories** is only open for monthly tours, though Steinbeck fans should plan ahead, as this was marine biologist Ed Ricketts' actual lab from 1928 to his death in 1948 (Ricketts was the model for several "Doc" characters in Steinbeck's novels). Docents tell illuminating stories about both men and about the "PBL" members who acquired the Lab in the mid-1950s and who helped found the Monterey Jazz Festival.

Monterey Bay Aquarium
886 Cannery Row • Generally daily 9.30am–6pm, but check website for seasonally varying hours • $49.95, child (3–12) $29.95 • ☎ 831 648 4800, ⓦ montereybayaquarium.org

Ride, walk or take the free trolley to the western end of Cannery Row, where sits the magnificent **Monterey Bay Aquarium** – one of the largest, most stunning displays of underwater life in the world, housed in a cannery dating back to 1916. The place can be very busy in summer, but making reservations online beforehand can save you a long wait. The aquarium's eastern end is largely devoted to the **Outer Bay** section, an enormous tank with vast windows providing matchless views of the species that populate the deep waters just beyond the bay. Lazy hammerhead sharks glide among foul-tempered tuna, while hungry barracuda dart about and massive sunfish make their stately circuit of the tank's perimeter.

Towards the middle of the building, the **sea otters** always draw a crowd, particularly at feeding time (10.30am, 1.30pm & 3.30pm). These playful creatures are now relatively

---

THE MONTEREY TROLLEY

To save the walk between Fisherman's Wharf and Cannery Row, take the free **MST trolley bus** (summer 10am–7pm; rest of year Sat & Sun 10am–7pm) that zips between Downtown Monterey, the wharf, Cannery Row and the aquarium every 10–15min.

6

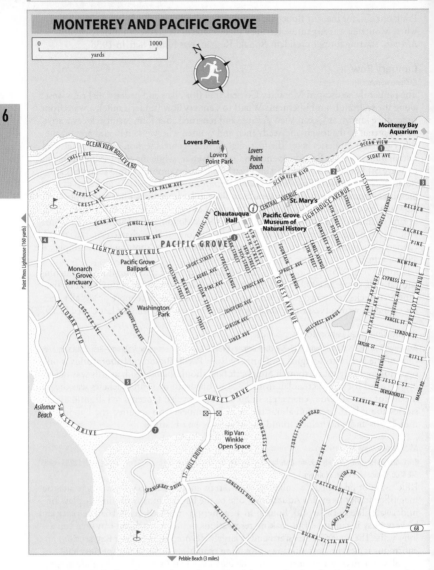

MONTEREY AND PACIFIC GROVE

common out in the bay, but were once hunted nearly to extinction for their uncommonly soft fur. At the western end of the aquarium, habitats close to shore are presented in the **kelp forest**, where mesmerizing, ever-circling schools of silver anchovies avoid the sharks.

The complex also opens directly onto the bay, allowing you to step out and peer into **wild tide pools** after observing the bevy of captive tanks.

Pacific Grove

Though it merges seamlessly into Monterey, **PACIFIC GROVE** – or "Butterfly Town USA", as it likes to call itself – stands curiously apart from the rest of the Peninsula, less

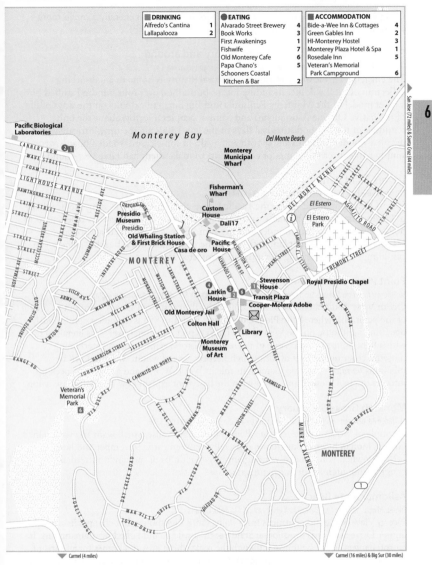

■ DRINKING	
Alfredo's Cantina	1
Lallapalooza	2

● EATING	
Alvarado Street Brewery	4
Book Works	3
First Awakenings	1
Fishwife	7
Old Monterey Cafe	6
Papa Chano's	5
Schooners Coastal Kitchen & Bar	2

■ ACCOMMODATION	
Bide-a-Wee Inn & Cottages	4
Green Gables Inn	2
HI-Monterey Hostel	3
Monterey Plaza Hotel & Spa	1
Rosedale Inn	5
Veteran's Memorial Park Campground	6

known but more impressively situated than its famous neighbours. The city began as a campground and Methodist retreat in 1875, a summertime tent city for revivalist Christians in which strong drink, naked flesh and reading the Sunday papers were firmly prohibited. The Methodists have long since moved on, but otherwise the city centre is little changed from that era. Its quiet streets, lined by pine trees and grand old **Victorian wooden homes** are enlivened by hundreds of thousands of orange-and-black **monarch butterflies**, which arrive here each winter from all over the western US and Canada. In fact, the migration of these butterflies is so crucial to the local economy that they're protected by local law: there's a $1000 fine for "molesting a butterfly in any way". **Downtown Pacific Grove** is centred along Lighthouse Avenue (between 12th and

Congress), two miles northwest of central Monterey, and is generally a much more pleasant place to eat and drink.

Pacific Grove Museum of Natural History and around

165 Forest Ave • Tues–Sun 10am–5pm • $8.95 • ☎ 831 648 5716, ⬤ pgmuseum.org

The engaging **Pacific Grove Museum of Natural History** is home to an absorbing collection of local wildlife, including lots of butterflies, over four hundred stuffed birds, a relief model of the Monterey Peninsula and Big Sur, and exhibits on the ways of life of the native Ohlone (Costanoan) and Salinan peoples. Nearby, about the only reminder of the Methodist revival days of the late 1800s are the tiny, intricately detailed **wooden cottages** along 16th and 17th; in some cases, wooden boards were simply nailed over the frames of canvas tents to make them habitable year-round.

Lovers Point Park

630 Ocean View Blvd, at 17th St • Daily 24hr • Free • ☎ 831 648 3100

Ocean View Boulevard circles the Pacific Grove along the coast, passing the headland of **Lovers Point Park** – originally called Lovers of Jesus Point – where preachers used to hold sunrise services. Surrounded in early summer by colourful red-and-purple blankets of blooming ice plants, it's one of the peninsula's finest **beaches**, where you can lounge and swim along the intimate, protected strand.

Point Pinos Lighthouse

80 Asilomar Ave • Mon & Thurs–Sun 1–4pm • Free (donation requested) • ☎ 831 648 3176, ⬤ pointpinoslighthouse.org

Ocean View Boulevard runs another mile along the coast from Lovers Point out to the tip of the peninsula, where **Point Pinos Lighthouse**, built in 1855 is the oldest continuously operating lighthouse on the West Coast. Don't expect a soaring tower – it's literally a house with a light on top – but it's one of the region's historic gems, with an entertaining museum covering the lives of former lightkeepers (one of whom was murdered by infamous *bandido* Anastasio García), its role in World War II, and a chance to peek up into the original Fresnel lens. Exhibits in the basement explain how the lighthouse works.

Monarch Grove Sanctuary

250 Ridge Rd, between Lighthouse Ave and Short St • Dawn–dusk • Free • ☎ 831 648 5716

A couple of blocks southeast from Point Pinos Lighthouse, you'll want to visit Pacific's Grove's **Monarch Grove Sanctuary**, especially between early November and late February when you can easily spot giant brown clumps of monarch butterflies congregating high in the eucalyptus treetops.

Asilomar State Beach

Sunset Drive, at Asilomar Ave • Dawn–dusk • Free • ☎ 831 646 6440, ⬤ parks.ca.gov

Ocean View Boulevard continues from Point Pinos Lighthouse, but changes its name to Sunset Drive as it leads to **Asilomar State Beach**, a wild strand lashed by dramatic surf. It's far too dangerous for swimming, though the rocky shore provides homes for all sorts of tide-pool life and the accessible **Asilomar Coast Trail** provides an easy one-mile (one-way) taster. The old camp buildings here (still in use as a conference centre and restaurant) were designed by renowned California architect Julia Morgan between 1913 and 1928.

17-Mile Drive

If you're at (or even near) Asilomar State Beach, it's logical to continue your explorations along **17-MILE DRIVE**, a scenic, privately owned toll road ($10 per car; motorcycles prohibited; ☎ 800 877 0597, ⬤ pebblebeach.com) that loops from Pacific Grove along the coast south to Carmel, swooping past the golf courses and country clubs of **Pebble Beach** along the way. Don't miss the trussed-up figure of the **Lone Cypress** halfway along the route, the subject of many a postcard; there are enough beautiful vistas of the rugged coastline to almost make it worth braving the hordes that pack the route most weekends.

Carmel and around

Set on gently rising bluffs above a rocky shore, the precious town of **CARMEL** is well known for its genteel air, neat rows of boutiques and miniature homes, and a largely untouched coastline. Besides all the rampant cuteness, Carmel's only real crime is its ridiculously inflated price scale; think of it as the West Coast's middle-aged answer to New York's Hamptons.

The town's reputation as an exclusive corner belies its origins, for there was nothing much here until the San Francisco earthquake and fire of 1906 led a number of artists and writers from the city to take refuge in the area, forming a **bohemian colony** on the wild and uninhabited slopes that soon became infamous throughout the state for its free-spirited excess. The figurehead of the group was poet George Sterling; part-time members included Jack London, Mary Austin and the young Sinclair Lewis. By the 1920s an influx of wealthy San Franciscans had put Carmel well on its way to becoming the **rich resort** it is today. Despite the continued growth of tourism in the area, Carmel – its official name is Carmel-by-the-Sea – still seems the epitome of parochial snobbishness, with an array of laws enacted to stringently maintain the gingerbread charm of the town's central district (parking meters and street addresses are prohibited, for instance). One long-term by-product of this bizarre rebellion against house numbers was that all post had to be picked up in person from the post office – at least until a local resident sued for home delivery and was rewarded with the chance to pay a premium to have post delivered.

Carmel's central business district is largely designer-shopping territory: Carmel Plaza Mall (Ocean Ave, at Mission St) holds branches of Tiffany and Louis Vuitton, and a number of tacky, overpriced art **galleries** are strung along Dolores Street.

Weston Gallery

6th St, between Dolores and Lincoln • Tues–Sun 10.30am–5.30pm • ☎ 831 624 4453, ⓦ westongallery.com

One exception to Carmel's otherwise overhyped gallery scene is the **Weston Gallery**, worth a look for its regular shows of top contemporary **photographers**, as well as its permanent display of works by Fox Talbot, Ansel Adams and Edward Weston (who lived in Carmel most of his life).

Carmel Beach

Carmel's inarguably best feature is its largely untouched coastline, among the most beautiful in California. City-managed **Carmel Beach** (dawn–dusk; free), at the foot of Ocean Avenue, is a tranquil cove of emerald-blue water bordered by soft, blindingly white sand and cypress-covered cliffs; its tides are deceptively strong and dangerous, however, so take extreme care if you chance a swim.

Tor House

26304 Ocean View Ave • Tours: hourly Fri & Sat 10am–3pm • $10 • ☎ 831 624 1813, ⓦ torhouse.org

Less than a mile south from Carmel Beach sits **Tor House**, which, when built in 1919, was the only building on the then treeless headland. Poet **Robinson Jeffers** (whose very long, starkly tragic narrative poems were far more popular in his time than they are today) built the small cottage and adjacent tower (loosely based on medieval Irish stone towers) on his own from granite boulders he hauled from the cove below. Guided tours of the house and surrounding gardens saddle visitors with an obsequious account of the now obscure writer's life and work, but the house itself is worth the overload. Tour sizes are capped at six people, so reserve well in advance. Note that the entrance is one block from the clifftop, and be sure to allow ample time for parking as very few street spaces exist in this residential neighbourhood.

Carmel River State Beach

Carmelo St • Dawn–dusk • Free • ☎ 831 649 2836, ⓦ parks.ca.gov

A quarter of a mile southeast from Tor House and around the tip of Carmel Point, you'll find idyllic, mile-long **Carmel River State Beach**. It's less visited than city-operated Carmel Beach (see p.403) and includes a bird sanctuary on a fresh-water lagoon, as well as the mouth of the Carmel River. Again, if you brave the frigid ocean waves, beware of strong tides and currents, especially at the south end of the beach, where the sand falls away at a very steep angle to cause potentially hazardous surf.

6

Carmel Mission

3080 Rio Rd • Mon–Sat 9.30am–5pm (7pm in summer), Sun 10.30am–5pm • $6.50 • ☎ 831 624 1271, ⓦ carmelmission.org

About a mile from Carmel town centre via Junípero Avenue, the Mission San Carlos Borromeo de Carmelo (commonly known as the **Carmel Mission**) is one of the most romantic of all Californian's Spanish remnants, a beautifully restored sandstone edifice in Colonial style, its gardens festooned with colourful blossoms. The complex includes three absorbing museums and the resting place of **Junípero Serra** himself, founder of the missions and canonized by Pope Francis in 2015.

Serra originally founded the church in Monterey in 1770 as the second of his California missions and the headquarters of the chain; a year later, it was moved to its current site in Carmel, to be closer to a major Native American village. Originally completed in 1797, the church has undergone one of the most painstakingly authentic restorations in the entire mission chain; by 1937, when reconstruction began, the facility had lain derelict for more than eighty years and was little more than its foundations and a few feet of wall. Today the church features an unusual catenary arch ceiling, and a grand *retablo* (altarpiece), with Serra buried under the sanctuary (he was reinterred in 1943 and remains of his original redwood coffin are displayed in a reliquary in front of the altar). The Harry Downie Museum shows videos (on loop) about Serra, while the Munras Museum offers a fascinating insight into the history of an Anglo-Spanish *Californio* family. The Mora Chapel Museum contains religious relics and period mission rooms (don't miss the **Espinosa Shield**, an aged piece of leather armour used during the 1769 Portola expedition), as well as a special gallery dedicated to (St) Junípero Serra.

Point Lobos State Natural Reserve

62 Hwy-1 • Daily 8am–7pm (docents staff the Information Station at the Sea Lion Point parking lot daily 9am–5pm) • $10/vehicle •
☎ 831 624 4909, ⓦ pointlobos.org

Two miles south of Carmel Mission along Hwy-1, **Point Lobos State Natural Reserve** boasts plenty of justification to support its humble claim of being "the greatest meeting of land and water in the world". There are over 250 bird and animal species that pepper its hiking trails, while the sea here is one of the richest underwater habitats in California.

Because Point Lobos itself juts so far out into the ocean, it contains some of the earth's most **undisturbed views** of the sea, as craggy granite pinnacles – landforms that helped inspire Robert Louis Stevenson's *Treasure Island* – reach out of jagged blue coves. Sea lions and otters frolic in the crashing surf, just below the many vantage points along the park's perimeter-hugging trails. Grey whales are often seen as close as one hundred yards away on their southerly migration route in January before returning with young calves in April and May. A small cabin built by Chinese abalone fishermen in the 1850s still remains at Whalers Cove and is now the **Whalers Cabin Museum** (daily 9am–5pm, volunteers permitting). The spectacular park, named after *lobos marinos* – the noisy, barking sea lions that group on the rocks off the reserve's tip – also protects some of the few remaining Monterey cypress trees on its knife-edged headland, despite being buffeted by tireless coastal gusts.

Finally, the park's Whalers and Bluefish coves are excellent **diving** spots for anyone with proper certification. Call ☎ 831 624 8413 or search online at ⓦ parks.ca.gov for information and reservations.

ARRIVAL AND DEPARTURE

By bus and train Amtrak and Greyhound avoid the Monterey Peninsula entirely, so you'll have to arrive by bus or train at the inland agricultural city of Salinas (p.385).

MONTEREY PENINSULA

From there, Monterey–Salinas Transit bus #20 ($2.50) makes the 55min trip to Monterey several times daily from the Transit Center at 110 Salinas St.

INFORMATION AND GETTING AROUND

Pacific Grove Chamber of Commerce 100 Central Ave, Pacific Grove (daily 10am–5pm; ☎831 324 4668, ⓦ pacificgrove.org).

Lake El Estero Visitors Center 401 Camino El Estero, Monterey (Mon–Sat 9am–6pm, Sun 9am–5pm; ☎888 221 1010, ⓦ seemonterey.com).

By bus MST buses (☎888 678 2871, ⓦmst.org) run between 7am and 6pm (11pm on some routes), radiating out from Transit Plaza in the historic core of Monterey and ranging as far afield as Nepenthe in Big Sur and San Jose.

Journeys within the Monterey Peninsula cost $1.50–2.50. Particularly useful routes are #1, which runs along Lighthouse Ave past the main sights and on out to Pacific Grove; #20, which runs between Monterey and both Amtrak and Greyhound in Salinas; and #22, which links Monterey with Carmel before continuing on down to Big Sur ($3.50).

By bike For bicycle rentals, try one of Adventures by the Sea's several locations around the peninsula, including 299 Cannery Row (☎831 648 7236, ⓦ adventuresbythesea .com). Rates are $25 for a half-day rental, $35 for a full day.

ACTIVITIES

Whale-watching trips Monterey Bay Whale Watch (from $41; ☎831 375 4658; ⓦ gowhales.com) offers trips from the end of Fisherman's Wharf in Monterey to see

humpbacks, orcas, blue whales and dolphins April to mid-December, and grey whales and dolphins mid-December to March.

ACCOMMODATION

The fact that the Monterey Peninsula is among the most **expensive** vacation destinations in California may prompt you to stay elsewhere – in Santa Cruz or Salinas, perhaps – and simply come here for the day. One budget lodging option, however, is to check in at one of the many **motels** lining North Fremont St or Munras Ave, about one mile from the city centre. Alternatively, try to visit in spring or the fall, when the peninsula is quieter, lodging is cheaper and the coastal weather is sunnier.

MONTEREY

HI-Monterey Hostel 778 Hawthorne St ☎831 649 0375, ⓦmontereyhostel.org; map pp.400–401. Right near Cannery Row, this well-managed hostel has a spacious common room and pleasant dorms. Dorms $39

Monterey Plaza Hotel & Spa 400 Cannery Row ☎831 646 1700, ⓦmontereyplazahotel.com; map pp.400–401. Sited amid Cannery Row's tourist-geared action – it's only three blocks from the Monterey Bay Aquarium – this four-star waterfront hotel boasts plush rooms, outstanding views and *Schooners Coastal Kitchen & Bar* (see p.406). $269

Veteran's Memorial Park Campground ☎831 646 3865, ⓦmonterey.org/rec; map pp.400–401. The Monterey Peninsula's only campground, on Jefferson St one mile west of Downtown Monterey in the hills above town, is the picturesque site of John Steinbeck's fictional *Tortilla Flat*. It's set among trees with picnic tables and fire rings at

all 40 sites, which are available on a first-come, first-served basis. $30

PACIFIC GROVE

Bide-a-Wee Inn & Cottages 221 Asilomar Blvd ☎831 372 2330, ⓦbideaweeinn.com; map pp.400–401. The nicely spruced-up rooms at this lush compound include modern, homely furnishings, as well as mini-fridges and microwaves; cottages with kitchenettes are also on offer. Doubles $139, cottages $169

Green Gables Inn 301 Ocean View Blvd ☎800 375 2095, ⓦgreengablesinnpg.com; map pp.400–401. Offering luxurious lodging in one of Pacific Grove's prettiest houses (built from redwood in 1888 by Englishman William Lacy), situated on the waterfront a few blocks from Monterey Bay Aquarium. Evening wine and buffet breakfast are served in the ocean-view lounge with fireplace. $225

CARMEL VALLEY WINERIES

For a wealth of information on Carmel area **wineries**, contact the Monterey County Vintners and Growers Association (☎831 375 9400, ⓦmontereywines.org). One of the top producers is Joullian, which operates a pleasant tasting room at 2 Village Drive in Carmel Valley Village (daily 11am–5pm; ☎831 659 8100, ⓦjoullian.com). The Bordeaux varietals are favourites here, with Cabernet Sauvignon and Merlot comprising more than seventy percent of the grapes grown in Carmel Valley.

6

★**Rosedale Inn** 775 Asilomar Blvd ☎831 655 1000, ⓦrosedaleinn.com; map pp.400–401. The cabin-like exteriors of the rooms at this delightful inn hide refreshingly modern interiors, where you'll find ceiling fans, pine furniture, fireplaces and jacuzzi baths. The real attraction here, though, are the affable staff. **$160**

CARMEL

Carmel Resort Inn & Cottages Carpenter Ave, between 1st and 2nd aves ☎831 293 8390, ⓦcarmelresortinncottages.com; map p.395. These motel-style cottage rooms, dating back to the early 1900s, include microwaves, mini-fridges and fireplaces; continental breakfast is also served. Perhaps best of all, it's a remarkably inexpensive place to stay (relatively). **$130**

Horizon Inn & Ocean View Lodge Junipero St and 3rd Ave ☎800 350 7723, ⓦhorizoninncarmel.com; map p.395. A relatively good deal in Carmel, this inn is set a few blocks north of the town centre and features cosy rooms, a continental breakfast basket delivered to your door and access to an outdoor hot tub. **$193**

EATING

MONTEREY

Alvarado Street Brewery 426 Alvarado St ☎831 655 2337, ⓦalvaradostreetbrewery.com; map pp.400–401. Craft beer (hoppy West Coast-style and Belgian-inspired ales), plus the best poutine ($11), burgers (including excellent veggie burgers; $14) and fish tacos ($14) in town. Mon–Thurs & Sun 11am–10pm, Fri & Sat 11am–11pm.

Old Monterey Cafe 489 Alvarado St ☎831 646 1021; map pp.400–401. Often bustling, this longtime favourite serves reasonably priced breakfasts (almost everything's under $12) and excellent sandwiches. Daily 6.45am–2.30pm.

Papa Chano's 462 Alvarado St ☎831 646 9587; map pp.400–401. One of Monterey's great bargains, this is the place to go for authentic Mexican specialities. In true California taqueria style, everything's under $10. Mon–Thurs 10am–10pm, Fri–Sun 10am–11pm.

Schooners Coastal Kitchen & Bar Monterey Plaza Hotel & Spa, 400 Cannery Row ☎831 646 1706, ⓦschoonersmonterey.com; map pp.400–401. This dignified restaurant, set in one of Monterey's finest hotels, claims stunning views over the bay and an adventurous seafood menu (mains $22–32) at dinner; breakfast and lunch are also available. Daily 6.30am–10pm.

PACIFIC GROVE

★**Book Works** 667 Lighthouse Ave ☎831 372 2242, ⓦbookworkspg.com; map pp.400–401. The best hangout in otherwise somnolent Pacific Grove this relaxed bookshop and café (with drinks from Santa Cruz Coffee Roasting Co) also hosts book signings and readings most Wed (5pm). Café daily 7am–6pm; bookshop daily 10am–6pm.

First Awakenings 125 Oceanview Blvd ☎831 372 1125, ⓦfirstawakenings.net; map pp.400–401. Located inside the American Tin Cannery building, this is an excellent spot for hearty breakfasts, salads and sandwiches ($11–14), served inside or out on the terrace. Mon–Fri 7am–2pm, Sat & Sun 7am–2.30pm.

★**Fishwife** 1996 Sunset Drive ☎831 375 7107, ⓦfishwife.com; map pp.400–401. A long-standing local favourite adjacent to Asilomar Beach, *Fishwife* serves peerless, Caribbean-tinged California cuisine amid unpretentious environs. Try the delicious "Prawns Belize" ($18.50) – large prawns sautéed with red onions, chillies, lime juice and cashews. Mon–Thurs & Sun 11am–9pm, Fri & Sat 11am–9.30pm.

CARMEL

Carmel Bakery Ocean Ave, at Lincoln St ☎831 626 8885; map p.395. A refreshing, low-key café on the village's main drag – with roots in 1899 – where browsing locals enjoy coffee and gooey, old-fashioned cakes. Mon–Thurs & Sun 7am–8pm, Fri & Sat 7am–10pm.

★**La Bicyclette** Dolores St, at 7th Ave ☎831 622 9899, ⓦlabicycletterestaurant.com; map p.395. Wooden tables and ceiling-hung copper pots help set a suitably rustic tone for this delightful, country-style French/Italian restaurant. Dinner mains are $25–31, with wood-fired pizzas from $16; the menu changes daily. Daily 8–10.45am, 11.45am–3.30pm & 5–10pm.

Mission Ranch 26270 Dolores St ☎831 625 9040, ⓦmissionranchcarmel.com; map p.395. Restored by Clint Eastwood, this plush ranch features an expensive inn and lauded restaurant, that really does match up to the hype; the hearty West Coast food is excellent (slow-roasted prime rib, char-broiled salmon; mains $24–44) and the views across the hills spectacular. Mon–Sat 4–9pm, Sun 10am–1.30pm & 5–9pm.

Robata Grill & Sake Bar 3658 The Barnyard ☎831 624 2643, ⓦrobata-barnyard.com; map p.395. *Robata*'s warm, wood-panelled setting is one of the most pleasant in Carmel; the likeably unpretentious place also has a heated patio. The tasty sushi and tempura here certainly isn't cheap– a two-piece order can cost over $10 – but it's the best in town. Mon–Thurs 11.30am–2pm & 5–8.30pm, Fri & Sat 11.30am–2pm & 5–9.30pm, Sun 5–8.30pm.

The Tuck Box Dolores St, at 7th Ave ☎831 624 6365, ⓦtuckbox.com; map p.395. Breakfast, lunch (sandwiches $9.25) and afternoon tea ($6.50) are served at this half-timbered, mock-Tudor Olde England cottage. It's kitsch (and cash-only), but fun. Daily 7.30am–2.30pm.

DRINKING AND NIGHTLIFE

The Monterey area has always been better known as a sleepy, romantic getaway than a hub of hip culture and nightlife. That said, the peninsula's best selection of bars is in Monterey itself on Alvarado St, while the **Monterey Jazz Festival** each September (ⓦmontereyjazzfestival.org) is the oldest continuous festival in the world and still draws crowds from afar. The best publication for what's on in the Monterey area is the widely available freebie *Monterey County Weekly* (ⓦmontereycountyweekly.com), which contains listings of movies, live music, art shows and so on.

Alfredo's Cantina 266 Pearl St, Monterey ☎831 375 0655; map pp.400–401. Classic, dimly lit dive bar, full of local characters, grouchy bar tenders and offering honest, cheap booze. Cash only (ATM inside). Daily 10am–2am.

Lallapalooza 474 Alvarado St, Monterey ☎831 645 9036, ⓦlalla-palooza.com; map pp.400–401. A smooth martini bar (with reasonable American-cuisine restaurant attached) featuring olive-themed art on the walls, a small pavement terrace and a stylish oval bar – the dressiest place in town for a drink. Daily 4pm–midnight.

My Attic Bar 414 Alvarado St, Monterey ☎831 647 1834, ⓦmyattic1937.com; map pp.400–401. Inviting lounge and cocktail bar, a real contrast from the rest of the pubs downtown, with a handful of bar stools in the historic Casa Sanchez – it's been a bar since 1937. Tues–Thurs 5pm–midnight, Fri & Sat 5pm–2am.

DIRECTORY

Internet Monterey Public Library, 625 Pacific St (Mon–Wed noon–8pm, Thurs–Sat 10am–6pm, Sun 1–5pm; ☎831 646 3932, ⓦmonterey.org/library).

Post office 565 Hartnell St, Monterey (Mon–Fri 8.30am–5pm, Sat 10am–2pm).

Santa Cruz

Seventy-five miles south of San Francisco, the edgy – and often maddening – city of **SANTA CRUZ** is an essential stop, though it can be a tough place to pin down. In many ways it's the quintessential California coastal town, with miles of beaches for sunning and superb **surfing**, huge swathes of mountainside forests for hiking and a historic seaside amusement park complete with a vintage wooden rollercoaster. It's also home to eagerly displayed wealth, as well as a great number of homeless people who benefit from the town's generous civic resources, joining with its hippie past to bring out the crustier side of local life. Indeed, rising rents, exacerbated by nearby Silicon Valley and a boom in airbnb rentals, have made it impossible for many low-income workers to remain in Santa Cruz, making the housing shortages and homeless epidemic here especially bad, even by California standards.

More than anything, however, the Santa Cruz area has a reputation as a 1960s cultural throwback and is still considered among the most politically and socially progressive in California – one reason Santa Cruz has become known in recent times as a **lesbian** haven (see box, p.415). The town also boasts a range of bookshops and coffeehouses, and also a number of lively bars and nightclubs where music varies from hardcore punk to psychedelic surf-guitar.

As if all this weren't enough, Santa Cruz is home to a particularly nonconformist branch of the **University of California**, while also containing a handful of quiet, family-oriented neighbourhoods. All this far-reaching cultural diversity is certainly cause for the town's underlying tension, so by no means should you expect a coastal resort town at ease with itself. In fact, Santa Cruz's motley mixture underscores why it's such an intriguingly complex place to visit.

Before it feeds into the Pacific Ocean, the sluggish San Lorenzo River wraps around the town centre two blocks east of **Pacific Avenue**, a landscaped and pedestrianized stretch that's Santa Cruz's principal business street – it's where dishevelled hippies share pavement space with students, dropout punks, well-heeled shoppers and gawking visitors.

Octagon Building and Santa Cruz Museum of Art & History

Octagon Building 118 Cooper St • Mon–Fri 7am–7pm, Sat & Sun 8am–7pm **Museum of Art & History** 705 Front St • Tues–Thurs, Sat & Sun 11am–5pm, Fri 11am–9pm • $5, free first Fri of month • ☎ 831 429 1964, ⓦ santacruzmah.org

At the north end of Pacific Avenue, the ornate brick-and-stone **Octagon Building** was completed in 1882 as the Santa Cruz County Hall of Records; it survived the devastating Loma Prieta Earthquake in 1989 and now houses a posh café, *Lulu Carpenter's*. Adjacent is the **Santa Cruz Museum of Art & History** and its spirited displays on the region's past, where the grounds include a sculpture garden, as well as a rooftop gallery with fine views of the city.

6

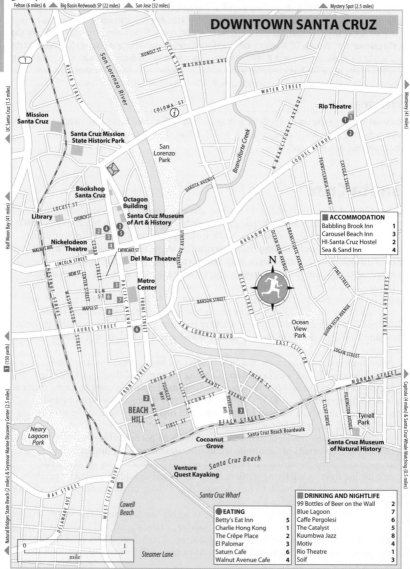

DOWNTOWN SANTA CRUZ

Felton (6 miles) & Big Basin Redwoods SP (22 miles) San Jose (32 miles) Mystery Spot (2.5 miles)

UC Santa Cruz (1.5 miles) Monterey (41 miles)

Half Moon Bay (41 miles) Capitola (4 miles) & Santa Cruz Whale Watching (0.5 miles)

Natural Bridges State Beach (2 miles) & Seymour Marine Discovery Center (2.5 miles)

ACCOMMODATION
Babbling Brook Inn	1
Carousel Beach Inn	3
HI-Santa Cruz Hostel	2
Sea & Sand Inn	4

EATING
Betty's Eat Inn	5
Charlie Hong Kong	1
The Crêpe Place	2
El Palomar	3
Saturn Cafe	6
Walnut Avenue Cafe	4

DRINKING AND NIGHTLIFE
99 Bottles of Beer on the Wall	2
Blue Lagoon	7
Caffe Pergolesi	6
The Catalyst	5
Kuumbwa Jazz	8
Motiv	4
Rio Theatre	1
Soif	3

Santa Cruz Mission State Historic Park

144 School St • Mon & Thurs–Sat 10am–4pm, Sun noon–4pm • Free • ☎ 831 425 5849, ⓦ parks.ca.gov

Set along Pacific Avenue in the northern reaches of downtown, **Santa Cruz Mission State Historic Park** displays fragments dating from the region's earlier Spanish colonial days. The complex includes the only building remaining from the **Misión la Exaltacion de la Santa Cruz,** founded by Father Fermín Lasuén in 1791; the simple adobe structure once housed the Ohlone and Yokuts residents of the mission, and exhibits inside tell their story. There's also a half-scale replica of the mission chapel (the original was destroyed by an earthquake in 1857).

Santa Cruz Beach and around

Santa Cruz's main local beach, known simply as **Santa Cruz Beach**, is wide and sandy, with lots of volleyball courts and water that's safe and warm enough for summer swimming. It can get crowded and rowdy here, so for some peace and quiet, or to catch the largest waves, simply follow the coastline east or west of town to one of the smaller beaches hidden away at the foot of the cliffs; most are undeveloped and fairly accessible.

Santa Cruz Beach Boardwalk

Hours vary seasonally • All-day unlimited rides $33.95, individual rides $3–6 • ☎ 831 423 5590, ⓦ beachboardwalk.com

Dominating the main beach area is the **Santa Cruz Beach Boardwalk**, an amusement park that stretches half a mile along the edge of the sand. Full of bumper cars, shooting galleries, corndog stands, log flume rides, rollercoasters, Ferris wheels and a vintage carousel, it's packed solid on summer days with local day-tripping families and teenagers on the prowl. While the latest thrill is the Undertow – a 50-foot-tall spinning-car rollercoaster – the star attraction will always be the circa-1924 **Giant Dipper** ($6) a wild wooden rollercoaster that's jolted the bones of over sixty million people and is the fifth-oldest such thrill ride in the US; you may recognize it from films such as *Sudden Impact* or *The Lost Boys*. The boardwalk first opened in 1907, and its oldest surviving structure, the elegant **Cocoanut Grove** at its west end, dates from that year.

Just west of the boardwalk, the century-old wooden **Municipal Pier** juts far out into Monterey Bay, and is crammed with fresh-fish shops, seafood grills and gift stores. You don't need a licence to join the crab fishermen at the end of the pier – simply rent tackle from one of the many bait shops close at hand.

Steamer Lane

West of the Santa Cruz Beach Boardwalk, along West Cliff Drive, the shore is pounded by some of the state's biggest waves, not least at Cowell Beach's **Steamer Lane**, beyond the Municipal Pier as the coast stretches toward Lighthouse Point. Santa Cruz surfers have garnered a reputation for being less than welcoming to non-locals over the years, and Cowell Beach can be notoriously dirty, but if you want to get in the water and give it a shot, Club Ed (see p.412), offers rentals and lessons.

Santa Cruz Surfing Museum

701 W Cliff Drive • Summer Thurs–Tues 10am–5pm; rest of year Mon & Thurs–Sun noon–4pm • Free, but donation requested • ☎ 831 420 6289

Ghosts of surfers past are animated at the evocative **Santa Cruz Surfing Museum**, housed in the old red-brick lighthouse building at Lighthouse Point near Cowell Beach. The tiny museum holds surfboards ranging from twelve-foot redwood planks used by the sport's local pioneers to modern, multi-finned cutters.

Santa Cruz Museum of Natural History

1305 E Cliff Drive • Tues–Fri 11am–4pm, Sat & Sun 10am–5pm • $4, free first Fri of month • ☎ 831 420 6115, ⓦ santacruzmuseums.org

Just east of the Beach Boardwalk and across the San Lorenzo River, the small **Santa Cruz Museum of Natural History** is marked by a concrete whale. Its concise displays

6

describe local animals and sea creatures and also include brief descriptions of local Native American culture, near which you can try your hand at grinding acorns with a mortar and pestle.

Natural Bridges State Beach

2531 West Cliff Drive • Daily 8am–sunset • $10/vehicle • ☎ 831 423 4609, ⓦ parks.ca.gov

Both a cliff-side bicycle path and West Cliff Drive run two miles west from Lighthouse Point to **Natural Bridges State Beach**. Near the sands, waves have cut holes through coastal cliffs to form delicate arches in the remaining stone; three of the four bridges after which the park was named have since collapsed, however, leaving large stacks of stone protruding from the surf. The park is also famous for its annual gathering of monarch butterflies, thousands of which arrive each winter.

Seymour Marine Discovery Center

100 Shaffer Rd • July & Aug daily 10am–5pm; Sept–June Tues–Sun 10am–5pm • $8 • ☎ 831 459 3800, ⓦ seymourcenter.ucsc.edu

A short distance from Natural Bridges State Beach, clifftop **Seymour Marine Discovery Center** is a working laboratory that offers kid-friendly insights into the region's undersea life through informative displays, windows into labs and touch tanks packed with starfish and anemones. Free 45-minute **tours** (hourly 1–3pm) interpret the centre's displays, and the 87ft-long blue whale skeleton outside never fails to impress.

UC Santa Cruz

1156 High St • Campus tours begin at Cook House at the foot of campus • Free (reservations required) • ⓦ admissions.ucsc.edu/visit/campus-tours.html

Stretching over three hilly square miles above the city, **UC Santa Cruz** is very much a product of the 1960s. Until the early 2000s, when the demands of graduate schools elsewhere forced change, students didn't take exams or get grades. Still, its academic programmes continue to stress individual exploration of topics rather than rote learning. Whereas other University of California branches have adopted a proud bear as a school mascot, it's a telltale sign that UC Santa Cruz's mascot, is a Plato-reading banana slug. Its campus design is even a deliberate attempt to stand apart from traditional university campuses, with its heavily wooded plots divided into small, autonomous colleges where deer stroll among the redwood trees overlooking Monterey Bay.

Arboretum

High St, at Arboretum Rd • Daily 9am–5pm • $5 • ☎ 831 427 2998, ⓦ arboretum.ucsc.edu

If you don't have time for a full look around UC Santa Cruz, pop by the university's fine **Arboretum**, highly regarded for its experimental cultivation techniques and collections of plants from New Zealand, South Africa, Australia and South America, all landscaped as they would be in their original habitats.

Mystery Spot

465 Mystery Spot Rd (off Branciforte Drive) • Mon–Fri 10am–4pm, Sat & Sun 10am–5pm; frequent 45min tours, reservations recommended at weekends and holidays • Tickets $8, parking $5 • ☎ 831 423 8897, ⓦ mysteryspot.com

About three miles up Branciforte Drive from Santa Cruz's city centre, there's a point within the woods where normal laws of gravity no longer apply. Here, trees grow at odd angles, pendulums swing counterclockwise and balls roll uphill – all thanks to the **Mystery Spot**. Tours of this freaky, inexplicable place are contrived but amusing, and

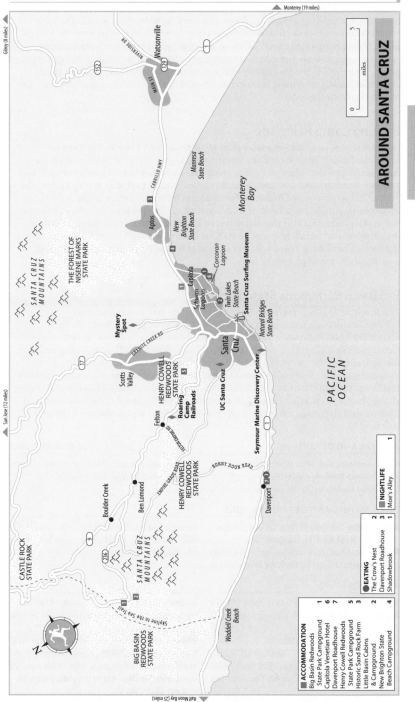

AROUND SANTA CRUZ

Monterey (19 miles)

Gilroy (8 miles)

San Jose (12 miles)

Half Moon Bay (25 miles)

6

PACIFIC OCEAN

Monterey Bay

CASTLE ROCK STATE PARK

BIG BASIN REDWOODS STATE PARK

SANTA CRUZ MOUNTAINS

THE FOREST OF NISENE MARKS STATE PARK

HENRY COWELL REDWOODS STATE PARK

Boulder Creek
Ben Lomond
Felton
Scotts Valley
Watsonville
Aptos
Capitola
Santa Cruz
Davenport

Mystery Spot
Roaring Camp Railroads
UC Santa Cruz
Seymour Marine Discovery Center
Santa Cruz Surfing Museum

Waddell Creek Beach
New Brighton State Beach
Manresa State Beach
Corcoran Lagoon
Twin Lakes State Beach
Natural Bridges State Beach
Schwan Lagoon

ACCOMMODATION
Big Basin Redwoods State Park Campground 1
Capitola Venetian Hotel 6
Davenport Roadhouse 7
Henry Cowell Redwoods State Park Campground 5
Historic Sand Rock Farm 3
Little Basin Cabins & Campground 2
New Brighton State Beach Campground 4

EATING
The Crow's Nest 2
Davenport Roadhouse 3
Shadowbrook 1

NIGHTLIFE
Moe's Alley 1

0 5 miles

involve guides leading groups up, down and every which way via a small shed that teeters on the edge of the hill, demonstrating in seven different ways how the laws of physics seem not to apply here. Much of the amusement is reliant more on canny perspective tricks than metaphysical skullduggery, but even so, it's a diverting treat as guides posit various theories about what caused the Mystery Spot's seeming taunts of gravity, including everything from extraterrestrial interference to excess carbon dioxide seeping up from the earth.

Roaring Camp Railroads

5401 Graham Hill Rd, Felton · Schedules vary seasonally · Tickets $27–29, parking $8 · ☎ 831 335 4484, ⓦ roaringcamp.com

Up in the Santa Cruz Mountains separating the region from the San Francisco Bay Area, you'll find the village of Felton, seven miles north of Santa Cruz on Hwy-9 and home to **Roaring Camp Railroads**, which is based around buildings dating back to the 1880s. The narrow-gauge **Redwood Forest Steam Train** ($27 return) departs from here and, over the course of an hour, trundles over trestle bridges on a six-mile run among the massive redwoods covering the slopes of Bear Mountain. From the same station, the diesel-hauled, standard-gauge **Santa Cruz Beach Train** ($29 return) powers down to the Santa Cruz Beach Boardwalk and back in three hours; you can also begin your journey at the beach end of the line.

Big Basin Redwoods State Park

21600 Big Basin Way (Hwy-236), Boulder Creek · Daily 6am–sunset · $10/vehicle · ☎ 831 338 8860, ⓦ parks.ca.gov

Further exploration into the Santa Cruz Mountains beyond Felton reveals divine **Big Basin Redwoods State Park**, about 23 winding miles northwest of Santa Cruz. Here at California's oldest state park (established 1902), over eighty miles of **hiking trails** (see box opposite) lead in every direction: into dense wilderness through scores of 300ft tall **redwood trees**; up ridges affording views across the bay to Monterey; and down to the Pacific Ocean at Waddell Beach, about twenty miles along Hwy-1 from Santa Cruz, and a favourite spot for watching windsurfers and kiteboarders negotiate the foamy currents. Camping is also available in the park (see p.414).

ARRIVAL AND DEPARTURE | SANTA CRUZ AND AROUND

By bus Greyhound stops at the Metro Center, 920 Pacific Ave, in between downtown and the beach.
Destinations Los Angeles (3 daily; 8hr 25min–9hr 5min);

Oakland (3 daily; 2hr–2hr 20min); San Francisco (2 daily; 2hr 30min–2hr 50min); San Jose (3 daily; 50min).

INFORMATION AND GETTING AROUND

Visitor Center 303 Water St (Mon–Sat 9am–5pm, Sun 10am–4pm; ☎ 831 425 1234, ⓦ santacruz.org).
By bus Santa Cruz has an excellent bus system, based around the Metro Center at 920 Pacific Ave and operated by

the Santa Cruz Metropolitan Transit District (☎ 831 425 8600, ⓦ scmtd.com). Basic fares are $2, while an all-day pass costs $6.

ACTIVITIES

Bike rental Santa Cruz Family Cycling Center, 914 41st Ave, (Mon–Sat 10am–6pm, Sun 10am–5pm ☎ 831 475 3883, ⓦ familycycling.com), rents hybrids and cruisers for $30/day and mountain bikes for $50–100.
Kayaking Venture Quest (☎ 831 427 2267, ⓦ santacruzkayak.com) rents kayak ($35/3hr; $55/day) and runs guided tours ($60) of the bay from Santa Cruz Wharf.

Surfing Club Ed (☎ 831 464 0177, ⓦ club-ed.com), in the beach parking lot, rents surfboards ($20/hr, $50/day) and wetsuits ($9/hr, $20/day). Surfing lessons cost $90/2hr.
Whale watching Santa Cruz Whale Watching, 1718 Brommer St (☎ 831 427 0230, ⓦ santacruzwhalewatching .com), runs 3–4hr whale and dolphin cruises from 789 Mariner Park Way (May–Nov for humpback whales; Dec–April grey whales; $48.95).

HIKING NEAR SANTA CRUZ

Helping form the backbone of California's Coast Range, the redwood-studded **Santa Cruz Mountains** reach nearly 4000ft, stretch almost as far north as San Francisco and provide extraordinary hiking opportunities at a trio of state parks close to Santa Cruz. **The Forest of Nisene Marks State Park** (daily sunrise to sunset; $8/vehicle; ☏ 831 763 7062, ⓦ parks.ca.gov), nine miles due east of central Santa Cruz on Aptos Creek Rd, covers the epicentre of the 1989 Loma Prieta Earthquake. To reach it from the Mary Easton Picnic Area just beyond the main entrance, follow the main road past the site of a former mill to the Aptos Creek Trail, off which a simple sign marks the spot; it's a gentle climb (about 200ft) over less than three miles. The rest of the park is laced with trails, with backcountry camping available six miles into the interior.

6

Larger and more developed than the Forest of Nisene Marks, **Big Basin Redwoods State Park** (see opposite) is another forested hiking paradise. Its signature amble is the Skyline to the Sea Trail, a thirty-mile route that begins in nearby Castle Rock State Park before winding its way through Big Basin Redwoods all the way to the ocean. Its final eleven miles – the trail's easiest section – begin near Big Basin Redwoods' visitor centre and pass by stunning Berry Creek Falls en route to Waddell Beach. If you're staying in Santa Cruz, you can complete this hike one-way by riding SCMTD bus #35 from Santa Cruz to the trailhead; once you reach the trail's end, hop aboard bus #40 at Waddell Beach back to Santa Cruz. Check ⓦ www.scmtd.com for exact timetables.

A little more than five miles north of Santa Cruz's city centre along Hwy-9, **Henry Cowell Redwoods State Park** (daily sunrise to sunset; $10/vehicle; ☏ 831 335 4598, ⓦ parks.ca.gov) is the best pick of the lot for a quick visit and a short hike; camping is available for those wishing to extend their stay (see p.414). The mostly flat, wheelchair-accessible Redwood Grove Loop Trail (about one mile in length), just past the entrance at the northern end of the park, is ideal for a slow stroll, on which you can expect to continually crane your neck as you contemplate the 1500-year-old trees that tower overhead.

ACCOMMODATION

Compared to most California beach resorts, **accommodation** in the Santa Cruz area can be moderately priced, but you should expect wildly varying seasonal rates, as a room that goes for $75 midweek in winter can easily cost two or even close to three times that amount on a July or August weekend. Also keep in mind that there's a clump of inexpensive motels along Ocean St.

HOTELS, INNS, B&BS AND HOSTELS

★**Babbling Brook Inn** 1025 Laurel St, Santa Cruz ☏ 831 427 2437, ⓦ babblingbrookinn.com; map p.408. Romantic, clapboard B&B (built as a corn grist mill in 1796), surrounded by lush gardens, with luxurious rooms with whirlpool tubs and adorned with famous works of art (reproductions). $191

Capitola Venetian Hotel 1500 Wharf Rd, Capitola ☏ 831 476 6471, ⓦ capitolavenetian.com; map p.411. A quirky, ageing beachfront hotel just across the bridge from Capitola's lively esplanade, where all rooms have kitchens with gas stoves; some are two-bedroom suites. $186

Carousel Beach Inn 110 Riverside Ave, Santa Cruz ☏ 831 425 7090, ⓦ carousel-beach-inn.com; map p.408. This sparklingly clean place has simple rooms fitted with blond wood furniture and loudly colourful bedcovers. All rooms have microwaves and there's free continental breakfast included. Conveniently for rollercoaster-riders, it's directly across from the Beach Boardwalk. $99

Davenport Roadhouse 1 Davenport Ave, Davenport ☏ 831 426 8801, ⓦ davenportroadhouse.com; map p.411. A boutique, yet shockingly inexpensive inn about

eleven miles northwest of Santa Cruz along Hwy-1, where rooms are small, but tastefully decorated; many feature ocean views. There's also a terrific downstairs restaurant (see p.414). $85

★**Historic Sand Rock Farm** 6901 Freedom Blvd, Aptos ☏ 831 688 8005, ⓦ sandrockfarm.com; map p.411. This secluded five-room guesthouse, eleven miles east of central Santa Cruz, has been lovingly restored and filled with arts-and-crafts antiques; multi-course, made-to-order breakfasts are lavish and delicious. $260

HI-Santa Cruz Hostel 321 Main St ☏ 831 423 8304, ⓦ hi-santacruz.org; map p.408. As informal as Santa Cruz itself, this hostel is set in a series of 1870s cottages just a couple of blocks from the beach and includes dorms and private rooms. It's closed between 10am–5pm and is often booked solid well in advance. Dorms $28 (non-members $31); doubles (shared bath) $65 (non-members $71); doubles (private bath) $140 (non-members $146)

Sea & Sand Inn 201 W Cliff Drive, Santa Cruz ☏ 831 427 3401, ⓦ seaandsandinn.com; map p.408. This small, upscale motel boasts fine sea views, fresh-baked cookies at 3pm and flower boxes bursting with colour under every window. $189

6

CAMPGROUNDS

Big Basin Redwoods State Park ☎ 800 444 7275, ⓦ reserveamerica.com; map p.411. This enormous, marvellously lush park in the Santa Cruz Mountains has a large campground adjacent to its visitor centre and several trailheads, as well as a couple of free walk-in campgrounds in the backcountry. $\overline{\$35}$

Henry Cowell Redwoods State Park ☎ 800 444 7275, ⓦ reserveamerica.com; map p.411. Abutting UC Santa Cruz directly to the northeast, this sizeable park is home to a wonderful campground set in a redwood grove near a pair of burbling creeks. Hike/bike-in $\overline{\$7}$, drive-in $\overline{\$35}$

Little Basin Cabins & Campground 21700 Little Basin Rd, Boulder Creek ☎ 831 338 3314, ⓦ littlebasin .org; map p.411. Set a few miles southeast of Big Basin Redwoods State Park's visitor centre, these excellent recent additions to the park's lodging scheme operate on a reservation-only basis. Pitches $\overline{\$45}$, cabins $\overline{\$105}$

New Brighton State Beach ☎ 800 444 7275, ⓦ reserveamerica.com; map p.411. Seven miles east of Santa Cruz on the edge of the beachfront village of Capitola, New Brighton's campground is set on bluffs above a lovely, lengthy strand; reservations are essential. $\overline{\$35}$

EATING

Restaurants in and around Santa Cruz are surprisingly diverse, encompassing vegetarian cafés, all-American burger joints, fine dining and a number of worthwhile seafood establishments on the wharf. The Wednesday **farmers' market** (1.30–4.30pm; ⓦ santacruzfarmersmarket.org) at Cedar and Lincoln downtown is immensely popular with locals.

Betty's Eat Inn 1222 Pacific Ave, Santa Cruz ☎ 831 600 7056, ⓦ bettyburgers.com; map p.408. The downtown location of local mini-chain *Betty Burgers* serves absolutely delicious, no-frills burgers served a variety of ways, from the Basic Betty ($6.99) to the Slammin' Salmon burger ($9.99). Mon–Thurs & Sun 11am–9.30pm, Fri & Sat 11am–11pm.

Charlie Hong Kong 1141 Soquel Ave, Santa Cruz ☎ 831 426 5664, ⓦ charliehongkong.com; map p.408. An innocent-looking hut with a small amount of outdoor seating where organic, mostly vegetarian noodle dishes – green curry, spicy noodles, stir-fries – cost $6.50–14. Vietnamese sandwiches ($6.75–9.45) are also available. Daily 11am–11pm.

★**The Crêpe Place** 1134 Soquel Ave, Santa Cruz ☎ 831 429 6994, ⓦ thecrepeplace.com; map p.408. This longtime local favourite cooks up its namesake item with savoury and sweet fillings ($9.50–17); try the Crêpe Gatsby, stuffed with tomato pesto, mushrooms, spinach, chicken and two kinds of cheese. The flower-filled back garden is a delightful spot in which to eat on a warm summer evening. The venue also hosts a range of bands and movie nights. Mon–Thurs 11am–midnight, Fri 11am–1am, Sat & Sun 9am–midnight.

The Crow's Nest 2218 E Cliff Drive, Santa Cruz ☎ 831 476 4560, ⓦ crowsnest-santacruz.com; map p.411. The modern American, fish-dominated menu at this harbour spot contains a number of tasty mains ($20–32), but the real reason to visit is for its spectacular views across the water, particularly at sunset. There's also a pub upstairs. Mon–Fri 7.30am–2.30pm & 5–9pm, Sat 7.30am–3pm & 4.30–9.30pm, Sun 11.30am–9.30pm.

Davenport Roadhouse 1 Davenport Ave, Davenport ☎ 831 426 8801, ⓦ davenportroadhouse.com; map p.411. A 15min drive up Hwy-1 from Santa Cruz brings you to this village gem and its unique dishes, many of them organic: artichoke leek lasagne ($14), pan-seared king salmon ($28), and wood-fired pizzas ($11–15), plus more conventional pasta, burger and chowder options. Mon 9am–3pm, Tues–Fri 8.30am–9pm, Sat 8am–9pm, Sun 8am–8.30pm.

★**El Palomar** 1336 Pacific Ave, Santa Cruz ☎ 831 425 7575, ⓦ elpalomarsantacruz.com; map p.408. Don't be put off by this restaurant's location – it's on the ground floor of a historic building that now houses government-subsidized apartments – for its Mexican dishes are likely the best in town. All the usuals (enchiladas, fajitas) are done well, along with several seafood specialities. Mains run $15–31. Daily 11am–3pm & 5–10pm.

Saturn Cafe 145 Laurel St, Santa Cruz ☎ 831 429 8505, ⓦ saturncafe.com; map p.408. Santa Cruz's wackiest diner is set in a round building and decked out with red vinyl banquettes, Formica tables and a space-age theme. The vegetarian menu ranges from burgers and sandwiches to vegan breakfasts, and just about everything's under $13. It's also one of the few late-night dining options in town. Mon–Thurs & Sun 10am–midnight, Fri & Sat 10am–3am.

Shadowbrook 1750 Wharf Rd, Capitola ☎ 831 475 1511, ⓦ shadowbrook-capitola.com; map p.411. A smart choice for a romantic (if pricey) meal, this upscale destination offers a variety of mains (including steak, seafood and vegan options) for $25–35, served on terraces that step down to the banks of Soquel Creek. Just beware of dodgy singers performing Gordon Lightfoot classics at weekends. Mon–Thurs 5–8.30pm, Fri 4.30–8.30pm, Sat 4–9.30pm, Sun 4–8.30pm.

Walnut Avenue Cafe 106 Walnut Ave, Santa Cruz ☎ 831 457 2307, ⓦ walnutavenuecafe.com; map p.408. A local institution, this diner has made its name on massive, delicious breakfasts and lunches (most $10–12) for the last two decades. Mon–Fri 7am–3pm, Sat & Sun 8am–4pm.

LGBT SANTA CRUZ

Over the last few decades, Santa Cruz has established itself as one of the country's hippest **lesbian** hangouts; it also boasts an increasingly sizeable gay population. Most local **accommodation** is gay-friendly, and *Saturn Café* (see opposite) is an especially popular gay and lesbian venue. For more information, contact or stop by the well-connected Diversity Center of Santa Cruz, 1117 Soquel Ave (Mon, Tues, Thurs, Fri 9am–6pm; Wed 2–6pm; ☎831 425 5422, ⓦ diversitycenter.org).

6

DRINKING AND NIGHTLIFE

Santa Cruz has the Central Coast's best and most varied **nightlife**, ranging from coffeehouses to bars and nightclubs where music careens between surf-thrash, reggae, hard rock and seemingly everything else. For simply hanging out, your best choices are the espresso bars and coffeehouses lining Pacific Ave; if you have your heart set on seeing a show or film, check the useful free weekly *Good Times* (ⓦ goodtimes.sc).

99 Bottles of Beer on the Wall 110 Walnut Ave ☎831 459 9999, ⓦ 99bottles.com; map p.408. This airy pub offers over forty beers on tap; the crowd's friendly and a bit more mainstream than in other local watering holes. There are also great California burgers, along with quiz, karaoke and live music nights (no cover). Mon–Thurs noon–1.30am, Fri & Sat 11.30am–2am, Sun 11.30am–midnight.

Blue Lagoon 923 Pacific Ave ☎831 423 7117, ⓦ thebluelagoon.com; map p.408. A lively bar and nightclub where DJs spin anything from Top 40 hits to industrial tunes; live bands frequently hold court as well. Daily 4pm–2am.

★**Caffe Pergolesi** 418 Cedar St ☎831 426 1775, ⓦ theperg.com; map p.408. Attractively set in an old wooden villa with a garden, this fun and friendly coffeehouse is often full of students hunched over laptops. Management regularly books a wide variety of live music. Daily 7am–11pm.

The Catalyst 1011 Pacific Ave ☎831 423 1338, ⓦ catalystclub.com; map p.408. The main venue in town for big-name touring artists, this medium-sized club has something happening almost nightly. Beware that staff can be brusque from time to time. Tickets $10–30. Hours vary.

Kuumbwa Jazz 320 Cedar St ☎831 427 2227, ⓦ kuumbwajazz.org; map p.408. The city's showcase for traditional and modern jazz, this club boasts a friendly and intimate garden setting tucked down a small alley. Don't be surprised to see a big name or two (Bobby Hutcherson, Terence Blanchard) come through each month. Tickets $15–35. Hours vary.

Moe's Alley 1535 Commercial Way ☎831 479 1854, ⓦ moesalley.com; map p.411. Reggae and blues are mainstays at this amiable venue six nights a week, but you can also expect salsa, jam rock and world music on any given night. Tickets $5–25. Tues–Sun 4pm–2am.

Motiv 1209 Pacific Ave ☎831 429 8070, ⓦ motivsc .com; map p.408. This hit-and-miss dance club is frequented by local hipsters and university students; it has a modern vibe and DJs spinning house, reggae and hip-hop, depending on the night. Daily 9.30pm–2am.

Rio Theatre 1205 Soquel Ave ☎831 423 8209, ⓦ riotheatre.com; map p.408. Opened in 1949 as a state-of-the-art movie theatre, the *Rio* now sees the likes of singer-songwriter Bruce Cockburn, alt-rock legends the Breeders and local psycho-surf legends the Mermen grace its stage. Tickets $25–35.

Soif 105 Walnut Ave ☎831 423 2020, ⓦ soifwine.com; map p.408. Popular with Santa Cruz's young sophisticates, this hotspot is bathed in warm light and has varnished wooden tables; the menu features small plates and over fifty wines by the glass. Mon–Thurs & Sun 5–9pm, Fri & Sat 5–10pm.

DIRECTORY

Santa Cruz Public Library There's internet access here at 224 Church St (Mon–Thurs 10am–7pm, Fri & Sat 10am–5pm, Sun 1–5pm; ☎831 427 7707, ⓦ santacruzpl.org).

Laundry Surf City Suds, 228 Cardiff Place (daily 7am–10pm; ☎831 334 8098), a green-certified laundrette located a couple of miles west of downtown and adjacent to UC Santa Cruz.

Post office 850 Front St (Mon–Fri 9am–5pm).

San Francisco and the Bay Area

GOLDEN GATE BRIDGE

San Francisco and the Bay Area

One of America's most stunningly sited cities, San Francisco sits poised on the northern tip of a slender peninsula along the California coast. Home of the Golden Gate, Alcatraz, Levi's, Twitter, a prominent LGBT scene and those loveable cable cars, it's arguably the most progressive major city in the US, and one of the most beautiful. Surprisingly compact and approachable, San Francisco's downtown streets rise on impossible gradients to reveal stunning views, and fog rolls in on a moment's notice to envelop everything in mist. This is not the California of monotonous blue skies and slothful warmth – in George Sterling's "cool grey city of love" the temperature rarely exceeds 80°F (27°C) and usually hovers in the 60s (15–20°C) between May and August, until summer weather finally arrives in fall's early weeks. The city proper occupies a mere 47 square miles, but the metropolitan Bay Area sprawls far beyond those narrow confines, its nine counties home to around eight million residents and growing.

San Franciscans like to think of their city as Northern California's cultured, idealistic counterpart to the mass entertainment capital of Los Angeles in the south, and to an extent they're right: this is where the United Nations originated, and the city boasts indissoluble connections to the Beat, hippie and gay rights movements. Still, despite its attempt to stand apart from the rest of the state (and often, the nation), it remains an undeniably Californian place – after all, blue jeans, topless waitressing and oversize burritos all got their start here. Today, along with **Silicon Valley** to the south, it's a city in the grip of a new Gold Rush, the internet boom that started in the 1990s. Jobs are

GOLDEN GATE PARK

Highlights

❶ Cable cars These glorious old trolleys have rattled their way up and down San Francisco's steepest hills since 1873. **See p.438**

❷ Golden Gate Bridge The city's signature sight is gorgeous in any light – or fog – and experiencing it first-hand (driving, cycling or walking) is a singular thrill. **See p.447**

❸ Mission District Bustling taquerias, iconic Mission Dolores and the collision of Anglo and Latino cultures make for one of San Francisco's liveliest neighbourhoods. **See p.453**

❹ Golden Gate Park The gardens and groves of this much-loved green expanse are home to some of the city's best attractions. **See p.455**

❺ San Francisco Pride Queer culture exuberantly takes over much of the city on a late June weekend, with boisterous parades, outlandish costumes and the colours of the rainbow flag all taking centre stage. **See p.483**

❻ University of California, Berkeley This attractive, park-like campus is bordered by fine book and music stores, as well as notable restaurants and cafés. **See p.498**

❼ Whale watching at Point Reyes The lighthouse at the southwestern tip of Point Reyes National Seashore is a great spot to glimpse migrating grey whales. **See p.533**

HIGHLIGHTS ARE MARKED ON THE MAP ON P.420

SAN FRANCISCO & THE BAY AREA

HIGHLIGHTS

1. Cable cars
2. Golden Gate Bridge
3. Mission District
4. Golden Gate Park
5. San Francisco Pride
6. University of California, Berkeley
7. Whale watching at Point Reyes

plentiful (the joke goes that dog walkers make more than teachers), but rents and house prices are shockingly high – it's a place where $1 million for a one-bedroom apartment is a bargain. And in a city that prides itself on high-quality, organic farm-to-table cuisine, and where bars sport hand-illustrated cocktail menus, a visit to *Starbucks* can be laden with guilt. Gentrification has even spread across the East Bay, where traditionally blue-collar **Oakland** and the university locus of **Berkeley** offer their own unique ensemble of sights and experiences. Yet despite the changes – and persistent challenges, such as a major homeless problem – the undeniable romance of San Francisco endures, whether it's the version evoked by Armistead Maupin's *Tales of the City* or that wistful 1967 anthem *San Francisco (Be Sure to Wear Flowers in Your Hair)*.

San Francisco

The financial and commercial heart of the Bay Area, **SAN FRANCISCO** is a blend of soaring skyscrapers, Victorian villas and wooden houses blanketing the tip of the hilly San Francisco Peninsula, separating the Pacific Ocean from San Francisco Bay. Though its major attractions – the **Golden Gate Bridge** and **Golden Gate Park**, the famed **cable cars**, **Alcatraz** and **Fisherman's Wharf** – are certainly worth braving the crowds, this is above all a city of discrete neighbourhoods. Experience the legacies of the Beats in **North Beach** and the hippies in **Haight-Ashbury**, the tastes and aromas of **Chinatown**, the gay icons of the **Castro** and the vibrant Latino flavour of the **Mission**. Indeed, the first thing likely to strike you about San Francisco is that it's a remarkably compact place of **hills** – some four dozen or so prominent ones. Walking is an ideal daytime mode for taking in its renowned museums, fine parks and stirring hilltop vistas – the best way to get to know San Francisco is to dawdle, unbound by itineraries.

Downtown is bisected by the wide, diagonal thoroughfare of **Market Street**, the city's main drag, lined with stores and office buildings. It begins across from the water's edge at the **Embarcadero** and runs southwest, brushing against the corporate high-rises of the **Financial District**, the shopping quarter of **Union Square**, the governmental locus of the **Civic Center** and chic **Hayes Valley** before finally reaching the Castro. It then spirals up around **Twin Peaks**, the most prominent of San Francisco's considerable heights. Below Market Street and jutting inland from the waterfront is **South of Market**, once an industrial enclave and now peppered with internet businesses, stylish restaurants, museums and popular nightclubs.

7

Brief history

The original inhabitants of the San Francisco area were the **Ohlone people**, who lived in roughly 35 villages spread out around the bay. Though Spanish explorer **Juan Rodríguez Cabrillo** had charted the west coast of North America in 1542, he missed San Francisco Bay – as did Francis Drake, sailing in 1579, who may have landed at Drake's Bay in Marin County. It wasn't until 1769 that Spanish explorer **Gaspar de Portolà** officially discovered San Francisco Bay, and in 1775 Spanish naval captain **Juan de Ayala** became the first to pass through what would become the Golden Gate. In 1776, **Mission Dolores**, the sixth in the chain of Spanish Catholic missions in California, was established by members of the **Juan Bautista de Anza** expedition, and the area was formally incorporated into the Spanish Empire. Harsh mission life, combined with the spread of European diseases, killed off the Ohlone within a few generations. Alta California became part of newly independent Mexico in 1821, but the Bay Area remained sparsely populated by Spanish-speaking and largely self-sufficient "Californios" until the 1840s, when the first major waves of American settlers arrived. The mission and the old Spanish fort (the Presidio) continued to be the focus of the settlement until the foundations of modern San Francisco were laid in 1835, when British sailor **William Richardson** got permission to settle at what was then known as

Yerba Buena Cove (Richardson had married the daughter of the local *commandante* and taken Mexican citizenship in the 1820s). The town was slowly laid out in subsequent years, its inhabitants trading hides and tallow with visiting ships, but by 1848 the population was little more than eight hundred.

Becoming American

The region finally came under American rule after the **Bear Flag Revolt** of 1846, which took place north of San Francisco in Sonoma. The bloodless coup was engineered by American immigrants who wanted to free themselves of the Mexicans, but the independent "Bear Flag Republic" barely lasted a month; overtaken by the start of the **Mexican–American War**, the coup brought US Marines, sailing on the USS *Portsmouth*, into San Francisco Bay, joining up with the forces of US army captain **John Frémont** (who is supposed to have christened the bay's spectacular entrance the "**Golden Gate**"). The Marines docked their boat at the tiny town plaza, renaming it **Portsmouth Square**, raising an American flag and claiming the city for the United States. The following year, the hamlet known as Yerba Buena was rechristened San Francisco, honouring the dying wish of Father Junípero Serra, the Franciscan founder of California's missions.

Gold Rush and boom

In 1848, San Francisco's population exploded when pioneer Sam Brannan bounded across Portsmouth Square waving bottles of gold dust he claimed came from the Sierra foothills, thereby igniting the **California Gold Rush**. Within a year, fifty thousand pioneers (the "forty-niners") had arrived from all over the country as well as overseas (especially China), turning San Francisco from a muddy village and wasteland of dunes into a thriving supply centre and transit town. When **Mark Twain** arrived in 1863, he described it as being made up of "decaying, smoke-grimed, wooden houses". By the time the **transcontinental railroad** was completed in 1869, San Francisco was a rowdy boomtown of bordellos and saloons, something the moneyed elite – who hit it big on the much more dependable silver Comstock Lode in western Nevada – worked hard to mend, constructing wide boulevards, parks, a cable car system and elaborate Victorian redwood mansions, the latter replacing local prostitutes as San Francisco's famed "Painted Ladies". The city also became the epicentre for anti-Chinese racism, precipitated by the **San Francisco riot of 1877**, a two-day orgy of violence which claimed at least four lives and destroyed swathes of Chinatown (the Chinese Exclusion Act of 1882 effectively ended Chinese immigration to the US).

The twentieth century

In 1906 a massive **earthquake**, followed by three days of fire, wiped out three-quarters of the city. Rebuilding began immediately, resulting in a city more magnificent than before, drawing writers, artists and free spirits. In the decades that followed, authors such as Frank Norris, Dashiell Hammett and Jack London lived and worked here, as did Diego Rivera and other WPA-sponsored artists. During the Great Depression of the 1930s, San Francisco's position as the nexus of trade with Asia, coupled with its engineering projects – including both the Bay and Golden Gate bridges – lessened the agonies of the Depression for its residents. In the 1950s the **Beat Generation** flourished in North Beach, while the **hippies** came to prominence during 1967's **Summer of Love** in the Haight-Ashbury neighbourhood. In the 1970s and 1980s the city was heavily affected by drugs, prostitution and crime (as depicted in the *Dirty Harry* movies), though it also was home to a fast-growing gay community – **Harvey Milk** was shot in 1978 (see p.453). In 1989 the city was rocked by the **Loma Prieta earthquake**, causing extensive damage and 63 deaths.

Contemporary San Francisco

Despite its fame as a hub of counterculture, San Francisco has always meant business and wealth, evinced today by a walk through the skyscraper-filled Financial District

(Bank of America, Charles Schwab and Wells Fargo Bank were all founded here). Fancy restaurants, art museums, designer malls and the creeping **gentrification** of neighbourhoods point to an unusually strong local economy in the last few years, with the cost of living escalating. The boom has been fed by San Francisco's role as a cradle of internet mania since the 1990s – Airbnb, Craigslist, Dropbox, Fitbit, Pinterest, Reddit, Twitter, Uber and Yelp are all based in the city, and many employees of Silicon Valley giants such as Apple, Google and Facebook also choose to live here.

Today, San Francisco also prides itself on being the **gay capital** of the world. One of the most prominent local politicians is openly gay former stand-up comedian **Tom Ammiano**; furthermore, former mayor (and current California Lieutenant Governor) **Gavin Newsom** made national headlines in 2004 as the first elected official in America to legalize gay weddings, albeit abortively. San Francisco basks in its reputation as a model of tolerance (there's almost nowhere in town you won't see gay couples walking hand-in-hand), and as a **progressive enclave**: in 2011, **Ed Lee** became the first Chinese American mayor in the city's history (he was re-elected in 2015). Ex-mayor (the first woman to hold the post) **Dianne Feinstein** is currently the senior US Senator from California, while local Congresswoman **Nancy Pelosi** is the only woman to have served as the House Speaker.

Nevertheless, the city remains troubled by a substantial **homeless** population, jarringly noticeable among the leafy affluence of Market Street: estimates suggest that a mind-boggling 7000–10,000 people live on the streets of the city.

Union Square

The retail focus of Downtown San Francisco, **UNION SQUARE** is a sixteen-block area filled with stores, hotels and flocks of tourists. The plaza itself, on the block north of Geary Street between Powell and Stockton, is anchored by a 97ft-tall Corinthian column commemorating Admiral Dewey's success in the Spanish-American War, while the voluptuous female figure on top of the monument was modelled on **Alma de Bretteville Spreckels**, who also founded the Legion of Honor art museum (see p.458). The square is remembered by many for the attempted assassination of President Gerald Ford outside the *Westin St Francis* hotel in 1975. The opulent hotel, opened in 1904, also featured prominently in many of Dashiell Hammett's detective stories, including *The Maltese Falcon* – in fact, during the 1920s, Hammett worked there as a Pinkerton detective,

---

FESTIVALS IN SAN FRANCISCO

San Francisco hosts a huge range of festivals – the biggest of which are detailed below. There are also year-round gay- and lesbian-geared events (see box, p.483).

Chinese New Year Festival & Parade ☎415 986 1370, ⓦchineseparade.com. Late Jan or early/mid-Feb. A massive, week-long celebration around the lunar New Year. Its main event is the Golden Dragon Parade, headed by the namesake 75ft-long dragon.

Cherry Blossom Festival ☎415 563 2313, ⓦsfcherryblossom.org. Late April. Otherwise-sedate Japantown is riotously transformed with a wide assortment of activities (including a beauty pageant) over two consecutive weekends; the festival culminates in a parade from Civic Center.

Bay to Breakers ☎415 359 2800, ⓦbaytobreakers.com. Third Sun in May. This legendarily campy event, disguised as a crosstown, 12km fun run, is an excuse for locals to don a costume – or in the case of some, no costume at all. Recent attempts to curtail drinking and debauchery along the race route have met with limited success.

Hardly Strictly Bluegrass ⓦhardlystrictlybluegrass.com. First weekend in Oct. Three-day music festival in Golden Gate Park featuring small- and big-name performers often playing acoustically – and for free – on multiple stages. Hugely popular, so arrive early to stake out space.

SAN FRANCISCO

Sausalito (4.5 miles), Muir Woods National Monument (11.5 miles), Point Reyes Station (35.5 miles)

● EATING
Arizmendi Bakery	7
Beach Chalet	
Brewery & Restaurant	5
Bellota	4
Chapeau!	3
Gordo Taqueria	6
Greens	1
Mandalay	2
Taqueria San Francisco	10
Thanh Long	8
Trouble Coffee and	
Coconut Club	9

■ ACCOMMODATION
Cow Hollow Motor Inn	2
HI-Fisherman's Wharf Hostel	1
Hotel Del Sol	3

● SHOPPING
Andronico's	3
Green Apple Books	2
Real Food Company	1

Golden
Gate
Bridge

Fort Point
National
Historic Site

GOLDEN GATE
NAT. RECREATION AREA

Golden Gate
Bridge Pavilion

Warming Hut

Crissy Field

MASON STREET

DOYLE DR

101

LINCOLN BLVD

Palace of
Fine Arts

THE PRESIDIO

Walt Disney
Family Museum

PACIFIC
OCEAN

Baker Beach

China
Beach

Lands End

Legion of Honor

Lincoln Park

EL CAMINO DEL MAR

SEACLIFF

LAKE STREET

CALIFORNIA STREET

CALIFORNIA STREET

Seal
Rocks
Sutro Baths
Cliff
House

Lands End
Lookout
Visitor Center

CLEMENT STREET

CLEMENT ST

GEARY BOULEVARD

ANZA STREET

BALBOA STREET

EUCLID AVENUE

ANZA STREET

University of
San Francisco

GOLDEN GATE AVE

WESTERN
ADDITION

Dutch
Windmill

Bison
Paddock

CABRILLO STREET

RICHMOND

FULTON STREET

CABRILLO STREET

FULTON STREET

de
Young
Museum

Japanese Tea Garden

California
Academy
of Sciences

Conservatory
of Flowers

Shakespeare
Garden

The Panhandle

UPPER
HAIGHT

Golden Gate Park

JOHN F. KENNEDY DRIVE

MIDDLE DR.

MARTIN LUTHER KING JR. DRIVE

San Francisco
Botanical Garden

KEZAR DR.

SEE 'HAYES VALLEY to
UPPER HAIGHT' MAP

LINCOLN WAY

IRVING STREET

IRVING STREET

7TH AVENUE

PARNASSUS AVE

17TH STREET

Ocean
Beach

JUDAH STREET

KIRKHAM STREET

LAWTON STREET

LAWTON ST

MORAGA STREET

NORIEGA STREET

SUNSET

ORTEGA STREET

Sunset
Reservoir
Solar Project

Laguna
Honda
Reservoir

Twin Peaks
Reservoir

TWIN
PEAKS

QUINTARA ST

QUINTARA STREET

TARAVAL STREET

PARKSIDE

ULLOA STREET

WEST
PORTAL

PORTOLA DRIVE

Mt
Davidson
Park

VICENTE STREET

Pine
Lake

Pine Lake Park

SLOAT BLVD

SLOAT BOULEVARD

MONTEREY BOULEVARD

City College
of San Francisco

San
Francisco
Zoo

San Francisco
State University

Lake
Merced
Park

Lake
Merced

INGLESIDE

Fort
Funston

PARK
MERCED

HOLLOWAY AVENUE

GARFIELD STREET

SARGENT STREET

San Jose (49 miles), Half Moon Bay (26 miles)

7

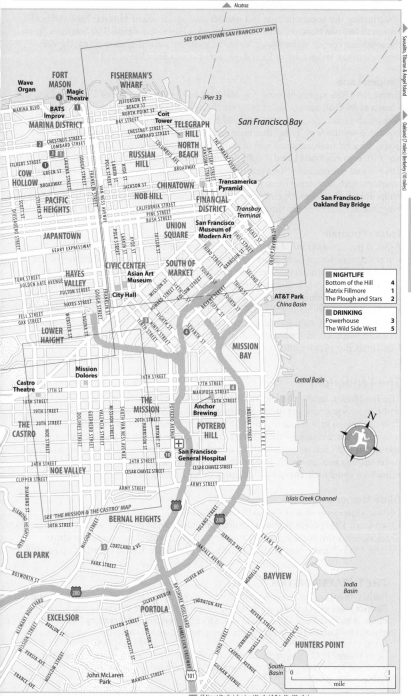

7

Alcatraz

SEE 'DOWNTOWN SAN FRANCISCO' MAP

Sausalito, Tiburon & Angel Island

Oakland (7 miles); Berkeley (10 miles)

Wave Organ

FORT MASON

Magic Theatre ❶

BATS Improv

MARINA DISTRICT

MARINA BLVD

CHESTNUT STREET ❷
LOMBARD STREET ❸❶

FILBERT STREET ❶

COW HOLLOW

GREEN ST
BROADWAY

PACIFIC HEIGHTS

SCOTT ST

DIVISADERO STREET

JAPANTOWN

GEARY EXPRESSWAY

HAYES VALLEY

TURK STREET
GOLDEN GATE AVENUE
FULTON STREET

HAYES STREET

FELL STREET
OAK STREET

LOWER HAIGHT

FISHERMAN'S WHARF

JEFFERSON ST
BEACH ST
NORTH POINT ST
BAY STREET

Pier 33

Coit Tower

CHESTNUT STREET
LOMBARD STREET

TELEGRAPH HILL

NORTH BEACH

RUSSIAN HILL

COLUMBUS AVE

BROADWAY

JACKSON ST

NOB HILL

CALIFORNIA STREET
PINE STREET
BUSH STREET

UNION SQUARE

CHINATOWN

Transamerica Pyramid

FINANCIAL DISTRICT

Transbay Terminal

San Francisco Museum of Modern Art

CIVIC CENTER

Asian Art Museum

City Hall

SOUTH OF MARKET

MISSION ST
HOWARD STREET
FOLSOM STREET
HARRISON ST
BRYANT STREET

AT&T Park
China Basin

MISSION BAY

San Francisco Bay

BATTERY STREET
SANSOME STREET

THE EMBARCADERO

FIRST STREET
BEALE ST
SECOND STREET
THIRD ST

THE EMBARCADERO

San Francisco–Oakland Bay Bridge

NIGHTLIFE	
Bottom of the Hill	4
Matrix Fillmore	1
The Plough and Stars	2

DRINKING	
Powerhouse	3
The Wild Side West	5

Mission Dolores

Castro Theatre

17TH ST
18TH STREET
19TH STREET
20TH STREET

THE CASTRO

24TH STREET

NOE VALLEY

CLIPPER STREET

GLEN PARK

BOSWORTH ST

16TH STREET

17TH STREET
MARIPOSA STREET
18TH STREET

Anchor Brewing

THE MISSION

20TH STREET

San Francisco General Hospital

CESAR CHAVEZ STREET

ARMY STREET

POTRERO HILL

Central Basin

INDIANA STREET

CESAR CHAVEZ STREET

ARMY STREET

Islais Creek Channel

THIRD STREET

SEE 'THE MISSION & THE CASTRO' MAP

30TH STREET

BERNAL HEIGHTS

CORTLAND AVE

PARK STREET

SILVER AVE

JERROLD AVE

EVANS AVE

OAKDALE AVENUE

BAYVIEW

India Basin

EXCELSIOR

PORTOLA

SILVER AVENUE

THORNTON AVE

REVERE STREET

HUNTERS POINT

South Basin

John McLaren Park

MANSELL STREET

JAMES LICK FREEWAY

N

0   1
mile

SF Airport (9 miles); San Jose (45 miles) & Palo Alto (29 miles)

investigating the notorious rape and murder case against silent film star Fatty Arbuckle. Pop in to **Neiman Marcus** (Mon–Sat 10am–7pm, Sun noon–6pm), 150 Stockton St, on the southeast corner of the square, to see its stunning stained-glass rotunda, the only remnant of the lavish City of Paris department store (demolished in 1981).

Maiden Lane

Before the 1906 earthquake and fire, **Maiden Lane**, on the east side of Union Square, was known as Morton Street, one of San Francisco's lowest-class red-light districts; an average of around ten murders a month occurred here, and prostitutes used to lean out of low-hung windows of "cribs" that bore signs reading, "Men taken in and done for". Today it's a far more subdued row of shops that includes the old **V.C. Morris Gift Shop** at no. 140, the only **Frank Lloyd Wright**-designed building in San Francisco, completed in 1949. From the outside, it's a squat orange-brick edifice, oddly lacking in Wright's usual obsession with horizontal lines; its interior is extraordinary, however, its sweeping, spiral ramp linking the floors is a clear ancestor of Wright's famed Guggenheim in New York. A longtime art gallery, at the time of research the building was seeking a new tenant.

Lotta's Fountain

Around the corner from Maiden Lane and marooned on a traffic island at the intersection of Kearny and Market, **Lotta's Fountain** remains one of the city's oldest landmarks. This ornate, caramel-coloured fountain served as a message centre after the 1906 earthquake, where distraught locals gathered to hear the latest damage reports. The fountain was donated to the city in 1875 by actress **Lotta Crabtree** (1847–1924), the daughter of British immigrants who made a fortune as an entertainer between the 1850s and 1880s (she was one of the world's first child stars). It enjoyed its greatest moment when world-renowned Italian opera diva Luisa Tetrazinni sang a free Christmas Eve performance atop it in 1910.

The Tenderloin

The **Tenderloin**, sandwiched on the north side of Market Street between Civic Center and Union Square, is one of the grittiest and most notorious areas in San Francisco. This uninviting area remains a blemish on the heart of the city and you're likely to be hassled for spare change – though you should be safe as long as you keep your wits about you and exercise extra caution after dark. Recent waves of South and Southeast Asian immigrants are slowly transforming the neighbourhood, however, establishing numerous spots for a cheap bowl of curry or Vietnamese pho.

Glide Memorial Church

330 Ellis St, at Taylor • Sun services 9am & 11am • ☏ 415 674 6000, ⓦ glide.org

Open since 1931, **Glide Memorial Church** provides a wide range of social services for the Tenderloin's downtrodden, but it's best known for its rollicking, one-hour-thirty-minute 11am Sunday service, which attracts a gloriously diverse crowd of up to 2000

THE THEATER DISTRICT

The area between Union Square and the gritty Tenderloin (see above) is known as the **Theater District** (though it's nothing like Broadway in New York or the West End in London). The district is anchored by two theatres along Geary St: **American Conservatory Theater** at no. 415 and the **Curran Theatre** at no. 445. Taking design cues from a Napoleonic palace, A.C.T.'s grand, colonnaded Neoclassical building opened in 1910 and was originally known as the Geary Theater. The Curran, immediately next door, dates from 1922 and first operated as a vaudeville stage; these days, it hosts crowd-pleasing productions such as *A Chorus Line* and *Hairspray* (see p.481).

people, ranging from pious locals to drag queens. Be sure to arrive at least an hour ahead if you want a seat in the main church, as overflow attendees usually have to make do with watching the proceedings via closed-captioned television in an adjacent room. Services feature its uplifting in-house gospel choir and band, Reverend Cecil Williams (who was marrying gay couples decades ago) and his wife, Janice Mirikitani, a former San Francisco poet laureate.

Civic Center

To the immediate southwest of the grubby Tenderloin stands San Francisco's grandest architectural gesture: the complex of Beaux Arts buildings known as the **Civic Center**. This cluster was the brainchild of famed Chicago-based urban planner Daniel Burnham – even before the calamities of 1906, he proposed levelling San Francisco and building a grand civic plaza, extensive subways and boulevard-like traffic arteries fanning out like spokes across the city. Unfortunately, after the earthquake, the city was choked in bureaucracy and his plan was heavily diluted until only the civic plaza was approved. Despite Burnham's beliefs that grand architectural solutions would help remedy social inequities, today's Civic Center is often simply an extension of the Tenderloin with bigger, more attractive buildings – the city's **homeless problem** is well in evidence across the main plaza.

7

United Nations Plaza

Heart of the City Farmers' Market Wed 7am–5.30pm, Sun 7am–5pm • ☎ 415 558 9455, ⓦ heartofthecity-farmersmar.squarespace.com

Sitting above the Civic Center Muni and BART station, the mostly unappealing **United Nations Plaza** was opened in 1975 to commemorate the founding of the UN here thirty years earlier – look for the UN Charter etched on a black stone shard. The space is filled with fountains, homeless people and little else; unless it's filled with vendors participating in the **Heart of the City Farmers' Market**, there's not much reason to dawdle here.

Main Library

100 Larkin St, at Grove • Mon & Sat 10am–6pm, Tues–Thurs 9am–8pm, Fri noon–6pm, Sun noon–5pm • ☎ 415 557 4400, ⓦ sfpl.org

As you approach **Civic Center Plaza** from UN Plaza, the first building you're likely to see is San Francisco's **Main Library** which moved to this airy, custom-built space in 1996 from its original site across the street, now the Asian Art Museum (see below). The building contains the James C. Hormel LGBTQIA Center (lesbian, gay, bisexual, transgender, queer, questioning, intersex and allies); it's topped by a dome with a mural depicting leading figures in gay rights and literary movements. There's usually a $1 book sale (dubbed "Steps Sales") just outside the library every Wednesday 11am–3pm (weather permitting).

Asian Art Museum

200 Larkin St, at McAllister • Tues, Wed & Fri–Sun 10am–5pm; late March–late Sept Thurs 10am–9pm; Oct–Jan Thurs 10am–5pm • $15, $10 after 5pm Thurs late March–late Sept • ☎ 415 581 3500, ⓦ asianart.org

Adjacent to the Main Library, the **Asian Art Museum** contains one of America's largest collections of paintings, sculptures, ceramics and textiles from Asia, with exhibits beautifully presented and labelled. Galleries are arranged by region and time period, beginning with ancient **South Asia** (India, Pakistan, Bangladesh and Sri Lanka) on the third floor. Much of this level is taken up with religious statuary, though the delicate jade cup in room 5, inscribed in Arabic and Persian, is a rare find from Central Asia, and there are also displays of Javanese puppets and precious gold jewellery from Indonesia (room 11). The **Chinese collection** begins with a fabulous room full of intricate jade objects (13), and ancient ritual bronze vessels from the Shang dynasty (14), one in the shape of a rhino. Room 16 contains the

Ferries to Sausalito, Angel Island & Tiburon

DOWNTOWN SAN FRANCISCO

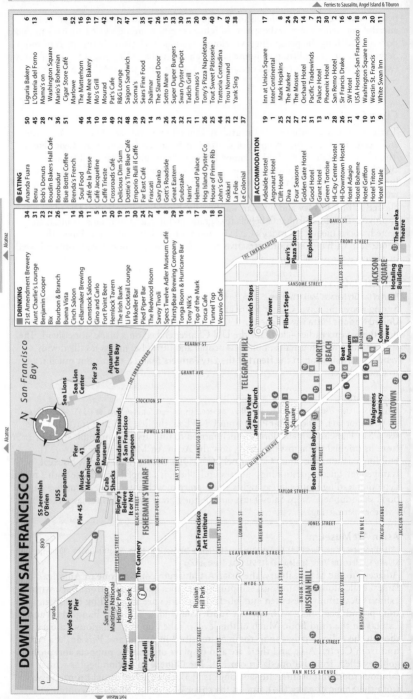

■ EATING

Ananda Fuara	50
Benu	45
Bob's Donuts	28
Boudin Bakers Hall Cafe	2
Borobudur	36
Blue Bottle Coffee	51
Brenda's French Soul Food	46
Café de la Presse	34
Café Jacqueline	11
Caffe Trieste	5
Crossroads Café	18
Delicious Dim Sum	49
Dottie's True Blue Café	22
Emporio Rulli il Caffè	48
Far East Café	13
Frascati	30
Gary Danko	27
Gott's Roadside	14
Great Eastern	3
Grubstake	26
Harris'	24
Helmand Palace	16
Hog Island Oyster Co	17
House of Prime Rib	26
John's Grill	44
Kokkari	23
La Folie	12
Le Colonial	37
Liguria Bakery	6
L'Osteria del Forno	13
Mama's on Washington Square	5
Mario's Bohemian Cigar Store Café	8
Marlowe	52
The Matterhorn	16
Mee Mee Bakery	19
Mo's Grill	17
Mourad	42
Pat's Cafe	4
R&G Lounge	27
Saigon Sandwich	47
Scoma's	1
Sears Fine Food	35
Shalimar	41
The Slanted Door	15
Sotto Mare	33
Super Duper Burgers	30
Swan Oyster Depot	31
Tadich Grill	20
Tommaso's	9
Tony's Pizza Napoletana	26
Tout Sweet Pâtisserie	40
Trattoria Contadina	7
Trou Normand	43
Yank Sing	38

■ DRINKING

21st Amendment Brewery	34
Aunt Charlie's Lounge	31
Benjamin Cooper	23
Bix	26
Bourbon & Branch	1
Buena Vista	14
Cinch Saloon	36
Cellarmaker Brewing	11
Comstock Saloon	5
Gino and Carlo	20
Fort Point Beer	13
Hemlock Tavern	30
The Irish Bank	27
Li Po Cocktail Lounge	3
Mikkeller Bar	17
Pied Piper Bar	18
The Redwood Room	10
Savoy Tivoli	29
Specs Twelve Adler Museum Café	8
ThirstyBear Brewing Company	9
Tonga Room & Hurricane Bar	16
Tony Nik's	17
Top of the Mark	18
Tosca Cafe	3
Tunnel Top	15
Vesuvio Cafe	10

■ ACCOMMODATION

Adelaide Hostel	19
Argonaut Hotel	1
Clift Hotel	25
Diva	27
Four Seasons	12
Golden Gate Hotel	31
Good Hotel	13
Grant Hotel	28
Green Tortoise Hostel	26
HI-City Center Hostel	21
HI-Downtown Hostel	4
Hotel Adagio	10
Hotel Boheme	15
Hotel Griffon	9
Hotel Triton	
Hotel Vitale	
Inn at Union Square	17
InterContinental	8
Mark Hopkins	24
The Marker	29
The Mosser	14
Orchard Hotel	7
Pacific Tradewinds	23
Palace Hotel	30
Phoenix Hotel	16
San Remo Hotel	6
Sir Francis Drake	18
SW Hotel	3
USA Hostels-San Francisco	20
Washington Square Inn	2
Westin St. Francis	11
White Swan Inn	

San Francisco Bay

Alcatraz

Sea Lions

Sea Lion Center

Pier 39

Aquarium of the Bay

SS Jeremiah O'Brien

USS Pampanito

Musée Mécanique

Crab Shacks

Pier 45

Pier 41

Boudin Bakery Museum

Madame Tussauds & San Francisco Dungeon

Ripley's Believe It or Not

Hyde Street Pier

San Francisco Maritime National Historic Park

Aquatic Park

Maritime Museum

Ghirardelli Square

The Cannery

FISHERMAN'S WHARF

San Francisco Art Institute

Russian Hill Park

RUSSIAN HILL

TELEGRAPH HILL

Coit Tower

Greenwich Steps

Filbert Steps

Saints Peter and Paul Church

Washington Square

NORTH BEACH

Beat Museum

Beach Blanket Babylon

Columbus Tower

CHINATOWN

Walgreens Pharmacy

JACKSON SQUARE

Hotaling Building

The Eureka Theatre

Levi's Plaza Store

Exploratorium

Fort Mason

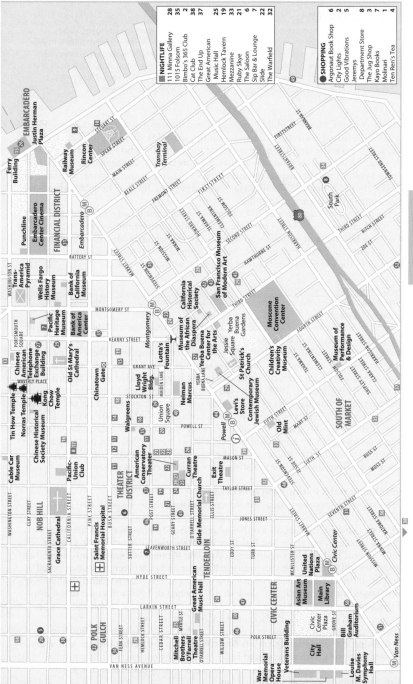

NIGHTLIFE

111 Minna Gallery	28
1015 Folsom	35
Bimbo's 365 Club	2
Cat Club	38
The End Up	37
Great American Music Hall	25
Hemlock Tavern	19
Mezzanine	33
Ruby Skye	21
The Saloon	6
Sip Bar & Lounge	7
Slide	22
The Warfield	32

● **SHOPPING**

Argonaut Book Shop	6
City Lights	2
Good Vibrations	5
Jeremys	8
Department Store	3
The Jug Shop	3
Kayo Books	1
Molinari	7
Ten Ren's Tea	4

7

HAYES VALLEY

Beyond the western boundary of Civic Center is the gentrified district of **Hayes Valley**, reborn when the earthquake-damaged freeway that once overshadowed it was demolished in the 1990s. Here, sleek boutiques sit alongside earthier remnants of the area's past, although a number of the former seem to encroach with each passing year. Lined with shady trees and cafés, as well as some of the funkiest homeware and clothing stores around (see p.485), the district's main business strip, Hayes St, is a fun place to wander and browse.

oldest known Chinese Buddha image, a gilded bronze statue dating back to 338 AD. The Chinese collection continues on the second floor with porcelain and scroll paintings from the later Qing dynasty and the Lingnan School, including the work of Chao Shao-an. This floor also houses the **Korean** and **Japanese** collections, the latter beginning with ancient Jōmon pottery (25) and featuring miniature sculptures (27), samurai armour (27) and screen paintings (28). The first floor usually hosts high-quality temporary exhibitions.

The museum opened here in 2003 after relocating from its original, earthquake-crippled quarters in Golden Gate Park. The building conversion was masterminded by Gae Aulenti, the same woman who transformed the fabulous Musée d'Orsay in Paris from a dingy old train station; here, Aulenti opened the musty, bookstack-crammed interior of the old library and created a modern, welcoming space.

City Hall

1 Dr Carlton B. Goodlett Place • Mon–Fri 8am–8pm; tours (45min) Mon–Fri 10am, noon & 2pm • Free • ☎ 415 554 6139, ⓦ sfgov.org/cityhall/city-hall-tours

Dominating spacious Civic Center Plaza is the imposingly grand **City Hall**. After San Francisco's first city hall was destroyed in 1906, a contest with a prize of $25,000 was announced for local architectural firms to design a new building. The winning design was by Bakewell & Brown, run by former students of the École des Beaux Arts in Paris, who wanted to create a structure inspired by the haughty, gilded dome of Paris' Les Invalides. Completed in 1915, City Hall cost an astonishing $3.5 million to build, and includes more than ten acres of marble that was shipped from New England and Italy. It was here in 1978 that conservative ex-Supervisor Dan White crawled through an open window on the mammoth building's north side and assassinated Mayor George Moscone and gay City Supervisor **Harvey Milk** (see box, p.453). The best way to see City Hall's grand interior is on one of the regularly offered **tours** – simply sign up at the Docent Tour kiosk in the Goodlett Place lobby next to the elevators.

War Memorial & Performing Arts Center

401 Van Ness Ave • Tours (from Grove St entrance of Davies Symphony Hall) Mon 10am–2pm (hourly) • $7 • ☎ 415 552 8338, ⓦ sfwmpac.org

Directly behind City Hall on Van Ness Avenue are San Francisco's cultural mainstays, managed collectively as the **San Francisco War Memorial & Performing Arts Center**. The most elegant building here is the Beaux-Arts **War Memorial Opera House** – opened in 1932, it's still home to both San Francisco's opera and ballet companies (see p.480), and its understated grandeur sits in sharp contrast to the giant Modernist fishbowl of the **Davies Symphony Hall**, one block south. Opened in 1980 and home to the San Francisco Symphony, the latter has some fans in the progressive architecture camp, though many feel it's out of place among Civic Center's otherwise tastefully harmonious scheme. To the north of the opera house lies the **Veterans Building**, containing the stunning Beaux-Arts **Green Room** and the **Herbst Theatre**, where the United Nations Charter was signed in 1945. The theatre's interior is beautifully adorned by a series of Frank Brangwyn murals originally painted for the 1915 Panama-Pacific International Exposition.

Financial District

Stretching along **Market Street** – the city's main drag – between Union Square and the waterfront, San Francisco's **Financial District** is the city's business hub. The area is home to San Francisco's two signature skyscrapers; the Transamerica Pyramid and 555 California St (aka the **Bank of America Center**). Note that by 2018 the city's tallest building should be César Pelli's **Salesforce Tower**, a 1070ft giant in the South of Market district.

Transamerica Pyramid

600 Montgomery St • **Point of Interest** Mon–Fri 10am–3pm • Free • ☎ 415 500 6637, Ⓦ pyramidcenter.com

The city's most recognizable high-rise, the **Transamerica Pyramid** is the tallest building in San Francisco (at 853ft), until 2018 at least (it's now barely in the top 40 tallest buildings in the US). The off-white, once-controversial structure – which more resembles a squared-off rocket than an actual pyramid – opened to business tenants in 1972. The "**Point of Interest**" on the ground floor is a small visitor centre and shop that chronicles the history of the building with videos and storyboards (higher floors are off-limits, but there's a live video from the top).

Pacific Heritage Museum

608 Commercial St • Tues–Sat 10am–4pm • Free • ☎ 415 399 1124

Just across the street from the Transamerica Pyramid, the **Pacific Heritage Museum** is housed in the old US Subtreasury Building, dating from 1875 and built on the site of the original **US Mint**. The exhibits inside chronicle the history of the building and its unique construction techniques – it's been incorporated into the modern United Commercial Bank skyscraper that surrounds it – and include vintage photographs, coins and revolving displays of Asian art.

Wells Fargo History Museum

420 Montgomery St • Mon–Fri 9am–5pm • Free • ☎ 415 396 2619, Ⓦ wellsfargohistory.com

Commemorating the establishment of Wells Fargo Bank's first office on this site in 1852, the slick **Wells Fargo History Museum** contains interactive displays exploring early communications championed by the bank, from stagecoaches and the Pony Express to the telegraph and railroads. There's a section on the Gold Rush and a real Concord stagecoach from 1867. Today Wells Fargo & Co is one of the world's biggest financial institutions, still headquartered in San Francisco.

Bank of California Museum

400 California St • Mon–Fri 9am–4.30pm • Free • ☎ 415 291 4653

The small, one-room **Bank of California Museum** sits in the basement of the oldest

---

THE BARBARY COAST

The area centred on Pacific Ave, between Montgomery and Stockton (roughly the neighbourhood known as **Jackson Square** today, just north of the Financial District) was once the notorious **Barbary Coast**, San Francisco's district of vice during the nineteenth century. In its earlier rough-and-tumble era, a constant stream of sailors provided unrivalled demand for illicit entertainment; the area was nicknamed "Baghdad by the Bay" for its unsavoury reputation as a nexus for shanghaiing, which involved hapless young males being given Mickey Finns (a drink laced with a drug) and, once unconscious, dragged aboard sailing ships for stints of involuntary servitude. Though buildings here remarkably survived the 1906 disaster, the relentless campaigning from William Randolph Hearst's *Examiner* newspaper against the district in 1913 soon put an end to the Barbary Coast's heyday. Today, some of the restored red-brick structures are preserved in the **Jackson Square Historical District**. The **Barbary Coast Trail** (Ⓦ barbarycoasttrail.org) is a 3.8-mile walking tour that connects the city's most important historic sites (it goes well beyond the original boundaries of the district).

branch of Union Bank of California, a Neoclassical, cavernous banking hall completed in 1908 and known as the "Grand Old Lady of California Street". On display is a series of gold nuggets from the Gold Rush days, old notes and coins (including Mormon currency from Utah) and exhibits on colourful locals such as "James King of William", a banker and newspaper editor shot dead by a rival in 1856.

555 California St (Bank of America Center)

555 California St • Closed to the public • Ⓦ 555cal.com

The 779ft-tall **555 California St building** (formerly known as **Bank of America Center**) is a broad-shouldered monolith of dark granite – depending on natural lighting and your vantage point, it can look either brown or vaguely reddish – that dominates the skyline (it's the second tallest building in the city). Its 1969 debut instantly divided the city into fans and those who would still like to see it razed; the latter doubtlessly cheered when it was used for exterior shots in the 1974 disaster film *The Towering Inferno*. No longer Bank of America's headquarters, the building is thirty percent owned by Donald Trump.

South of Market

Distinctly urban **South of Market** stretches diagonally from the Embarcadero in the northeast to the Mission in the southwest ("south of Market Street"). The once-derelict district has taken a surprising upswing in the last two decades, thanks in part to internet start-up companies and **Yerba Buena Gardens**, a museum and entertainment complex.

Rincon Center

101 Spear St, at Mission • Mon–Fri 8.30am–5.30pm • Free • ☎ 415 777 4100

One block inland from the bayfront and completed in 1940 as a US Post Office complex, the **Rincon Center**'s smooth and imposing lines, outer simplicity and ornamented interior make it a fine example of Streamline Moderne architecture. The main attraction inside is the lobby, lavishly decorated with the **History of California** mural, comprising 27 individual watercolour panels painted by the Russian artist **Anton Refregier** (from 1941 to 1948), commissioned by the WPA.

Museum of the African Diaspora

685 Mission St, at 3rd • Wed–Sat 11am–6pm, Sun noon–5pm • $10 • ☎ 415 358 7200, Ⓦ moadsf.org

The intriguing **Museum of the African Diaspora** spotlights everything from traditional African art, to work inspired by the horrors of slavery and modern pieces in a range of media. Opened in 2005 in this stunning, modern space, the museum places a particular emphasis on hosting educational events and fostering community discussions about history and racism.

California Historical Society

678 Mission St • Tues–Sun 11am–5pm • $5 • ☎ 415 357 1848, Ⓦ californiahistoricalsociety.org

Just across Mission Street from the Museum of the African Diaspora, the **California Historical Society** hosts revolving exhibitions on aspects of the state's history; recent themes have been "Photographing South of Market" and "The People of Klamath". The society's current premises once served as the San Francisco Builders Exchange and Nancy Pelosi's first campaign headquarters.

Yerba Buena Gardens

750 Howard St • Daily 6am–10pm • Free • ☎ 415 820 3550, Ⓦ yerbabuenagardens.com

A symbol of the neighbourhood's regeneration, **Yerba Buena Gardens** boasts inviting lawns and benches that are often packed with office workers during lunchtime. Look

CLOCKWISE FROM TOP ALAMO SQUARE (P.450); *NOPA* (P.471); *TONY'S PIZZA NAPOLETANA* (P.470) >

for the 50ft granite waterfall memorial to **Martin Luther King Jr** inscribed with extracts from his speeches, and on the terrace above it, the **Sister Cities garden** featuring flora from each of the thirteen cities worldwide that are twinned with San Francisco – there are camellias from Shanghai and cyclamen from Haifa, among others. The Gardens extend across Howard Street, where there's the **Children's Creativity Museum** at 221 Fourth St (Wed–Sun 10am–4pm; $12; ☎415 820 3320, ⓦcreativity.org) and the vintage **LeRoy King Carousel** (daily 10am–5pm; $4 or $3 with museum admission), dating back to 1906.

Yerba Buena Center for the Arts

701 Mission St, at 3rd · **Galleries** Tues– Sun 11am–6pm (Thurs till 8pm) · $10, free first Tues of month · ☎415 978 2700, ⓦybca.org

On the northeast fringe of Yerba Buena Gardens stands **Yerba Buena Center for the Arts**, initially conceived as a forum for community art projects but now expanded to host international touring exhibitions and performances in its two main spaces. The small second-floor screening room shows works by local experimental film-makers – check the website for a schedule of upcoming screenings.

San Francisco Museum of Modern Art

151 3rd St, at Howard · Daily 10am–5pm (Thurs till 9pm) · $25 · ☎415 357 4000, ⓦsfmoma.org

Across Third Street from Yerba Buena Gardens, the **San Francisco Museum of Modern Art** reopened in 2016 after a major three-year renovation to become one of the Bay Area's landmark museums. Most of its vast gallery space will be taken up with changing exhibitions, but the fourth floor will display a revolving selection of American abstract art from the permanent collection (from the likes of Lee Krasner and Ellsworth Kelly); the fifth floor will display pop, minimal and figurative art, from Chuck Close and Sol LeWitt, to Roy Lichtenstein and Andy Warhol; the sixth floor covers German art after 1960 (Georg Baselitz, Sigmar Polke and Gerhard Richter); with contemporary art on the seventh floor. Floor two is dedicated to painting and sculpture since 1900 (the museum owns work by Matisse, Magritte, Paul Klee and Picasso). On the third floor, the **Pritzker Center for Photography** is the largest space dedicated to the medium in the nation.

St Patrick Church

756 Mission St · Mon–Fri 6am–6.15pm, Sat & Sun 6am–6.45pm · Free · ☎415 421 3730, ⓦstpatricksf.org

On the north side of Yerba Buena Gardens lies **St Patrick Church**, a red-brick remnant of early San Francisco and its Irish Catholic community. Though the present Neo-Gothic edifice was completed in 1914, it was built on the earthquake-ravaged ruins of a church that served Irish gold miners in the 1850s. Inside, Irish green is represented by emerald Connemara marble pillars, and each of the patron saints of the thirty-two counties of Ireland is showcased on the Tiffany-style stained-glass windows.

Contemporary Jewish Museum

736 Mission St, at 3rd · Mon, Tues & Fri–Sun 11am–5pm, Thurs 11am–8pm · $12 · ☎415 655 7800, ⓦthecjm.org

Just behind St Patrick Church, you'll see a striking, askew blue stainless-steel cube: the "Yud" gallery attached to the **Contemporary Jewish Museum**, designed by Daniel Libeskind in 2008. The museum has no permanent collection; instead, it hosts smartly curated exhibitions spanning Jewish history and culture, such as retrospectives of Oakland-raised Gertrude Stein and *Shrek* creator William Steig.

Old United States Mint

88 5th St, at Mission

Completed in 1874, the **Old United States Mint** replaced the original building that had served the mines of the California Gold Rush. The stately Greek Revival-style edifice was in use until 1937 – for the last decade it's been mostly derelict, requiring upwards of $100 million in repairs. In 2016 the California Historical Society was chosen to transform the building into a cultural centre, but this is likely to take many years – in the meantime local production company **Activate San Francisco Events** has been mandated to host public events at the building through 2017. Check ⓦ oewd.org for the latest.

Museum of Performance & Design

893 Folsom St, between 4th & 5th • Wed & Fri–Sat 12.30–5.30pm, Thurs 12.30–7.30pm • Free (suggested donation $5) • ☎ 415 741 3531, ⓦ mpdsf.org

Founded in 1947, the small but illuminating **Museum of Performance & Design** offers several exhibitions on aspects of the performing arts (especially in the Bay Area) a year, plus holding an important library of over 3.5 million items on the history of performances in the region.

The Embarcadero

The thin, long waterfront district known as **THE EMBARCADERO** is centred on the Ferry Building and extends from Mission Bay up to Fisherman's Wharf. For over thirty years beginning in the late 1950s, the wide boulevard was topped by the ugly double-decker Embarcadero Skyway; however, the overhead highway was fatally damaged in the 1989 earthquake and subsequently demolished a few years later, kick-starting a reflowering of the Embarcadero as a view-laden, pedestrian-friendly promenade on San Francisco Bay.

7

Ferry Building

1 Ferry Building (Market St, at Embarcadero) • Mon–Fri 10am–6pm, Sat 9am–6pm, Sun 11am–6pm • ☎ 415 983 8030, ⓦ ferrybuildingmarketplace.com • **Farmers Market** Sat 8am–2pm, Tues & Thurs 10am–2pm • ☎ 415 291 3276, ⓦ cuesa.org

The graceful **Ferry Building**, at the foot of Market Street, was designed after the Giralda in Seville, Spain, in 1892. Before San Francisco's bridges were built in the 1930s, it was the arrival point for fifty thousand daily cross-bay commuters; following a long period of neglect beginning in the 1940s, which eventually saw it cut off from Downtown for decades by the bygone Embarcadero Skyway, it's once again a working ferry terminus for a revitalized commuter service. In 2003, following a multimillion-dollar facelift, its grand nave reopened as a gourmet **food marketplace** (see box, p.485), now one of the city's premier attractions for locals and visitors alike. A good time to stop by is during the **Ferry Plaza Farmers Market**, where local produce is sold from numerous stalls set up around the building.

Railway Museum

77 Steuart St • Tues–Sun 10am–5pm • Free • ☎ 415 974 1948, ⓦ streetcar.org/museum

Just south of the Ferry Building, the **Railway Museum** offers a quick overview of the history of streetcars and cable cars in the city, with displays of historic photos, film and railroad memorabilia, including a full-sized replica of a 1911 San Francisco streetcar.

HOW ABOUT THOSE GIANTS?

Its name may not be pretty, but **AT&T Park**, the San Francisco Giants' baseball park, is beautifully sited along the water in one of the sunniest parts of town. The Giants' season stretches from April to September and if you want to catch a game you'll find that tickets are fairly easy to come by (see p.41). Don't miss the concession stands featuring the ballpark's signature garlic fries. If you just want to see the ballpark, terrific one-hour-thirty-minute **tours** (daily 10.30am & 12.30pm; also 11.30am & 1.30pm June–Aug; $22; ☎ 415 972 2400, ⓦ sanfrancisco.giants.mlb.com) leave from the Giants Dugout Store on the Third St side of the ballpark. You'll not only get to sit in the dugout and wander onto the field, but also be able to avail yourself of superb views out across the city to the Bay Bridge from the ballpark's upper level.

LEVI'S JEANS

In 1853, a Jewish peddler from Bavaria named **Levi Strauss** (1829–1902) started selling tents in San Francisco, made with imported cloth from Nîmes (France) to Gold Rush miners – "de nimes" became denim. By the 1870s, tailor Jacob W. Davis was making trousers from this material, supplied by Strauss, and after he reinforced them with copper rivets he asked Levi to support his patent in 1873; a legend was born. Levi Strauss & Co global headquarters (and the Levi's Plaza Store) is at 1155 Battery St, just off the Embarcadero (Mon–Fri 9am–7pm, Sat & Sun noon–5pm; ☎ 415 677 9927). Inside there's a visitor centre and displays of some of the oldest jeans in the world in "The Vault", the lobby exhibition space. The Levi's Store at 815 Market St (Mon–Sat 9am–9pm, Sun 10am–8pm) also offers special products unique to the location (like Lot #1 jeans).

Exploratorium

Pier 15 • Tues–Sun 10am–5pm (Thurs also 6–10pm, 18 and over only) • $29.95, youth (13–17) $24.95, kids (4–12) $19.95 • ☎ 415 528 4360, ⓦ exploratorium.edu

The hugely popular **Exploratorium** is the best participatory science museum in the Bay Area, with hundreds of hands-on exhibits that engagingly explain scientific principles such as electricity and sound waves. A major draw is the **Tactile Dome** (reservations essential; ☎ 415 528 4444), a complete sensory-deprivation space explored on hands and knees that's huge fun for anyone not claustrophobic. The museum's Thursday night programming is geared towards adults, with bars serving drinks and live performances regularly scheduled.

Chinatown

CHINATOWN's twenty-four square blocks make up one of the largest Chinese communities in the world outside Asia; it's also the oldest such enclave in the US. Its roots lie in the migration of Chinese labourers to San Francisco after the completion of the transcontinental railroad, and the arrival of Chinese sailors keen to benefit from the Gold Rush. San Francisco is still known in China as "Old Gold Mountain" (*Jiùjīnshān*), its storied moniker from the nineteenth century, but the city didn't extend much of a welcome; rather, Chinese immigrants were met not only by a tide of vicious racial attacks, but also the unapologetically racist **1882 Chinese Exclusion Act**, a US federal law that banned new immigration and forbade thousands of single Chinese men from dating local women or bringing wives from China. A rip-roaring prostitution and gambling quarter thus developed, controlled by gangs known as *tongs*. However, with the loosening of immigration laws due to China's partnership with the US during World War II, and decades of hard work by its residents, Chinatown has grown into a self-made success. Today's population, descendants of Cantonese- and Fujianese-speaking southern mainlanders, as well as Taiwanese, has been joined by Mandarin-speaking northerners, Vietnamese, Koreans, Thais and Laotians, turning the area into a virtual Asiatown.

Chinatown Gate

The best way to approach Chinatown is through **Chinatown Gate**, built in 1970 in traditional style, where Grant Avenue meets Bush Street. Facing south, per *feng shui* precepts, it's a large dragon-clad arch adorned with a four-character inscription that translates to "All under heaven is for the good of the people".

Grant Avenue and Stockton Street

One of San Francisco's oldest thoroughfares, **Grant Avenue** – originally called Dupont Street – was once a wicked ensemble of opium dens, bordellos and gambling huts policed, if not terrorized, by *tong* hatchet-men. After the 1906 fire, the city decided to rename it in honour of president and Civil War hero Ulysses S. Grant, and in the process helped excise the seedy excesses for which it had become infamous. Note the two pagoda-topped buildings at the corner of Grant Avenue and California Street, the **Sing**

Fat and **Sing Chong**, originally oriental art stores – important because they were the first to be constructed after the 1906 fire, signalling Chinese resolve to remain on their much-coveted land. Running parallel to Grant Avenue one city block west, **Stockton Street** is a commercial artery for Chinatown locals, packed with grocery stores and dim sum shops, as well as herbalists and fishmongers. Between Stockton Street and Grant Avenue, narrow **Waverly Place** also runs north–south and holds two opulent, but skilfully hidden Cantonese temples (see box below).

Old St Mary's Cathedral

660 California St • Mon–Fri 7am–2pm, Sat noon–6.30pm, Sun 8am–2.30pm (concerts Tues 12.30pm) • Free • ☎ 415 288 3800, ⓦ oldsaintmarys.org

Built in 1854 as California's first Catholic cathedral (just across the street from the Sing Fat and Sing Chong buildings), with granite quarried in China and bricks from New England, **Old St Mary's Cathedral** barely survived the 1906 earthquake. Pop inside to see photos of the damage, and its array of beautiful stained-glass windows.

Portsmouth Square

Set between Washington, Clay and Kearny, **Portsmouth Square** was San Francisco's original city centre and its first port of entry; it was here that English mariner William Richardson established his trading post in 1835 (see p.421). The plaza has since become, for all intents and purposes, Chinatown's living room, with spirited card games played atop cardboard boxes and other makeshift tables as children let off steam in the adjacent playground. When US naval officer John Montgomery came ashore in 1846 to claim the land for the United States, he raised his flag here and named the square after his ship; the spot where he first planted the Stars and Stripes is marked by the one flying in the square today. Near Montgomery's flagpole is a replica of the galleon *Hispaniola* from the novel *Treasure Island*, a monument to writer **Robert Louis Stevenson**, who spent much time observing the locals in Portsmouth Square during his brief sojourn in San Francisco (he lived here 1879 to 1880, sick and impoverished, while courting his future wife Fanny). The most recent addition to the square is the already weathered bronze *Goddess of Democracy* statue near the playground, a replica of the sculpture that famously graced Beijing's Tiananmen Square during the protests of 1989.

7

CHINATOWN'S TEMPLES

Chinatown's traditional temples offer a small window into the neighbourhood's spiritual life, a stark contrast to the frantic commercial activity outside. Buddhist **Norra's Temple** (daily 10am–4pm; ☎ 415 362 1993) on the third floor of 109 Waverly Place, is a serene space with an altar of gold Buddha statues. It's dedicated to Norlha Hotogtu (pronounced "No-ra" in Cantonese), a Tibetan lama who died trying to expand Tibetan Buddhism in China in 1936. **Tin How Temple** on the fourth floor of 125 Waverly Place (daily 9.30am–3.30pm) is a Taoist temple opened here in 1910 and dedicated to Mazu, a semi-historical figure also known as the Goddess of Heaven ("Tin Hau" in Cantonese), represented by the main statue behind the altar. The shrine's ornate interior is splashed with gold and vermilion, its ceiling dripping with tassels and red lanterns (the names of temple donors are written on slips of red paper and attached to the latter). Further along at 855 Stockton St (take the elevator to the fourth floor), similarly lavish **Kong Chow Temple** (daily 9am–4pm; ☎ 415 788 1339) has roots in the 1850s, though this location was established in 1977. The temple is dedicated to red-faced Guan Di, usually described as the God of War, but originally more like a patron of chivalrous warriors, based on Guan Yu, a real-life general featured in the Chinese classic *Romance of the Three Kingdoms* – today he is worshipped by executives, police, restaurant owners and criminal gangs, as well as being revered as a god of wealth and literature. Bess Truman visited the temple in 1948 to consult its fortune-telling "kau cim sticks" – pinned to the wall is the slip she received that predicted her husband's victory in the presidential election that year. Although the temples don't charge admission, it's respectful to leave a donation and not use cameras inside.

Chinese American Telephone Exchange

743 Washington St • Mon–Thurs 9am–5pm, Fri 9am–6pm, Sat 9am–4pm

Just beyond Portsmouth Square stands a red, three-storey pagoda-like structure built in 1909 for the **Chinese American Telephone Exchange**. A team of telephone operators worked here until 1949, routing calls solely by memory; it was restored in 1960 and serves as a branch of East West Bank today. Strangely enough, the building was a tourist attraction when it was still an exchange, visitors peering in to watch the stylish female operators, clad in embroidered silk cheongsams, at work.

Golden Gate Fortune Cookie Factory

56 Ross Alley • Daily 9am–6pm • Free • ☎ 415 781 3956

Anyone with even a moderately sweet tooth will want to duck into fragrant **Golden Gate Fortune Cookie Factory**, where, true to its name, the cramped plant has been churning out 20,000 fresh fortune cookies a day since 1962 – all by hand. A bag of forty cookies is no more than $5, but it costs 50¢ to snap a photo. The Chinese "tradition" of fortune cookies is said to have originated at Golden Gate Park's Japanese Tea Garden (see p.457).

Chinese Historical Society of America Museum

965 Clay St • Tues–Fri noon–5pm, Sat 11am–4pm • Free • ☎ 415 391 1188, ⊛ chsa.org

Housed in the old Chinese YWCA building designed by Julia Morgan (the architect responsible for Hearst Castle) in 1932, the **Chinese Historical Society of America Museum** chronicles the history of the Chinese in America from the Gold Rush to modern times, with old photos, rare artefacts and changing exhibits. Highlights include *One Hundred Years' History of the Chinese in America*, a vibrant 1952 mural by local Chinese American artist James Leong.

Cable Car Museum

1201 Mason St • Daily: April–Oct 10am–6pm; Nov–March 10am–5pm • Free • ☎ 415 474 1887, ⊛ cablecarmuseum.org

Technically in Nob Hill but just a few blocks west of the Chinese Historical Society, the **Cable Car Museum** is housed in a large Victorian workshop dating from 1887, a

---

HALLIDIE'S FOLLY: SAN FRANCISCO'S CABLE CARS

San Francisco's **cable cars** first appeared in 1873, the brainchild of Andrew Hallidie, an enterprising engineer with a taste for moneymaking schemes. The Scotland-born Hallidie is said to have been inspired to find an alternative to horse-drawn carriages when he saw a team of horses badly injured while trying to pull a dray up a steep hill in the rain. More than equine welfare was under threat – his father had patented a strong wire rope that had been extensively used in the mines of eastern California, but once the Gold Rush slowed, Hallidie needed a new application for his family's signature product, and a privately owned transit system reliant upon strong cable seemed the ideal solution.

The **pulley system** employed to run San Francisco's cable car system was dubbed "Hallidie's Folly" by unconvinced locals, but doubters were soon proved wrong as elevated neighbourhoods such as Nob Hill became accessible; businesses and homes were suddenly constructed along cable car routes. At their peak, just before the 1906 earthquake, more than six hundred trolleys plied eight lines and 112 miles of track throughout the city, travelling at a maximum of 9.5mph.

Unfortunately, the system was hit hard by a pair of obstacles: the devastation wrought by the 1906 earthquake – which wrecked large chunks of track – and the eventual onset of the automobile. However, when it was rumoured in 1947 that the ailing system would be phased out altogether, a local activist named Friedel Klussmann organized a citizens' committee to save the cable cars. Protests worked, and seventeen years later the beloved cars were placed on the National Register of Historic Places, at which time the remaining few miles of track were saved. Today there are around 40 cars in use – each unique – and about 23 miles of moving cable underground.

still-working powerhouse of whirring wheels and giant cable mechanisms in action. Inside are also vintage cable cars from the 1870s and exhibits on the history and workings of the system (see box opposite).

Nob Hill

The posh hotels and Masonic institutions of **Nob Hill**, west of Chinatown, exemplify San Francisco's old money. Once you've made the stiff climb up (or taken the California cable car line), there are very few real sights as such, apart from the astounding views over the city and beyond.

Originally called California Street Hill, the 376ft knoll was once scrubland occupied by sheep. The invention of the cable car in the late nineteenth century made it more accessible to Gold Rush millionaires, and the area soon became known as Nob Hill (from "nabob", a Moghul prince; or "knob" as in rounded hill) after the **Big Four** – Central Pacific Railroad barons Leland Stanford, Collis P. Huntington, Mark Hopkins and Charles Crocker – built their mansions here.

Ostentatious designs built out of Marin County redwood were the fashion, but unfortunately, after the earthquake and fire of 1906, almost all the mansions on Nob Hill had burned to the ground. The single exception can be viewed at 1000 California St, at Mason, where James C. Flood bucked local fashions and instead emulated the brownstone style popular in New York; the **Flood Mansion**, constructed in 1886 at the cost of a cool $1 million, is now home to the private **Pacific Union Club**. Across California Street, you'll find another jaw-dropping view – and even more startling prices – at San Francisco's most famous vista-bar, the *Top of the Mark* (see p.477), atop the *InterContinental Mark Hopkins*, completed in 1926 on the site of the old Hopkins mansion. The nearby and equally luxurious *Fairmont San Francisco* at 950 Mason St was completed in Italian Renaissance style just after the earthquake by Julia Morgan, and its Venetian Room was where Tony Bennett first sang *I Left My Heart in San Francisco* in 1961.

Grace Cathedral

1100 California St • Mon–Fri 7am–6pm, Sat 8am–6pm, Sun 8am–7pm; 1hr 30min tours Wed–Fri 10am • Free; tours $25 • ☎ 415 749 6300, ⟨ʷ⟩ gracecathedral.org

Overlooking Huntington Park, the manicured green space at the summit of Nob Hill, is the Episcopal **Grace Cathedral**, one of the biggest hunks of sham-Gothic architecture in the US. Although this pale copy of Paris's Notre Dame was begun in 1928 on the site of the old Crocker mansion, it took until 1964 to finish – and it suffers from a hodgepodge of styles as a result. The building offers an impression of unloved hugeness, despite florid (if hopelessly out of place) touches like the faithful replicas of Ghiberti's Renaissance doors from the Florence Baptistery adorning the main entrance. Inside, the moving **AIDS Interfaith Chapel** to the right of the main entrance features a cast-bronze altar as centrepiece, picked out in gold and silver leaf and designed by the late pop artist Keith Haring. If you fancy joining one of the tours, be sure to book in advance.

North Beach

Sandwiched by Chinatown to the south and Fisherman's Wharf to the north, inland **NORTH BEACH** has always been a gateway for newcomers to San Francisco and, indeed, the US. Italian immigration to the city was ignited, unsurprisingly, by the Gold Rush, although it gained momentum at the end of the nineteenth century, when this area began to develop the characteristics – focaccia bakeries, salami grocers – of a true *Piccola Italia*. Italian-American baseball hero **Joe DiMaggio** grew up here in the 1920s (after he married Marilyn Monroe at City Hall in 1954, the couple took wedding photos at Washington Square Park in North Beach). The freewheeling European flavour here, coupled with robust nightlife and wide availability of housing, attracted rebel writers like Lawrence Ferlinghetti, Allen Ginsberg and Jack Kerouac in the 1950s, making North Beach the nexus of the **Beat movement** (see box opposite).

Columbus Avenue

The main route through North Beach is **Columbus Avenue**, proudly tagged by the colours of the Italian flag painted on each lamppost and now one of San Francisco's liveliest nocturnal drags. At its southern end you'll find the distinctive green-copper siding of the **Columbus Tower** (916 Kearny St). Built in 1907, it's owned by director and Bay Area resident Francis Ford Coppola, and houses on its ground floor *Café Zoetrope* (named for Coppola's production company, American Zoetrope), decorated with Italian paraphernalia and mementoes from Coppola's career.

The biggest draw near the intersection of Columbus and Broadway is **City Lights**, 261 Columbus Ave (see p.484), a bookstore opened in 1953 by poet **Lawrence Ferlinghetti** – and still owned by him today – that perseveres as a beacon of San Francisco culture (Ferlinghetti turned 97 in 2016). Just off Columbus, at 540 Broadway, the **Beat Museum** (daily 10am–7pm; $8; ☎405 399 9626, ⓦkerouac.com) is a modest but enthusiastic attempt to commemorate the legacy of the Beats, with a respectable collection of Beat memorabilia (such as one of Kerouac's shirts and Neal Cassady's car), original manuscripts, first editions, letters (including a rare missive from Kerouac to Marlon Brando) and personal effects (it also holds an annual poetry festival every September).

Also at the crossroads of Columbus and Broadway, you'll find a handful of euphemistically named "gentlemen's clubs". In fact, one of the city's legacies is the topless waitress phenomenon: it was at the *Condor Club*, 300 Columbus Ave, one night in 1964 that Carol "44 Inches" Doda slipped out of her top and into the history books.

Along Grant Avenue

The area grows more Italian as you head north from Broadway – expect plenty of delis, cafés and restaurants selling cured meats, strong coffee and plates of tagliatelle, respectively. One exception is the section of **Grant Avenue** north of Vallejo, where you'll find one of the best shopping streets in the city, lined with clothing stores and various other boutiques. Grant Avenue is also the site of two neighbourhood landmarks: San Francisco's oldest bar, *The Saloon*, at no. 1232 (see p.480), a rare North Beach survivor of the 1906 fire; and, *Caffè Trieste*, at the corner of Grant and Vallejo (see p.474). Opening in 1956, Coppola supposedly penned his *Godfather* script here, and it claims to have been the first West Coast café to serve real espresso.

Washington Square Park

The soul of North Beach is **Washington Square Park**, a grassy gathering spot and public backyard that plays host to dozens of older, local Chinese each morning practising tai chi; oddly, it's anchored by a statue of Benjamin Franklin (erected in 1897), not George Washington.

On the north side of the park, the white lacy spires of **Saints Peter and Paul Church** (Mon–Fri 7.30am–12.30pm, Sat & Sun 7.30am–5pm) look like a pair of fairy-tale castles. Completed in 1924 to serve the Italian Catholic community, the interior is a vast wedding-cake confection, with a lavish altar of Carrara marble and gorgeous rose window. Joe DiMaggio's funeral was held here in 1999.

Russian Hill

West of North Beach lies elegant **Russian Hill**, named for six Russian sailors who died on an expedition here in the early 1800s. It's easy to get your bearings as the cable car tracks along **Hyde Street** neatly divide the district in two. Most people, though, come

THE BEATS IN NORTH BEACH

Beat literature didn't begin in San Francisco; rather, it emerged in 1940s New York, where bohemian **Jack Kerouac** had joined with Ivy League-educated **Allen Ginsberg**, as well as **William Burroughs**, to bemoan the conservative political climate there. The group soon moved out West, where they settled in North Beach and secured jobs at the docks to help longshoremen unload fishing boats. The initial rumblings of interest in the movement were signalled by the 1953 opening of the first bookstore in America dedicated solely to paperbacks: **Lawrence Ferlinghetti**'s City Lights bookstore (see p.480) drew attention to the area as the latest literary capital of California.

But it wasn't until the publication in 1956 of Ginsberg's pornographic protest poem *Howl* – originally written simply for his own pleasure rather than for printing – that mainstream America took notice. Police moved in on City Lights to prevent the sale of the book, inadvertently catapulting the Beats to national notoriety – assisted by press hysteria over their hedonistic antics, including heavy drinking and an immense fondness for pot – matching the fame earned by the literary merits of their work. Ginsberg's case went all the way to the California State Superior Court, which ruled in 1957 that so long as a work has "redeeming social value", it could not be considered pornographic. Within six months, Jack Kerouac's *On the Road*, inspired by his friend Neal Cassady's benzedrine monologues and several cross-country trips, had shot to the top of the bestseller lists, cementing the Beats' fame.

It's said that the word Beatnik was jokily coined by legendary San Francisco newspaper columnist Herb Caen, who noted that the writers were as far out as the then recently launched Soviet rocket, Sputnik. Soon, North Beach was synonymous across America with a wild and subversive lifestyle, an image that drove away the original artsy intelligentsia, many of whom ended up in **Haight-Ashbury**. In their place, heat-seeking libertines swamped the area, accompanied by tourists on "Beatnik Tours" who were promised pavements clogged with black-bereted, goateed trendsetters banging bongos. (The more enterprising fringes of bohemia responded in kind with "The Squaresville Tour" of the neighbouring Financial District, dressed in Bermuda shorts and carrying plaques that read "Hi, Squares".) Soon enough, of course, the Italians who'd once dominated North Beach reclaimed it from the dwindling Beat movement.

The legend of the Beats, though, has yet to die. It's been significantly aided by Ferlinghetti's successful campaign to rename certain smaller North Beach streets after local literary figures – the alley next to City Lights, for example, is now known as Jack Kerouac Alley.

7

here for the white-knuckle drive down **Lombard Street**, a terracotta-tiled waterchute for cars. Its tight, narrow curves swoop down one block, and there's a 5mph speed limit here – not that you'll be able to drive much faster, given the usual queue. The best time to enjoy it is early morning or, better still, late at night when the city lights twinkle below and most of the tourists have disappeared.

San Francisco Art Institute

800 Chestnut St, at Jones • **Diego Rivera Gallery** daily 9am–7pm • Free • ☎ 415 771 7020, ⓦ sfai.edu

Just around the corner from the bottom of Lombard Street's twisty block, the low-rise mission-style building of the **San Francisco Art Institute** clings to the side of a steep incline. It's easy to miss the place, which is in fact the oldest art school in the West; Jerry Garcia and Lawrence Ferlinghetti passed through the school's open studios and Ansel Adams started its photography department. Its one unmissable sight is the **Diego Rivera Gallery** and its outstanding mural, *The Making of a Fresco Showing the Building of a City*. Executed by the Mexican painter at the height of his fame in 1931, the fresco cleverly includes Rivera himself sitting with his back to the viewer in the centre of the painting – find the chubby figure looking on as others construct a giant human being in front of him.

Telegraph Hill

Due east of North Beach and dominated by Coit Tower, **Telegraph Hill** is a quiet cluster of slope-hugging homes. The most direct path up its slope is Filbert Street, but be

---

SAN FRANCISCO'S STEEPEST (AND TWISTIEST) STREETS

Though no San Francisco street can match **Lombard** for its fabled curves, there's another, lesser-known auto twistathon in town, adjacent to the US-101 freeway in the Potrero Hill neighbourhood: **Vermont St** between 20th and 22nd. Its scenery may not be as picturesque as its Russian Hill counterpart, but it's virtually guaranteed that you won't have to wait in a queue to trundle down its one-way turns.

Another uniquely San Francisco thrill – provided your car's brakes and clutch are up to it – is to plummet down (or in certain cases when the streets aren't one-way, slog up) any of the city's **steepest streets**. Much pride among locals hinges on a driver's ability to negotiate San Francisco's most precipitous climbs and drops, particularly with a manual transmission vehicle.

Here's a quick rundown of the sharpest driveable grades in town, including degree of steepness.
• Filbert St between Leavenworth and Hyde, Russian Hill (31.5°)
• 22nd St between Church and Vicksburg, Noe Valley (31.5°)
• Jones St between Filbert and Union, Russian Hill (29.0°)
• Duboce St between Alpine and Buena Vista Ave East, Roosevelt Terrace (27.9°)
• Jones St between Union and Green, Russian Hill (26.0°)

---

aware that the gradient east of Grant Avenue is very steep; since there are few parking spots up at the tower, non-walkers are better off waiting for the #39-Coit Muni bus to the top. Once you reach **Pioneer Park** at the summit, it's easy to see why the peak was used as a signal tower for ships entering the Golden Gate.

Coit Tower

1 Telegraph Hill Blvd • Daily: April–Oct 10am–6pm; Nov–March 10am–5pm • Lobby free, elevator to top $8 • ☎ 415 249 0995, ⓦ coittowertours.com • Bus #39 from Fisherman's Wharf

Dominating the summit of Telegraph Hill is **Coit Tower**, a 210ft-tall pillar built in 1933 with a chunk of firefighter-benefactor Lillie Coit's money after her death. Provided there isn't too long a queue for the cramped elevator, the trip to the open-air viewing platform is well worth it – a stunning panorama with unimpeded vistas in every direction.

While waiting to ascend to the top, take some time to admire the **frescoes** draped around the interior's base, painted in 1934. These were an early project overseen by the Public Works of Art Authority, a predecessor of the better-known Works Progress Administration that employed artists to decorate public and government buildings during the Depression. Those chosen for this project were students of **Diego Rivera**, and the figures are typically muscular and sombre, emphasizing the glory of labour, although there's a wide variation in style and quality between panels, despite their thematic cohesion. San Francisco City Guides (see box, p.463) leads a free, twice-weekly **tour** of the murals (Wed & Sat 11am) – meet at the tower's main entrance.

Greenwich steps

The first of a pair of canopied **pedestrian paths** clinging to Telegraph Hill's eastern flank, the brick **Greenwich steps** drop from the east side of the small Pioneer Park parking lot (look for the street sign) down to a hillside block of Montgomery Street; at no. 1440 Montgomery St, the steps continue down the sharp slope to Sansome Street. As you descend look and listen for the famed flock of parrots, primarily **red-masked parakeets**, descended from escaped or released pets – at least 200 strong (it's impossible to know the exact number) – that now calls this side of Telegraph Hill home. The birds' green plumage sometimes makes them difficult to spot in the tall trees, but you can't miss their squawking.

Filbert steps

One block south of the Greenwich steps, another steep walkway passes between oversized bungalows and gardens both wild and manicured: the **Filbert steps** trace an even steeper path up and down Telegraph Hill, with the lengthy stretch of the footpath between Sansome and Montgomery still laid with wooden planks. There's also a boardwalk on the route's most florid offshoot, Napier Lane, which overflows with foliage and is exhilaratingly fragrant with honeysuckle and roses in spring. The cottage at 224 Filbert dates from the 1860s and was thoroughly restored in the late 1970s, while many of the other small homes in the immediate area are equally charming, helping bring the true identity of this urban peak into focus.

Fisherman's Wharf

Embarcadero, from Pier 35 (Kearny St) to Van Ness Ave • ⓦ fishermanswharf.org

An essential part of the San Francisco experience, despite being universally loathed by locals, **Fisherman's Wharf** is a fun but tacky zone of souvenir shops, kitsch attractions such as the ubiquitous **Madame Tussauds** and **Ripley's Believe It or Not** and overpriced restaurants squarely aimed at tourists. The waterfront district flourished as a serious fishing port well into the twentieth century, and its few genuinely historic remnants are well worth checking out – as well as the pricey but tasty **crab shacks** on Taylor Street (see p.467).

Sea Lion Center

Pier 39 • Sun–Thurs 10am–4pm, Fri & Sat 10am–5pm • Free • ☎ 415 262 4734, ⓦ sealioncenter.org

Aside from embarking on a bay cruise (see p.461), the most endearing attraction at Fisherman's Wharf is the large colony of barking **sea lions** that often take over a number of floating platforms between piers 39 and 41. Operated by the nearby aquarium (see below), the **Sea Lion Center** has exhibits on the playful sea mammals above their regular hangout on Pier 39. Check the website to learn more about the centre's free interpretive programmes.

Aquarium of the Bay

Pier 39 • March–May & Sept–Oct daily 10am–7pm; June–Aug daily 9am–8pm; Nov–Feb Mon–Thurs 10am–6pm, Fri–Sun 10am–7pm • $22.95, kids (4–12) $13.95; tours (daily 1pm, plus Fri–Sun 4pm) additional $12 • ☎ 415 623 5300, ⓦ aquariumofthebay.org

Along with the sea lions of Fisherman's Wharf, another sure bet for viewing aquatic life is the **Aquarium of the Bay** at Pier 39. Exhibits here are standard fare for sea-life museums, although the petting pool with bat rays makes this a big favourite with kids. Highlights include a river otter exhibit and two lengthy viewing tunnels under the main tanks, affording close-up views of numerous species of fish and crustaceans. Behind-the-scenes tours, which offer visitors the chance to feed the marine animals, are also available.

The San Francisco Dungeon

145 Jefferson St • Mon–Thurs 11.30am–8pm, Fri & Sat 11.30am–10pm, Sun 11.30am–9pm • $23.75 ($19.75 online); kids 3–12 from $15 • ☎ 855 753 9999, ⓦ sanfrancisco.thedungeons.com

---

SOURDOUGH OF SAN FRANCISCO

Isidore Boudin arrived in San Francisco in 1849, a master baker from Burgundy, France, hoping to make it rich off Gold Rush miners. Experimenting with local ingredients and French techniques, he pioneered modern sourdough bread (with that genuinely sour taste) in the 1850s, spawning a network of "Boudin" ("boo-DEEN") bakeries all over the state. Today you can learn about the iconic San Francisco loaf at the **Boudin Bakery Museum**, 160 Jefferson St, on Fisherman's Wharf (daily 11.30am–7.30pm; $3; ☎ 415 928 1849, ⓦ boudinbakery.com), observe the bakery in action and see how the original starter yeast-bacteria culture, developed during the Gold Rush, is still used. The on-site Bakers Hall sells Boudin products and operates a café (see p.473). More recently, San Francisco's **Tartine Bakery** (p.474) has pioneered its own long-fermented country loaf, inspiring a whole new generation of artisanal bread makers.

7

On a strip dominated by kitsch attractions, the **San Francisco Dungeon** at least stands out with its series of nine live-actor-led shows bringing to life the city's dark past, through fairly gripping skits and special effects. The one-hour programme begins with "Gold Rush Greed" and runs through tales about the Barbary Coast criminal gangs and Shanghai Kelly (which involves a boat ride), concluding with the "Ghosts of Alcatraz". There are similar attractions in many European cities (London, Edinburgh, Berlin), but this is the first "dungeon" experience in North America.

Musée Méchanique
Pier 45 (Shed A) • Mon–Fri 10am–7pm, Sat & Sun 10am–8pm • Free • ☎ 415 346 2000, ⓦ museemechanique.org

Another entertaining pick at Fisherman's Wharf is the **Musée Méchanique**, an amusing collection of vintage arcade machines. Set in an enormous shed, this paean to all sorts of gaming – from 1920s analogue to 1980s digital – is home to a number of antique, hand-operated games that are relics from Playland-at-the-Beach, the city's bygone amusement park that closed in 1972. If you dare, follow the booming cackling you hear to the giant fibreglass case housing Laffing Sal, a freakish, gap-toothed veteran of Playland who'll howl forever for a mere quarter.

USS Pampanito
Pier 45 • Daily 9am–8pm (check website for seasonal changes) • $16, kids (6–12) $10 • ☎ 415 775 194, ⓦ maritime.org

The **USS Pampanito**, a World War II submarine museum and memorial, is managed by the Maritime Park Association separately to the boats on Hyde Street Pier (see opposite). It's one of the more intriguing vessels on the Wharf and a rare chance to experience the cramped conditions withstood by US submariners.

ALCATRAZ

Before the rocky islet of **Alcatraz** became America's most dreaded high-security prison in 1934, it had already served as a fortress and military jail since the 1850s. Surrounded by the bone-chilling water of San Francisco Bay, it made an ideal place to hold the nation's most wanted criminals, including Al Capone and Machine Gun Kelly. Conditions were inhumane: inmates were kept in solitary confinement, in cells no larger than nine by five feet, most without light; they were not allowed to eat together, read newspapers, play cards or even talk; relatives could visit for only two hours each month. Escape really was impossible: nine men managed to get off "The Rock", but none gained his freedom, and the only two to reach the mainland (using a jacket stuffed with inflated surgical rings as a raft) were soon apprehended.

Due to its massive running costs, the prison finally closed in 1963. The island remained abandoned until 1969, when a group of **Native Americans** under the umbrella "**Indians of All Tribes**" staged an occupation as part of a peaceful attempt to claim the island for their people, citing treaties designating that all federal land not in use automatically reverts to their ownership. Using all the bureaucratic trickery it could muster, the US government finally ousted them in 1971, claiming that the operative lighthouse qualified Alcatraz as active. Today, the island is managed by the National Park Service (☎ 415 561 4900, ⓦ nps.gov/alca), and is open daily (except Christmas, Thanksgiving and New Year's Day). Nearly one million tourists annually take the excellent hour-long, self-guided audio tour of the abandoned prison, which includes sharp anecdotal commentary, as well as re-enactments of prison life featuring improvised voices of the likes of Capone and Kelly; the price of the ferry ticket includes the audio tour and the Federal Lands Recreation Enhancement Act fee for landing on the island (there's no separate entrance fee).

Ferries to Alcatraz leave from Piers 31–33 (frequent departures 8.45am–3.50pm, last boat back 6.30pm; night tour departs at 5.55pm and 6.30pm mid-May to late Oct, returning 8.40pm & 9.25pm; departures 4.20pm rest of year; day tour $33, night tour $40; ☎ 415 981 7625, ⓦ alcatrazcruises.com); allow at least three hours for a visit, including cruise time. Advance **reservations** (up to 90 days) are essential – in peak season, it's nearly impossible to snag a ticket for a same-day visit.

SS Jeremiah O'Brien

Pier 45 • Daily 9am–4pm • $20 • ☎ 415 544 0100, ⓦ ssjeremiahobrien.org

The **SS Jeremiah O'Brien**, one of the World War II "Liberty Ships" built in 1943, has been fully restored and now serves as the National Liberty Ship Memorial. It commemorates the merchant seamen who served on over 2700 of these support ships throughout the war, though it remains seaworthy and often departs Pier 45 on cruises. When it's docked, you can explore its decks from engine room to flying bridge.

San Francisco Maritime National Historic Park

Visitor Center: 499 Jefferson, at Hyde St • Daily: June–Aug 9.30am–5.30pm; Sept–May 9.30am–5pm • Free • ☎ 415 447 5000, ⓦ nps.gov/safr

West of Hyde Street, the pandering tourist trade at Fisherman's Wharf recedes, although pockets persist next to **Aquatic Park**. This area's best asset is **San Francisco Maritime National Historic Park**, a low-key complex that includes restored sailing vessels, curving jetties, impressive nautical architecture and a sandy spit. Be sure to drop into the fine **Visitor Center**, which offers an extensive display of local maritime history in the red-brick Haslett Warehouse, built in 1907 and now the posh *Argonaut Hotel*.

7

Hyde Street Pier

Hyde St Pier • Daily: June–Aug 9.30am–5.30pm; Sept–May 9.30am–5pm • Ship entry $10 (free for children 15 and under)

Hyde Street Pier, in its working heyday, served numerous ferries that shuttled passengers (and in later years, their cars) between San Francisco and the Marin County communities of Sausalito and Tiburon. Today, there's no charge to wander down the wooden slats perched over the bay and peruse the exhibits, and free ranger tours meet regularly throughout the day at the foot of the pier. To board one of the painstakingly preserved ships, though, you'll need to pick up a ticket at the visitor centre (see p.461). These range from the 1886 square-rigger **Balclutha**, to the 1914 paddlewheel tug **Eppleton Hall**.

Aquatic Park

Aquatic Park sits at the end of Jefferson Street, established in the 1930s overlooking a small cove created by the curving Municipal Pier. Plenty of benches and gardens make this a pleasant spot for a picnic if the weather's agreeable (the **beach** is well maintained but the water is usually freezing), while the park's southeast corner is the terminus for the Powell-Hyde cable car line, the city's steepest.

Maritime Museum

900 Beach St, at Polk • Daily 10am–4pm • Free • ☎ 415 561 7100

The Streamline Moderne-styled Aquatic Park Bathhouse directly behind Aquatic Park is now the **Maritime Museum**. Originally opened in 1939, near the tail end of the Art Deco era, its gently sloping corners and clean lines emulate the sleek ocean liners of the day; throughout the ensuing years, it served as a public bathhouse and World War II troop centre. The museum contains changing exhibits on West Coast maritime history, with its ground-floor lobby full of extensive WPA murals portraying real and mythical sea creatures.

Golden Gate National Recreation Area

It's possible to stroll or bike along the waterfront all the way from Fisherman's Wharf to the Golden Gate Bridge (around 3.5 miles), with most of the shoreline falling under the **Golden Gate National Recreation Area** umbrella. Allow a couple of hours for the walk, longer if you intend to head inland to explore the **Presidio** (see p.448).

CHOCOLATE CITY

Chocolate lovers are in for a real treat in San Francisco, where Ghirardelli (w ghirardelli.com) has been making high-quality bars, caramels and cocoa since the Gold Rush. Born in Rapallo, Italy, **Domenico Ghirardelli** was a failed gold miner who started a candy business in a tent in 1849. In 1852 he imported 200 pounds of cacao beans from Peru, gambling that the gold-rich miners were starved of luxuries. Originally constructed in 1864 as the Pioneer Woolen Mill, Ghirardelli Square in Fisherman's Wharf (900 North Point St; w ghirardellisq.com) became the booming company's headquarters in 1893, and though it's no longer based here, the complex of buildings still retains a factory-themed Ghirardelli café, the Original Chocolate Manufactory (Sun–Thurs 9am–11pm, Fri & Sat 9am–midnight), with an ice-cream fountain; and a massive chocolate shop, the Ghirardelli Chocolate Marketplace (daily 8.30am–10pm).

Fort Mason

2 Marina Blvd • **Fort Mason Center Office** Daily 9am–8pm ☎ 415 345 7500, w fortmason.org • **Visitor Information Center (Upper Fort Mason)** Mon–Fri 8.30am–4.30pm • ☎ 415 561 7500, w nps.gov/goga

At the west end of Aquatic Park, a trail rises above the waterfront to skirt around Black Point, a promontory topped by **Fort Mason**. The point has a long military history, beginning with a Spanish gun battery located here in 1797. The US army fortified the site in 1861 at the outbreak of the Civil War, calling it Point San Jose (it was renamed in 1882 after an early military governor of California, Colonel Richard Mason). Today the bucolic **Upper Fort Mason** section is rich with the scent of eucalyptus trees and boasts the enormous Great Meadow, hidden picnic areas, excellent bay views and even *Fisherman's Wharf Hostel* housed in a converted barracks (see p.466). The remnants of the Black Point Battery (1864) lie at the end of the headland. Below the headland (connected by a steep footpath), **Lower Fort Mason** is now occupied by around two dozen nonprofit groups collectively dubbed **Fort Mason Center.** Comprising three piers, sheds and warehouses built in 1915 as the "San Francisco Port of Embarkation" for the military in the region, residents include the Magic Theatre, BATS Improv, the **SFMOMA Artists Gallery** (Tues–Sat 10.30am–5pm) and *Greens Restaurant* (see p.470).

Museo Italo Americano

Fort Mason Center, 2 Marina Blvd, Building C • Tues–Sun noon–4pm • Free • ☎ 415 673 2200, w museoitaloamericano.org

The nation's Italian-American heritage is celebrated at the **Museo Italo Americano**, with changing exhibits that feature everything from contemporary art to rare photographs of Italian neighbourhoods.

Mexican Museum

Fort Mason Center, 2 Marina Blvd, Building D • Thurs–Sun noon–4pm • Free • ☎ 415 202 9700, w mexicanmuseum.org

Focusing on Mexican and Mexican-American art, the **Mexican Museum** displays a rotation of travelling exhibits and pieces from its permanent collection, a cache of 16,000 artworks that includes Chicano artists such as Alejandro Colunga and Gronk (aka Glugio Nicandro), and Mexican heavyweights Diego Rivera and José Orozco.

Palace of Fine Arts

3601 Lyon St, at Marina Blvd

San Francisco's most theatrical piece of architecture sits a short walk west of Fort Mason, just beyond the Marina Green: the **Palace of Fine Arts** is not the museum its name suggests, but a huge, freely interpreted Greek- and Roman-style rotunda designed by Bernard Maybeck that's free to wander round. It was erected for the **Panama Pacific International Exhibition** in 1915, but when all the other buildings from the grand fair were torn down, the palace was saved simply because locals thought it too beautiful to destroy. Unfortunately, since it was built of wood, plaster and burlap, it crumbled with dignity until the late 1950s, when a wealthy resident put up money for the structure to be recast in reinforced concrete; the Palace and its lovely surrounding swan lagoon have since undergone another major refit, completed in 2011. To the modern eye, the palace is a spectacular if mournfully sentimental piece of Victoriana, complete with weeping figures on the colonnade by sculptor Ulric Ellerhusen, said to represent the melancholy of life without art. The shed-like **Palace of Fine Arts Building** behind the rotunda is set to be redeveloped with a posh hotel and restaurants in the next few years.

Crissy Field

From the Palace of Fine Arts, the waterfront stretches west along **Crissy Field**, a former 1919 military airfield now popular with picnickers who come to enjoy some of the city's best views of the Golden Gate Bridge (see box below). Walk along the narrow promontory north of the Palace of Fine Arts to see the **Wave Organ**, an acoustic sculpture constructed in 1986 by the Exploratorium (see p.436). At the field's western edge is the **Warming Hut** (daily 9am–5pm; ☎415 561 3040), an old army shed turned café and bookstore where you can recharge with coffee and a sandwich.

Greater Farallones National Marine Sanctuary Visitor Center

991 Marine Drive • Wed–Sun 10am–4pm • Free • ☎ 415 561 6622, ⓦ farallones.noaa.gov

Located inside a historic coastguard station on the northwest side of Crissy Field, the **Greater Farallones National Marine Sanctuary Visitor Center** contains exhibits on the wildlife and conservation of its namesake reserve, spanning over three thousand square miles of ocean, beaches and wetlands just north and west of San Francisco Bay.

Fort Point National Historic Site

Marine Drive • Fri–Sun 10am–5pm • Free • ☎ 415 556 1693, ⓦ nps.gov/fopo

Directly beneath the southern terminus of the Golden Gate Bridge (see box below) is **Fort Point National Historic Site**, a brick fortress built in the 1850s on the site of an older Spanish gun battery. It's a dramatic site with surf pounding away, a view made famous by Kim Novak's near-fatal leap into the bay in Alfred Hitchcock's

---

THE GOLDEN GATE BRIDGE

The orange towers of the **Golden Gate Bridge** – likely the most photographed bridge in the world – are visible from several of San Francisco's highest points. As much an architectural feat as an engineering one, construction on the Golden Gate was begun in January 1933 and completed in May 1937. Overseen by Chicago-born Joseph Strauss, the final design was in fact the brainchild of his locally born assistant, Irving Morrow. The first massive suspension bridge in the world, with a main span of 4200ft, it ranked until 1959 as the world's longest; it was designed to withstand winds of up to one hundred miles an hour and swing as much as 27 feet (and sag as many as ten) in high winds. It's only been closed for weather three times, most recently one day in 1983 when 75mph gusts blew through the channel.

Handsome on a clear day, the bridge takes on an eerie quality when thick white fogs pour in and hide it almost completely. Interestingly, its ruddy colour was originally intended as a temporary undercoat before the grey topcoat was applied; locals liked it so much, however, that the bridge has remained swathed in "international orange" ever since – and it takes more than five thousand gallons of paint annually to keep it that way.

To **visit the bridge**, take a GGT bus (#10, #70, #101) from Downtown San Francisco (or walk/bike from Fisherman's Wharf). The bus drops off at the **Golden Gate Bridge Pavilion** (daily 9am–6pm; ☎415 426 5220) at the southern end of the bridge, which contains a store, interpretive panels and a 12-foot bridge "test tower" used in 1933. Outside there are numerous viewpoints and the remains of old gun batteries.

You can either drive, cycle or walk across the bridge; an automatic **toll** is collected from southbound drivers only and is $7.50/car. The walk across its 1.7-mile span, however gusty and noisy from traffic, offers the best opportunity to take in the bridge's enormous size and absorb views of San Francisco and the bay, the Pacific Ocean, the Marin Headlands and the East Bay.

Vertigo. The first-floor exhibits focus on the fort's construction, while photos on the second floor highlight the roles of African American soldiers in the US military. The third floor contains an exhibit about the construction of the bridge – the fort was to have been demolished to make way for the great span of the bridge high above, but the clever design of the southern approach – note the additional arch overhead – ultimately left it intact. If you're visiting in winter and up for some eerie exploration, be sure to reserve one of the fortress's Saturday night candlelight tours (Nov–Feb only).

The Presidio

Presidio Officers' Club 50 Moraga Ave • Tues–Sun 10am–6pm • Free • ☎ 415 561 5300, ⓦ presidio.gov **Visitor Center** 36 Lincoln Blvd • Thurs–Sun 10am–4pm • Free • ☎ 415 561 4323, ⓦ nps.gov/prsf • For Getting there, see p.462

South of Golden Gate Bridge, the forested hills of the **Presidio** are named for the Spanish garrison founded here in 1776, though the original fort is long gone. It served as a military base until 1994, and since then has been developed as a mix of parkland (with 24 miles of trails), homes, museums and private businesses. The landscaped grounds of **Main Post** is the heart of the Presidio, with the **Presidio Visitor Center** containing a small history museum and the **Presidio Officers' Club** (which incorporates the adobe walls of the old Spanish fort) hosting changing exhibits about the history of the area. George Lucas's film company is based in the **Letterman Digital Arts Center**, just east of the Main Post, its main entrance marked by the iconic **Yoda fountain** (the lobby of Building B is usually open Mon–Fri 9am–5pm and contains Lucasfilm memorabilia including costumes from *Star Wars*).

Walt Disney Family Museum

104 Montgomery St • Mon & Wed–Sun 10am–6pm • $20, kids 6–17 $12 • ☎ 415 345 6800, ⓦ waltdisney.com

The highly entertaining **Walt Disney Family Museum**, on the west side of the Presidio's Main Post, chronicles the life and work of the iconic movie- and cartoon maker, its interactive exhibits (including a 12-foot model of Disneyland) deserving several hours. The museum's Fantasia-themed theatre shows Disney movies daily.

Society of California Pioneers Museum

101 Montgomery St • Wed–Sat 10am–5pm • Free • ☎ 415 957 1849, ⓦ californiapioneers.org

The **Society of California Pioneers Museum** (next door to the Walt Disney museum) hosts high-quality, changing exhibits on California's early history, from the Gold Rush to the Panama-Pacific International Exposition.

Pacific Heights

Southeast of the Presidio, wealthy **PACIFIC HEIGHTS** is home to some of the city's most monumental Victorian piles and stone mansions – a millionaires' ghetto poised around two windswept parks. The neighbourhood is neatly divided by north–south **Fillmore Street**, an upscale shopping and dining corridor. To its west lies **Alta Plaza Park**, at Clay and Steiner, while east of Fillmore are swanky Art Deco apartment buildings and **Spreckels Mansion** at 2080 Washington St (at Octavia), facing the cypress-dotted peak of **Lafayette Park**. This gaudily decadent white-stone chateau (now surrounded by a

---

GOLDSWORTHY AT THE PRESIDIO

British artist **Andy Goldsworthy** has been contributing works of art to the Presidio since 2008. Inside the old Powder Magazine (Sat & Sun 10am–4pm; free) on the Main Post stands his captivating *Tree Fall* installation, a felled eucalyptus tree combined with clay. Goldsworthy's stunning 95-foot *Spire*, constructed from the trunks of 37 Monterey cypress trees, can be found on the Bay Area Ridge Trail south of Main Post.

massive hedge) was constructed in 1912 for sugar magnate Adolph Spreckels and his wayward wife, Alma, a former nude model who posed for the statue at the centre of Union Square (see p.423); these days, she's mainly remembered for being Auguste Rodin's first US patron and filling the local art museum she built, the Legion of Honor (see p.458), with her collection of his work. The home she shared with her husband is now owned by bestselling novelist Danielle Steel, who has pumped a fortune into the structure's restoration and upkeep.

Haas-Lilienthal House

2007 Franklin St, at Jackson • Tours every 20–30min, Wed & Sat noon–3pm, Sun 11am–4pm • $8 • ☎ 415 441 3000, ⓦ sfheritage.org • Bus #1, #10, #47, #49

To see the interior of a Pacific Heights home, head one and a half blocks northeast of Lafayette Park to the ornate **Haas-Lilienthal House**. This double-sized Queen Anne-style Victorian home was built by wealthy merchant William Haas in 1886, and the one-hour tours are more illuminating about his family's day-to-day life than the architecture of the building. Even so, the place is a grand symbol of old wealth, with intricate wooden towers outside and Tiffany-designed glass and stencilled leather panelling inside.

Japantown

Those looking to satisfy a craving for a steaming bowl of ramen or Hello Kitty contraband can push south from Pacific Heights and into **Japantown**, a once-thriving neighbourhood that never recovered from World War II, when its entire community was hauled off to internment camps. Although a small handful of the district's shops have roots in the early 1900s, the Japantown of today is centred on an unattractive, late 1960s indoor shopping complex with an eastern flavour, the **Japan Center Malls**. Its one notable sight is the 100ft-tall **Peace Pagoda**, a gift from San Francisco's sister city of Osaka in 1968 that stands in the central plaza looking like a stack of poured-concrete space-age mushrooms – although its design implies an atomic bomb cloud to some.

Kabuki Springs & Spa

1750 Geary Blvd, at Fillmore St • Daily 10am–10pm • $25 • ☎ 415 922 6001, ⓦ kabukisprings.com

Accessed via a low-profile entrance just east of Fillmore Street, **Kabuki Springs & Spa** is an island of respite where the communal baths alternate days for men and women, with Tuesday set aside for co-ed bathing. The Japanese-style spa features a full slate of treatments (including massages), but its most popular elements are the steam room, dry sauna, small cold plunge pool and larger hot soaking pool.

Western Addition

South of Pacific Heights, the sizeable **WESTERN ADDITION** comprises a complex mix of Victorian charm (Alamo Square), dynamic dining and nightlife (along Divisadero St) and tension (public-housing projects in its eastern reaches). It's certainly endured its share of ups and downs through the decades, the nadir coming in the wake of World War II, when the dual forces of urban renewal and blunderheaded civic planner Justin Herman had led to the demolition of a chunk of the area's precious Victorian housing by the 1960s. The **Fillmore District** (adjacent to Japantown) – dubbed the "Harlem of the West" in the 1920s – was especially affected, with thousands of African Americans displaced. Attempts to commemorate this heritage have had mixed success; opened in 2007, the swish **Fillmore Heritage Center**, 1320 Fillmore St, had become a debt-ridden white elephant by 2016, with the city desperately looking for new owners.

Alamo Square

A primary stopping point for every tour bus trundling its way around San Francisco is **Alamo Square**, a hilltop park surrounded by Hayes, Scott, Fulton and Steiner streets. The park's southeast slope sees daily flocks of visitors who are eager to see and snap pictures of the so-called **Painted Ladies**. These seven Italianate Victorian houses, originally built between 1892 and 1896 and colourfully and attractively restored, have been postcard subjects for years; the largest of the lot, on the corner of Steiner and Grove, was sold for $3.1 million in 2014. Even if you're without a camera, it's still worth a visit for picnicking opportunities and brilliant eastward **views** that, on a clear day, stretch across the city, the bay and beyond.

Haight-Ashbury (Upper Haight)

Two miles west of the city's downtown core, **HAIGHT-ASHBURY** – invariably known among locals these days as the **Upper Haight**, or simply "the Haight" – lent its name to an entire era, receiving in return a fame on which it has traded mercilessly ever since. Originally part of the Western Addition (see p.449), the neighbourhood was unofficially carved off following the widespread publication of a picture of the **Grateful Dead** posing at the sign denoting the intersection of Haight and Ashbury. Stretching between Golden Gate Park in the west and Divisadero Street at its eastern boundary, the neighbourhood has changed dramatically since the heady era of the 1960s. Even with its attractive strips of Edwardian and Victorian buildings and playing host to one of San Francisco's most compelling shopping scenes, today's version feels like a tie-dyed theme park of sorts, with **Haight Street** itself full of young and itinerant homeless, shops offering hippie-themed souvenirs and secondhand vintage clothes, with a confrontational vibe hanging over its pavements and sullying the district's love-is-all sloganeering.

Away from the begging and patchouli that characterize its main drag, the Upper Haight becomes a somewhat quieter affair once you begin wandering its tree-lined side streets. The **Grateful Dead**'s former house – where the band was busted for drugs in 1967 – still stands at 710 Ashbury St; right across the street, the **Hell's Angels**' house at no. 719 (it's unnumbered, between no. 715 and no. 721) surely did even more to add to this block's living-outside-the-law volatility during that era. Continuing further east along Haight Street, you'll soon come to the base of **Buena Vista Park**, a mountainous forest full of pines and other foliage. Enjoyed by dog walkers in the daylight hours, it's best to avoid the park after dark.

The Castro

Directly west of the Mission, the **CASTRO** has been the spiritual heart of San Francisco's gay and now LGBT community since the 1970s. Initially known for its bacchanalian atmosphere, the assassination of gay City Supervisor Harvey Milk in 1978 (see box, p.453) and the onset of the AIDS epidemic motivated many in the community to focus their energies on political organizing instead of the wild life. As a result, the

---

LOWER HAIGHT

Long an African American stronghold (and culturally part of the Fillmore District), the Lower Haight was transformed in the 1990s into a centre of the city's DJ culture, and while that moment has certainly passed, today it seems perfectly happy to lurk in the shadow of the higher-profile Mission district as San Francisco's second-hippest neighbourhood. Lower key and more authentic than the Upper Haight to the west, the area remains torn between its old and new identities – a conflict that has occasionally led to tensions. It remains a great place to eat and drink (see p.471), but it's best to exercise caution at night, particularly in the vicinity of Webster St.

HAYES VALLEY TO UPPER HAIGHT

ACCOMMODATION

The Buchanan	3
Chateau Tivoli	5
Hotel Drisco	1
Laurel Inn	2
Queen Anne Hotel	4
The Red Victorian	6
Stanyan Park Hotel	7

DRINKING

The Alembic	9
Aub Zam Zam	10
Hotel Biron	7
Kezar Pub	13
Mad Dog in the Fog	8
Noc Noc	12
Smuggler's Cove	3
Trax	11

NIGHTLIFE

Boom Boom Room	1
The Fillmore	2
The Independent	4
Rickshaw Stop	6
SF Jazz Center	5

EATING

Benkyodo	5	Kiss Seafood	4	Rosamunde	
b. patisserie	3	The Little Chihuahua	12	Sausage Grill	14
Burgermeister	17	Little Star Pizza	8	Smitten Ice Cream	2
Green Chile Kitchen	7	Magnolia Gastropub		Sociale	1
Jardinière	9	& Brewery	13	State Bird Provisions	3
Kate's Kitchen	15	Nopa	10	Thep Phanom	16
				Zuni	11

SHOPPING

Amoeba Music	6	Rooky Ricardo's	
The Booksmith	3	Records	5
Flight 001	2	Upper Playground	8
Goorin Brothers	4		
Paolo Shoes	1		
Recycled Records	7		

community now finds itself increasingly wealthy, politically influential and mellowed, adopting the self-consciously enlightened demeanour of what is probably the world's most prominent gay community.

The heart of the district, along **Castro Street**, is filled with stores, restaurants and bars all proudly flying the rainbow flag (**Rainbow Honor Walk** between 18th and 19th is the gay version of Hollywood's Walk of Fame), and it's usually packed with people anytime of day; it's especially vibrant on a Sunday afternoon (or during **Pride Month**; see p.483), full of men strolling, cruising and sipping coffee at pavement cafés. You might even spot one of the **Sisters of Perpetual Indulgence**, volunteers who dress as white-faced nuns to promote safe-sex and HIV awareness in a camp parody of Catholic pageantry. Landmarks include **Harvey Milk Plaza**, at Castro and Market, marked by a huge rainbow flag and displays on Harvey Milk on its lower level. Across the street is the legendary *Twin Peaks Tavern* (see p.483), and the **Castro Theatre**.

Castro Theatre

429 Castro St, at 17th • ☎ 415 621 6120, ⓦ castrotheatre.com

With its lovely Art Deco neon sign rising high above Castro Street, the **Castro Theatre** opened here in 1922, a landmark that shines brightly in a neighbourhood where people, not places, are the star attractions. Screening a well-curated schedule of classic film revivals and unusual premieres, the unofficial "Castro Cathedral" manages to find quality cinema that's more than a match for the theatre itself, a stunning example of the Mediterranean Revival style. Its foamy balconies, Wurlitzer pipe organ (played before every screening), wall-mounted busts of heroic figures and massive ceiling ornamentation lend an air of glamour, though you'll have to come for a movie showing to get in (see p.482) – the world premiere of *Milk* was held here in 2008.

GLBT History Museum

4127 18th St • Mon–Sat 11am–7pm, Sun noon–5pm • $5 • ☎ 415 621 1107, 🖰 glbthistory.org

Located in the heart of the Castro, the **GLBT History Museum** offers a poignant reminder of just how hard it was to create the successful community outside. The multimedia exhibits include Harvey Milk artefacts, historic lesbian and gay posters from the museum's extensive collection and displays on pioneers such as **José Sarria**, drag queen and political activist who, in 1961, became the first openly gay candidate for public office in the US (though he lost his bid for the San Francisco Board of Supervisors, gay voters came out in droves, establishing the concept of a gay voting bloc for the first time).

7

HIPPIES

The first **hippies** were an offshoot of the Beats, many of whom had moved out of their increasingly expensive North Beach flats to take advantage of the low rents and large spaces in the Victorian houses spread about what later became known as Haight-Ashbury. The post-Beat bohemia that subsequently began to develop here in the early 1960s was initially a small affair, involving psychedelic drug use and the embrace of Eastern religion and philosophy, together with a marked anti-American political stance and a desire for world peace. Where Beat philosophy had emphasized self-indulgence, the hippies – on the face of it at least – attempted to be more embracing, focusing on self-coined concepts such as "universal truth" and "cosmic awareness". Naturally, it took a few big names to get the ball rolling, and characters such as **Ken Kesey** and his Merry Pranksters soon set a precedent of wild living, challenging authority and dropping out (as they saw it) of the established norms of society. **Drugs** were particularly important and considered an integral part of the movement, and experiences through taking LSD, the effects of which were just being discovered – and which at the time was not yet illegal – were themselves claimed to be avant-garde art forms as such. Tabs of LSD were pumped out in private laboratories and distributed by Timothy Leary and his network of supporters with a prescription – "Turn on, tune in, drop out" – that galvanized a generation into inactivity.

Before long, life in Haight-Ashbury began to take on a theatrical quality: pop art found mass appeal, light shows became legion, fashion turned colourfully flamboyant, and the Grateful Dead, Jefferson Airplane and Janis Joplin all made international names for themselves. Backed by the business weight of irascible local promoter Bill Graham, San Francisco's **psychedelic music** scene became a genuine force nationwide, and it wasn't long before kids from all over America started turning up in Haight-Ashbury for the free food, free drugs and free love. In no time, "money" became a dirty word, the hip became "heads" and the rest of the world were "straights".

Among other illustrious tenants of the Haight in the 1960s, writer Kenneth Rexroth hosted a popular radio show and wrote for the *San Francisco Examiner*. Hunter S. Thompson, too, spent time here researching and writing his book *Hell's Angels*, becoming instantly unpopular with neighbours for inviting his biker subjects round to his apartment on Parnassus St for noisy, long and occasionally dangerous drinking and drug-taking sessions.

Things inevitably turned sour towards the end of the decade, but during the heady era of the massive "Human Be-in" in 1967 (see box, p.456) – and especially the so-called **Summer of Love** that soon followed – the area became home to no fewer than 75,000 transitory pilgrims who saw it as the headquarters of a burgeoning alternative culture.

THE ASSASSINATION OF HARVEY MILK

In 1977, eight years after New York's Stonewall riots brought gay political activism into the spotlight, Castro camera-shop owner **Harvey Milk** won election as San Francisco's first openly gay City Supervisor (or councillor), and quickly became one of the most prominent gay officials in the country. Milk was a celebrated figure for the city's gay community, nicknamed the "Mayor of Castro Street", so it came as a horrifying shock when, just the following year, former Supervisor **Dan White** snuck into City Hall and shot both Milk and Mayor George Moscone dead.

White was an ex-cop who had resigned from the Board of Supervisors, claiming he couldn't live on the small salary. In fact, he was angered that the liberal policies of Moscone and Milk didn't accord with his conservative views. A staunch Catholic, White saw himself as a spokesman for San Francisco's many blue-collar Irish families and, as an ex-policeman, the defender of the family values he believed gay rights were damaging. During his 1979 trial, White's attorneys claimed that harmful additives in his junk-food-laden diet had driven him temporarily insane – a plea which came to be known as the infamous "**Twinkie defense**" (Twinkies being synthetic-cream snack cakes) – and was sentenced to five years' imprisonment for manslaughter. The gay community exploded when the news of White's light sentence was announced, and the "White Night" riots that followed were among the most violent San Francisco has ever witnessed, as protesters turned over and burned police cars en route to storming City Hall. White was released from prison in 1985 and moved to Los Angeles, where he committed suicide shortly after.

Milk's home and shop – Castro Camera at 575 Castro St – now operates as the **Human Rights Campaign Action Center & Store** (Mon–Sat 10am–8pm, Sun 10am–7pm; ☎415 431 2200, ⊛hrc.org), which sells LGBT merchandise and items emblazoned with the words and images of Harvey Milk.

Twin Peaks

501 Twin Peaks Blvd • Daily 5am–midnight • Free • Bus #37 stops on Crestline Drive; #48 stops on Portola Drive

After leaving the Castro, make an effort to ascend **TWIN PEAKS**, about a mile and a half uphill along Market Street from its intersection with Castro. Very nearly the highest points in the city (at 922ft), Twin Peaks offer a terrific view of San Francisco's peninsula; during the day, busloads of tourists arrive at **Christmas Tree Point Viewing Area** (where a trail leads over both peaks) to point their cameras; in summer crowds often build up waiting (sometimes futilely) for the fog to lift. Instead, try visiting on a clear night to pick out landmarks along either side of the shimmering artery of Market Street below.

The Mission

Home of San Francisco's earliest Spanish settlement and church, the **MISSION** district remains one of the city's hippest and most creative neighbourhoods, despite years of gentrification and high rents that have seen much of its large Latino population move away (Carlos Santana spent his teenage years here in the 1960s). Though a sizeable Central American presence remains, today it's primarily a destination for revellers who head to trendy bars and restaurants – notably along **Valencia Street** (between 14th and 25th) – that jostle for space with old taquerias, the home of the legendary **Mission burrito** (see box, p.471). If Valencia Street is the hipster heart of the Mission, then **Mission Street**, one city block east, is the commercial hub of San Francisco's Latino community, lined with numerous produce and meat markets, as well as retailers selling a virtually identical stock of clothing and kitschy religious items.

Mission Dolores

3321 16th St, at Dolores • Daily: May–Oct 9am–4.30pm; Nov–April 9am–4pm • $5 donation • ☎415 621 8203, ⊛missiondolores.org

The Mission district gets its name from the oldest building in the city – and one of its finest historical icons – Misión San Francisco de Asis, more commonly known as

Mission Dolores. The first Mass celebrated near here, on June 29, 1776, marks the official founding of the city by the Spanish under José Joaquín Moraga, though the community was then known as Yerba Buena (Moraga's tombstone lies within the original chapel). The evolution of San Francisco is reflected in the mission's architecture: the original building, completed around 1791, is squat and relatively spare, while the more prominent **basilica** next door, opened in 1918, is a riot of ornate churrigueresque design. Aside from periodic tour-bus herds, the building can be quite

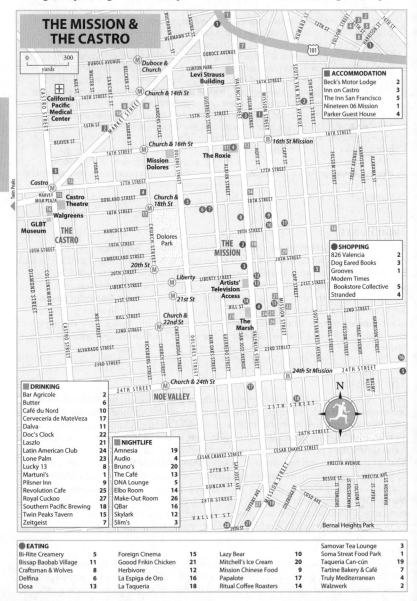

THE MISSION & THE CASTRO

0   300
yards

■ ACCOMMODATION	
Beck's Motor Lodge	2
Inn on Castro	3
The Inn San Francisco	5
Nineteen 06 Mission	1
Parker Guest House	4

● SHOPPING	
826 Valencia	2
Dog Eared Books	3
Grooves	1
Modern Times Bookstore Collective	5
Stranded	4

■ DRINKING	
Bar Agricole	2
Butter	6
Café du Nord	10
Cervecería de MateVeza	17
Dalva	11
Doc's Clock	22
Laszlo	21
Latin American Club	24
Lone Palm	23
Lucky 13	8
Martuni's	1
Pilsner Inn	9
Revolution Cafe	25
Royal Cuckoo	27
Southern Pacific Brewing	18
Twin Peaks Tavern	15
Zeitgeist	7

■ NIGHTLIFE	
Amnesia	19
Audio	4
Bruno's	20
The Café	13
DNA Lounge	5
Elbo Room	14
Make-Out Room	26
QBar	16
Skylark	12
Slim's	3

● EATING					
Bi-Rite Creamery	5	Foreign Cinema	15	Lazy Bear	10
Bissap Baobab Village	11	Goood Frikin Chicken	21	Mitchell's Ice Cream	20
Craftsman & Wolves	8	Herbivore	12	Mission Chinese Food	9
Delfina	6	La Espiga de Oro	16	Papalote	17
Dosa	13	La Taqueria	18	Ritual Coffee Roasters	14

Samovar Tea Lounge	3
Soma Streat Food Park	1
Taqueria Can-cún	19
Tartine Bakery & Café	7
Truly Mediterranean	4
Walzwerk	2

MISSION DISTRICT MURALS

The hundreds of **murals** around the Mission underscore a strong sense of community pride and Hispanic heritage. The greatest concentration of work can be found on Balmy Alley, an unassuming back way between 24th, Harrison, 25th and Treat in the neighbourhood's southern section, where's there barely an inch of wall unadorned. The murals here are painted on wooden fences, rather than stucco walls, and are regularly refreshed and replaced. The earliest murals date back to 1972, but in the decades since, the tiny street has become the spiritual centre of a burgeoning Latino arts movement. While some of the murals are more heartfelt than either skilled or beautiful, it's still worth stopping by for a peek, although the heavy-handed political imagery can be wearying.

For an informed tour of the artwork, contact Precita Eyes Mural Arts and Visitors Center, 2981 24th St, at Harrison (tours Sat & Sun 1.30pm; 2hr 15min; $20; ☎ 415 285 2287, ⓦ precitaeyes .org), which has sponsored most of the paintings since its founding in 1977; the organization also sells maps of the neighbourhood's murals.

7

serene, with a stained-glass-lit interior offering a pleasant opportunity to gaze into the city's long-erased past. The small **museum** contains a handful of artefacts, including replicas of gifts from founder Father Junípero Serra himself, and a revolving tabernacle from the Philippines. The backyard **cemetery** (made famous in Hitchcock's *Vertigo*) holds the graves of the mission's Spanish founders, as well as later Irish Catholic immigrants of the Gold Rush era – many of whom died tragically young. Once much larger, the cemetery is thought to also contain over five thousand "converted" Native Americans.

Golden Gate Park

Daily 5am–midnight • Free • ☎ 415 831 2700, ⓦ goldengatepark.com • Shuttle bus service (free) runs through the park Sat & Sun 9am–6pm

San Francisco is not short on green space, and **GOLDEN GATE PARK** is its largest, a civic treasure simultaneously rich with museums and quiet natural environments that would require days to fully explore. Spreading three miles west from the Upper Haight as far as the shore of the Pacific Ocean, Golden Gate Park was designed in 1871 by Park Commissioner William Hall in the style of Frederick Law Olmsted, the man behind Central Park in New York; it was ultimately completed – on what was then an area of wild sand dunes buffeted by the sea's spray – by Scottish horticulturalist John McLaren who designed a dike to protect the western side from the sea. Inconveniently, the area's famous fog fails to stick to any sort of daily schedule or pattern, so a late morning gripped in the clutch of grey skies can turn into a sunny afternoon by lunchtime – and vice versa – so be sure to dress in layers.

Its eastern half is dotted with striking structures holding must-see sights such as the California Academy of Sciences and the Conservatory of Flowers. Some date from the 1894 California Midwinter Exposition, the first World's Fair held in California, which was designed as a recession-busting sideshow by local newspaperman M.H. de Young; it was so successful that de Young was honoured with a permanent museum in his name (see p.456). Also in the eastern half is the poignant **National AIDS Memorial Grove** (ⓦ aidsmemorial.org) created in 1991 to commemorate all those lost to the disease. Names of those who have passed away are inscribed every year in the **Circle of Friends** (though each name incurs a donation of $1000). On the far western edge of the park stand two wooden windmills that were built to pump groundwater for the park's lawns and gardens; the **Dutch Windmill** built in 1902 and the **Murphy Windmill** completed in 1907. Stop by **McLaren Lodge** (daily 8am–5pm), at the eastern entrance (501 Stanyan St) for maps and information.

TURN ON, TUNE IN, AND GET HIGH

Triggered by LSD being made illegal, in 1967 the polo field at Golden Gate Park was the site of the **Human Be-In**, where the Grateful Dead played, Allen Ginsberg chanted mantras and Timothy Leary encouraged the 30,000-strong crowd of hippies to "tune in, turn on, and drop out". These days it's the location of the comparatively tame annual **Hardly Strictly Bluegrass Festival** (p.423), though pot smokers still congregate at "Hippie Hill" near the "Janis Joplin Tree", especially on April 20th (**"420 in the Park"**), when 15,000 turn up to get high (4/20 has been a codeword for smoking marijuana since the 1970s). Note, however, though police usually leave 420 festival-goers alone, officially the park is a drug- and alcohol-free zone.

Conservatory of Flowers

100 John F. Kennedy Drive • Tues–Sun 10am–4pm • $8 • ☎ 415 831 2090, ⓦ conservatoryofflowers.org

A ten-minute walk from the McLaren Lodge, the whitewashed wooden frame of the delightful **Conservatory of Flowers** was modelled on the greenhouse at Kew Gardens in London. It was manufactured in Ireland for San Jose millionaire James Lick, who died before he could take possession of it; the building was eventually donated and shipped piecemeal to San Francisco after Lick's death in 1876. The attractive space is divided into several sections, including a temporary exhibition space, a room filled with Victorian-style potted plants, lowland and highland tropics areas (in the latter, look for the spindly orchids from the Andes) and, best of all, a cool, aquatic-plant room boasting tractor-wheel-sized Victoria water lilies.

California Academy of Sciences

55 Music Concourse Drive • Mon–Sat 9.30am–5pm, Sun 11am–5pm • $34.95, kids $24.95–29.95 • ☎ 415 379 8000, ⓦ calacademy.org

The park's star attraction is the pricey but hugely popular **California Academy of Sciences**, whose grass-roofed, Renzo Piano-designed structure is a high-profile nod towards sustainable building practices. Inside the grand entrance, you're immediately struck by the glass-encased **tropical rainforest** consisting of four spherical storeys of humidity-enhanced life, including bat caves and butterflies galore as well as a host of rainforest foliage. Elsewhere in the complex, the **Steinhart Aquarium** is home to nearly forty thousand marine creatures, from African penguins and giant Pacific octopuses to stingrays and piranhas, while the **Morrison Planetarium**, housed in a gigantic dome, presents two lively shows on its 75ft projection screen – check the website for times. Also be sure to take the lift up to the **Living Roof**, which includes a variety of native wildflowers and seven grassy hillocks that pay homage to San Francisco's seven major hills.

de Young Museum

50 Hagiwara Tea Garden Drive • Tues–Thurs, Sat & Sun 9.30am–5.15pm, Fri 9.30am–8.45pm • $10, free first Tues of each month • Entry includes same-day general admission to the Legion of Honor (see p.458) • ☎ 415 750 3600, ⓦ deyoung.famsf.org

Flashily rebuilt from the ground up in 2005, the **de Young Museum** is now the largest copper-clad building in the world and the city's primary **fine arts** museum. It lends almost as much space to major touring shows as to its own varied collection, which wanders through sub-Saharan Africa and the Americas and includes some four hundred works of art from New Guinea. The de Young's acknowledged highlights are its **American paintings** – with more than a thousand on display, they make up one of the best collections of their kind, and include works by Georgia O'Keeffe, Edward Hopper, Thomas Eakins and George Caleb Bingham – Thomas Moran's *Grand Canyon With Rainbow* is one of the standouts. Still, its striking structure vies for equal attention, with the interplay between Modernist behemoth and outdoor public space cleverly designed, with interior courts filled with the park's trademark ferns. The museum deserves an entire morning, capped by lunch in the excellent *de Young Café*, which has outdoor seating next to a sculpture garden. Finally, don't leave without visiting the 144ft Hamon Tower (free) for sweeping views across the park and city.

Japanese Tea Garden

75 Hagiwara Tea Garden Drive • Daily: March–Oct 9am–6pm; Nov–Feb 9am–4.45pm • $8, free Mon, Wed & Fri before 10am • ☎ 415 752 1171, 🌐 japaneseteagardensf.com

Immediately next to the de Young, the popular **Japanese Tea Garden** is a legacy from the Midwinter Fair of 1894. It was beautifully landscaped by the Hagiwara family, who were also responsible for the invention of the fortune cookie during the Pan-Pacific Exposition of 1915 (despite the prevailing belief that fortune cookies are Chinese). The Hagiwaras looked after the garden until World War II, when, along with all other Japanese-Americans, they were sent to internment camps (the city refused to let them return after the war). The best way to enjoy the garden is to arrive right when it opens for tea and fortune cookies in the teahouse; then, wander among the bridges, statues (including a massive bronze Buddha), footpaths, pools filled with shiny oversized carp, and bonsai and cherry trees before the inevitable busloads of tourists descend later in the morning.

San Francisco Botanical Garden

7

9th Ave, at Lincoln Way (Main Gate); Martin L. King, Jr Drive, off the Music Concourse (Friend/North Gate) • Daily: March–Sept 7.30am–6pm; Oct & Feb 7.30am–5pm; Nov–Jan 7.30am–4pm • $8 • ☎ 415 661 1316, 🌐 sfbotanicalgarden.org

A short walk south of the de Young Museum, 75-acre **San Francisco Botanical Garden** is home to more than seven thousand varieties of plants, with miniature gardens focusing on specimens from regions ranging from desert to tropical; especially appealing is the headily scented garden of fragrance, as well as the towering grove of redwoods towards the garden's west end. For a free tour, head to the Main Gate (daily 1.30pm) or North Gate (May–Sept Fri–Sun 2pm).

Shakespeare Garden

Martin L. King, Jr Drive and Middle Drive E • Dawn–dusk • Free

Near the Botanical Garden's Main Gate is the tiny, hedged green space known as the **Shakespeare Garden**. Centred on an old-fashioned sundial and dotted with benches, it showcases every flower and plant mentioned in Shakespeare's plays and poems, with a metal plaque full of the relevant quotations on a brick wall at the edge of the lawn.

Bison Paddock

1237 John F. Kennedy Drive • Daily 5am–midnight • Free

Perhaps the most unusual sight in Golden Gate Park is the **Bison Paddock**, where a small herd of the stately, massively heavy beasts roam a field far from their native land over one thousand miles east of San Francisco – they've been kept at the park since 1892, when American bison had been almost driven to extinction. They're fenced in by hefty metal railings, so the closest you can get to the grunting giants is in their feeding area at the far west end.

Beach Chalet

1000 Great Highway • Mon–Thurs 9am–10pm, Fri 9am–11pm, Sat 8am–11pm, Sun 8am–10pm • ☎ 415 386 8439, 🌐 beachchalet.com

At the far western edge of the park across the Great Highway from Ocean Beach, you'll find the **Beach Chalet**. This 1925 Spanish Revival-style building, designed by renowned architect Willis Polk, originally served as a changing room for Ocean Beach swimmers. Added 1936 to 1937 (yet another project funded by the WPA), the frescoes in its lobby by Lucien Labaudt depict both the growth of San Francisco and the creation of Golden Gate Park. It also holds a small **visitor centre** that provides information about the park's numerous guided walking tours, as well as a pair of lively bar-restaurants (see p.473).

Lands End

Lands End Lookout 680 Point Lobos Ave • Daily 9am–5pm • ☎ 415 426 5240, ⓦ nps.gov/goga

Part of the Golden Gate National Recreation Area (see p.445), **Lands End** is a refreshingly wild park that covers the rocky and windswept shoreline south of the Presidio and the Golden Gate itself. The Coastal Trail runs along the shore, from the Golden Gate Bridge to **Lands End Lookout**, the park visitor centre. En route lies the **USS San Francisco Memorial**, commemorating the World War II cruiser that sustained 45 hits and 25 fires during the Battle of Guadalcanal in 1942.

Legion of Honor

100 34th Ave, at Clement St • Tues–Sun 9.30am–5.15pm • $10, free first Tues of each month • Entry includes same-day general admission to the de Young Museum in Golden Gate Park • ☎ 415 750 3600, ⓦ legionofhonor.famsf.org • Muni bus #18-46th Ave

Just above the Coastal Trail in Lincoln Park, the stately **Legion of Honor** is one of the most intriguing museums in San Francisco. The Beaux-Arts building itself, completed in 1924 thanks to local patron Alma de Bretteville Spreckels (see p.423), is no less staggering than its hilltop setting far above the Golden Gate – it's a three-quarter scale model of the Palais de la Légion d'Honneur in Paris. The museum's **Rodin holdings** are breathtaking in their depth and range, all the way down to a cast of *The Thinker* set dramatically on a pedestal in the centre of the front courtyard; with around seventy pieces on display, it's one of the best collections of its kind in the world. One of the highlights of the paintings – primarily a once unfashionable cache of French, Italian and Dutch works from the seventeenth to nineteenth centuries – is Fragonard's dreamy *The Useless Resistance (La Resistance Inutile)* in Gallery 7, with a pretty young woman batting away her would-be seducer with a feather pillow, in a scene right out of *Dangerous Liaisons*. There's an especially luminous *Water Lilies* by Monet in Gallery 9, and an intriguing Rubens, *The Tribute Money* in Gallery 14.

Cliff House

1090 Point Lobos Ave • **Gift Shop** Sun–Thurs 9am–6pm, Fri & Sat 9am–9pm • ☎ 415 386 3330, ⓦ cliffhouse.com

Perched precipitously on the western edge of Lands End, the original **Cliff House** was built in 1863 and became a popular seaside resort for the city's wealthiest families. Twice destroyed by fire, the current 1907 incarnation now consists primarily of restaurants, with a National Park Service gift shop thrown in for good measure – don't miss the arresting photographic display of the numerous ships that have run aground on the rocks below.

Camera Obscura

1090 Point Lobos Ave • Daily 11am–5pm (but opening times can be erratic) • $3 • ☎ 415 750 0415

On the terrace of Cliff House stands the **Camera Obscura**, a longtime oddity built in 1946. Using a rotating mirror and a trick of light, the camera affords entrants a panoramic view of the surrounding area, including the birds on nearby Seal Rock.

Sutro Baths

Far below the Cliff House complex are the ruins of a bygone local recreation area: **Sutro Baths**. The baths were a legacy of Adolph Sutro (1830–1898), a Prussian-born engineer who made a fortune in the Nevada mines and became the city's first Jewish mayor in 1895. In 1896 he spent $1 million on a collection of opulent recreational pools, gardens and elegant sculptures at Lands End, all covered with one hundred thousand feet of stained glass in its day – sadly, it was destroyed by fire in 1966, although it had long been shuttered by that time.

Ocean Beach

Stretching towards the city's southern border from Lands End and endlessly buffeted by sea breezes and fog, **Ocean Beach** seems constantly on the brink of being either washed out or blown into locals' backyards. Aside from a small community of particularly hearty surfers, the strand is the near-exclusive territory of joggers and dog walkers.

San Francisco Zoo

Sloat Blvd, at the Great Highway • Daily: March–Oct 10am–5pm; Nov–Feb 10am–4pm • $20, children (4–14) $14 • ☎ 415 753 7080, Ⓦ sfzoo.org

Towards the southern end of Ocean Beach is the **San Francisco Zoo**, where the top draws are the Children's Zoo (complete with a beautifully restored carousel), lush Lemur Forest, and the three-acre African Savannah containing giraffes, zebras, dik-diks and kudus.

ARRIVAL AND DEPARTURE   SAN FRANCISCO

BY PLANE

SAN FRANCISCO INTERNATIONAL AIRPORT

All international and most domestic flights arrive at San Francisco International Airport (SFO; ☎ 650 821 8211, Ⓦ flysfo.com), located about fifteen miles south of the city. **BART** BART (Ⓦ bart.gov) trains whisk you from the airport to the heart of downtown for $8.95 in under 40min, with regular departures.

San Mateo County Transit The KX express ($4) operated by SamTrans (☎ 800 660 4287, Ⓦ samtrans.com) leaves from the lower level of the airport; it takes around 35min to reach Downtown San Francisco (main bus station on Market St), but only has four departures 6–9am and four returns 3.30–6.50pm Mon–Fri.

Minibus shuttles A number of private minibus shuttles depart every 5–10min from the lower level of SFO's circular road and take passengers to any San Francisco destination. SuperShuttle (☎ 800 258 3826, Ⓦ supershuttle.com) charges $17 per person for shared rides but only $10 for each additional person in your party.

Taxis You can expect a taxi from SFO to any downtown location to cost $45–62 (plus customary 15 percent tip), and more for the East Bay and Marin County. If you're planning to drive, note that the usual **car rental** agencies operate free shuttle buses from the upper level to their car lots.

OAKLAND INTERNATIONAL AIRPORT

Several domestic airlines fly into compact Oakland International Airport – OAK (see p.494) – across the bay. It's efficiently connected with San Francisco via BART's new airport connector tram, which drops you at the Coliseum/Oakland Airport BART station (8 min); once there, board BART for San Francisco to complete your 35min journey ($10.20). Taxis will be around $65 plus tip (metered).

BY BUS

Greyhound and Bolt Bus services will use the temporary station at 200 Folsom St until the new Transbay Transit Center (Ⓦ transbaycenter.org) opens in late 2017, extending just south of Mission St from Second to Beale. Megabus (for Los Angeles, Reno and Sacramento) stops at

Townsend St, between 4th and 5th.

Destinations Eureka (2 daily; 7hr–7hr 25min); Los Angeles (12 daily; 7hr 30min–12hr 30min); Reno (5 daily; 5hr 10min–6hr 40min); Sacramento (9 daily; 2hr–2hr 40min); Salinas (3 daily; 4hr–4hr 10min); San Jose (8 daily; 1hr–1hr 50min); Santa Barbara (3 daily; 8hr 40min–9hr 5min); Santa Cruz (3 daily; 2hr 45min–2hr 55min).

BY TRAIN

Amtrak (☎ 800 872 7245, Ⓦ amtrak.com) trains stop across the bay in Richmond (the most efficient BART transfer point) and continue to Emeryville, from where free shuttle buses run across the Bay Bridge to the main bus station (see above) in Downtown San Francisco.

Caltrain (see p.462) is the best option for Palo Alto (Stanford; $7.75) and San Jose ($9.75). About fifty trains make the trip to San Jose each way daily, taking 1hr on the Baby Bullet (40min to Palo Alto) or 1hr 30min (or longer) on the local (55min to Palo Alto). Caltrain's main San Francisco station is at 700 4th St, at King (around 1 mile south of Market), where you'll have to take a taxi or transfer to Muni (bus #30) for downtown.

Destinations (Amtrak) Fresno (daily; 4hr 20min); Los Angeles (daily; 8hr 50min); Reno (daily; 7hr 20min); Sacramento (daily; 2hr 20min); Salinas (daily; 4hr 20min); San Diego (daily; 11hr 40min).

BY CAR

From the east, the only route by car into San Francisco is across the Bay Bridge ($4–6 toll, depending on time and day) on I-80, which traces a path clear across the US via Sacramento, Chicago and New York. If you're approaching from San Jose in the south, workaday US-101 or verdant I-280 will be your bridgeless (and free) points of entry. The sole gateway along the city's north shore is US-101's Golden Gate Bridge ($7.50 toll) from neighbouring Marin County.

BY FERRY

The most picturesque way of crossing San Francisco Bay – assuming fog isn't suffocating the region – is by boat. A few companies operate regular ferry services into and out

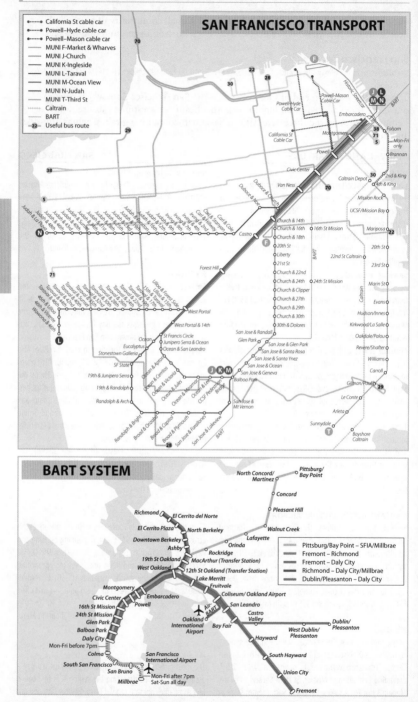

of San Francisco: Golden Gate Ferry (☎415 455 2000, ⓦgoldengateferry.org) runs during commuter hours to Sausalito ($11.75) and Larkspur ($11) in Marin County and calls in at the Ferry Building; Blue & Gold Fleet (☎415 705 8200, ⓦblueandgoldfleet.com) operates boats to Angel Island ($8), Sausalito ($10) and Tiburon ($10) from Pier 39

at Fisherman's Wharf; and San Francisco Bay Ferry (☎415 705 8291, ⓦsanfranciscobayferry.com), best for trips between Oakland ($6.60), Alameda ($6.60) and Vallejo ($13.80) and several points along the San Francisco waterfront from the Ferry Building and Pier 41. Ferries to Alcatraz leave from Pier 33 (see box, p.444).

INFORMATION AND TOURS

San Francisco Visitor Information Center On the lower level of Hallidie Plaza (900 Market St at Powell, Mon–Fri 9am–5pm, Sat & Sun 9am–3pm; Nov–April closed Sun; ☎415 391 2000, ⓦsanfrancisco.travel). This sizeable information centre has free maps of the city and the Bay Area, and can help with lodging and travel plans. They also offer the good-value City Pass ($94; ⓦcitypass.com/san-francisco), which pays for entry into several top local museums – California Academy of Sciences and the Exploratorium, among others – and also acts as a seven-day Muni pass, including cable car fares.

Blue & Gold Fleet (☎415 705 8200, ⓦblueandgoldfleet.com) operate bay cruises from Pier 39, though be warned that everything may be shrouded in fog, making the price ($30) less than worth it.

City Sightseeing San Francisco (☎415 440 8687, ⓦcity-sightseeing.us; $33 and upwards) and its red open-top double-decker buses trundle along several routes around the city.

San Francisco Helicopter Tours (☎800 400 2404, ⓦsfhelicoptertours.com) Undoubtedly, the most exciting – and expensive – tours are aerial: this is the best local operator, who offer a variety of spectacular options over the Bay Area beginning at $195/passenger for a 20min flight.

GETTING AROUND

San Francisco's **public transport** system, Muni, covers every neighbourhood relatively inexpensively. **Cycling** is also an option, though you'll need to be continually alert for wayward drivers and have strong legs to tackle the city's punishing hills. If you can budget the time, **walking** is often your best bet, with each turn revealing surprises.

For a wealth of information on all forms of Bay Area transport, including real-time traffic maps, visit ⓦ511.org. Purchase all transport passes and a handy Muni map at the San Francisco Visitor Information Center (see above), or visit ⓦsfmta.com for other sellers.

MUNI

San Francisco public transport is provided by often-beleaguered Muni (☎511, ⓦsfmta.com), which operates a comprehensive network of buses, streetcars and cable cars that trundle up and around (and tunnel through) the city's hills. The flat fare is $2.25 on buses and trains (exact change only); with each ticket you buy, make sure you get a free transfer – good on all lines (except cable cars) for at least 1hr 30min from the time you receive it. Muni streetcars run until about 1am nightly; after that, owl buses run sporadically between 1–5am. A single cable car fare is $7, with no free transfers.

USEFUL BUS ROUTES

#5-Fulton Begins downtown; heads near Upper Haight and alongside Golden Gate Park; terminates near Ocean Beach.

#12-Folsom Begins in the Mission; heads through South of Market and along Embarcadero; terminates in Russian Hill.

#22-Fillmore Begins in Potrero Hill; heads through the Mission, Western Addition and Pacific Heights; terminates in the Marina.

#28-19th Ave Begins in the Marina; heads through Presidio to Golden Gate Bridge, and through the Richmond and Sunset; terminates at Daly City BART.

#30-Stockton Begins downtown; heads through Chinatown and North Beach; terminates in the Marina.

#38-Geary Begins downtown; heads through the

SAN FRANCISCO NEWS AND EVENTS

The city's main newspaper is the *San Francisco Chronicle* (ⓦsfgate.com), handy for getting up to speed on life in the Bay Area; for comprehensive arts and food listings, check *96Hours*, a four-day weekend entertainment guide available in each Thursday's edition, as well as the Sunday edition's pink-coloured *Datebook*, which contains listings and picks for the coming week. The city's alternative press includes the *San Francisco Bay Guardian* (ⓦsfbg.com), re-launched as a solely online publication in 2016, and *SF Weekly* (ⓦsfweekly.com), which is available in pavement boxes all around town. Both offer muck-raking political coverage, in-depth features on local life and full music and club listings.

SAN FRANCISCO TRANSPORT PASSES

The **Muni Passport** is well suited for city visitors staying a few days, allowing unlimited rides on Muni buses, trains and cable cars; it's available in one- ($20), three- ($31) or seven-day ($40) denominations. If you'll be using multiple transport services during a shorter visit, you may want to consider purchasing a stored-value **Clipper** card (☎877 878 8883, ⊚clippercard.com), available for $3 via vending machines on the concourse of Market St Subway stations. It can be topped up at machines in most stations and is accepted by all major Bay Area transport agencies (excluding Blue & Gold Fleet ferries), making for hassle-free transfers.

Tenderloin, Western Addition and the Richmond; terminates near Ocean Beach.

#47-Van Ness Begins at Caltrain Depot; heads through Civic Center; terminates at Fisherman's Wharf.

USEFUL STREETCAR LINES

F-Market Restored vintage trolleys from around the world begin in the Castro, head downtown, and terminate at Fisherman's Wharf. It always has a colourful dynamic for its popularity with local commuters and visitors alike.

J-Church Begins at Embarcadero; heads along edge of the Castro and Mission; terminates at Balboa Park.

L-Taraval Begins at Embarcadero; heads to the Castro and West Portal; terminates near San Francisco Zoo.

N-Judah Begins near Caltrain Depot; heads through downtown subway, along edge of the Castro and Upper Haight and through Cole Valley and the Sunset; terminates at Ocean Beach.

CABLE CAR ROUTES

California St Begins downtown at foot of California St at Market; heads up and over Nob Hill; terminates at California St and Van Ness Ave.

Powell-Mason Begins downtown at foot of Powell St at Market; heads along edge of North Beach; terminates at Taylor and Bay near Fisherman's Wharf.

Powell-Hyde Begins downtown at foot of Powell St at Market; heads through Union Square and Russian Hill; terminates at end of Hyde St at Beach near Fisherman's Wharf.

GGT AND PRESIDIGO SHUTTLE

Operated separately to Muni, Golden Gate Transit (GGT)

buses (⊚goldengatetransit.org) offer quick links between downtown and the Golden Gate Bridge (#10, #70, #101), plus destinations in Marin (p.522) and Sonoma (p.599) counties. PresidiGo Shuttle (free; ⊚presidio.gov/transportation/presidigo) runs between the Presidio and downtown (Transbay Terminal and Embarcadero BART station) every 30min–1hr Mon–Fri 9.30am–4pm & 7.30–9.30pm, Sat & Sun 10am–7pm, and offers hop-on/hop-off routes around the Presidio site.

BART AND CALTRAIN

BART – short for Bay Area Rapid Transit (☎415 989 2278, ⊚bart.gov) – is the region's electric rail transport system. Although access is limited within San Francisco to Market and Mission sts and a few neighbourhoods in the southern part of the city, it does a good job of connecting San Francisco with myriad East Bay communities and the airports on each side of the bay. Tickets are $1.95–15.70 one-way, depending how far you ride, and the system features clean and comfortable trains that follow a fixed schedule. Tickets can be purchased on the station concourse, or you can use a Clipper card (see above); save your ticket after entering the station, as you'll also need it when exiting your destination station. Note that the system shuts down for maintenance each night between about 1–5am.

Caltrain (see p.459) is a good option if you're travelling beyond the final Peninsula BART stop at Millbrae.

TAXIS AND DRIVING

By taxi Taxi cabs roam San Francisco's streets, although they can be quite expensive and difficult to find outside of downtown, especially at weekends. Ridesharing services Uber (⊚uber.com) and Lyft (⊚lyft.com) were both founded

AVOIDING CABLE CAR QUEUES

The Powell-Mason and Powell-Hyde **cable car** lines run along the west edge of Union Square, although the queue to board the trolleys is often interminably long at both lines' **Hallidie Plaza** southern terminus. A couple of queue-dodging tips: come late in the day (7pm or so), when crowds lessen somewhat; if you must come at peak time, board a block or two north along Powell St, since drivers try to leave a bit of extra room on board at the start of the journey. Note that if the two Powell St lines are still too busy, the California St line that crawls up and over Nob Hill from the intersection of California and Market is usually less thronged with crowds of visitors.

WALKING TOURS

A great way to get to know the quieter, historical side of San Francisco is to take a **walking tour**. The better ones keep group sizes small and are run by locals who know their subject matter inside out. Some, like those sponsored by the library, are free; reservations are recommended for all walks.

City Guides ☎415 557 4266, ⓦsfcityguides.org. A terrific series sponsored by the library and covering several San Francisco neighbourhoods, also offering themed walks on topics ranging from the Gold Rush to the Beat Generation. Its wide-ranging subject matter means you'll often trek alongside locals instead of fellow tourists. Free, but small donations solicited.

Cruisin' the Castro ☎415 255 1821, ⓦcruisin thecastro.com. Founded by the grand dame of San Francisco walks, Ms Trevor Hailey, this tour (2hr) explains how and why San Francisco became the gay capital of the world. It's as much a history lesson as a sightseeing stroll. $30.

Haight-Ashbury Flower Power Walking Tour ☎415 863 1621, ⓦhippygourmet.com. A quite thorough rundown of the Human Be-in, Grateful Dead, the Summer of Love and the Haight's distant past as a Victorian resort destination (2hr 30min). $20.

HobNob Tours ☎650 814 6303, ⓦwww .hobnobtours.com. Terrific, information-packed (2hr) ramble around the haunts of Silver Kings and Robber Barons, mostly in and around Grace Cathedral. $30.

Mission Mural Walk ☎415 285 2287, ⓦprecitaeyes .org. Two-hour stroll hosted by mural artists that leads around the Mission's famed outdoor wall paintings. Sat & Sun 1.30pm; $20.

Victorian Home Walk ☎415 252 9485, ⓦvictorian homewalk.com. Leisurely tour (2hr 30min) through Pacific Heights, where you'll learn to tell the difference between a Queen Anne, Italianate and San Francisco Stick. $25.

Wok Wiz Tours ☎650 355 9657, ⓦwokwiz.com. A two-hour walk through Chinatown run by chef-writer Shirley Fong-Torres and her team. Plenty of anecdotes but a little thin on historical information. $35, or $50 for tour and dim sum lunch.

7

here, and are safe and easy to use assuming you have a smartphone. Traditional taxi companies include white-painted Luxor Cabs (☎415 282 4141) and Yellow Cab (☎415 333 3333). Meters start at $3.50, plus $0.55/1/5 mile.

By car The only reason to rent a car in San Francisco is if you plan to explore the outlying Bay Area, Wine Country or north or south along the coast. Driving among San Francisco's tangle of transit vehicles, cyclists and pedestrians – to say nothing of its hair-raising hills – can be a real headache for first-timers, while looking for available parking often requires a monk's patience. Still, if you accept the challenge, pay attention to posted speed limits (often no higher than 35mph), don't speed through yellow lights and always yield to pedestrians waiting at a pedestrian crossing. Take equal care to observe the city's law of kerbing wheels – turn wheels into the kerb if the car points downhill, away from the kerb if uphill; violators are subject to citation and fines.

CYCLING

The Bay Area Bike Share service (ⓦbayareabikeshare.com) maintains bike stations all over the city: buy a 24hr ($9) or 3-day membership ($22) from any station kiosk to get free 30min trips ($4 for 30–60min, then $7 for each additional 30min). Blazing Saddles (☎415 202 8888, ⓦblazing saddles.com) rents bikes from $8/hr and $32/day, with several locations (including 433 Mason St, Union Square; and Pier 41 at Fisherman's Wharf). Bikes are allowed on Muni buses equipped with bicycle racks (on the front of the bus) and on BART (except during peak hours). For a tranquil trek through undeveloped nature, head north over the Golden Gate Bridge – its western side is reserved solely for bikes – into the Marin Headlands (see p.524) for trails that follow seaside cliffs into verdant valleys; alternatively, ride across the bridge to Sausalito (see p.525), then catch a ferry back to the city.

ACCOMMODATION

Expect accommodation to cost upwards of $200/night in a reasonable hotel or motel, and less out of high season, although keep in mind that rates can fluctuate wildly at any time based on demand. To get the best deal, be sure to reserve well in advance, especially for summer and early fall visits. The San Francisco Visitor Information Center (see p.461) can provide help with finding accommodation, while ⓦairbnb.com – founded here in 2008 – offers hundreds of listings in the city (ⓦcouchsurfing.com was also established in San Francisco). For tradional B&Bs, you can also try Bed and Breakfast San Francisco (☎415 899 0060, ⓦbbsf.com). Bear in mind that all quoted room rates (including airbnb) are subject to a 14 percent local occupancy tax. We have listed specific LGBT accommodation separately (see p.482).

Finally, other than a group-only campground in the Presidio, there's nowhere legal to camp in San Francisco itself, so if you're determined to sleep under the stars, head to any number of parks in the East Bay, down the Peninsula or in Marin County.

HOTELS, MOTELS AND B&BS
UNION SQUARE

★**Golden Gate Hotel** 775 Bush, at Mason ☎415 392 3702, ⓦgoldengatehotel.com; map pp.428–429. Friendly, European-style B&B with warmly furnished rooms, some with shared bathrooms. Beautiful, original iron elevator and Edwardian interior. Shared bath $\underline{\$145}$, en suite $\underline{\$215}$

Grant Hotel 753 Bush, at Mason ☎415 421 7540; map pp.428–429. A good deal for its location, this hotel has small but clean rooms, overpowered a little by the relentlessly maroon carpets. Basic but convenient. $\underline{\$145}$

Hotel Triton 342 Grant Ave, at Bush St ☎415 394 0500, ⓦhoteltriton.com; map pp.428–429. Trippy, eco-friendly hotel that offers modern amenities such as a 24hr gym, as well as more unusual services like nightly tarot-card readings and a round-the-clock yoga channel. The rooms themselves are stylish but gaudy, painted in rich, clashing colours and plenty of gold. $\underline{\$271}$

★**Inn at Union Square** 440 Post St ☎415 397 3510, ⓦunionsquare.com; map pp.428–429. Comfortable boutique hotel steps from Union Square, with stylish modern rooms and deep-red colour scheme, nightly wine and cheese receptions and freshly baked cookies. $\underline{\$299}$

Orchard Hotel 665 Bush St, at Powell ☎415 362 8878, ⓦtheorchardhotel.com; map pp.428–429. A little-known gem, with ample amenities that include DVD player (with free movies on loan) and rooms that are surprisingly spacious, decorated like a clubby study in light teak woods, white linens and striped wallpaper. $\underline{\$260}$

Sir Francis Drake 450 Powell St, at Sutter ☎415 392 7755, ⓦsirfrancisdrake.com; map pp.428–429. This hotel's lobby is a hallucinogenic evocation of all things heraldic, crammed with faux British memorabilia, chandeliers and drippingly ornate gold plasterwork. Thankfully, the rooms are calmer, with a gentle apple-green colour scheme and full facilities. $\underline{\$255}$

Westin St. Francis 335 Powell St, at Sutter ☎415 397 7000, ⓦwestinstfrancis.com; map pp.428–429. This historic hotel has a sumptuous lobby, four restaurants and lounges, a fitness centre and a spa. The rooms in the historic main building, which dates to the early 1900s, have high ceilings and chandeliers, while those in the newer tower are contemporary, with views across the city. $\underline{\$345}$

THEATER DISTRICT

Clift Hotel 495 Geary St, at Taylor ☎415 775 4700, ⓦmorganshotelgroup.com; map pp.428–429. The old-school *Clift* is a postmodern Ian Schrager–Philippe Starck conversion, where expensive rooms are vaguely oriental and feature quirky touches like sleigh beds and Louis XIV-style chairs with mirrors on the seat and back. $\underline{\$280}$

Diva 440 Geary St, at Mason ☎415 885 0200, ⓦhoteldiva.com; map pp.428–429. Trendy, modern art hotel with spacious rooms, as well as sleek metal and leather furniture. Particularly well positioned if you're planning to see theatre, with A.C.T. and the Curran directly across the street. $\underline{\$305}$

Hotel Adagio 550 Geary St, at Jones ☎415 775 5000, ⓦhoteladagiosf.com; map pp.428–429. The decor at this pricey hotel echoes its ornate Spanish Revival façade with deep reds and ochres. Rooms are spacious and feature a contemporary spin on traditional style, with rich wood decor and splashes of colour. $\underline{\$350}$

The Marker 501 Geary St, at Taylor ☎415 292 0100, ⓦthemarkersanfrancisco.com; map pp.428–429. Quirky boutique hotel housed in a historic Beaux Arts building. Eclectic furnishings grace each room – Indian enamel tables, 1960s ottomans, Chinese cushion covers – and the rest of the decor is equally riotous, colourful and a little over the top. $\underline{\$210}$

TENDERLOIN

Phoenix Hotel 601 Eddy St, at Larkin ☎415 776 1380, ⓦjdvhotels.com; map pp.428–429. A favourite with touring bands, this raucous retro motel conversion feels more Los Angeles than San Francisco and features a small pool. Its 44 rooms are eclectically decorated in tropical colours with a rotation of local artwork on the walls. $\underline{\$269}$

SOUTH OF MARKET

Four Seasons 757 Market St, at 3rd ☎415 633 3000, ⓦfourseasons.com/sanfrancisco; map pp.428–429. Sparkling hotel with spectacular views over the city, where plush rooms are the ultimate indulgence, from the soft, luxurious quilts to the stand-alone two-person shower stocked with Bulgari beauty products. Definitely the place to stay if someone else is paying. $\underline{\$765}$

★ **Good Hotel** 112 7th St, at Mission ☎415 621 7001, ⓦhaiyihotels.com/thegoodhotel; map pp.428–429. Fun, eco-aware hotel within walking distance of several museums, featuring pet-friendly accommodation and free bicycle rental. $\underline{\$211}$

★**The Mosser** 54 4th St, at Market ☎1415 986 4400, ⓦthemosser.com; map pp.428–429. This hotel is a funky conversion fusing Victorian touches with mod leather sofas. The chocolate-and-olive rooms may be tiny, but the place is one of the best-value lodging options in town, especially given its central location. $\underline{\$236}$

Palace Hotel 2 New Montgomery St, at Market ☎415 512 1111, ⓦsfpalace.com; map pp.428–429. Hushed, opulent landmark known for, among other things, its fabulous *Garden Court* tearoom and the fact that US President Warren Harding died here in 1923. The grand lobby and corridors are mismatched with small rooms decorated in lush golds and greens like an English country house. $\underline{\$395}$

THE EMBARCADERO

Hotel Griffon 155 Steuart St, at Mission ☎415 495 3522, ⓦhotelgriffon.com; map pp.428–429. Secluded hotel close to the waterfront; rooms are elegant and understated, with exposed brick walls and window seats. **$309**

Hotel Vitale 8 Mission St, at the Embarcadero ☎415 278 3700, ⓦjdvhotels.com; map pp.428–429. Steps from the Ferry Building, this luxury boutique hotel boasts 199 well-insulated, elegantly decorated contemporary rooms (many with bay views) and an on-site spa with rooftop soaking tubs. Bathrooms are decked out in limestone and feature oversized shower heads. **$445**

NOB HILL

InterContinental Mark Hopkins One Nob Hill Circle (California St, at Mason) ☎415 392 3434, ⓦinter continentalmarkhopkins.com; map pp.428–429. Grand, castle-like hotel that was once the chic choice of writers and movie stars: it's more corporate these days in both clientele and design, although its rates are surprisingly reasonable. All rooms are identical, but room prices rise as the floors do. It's also known for its *Top of the Mark* rooftop bar (see p.477). **$242**

White Swan Inn 845 Bush St ☎415 775 1755, ⓦwhiteswaninnsf.com; map pp.428–429. Central hotel with a theme that blends English country inn and 1960s London decor; chintzy wallpaper combined with pop art, antique beds and modern furniture. **$240**

NORTH BEACH

Hotel Boheme 444 Columbus Ave, at Vallejo St ☎415 433 9111, ⓦhotelboheme.com; map pp.428–429. Set amid the heartland of North Beach (Ginsberg often stayed here), this small, 15-room hotel has tiny but dramatic rooms done in rich, dark colours, with Art Deco-ish bathrooms. Columbus Ave can be noisy, so if you're a light sleeper, ask for a room at the back. **$230**

San Remo Hotel 2237 Mason St, at Chestnut ☎415 776 8688, ⓦsanremohotel.com; map pp.428–429. A quirky, warren-like option set in a clapboard 1906 property on the neighbourhood's edge, close to Fisherman's Wharf. Rooms are cosy and chintzy – all share spotless bathrooms and only a few have sinks. There are no phones or TVs in the rooms, and no elevator. **$139**

SW Hotel 615 Broadway, at Grant Ave ☎415 362 2999, ⓦswhotel.com; map pp.428–429. Set on the boundary dividing North Beach and Chinatown, this boutique hotel features large rooms full of modern Asian decor, including bright bedspreads and carved armoires and headboards. **$190**

Washington Square Inn 1660 Stockton St, at Union ☎415 981 4220, ⓦwsisf.com; map pp.428–429. This B&B-style hotel overlooking Washington Square has large, airy rooms decorated in modern shades of taupe and cream; staff are friendly and amenable. **$209**

FISHERMAN'S WHARF

Argonaut Hotel 495 Jefferson St, at Hyde ☎415 563 0800, ⓦargonauthotel.com; map pp.428–429. This nautical-themed hotel in the Cannery complex has large, lush rooms decorated in pleasant blue and gold colours. Amenities and impressive views abound, and it's surprisingly quiet for its location. **$369**

COW HOLLOW

Cow Hollow Motor Inn 2190 Lombard St, at Steiner ☎415 921 5800, ⓦcowhollowmotorinn.com; map pp.424–425. Swiss-chalet-style inn, with plentiful parking and charmingly dated common areas. The rooms, though, are bland, if enormous for San Francisco. **$185**

★**Hotel Del Sol** 3100 Webster St, at Lombard ☎415 921 5520, ⓦjdvhotels.com; map pp.424–425. Funky, offbeat 1950s motor lodge turned boutique, with a tropical theme, plus a swimming pool. The colour scheme combines zesty walls with chunky mosaics and palm trees wrapped in fairy lights. **$300**

PACIFIC HEIGHTS

Hotel Drisco 2901 Pacific Ave ☎415 346 2880, ⓦhoteldrisco.com; map p.451. Popular luxury hotel since 1903, an elegant Edwardian throwback with rooms in a tradional style, gourmet buffet breakfast, nightly wine receptions and exceptional service. **$410**

Laurel Inn 444 Presidio Ave, at California St ☎415 567 8467, ⓦjdvhotels.com; map p.451. Located one block from Sacramento St's antique shops and eight blocks west of Fillmore St's bustling strip of cafés and retailers. Decor is a stylish update of 1950s Americana, with muted graphic prints and simple fixtures. **$349**

Queen Anne Hotel 1590 Sutter St, at Octavia ☎415 441 2828, ⓦqueenanne.com; map p.451. Gloriously restored Victorian building enjoying its second life as a boutique B&B. Each room is stuffed with gold-accented Rococo furniture and bunches of silk flowers, while some have fireplaces; the parlour (where afternoon tea and sherry is served) is packed with museum-quality period furniture. **$245**

JAPANTOWN

The Buchanan 1800 Sutter St, at Buchanan ☎415 921 4000, ⓦthebuchananhotel.com; map p.451. Posh hotel with a "zen-meets-boutique chic" theme, its spacious rooms featuring a blend of local historic pieces, contemporary minimalism and Asian furnishings. It's across the street from the Japan Center and convenient to Fillmore St's boutiques and restaurants. **$375**

7

ALAMO SQUARE

Chateau Tivoli 1057 Steiner St, at Fulton ☎ 415 776 5462, ⊚ chateautivoli.com; map p.451. History figures prominently here, whether in the furniture (one of the beds was owned by Charles de Gaulle), the rooms named for Jack London and Isadora Duncan (among others) or the building itself (built for an early local lumber baron). It's grand and quite serious accommodation, but a solid alternative to many of the overly cosy B&Bs elsewhere in town. Shared bath $130, en suite $175

THE MISSION

★ **The Inn San Francisco** 943 S Van Ness Ave, at 20th St ☎ 415 641 0188, ⊚ innsf.com; map p.454. Superb, sprawling B&B spread across two adjoining Victorians. The 1872 mansion has fifteen dark and stylish rooms; the 1904 extension next door holds six more. The breakfast buffet, redwood hot tub, on-site parking and rooftop sun deck with stunning views all help make for a delightful stay. $185

Nineteen 06 Mission 1906 Mission St ☎ 415 801 5000, ⊚ 1906mission.com; map p.454. Refurbished property dating back to 1906, a B&B with simple, compact rooms featuring bright colours and artsy wooden headboards. Excellent showers – though none are en suite. $199

THE CASTRO

Beck's Motor Lodge 2222 Market St, at Sanchez ☎ 415 621 8212, ⊚ becksmotorlodge.com; map p.454. The clientele at this old-fashioned drive-in motel is more mixed than you'd expect from its heart-of-the-Castro location, and the soft, bluish rooms are plusher than the gaudy yellow exterior might suggest. If you're a light sleeper, ask for a room well away from hectic Market St. One of only a few non-B&B accommodation options in the neighbourhood. $229

HAIGHT-ASHBURY

The Red Victorian 1665 Haight St, at Cole ☎ 415 864 1978, ⊚ embassynetwork.com; map p.451. This quirky 1904 B&B was completely renovated in 2014 and now forms part of a community space decorated with Sami Sunchild's artwork. Simple hostel rooms and private rooms available, as well as the chance to participate in ground-floor arts events. Dorms $63, doubles $143

Stanyan Park Hotel 750 Stanyan St, at Waller ☎ 415 751 1000, ⊚ stanyanpark.com; map p.451. Right across from Golden Gate Park, this small hotel has 35 sumptuous rooms busily decorated in country florals, with heavy drapes and junior four-poster beds. $224

HOSTELS

★ **Adelaide Hostel** 5 Isadora Duncan St (off Taylor between Geary and Post), Theater District ☎ 877 359 1915, ⊚ adelaidehostel.com; map pp.428–429. This

100-bed hostel includes both multi-person dorms and private rooms. There's a big, sofa-filled lounge, backyard deck and clean kitchen; also hefty continental breakfasts and cheap laundry. Dorms $53, doubles $159

HI-City Center Hostel 685 Ellis St, at Larkin, Tenderloin ☎ 415 474 5721, ⊚ sfhostels.com/city-center; map pp.428–429. Smart hostel with 272 beds divided into four-person dorms, each with an en-suite bathroom. With plenty of activities laid on (such as nightly movies and communal pancake breakfasts), it's good for meeting other travellers; its only downside is the location in a dodgy part of the Tenderloin, so women in particular should exercise caution after dark. There's no curfew, and overall it's friendly and funky. Dorms $48, doubles $145

HI-Downtown Hostel 312 Mason St, at Geary, Theater District ☎ 415 788 5604, ⊚ sfhostels.org/downtown; map pp.428–429. This hostel fills up quickly in peak season due to its very central location. Its four-person dorms are spotless, sharing bathroom facilities among eight people. There's a kitchen with microwave and vending machines and a small reading room. Dorms $55, doubles with shared bath $145, doubles with en suite $170

★ **HI-Fisherman's Wharf Hostel** Building 240, Fort Mason ☎ 415 771 7277, ⊚ sfhostels.org/fishermans-wharf; map pp.424–425. High above the waterfront with cosy dorms and spacious common areas, this is a choice option for the outdoorsy traveller, mostly thanks to its location on the edge of Fort Mason's rolling meadow. Be aware that although public transport connects the hostel with the city's main sights, it's nonetheless a little out of the way. Dorms $46, doubles $110

Green Tortoise 494 Broadway, at Kearny St, North Beach ☎ 415 834 1000, ⊚ greentortoisesf.com; map pp.428–429. Laidback destination with luggage storage, complimentary breakfast daily (and dinner three nights a week) and use of the small sauna. No curfew. *Green Tortoise* also runs popular bus trips around the state (see p.33). Dorms $52, doubles $130

Pacific Tradewinds 680 Sacramento St, at Kearny, Financial District ☎ 415 433 7970, ⊚ san-francisco-hostel.com; map pp.428–429. Small hostel (fewer than 40 beds) offering free internet access, a clean kitchen and a large communal dining table that makes meeting fellow travellers easy. It's certainly an international hub – house rules are posted in almost 40 languages, including Afrikaans and Catalan. Book well ahead in high season. $39.50

USA Hostels-San Francisco 711 Post St, at Jones, Union Square ☎ 415 440 5600, ⊚ usahostels.com; map pp.428–429. A friendly and fun place with a 45-seat cinema (with complimentary popcorn) on site, along with free all-you-can-make pancakes and oatmeal in the morning. Large lockers are available. Dorms $57, doubles with shared bath $139, en suite $154

EATING

San Francisco has long been known for its fine-dining restaurant experiences, and more recently for its wealth of low-end marvels such as taquerias, dim sum eateries, green goddess dressing, Mission-style burritos and of course, farm-to-table everything. Adding to all this has been an explosion of mobile vendors – chefs behind the wheel of catering trucks serving so-called street food, encompassing crêpes to barbecue to waffles – in Soma Streat Food Park (see p.468), as well as in day-to-day locations and hours of operation advertised on websites and Twitter feeds.

RESTAURANTS
UNION SQUARE

Borobudur 700 Post St, at Jones ☎415 775 1512, ⓦborobudursf.com; map pp.428–429 Indonesian powerhouse that fuses Indian and Thai influences with often extraordinary results. Don't pass up the *roti prata* (grilled, flaky bread) and curry dipping sauce appetizer. Mains $10–18. Mon–Thurs 11.30am–10pm, Fri & Sat 11.30am–11pm, Sun 1–10pm.

John's Grill 63 Ellis St ☎415 986 0069, ⓦjohnsgrill.com; map pp.428–429. Open since 1908, this touristy but classic steak and seafood joint is famed for being a key setting in Dashiell Hammett's *The Maltese Falcon*. Live jazz nightly. Mains $27–40. Mon–Sat 11am–10pm, Sun noon–10pm.

Le Colonial 20 Cosmo Place, at Taylor St ☎415 931 3600, ⓦlecolonialsf.com; map pp.428–429. Swish Vietnamese restaurant with a quiet French influence, boasting lush, 1920s-themed dining quarters decked out with tile floors, palm fronds and ceiling fans. Mains $24–37. Mon–Thurs & Sun 5.30–10pm, Fri & Sat 5.30–11pm.

★**Sears Fine Food** 439 Powell St, at Post ☎415 986 0700; map pp.428–429. Local old-timers claim *Sears'* signature breakfast dish – 18 little Swedish pancakes for $11.95 (plus warm maple syrup and soft butter; add lingonberries), eleven thousand of which are made daily – hasn't changed at all since it opened in 1938. Amber chairs and tiled flooring add to the ambience. Daily 6.30am–10pm.

THE TENDERLOIN

Brenda's French Soul Food 652 Polk St, at Eddy ☎415 345 8100, ⓦfrenchsoulfood.com; map pp.428–429. Deeply flavourful Cajun food from New Orleans' native Brenda Buenviaje, featuring sweet potato dumplings ($12.75), shrimp and grits ($13.75) and crawfish beignets ($3.50). Mon & Tues 8am–3pm, Wed–Sat 8am–10pm, Sun 8am–8pm.

Grubstake 1525 Pine St, at Polk, Polk Gulch ☎415 673 8268, ⓦsfgrubstake.com; map pp.428–429. Its dining counter set in an old railcar, this classic diner dishes out all the American basics (and breakfast all night); what really sets it apart, however, are all the Portuguese specialities on the menu, including *caldo verde* soup ($8). Mains $17–23. Mon–Fri 5pm–4am, Sat & Sun 11am–4pm.

Saigon Sandwich 560 Larkin St, at Eddy ☎415 474 5698; map pp.428–429. Cupboard-sized shop selling sizeable, made-to-order *bahn mi* (Vietnamese sandwiches) for no more than $3.75; ask the hard-working ladies behind the counter to add lashings of fresh carrot and bundles of coriander (cilantro). Expect a queue out the door every afternoon. Daily 7am–5pm.

★**Shalimar** 532 Jones St, at O'Farrell ☎415 928 0333, ⓦshalimarsf.com; map pp.428–429. The chicken tikka masala is the main attraction at this austere South Asian joint, although the lamb saag is just as exceptional (and generous in its portion). Mains under $10. Daily noon–midnight.

CIVIC CENTER

Ananda Fuara 1298 Market St, at Larkin ☎415 621 1994, ⓦanandafuara.com; map pp.428–429. This affordable and popular vegetarian restaurant casts a wide net – a group of four could easily sample meatless dishes spanning the culinary styles of Mexico, the Middle East, the American South and South Asia. Mains $12–13. Tues–Sat 11am–8pm, Sun 11am–3pm.

Jardinière 300 Grove St, at Franklin ☎415 861 5555, ⓦjardiniere.com; map p.451. This two-storey brick space makes for an indulgent splurge, but it's worth it for every impeccable plate passed your way. Most of the French-inspired Californian menu changes regularly (although thankfully, the aged-cheese platter is a constant), but you can expect peerless dishes like Alaskan coho salmon ($33). Daily 5–9.30pm.

CHOWDER AND CRAB STANDS

The no-frills seafood stands at Fisherman's Wharf (at the end of Taylor St) offering fresh steamed Dungeness crab, delicious seafood cocktails, clam chowder, fried fish and shrimp salad sandwiches daily (usually 10am–10pm) are an essential San Francisco experience. Just peruse the stalls, then pick what you want before munching somewhere along the pier. Most spots also have cramped dining rooms behind the stalls, including Nick's Lighthouse (ⓦnickslighthouse.com), here since 1934, and Alioto's (since 1925; ⓦaliotos.com), both solid options. It's not cheap, though: expect to pay around $7–8 for a bowl of chowder, and $15–16 for a crab sandwich (fresh crabs are sold by weight).

7

Zuni 1658 Market St, at Gough ☎ 415 552 2522, ⓦ zunicafe.com; map p.451. Once nouveau, now a staple, this light-filled triangular restaurant boasts the most famous Caesar salad ($12) in town – made with home-cured anchovies – and an equally legendary focaccia hamburger ($18). If you decide on the custom-roasted chicken ($58), be sure you enjoy the company you're with – you're likely to wait an hour for it to emerge from the kitchen. Tues–Thurs 11.30am–11pm, Fri & Sat 11.30am–midnight, Sun 11am–11pm.

FINANCIAL DISTRICT AND JACKSON SQUARE

★**Kokkari** 200 Jackson St, at Front ☎ 415 981 0983, ⓦ kokkari.com; map pp.428–429. This bustling restaurant's Greek influence runs deep, relying as it does on Hellenic staples such as lamb and eggplant. Its huge open fireplace heats two dazzling dining rooms decorated with oriental rugs and goatskin lampshades. Mains $24–53. Mon–Thurs 11.30am–2.30pm & 5.30–10pm, Fri 11.30am–2.30pm & 5.30–11pm, Sat 5–11pm, Sun 5–10pm.

Super Duper Burgers 346 Kearny St, at Pine ☎ 415 677 9936; map pp.428–429. This mini chain specializes in locally sourced burgers ($7.75), organic shakes ($4.75) and garlic fries ($3.25), plus the famously free house-made pickles . Mon–Fri 7am–10pm, Sat 10am–7pm.

Tadich Grill 240 California St, at Front ☎ 415 391 1849, ⓦ tadichgrill.com; map pp.428–429. Founded during the '49 Gold Rush and specializing in seafood, this Downtown classic is half-diner, half-gentleman's club, with a seasoned group of waiters nearly as stiff as their white jackets. Try the iconic cioppino (fish stew) or the notorious Hangtown Fry, a bacon and fried oyster frittata. Most mains $23–32. Mon–Fri 11am–9.30pm, Sat 11.30am–9.30pm.

SOUTH OF MARKET

★**Bellota** 888 Brannan St, at 8th ☎ 415 430 6580, ⓦ bellotasf.com; map pp.424–425. One of the hottest restaurants in the city, serving beautifully crafted Spanish cuisine (paella, tapas, wood-fire-grilled options and a wholly Spanish wine list) in a rustic-chic dining room. Mains $20–45, tapas from $6. Mon–Wed 4–10pm, Thurs–Sat 4–11pm.

Benu 22 Hawthorne St, at Howard ☎ 415 685 4860, ⓦ benusf.com; map pp.428–429. San Francisco's three-Michelin-star showcase, featuring innovative Californian-Asian fusion cuisine in an elegant, minimalist space; think smoked quail with nasturtium, beef rib steak and sesame leaf ice cream. Tasting menu only ($268 per person, plus 20 percent service). Tues–Sat 6–9pm.

Dottie's True Blue Café 28 6th St, at Market ☎ 415 885 2767; map pp.428–429. An inexpensive spot that's become immensely popular with locals and visitors. The oversize pastries and breads (don't leave without trying the chilli cornbread), as well as generous platters of breakfast favourites, make it worth waiting for a place to sit (up to

1hr). Mon & Thurs–Fri 7.30am–3pm, Sat & Sun 7.30am–4pm.

Marlowe 500 Brannan St, at 4th ☎ 415 777 1413, ⓦ marlowesf.com; map pp.428–429. Stylish American bistro with a butcher shop theme and meat-centric menu serving excellent burgers ($16), but also specials such as devilled eggs ($3), English pea pancakes ($13), Brussels sprout chips ($9.50) and roasted bone marrow ($17). Mon–Wed 11.30am–10pm, Thurs & Fri 11.30am–11pm, Sat 10am–11pm, Sun 10am–10pm.

Mourad 140 New Montgomery St, at Minna ☎ 415 660 2500, ⓦ mouradsf.com; map pp.428–429. Exquisite (and pricey) Moroccan-inspired restaurant helmed by chef Mourad Lahlou, in an elegant dining room with a menu featuring duck basteeya ($22), couscous ($24), huge plates of lamb and short rib served family-style ($145–165), as well as inventive cocktails ($14). Mon–Fri 11.30am–9.30pm, Sat & Sun 5–10pm.

★**Soma Streat Food Park** 428 11th St, at Division ⓦ somastreatfoodpark.com; map p.454. A former parking lot now brilliantly re-imagined as a mobile food vendor oasis. Choose from a daily rotation of trucks offering everything from kim-chi wraps and seafood salads to sausages and cupcakes; there's also a covered beer garden. Check the website for that day's roster. Mon–Fri 11am–3pm & 5–9pm, Sat 11am–9pm, Sun 11am–5pm.

★**Trou Normand** 140 New Montgomery St, at Minna ☎ 415 975 0876, ⓦ trounormandsf.com; map pp.428–429. Fashionable minimalist lounge and restaurant in an Art Deco high-rise, with an elegant marble bar serving forty types of house-made charcuterie (plates from $12), craft cocktails and calvados, plus tables on the back patio for pasta and chophouse style cuts of meat (mains $23–29). Mon–Fri 11.30am–3.30pm & 5.30–10.30pm, Sat 10.30am–3.30pm & 5.30–10.30pm, Sun 10.30am–3.30pm & 5.30–9.30pm.

Yank Sing 49 Stevenson St, at 1st ☎ 415 541 4949, ⓦ yanksing.com; map pp.428–429. One of the better (if more expensive) places for dim sum in the city. Though it's routinely packed, the staff can almost always find a spot for you; come early to select from left-field varieties such as snow-pea-shoot dumplings that populate the circulating carts. Mon–Fri 11am–3pm, Sat & Sun 10am–4pm.

THE EMBARCADERO

Gott's Roadside Ferry Building Marketplace ☎ 415 318 3423, ⓦ gotts.com; map pp.428–429. Fancified, yet inexpensive burger stand with an immense alfresco dining area off the Embarcadero pedestrian path that's a major draw on sunny afternoons. Burgers ($7–13), sweet-potato fries ($4) and super-thick milk shakes ($6) are all made from fresh ingredients. Daily 10am–10pm.

Hog Island Oyster Co Ferry Building Marketplace ☎ 415 391 7117, ⓦ hogislandoysters.com; map pp.428–429.

This outpost of the Tomales Bay (Marin County) farm hosts mollusc devotees who sit elbow to elbow at the wraparound granite bar. The lists of available oysters (about $18 for six, $33 for a dozen), wines and beers are equally impressive, while the creamy oyster stew is a perennial hit. Daily 11am–9pm.

The Slanted Door Ferry Building Marketplace ☎ 415 861 8032, ⓦ slanteddoor.com; map pp.428–429. The daily-changing menu at this gorgeously sited, continually buzzing restaurant is light French-Vietnamese. There's a raw bar and several deliciously fragrant chicken dishes available, and the tea list is remarkably diverse. Mains cost around $20–48, and you'll definitely want to make reservations in advance. Mon–Sat 11am–2.30pm & 5.30–10pm, Sun 11.30am–3pm & 5.30–10pm.

CHINATOWN

Delicious Dim Sum 752 Jackson St, at Stockton ☎ 415 781 0721; map pp.428–429. Come to this tiny Cantonese place to ogle – and then devour – glistening, pearly dumplings ($4–5) arranged in layers of steamers. Mon–Tues & Thurs–Sun 7am–6pm.

Far East Cafe 631 Grant Ave ☎ 415 982 3245, ⓦ fareastcafesf.com; map pp.428–429. Classic Chinese joint since 1920, with kitsch American decor, curtained mahogany booths and all the American-Chinese favourites: kungpao chicken, hot and sour soup and the notorious General Chou's chicken. Mains $9–16. Daily 11.30am–10pm.

Great Eastern 649 Jackson St, at Kearny ☎ 415 986 2500, ⓦ greateasternsf.com; map pp.428–429. Elegant and traditional Cantonese restaurant serving favourites such as sautéed squab with Chinese broccoli. Most mains about $20. President Obama ate dim sum here in 2012. Mon–Fri 10am–11pm, Sat & Sun 9am–11pm.

R&G Lounge 631 Kearny St, at Commercial ☎ 415 982 7877, ⓦ rnglounge.com; map pp.428–429. Behind frosted windows looms this enormous, Hong Kong-style restaurant that draws a diverse crowd. The fairly priced dishes (most $17–22) are presented family-style and there's a heavy slant towards seafood. Daily 11am–9.30pm.

NOB HILL

Harris' 2100 Van Ness Ave, at Pacific ☎ 415 673 1888, ⓦ harrisrestaurant.com; map pp.428–429. Proudly old-fashioned and one of the premier steakhouses in the city, *Harris'* decor includes padded chairs, cushy leather booths and thick velvet curtains. There's practically every cut of beef imaginable on the menu – from filet mignon to Kobe rib-eye – and all are buttery-sweet and tender. Just be sure to pack your credit card, as steak dinners begin at $48. Mon–Fri 5.30–9.30pm, Sat & Sun 5–9.30pm.

★ **House of Prime Rib** 1906 Van Ness Ave ☎ 415 885 4605, ⓦ houseofprimerib.net; map pp.428–429. This 1940s San Francisco classic is a real throwback, serving essentially one item – exceptional roast beef (served from roving steel carts to your required tenderness and thickness, and with mashed or loaded baked potatoes). Each dish comes with a salad prepared tableside, creamed spinach and real Yorkshire pudding (dinners $30–50). Order a martini for the finishing touch. Mon–Thurs 5.30–10pm, Fri 5–10pm, Sat & Sun 4–10pm.

★ **Swan Oyster Depot** 1517 Polk St, at California ☎ 415 673 1101, ⓦ sfswanoysterdepot.com; map pp.428–429. Expect no frills at this legendary seafood joint with its huge marble countertop and tiled walls. Endure the inevitable wait, grab a stool and hang onto it, and suck down some cheap shellfish (from $12) or a bowl of chowder ($2.75). Mon–Sat 10.30am–5.30pm.

NORTH BEACH

Café Jacqueline 1454 Grant Ave, at Union St ☎ 415 981 5565; map pp.428–429. A romantic, candlelit gourmet experience in an inviting dining room that feels like a French country cottage. The menu here is entirely made up of soufflés ($30 and up), both savoury and sweet; since every dish is made to order, plan on making an evening of it. Wed–Sun 5.30–11pm.

L'Osteria del Forno 519 Columbus Ave, at Green St ☎ 415 982 1124, ⓦ losteriadelforno.com; map pp.428–429. This postage-stamp-sized nook is a humble refuge from the gaudy tourist traps all along Columbus Ave. The menu's short and driven by whatever's freshest at the market, although pizzas ($3–24) are an excellent standby. Reservations aren't taken, so a wait may be inevitable even at off-peak times. Mon, Wed, Thurs & Sun 11.30am–10pm, Fri & Sat 11.30am–10.30pm.

★ **Mama's on Washington Square** 1701 Stockton St, at Filbert ☎ 415 362 6421, ⓦ mamas-sf.com; map pp.428–429. Justly popular all-day breakfast and brunch spot overlooking the park, especially famed for its omelettes (from $10.50), French toast (from $8.95) and benedicts (from $12.50) . No credit cards. Tues–Sun 8am–3pm.

Mo's Grill 1322 Grant Ave, at Vallejo St ☎ 415 788 3779, ⓦ mosgourmethamburgers.com; map pp.428–429. This no-frills joint cooks beef over a volcanic rock grill to produce some of San Francisco's best (and chunkiest) hamburgers (from $11). The house fries are also noteworthy, and good breakfasts are available until mid-afternoon each day. Mon–Thurs & Sun 8.30am–10.30pm, Fri & Sat 8.30am–11pm.

Pat's Cafe 2330 Taylor St, at Chestnut St ☎ 415 776 8735, ⓦ patscafesf.com; map pp.428–429. Eminently inviting spot right along the Powell-Mason cable car line. It's bright and comfortable, but the charming decor can't overshadow the delicious, affordable and occasionally rich breakfasts – the peppery home fries ($3.90) and Belgian waffles ($10.55) are especially recommended. Daily 7.30am–2.30pm.

Sotto Mare 552 Green St, at Jasper Place ☎ 415 398 3181, ⓦ sottomaresf.com; map pp.428–429. Classic seafood joint, especially known for its cioppino (fish stew;

7

$41 for two), perhaps the best in the city (it's a San Francisco creation) and fresh oysters ($1.50). Mon–Sat 11.30am–9.30pm.

Tommaso's 1042 Kearny St, at Pacific St ☎ 415 398 9696, ⓦ tommasos.com; map pp.428–429. Claiming to be the West Coast birthplace of the wood-fired pizza oven, this neighbourhood stalwart hasn't lost a step in popularity since opening in 1935 as *Lupo's*. And for good reason: the thin-crust pizzas ($24–30 for a 15-inch large) are terrific, while the seven-layer lasagne is wonderfully gooey. Tues–Sat 5–10.30pm, Sun 4–9.30pm.

★**Tony's Pizza Napoletana** 1570 Stockton St, at Union ☎ 415 835 9888, ⓦ tonyspizzanapoletana.com; map pp.428–429. World Pizza Cup champion Tony Gemignani's corner pizzeria bakes up to 600 pizzas in several styles daily, from his prized, gossamer-thin-crusted Margherita ($21; only 73 made each day) to an extra-saucy New Jersey version ($19). Service is remarkably attentive, and it's nice to sit near the brick oven to watch the chefs in action. Mon noon–1pm, Wed–Sun noon–11pm.

Trattoria Contadina 1800 Mason St, at Union ☎ 415 982 5728, ⓦ trattoriacontadina.com; map pp.428–429. Family-owned, warm and charming, with white-cloth-swathed tables and photograph-covered walls. The rigatoni with eggplant and smoked mozzarella is a top option, and the Powell-Mason cable car will drop you off steps from the front door. Pasta $17–23, *secondi* $27–35. Mon–Thurs 5–9pm, Fri 5–9.30pm, Sat & Sun 4–9.30pm.

RUSSIAN HILL

Frascati 1901 Hyde St, at Green ☎ 415 928 1406, ⓦ frascati.ipower.com/new; map pp.428–429. Vividly romantic, Mediterranean-style bistro on a prime Russian Hill corner. Expect uniquely paired California dishes such as maple-leaf duck breast with herb and huckleberry sauce, and an extensive wine list. Mains $26–31. Mon–Sat 5.30–9.45pm, Sun 5.30–9pm.

Helmand Palace 2424 Van Ness Ave, at Green St ☎ 415 345 0072, ⓦ helmandpalacesf.com; map pp.428–429. The menu at this popular Afghani restaurant is filled with tangy and spicy staples – try the *kaddo* (caramelized pumpkin on a bed of yoghurt) or the *chapandaz* (grilled beef tenderloin). Plenty of vegetarian items are also available. Most mains $14–23. Mon–Thurs & Sun 5.30–10pm, Fri & Sat 5.30–11pm.

La Folie 2316 Polk St, at Green St ☎ 415 776 5577, ⓦ lafolie.com; map pp.428–429. Magnificent Provençal food served *sans* attitude or pretension. There are typically three *prix fixe* options ($100–150) available to choose from, so make a reservation if you fancy duck confit or a trio of rabbit. Tues–Sat 5.30–10pm.

The Matterhorn 2323 Van Ness Ave, at Vallejo St ☎ 415 885 6116, ⓦ thematterhornrestaurant.com; map pp.428–429. Lurking at the foot of a nondescript apartment building, this restaurant is known for cheese, beef and chocolate fondues; its ski-lodge decor was shipped in pieces from the Swiss motherland and reassembled on site. Beef fondues for two are $51; cheese fondues for two, $45.50. Tues–Sun 5–9.30pm.

FISHERMAN'S WHARF AND FORT MASON

Gary Danko 800 North Point St, at Hyde ☎ 415 749 2060, ⓦ garydanko.com; map pp.428–429. This understated oasis regularly vies for the title of best restaurant in food-obsessed San Francisco. Granted, this is performance food served with a flourish, but its *prix fixe* menus ($83–119) are utterly splurge-worthy. Reserve well ahead. Daily 5.30–10pm.

Greens Building A, Fort Mason Center, 2 Marina Blvd ☎ 415 771 6222, ⓦ greensrestaurant.com; map pp.424–425. San Francisco's original vegetarian restaurant remains popular thanks to its continually inventive menu, picturesque pier setting and airy interior. It's surprisingly casual, given the quality and price of the food. Mains $19–28. Tues–Fri 11.45am–2.30pm & 5.30–9pm, Sat 11am–2.30pm & 5.30–9pm, Sun 10.30am–2pm & 5.30–9pm.

Scoma's 1965 Al Scoma Way (Pier 47) ☎ 415 929 1730, ⓦ scomas.com; map pp.428–429. If you can't resist the allure of the tourist-targeting seafood palaces that crowd the Wharf, *Scoma's* is likely your safest choice. Just steel yourself for high prices and be sure to make a reservation, as this is reportedly the highest-volume restaurant west of the Mississippi. Mains $25–39. Mon–Thurs & Sun 11.30am–10pm, Fri & Sat 11.30am–10.30pm.

PACIFIC HEIGHTS AND JAPANTOWN

Kiss Seafood 1700 Laguna St, at Sutter ☎ 415 474 2866, ⓦ kissseafoodsf.com; map p.451. You'll need to reserve well ahead to get into this unsigned, blink-and-you'll-miss-it Japanese restaurant; it's also quite expensive, with a full meal running to $70 per person. Once in the door, expect as many as eight courses if you order the *omakase* (chef's choice; $60–78). Wed–Sun 5.30–9.30pm.

★**Sociale** 3665 Sacramento St, at Spruce ☎ 415 921 3200, ⓦ sfsociale.com; map p.451. Intimate, pricey Northern Italian bistro worth seeking out at the end of its verdant pedestrian lane. Go for the heated dining courtyard, cosy atmosphere and fontina-cheese-crammed fried olives appetizer ($11). Mains $23–30. Mon 5.30–10pm, Tues–Sat 11.30am–2.30pm & 5.30–10pm.

WESTERN ADDITION

Green Chile Kitchen 1801 McAllister St, at Baker ☎ 415 440 9411, ⓦ greenchilekitchen.com; map p.451. Extraordinarily flavourful cuisine from the state of New Mexico, further enhanced by robust chillies – request "Christmas" sauce for a dollar extra, and you'll get both red and green chillies on (or in) your meal. Mains $13–18.

SAN FRANCISCO'S SUPER BURRITO

Philadelphia has its cheesesteaks, New York its pastrami sandwiches and Texas its barbecue. In San Francisco, the **super burrito** is not only the premier bargain food, but truly a local phenomenon. The city is home to something approaching two hundred **taquerias** – informal Mexican restaurants specializing in tacos, quesadillas, tortas and, of course, burritos – and locals are often heard debating their favourites effusively.

San Francisco's take on the burrito differs from its Southern California cousin not only in its comparatively gargantuan size, but also in its ingredient list. Whereas a San Diego-style burrito can be an austere meal of meat, cheese and salsa scattered about a standard-size tortilla, the San Francisco version stuffs a jumbo tortilla with any number of grilled or barbecued meats, Spanish rice, beans (choices include whole pinto, black or refried), melted cheese, *pico de gallo* (a splashy mix of diced tomato, onion, jalapeño and cilantro), guacamole or slices of avocado, a splatter of salsa and even sour cream. And with its emphasis on vegetables, grains and legumes, the burrito also easily lends itself to vegetarian and vegan variants.

Most San Francisco taquerias wrap their goods in aluminium foil for easy handling, as the majority of locals eat burritos by hand. Expect to pay $6–10 for a super burrito and to not have much of an appetite for hours afterwards. Forgo the utensils, order a Mexican beer or non-alcoholic *agua fresca* (fruit drink) with your foiled meal and you'll fit right in.

7

Mon–Thurs & Sun 9am–9.30pm, Fri & Sat 9am–10pm.
Little Star Pizza 846 Divisadero St, at McAllister ☎ 415 441 1118, ⓦ littlestarpizza.com; map p.451. One of San Francisco's top pizzerias, dimly lit and packed nightly with hipsters enjoying its lively bar and jukebox blasting American and British indie rock. The kitchen bakes deep-dish and thin-crust pizzas (large $17.75–27.50) with equal aplomb. Mon–Thurs 5–10pm, Fri 4–10.30pm, Sat 3–10.30pm, Sun 3–10pm.

★ **Nopa** 560 Divisadero St, at Hayes ☎ 415 864 8643, ⓦ nopasf.com; map p.451. Buzzing, impossibly popular hotspot which focuses on a number of cuisine styles, from New American (country pork chop, rotisserie herbed chicken) to further afield (Moroccan vegetable tagine, baked pastas). Mains $17–30. Mon–Fri 5pm–1am, Sat & Sun 11am–1am.

★ **State Bird Provisions** 1529 Fillmore St, at Geary Blvd ☎ 415 795 1272, ⓦ statebirdsf.com; map p.451. Expect long queues at this popular spot, serving small plates of Californian fusion cuisine, dim sum style; guinea hen dumpling with aromatic broth ($3), cauliflower falafel ($6), halibut spring roll ($8) and summer squash goat cheese toast ($4). Mon–Thurs & Sun 5.30–10pm, Fri & Sat 5.30–11pm.

LOWER HAIGHT

Kate's Kitchen 471 Haight St, at Fillmore ☎ 415 626 3984; map p.451. When you first stare down at the monstrous plates of budget breakfast fare served here, it's a little hard to think about saving room for extras. But treat yourself to six hush puppies ($5) to take away – deep-fried lumps of cornmeal served with honey-touched "pooh butter". Daily 9am–2.30pm.

The Little Chihuahua 292 Divisadero St, at Page ☎ 415 255 8225, ⓦ thelittlechihuahua.com; map

p.451. Not your garden variety taqueria at all – look for unique menu items such as Mexican French toast and fried plantain burritos alongside standard favourites such as tortilla soup and enchiladas. Just about everything's under $13. Mon–Fri 11am–11pm, Sat & Sun 10am–11pm.

Rosamunde Sausage Grill 545 Haight St, at Fillmore ☎ 415 437 6851, ⓦ rosamundesausagegrill.com; map p.451. Tiny storefront serving terrific, inexpensive grilled sausages on sesame rolls ($8). Options range from Hungarian pork to tequila-smoked chicken *habanero*. Mon–Wed & Sun 11.30am–10pm, Thurs–Sat 11.30am–11pm.

Thep Phanom 400 Waller St, at Fillmore ☎ 415 431 2526, ⓦ thepphanom.com; map p.451. This corner Thai spot pulls in diners from all over town for its fragrant curries ($15–16). The spinach with peanut sauce is sweet and sharp, while the "Three's Company" seafood medley in coconut sauce is equally divine. Mon–Fri 5.30–10.30pm, Sat & Sun 11.30am–10.30pm.

HAIGHT-ASHBURY (UPPER HAIGHT)

Burgermeister 86 Carl St, at Cole ☎ 415 566 1274, ⓦ burgermeistersf.com; map p.451. Popular spot bang on the N-Judah streetcar line that grills excellent gourmet half-pound burgers ($9.50–14.25). All the mainstream choices are available, as well as a handful of unusual options (such as the mango burger) for the adventurous. Daily 11am–10pm.

Magnolia Gastropub & Brewery 1398 Haight St, at Masonic Ave ☎ 415 864 7468, ⓦ magnoliapub.com; map p.451. The menu at this popular corner spot goes beyond standard pub food – although there's a good burger ($16) and plenty of sausages ($12) to choose from – to include roasted king salmon ($28) and full English breakfast ($17). An on-site brewery produces American riffs on classic British ales. Mon–Thurs 11am–11pm, Fri 11am–midnight, Sat 10am–midnight, Sun 10am–11pm.

7

THE MISSION

Bissap Baobab Village 3372 19th St, at Mission ☎415 826 9287, ⓦbissapbaobab.com; map p.545. This Senegalese restaurant attracts a diverse crowd of Mission hipsters and African expats, and its vegetarian-friendly menu features vegetable and peanut *mafe* stew, as well as meatier choices including *niebe thies* (black-eyed peas with chicken in spice sauce). Mains $8.50–14.75. Also features weekly, monthly and special events from DJ parties to live music and dance performances. Wed–Sat 5.30pm–2am.

★ **Delfina** 3621 18th St, at Guerrero ☎415 552 4055, ⓦdelfinasf.com; map p.545. This continually buzzing hotspot attracts nearly every sort of San Franciscan. *Delfina's* light Cal-Ital dishes rarely miss the mark, while its pizzeria next door (open for lunch and dinner) is just as terrific. Mains $11–30. Mon–Thurs 5.30–10pm, Fri & Sat 5.30–11pm, Sun 5–10pm.

Dosa 995 Valencia St, at 21st ☎415 642 3672, ⓦdosasf.com; map p.545. *Dosa's* crêpe-like namesake item ($10.50–15.40) – and its close cousin, the thicker *uttapam* – dominate its South Indian menu, while the terracotta dining room is welcoming and not too noisy. Mon–Thurs 5.30–10pm, Fri 5.30–10pm, Sat 11am–3pm & 5.30–11pm, Sun 11am–3pm & 5.30–10pm.

Foreign Cinema 2534 Mission St, at 21st ☎415 648 7600, ⓦforeigncinema.com; map p.545. The "dinner and a movie" concept is redefined at this upscale, romantic restaurant, where films are projected onto a large outdoor wall. The menu, with North African and Mediterranean leanings, is as noteworthy as the offbeat concept, with the exhaustive oyster-heavy raw bar making for showy opening credits. Mains $23–32. Mon–Wed 5.30–10pm, Thurs & Fri 5.30–11pm, Sat 11am–2.30pm & 5.30–11pm, Sun 11am–2.30pm & 5.30–10pm.

Goood Frikin Chicken 10 29th St, at Mission ☎415 970 2428, ⓦgooodfrickinchicken.com; map p.545. Superbly seasoned poultry that warrants the extra "o" in this airy restaurant's goofy name. The dining room is cast in various earth tones, with the ceiling and walls covered in soothing landscape murals. The best bet is the rotisserie half-chicken, served with tasty sides for $9.50. Daily 11am–9pm.

Herbivore 983 Valencia St, at 21st ☎415 826 5657, ⓦherbivorerestaurant.com; map p.545. There's no meat or dairy in sight at this all-vegan restaurant, which boasts popular dishes such as lentil loaf with mashed potatoes and giant bowls of coconut noodle soup. Everything's $10–14, with breakfast available daily. Mon–Thurs & Sun 9am–10pm, Fri & Sat 9am–11pm.

La Espiga de Oro 2916 24th St, at Florida ☎415 826 1363; map p.545. As authentic a place as you'll find in San Francisco's Latino stronghold, this informal, open-air spot makes its own delectable tortillas; when grilled, they're often the best part of any meal here. Mains under $10. Daily 6am–7pm.

★ **La Taqueria** 2889 Mission St, at 25th ☎415 285 7117; map p.545. Though it is famed for its burritos ($6), head straight for this Mission stalwart menu's true strength: the super taco (around $6, including guacamole). Mon–Sat 11am–9pm, Sun 11am–8pm.

★ **Lazy Bear** 3416 19th St, at San Carlos ☎415 931 1475, ⓦlazybearsf.com; map p.545. Chef David Barzelay's trendsetting New American restaurant features a nightly cocktail hour of shared appetizers in the mezzanine before dinner is served in the main dining room with communal seating at two elm tables – it's a bit like a big dinner party. The tasting menu (rabbit, lamb, rhubarb) varies between $155 and $185 per person, and tickets must be purchased in advance. Tues–Sat seatings at 6pm & 8.30pm.

Mission Chinese Food 2234 Mission St ☎415 863 2800, ⓦmissionchinesefood.com; map p.545. Hidden within the "Lung Shan Restaurant", *Mission* has lost some of its lustre since Korean-American celebrity chef Danny Bowien decamped to New York, but the contemporary Sichuan-fusion food still has a cult following; try the kung pao pastrami ($16), tiki pork belly ($14) and thrice-cooked bacon and rice cakes ($16). Mains $8.50–14.75. Mon & Thurs–Sun 11.30am–3pm & 5–10.30pm, Tues & Wed 5–10.30pm.

★ **Papalote** 3409 24th St, at Valencia ☎415 970 8815, ⓦpapalote-sf.com; map p.545. Peerless Cal-Mex cuisine – there's nary a poor menu choice to be made, from the top-grade nachos to anything that includes the perfectly grilled *carne asada* (tacos $8.75). The warm chips and otherworldly salsa make for an ideal pairing. Most things $10 or less. Mon–Sat 11am–10pm, Sun 11am–9pm

Taqueria Can-cún 3211 Mission St, at Fair Ave ☎415 550 1414; map p.545. Standby taqueria featuring some of the finest cheap eats in the neighbourhood. Go for a terrific, budget-priced super burrito ($6–7), or, for a belt-busting eye-opener, drop in for breakfast. Mon–Thurs 10am–1am, Fri & Sat 10am–2am, Sun 10am–1.30am.

Taqueria San Francisco 2794 24th St, at York ☎415 641 1770, ⓦtaqueriasanfrancisco.com; map pp.424–425. The quintessential San Francisco taqueria (look no further than its name), where burritos are weighty and characterized by flaky grilled tortillas and rustic meats such as *al pastor* (rotisserie-grilled pork). Expect bouncy tuba-pop from the jukebox. Burritos ($9–11) and plate meals under $12. Daily 11am–9.30pm.

Truly Mediterranean 3109 16th St, at Valencia ☎415 252 7482, ⓦtrulymedsf.com; map p.545. *Truly Med's* inexpensive *shawarmas* ($10) are wrapped in thin, crispy lavash bread – though there's barely anywhere to sit and enjoy them in this tiny Middle Eastern restaurant. Mon–Thurs 11am–11pm, Fri & Sat 11am–midnight, Sun 11am–10pm.

Walzwerk 381 S Van Ness Ave, at 15th St ☎415 551 7181, ⓦwalzwerk.com; map p.545. Cramped spot serving hearty German comfort food such as pork schnitzel with seasonal vegetables ($16) or bratwurst with mashed potatoes and sauerkraut ($16). Framed East German pop records and large portraits of twentieth-century Eastern Bloc industry evoke past eras behind the Iron Curtain. Tues–Sun 5.30–10pm.

GOLDEN GATE PARK

★**Beach Chalet Brewery & Restaurant** 1000 Great Highway, at John F. Kennedy Drive ☎ 415 386 8439, ⓦ beachchalet.com; map pp.424–425. Although the *Beach Chalet*'s singular setting will always be its star attraction, this upstairs restaurant's food is eminently enjoyable in its own right. A variety of fish, meat and vegetarian mains ($16–30) pair well with any of the several beers brewed on site. There's a popular brunch on weekends, both here and in the adjacent, more informal *Park Chalet* in the rear of the historic building. Mon–Thurs 9am–11pm, Fri 9am–midnight, Sat 8am–midnight, Sun 8am–11pm.

RICHMOND AND SUNSET

Primarily residential neighbourhoods, Richmond and Sunset districts lie at the western end of the city, divided by Golden Gate Park. Though there's little here in the way of sights, their multi-ethnic flavour (and especially their Asian population) means there are plenty of culinary gems to seek out.

Chapeau! 126 Clement St, at 2nd Ave ☎ 415 750 9787; map pp.424–425. Exceptional, Provençal-inspired meats and seafood served amid the neighbourhood's raft of Asian restaurants; there's a terrific three-course *prix fixe* for $44.50. Mon–Thurs & Sun 5–10pm, Fri & Sat 5–10.30pm.

Gordo Taqueria 1233 9th Ave, at Lincoln Way ☎ 415 566 6011; map pp.424–425. Efficient burrito shop that lives up to its name (which translates to "fat" in English) by specializing in hefty, stumpy slabs on a par with any in town. The menu's as simple as can be, including only tacos, burritos and quesadillas, and everything's around $6–7. Daily 10am–10pm.

Mandalay 4344 California St, at 6th Ave ☎ 415 386 3895, ⓦ mandalaysf.com; map pp.424–425. The go-to appetizer here is *balada*, a crispy pancake tailor-made for dipping in its accompanying curry sauce. Although the menu features chow mein and Singapore-style noodles, overall the choices here are Burmese. Most mains top out around $14. Mon–Thurs 11.30am–2.30pm & 5–9.30pm, Fri 11.30am–2.30pm & 5–10pm, Sat & Sun 11.30am–10pm.

★**Thanh Long** 4101 Judah St, at 46th Ave ☎ 415 665 1146, ⓦ thanhlongsf.com; map pp.424–425. An unlikely destination restaurant far from San Francisco's core, *Thanh Long* was the city's first Vietnamese restaurant in the early 1970s (during the Vietnam War, in fact); it's become increasingly French-inspired and upscale in the years since. Its soothing dining room is bedecked in

blonde-wood panelling and earth tones. Most mains $15–25. Tues–Thurs & Sun 5–9.30pm, Fri & Sat 5–10pm.

CAFÉS AND BAKERIES

A coffee-loving city like few others, San Francisco is liberally dotted with excellent cafés serving first-rate blends, along with other assorted beverages (often including beer and wine). More social than utilitarian, people hang out in these generally lively venues as much to pass time as to refresh themselves, although an ever-increasing number of wi-fi cafés cater to industrious laptop users. And in the city that invented sourdough bread (p.443), the bakeries are just as inventive.

★**Arizmendi Bakery** 1331 9th Ave, at Irving St, Sunset ☎ 415 566 3117, ⓦ arizmendibakery.com; map pp.424–425. The daily rotation of artisanal breads and pastries are reason enough to head to this small, earthy and inexpensive bakery (a worker-owned cooperative), but its gourmet pizza slices ($2.75) are the true surprise treat. Tues–Fri 7am–7pm, Sat & Sun 7.30am–6pm.

Benkyodo 1747 Buchanan St, at Sutter, Japantown ☎ 415 922 1244, ⓦ benkyodocompany.com; map p.451. Selling hundreds of confectionery snacks daily, this popular Japanese bakery is inexpensive, so it's easy to fill up on dessert for a small sum. Founded here in 1906, it's one of Japantown's original businesses. Mon–Sat 8am–5pm.

★**Blue Bottle Coffee** 1355 Market St (10th and Stevenson), South of Market ☎ 415 252 7535, ⓦ bluebottlecoffee.com; map pp.428–429. Tucked away in Art Deco Market Square (the home of Twitter), just off the main drag, this quirky spot offers its own roasted coffee that has taken San Francisco by storm. Cold brews also grace the menu, as do a few milk-based beverages. Mon–Fri 7am–5.30pm, Sat & Sun 8.30am–3pm.

★**Bob's Donuts** 1621 Polk St, Nob Hill ☎ 415 776 3141, ⓦ bobsdonutssf.com; map pp.428–429. Old-school doughnut shop since 1960, now open 24 hours, perfect for that late-night, post-boozing sweet snack – all the doughnut are good, but locals opt for the crispy apple fritter, frosted coated and laced with cinnamon. Daily 24hr.

Boudin Bakers Hall Cafe 160 Jefferson St, at Mason, Fisherman's Wharf ☎ 415 928 1849, ⓦ boudinbakery .com; map pp.428–429. Café serving some of the finest sourdough around, made using yeast descended from the first batch from Gold Rush times (see p.443). A variety of cheap salads, sandwiches and sourdough pizzas are available, in addition to the inevitable chowder in a bread bowl. Sun–Thurs 8am–8.30pm, Fri & Sat 8am–10pm.

★**b. patisserie** 2821 California St, Pacific Heights ☎ 415 440 1700, ⓦ bpatisserie.com; map p.451. This authentic French bakery has gained a cult following since opening in 2013, serving superb pastries and viennoise a match to anything you'll find in Paris. Try the *kouign* *amman* ($4), a croissant-like treat from Brittany. Tues–Sun 8am–6pm.

Café de la Presse 352 Grant Ave, at Bush St, Union Square ☎415 398 2680, ⍺cafedelapresse.com; map pp.428–429. Location just down the block from Chinatown Gate, this Parisian-inspired café has a good selection of European magazines and newspapers. Daily 7.30am–10pm.

Caffè Trieste 601 Vallejo St, at Grant Ave, North Beach ☎415 392 6739, ⍺caffetrieste.com; map pp.428–429. This local institution is where espresso made its West Coast debut in 1956. Today, it's known almost as much for its mandolin sessions and opera recitals as for its own-roasted, thick-bodied coffee. Cash only. Mon–Thurs & Sun 6.30am–10pm, Fri & Sat 6.30am–11pm.

Craftsman & Wolves 746 Valencia St between 19th & 18th, Mission ☎415 913 7713, ⍺craftsman-wolves.com; map p.454. Hip pastry shop that knocks out irresistible creations: Thai crumble, raspberry corn scone, valrhona chocolate croissant and violet vanilla cheesecake among them. Mon–Thurs 7am–6pm, Fri 7am–7pm, Sat 8am–7pm, Sun 8am–6pm.

★**Crossroads Café** 699 Delancey St, at Brannan, South of Market ☎415 836 5624; map pp.428–429. The sprawling, inexpensive menu here covers all three meals and ranges from fruit smoothies and egg sandwiches to creative salads and tapas dishes. What's more, the relaxed, waterfront-adjacent setting encourages lingering – you could easily spend the better part of a morning or afternoon enjoying the sunny courtyard along the Embarcadero. Mon–Fri 7am–10pm, Sat 8am–10pm, Sun 8am–5pm.

Emporio Rulli il Caffè 225 Stockton St, at Post, Union Square ☎415 433 1122, ⍺rulli.com; map pp.428–429. A popular shopping pit stop with mandolin-drenched Italian ballads spilling out of its speakers, this café on Union Square itself serves bracingly strong coffee, as well as breakfast and lunch panini starting around $8. Most tables are set outside on the square, ideal for lounging. Daily 7am–7pm.

Liguria Bakery 1700 Stockton St, at Filbert, North Beach ☎415 421 3786; map pp.428–429. Marvellous old-world bakery, founded in 1911, with vintage scales and cash registers in its front display windows. Fresh focaccia ($4–5; cash only) is the smart order here, and there's no shortage of choices: onion, garlic, rosemary and mushroom, among others. It's best to arrive earlier than later, as it simply closes when the day's goods are sold out. Tues–Fri 8am–2pm, Sat 7am–2pm.

Mario's Bohemian Cigar Store Café 566 Columbus Ave, at Union St, North Beach ☎415 362 0536; map pp.428–429. Stogies haven't been sold on these premises for ages, but the chunky, home-made focaccia sandwiches and corner location make this local institution a terrific place to grab a cheap bite and absorb the neighbourhood

scene – its bar is a great spot for an unpretentious nightcap. Daily 10am–11pm.

Mee Mee Bakery 1328 Stockton St, at Broadway, Chinatown ☎415 362 3204, ⍺meemeebakery.com; map pp.428–429. From morning until evening each day since 1950, this under-the-radar gem bakes heaps of fragrant fortune cookies, mooncakes and Chinese pastries that fill the space with a sweet aroma. Daily 8am–6pm.

Ritual Coffee Roasters 1026 Valencia St, at 21st, Mission ☎415 641 1011, ⍺ritualroasters.com; map p.454. The impossibly hipster-chic clientele at this vaunted café can't overshadow the outstanding coffee, roasted on the premises using the company's own beans. Try the intense espresso, which boasts flavours of hazelnut and caramel. Mon–Thurs 6am–8pm, Fri 6am–10pm, Sat 7am–10pm, Sun 7am–8pm.

Samovar Tea Lounge 411 Valencia St, Mission ☎415 626 4700, ⍺samovartea.com; map p.454. Earthy, cushion-filled café chain that serves more than a hundred varieties of tea, as well as tasty Asian snacks such as baked tofu with miso chutney. The overstuffed wicker chairs are a great place to curl up with a book for an afternoon. Daily 7am–7pm.

★**Tartine Bakery & Café** 600 Guerrero St, at 18th, Mission ☎415 487 2600, ⍺tartinebakery.com; map p.454. Quite possibly San Francisco's most popular bakery, and with good reason: this *boulangerie*'s pies, pastries, hot-pressed sandwiches and fresh breads are some of the finest around, and consequently, queues often twist out the door. Mon 8am–7pm, Tues & Wed 7.30am–7pm, Thurs & Fri 7.30am–8pm, Sat & Sun 8am–8pm.

Tout Sweet Pâtisserie 170 O'Farrell St, 3/F Macy's (Geary St entrance) ☎415 385 1679, ⍺toutsweetsf.com; map pp.428–429. Bright, modern bakery serving up creatively flavoured pastries inside Macy's; multicoloured macaroons, cookies plus savoury sandwiches. Mon–Wed 10am–7pm, Thurs & Fri 10am–8pm, Sat 10am–9pm, Sun 11am–7pm.

Trouble Coffee and Coconut Club 4033 Judah St, at 45th Ave, Sunset ☎415 665 1146; map pp.424–425. A few blocks in from the coastline sits this pint-sized powerhouse, operated by young eccentrics remarkably passionate about their trade. The menu's simple: coffee, grapefruit juice, whole Thai coconuts, toast ($4.50). Yep, this place is responsible for that ultimate hipster trend, "artisanal toast". Daily 7am–7pm.

ICE CREAM

★**Bi-Rite Creamery** 3692 18th St, at Dolores, Mission ☎415 626 5600, ⍺biritecreamery.com; map p.454. Tiny, inexpensive ice-cream shop that hits all the right notes with its artisanal flavours. Usual suspects like mint-choc-chip share freezer space with unique concoctions such as toasted coconut and honey lavender. Mon–Thurs & Sun 11am–10pm, Fri & Sat 11am–11pm.

Mitchell's Ice Cream 688 San Jose Ave, at 29th St, Mission ☎ 415 648 2300, �🖱 mitchellsicecream.com; map p.454. Local legend that produces its extensive selection of flavours on site, from the mainstream (French vanilla, strawberry) to the far left-field (avocado, sweet bean). Daily 11am–11pm.

★**Smitten Ice Cream** 2404 California St, Pacific Heights ☎ 415 872 9414; map p.451. Mini-chain justly celebrated for its unique-tasting liquid nitrogen ice cream (in flavours such as salted caramel, nectarines and cream, Earl Grey and lemon gingersnap), rustic wagon benches and a tranquil patio adorned with hand-painted murals. Mon–Thurs noon–11.30pm, Fri & Sat 11.30am–11.30pm, Sun 11.30am–11pm.

DRINKING

San Francisco is a great drinking town, with a huge number of **bars** ranging from comfortably scruffy jukebox joints to chic lounges and clubby watering holes. Though spread fairly evenly over the city, top choices are particularly numerous in the Mission and the area between Hayes Valley and Upper Haight, where bars seem to line up one after the other, while slick lounges speckle downtown and South of Market. Of course, the city has many specifically **LGBT bars** (see p.482), most plentifully in the Castro and South of Market, with a few scattered in the Mission. According to California law, there's **no smoking** allowed in any bar unless its sole employees are the owners; to assuage all concerned parties, a clever handful of San Francisco taverns have constructed enclosed spaces expressly built for puffing.

7

UNION SQUARE

★**Benjamin Cooper** 398 Geary St, at Mason ☎ 415 788 7152, �🖱 benjamincoopersf.com; map pp.428–429. Fashionable cocktail and oyster bar; it might be tough to find a seat (only 14 bar seats and a few more off to the side), but it's worth the wait. Mon–Fri 5pm–2am, Sat 6pm–2am.

The Irish Bank 10 Mark Lane, at Bush St ☎ 415 788 7152, �🖱 theirishbank.com; map pp.428–429. An appealing respite from the nearby shopping district, with plenty of alfresco alley seating, pub fare and all the requisite Irish artefacts. Daily 11.30am–2am.

The Redwood Room Clift Hotel, 495 Geary St, at Taylor St ☎ 415 929 2372; map pp.428–429. This clubby landmark bar from the 1930s has been made over to include lightboxes on the walls that display shifting, fading portraits, with DJs spinning Thurs–Sat. It's posey fun – just don't choke on the comically high drink prices (around

$15). Mon–Thurs & Sun 5pm–2am, Fri–Sat 4pm–2am.

Tunnel Top 601 Bush St, at Stockton ☎ 415 722 6620; map pp.428–429. Fun spot atop the Stockton Tunnel where you can expect stiff drinks, a terrific balcony and nightly entertainment (usually DJs). Daily 5pm–2am.

THE TENDERLOIN

★**Bourbon & Branch** 501 Jones St, at O'Farrell ☎ 415 346 1735, �🖱 bourbonandbranch.com; map pp.428–429. A reservations-only bar (book online) that's garnered plenty of buzz for its re-creation of a Prohibition-era speakeasy; indeed, this fiercely retro spot is not the place to order a vodka and Red Bull (it's a whiskey, rum and tequila all the way). Give the password at the unmarked door and you'll be whisked into a dimly lit space with wooden booths, burgundy velvet wallpaper and a pressed-tin ceiling. Daily 6pm–2am.

SAN FRANCISCO BEERS

While its surrounding countryside may be internationally known for wine-making, the city of San Francisco is renowned for its **craft beers**. The best-known local product is so-called **steam** beer, a lager-bitter hybrid invented when early local brewers, finding the ice needed for lager production too expensive, instead fermented their yeast at room temperature like an ale. The result was a beer with the lower ABV of lager but the hearty flavour of bitter. (The precise origin of the odd name, unfortunately, has never been established.) To find out more, take one of the engaging, one-hour-thirty-minute tours at **Anchor Brewing**, 1705 Mariposa St at Carolina, Potrero Hill (Mon–Fri 10am & 1pm, Sat & Sun 11am & 2pm; $20; happy hour tours Fri–Sun 4.30pm; $25; reservations essential; ☎ 415 863 8350, �🖱 anchorbrewing.com), whose namesake product is a local treasure and universally available at bars and stores. The pick of San Francisco brewpubs:

21st Amendment Brewery South of Market. See p.476.
Cellarmaker Brewing South of Market. See p.476.
Cervecería de MateVeza Mission. See p.478.
Southern Pacific Brewing Mission. See p.478.
ThirstyBear Brewing Company South of Market. See p.476.

★Hemlock Tavern 1131 Polk St, at Post ☎415 923 0923, ⊛hemlocktavern.com; map pp.428–429. The coolest bar along Polk St has a free jukebox heavy on punk, fresh peanut shells on the floor, live music in its back room (see p.480) and a handy, enclosed patio where smokers can puff and sip in peace. Daily 4pm–2am.

Mikkeller Bar 34 Mason St, between Eddy and Turk ☎415 984 0279, ⊛mikkellerbar.com; map pp.428–429. Congenial beer hall in a 1907 building, with a stunning 42 taps and a host of bottle beers from around the world. Mon–Wed & Sun noon–midnight, Thurs–Sat noon–2am.

HAYES VALLEY

Hotel Biron 45 Rose St, at Gough ☎415 703 0403, ⊛hotelbiron.com; map p.451. Tucked away down an alley, this intimate wine bar – it's only a hotel in name – has a quality selection of California and European wines, as well as a small menu of cheeses and olives. Revolving exhibitions of local art adorn the walls. Daily 5pm–2am.

Smuggler's Cove 650 Gough St ☎415 869 1900, ⊛smugglerscovesf.com; map p.451. Fun tiki bar with a shipwreck/pirate theme and often queues to get in (only 49 people maximum), for its massive selection of rums (550 at any time) and 80 exotic cocktails. Daily 5pm–1.15am.

FINANCIAL DISTRICT

Bix 56 Gold St, at Montgomery ☎415 433 6300, ⊛bixrestaurant.com; map pp.428–429. Hidden on a tiny side street, this bar-restaurant's decor maintains a touch of 1940s glamour. It's often packed after work with a somewhat formal downtown crowd enjoying the mahogany bar's famed gin martinis ($13). Mon–Thurs & Sat–Sun 4.30–11pm, Fri 11.30am–2pm & 4.30–11pm.

SOUTH OF MARKET

21st Amendment Brewery 563 2nd St, at Brannan ☎415 369 0900, ⊛21st-amendment.com; map pp.428–429. This bright, lively brewpub, across from South Park and two blocks from the ballpark, turns out a dozen or so tasty microbrews, which it serves alongside decent burgers and other pub fare to a nightly throng. Mon–Sat 11.30am–midnight, Sun 10am–midnight.

★Bar Agricole 355 11th St between Harrison and Folsom ☎415 355 9400, ⊛baragricole.co; map p.454. Most celebrated cocktail bar in the city, with spectacular creations (using house-made tinctures and herbs grown in the courtyard garden) ranging from the Bingo Bango, with white rum, lime, sloe gin, pineapple gum and bitters, to the House Old Fashioned with Ravignan armagnac and maraschino ($13 to $17). Mon–Sat 5–10pm, Fri & Sat 5–11pm.

Butter 354 11th St, at Folsom ☎415 863 5964, ⊛smoothasbutter.com; map p.454. Fun, stylized "white trash" bar that's a hopeless case of forced irony in this

warehouse-and-lofts neighbourhood. It's full of imitation trailer-park decor, serves Pabst Blue Ribbon on tap (and yes, Red Bull & vodka), and has a food window that serves only microwaveable junk food and "nutritious grape and strawberry sodas for our increasingly health conscious clientele". Karaoke on Sundays. Wed–Sat 6pm–2am, Sun 8pm–2am.

★Cellarmaker Brewing 1150 Howard St, at Rausch ☎415 863 3940, ⊛cellarmakerbrewing.com; map pp.428–429. One of the city's best up-and-coming small-batch microbreweries, with plenty of bold experimental ales such as the extra-strong "Are you afraid of the dank?", "Vanilla Vastness" and "Coffee Sessions". Tues–Thurs 3–11pm, Fri & Sat noon–11pm, Sun 1–8pm.

Pied Piper Bar Palace Hotel 2 New Montgomery St, at Market ☎415 546 5089; map pp.428–429. Named for its striking Maxfield Parrish 1909 mural hovering behind its bar, this mahogany-panelled room within one of San Francisco's fanciest hotels is a secluded, elegant place for a martini. Mon–Fri 4–11pm, Sat 11.30am–11pm, Sun 10am–11pm.

★ThirstyBear Brewing Company 661 Howard St, at 2nd ☎415 974 0905, ⊛thirstybear.com; map pp.428–429. A combination brewpub and tapas bar that's packed in the evenings with local tech workers; the Spanish food's fairly priced ($1.50–12 a plate) and tasty – try the fried calamari. Mon–Fri 11.30am–2am, Sat noon–2am, Sun 5–11pm.

EMBARCADERO

Fort Point Beer Ferry Building (kiosk 54) ☎415 818 3993, ⊛fortpointbeer.com; map pp.428–429. Presidio-based microbrewery churning out beers made with Munich and Vienna malts (especially the Westfalia red ale), served at this kiosk with six rotating taps ($7–8). Golden Gate Meat Co hot dogs and Firebrand pretzels sold to wash the beer down. Daily 11am–8pm.

CHINATOWN

Li Po Cocktail Lounge 916 Grant Ave, at Jackson St ☎415 982 0072, ⊛lipolounge.com; map pp.428–429. Named after the Chinese poet, charmingly grotty *Li Po* is one of the few places to drink in Chinatown. Enter through the false cavern front and grab a Chinese mai tai among the many regular patrons. Daily 2pm–2am.

NOB HILL

Tonga Room & Hurricane Bar The Fairmont, 950 Mason St, at California ☎415 772 5278, ⊛tonga room.com; map pp.428–429. Ultra-campy tiki bar styled like a Polynesian village, complete with pond, simulated rainstorms and grass-skirted band murdering jazz and pop covers upon a floating raft. Cocktails are predictably overpriced (the famous mai tai has been served here since

1945), but the happy-hour buffet (Wed–Fri 5–7pm; $15) helps make up for it. Wed, Thurs & Sun 5–11.30pm, Fri & Sat 5pm–12.30am.

★**Top of the Mark** InterContinental Mark Hopkins, 999 California St, at Mason St ☎415 616 6916; map pp.428–429. Panoramic views of the city (on the 19/F) make the pricey cocktails ($15) at this 1939 landmark worthwhile. Reserve in advance for the Sunday champagne brunch (10am–1pm; $89). Mon–Thurs 4.30–11.30pm, Fri & Sat 4.30pm–12.30am, Sun 10am–1pm & 5–11.30pm.

NORTH BEACH

Comstock Saloon 155 Columbus Ave, at Kearny St ☎415 617 0071, ⓦcomstocksaloon.com; map pp.428–429. Historic tavern dating back to 1907 – the tile floors and mahogany bar are all original. Mixes up classic cocktails ($9–13), bamboo cocktails, pisco punch, and the infamous barkeep's whimsy (the bartender decides). Tues–Thurs & Sat 4pm–2am, Fri noon–2am, Sun & Mon 4pm–midnight.

Gino and Carlo 548 Green St, at Grant Ave ☎415 421 0896, ⓦginoandcarlo.com; map pp.428–429. Neighbourhood watering hole since 1942 once popular with night-shift-working pressmen, now with longtime regulars and sports fans. A welcoming place overall, with pinball and pool available. Daily 6am–2am.

Savoy Tivoli 1434 Grant Ave, at Union St ☎415 361 7023; map pp.428–429. Sprawling North Beach landmark dating back to 1907 with a smoker-friendly open-air patio, a couple of pool tables, a beautiful dark-wood bar and bizarre decor dotted around the main room. Strangely, the post-collegiate crowd it draws on weekends belies its bohemian vibe. Tues & Wed 6pm–2am, Thurs & Fri 5pm–2am, Sat 3pm–2am.

Specs Twelve Adler Museum Café 12 Saroyan Place, at Columbus Ave ☎415 421 4112; map pp.428–429. Known locally as simply "Specs", this friendly dive set just off North Beach's main drag is known for its chatty bar staff and is decked out with loads of oddities from the high seas. Its regulars may be older eccentrics, but it's popular with just about everybody. Mon–Fri 4.30pm–2am, Sat & Sun 5pm–2am.

★**Tony Nik's** 1534 Stockton St, at Union ☎415 693 0990, ⓦtonyniks.com; map pp.428–429. A legendary watering hole, *Tony Nik's* dim, sulky interior and stiff drinks have been summoning North Beach denizens since 1933. The bar area is the liveliest spot, while the even darker back area is great for intimate chats. Mon–Fri 4pm–2am, Sat & Sun 2am–2pm.

Tosca Cafe 242 Columbus Ave, at Pacific ☎415 986 9651, ⓦtoscacafesf.com; map pp.428–429. A bar so classic it feels like a Hollywood set: bartenders in white waistcoats, arias (or perhaps Sinatra) wafting out of the jukebox and a long line of cocktail glasses along the bar filled with the house drink, a brandy-laced "cappuccino"

(there's no coffee in it). Even the average teetotalling San Franciscan has been here at least once. Daily 5pm–2am.

Vesuvio Cafe 255 Columbus Ave, at Jack Kerouac Alley ☎415 362 3370, ⓦvesuvio.com; map pp.428–429. Even if it weren't once the regular hangout of Kerouac and company, North Beach's most famous bar since 1948 would still merit a visit for at least one drink for its inviting atmosphere. Daily 6am–2am.

FISHERMAN'S WHARF

Buena Vista 2765 Hyde St, at Beach ☎415 474 5044, ⓦthebuenavista.com; map pp.428–429. Ever crowded with tourists (and the occasional local), this 1916 San Francisco landmark has been churning out its famed concoction, Irish coffee (based on the Shannon Airport original), since 1952. Mon–Fri 9am–2am, Sat & Sun 8am–2am.

LOWER HAIGHT

Mad Dog in the Fog 530 Haight St, at Fillmore ☎415 626 7279, ⓦthemaddoginthefog.com; map p.451. Aptly named tavern that's one of the Lower Haight's most loyally patronized bars, with darts, English beer, footie on TV – it opens early at weekends to show Premier League matches – and a popular trivia night each Thursday. Mon–Fri 11.30am–2am, Sat & Sun 7am–2am.

Noc Noc 557 Haight St, at Steiner ☎415 861 5811; map p.451. Dark, super-groovy spot with bizarre decor befitting a post-apocalyptic tribal cave. The bar doesn't have a licence to sell hard liquor, but it makes mean *saké* cocktails and boasts a fairly wide range of beers ($3 pints until 7pm) and wine. Mon–Thurs 5pm–2am, Fri 3.30pm–2am, Sat & Sun 3pm–2am.

HAIGHT-ASHBURY (UPPER HAIGHT)

★**The Alembic** 1725 Haight St, at Cole ☎415 666 0822, ⓦalembicbar.com; map p.451. Offering a refreshing break from the dog-eared Haight scene, this small, stylish spot is serious about its liquor, with a wide selection of small-batch bourbons, ryes and gins poured by knowledgeable, friendly bartenders. Mon–Wed 4pm–midnight, Thurs & Fri 4pm–2am, Sat 2pm–2am, Sun 2pm–midnight.

Aub Zam Zam 1663 Haight St, at Clayton ☎415 861 2545; map p.451. Bar regulars purchased this Persian-themed cocktail lounge after the death of its ornery Iranian owner, Bruno, and have just about managed to retain its alternately surly/warm vibe. There's a great jazz jukebox to boot. Mon–Fri 3pm–2am, Sat & Sun 1pm–2am.

Kezar Pub 770 Stanyan St, at Beulah ☎415 386 9292, ⓦthekezarpub.com; map p.451. Lively neighbourhood pub with pool, darts and all kinds of sports shown on a slew of overhead TVs. Mon–Fri 11.30am–2am, Sat & Sun 6am–2am.

7

THE CASTRO

★**Café du Nord** 2170 Market St, at Sanchez ☎415 861 5016, ⓦcafedunord.com; map p.454. This old subterranean speakeasy (which dates back to 1907) is a terrific place to enjoy bar bites, cocktails and the odd touring or local rock bands, with the occasional comedy act booked for good measure. The amber-walled Swedish American Hall upstairs also regularly features shows. Daily 5pm–2am.

Lucky 13 2140 Market St, at Church ☎415 487 1313; map p.454. Straight bar on the outskirts of the Castro with an extensive selection of international beers. It's filled with pool-players chomping on free popcorn; there's a loud jukebox inside and a humble patio out back. Daily 11am–2am.

THE MISSION

★**Cervecería de MateVeza** 3801 18th St, at Dolores Park ☎415 923 0923, ⓦwoodsbeer.com/cerveceria; map p.454. This tiny taproom serves house-made Woods beers (brewed with yerba maté), guest taps and El Porteño empanadas. Famed for its series of Girl Scout-cookie-flavoured beers. Mon 3–10pm, Tues & Wed noon–10pm, Thurs noon–11pm, Fri & Sat noon–midnight, Sun noon–10pm.

Dalva 3121 16th St, at Valencia ☎415 252 7740, ⓦdalvasf.com; map p.454. Wonderfully divey and dark, but easy to miss along 16th St's glut of bars, this wafer-thin space brings in a diverse crowd. Daily 4pm–2am.

Doc's Clock 2575 Mission St, at 21st ☎415 824 3627, ⓦdocsclock.com; map p.454. Art Deco-styled watering hole that's easy to spot thanks to the hot-pink neon sign blazing out front. Its long bar and shuffleboard games are consistently popular with neighbourhood denizens. Mon–Thurs 5pm–2am, Fri & Sat 4pm–2am, Sun 3pm–2am.

Laszlo 2526 Mission St, at 21st ☎415 401 0810, ⓦlaszlobar.com; map p.454. This industrial-chic bar, attached to film-themed restaurant *Foreign Cinema* (see p.472) next door, is itself, unsurprisingly, named in homage to the movies (Jean-Paul Belmondo's character in *À Bout de Souffle*). DJs spin nightly, while the cocktails ($12) – especially the mojitos – are outstanding. Mon–Wed 5.30pm–midnight, Thurs 5.30pm–2am, Fri 3pm–2am, Sat 11am–2am, Sun 11am–midnight.

★**Latin American Club** 3286 22nd St, at Valencia ☎415 647 2732; map p.454. Cosy place with a warm vibe – great for an early chat over margaritas before the crowds arrive later in the evening. The loft space above the entrance is full of piñatas, Mexican streamers and assorted trinkets. Mon–Fri 5pm–2am, Sat 1pm–2am, Sun 2pm–2am.

Lone Palm 3394 22nd St, at Guerrero ☎415 648 0109; map p.454. Like some forgotten Las Vegas revue bar from the 1950s, this candlelit cocktail lounge – less than a block off the well-trodden Valencia corridor – is a gem. White cloths cover the raised tables and a TV above the bar plays classic American movies. Daily 4pm–2am.

Revolution Cafe 3248 22nd St, at Bartlett ☎415 642 0474, ⓦrevolutioncafesf.com; map p.454. This hybrid bar and café boasts alfresco drinking, ginger lattes, an upright piano available to any and all comers, and nightly live music that includes (but isn't limited to) jazz, Brazilian and classical. Despite constant throngs packing the small space, its atmosphere is laidback and resolutely bohemian. Mon–Thurs & Sun 9am–midnight, Fri & Sat 9am–2am.

★**Royal Cuckoo** 3202 Mission St, at Valencia ☎415 550 8667, ⓦroyalcuckoo.com; map p.454. Dimly lit nightspot where a live Hammond organ player sits in five nights a week (Wed–Sun), sometimes with an accompanying vocalist or band; Mon & Tues see all-vinyl DJs manning the lo-fi house stereo. The drink menu is suitably sophisticated: lots and lots of craft cocktails plus the requisite wine and beer. Mon–Thurs 4pm–2am, Fri–Sun 3pm–2am.

★ **Southern Pacific Brewing** 620 Treat Ave, at 19th St ☎415 341 0152, ⓦsouthernpacificbrewing.com; map p.454. Huge microbrewery in a former factory, with plenty of patio seating, at least 21 beers on tap ($3 to $5), including an excellent German wheat beer, and a decent menu of bar food (sage fries $5; burgers $11.50). Mon–Wed & Sun 11am–midnight, Thurs–Sat 11am–2am.

Zeitgeist 199 Valencia St, at Duboce ☎415 255 5505, ⓦzeitgeistsf.com; map p.454. This cyclist bar is a Mission institution, with an enormous outdoor beer garden that's wildly popular on sunny afternoons. Come for punk tunes, tattooed bartenders, afternoon cookouts at weekends, famously powerful Bloody Marys and lots of beer on tap. Daily 9am–2am.

NIGHTLIFE

A night out in San Francisco is more of a party than a feverish pose, so while the city's collection of **clubs** will never be confused with more celebrated scenes in Miami or New York, there are a few upsides to its humbler scope: namely that you'll be hard-pressed to encounter high cover charges, ridiculously priced drinks or long queues. Unlike most other major cities, where the action never gets going until after midnight, many San Francisco clubs close at 2am, so you can usually be sure of finding things well under way around 10pm. Note that some operate dress codes, with jeans, T-shirts and team gear barred – call or check venue websites for details, as well as current hours, as they can frequently change.

San Francisco's live music scene reflects the character of the city: laidback, eclectic and just a little nostalgic. This was the home of the Grateful Dead, Santana and Sly and the Family Stone, with artists currently attracting lots of buzz Jay Som (Melina Duterte), Motor Inn, Heron Oblivion and old-timers Thee Oh Sees.

CLUBS

111 Minna Gallery 111 Minna St, at 2nd, South of Market ☎ 415 974 1719, ⓦ 111minnagallery.com; map pp.428–429. Combination bar, art gallery and DJ venue set a short way down an alley. It gets busier, noisier and more raucous as the evening wears on. Free–$10. Hours vary.

1015 Folsom 1015 Folsom St, at 6th, South of Market ☎ 415 991 1015, ⓦ 1015.com; map pp.428–429. Multilevel megaclub that's popular across the board for late-night dancing. The music's largely house and trance with big names often spinning on the main floor. $15–20. Thurs & Fri 10pm–3am (also occasional Sun).

Audio 316 11th St, at Folsom, South of Market ☎ 415 481 0556, ⓦ audiosf.com; map p.454. The place to get your 1970s groove on, with a sunken dancefloor, retro decor, amazing sound system and a focus on international DJs. Cover $10. Fri & Sat 9.30pm–2am.

Bruno's 2389 Mission St, at 20th, Mission ☎ 415 643 5200, ⓦ brunossf.com; map p.454. Like something from a Scorsese film, this weekends-only retro dance venue is filled with 1960s-style furniture. If it's danceable – hip-hop, R&B, soul, funk – you'll hear it here at some point. Cover $10. Fri & Sat 9pm–2am.

Cat Club 1190 Folsom St, at 8th, South of Market ☎ 415 703 8965, ⓦ sfcatclub.com; map pp.428–429. With free karaoke every Tuesday and dancing every other night of the week in a pair of separate rooms, there's something for practically every clubgoer here: electro, darkwave, goth, Britpop. Free–$10. Hours vary.

DNA Lounge 375 11th St, at Harrison, South of Market ☎ 415 626 1409, ⓦ dnalounge.com; map p.454. Longtime club that changes its music style nightly but consistently draws a young, mixed gay/straight crowd. Downstairs is a large dancefloor, while the mezzanine is a sofa-packed lounge ideal for chilling. Cover $5–25. Mon 9.30pm–2am, Tues 7pm–2am, Thurs 8pm–5am, Fri 8.30pm–5am, Sat 9pm–5am.

The End Up 401 6th St, at Harrison, South of Market ☎ 415 646 0999, ⓦ facebook.com/theendup; map pp.428–429. Best known as the home of Sunday's all-day party (2–9pm), this stalwart club attracts a mixed bag of hardcore clubbers for after-hours dancing on the cramped dancefloor; if you need a break from the beat assault, head for the outdoor patio with plenty of seating. Cover $7 and up. Hours vary.

★**Matrix Fillmore** 3138 Fillmore St, at Pixley, Marina District ☎ 415 563 4180, ⓦ matrixfillmore.com; map pp.424–425. Current hotspot with excellent house DJs playing everything from 1970s funk to house, a stylish interior and handcrafted cocktails. Usually no cover. Daily 6pm–2am.

Mezzanine 444 Jessie St, at 5th, South of Market ☎ 415 625 8880, ⓦ mezzaninesf.com; map pp.428–429. Massive megaclub featuring mainstream, brand-name DJs, as well as gigs by indie-rock, reggae and hip-hop acts, although the space's acoustics benefit DJs rather than live bands. Cover varies wildly depending on headliner and event. Hours vary.

Rickshaw Stop 155 Fell St, at Van Ness Ave, Hayes Valley ☎ 415 861 2011, ⓦ rickshawstop.com; map p.451. Hayes Valley bar-club known for live indie-rock shows, as well as its queer "Cockblock" dance party on alternating Saturdays. Cover $8–25. Tues–Sun from 8pm.

Ruby Skye 420 Mason St, at Geary, Union Square ☎ 415 693 0777, ⓦ rubyskye.com; map pp.428–429. The biggest mainstream DJs tend to stop through this gorgeous, spacious Victorian dance hall, where programming skews towards trance, house and techno. Cover $15 and up. Thurs–Sat 9pm–2am.

Sip Bar & Lounge 787 Broadway, at Powell St, North Beach ☎ 415 699 6545, ⓦ siploungesf.com; map pp.428–429. Adding a splash of amber-hued moodiness to the North Beach scene, this friendly weekends-only lounge has nightly DJs spinning everything from hip-hop to Top-40. Fri & Sat 9pm–1.30am.

★**Skylark** 3089 16th St, at Valencia, Mission ☎ 415 621 9294, ⓦ skylarkbar.com; map p.454. Popular for its intimate vibe, low lighting, strong drinks and varied DJs, this spot makes for an inexpensive night out, with primarily reggae, dancehall and hip-hop DJs. No cover. Mon & Tues 6pm–2am, Wed–Fri 4pm–2am, Sat 2pm–2am, Sun 2–10pm.

Slide 430 Mason St, at Geary ☎ 415 421 1916, ⓦ slidesf.com; map pp.428–429. The main access to this underground homage to the 1920s is via a serpentine slide, but if you'd rather not arrive at the swish, mahogany-clad lounge/club via your hind quarters, stairs are also available. Club nights include Gold on Thurs (hip-hop) and Replay Sundays. Wed–Sun 9pm–3am.

MAJOR LIVE MUSIC VENUES

Bimbo's 365 Club 1025 Columbus Ave, at Chestnut St, North Beach ☎ 415 474 0365, ⓦ bimbos365club.com; map pp.428–429. Dating back to the 1930s, this elegant, intimate club schedules underground European acts, kitschy tribute bands and big-name rock acts in equal proportion. Tickets $20 and up.

★ **The Fillmore** 1805 Geary Blvd, at Fillmore St, Western Addition ☎ 415 346 6000, ⓦ thefillmore.com; map p.451. This ballroom auditorium was at the heart of 1960s counterculture, masterminded by legendary local promoter Bill Graham. It's still a terrific spot for catching up-and-comers and longtime favourites alike. $20 and up. Hours vary.

★**Great American Music Hall** 859 O'Farrell St, at Polk, Tenderloin ☎ 415 885 0750, ⓦ slimspresents.com; map pp.428–429. A former bordello converted long ago into a beloved venue for rock, blues and international acts. The ornately moulded balcony offers seats with terrific views for those who arrive early. $15 and up. Hours vary.

7

7

SFJazz Center 201 Franklin St, at Fell, Hayes Valley ☎866 920 5299, ⊛sfjazz.org; map p.451. With incomparable acoustics and a central location adjacent to the Civic Center, this venue has drawn major figures in jazz (Bill Frisell and Brad Mehldau, among many others) to its stage for multinight residencies. $20 and up. Hours vary.

The Warfield 982 Market St, at 6th, Tenderloin ☎415 775 7722, ⊛thewarfieldtheatre.com; map pp.428–429. Classic theatre offering a grand setting for enjoying top-tier touring artists. There's reserved balcony seating, as well as general admission tickets that put you close to the stage. Tickets $25 and up.

SMALLER LIVE MUSIC VENUES

Amnesia 853 Valencia St, at 19th, Mission ☎415 970 0012, ⊛amnesiathebar.com; map p.454. Red-lit venue serving wine, craft beers and *soju* cocktails. Entertainment varies wildly from night to night: bluegrass bands and hip-hop DJs to karaoke and politically charged puppet shows. Free–$10. Times vary; usually daily from 6pm.

Boom Boom Room 1601 Fillmore St, at Geary Blvd, Western Addition ☎415 673 8000, ⊛boomboomroom .com; map p.451. The current owner of this bar – which has roots in the 1930s – made late blues legend John Lee Hooker a partner in the 1990s (a leather booth remains permanently reserved in his honour), and this small, intimate space with a chequerboard floor still delivers blues and roots acts nightly. Cover $5–20. Tues–Thurs & Sun 4pm–2am, Fri & Sat 4pm–3am.

Bottom of the Hill 1233 17th St, at Missouri, Potrero Hill ☎415 621 4455, ⊛bottomofthehill.com; map pp.424–425. Well off the beaten path, San Francisco's celebrated indie-rock stronghold draws crowds nightly for local and nationally touring acts. $10–15. Tues–Sun 8.30pm–2am.

Elbo Room 647 Valencia St, at 17th, Mission ☎415 552 7788, ⊛elbo.com; map p.454. A local cradle of acid jazz in the early 1990s, this neighbourhood spot now hosts a smorgasbord of bands and DJs, from rock to reggae to soul. Tickets $5–20. Daily 5pm–2am.

Hemlock Tavern 1131 Polk St, at Post, Polk Gulch ☎415 923 0923, ⊛hemlocktavern.com; map pp.428–429. A variety of hipster-approved music is performed in the shoebox-sized room inside this popular bar, from underground pop to arty noise to electro-punk-disco to ukulele country. Tickets free–$15. Daily 4pm–2am.

The Independent 628 Divisadero St, at Hayes, Western Addition ☎415 771 1421, ⊛theindependentsf.com; map p.451. This mid-sized club with friendly staff and exceptional sound books top acts from near and far. Tickets usually $12–35. Hours vary, usually daily 8pm–midnight.

Make-Out Room 3225 22nd St, at Mission, Mission ☎415 647 2888, ⊛makeoutroom.com; map p.454. A combination watering hole and music venue, with curved vinyl booths, streamers aplenty dangling from the ceiling and nightly entertainment – typically features soul DJs or local indie bands. Tickets free–$7. Daily 6pm–2am.

The Plough and Stars 116 Clement St, at 2nd Ave, Richmond ☎415 751 1122, ⊛theploughandstars.com; map pp.424–425. Local Irish expats cram into this terrific pub for pints and live folk, bluegrass and Americana music nightly. Minimal cover on weekends, no cover on weeknights. Mon–Thurs 3pm–2am, Fri–Sun 2pm–2am.

The Saloon 1232 Grant Ave, at Vallejo St, North Beach ☎415 989 7666, ⊛sfblues.net/Saloon.html; map pp.428–429. Lively hardcore blues venue that's wonderfully anachronistic among the encroaching boutiques along upper Grant's shopping and dining strip; the bar opened in 1861, making it the city's oldest. Cover $5 and up. Daily noon–1.30am.

Slim's 333 11th St, at Folsom, South of Market ☎415 255 0333, ⊛slimspresents.com; map p.454. Owned by local 1970s hit-maker Boz Scaggs, this cavernous brick space is a prime venue to catch an array of punk, alternative and international music. Tickets $15–30. Most shows Tues–Sun 8pm.

ENTERTAINMENT

San Francisco has a top reputation for embracing the highbrow arts: patrons flock to **opera** and **classical music** performances, while the city's symphony orchestra is considered among the best in the US. **Tickets** can be purchased either through the individual theatre's box offices or often through Ticketmaster (☎415 421 8497, ⊛ticketmaster.com); for last-minute bargains, try the Tix booth (Sun–Thurs 8am–4pm, Fri & Sat 8am–5pm; ☎415 430 1140, ⊛tixbayarea.org) located on the west side of Union Square. For live venues, see above.

BALLET, OPERA AND SYMPHONY

San Francisco Ballet War Memorial Opera House, 301 Van Ness Ave, at Grove St, Civic Center ☎415 865 2000, ⊛sfballet.org. The city's ballet company puts on an ambitious annual programme (Dec–May) of both classical and contemporary dance. Tickets begin at around $45.

San Francisco Opera War Memorial Opera House, 301 Van Ness Ave, at Grove St, Civic Center ☎415 864 3330, ⊛sfopera.org. A typical season (Sept–Dec, with a short run June & July) for this internationally regarded company offers a mixture of avant-garde stagings along with acclaimed productions of perennial favourites by Wagner or Puccini. Tickets start at around $45, with prices rising dramatically from there.

★**San Francisco Symphony** Louise M. Davies Symphony Hall, 201 Van Ness Ave, at Grove St, Civic

SAN FRANCISCO ARTS FESTIVALS

Each September, the **San Francisco Fringe Festival** (☎ 415 931 1094, ⓦ sffringe.org), featuring over 250 experimental performances, is held at several venues – the Exit Theatre (see below) is often a primary location; tickets generally cost $13–25.

The **Stern Grove Festival** (☎ 415 252 6252, ⓦ sterngrove.org) presents free, open-air performances by San Francisco's symphony orchestra, opera and ballet companies (with jazz, blues, hip-hop and rock acts also booked) on summer Sundays at 2pm at its namesake park at 19th Ave and Sloat Blvd. Arrive early to secure a spot on the lawn; public transport (Muni lines #K, #L, #M, #23 and #28) is recommended.

Held each spring, the **San Francisco International Film Festival** (☎ 415 931 3456, ⓦ sffs .org) offers an eclectic and oddball selection, mainly at the Castro Theatre and Sundance Kabuki. Tickets can go quickly, so book well in advance for all but the most obscure selections.

Center ☎ 415 864 6000, ⓦ sfsymphony.org. Since the 1995 arrival of musical director Michael Tilson Thomas, this once-musty institution has catapulted to the first rank of American symphony orchestras. The season runs Sept–May and tickets range from $45 far upwards, with day-of-performance rush tickets sometimes available for $20.

MAJOR THEATRES

★ **American Conservatory Theater (ACT)** 415 Geary St, at Taylor, Theater District ☎ 415 749 2228, ⓦ act-sf .org. Leading resident group that mixes newly commissioned works and innovative renditions of the classics, with inventive set design and staging. Most productions take place at the ACT Theater (also the Strand Theater at 1127 Market St). Tickets $35–80, although preview shows can cost as little as $15.

Curran Theatre 445 Geary St, at Mason, Theater District ☎ 415 551 2000, ⓦ sfcurran.com. Former vaudeville theatre that now presents both hit Broadway plays and musicals. Pre-Broadway trial runs are common here: Tony magnet *Wicked* was workshopped for several weeks at the Curran before hitting New York. Tickets $35–90.

Yerba Buena Center for the Arts 701 Mission St, at 3rd, South of Market ☎ 415 978 2787, ⓦ ybca.org. This modern, 750-seat performance space showcases local talents in programmes like the Hip-Hop Theater Festival, as well as touring shows. Tickets $15–50.

SMALLER THEATRES

★ **BATS Improv** Bayfront Theater, Fort Mason Center ☎ 415 474 6776, ⓦ improv.org. Celebrated long-form improv company (its titular acronym stands for Bay Area Theatresports) that stages shows such as *Improvised Elvis: The Musical* year-round. Tickets $18–25.

★ **Beach Blanket Babylon** Club Fugazi, 678 Green St, at Powell, North Beach ☎ 415 421 4222, ⓦ beach blanketbabylon.com. This locally legendary musical revue has been running continuously since 1974, though it regularly incorporates new spoofs of current events. Expect celebrity impersonations and towering hats, and be sure to

reserve in advance. Tickets $30–155.

Exit Theatre 156 Eddy St, at Taylor, Tenderloin ☎ 415 673 3847, ⓦ theexit.org. One of the best spots in town for cutting-edge theatre, the Exit is best known for its women-centric plays and spring DivaFest season; it's also a central location for the annual San Francisco Fringe Festival. Most tickets $20–25.

Magic Theatre Building D, Fort Mason Center ☎ 415 441 8822, ⓦ magictheatre.org. The busiest and largest local company after ACT specializes in the works of contemporary playwrights, as well as those by emerging new talents. Tickets $25–55.

The Marsh 1062 Valencia St, at 22nd, Mission ☎ 800 838 3006, ⓦ themarsh.org. This long-standing alternative space hosts fine solo shows, many with an offbeat bent; Mon is often a good night to catch works in progress. Tickets $15–35.

Theatre Rhinoceros ☎ 800 838 3006, ⓦ therhino.org. The city's prime LGBT company presents productions that range from heartfelt political drama to raunchy cabaret acts. Formerly based in the Mission, shows are currently held all over the city. Tickets $15–25.

COMEDY

Cobb's Comedy Club 915 Columbus Ave, at Lombard St, North Beach ☎ 415 928 4320, ⓦ cobbscomedy.com. A 400-seat room not far from Fisherman's Wharf that consistently hosts mid-profile touring comedians. Tickets $12.50–35, plus two-drink minimum.

Punch Line 444 Battery St, at Clay, Financial District ☎ 415 397 7573, ⓦ punchlinecomedyclub.com. Still a frontrunner in name cachet among San Francisco's few full-scale comedy venues, this strangely located cabaret books nightly shows featuring well-known headliners. Tickets $15–25, with two-drink minimum.

FILM

Artists' Television Access 992 Valencia St, at 21st, Mission ☎ 415 824 3890, ⓦ atasite.org. A scrappy, nonprofit storefront space that shows underground films

7

(often with a political or social theme) a few nights a week.
★ **Castro Theatre** 429 Castro St, at 17th, Castro ☎ 415
621 6120, ⓦ castrotheatre.com. San Francisco's
signature, circa-1922 movie palace offers foreign films,
classic revivals, seating for over 1400 and the most
enthusiastic audience in town. Arrive early to gaze up at
the spectacular chandelier and, at evening screenings,
listen to the Wurlitzer organ.

Clay Theatre 2261 Fillmore St, at Sacramento, Pacific
Heights ☎ 415 267 4893, ⓦ landmarktheatres.com.
Circa-1910 single-screen cinema showing art-house and
foreign films along the heart of Fillmore St's upscale
commercial drag.

Embarcadero Center Cinema 1 Embarcadero Center
(Front and Clay), Financial District ☎ 415 267 4893,
ⓦ landmarktheatres.com. Popular Downtown complex
showing both first-run independents and Oscar contenders.

The Roxie 3117 16th St, at Valencia, Mission ☎ 415 863
1087, ⓦ roxie.com. Venerable, pugnacious indie
moviehouse that's always been willing to take a risk on
documentaries and little-known foreign directors –
although it's not above screening old Cheech & Chong
favourites.

Sundance Kabuki 1881 Post St, at Fillmore,
Japantown ☎ 415 346 3243, ⓦ sundancecinemas.com.
With advance reserved seating, sustainable-living details
like "spudware" utensils and three eating/drinking
destinations inside, this facility is like few other cinemas in
the US. Programming varies from the mainstream fare to
more eclectic choices.

7

LGBT SAN FRANCISCO

Though still considered by most to be the gay capital of the world, San Francisco's LGBT community has made a definite move
from the outrageous to the mainstream – a measure of its political success. The exuberant energy that went into the
parading of the 1970s has taken on a much more sober, down-to-business attitude, and these days you'll find more political
activists organizing conferences than drag queens throwing parties. San Francisco's **gay scene** has also mellowed socially,
though gay parties, parades and street fairs here still swing better than most. Like any well-organized section of society, the
gay scene definitely has its social season and established events (see box opposite). Though **lesbian culture** flowered here
in the 1980s and women's club nights still exist, San Francisco's scene is a shadow of its former self. Many lesbians have now
claimed Oakland for their own, though Bernal Heights and the Mission continue to have strong lesbian communities.

INFORMATION AND RESOURCES

For LGBT-focused news, information and event listings,
visit the online homes of the *Bay Times* (ⓦ sfbaytimes.com)
and *Bay Area Reporter* (ⓦ ebar.com); regular print editions
are also available in the Castro and other neighbourhoods.

San Francisco LGBT Community Center 1800 Market
St, at Octavia, Hayes Valley ☎ 415 865 5555, ⓦ sfcenter
.org. Located along the Castro district's main artery, "the
Center" is San Francisco's leading gay and lesbian
community resource, with knowledgeable staff and plenty
of information available at its first-floor information desk.
Mon–Fri noon–10pm, Sat 10am–6pm.

ACCOMMODATION

Choose almost any hotel in San Francisco and a same-sex
couple won't raise an eyebrow at check-in; some, like the
Queen Anne (see p.465), attract equal numbers of gay and
straight visitors. Listed below are a few places that cater
especially to gay and lesbian travellers.

Inn on Castro 321 Castro St, at Market, Castro ☎ 415
861 0321, ⓦ innoncastro.com; map p.454. This luxurious
B&B is spread across two adjacent houses, with eight
rooms and three apartments available – all of which are
brightly decorated in individual styles and have private
baths. There's also a funky lounge where you can meet
other guests. Shared bath **$170**, en suite **$240**

★ **Parker Guest House** 520 Church St, at 17th, Castro
☎ 888 520 7275, ⓦ parkerguesthouse.com; map p.454.
Popular with gay visitors, this 21-room converted mansion
is set amid beautiful gardens and features ample common
areas (including a living room with fireplace), a sunny
breakfast room and a sauna. **$179**

NIGHTLIFE

San Francisco's gay bars are many and varied, ranging from
cosy cocktail lounges to no-holds-barred leather-and-chain
hangouts. Yet bars across the city have faced increasing
pressure as rents rise and neighbourhoods change – the city's
last old-school lesbian bar, the *Lexington Club*, closed in 2015;
gay legend *Esta Noche* closed in 2014 and *The Stud* was
expected to close at the time of writing.

Aunt Charlie's Lounge 133 Turk St, at Taylor,
Tenderloin ☎ 415 861 3846, ⓦ auntcharlieslounge
.com; map pp.428–429. Popular Tenderloin dive bar
known for cheap drinks and the Hot Boxxx Girls Drag Show
Fri & Sat from 10pm (cover $5). Mon–Fri noon–2am, Sat
10am–2am, Sun 10am–midnight.

The Café 2369 Market St, at 17th, Castro ☎ 415 861 3846,
ⓦ cafesf.com; map p.454. With its mainstream house DJs,
cheap cover and nightly happy hour until 9pm, this longtime
staple of the gay club scene remains a crowd-pleaser. It's
classic out-and-proud Castro, from the thump-ing beats to the
rainbow-coloured socks strategically placed on male dancers.
Mon–Fri 5pm–2am, Sat & Sun 3pm–2am.

Cinch Saloon 1723 Polk St, between Washington and
Clay, Nob Hill ☎ 415 776 4162, ⓦ cinchsf.com; map

LGBT EVENTS

AIDS Candlelight Memorial ⓦ www.candlelightmemorial.org. May. Almost as much of an awareness and mobilization event as it is a memorial procession, this moving vigil attracts thousands and leads from the heart of the Castro up Market St to Civic Center.

Frameline ⓣ 415 703 8650, ⓦ frameline.org. June. Short films and features from amateurs and auteurs, generally shown at the Castro Theatre, as well as the Roxie and Victoria theatres in the Mission. The oldest and largest event of its kind in the world.

San Francisco Pride ⓣ 415 864 0831, ⓦ sfpride.org. June. One of the largest Pride festivals in the world, with an all-day parade to match. The Saturday-night Dyke March is more homespun than the increasingly corporate Pride parade the following afternoon, but the whole weekend is one giant celebration of queer culture.

Up Your Alley Fair ⓣ 415 777 3247, ⓦ folsomstreetevents.org/upyouralley. July. The hardcore brother of Folsom Street Fair (see below) takes place on nearby Dore Alley; it's a more sex-driven event, with fewer onlookers and plenty of S&M.

Folsom Street Fair ⓣ 415 777 3247, ⓦ folsomstreetfair.com. September. Legendary leather street fair that seems to get more and more popular with curious voyeurs every year. Nevertheless, it's a friendly event full of unwholesome fun, held at the peak of San Francisco's good-weather season.

Castro Street Fair ⓣ 415 841 1824, ⓦ castrostreetfair.org. October. The Castro's annual street fair is one of the best. It's as much about arts and crafts as it is ass and chaps, with locally handmade wares for sale amid food vendors and live performances.

7

pp.428–429. Old-school leather bar since the 1970s, with weekly events such as the Big Gay Beer Bust on Sundays 3–7pm ($15 for all-you-can-drink beer). Daily 9am–2am.

Martuni's 4 Valencia St, at Market, Mission ⓣ 415 241 0205, ⓦ martunis.ypguides.net; map p.454. Serving kitschy drinks on the edge of the Mission, Castro and Hayes Valley, this two-room piano bar attracts a fun and diverse crowd, with many keen to sing along to classics by Judy, Liza and Edith. Daily 2pm–2am.

Pilsner Inn 225 Church St, at Market, Castro ⓣ 415 621 7058, ⓦ pilsnerinn.com; map p.454. Mature neighbourhood bar that fills nightly with a wide-ranging crowd playing pool and darts. There's a large patio out back, and a generally welcoming, open vibe. Mon–Fri noon–2am, Sat & Sun 10–2am.

Powerhouse 1347 Folsom St, at Dore Alley, South of Market ⓣ 415 552 8689, ⓦ powerhousebar.com; map pp.424–425. One of the prime pick-up joints in the city, this cruisey bar boasts a patio and plenty of convenient dark corners inside. Daily 4pm–2am.

QBar 456 Castro St, between 17th and 18th, Castro ⓣ 415 864 2877, ⓦ qbarsf.com; map p.454. With its mainstream house DJs and young clientele, drag queens

and LGBT events, this bar becomes more like a club as the night goes on. There's also a popular lesbian night on Tuesdays. Daily noon–2am.

Trax 1437 Haight St, at Masonic Ave, Upper Haight ⓣ 415 864 4213; map p.451. The Haight's only gay bar is a bit of a dive, though it's been smartened up slightly from its grungy yesteryear. There's a mix of gays and straights, so it's much less cruisey than other bars. Daily noon–2am.

Twin Peaks Tavern 401 Castro St, at 17th, Castro ⓣ 415 864 9470, ⓦ twinpeakstavern.com; map p.454. A great spot for watching the lively Castro pavement scene, this corner saloon is famous for being the first gay bar in America (in 1973) to install transparent picture windows rather than blacked-out barriers. These days, it's laidback and filled with middle-class, older white men. Mon–Wed noon–2am, Thurs & Sun 10am–2am, Fri & Sat 8am–2am.

★ **The Wild Side West** 424 Cortland Ave, at Andover St, Bernal Heights ⓣ 415 647 3099, ⓦ wildsidewest.com; pp.424–425. Unpretentious and friendly tavern at the centre of the Bernal Heights lesbian scene, with plenty of kitsch Americana to gaze at. There's a lovely, quirky art-filled garden out back, but without heat lamps, you'd be well advised to stay inside on a cold evening. Daily 2pm–2am.

SHOPPING

Aside from the retail palaces around Union Square (including Macy's, Saks and practically every major designer label), San Francisco's shopping scene is refreshingly edgy, peppered with stylish homeware stores and one-off boutiques selling locally designed clothes. There's also a brilliantly varied (if thinning) selection of **independent book** and **music shops**. It's worth remembering that, unlike in many other American cities, shops in San Francisco close relatively early – 6pm Monday to Saturday and 5pm on Sunday isn't unusual – so start your major shopping expeditions early. For Levi's, see box, p.436.

BOOKSHOPS

Unsurprisingly, for a city with such a rich literary history,

San Francisco is home to numerous terrific speciality bookstores, from legendary City Lights in North Beach to the Mission, where you'll find some of the city's most energized – and politicized – bookstores.

GENERAL

The Booksmith 1644 Haight St, at Cole, Upper Haight ☎415 863 8688, ⓦbooksmith.com; map p.451. Solid neighbourhood shop stocking mainstream as well as countercultural titles; it's notable for its high-profile author readings and other events. Mon–Sat 10am–10pm, Sun 10am–8pm.

City Lights 261 Columbus Ave, at Broadway, North Beach ☎415 362 8193, ⓦcitylights.com; map pp.428–429. Internationally known bookstore with oddball sections such as "Stolen Continents" and "Muckraking" scattered about, and an excellent poetry room upstairs. Daily 10am–midnight.

★**Green Apple Books** 506 Clement St, at 6th Ave, Richmond ☎415 387 2272, ⓦgreenapplebooks.com; map pp.424–425. Wonderfully browseable store with deftly amusing touches like the regular section called "Books That Will Never Be Oprah's Picks". Daily 10am–10.30pm.

SPECIALIST AND SECONDHAND

Argonaut Book Shop 786 Sutter St, at Jones, Tenderloin ☎415 474 9067; map pp.428–429. San Francisco's finest history-focused bookseller, specializing in volumes on California and the West, from the Gold Rush to contemporary times. Mon–Fri 9am–5pm, Sat 10.30am–4pm.

Dog Eared Books 900 Valencia St, at 20th, Mission ☎415 282 1901, ⓦdogearedbooks.com; map p.454. Corner bookstore along Valencia's shopping strip with a sharp selection of budget-priced remainders, as well as an eclectic range of secondhand titles, most in terrific condition. Daily 10am–10pm.

Kayo Books 814 Post St, at Leavenworth, Tenderloin ☎415 749 0554, ⓦkayobooks.com; map pp.428–429. Glorious vintage paperback store full of bargain classics, from pulpy mysteries and sci-fi to campy sleaze fiction. Thurs–Sat 11am–6pm; also by appointment.

Modern Times Bookstore Collective 2919 24th St, at Florida, Mission ☎415 282 9246, ⓦmoderntimes bookstore.com; map p.454. Hefty stock of Latin American literature and progressive political publications, as well as a small but well-chosen selection of gay and lesbian literature and radical feminist magazines. Also stages regular readings of authors' works. Daily noon–8pm.

RECORD SHOPS

Despite the predicted extinction of brick-and-mortar music retailers, several excellent speciality record shops soldier on in San Francisco, including several excellent shops specializing in underground genres and vinyl.

★**Amoeba Music** 1855 Haight St, at Stanyan, Upper Haight ☎415 831 1200, ⓦamoeba.com; map p.451. Enormously housed in a former bowling alley, this renowned emporium is one of the largest independent music retailers in the US. Its encyclopedic selection of modern music is a treasure-trove for all stripes of music fans, where ploughing through the stacks of new and used vinyl, CDs, DVDs and assorted memorabilia can while away a full afternoon. Daily 11am–8pm.

Grooves 1797 Market St, at Octavia, Hayes Valley ☎415 436 9933; map p.454. Adorned with coloured LPs on the walls, this speciality store is crammed with collectable items in all imaginable genres – jazz, classical,

---

SHOPPING NEIGHBOURHOODS

San Francisco's prime **shopping streets**, arranged by neighbourhood and detailed below, are sure to provide a heaping (and potentially costly) dose of retail therapy to even the most inveterate shopaholics.

The Castro Castro St between 17th and 19th; Market St between Castro and Church. Gay-oriented boutiques, clubwear and shoes.

Cow Hollow Union St between Steiner and Gough. Sweet – if rather conservative – boutiques, shoe stores and homeware retailers.

Upper Haight Haight St between Stanyan St and Masonic Ave. Clothing (men's and women's), especially vintage and secondhand.

Hayes Valley Hayes St between Franklin and Laguna. Trendy but quite expensive, with edgy boutiques for men and women, as well as jewellery galleries and other high-end goodies.

The Marina Chestnut St between Broderick and Fillmore. Hopelessly yuppified strip of health-food stores, wine shops and women's clothing boutiques.

The Mission Valencia St between 16th and 21st. The best choice for urban hipsters, with lots of used furniture and clothing stores, bookshops and even the odd pirate-gear retailer.

North Beach Grant Ave between Filbert and Vallejo. Inviting boutiques, jewellers, homeware retailers and shops specializing in rare maps; also one of the newest and freshest places to find cool clothes.

blues, comedy, lounge and polka. Daily noon–7pm.

Recycled Records 1377 Haight St, at Masonic Ave, Upper Haight ☎ 415 626 4075, ⓦ recycled-records.com; map p.451. While mediocre for CDs, this longtime neighbourhood favourite shines best with its extensive vinyl selection, from old film soundtracks to good-condition Stones and Dylan records. Everything's secondhand, the staff are usually good for a gab and prices are often negotiable. Mon–Fri 10am–8pm, Sat 10am–9pm, Sun 11am–7pm.

Rooky Ricardo's Records 448 Haight St, at Webster, Lower Haight ☎ 415 864 7526, ⓦ www.rookyricardos .com; map p.451. With a lifetime of LPs and 45s to sift through, this fun shop leans heavily on old-school soul and R&B, but it's entirely possible you may unearth a rock or jazz gem if you dig long enough. Daily noon–6pm.

Stranded 1055 Valencia St, at 21st, Mission ☎ 415 647 2272, ⓦ stranded-shop.com; map p.454. The former Aquarius Records was taken over in 2016 by this Oakland outfit, which will hopefully maintain the tradition of indie record labels with hip, but friendly staff and an emphasis on all kinds of underground styles, from noise-rock to experimental and electronic. Mon–Wed & Sun 10am–9pm, Thurs–Sat 10am–10pm.

FOOD AND DRINK

Andronico's 1200 Irving St, at Funston Ave, Sunset ☎ 415 661 3220, ⓦ andronicos.com; map pp.424–425. Pricey supermarket selling gorgeous produce, as well as craft beer, top wine, artisan bread and lots of cheese; there's even an olive bar and a terrific deli. Daily 7am–10pm.

The Jug Shop 1590 Pacific Ave, at Polk St, Russian Hill ☎ 415 885 2922, ⓦ thejugshop.com; map pp.428–429. Large wine retailer best known for its inexpensive California varietals and interesting range of New World vintages; it also has more than two hundred varieties of similarly well-priced beers. Mon–Sat 9am–9pm, Sun 10am–7pm.

★**Molinari** 373 Columbus Ave, at Vallejo St, North Beach ☎ 415 421 2337, ⓦ molinarisalame.com; map pp.428–429. Rich with the singular aroma of cured meats, this bustling North Beach delicatessen opened in 1896, and is jammed with Italian goodies, both familiar and exotic. Pick the bread of your choice and order a doorstop sandwich to take away. Mon–Fri 9am–5.30pm, Sat 7.30am–5.30pm.

Real Food Company 3060 Fillmore St, at Filbert, Cow Hollow ☎ 415 567 6900, ⓦ realfoodco.com; map pp.424–425. Smallish, artsy grocery store with an excellent gourmet meat counter and delicious whole-wheat pastries; it also carries potions, vitamins and myriad health foods. Daily 8am–9pm.

Ten Ren's Tea 949 Grant Ave, at Jackson St, Chinatown ☎ 415 362 0656, ⓦ tenren.com; map pp.428–429. Large, inexpensive and well-stocked Taiwanese tea emporium where you can stop in for tea by the pound or a fresh brew to go. The scented iced teas, thick with gloopy tapioca balls, are particularly delicious. Daily 9am–9pm.

SPECIALITY SHOPS

★**826 Valencia** 826 Valencia St, at 19th, Mission ☎ 415 642 5905, ⓦ 826valencia.org/store; map p.454. A front for writer/publisher Dave Eggers' nonprofit youth writing workshop, this pirate supply store – seriously – offers everything a would-be swashbuckler could need, from eye patches to message bottles; naturally, all of Eggers' publications are on sale as well. The store is an adventure unto itself, with treasures scattered about and a wonderful fish-tank room that's home to Vaclav the porcupine pufferfish. Daily noon–6pm.

Flight 001 525 Hayes St, at Octavia, Hayes Valley ☎ 415 487 1001, ⓦ flight001.com; map p.451. This sleek, futuristic travel store sells books, funky accessories (think chunky, Day-Glo luggage tags and all-in-one shaving kits) and dapper carry-on bags. The place to stock

7

FERRY BUILDING MARKETPLACE

The Ferry Building, across the Embarcadero and Harry Bridges Plaza from the foot of Market St, offers a one-stop place to graze goods from some of Northern California's best specialist food producers. Everything from bread and cheese to wine and tea is on offer, with a few of the top shops listed below. The Ferry Building's outside plaza is home to the area's biggest farmers' market (Sat 8am–2pm, Tues & Thurs 10am–2pm).

Cowgirl Creamery Cheese Shop ☎ 415 362 9354, ⓦ cowgirlcreamery.com. Top-notch cheesery featuring selections from small producers around the world, as well as the Point Reyes Station creamery's own award-winning concoctions, such as crème fraîche. Mon–Fri 10am–7pm, Sat 8am–6pm, Sun 10am–5pm.

Golden Gate Meat Company ☎ 415 983 7800. Butcher shop and charcuterie carving organic meats daily, from the usual suspects (beef, poultry) all the way

to exotic game and offal. Exceptional, reasonably priced sandwiches are also available to take away. Mon–Fri 6.30am–7pm, Sat 7am–5.30pm, Sun 11am–5pm.

Stonehouse Olive Oil ☎ 415 765 0405, ⓦ stonehouseoliveoil.com. High-quality Californian virgin olive oils, including citrus olive oils such as Blood Orange, Lisbon Lemon and Persian Lime. Mon–Fri 9am–7pm, Sat 7am–6pm, Sun 11am–5pm.

up if you only travel first-class – or at least want to look like it. Mon–Sat 11am–7pm, Sun 11am–6pm.

★**Good Vibrations** 1620 Polk St, at Sacramento, Polk Gulch ☎ 415 345 0400, ⓦ goodvibes.com; map pp.428–429. Gloriously erotic store that's a co-op, where the mission is to destigmatize sex shops and make browsing fun and comfortable. It's packed with every imaginable sex toy, plus racks of erotica and candy-store-style jars of condoms; be sure to give the antique vibrator museum a look. Mon–Thurs & Sun 10am–9pm, Fri & Sat 10am–10pm.

Goorin Brothers 1446 Haight St, at Masonic Ave, Upper Haight ☎ 415 436 9450, ⓦ goorin.com; map p.451. This San Francisco-based haberdasher has been producing its own extensive line of hats for well over a century, but one step inside reveals that its designs have moved with the times. Caps ranging from conservative to brash line the shelves, as do fedoras and a cache of women's hats. Mon–Thurs & Sun 11am–7pm, Fri & Sat 10am–7pm.

Jeremys Department Store 2 South Park, at Second St, South of Market ☎ 415 882 4929, ⓦ jeremys.com; map pp.428–429. Local designer discount boutique where you might find last spring's Prada dress at a fraction of the original price; there are also plenty of men's clothes to browse through. Mon–Wed, Fri & Sat 11am–6pm, Thurs 11am–8pm, Sun noon–6pm.

Paolo Shoes 524 Hayes St, at Laguna, Hayes Valley ☎ 415 552 4580, ⓦ paoloshoes.com; map p.451. Local gem where designer Paolo Iantorno sells his edgy, yet wearable – if extremely expensive – limited-edition men's and women's shoe designs, which are otherwise only sold in Italy. Mon–Sat 11am–7pm, Sun 11am–6pm.

Upper Playground 220 Fillmore St, at Waller, Lower Haight ☎ 415 861 1960, ⓦ upperplayground.com; map p.451. Fiercely San Francisco-based clothing and hip-hop culture boutique whose racks and shelves are full of caps and other streetwear, including no shortage of clever, locally referenced T-shirts. There's artwork for sale in a separate room. Daily noon–7pm.

DIRECTORY

Car rental All major firms have branches at SFO, as well as within the city itself. Alamo: 750 Bush St, at Powell, Union Square ☎ 888 826 6893; Avis: 675 Post St, at Jones, Union Square ☎ 415 929 2555; Budget: 821 Howard St, at 4th, South of Market ☎ 415 957 9988; Dollar: 364 O'Farrell St, at Taylor, Union Square ☎ 866 434 2226; Enterprise: 550 Turk St, at Larkin, Tenderloin ☎ 415 447 0520; Hertz: 325 Mason St, at O'Farrell, Tenderloin ☎ 415 771 2200.

Consulates Australia: 575 Market St, at 2nd, Financial District ☎ 415 644 3620, ⓦ usa.embassy.gov.au. Canada: 580 California St, at Kearny, Financial District ☎ 415 834 3180, ⓦ can-am.gc.ca/san-francisco. Ireland: 100 Pine St, at Front, Financial District ☎ 415 392 4214, ⓦ dfa.ie. UK: 1 Sansome St, at Market, Financial District ☎ 415 617 1300, ⓦ gov.uk.

Dental treatment For a free referral, call the San Francisco Dental Society (☎ 415 928 7337, ⓦ sfds.org) or visit the California Dental Association's website (ⓦ cda.org/find-a-dentist).

Disabled access Steep hills aside, the Bay Area is generally considered one of the most barrier-free regions around. Most public buildings have been built (or modified) for disabled access, all BART stations are accessible and most buses have lowering platforms for wheelchairs. For more information, visit ⓦ accessnca.org.

Hospitals Saint Francis Memorial Hospital, 900 Hyde St, at Pine, Nob Hill (☎ 415 353 6000, ⓦ saintfrancismemorial.org); California Pacific Medical Center, 45 Castro St, at Duboce, Castro (☎ 415 600 0257, ⓦ cpmc.org); and San Francisco General Hospital, 1001 Potrero Ave, at 22nd St, Mission (☎ 415 206 8000, ⓦ sfdph.org).

Internet Travellers with laptops will be able to find a café with free or low-cost access in any neighbourhood, if not at their hotel or hostel.

Library Main Library: 100 Larkin St, at Grove, Civic Center ☎ 415 557 4400, ⓦ sfpl.org (see p.427). All 28 San Francisco libraries offer free wi-fi.

Passport and visa US Bureau of Citizenship and Immigration Services, 630 Sansome St, at Washington, Financial District ☎ 415 844 5110, ⓦ uscis.gov.

Pharmacies Walgreens 24hr pharmacies: 459 Powell St, at Sutter (☎ 415 984 0793); 498 Castro St, at 18th (☎ 415 861 6276); 1344 Stockton St, at Broadway (☎ 415 981 6274).

Post offices For a list of local post offices, consult ⓦ usps.com.

Sales tax San Francisco imposes a sales tax of 8.75 percent – seldom included in any quoted price – on almost all purchased goods other than groceries and prescription drugs. The city's hotel occupancy tax is 14 percent (not included in room rates quoted by hotels).

The East Bay

Across the steel **Bay Bridge**, eight miles from Downtown San Francisco and generally sunnier and warmer, the **East Bay** is home to the lively, left-leaning cities of **Oakland** and **Berkeley**. A hard-working, blue-collar city at the heart of the East Bay, Oakland traditionally earned its livelihood from shipping and transport services, as evidenced by the enormous cranes in the massive Port of Oakland, but the city has undergone something of a renaissance by attracting businesses and workers from the information technology industry. Oakland spreads north along wooded foothills to **Berkeley**, an image-conscious university town that looks out to the Golden Gate and collects a mixed bag of earnest young students, much-pierced dropouts, ageing 1960s radicals and Nobel Prize-winning nuclear physicists in its cafés and bookshops.

Berkeley, Oakland and the less inspiring bayside towns to the north blend together so much as to be virtually the same city; the hills above them are topped by a twenty-mile string of **regional parks**, providing much-needed fresh air and quick relief from the populated grids below. Spreading east and north of the hills is Contra Costa County, a huge area that contains some intriguing, historically important waterfront towns – well worth a stop if you're passing through on the way to the Wine Country – as well as some of the Bay Area's most inward-looking suburban sprawl. For convenience, we have included Benicia, the one worthwhile town north of the Carquinez Strait, in this section.

In contrast, standing out from the soulless dormitory communities that fill the often baking-hot **inland valleys** are the preserved homes of an unlikely pair of influential writers: the naturalist John Muir, who, when not out hiking around Yosemite and the High Sierra, lived most of his life near **Martinez**, and the playwright Eugene O'Neill, who wrote many of his angst-ridden works at the foot of **Mount Diablo**, the Bay Area's most significant peak.

7

GETTING AROUND   THE EAST BAY

By subway The East Bay is linked to San Francisco (including the airport) via the underground BART Transbay subway (see p.462). Four lines run underneath the bay, while a fifth line operates its entire length in the East Bay between Richmond (see p.507) and Fremont. To phone BART from the East Bay call ☎ 510 465 2278, or check ⌨ bart.gov.

By bus From East Bay BART stations, pick up a free transfer, saving you 25¢ on the $2.10 fares of the efficient AC Transit (☎ 510 817 1717 ext 1111, ⌨ actransit.org) bus service, which covers the entire East Bay. AC Transit also runs buses on a number of routes to Oakland and Berkeley from the Transbay Terminal in San Francisco. These operate all night and are the only way of getting across the bay by public transport once BART has shut down. A smaller-scale bus company that also proves useful is the Contra Costa County Connection (☎ 925 676 7500, ⌨ cccta.org), running buses

to most of the inland areas, including the John Muir and Eugene O'Neill historic houses.

By bike One of the best ways to get around the East Bay is by bike. A fine cycle route follows Skyline and Grizzly Peak blvds along the wooded crest of the hills between Berkeley and Lake Chabot. Within Berkeley itself, the Ohlone Greenway makes for a pleasant cycling or walking route up through North Berkeley to El Cerrito (see p.507). Bike rental is available in Oakland (see p.495) and Berkeley (see p.503).

By car If you're driving, allow yourself plenty of time to get anywhere: the East Bay has some of California's worst traffic, with the Bay Bridge and I-80 in particular jam-packed sixteen hours a day. Car-pool lanes are becoming increasingly popular, so having at least two or three people in your vehicle (minimum number varies) can speed things up, at least slightly.

Oakland

What was the use of me having come from Oakland, it was not natural for me to have come from there yes write about it if I like or anything if I like but not there, there is no there there.

Gertrude Stein, *Everybody's Autobiography*

As the workhorse of the Bay Area, **OAKLAND** is commonly known as a place of little or no play. One of the busiest ports on the West Coast and the western terminal of the country's rail network, it's also the spawning ground of some of America's most unabashedly revolutionary **political movements**, such as the militant **Black Panthers**, who gave a radical voice to the African American population, and the **Symbionese Liberation Army**, who demanded a ransom for kidnapped heiress Patty Hearst in the form of free food distribution to the poor.

The city is also the birthplace of literary legends **Gertrude Stein** and **Jack London**, who grew up here at approximately the same time, though in entirely different circumstances – Stein was a stockbroker's daughter, while London was an orphaned delinquent. Most of the waterfront where London used to steal oysters and lobsters is

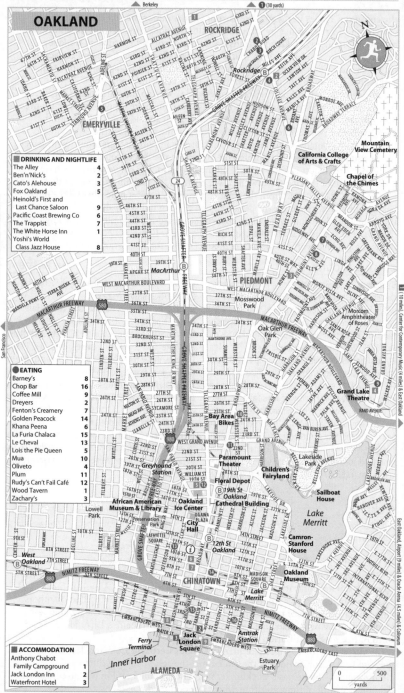

OAKLAND

DRINKING AND NIGHTLIFE

The Alley	4
Ben'n'Nick's	2
Cato's Alehouse	3
Fox Oakland	5
Heinold's First and	
Last Chance Saloon	9
Pacific Coast Brewing Co	6
The Trappist	7
The White Horse Inn	1
Yoshi's World	
Class Jazz House	8

EATING

Barney's	8
Chop Bar	16
Coffee Mill	9
Dreyers	2
Fenton's Creamery	7
Golden Peacock	14
Khana Peena	6
La Furia Chalaca	15
Le Cheval	13
Lois the Pie Queen	5
Mua	10
Oliveto	4
Plum	11
Rudy's Can't Fail Café	12
Wood Tavern	1
Zachary's	3

ACCOMMODATION

Anthony Chabot	
Family Campground	1
Jack London Inn	2
Waterfront Hotel	3

THE BAY BRIDGE AND TREASURE ISLAND

The largest and most travelled bridge in California, connecting Downtown San Francisco to the East Bay, the **Bay Bridge** is part graceful suspension bridge and part heavy-duty steel truss. Built in 1933 as an economic booster during the Depression, the bridge is made from enough steel cable to wrap around the earth three times. Completed just seven months before the more famous Golden Gate, it works a lot harder for a lot less respect: a hundred million vehicles cross it each year. Local scribe Herb Caen dubbed it "the car-strangled spanner", a reflection of its often-clogged lanes. Indeed, the bridge's only claim to fame – apart from the much-broadcast videotape of its partial collapse during the 1989 earthquake – is that **Treasure Island**, adjoined to Yerba Buena Island where the two halves of the bridge meet, hosted the 1939 World's Fair. The ultra-expensive project to replace the bridge's eastern span was finally completed in September 2013, well behind schedule and over budget.

now named in his memory, while Stein, who was actually born in East Oakland, is all but ignored here, not surprising given her famously unflattering quote about the place.

7

Indeed it's only since the millennium that the city has begun to shake off its negative image through efforts to revitalize (some say gentrify) the town and slash its infamous crime rate. These were initiated by former Mayor **Jerry "Moonbeam" Brown**, who drew in thousands of new residents by advertising the city's lower rents and consistently sunny climate, and have been continued in less flamboyant style by his three successors, the latest being Libby Schaaf. A significant number of lesbians left San Francisco's Castro and Mission for Oakland, as well as a great number of artists who were pushed from their South of Market lofts by sky-high rents into the warehouses of West Oakland. Recent years, however, have seen rents in the increasingly popular **Rockridge** and **Lake Merritt** districts rival San Francisco prices – and adversely there's been an increase in the number of homeless sleeping under the elevated freeways of Emeryville and West Oakland especially.

For the casual visitor there are enough museums, activities, restaurants and musical venues to keep everybody happy.

Downtown Oakland

If you come by BART from San Francisco, get off at the Twelfth Street–Civic Center station and you'll find yourself at the open-air shopping and office space of **City Center** in the heart of **DOWNTOWN OAKLAND**. Bustling on weekdays with the nine-to-five contingent, the area can seem eerily deserted at other times. Downtown's compact district of spruced-up Victorian storefronts, overlooked by modern hotels and office buildings, has undergone an ambitious programme of restoration and redevelopment for well over a decade. Fraught with allegations of illegal dealings and incompetent planning, the initiative has not been an unqualified success. One of the more controversial projects was the moat-like I-980 freeway, the main route through Oakland since the collapse of the Cypress Freeway in the 1989 earthquake; to make room, entire blocks were cleared of houses. Yet there were efforts to maintain the city's architectural heritage, most noticeably in the collection of charming properties of **Preservation Park** at Twelfth Street and Martin Luther King Jr Way. The late nineteenth-century commercial centre along Ninth Street west of Broadway, now tagged **Old Oakland**, also underwent a major restoration some years ago, and nearly all premises are now occupied by tenants such as architecture and design firms. Even better, the section between Broadway and Clay is home to a fine **farmers' market** every Friday between 8am and 2pm.

By way of contrast with the generally subdued Old Oakland area, stroll a block east of Broadway, between Seventh and Ninth to Oakland's **Chinatown**, whose bakeries and restaurants are more authentic and less tourist-trodden than their counterparts across the bay, though not as lively nor as picturesque.

Frank Ogawa Plaza and City Hall

The city experienced its greatest period of growth in the early twentieth century, and many of the grand buildings of this era survive a few blocks north along Broadway, centred on the gigantic grass triangle of **Frank Ogawa Plaza** and the awkwardly imposing 1914 **City Hall** on 14th Street. This area hosts the annual **Art and Soul Festival** (Ⓦartandsouloakland.com) over Labor Day weekend, featuring live music and art displays. Two blocks away at 13th and Franklin stands Oakland's most unmistakeable landmark, the chateauesque lantern of the **Tribune Tower**, the 1920s former home of the *Oakland Tribune* newspaper.

African American Museum & Library

659 14th St • Tues–Sat noon–5.30pm • Free • ☎ 510 238 6716, Ⓦ oaklandlibrary.org

A few blocks west of Frank Ogawa Plaza, the **African American Museum & Library** is housed in an elegant Neoclassical building whose upper floor has a permanent display on the history of African Americans in California from 1775 to 1900, and revolving art and photo exhibitions.

7

Paramount Theatre and around

2025 Broadway • Tours 10am first and third Sat of the month • $5 • ☎ 510 465 6400, Ⓦ paramounttheatre.com

Some of the Bay Area's finest early twentieth-century buildings are to be found around the 19th Street BART station, highlighted by the outstanding Art Deco interior of the 1931 **Paramount Theatre**. The West Coast's answer to New York's Radio City Music Hall, the Paramount shows Hollywood classics and hosts occasional concerts by diverse musicians such as Neil Young and Norah Jones, as well as performances by stand-up comedians, ballet troupes and the Oakland Symphony.

Other buildings close to the Paramount Theatre are equally flamboyant, ranging from the wafer-thin Gothic "flatiron" office tower of the **Cathedral Building** at Broadway and Telegraph, to the Hindu-temple-like façade of the magnificent 3500-seat **Fox Oakland** at 1807 Telegraph Ave (see p.497), the largest moviehouse west of Chicago when it was built in 1928. Across the street, the 1931 **Floral Depot** is a group of small modern storefronts faced in black-and-blue terracotta tiles with shiny silver highlights. If you want to get your skates on, lace up at the nearby **Oakland Ice Center** (see p.495).

Lake Merritt

Five blocks east of Broadway, the eastern third of Downtown Oakland comprises **Lake Merritt**, a three-mile-circumference tidal lagoon that was bridged and dammed in the 1860s to become the centrepiece of Oakland's most desirable neighbourhood. All that remains of the many fine houses that once circled the lake is the elegant **Camron-Stanford House**, on the southwest shore at 1418 Lakeside Drive, a graceful Italianate mansion whose sumptuous interior is open for visits (Sun 1pm, 2pm & 3pm; $5; ☎ 510 874 7802, Ⓦ cshouse.org). The lake is also the nation's oldest wildlife refuge, with migrating flocks of ducks, geese and herons breaking their journeys here. **Lakeside Park** lines the north shore, where you can engage in various boating and watersports activities (see p.495).

Children's Fairyland

Summer Mon–Fri 10am–4pm, Sat & Sun 10am–5pm; times vary through rest of year • $10 • ☎ 510 452 2259, Ⓦ fairyland.org

Kids will like the puppet shows and pony rides at the **Children's Fairyland**, along Grand Avenue on the northwest edge of the park. At night, the lake is lit up by the "Necklace of Lights", an elegant source of local pride. Once you reach the north side of the lake, be sure to stroll under the MacArthur Freeway to soak up the relaxed atmosphere of the cafés and shops along Grand and Lakeshore avenues. Note the huge Art Deco-cum-mock-classical façade of the still-functioning **Grand Lake Movie Theater**, a bastion of subversive political films.

Oakland Museum

1000 Oak St • Wed–Fri 11am–5pm, Sat & Sun 10am–6pm • $15.95, free first Sun of the month • ☎ 510 238 2200, ⓦ museumca.org

Two blocks south of Lake Merritt, only a block up from the Lake Merritt BART station, the **Oakland Museum** is undoubtedly Oakland's most worthwhile stop, not only for the exhibits but also for the superb modern building in which they are housed, topped by a terraced rooftop sculpture garden that gives great views out over the lake and the city. The museum covers many diverse areas: displays on the **ecology** of California, including a simulated walk from the seaside through various natural habitats up to the 14,000ft summits of the Sierra Nevada mountains; state history, ranging from old mining equipment to the guitar that Berkeley-born Country Joe MacDonald played at the Woodstock Festival in 1969; and a broad survey of works by California artists and craftspeople, highlights of which include turn-of-the-twentieth-century **furniture**. There's also an excellent collection of **photography** by Edward Muybridge, Dorothea Lange, Imogen Cunningham and many others, as well as a collector's gallery that rents and sells works by California artists.

Jack London Square

Half a mile south of Downtown Oakland at the foot of Broadway, waterfront **Jack London Square** is Oakland's major concession to the tourist trade. Also accessible by direct ferry from San Francisco (see p.495), this somewhat sterile complex of boutiques and restaurants was named after the self-taught writer who grew up pirating shellfish around here but is about as distant from the spirit of the man as it's possible to get. Jack London's best story, *The Call of the Wild*, was written about his adventures in the Alaskan Yukon, where he carved his initials in a small cabin that has been reconstructed here. The one sight worth stopping at is **Heinold's First and Last Chance Saloon** (see p.497), built in 1883 from the hull of a whaling ship. Jack London really did drink here, and the collection of yellowed portraits of him on the wall are the only genuine thing about the writer you'll find on the square.

Aside from London memorabilia, there are a few other interesting things to see here. At the western end of the square you can visit a couple of **historical vessels**; dockside tours are available for both the Lightship *Relief* (Wed 1–4pm, Sat & Sun 11am–4pm; $5; ☎510 685 2346, ⓦ uslhs.org/about/lightship) and the USS *Potomac* (Wed, Fri & Sun 11am–2.30pm; $10; ☎510 627 1215, ⓦ usspotomac.org), Franklin D. Roosevelt's famous "floating White House", which also offers occasional cruises. On Sunday, the square bustles with the weekly farmers' market and in late September it hosts the **Eat Real Festival** (ⓦ eatrealfest.com), which focuses on quality organic food, craft beer and local wines.

A few short blocks inland, along Third and Fourth, there's a good **Produce Market**. This bustling warehouse district has fruit and vegetables by the forklift-load, and is at its liveliest early in the morning, from about 5am.

East Oakland

The bulk of Oakland spreads along foothills and flatlands to the east of downtown, in neighbourhoods running down the main thoroughfares of Foothill and MacArthur boulevards. Gertrude Stein grew up here, though her childhood home was long ago torn down and replaced by a dozen Craftsman-style bungalows – the simple 1920s wooden houses that cover most of **East Oakland**, each fronted by a patch of lawn and divided from its neighbour by a narrow concrete driveway. The main artery through the area is East 14th Street, whose string of cheap Mexican restaurants and Latino shops sums up its international ambience.

Joaquin Miller Park

AC Transit buses #39 & #339 from the Fruitvale BART station

A quick way out from the gridded streets of the city is to head east up into the hills to **Joaquin Miller Park**, the most easily accessible of Oakland's hilltop open spaces. It stands on the former grounds of "The Hights", the misspelled home of the "Poet of the Sierras", Joaquin Miller, who made his name playing the eccentric frontier American in the literary salons of 1870s London. Renowned more for his outrageous behaviour than his literary prowess, he became famous by wearing bizarre clothes and biting debutantes on the ankle. For years, Japanese poet Yone Noguchi also lived here, working the sprinkler as Miller impressed lady visitors with a rain dance he claimed to have learned from Native Americans.

Mormon Temple

4766 Lincoln Ave • **Museum** Daily 9am–9pm • Free • ☎ 510 531 3200, ⓦ ldschurchtemples.com/oakland

Perched in the hills at the foot of Joaquin Miller Park, the pointed towers of the **Mormon Temple** look like missile-launchers designed by the Wizard of Oz – impossible to miss by day or floodlit night. In December, speakers hidden in the landscaping make it seem as if the plants are singing Christmas carols. Though you can't go inside the main temple unless you're a confirmed Mormon, there are great views from its courtyard out over the entire Bay Area, and a small museum explains the tenets of the faith; expect to be greeted and offered a free personalized tour of the museum by one of the faithful upon entering.

Chabot Space & Science Center

10,000 Skyline Blvd • Wed–Sun 10am–5pm • $18 • ☎ 510 336 7300, ⓦ chabotspace.org • AC Transit bus #339 from the Fruitvale BART station

Several miles up in the hills behind the Mormon temple is the gigantic **Chabot Space & Science Center**, a state-of-the-art museum with permanent interactive displays, temporary exhibitions, working telescopes and a fine **planetarium** – daytime shows are included in the admission but special evening events cost extra, as do evening telescope viewings, which are weather permitting.

Oakland Zoo

Summer Mon–Fri 10am–4pm, Sat & Sun 10am–5.30pm; winter daily 10am–4pm • $17.75; parking $9 • ☎ 510 632 9525, ⓦ oaklandzoo.org • AC Transit bus #46 from the Coliseum BART station

Out past the airport in the suburb of San Leandro, the **Oakland Zoo** is home to over three hundred species of animals, comfortably nestled in the rolling hills of 525-acre Knowland Park. Aside from the creatures on show, there are various rides to enjoy, and you can check the public feeding times online.

Mission San Jose de Guadalupe

Daily 10am–5pm • Donation

The only other place of interest southeast of Oakland is in **Fremont**, at the end of the BART line, where the peaceful and leafy **Mission San Jose de Guadalupe**, which was completely rebuilt some years ago, stands on Mission Boulevard south of the I-680 freeway.

North Oakland

The high-priced hills of **North Oakland**, which lost three thousand homes and 26 people in a horrific fire in 1991, are still lush and green, though the thick foliage that made the area so attractive has never been allowed to grow back fully in order to prevent more fires. These bay-view homes, some of the area's most valuable real estate, look out across some of its poorest – the neglected flatlands below, which in the 1960s were the proving grounds of Black Panthers Bobby Seale and Huey Newton.

Broadway is the dividing line between the two halves of North Oakland, and also gives access (via the handy AC Transit #51A bus) to most sights and activities. East of Broadway, **Piedmont Avenue**, one of Oakland's most neighbourly streets, is lined by a number of small bookstores and cafés.

Mountain View Cemetery

At the north end of Piedmont Avenue, the **Mountain View Cemetery** was laid out in 1863 by Frederick Law Olmsted (designer of New York's Central Park) and holds the elaborate dynastic tombs of San Francisco's most powerful families – the Crockers, the Bechtels and the Ghirardellis.

Chapel of the Chimes

4499 Piedmont Ave • Daily 9am–5pm • Free • ☎ 510 768 8462, ⓦ oakland.chapelofthechimes.com

Just outside Mount View Cemetery, the columbarium, known as the **Chapel of the Chimes**, was designed by Julia Morgan of Hearst Castle fame during her decade-long involvement with the chapel, beginning in 1921. The structure is remarkable for its seemingly endless series of urn-filled rooms, grouped together around skylit courtyards, bubbling fountains and intimate sanctuaries – all connected by ornate staircases of every conceivable length. Morgan wanted the space to sing of life, not death, and she's succeeded – there's no better place in Oakland to wander about in peace, or even plop down with a book. Try to visit during one of the regular concerts held here for a completely unique – and distinctly Californian – experience.

Lake Temescal and Robert Sibley Regional Preserve

From just north of the junction of Broadway and College Avenue, Broadway Terrace climbs up along the edge of the fire area to small **Lake Temescal**, where you can swim in summer, then continues on up to the forested ridge at the **Robert Sibley Regional Preserve**. This includes the 1761ft volcanic cone of Round Top Peak and offers panoramas of the entire Bay Area. The peak has been dubbed the "Volcanic Witch Project" by the local media due to the five mysterious mazes, carved into the dirt and lined with stones, located in the canyons around the crater. Nobody knows where they came from, but navigating the designs leads to their centre, where visitors add to the pile of diverse offerings. Skyline Boulevard runs through the park, connecting to Lake Chabot twelve miles south and Grizzly Peak Boulevard, which winds five miles north through the Berkeley Hills to Tilden Park.

Rockridge

The majority of the Broadway traffic, including the AC Transit #51A bus, cuts off onto College Avenue through Oakland's most upscale shopping district, **Rockridge**, whose upper reaches merge into Berkeley. Spreading for half a mile on either side of the Rockridge BART station, the quirky stores and restaurants here, despite their undeniable yuppie overtones, surpass Piedmont's in variety and volume.

ARRIVAL AND DEPARTURE   OAKLAND

By plane Oakland International Airport (☎ 510 577 4015, automated flight info ☎ 800 992 7433, ⓦ oaklandairport .com) is served by most major domestic airlines, but is less crowded than its San Francisco counterpart and just as easy to access the whole Bay Area from. The AirBART shuttle bus (every 15min; $3; ☎ 510 569 8310) runs to the Coliseum BART station, from where you can hop on a train to Berkeley, Oakland or San Francisco. Numerous door-to-door shuttle buses run from the airport to East Bay stops and into the city, such as A1 American (☎ 877 378 3596 or 510 300 7979, ⓦ a1americanshuttle.com) – expect to pay around $20 to Downtown Oakland, $35–40 to San Francisco. Taxis charge $30–35 into Oakland and around $65 (plus tip) into Downtown San Francisco.

By bus The Greyhound station is in an insalubrious part of

northern Oakland, alongside the I-980 freeway at 2103 San Pablo Ave (☎ 510 832 4730). Local bus services AC Transit operate to and from San Francisco and Berkeley (see p.487). Destinations include: Bakersfield (2 daily; 5hr 30min–7hr 35min); Eureka (2 daily; 6hr 30min); Fresno (3 daily; 3hr 20min–5hr); Los Angeles (10 daily; 7hr 5min–11hr 55min); Reno (5 daily; 4hr 40min–6hr 5min); Sacramento (9 daily; 1hr 30min–2hr 10min); San Jose (8 daily; 1hr–1hr 35min); Santa Barbara (3 daily; 8hr 10min–8hr 50min); Santa Cruz (3 daily; 2hr 20min); Truckee (5 daily; 4hr 50min–7hr).

By train Amtrak trains terminate at 2nd St near Jack London Square, where a free Thruway shuttle bus heads across the Bay Bridge to the Transbay Terminal. A better option for heading into San Francisco, though, is to get off at Richmond and change onto the nearby BART trains.

Some of the trains below depart from nearby Emeryville, connected to Oakland by Thruway shuttle bus; other routes are partly served by bus.

Destinations include: Bakersfield (5 daily; 6hr–6hr 15min); Fresno (5 daily; 4hr–4hr 5min); Los Angeles (10 daily; 8hr 40min–12hr 10min); Reno (5 daily; 5hr 30min–6hr 50min); Sacramento (13–16 daily; 1hr 50min–2hr 5min); San Jose (7 daily; 1hr 15min–1hr 55min); San Luis Obispo (5 daily; 6hr 15min–7hr 30min); Santa Barbara (7 daily; 9hr 5min–10hr 40min); Stockton (7 daily; 1hr 40min–1hr 50min); Truckee (5 daily; 4hr 50min–7hr).

By subway Oakland is linked to San Francisco and other points in the East Bay via the BART subway (☎ 510 465 2278, ⓦ bart.gov). The best stops for Downtown are 12th St and 19th St.

By ferry The most enjoyable way to arrive in the East Bay is aboard an Alameda–Oakland ferry (every 35min–1hr 45min; $6.60 one-way; ☎ 510 522 3300, ⓦ sanfranciscobayferry .com), which sails from San Francisco's Ferry Building and Pier 41 to Oakland's Jack London Square.

INFORMATION

Visit Oakland The office is at 481 Water St, Jack London Square (Mon–Fri 9am–5pm, Sat & Sun 10am–4pm; ☎ 510 500 9235, ⓦ visitoakland.org) and there's a good downloadable brochure available on their website too.

East Bay Regional Parks The district office at 2950 Peralta Oaks Court, Oakland (☎ 510 562 7275, ⓦ ebparks .org) has plenty of info on the huge network of parks.

Listings The widely available *East Bay Express* (issued every Wed; free; ⓦ eastbayexpress.com) has the most comprehensive listings of what's on in the vibrant East Bay music and arts scene and the daily *East Bay Times* (75¢; ⓦ eastbaytimes.com) is also worth a look for its coverage of local politics and sporting events.

ACTIVITIES AND TOURS

Bay Area Bikes 2400 Broadway (☎ 510 823 2555, ⓦ bayareabikes.com). Standard bikes to rent for $35/day or $140/week, more for a sports or mountain model.

Ice Skating You can skate at Oakland Ice Center, 519 18th St (times vary; $8.25–10.50 plus $4.50 skate rental; ☎ 510 268 9000, ⓦ oaklandice.com). Lessons available.

Walking tours The City of Oakland sponsors free "discovery tours" (May–Oct Wed & Sat 10am; ☎ 510 238 3234) of various neighbourhoods.

Watersports At Sailboat House on Lake Merritt you can rent canoes, rowing boats, kayaks, pedal boats, sailboats and catamarans ($12–24/hr, $20–30 deposit; March–June, Sept & Oct Mon–Fri 11am–5pm, Sat & Sun 10.30am–5pm; July & Aug Mon–Fri 10am–6pm, Sat & Sun 10.30am–6pm; ☎ 510 238 2196, ⓦ sailoakland.com). You can also be serenaded on the overpriced but romantic Gondola Servizio (from $60/30min; ☎ 510 663 6603, ⓦ gondolaservizio.com). On the waterfront by Jack London Square you can rent canoes and kayaks at California Canoe & Kayak (☎ 510 893 7833, ⓦ calkayak.com) from $75/day.

ACCOMMODATION

Oaklands's **motels** and **hotels** are slightly better value than their San Francisco equivalents, thus worth considering as a base. The occasional **campground** is to be found in the outer suburbs and beyond.

Anthony Chabot Family Campground 9999 Redwood Rd, Castro Valley, approx 10 miles southeast of Oakland ☎ 888 327 2757 or ☎ 510 544 3196, ⓦ ebparks.org. Over 60 tent sites and a dozen RV spots with hookups. Clean facilities with hot showers and lots of good hiking nearby. Reservations wise in summer. Pitches $25, hookup $35

Jack London Inn 444 Embarcadero West, Jack London Square ☎ 800 549 8780, ⓦ jacklondoninnoakland.com. Kitschy but great-value 1950s-style motor lodge next to Jack London Square. The rooms are fully modernized, plus there's a decent restaurant and seasonal outdoor pool. $90

Waterfront Hotel 10 Washington St, Jack London Square ☎ 510 836 3800, ⓦ jdvhotels.com. Plush, modern hotel with brightly decorated rooms, moored on the best stretch of the Oakland waterfront. Outdoor pool, plus complimentary wine and cheese hour. $149

EATING

Oakland is best for plain **American food** such as barbecued ribs, grilled steaks or deli sandwiches, for which it's unbeatable. There are also some excellent Asian restaurants, mostly around Chinatown, while trendy Rockridge offers some finer dining.

CAFÉS, DELIS AND DINERS

Barney's 4162 Piedmont Ave, North Oakland ☎ 510 655 7180, ⓦ barneyshamburgers.com. The Bay Area's most popular burgers – including meatless ones – smothered in dozens of different toppings, all around $10. Check the website for other locations in Rockridge and Berkeley. Mon–Thurs 11am–10pm, Fri & Sat 11am–10.30pm, Sun 11am–9.30pm.

Coffee Mill 3363 Grand Ave, North Oakland ☎ 510 465 4224. A range of great coffee and tasty pastries is served in

7

a spacious room that doubles as an art gallery and often hosts poetry readings. Daily 7am–3pm.

Dreyers 5925 College Ave, Rockridge ☎ 510 594 9466, ⓦ dreyers.com. Oakland's own rich ice cream, which is distributed throughout California, is served at this small, slightly dull Rockridge café. Mon–Sat noon–7pm, Sun noon–6pm.

Fenton's Creamery 4226 Piedmont Ave, North Oakland ☎ 510 658 7000, ⓦ fentonscreamery.com. A brightly lit, 1950s ice-cream parlour, specializing in extravagant sundaes costing nearly $10, more than the filling breakfasts, sandwiches and burgers also on the menu. Mon–Thurs 11am–11pm, Fri & Sat 9am–midnight, Sun 9am–11pm.

Lois the Pie Queen 851 60th St at Adeline, North Oakland ☎ 510 658 5616. Famous around the bay for its southern-style sweet potato and fresh fruit pies, this cosy diner also serves massive breakfasts and Sunday lunches, all for $12 or less. Mon–Fri 8am–2pm, Sat 7am–3pm, Sun 7am–4pm.

Rudy's Can't Fail Café 1805 Telegraph Ave, downtown ☎ 510 251 9400, ⓦ iamrudy.com. Unique Clash-themed diner with a predictably rocking soundtrack and full bar. All-day breakfasts and daily specials like Give'em Enough meatloaf go for $12–15. See website for Emeryville location. Daily 7am–1am.

RESTAURANTS

Chop Bar 247 4th St, Jack London Square ☎ 510 834 2467, ⓦ oaklandchopbar.com. Smart new restaurant in a converted warehouse, whose curved bar also serves fine ales. Main dishes such as pork confit are decent value at around $20. Mon–Thurs 8am–3pm & 5.30–10pm, Fri 8am–3pm & 5.30–11pm, Sat 9am–3pm & 5.30–11pm, Sun 9am–3pm & 5.30–10pm.

Golden Peacock 825 Webster St, downtown ☎ 510 763 0338, ⓦ goldenpeacockrestaurant.com. One of the most popular places in Chinatown, famous for its wonton soups, clay pot and *mu shu* dishes. Even seafood dishes cost under $10. Daily 11am–9pm.

Khana Peena 5316 College Ave, Rockridge ☎ 510 658 2300, ⓦ khanapeenaindianfood.com. Fine Indian restaurant in terms of both decor and quality of cuisine. A wide range of curries and tandoori dishes is available for $12–20. See website for Berkeley location. Daily

11.30am–3.30pm & 5–9.30pm.

La Furia Chalaca 310 Broadway, downtown ☎ 510 451 4206, ⓦ lafuriachalaca.com. Great range of ceviche and seafood in various Peruvian sauces for $21–27, plus meat dishes such as pork stew. Mon, Wed & Thurs 11.30am–3pm & 5–10pm, Tues 5–10pm, Fri & Sat 11.30am–10pm, Sun 11.30am–9pm.

★**Le Cheval** 1007 Clay St, downtown ☎ 510 763 8495, ⓦ lecheval.com. Huge downtown Vietnamese place serving exquisitely spiced dishes like imperial beef sausage, mostly around $15, in comfortable, stylishly decorated surroundings. Mon–Thurs 11am–9pm, Fri & Sat 11am–9.30pm, Sun 4–9pm.

Mua 2442A Webster St, Lake Merritt ☎ 510 238 1100, ⓦ muaoakland.com. A few blocks northwest of the lake itself, this sleek modern Spanish restaurant does a good range of tasty tapas such as crispy polenta and smoked trout salad. $20 per person minimum. Mon–Thurs 5.30–9pm, Fri 11.30am–2.30pm & 5.30pm–midnight, Sat 5.30pm–midnight, Sun 5–10pm.

Oliveto 5655 College Ave, Rockridge ☎ 510 547 5356, ⓦ oliveto.com. Gourmet Italian main courses for $26–34 are served in the main dining room but there's a less pricey basement café with a more basic menu. Mon–Fri 11.30am–2pm; Mon–Thurs & Sun 5.30–9pm, Fri & Sat 5.30–9.30pm.

Plum 2214 Broadway, downtown ☎ 510 444 7586, ⓦ plumoakland.com. This highly rated place with a lively bar serves up a range of delights ranging from burgers to braised beef for $12–25. Also tasting menus from $18. Mon–Thurs 3.30pm–midnight, Fri 3.30pm–2am, Sat 5pm–2am.

★**Wood Tavern** 6317 College Ave, North Oakland ☎ 510 654 6607, ⓦ woodtavern.net. Slick American restaurant whose menu includes charcuterie and cheese boards, starters such as risotto with wild lobster mushrooms, and mains like seafood stew for $27–33. Mon–Thurs 11.30am–10pm, Fri & Sat 11.30am–10.30pm, Sun 11.30am–9pm.

Zachary's 5801 College Ave, Rockridge ☎ 510 655 6385, ⓦ zacharys.com. Zealously defended as the best pizza in the Bay Area, *Zachary's* is also one of the only places offering the rich, deep-dish Chicago-style pies from $16 up. See website for Berkeley location. Mon–Thurs & Sun 11am–10pm, Fri & Sat 11am–10.30pm.

DRINKING AND NIGHTLIFE

Oakland's bars are grittier versions of what you'd find in San Francisco; they're mostly blue-collar, convivial and invariably cheaper. **Nightlife** is where Oakland really comes into its own. There are numerous **live music** venues, covering a range of musical tastes and styles – from small, unpretentious jazz clubs to buzzing R&B venues.

BARS

The Alley 3325 Grand Ave, North Oakland ☎ 510 444 8505. Ramshackle, black-timber piano bar, decorated with

business cards and with live old-time blues musicians on the keyboards. Mon & Sun 6pm–midnight, Tues–Sat 4pm–2am.

Ben'n'Nick's 5612 College Ave, Rockridge ☎ 510 933 0327, ⓦ benandnicks.com. Lively and welcoming bar, popular with the student crowd, playing good recorded rock music; tasty food, too, if you're hungry. Daily 11.30am–2am.

Cato's Alehouse 3891 Piedmont Ave, North Oakland ☎ 510 655 3349, ⓦ catosalehouse.com. Local alehouse with a good beer selection, as well as pizza and sandwiches. Live music several times a week. Mon–Thurs & Sat 11.30am–midnight, Fri 11.30am–1am, Sun 11.30am–10pm.

Heinold's First and Last Chance Saloon 56 Jack London Square ☎ 510 839 6761, ⓦ heinolds.com. Authentic waterfront bar that's hardly changed since Jack London was a regular. It still has the slanted floor caused by the 1906 earthquake. Mon–Thurs & Sun noon–11pm, Fri & Sat noon–1am.

★ **Pacific Coast Brewing Co** 906 Washington St, downtown ☎ 510 836 2739, ⓦ pacificcoastbrewing.com. The only real microbrewery downtown, featuring a good selection of ales, which you can wash down with ample portions of pub grub: note that the kitchen closes earlier than the bar. Mon 11.30am–11.30pm, Tues–Thurs 11.30am–midnight, Fri & Sat 11.30am–1am, Sun 11am–11pm.

★ **The Trappist** 460 8th St, downtown ☎ 510 238 8900, ⓦ thetrappist.com. As the name suggests, this place specializes in Belgian and other European beers but also serves local microbrews, along with tasty bar meals. Note there are two bars with separate beer lists. Mon–Thurs & Sun noon–12.30am, Fri & Sat noon–1.30am.

The White Horse Inn 6551 Telegraph Ave, at 66th St, North Oakland ☎ 510 652 3820, ⓦ whitehorsebar.com. Oakland's oldest gay bar – a small, friendly place with mixed dancing for men and women, plus comedy nights. Wed–Sun 1pm–2am.

LIVE MUSIC VENUES

Fox Oakland 1807 Telegraph Ave, downtown ☎ 510 302 2277, ⓦ thefoxoakland.com. Recently renovated, this classic old theatre is now a great venue for established and up-and-coming live acts, mostly rock.

Yoshi's World Class Jazz House 510 Embarcadero West, Jack London Square ☎ 510 238 9200, ⓦ yoshis.com. The West Coast's premier jazz club near Jack London Square attracts an impressive roster of performers nightly. The place is almost always full. Most shows $15–55.

7

ENTERTAINMENT

Tickets for most venues are available at their box office or online through the usual agents. Check the free *East Bay Express* (ⓦ eastbayexpress.com) or the *SF Weekly* (ⓦ sfweekly.com) for details of what's on.

PERFORMING ARTS

Center for Contemporary Music Mills College, 5000 MacArthur Blvd, North Oakland ☎ 510 430 2191, ⓦ mills.edu. This college performing space is one of the prime centres in the world for experimental music.

Oracle Arena & Coliseum 7000 Coliseum Way, near Coliseum BART ☎ 510 639 7700, ⓦ coliseum.com. Mostly stadium shows, inside the 18,000-seat arena or outdoors in the adjacent 55,000-seat Coliseum. Used to be one of the Grateful Dead's favourite venues.

Paramount Theatre 2025 Broadway, downtown ☎ 510 465 6400, ⓦ paramounttheatre.com. Beautifully restored Art Deco masterpiece, hosting classical concerts, big-name crooners, ballets, operas and a growing number of rap and rock shows. Ticket office Tues–Sat noon–5pm; tickets $20–90. Some nights they play old Hollywood classics for $5.

FILM

Grand Lake Theater 3200 Grand Ave ☎ 510 452 3556, ⓦ renaissancerialto.com. The *grande dame* of East Bay picture palaces, just northeast of Lake Merritt, showing the best of the current major releases, with special emphasis on politically alternative works.

Berkeley

This Berkeley was like no somnolent Siwash out of her own past at all, but more akin to those Far Eastern or Latin American universities you read about, those autonomous culture media where the most beloved of folklores may be brought into doubt, cataclysmic of dissents voiced, suicidal of commitments chosen – the sort that bring governments down.   Thomas Pynchon, *The Crying of Lot 49*

More than any other American city, **BERKELEY** conjures up an image of 1960s student dissent. When college campuses across the nation were **protesting** the Vietnam War, it was the students of the University of California, Berkeley, who led the charge – gaining a name as the vanguard of what was increasingly seen as a challenge to the authority of the state. Full-scale battles were fought almost daily here at one point, on the campus and its surrounding streets, and there were times when Berkeley looked almost on the brink of revolution itself: students (and others) throwing stones and gas bombs were met with tear-gas volleys and truncheons by National Guard troops under the nominal command of then-Governor Ronald Reagan.

Such action was inspired by the mood of the time and continued well into the 1970s, although during the conservative 1980s and Clinton-dominated 1990s, Berkeley politics became far less confrontational. Yet despite an influx of more conformist students, a surge in the number of exclusive restaurants and the dismantling of the city's rent-control programme, the progressive legacy has remained in Berkeley's independent **bookshops** (see box, p.500) and at sporadic political demonstrations.

Even though such an obvious target for bile as George W. Bush is long gone, Berkeley remains a bastion of the **antiwar movement** and streets like Telegraph Avenue are festooned with posters, stickers, badges and T-shirts questioning the occupation of Iraq and the war in Afghanistan.

The **University of California**, right in the centre of town, completely dominates Berkeley and makes a logical starting point for a visit. Its many grand buildings and over 30,000 students give off a definite energy, which spills down the raucous stretch of Telegraph Avenue that runs south from the campus and holds most of the student hangouts. Older students, and a good percentage of the faculty, congregate in the **Northside** area, the part of **North Berkeley** just above the campus, popping down from their hillside homes to partake of goodies from the **Gourmet Ghetto**, a stretch of Shattuck Avenue crammed with restaurants, delis and bakeries. Of quite distinct character are the flatlands that spread through **West Berkeley** down to the bay, a poorer but increasingly gentrified district that mixes old Victorian houses with builders' yards and light-industrial premises. Along the bay itself is the **Berkeley Marina**, where you can rent sailboards and sailboats or just watch the sun set behind the Golden Gate.

The University of California

Student tours: Mon–Sat 10am, Sun 1pm, from the Campanile (see p.500) at weekends and during holidays, from the University Visitor Center (see p.503) during weekdays in term • 1hr 30min • ☎ 510 642 5215, ⓦ berkeley.edu

Caught up in the frantic crush of students who pack the **UNIVERSITY OF CALIFORNIA** campus during the semesters, it's nearly impossible to imagine the bucolic learning environment envisaged by the school's high-minded founders. When the Reverend Henry Durant and other East Coast academics decided to set up shop here in the 1860s, these rolling foothills were still largely given over to dairy herds and wheatfields. In 1866, while surveying the land, a trustee recited "Westward the course of the empire takes its way", from a poem by George Berkeley. Moved by the moment, all assembled agreed to name their school after the bishop. Construction work on the two campus buildings – imaginatively named North Hall and South Hall – was still going on when the first 200 students, including 22 women, moved here from Oakland in 1873. Since then an increasing number of buildings have been squeezed into the half-mile-square main campus, and the state-funded university has become one of America's most prestigious, with so many Nobel laureates on the faculty that it's said you have to win one just to get a parking permit. University physicists built the first cyclotron, and plutonium was discovered here in 1941, along with thirteen other synthetic elements (including berkelium and californium). As such, sketches for the first atomic bomb began here.

Nuclear weaponry and overcrowding aside, the beautifully landscaped campus, stepping down from the eucalyptus-covered Berkeley Hills towards the Golden Gate, is eminently strollable. With maps posted everywhere, you'd have to try hard to get lost – though enthusiastic students will show you around on a free **tour**, explaining the campus's history, architecture and flavour. Be sure to take one if you want a fuller picture of Berkeley beyond looking at façades and the faces of passing students.

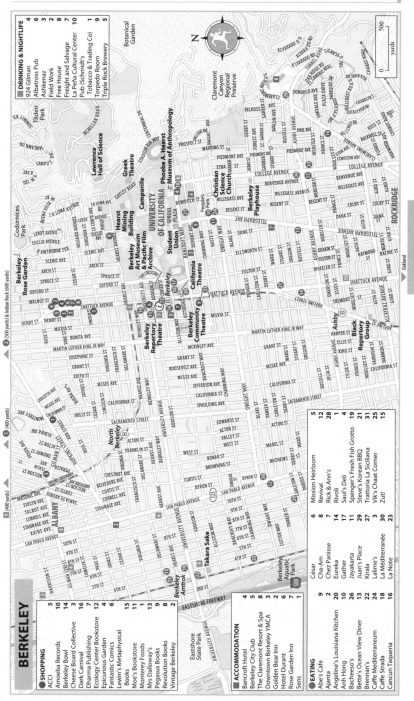

BERKELEY

● SHOPPING
ACCI	5
Amoeba Records	10
Berkeley Bowl	14
Cheese Board Collective	3
Dark Carnival	16
Dharma Publishing	7
Ecology Center Bookstore	12
Epicurious Garden	4
Fantastic Comics	6
Lewin's Metaphysical Books	15
Moe's Bookstore	11
Monterey Foods	1
Mrs Dalloway's	13
Pegasus Books	9
Revolution Books	8
Vintage Berkeley	2

■ ACCOMMODATION
Bancroft Hotel	4
Berkeley City Club	5
The Claremont Resort & Spa	8
Downtown Berkeley YMCA	3
Golden Bear Inn	2
Hotel Durant	6
Rose Garden Inn	7
Sens	1

● EATING
Abe's Cafe	9
Ajanta	10
Angeline's Louisiana Kitchen	20
Anh Hong	10
Bacheeso's	26
Bette's Ocean View Diner	13
Brennan's	22
Caffe Mediterraneum	24
Caffe Strada	18
Cancun Taqueria	16
César	9
Cha-Am	2
Chez Panisse	7
Eureka	14
Gather	17
Jayakarta	11
Juan's Place	29
Kirala	27
Lalime's	3
La Méditerranée	24
La Note	23
Mission Heirloom	6
Revival	8
Rick & Ann's	28
Rivoli	1
Saul's Deli	4
Spenger's Fresh Fish Grotto	19
Steve's Korean BBQ	21
Trattoria La Siciliana	31
Vik's Chaat Corner	25
Zut!	15

■ DRINKING & NIGHTLIFE
924 Gilman	4
Albatross Pub	6
Ashkenaz	3
Field Work	2
Free House	8
Freight and Salvage	7
La Peña Cultural Center	10
Pub (Schmidt's)	1
Tobacco & Trading Co)	9
Torpedo Room	9
Triple Rock Brewery	5

BERKELEY'S BOOKSHOPS

Unsurprisingly for a university town, Berkeley's **bookshops** are as exhaustive as they are exhausting. Perfect for browsing and taking your time, you won't be made to feel guilty or obliged to buy a book you've been poring over for ages. The Visit Berkeley tourist office (see p.503) has a useful list of over fifty shops, of which the following are a representative selection:

Dark Carnival 3086 Claremont Ave ☎510 654 7323, ⓦdarkcarnival.com. The place to come for titles on the cutting edge of imaginative fiction. Mon–Sat 10.30am–7pm, Sun noon–6pm.

Dharma Publishing Bookstore 2210 Harold Way ☎510 809 1540, ⓦdharmapublishingbookstore.com. Lots of new books on Buddhism, meditation and healing, as well as Eastern gifts and cards. Daily 11am–7pm.

Ecology Center Bookstore 2530 San Pablo Ave ☎510 548 3402, ⓦecologycenter.org. A wealth of books on ecology, environment and practical subjects like gardening. Tues–Sun 11am–6pm.

Fantastic Comics 2026 Shattuck Ave ☎510 848 2988, ⓦcomicrelief.net. Huge selection of comics and graphic novels, plus self-published mini-comics by locals. Mon, Tues & Sun 11am–7pm, Wed–Sat 10am–10pm.

Lewin's Metaphysical Books 2644 Ashby Ave ☎510 843 4491. The place to come for the best selection on spirituality, religion, astrology and other arcane subjects. Mon–Sat 11am–6pm.

Moe's Bookstore 2476 Telegraph Ave ☎510 849 2087, ⓦmoesbooks.com. An enormous selection of new and used books on four floors, with esoteric surprises in every field of study; perfect for academics, book collectors and browsers. Daily 10am–10pm.

Mrs Dalloway's 2904 College Ave ☎510 704 8222, ⓦmrsdalloways.com. Interesting shop specializing in literature and gardening. Hosts regular readings and slide shows. Mon & Tues 10am–7pm, Wed 10am–Sat 10am–9pm, Sun 11am–6pm.

Pegasus Books 2349 Shattuck Ave ☎510 649 1320, ⓦpegasusbookstore.com. Vast collection of used and new books on a wide range of subjects. Check website for second branch in North Berkeley. Mon–Thurs 9am–10pm, Fri & Sat 9am–10.45pm, Sun 10am–10pm.

Revolution Books 2444 Durant Ave ☎510 848 1196, ⓦrevolutionbooks.org. Wide range of books on political themes with, as you might expect, an emphasis on leftist and anarchist thought. Mon–Fri 10am–7pm, Sat 11am–6pm, Sun 1–6pm.

Sproul Plaza

A number of footpaths climb the hill from the Berkeley BART station on Shattuck Avenue, but the best way to get a feel for the place is to follow Strawberry Creek from the top of Center Street across the southeast corner of the campus, emerging from the groves of redwood and eucalyptus trees at **Sproul Plaza**. The largest public space on campus, it's often enlivened by street musicians playing for change on the steps of the **Student Union** building. Sather Gate, which bridges Strawberry Creek at the north end of Sproul Plaza, marks the entrance to the older part of the campus.

Campanile

Mon–Fri 10am–3.45pm, Sat 10am–4.45pm, Sun 10am–1.30pm & 3–4.45pm • $3

Up the hill, past the imposing façade of Wheeler Hall, the 1914 landmark **Campanile**, officially Sather Tower, is modelled after the one in the Piazza San Marco in Venice; take an elevator to the top for a great view of the campus and the entire Bay Area. At the foot of the tower stands the red-brick **South Hall**, the sole survivor of the original pair of buildings.

Phoebe Hearst Museum of Anthropology

Wed–Sat 10am–4.30pm, Sun noon–4pm • Free • ☎510 642 3682, ⓦhearstmuseum.berkeley.edu

In the southeast corner of the UC Berkeley campus, the **Phoebe Hearst Museum of Anthropology** in the extensively renovated Kroeber Hall holds a variety of changing exhibits as well as an intriguing display of artefacts made by Ishi, the last surviving Yahi Native American who was found near Mount Lassen in Northern California in 1911.

Anthropologist (and father of writer Ursula Le Guin) Alfred Kroeber brought Ishi to the museum, then located on the UC San Francisco campus, where he lived under the scrutiny of scientists and journalists – in effect, in a state of captivity – until his death from tuberculosis a few years later.

Lawrence Hall of Science

Daily 10am–5pm • $12 • ☎ 510 642 5132, ⓦ lawrencehallofscience.org • Accessible Mon–Fri via the free UC Berkeley Shuttle bus from the campus or the Berkeley BART station

Towards the northeastern crest of the hilly campus, with great views out over the bay, a full-sized fibreglass sculpture of a whale stretches out in front of the space-age **Lawrence Hall of Science**. This excellent museum and learning centre features earthquake simulations, model dinosaurs and a planetarium, plus hands-on exhibits for kids in the Wizard's Lab.

Botanical Garden

200 Centennial Drive • Daily 9am–5pm, closed first Tues of month • $10, free on first Wed of month • ☎ 510 643 2755, ⓦ botanicalgarden .berkeley.edu • Accessible Mon–Fri via the free UC Berkeley Shuttle bus from the campus or the Berkeley BART station

In the furthest southeastern reaches of the campus hills, above the 80,000-seat Memorial Stadium, the lushly landscaped **Botanical Garden** defeats on-campus claustrophobia with its thirty acres of plants and cacti. There is a huge diversity of species on display, with tropical plants in carefully heated greenhouses.

Berkeley Art Museum and Pacific Film Archive (BAMPFA)

2155 Center St • Wed, Thurs & Sun 11am–7pm, Fri & Sat 11am–9pm • $12, free on first Thurs of month • ☎ 510 642 0808, ⓦ bampfa.berkeley.edu

The stunning new home of the **Berkeley Art Museum** opened just to the west of the campus to great fanfare in January 2016. The sleek concrete, steel and glass edifice was adapted from a print works, whose original Art Deco building and sawtooth roof was augmented by a new structure. The museum is renowned for its cutting-edge, changing exhibitions: the various wide-open spaces within host a range of major shows – some on specific themes, others showcasing local and international artists. In the same complex, the **Pacific Film Archive** (see p.506) features nightly showings of classics and obscurities. The two entities are known collectively as BAMPFA.

Telegraph Avenue

Downtown Berkeley – basically two department stores, a few banks, a post office and the City Hall building – lies west of the university campus around the Berkeley BART station on Shattuck Avenue, but the real activity centres on **Telegraph Avenue**, which runs south of the university from Sproul Plaza. This thoroughfare saw some of the worst of the 1960s riots and is still a frenetic bustle, especially the four short blocks closest to the university, which are packed with lively cafés and secondhand bookshops. Street vendors selling jewellery and subversive souvenirs are not as ubiquitous as they used to be but down-and-outs still hustle for spare change and spout psychotic poetry. Telegraph Avenue is also home to the original branch of legendary Amoeba Records (see p.507).

People's Park

Half a block up from Telegraph Ave between Haste St and Dwight Way

People's Park, now a slightly seedy and partly overgrown plot of land, was another battleground in the late 1960s, when organized and spirited resistance to the university's plans to develop the site into dormitories brought out the troops, who shot dead an onlooker by mistake. To many, the fact that the park is still a community-controlled open space (and outdoor flophouse for Berkeley's legions of pushers and homeless) symbolizes a small victory in the battle against the Establishment, though it's not a pleasant or particularly safe place to hang about, at least after dark. Though its message is rather undermined by its insalubrious surroundings, a mural along Haste Street recalls some of the reasons why the battles were fought, in the words of student leader Mario Savio: "There's a time when the operation of the machine becomes so odious, makes you so sick at heart, that you can't take part, you can't even tacitly take part. And you've got to put your bodies upon the gears and upon the wheels, upon the levers, upon all the apparatus, and you've got to make it stop."

7

Christian Science Church

Directly across Bowditch St from People's Park • Open Sun for worship; free tours Mon–Sat at 11am

Bernard Maybeck's **Christian Science Church** is one of the finest buildings in the Bay Area. Built in 1910, it's an eclectic and thoroughly modern structure, laid out in a simple Greek-cross floor plan and spanned by a massive redwood truss with carved Gothic tracery and Byzantine painted decoration. The interior is only open limited hours, but the outside is worth lingering over, its cascade of gently pitched roofs and porticoes carrying the eye from one handcrafted detail to another.

North Berkeley

North Berkeley is a subdued neighbourhood of professors and postgraduate students, spreading from the flat leafy blocks around the BART lines to the steep, twisting streets that climb up the lushly overgrown hills north of the campus. At the foot of the hills, some of the Bay Area's finest **restaurants** and **delis** – most famously *Chez Panisse* (see p.504) – have sprung up along **Shattuck Avenue** to form the so-called Gourmet Ghetto. There are also a few **galleries**, most notably ACCI (see p.507). Over a mile further northwest, where Berkeley meets Albany, **Solano Avenue** is another trendy shopping and dining area, with a dazzling array of outlets, such as Tibetan craft shops, draped along its curved length.

Euclid Avenue, off Hearst and next to the north gate of the university, is a sort of antidote to Telegraph Avenue, a quiet grove of coffee joints and pizza parlours frequented by grad students and the focal point of the largely academic enclave known as **Northside**. Above Euclid (if you want to avoid the fairly steep walk, take the #65 bus) there are few more pleasant places for a picnic than the **Berkeley Rose Garden** at Euclid Avenue and Bayview Place (daily dawn–dusk; free), a terraced amphitheatre filled with some three thousand varieties of rose and looking out across the bay to San Francisco. Built as part of a WPA job-creation scheme during the Depression, a wooden pergola rings the top, with steps down to a small spring.

Between the north end of Shattuck and the east end of Solano, the grey basalt knob of **Indian Rock** stands out from the foothills, challenging rock climbers who hone their skills on its forty-foot vertical faces. Carved into similarly hard volcanic stone across the street are the mortar holes used by the Ohlone to grind acorns into flour. Those who just want to appreciate the extraordinary view from the rock can take the steps around its back.

Tilden Park

Tucked among the ridges of the Berkeley Hills, a number of enticing parks give great views over the flatlands and the bay. The largest and highest of them, **Tilden Park**, spreads along the crest of the hills, encompassing over two thousand acres of near wilderness. Kids can enjoy a ride on the carved wooden horses of the carousel or through the redwood trees on the 1950s mini steam train. In the warmer months, don't miss a swim in soothing **Lake Anza** (lifeguard on duty May–Sept daily, some weekends in April & Oct 11am–6pm; $3.50).

West Berkeley

From Downtown Berkeley and the UC campus, **University Avenue** runs in an almost imperceptible gradient downhill towards the bay, and is lined by increasingly shabby frontages of motels and massage parlours. The liveliest part of this **West Berkeley** area is around the intersection of University and San Pablo, where a community of recent immigrants from India and Pakistan have set up stores and restaurants that serve some of the best of the Bay Area's curries.

The area between San Pablo Avenue and the bay is the oldest part of Berkeley and a handful of hundred-year-old houses and churches – such as the two white-spired Gothic Revival structures on Hearst Avenue – survive from the time when this district was a separate city, known as Ocean View. The neighbourhood also holds remnants of Berkeley's industrial past and many of the old warehouses and factory premises have been converted into living and working spaces for artists, craftspeople and software companies. The newly polished and yuppified stretch of **Fourth Street** between Gilman and University features upscale furniture outlets and quaint gourmet delis, as well as some outstanding restaurants (see p.505). Just to the south of here at 708 Addison St, you can take a tour of the huge Takara Sake USA Inc. brewery, whose tasting room and museum grant the opportunity to sample the company's products in elegant Japanese surroundings and learn about the process of sake-making (daily noon–6pm; $5–10; ☎510 540 8250, ⓦtakarasake.com).

ARRIVAL AND GETTING AROUND
BERKELEY

By subway Berkeley is linked to San Francisco and other points in the East Bay via the BART subway (☎510 465 2278, ⓦbart.com).
By bus Local bus services AC Transit operate to and from San Francisco and Oakland (see p.487).

Lulu's Cyclery 3089 Telegraph Ave (☎510 841 1849, ⓦluluscyclery.com). Rents different models, including road and mountain bikes, for around $150/week.

INFORMATION

University of California Visitor Center 101 Sproul Hall (Mon–Fri 8.30am–4.30pm; ☎510 642 5215, ⓦvisitors.berkeley.edu). Visitor Services, on Sproul Plaza, has plenty of information about the Berkeley campus,

hands out free self-guided tour brochures and conducts 1hr 30min tours (see p.498).
Visit Berkeley 2030 Addison St (Mon–Fri 9am–1pm & 2–5pm; ☎510 549 7040, ⓦvisitberkeley.com).

ACCOMMODATION

Berkeley offers a convenient but quieter base for the whole Bay Area. **Bed and breakfasts** often represent the best deals, tucked away as they are in the leafy hills. Check with the Berkeley & Oakland Bed and Breakfast Network (☎510 547 6380, ⓦbbonline.com/ca/berkeley-oakland) for a complete list. **Dorm beds** are available in summertime, such as the summer-only student rooms in Stern Hall, through the Summer Visitor Housing agency at 2601 Warring St, Berkeley (☎510 642 4444, ⓦconferenceservices.berkeley.edu).

★**Bancroft Hotel** 2680 Bancroft Way, downtown ☎510 549 1000 or ☎800 549 1002, ⓦbancrofthotel.com. Small and extremely welcoming boutique hotel with 22 rooms with queen beds, a good location right by the UC campus and fine service. Bay views from the upper rooms and roof terrace. Breakfast included. $159
Berkeley City Club 2315 Durant Ave, downtown ☎510 848 7800, ⓦberkeleycityclub.com. Two blocks from the UC campus, this engaging B&B was designed by Hearst Castle architect Julia Morgan, with an indoor swimming pool, exercise room and quality restaurant. Each of the spacious rooms has a private bathroom. $199
★**The Claremont Resort & Spa** 41 Tunnel Rd, downtown ☎510 843 3000, ⓦclaremontresort.com. The lap of luxury among Berkeley hotels in a 1915 building. Even the basic rooms are a treat, but you'll pay for the privilege. Spa sessions start around $100/hr for facials or massages. $237
Downtown Berkeley YMCA 2001 Allston Way, downtown ☎ 510 848 9622, ⓦbaymca.org. Downtown Berkeley's best bargain accommodation, especially for

singles, just one block from the Berkeley BART stop. Rates include use of gym and pool. $90
Golden Bear Inn 1620 San Pablo Ave, West Berkeley ☎510 525 6770, ⓦgoldenbearinn.com. The most pleasant of the many motels in the "flatlands" towards the bay, whose decent rooms have smart furnishings. $90
Hotel Durant 2600 Durant Ave, downtown ☎510 845 8981, ⓦhoteldurantberkeley.com. Just a block from campus, this large boutique hotel has saucy touches such as bong lamps and nude art in its very well-appointed rooms. Good bar-restaurant on the ground floor. $169
Rose Garden Inn 2740 Telegraph Ave, downtown ☎800 992 9005, ⓦrosegardeninn.com. Forty stylishly decorated rooms of varying sizes but all with fireplaces, in a mock-Tudor mansion near the university. Hot buffet breakfast included. $138
Sens 1538 Shattuck Ave, North Berkeley ☎510 548 9930, ⓦsenshotelberkeley.com. There's a touch of European class about this small hotel with eighteen simple but pleasant rooms in the heart of Berkeley's Gourmet Ghetto. The new ownership have added a good bistro. $105

EATING

Home to **California cuisine** and some of the best restaurants in the state, Berkeley is an upmarket diner's paradise. But it's also a college town, so you can eat cheaply and well, especially around the campus and along Telegraph Ave. Concentrated most densely around the UC Berkeley campus, the town's **cafés** are on a par with the best of San Francisco's North Beach.

RESTAURANTS

DOWNTOWN

Angeline's Louisiana Kitchen 2261 Shattuck Ave ☎510 548 6900, ⓦangelineskitchen.com. Classic New Orleans' dishes such as voodoo shrimp and fried catfish are rustled up for $14–19 in this lively place that also has great sounds. Mon 5.30–9pm, Tues–Thurs & Sun 11.30am–9pm, Fri & Sat 11.30am–10pm.

Anh Hong 2067 University Ave ☎510 981 1789, ⓦanhhong.com. Smart and spacious Vietnamese restaurant, serving gigantic bowls of beef pho and a full range of other favourites. The gut-busting seven courses of beef costs only $19.95. Mon–Sat 11am–2.30pm, daily 5–10.30pm.

Cancun Taqueria 2134 Allston Way ☎510 549 0964, ⓦsabormexicano.com. Popular downtown burrito and taco joint. Self-service but huge portions of tasty food in lively and colourful surroundings, costing $6–14. Mon–Thurs 10.30am–9pm, Fri & Sat 10.30am–10.30pm, Sun noon–9pm.

Eureka 2068 Center St ☎510 809 8282, ⓦeureka restaurantgroup.com. This branch of the trendy California chain serves gourmet burgers for $10–13, as well as tacos and other snacks, in an industrial brick and steel pipe setting. Mon–Thurs 11am–midnight, Fri & Sat 11am–1am, Sun 10am–midnight.

Gather 2200 Oxford St ☎510 809 0400, ⓦgather restaurant.com. Trendy restaurant with menus based on local produce and sustainability, half vegetarian, half top-quality meat and fish. Great lunch deals for $12. Mon–Thurs 11.30am–2pm & 5–9.30pm, Fri 11.30am–2pm & 5–10pm, Sat 10am–2.30pm & 5–10pm, Sun 10am–2.30pm & 5–9.30pm.

Jayakarta 2026 University Ave ☎510 841 0884, ⓦjayakartarestaurant.com. Eat well for $10–15 at this authentic Indonesian joint that serves specialities such as *nasi padang*, a mixture of boiled egg, chicken hearts, pork and stinky beans in chilli. Tues–Sun 11am–9pm.

Kirala 2100 Ward St ☎510 549 3486, ⓦkiralaberkeley .com. Many argue that *Kirala* serves the best sushi in the Bay Area. Moderate pricing, too – but it will cost at least $20 to get your fill. Mon–Fri 11.30am–2pm & 5.30–9.30pm, Sat 5.30–9.30pm, Sun 5–9pm.

La Note 2377 Shattuck Ave ☎510 843 1535, ⓦlanote restaurant.com. Delicious main courses from Provence such as *bouillabaise Marseillaise* (fish stew; $19.95) are complemented by *bagnat* sandwiches and fluffy omelette breakfasts. Mon–Wed 8am–2.30pm, Thurs & Fri 8am–2.30pm & 6–10pm, Sat 8am–3pm & 6–10pm, Sun 8am–3pm.

★Mission Heirloom 2085 Vine St ☎510 900 1307, ⓦmissionheirloom.com. Highly rated multicuisine newcomer, which serves everything from Brazilian breakfast to chicken curry ($14) and roasted pineapple lamb neck ($35). Mon–Thurs & Sun 10am–4pm, Fri 10am–8pm, Sat 9am–8pm.

Revival 2102 Shattuck Ave ☎510 549 9950, ⓦrevivalbarandkitchen.com. This snazzy restaurant serves the likes of *zatar*-braised McCormick ranch goat and roasted Sonoma duck breast in classily understated surroundings. Main courses in the $20–25 range. Tues–Sat 5–10pm, Sun 5–9.30pm; bar till late.

Steve's Korean BBQ Durant Center, 2521 Durant Ave ☎510 848 6166, ⓦsteveskbbq.com. Excellent Korean food (the *kimchee* is superb) that costs no more than $10, not to mention bargain pitchers of beer. Daily 11am–11pm.

NORTH BERKELEY

Ajanta 1888 Solano Ave ☎510 526 4373, ⓦajanta restaurant.com. The chef rotates dishes from different regions of India every month, such as Goa lamb curry or Kashmiri *dhanwala murg* for $15–20. Tasting menus from $26. Daily 11.30am–2.30pm & 5.30–9pm.

César 1515 Shattuck Ave ☎510 883 0222, ⓦcesar berkeley.com. Perpetually crowded tapas bar serving small dishes overflowing with taste. Its combination of quality and a relaxed atmosphere has made this a cultish destination for locals. Can easily add up to $25–30 per person, however. Daily noon–midnight.

Cha-Am 1543 Shattuck Ave, North Berkeley ☎510 848 9664, ⓦchaamberkeley.com. Climb the stairs to this unlikely and always crowded small restaurant. Deliciously spicy Thai food such as *gaeng massaman* curry for $9.50. Mon–Thurs & Sun 11.30am–9.15pm, Fri & Sat 11.30am–9.45pm.

★Chez Panisse 1517 Shattuck Ave ☎510 548 5525, ⓦchezpanisse.com. First and still the best of the California cuisine restaurants, overseen by legendary chef Alice Waters. The main restaurant's *prix fixe* menu costs $75–125 depending on the day of the week. The café upstairs is comparatively inexpensive. Reservations recommended for the café, essential for the main restaurant. Restaurant sittings Mon–Sat 6pm & 8.30pm; café Mon–Thurs 11.30am–2.45pm & 5–10pm, Fri & Sat 11.30am–3pm & 5–11.30pm.

Lalime's 1329 Gilman St ☎510 527 9838, ⓦlalimes .com. A culinary dissertation on irony, as rich leftist Berkeley professors chow down on veal, pâté de foie gras, and other distinctly un-PC fare, in a casual setting. Expect to pay at least $40 per head. Mon–Thurs 5.30–9.30pm, Fri 5.30–10pm, Sat 5–10pm, Sun 10am–2pm & 5–9pm.

Rivoli 1539 Solano Ave ☎510 526 2542, ⓦrivoli restaurant.com. A fine place for first-rate fresh food based on Italian and French cuisine, courteous service and a casual, friendly atmosphere. Main dishes such as swordfish or Dungeness crab ravioli cost $20–38. Mon–Thurs 5.30–9pm, Fri 5.30–9.30pm, Sat 5–9.30pm, Sun 5–9pm.

Saul's Deli 1475 Shattuck Ave 📞 510 848 3354, 🌐 saulsdeli.com. For pastrami, corned beef, *kreplach*, or knishes, this is the place. Great sandwiches and picnic fixings to take away, plus a full range of sit-down evening meals for $15–18. Closed major Jewish holidays. Mon–Thurs & Sun 8am–9pm, Fri & Sat 8am–10pm.

WEST BERKELEY

Bette's Ocean View Diner 1807 4th St, West Berkeley 📞 510 644 3932, 🌐 bettesdiner.com. No views but this popular joint serves up great breakfasts and lunches for $8–13. Queues at weekends can take up to an hour. Mon–Fri 6.30am–2.30pm, Sat–Sun 6.30am–4pm.

Brennan's 700 University Ave, West Berkeley 📞 510 841 0960, 🌐 brennansberkeley.com. Great simple self-service meals like roast beef and mash for $7–15. Also a solidly blue-collar hangout that's a great place for drinking inexpensive beers and watching sports on TV, including European soccer. Mon–Wed & Sun 11am–9.30pm, Thurs–Sat 11am–10.30pm; bar till 2am.

Juan's Place 941 Carleton St, West Berkeley 📞 510 845 6904. The original Berkeley Mexican restaurant, with huge portions of all the favourites for $10 or less, as well as an interesting mix of people. Mon–Fri 11am–10pm, Sat & Sun 2–10pm.

Spenger's Fresh Fish Grotto 1919 4th St, West Berkeley 📞 510 845 7771, 🌐 spengers.com. Local institution with a spacious sit-down restaurant and cheaper takeaway counter. The restaurant serves up heaps of seafood, pasta and choice steaks for $20–40. Sun–Thurs 11.30am–10pm, Fri–Sat 11.30am–11pm.

★**Vik's Chaat Corner** 2390 4th St, West Berkeley 📞 510 644 4432, 🌐 vikschaatcorner.com. Fantastic daytime spot, where you can feast on authentic South Indian dishes such as masala dosa for well under $10 in a huge, saffron-coloured self-service canteen. Mon–Thurs 11am–6pm, Fri–Sun 11am–8pm.

Zut! 1820 4th St, West Berkeley 📞 510 644 6444, 🌐 zutonfourth.com. This smart modern place offers a decent range of Mediterranean favourites such as pizza and *meze* platters to more innovative mains like charred Spanish octopus for $26. Mon–Thurs 11.30am–9pm, Fri 11.30am–9.30pm, Sat 11am–9.30pm, Sun 11am–9pm.

SOUTH BERKELEY

La Mediterranée 2936 College Ave 📞 510 540 7773, 🌐 cafelamed.com. Good Greek and Middle Eastern dishes, such as Levantine meat tart or various kebabs for $12–24, served indoors or on the large patio. Mon–Thurs & Sun 10am–9.30pm, Fri & Sat 10am–10.30pm.

Rick & Ann's 2922 Domingo Ave 📞 510 649 8538, 🌐 rickandanns.com. Crowds line up outside this neighbourhood diner every weekend for a hearty breakfast or filling lunchtime sandwich or burger for $10–13. Daily 8am–2pm & Tues–Sat 5.30–9.30pm, Sun 5.30–8.30pm.

Trattoria La Siciliana 2993 College Ave 📞 510 704 1474, 🌐 trattorialasiciliana.com. Intimate, family-run Italian place with a wide range of antipasti, pastas, risotti and specialities like stuffed beef roll for under $20. Daily 5–10pm.

CAFÉS

Abe's Cafe 1842 Euclid Ave, North Berkeley 📞 510 529 4913. Welcoming coffeehouse with a gentle academic atmosphere and good selection of savoury and sweet treats. Mon–Fri 7.30am–5pm.

Bacheeso's 2501 San Pablo Ave, West Berkeley 📞 510 644 2035, 🌐 bacheesos.net. Imaginative breakfasts such as egg with artichokes and more filling snacks, as well as a full range of hot beverages, all served with a smile in brightly decorated surroundings. Mon–Thurs 8am–4pm,

BERKELEY FOOD SHOPS AND MARKETS

Berkeley Bowl 2020 Oregon St, South Berkeley 📞 510 898 9555, 🌐 berkeleybowl.com. Only in Berkeley would such an enormous produce, bulk and health-food market take over premises from Safeway. The least expensive groceries in town, with the largest selection of fresh food. Mon–Sat 9am–8pm, Sun 10am–7pm.

The Cheese Board Collective 1504-12 Shattuck Ave, North Berkeley 📞 510 549 3183, 🌐 cheeseboard collective.coop. Collectively owned and operated since 1967, offering over 200 varieties of cheese and a range of delicious breads. Great pizzas at the attached restaurant. Mon 7am–1pm, Tues–Fri 7am–6pm, Sat 8am–5pm.

Epicurious Garden 1511 Shattuck Ave, North Berkeley 📞 510 548 2466, 🌐 epicuriousgarden.com. This indoor mall of top-notch produce and takeaway snacks includes half a dozen independent outlets, such as Alegio chocolate and Guacamole 61 Mexican, as well as a Japanese tea garden at the back. Daily hours vary.

Monterey Foods 1550 Hopkins St, North Berkeley 📞 510 526 6042, 🌐 montereymarket.com. The main supplier of exotic produce to Berkeley's gourmet restaurants, this boisterous market also has the highest-quality fresh fruit and vegetables available. Mon–Fri 9am–7pm, Sat & Sun 8.30am–6pm.

Vintage Berkeley 2113 Vine St, North Berkeley 📞 510 665 8600, 🌐 vintageberkeley.com. Excellent outlet for quality domestic and imported wines, mostly under $20, housed in a cute old pump station. Wine tasting during the afternoons. Mon–Wed 11am–8pm, Thurs–Sat 11am–9pm, Sun noon–6pm.

Fri & Sat 8am–8pm, Sun 8am–5pm.

Caffe Mediterraneum 2475 Telegraph Ave, downtown ☎ 510 841 5634, ⓦ caffemed.com. Berkeley's oldest café featuring pavement seating. Straight out of the Beat archives: beards and berets optional, battered paperbacks de

rigueur. Daily 7am–midnight.

Caffe Strada 2300 College Ave, downtown ☎ 510 843 5282. Delightful open-air café, right opposite the campus, which serves freshly made pastries as well as a range of coffee and tea. Daily 6am–midnight.

DRINKING AND NIGHTLIFE

Most of Berkeley's **bars** are predictably student-oriented, while its **music venues** tend more towards folk and world music, with other places dedicated to underground rock.

BARS

Albatross Pub 1822 San Pablo Ave, West Berkeley ☎ 510 843 2473, ⓦ albatrosspub.com. Popular student super-bar, replete with darts, pool, board games and fireplace. Serves a large selection of ales from around the world. Live jazz, flamenco and blues music at weekends (free–$5). Sun–Tues 6pm–2am, Wed–Sat 4.30pm–2am.

★ **Field Work** 1160 6th St, West Berkeley ☎ 510 898 1203, ⓦ fieldworkbrewing.com. The best of the new crop of microbreweries occupies a converted warehouse and brews superb ales. Try the $13 IPA flight while munching on a meat pasty. Mon–Thurs & Sun 11am–10pm, Fri & Sat 11am–11pm.

Free House 2700 Bancroft Ave, downtown ☎ 510 647 2300, ⓦ berkeleyfreehouse.com. Housed in an atmospheric dark-wood-panelled hall with a huge fireplace, this place has a wide range of draught and bottled beer, as well as fine food. Mon–Fri 11.30am–midnight, Sat 5pm–midnight.

★ **Pub (Schmidt's Tobacco & Trading Co)** 1492 Solano Ave, North Berkeley ☎ 510 525 1900. This small, relaxed bar lures a mixture of bookworms and game players with a good selection of beers. Their other speciality is tobacco, so they even get away with a semi-open smoking area out back. Mon–Wed & Sun noon–midnight, Thurs–Sat noon–1am.

Torpedo Room 2031 4th St, West Berkeley ☎ 510 647 3439, ⓦ sierranevada.com. This huge post-industrial

space has been converted into Sierra Nevada Brewery's first taproom outside of Chico. Great range of ales to sup on site or take away. Tues–Fri noon–9pm, Sat 11am–9pm, Sun noon–6pm.

Triple Rock Brewery 1920 Shattuck Ave, downtown ☎ 510 843 2739, ⓦ triplerock.com. Newly expanded, this lively student bar offers fine burgers and beers, including cask-conditioned ales at weekends. Mon–Wed 11.30am–1am, Thurs–Sat 11.30am–2am, Sun 11.30am–midnight.

LIVE MUSIC VENUES

★ **924 Gilman** 924 Gilman St, West Berkeley ☎ 510 525 9926, ⓦ 924gilman.org. On the outer edge of the hardcore punk, indie and experimental scene, this institution helped launch Green Day and Sleater-Kinney. No alcohol, all ages. Weekends only; cover $5–10.

Ashkenaz 1317 San Pablo Ave, West Berkeley ☎ 510 525 5054, ⓦ ashkenaz.com. World music and dance café hosting acts from modern Afro-beat to the best of the Balkans. Kids and under-21s welcome. Cover $10–25.

Freight and Salvage 2020 Addison St, downtown ☎ 510 644 2020, ⓦ freightandsalvage.org. Singer-songwriters and folkies perform in a smooth coffeehouse setting. Tickets mostly under $20, open-mike nights $5.

La Peña Cultural Center 3105 Shattuck Ave, near Ashby BART ☎ 510 849 2568, ⓦ lapena.org. More folk than rock, and some Latin, often politically charged – the website encourages cultural activism for social change. $10–30.

ENTERTAINMENT

MAJOR PERFORMANCE VENUES

The UC Theatre Taube Family Music Hall 2036 University Ave ☎ 510 356 4000, ⓦ theuctheatre.org. Reopened in 2016, this former cinema has become a hot venue for well-known, mostly alternative rock acts such as Green Day and Cat Power. $20–40.

Zellerbach Hall/Greek Theatre UC Berkeley campus ☎ 510 642 9988, ⓦ calperfs.berkeley.edu. Two of the top spots for catching big names touring the Bay Area during the academic year. Zellerbach showcases drama, classical and world music and dance, while the Greek welcomes more popular acts. Tickets $20–100.

FILM

Pacific Film Archive 2155 Center St ☎ 510 642 0808, ⓦ bampfa.berkeley.edu. Now housed in the brand new Barbro Osher Theater, the exhaustive archive features two nightly showings of classics, developing world and experimental films, plus revivals of otherwise forgotten favourites. Same-day gallery admission with ticket.

Shattuck Cinemas 2230 Shattuck Ave ☎ 510 644 2992, ⓦ landmarktheatres.com. Ten screens in this large complex near the campus show a mixture of big releases and more offbeat films. Landmark also operates the California Theatre around the corner.

THEATRE

Berkeley Playhouse 2640 College Ave ☎ 510 845 8542, ⓦ berkeleyplayhouse.org. A variety of touring shows stop off in this cunningly converted old church. Tickets usually $20–65.

Berkeley Repertory Theater 2025 Addison St ☎ 510 845 4700, ⓦ berkeleyrep.org. One of the West Coast's most highly respected theatre companies, presenting updated classics and contemporary plays in an intimate modern theatre. Tickets $30–75; fifty percent discounts for students and under-30s with advance booking.

Black Repertory Group 3201 Adeline St ☎ 510 652 2120, ⓦ blackrepertorygroup.com. Now well established, this politically conscious company, with its own home near Ashby BART, encourages new talent with great success. Tickets $15–30.

SHOPPING

ACCI 1652 Shattuck Ave ☎ 510 843 2527, ⓦ accigallery .com. An arts-and-crafts cooperative designed to exhibit and sell the work of local artists. Entry is free. Mon–Sat 11am–6pm, Sun noon–5pm.

Amoeba Records 2455 Telegraph Ave ☎ 510 549 1125, ⓦ amoeba.com. This venerable emporium, whose vast younger sister is across the bay in Haight-Ashbury (see p.484), still houses the East Bay's widest selection of used and new music, on CD and vinyl. Mon–Thurs & Sun 11am–8pm, Fri & Sat 11am–10pm.

7

Northern East Bay

Compared to the absorbing cities of Oakland and Berkeley, the rest of the East Bay is generally less attractive, and places of interest are few and far between, especially in the more sparsely populated inland reaches. The **Northern East Bay** is home to some of the Bay Area's heaviest industry – oil refineries and chemical plants dominate the landscape – but also holds a few remarkably unchanged waterfront towns that merit a side-trip if you're passing by. Across the narrow Carquinez Strait, further around the North Bay from the oil-refinery landscape of **Richmond**, lies the sleepy and little-visited former state capital of **Benicia**, vitally important during California's first twenty years of existence after the 1849 Gold Rush.

Albany and El Cerrito

Off the Eastshore Freeway in mostly mundane **Albany**, Golden Gate Fields has **horse racing** from October to June, and beyond it, the **Albany Mud Flats** are a fascinating place to stroll; impromptu works of art made from discarded materials vie with wild irises to attract the passer-by's eye in this reclaimed landfill jutting out into the bay. About a mile from Albany, **El Cerrito**'s main contribution to world culture was the band Creedence Clearwater Revival, who staged most of their *Born on the Bayou* publicity photographs in the wilds of Tilden Park in the hills above. The town is still home to one of the best record stores in California, Down Home Music, at 10341 San Pablo Ave (Thurs–Sun 11am–7pm; ☎ 510 525 2129).

Richmond

Rough and depressing **Richmond**, at the top of the bay, was once a boomtown, whose Kaiser Shipyards built ships during World War II and employed 100,000 workers between 1940 and its closure in 1945. Now it's the proud home of the gigantic Standard Oil refinery, which you drive through before crossing the **Richmond–San Rafael Bridge** ($5) to Marin County. About the only reason to stop in Richmond is that it marks the north end of the BART line, and the adjacent Amtrak station is a better changing point for journeys to and from San Francisco than the terminal in West Oakland. Jutting out into the bay, posh and leafy **Point Richmond** is a world apart and worth a wander if you accidentally end up here.

ACCOMMODATION   **RICHMOND**

East Brother Light Station 117 Park Place, Point Richmond ☎ 510 233 2385, ⓦ ebls.org. Five rooms in a converted lighthouse, on an island in the straits linking the San Francisco and San Pablo bays, making it a unique retreat. Prices include highly rated gourmet dinners with wine as well as breakfast. Thursday to Sunday nights only. **$345**

Benicia

On the north side of the Carquinez Strait, connected by the Carquinez Bridge and hard to get to without a car, **Benicia** is the most substantial of the Bay Area's historic waterfront towns, but one that has definitely seen better days. Founded in 1847, it initially rivalled San Francisco as the major Bay Area port and was even the state capital for a time. Despite Benicia's better weather and fine deep-water harbour, San Francisco, which is closer to the ocean, eventually became the main transport point for the fortunes of the Gold Rush and Benicia very nearly faded away altogether.

The town is pleasant to stroll around and a walking-tour map of its many intact Victorian houses, churches and several glass studios is available from the Chamber of Commerce (see below). Included on the itinerary are the steeply pitched roofs and gingerbread eaves of the **Frisbie-Walsh house** at 235 East L St, a prefabricated Gothic Revival building shipped here in pieces from Boston in 1849. Across the City Hall park, the arched ceiling beams of **St Paul's Episcopal Church** look like an upturned ship's hull; it was built by shipwrights from the Pacific Mail Steamship Company, one of Benicia's many successful nineteenth-century shipyards.

Benicia Capitol State Historic Park

115 West G St • Thurs noon–4pm, Fri–Sun 10am–5pm • $3 • ☎ 707 745 3385, ⓦ parks.ca.gov

Examples of Benicia's efforts to become a major city stand poignantly around the very compact downtown area, most conspicuously the 1852 Greek Revival structure that was used as the **first State Capitol** for just thirteen months. Now designated as **Benicia Capitol State Historic Park**, the building has been restored as a **museum** and furnished in the legislative style of the time, complete with top hats on the tables and shining spittoons every few feet.

Benicia Arsenal

The Arsenal Open studios first weekend of May and first weekend of December • Free • ⓦ beniciaarsenal.com **Museum** Wed–Sun 1–4pm • $5 • ☎ 707 745 5435, ⓦ beniciahistoricalmuseum.org

Feminist artist Judy Chicago and sculptor Robert Arneson are among those who have worked in the converted studios and modern light-industrial parks around the sprawling fortifications of the old **Benicia Arsenal**, whose thickly walled sandstone buildings east of the downtown area formed the main army storage facility for weapons and ammunition from 1851 until the Korean War.

One of the oddest parts of the complex is the **Camel Barn** in the **Benicia Historical Museum**: the structure used to house camels that the army imported in 1856 to transport supplies across the deserts of the southwestern US. The experiment failed and the camels were kept here until they were sold off in 1864.

ARRIVAL AND INFORMATION   BENICIA

By car Take the Carquinez Bridge ($5) across the strait from the East Bay and turn right onto I-780.

By ferry and bus There is no direct public transport connection to San Francisco or the East Bay but you can take the San Francisco Bay Ferry service (☎ 415 705 8291, ⓦ sanfranciscobayferry.com) to Vallejo and transfer onto Soltrans bus #78 (☎ 707 648 4666, ⓦ soltransride.com).

Chamber of Commerce 601 1st St (Mon–Fri 9am–5pm; ☎ 707 745 2120, ⓦ beniciachamber.com).

ACCOMMODATION AND EATING

Mai Thai 807 1st St ☎ 707 747 1868, ⓦ maithaibenicia .com. Exquisitely prepared Thai food for $6–16. The *som tum* papaya salad is a spicy winner and the curries are great too. Mon–Fri 11am–3pm & 5–10pm, Sat 11am–10pm.

Nine O Seven Grill 907 1st St ☎ 707 746 0505, ⓦ 907grill.com. Typical modern American restaurant, serving huge portions of burgers, steaks and the odd Mexican dish for $10–29. Mon–Fri 11am–9pm, Sat & Sun 9am–9pm.

Union Hotel and Gardens 401 1st St ☎ 707 746 0100, ⓦ unionhotelbenicia.com. Historic hotel and once a bordello, now converted into a classy bed and breakfast with twelve rooms, all featuring a jacuzzi and named after plants. **$129**

NEMESIS AT ALTAMONT

Uncannily timed at the dying embers of the Sixties and often referred to as "the nemesis of the Woodstock generation", the concert headlined by the **Rolling Stones** at the **Altamont Speedway**, fifteen miles southeast of Mount Diablo, on December 6, 1969, ended in total disaster. The free event was conceived to be a sort of second Woodstock, staged in order to counter allegations that the Stones had ripped off their fans during a long US tour. The band, however, inadvisably hired a chapter of Hell's Angels instead of professional security to maintain order and the result, predictably enough, was chaos. Three people ended up dead, one kicked and stabbed to death by the Hell's Angels themselves.

The whole sorry tale was remarkably captured on film by brothers David and Albert Maysles (plus co-director Charlotte Zerwin) and released the following year as their documentary *Gimme Shelter*. The footage of the concert clearly shows the deteriorating mood and growing menace in the crowd, exemplified by the scene when Jefferson Airplane vocalist Marty Balin jumped down into the fray to break up a fight, earning himself a broken jaw. By the time the Stones came on stage matters were patently out of hand, and after several interruptions and pleas for sanity by Mick Jagger, all hell broke loose during, ironically, *Sympathy for the Devil*. Jagger, Richards and company are later shown watching footage of the incident with numb looks on their faces as the glint of a knife signals the fatal stabbing during the following number.

The speedway itself continued operating under various names for four more decades until its closure in 2008 but for most people it will forever be associated with that dark day in the late Sixties.

Inland valleys

At the northern head of the **inland valleys**, nudging the Carquinez Strait, Contra Costa's county seat **Martinez** is an uninspiring industrial town and major railroad depot, saved only by its proximity to the birthplace of John Muir. Further south and inland, a whole other world of dry rolling hills is dominated by the towering peak of **Mount Diablo**.

Dozens of tract-home developments have made commuter suburbs out of what were once cattle ranches and farms but so far the region has been able to absorb the numbers and still feels rural, despite having doubled in population in the past few decades. BART's yellow line tunnels a direct route from Oakland through the Berkeley Hills to the leafy-green stockbroker settlements of **Orinda**, home of the summer-long California Shakespeare festival (☎510 548 9666, ⓦcalshakes.org), and **Walnut Creek**. En route to its terminal just beyond Martinez, it continues northeast through the increasingly hot and dry landscape to **Concord**, site of a controversial nuclear-weapons depot. In 1987 a civil disobedience blockade here ended in protester Brian Willson losing his legs under the wheels of a slow-moving munitions train. The event raised public awareness of the atomic activities and earned Willson a place in the Lawrence Ferlinghetti poem *A Buddha in the Woodpile*. These days, however, it's business as usual at the depot.

John Muir National Historic Site

4202 Alhambra Ave • Daily 10am–5pm • Free • ☎925 228 8860, ⓦnps.gov/jomu • Contra Costa County Connection buses leave every 30min from Pleasant Hill BART station

The preserved home of naturalist **John Muir** is just off Hwy-4 two miles south of Martinez. Muir, an articulate, persuasive Scot whose writings and political activism were of vital importance in the preservation of America's wilderness, spent much of his life exploring and writing about the majestic Sierra Nevada, particularly Yosemite. He was also one of the founders of the **Sierra Club** – a wilderness lobby and education organization that retains a strong presence today (see p.43). Anyone familiar with the image of this thin, bearded man wandering the mountains with his knapsack, notebook and packet of tea might be surprised to see his very conventional, upper-class Victorian home, now restored to its appearance when Muir died in 1914. The bulk of Muir's personal belongings and artefacts are displayed in his study on the upper floor and in the adjacent room an exhibition documents the history of the Sierra Club and

7

Muir's battles to protect America's wilderness. You can also visit the still-productive orchards and the 1849 **Martinez Adobe**, homestead of the original Spanish land-grant settlers and now a small **museum** of Mexican colonial culture.

Tao House

Tours: guided by reservation only Wed–Fri & Sun 10am & 2pm, self-guided Sat 10.15am, 12.15pm & 2.15pm • Free • ☎ 925 838 0249, ⓦ nps.gov/euon • Shuttles operate from Museum of the San Ramon Valley in nearby downtown Danville at 205 Railroad Ave

At the foot of Mount Diablo, fifteen miles south of Martinez, playwright **Eugene O'Neill** (1888–1953) used the money he received for winning the Nobel Prize for Literature in 1936 to build a home and sanctuary for himself, which he named **Tao House**. It was here, when he was suffering with Parkinson's disease, that he wrote many of his best-known plays: *The Iceman Cometh*, *A Moon for the Misbegotten* and *Long Day's Journey into Night*. Readings and performances of his works are sometimes given in the house, which is open to visitors on guided or self-guided **tours**. As it's protected National Park Service land, there's no parking on site, so the tours pick you up nearby.

Blackhawk Automotive Museum

3700 Blackhawk Plaza Circle • Wed–Sun 10am–5pm • $15 • ☎ 925 736 2277, ⓦ blackhawkmuseum.org

Danville's richest neighbourhood, Blackhawk, is the home of the **Blackhawk Automotive Museum** where you'll find an impressive collection of classic cars from Britain, Germany, Italy and the US, along with artwork inspired by them. The adjacent plaza is worth visiting for its array of galleries, boutiques and restaurants.

Mount Diablo State Park

Daily 8am–sunset • $10/vehicle • ☎ 925 837 2525, ⓦ parks.ca.gov • There's no public transport, though the Sierra Club sometimes organizes day-trips (see p.43)

Majestic **Mount Diablo** rises up from the rolling ranch-lands at its foot to a height of nearly four thousand feet, its summit and flanks preserved within **Mount Diablo State Park**. North Gate, the main road through the park, comes within three hundred feet of the top, so it's a popular place for an outing and you're unlikely to be alone to enjoy the marvellous view: on a clear day you can see over two hundred miles in every direction.

Two main entrances lead into the park, both well marked off I-680. The one from the southwest by way of Danville passes by the **ranger station**, where you can pick up a trail map ($5) listing the best day-hikes. The other runs from the northwest by way of Walnut Creek, and the routes join together five miles from the summit, beside which the attractive **visitor centre** (daily summer 8am–4pm, rest of year 10am–2pm) contains a free interpretive museum and observation deck. March and April, when the wildflowers are out, are the best months to come and since mornings are ideal for getting the clearest view, you should drive to the top first and then head back down to a trailhead for a hike, or to one of the many picnic spots for a leisurely lunch. In summer it can get desperately hot and dry, with parts of the park closed due to fire danger.

ACCOMMODATION	MOUNT DIABLO STATE PARK
Mount Diablo State Park Campground 20 miles east of Oakland off I-680 in Contra Costa County ☎ 800 444	7275, ⓦ reserveamerica.com. Year-round tent pitches in two separate sites, both with good facilities. $30

The Peninsula

The city of San Francisco sits at the tip of a five-mile-wide neck of land commonly referred to as **The Peninsula**. Home to old money and new technology, the Peninsula stretches along the bay for fifty miles of relentless suburbia south from San Francisco, ending up in the futuristic roadside landscape of the "**Silicon Valley**" around **San Jose**, the fastest-growing city in California and now tenth-largest in the US.

There was a time when the region was largely agricultural, but the computer boom – spurred by Stanford University in **Palo Alto** – has replaced orange groves and fig trees with office complexes and parking lots. Surprisingly, however, most of the land along the **coast** – separated from the bayfront sprawl by a spur of redwood-covered ridges – remains rural and largely undeveloped; it also contains some excellent **beaches** and a couple of affably down-to-earth communities, all well served by public transport.

GETTING AROUND   **THE PENINSULA**

By subway BART only runs as far as Millbrae. An extension from the East Bay to San Jose is under construction.
By bus SamTrans buses (☎ 800 660 4287, ⌨ samtrans .com) run south to Palo Alto or along the coast to Half Moon Bay.
By train Caltrain (☎ 650 817 1717 or ☎ 800 660 4287, ⌨ caltrain.com) offers an hourly rail service, stopping at most bayside towns between San Francisco and San Jose.

The I-280 corridor

Six-lane freeways don't usually qualify as scenic routes, but an exception is **I-280**, one of the most recent and expensive freeways in California. It runs parallel to US-101 but avoids the worst of the bayside mess by cutting through wooded valleys down the centre of the Peninsula. Just beyond the San Francisco city limits the road passes through **Colma**, a unique place filled with cemeteries, which, other than the military burial grounds in the Presidio, are prohibited within San Francisco. Besides the expected roll call of deceased San Francisco luminaries, including Levi Strauss and William Hearst, are a few surprises, such as Wild West gunman Wyatt Earp. From here the scenery improves dramatically as you pass the enormous **Crystal Springs Reservoir**, whose water is pumped all the way from Yosemite to provide San Francisco's water supply.

CuriOdyssey at Coyote Point

1651 Coyote Point Drive • Tues–Sun 10am–5pm • $9 • ☎ 650 342 7755, ⌨ curiodyssey.org

The first place worth a visit heading out of San Francisco is the museum of **CuriOdyssey at Coyote Point**, four miles south of the airport, off Poplar Avenue. Surrounded by a large bayfront park, the museum showcases examples of the natural life of the San Francisco Bay, from tidal insects to birds of prey, all exhibited in engaging and informative displays and enhanced by interactive computers and documentary films.

Filoli Estate

Early Feb to late Oct Tues–Sun 10am–3.30pm, Sun 11am–3.30pm, last admission 2.30pm • $20 • ☎ 650 364 8300 ext 507, ⌨ filoli.org

Just off I-280 on Canada Road near the well-heeled town of **Woodside**, luscious gardens surround the palatial **Filoli Estate**. The 45-room mansion, designed in 1915 in Neo-Palladian style by architect Willis Polk, may look familiar – it was used in the TV series *Dynasty* as the Denver home of the Carrington clan. The gardens, however, are the real draw, especially in the spring when everything's in bloom.

Palo Alto and Stanford University

PALO ALTO, just south and three miles east of Woodside between I-280 and US-101, is a small, leafy community, which, despite its proximity to Stanford, exudes little of the college-town vigour of its northern rival, Berkeley. Home to Facebook creator Mark Zuckerberg and Google's Larry Page, Palo Alto has become something of a social centre for Silicon Valley's nouveau riche, as evidenced by the trendy cafés and chic new restaurants that have popped up along its main drag, **University Avenue**. The computer-industry-boom job market made more than just those two rich and even small houses in the quaint neighbourhoods surrounding downtown can cost over a million dollars.

In terms of sights, the town doesn't have a lot to offer other than Spanish Colonial homes, but it's a great place for a lazy stroll and a gourmet meal. Monthly historic tours of Palo Alto's neighbourhoods take place during summer (❶650 299 8878), but you can easily see the best of the city's designs for yourself along **Ramona Street**. These days even **East Palo Alto**, on the bay side of US-101, once notorious as America's per capita murder capital due to gang- and drug-related violence, has started on the road to gentrification. This is an ironic return to its foundation in the 1920s as the utopian Runnymeade Colony, an agricultural, poultry-raising cooperative. There is nothing to see though, and Grateful Dead guitarist Jerry Garcia's hometown remains resolutely off the San Francisco tourist trail.

Stanford University

❶ 650 723 2300, Ⓦ stanford.edu • The University Visitor Center (see opposite) organizes various tours of the campus – keep in mind that it's fairly big and best seen by car or bike

STANFORD UNIVERSITY, spreading out from the west end of University Avenue, is among the top – and most expensive – in the US, though when it opened in 1891, founded by railroad magnate Leland Stanford in memory of his dead son, it offered free tuition. Stanford's reputation as an arch-conservative think-tank was enhanced by Ronald Reagan's offer to donate his video library to the school (though Stanford politely declined) but it hasn't always been an entirely boring place. Ken Kesey came here from Oregon in 1958 on a writing fellowship, working nights as an orderly on the psychiatric ward of one local hospital, and getting paid $75 a day to test experimental drugs such as LSD in another. Drawing on both experiences, Kesey wrote *One Flew Over the Cuckoo's Nest* in 1960 and quickly became a counterculture hero. The period is admirably chronicled by Tom Wolfe in *The Electric Kool-aid Acid Test*. In keeping with that spirit, Stanford is now the home of the Center for the Explanation of Consciousness, which conducts various experiments in human consciousness and is bridging the gap between the physical and metaphysical.

Approaching from the Palo Alto CalTrain and SamTrans bus station, which acts as a buffer between the town and the university, you enter the campus via a half-mile-long, palm-tree-lined boulevard which deposits you at its heart, the **Quadrangle**, bordered by the colourful gold-leaf mosaics of the **Memorial Church** and the phallic **Hoover Tower**, whose observation platform (daily 10am–4pm; $3) is worth ascending for the view.

Iris and B. Gerald Cantor Center for Visual Arts

Corner of Lomita Drive & Museum Way • Daily except Tues 11am–5pm, Thurs till 8pm • Free • ❶ 650 723 4177, Ⓦ museum.stanford.edu

One of the finest museums in the Bay Area, the **Iris and B. Gerald Cantor Center for Visual Arts** comprises 27 galleries (spread over 120,000 square feet) of treasures from six continents, dating from 500 BC to the present. Housed in the old Stanford Museum of Art, the Cantor Center incorporates the earthquake-damaged former structure with a new wing, including a bookshop and café. One of the finest pieces in the permanent collection is the stunning *Plum Garden, Kameido*, by Japanese artist Hiroshige. Be sure to have a look at the distinguished collection of over two hundred **Rodin sculptures**, including a *Gates of Hell* flanked by a shamed *Adam and Eve*, displayed in an attractive outdoor setting on the museum's south side, plus a version of *The Thinker*.

Anderson Collection at Stanford University

315 Lomita Drive • Daily except Tues 11am–5pm, Thurs till 8pm • Free • ❶ 650 721 6055, Ⓦ anderson.stanford.edu

The newest art gallery on campus is the sharply designed structure of the **Anderson Collection at Stanford University**. The permanent works of modern art from 1941 on display include paintings by the likes of Mark Rothko and Nathan Oliveira, while temporary exhibitions showcase cutting-edge works such as musician Nick Cave's *Soundsuits*, full-body-sized sculptures of various materials.

ARRIVAL AND INFORMATION

By train or bus The Caltrain and SamTrans stations are next to each other just above the University Ave underpass. Both offer frequent connections to San Francisco and the former to San Jose too.

Listings To find out what's on in the area and where, pick up a free copy of the *Palo Alto Weekly* (paloaltoonline.com), or get a copy of the free *Stanford Daily* (published weekdays), available at most local shops.

Palo Alto Chamber of Commerce 355 Alma St, opposite the SamTrans station (Mon–Thurs 9am–5pm, Fri 9am–noon; 650 324 3121, paloaltochamber.com), has lists of local restaurants and cycle routes.

Stanford University Visitor Center 295 Galvez St (Mon–Fri 8.30am–5pm, Sat & Sun 10am–5pm; 650 723 2560, stanford.edu) is a helpful new facility. Free 1hr walking tours of the campus leave from here daily at 11am and 3.15pm, and driving tours ($5) in a golf cart are offered daily at 10am and 1pm during term (and some of the holidays) from Memorial Auditorium.

PALO ALTO AND STANFORD UNIVERSITY

ACCOMMODATION

The environs of Palo Alto contain a range of **accommodation** to suit most budgets, mainly used by parents and academics visiting Stanford. Dozens of $60–75/night **motels** line El Camino Real (Hwy-82, the old main highway).

Cardinal Hotel 235 Hamilton Ave 650 323 5101, cardinalhotel.com. Reasonably affordable and comfortable rooms, the cheaper ones with shared bathrooms, are available at this downtown institution with a posh lobby. **$139**

Cowper Inn 705 Cowper St 650 327 4475, cowperinn.com. Restored Victorian house with attractive and cosy rooms, two with a shared bathroom, close to University Ave. Excellent hot buffet breakfast included. **$179**

Garden Court Hotel 520 Cowper St 650 322 9000 or 800 824 9028, gardencourt.com. Downtown's prime luxury boutique hotel features beautiful design, furniture and decoration in the fancy rooms and common areas. Fine restaurant and bar too. **$319**

The Zen Hotel 4164 El Camino Real 650 493 4492 or 800 thezenhotel.com. Asian touches in the design reflect the name of this smart modern hotel with spacious rooms and quality facilities. Complimentary hot breakfast and cookies. **$139**

EATING

For a college town, most **places to eat** in downtown Palo Alto around University Ave are on the chic side, though that's not so surprising, given the exclusive nature of the university. Cheaper alternatives tend to cluster around El Camino Real.

RESTAURANTS

Bistro Elan 2363A Birch St 650 327 0284, bistroelan.com. Elegant California cuisine dishes such as Sonoma duck leg confit and MA sea scallops go for $26–36 at this swanky place. Tues & Wed 5.30–11pm, Thurs & Fri 11.30am–1.30pm & 5.30–11pm, Sat 5.30–11pm.

Café Brioche 445 S California Ave 650 336 8640, cafebrioche-paloalto.com. Classic Gallic fare such as *coq au vin* and *bouillabaisse* are among the delights at this French bistro. Mostly under $25/main course. Daily 9am–3pm & 5.30–9.30pm.

Coconuts 642 Ramona St 650 329 9533, coconutspaloalto.com. This colourful Caribbean restaurant and bar rustles up all the West Indian favourites such as curried goat and jerk chicken for $13–16, as well as great cocktails. Tues–Thurs 11.30am–2.30pm & 5–9.30pm, Fri 11.30am–10.30pm, Sat noon–10.30pm, Sun noon–8pm.

★ **Evvia** 420 Emerson St 650 326 0983, evvia.net. California-style Greek dishes such as braised *paidakia* (small grilled lamb chops) cost $25–45 at this highly rated upmarket place. Mon–Fri 11.30am–2pm & 5.30–10pm, Sat 5–11pm, Sun 5–9pm.

Joanie's Café 447 California Ave 650 326 6505, joaniescafepaloalto.com. Home-style eggy breakfasts and burger or sandwich lunches are the hallmarks of this comfortable neighbourhood restaurant. Most items under $13. Daily 7.30am–2.15pm.

Oren's Hummus 261 University Ave 650 752 6492, orenshummus.com. Excellent Middle Eastern restaurant, serving filling wraps and huge wads of fluffy pitta bread with which to mop up a plethora of dips, mostly under $12. Daily 11am–11pm.

St Michael's Alley 806 Emerson St 650 326 2530, stmikes.com. One of Palo Alto's hottest bistros features "casual California" cuisine such as red curry duck breast ($28) and weekend brunch specials for $13–18. An extensive wine list too. Tues–Fri 11.30am–2pm & 5.30–10pm, Sat 5.30–10pm.

CAFÉS

Café Venetia 419 University Ave 650 323 3600, cafevenetia.com. Relaxing student hangout, serving fine coffee from Italy and elsewhere. There's another branch by the Caltrain station. Mon–Thurs 7am–11pm, Fri & Sat 7am–midnight, Sun 8am–11pm.

Coupa Café 538 Ramona St 650 322 6872, coupacafe.com. Colourful, laidback spot with a huge range of coffee and tea from around the world, as well as plenty of

international sweet and savoury snacks. Daily 7am–11pm.
Printer's Inc Cafe 320 S California Ave ☎ 650 323 3347, ⓦ printerscafe.com. Great coffees and smoothies, plus a range of meals, served indoors or on the sunny patio. Adjacent to Palo Alto's best bookshop. Mon 7am–4pm, Tues–Fri 7am–6pm, Sat 8am–6pm, Sun 8am–4pm.

DRINKING

Rose and Crown 547 Emerson St ☎ 650 327 7673, ⓦ roseandcrownpa.com. British-style pub with a mock Tudor façade and festooned inside with European soccer paraphernalia; games are shown on TV too. Huge range of beers. Daily 11.30am–late.

Vino Locale 431 Kipling St ☎ 650 328 0450, ⓦ vinolocale .com. European-style wine bar specializing in local appelations, as the name suggests, and serving fine food. It also has live music and art exhibitions, plus there's a garden. Sun–Thurs 11.30am–1am, Fri & Sat 11.30am–2am.

San Jose

Burt Bacharach wouldn't need to ask the way to **SAN JOSE** today – heading south from San Francisco, it should take under an hour (avoiding peak times) to reach the heart of the heat and smog that collects below the bay. Sitting at the southern end of the Peninsula, San Jose has in the past three decades emerged as the civic heart of Silicon Valley, spurred by the growth of local behemoths Apple, Cisco, Intel and Hewlett-Packard. San Jose's priority of late has been the development of a culture beyond that of geeks, so new museums, shopping centres, restaurants, clubs and performing-arts companies have mushroomed throughout the compact downtown area. While the nightlife and cultural scene here can't begin to compete with San Francisco, there are enough attractions around the city's clean and sunny streets to warrant a short stay.

Downtown San Jose

Though now rooted in the modern high-tech world, San Jose's 1777 founding actually makes it one of the oldest settlements – and the oldest city – in California. The only sign of that **downtown** is the 1797 **Peralta Adobe**, at 184 W St John St (tours by arrangement, minimum 5 people; $8; ☎ 408 287 2290, ⓦ historysanjose.org), notable more for having survived the encroaching suburbia than for anything on display in its sparse, whitewashed interior. Admission includes a tour of the **Fallon House**, a Victorian mansion across the street, built by the city's seventh mayor in 1855, a frontiersman in the Fremont expedition.

The two blocks of San Pedro Street that run south of the adobe form a restaurant row known as **San Pedro Square**. There's no central plaza as such, just a collection of some of San Jose's best eateries (see p.517). Further south, down Market Street, lies the pleasant and palm-dotted **Plaza de César Chávez**. The plaza is San Jose's town square and there's no better place to lounge on the grass, read on one of the many wooden benches or play in the unique **fountain** whose shooting spumes are a favourite hangout for kids.

Cathedral Basilica of St Joseph

80 S Market St • Hours vary • Free • ☎ 408 283 8100, ⓦ stjosephcathedral.org

A block north of the plaza, the **Cathedral Basilica of St Joseph** stands on the site of the first Catholic parish in California, circa 1803. The present building was dedicated in 1997 and you should duck inside to see its painted cupola, stained-glass windows and Stations of the Cross. Masses are held daily, often in Spanish.

San Jose Museum of Art

110 S Market St • Tues–Sun 11am–5pm • $10 • ☎ 408 271 6840 • ⓦ sjmusart.org

Next door to St Joseph's Cathedral, the fantastic **San Jose Museum of Art** is set in the old post office building built in 1892, to which a new wing was added in 1991. The museum contains more than one thousand works of art, with the spotlight falling on post-1980 Bay Area artists. A relationship with New York's Whitney Museum of American Art allows the museum to exhibit works from the Whitney's vast permanent collection. The sweeping, open galleries are flooded with light, as is the attached café, including its outdoor patio with a plaza view.

Tech Museum of Innovation
201 S Market St • Daily 10am–5pm • $24 • ☎ 408 294 8324, ⓦ thetech.org

Facing the southwest corner of the Plaza de César Chávez, downtown's biggest draw is the **Tech Museum of Innovation** with its hands-on displays of high-tech engineering.

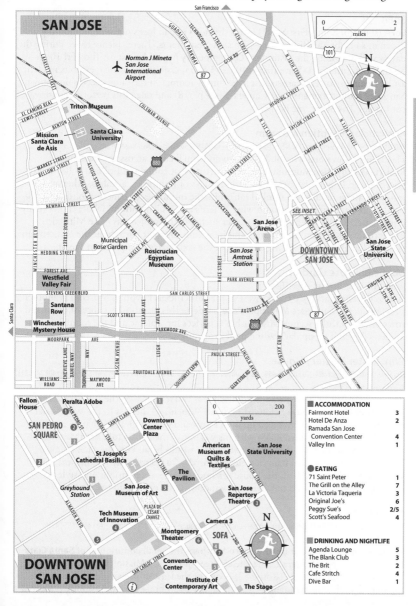

■ ACCOMMODATION	
Fairmont Hotel	3
Hotel De Anza	2
Ramada San Jose Convention Center	4
Valley Inn	1

● EATING	
71 Saint Peter	1
The Grill on the Alley	7
La Victoria Taqueria	3
Original Joe's	6
Peggy Sue's	2/5
Scott's Seafood	4

■ DRINKING AND NIGHTLIFE	
Agenda Lounge	5
The Blank Club	3
The Brit	2
Cafe Stritch	4
Dive Bar	1

There are three floors of interactive exhibits, as well as the inevitable IMAX theatre ($10; $5 with museum entry). Highlights include the Body Metrics and Innovations in Health Care sections, both of which allow you to delve into the relationship between high-tech and living organisms, and Social Robots, which gives you the chance to design, build and programme a robot. Unfortunately, the queues to access many of the best exhibits can seem like a virtual hell, and, unless you're a geek, you may feel the effort does not warrant the hefty entry fee.

SoFA

SoFA (short for South First Street) forms the heart of San Jose's nightlife, comprising a dozen or so clubs and discos along with some restaurants. There's plenty to see during the day as well, including the **Institute of Contemporary Art** (451 S 1st St; Tues–Fri 10am–5pm, Sat & Sun noon–5pm; free; ☎408 283 8155, ⓦsjica.org), which, exhibits modern art by (mainly) Bay Area artists in a large, sunny room. On the same street is downtown San Jose's **arthouse cinema**, the Camera 3 (see p.518) and one of its performing-arts companies, **The Stage** (see p.518).

Rosicrucian Egyptian Museum

1600 Park Ave • Wed–Fri 9am–5pm, Sat & Sun 10am–6pm • $9 • ☎ 408 947 3636, ⓦ egyptianmuseum.org

Head four miles northwest of downtown and you'll come across the intriguing **Rosicrucian Egyptian Museum**, a grand structure that contains a brilliant collection of Assyrian and Babylonian artefacts, with displays of mummies, amulets, other ancient jewellery and a replica of a tomb. Don't miss the mummies of baboons, birds and fish on the left-hand side of the tomb wing. There's also a **planetarium**, whose shows (daily 2pm, Sat & Sun also 3.30pm; free) cover such esoteric subjects as "The Mithraic Mysteries". Aside from fascinating exhibits within, the best part about the Rosicrucian is its garden grounds, featuring a replica of the Akhenaten Temple from Luxor.

Municipal Rose Garden

Naglee Ave, at Diana • Daily 8am–sunset • Free

Across the street and two blocks west of the Rosicrucian Egyptian Museum is another peaceful locale, San Jose's **Municipal Rose Garden**. This beautiful expanse of green and rows of wonderfully scented rose bushes is perfect for a picnic and the fountain in the garden's centre is a popular wading pool for youngsters.

Winchester Mystery House

525 S Winchester Blvd, just off I-280 near Hwy-17 • Daily summer 9am–7pm, winter 9am–5pm • Various tours $30–44 • ☎ 408 247 1313, ⓦ winchestermysteryhouse.com

This true American tourist trap is unmissable if you're into over-the-top yarns. The **Winchester Mystery House** belonged to Sarah Winchester, heiress to the Winchester rifle fortune, who was convinced upon her husband's death in 1884 that he had been taken by the spirits of men killed with his weapons. The ghosts told her that unless a room was built for each of them, the same fate would befall her. She took them so literally that the sound of hammers never ceased – 24 hours a day for the next thirty years. Now, still unfinished, the house is a hodgepodge of extensions and styles: extravagant staircases lead nowhere and windows open onto solid brick walls.

Santa Clara

University: 500 El Camino Real **Mission**: Daily sunrise–sunset • Free **Museum**: Tues–Sun 11am–4pm • Free • ☎ 408 554 4528, ⓦ scu.edu/desaisset

Engulfed in the sprawl of northwestern San Jose, the small community of **Santa Clara** holds its own area of interest. The late eighteenth-century **Mission Santa Clara de Asis**, just south of The Alameda (Route 82) is one of the least impressive structures in the mission chain but its remnants – it burned in a 1926 fire – have been subtly preserved and integrated into the campus of the Jesuit-run **University of Santa Clara**. The **de Saisset Museum** within the university complex traces the history of the mission through a permanent display of objects recovered from its ruins, along with changing shows of contemporary art. The bell in the belfry is original, a gift from King Carlos IV of Spain in 1798. Overall, the university is a green, quiet place to stroll around and pass an afternoon.

ARRIVAL AND DEPARTURE   SAN JOSE

By plane Most major domestic airlines fly direct into Norman J. Mineta San Jose International Airport (☎ 408 501 7600, ⓦ flysanjose.com), close to Downtown San Jose; the VTA SJC Airport Flyer express bus runs to downtown and Santa Clara for $4 and there is the usual choice of taxis, limos and shuttles.

By train Caltrain (see p.459) offers an hourly rail connection to San Francisco from San Jose Diridon station at 65 Cahill St.

By bus Greyhound runs regular services to other major Californian cities from its Downtown San Jose terminal at 70 S Almaden Ave.

GETTING AROUND AND INFORMATION

For local news and events, pick up a copy of the excellent *San Jose Mercury* (ⓦ mercurynews.com) or the free weekly *Metro* (ⓦ metroactive.com).

By bus and trolley Santa Clara Valley Transit Authority (VTA) ($2, day-pass $6; ☎ 408 321 2300, ⓦ vta.org) runs buses and modern trolleys around metropolitan San Jose.
Convention & Visitors Bureau The Team San Jose office is inside the Convention Center at 408 S Almaden Blvd (Mon–Fri 8am–5pm; ☎ 408 295 9600 or ☎ 800 726 5673, ⓦ sanjose.org), although it is more geared towards helping visiting businesspeople than the casual traveller.

ACCOMMODATION

San Jose's **hotels** are mainly aimed at business travellers and thus mostly functional. Rates also tend to be much pricier during the week but there are often great deals at weekends.

Fairmont Hotel 170 S Market St ☎ 408 998 1900 or ☎ 800 527 4727, ⓦ fairmont.com. San Jose's finest hotel is part of the luxury chain which began in San Francisco. It has all the amenities, such as room service, swimming pool and lounge, to go with sparkling service. <u>$179</u>
Hotel De Anza 233 W Santa Clara St ☎ 408 286 1000, ⓦ hoteldeanza.com. Smart business hotel in one of the livelier parts of town, which sometimes offers good internet deals at weekends. All rooms have king beds. <u>$209</u>

Ramada San Jose Convention Center 455 S 2nd St ☎ 408 298 3500 or ☎ 888 637 4861, ⓦ ramada.com. Fairly new branch of the trusty chain with bright but characterless rooms, conveniently situated near the city's main nightlife strip. <u>$159</u>
Valley Inn 2155 The Alameda ☎ 408 241 8500, ⓦ valleyinnsanjose.com. Above-average motel with compact, well-kept and brightly decorated rooms. Conveniently located for the Rosicrucian Museum and the western suburbs. <u>$119</u>

EATING

71 Saint Peter 71 N San Pedro St ☎ 408 971 8523, ⓦ 71saintpeter.com. Patio dining and oyster bar centred on a menu of filet mignon, pork loin, chicken and salads. Mains mostly $18–30. A hotspot with the in-crowd. Mon–Fri 11.30am–2pm & 5–9.30pm, Sat 5–9.30pm.
The Grill on the Alley 172 S Market St ☎ 408 294 2244, ⓦ thegrill.com. Smart modern steakhouse franchise, where businessmen on fat company accounts tuck into undeniably juicy steaks for at least $50 a pop. Mon–Thurs 11.30am–10pm, Fri 11.30am–11pm, Sat 5–11pm, Sun 5–9pm.
La Victoria Taqueria 140 E San Carlos St ☎ 408 298 5335, ⓦ lavicsj.com. Cheap-and-cheerful Mexican franchise, featuring all the favourites such as burritos and

tacos for under $10 and open until late. Daily 7am–3am.
★**Original Joe's** 301 S 1st St ☎ 408 292 7030, ⓦ originaljoes.com. San Jose institution, serving quality Italian specialities such as sauteed calf's liver in the $15–30 range, plus cheaper snacks. Mon–Thurs & Sun 11am–11pm, Fri & Sat 11am–midnight.
Peggy Sue's 29 N San Pedro St ☎ 408 298 6750 & 183 Park Ave ☎ 480 294 0252, ⓦ peggysues.com. Inexpensive milk shakes, burgers and fries (all under $10) served in a 1950s setting. Also has a vegetarian and kids' menu. Sun–Thurs 8am–midnight, Fri & Sat 8am–2am.
Scott's Seafood 185 Park Ave ☎ 408 971 1700, ⓦ scottsseafoodsj.com. Popular place near the Tech Museum, where you can enjoy seafood such as crab-stuffed

7

sustainable salmon for around $30 on the romantic rooftop patio. Mon–Wed 11.30am–1.30pm & 4.30–9pm, Thurs & Fri 11.30am–1.30pm & 4.30–9.30pm, Sat 5–9.30pm, Sun 10.30am–2pm & 4.30–9pm.

DRINKING AND NIGHTLIFE

Agenda Lounge 399 S 1st St ☎480 287 3991, ⓦagendalounge.com. The bar/restaurant/lounge in SoFA that heralded the arrival of nightlife in San Jose. DJ dancing and live jazz nightly. Reggae night on Sunday. Wed–Sat 5.30pm–2am, Sun 9pm–2am.

★**The Blank Club** 44 S Almaden Ave ☎408 292 5265, ⓦtheblankclub.com. Live shows most nights and the only regular local space for indie, punk and alternative sounds. Mon–Sat 9pm–2am.

The Brit 173 W Santa Clara St ☎480 266 0550, ⓦbritanniaarmsdowntown.com. One of the growing chain of British-themed pubs with fish'n'chips, real ale,

footie (meaning soccer) on TV and a trivia quiz night. Daily 11am–2am.

Cafe Stritch 374 S 1st St ☎480 280 6161, ⓦcafestritch.com. This up-and-coming place does a decent line in beers, cocktails and bar snacks. Also features live pop and rock shows some nights. Wed–Sat 4pm–2am, Sun 4pm–midnight.

Dive Bar 78 E Santa Clara St ☎480 288 5252, ⓦsjdivebar.com. The name is rather misleading as the premises are actually smart with brick walls and leather chairs. A fun hangout nonetheless, with billiard tables and frequent live music. Daily 4pm–2am.

ENTERTAINMENT AND THEATRE

Camera 3 288 S 1st St ☎408 294 3334, ⓦcameracinemas.com. This is the South Bay's premier cinema for independent and foreign film showings. It also has space for live comedy and a hip café.

The Stage 490 S 1st St ☎408 283 7142, ⓦsanjosestage.com. This theatre showcases serious contemporary dramas by established and up-and-coming writers, both local and internationally renowned. Performances Wed–Sat; tickets $20–50.

The Peninsula coast

The largely undeveloped **coastline** of the Peninsula south of San Francisco is worlds away from the inland valleys. A few small towns, countless beaches and salty prides of sea lions trace the way 75 miles south to the mellow summer fun of Santa Cruz and Capitola. Bluffs protect the few **nudist beaches** from prying eyes and make a popular launching pad for hang-glider pilots, particularly at **Fort Funston**, a mile south of the San Francisco Zoo, which is also the point where the earthquake-causing San Andreas Fault enters the sea, not to surface again until Point Reyes. **Skyline Boulevard** follows the coast from here past the repetitious tracts of proverbial ticky-tacky houses that make up Daly City, before heading inland towards Woodside at its intersection with Hwy-1, which continues south along the coast. Driving **Hwy-1** can be a relaxing jaunt providing jaw-dropping views of the ocean, as long as you avoid the summer-weekend traffic jams. Try hitting the road at sunrise if you can manage it and, provided the fog isn't obscuring everything, expect a magical ride.

Pacifica and around

San Pedro Point, a popular surfing beach fifteen miles south of San Francisco proper, and the town of **Pacifica** mark the southern extent of the city's suburban sprawl. Pacifica is a pleasant stopover for lunch and wave-gazing around Rockaway Beach. It exudes the feeling of an old-time resort and seems a million miles away from San Francisco.

  Sweeney Ridge, south of Pacifica, is the point from where Spanish explorer Gaspar de Portola discovered the San Francisco Bay in 1769. In the nineteenth century Pacifica's **Ocean Shore Railroad Depot**, now a private residence, was built here and is one of the few surviving remnants of an ill-advised train line between San Francisco and Santa Cruz. Wiped out during the 1906 earthquake, the line was in any case never more than a third complete. Its few patrons had to transfer back and forth by ferry to connect the stretches of track that were built, traces of which you can still see scarring the face of the bluffs.

  The continually eroding cliffs make construction of any route along the coast difficult, as evidenced a mile south by the **Devil's Slide**, which required constant repairs over the decades until it finally closed to motorized traffic in 2013, when the new Tom

Lantos tunnels opened. The old road has been converted into a fine hiker/biker trail. The slide area was a popular dumping spot for corpses of those who fell foul of rum-runners during Prohibition and is featured under various names in many of Dashiell Hammett's detective stories.

Just south of the Devil's Slide, **Gray Whale Cove State Beach** (daily 8am–sunset; free) is clothing-optional. Despite the name, it's not an especially great place to look for migrating grey whales, but the stairway at the bus stop does lead down to a lovely strand.

Montara and around

Around five miles south of Pacifica, the small and sleepy town of **Montara** is draped across a leafy hillside. A good half-mile west of Hwy-1, the red-roofed buildings of the 1875 **Montara Lighthouse**, set among the windswept Monterey pine trees at the top of a steep cliff, have been converted into a youth hostel (see p.521).

Just south of the turn to the Montara lighthouse, at the end of California Street, the **Fitzgerald Marine Reserve** (8am–sunset; free; ☎650 728 3584, ⊕fitzgeraldreserve.org) offers three miles of diverse oceanic habitat, peaceful trails and, at low tide, the best tide pools in the Bay Area. The ranger often gives free interpretive walks through the reserve at low tide, the best time to explore, so call ahead or ask at one of the coast's tourist offices for low-tide times. The reserve encompasses tranquil **Moss Beach** and the eponymous community behind it.

7

Half Moon Bay

Just beyond the south end of Fitzgerald Marine Reserve, **Pillar Point** juts out into the Pacific, marking the northern end of gently curving **Half Moon Bay**, whose crescent shape gives it its name. **Mavericks Beach**, just off Pillar Point beyond the enormous communications dish, is the first of its splendid beaches and boasts the largest waves in North America. It attracts some of the world's best (and craziest) surfers when conditions are right and was captured in all its raging glory in the surfing documentary *Riding Giants*. Just watching them can be an exhilarating way to spend an hour or so and hundreds of people do just that every day. There's a long breakwater you can walk out on, too, but remember never to turn your back to the ocean – rogue waves have crashed in and swept unsuspecting tourists to their deaths.

Immediately to the south, the neighbouring villages of **Princeton-by-the-Sea**, whose main drag beside the marina has become extremely trendy, and **El Grenada** both have good restaurants serving freshly caught fish and seafood. Further along, surfers also frequent the waters just offshore from the splendid long stretch of **Miramar Beach**.

The delightful **town of Half Moon Bay** itself lies just over twenty miles from the southern reaches of San Francisco and is the largest place between there and Santa Cruz. It was originally called Spanishtown, as it was founded when Spanish settlers forced the native Costona off the land in the 1840s and is thus the oldest European settlement in San Mateo County. Lined by miles of sandy beaches, the town is surprisingly rural considering its proximity to San Francisco and Silicon Valley and sports a number of ornate Victorian wooden houses clustered around its centre. The oldest of these, at the north end of Main Street, was built in 1849 just across a little stone bridge over Pillarcitos Creek.

RIDING BY THE WAVES

If you fancy an equestrian experience beside the Pacific, Sea Horse Ranch and Friendly Acres, one mile north of Half Moon Bay at 2150 N Cabrillo Hwy (daily 8am–5.30pm; ☎650 726 9903, ⊕seahorseranch.org), operate **trail rides** for $55/hour and one-hour-thirty-minute beach rides for $65, or you can combine the two and get two hours for $75. Reservations (by phone only) are essential for individuals and small groups alike.

The town hosts two popular festivals, the first being the **Holy Ghost and Pentecost Festival**, a parade and barbecue held on the seventh Sunday after Easter; the other is the **Pumpkin Festival**, which celebrates the harvest of the area's many pumpkin farms just in time for Halloween, when the fields around town are full of families searching for the perfect jack-o'-lantern to greet the hordes of trick-or-treaters. **Half Moon Bay State Park** (daily 8am–sunset; $10 parking), half a mile west of the town, has a great stretch of beach and good camping (see opposite).

Butano Redwood Forest and Butano State Park
If you've got a car and it's not a great day for the beach, head up into the hills above the coast, where the thousands of acres of the **Butano Redwood Forest** feel at their most ancient and primeval in the greyest, gloomiest weather. About half of the land between San Jose and the coast is protected from development in a variety of state and county parks, all of which are virtually deserted despite being within a thirty-minute drive of the Silicon Valley sprawl. Any one of a dozen roads heads through endless stands of untouched forest and even the briefest of walks will take you seemingly miles from any sign of civilization. Hwy-84 climbs up from San Gregorio through the Sam McDonald County Park to the hamlet of **La Honda**, where Ken Kesey had his ranch during the Sixties and once notoriously invited the Hell's Angels to an acid-fuelled party. From here, you can continue on to Palo Alto or loop back to the coast via Pescadero Road. A mile east of Pescadero, Cloverdale Road heads south to **Butano State Park**, where you can hike and camp (see opposite) overlooking the Pacific.

Pescadero and around
Tiny **Pescadero** itself has one of the best places to eat on the Peninsula – *Duarte's Tavern* (see p.522) – as well as a gas station, just about the last place to fill up north of Santa Cruz. Just north of the turn-off to the village from Hwy-1, **Pescadero State Beach** is yet another fine spot for a dip, with no time restrictions or parking fee. The marsh between the beach and the town is a great place for watching waterfowl, especially at high tide. Pescadero, which was founded by Portuguese fishermen, celebrates the same **Holy Ghost Festival** as Half Moon Bay but a week earlier, on the sixth Sunday after Easter. The festival is also known by its Portuguese name of Chamarita.

Five miles south of Pescadero, you can visit the grounds of the **Pigeon Point Lighthouse** (daily 8am–sunset; free; ☎650 879 2120) but the structure itself is closed, pending a proposed $11 million renovation into an education centre. The old lighthouse-keeper's quarters function as the memorable *HI-Pigeon Point Lighthouse Hostel* (see opposite). The calmest, most pleasant beach for wading is **Bean Hollow State Beach**, a mile north of the hostel; it's free but has very limited parking.

The Año Nuevo State Reserve
13 miles south of Pescadero • Elephant seal tours: hourly 8am–4pm • $7 per person, $10 parking • ☎ 650 879 2025, ⓦ parks.ca.gov/anonuevo
If you're here between mid-December and the end of March visit the **Año Nuevo State Reserve** for a chance to see one of nature's most bizarre spectacles – the mating rituals of **northern elephant seals**. These massive, ungainly creatures, fifteen feet long and weighing up to three tonnes, were once found all along the coast, though they were nearly hunted to extinction by whalers in the nineteenth century. During the mating season, the beach is literally a seething mass of blubbery bodies, with the trunk-nosed males fighting it out for the right to sire as many as fifty pups in a season. At any time of the year, you're likely to see half a dozen or so dozing in the sands. The reserve is also good for birding, and in March you might even catch sight of migrating grey whales.

The slowly resurgent Año Nuevo elephant seal population is still carefully protected and during the breeding season the obligatory guided tours – designed to protect spectators as much as to give the seals some privacy – begin booking in October. Otherwise tickets are usually made available to people staying at the *Pigeon Point*

Lighthouse Hostel, and from April to November you can get a free permit from the park entrance to visit the point. The reserve is closed during the first half of December.

ARRIVAL AND INFORMATION

By bus BART only travels down the Peninsula as far as Millbrae but you can connect onto SamTrans (see p.511) buses south along the coast to Half Moon Bay.

Pacifica Chamber of Commerce 225 Rockaway Beach Ave (Mon–Fri 9am–5pm; ☎650 355 4122,

THE PENINSULA COAST

ⓦ pacificachamber.com).

Half Moon Bay Chamber of Commerce 235 Main St (Mon–Fri 9am–5pm, Sat & Sun 10am–3pm; ☎650 726 8380, ⓦ halfmoonbaychamber.com).

ACCOMMODATION

PACIFICA

Pacifica Motor Inn 200 Rockaway Beach Ave ☎650 359 7700 or ☎800 522 3772, ⓦ pacificamotorinn.com. Simple but large pet-friendly motel rooms just a block inland from the beach. Complimentary continental breakfasts. **$149**

Sea Breeze Motel 100 Rockaway Beach Ave ☎650 359 3903, ⓦ nicksrestaurant.net. These small rooms, attached to *Nick's* (see below), have the advantage of ocean views. It's also just a few yards to the small but pretty black-sand beach. **$130**

MONTARA AND AROUND

Goose & Turrets 835 George St ☎650 728 5451, ⓦ gooseandturretsbandb.com. Quirky and cosy Victorian house run by an engaging older couple. Great gourmet breakfasts and afternoon tea included. **$200**

HI Point Montara Lighthouse Off Hwy-1, SamTrans bus #294 from Pacifica ☎650 728 7177, ⓦ norcalhostels.org. Dorms and rooms are in the converted outhouses of an 1875 lighthouse. Office hours 7.30am–10pm. Small discount for HI members. Dorms **$30**, doubles **$80**

Seal Cove Inn 221 Cypress Ave, Moss Beach ☎650 728 4114 or ☎800 884 4431, ⓦ sealcoveinn.com. Splendid inn with the style of an opulent hotel but B&B friendliness. Has a path to the Fitzgerald Marine Reserve. **$325**

HALF MOON BAY

Beach House 4100 N Cabrillo Hwy (Hwy-1), El Granada ☎650 712 0220 or ☎800 315 9366, ⓦ beach-house .com. Huge modern boutique hotel, where all 54 junior suites are spacious, well furnished and most look out on the ocean. **$235**

Cypress Inn on Miramar Beach 407 Mirada Rd, Miramar Beach ☎650 726 6002, ⓦ cypressinn.com. Fine set of three modern clapboard buildings some of whose luxurious rooms have balconies right on the ocean. Great buffet breakfast and evening wine & cheese included. **$229**

Half Moon Bay State Beach Campground 95 Kelly Ave, 1 mile west of Half Moon Bay ☎800 444 7275, ⓦ parks.ca.gov. Plenty of tent and RV sites in the woods, right behind the splendid beach. Decent shared facilities. Pitches **$35**, plus hike/bike-in **$7**, hookup **$50**

★ **Mill Rose Inn** 615 Mill St, Half Moon Bay ☎650 726 8750, ⓦ millroseinn.com. Top of the B&Bs in town is this intricately designed place with luxurious rooms. The gazebo in the beautiful garden contains a huge hot tub. **$230**

Nantucket Whale Inn 779 Main St, Half Moon Bay ☎650 726 1616, ⓦ nantucketwhaleinn.com. Thoroughly renovated Victorian house with cosy and beautifully furnished rooms, the pricier ones with hot tubs. It's an easy walk to the town's restaurants and facilities. **$169**

Oceano Hotel & Spa 280 Capistrano Rd, Princeton-by-the-Sea ☎650 726 5400, ⓦ oceanohalfmoonbay.com. Latching itself onto the cachet of Half Moon Bay, this modern luxury hotel offers superbly fitted out rooms with harbour views and full spa facilities. Also boasts a good bar and grill. **$259**

PESCADERO AND AROUND

Butano State Park Campground 1500 Cloverdale Rd ☎800 444 7275, ⓦ reserveamerica.com. Tent spaces located in a beautiful redwood forest. Clean bathrooms and cooking facilities. **$35**

Costanoa Coastal Lodge & Camp 2001 Rossi Rd, just south of Pescadero ☎650 879 1100 or ☎877 262 7848, ⓦ costanoa.com. Offers a pampered night under the stars with accommodation ranging from smart pre-erected tents, through cabins to luxury suites. Spa on site. Tents **$97**, doubles **$193**

★ **HI Pigeon Point Lighthouse Hostel** 5 miles south of Pescadero ☎650 879 0633, ⓦ norcalhostels.org. Stay in the well-kept old lighthouse-keeper's quarters and enjoy the ocean view and breeze. Check-in from 3pm, curfew 11pm; reservations essential in summer. Discount for HI members. Dorms from **$28.50**, doubles **$80**

EATING AND DRINKING

PACIFICA

Nick's Seashore Restaurant 101 Rockaway Beach Ave ☎650 359 3903, ⓦ nicksrestaurant.net. An all-purpose

joint providing cheap breakfasts, moderate pasta options, and pricier steak/seafood dishes, all at around $16–38. Mon–Thurs 11am–10pm, Fri 9am–10pm, Sat & Sun

7

8am–10pm, bar till 1am.

Rock'n'Rob's 450 Dondee St ☎ 650 359 3663. Tucked in a small mall close to the seafront, this simple diner is recommended for its filling burgers and other classic American favourites. Mon & Wed–Sun 11.30am–8pm.

MONTARA

★ **La Costanera** 8150 Cabrillo Hwy (Hwy-1) ☎ 650 728 1600, ⓦ lacostanerarestaurant.com. One of the most highly rated venues on the coast, serving traditional Peruvian cuisine and lovely Pisco sours in the smart interior or on the breezy deck. Tues–Thurs & Sun 5–9pm, Fri & Sat 5–10pm.

Moss Beach Distillery 140 Beach Way, Moss Beach ☎ 650 728 5595, ⓦ mossbeachdistillery.com. Top-quality seafood and meat dishes go for $22–36/main course at the popular restaurant but there's a cheaper bar menu or you can enjoy a sunset cocktail from the patio overlooking the ocean. Mon–Thurs noon–8.30pm, Fri & Sat noon–9pm, Sun 11am–8.30pm.

HALF MOON BAY

Barbara's Fish Trap 281 Capistrano Rd, Princeton-by-the-Sea ☎ 650 728 7049, ⓦ barbarasfishtrap.com. This oceanfront place has an unbeatable view and serves excellent fish, seafood and pasta dishes for around $20–25. Don't miss their delicious clam chowder. Mon–Thurs & Sun 11am–8.30pm, Fri & Sat 11am–9pm.

Cameron's Inn 1410 S Cabrillo Hwy (Hwy-1), 1 mile south of Half Moon Bay ☎ 650 726 5705, ⓦ cameronsinn .com. Decent pub grub for $10–16, over 20 draught beers from English ales to local microbrews, British football on TV and a unique double-decker bus make this a top spot. Three rooms available too. Daily 11am–11pm.

Cetrella 845 Main St, Half Moon Bay ☎ 650 726 4090, ⓦ cetrella.com. One of the best options right in town is this award-winning Mediterranean restaurant, with delights such as braised Atkins Ranch lamb shank for $29; live jazz Sat & Sun evenings. Wed, Thurs & Sun 5.30–9.30pm, Fri & Sat 5.30–10pm; bar opens later.

Half Moon Bay Brewing Company 390 Capistrano Ave, Princeton-by-the-Sea ☎ 650 728 2739, ⓦ hmbbrewingco.com. An excellent option where you can wash down a full meal, mostly under $20, or cheaper bar snack with their own finely crafted ales. Mon–Thurs 11am–9pm, Fri 11am–11pm, Sat 10am–11pm, Sun 10am–10pm; bar opens later.

Old Princeton Landing 460 Capistrano Ave, Princeton-by-the-Sea ☎ 650 728 7096, ⓦ oplhmb.com. Nothing fancy about this bar, which is how the predominantly local clientele like it. Decent beers and pub grub for $10–16 though. Mon–Sat 11am–2am, Sun 10am–2am; food until 9pm.

Pasta Moon 315 Main St, Half Moon Bay ☎ 650 726 5125, ⓦ pastamoon.com. Elegant but unpretentious Italian place that serves excellent pizza, pasta and mouthwatering dishes such as seafood spiedini. Mains $20–38. Mon–Fri 11.30am–2pm & 5.30–10pm, Sat–Sun noon–3pm & 5.30–10pm.

★ **Sam's Chowder House** 4210 Cabrillo Hwy (Hwy-1), El Granada ☎ 650 712 0245, ⓦ samschowderhouse.com. One of the Peninsula's prime restaurants, serving New England-style seafood, as well as meat dishes, for $20–30. Now there's a mobile truck and a new location in Palo Alto. Mon–Thurs 11.30am–9pm, Fri 11.30am–9.30pm, Sat 11am–9.30pm, Sun 11am–9pm.

Via Uno 2810 N Cabrillo Hwy (Hwy-1), 2 miles north of Half Moon Bay ☎ 650 560 8858, ⓦ viaunorestaurant .com. With a pizza oven made in Naples, sunset views and friendly, attentive service, this is a great choice. Authentic Italian mains cost $20–25. Mon–Thurs 11.30am–2.30pm & 5–9.30pm, Fri 11.30am–2.30pm & 5–10pm, Sat 11.30am–10pm, Sun 11.30am–9pm.

PESCADERO

★ **Duarte's Tavern** 202 Stage Rd ☎ 650 879 0464, ⓦ duartestavern.com. Open since 1894 and still one of the best places to eat on the Peninsula. Feast on artichoke soup and huge portions of fish ($22–26) in a relaxed atmosphere. Great breakfasts too. Daily 7am–8pm.

Marin County

Across the Golden Gate from San Francisco, **Marin County** (pronounced "Ma-RINN") is an unabashed introduction to California self-indulgence: an elitist pleasure zone of conspicuous luxury and abundant natural beauty, with sunshine, high mountains, thick redwood forests and sandy if often fog-bound beaches. Often ranked as the wealthiest county in the US, Marin has attracted a sizeable contingent of Northern California's rich professionals, many of whom grew up during the Flower Power years of the 1960s, and lend the place its New Age feel and reputation. Indeed, the fact that numerous 60s musical heroes still live in the county means that they can occasionally still be found performing in the intimate surroundings of friendly local bars and small venues. Though many of the cocaine-and-hot-tub devotees who seemed to populate the swanky waterside towns in the 1970s have traded in their drug habits for mountain bikes – which were invented here – life in Marin still centres on personal pleasure and the throngs you see hiking and cycling at weekends, not to mention the hundreds of esoteric self-help practitioners (rolfing, rebirthing and soul-travel therapists fill up the classified ads of the local papers) prove that residents of Marin work hard to maintain their easy air of physical and mental wellbeing.

Flashy modern ferries, appointed with fully stocked bars, sail across the bay from San Francisco and present a marvellous initial view of the county. As you head past desolate Alcatraz Island, curvaceous **Mount Tamalpais** looms larger until you land near its foot in one of the chic bayside settlements of **Sausalito** or **Tiburon**. **Angel Island**, in the middle of the bay but most easily accessed from Tiburon, provides relief from the excessive style-consciousness of both towns, retaining a wild, untouched feeling among the eerie ruins of derelict military fortifications.

The bulk of Marin County rests on the slopes of the ridges that divide the Peninsula down the middle, separating the sophisticated harbourside towns in the east from the untrammelled wilderness of the Pacific Coast in the west. The **Marin Headlands**, just across the Golden Gate Bridge from San Francisco, hold time-warped old battlements and gun emplacements that once protected San Francisco's harbour from would-be invaders. Along the coastline that spreads north, the broad shore of **Stinson Beach** is the Bay Area's finest and widest stretch of sand, beyond which Hwy-1 clings to the coast past the counterculture village of **Bolinas** to seascapes around **Point Reyes**, where it's thought Sir Francis Drake may have landed in 1579. Whale- and seal-watchers congregate here year-round for glimpses of migrations and matings.

7

Inland, the heights of Mount Tamalpais, and specifically **Muir Woods**, are a magnet to sightseers and nature lovers, who come to wander through one of the county's few surviving stands of the native coastal redwood trees. Such trees covered most of Marin before they were chopped down to build and rebuild the wooden houses of San Francisco. The long-vanished lumber mills of the rustic town of **Mill Valley**, whose upper reaches overlook the bay from the slopes of Mount Tam, as it's locally known, bear the guilt for much of this destruction; the oldest town in Marin County is now home to an eclectic bunch of art galleries and cafés, as well as 60s legends like Grace Slick and Phil Lesh. Further north, Marin's largest town, **San Rafael**, is rather bland, though its outskirts contain two of the most unusual attractions in the county: **Frank Lloyd Wright**'s peculiar Civic Center complex and the preserved remnants of an old Chinese fishing village in **China Camp State Park**.

ARRIVAL AND DEPARTURE   MARIN COUNTY

By car It's definitely easiest to get to and around Marin County by car. US-101 enters it across the Golden Gate Bridge from San Francisco (outbound free; $7 city-bound toll must be paid electronically), while I-580 comes in from the East Bay via the San Rafael Bridge ($5 towards Marin, cash payment allowed; return free). Once in Marin, scenic Hwy-1 weaves its way over the lower reaches of Mt Tamalpais to the coastal beaches and towns.

By bus Golden Gate Transit (☎415 923 2000, ⓦgoldengatetransit.org) offers a comprehensive bus service around Marin County and across the Golden Gate Bridge from the Transbay Terminal in San Francisco. Every 30min throughout the day, hourly late at night; some areas can only be reached by rush-hour commuter services. Route #40, the only service between Marin County and the East Bay, runs from the San Rafael Transit Center to the Del

Norte BART station in El Cerrito.

By ferry To Sausalito, Larkspur and Tiburon There are frequent connections by smart modern ferries to Sausalito, Larkspur and Tiburon from San Francisco's Ferry Building every 30–40min during the rush hour, roughly hourly during the rest of the day and about every 1hr30min–2hr on weekends and holidays. These are run by Golden Gate Ferry (see p.461) from $11 each way and by Blue & Gold Fleet ferries (see p.461) for $10 each way. To Angel Island Blue & Gold Fleet provides a service direct to Angel Island from Pier 41 (Mon–Fri 2 daily Sat–Sun 4 daily; $8 one-way). From Tiburon, there's the Angel Island ferry ($13.50 return, $1/bicycle; ☎415 435 2131, ⓦangelislandferry .com; Jan, Feb, Nov & Dec weekends only 4 daily, March 2–4 daily, April 2–7 daily, May–Sept 4–8 daily, Oct 2–8 daily).

INFORMATION AND TOURS

Information on cultural events can be found in the widely available free local papers, the down-to-earth *Coastal Post* (ⓦcoastalpost.com) or New Age *Pacific Sun* (ⓦpacificsun.com).

Marin County Visitors Bureau Signposted off US-101 at 1 Mitchell Blvd (Mon–Fri 9am–5pm; ☎415 925 2060 or ☎866 925 2060, ⓦvisitmarin.org).
Gray Line ☎415 558 9400, ⓦgrayline.com. Offers 4–5hr guided bus tours from the Transbay Terminal in San Francisco, taking in Sausalito and Muir Woods (daily 9.15am & 2.15pm; $62, $91 with bay cruise).

Blue & Gold Fleet ☎415 705 8200, ⓦblueandgoldfleet .com. Offers a bus trip to Muir Woods (daily 9am & 2pm; 4hr; $59), with an option to return to San Francisco by ferry from Tiburon.
Angel Island Company ☎415 897 0715, ⓦangelisland .com. Offers tram tours for $15.50; you can also take a Segway tour for $71.

The Marin Headlands

Muni bus #76 from San Francisco (Sat, Sun & holidays only)

The largely undeveloped **MARIN HEADLANDS** of the Golden Gate National Recreation Area, across the Golden Gate Bridge from San Francisco, afford some of the most impressive views of the bridge and the city behind. As the regular fog rolls in, the breathtaking image of the bridge's stanchions tantalizingly drifting in and out of sight and the fleeting glimpses of downtown skyscrapers will abide long in the memory. If you're driving, take the first turn as you exit the bridge (Alexander Ave) and follow the sign back to San Francisco – the one-way circle trip back to the bridge heads first to the west along Conzelman Road and up a steep hill. You'll pass through a largely undeveloped land, dotted with the concrete remains of Civil War and World War II old forts and gun emplacements standing guard over the entrance to the bay. The coastline here is much more rugged than it is on the San Francisco side, making it a great place for an aimless clifftop hike or a stroll along one of the beaches at the bottom of treacherous footpaths.

Battery Wallace

The first installation as you climb the steep Marin Headlands is **Battery Wallace**, the largest and most impressive of the artillery sites along the rocky coast here, cut through a hillside above the southwestern tip of the Peninsula. The angular military geometry survives, framing views of the Pacific Ocean and the Golden Gate Bridge. Otherwise, continue along Conzelman for incredible views of the city from any of the many lay-bys. For birdwatching, walk from the Battery Wallace parking lot through tunnels that lead five hundred yards to the opposite bluff, from where various sea birds and birds of prey can be seen in large numbers.

Point Bonita Lighthouse

Mon, Sat & Sun 12.30–3.30pm • Free • ☎415 331 1540, ⓦnps.gov/goga

To approach **Point Bonita Lighthouse** by vehicle, keep winding all the way down Conzelman from Battery Wallace, as it becomes one-way. The structure stands sentry at the very end of the headlands and is open for tours. Conzelman comes to a "T" in the road; turn left and park your car on the side of the road or at the parking lot three hundred yards west, at the end of the drive. To reach the lighthouse, you have to walk the half-mile pathway down, a beautiful stroll that takes you through a tunnel cut into the cliff, and across a precarious suspension bridge.

The outer headlands

Nike Missile Site Thurs–Sat 12.30–3.30pm • Free • ☎415 331 1540, ⓦnps.gov/goga

If you really want to relive holocaustic Cold War nightmares, you can visit the **Nike Missile Site** at **Fort Barry** (Thurs–Sat 12.30–3.30pm; ⓦnps.gov/goga) and take a free guided tour of an abandoned 1950s ballistic-missile launch pad, complete with disarmed nuclear missiles.

SEA-KAYAKING AT SAUSALITO

If you want to get on the waters around Sausalito yourself, a good energetic diversion is sea-kayaking. **Sea Trek** (April–Oct Mon–Fri 9am–5pm, Sat & Sun 8.30am–5pm; ☎415 332 8494, ⓦseatrek.com) rents single or double sea-kayaks beginning at $25/40 for one hour's worth of superb paddling around the bay. They offer sit-on-top kayaks, lessons and safe routes for first-timers, or closed kayaks and directions around Angel Island for the more experienced.

If you're after a more pacifistic pastime, stop off at the **Marin Headlands Visitor Center** (see below) alongside Rodeo Lagoon for free maps of popular hiking trails in the area. Across the road and a bit further along, one of the largest of Fort Barry's old residential buildings has been converted into the spacious but homely *HI–Marin Headlands* hostel (see below), an excellent base for more extended explorations of the inland ridges and valleys.

Rodeo Beach

Turn off to the left where Bunker Road snakes down to wide, sandy **Rodeo Beach**. The beach separates the chilly ocean from the marshy warm water of **Rodeo Lagoon**, where swimming is prohibited to protect nesting sea birds.

Marine Mammal Center

2000 Bunker Rd • Daily 10am–5pm • Free • ☎415 289 7325, ⓦmarinemammalcenter.org

North of the Rodeo Lagoon, you can visit the **Marine Mammal Center** which rescues and rehabilitates injured and orphaned sea creatures, including dolphins and sea otters. There are docent-led tours and, for those with more time on their hands, opportunities to get involved as a volunteer.

INFORMATION   **MARIN HEADLANDS**

Marin Headlands Visitor Center Fort Barry Chapel, Field Rd, at Bunker (daily 9.30am–4.30pm; ☎415 331 1540, ⓦnps.gov/goga).

ACCOMMODATION

★**HI-Marin Headlands** Building 941, Fort Barry ☎415 331 2777, ⓦnorcalhostels.org. Worth the effort for its setting, in cosy old army barracks near the ocean. On weekends and hols only, Muni bus #76 from San Francisco stops right outside. The whole place is closed 10am–3.30pm, except for check-in. Dorms $28, doubles $82

Marin Headlands campgrounds ☎877 444 6777, ⓦrecreation.gov. Five campgrounds, the best of which is the very popular *Kirby Cove* (open April–Oct only), at the northern foot of the Golden Gate Bridge. Of the remaining sites, one is a group campground and the other three are free. Kirby Cove $25

Sausalito

SAUSALITO, fronting the bay below US-101, is a picturesque, snug little town of exclusive restaurants and pricey boutiques along a pretty waterfront promenade. Expensive, quirkily designed houses climb the overgrown cliffs above **Bridgeway Avenue**, the main route through town. Sausalito used to be a fairly gritty community of fishermen and sea-traders, full of bars and bordellos, and despite its upscale modern face it still makes a fun day out from San Francisco by ferry; boats arrive next to the Sausalito Yacht Club in the centre of town. Hang out in one of the waterfront bars and watch the crowds strolling along the esplanade or climb the stairways above Bridgeway Avenue and amble around the leafy hills.

Many of the old working wharves and warehouses that made Sausalito a haven for smugglers and Prohibition-era rum-runners are long gone; most have been taken over by dull strip malls, though some stretches have survived the tourist onslaught. A mile north of the town centre along Bridgeway Avenue, an ad hoc community of exotic **barges** and **houseboats**, some of which have been moored here since the 1950s, are staving off eviction to make room for yet another luxury marina. For now, many of the boats – one looks like a South Pacific island, another like the Taj Mahal – can still be viewed at Waldo Point.

Bay Model Visitor Center

2100 Bridgeway Ave • Summer Tues–Fri 9am–4pm, Sat 10am–5pm; rest of year Tues–Sat 9am–4pm • Free • ☎ 415 332 3870, ⊕ baymodelalliance.org

Half a mile south of Waldo Point, the cavernous concrete **Bay Model Visitor Center** is perhaps Sausalito's most unique attraction. Inside the huge building, elevated walkways lead you around a scale model of the bay and its surrounding deltas and aquatic inhabitants, offering insight on the enormity and diversity of this area.

Bay Area Discovery Museum

557 McReynolds Rd • Summer daily 9am–5pm; rest of year Tues–Fri 9am–4pm, Sat & Sun 9am–5pm • $13.95, free every first Wed • ☎ 415 339 3900, ⊕ baykidsmuseum.org

South of Sausalito towards the Golden Gate Bridge is the **Bay Area Discovery Museum**. Within the remodelled barracks of **Fort Baker**, it holds a series of activities and workshops for youngsters up to around age 10, including art and media rooms as well as the outdoor Lookout Cove area. Here kids can play in a mini-tide pool, on a shipwreck or on the model of the Golden Gate Bridge as it was during construction – pretty cool, as the real one is visible in the distance if it's clear.

INFORMATION   SAUSALITO

Sausalito Chamber of Commerce 1913 Bridgeway Ave (Tues–Sun 11.30am–4pm; ☎ 415 331 7262, ⊕ sausalito.org).

ACCOMMODATION

Casa Madrona 801 Bridgeway Ave ☎ 415 332 0502 or ☎ 800 567 9524, ⊕ casamadrona.com. Deluxe, all mod cons hotel with an extension spreading up the hill above the bay. All rooms are tastefully decorated. Spa facilities available. **$199**

Hotel Sausalito 16 El Portal ☎ 415 332 0700 or ☎ 888 442 0700, ⊕ hotelsausalito.com. Sixteen rooms, decorated in French Riviera style, with views across the park and harbour. Owned and run by an entertaining Scot. **$175**

EATING AND DRINKING

Bridgeway Café 633 Bridgeway Ave ☎ 415 332 3426, ⊕ bridgeway-cafe.4t.com. A good place to relax over a coffee or grab a gourmet egg breakfast at reasonable prices by local standards. Daily 7.30am–5pm.

★ **Fish** 350 Harbor Drive ☎ 415 331 3474, ⊕ 331fish .com. This place makes a point of serving sustainable fish and seafood in undoubted style. Follow the Portuguese red chowder with a tuna melt for $17. Good beers available. Daily 11.30am–8.30pm.

No Name Bar 757 Bridgeway Ave ☎ 415 332 1392, ⊕ thenonamebar.com. An ex-haunt of the Beats; hosts live music, mostly jazz, every night beginning at 8pm and on Sundays 3–7pm. Mon–Fri 11am–midnight, Sat & Sun 11am–1am.

Poggio 777 Bridgeway Ave ☎ 415 332 7771, ⊕ poggiotrattoria.com. Excellent Italian cuisine, cooked

from many ingredients imported from Italy. Meat and fish main courses range in price from $22 to $69 for a Porterhouse steak – breakfast options include waffles and bagels. Daily 6.30–11am & 11.30am–11pm.

Sweet Ginger 400 Caledonia St ☎ 415 332 1683, ⊕ sweetgingersausalito.com. Small Japanese restaurant that serves sushi, sashimi and main courses like tempura and teriyaki in the $15–20 range. Tues–Thurs 11.30am–3pm & 5–10pm, Fri 11.30am–3pm & 5–10.30pm, Sat noon–3pm & 5–10.30pm, Sun 4.30–9.30pm.

Tommy's Wok 3001 Bridgeway ☎ 415 332 5818, ⊕ tommyswok.com. This Chinese spot specializes in organic vegetables, free-range meats, and fresh seafood, cooked using Mandarin, Hunan and Szechuan recipes. Most items under $10. Mon–Thurs 11.30am–3pm & 4–9pm, Fri & Sat 11.30am–3pm & 4–9.30pm.

The Marin County Coast to Bolinas

Marin Transit (☎ 415 226 0855, ⊕ marintransit.org) operates route #61 (4–12 daily) from Marin City (starts at Sausalito at weekends) via Mill Valley and Panoramic Hwy to Stinson Beach and finally Bolinas

FROM TOP NORTHERN ELEPHANT SEALS, AÑO NUEVO STATE RESERVE (P.520); POINT REYES NATIONAL SEASHORE (P.533) >

The **Shoreline Highway**, Hwy-1, cuts off west from US-101 just north of Sausalito, following the old main highway towards Mill Valley (see p.530). The first turn on the left leads up to the less-visited northern expanses of the Golden Gate National Recreation Area. You can take a beautiful three-mile hike from the parking lot at the end of the road, heading down along the secluded and lushly green **Tennessee Valley** to a small beach along a rocky cove, or you can take a trail-ride lesson on horseback from Miwok Livery, 701 Tennessee Valley Rd (Sat 10.30am & 1.30pm; $100/1hr 30min; ☎415 383 8048, ⊚miwokstables.com). From the head of the valley, **Panoramic Highway** spears off Hwy-1 to the right, following the ridge north to Muir Woods and Mount Tamalpais; Marin Transit # 61 to Stinson Beach follows this route (see below). Be warned, however, that the hillsides are usually choked with fog until 11am and most of the day in summer, making the approach from San Francisco to Stinson Beach/ Bolinas via Hwy-1 both dangerous and uninteresting – go later in the day.

Green Gulch Farm Zen Centre

1601 Shoreline Hwy • **Welcome Center** Mon–Sat 9am–noon & 1.30–1.45pm, Sun 9am–5.45pm • ☎ 415 383 3134 • ⊚ sfzc.org

Two miles below the crest of the Panoramic Highway that climbs Mount Tamalpais (see opposite), a small paved lane cuts off to the left, dropping down to the bottom of the broad canyon to the **Green Gulch Farm Zen Center**, an organic farm and Buddhist retreat with an authentic Japanese teahouse and a simple but refined prayer hall. On Sundays the centre has a public meditation period at 8.15am, followed by an informal talk on Zen Buddhism at 10am (suggested donation $10–20) and tea, after which you can stroll down to Muir Beach or stay for lunch (donation $10–15). If you're interested in learning more about Zen, enquire about the centre's Guest Student Program.

Muir and Stinson beaches

Marin Transit #61 to Stinson Beach; 4–12 daily

Accessible either from Muir Woods or Hwy-1, **Muir Beach** is usually uncrowded and its location is beautifully secluded in a semicircular cove. Three miles north, **Steep Ravine** drops sharply down the cliffs to a small beach, past very rustic cabins and a campground, bookable through Mount Tamalpais State Park (see p.530). A mile on is the small and lovely **Red Rocks** nudist beach, down a steep trail from a parking area along the highway. **Stinson Beach**, whose wide strand is stunning and justifiably the most popular in the county despite the rather cold water, is a mile further. Unfortunately, it gets packed at weekends in summer.

ACCOMMODATION	MUIR AND STINSON BEACHES

Lindisfarne Guest House Green Gulch Zen Center, Muir Beach ☎415 383 3134, ⊚sfzc.org. Restful rooms in a meditation retreat set in a secluded valley above Muir Beach. Price includes excellent vegetarian meals. **$243**

★**Pelican Inn** 10 Pacific Way, Muir Beach ☎415 383 6000, ⊚pelicaninn.com. Very comfortable rooms in a romantic pseudo-English country inn, with good bar and restaurant downstairs. Two-minute walk from the beautiful beach. **$215**

Stinson Beach Motel 3416 Shoreline Hwy, Stinson Beach ☎415 868 1712, ⊚stinsonbeachmotel.com. Basic roadside motel right on Hwy-1, with tiny but perfectly adequate rooms. A 5min walk to the beach. **$110**

Bolinas

At the tip of the headland, due west from Stinson Beach, is the laidback village of **Bolinas**, though you may have a hard time finding it – road signs marking the turn-off from Hwy-1 are removed as soon as they're put up by locals hoping to keep the place to themselves. The campaign may have backfired, though, since press coverage of the "sign war" has done more to publicize the town than any road sign ever did. To get there, take the first left beyond the estuary and follow the road to the end. Bolinas is completely surrounded by federal property – the Golden Gate National Recreation

Area and Point Reyes National Seashore – and even the lagoon has been declared a National Bird Sanctuary. Known for its leftist hippie culture, the village itself has been home at different times to Grace Slick and the late Paul Kantner, a regular colony of artists, bearded handymen, writers (the late trout-fishing author Richard Brautigan and basketball diarist Jim Carroll among them), and stray dogs.

Bolinas Museum
48 Wharf Rd • Fri 1–5pm, Sat & Sun noon–5pm • Free • ☎ 415 868 0330, ⓦ bolinasmuseum.org

There's not a lot to see in Bolinas apart from the small **Bolinas Museum**, which has a few historical displays and works by local artists in a set of converted cottages around a courtyard. Mostly, it's more fun just people watching and taking in the relaxed atmosphere.

ACCOMMODATION   BOLINAS

Grand Hotel 15 Brighton Ave ☎ 415 868 1757. Just two budget rooms in a funky, run-down old hotel above a secondhand shop. Shared bathroom. Unbeatable character, including the quirky owner. **$80**

Smiley's Saloon & Hotel 41 Wharf Rd ☎ 415 868 1311. Half a dozen compact and simply furnished rooms. Decent value but don't expect a quiet night, as they are over the town's only saloon (see below). **$100**

EATING AND DRINKING

Coast Café 46 Wharf Rd ☎ 415 868 2298. The only real restaurant in town does a good range of seafood and meat dishes such as meatloaf, mostly in the $20–30 range, as well as cheaper snacks. Tues–Thurs 11.30am–3pm & 5–8pm, Fri 11.30am–3pm & 5–9pm, Sat 8am–3pm & 5–9pm, Sun 8am–3pm & 5–8pm.

Smileys Saloon 41 Wharf Rd ☎ 415 868 1311, ⓦ smileyssaloon.com. The bartender calls the regulars by name at one of the oldest continually operating bars in the state. Live music Thursday to Saturday and open-mike Sunday. Mon–Fri 8am–2am, Sat & Sun 9am–2am.

Southern Point Reyes

Beyond Bolinas, there's a rocky beach at the end of Wharf Road west of the village and, half a mile west at the end of Elm Road, Duxbury Reef Nature Reserve lures visitors to its tide pools, full of sea stars, crabs and sea anemones. Otherwise, Mesa Road heads north from Bolinas past the Point Reyes Bird Observatory on Mesa Road (☎ 415 868 1221, ⓦ prbo.org), open for informal tours all day, though best visited in the morning. The first bird observatory in the US, this is still an important research and study centre and if you time it right you may be able to watch, or even help, the staff as they put coloured bands on the birds, such as cormorants and sandpipers, to keep track of them.

Beyond here, the unpaved road leads on to the **Palomarin Trailhead**, the southern access into the Point Reyes National Seashore (see p.533). The best of the many beautiful hikes around the area takes you past a number of small lakes and meadows for three miles to **Alamere Falls**, which throughout the winter and spring cascade down the cliffs onto Wildcat Beach. **Bass Lake**, the first along the trail, is a great spot for a swim and is best entered from one of the two rope-swings that hang above its shore.

At the junction of Bolinas Road and Hwy-1, cross the highway and head due east. If the road is open (landslides cause frequent closures), continue up this route, the **Bolinas–Fairfax Road**, for a superb, winding drive through redwoods and grassy hillsides. When you reach the "T" in the road, turn left to get to Fairfax, or right to scale Mount Tamalpais.

Mount Tamalpais
State Park: 7am–sunset • Free • ☎ 415 388 2070, ⓦ parks.ca.gov

Mount Tamalpais, fondly known as Mount Tam, dominates the skyline of Marin County, hulking over the cool canyons of the rest of the county and dividing it into two distinct parts: the wild western slopes above the Pacific Coast and the increasingly suburban communities along the calmer bay frontage. Panoramic Highway branches off from Hwy-1 along the crest through the centre of **Mount Tamalpais State Park** which has some thirty miles of hiking trails and many campgrounds, though most of the redwoods which once covered its slopes have long since been chopped down to form the posts and beams of San Francisco's Victorian houses.

INFORMATION   MOUNT TAMALPAIS

Mount Tamalpais State Park Visitor Center 801 Panoramic Hwy, Mill Valley (daily 8am–5.30pm; ☎ 415 388 2070, ⓦ parks.ca.gov).

ACCOMMODATION

Mount Tamalpais State Park campgrounds ☎ 800 444 7275, ⓦ reserveamerica.com. Two separate campgrounds for backpackers, one on the slopes of the mountain and the other towards the coast at Steep Ravine, which also has a few rustic cabins. Pitches $25, cabins $100

Mountain Home Inn 810 Panoramic Hwy ☎ 415 381 9000 or ☎ 877 381 9001, ⓦ mtnhomeinn.com. Romantically located on the crest of Mount Tamalpais, this B&B offers great views and endless hiking. Some rooms with hot tubs. Ample cooked breakfasts included and a great restaurant. $195

Muir Woods National Monument

Daily 8am–sunset • $10 • ☎ 415 388 2595, ⓦ nps.gov/muwo • Marin Transit (☎ 415 226 0855, ⓦ marintransit.org) #66 from Sausalito ferry to Muir Woods (summer 4–5 daily, winter select holidays only)

One thick grove of towering redwood trees remains in Marin, protected as the **Muir Woods National Monument**, a mile down Muir Woods Road from Panoramic Highway. It's a tranquil and majestic spot, with sunlight filtering through the 300ft trees down to the laurel- and fern-covered canyon below. The canyon's steep sides are what saved it from Mill Valley's lumbermen, and today it's one of the few first-growth redwood groves between San Francisco and the fantastic forests of Redwood National Park (see p.632), up the coast towards the Oregon border.

One way to avoid the crowds that descend here at weekends, and the only way to get here on public transport, is to enter the woods from the top by way of a two-mile hike from the **Pan Toll Ranger Station** (☎ 415 388 2070) on Panoramic Highway – which is a stop on the bus route. As the state park headquarters, the station has maps and information on hiking and camping, and rangers can suggest hikes to suit your mood and interests. From here the **Pan Toll Road** turns off to the right along the ridge to within a hundred yards of the 2571ft summit of Mount Tamalpais, where red-necked turkey vultures listlessly circle against breathtaking views of the distant Sierra Nevada.

Mill Valley

Golden Gate Transit bus #10 every 30min from San Francisco and Sausalito

From the east peak of Mount Tamalpais, a quick two-mile hike downhill follows the **Temelpa Trail** through velvety shrubs of chaparral to **Mill Valley**, the oldest and most enticing of Marin County's inland towns. Originally a logging centre, it was from here that the destruction of the surrounding redwoods was organized. You can still follow the route of the defunct **Mill Valley and Mount Tamalpais Scenic Railroad** from the end of Summit Avenue in Mill Valley, a popular trip with daredevils on mountain bikes, which, incidentally, originated here.

Though much of Mill Valley's attraction lies in its easy access to hiking and mountain-bike trails up Mount Tam, its compact yet relaxed centre has a number of cafés and some good shops and galleries. If you're in the area in early October, don't miss the **Mill Valley Film Festival** (☎ 415 383 5256, ⓦ mvff.com) a world-class event that draws a host of up-and-coming directors, and is attended by stars such as Ewan McGregor and Amy Adams.

INFORMATION   **MILL VALLEY**

Chamber of Commerce & Visitor Center 85 Throckmorton Ave (Tues–Fri 10am–4pm; ☎ 415 388 9700, ⊚ millvalley.org).

ACCOMMODATION

Acqua Hotel 555 Redwood Hwy ☎ 415 380 0400 or ☎ 888 662 9555, ⊚ marinhotels.com. Sumptuous hotel at the Richardson Bay end of sprawling Mill Valley, with fifty luxurious rooms and oriental touches in its stylish decor. **$249**

★**Mill Valley Inn** 165 Throckmorton Ave ☎ 415 389 6608 or ☎ 800 595 2100, ⊚ millvalleyinn.com. One of the county's top establishments, this gorgeous European-style inn offers elegant rooms, lavishly furnished in period style, as well as two private cottages (at $263 they are cheaper than the bigger suites). Free use of mountain bikes. **$239**

EATING

★**Avatar's Punjabi Burritos** 15 Madrona St ☎ 415 381 8293, ⊚ enjoyavatars.com. A dastardly simple cross-cultural innovation: burritos stuffed with delicious spicy curries for $8–10. Does a brisk takeaway trade, as there are only two tables inside. Mon–Sat 11am–8pm.

The Dipsea Café 200 Shoreline Hwy ☎ 415 381 0298, ⊚ dipseacafe.com. Hearty pancakes, omelettes or sandwiches for breakfast, followed by a wide range of salads and Greek classics such as moussaka or spanakopita, nearly all under $20. Mon–Fri 7am–3pm, Sat & Sun 7am–4pm.

Small Shed Flatbreads 17 Madrona St ☎ 415 383 4200, ⊚ smallshed.com. Unusual place that serves a tasty range of cheesy toppings on organic stoneground flatbreads, as well as burgers and quiches, all $12–15. Mon–Wed & Sun 11am–9pm, Thurs 11am–9.30pm, Fri & Sat 11am–10pm.

NIGHTLIFE AND DRINKING

Mill Valley Beerworks 173 Throckmorton Ave ☎ 415 888 8218, ⊚ millvalleybeerworks.com. This sleek modern bar with handcrafted draught beers and bottled imports would look more at home in the big city. Coffee in the mornings and locally sourced food served till 10pm. Daily 8am–midnight.

Sweetwater Music Hall 19 Corte Madera Ave ☎ 415 388 3850, ⊚ sweetwatermusichall.com. Happily relocated back in Mill Valley in an old theatre, this legendary Marin venue has live rock, folk and blues most nights. Tickets mainly $20–50. Hours vary.

Throckmorton Theatre 142 Throckmorton Ave ☎ 415 383 9600, ⊚ throckmortontheatre.org. One of the most diverse entertainment venues in Marin, showcasing everything from stand-up comedy and film to jazz and folk.

Tiburon

Tiburon, at the tip of a narrow peninsula three miles east of US-101 and five miles from Mill Valley, is, like Sausalito, a ritzy harbourside village to which hundreds of people come each weekend, many of them via direct Blue & Gold Fleet **ferries** from San Francisco's Fisherman's Wharf (see p.461). It's a relaxed place, less touristy than Sausalito, and if you're in the mood to take it easy and watch the boats sail across the bay, sitting out on the sunny deck of one of the many cafés and bars can be idyllic. There are few specific sights to look out for here, but it's pleasant enough to simply wander around, browsing the galleries and antique shops. The best of these are grouped together in **Ark Row**, at the west end of Main Street, where the quirky buildings are actually old houseboats that were beached here early in the century. On a hill above the town stands **Old St Hilary's Church** (April–Oct Wed–Sun 1–4pm; ☎ 415 789 0066), a Carpenter Gothic beauty best seen in the spring, when the surrounding fields are covered with multicoloured buckwheat, flax and paintbrush.

Cyclists can cruise around the many plush houses of **Belvedere Island**, just across the Beach Road Bridge from the west end of Main Street, enjoying the fine views of the bay and Golden Gate Bridge. More ambitious bikers can continue along the waterfront bike path, which winds from the bijou shops and galleries three miles west along the undeveloped Richardson Bay frontage to a bird sanctuary at **Greenwood Cove**. The pristine Victorian house here is now the western headquarters of the National Audubon Society and open for tours on Sundays (10am–4pm; free; ☎ 415 388 2524, ⊚ audubon .org); a small interpretive centre has displays on local and migratory birds and wildlife.

ACCOMMODATION	TIBURON

The Lodge At Tiburon 1651 Tiburon Blvd ☎ 415 435 3133, ⊛ thelodgeattiburon.com. Smart modern hotel with a rustic feel. Comfortable rooms, all with CD/DVD players, some with jacuzzis. $\overline{\$269}$

EATING

Guaymas 5 Main St ☎ 415 435 6300, ⊛ guaymas restaurant.com. Some of the most unique, inventive but pricey Cal-Mex cuisine in the Bay Area, along with spectacular city views. The tamales are especially worth trying for around $15. Mon–Thurs & Sun 11.30am–9pm, Fri & Sat 11.30am–10pm.

New Morning Café 1696 Tiburon Blvd ☎ 415 435 4315. Lots of healthy wholegrain sandwiches with a range of tasty fillings, plus salads and omelettes, all around $10 or less. Quite a selection of coffee too. Mon–Fri 6.30am–2.30pm, Sat–Sun 6.30am–4pm.

Sam's Anchor Cafe 27 Main St ☎ 415 435 4527, ⊛ samscafe.com. Popular waterfront spot which serves eggy brekkies, filling lunches and a variety of fish, meat and veg dinners for $17–32. Mon–Fri 11am–9.30pm, Sat–Sun 9.30am–9.30pm; bar till midnight.

7 Angel Island

The largest island in the San Francisco Bay, ten times the size of Alcatraz, **Angel Island** is officially a state park but over the years it has served a variety of purposes, everything from a home for Miwok Native Americans to a World War II prisoner-of-war camp. It's full of ghostly ruins of old military installations, but it's the nature that lures people to Angel Island nowadays, with its oak and eucalyptus trees and sagebrush covering the hills above rocky coves and sandy beaches, giving the island a feel quite apart from the mainland. It offers some pleasant biking opportunities as well: a five-mile road rings the island, and an unpaved track, along with a number of hiking trails, leads up to the 800ft hump of **Mount Livermore**, with panoramic views of the Bay Area.

The ferry arrives at **Ayala Cove**, where a small snack bar selling hot dogs and cold drinks provides the only sustenance available on the island – bring a picnic if you plan to spend the day here. The nearby **visitor centre** (see below), in an old building that was built as a quarantine facility for soldiers returning from the Philippines after the Spanish–American War, has displays on the island's history. Around the point on the northwest corner of the island the **North Garrison**, built in 1905, was the site of a prisoner-of-war camp during World War II; while the larger **East Garrison**, on the bay half a mile beyond, was the major transfer point for soldiers bound for the South Pacific.

Quarry Beach around the point is the best on the island, a clean sandy shore that's protected from the winds blowing in through the Golden Gate; it's also a popular landing spot for kayakers and canoeists who paddle across the bay from Berkeley. **Camping** on Angel Island (see below) is well worth considering for the views of San Francisco and the East Bay at night, if you can bag a place. For one-hour **tours** of Angel Island, contact Angel Island TramTours through the visitor centre (see below).

INFORMATION	ANGEL ISLAND

Angel Island Visitor Center Near Ayala Cove (daily 9am–4pm; ☎ 415 435 1915, ⊛ angelisland.org).

ACCOMMODATION

Angel Island State Park Campground ☎ 800 444 7275, ⊛ reserveamerica.com. Camping on Angel Island affords glittering views of San Francisco and the East Bay by night. The campground's nine walk-in (and one pricier kayak-in) sites fill up fast, so reserve well in advance. Open year-round, $10 discount in winter. $\overline{\$30}$

Sir Francis Drake Boulevard and Central Marin County

The quickest route from the East Bay to the wilds of the Point Reyes National Seashore and the only way to get there on public transport is by way of **Sir Francis Drake Boulevard**, which cuts across central Marin County, reaching the coast thirty miles west at a crescent-shaped bay where, in 1579, Drake supposedly landed and claimed all of what he called Nova Albion for England. The route makes an excellent day-long cycling tour, with the reward of good beaches, a youth hostel and some tasty restaurants at its western end.

At the eastern end, right off the San Rafael Bridge that connects Marin to the East Bay, you pass the ominous red-tile-roofed complex of the maximum-security **San Quentin State Prison**, which houses the state's most violent and notorious criminals. No longer open for tours, it was of here that Johnny Cash sang so resonantly "I hate every stone of you". Just beyond it you will see the busy ferry terminal at otherwise nondescript **Larkspur**.

San Anselmo and around

Further west is **San Anselmo**, set in a broad valley two miles north of Mount Tam, which calls itself "the antiques capital of Northern California" and sports a tiny centre of speciality shops, furniture stores and cafés. The ivy-covered **San Francisco Theological Seminary** off Bolinas Avenue (105 Seminary Rd; free; ☎415 451 2800, ⓦsfts.edu), which dominates the town from the hill above, is worth a quick peek for the view and mission-styled architecture. At serene **Robson-Harrington Park** on Crescent Avenue you can picnic among well-tended gardens, while the very green and leafy **Creek Park** follows the creek that snakes through the town centre.

Ten miles beyond fairly nondescript Fairfax, which San Anselmo merges into, Sir Francis Drake Boulevard winds through gentle and increasingly pastoral hills, passing **Samuel P. Taylor State Park**, which has excellent camping.

7

DRINKING   **LARKSPUR**

Marin Brewing Company 1809 Larkspur Landing, Larkspur ☎415 461 4677, ⓦmarinbrewing.com. Lively pub that serves a dozen or so tasty draught ales – try the malty Albion Amber or the Raspberry Trail Ale – all brewed on the premises. Mon–Thurs & Sun 11.30am–midnight, Fri & Sat 11.30am–1am.

Point Reyes National Seashore

Fifteen miles west of Fairfax, Sir Francis Drake Boulevard meets coastal Hwy-1 at the hamlet of **Olema**, which has good food and lodging, as does nearby **Inverness**. A mile north of Olema sits the quaint service town of **Point Reyes Station**, another good place to stop for refreshment before heading off to enjoy the wide open spaces of **Point Reyes National Seashore** just beyond. This near-island of wilderness is surrounded on three sides by more than fifty miles of isolated coastline, with pine forests and sunny meadows bordered by rocky cliffs and sandy, windswept beaches.

This wing-shaped landmass, something of an aberration along the generally straight coastline north of San Francisco, is in fact a rogue piece of the earth's crust that has

---

GREY WHALES

The most commonly spotted whale along California's coast, the **grey whale** migrates annually from its summer feeding grounds near Alaska to its winter breeding grounds off Baja California and back again. Some 23,000 whales make the 13,000-mile round-trip, swimming just a half-mile from the shoreline in small groups, with pregnant females leading the way on the southbound journey. Protected by an international treaty from hunters since 1938, the grey whale population has been increasing steadily each year and its migration brings out thousands of humans hoping to catch a glimpse of their fellow mammals. Mid-March to April is the best time, as the whales swim closer to the shore on the northbound journey. Point Reyes is a favourite watching spot, as are the beaches along Hwy-1 south to Santa Cruz. For information on **whale-watching expeditions** or the latest information on the migration, contact Oceanic Society Expeditions (☎415 441 1106, ⓦoceanicsociety.org).

been drifting steadily northward along the San Andreas Fault, having started some six million years ago as a suburb of Los Angeles. When the great earthquake of 1906 shattered San Francisco, the land here – the quake's epicentre – shifted over sixteen feet in an instant, though damage was confined to a few skewed cattle fences.

Two miles southwest of Point Reyes Station, at the park's headquarters, **Bear Valley Visitor Center** (see below) holds engaging displays on the geology and natural history of the region. Rangers dish out excellent hiking and cycling itineraries, and have up-to-date information on the weather, which can change quickly and be cold and windy along the coast even when it's hot and sunny here, three miles inland. They also handle permits and reservations for the various hike-in **campgrounds** within the park.

Nearby, a replica of a native Miwok village has an authentic religious **roundhouse**, and a popular hike follows the Bear Valley Trail along Coast Creek four miles to **Arch Rock**, a large tunnel in the seaside cliffs that you can walk through at low tide.

The western Seashore

North of the visitor centre, Limantour Road heads west six miles to the *HI-Point Reyes Hostel* (see opposite), continuing on another two miles to the coast at **Limantour Beach**, one of the best protected swimming beaches and a good place to watch the sea birds in the adjacent estuary. Bear Valley Road rejoins Sir Francis Drake Boulevard just past Limantour Road, leading north along Tomales Bay through the village of **Inverness**, so named because the landscape reminded an early settler of his home in the Scottish Highlands. Eight miles west of Inverness, a turn leads down to **Drake's Beach**, the presumed landing spot of Sir Francis in 1579 (his voyage journal makes the exact location unclear). Appropriately, the coastline here resembles the southern coast of England, often cold, wet and windy, with chalk-white cliffs rising above the wide, sandy beach.

The road continues southwest another eight miles to the very tip of Point Reyes. A precarious-looking **lighthouse** (Mon & Fri–Sun 10am–4.30pm; free; ☏415 669 1534, ⓦnps.gov/pore) stands firm against the crashing surf, and the bluffs are excellent for watching migrating **grey whales** from mid-March to April and late December to early February. Just over a mile back from the lighthouse a narrow road leads to **Chimney Rock**, where you can often see basking **elephant seals** or **sea lions** from the overlook. Keep in mind the distance and slow speeds it takes to reach these spots, which is hard to judge on a map. From the visitor centre, it's 15 miles to Drake's Beach and 23 miles to the lighthouse. Check with the rangers on weather conditions before setting out. From late December through to April a shuttle bus (9.45am–3.30pm; $7) runs roughly every twenty minutes on weekends and holidays from Drake's Beach out to the lighthouse and Chimney Rock, and the roads are closed to private vehicles to avoid congestion.

The northern Seashore

The northern tip of the Point Reyes National Seashore, **Tomales Point**, is accessible via Pierce Point Road, which turns off Sir Francis Drake Boulevard two miles north of Inverness. Jutting out into Tomales Bay, it's the least-visited section of the park and a refuge for hefty **tule elk**; it's also a great place to admire the lupins, poppies and other wildflowers that appear in the spring. The best swimming (or rather least freezing water) is at **Heart's Desire Beach**, just before the end of the road. Down the bluffs from where the road comes to a dead end, there are excellent tidal pools at rocky **McClure's Beach**. North of Point Reyes Station, Hwy-1 continues past the famed oyster beds of Tomales Bay north along the crashing surf and up the Northern California coast.

INFORMATION   **POINT REYES NATIONAL SEASHORE**

Bear Valley Visitor Center Just off Hwy-1 on Bear Valley Rd (Mon–Fri 10am–5pm, Sat & Sun 9am–5pm; ☏415 464   5100, ⓦnps.gov/pore).

ACCOMMODATION

HI-Point Reyes 1390 Limantour Spit Rd, 6 miles west of the visitor centre ☎415 663 8811, ⓦnorcalhostels .org. Located in an old ranch house and surrounded by meadows and forests. Office hours 7.30–10am & 4.30–9pm; no check-in after 9.30pm. Dorms from $\overline{\$29}$, doubles from $\overline{\$87}$

Olema Cottages 9970 Sir Francis Drake Blvd, Olema ☎415 663 1288, ⓦvacationrentalspointreyes.com. Five delightful and comfortable cottages in flower-filled grounds amid farmland. Minimum 2–3-night stay, depending on the season. $\overline{\$170}$

Point Reyes National Seashore campgrounds ☎415 663 8054, ⓦnps.gov/pore. A wide range of hike-in sites for backpackers, near the beach or in the forest. Reserve sites up to two months in advance. $\overline{\$20}$

Point Reyes Seashore Lodge 10021 Hwy-1, Olema ☎415 663 9000 or ☎800 404 5634, ⓦpointreyes seashore.com. Attractive, largely wooden lodge that's the size of a hotel but with the personal touch of a B&B. All rooms overlook the garden and brook. $\overline{\$155}$

Ten Inverness Way 10 Inverness Way, Inverness ☎415 669 1648, ⓦteninvernessway.com. Quiet and restful lodging, with a hot tub and complimentary evening wine, in a small village of good restaurants and bakeries on the fringes of Point Reyes. $\overline{\$195}$

EATING

Station House Café 11180 Hwy-1 (Main St), Point Reyes Station ☎415 663 1515, ⓦstationhousecafe .com. Serving breakfast, lunch and dinner daily, this friendly local favourite entices diners from miles around to sample their grilled seafood and top-notch steaks for $15–30. Mon, Tues & Thurs–Sun 8am–9pm.

Vladimir's Czech Restaurant 12785 Sir Francis Drake Blvd, Inverness ☎415 669 1021. This relic of rural Bohemia in the far West has been serving up tasty items like Moravian cabbage roll, roast duckling and apple strudel since 1960. Main courses $20–30. Tues 4–10pm, Wed noon to 9pm, Thurs–Sun noon–10pm.

San Rafael and around

You may pass through **San Rafael** on your way north from San Francisco on US-101 but there's little to detain you. The county seat and the only sizeable city in Marin County, it has none of the rural qualities that make the other towns special, though you'll come across a couple of good restaurants and bars along Fourth Street, the main drag. Downtown's lone attraction is the old **Mission San Rafael Arcangel** (daily 11am–4pm; free; ☎415 454 8141, ⓦsaintraphael.com), in fact a 1949 replica that was built near the site of the 1817 original on Fifth Avenue at A Street.

Marin County Civic Center

Mon–Fri 9am–5pm; tours depart from 2nd-floor café Wed 10.30am • $10 • ☎415 499 6646, ⓦmarincounty.org

San Rafael's main point of interest is the **Marin County Civic Center**, spanning the hills just east of US-101 a mile north of central San Rafael. It is a strange, otherworldly complex of administrative offices, plus an excellent performance space that resembles a giant viaduct capped by a bright-blue-tiled roof. These buildings were architect **Frank Lloyd Wright**'s one and only government project, and although the huge circus tents and amusement park at the core of the designer's conception were never built, it does have some interesting touches, such as the atrium lobbies that open directly to the outdoors.

Six miles north of San Rafael, the **Lucas Valley Road** turns off west, twisting across Marin towards Point Reyes. Although he lives and works here, it was not named after *Star Wars* film-maker George Lucas, whose sprawling **Skywalker Ranch** studios are well hidden off the road.

| ACCOMMODATION AND NIGHTLIFE | SAN RAFAEL |

★**Sol Food** 901 Lincoln Ave ☎415 451 4765, ⓦsolfoodrestaurant.com. It's worth making a detour just to try the exquisite Puerto Rican dishes such as *pollo al horno*. Most dishes $10–20. Check website for Mill Valley branch. Mon–Thurs & Sun 8am–11pm, Fri & Sat 9am–1am.

★**Terrapin Crossroads** 100 Yacht Club Drive ☎415 524 2773, ⓦterrapincrossroads.net. Owned by the Grateful Dead's bassist Phil Lesh, this has become a popular hangout for those wanting to hear top-notch old-style rock. Also has a fine restaurant. Hours vary.

The Gold Country and Lake Tahoe

LAKE TAHOE

The Gold Country and Lake Tahoe

About 150 years before techies from all over the world rushed to California in search of Silicon Valley gold, the rough-and-ready forty-niners invaded the Gold Country of the Sierra Nevada to pan for the real thing. The first prospectors on the scene – about 150 miles northeast of San Francisco – sometimes found large nuggets of solid gold sitting along the riverbanks. They worked all day in the hot sun, wading through fast-flowing, ice-cold rivers to recover trace amounts of the precious metal that had been eroded out of the hard-rock veins of the Mother Lode – the name miners gave to the rich sources of gold at the heart of the mining district. These days the old-fashioned towns and many of the mines they left behind have become attractive pieces of living history, set against the backdrop of the majestic Sierra Nevada.

The region ranges from the foothills near Yosemite National Park to the deep gorge of the Yuba River, two hundred miles north. In many parts throughout this area, little seems to have changed since the argonauts began their digging and even in the air-conditioned comfort of your rental car – without one it's nearly impossible to navigate the area – distances from one town to the next may seem exponentially greater than they appear on the map: count on plenty of hairpin bends and steep climbs.

The **Mother Lode** was first discovered in 1848 at Sutter's Mill in **Coloma**, forty miles east of **Sacramento**, the largest city in the Gold Country and the state capital. Once a tiny military outpost and farming community that boomed as a supply town for miners, Sacramento, now a busy and largely modern state capital, acts as a gateway to the two distinct mining areas to the north and south. The **northern mines**, around the twin towns of **Grass Valley** and **Nevada City**, were the richest fields and today retain most of their Gold Rush buildings in an unspoiled, near-alpine setting halfway up the towering peaks of the Sierra Nevada. The hot and dusty **southern mines**, on the other hand, became depopulated faster than their northern neighbours. These towns were the rowdiest and wildest of all and it's not too hard to imagine that many of the abandoned towns sprinkled over the area once supported upwards of fifty saloons and gambling parlours, each with its own cast of cardsharps and thieves, as immortalized by writers including Bret Harte and Mark Twain.

Most of the mountainous forest along the Sierra crest is preserved as near-pristine wilderness, with excellent hiking, camping and backpacking. There's great skiing in winter around the mountainous rim of **Lake Tahoe** on the border between California and Nevada,

SACRAMENTO CAPITOL BUILDING

Highlights

❶ **Sacramento Capitol building** An elegant Classical Revival structure that has some spectacular architectural detailing, and whose comprehensive tours provide a glimpse into California's government. **See p.544**

❷ **Indian Grinding Rock** In this State Historic Park nine miles from Jackson, the Miwok Indians once carved hundreds of small cups into the limestone, still visible today. **See p.553**

❸ **Jamestown's Railtown 1897 State Historic Park** Even if you're not a trainspotter, it's worth stopping by to see the old engines, thanks to the enthusiastic, endlessly knowledgeable guides. **See p.560**

❹ **Empire Mine State Park** Now retired among thick stands of pine, the impressive array of mining equipment here is a contemplative reflection on California's Gold Rush heyday. **See p.562**

❺ **Lake Tahoe** A stunning region that guarantees beautiful scenery at any time of year, whether you're skiing the slopes or paddling in the lake itself. **See p.568**

❻ **Virginia City, Nevada** This mining town exudes a more tangible Wild West atmosphere than most of its California counterparts. **See p.584**

HIGHLIGHTS ARE MARKED ON THE MAP ON P.540

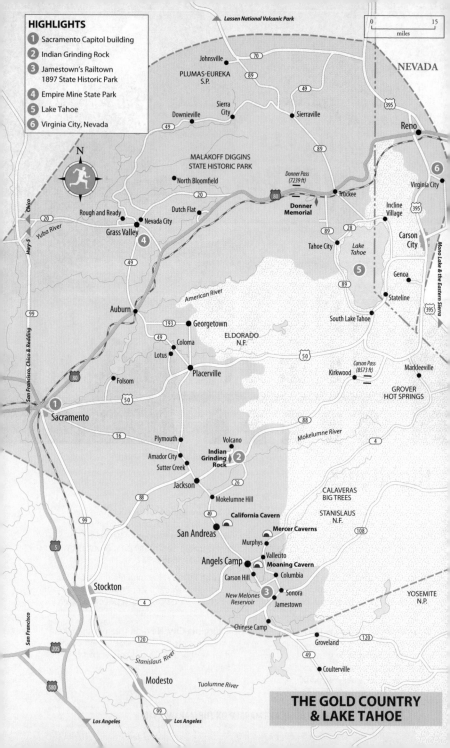

HIGHLIGHTS

1. Sacramento Capitol building
2. Indian Grinding Rock
3. Jamestown's Railtown 1897 State Historic Park
4. Empire Mine State Park
5. Lake Tahoe
6. Virginia City, Nevada

Lassen National Volcanic Park

NEVADA

N

Johnsville
70
89
PLUMAS-EUREKA S.P.
49
Sierraville
Downieville
Sierra City
49
89
Reno
395

MALAKOFF DIGGINS STATE HISTORIC PARK

Donner Pass (7239 ft)
North Bloomfield
80
Truckee
Virginia City ⑥
20
Dutch Flat
Donner Memorial
Incline Village
395
Rough and Ready
Nevada City
Grass Valley ④
89
28
Carson City
49
Tahoe City
Lake Tahoe
Genoa

American River
Auburn
89
Stateline
193
Georgetown
ELDORADO N.F.
South Lake Tahoe
395
49
Coloma
Lotus
50
Placerville
Carson Pass (8573 ft)
Markleeville
Folsom
Kirkwood
80
50
GROVER HOT SPRINGS
Sacramento ①
88
16
Plymouth
Volcano
Mokelumne River
4
Amador City
Indian Grinding Rock ②
Sutter Creek
26
Jackson
88
Mokelumne Hill
CALAVERAS BIG TREES
99
49
California Cavern
STANISLAUS N.F.
San Andreas
Mercer Caverns
108
Murphys
Angels Camp
Vallecito
Moaning Cavern
Stockton
Carson Hill
Columbia
5
New Melones Reservoir
③ Sonora
Jamestown
YOSEMITE N.P.
4
Chinese Camp
San Francisco
120
Groveland
120
205
49
Coulterville
Stanislaus River
Modesto
Tuolumne River
580
99
Los Angeles
Los Angeles

San Francisco, Chico & Redding
Chico
Yuba River
20
99
Hwy-5
Mono Lake & the Eastern Sierra

0 miles 15

THE GOLD COUNTRY & LAKE TAHOE

aglow under the bright lights of the casinos that line its southeastern shore. East of the mountains, in the dry Nevada desert but very much part of the Tahoe circuit, sit the highway towns of **Reno**, famed for low-budget weddings and speedy divorces, and **Carson City**, the Nevada state capital and one-time boomtown of the Comstock silver mines.

GETTING AROUND

By car To get a real feel for the Gold Country, and to reach the most evocative ghost towns, you'll need a car. Though it's all very scenic, cycling is not a viable option: the distances between the sights are long and the roads are far too hilly and narrow for comfort. Hwy-49 runs north to south, linking most of the sights of the Gold Country; two main highways, US-50 and I-80 run east from Sacramento across the Sierra Nevada to opposite ends of Lake Tahoe and on into Nevada.

By public transport A daily Amtrak train follows the transcontinental route from Sacramento, via Auburn and Truckee, to Reno and points east. Greyhound operates a scant bus service connecting the major towns along I-80, while an Amtrak Thruway bus runs along US-50 to South Lake Tahoe. Long-distance connections beyond these corridors are almost nonexistent.

Sacramento

Roughly midway between San Francisco and the crest of the Sierra Nevada and well connected by Greyhound, Amtrak and the arterial I-5 highway, **SACRAMENTO** is likely to be your first stop in the Gold Country. It's the quintessential American state capital, with sleepy tree-lined streets fanning out from the elegant State Capitol building. The city's waterfront quarter, restored to the style of Pony Express days, contains the region's largest collection of Gold Rush-era buildings.

Until recently, Sacramento had the reputation of being decidedly dull, a suburban enclave of politicians and bureaucrats surrounded by miles of marshes and farmland. The government has long loomed large over the city, filling its streets on weekdays and emptying the centre at weekends; but in recent years residential neighbourhoods have reawakened, especially around the Midtown area, thanks to the cafés and restaurants that have mushroomed on many of the leafier blocks. A dash of Hollywood pizzazz (and Kennedy-grade connections courtesy of his wife, TV anchor Maria Shriver) was added to the mix by the tenure of Arnold "the Governator" Schwarzenegger as a relatively moderate Republican governor between 2003 and 2011. Both he and his colourful Democrat successor Jerry "Moonbeam" Brown have seized on increasing local pride in the city's Gold Rush history by overseeing important historic preservation and restoration projects, injecting some much-needed tourist dollars into the local economy during the ongoing recession.

Most of the local attractions in Sacramento are close together, in one of the three main areas that together comprise the city centre: the I-5 highway quarantines **Old Sacramento** from the commercial hub of **Downtown**, centred on K Street Mall, as well as the funkier, residential **Midtown** district further east.

Brief history

Before gold was discovered in 1848, the area around Sacramento belonged entirely to one man, **John Sutter**. He came here from Switzerland in 1839 to farm the flat, marshy lands at the foot of the Sierra Nevada, which were then within Mexican California. Sacramento, the prosperous community he founded, became a main stopping place for the few trappers and travellers who made their way inland or across the range of peaks. Yet it was after the discovery of flakes of **gold** in the foothills forty miles east that things really took off and the small trading post was transformed.

Sutter's 50,000-acre settlement, set at the confluence of the Sacramento and American rivers in the flatlands of the northern San Joaquin Valley, was granted to him by the Mexican government and he worked hard to build the colony into a busy trading centre and cattle ranch. He was poised to become a wealthy man when his hopes were thwarted by the discovery of gold at a nearby sawmill. His workers quit their jobs to go prospecting and many thousands more flocked to the goldfields, trampling over Sutter's land. The small colony was soon overrun: since ships could sail upriver from the San Francisco Bay, Sacramento quickly became the main supply point for miners bound for the isolated camps in the foothills above.

The city prospered, and in 1854 Sacramento snagged the title of **California state capital**, thanks to its equidistance between the gold mines, the rich farmlands of the San Joaquin Valley and the financial centre of San Francisco. As the Gold Rush faded, Sacramento remained important as a transport hub, first as the western terminus of the Pony Express and later as the western headquarters of the transcontinental railroad. Although its administrative role saved the city when mining dollars dwindled, it also

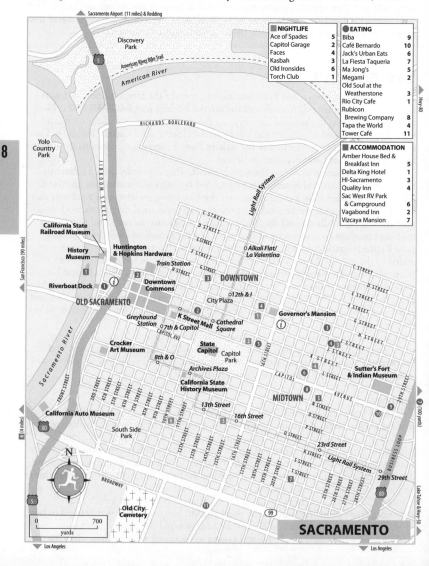

■ NIGHTLIFE	
Ace of Spades	5
Capitol Garage	2
Faces	4
Kasbah	3
Old Ironsides	6
Torch Club	1

● EATING	
Biba	9
Café Bernardo	10
Jack's Urban Eats	6
La Fiesta Taqueria	7
Ma Jong's	5
Megami	2
Old Soul at the Weatherstone	3
Rio City Cafe	1
Rubicon Brewing Company	8
Tapa the World	4
Tower Café	11

■ ACCOMMODATION	
Amber House Bed & Breakfast Inn	5
Delta King Hotel	1
HI-Sacramento	3
Quality Inn	4
Sac West RV Park & Campground	6
Vagabond Inn	2
Vizcaya Mansion	7

SACRAMENTO

smothered much of its rough, pioneer edges and it has taken a long time to develop a distinct, urban personality.

Old Sacramento and the riverfront

Sacramento grew up along the **riverfront**, where the wharves, warehouses, saloons and stores of the city's historic core have been restored and converted into the novelty shops and theme restaurants of **OLD SACRAMENTO**. It's a shame that such a large collection of authentic Gold Rush-era architecture should be choked with such relentless fakery: costumed sales staff hawking souvenirs and tourist-chasing bars dressed up as faux Wild West saloons. In fact, although most of the buildings are original, some stood elsewhere until they were forcibly relocated here in the 1960s to make way for the massive I-5 highway that carves this area off from the rest of the city centre. To avoid the stampede of tourists in search of tacky souvenirs, it's best to avoid Old Sacramento completely at weekends, since that's when the place seems most inauthentic, its streets more like a Hollywood backlot than the real thing.

Huntington & Hopkins Hardware

113 I St • Thurs–Sun 11am–4pm • Free • ☎ 916 323 7234

The area's three main historical attractions stand in a row along **I Street**: the smallest is **Huntington & Hopkins Hardware**, a store-turned-museum. Here, the **Big Four** – Leland Stanford, Mark Hopkins, Collis P. Huntington and Charles Crocker – held their first meeting to mastermind the Central Pacific and later Southern Pacific railroads (see box below). It's now decked out as a spartan 1840s supply store, highlighting the humble beginnings of the ruthless Huntington and the henpecked Hopkins. Upstairs there's a low-key homage to the men, with a re-creation of their boardroom and an archive of rail history.

California State Railroad Museum

125 I St • Museum daily 10am–5pm; train rides April–Sept Sat & Sun hourly 11am–4pm • Museum $10, train rides $12–20 • ☎ 916 445 6645, ⓦ csrmf.org

Railway history is fully chronicled at the **California State Railroad Museum**, which boasts a range of lavishly restored 1860s locomotives with "cow-catcher" front grilles and huge

---

THE BIG FOUR AND CALIFORNIA'S EARLY RAILROADS

Starting in 1861, the **Central Pacific** and **Southern Pacific railroads** monopolized transportation and dominated the economy and politics of California and the western US for over twenty years. These companies were the creation of just four men – Leland Stanford, Mark Hopkins, Collis P. Huntington and Charles Crocker – known collectively as the **Big Four**.

For an initial investment of $15,000, the four financiers, along with the railroad designer and engineer Theodore Judah who died before its completion in 1883, received federal subsidies of $50,000 per mile of track laid – twice what it actually cost. On top of this, they were granted half the land in a forty-mile strip bordering the railroad: as the network expanded, the Southern Pacific became the largest landowner in California, owning over twenty percent of the state. This unregulated monopoly – caricatured in the liberal press as a grasping **octopus** – had the power to make or break farmers and manufacturers dependent upon it for the transportation of goods. In the cities, particularly Oakland and Los Angeles, it was able to demand massive concessions from local government as an inducement for rail connections. By the end of the nineteenth century, the Big Four had extracted and extorted a fortune worth over $200 million each and ran a network that stretched across the country to New Orleans.

Although the Big Four all built fabulous mansions on San Francisco's swanky Nob Hill (see p.439), those palaces were destroyed by the 1906 earthquake and fire soon after the men's deaths. The four's most enduring monument is arguably the prestigious university that Leland Stanford endowed in honour of his namesake and only son after the boy's early death.

bulbous smokestacks. Perhaps due to its exhaustive exhibits on early railroad technology, it's more suited to dedicated trainspotters than casual tourists. The best part is the old passenger station and freight depot a block south, which is also part of the museum. From here you can take a seven-mile, 45-minute **ride** beside the river on a vintage train.

Sacramento History Museum
101 I St • Daily 10am–5pm • $6 • ☎ 916 808 7057, ⓦ historicoldsac.org

The **Sacramento History Museum** features a hands-on display about early newspapers in California (including the *Sacramento Bee*, founded in 1857), as well as coverage of more recent history, like the Depression-era diner run by the pioneering African American Dunlap family. There are regular special exhibitions too.

Crocker Art Museum
216 O St • Tues–Sun 10am–5pm, Thurs till 9pm • $10 • ☎ 916 808 7000, ⓦ crockerartmuseum.org

The **Crocker Art Museum** houses paintings collected by Supreme Court judge Edwin Crocker, brother of railroad baron Charles. There are a few pictures of early California life amid the works by mainly European artists, including drawings by Dürer, Rembrandt, Boucher and Fragonard.

California Auto Museum
2200 Front St • Daily except Tues 10am–5pm, last admission 4pm • $9 • ☎ 916 442 6802, ⓦ calautomuseum.org

Appropriately enough, given its setting in the shadow of the massive I-5 and I-80 interchange, the **California Auto Museum** offers an impressive collection of antique cars and trucks, from Model Ts and As to classic '57 T-birds and "woody" station wagons. Displays on the evolution of the automobile are particularly informative.

Downtown

Running east from the riverfront and Old Sacramento, past the Greyhound and Amtrak stations, the **K Street Mall** is the commercial heart of **DOWNTOWN SACRAMENTO**, with the end of the light rail network running through the centre of a pedestrianized shopping precinct. While its western reaches are rather drab, the street grows livelier the closer it gets to the massive, open-air **Downtown Commons** shopping and entertainment complex, which centres on the brand-new Golden 1 Center (see p.547), a major performance venue and now home of the Sacramento Kings basketball team. At its western end is a tunnel that takes pedestrians under the highway to connect with Old Sacramento.

State Capitol
10th & L St • Tours hourly Mon–Fri 8am–4pm, Sat & Sun 9am–4pm • ☎ 916 324 0333, ⓦ capitolmuseum.ca.gov

The city's most imposing edifice is the **State Capitol**, with its Classical Revival dome, which was built in the 1860s, although there have been several significant, if insensitive, additions since then. It was restored to nineteenth-century opulence in 1976 in what was then the largest such project in US history; it underwent another heavy restoration following a bizarre incident in early 2001 when a mentally unstable truck driver ploughed his milk tanker into the southern façade and caused almost $15 million of damage.

Now, in the post 9/11 and milk truck world, you need photo ID to enter the building; once inside, you're free to ramble around the main floor using the self-guided leaflets on offer in the rotunda. You'll see more, though, if you take one of the free **tours** that leave hourly from Room B-27 on the lower ground floor. The tours will take you through administrative rooms set up as if it were April 1906, when the devastating San Francisco earthquake occurred. You'll also visit the salmon-pink Senate Gallery and lush green Assembly Room; in the latter, note the gargoyle's face in the egg-and-dart ceiling moulding, sticking its tongue out at whoever's at the podium. Outside, the popular **park** around the Capitol is delightful, filled with dazzling flowerbeds, enormous trees and a plague of friendly squirrels.

Governor's Mansion
1526 H St

Northeast of the K Street Mall stands the meringue-like **Governor's Mansion**, home since 2016 to Jerry Brown. Built in 1877 as a private home, the enormous and elaborate building soon became the official residence of California's governors, a role it filled for more than sixty years until 1967, when then-governor Ronald Reagan abandoned its high ceilings and narrow staircases in favour of a ranch-style house on the outskirts of town. It was open to the public for many years, but now that it is once more an official residence you can only admire it from the street.

The California Museum
1020 O St • Tues–Sat 10am–5pm, Sun noon–5pm • $9 • ☎ 916 653 0650, ⓦ californiamuseum.org

The California Museum is an enormous, cutting-edge facility that focuses on both the state's physical history and the development of the often lampooned, laidback world-view of its inhabitants. The layout is rather confusing, since each exhibit bleeds into the next, but don't miss the eye-catching re-creation of an early Chinese herbalist store or the perky TV montage showing Californians' often amusing reflections on their home state. It is also worth checking out the regularly changing exhibitions.

Midtown
8

Sacramento's trendiest district is **Midtown**, a pleasant area for a leisurely, leafy stroll; city planners planted trees on almost every street, so there's ample shade from the relentless sunshine. Although there are few actual attractions, you'll find dozens of hip restaurants and cafés (see p.546) dotted among the old Victorian mansions, especially along Capitol Avenue, not to mention one of the city's best sights: Sutter's Fort.

Sutter's Fort State Historic Park
2701 L St • Daily 10am–5pm • $5 • ☎ 916 445 4422, ⓦ suttersfort.org

This re-creation of Sacramento's original settlement provides a very interesting glimpse into the city's early history. Inside, motion-triggered audio commentary describes each room, like the blacksmith's and the bakery, and an adobe house exhibits relics from the Gold Rush; its quiet atmosphere gives a vivid sense of early European life in California.

California State Indian Museum
2618 K St • Daily 10am–5pm • $5 • ☎ 916 324 0971, ⓦ www.parks.ca.gov

In the northwest corner of the two-block area surrounding Sutter's Fort State Historic Park, the small **California State Indian Museum** has a scant and poorly laid out collection of tools, handicrafts and ceremonial objects of the Native Americans of the Central Valley and the Sierra Nevada. It also recounts the story of Ishi, the last of the Yahi Native Americans, who was paraded around towns as a curiosity in the early twentieth century.

ARRIVAL AND DEPARTURE   **SACRAMENTO**

By plane Sacramento International airport (☎ 916 874 0700, ⓦ sacairports.org), 12 miles northwest of downtown, is served by most major domestic airlines. SuperShuttle Sacramento vans (☎ 800 258 3826, ⓦ supershuttle.com) can take you directly to any downtown destination for $12–16.

By train Numerous daily Amtrak trains connect Sacramento with the Bay Area and further afield; these stop at the station at 4th and I streets, near Old Sacramento.

Destinations Oakland/Emeryville (12–16 daily; 1hr 50min–2hr); Reno (1 daily; 4hr 45min); Truckee (1 daily; 3hr 30min).

By bus Frequent Greyhound buses pull into the bus depot at 715 L St, a block from the K Street Mall.

Destinations Los Angeles (8 daily; 7hr 20min–10hr); Reno (5 daily; 2hr 40min–3hr 25min); San Francisco (7 daily; 2hr–2hr 45min); Truckee (3 daily; 2hr 10min–2hr 40min).

GETTING AROUND

By bus and light rail An extensive network of buses and light rail cars is run by Regional Transit, 1225 R St (Mon–Fri 9am–5.30pm; ☎916 321 2877, ⊛sacrt.com). The service you're most likely to use is #30, connecting the Amtrak station, K Street Mall, the State Capitol and Old Sacramento (flat fare $2.75, day-pass $7).

By bike The city is compact, flat and largely walkable,

though you can rent a cycle from Practical Cycle, 114 J St (daily: summer 10am–7pm, rest of year 10am–6pm; ☎916 706 0077, ⊛practicalcycle.com), from $10/hr or $50/day.

By boat Hornblower Cruises run popular 1hr trips along the Sacramento River (from $20; ☎888 467 6256, ⊛hornblower.com), departing from the L St dock in Old Sacramento.

INFORMATION

Visitor centres 1002 2nd St in Old Sacramento (daily 10am–5pm; ☎916 442 7644 or ☎800 292 2334, ⊛visitsacramento.com) and 1608 I St, near the State Capitol (Mon–Fri 8am–5pm; ☎916 808 7777). Both offices hand out plenty of brochures and an informative self-guided walking tour leaflet.

Website Other than the visitor centre site, try ⊛sacramento365.com.

Listings Check out the free *Sacramento News & Review* (⊛newsreview.com), or *Ticket*, the Friday supplement to the *Sacramento Bee* newspaper (⊛sacbee.com). The city's LGBT scene is covered by *Outword* (⊛outwordmagazine.com).

ACCOMMODATION

Sacramento has plenty of reasonably priced **places to stay**, all within easy walking distance of the centre. Choices are limited primarily to unexciting chains with a few B&Bs thrown in, with **weekend rates** often steeply discounted.

★**Amber House Bed & Breakfast Inn** 1315 22nd St, Midtown ☎916 444 8085, ⊛amberhouse.com. The pick of the city's B&Bs, with luxurious rooms, including marble baths, and sumptuous breakfasts. A worthwhile treat to avoid the endless chain motels nearby. $179

Delta King Hotel 1000 Front St, Old Sacramento ☎916 444 5464, ⊛deltaking.com. A 1926 paddlewheel riverboat now permanently moored on the waterfront. Although the rooms fail to justify their "stateroom" advertising, the vessel makes an enjoyably unusual place to stay. Unlike most places in Sacramento, prices rise at weekends; they also fluctuate wildly. $163

HI-Sacramento 925 H St, downtown ☎916 443 1691, ⊛norcalhostels.org. This hostel is housed in a rambling 1885 mansion with all the usual facilities, plus free bike rental, but there's a daytime lockout and 11pm curfew. Dorms $33, doubles $85

Quality Inn 818 15th St, downtown ☎916 444 3980, ⊛qualityinn.com. Refurbished rooms near the Governor's Mansion in a standard chain hotel equipped with a pool. Invariably one of the best deals at the budget end. $87

Sac West RV Park & Campground 3951 Lake Rd, 4 miles west of downtown ☎800 562 2747, ⊛sacramentokoa.com. This RV-heavy location with the usual excellent facilities is the closest campground to downtown and has some cabins. Pitches $35, cabins $50

Vagabond Inn 909 3rd St, Old Town ☎800 522 1555, ⊛vagabondinn.com. Motor-lodge-style accommodation near the river and Old Sacramento. There's a pool and free shuttle to public transport hubs. $79

Vizcaya Mansion 2019 21st St, Midtown ☎916 594 9285, ⊛vizcayasacramento.com. A lavish, historic property with elegantly furnished rooms and marble-tiled bathrooms. Pretty good value. $139

EATING

Many downtown **restaurants** cater primarily to office workers and are therefore closed in the evening; for dinner, it's better to stroll over to Midtown, around 20th St and Capitol Ave.

★**Biba** 1806 Capitol Ave, Midtown ☎916 447 8646, ⊛paesanos.biz. Quality Italian restaurant run by an award-winning cookbook author. Pastas and main courses run from $18–45 or try the fine $35 *prix fixe* dinner Mon–Wed. Mon 5.30–9pm, Tues–Thurs 11.30am–2pm & 5.30–9pm, Fri 11.30am–2pm & 5.30–10pm, Sat 5.30–10pm.

Café Bernardo 2726 Capitol Ave, Midtown ☎916 443 1180, ⊛cafebernado.com. Large, Tuscan-style dining room with a mixed menu of pizzas, sandwiches, burgers, plus some Thai and Mexican dishes for $9–18, although breakfast is more classically American. Check the website

for other local branches. Mon–Thurs 7am–9pm, Fri 7am–10pm, Sat 8am–10pm, Sun 8am–9pm.

Jack's Urban Eats 1230 20th St, Midtown ☎916 444 0307, ⊛jacksurbaneats.com. Bargain rotisserie, serving slab-like sandwiches of juicy herbed chicken or steak for around $10 and great urban-style fries, with blue cheese and spicy chilli oil. Chic ambience and a few canvases by local artists on the walls. Mon & Sun 11am–8pm, Tues–Sat 11am–9pm.

La Fiesta Taqueria 1105 Alhambra Blvd, Midtown ☎916 454 5616, ⊛lafiestataqueria.com. Near Sutter's Fort, this authentic place bashes out marvellous super burritos and tacos with some unusual meat selections like *lengua* (tongue) for $5–15. Good help-yourself salsa-and-chips bar too. Mon–Thurs & Sun 9am–10pm, Fri & Sat 9am–11pm.

★**Ma Jong's** 1116 15th St, downtown ☎ 916 442 7555, ⓦ majongs.com. Great value pan-Asian diner set in the modern Park Downtown complex. You can get a choice of meat, prawns or veg in different styles such as Thai basil special or Mongolian, all for $10 or under. Mon–Thurs & Sun 11am–9pm, Fri & Sat 11am–2.30am.

Megami 1010 10th St, downtown ☎ 916 448 4512, ⓦ megamirestaurant.com. A bargain Japanese restaurant with many mains, such as sesame chicken and teriyaki salmon, for little over $10. Good-value sushi plates are also available. Mon–Fri 11am–9pm.

Old Soul at the Weatherstone 812 21st St, Midtown ☎ 916 443 6340, ⓦ oldsoulco.com. Sacramento's standout café, with a large interior space and huge courtyard, serving great coffee and pastries. Daily 6am–11pm.

Rio City Cafe 1110 Front St, Old Sacramento ☎ 916 442 8226, ⓦ riocitycafe.com. One of the most pleasant options in the tourist quarter, with river views. Lots of appetizers, such as coconut prawns, while mains such as bacon and bleu rib-eye cost $23–38. Mon–Thurs 11am–9pm, Fri 11am–10pm, Sat 10am–10pm, Sun 10am–9pm.

Rubicon Brewing Company 2004 Capitol Ave, Midtown ☎ 916 448 7032, ⓦ rubiconbrewing.com. Don't miss the flagship Rubicon IPA, which is brewed right here along with a range of amber ales, pilsners and stouts. Good wings, burgers, sandwiches and meals also available. Mon–Thurs 11am–11pm, Fri & Sat 11am–midnight, Sun 11am–10pm.

Tapa the World 2115 J St, Midtown ☎ 916 442 4353, ⓦ tapatheworld.com. Choose from twenty different tapas such as *chorizo con papas*, all $4.50–12, or enjoy a full meal of paella, lamb or fresh fish, while being serenaded by a flamenco guitar. Daily 11.30am–midnight.

★**Tower Café** 1518 Broadway, downtown ☎ 916 441 0222, ⓦ towercafe.com. The furnishings at this casual restaurant are as eclectic as the food, with walls covered in masks and tapestries. The menu features dishes from all over the world such as Jamaican jerk chicken, Florentine ravioli and Thai green curry, all in the $17–22 range. Mon–Thurs & Sun 8am–10pm, Fri & Sat 8am–midnight.

DRINKING AND NIGHTLIFE

Sacramento's **nightlife** can be rather flat, especially in the centre of the city once the office workers have headed home to the suburbs. Still, there are some lively **bars**, mostly in Midtown.

Ace of Spades 1417 R St, downtown ☎ 916 930 0220, ⓦ aceofspadessac.com. The best place to catch international rock acts such as Savages and Echo & The Bunnymen. The venue has four bars and food is available. Tickets mostly $20–40. Hours vary.

Capitol Garage 1500 K St, downtown ☎ 916 444 3633, ⓦ capitolgarage.com. A restaurant-cum-club, featuring occasional local bands and regular karaoke and dub/reggae nights. Nominal cover. Mon–Thurs 6am–midnight, Fri 6am–1am, Sat & Sun 8am–1am.

Faces 2000 K St, Midtown ☎ 916 448 7798, ⓦ faces.net. The city's largest and predominantly gay (male) nightclub with three dancefloors, four patios and nine bars; cover $5–10. Mon–Thurs 7pm–2am, Fri 4pm–2am, Sat 3pm–2am, Sun 2pm–2am.

Golden 1 Center 500 David J Stern Walk, downtown ☎ 916 928 0000, ⓦ golden1center.com. The centrepiece of the remodelled Downtown Commons is a large arena that hosts major bands as well as more theatrical events and basketball games. Hours vary.

Kasbah 2115 J St, Midtown ☎ 916 442 4388, ⓦ kasbahlounge.com. Run by the brother-and-sister team who own *Tapa the World* next door (see above), this unique bar draped in exotic fabrics is a fun place to sip a top-drawer cocktail while watching the nightly belly dancers. Tues–Thurs & Sun 5pm–midnight, Fri & Sat 5pm–2am.

Old Ironsides 1901 10th St, downtown ☎ 916 443 9751, ⓦ theoldironsides.com. A good spot for offbeat live music, mostly indie rock. Also has open-mike and dance-club nights, plus there's decent food, including weekday lunchtime. Most events are free, though some cost $5–8. Mon–Fri 11.30am–2pm & 8pm–2am, Sat 6pm–2am.

Torch Club 904 15th St, downtown ☎ 916 443 2797, ⓦ torchclub.net. The town's oldest blues and rock haunt, located in atmospheric premises and featuring local and national acts for $10 or less. Tues–Sun 2pm–2am.

The Central Mother Lode

From Sacramento, US-50 and I-80 head east through the traditional heart of the Gold Country, known as the **Central Mother Lode**, then up and over the mountains past Lake Tahoe and into the state of Nevada. The roads closely follow the old stagecoach routes over the Donner Pass, named in honour of the gruesomely tragic exploration (see box, p.579). In the mid-1860s, local citizens, seeking to improve dwindling fortunes after the Gold Rush subsided, joined forces with railroad engineer Theodore Judah to finance and build the first railroad crossing of the Sierra Nevada over much the same route – even along much of the same track – that Amtrak uses today. The area is less well-trodden than the northern or southern mines: either **Placerville** or **Auburn** make good bases, with affordable accommodation and some local points of interest in each. Placerville's especially handy if you want to sample some of the vintages produced locally in the El Dorado wine country. And while they may not be nearly as postcard-perfect as the towns elsewhere in the region, **Folsom** and **Coloma**, in between the two highways on the American River, are both worth exploring for their less-touristy Gold Rush feel.

Folsom

Most people know of **Folsom** thanks to the Johnny Cash song about being "stuck in Folsom Prison" after having "shot a man in Reno, just to watch him die". The town itself is attractive enough, with a single main street, Sutter Street, of restored homes and buildings that date from the days of the Pony Express.

Folsom State Prison

Two miles north of town at 300 Prison Rd, Represa • Daily: gallery 8am–5pm, museum 10am–4pm • $2 • ☎916 985 2561 ext 4589, ⓦ folsomprisonmuseum.org

The stone-faced **Folsom State Prison** has an arts-and-crafts gallery selling works by prisoners, who get the proceeds when released. The small **Folsom Prison Museum** across

8

EL DORADO WINE COUNTRY

In the 1860s, when the now-famous and over-commercialized Napa and Sonoma valleys were growing potatoes, **vineyards** flourished in El Dorado County. However, the fields were neglected after the Gold Rush and killed off by phylloxera, a nasty yellow aphid that gorges itself on vine roots; it wasn't until 1972 that vineyards were systematically re-established. Since then, however, the **wineries** in El Dorado County, especially around Placerville, have rapidly gained a reputation that belies their diminutive size. Most are low-key affairs where no charge or only a nominal one is levied for tasting or tours and you're encouraged to enjoy a bottle out on the veranda. At quiet times, you may even be shown around by the wine-maker.

The differences in altitude and soil types throughout the region lend themselves to a broad range of grape varieties and the producers here are often criticized for being unfocused; regardless, in recent years local wineries have regularly snagged awards. Zinfandel and Sauvignon Blanc are big, but it's the Syrah/Merlot blends that attract the attention and the Barbera (from a Piedmontese grape) is said to be one of the best in the world.

TOURS AND TASTINGS

If you're out for a relaxed day's tasting, avoid the two consecutive **Passport Weekends** ($85; ☎800 306 3956, ⓦeldoradowines.org), which take place in April and get booked out months in advance, although the purchase of this passport does entitle you to all manner of foodie extravagances to complement the tastings. Better to pick up the **El Dorado Wine Country Tour** leaflet from the El Dorado Chamber of Commerce in Placerville (see opposite) and make your way to the Boeger Vineyard, 1709 Carson Rd (daily 10am–5pm; tasting $5; ☎530 622 8094, ⓦboegerwinery.com), less than a mile from downtown, where you can sit in an arbour of apples and pears. Also try the Lava Cap Vineyard, 2221 Fruitridge Rd (daily 11am–5pm; tasting free; ☎530 621 0175, ⓦlavacap.com), which in recent years has won awards for its Sauvignon Blanc and Chardonnay.

The quality of the local produce – not only grapes, but also apples, pears, peaches, cherries and berries – is celebrated around the district, especially during **Johnny Appleseed Day** (☎530 644 7692, ⓦapplehill.com) in September, when a bus runs from Placerville to the majority of the orchards and wineries in the Apple Hill region. At other times during harvest, you can make your own way along the roads just north of I-50 and east of town to pick your own apples.

the road makes a more interesting stop: it's filled with grisly photographs, the medical records of murderers and thieves who were hanged for their crimes, as well as a whole arsenal of handmade escape tools recovered from prisoners over the years.

Folsom History Museum

823 Sutter St • Tues–Sun 11am–4pm • $10 • ☎ 916 985 2707, ⓦ folsomhistoricalsociety.org

A handsome reconstruction of the 1860 Wells Fargo office makes an imposing setting for the **Folsom History Museum**, whose prized possessions include a working scale model of a steam-powered gold dredge; artefacts from the Chinese community that settled here in the 1850s; and a huge mural depicting the area's main native people, the Maidu. There are also temporary exhibitions.

ARRIVAL AND INFORMATION   FOLSOM

By train Folsom is at the end of Sacramento Regional Transit's (see p.546) Gold Line (every 30min; 45min–1hr).

Chamber of Commerce 200 Wool St (Mon–Fri 10am–4pm, Sat 11am–4pm; ☎ 916 985 2698, ⓦ folsomchamber.com).

ACCOMMODATION AND EATING

Bacchus House Bistro 1004 E Bidwell St ☎ 916 984 7500, ⓦ bacchushousebistro.com. The best place to eat in town, serving a range of tasty starters and main courses such as vegetable risotto and prime rib for $16–32. Tues–Fri 11.30am–2pm & 5–9pm, Sat 5–9pm.

Lake Natoma Inn 702 Gold Lake Drive ☎ 916 351 1500, ⓦ lakenatomainn.com. Surprisingly snazzy but good-value retreat, boasting huge rooms and lovely grounds with a pool, plus a restaurant and a spa. $99

Placerville

PLACERVILLE, twenty miles east of Folsom, takes a perverse delight in having been known originally as Hangtown for its practice of lynching alleged criminals in pairs and stringing them up from a tree in the centre of town. Despite these gruesome beginnings, Placerville has always been more of a market than a mining town and is now a major crossroads, halfway between Sacramento and Lake Tahoe at the junction of US-50 and Hwy-49. For a time in the mid-1850s it was the third largest city in California and many of the state's most powerful historical figures got their start here: railroad magnates Mark Hopkins and Collis P. Huntington were local merchants, while car mogul John Studebaker made wheelbarrows for the miners.

The modern town spreads out along the highways in a string of fast-food restaurants, gas stations and motels. The old Main Street, running parallel to US-50, retains some of the Gold Rush architecture, with an effigy dangling by the neck in front of the *Hangman's Tree* bar, built over the site where the town's infamous tree once grew. The oldest continuously operating hardware store west of the Mississippi, is at 441 Main St and you'll see many fine old houses scattered among the pine trees in the steep valleys to the north and south of the centre.

El Dorado County Historical Museum

104 Placerville Drive • Wed–Sat 10am–4pm, Sun noon–4pm • Free • ☎ 530 621 5865, ⓦ museum.edcgov.us

One of the best of the Gold Country museums lies within the sprawling El Dorado County Fairgrounds, just north of US-50. The **El Dorado County Historical Museum** gives a broad historical overview of the county from the Miwok to the modern day, including logging trains and a mock-up of a general store, plus pioneer wagons and Native American handicrafts.

Gold Bug Mine Park

Bedford Ave • April–Oct daily 10am–4pm; Nov–March Sat & Sun noon–4pm • $7 • ☎ 530 642 5207, ⓦ goldbugpark.org

For more on the days of the argonauts, head across US-50 to the **Gold Bug Mine Park**; admission includes an audio tour of this typical Mother Lode mine, including a hard-rock mining site and a stamp mill showing the ore extraction process. If you want to try your luck hunting for gold, rent a pan for $2 an hour – though don't expect to find anything.

ARRIVAL, GETTING AROUND AND INFORMATION   PLACERVILLE

By bus Placerville is on the route of the once-daily Amtrak Thruway service between Sacramento (1hr 30min) and South Lake Tahoe (1hr 20min). El Dorado Transit ($1.50; ☎ 530 642 5383, ⓦ eldoradotransit.com) buses provide local transport.

El Dorado County Chamber of Commerce 542 Main St (Mon–Fri: summer 9am–5pm, rest of year 11am–3pm; ☎ 530 621 5885, ⓦ eldoradocounty.org). This office has local information and can help set up river-rafting trips in Coloma (see box opposite).

ACCOMMODATION AND EATING

The Albert Shafsky House 2942 Coloma St ☎ 530 642 2776, ⓦ shafsky.com. The area's most romantic getaway is this historic B&B with period furnishings and gourmet breakfasts, on the north side of town. **$175**

★ **Cozmic Café & Pub** 594 Main St ☎ 530 642 8481, ⓦ ourcoz.com. There's a real community feel about this place, which serves breakfasts, sandwiches and specialities like "Nacho Nirvana" for less than $10. Live events such as belly dancing and bands at different times of day. Tues, Wed & Sun 7am–8pm, Thurs–Sat 7am–midnight.

Heyday Café 325 Main St ☎ 530 626 9700, ⓦ heydaycafe.com. Small, nicely designed dining room with a menu of fine Italian food, with Mediterranean and

Californian touches, such as chicken *piccata* for $22. Mon 11am–2.30pm, Tues–Thurs 11am–9pm, Fri & Sat 11am–10pm, Sun 11am–8pm.

Mother Lode Motel 1940 Broadway ☎ 530 622 0895, ⓦ motherlodemotel.com. Classic old-style motel whose cosy rooms are decked out with floral wallpaper and bedspreads – and at old-time prices too. There's a small outdoor pool. **$64**

Sweetie Pie's 577 Main St ☎ 530 642 0128, ⓦ sweetiepies.biz. Friendly spot serving great breakfasts and filling sandwiches at lunchtime, all under $10. The bakery also dispenses fine cinnamon rolls and the like. Mon–Fri 6.30am–3pm, Sat 7am–3pm, Sun 7am–1pm.

Coloma

Sights along Hwy-49, the Gold Country's main north–south artery on the north side of Placerville, are few and far between but it was here that gold fever began on January 24, 1848, when James Marshall discovered flakes of gold in the tailrace of a mill he was building for John Sutter along the south fork of the American River at **Coloma**. By the summer of that year, thousands had flocked to the area, and by the following year Coloma was a town of ten thousand – though most left quickly following news of richer strikes elsewhere in the region and the town all but disappeared within a few years. These days Coloma attracts people after a different kind of rush: it's the best place to begin a **whitewater-rafting** journey on the American River (see opposite).

Marshall Gold Discovery State Historic Park

310 Back St • Daily: park 8am–sunset; museum March–Oct 10am–5pm; Nov–Feb 10am–4pm • $8/vehicle • ☎ 530 622 3470, ⓦ parks.ca.gov

Some of the few surviving buildings from Coloma's heyday, including two Chinese stores and the cabin where James Marshall lived, have been preserved as the **Marshall Gold Discovery State Historic Park**. A reconstruction of **Sutter's Mill** stands along the river within the park and working demonstrations are held on most weekends at 10am and 1pm. There's a small historical museum on one side of the site, and on a hill overlooking the town a statue marks the spot where Marshall is buried. Marshall never profited from his discovery and he spent most of his later years in poverty, claiming that supernatural powers had helped him to find gold.

ACCOMMODATION AND EATING   COLOMA

American River Resort 6091 New River Rd ☎ 530 622 6700, ⓦ americanriverresort.com. With a fine riverside location close to the state park, this campground offers spacious pitches, RV slots, cabins and rafting trips. Pitches **$35**, cabins **$55**

★ **Café Mahjaic** 1006 Lotus Rd, 1 mile west of Coloma ☎ 530 622 9587, ⓦ cafemahjaic.com. An unexpected location for one of the region's finest restaurants: here you can savour delights such as chocolate chipotle prawns and *coulotte* steak for $17–23. Wed–Sun 5–10pm.

RIVER RAFTING IN THE GOLD COUNTRY

Although plenty of people come through the area to see the Gold Rush sights, a good many come to enjoy the thrills and spills of **whitewater rafting** and **kayaking** on the various forks of the American, Stanislaus, Tuolumne and Merced rivers, which wind down through the region from the Sierra crest. Trips run from late spring through to early fall and start at about $78 per person/half-day midweek and sometimes include free camping.

American River Recreation ☎800 333 7238, ⓦarrafting.com

Tributary Whitewater Tours ☎800 672 3846, ⓦwhitewatertours.com

O.A.R.S. ☎800 346 6277, ⓦoars.com

Auburn

The town of **Auburn**, built into a hillside on three levels, manages to preserve its Gold Rush-era charm, even though it's right at the crossroads of Hwy-49 and I-80. The outskirts are sprawling and modern but the Old Town, on Auburn's lowest level just off Hwy-49, is one of the best preserved and most picturesque of the Gold Rush sights, with antique stores and saloons clustered around a Spanish-style plaza. You'll also find California's oldest post office, in continuous use since 1848, and the unmissable red-and-white tower of the 1891 **firehouse**. There are also a number of under-visited museums like the **Gold Country Museum** at 1273 High St (Tues–Sun 11am–4pm; free), which has an authentic tunnel on site and a replica of a miners' camp. More offbeat is the **Bernhard Museum Complex** at 291 Auburn-Folsom Rd (Tues–Sun 11am–4pm; free; ☎530 889 6500, ⓦplacer.ca.gov), whose former owner was looking for liquid, rather than nugget, gold: come here for guided tours of an amateur viticulturist's 1851 home, as well as his carriage barn and modest winery.

ARRIVAL AND INFORMATION   AUBURN

By bus Greyhound buses between Sacramento and Reno stop at 246 Palm Ave.

By train Amtrak trains use the unmanned station at 277 Nevada St.

Placer County Visitors Bureau & California Welcome Center 1103 High St (Mon–Sat 9.30am–4.30pm, Sun 11am–4.30pm; ☎530 887 2111 or ☎866 752 2371, ⓦvisitplacer.com).

ACCOMMODATION AND EATING

Bootlegger's Old Town Tavern and Grill 210 Washington St ☎530 889 2229, ⓦbootleggersauburn .com. The menu features a good range from sandwiches and hamburgers to Korean skirt steak, with prices mostly $12–30. Tues–Thurs 11am–9pm, Fri & Sat 11am–10pm, Sun 4–9pm.

Monkey Cat 805 Lincoln Way ☎530 888 8492, ⓦmonkeycat.com. Curiously decorated in part as a thatched hut with marine murals, this fusion restaurant does delicious dishes like duck breast or shrimp stir-fry for $20–25. Mon–Wed 11.30am–2pm & 5–8.30pm, Thurs & Fri 11.30am–2pm & 5–9pm, Sat 5–9pm, Sun 5–8.30pm.

Super 8 Motel 140 E Hillcrest Drive ☎530 888 8808, ⓦsuper8.com. Reliable if unspectacular chain franchise, whose simple, modern rooms are spacious enough and spotlessly clean. $64

Southern Gold Country

South from Placerville, Hwy-49 passes through **Jackson**, which makes a convenient, if unattractive, base for exploring the many dainty villages scattered around the wine-growing countryside of **Amador County**; then the highway continues on through the mining towns of **Calaveras County**. The centre of **Tuolumne County** and the southern mining district is **Sonora**, a small, prosperous town of ornate Victorian houses set on ridges above steep gorges. Once an arch rival but now a ghost town, neighbouring **Columbia** has a carefully restored Gold Rush-era Main Street.

The gold-mining district actually extended as far south as **Mariposa** but little remains to make it worth the trip unless you are passing through en route to Yosemite National Park (see p.329). Drivers should note that **speed traps** are rampant around the southern mines, particularly in Amador County and on any roads leading to Yosemite, where the speed limits tend to be low and regional traffic police await to rake in tourist revenue.

Amador County

South from Placerville and US-50, the old mining landscape of **AMADOR COUNTY** has been given over to the vineyards of one of California's up-and-coming **wine-growing** regions, best known for its robust Zinfandel, a full-flavoured vintage that thrives in the sun-baked soil. Most of the wineries are located above Hwy-49 in the Shenandoah Valley, near **Plymouth** on the north edge of the county (ⓦamadorwine.com).

Amador City and Sutter Creek

About thirty miles east of Sacramento, Hwy-16 joins Hwy-49 at **Amador City**, whose short strip of antique shops gives it a cutesy Old West look. **Sutter Creek**, two miles south, is much larger, but still little more than a row of tidy antiques shops and restaurants catering to tourists. Though there are a number of surprisingly large Victorian wooden homes – many styled after Puritan New England farmhouses – the town lacks the dishevelled spontaneity that animates many of the other Gold Rush towns, perhaps because its livelihood was never based on independent prospectors panning for placer gold but on hired hands working in the more organized and capital-intensive hard-rock mines. It was a lucrative business for the mine owners: Hetty Green, who owned the **Eureka Mine**, was at one time the richest woman in the world, while Leland Stanford, owner of the **Lincoln Mine**, used a chunk of his fortune to endow Stanford University.

8

PANNING, GAMBLING AND GUNFIGHTING

The gold of California is a touchstone which has betrayed the rottenness, the baseness, of mankind. Satan, from one of his elevations, showed mankind the kingdom of California, and they entered into a compact with him at once. Henry David Thoreau, *Journal*, February 1, 1852

Though never as rich or successful as the diggings further north, the camps of the **southern mines** had a reputation for being the liveliest and most uproarious of all the Gold Rush settlements and inspired most of the popular images of the era: Wild West towns full of gambling halls, saloons and gunfights in the streets. Certainly the southern settlements were more ethnically varied than those to the north, even if most groups stuck firmly with their own. The mining methods here were also very different from those used to the north. Instead of digging out gold-bearing ore from deep underground, claims here were more often worked by itinerant, roving prospectors searching for bits of gold washed out of rocks by rivers and streams, known as **placer** gold (from the Spanish word meaning both "sand bar", where much of the gold was found, and – appropriately – "pleasure"). Nuggets were sometimes found sitting on the riverbanks, though most of the gold had to be laboriously separated from mud and gravel using hand-held pans or larger sluices.

Mining wasn't a particularly lucrative existence: freelance miners roamed the countryside until they found a likely spot, then quickly blew most of their earnings, either in celebration or on the expensive supplies needed to carry on digging. Unsurprisingly, the boomtowns that sprang up around the richest deposits were abandoned as soon as the gold ran out but a few slowly decaying **ghost towns** have managed to survive more or less intact to the present day, hidden among the forests and rolling ranchland that in spring are covered in fresh green grasses and brightly coloured wildflowers. Other sites were buried under the many **reservoirs** – built in the 1960s to provide a stable source of water for the agricultural San Joaquin Valley – that cover much of the lower elevations.

Jackson

In comparison with Sutter Creek, the town of **Jackson**, four miles south, can seem distinctly blue-collar, mainly because of the huge Georgia Pacific lumber mill that serves as its northern gateway. Nevertheless, it's a more affordable base for exploring the surrounding countryside. Most of the well-preserved buildings in the small, historic downtown area were erected after a large fire in 1862 but today seem a bit lost amid the encroaching modern businesses. Note the lovely, if architecturally inappropriate, 1939 Art Deco front on the **County Courthouse** at the top of the hill.

Amador County Museum

225 Church St • Fri–Sun 11am–3pm • Donation • ☎ 209 257 1485, ⓦ amadorcountyhistoricalsociety.org

The extensively renovated **Amador County Museum** has displays of all the usual Gold Rush artefacts, but is worth a look most of all for its detailed models of the local hard-rock mines – with shafts over a mile deep – that were in use up until World War II.

Kennedy Tailing Wheels Park

Jackson Gate Rd • Daily 8am–sunset • Free • ☎ 209 223 1646

In the **Kennedy Tailing Wheels Park**, two 60ft-diameter tailing wheels, which carried away the waste from the Kennedy Mine, are accessible by way of short trails that lead up from a well-signposted parking area. The headframe of the 6000ft shaft, the deepest in North America, stands out at the top of the slope, along Hwy-49. The other major mine in Jackson, the **Argonaut Mine** (of which nothing remains), was the scene of a tragedy in 1922, when 47 men were killed in an underground fire.

Indian Grinding Rock State Historic Park

Off Hwy-88 • Daily sunrise–sunset • $8/car • ☎ 209 296 7488, ⓦ parks.ca.gov

Hwy-88 heads east from Jackson up the Sierra crest, through hills that contain one of the most fitting memorials to the Native Americans who lived here for thousands of years before the Gold Rush all but wiped them out. Nine miles from Jackson, a side road passes by the **Indian Grinding Rock State Historic Park**, where eleven hundred small cups – *Chaw'Se* in Miwok – were carved into the marbleized limestone outcropping to be used as mortars for grinding acorns into flour; it's the largest collection of bedrock mortars in North America. If you arrive near dawn or dusk and look closely from the small elevated platform next to the biggest of the flat rocks, you can just detect the faint outline of some of the 360 **petroglyphs** here. The state has developed the site into an interpretive centre and has, with the close participation of tribal elders and community leaders, constructed replicas of Miwok dwellings and religious buildings. Descendants of the Miwok gather here during the weekend following the fourth Friday in September for **Big Time**, a celebration of the survival of their culture with traditional arts, crafts and games.

Chaw'Se Regional Indian Museum

Mon, Thurs & Fri 11am–2.30pm, Sat & Sun 10am–3.30pm

At the entrance to the site, the **Chaw'Se Regional Indian Museum** explores the past and present state of the ten Sierra Nevada native groups in a building said to simulate a Miwok roundhouse. The full process of producing acorn flour is covered but the lack of information on modern Miwok life is a sad testament to the extent of the devastation done to the culture.

Volcano

Named after the crater-like bowl in which it sits, **Volcano**, a tiny village a mile and a half north of Indian Grinding Rock, once boasted over thirty saloons and dance halls. Today, it claims nearly as many historic sites as Jackson but has been mercifully bypassed by all the latter's development and traffic. The densely forested countryside around the village makes it well worth a visit, especially from mid-March to mid-April,

BLACK BART

The mysterious man known as **Black Bart** made an unlikely highwayman: Charles E. Bowles – sometimes Bolton – was a prominent and respectable San Francisco citizen in his 50s who claimed to be a wealthy mining engineer. In fact, Charles's background was rather more chequered: born to a farmer father in England, he'd emigrated to America as a child and moved to California to try his luck in the Gold Rush. His luck failed and, now married with children, Bowles enlisted in the Union Army, fighting through the Civil War.

Unsurprisingly, it left him a changed man. Once discharged, he drifted around the West Coast, losing contact with his family and trying his hand at silver mining. Finally, in 1875, Charlie turned to crime: over the next eight years, he committed almost thirty **stagecoach robberies**, which yielded a then-staggering income of $6000 a year. But what set Bart apart wasn't his money but his manners. No brutal thug, he instead always addressed his victims as "Sir" and "Madam", never shot them, and in a waggish touch, sometimes recited fragments of poetry before escaping with the loot. His name, incidentally, was pinched from a fictional story published in a local paper that mythologized a merciless criminal known as Black Bart.

But Bart's luck only held so long: he was finally discovered after dropping a handkerchief at the scene of a hold-up, the police nabbing him by tracing the laundry mark back to a San Francisco laundry and from there to Bowles. He spent four years of a six-year sentence in **San Quentin**. Of course, it was commuted for good behaviour and, after his release, he disappeared without trace.

---

when **Daffodil Hill**, three miles north of Volcano, is carpeted with more than 300,000 of the bobbing yellow heads. Its other notable attraction is the creaky cannon known as "Old Abe": locals threatened to fire it at a rebellious band of Confederate sympathizers during the Civil War – the sole threat of aggression to take place in California, even though not a single shot was actually exchanged.

ARRIVAL AND INFORMATION AMADOR COUNTY

By car The best way to travel through this area is by car, as the local bus system can be patchy.

By bus There are two weekday commuter services into Sacramento and back from Sutter Creek with Amador Transit (☎ 209 267 9395, ⓦ amadortransit.com), which also operates local buses to Plymouth and Jackson.

Amador County Chamber of Commerce 115 Main St, Jackson (Mon–Fri 8am–4pm, Sat 10am–2pm; ☎ 800 726 4667, ⓦ amadorcountychamber.com).

Sutter Creek visitor centre 71A Main St, Sutter Creek (Mon–Thurs 11am–3pm, Fri–Sun 10am–4pm; ☎ 209 267 1344 or ☎ 800 400 0305, ⓦ suttercreek.org).

ACCOMMODATION AND EATING

PLYMOUTH

Rancho Cicada Retreat 10001 Bell Rd ☎ 209 245 4841, ⓦ ranchocicadaretreat.com. Smart yet rustic cabins of different styles in a lovely forested area, with shared facilities such as a hot tub. Nature walks and group activities are also organized. **$85**

★Taste 9402 Main St ☎ 209 245 3463, ⓦ restauranttaste.com. One of the best restaurants in all of the Gold Country, serving delights such as Grimaud Farms guinea hen for $33, as well as intriguing-sounding starters such as mushroom cigars for $10.50. Mon, Tues & Thurs 5–9pm, Fri–Sun 11.30am–2pm & 4.30–9pm.

AMADOR CITY

Andrae's Bakery & Cheese Shop 14141 Old Hwy-49 ☎ 209 267 1352, ⓦ andraesbakery.com. Gourmet sandwiches, savouries, cakes and cookies are all available, as are quality cheeses, beer and wine. Thurs–Sun

7.30am–4pm.

Imperial Hotel 14202 Old Hwy-49 ☎ 209 267 9172, ⓦ imperialamador.com. Dominating the northern edge of town, this 1879 hotel with 4ft-thick brick walls has quaintly furnished rooms. Complimentary gourmet breakfast. **$120**

SUTTER CREEK

The Foxes Inn 77 Main St ☎ 209 267 5882, ⓦ foxesinn .com. Fairly luxurious and well-appointed rooms with claw-foot baths are available at this quaint Victorian inn. Excellent two-course breakfast included. **$160**

Hotel Sutter 53 Main St ☎ 209 267 0242, ⓦ hotelsutter .com. Still boasting its attractive wooden façade but completely renovated inside, this fine hotel also has a quality restaurant and a cellar bar with live music. **$120**

Sina's Back Roads Café 74 Main St ☎ 209 267 0440, ⓦ sinasbackroadscafe.com. Bright-and-breezy café serving huge breakfasts, sandwiches, wraps, salads and

baked items such as chunky cookies, all well under $10. Mon, Tues, Thurs & Fri 7.30am–3pm, Sat & Sun 7.30am–4pm.
Sutter Creek Ice Cream Emporium 51 Main St ☏ 209 267 0543. Delightful old-style ice-cream parlour, where the friendly owner may well play Scott Joplin tunes on the piano while you sip a milk shake. Mon–Fri & Sun 9am–8pm, Sat 9am–10pm.

JACKSON
Fargo Club 2 Main St ☏ 209 223 3859. Behind an unmarked door, this is the modern equivalent of a Wild West saloon, with cheap if uninspiring beers and late-night poker games. It can get rowdy late at weekend nights. Mon–Thurs & Sun 6am–10pm, Fri & Sat 6am–2am.
Jackson Lodge 850 N Hwy-49 ☏ 888 333 0486, ⓦ thejacksonlodge.com. Functional, simply furnished rooms and more spacious private cabins are available at this motel-style place just north of town with a decent outdoor pool. Doubles $79, cabins $125
Mel and Faye's Diner 31 Hwy-49 ☏ 209 223 0853, ⓦ melandfayes.homestead.com. Classic 1956 roadside

diner where the waitresses dish up filling breakfasts and sandwiches for around $10, plus steak dinners for only $13. Daily 7am–9pm.

INDIAN GRINDING ROCK
Indian Grinding Rock State Historic Park campground 14481 Pine Grove-Volcano Rd ☏ 209 296 7488, ⓦ parks.ca.gov. Plenty of tent sites on shady ground overlooking the grinding rocks. Closed occasionally for Native American festivals. Pitches $30

VOLCANO
St George Hotel 16104 Main St ☏ 209 296 4458, ⓦ stgeorgevolcano.com. Most rooms at this three-storey hotel with wooden balconies have shared bathrooms. The restaurant serves great rib-eye steaks for $25. $75
★ **Union Inn & Pub** 21375 Consolation St ☏ 209 296 4458, ⓦ volcanounion.com. The rooms in this 1880 structure are perfectly comfortable, some with tubs, and the lively pub-restaurant (closed Tues & Wed) is the sister to *Taste* in Plymouth (see opposite). $89

Calaveras County

8

CALAVERAS COUNTY lies across the Mokelumne River, eight miles south of Jackson, and is best known for being the setting of Mark Twain's first published story, *The Celebrated Jumping Frog of Calaveras County*. Today, precious few sights of historic interest remain, though there are plenty of options in the county for rugged outdoor activities.

Mokelumne Hill
The most northerly town in the county, **Mokelumne Hill**, or "Moke Hill", was as action-packed in its time as any of the southern Gold Rush towns but tourism has been slower to take hold here and today the town is just an all-but-abandoned cluster of ruined and half-restored buildings, not without a certain melancholy appeal.

The **Mokelumne Hill Library & History Center** on Main Street (Tues & Thurs 1.30–6pm, Wed 10am–6pm, Fri 9am–1.30pm; free; ☏ 209 286 0507) has a modest exhibit on the history of the immediate area, once home to almost ten thousand people. The range of names and languages on the headstones of the **Protestant Cemetery**, on a hill a hundred yards west of town, gives a good idea of the mix of people who came from all over the world to the California mines.

San Andreas
San Andreas hardly seems to warrant a second look: the biggest town for miles, it's now the Calaveras County seat, and has sacrificed historic character for commercial sprawl. What remains of old San Andreas survives along narrow Main Street, on a steep hill just east of the highway.

Calaveras County Museum
30 N Main St • Daily 10am–4pm • $3 • ☏ 209 754 1058, ⓦ calaverascohistorical.com
The 1893 granite-and-brick County Courthouse has been restored as the **Calaveras County Museum** and now houses an interesting collection of Gold Rush memorabilia. There's a diverse collection of gold nuggets and miners' tools, such as sluice boxes and baskets, as well as Miwok artefacts and a replica of an 1880s general store.

Angels Camp

The mining camps of southern Calaveras County were some of the richest in this part of the Gold Country, both for the size of their nuggets and for the imaginations of their residents. The author Bret Harte spent an unhappy few years teaching in and around the mines in the mid-1850s and based his short story, *The Luck of Roaring Camp*, on his stay in **Angels Camp**, thirty miles south of Jackson. There isn't much to see here these days, though the downtown feels mildly authentic.

The saloon in the *Angels Hotel* on Main Street is where 29-year-old Twain heard a tale that inspired him to write his famous story, *The Celebrated Jumping Frog of Calaveras County*, about a frog-jumping competition (the saloon is now a discount tyre store). Aside from the relentless onslaught of frog-themed souvenirs, the longest lasting legacy of Twain's story is the **Jumping Frog Jubilee**; it's held along with the local state fair on the third weekend in May each year and attended by thousands of people who come to watch as pet amphibians compete to see who can jump furthest.

Angels Camp Museum

753 S Main St • March–Nov Mon & Thurs–Sun 10am–4pm; Dec–Feb Sat & Sun 10am–4pm • $5 • ☎ 209 736 2963, ⓦ angelscampmuseumfoundation.org

On the north side of town, the **Angels Camp Museum** presents a cornucopia of gold-excavating equipment and memorabilia, as well as a carriage barn filled with historic horse-drawn vehicles. There is also an absorbing Mark Twain exhibit, which chronicles how he heard and ultimately wrote the story about the jumping frog (see above).

Carson Hill

Carson Hill, now a ghost town along Hwy-49 four miles south of Angels Camp, boasted the largest single nugget ever unearthed in California: 195 pounds of solid gold fifteen inches long and six inches thick, worth $43,000 when it was discovered in 1854 and well over a million dollars today.

New Melones Reservoir

Near Carson Hill, **New Melones Reservoir** is the third largest reservoir in California and has all the camping, swimming, hiking, boating and other recreational possibilities you could hope for, not to mention spectacular, if man-made, views. It's all the more

---

LIMESTONE CAVERN TOURS

Limestone caverns abound in the southern Gold Country; three have been developed expressly for public tours.

California Cavern Calaveras ☎ 866 762 2837, ⓦ caverntours.com. California Cavern is a horizontal network of caves that's a better choice for vertigo sufferers than the precipitous stairs at Moaning Cavern. You might also enjoy the Black Chasm Cavern tour. Mid-May to mid-Sept daily 10am–5pm; mid-Sept to mid-May Sat & Sun 11am–4pm, Mon–Fri by appointment; $17.50.

Mercer Caverns A mile north of Murphys on Sheep Ranch Rd ☎ 209 728 2101, ⓦ mercercaverns.com. Known for the spectacular stalagmite and stalactite formations in its 800ft-long gallery, resembling swooping angels' wings and giant flowers. Summer daily 9am–5pm; rest of year daily 10am–4.30pm; $16.

Moaning Cavern Vallecito, just south of Hwy-4 and 5 miles east of Angels Camp off Parrots Ferry Rd ☎ 866 762 2837, ⓦ caverntours.com. Although discovered by gold miners in 1851, bones have been found here dating back 13,000 years. It didn't take long for locals to recognize the lucrative potential of the eerie, lacy rock formations and the caves were opened as a tourist attraction in 1919. The owners first inserted a 234-step spiral staircase to facilitate access and then corked the cavern's opening by building a gift shop on top of it: ironically, these renovations wrecked the cave's natural acoustics and muted the moaning sounds after which it's named. Various adventure activities are possible. Mid-May to mid-Sept daily 9am–6pm; mid-Sept to mid-May Mon–Fri 10–5pm, Sat & Sun 9am–5pm; walking tour $17.50, zip line $45, rappel $72.

attractive for the fact that it is seldom visited by the throngs who fly through the Gold Country on their way to pricier recreational areas.

Murphys

Up the fairly steep Hwy-4, **Murphys**' one and only street is shaded by locust trees and graced by rows of delightfully rickety monumental buildings. One of the Gold Country's few surviving wooden water flumes still stands on the town's northern edge, while the oldest structure here now houses the **Old Timer's Museum** (470 Main St; Mon & Fri–Sun noon–4pm; donation; ☎209 728 1160, ⓦmurphysoldtimersmuseum.com), a small gathering of documents with a wall full of rifles. You can take a free one-hour walking tour from here at 10am on Sundays.

Calaveras Big Trees State Park

Daily dawn–dusk · $8/vehicle · ☎ 209 795 3840, ⓦ parks.ca.gov

Extensive **Calaveras Big Trees State Park** covers six thousand acres of gigantic sequoia trees, threaded with trails. It makes for fine ski-touring in winter and is a great place for hiking and camping the rest of the year, or just enjoying a picnic under the shade of the ancient boughs.

ARRIVAL AND INFORMATION

By bus Calaveras Transit (☎209 754 4450, ⓦtransit .calaverasgov.us) runs several daily services between all the towns within the county and to Jackson and Columbia in the neighbouring counties.

Calaveras County Visitors Bureau 1192 S Main St,

CALAVERAS COUNTY

Angels Camp (Mon–Fri 9am–5pm, Sat 10am–5pm, Sun 11am–3pm; ☎209 736 0049 or ☎800 225 3764, ⓦvisitcalaveras.org). It has copious frog-related memorabilia in honour of Mark Twain, as well as information.

ACCOMMODATION AND EATING

SAN ANDREAS

Black Bart Inn 35 N Main St ☎209 754 3808, ⓦblackbartinn.net. Named after the gentleman stagecoach robber (see box, p.554), only the rather down-at-heel motel section remains open but the rooms are among the cheapest in the Gold Country. $55

ANGELS CAMP

Jumping Frog Motel 330 Murphy's Grade Rd ☎209 736 219, ⓦmagnusonhotels.com. This standard motel wins no prizes for architectural style but the rooms are well maintained and as good value as you are likely to find anywhere. $65

MURPHYS

Alchemy 191 Main St ☎209 728 0703, ⓦalchemymarket

.com. Fancy and sleek restaurant attached to a gourmet market. You can enjoy an early dinner such as cranberry-balsamic-glazed salmon for $25–30. Mon, Tues, Thurs & Fri 11am–8pm, Sat & Sun 10.30am–8pm.

Grounds 412 Main St ☎209 728 8663, ⓦgrounds restaurant.com. Try the seared swordfish steak, steamed mussels or fresh medallions of elk, all in the $20–30 range, at this extremely popular restaurant. Daily 7am–3pm; also Wed & Thurs 5–8.30pm, Fri & Sat 5–10pm, Sun 5–8pm.

★**Murphys Hotel** 457 Main St ☎209 728 3444 or ☎800 532 7684, ⓦmurphyshotel.com. A charming hotel with colourful rustic doubles, all boasting traditional wooden shutters, and cheaper lodge rooms. The elegant restaurant does fine California cuisine. $95

Tuolomne County

The mountains get a little taller, the ravines sharper and the scenery even more picturesque as Hwy-49 presses on south through **TUOLOMNE COUNTY**, which contains several more fascinating towns from the gold heyday, including the region's traditional hub of **Sonora**, as well as **Columbia**, one of the most self-consciously touristic but entertaining places of all.

Sonora

Sonora is the centre of the southern mining district: it was the site of the **Bonanza Mine**, one of the most lucrative Gold Rush digs. Now a logging town set on steep ravines, it makes a good base for exploring the southern region: there are two settlement clusters, Historic Sonora and the commercial district known as East Sonora. There's little to see beyond the false-fronted buildings and Victorian houses on the main **Washington Street** and the Gothic **St James Episcopal Church** at its far end, but it's a friendly, animated place. The small **Tuolumne County Museum** (Mon–Fri 10am–4pm, Sat 10am–3.30pm; free; ☎209 532 1317, ⓦtchistory.org), in the old County Jail at 158 Bradford St, is mainly worth a look for the restored cellblock.

Columbia State Historic Park

Sonora's one-time arch rival, tourist-loving Columbia, three miles north on Parrots Ferry Road, now passes itself off as a ghost town with a carefully restored Main Street that gives an excellent – if contrived – idea of what Gold Rush life might have been like, complete with period-costumed staff in the local hotels and restaurants. Thanks to agitation from locals, the entire town is now preserved as **Columbia State Historic Park**.

Brief history

Columbia experienced a brief burst of riches after Dr Thaddeus Hildreth and his party picked up thirty pounds of gold in just two days in March 1850. Within a month, more than five thousand miners were working claims limited by local law to ten square feet, and by 1854 Columbia was California's second largest city, with fifteen thousand inhabitants supporting some forty saloons, eight hotels and one school. Legend has it that the town missed becoming the state capital by two votes – just as well, since by 1870 the gold had run out and Columbia was almost totally abandoned, but only after over two and a half million ounces of gold (worth nearly a billion dollars at today's prices) had been taken out of the surrounding area.

Main Street

Open access; stagecoach ride hourly April–Sept Tues–Sun 10am–4.45pm; Oct–March Fri–Sun same hours • Free; stagecoach ride $7 • ☎ 209 588 9128, ⓦ parks.ca.gov

Though designated a State Historic Park, Columbia is also a genuine town with an active **Main Street** and year-round residents. Most of the surviving buildings date from the late 1850s, rebuilt in brick after fire destroyed the town a second time. Roughly half of them house historical exhibits – including a dramatized visit to the frontier dentist's office, complete with a 200-proof anaesthetic and tape-recorded screams. The rest have been converted into shops, restaurants and saloons, where you can sip a sarsaparilla or munch on a hot dog. Two notable structures are the **Claverie Mason Building**, once the heart of Columbia's Chinatown, and the atmospheric ruins of the **Bixel Brewery**, a mile or so north along Main Street from downtown: although there's little to see now, it's an evocative change from the staged Victoriana in the centre. As you might imagine, the park/town can be nightmarishly crowded, especially on **Living History Days** (early June), when volunteers dress up and act out scenes from old times. If you want to escape the crowds, take the corny but fun **stagecoach ride** which leaves hourly from the Wells Fargo Building and zips along the old mining trails around the town.

Hidden Treasure gold mine

Tours: hours vary; 1hr 30min • $10 • ☎ 209 532 9693, ⓦ hiddentreasuregoldmine.com

At the southern end of the park is the **Hidden Treasure gold mine**, where microscopic nuggets are still occasionally found. **Tours**, including the opportunity to do some panning, start from the shack at the south end of Main Street and are hosted by amusingly crabby former miners.

Jamestown

Three miles south of Sonora on Hwy-49, **Jamestown** serves as the southern gateway to the Gold Country for drivers entering on Hwy-120 from the San Francisco Bay Area.

Before 1966, when much of Jamestown burned down in a fire, it was used as a location for many well-known Westerns: later the classic TV series *Little House on the Prairie* spent several seasons filming in town and Clint Eastwood shot scenes for his Oscar-winning *Unforgiven* here. It is one of the few Gold Country towns with a working mine – the huge open-pit **Sonora Mining Corporation** just to the west. **Gold Prospecting Adventures** at 18170 Main St (from $25/hr; ☎ 800 596 0009, ⓦ goldprospecting.com) gives brief instruction in the arts of panning, sluicing and sniping, allowing you to scrape what minuscule traces you can from its local stream. Unless, of course, you are as fortunate as Oscar Espinoza from Modesto, who discovered a large nugget weighing over a pound and worth at least $20,000 in nearby Woods Creek in August 2016.

Railtown 1897 State Historic Park

5th Ave, at Reservoir St · Daily: April–Oct 9.30am–4.30pm; Nov–March 10am–3pm · $5 · **Train rides** April–Oct Sat & Sun 10.30am, noon, 1.30pm & 3pm · $15 · ☎ 209 984 3953, ⓦ railtown1897.org

The train from *Unforgiven* – also used forty years earlier in *High Noon*, starring Gary Cooper – can be found among many other steam giants in the **Railtown 1897 State Historic Park**, Jamestown's biggest attraction. You can ride one of the vintage trains for an additional fee at weekends.

ARRIVAL AND INFORMATION

TUOLOMNE COUNTY

By bus The only out-of-county bus service is the connection from Columbia to San Andreas in neighbouring Calaveras County on Calaveras Transit (see p.557), while Tuolumne County Transit (☎ 209 532 0404, ⓦ tuolumnecountytransit.com) links Columbia, Sonora and Jamestown.

Tuolumne County Visitors Bureau 542 W Stockton Rd, Sonora (Mon–Sat 9am–5pm; ☎ 209 533 4420, ⓦ yosemitegoldcountry.com).

ACCOMMODATION AND EATING

SONORA

★ **Diamondback Grill** 93 S Washington St ☎ 209 532 6661, ⓦ thediamondbackgrill.com. Very reliable option for sandwiches, huge burgers and hefty portions of meat for $11–18. Also has a convivial wine bar. Mon–Thurs 11am–9pm, Fri & Sat 11am–9.30pm, Sun 11am–8pm.

Gunn House 286 S Washington St ☎ 209 532 3421, ⓦ gunnhousehotel.com. The expanded old adobe house of the Mother Lode's first newspaper proprietor, Dr Gunn, has large, slightly dark rooms. **$140**

Sonora Thai 51 S Washington St ☎ 209 532 2355. All the Siamese favourites from stir-fries to spicy red and green curries can be enjoyed at this simple place for $10–15. Mon–Thurs 11am–9pm, Fri & Sat 11am–9.30pm.

Zane Iron Horse Lounge 97 S Washington St ☎ 209 532 4482. This is the best place to find a hint of the Wild West and drink with the locals. The beers are unremarkable but the spirits are cheap and strong. Daily noon–late.

COLUMBIA

Columbia City Hotel 22768 Main St, Columbia ☎ 209 588 7234, ⓦ parks.ca.gov. State-run hotel, subtly refurbished to maintain its nineteenth-century character while providing well-appointed rooms. Those with balconies cost more. **$85**

Columbia House Restaurant 22738 Main St, Columbia ☎ 209 532 0663. Filling comfort food such as eggy breakfast, onion rings, garlic fries, deep-fried

---

CHINESE CAMP

Hwy-49 winds south from Sonora through some sixty miles of the sparsely populated, rolling foothills of **Mariposa County**, but first it passes the scant remains of the town of **Chinese Camp**. It was here that the worst of the Tong Wars between rival factions of Chinese miners took place in 1856, after the Chinese had been excluded from other mining camps in the area by white miners. Prejudice against all foreigners was rampant in the southern Gold Country, which accounts for its most enduring legend, that of the so-called Robin Hood of the Mother Lode, **Joaquin Murieta**. Though it's unlikely he ever existed, Murieta was an archetype representing the dispossessed Mexican miners driven to banditry by racist abuse at the hands of newly arrived white Americans. Today, amid the run-down shacks and trailers, there's little evidence of Chinese Camp's violent past, other than a historic marker on the main road.

artichoke hearts, burgers and sandwiches are served for $10–13. Daily 8am–6pm.

JAMESTOWN
Jamestown Hotel 18153 Main St ☎209 984 3902, ⓦthejamestownhotel.com. Historic building with a blue and white wooden colonnade and balconies outside some of the renovated period rooms with smart new bathrooms. Good restaurant downstairs. **$125**

Miner's Motel 18740 Hwy-108 ☎209 532 7850, ⓦsonoraminersmotel.com. Bright, simply furnished rooms with some interesting touches – such as lamp bases in the shape of old miners – are available at bargain rates at this motel halfway towards Sonora. Sizeable outdoor pool. **$75**

★**National Hotel** 18183 Main St ☎209 984 3446, ⓦnational-hotel.com. All nine rooms are furnished with antiques and decorated with period flock wallpaper. There is also a casually elegant restaurant and an atmospheric saloon bar. **$160**

The Willow Steakhouse 18723 Main St ☎209 984 3998. Smart high-ceilinged place, where you can tuck into generous portions of steak, seafood and pasta from $16.95. Plenty of appetizers too. Mon–Fri 11am–3pm & 5–10pm, Sat 5–10pm, Sun 5–9pm.

Northern Gold Country

The **northern section** of the Gold Country includes some of the most spectacularly beautiful scenery in California. Fast-flowing rivers cascade through steeply walled canyons whose slopes are covered with the flaming reds and golds of poplars and sugar maples in fall, highlighted against an evergreen background of pine and fir trees. Unlike the freelance placer mines of the south, where wandering prospectors picked nuggets of gold out of the streams and rivers, the gold here was (and some still is) buried deep underground and had, therefore, to be pounded out of hard-rock ore.

Twenty-five miles north of Auburn and I-80, the neighbouring towns of **Grass Valley** and **Nevada City** were the most prosperous and substantial of the gold-mining towns and are still thriving communities, just four miles apart in beautiful surroundings in the lower reaches of the Sierra Nevada. Gold was the lifeblood of the area as recently as the mid-1950s, and both towns look largely unchanged since the Gold Rush. These **northern mines** were the most profitable, more than half of California's gold originating in the mines of **Nevada County** and most of that from Grass Valley's Empire Mine (see p.562).

A few miles from Nevada City, at the end of a steep and twisting backroad, the scarred yet curiously beautiful landforms of the **Malakoff Diggins** stand as an exotic reminder of the destruction wrought by overzealous miners. Hwy-49 winds further up into the mountains, along the Yuba River to the High Sierra hamlet of **Downieville**, at the foot of the towering Sierra Buttes, and even smaller **Sierra City**. From here you're within striking distance of the northernmost Gold Rush ghost town of **Johnsville**, which stands in an evocative state of arrested decay in the middle of the forests of **Plumas-Eureka State Park**, on the crest of the Sierra Nevada.

Grass Valley

The inviting town of **GRASS VALLEY** makes a worthwhile stop on any tour of the Gold Country. Although there has been a fair amount of new construction – it's less well preserved than close neighbour Nevada City – plenty of Victorian buildings have survived, and the town is compact enough for them to be viewed during a short stroll.

The North Star Mining Museum & Pelton Wheel Exhibit

933 Allison Ranch Rd • May–Oct Tues–Sat 10am–4pm, Sun noon–4pm; Nov–April by appointment • Donation • ☎530 273 4255, ⓦnevadacountyhistory.org

The **North Star Mining Museum & Pelton Wheel Exhibit**, at the south end of Mill Street, is one of the most evocative Gold Country museums, with enthusiastic guides and interesting exhibits illustrating Grass Valley's glory days. Housed in what used to be the power station for the North Star Mine, the centrepiece is the giant **Pelton wheel**. Patented in 1878 and resembling nothing so much as a 30ft-diameter bicycle wheel, the wheel became one of the most important inventions to come out of the Gold Country. Many Pelton wheels were used to generate electricity, though the one here drove an air compressor that powered the drills and hoists of the mine.

A series of dioramas in the museum describes the day-to-day working life of the miners, three-quarters of whom had emigrated here from the depressed tin mines of Cornwall in England. Besides their expertise at working deep underground, the "Cousin Jacks", as they were called by the non-Cornish miners, introduced the **Cornish pump** (not to mention the Cornish pasty, a traditional savoury pie) to the mines. You can see a mock-up of one of these mammoth beasts, which were designed to extract water from underground, as well as a scaled-down version of a noisy stamp mill, used for pulverizing gold-bearing quartz ore.

Empire Mine State Park

10791 E Empire St · Daily 10am–5pm; Empire Cottage tour times vary · $7 · ☏ 530 273 8522, ⓦ empiremine.org

The largest and richest gold mine in the state was the **Empire Mine**, now preserved as a state park a mile southeast of Grass Valley, just off Hwy-174 at the top of Empire Street. The 800-acre **park** is surrounded by pines, among which are vast quantities of mining equipment and machinery. Standing among the machines, it's easy to imagine the din that shook the ground 24 hours a day or the skips of fifty men descending the now-desolate shaft into the 350 miles of underground tunnels. After more than six million ounces of gold had been recovered, the cost of getting the gold out of the ground exceeded $35 an ounce – the government-controlled price at the time – and production ceased. Most of the mine has been dismantled but there's a small, very informative **museum** at the entrance with a superb model of the whole underground system, built secretly to help predict the location of lucrative veins of gold.

8

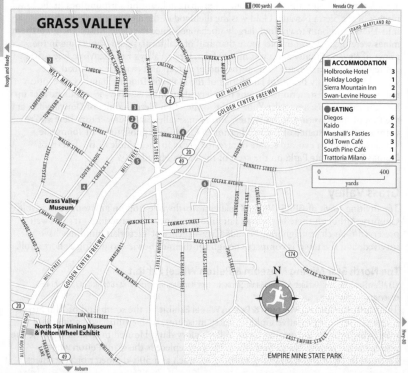

GRASS VALLEY

■ **ACCOMMODATION**
Holbrooke Hotel	3
Holiday Lodge	1
Sierra Mountain Inn	2
Swan-Levine House	4

● **EATING**
Diegos	6
Kaido	2
Marshall's Pasties	5
Old Town Café	3
South Pine Café	1
Trattoria Milano	4

THE LOLA MONTEZ STORY

There's nothing Gold Country folk love better than telling a long tale about their town's toughest days, making it virtually impossible to pass through Grass Valley without getting at least one rendition of the **Lola Montez** story. This Irish dancer and entertainer – the former mistress of Ludwig of Bavaria and friend of Victor Hugo and Franz Liszt – embarked on a highly successful tour of America in the 1850s, playing to packed houses from New York to San Francisco. Her provocative "Spider Dance", in which she wriggled about the stage shaking cork spiders out of her dress, didn't much impress the miners, but she liked the wild lifestyle of the town, gave up dancing, and retired to Grass Valley with her pet grizzly bear, which she kept tied up in the front yard. A few mementoes of Lola's life, such as clothes and accessories, are displayed in the otherwise uninspiring **Grass Valley Museum**, located in the Old St Mary's Academy (410 S Church St; Tues–Fri 12.30–3.30pm; donation; ☎ 530 273 5509).

You can get some sense of the mine's prosperity by taking one of the **tours** of the owner's house, the **Empire Cottage** at the north end of the park – a vaguely English stone-and-brick manor house with a glowing, redwood-panelled interior overlooking a formal garden.

ARRIVAL AND INFORMATION   GRASS VALLEY

By bus Grass Valley is connected to Nevada City every 30min by the Gold Country Stage minibus (Mon–Fri 8am–7pm, Sat 10am–5pm; $1.50, $4.50 for a day-pass; ☎ 530 477 0103, ⓦ goldcountrystage.com). For more distant connections, the nearest Greyhound and Amtrak stops are at Colfax, around 10 miles away.

Chamber of Commerce 128 E Main St (Mon–Fri 10am–4pm, Sat & Sun 11am–3pm; ☎ 530 273 4667, ⓦ grassvalleychamber.com).

ACCOMMODATION

★ **Holbrooke Hotel** 212 W Main St ☎ 530 273 1353, ⓦ holbrooke.com. Right in the centre of town, this historic hotel, where Mark Twain once stayed, has stylish rooms, an opulent lobby and a highly rated bar-cum-restaurant. $114

Holiday Lodge 1221 E Main St ☎ 530 273 4406 or ☎ 800 742 7125, ⓦ holidaylodge.biz. Reasonable, no-frills rooms in a lodge whose main advantages are a heated swimming pool and free local calls. $89

Sierra Mountain Inn 816 W Main St ☎ 530 273 8133, ⓦ sierramountaininn.com. Cosy and tastefully decorated rooms, all with kitchenettes, in a pleasant clapboard house dating from the 1930s. $120

Swan-Levine House 328 S Church St ☎ 530 272 1873, ⓦ swanlevinehouse.com. Attractively decorated, sunny en-suite rooms in an old Victorian hospital. There's original artwork on display and the friendly owners give printmaking lessons. $125

EATING

★ **Diegos** 217 Colfax Ave ☎ 530 477 1460, ⓦ diegos restaurant.com. Stunningly decorated with colourful wall mosaics, this Central and South American restaurant serves tasty delights such as *achiote de pollo* for $16.95. You can wash your meal down with Latin beers or sangria. Daily 11am–9pm.

Kaido 207 W Main St ☎ 530 274 0144, ⓦ kaidosushi.com. Smart Japanese restaurant serving excellent sushi combos for $30–39 and mains for $21–25 in authentic surroundings. The owner used to be a chef at the Japanese embassy in London. Tues–Thurs 5.30–9pm, Fri 5.30–9.30pm, Sat 5–9.30pm.

★ **Marshall's Pasties** 203 Mill St ☎ 530 272 2844. Mind-boggling array of fresh filled Cornish pasties for just over $5, a legacy of the immigrant Cornish miners. Only several cramped tables inside so best for takeaway. Mon–Fri 9.30am–6pm, Sat 10am–6pm.

Old Town Café 110 Mill St ☎ 530 273 4304. Classic diner in a sharp renovation of what claims to be the oldest continuously operating restaurant in town. The breakfasts are especially good value at under $10. Mon–Sat 7am–3pm, Sun 7.30am–2.30pm.

South Pine Café 102 Richardson St ☎ 530 274 0261, ⓦ southpinecafe.com. Relaxing, bright place which specializes in fine eggy breakfasts including a Mexican one with meat, plus vegetarian options such as spicy Jamaican tofu for $10.50. Daily 8am–3pm.

Trattoria Milano 124 Bank St ☎ 530 273 3555, ⓦ trattoria-milano.com. Quality Italian restaurant in an attractive building a short way off Main St. Plenty of fine salads and pasta, as well as tasty mains such as Milanese braised veal shank for $29. Tues–Sat 5–9pm, Sun 4.30–8.30pm.

8

Nevada City

Towns don't get much quainter than **NEVADA CITY**, four miles north of Grass Valley, with its crooked rows of elaborate Victorian homes set on the winding, narrow, maple-tree-lined streets, which rise up from Hwy-49. It gets away with its cuteness by being one of the least changed of all the Gold Country towns, and the cluster of excellent shops and restaurants in the town centre make it a good, if pricey, base for the surrounding area.

There aren't many set-piece sights other than the restored, lacy-balconied and bell-towered **Firehouse Museum #1**, 214 Main St (May–Oct Tues–Sun 1–4pm; Nov–March by appointment; donation; ☎530 265 5468, ⊛nevadacountyhistory.org), which describes the social history of the region. The heart of town is Broad Street, which climbs up from the highway past the imposing 1854 **National Hotel** (see opposite) and a number of antiques shops and restaurants, all boasting Gold Country balconies and wooden awnings. Almost the only exception to the rule of picturesque nostalgia is the Art Deco 1937 **City Hall**.

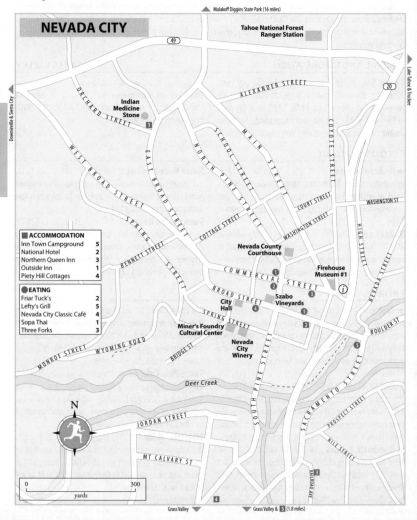

WINERIES IN NEVADA CITY

Some of the region's wineries have tasting rooms right in town. One such is **Nevada City Winery**, 321 Spring St (Mon–Thurs & Sun noon–5pm, Fri & Sat noon–7pm; ☏ 530 265 9463, ⓦ ncwinery .com), where you can taste the produce of one of the state's oldest vineyards. If you'd like to sample some more, stop by **Szabo Vineyards**, whose tasting room is at 316 Broad St (Thurs 2–8pm, Fri & Sat noon–7pm, Sun noon–6pm; ☏ 530 265 8792, ⓦ szabovineyards.com). Both wineries sell their product at very modest prices in comparison to those of the Wine Country.

The **Miner's Foundry Cultural Center** (Mon–Fri 10am–3pm; free; ☏ 530 265 5040, ⓦ minersfoundry.org), close to the Deer Creek Canyon at 325 Spring St, is an old tool foundry converted into a cultural centre, art gallery, performance space and the KVMR radio studios.

Above the town at the top of Pine Street, a small plaque marks **Indian Medicine Stone**, a granite boulder with sun-beds worn into the hollows of the rock by Native Americans who valued the healing power of sunshine.

ARRIVAL AND INFORMATION NEVADA CITY

By bus Nevada City is connected to Grass Valley every 30min by the Gold Country Stage minibus (see p.563).

Nevada City tourist office 132 Main St, a block north of Hwy-49, (Mon–Fri 9am–5pm, Sat 11am–4pm; ☏ 530 265 2692 or ☏ 800 655 6569, ⓦ nevadacitychamber.com). A smart first stop, where you can pick up a free walking-tour map of the town.

Website ⓦ ncgold.com.

ACCOMMODATION

8

Inn Town Campground 9 Kidder Court, 2 miles from downtown ☏ 530 265 9900, ⓦ inntowncampground .com. The *Outside Inn* (see below) owners have opened this year-round campground with excellent facilities, including deluxe glamping tents. Pitches $45, RVs $50, glamping $90

★ **National Hotel** 211 Broad St ☏ 530 265 4551, ⓦ thenationalhotel.com. The oldest continuously operated hotel in the West and a state historic landmark, with plenty of Gold Rush charm in the rooms and lobby, which boasts original photographs, period wallpaper and a grand staircase. $80

Northern Queen Inn 400 Railroad Ave ☏ 530 265 5824, ⓦ northernqueeninn.com. This decent-value hotel with an outdoor heated pool offers attractive woodland cabins and chalets, along with simpler rooms in a motel-style wing. Doubles $107, cabins $119, chalets $149

Outside Inn 575 E Broad St ☏ 530 265 2233, ⓦ outsideinn.com. Quiet 1940s motel with a wide range of simple but comfortable rooms and a swimming pool, only a 10min walk from the centre of town. $89

Piety Hill Cottages 523 Sacramento St ☏ 530 265 2245, ⓦ pietyhillcottages.com. Cottages with kitchenettes, decorated in period furnishings in a garden setting; the smaller ones are an especially good deal. Gazebo-covered spa open April–Nov. $95

EATING

★ **Friar Tuck's** 111 N Pine St ☏ 530 265 9093, ⓦ friartucks.com. Quality American, European and Pacific Rim cuisine, including fondue dinners for $26–32, is served at this classy establishment. Live, mostly acoustic music every night. Daily 4–10pm.

Lefty's Grill 101 Broad St ☏ 530 265 5838, ⓦ leftysgrill .com. You can feast on large portions of main courses such as shrimp and pork belly pasta, as well as crêpes, burgers, sandwiches, pizzas and desserts in the spacious and classy dining room. Tues–Thurs, Sat & Sun 11.30am–9pm, Fri 11.30am–9.30pm.

Nevada City Classic Café 216 Broad St ☏ 530 265 9440, ⓦ ncclassiccafe.com. Plain-looking all-American diner with eggs, bacon and more for breakfast, all under $10, burgers for lunch, and tapas on Friday evenings. Daily 8.30am–2.30pm & Fri 6–9pm.

Sopa Thai 312–316 Commercial St ☏ 530 470 0101, ⓦ sopathai.com. Wonderful, tasty and moderately priced Thai fare, served with a smile in a pleasantly decorated dining room. The green curry is superb for $14.95. Mon–Fri 11am–3pm & 5–9.30pm, Sat & Sun noon–9.30pm.

★ **Three Forks** 211 Commercial St ☏ 530 470 8333, ⓦ threeforksnc.com. This hip place bills itself as a baking and brewing company, thus it is equally good for quality coffee and pastries or ale and food such as sandwiches or pizza for $5–15. Mon, Wed & Thurs 7am–10pm, Fri 7am–11pm, Sat 8am–11pm, Sun 8am–10pm.

Nevada County

The rest of the **NEVADA COUNTY** foothills are as attractive now as they were productive in the gold heyday. Before the deep, hard-rock mines were established in the late 1860s, there were mining camps spread all over the northern Gold Country, with evocative names like "Red Dog" and "You Bet", that disappeared as soon as the easily recovered surface deposits gave out.

Rough and Ready

Rough and Ready, five miles west of Grass Valley, survives on the tourist trade alone – visitors come to take a look at the only mining town ever to secede from the United States, which Rough and Ready did in 1850. The band of veterans who founded the town, fresh from the Mexican–American War, opted to quit the Union in protest against unfair taxation by the federal government and although they declared their renewed allegiance in time for that summer's Fourth of July celebrations, the conflict was not officially resolved until 1948. Now the handful of ramshackle buildings, including a gas station and a general store, only warrants the briefest of visits.

Bridgeport covered bridge

Off the winding Bitney Springs Road in the **South Yuba River State Park**, stands the **Bridgeport covered bridge**, the longest single-span, wood-truss covered bridge in the world, spanning the Yuba River. The swimming spot underneath offers some relief from a hot summer's day, and the area's many hiking trails are abundant in wildflowers and birdlife.

Malakoff Diggins State Park

16 miles up North Bloomfield Rd from Nevada City, or accessible via the 16-mile Tyler Foote Crossing Rd, off Hwy-49 12 miles northwest of Nevada City • Park: summer daily sunrise–sunset; rest of year Sat & Sun sunrise–sunset; museum: June–Aug daily; May & Sept Fri–Sun 10am–4pm • $8/car • ☎ 530 265 2740, ✪ parks.ca.gov

One of the most moving and, in some ways, disconcerting of all the places you can visit in Gold Country is **Malakoff Diggins State Park**, site of the worst excesses caused by hydraulic mining (see box below). Here, a canyon more than a mile long, half a mile wide and over six hundred feet deep was carved out of the red-and-gold earthen slopes. Natural erosion has softened the scars somewhat, sculpting pinnacles and towers into a miniature Grand Canyon, now preserved as a 3000-acre **state park**. While the park may seem just a short detour from Hwy-49 on your map, its interminable unmarked gravel roads and snaking bends can make it feel eerily isolated. Old buildings from ghost towns around the Gold Country have been moved to the restored settlement of **North Bloomfield**, inside the park, where a small **museum** shows a twenty-minute film on hydraulic mining.

HYDRAULICKING

The waters of the Yuba River are now crisp and clear, but when the Bridgeport bridge was completed in 1862 they were being choked with mud and residue from the many **hydraulic mining** – or "hydraulicking" – operations upstream. Hydraulic mining was used here in the late 1850s to get at the trace deposits of gold that weren't worth recovering by orthodox methods. It was an unsophisticated technique: giant nozzles or monitors sprayed powerful jets of water against the gold-bearing hillsides, washing away tonnes of gravel, mud and trees just to recover a few ounces of gold. It also required an elaborate system of flumes and canals – some still used to supply water to local communities – to collect the water, which was sprayed at a rate of over thirty thousand gallons a minute. Worst of all, apart from the obvious destruction of the landscape, was the waste it caused, silting up rivers, causing floods, impairing navigation and eventually turning the San Francisco Bay, nearly 150 miles away, a muddy brown. The practice was finally outlawed in 1884.

Ananda's Retreat Center

14618 Tyler-Foote Rd • ☎ 530 478 7518 or ☎ 800 346 5350, ⓦ expandinglight.org

While in Nevada County, those interested in yoga and spirituality mustn't miss **Ananda's Retreat Center**, which occupies expansive mountainside grounds close to Malakoff Diggins State Park. Most of the beautifully landscaped grounds, shrines and the visitor centre are open to the public, and regular courses are scheduled.

ACCOMMODATION	NEVADA COUNTY
Malakoff Diggins State Park campground Chute Hill ☎ 800 444 7275, ⓦ reserveamerica.com. Standard state park campground with spacious pitches and decent shared facilities. Located underneath some spooky cliffs. Pitches $35	**Scott's Flat Lake Resort** 23333 Scotts Flat Rd, Scotts Flat Lake ☎ 530 265 5302, ⓦ scottsflatlake.net. Privately operated campground near the shores of a huge man-made reservoir, whose facilities include yurts, boats, kayaks and canoes for rent. Pitches from $25, yurts $49

The High Sierra towns

Hwy-49 climbs up along the Yuba River Gorge into some of the highest and most marvellous scenery in the Gold Country, where waterfalls tumble over sharp, black rocks bordered by tall pines and maple trees. In the middle of this wilderness, an hour's drive from Nevada City, **Downieville**, the most picturesque of the Gold Rush towns, spreads out along both banks of the river, crisscrossed by an assortment of narrow bridges. Still further up in the hills, **Sierra City** is another attractive town that deserves a look, but you are only likely to encounter tiny **Sierraville** if you're heading up into Plumas County (see p.640), a route that will take you close to the fascinating ghost town of **Johnsville**.

Downieville

Hwy-49 runs right through the centre of **Downieville**, slowing to a near-stop to negotiate tight curves that have not been widened since stagecoaches passed through. Thick stone buildings, some enhanced with delicate wooden balconies and porches, others with heavy iron doors and shutters, face raised wooden pavements, as their backs dangle precipitously over the steep banks of the river.

For what is now a peaceful and quiet little hamlet of three hundred people, Downieville seems strangely proud of its fairly nasty history. It has the distinction of being the only mining camp ever to have hanged a woman, Juanita, "a fiery Mexican dancehall girl" who stabbed a miner in self-defence. A restored wooden gallows, last used in 1885, still stands next to the County Jail on the south bank of the river to mark this ghastly heritage.

Downieville Museum

330 Main St • May–Oct daily 11am–4pm • Donation • ☎ 530 289 3423

Across the river and two blocks north, at the end of a row of 1850s storefronts, the **Downieville Museum** is packed full of odd bits and historical artefacts, including a set of snowshoes for horses and a scaled-down model of the local stamp mill.

Sierra City

Delightful **Sierra City** does not offer much in the way of sights but oozes old-time Gold Country charm. Beyond the town, Hwy-49 continues east through the **Tahoe National Forest**, passing over the 6700ft **Yuba Pass** on its way to join forces with Hwy-89 just north of Sattley at Bassett Junction.

Kentucky Mine Historic Park and Museum

One mile east of Sierra City on Hwy-49 • Summer Wed–Sun 10am–4pm; tours 11am & 2pm • $1, tours $7 • ☎ 530 862 1310, ⓦ sierracountyhistory.org

The full-sized model of Sierra City's original stamp mill is maintained in working order at the **Kentucky Mine Historic Park and Museum**, where a guided tour takes you inside a reconstructed miner's cabin and down a mineshaft to give you a look at various pieces of equipment used for retrieving gold-bearing ore. Until the mine was shut down during World War II, the ore was dug out from tunnels under the massive **Sierra Buttes**, the craggy granite peaks that dominate the surrounding landscape. The museum hosts concerts during the summer.

Johnsville

Founded in 1870, **Johnsville** is, after Bodie (see p.291), the best preserved and most isolated old mining town in California. Located 25 miles north of Bassett Junction and five miles off Hwy-89, the ghost town is surrounded by over seven thousand acres of pine forest and magnificent scenery and lies at the centre of the **Plumas-Eureka State Park**. Johnsville's huge stamp mill and mine buildings are gradually being restored; in the meantime, a small **museum** (June–Sept daily 9am–4pm; donation; ☎530 836 2380, ⓦparks.ca.gov) describes the difficult task of digging for gold in the High Sierra winters.

ARRIVAL AND DEPARTURE	THE HIGH SIERRA TOWNS

By car As there is no public transport to any of the High Sierra towns, the only way to reach them is by car along Hwy-49 or Hwy-89, in the case of Johnsville.

ACCOMMODATION AND EATING

DOWNIEVILLE

Carriage House Inn 110 Commercial St ☎800 296 2289, ⓦdownievillecarriagehouse.com. Nicely refurbished property, with smart rooms and wooden decks overlooking the river. They also have a couple of larger houses to rent nearby. **$90**

Riverside Inn 206 Commercial St ☎888 883 5100, ⓦdownieville.us. Welcoming family-run place, with huge range of rooms, some with fully equipped kitchens and most with balconies overlooking the river. **$90**

Sierra Shangri-La 2.5 miles northeast of town on Hwy-49 ☎530 289 3455, ⓦsierrashangrila.com. Set in thick woods above the river, this secluded spot has B&B rooms and fully furnished cottages, the latter available by the week in summer. **$115**

Two Rivers Cafe 116 Main St ☎530 289 3540. There's nothing fancy about this place but you can tuck into filling pizza or succulent burgers for around $10 inside or on the river-facing wooden deck. Daily noon–9pm.

SIERRA CITY

Herrington's Sierra Pines Resort 104 Main St ☎530 862 1151, ⓦherringtonssierrapines.com. The rooms here are comfortable, the larger ones featuring kitchens.

The resort's most attractive aspects are the private meadow and illuminated waterfall. Open May–Oct. **$79**

Red Moose Cafe 224 Main St ☎530 862 1024, ⓦredmoosecafe.com. English-run place, which serves huge stacker pancake breakfasts, plus fish'n'chips for $12 and filling sandwiches. Rents a couple of rooms upstairs. May–Sept daily except Tues 7am–2pm.

The Yuba River Inn Cabins Junction of Hwy-49 & Wild Plum Rd ☎530 862 1122, ⓦyubariverinn.com. Spacious cabins spread out over 22 acres of forest beside the river. The interiors are suitably rustic but perfectly comfortable. **$90**

JOHNSVILLE

★**Iron Door** 5417 Main St ☎530 836 2376. Occupying the old general store, this excellent restaurant would not be out of place in San Francisco. From the lentil curry soup or clam chowder to the main courses ($15–30) such as the pepper steak diablo, high quality is guaranteed. 5–10pm; closed Tues.

Plumas-Eureka State Park campgrounds Plumas-Eureka State Park ☎800 444 7275, ⓦreserveamerica .com. There are a number of campgrounds spread throughout the vast tracts of forest, all with good facilities. Open May–Sept. **$35**

Lake Tahoe and around

High above the Gold Country, just east of the Sierra ridge, **Lake Tahoe** sits placidly in a dramatic alpine bowl, surrounded by high granite peaks and miles of thickly wooded forest. Its name means "lake of the sky" in the native Washoe language. Now it's a major tourist area; the sandy beaches and surrounding pine-tree wilderness are overrun with thousands of fun-lovers (predominantly families) throughout the summer, and in winter the snow-covered slopes of the nearby peaks are packed with skiers. The eastern third of the lake lies in Nevada, where gambling is legal, and therefore glows with light from the neon signs of the inevitable **Stateline casinos**.

Little visited beyond an influx of winter skiers, **Truckee**, fifteen miles north of Lake Tahoe, ranges along the Truckee River, which flows out of Lake Tahoe down into the desert of Nevada's Great Basin. **Donner Lake**, just west of town, was named in memory of the pioneer Donner family, many of whom lost their lives here (see box, p.579).

Lake Tahoe

Fault-formed **LAKE TAHOE** is one of the highest, deepest, cleanest, coldest and most beautiful lakes in the world. More than 1600ft deep, it is allegedly so cold that cowboys who drowned over a century ago have been recovered from its depths in perfectly preserved condition, gun holsters and all. The lake's position, straddling the border between California and Nevada, lends it a contradictory air, the dichotomy most evident at **South Lake Tahoe**, the lakeside's largest community, where ranks of restaurants, modest motels and pine-bound cottages stand cheek by jowl with the high-rise gambling dens of **Stateline**, just across the border. **Tahoe City**, the hub of the lake's northwestern shore, does not escape the tourists but manages to retain a more relaxed, if somewhat exclusive, attitude. Expensive holiday homes and shabby family-oriented mini-resorts line much of the remainder of the lake. Tahoe is never truly offseason, luring weekenders from the Bay Area and beyond with clear, cool waters in the summer, snow-covered slopes in the winter, and gambling all year round. On holiday weekends, expect traffic to reach maddening levels; convoys of cars and trucks spilling over with ski equipment or mountain bikes clog the roads throughout the area.

South Lake Tahoe and Stateline

Most of Tahoe's lakeshore is developed in some way or another, but nowhere is it as concentrated and overbearing as at the contiguous settlements of **South Lake Tahoe** and **Stateline**. The latter is compact, a clutch of gambling houses huddled, as you might expect, along the Nevada–California border. The half-dozen or so casinos compete for the attention of tourists, almost all of whom base themselves in the much larger South Lake Tahoe on the California side. This is the best place to organize one of the many **outdoor activities** the lake has to offer. Power-boating, waterskiing, surfing, parasailing, scuba diving, canoeing and mountain biking are just a few of the options on the menus of local equipment-rental offices. If you happen to lose your holiday allowance at the tables and slot machines, you can always explore the beautiful hiking trails, parks and beaches that adorn the surrounding area.

BOATING, RAFTING, KAYAKING AND CRUISING LAKE TAHOE

Though many stretches of the route around Lake Tahoe are stunning, the entire 72-mile **drive** is perhaps not the most beautiful in America, as at least one locally produced brochure touts. A good way to see the south side of the lake is to take a paddlewheel **boat cruise** on the *MS Dixie II* from Zephyr Cove, reached on a free shuttle from South Lake Tahoe, or *Tahoe Queen* from Ski Run Marina in South Lake Tahoe itself (timetable varies; $55–85; ☎775 589 4906, ⓦzephyrcove.com); the more expensive cruises include dinner. Even more impressive is the view of the lake from above, in one of the neighbouring ski resort's **aerial trams**; the most convenient and popular is the Gondola at Heavenly (see p.572), which runs from a smart terminal only a couple of blocks from Stateline.

Rafting down the Truckee is the thing to do on warm summer days at the north end of the lake, though it's really more of a relaxing social affair than a serious or challenging adventure. Call Tahoe Whitewater Tours (half-day trips from $68; ☎530 587 5777 or ☎800 442 7238, ⓦtruckee whitewaterrafting.com) to book. On the lake itself, **kayaking** is an increasingly popular activity – try West Shore Sports at 1785 West Lake Blvd (☎530 583 9920, ⓦwestshoresports.com). An even more relaxed excursion is a **cruise** with the *Tahoe Gal* ($25–48; ☎800 218 2464, ⓦtahoegal .com). All cruises leave from the jetty at 850 N Lake Blvd and some include dinner.

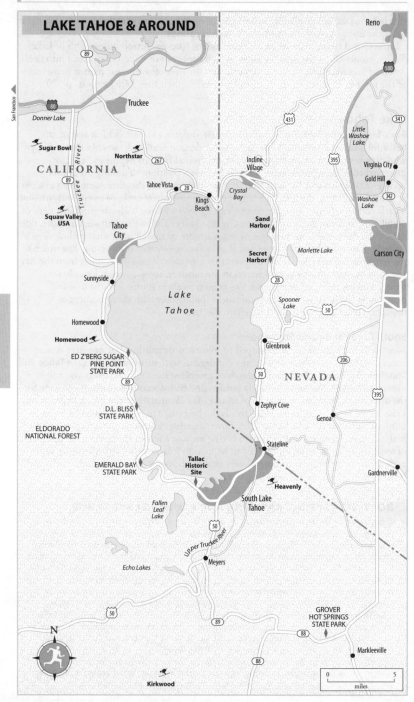

In bad weather you can visit the modest **Lake Tahoe Historical Museum**, next to the visitor centre at 3058 US-50 (summer Wed–Sun 11am–3pm; rest of year Sat 11am–3pm; free; ☎530 541 5458, ⊚laketahoemuseum.org), which has a small collection of local artefacts and historical displays.

Tallac Historic Site

Mid-June to mid-Sept daily dawn–dusk; museum 10am–4pm • Prices vary; museum free • ☎ 530 544 7383, ⊚ tahoeheritage.org

In summer, many enjoyable music and arts events take place at the **Tallac Historic Site**, beside Hwy-89 on the western side of the lake just northwest of the "Y" (where Hwy-89 and US-50 separate to the west and east). Even when there's nothing special going on, the site's sumptuous wooden homes – constructed by wealthy San Franciscans as lakeside vacation retreats in the late 1800s – are well worth a look. You can also see the remains of the lavish casino-hotel erected by Elias "Lucky" Baldwin, which brought the rich and famous to Lake Tahoe's shores until it was destroyed by fire in 1914. Inside the former Baldwin house, the **Baldwin Museum at the Tallac Site** records the family's impact on the region.

Emerald Bay State Park

Daily 8am–dusk; Vikingsholm tours summer 10.30am–3.30pm • $10/vehicle; tours $10 • ☎ 530 541 3030, ⊚ parks.ca.gov

The prettiest part of the lake is along the southwest shore, where **Emerald Bay State Park**, ten miles from South Lake Tahoe, surrounds a narrow, rock-strewn inlet. In the park, at the end of a steep, mile-long trail from the parking lot, is **Vikingsholm** (⊚vikingsholm.com), an authentic reproduction of a Viking castle built as a summer home in 1929 and open for hourly **tours**.

A short way out in the bay, diminutive **Fanette**, Lake Tahoe's only island, pokes pine-clad above the water. Its only structure is the defunct 1929 teahouse built by Vikingsholm's original owner, Lara Knight. From Vikingsholm, the stunning **Rubicon Trail** runs two miles north along the lakeside to **Rubicon Bay**, flanked by other grand old mansions dating from the days when Lake Tahoe was accessible only to the most well-heeled of travellers. You can also drive here on Hwy-89 and enter through the **D.L. Bliss State Park** (daily 8am–dusk; very limited parking $8), just to the north.

Ed Z'berg Sugar Pine Point State Park

Daily 8am–dusk; mansion tours daily 10am–3pm on the hour • $10/vehicle; tours $10 • ☎ 530 525 7982, ⊚ parks.ca.gov

Less than five miles north of Emerald Bay, thickly pined **Ed Z'berg Sugar Pine Point State Park** offers more lakeside relaxation and has one of only two year-round campgrounds in the area (see p.575). It also attracts crowds to see the vast **Hellman-Ehrman Mansion,** decorated in a happy blend of 1930s opulence and backcountry rustic, and surrounded by extensive lakefront grounds.

Tahoe City

Tahoe City, at the north end of the lake, is less developed and more compact than South Lake Tahoe, and a close-knit population of permanent residents coupled with a family-oriented atmosphere give it a more relaxed, peaceful disposition. Still, you're never far from the tourist crowds, who flock here all year long. At the western end of town, Hwy-89 meets Hwy-28 at Fanny Bridge, named after the body part (posterior rather than anterior in American English) that greets drivers as people lean over the edge to view the giant trout in the **Truckee River**. Flow-regulating sluice gates at the mouth of the river are remotely controlled from Reno, but were once operated by a gatekeeper who lived in what is now the **Gatekeeper's Museum** (May–Sept daily except Tues 10am–5pm; Oct–April Sat & Sun 11am–3pm; $5; ☎530 583 1762, ⊚northtahoemuseums.org), containing a well-presented array of artefacts from the nineteenth century, and a good collection of native basketware. Nearby, the **Truckee**

River Bike Trail begins its three-mile waterside meander west to the *River Ranch Lodge* (see p.574), which is also the end of a popular river-rafting route.

Eagle Rock

A couple of miles south of Tahoe City along Hwy-89, five hundred yards past the Kaspian picnic grounds, it's well worth **hiking** ten minutes up the unmarked trail to the top of **Eagle Rock**. The amazing panoramic views that surround you as you look down on the expansive royal-blue lake make this one of the world's greatest picnic spots.

Squaw Valley

The site of the 1960 Winter Olympics, **Squaw Valley** lies five miles west of Tahoe City off Hwy-89, although the original facilities (except the flame and the Olympic rings) are now swamped by the rampant development that has made this California's largest ski resort (see box below). In the valley below, **hiking**, **horseriding** and **mountain biking** are all popular summertime activities.

TAHOE SKIING AND SNOWBOARDING

Lake Tahoe has some of the best **downhill skiing** in North America and its larger resorts rival their Rocky Mountain counterparts. **Snowboarding** is equally popular and most resorts have massive snow parks with radical halfpipes and jumps. The slopes are usually open from mid-November to April or later, with peak season being January to March. Although skiing is certainly not cheap – the largest ski areas charge over $80 for the privilege of using their mountain for a single day at the busiest times – many resorts offer decent-value rental/lift ticket/lesson packages, as well as multi-day and online discounts. **Cross-country skiing** is harder work but also cheaper for rentals, lessons and trail fees, which are in the $25–40 range.

The following list of ski resorts is not exhaustive, but highlights the best options for skiers of varying ability and budget. Skis can be rented at the resorts for $30–70, depending on equipment quality, and snowboards for $45–60, although better deals for both can be found in the rental stores around town, especially if booked in advance online. Pick up the *Reno–Tahoe Winter Vacation Guide for Skiers and Boarders* at any of the visitor centres for a complete listing of resorts, along with prices and amenities.

DOWNHILL SKIING AND SNOWBOARDING

Heavenly Reachable by shuttle from South Shore, 2 miles from Stateline ☎ 775 586 7000, ⓦ skiheavenly .com. Prime location and sheer scale (82 runs, 27 lifts, 3500 vertical feet) make this one of the lake's most frequented resorts. Those not seeking to ski or snowboard can take the aerial Gondola for the view from the 8200ft summit ($46), also open in summer.

Homewood 6 miles south of Tahoe City on Hwy-89 ☎ 530 525 2992 or ☎ 800 824 6348, ⓦ skihomewood .com. Smaller and more relaxed than its massive neighbours, Homewood boasts some surprisingly good skiing with unbeatable views of the lake and reasonable prices. Offers good beginner packages that include equipment rental, a lesson and lift ticket.

Kirkwood Ski Resort 30 miles south of Lake Tahoe on Hwy-88 ☎ 209 258 6000 or ☎ 877 547 5966, ⓦ kirkwood.com. Kirkwood manages to escape the overdeveloped feel of many of the Tahoe resorts while still providing some amazing skiing. Also has a cross-country operation.

Squaw Valley USA Squaw Valley Rd, between Truckee and Tahoe City ☎ 800 403 0206, ⓦ squaw .com. Thirty-three lifts service over 4000 acres of unbeatable terrain at the site of the 1960 Winter Olympics. Non-skiers can take the cable car ($34) and use the ice-skating/swimming pool complex for minimal extra cost.

Sugar Bowl 10 miles west of Truckee at the Soda Springs–Norden exit ☎ 530 426 9000, ⓦ sugarbowl .com. The closest ski area to San Francisco has ten lifts and newly expanded terrain. Inexplicably, this excellent mountain is often less crowded than others in the area.

CROSS-COUNTRY SKIING

Royal Gorge Soda Springs, 10 miles west of Truckee ☎ 800 500 3871, ⓦ royalgorge.com. The largest and best of Tahoe's cross-country resorts has 204 miles of groomed trails. Good midweek discounts.

Spooner Lake Nevada, at the intersection of Hwy-50 and Hwy-28 ☎ 775 749 5349, ⓦ spoonerlake .com. The closest cross-country resort to South Lake Tahoe has lake views and 63 miles of groomed trails.

Northeast Lake Tahoe

East from Tahoe City are some unremarkable settlements but decent stretches of beach at **Tahoe Vista** and **King's Beach** on Carnelian Bay. As soon as you cross the Nevada state line from King's Beach into **Incline Village**, you're greeted by the predictable huddle of **casinos**, though they're not as numerous or in-your-face as at the south end of the lake: the casual visitor might find having a flutter at the Crystal Bay or Cal-Neva somewhat less sordid and garish. Unfortunately the beaches here only open to guests at the casino hotels, but better swimming options are close at hand. Once you leave the buildings behind at the northeast corner of the lake and bear south, you enter one of the most appealing and quietest stretches. **Lake Tahoe Nevada State Park** boasts a great beach at **Sand Harbor** – though the water is always prohibitively cold – and has trails winding up through the backcountry to the Tahoe Rim Trail. Just south, **Secret Harbor** is an appropriate location for an idyllic nudist beach, where gawkers are not tolerated.

ARRIVAL AND INFORMATION
LAKE TAHOE

BY BUS

Lake Tahoe is not served directly by Greyhound or Amtrak Thruway buses. Coming from the Bay Area or Sacramento, you'll have to travel via Truckee (see p.577). South Tahoe Express buses (9 daily; $29.75 one-way, $53 return; ☏775 324 4444 or ☏866 898 2463, ⍟southtahoeexpress .com) run between Reno Airport and the Stateline casinos, while the North Lake Tahoe Express (9–11 daily; from $32 one-way, depending on the number of passengers; ☏775 786 3706 or ☏866 216 5222, ⍟northlaketahoeexpress .com) links Reno Airport with Truckee, Tahoe City and other North Shore destinations.

BY CAR

If you're driving, expect to get here in a little over 3hr from San Francisco, unless you join the Friday-night exodus, in which case you can add an hour or two, more in winter when you'll need to carry chains; call the Caltrans road

phone (☏800 427 7623) to check on road conditions before you depart.

TOURIST INFORMATION

Incline Village/Crystal Bay Visitors Bureau 969 Tahoe Blvd (Mon–Fri 8am–5pm, Sat & Sun 10am–4pm; ☏800 468 2463, ⍟gotahoenorth.com). On the Nevada side of the North Shore.

Lake Tahoe Visitors Authority This is a cross-border organization with two offices: in California at 3066 US-50, South Lake Tahoe (daily 9am–5pm; ☏530 541 5255, ⍟tahoesouth.com), just before US-50 reaches the lake at El Dorado Beach, while the Nevada branch is just beyond Stateline at 195 US-50 (daily 9am–5pm; ☏775 588 4591).

Tahoe City Visitors Information Center 100 North Lake Blvd, Tahoe City (daily 9am–5pm; ☏530 581 6900 or ☏888 824 6348, ⍟gotahoenorth.com). The best bet for information on the Californian North Shore region.

GETTING AROUND

By bus BlueGo buses (☏530 541 7149, ⍟bluego.org) run within a 10-mile radius of South Lake Tahoe for a flat $2 fare (all-day pass $5); the company operates trolleys for the same fares in summer. In the north, TART buses (roughly 6am–6pm; $2.50 flat fare, $5 all-day pass; ☏530 582 4964 or ☏800 736 6365, ⍟laketahoetransit.com) run between Sugar Pine Point and Incline Village, with a branch route from Tahoe City up to Truckee. In addition, the Tahoe Trolley (same contacts and fares as TART) runs between Tahoe City and Crystal Bay (6am–6pm), and also between Sugar Pine Point and Emerald Bay (9am–6pm); on summer evenings

there's a free service between Squaw Valley and Incline Village (6pm–midnight), with a short extra route between Sunnyside and Crystal Bay (7–10.30pm).

By car Starting at about $30/day, car rental is available through the Stateline outlets of most national chains (see p.569).

By bike You can rent a bike for $30–70 a day from a number of outlets, such as the Tahoe Bike Company, 2277 S Lake Blvd, South Lake Tahoe (☏530 600 0267, ⍟tahoebikecompany.com); or the Olympic Bike Shop, 620 N Lake Blvd (☏530 581 2500, ⍟olympicbikeshop.com).

ACCOMMODATION

Most Tahoe **motels** are clustered along or just off US-50 in South Lake Tahoe. During the week, except in summer, many have bargain rates, from around $60 for a double; however, these rates can more than double at weekends or in summer. Don't expect great deals at the Stateline **casinos**, as there are fewer than in Las Vegas or Reno. North Shore accommodation is generally somewhat more expensive but quieter and of higher quality. **Camping** (see p.574) is only an option during summer.

8

SOUTH SHORE
HOTELS, MOTELS AND RESORTS

7 Seas Inn 4145 Manzanita Ave, South Lake Tahoe ☎530 544 7031, ⓦ7seasinn.com. Right by the state line and only a few blocks from the beach, this glorified motel offers brightly decorated rooms and an outdoor hot tub. **$100**

★ **Basecamp Hotel** 4143 Cedar Ave, South Lake Tahoe ☎530 208 0180, ⓦbasecamphotels.com. Slick sports hotel created out of an old motel, with smart, imaginatively designed rooms and a convivial bar. Staff can advise on outdoor activities. New sister hotel on North Shore. **$169**

Camp Richardson Resort Hwy-89 between Emerald Bay and South Lake Tahoe ☎530 541 1801, ⓦcamp richardson.com. Hotel-style rooms and comfortable cabins with full kitchens on a 150-acre resort that also offers camping. In summer, cabins are available by the week only. Pitches **$40**, cabins **$125**

Harveys Lake Tahoe US-50, Stateline, Nevada ☎800 648 3353, ⓦharrahs.com. Deluxe casino and resort whose more expensive rooms overlook the lake. It's worth looking for packages that include buffet brunches and spa discounts. **$149**

Inn by the Lake 3300 Lake Tahoe Blvd, South Lake Tahoe ☎530 542 0330 or ☎800 877 1466, ⓦinnbythelake.com. Nicely furnished rooms, a heated swimming pool and jacuzzi, plus use of bicycles render this relaxing spot reasonable value for money. Free shuttle bus to the casinos. **$160**

Meeks Bay Resort 7941 Emerald Bay Rd, Meeks Bay ☎530 525 6946, ⓦmeeksbayresort.com. Set in wooded ancestral Washoe grounds on the scenic southwest shore, this relaxed resort offers camping, cabins and lodge rooms, as well as a good grill and various lake activities. Pitches **$30**, doubles **$110**, cabins **$130**

Paradice Motel 953 Park Ave, South Lake Tahoe ☎530 544 6800, ⓦparadicemoteltahoe.com. The play on words in the name of this "boutique" motel indicates its proximity to the Stateline casinos, yet the street is quiet and the rooms a cut above the usual. There are four larger suites too. **$125**

Zephyr Cove Resort 760 US-50, Zephyr Cove, Nevada ☎775 589 4906 or ☎800 238 2463, ⓦzephyrcove.com. Run by the same management as the *MS Dixie II* (see p.569), its deluxe lodge rooms and lakeside cabins are away from the hubbub in a quiet, pine-clad nook. It also has expensive tent and RV sites. Pitches **$50**, RV **$75**, doubles **$180**, cabins **$210**

CAMPGROUNDS

The *Camp Richardson*, *Meeks Bay* and *Zephyr Cove* resorts also have pitches (see above).

Campground by the Lake 1150 Rufus Allen Blvd, South Lake Tahoe ☎530 542 6096, ⓦcityofslt.us. Lake Tahoe's best and certainly most conveniently located campground, with ample sites in the shade of the pines, plus some cabins. Open April–Oct. Pitches **$30**, cabins **$80**

Fallen Leaf 2165 Fallen Leaf Rd, 3 miles south of South Lake Tahoe ☎530 544 0426, reserve on ☎877 444 6777, ⓦreserveusa.com. Pleasant campground with good facilities, within walking distance of Tahoe's tiny neighbour, Fallen Leaf Lake. Open April–Oct. Pitches **$35**

NORTH SHORE
MOTELS, LODGES AND RESORTS

Cedar Glen Lodge 6589 N Lake Blvd, Tahoe Vista ☎530 546 4281, ⓦtahoecedarglen.com. Beautifully designed lodge, set in a fine rustic location on the northernmost shore, with luxury cabins of various sizes, a hot tub, pool and fine-dining restaurant. **$199**

★ **Granlibakken** 725 Granlibakken Rd, 1 mile south of Tahoe City ☎800 543 3221, ⓦgranlibakken.com. More like a rural village than a resort, with 74 acres of smart accommodation, sports facilities, a pool and direct trail access. Hot buffet breakfast with wide choice included. **$161**

Parkside Inn at Incline 1003 Tahoe Blvd, Incline Village ☎775 831 1052 or ☎800 824 6391, ⓦinnatincline.com. Nestled in a secluded forest setting, with private beach access, indoor pool, spa and sauna, this is a good-value option. **$134**

Pepper Tree Inn 645 N Lake Blvd, Tahoe City ☎530 583 3711 or ☎800 624 8580, ⓦpeppertreetahoe.com. Heated pool and standard hotel accommodation in an otherwise rather characterless high-rise. The upper-storey rooms with lake views are not much costlier. **$110**

Resort at Squaw Creek 400 Squaw Creek Rd, Olympic Valley ☎530 583 6300 or ☎800 327 3353, ⓦsquawcreek.com. The area's most lavish resort has sweeping mountain views and luxurious rooms, though rather a stilted atmosphere. There's a golf course, private ski-lift and shopping mall thrown in too. **$259**

River Ranch Lodge 2285 River Rd, Alpine Meadows ☎530 583 4263 or ☎800 535 9900, ⓦriverranchlodge .com. Historic and casual lodge on the Truckee River with one of the lake's best restaurants (see p.576); the cheapest rooms are right above the dining room. **$132**

★ **Sunnyside** 1850 W Lake Blvd, 1 mile south of Tahoe City ☎530 583 7200, ⓦsunnysideresort.com. A large, comfortable mountain lodge right on the lakeshore with unbeatable views of the lake from many rooms and a popular restaurant and cocktail deck on the ground floor. **$180**

Tahoma Meadows Cottages 6821 W Lake Blvd, Tahoma ☎866 525 1553, ⓦtahomameadows.com. Well-furnished and homely B&B cottages in a lovely setting on the west shore, 7 miles south of Tahoe City. **$149**

Tamarack Lodge 2311 N Lake Blvd, 1 mile northeast of Tahoe City ☎530 583 3350, ⓦtamarackattahoe .com. Nestled on a pleasant wooded knoll, you'll get more for your money at this comfortable and clean lodging than almost anywhere else on the lake. Some larger cabins are available too. **$79**

CAMPGROUNDS

Lake Forest Lake Forest Rd, 1.5 miles east of Tahoe City ☎ 530 583 3440, ⓦ tahoecitypud.com. Belonging to the Public Utility Dept, this is the cheapest site in the whole lake area, though it's some way from the beach and cannot be reserved. Pitches $20

Sugar Pine Point Halfway down the west shore ☎ 530 525 7982, reserve on ☎ 800 444 7275, ⓦ reserveamerica .com. Lovely sites in thick pine forest. Pitches $35, RV $50

Tahoe State Recreation Area On Hwy-28, just east of Tahoe City ☎ 530 583 3074, reserve on ☎ 800 444 7275, ⓦ reserveamerica.com. Nicely located, almost in the centre of Tahoe City and consequently just as crowded as you would expect. Late May to mid-Sept. Pitches $35

William Kent 1995 W Lake Blvd, 2 miles southwest of Tahoe City ☎ 530 583 3642, reserve through NRRS on ☎ 877 444 6777. Fine shady campground with good facilities, not far from good eating options, especially *Sunnyside* (see opposite). Pitches $30

EATING AND DRINKING

South Lake Tahoe has few exceptional **restaurants**; average burger-and-steak places, rustic in decor with raging fireplaces, are commonplace. Far better are the **buffets** at the Nevada **casinos**, which can cost as little as $12.95. The casinos are also good places to **drink** and hold most of the region's **entertainment** options: low-budget Vegas-style revues, by and large. For its size, Tahoe City has a fair range of moderately priced restaurants as well as a couple of trendy **bars**.

SOUTH SHORE

The Brewery at Lake Tahoe 3542 Lake Tahoe Blvd, South Lake Tahoe ☎ 530 544 2739, ⓦ brewery laketahoe.com. Microbrewery with decent ales ranging from pale to porter, including their signature Bad Ass, plus food specials such as beer-steamed shrimp and a full rack of barbecue ribs for $29. Daily 8am–late.

Chimayó Sreet Grill 1142 Ski Run Blvd, South Lake Tahoe ☎ 530 600 3900, ⓦ chimayotahoe.com. Sleek modern Mexican near Heavenly, where you can enjoy an après-ski margarita and unusual creations such as mahi-mahi tacos for $12, as well as all the classics. Mon, Wed, Thurs 3–9pm, Fri & Sat 11.30am–9.30pm, Sun 11.30am–9pm.

★**Cold Water Brewery & Grill** 2544 Lake Tahoe Blvd, South Lake Tahoe ☎ 530 544 4677, ⓦ tahoecoldwater brewery.com. Finely crafted ales such as Tahoe Cross IPA, above-average pub grub and regular live music make this microbrewery a popular choice. Mon–Thurs 11am–9pm, Fri & Sat 11am–10pm, Sun 10am–9pm.

Nephele's 1169 Ski Run Blvd, South Lake Tahoe ☎ 530 544 8130, ⓦ nepheles.com. Long-standing restaurant at the foot of the Heavenly ski resort, with a great selection of California cuisine: grilled meat, fish and pasta dishes cost $23–38. Spa on site. Daily 2pm–2am.

Nikki's Indian Cuisine 3469 Lake Tahoe Blvd, South Lake Tahoe ☎ 530 541 3354, ⓦ tajmahaltahoe.com. Good subcontinental cuisine, including masala dosa and other breakfast items from South India, plus *chaat* and *puri* dishes from the north, all $10 or under. Buffets and pricier main courses also available. Mon–Fri 9am–3pm & 5–9pm, Sat & Sun 9am–9pm.

Rojo's Tavern 3091 Harrison Ave, South Lake Tahoe ☎ 530 541 4960, ⓦ rojostavern.com. Popular joint with all the American classics, from lunchtime sandwiches and salads to evening specials such as ribs and pasta dishes, which hover around $20. Daily 11am–10pm.

Sprouts Natural Food Café 3123 Harrison Ave, South Lake Tahoe ☎ 530 541 6969, ⓦ sproutscafetahoe.com. Almost, but not completely vegetarian, with excellent organic sandwiches, burritos and smoothies, all under $10. Sunny outdoor seating available. Daily 8am–9pm.

Tep's Villa Roma 3450 Lake Tahoe Blvd, South Lake Tahoe ☎ 530 541 8227, ⓦ tepsvillaroma.com. South Shore institution serving up generous portions of hearty Italian cuisine, including several simple yet superb vegetarian pasta dishes, for $12–23. Daily 4–10pm.

NORTH SHORE

★**Bridgetender Bar & Grill** 65 W Lake Blvd, Tahoe City ☎ 530 583 3342, ⓦ tahoebridgetender.com. Friendly, rustic bar with good music, a fine range of beers and huge portions of ribs, burgers, fish and more for $9–15. Mon–Thurs & Sun 11am–11pm, Fri & Sat 11am–midnight.

GarWoods 5000 N Lake Blvd, Carnelian Bay ☎ 530 546 3366, ⓦ garwoods.com. Popular wooden restaurant on a quieter section of the north shore. Grills such as pistachio-crusted halibut and filet mignon go for $30–45. Live music at weekend evenings (Fri & Sat). Mon–Thurs & Sun 11.30am–9.30pm, Fri & Sat 11.30am–10pm.

Hacienda del Lago 760 N Lake Blvd, Tahoe City ☎ 530 583 0358, ⓦ hacdellago.com. Tasty Mexican cuisine is served for $12–16 in this colourful spot on the upper level of the Boatworks Mall, with an open deck from which to gaze at the lake views as you sip your margarita. Regular Latin or jazz music in the evening. Daily 4–10pm.

Jason's Beachside Grille 8338 N Lake Blvd, Kings Beach ☎ 530 546 3315, ⓦ jasonsbeachsidegrille.com. Classic American goodies such as gourmet burgers for around $12–13, plus pricier seafood, pasta, a salad bar and great desserts. Outside deck with lake views and occasional live music. Daily 11am–10pm.

8

River Ranch 2285 River Rd, Tahoe City ☎530 583 4264, ⒲riverranchlodge.com. Great curved dining room to maximize the Truckee River views and an outdoor patio in summer. Delicious braised bison short ribs will set you back $34 but there is also a cheaper tavern menu. Daily noon–10pm.

★**The Soule Domain** 9983 Cove Ave, King's Beach ☎530 546 7529, ⒲souledomain.com. Typical Tahoe rustic elegance in unexpected surroundings. Lots of seafood and ethnic dishes, such as curried almond chicken, plus other seafood and meaty delights for $22–39. Daily 6–11pm.

Spindleshanks 400 Brassie Ave, King's Beach ☎530 546 2191, ⒲spindleshankstahoe.com. In a quiet location by the lake, this American bistro and wine bar serves imaginative dishes like pan-roasted artichokes and ginger lemongrass brick chicken for $17–29. Mon–Thurs 11am–9pm, Fri–Sun 11am–10pm.

Tahoe House 625 West Lake Blvd, Tahoe City ☎530 583 1377, ⒲tahoe-house.com. Family-style bakery and gourmet store with lots of deli items for picnics, such as high-quality salads and sauces, plus great cakes. Popular with locals. Mon–Thurs & Sun 6am–4pm, Fri & Sat 6am–6pm.

Tahoe Mountain Brewing Company 479 North Lake Blvd, Tahoe City ☎530 581 4677, ⒲tahoebrewing .com. Great new microbrewery taproom, where you can wash down a simple $11–18 pub meal with a fine ale such as Hop Dragon Double IPA or Ranch Dog Red. Mon, Thurs & Sun noon–8pm, Tues & Wed noon–4pm, Fri & Sat noon–9pm.

Za's 395 North Lake Blvd, Tahoe City ☎530 583 1812, ⒲zastahoe.com. In a colourfully decorated room at the back of the friendly *Pete and Peter's* bar, this relaxed pizzeria also has a wide variety of pasta dishes for $14–18. Mon–Sat 5–9pm, Sun 10am–3pm & 5–9pm.

Kirkwood and around

To take advantage of Lake Tahoe's natural resources and still avoid at least some of the crowds, you might consider staying south of the lake near **Kirkwood**, though during peak times even this area can fill up quickly.

Located around thirty miles south of Tahoe by road, Kirkwood is home to a popular ski resort (see box, p.572) and is a destination in its own right, with plenty of **outdoor recreation** possibilities without all the Tahoe hype. Stop by the adventure centre in Kirkwood Village (Mon–Fri 9am–5pm, Sat & Sun 9am–6pm; ☎209 258 6000) for information on accommodation, equipment rental and hiking in the surrounding area, which holds nearly a dozen lakes, such as Winnemucca and Woods.

HIKING AND BIKING AROUND LAKE TAHOE

Of the many wonderful hikes in the Lake Tahoe area, only one – the 150-mile **Tahoe Rim Trail** – makes the circuit of the lake, some of it on the **Pacific Crest Trail**, which follows the Sierra ridge from Canada to the Mexican border. Most people tackle only a tiny section of it, such as **Kingsbury Grade** to **Big Meadows** (22 miles), starting off at Hwy-207 northwest of South Lake Tahoe and finishing on US-50, south of the lake.

Along the western side of the lake, the Tahoe Rim Trail follows the Pacific Crest Trail through the glaciated valleys and granite peaks of the **Desolation Wilderness**. Here, **wilderness permits** ($5) are required by all users, though for day-users these are self-issued. For overnighters, a quota system operates in summer: fifty percent of these are first-come, first-served on the day of entry from the Forest Service visitor centre; the remainder can be reserved up to ninety days in advance (☎530 644 6048). Among the most strenuous trails here is the five-mile Bayview Trail to Fontanillis Lake. The other wilderness areas around Tahoe – Granite Chief to the northwest and Mount Rose to the northeast – are used much less and consequently no wilderness permits are needed, though campfire permits are.

There are also many **mountain-biking** trails around the lake: **Meiss County**, between Hwy-89 and Hwy-88 twenty miles south of South Lake Tahoe, is a favoured area, where several beautiful lakes that escape most tourist itineraries are located. **Fallen Leaf Lake**, **Echo Lakes**, and **Angora Lake** are all pleasant, somewhat remote alternatives to the big T. Biking trails near the south shore include the three-mile loop of the **Pope-Baldwin Trail**, and you can pick up the popular **Marlett Lake/Flume Trail** in the Nevada State Park.

Most of the state and federal park areas that surround Lake Tahoe offer great opportunities for **camping** (see pp.574–575), at least during the warm summer months.

Grover Hot Springs State Park

4 miles west of Markleeville • May to mid-Sept daily 9am–9pm; closed last two weeks in Sept; reduced hours in winter • $8/vehicle, $5 pool use

A dozen miles southeast from the junction of Hwy-89 and Hwy-88 is **Markleeville**, a town of two hundred people on the Sierra crest. The major attraction here is the **Grover Hot Springs State Park**, with two concrete, spring-filled tubs – one hot, one tepid – in which the water appears yellow-green due to mineral deposits on the pool bottom.

ARRIVAL AND DEPARTURE

By car and shuttle bus The only way to get here for most of the year is by car via Hwy-89 and then Hwy-88, though during

KIRKWOOD AND AROUND

the skiing season there are some shuttle services such as the Bay Area Ski Bus (☎ 925 680 4386, ⓦ bayareaskibus.com).

ACCOMMODATION

Grover Hot Springs State Park campground Grover Hot Springs State Park ☎800 444 7275, ⓦ reserveamerica.com. Typical state park campground in terms of pitch size and quality of shared facilities but often less crowded than those nearer Lake Tahoe. Pitches $35

Lodge at Kirkwood 1501 Kirkwood Meadows Drive, Kirkwood ☎800 967 7500, ⓦ kirkwood.com. This relaxed, year-round resort has a wide range of smartly furnished and well-equipped rooms and suites. $101

Truckee

Just off I-80 along the main transcontinental Amtrak route, **TRUCKEE**, fifteen miles north of Lake Tahoe, makes a refreshing change from the tourist-dependent towns around the lake. A small town mostly lining the north bank of the Truckee River, it retains a fair amount of its late nineteenth-century wooden architecture along the main section of Donner Pass Road, which many locals still refer to as Commercial Row; some of it appeared as backdrop in Charlie Chaplin's *The Gold Rush*. Truckee, with a livelihood dependent on the logging industry and the railroad, is usually viewed as more of a stopover than a destination in its own right. However, the town's rough, lively edge makes it as good a base as any from which to see the Lake Tahoe area. On Thursday evenings from June to August, the downtown section of Donner Pass Road is closed to traffic for **Truckee Thursdays**, when a host of stalls and food trucks appear, and the parking lot in front of the visitor centre is turned into a beer garden with live music.

ARRIVAL AND INFORMATION

By bus Greyhound services connect Truckee with Reno (3 daily; 50min) and San Francisco (2 daily; 5hr 40min–5hr 55min). There are up to ten daily TART buses (see p.573) from Tahoe City (45min).
By train There's one daily Amtrak service in each direction,

TRUCKEE

towards Reno (1hr 20min) and further east, or west to Oakland (6hr 30min), from the station on Commercial Row in the middle of town.
California Welcome Center 10065 Donner Pass Rd (daily 9am–5.30pm; ☎ 530 587 2757, ⓦ truckee.com).

ACCOMMODATION

★**Cedar House Sport Hotel** 10918 Brockway Rd ☎530 582 5655, ⓦ cedarhousesporthotel.com. The rustic alpine style of the building gives way to San Francisco chic in the snazzily designed rooms of this trendy sport hotel. A lavish buffet breakfast is included and there's a fine restaurant too. $180

Goose Meadow campground 4 miles south of Truckee on Hwy-89 ☎800 444 7275, ⓦ reserveamerica.com. Tucked in a pine grove far enough off the road to be peaceful, there are only 25 tent pitches and basic vault toilets here. Drinkable water is available. Open May–Oct. Pitches $22

Granite Flat campground 1.5 miles south of Truckee on Hwy-89 ☎800 444 7275, ⓦ reserveamerica.com.

Located in between the highway and the Truckee River, this campground has a handful of quiet tent spaces and clean toilets but no showers. Drinkable water is available. Open May–Oct. Pitches $22

Hampton Inn & Suites 11951 Hwy-267 ☎530 587 1197 or ☎888 587 1197, ⓦ hamptoninntruckee.com. This large new hotel is as fine a franchise of the national chain as you will find. Elegantly designed in local cedarwood with spacious rooms and an outdoor pool. $164

River Street Inn 10009 E River St ☎530 550 9290, ⓦ riverstreetinntruckee.com. This quaint brick-and-wood Victorian building with attractive multi-pitched roof offers cosy refurbished rooms. Its *1882 Bar & Grill* does decent food. $145

The Truckee Hotel 10007 Bridge St ☎ 800 659 6921, ⓦ truckeehotel.com. Decked out in Victorian style, this venerable hotel near the station offers bargain rooms and an excellent bistro (see below). $109

EATING AND DRINKING

Bar of America 10040 Donner Pass Rd ☎ 530 587 2626, ⓦ barofamerica.com. Grills are the speciality here – try the blackened shrimp couscous for $32 or Big Ass pork chop for $36. Live music Thurs–Sat. Mon–Fri 11.30am–10pm, Sat 11am–10pm, Sun 11am–3pm.

Cottonwood 10142 Rue Hilltop Rd ☎ 530 587 5711, ⓦ cottonwoodrestaurant.com. The creative menu here includes starters such as pork medallions with brie ($15) and main courses such as seafood stew with sausage and a saffron tomato sauce ($31). Live acoustic music Thurs & Fri. Daily 4.30–9pm.

El Toro Bravo 10186 Donner Pass Rd ☎ 530 587 3557. This decent taqueria offers the full range of Mexican favourites from crispy tacos to filling burritos, mostly for $10 or less. Mon–Thurs & Sun 11.30am–9.30pm, Fri & Sat 11.30am–10pm.

Jax 10144 W River St ☎ 530 550 7450, ⓦ jaxtruckee .com. Recently renovated, this classic 1950s diner has retained its character and pumps out great breakfasts,

snacks and full meals for $11–19. Limited beer and wine selection. Daily 7am–10pm.

★**The Lodge at Tahoe Donner** 12850 Northwoods Blvd ☎ 530 587 9455, ⓦ tahoedonner.com/the-lodge. It's worth the trek north of town to eat quality California cuisine, such as pork tenderloin *gremolata* for $25 or a cheaper lunch on the deck overlooking the complex's golf course. Daily 11.30am–4pm & 5–9pm.

★**Mellow Fellow Pub** 10192 Donner Pass Rd ☎ 530 214 8927, ⓦ mellowfellowpub.com. Truckee's best watering hole has a huge range of fine draught ales and bottled beers, tasty snacks such as sausages and a dartboard. New branch at King's Beach, Tahoe. Mon–Thurs 3–10pm, Fri & Sat noon–midnight, Sun noon–10pm.

Moody's Bistro 10007 Bridge St ☎ 530 587 8688, ⓦ moodysbistro.com. This hotel restaurant is an excellent choice for a lunchtime pizza or sandwich, or quality dinners such as fried chicken roulade for $28. Live music Thurs–Sat. Daily 11.30am–9.30pm.

Donner Lake

Two miles west of Truckee, surrounded by alpine cliffs of silver-grey granite, **Donner Lake** was the site of one of the most gruesome and notorious tragedies of early California, when pioneers trapped by winter snows were forced to eat the bodies of their dead companions (see box opposite). The horrific tale of the Donner party is recounted in some detail in the small but newly refurbished **Emigrant Trail Museum** (daily: summer 9am–5pm; rest of year 9am–4pm; donation; ☎ 530 582 7892) – just off Donner Pass Road, three miles west of Truckee in **Donner Memorial State Park** (8am–sunset; $8/vehicle; ☎ 530 582 7892, ⓦ parks .ca.gov) – which shows a re-enactment of the events in an hourly, over-the-top 26-minute video. Outside, the **Pioneer Monument** stands on a plinth as high as the snow was deep that fateful winter of 1846 – 22ft. From the museum, an easy nature trail winds through the forest past a memorial plaque marking the site where the majority of the Donner party built its simple cabins.

Above Donner Lake, the Southern Pacific Railroad tracks climb west over the **Donner Pass** through tunnels built by Chinese labourers during the nineteenth century – still one of the main rail routes across the Sierra Nevada. For much of the way, the tracks are protected from the usually heavy winter snow by a series of wooden sheds, which you can see from across the valley, where Donner Pass Road snakes up the steep cliffs. On well-signposted Hwy-40, there's a scenic overlook where you can get that prize-winning photo of Donner Lake and possibly a glimpse beyond to Tahoe. Further on, rock climbers from the nearby Alpine Skills Institute (☎ 530 426 9108, ⓦ alpineskills .com) can often be seen honing their talents on the 200ft granite faces; the institute offers a variety of climbing and mountaineering courses and trips. At the crest, the road passes the Soda Springs, Sugar Bowl and Royal Gorge **ski areas** before rejoining I-80.

ACCOMMODATION   DONNER LAKE

★**Donner Lake Village Resort** 15695 Donner Pass Rd ☎ 530 587 6081 or ☎ 855 979 0402, ⓦ donner lakevillage.com. With its own little marina and stretch of beach, this excellent resort makes a fine retreat. The rooms

THE DONNER PARTY

The 91-member **Donner party**, named after one of the pioneer families among the group, set off for California in April 1846 from Illinois across the Great Plains, following a short cut recommended by the first traveller's guide to the West Coast (the 1845 *Emigrant's Guide to California and Oregon*), which actually took three weeks longer than the established route. By October, they had reached what is now Reno and decided to rest a week to regain their strength for the arduous crossing of the Sierra Nevada mountains – a delay that proved fatal. When at last they set off, early snowfall blocked their route beyond Donner Lake, and the group was forced to stop and build crude shelters, hoping that the snow would melt and allow them to complete their crossing; it didn't, and they were stuck.

Within a month, the pioneers were running out of provisions, and a party of fifteen set out across the mountains to try to reach **Sutter's Fort** in Sacramento. They struggled through yet another storm and, a month later, two men and five women stumbled into the fort, having survived by eating the bodies of the men who had died. A rescue party set off from Sutter's Fort immediately, only to find more of the same: thirty or so half-crazed survivors, living off the meat of their fellow travellers.

are all well appointed, spread across several modern two-storey blocks. $128

Donner Memorial State Park campground On the southeastern shore of the lake ☎ 800 444 7275, ⓦ reserveamerica.com. This summer-only campground has nice shady tent pitches in a beautiful lakeside location, although the facilities are quite basic. Pitches $35

Reno and around

Across the border in **Nevada**, **Reno** is a downmarket version of Las Vegas, popular with slot-machine junkies and elderly gamblers; others come to take advantage of Nevada's lax marriage and divorce laws. Though far smaller than Reno, **Carson City**, thirty miles south, is the Nevada state capital. A little deeper into Nevada, and up into the arid mountains to the east, are the silver mines of the **Comstock Lode** – whose wealth paid for the building of much of San Francisco – and which are buried below the evocative, if touristy, **Virginia City**.

Reno

On I-80 at the foot of the Sierra Nevada, thirty miles east of Truckee, **RENO, NEVADA** has plenty of bargain places to stay and eat, making it a reasonable stopoff, especially if you enjoy **gambling** (see box, p.581). The town itself, apart from the stream of blazing casino neon, is not much to look at, having sprung up out of nowhere in the middle of the desert in the hope that the gambling industry alone could sustain its existence. Nevertheless, its setting – with the snowcapped Sierra peaks as a distant backdrop and the Truckee River winding through – is nice enough and, unlike Las Vegas, Reno maintains a small-town feel that residents are proud of. As the locals love to say – over and over again – Reno is the "biggest little city in the world".

Once you're ready to cash in all the casino clatter and any remaining chips for some peace and quiet, take refuge in one of Reno's many **museums**, or just pass a pleasant afternoon ambling in the dry desert heat. Reno also makes an alternative base from which to visit Lake Tahoe, as well as the evocative mining towns of **Carson City** and **Virginia City**.

The casinos

While nowhere near as grand as the Vegas gambling institutions, most of Reno's **casinos** still warrant a quick tour. If you can only handle visiting a couple, the best of the lot are: **Circus Circus**, 500 N Sierra St, where a small circus performs every half-hour, giving patrons a reason to look up from their dwindling savings; it runs seamlessly into **Silver Legacy**,

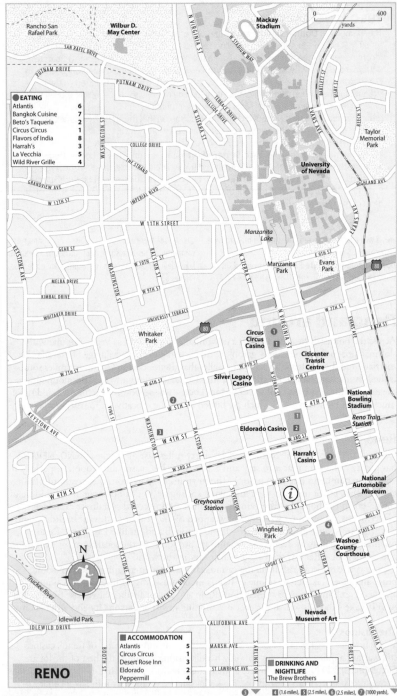

Mackay
Stadium

0   400
yards

Rancho San
Rafael Park

Wilbur D.
May Center

SAN RAFAEL DRIVE

PUTNAM DRIVE

PUTNAM DRIVE

●EATING
Atlantis   6
Bangkok Cuisine   7
Beto's Taqueria   2
Circus Circus   1
Flavors of India   8
Harrah's   3
La Vecchia   5
Wild River Grille   4

COLLEGE DRIVE

GRANDVIEW AVE

W 12TH ST

Taylor
Memorial
Park

University
of Nevada

HIGHLAND AVE

IMPERIAL BLVD

W 11TH STREET

Manzanita
Lake

GEAR ST

W 10TH ST

E 9TH ST

8

MELBA DRIVE

W 9TH ST

Manzanita
Park

Evans
Park

KIMBAL DRIVE

WHITAKER DRIVE

UNIVERSITY TERRACE

80

W 7TH ST

Whitaker
Park

80

Circus
Circus
Casino

Citicenter
Transit
Centre

W 6TH ST

W 6TH ST

W 5TH ST

Silver Legacy
Casino

W 5TH ST

National
Bowling
Stadium

E 4TH ST

Reno Train
Station

W 4TH ST

Eldorado Casino

W 3RD ST

W 3RD ST

Harrah's
Casino

W 2ND ST

National
Automobile
Museum

W 4TH ST

W 2ND ST

Greyhound
Station

W 1ST ST

ⓘ

W 2ND ST

W 1ST STREET

Wingfield
Park

Washoe
County
Courthouse

JONES ST

RIVERSIDE DRIVE

COURT ST

Truckee River

RIDGE ST

W LIBERTY ST

Idlewild Park

IDLEWILD DRIVE

CALIFORNIA AVE

Nevada
Museum of Art

N

■ ACCOMMODATION
Atlantis   5
Circus Circus   1
Desert Rose Inn   3
Eldorado   2
Peppermill   4

MARSH AVE

ST LAWRENCE ST

■ DRINKING AND
NIGHTLIFE
The Brew Brothers   1

RENO

❸ ▼   ❹ (1.6 miles), ❺ (2.5 miles), ❻ (2.5 miles), ❼ (1000 yards),

(1 mile)& Airport (4 miles)

whose main entrance is around the corner at 407 N Virginia St, revealing a planetarium-style dome with a makeshift 120ft mining derrick underneath, appearing to draw silver ore out of the ground and spilling cascades of coins in the process. This is joined in turn with **Eldorado** and you can quite unwittingly wander between all three. The other main attraction for punters is **Harrah's**, a few blocks south at 219 N Center St, the classiest casino downtown with row upon row of high-stakes slot machines and the occasional big-name entertainer. If you want to compare these with one of the newer establishments further out, head south towards the brash opulence of **Peppermill** at 2707 S Virginia St. **The Nugget**, several miles east in the twin town of Sparks, is another gambling behemoth.

National Automobile Museum

10 S Lake St • Mon–Sat 9.30am–5.30pm, Sun 10am–4pm • $10 • ☎ 775 333 9300, ⓦ automuseum.org

The largest and most significant of Reno's museums is the **National Automobile Museum** (The Harrah Collection), which holds the most comprehensive public display of automobiles in the western hemisphere. The sheer scale of the collection, with more than two hundred vintage and classic cars, some artfully arranged along re-created city streets of bygone decades, can't help but impress. The one time it's guaranteed to get crowded is during the **Hot August Nites** classic cars festival, when famous twentieth-century automobiles go on show.

Nevada Museum of Art

160 W Liberty St • Wed–Sun 10am–6pm, till 8pm on Thurs • $10 • ☎ 775 329 3333, ⓦ nevadaart.org

The inventive contemporary exhibitions at the **Nevada Museum of Art** are well worth a visit for art lovers. The permanent collection focuses on four themes: contemporary art, art of the Greater West, altered landscape photography, and the work ethic. In addition, there can be half a dozen or more temporary exhibitions spread throughout the various galleries.

Wilbur D. May Center

1595 N Sierra St • Wed–Sat 10am–4pm, Sun noon–4pm • $9 • ☎ 775 785 5961, ⓦ maycenter.com

You'll find Reno's most curious trove at the **Wilbur D. May Center**, which sits on the edge of **Rancho San Rafael Park**, a mile north of downtown Reno off North Sierra Street. The collection outlines the eventful life of Wilbur May (1898–1982) – a traveller, hunter, military aviator, cattle-breeder and heir to the May department store fortunes – with several rooms of furnishings, mounted animal heads and plunder from his trips to Africa and South America. The museum also houses temporary exhibitions.

Fleischmann Planetarium

1664 N Virginia St • Mon–Thurs noon–8pm, Fri noon–9pm, Sat 10am–9pm, Sun 10am–6pm; films screened 3–4 times daily • Free; films $8 • ☎ 775 784 4811, ⓦ planetarium.unr.edu

The **Fleischmann Planetarium**, part of the University of Nevada campus, has a fine collection of telescopes and galleries describing various aspects of the solar system, as well as all four meteorites recovered in Nevada and impressive 6ft globes of Earth and the moon. A gallery in the basement displays astronomy-themed artwork. The **Star Theater** shows IMAX-style films, projected onto a huge dome.

RENO'S GAMBLING ROOTS

It may lack the glitz and the glamour that make Vegas a global draw, but Reno is northern Nevada's number-one **gambling** spot, offering a 24-hour diet of slot machines, blackjack, craps, keno, roulette and many more ways to win and lose a bundle. Gaming was only legalized in Nevada in 1931, but silver miners in Virginia City and Gold Hill regularly tried their hands at fortune's wheel back in the mid-nineteenth century, when a deck of cards was an almost mandatory part of a miner's kit. This tradition was revived with a vengeance when Reno came into being the following century.

ARRIVAL AND INFORMATION

By plane Reno's Cannon International Airport (☎775 328 6400, ⓦrenoairport.com) is served by most major domestic carriers. RTC bus #13 (daily 6am–1am; $2 flat fare, $5 day-pass; ☎775 348 0480, ⓦrtcwashoe.com) makes the 20min journey from the terminals to Reno's downtown Citicenter transit centre, where you can connect to many of the company's other routes.

By bus Greyhound buses use the terminal at 155 Stevenson St. The South Lake Tahoe Express and North Lake Tahoe Express services (see p.573) connect Reno airport with their respective Lake Tahoe areas.

Destinations Reno: Los Angeles (4 daily; 12hr 45min–15hr

RENO

55); Sacramento (5 daily; 2hr 40min–3hr 25min); San Francisco (5 daily; 5hr–6hr 45min). Reno airport: South Lake Tahoe/Stateline (9 daily; 1hr 30min), Tahoe City (9–11 daily; 1hr 30min).

By train The Amtrak *California Zephyr* train from Chicago stops in the centre of town at 135 Commercial Row.

Destinations Oakland/Emeryville (1 daily; 7hr 35min); Sacramento (1 daily; 5hr 35min); Truckee (1 daily; 1hr).

Visit Reno Tahoe 135 N Sierra St, downtown (daily 10am–6pm; ☎800 367 7366, ⓦvisitrenotahoe.com).

ACCOMMODATION

Very competitive **accommodation** prices are plentiful midweek, at least outside the peak summer season, but if you arrive at the weekend you should book ahead and be prepared for rates to quadruple. This especially applies to the **casinos**, which often impose a two-night-minimum weekend stay. You can also call the **Reno-Sparks Visitor and Convention Association**'s toll-free reservation line (☎800 367 7366) for help with finding a place to stay.

Atlantis 3800 S Virginia St ☎800 723 6500, ⓦatlantiscasino.com. One of the newer casinos on the scene, *Atlantis* offers plusher amenities but costs more than the older casinos in the centre of town. Ask for an upper-storey room for splendid views. **$149**

Circus Circus 500 N Sierra St ☎800 648 5010, ⓦcircuscircusreno.com. One of the largest and tackiest casinos, with over 1500 popular rooms – check online for very low rates at slow times. **$65**

Desert Rose Inn 655 W 4th St ☎775 321 3451, ⓦdesertroseinnreno.com. Simple downtown motel with

basic rooms and few other trimmings but invariably better prices when the casinos hike theirs. **$69**

Eldorado 345 N Virginia St ☎800 777 5325, ⓦeldoradoreno.com. The nicer rooms are on the upper floors, while those lower down are cheaper in this bustling downtown casino. Lots of online specials. **$75**

Peppermill 2707 S Virginia St ☎866 821 9996, ⓦpeppermillreno.com. Another large casino, slightly outside the centre of town, and cushier than most with lavishly furnished bedrooms. Check for special online rates. **$109**

EATING AND DRINKING

All-you-can-eat **casino buffets** can be fun and of surprisingly good quality; the best are listed here along with locals' favourite alternatives, most of which are awkwardly spread over the south of the city.

GETTING MARRIED (AND DIVORCED) IN RENO

Many people come to Reno to get **married**, as it's so easy and inexpensive. If you decide to get hitched, you and your intended must be at least 18 years old and able to prove it, swear that you're not already married and appear before a judge at the **Washoe County Court** (daily 8am–midnight; ☎775 328 3275), south of the main casino district at South Virginia and Court streets, to obtain a **marriage licence** ($60). There is no waiting period or blood test required. Civil services are performed for an additional $50 at the **Commissioner for Civil Marriages**, 350 S Center St (☎775 328 3461). If you want something a bit more special, however, **wedding chapels** all around the city will help you tie the knot, although they tend to be on the kitsch side. Arch of Reno at 155 N Virginia St (from $90; ☎775 786 6882, ⓦarchofreno.com) and the cutely named Antique Angels Wedding Chapel, a block away at 15 N Virginia St (from $85; ☎775 337 1655, ⓦantiqueangelchapel.com), are two such places where you can get spliced with minimum fuss and cost. If it doesn't work out, you'll have to stay in Nevada for another six weeks before you can get a **divorce**. Having this short residency requirement also meant that people who were married in another state used to flock here to get divorced, especially in the 1940s and 1950s, but the increased ease of filing elsewhere means it is no longer America's "divorce capital".

BUFFETS

★**Atlantis** 3800 S Virginia St ☎775 825 4700, Ⓦatlantiscasino.com. *Toucan Charlie's* is consistently and justifiably voted Best Buffet by locals – well worth the extra few bucks at $24.99 for dinner. Among the other restaurants here are the moderately priced *Café Alfresco* and more upscale *Atlantis Steakhouse*, which has exceptional food, wine list and service. Daily 8am–3pm & 4.30–9pm.

Circus Circus 500 N Sierra St ☎800 648 5010, Ⓦcircuscircusreno.com. The place to go for a buffet meal if your budget is of greater concern than your stomach, with all-you-can-eat dinners for around $13 at weekends. Fri 4–10pm, Sat 8am–10pm, Sun 8am–4pm.

Harrah's 219 N Center St ☎775 786 3232, Ⓦharrahsreno.com. The most lavish downtown casino buffet includes multiple mains such as prime rib, crab legs, shrimp and a fine Asian section for around $18 most days. Their à la carte *Harrah's Steakhouse* is also recommended. Daily 10am–2pm & 4.30–9pm.

RESTAURANTS

Bangkok Cuisine 55 Mt Rose St ☎775 322 0299, Ⓦthaifoodreno.com. Cosy Thai family restaurant with a vast menu of spicy favourites such as green curries and pad thai noodles for $10–16. Also does filling lunch specials for around $7. Mon–Sat 11am–10pm.

Beto's Taqueria 575 W 5th St. Excellent and authentic self-service Mexican canteen, one of the best-value places to eat downtown outside of the casinos, with tacos, burritos and empanadas costing $8 or under. Daily 10am–10pm.

Flavors of India 1885 S Virginia St ☎775 323 4100, Ⓦflavorsofindiarenonevada.com. A range of cuisine from different parts of India, from northern dishes such as mutton korma to South India *dosas*, all $8–15, plus a good lunch buffet for only $9. Daily 11am–10pm.

La Vecchia 3005 Skyline Blvd ☎775 825 1113, Ⓦlavecchiareno.com. Relocated from its humble downtown beginnings, this gourmet Italian restaurant offers several vegetarian choices as well as all the meaty favourites, such as veal *scaloppine*, for around $20. Mon–Thurs 11am–2pm & 5–9pm, Fri 11am–2pm & 5–10pm, Sat 5–10pm, Sun 5–9pm.

Wild River Grille 17 S Virginia St ☎775 284 7455, Ⓦbestrenorestaurant.com. The boast of the website address, taken from a local vote, may be subject to debate but the starters, seafood and steaks are well prepared and very tasty. Mains $25–35. Mon–Thurs & Sun 11am–11pm, Fri & Sat 11am–midnight.

DRINKING AND NIGHTLIFE

Tourists tend to stick to the **shows** in the casinos for nightlife but occasionally the city holds an art or music festival and the Pioneer Center for the Performing Arts at 100 S Virginia St (☎775 686 6610, Ⓦpioneercenter.com) is the regular spot for highbrow culture. Check Reno's free independent weekly *Reno News and Review* (Ⓦnewsreview.com) for other listings.

The Brew Brothers Eldorado casino, 345 N Virginia St ☎775 786 5700, Ⓦeldoradoreno.com. A casino might seem an unlikely place to find a quality microbrewery but this one offers eight custom ales, a good range of pub grub and regular live music. Mon–Fri 11.30am–late, Sat & Sun 11am–late.

Carson City

US-395 heads south from Reno along the jagged spires of the High Sierra past Mono Lake, Mount Whitney and Death Valley (see Chapter Four). Just thirty miles south of Reno, it briefly becomes Carson Street as it passes through **CARSON CITY**, the state capital of Nevada. It's small compared to Reno and despite the sprawling mess of fast-food joints, strip malls and car dealerships that surround its centre, it's well worth a visit, especially if you're interested in the history of mining. Named after frontier explorer Kit Carson in 1858, even though he never came here, Carson City is still redolent with Wild West history. The city has a number of elegant buildings, excellent historical museums and a few world-weary casinos, populated mainly by old ladies. The fifteen-block downtown area has been redeveloped with many new pedestrian and bicycle routes.

Nevada State Museum

600 N Carson St • Tues–Sun 8.30am–4.30pm • $8 • ☎775 687 4810, Ⓦmuseums.nevadaculture.org

A good introduction to the area's history can be found at the **Nevada State Museum**. Housed in a sandstone structure built during the Civil War as the Carson Mint, the museum's exhibits deal with the geology and natural history of the Great Basin desert region, from prehistoric days up through the heyday of the 1860s, when the silver

8

mines of the nearby Comstock Lode were at their peak. Amid the many guns and artefacts, the two best features of the museum are the reconstructed **Ghost Town** and a full-scale model of an **underground mine**, connected to the former by a tunnel and giving some sense of the cramped conditions in which miners worked. The **North Building** is home to the **Under One Sky** exhibition, featuring material about cowboys and Native Americans, natural history and children's interactive displays.

State Capitol

101 N Carson St • Mon–Fri 8am–5pm • Free

Four blocks from the State Museum on the other side of Carson Street, the impressively restored **State Capitol**, dating from 1871, merits a look for its stylish Neoclassical architecture and artefacts relating to Nevada's past.

Nevada State Railway Museum

2180 S Carson St • Mon & Thurs–Sun 9am–5pm • $6 • ☎ 775 687 6953, ⓦ museums.nevadaculture.org

The **Nevada State Railway Museum**, a stone's throw from the visitor centre (see below), displays carefully restored locomotives and carriages, several of them from the long since defunct but fondly remembered Virginia & Truckee Railroad, founded in the nineteenth century.

ARRIVAL AND INFORMATION   CARSON CITY

By bus Carson City is connected to Reno by several weekday commuter services on the RTC network (see p.582).

CVBs The main CVB is at 1900 S Carson St (daily 9am–6pm; ☎ 775 687 7410 or ☎ 800 638 2321, ⓦ visitcarsoncity .com), plus there's a new branch at 716 N Carson St (same hours and details). You can buy the *Kit Carson Trail Map* ($2.50), a leaflet detailing a walking tour of the town, at either or download it free from the website.

ACCOMMODATION AND EATING

Firkin & Fox 310 S Carson St ☎ 775 883 1369, ⓦ thefirkinandfox.com. British-style pub, with some fifteen beers on tap and a range of food, from nachos and pizza to 25 wings with five different dips for $22.95. Daily 11am–midnight.

Gold Dust West Casino 2171 US-50 ☎ 775 885 9000, ⓦ gdwcasino.com. Standard high-rise casino with functional rooms, whose prices rise at weekends but not by anything as much as Reno. RV $\underline{\$30}$, doubles $\underline{\$90}$

Plaza Hotel 801 S Carson St ☎ 775 883 9500, ⓦ carsoncityplaza.com. Not far from the Capitol, this is more of a motel than a hotel but the rooms are pleasantly colourful. There are some larger rooms with kitchenettes too. $\underline{\$79}$

Red's Old 395 Grill 1055 S Carson St ☎ 775 887 0395, ⓦ reds395.com. Named after the highway, this popular place does a range of mainly grilled meat and fish dishes, such as wood-fired salmon for $18.50. You get $5 free play on the slot machines with a meal. Mon–Thurs 11am–9pm, Fri & Sat 11am–10pm.

Virginia City

Much of the wealth on which Carson City – and indeed San Francisco – was built came from the silver mines of the Comstock Lode, a solid seam of pure silver

MARK TWAIN IN VIRGINIA CITY

A young writer named Samuel Clemens made his way to Virginia City in the 1860s with his older brother, who'd been appointed acting secretary to the governor of the Nevada Territory, to see what all the fuss was about. His descriptions of the wild life of the mining camp and of the desperately hard work men put in to get at the valuable ore were published years later under his adopted pseudonym, **Mark Twain**. Twain also spent some time in the declining Gold Rush towns of California's Mother Lode on the other side of the Sierra but his accounts of Virginia City life, collected in *Roughing It*, offer a hilarious eyewitness account of the hard-drinking life of the frontier miners.

VIRGINIA CITY RAILROAD EXCURSIONS

A fun Virginia City activity is to take the 35-minute train ride on the **Virginia & Truckee Railroad** (late May to late Oct 10.30am–4pm; return $10 diesel or $12 steam; ☎775 847 0380, ⓦvirginiatruckee.com) from the depot at 370 F St, a little over a mile up to the all-but-extinct town of **Gold Hill**, the location of Nevada's oldest hotel (see below).

---

discovered in 1859 underneath Mount Hamilton, fourteen miles east of Carson City off US-50. **VIRGINIA CITY** grew up on the steep slopes above the mines – the hard life of its miners was documented by a young Mark Twain (see box opposite) – and the town still exploits a rich vein, one which taps the pockets of tour parties bussed up here from Reno. But despite the camera-clicking throngs, there's a sense of authenticity to Virginia City that's missing from even the most evocative of the California mining towns; perhaps it's the town's location, encircled by the barren Nevada Desert that so sharply contrasts with the diverse countryside of California's Gold Country. It's hard not to get caught up in the infectious Wild West atmosphere and stay longer than you'd intended, sampling the town's quirky **museums**. Still, not everyone who floods into town is here for the Gold Rush nostalgia – many visitors are here to frequent the **legal brothels**, another reminder of the town's frontier days.

The museums

Historic highlights include the **Mackay Mansion Museum**, 129 South D St (daily 10am–6pm; $6; ☎775 847 0373, ⓦuniquitiesmackaymansion.com), a painstakingly preserved 1860s residence, and the **Nevada Gambling Museum**, 50 South C St (daily: April–Sept 10.30am–5pm; Oct–March 10.30am–4pm; $3; ☎775 847 0789), with its historic roulette wheel and other period game-room accessories. You can also poke your head into the **Bucket of Blood Saloon** at 1 South C St, which is delightfully crowded with period fixtures and crooked old furnishings. The mood of the era and current desire to cash in on it is summed up in **The Way It Was Museum**, 113 North C St (daily 10am–4.30pm; $3; ☎775 847 0766), with its collection of mining equipment, rare photos and maps, and fully stocked gift shop.

8

ARRIVAL AND INFORMATION   VIRGINIA CITY

By car The only way to reach Virginia City is by car on steeply winding Rte-341.
Chamber of Commerce 86 South C St (Mon–Sat

9am–5pm, Sun 10am–4pm; ☎775 847 7500 or ☎800 718 7567, ⓦvisitvirginiacitynv.com); occupies the disused premises of the old *Crystal Bar Saloon*.

ACCOMMODATION AND EATING

★ **Gold Hill Hotel** 1540 Main St, Gold Hill ☎775 847 0111, ⓦgoldhillhotel.net. Nevada's oldest hotel, with good rates and atmosphere, especially in its restaurant and tavern. It also lets out five more expensive lodges in ex-miners' houses around the tiny town. $60
Sawdust Corner Restaurant 18 South C St ☎775 847 0789, ⓦsawdustcatering.com. Simple, no-nonsense snacks and meals, from sandwiches and omelettes to buffalo wings and some Mexican dishes, all cost less than $10 here. Daily 7am–9pm.

Silver Queen Hotel & Wedding Chapel 28 North C St ☎775 847 0440, ⓦsilverqueenhotel.net. Delightfully cheesy hotel with lots of period furniture and decor in the rooms and ornate saloon. Apart from putting on weddings, it also organizes ghost tours and sells antiques. $55
★ **Virginia City Brewery & Taphouse** 62 North C St ☎775 847 7064. Great new microbrewery that comes up with creations such as Steampunk Extra Pale Ale and Dirty Mucker Stout. Mon & Tues 1–7pm, Wed & Thurs noon–8pm, Fri & Sat 11am–late, Sun 11am–7pm.

Northern California

KLAMATH OVERLOOK

9

Northern California

The northern coast and interior of California covers around a third of the state, a gigantic area over three hundred and fifty miles long and two hundred wide, with a rugged rural landscape and an ethic far removed from the urban lifestyles to the south. It's a schizophrenic region of a schizophrenic state, coupling volcanoes with vineyards, fog-shrouded redwoods with scorched olive trees, loggers with environmentalists and legends of Bigfoot with movies of Ewoks. Northern Californians are tied to the land, and agriculture dominates the economy as well as the vistas. Deep-rooted forestry, fishing and cattle industries are also ever-present (even though the first two are in decline), along with the wild, crashing Pacific Coast and steady rain that supports a marijuana-growing region called the Emerald Triangle. Add only two major highways and the lack of a metropolis in favour of small, Main Street towns, and you have a region that has more in common with Oregon and Washington than Los Angeles or San Francisco.

Immediately north of the Bay Area, the **Wine Country** might be your first – indeed your only – taste of Northern California, though it's by no means typical. The two valleys of **Napa** and **Sonoma** unfold along thirty miles of rolling hills and premium real estate, home to the California wine barons and San Franciscan weekenders wanting to escape in style. Napa is the reigning king of indulgence and high-calibre vintages, while Sonoma caters to a funkier set, with its interesting history and outdoor tours. The northwest corner of Sonoma County is the Wine Country's other "grape escape", an area of six varieties and resorts clustered around the **Russian River** and its tributaries.

It's the **northern coast** which provides the most appealing, and slowest, route through the region, beginning just north of Marin County and continuing for three hundred miles on Hwy-1 and US-101 along rugged bluffs and through dense forests as far as the Oregon border. The landscape varies little at first, but given time reveals tangible shifts from the flat oyster beds of **Sonoma County**, to the seal and surfer breeding grounds around the coastal elegance of **Mendocino**, and to the big logging country further north in **Humboldt**. Trees are the main attraction up here: some thousands of

LASSEN VOLCANIC NATIONAL PARK

Highlights

❶ Russian River Valley wineries
Opportunities for leisurely wine-tasting against a glorious backdrop of vineyards and redwoods abound in this less commercialized part of Wine Country. **See p.610**

❷ Avenue of the Giants Wonder at the sheer scale of the ancient trees in the atmospheric forest on this magnificent detour through Humboldt Redwoods State Park. **See p.624**

❸ Klamath Overlook Where the Klamath River empties into the Pacific, take in the marvellous vistas at this dramatic stop on the rugged Coastal Trail. **See p.634**

❹ Lassen Volcanic National Park Visit this top wilderness area to enjoy steaming geysers, high-altitude lakes, bracing walks and exhilarating campsites. **See p.642**

❺ Mount Shasta This huge volcanic peak is at the heart of spirituality and legends, as well as a haven for cross-country skiing in winter and hiking or mountaineering in summer. **See p.653**

❻ Lava Beds National Monument Admire the black volcanic rock, crawl through tubular caves, or indulge in excellent birding at California's northernmost attraction. **See p.662**

HIGHLIGHTS ARE MARKED ON THE MAP ON P.590

9

years old and hundreds of feet high, dominating a very sparsely populated landscape swathed in swirling mists. In summer, areas like **Redwood National Park**, stretching into the most northerly **Del Norte County**, teem with campers and hikers but out of season they can provide idyllic experiences and an opportunity to coexist with the area's woodland creatures – including, legend has it, Bigfoot.

The **interior** is more remote still, an enchanting land whose mystery and sheer physical enormity can't help but leave a lasting impression. The I-5 neatly divides the region, cutting north to the **Shasta Cascades**, a mountainous area of isolated towns, massive lakes and a forbidding climate. The largest town and transport hub of **Redding** is a major crossroads serving **Whiskeytown-Shasta-Trinity National Recreation Area**,

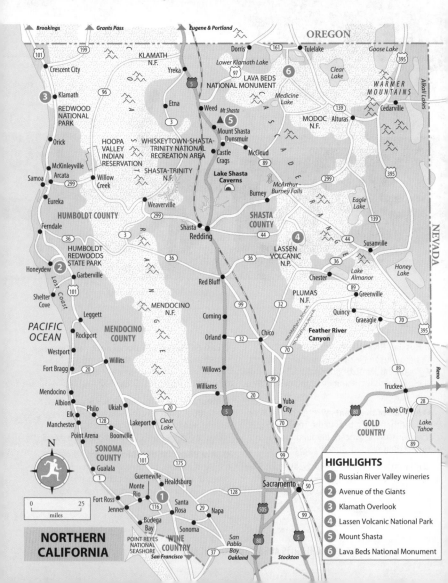

HIGHLIGHTS

1. Russian River Valley wineries
2. Avenue of the Giants
3. Klamath Overlook
4. Lassen Volcanic National Park
5. Mount Shasta
6. Lava Beds National Monument

NORTHERN CALIFORNIA

Lassen Volcanic National Park, McArthur-Burney Falls State Park and, northward, the railroad towns in the shadows of towering **Mount Shasta**. Up at the top of the interior, the eerie, moonlike terrain of the **Lava Beds National Monument** rewards those who make the effort to get there.

9

Unlike the Wine Country and the coast, locals all over the Shasta Cascades are actually glad to see tourists. Parts of the region fill up in summer but given the sheer enormity of the forests and the plethora of lakes, waterfalls, parks and bird sanctuaries, escaping the masses and finding peace is easy enough. Out of season, you may feel like you're the only one here at all.

Brief history

As with elsewhere in California, the first inhabitants of the north were **Native Americans**, whose past has been all but erased, leaving only the odd desolate reservation or crafts museum. Much later, the **Russians** figured briefly in the region's history, when they had a modest nineteenth-century settlement at Fort Ross on the coast, ostensibly to protect their interests in otter hunting and fur trading, though more likely to promote territorial claims. **Mexican** explorers and maintenance costs that exceeded revenues prevented them from extending their hunting activities further south and in the 1840s they sold the fort to the **Americans**. It was the discovery of **gold** just to the south in 1848 that really helped put the north on the map. Not a lot has happened since, although in the 1980s New Ageism triggered a kind of future for the region, with low land prices pulling more and more devotees up here to sample the delights of a landscape they see as rich in rural symbolism. Hollywood has also been drawn to the region, using the north as a cost-effective way to travel to another place and time. *Robin Hood*, *Gone With the Wind*, *The Birds*, *The Return of the Jedi* and *Jurassic Park: The Lost World* are just a few examples of movies filmed amid the frozen-in-time beauty.

Over the last two decades the spiralling rise in Bay Area property prices has led to a small but steady movement of more mainstream folk and retirees into some areas, searching for better value for money or a spacious second home. Many diehard locals are fearful of this influx spoiling the coast, in particular, and property prices have been creeping up as far north as Mendocino, though the Coastal Commission tightly controls development and farmers have so far resisted selling out on a large scale.

GETTING AROUND

By car As with most of the state, to get to the more remote locations and make the most of the region, you really need a car. It is more enjoyable to avoid the main interior I-5 freeway as much as possible. Towards the coast, US-101 has some beautiful sections but by far the most scenic driving is to be had on winding Hwy-1. A good network of routes links these main arteries but note that all roads can be clogged up with slow-moving RVs in summer.

By bus Greyhound only stops at Chico, Redding and Weed on the I-5 corridor and at Garberville, Eureka and Arcata on US-101. There are some inter-county and local services outlined in the chapter but overall services are pretty sparse.

By train Amtrak's Coastal Starlight service makes stops at Chico, Redding and Dunsmuir but only at the most inconvenient times of night in each direction.

The Wine Country

"The coldest winter I ever spent was summer in San Francisco", quipped Mark Twain. Like Twain, many visitors to San Francisco can't get over the daily fog and winds that chill even the most promising August day. For this reason, heading into the golden, arid and balmy **Napa and Sonoma valleys**, barely an hour's drive north of San Francisco, can feel like entering another country. Here, around thirty thousand acres of vineyards, feeding hundreds of **wineries** and their upscale patrons, make the area the heart of the American wine industry in reputation, if not in volume. In truth, less than

9

five percent of California's wine comes from the region, but what it does produce is some of America's best.

Predictably, the region is also one of America's wealthiest and most provincial, a fact that draws – and repels – a steady stream of tourists. There seems to be a bed and breakfast or spa for every grape on the vine, and tourism is gaining on wine production as the Wine Country's leading industry. Expect clogged highways and full hotels during much of **peak season** (May–Oct), especially at weekends, as well as packed tastings in the more popular wineries.

However, there are two sides to the Napa and Sonoma valleys. One, of course, is their prominence for serious, quality wine experiences. Almost all of the region's many wineries offer **tours and tastings**, usually for a variable charge (typically $20–50 but sometimes even more); this sometimes includes the wine glass and usually a credit towards the purchase of a bottle or case. Aside from the type and flavour of the drink, wineries all differ in what they offer visitors. Some delight oenologists by explaining the process of growing grapes, some excite kids with tractor rides through the vineyard and some please thirsty patrons with generous samples. The other side to the Wine Country is its **natural landscape**. Separated by the Mayacamas Mountains, the Napa and Sonoma valleys feature some of the most gently beautiful geography in the state, from the Valley of the Moon to Mount St Helena. Once you've tired of sipping, check out ballooning, biking, horseriding, hiking and myriad historical sights, including Spanish missions and Jack London's homestead.

Nothing comes cheap around **Napa** and the town itself can be quickly done with unless you want to board the over-hyped Wine Train. But many small towns further up the valley, particularly **St Helena**, have retained enough of their early twentieth-century-homestead character to be a welcome relief. **Calistoga**, at the top of the valley, is famous for its hot springs, massages and spas. On the western side of the dividing Mayacamas Mountains, the smaller backroad wineries of the Sonoma Valley reflect the down-to-earth nature of the place, which is more beautiful and less crowded than its easterly neighbour. The town of **Sonoma** itself is by far the prettiest of the Wine Country communities, retaining a number of fine Mission-era structures around its gracious central plaza. **Santa Rosa**, at the north end of the valley, is the region's sole urban centre, handy for budget lodgings but otherwise unremarkable.

Napa Valley

A thirty-mile strip of gently landscaped corridors and lush hillsides, **NAPA VALLEY** looks more like southern France than a near-neighbour of the Pacific Ocean. In spring, the valley floor is covered with brilliant wildflowers that mellow into fall shades by grape-harvest time. The main route through the valley is Hwy-29, along which all the towns described here are strung, but for a quieter alternative route between Napa and Calistoga, the **Silverado Trail** to the east is highly recommended.

Brief history

Local Native Americans named the fish-rich river that flows through the valley "Napa", meaning "plenty"; the name was adopted by Spanish missionaries in the early nineteenth century but the natives themselves were soon wiped out. The few ranches the Spanish and Mexicans managed to establish were in turn taken over by Yankee traders, and by the 1850s, with California part of the US, the town of Napa was soon swallowed by the Gold Rush. Its location also made it a thriving river port, sending agricultural goods to San Francisco and serving as a supply point for farmers and ranchers. The opening of White Sulphur Springs in 1852, California's first mineral-springs resort, made Napa the vacation choice for San Francisco's elite. Settlers came, too, including Jacob Beringer in 1870. The rocky, well-drained soil he saw resembled that of his hometown of Mainz, Germany, and by 1875 he and his brother had

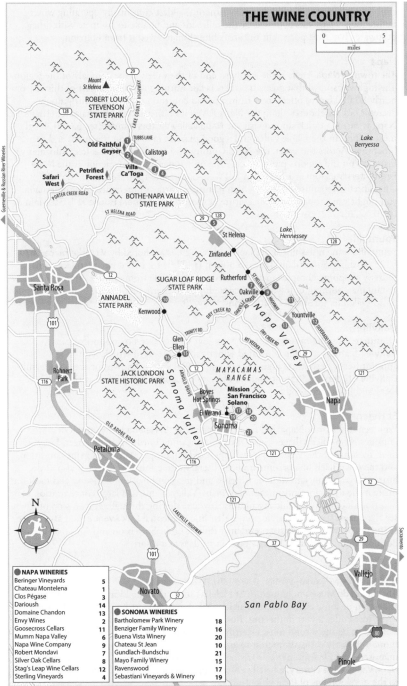

THE WINE COUNTRY

0 ——————— 5
miles

Mount St Helena ▲

ROBERT LOUIS STEVENSON STATE PARK

Old Faithful Geyser

Calistoga

Villa Ca'Toga

Lake Berryessa

Safari West

Petrified Forest

PORTER CREEK ROAD

BOTHE-NAPA VALLEY STATE PARK

ST HELENA ROAD

Lake Hennessey

St Helena

Zinfandel

SUGAR LOAF RIDGE STATE PARK

Rutherford

Santa Rosa

ANNADEL STATE PARK

Oakville

Kenwood

Yountville

Napa Valley

Glen Ellen

TRINITY RD

MT VEEDER RD

DRY CREEK RD

Rohnert Park

JACK LONDON STATE HISTORIC PARK

Sonoma Valley

MAYACAMAS RANGE

Boyes Hot Springs

Mission San Francisco Solano

El Verano

Napa

Sonoma

Petaluma

OLD ADOBE ROAD

N

Novato

San Pablo Bay

Vallejo

Pinole

LAKEVILLE HIGHWAY

Guerneville & Russian River Wineries

Sacramento

San Francisco

East Bay

NAPA WINERIES

Beringer Vineyards	5
Chateau Montelena	1
Clos Pégase	3
Darioush	14
Domaine Chandon	13
Envy Wines	2
Goosecross Cellars	11
Mumm Napa Valley	6
Napa Wine Company	9
Robert Mondavi	7
Silver Oak Cellars	8
Stag's Leap Wine Cellars	12
Sterling Vineyards	4

SONOMA WINERIES

Bartholomew Park Winery	18
Benziger Family Winery	16
Buena Vista Winery	20
Chateau St Jean	10
Gundlach-Bundschu	21
Mayo Family Winery	15
Ravenswood	17
Sebastiani Vineyards & Winery	19

9

established Beringer Vineyards, today America's oldest continually operating winery. Before long, Napa was bypassed by the railroads and unable to compete with other deepwater Bay Area ports, but the area's fine climate saved it from oblivion.

Napa

The town of **Napa** itself, at the southern end of the valley, is the anomaly of the region. The highway sprawl that greets travellers is fair warning to what the rest of this city of nearly 80,000 has to offer: apart from a proud courthouse and some intriguingly decrepit old warehouses along the Napa River, it's rather lacking in character. That said, Napa is worth a quick stop to visit the **Napa Valley Visitors Bureau** (see p.602). It's the most helpful in the whole valley and a good place to load up on free maps and brochures. Across the street, the Napa County Historical Society has free, informative materials on the region's pre-wine era. The only other minor attraction is the **Napa Firefighters Museum** at 1201 Main St (Wed–Sat 11am–4pm; free; ☎707 259 0609, ⒲napafirefightersmuseum.org), which features an array of firefighting paraphernalia, or you might want to take in some culture at the attractive **Opera House** at 1030 Main St (☎707 226 7372, ⒲nvoh.org).

Yountville

Yountville, nine miles north of Napa on Hwy-29, is anchored by **V Marketplace 1870**, 6525 Washington St (daily 10am–5.30pm; ☎707 944 2451, ⒲vmarketplace.com), a touristy shopping complex in a converted winery. Aside from antiques shops and a few restaurants, nothing in town exerts enough pull to merit a long stop, so it's best to push on to Oakville, three miles north along Hwy-29.

Oakville

Dominated by the massive Robert Mondavi winery (see box opposite), tiny **Oakville** features a dozen top-rated **wineries**, almost all of which require an appointment. Besides its high-calibre wines, Oakville is known for the wonderful **Oakville Grocery** at 7856 St Helena Hwy, an excellent deli packed with the finest local and imported foods.

St Helena

Eighteen miles from Napa and far more appealing, **St Helena** is the largest of all the antiques-shop-filled villages you'll encounter heading north. Its main street, Hwy-29, is lined by some of the Wine Country's finest old buildings, many in pristine condition, and the town itself boasts some unlikely literary attractions. St Helena is also at the heart of a large concentration of wineries and this combination of history and location make it the de facto tourism capital of Napa Valley, home to a large concentration of luxurious lodgings and chic restaurants. If you're driving through, at least stop off to see the quaint Craftsman-style homes that line residential **Oak Avenue**, and also to see remnants of two unlikely past residents: Robert Louis Stevenson and Ambrose Bierce, both of whom lived in St Helena back in its days as a resort.

Silverado Museum

1490 Library Lane • Tues–Sat noon–4pm • Free • ☎ 707 963 3757, ⒲ silveradomuseum.org

The **Silverado Museum**, housed in St Helena's former Public Library building, has a collection of some eight thousand articles relating to Robert Louis Stevenson, who spent just under a year in the area, honeymooning and recovering from an illness. It's claimed to be the second most extensive collection of Stevenson artefacts in the US, though the only thing of interest to any but the most obsessed fan is a scribbled-on manuscript of *Dr Jekyll and Mr Hyde*. The other half of the building is taken up by the **Napa Valley Wine Library**, a briefly entertaining barrage of photos and clippings relating to the development of local viticulture.

NAPA VALLEY WINERIES

Almost all of Napa Valley's **wineries** offer **tastings**, though not all have tours. The following selections are some long-standing favourites, plus a few lesser-known hopefuls. If you want to buy a bottle, particularly from the larger producers, you can usually get it cheaper in supermarkets than at the wineries themselves, unless you ship in bulk.

Beringer Vineyards 2000 Main St, St Helena ☎ 707 963 7115, ⓦ beringer.com. Napa Valley's most famous piece of architecture, the Gothic "Rhine House", modelled on the ancestral Rhine Valley home of Jacob Beringer, graces the cover of many a wine magazine. Expansive lawns and a grand tasting room, heavy on dark wood, make for a regal experience. Tasting $25–125, tours $30–50. Daily 10am–5.30pm.

Chateau Montelena 1429 Tubbs Lane, 2 miles north of Calistoga ☎ 707 942 9105, ⓦ montelena .com. Smaller but highly rated winery, below Mount St Helena. The Cabernet Sauvignon is acquiring a fine reputation. Tasting $25–50, tours $40. Daily 9.30am–4pm.

Clos Pégase 1060 Dunaweal Lane, Calistoga ☎ 707 942 4981, ⓦ clospegase.com. A flamboyant upstart, this high-profile winery amalgamates fine wine and fine art, with a sculpture garden around buildings designed by architect Michael Graves. Tasting $20–30, including tour $50–60. Daily 10.30am–5pm.

Darioush 4240 Silverado Trail, northeast of Napa ☎ 707 257 2345, ⓦ darioush.com. Grandiose new winery modelled on Persepolis and constructed with stone blocks imported by the owner from his native Iran. Cabernet Sauvignon and Shiraz are the signature wines. Tasting $20–75, tours by appointment ($150–300). Daily 10.30am–5pm.

Domaine Chandon 1 California Drive, Yountville ☎ 707 944 2280, ⓦ chandon.com. Sparkling wines from this progeny of France's Moët & Chandon can challenge the authentic French champagnes. Vast and modern, this winery and gallery is popular with connoisseurs and features a top-notch restaurant. Tasting $20–25, tours $20–40. Daily 10am–5pm.

Envy Wines 1170 Tubbs Lane, north of Calistoga ☎ 707 942 4670, ⓦ envywines.com. This friendly newcomer, a co-creation of veteran wine-maker Nils Venge and longtime wine collector Mark Carter, first bottled its produce as recently as 2007 but has already received awards. Tasting $25 (waived with purchase over $45). Daily 10am–4.30pm.

★**Goosecross Cellars** 1119 State Lane, east of Yountville ☎ 707 944 1986, ⓦ goosecross.com. It's well worth taking time to locate this friendly family-run winery, tucked away off Yountville Cross Rd. Crush-time is fun and their Chardonnay especially good. Tasting by appointment $25. Daily 10am–4.30pm.

Mumm Napa Valley 8445 Silverado Trail, Rutherford ☎ 800 686 6272, ⓦ mummnapa.com. Opened in 1986 by G.H. Mumm, France's renowned champagne house, and Seagrams, the sparkling wines from this beautifully situated winery are good but superseded by sweeping views of the surrounding valleys. The tours are particularly engaging and fun, led by witty and informative guides. Tasting $20–50, tours $40. Daily 10am–4.45pm; tours at 10am, 11am, 1pm & 3pm.

Napa Wine Company 7830-40 St Helena Hwy, Oakville ☎ 800 848 9630, ⓦ trnapawineco.com. Modelled on the cooperative wineries of France, the Napa Wine Company offers 28 small-vineyard owners access to state-of-the-art crushing and fermentation machinery, and also acts as a sales outlet for their vintages. Their tasting room is one of the best – and certainly the broadest – in Wine Country. Tasting $25. Daily 10am–3.30pm.

Robert Mondavi 7801 St Helena Hwy, Oakville ☎ 707 226 1395, ⓦ robertmondaviwinery.com. Long the standard-bearer for Napa Valley wines ("Bob Red" and "Bob White" are house wines at many California restaurants), they have one of the most informative and least hard-sell tours. Tasting $5–30, tours $20–55. Daily 10am–5pm.

Silver Oak Cellars 915 Oakville Cross Rd, Oakville ☎ 800 273 8809, ⓦ silveroak.com. Lovers of Cabernet Sauvignon mustn't miss a stop at Silver Oak, the crème de la crème of the heady red that costs over $100 a bottle in some San Francisco restaurants. Tasting $25–50, tours from $20. Mon–Sat 9am–5pm, Sun 11am–5pm; tour times vary.

Stag's Leap Wine Cellars 5766 Silverado Trail, east of Yountville ☎ 866 422 7523, ⓦ cask23.com. The winery that put Napa Valley on the international map by beating a bottle of Château Lafitte-Rothschild at a Paris tasting in 1976. Still quite highly rated. Tasting $40, tours with tasting by appointment $60–95. Daily 10am–4.30pm.

Sterling Vineyards 1111 Dunaweal Lane, Calistoga ☎ 800 726 6136, ⓦ sterlingvineyards.com. Famous for the aerial tram ride that brings visitors up the 300ft knoll to the tasting room. The extravagant white mansion, modelled after a monastery on Mykonos, is Napa's most recognizable. Tasting wines on the View Terrace is a memorable experience. Aerial tram, tasting, self-guided tour $29–39. Mon–Fri 10.30am–5pm, Sat & Sun 10am–5pm.

9

Calistoga

Beyond St Helena, towards the far northern end of the valley, the wineries become prettier and the traffic a little thinner. At the very tip of the valley, nestling at the foot of Mount St Helena, **Calistoga** is easily the most enjoyable Napa community, featuring around twenty wineries and some fancy bistros. The town, though, is better known for its **mud baths** and **hot springs** (see box below) – and the mineral water that adorns every California supermarket shelf. Sam Brannan, a young Mormon entrepreneur who made a mint out of the Gold Rush, established a resort community here in 1860. In his groundbreaking speech he attempted to assert his desire to create the "Saratoga of California", modelled upon the Adirondack gem, but in the event got tongue-tied and coined the town's unique name.

Sharpsteen Museum and Sam Brannan Cottage

1113 Washington St • Daily 11am–4pm • Suggested donation $3 • ☎ 707 942 5911, ⓦ sharpsteenmuseum.org

Calistoga has one standard tourist attraction in the shape of the **Sharpsteen Museum and Sam Brannan Cottage**. Founded by long-serving Disney producer Ben Sharpsteen, the quaint little museum contains some of his personal effects, including his Oscar for the pearl-diving film *Ama Girls*, as well as a model of the original resort and lots of biographical material on Sam Brannan, the founder of Calistoga, plus a full-size re-creation of his cottage.

Old Faithful Geyser

1299 Tubbs Lane • Daily: summer 8.30am–6pm; rest of year 8.30am–5.30pm • $15 • ☎ 707 942 6463, ⓦ oldfaithfulgeyser.com

Two miles north of Calistoga, the **Old Faithful Geyser** spurts boiling water 60ft into the air at nine- to forty-minute intervals, depending on the time of year. The water source was discovered during oil-drilling here in the 1920s, when search equipment struck a force estimated to be up to a thousand pounds per square foot; the equipment was blown away and, despite heroic efforts to control it, the geyser has continued to go off like clockwork ever since. Northwest beyond the Tubbs Lane turning, Hwy-128 takes you up the ridge of the **Mayacamas**, a picturesque and steep drive that winds to the summit and spirals southwest towards Geyserville (see p.611).

CALISTOGA SPAS AND MUD BATHS

Calistoga's main attraction is the opportunity to soak in the soothing hot water that bubbles up here from deep in the earth. A multitude of **spas** and volcanic **mud baths**, together with a homely and health-conscious atmosphere, beckon city dwellers and tourists alike. Prices vary but if they are all out of your budget, ask a local resident to spray you down with their garden hose – although even that might cost a few bucks given Calistoga water's restorative reputation.

Calistoga Spa 1006 Washington St ☎ 866 822 5772, ⓦ calistogaspa.com. With four geothermally heated pools, a spa, fitness centre and huge outdoor patio, this is a great place to pamper yourself. Mineral bath $45, mud bath $65, massage treatments from $57.
Dr Wilkinson's Hot Springs 1507 Lincoln Ave ☎ 707 942 4102, ⓦ drwilkinson.com. Legendary health spa and hotel whose heated mineral water and volcanic ash tension-relieving treatments have been overseen by the same family for almost fifty years. Baths from $77, massages from $74.

Indian Springs 1712 Lincoln Ave ☎ 707 942 4913, ⓦ indianspringscalistoga.com. Fully renovated premises include an Olympic-size mineral pool, the leafy Buddha meditation pool and a complete panoply of treatments and massages from $140.
Mount View Spa 1457 Lincoln Ave ☎ 707 942 6877, ⓦ mountviewspa.com. This place can soothe you with a variety of combined herbal therapies; it also has mud treatments costing over $100, as well as cheaper and shorter bath and hydrotherapy sessions.

9

Villa Ca'Toga

3061 Myrtledale Rd • Tours May–Oct Sat at 11am • $30 • ☏ 707 942 3900, ⓦ catoga.com

Just south of Old Faithful, stylish Venetian artist Carlo Marchiori conducts weekly guided tours of his imaginatively decorated house, **Villa Ca'Toga**. The Palladian villa is full of delicate whimsy – one room is painted as if you are a bird in a cage, another is adorned with painted cows – and the grounds secrete mock ruined temples, a Buddhist corner, and a shell-encrusted cave. An idea of his art can be gleaned, and tours arranged, through his impressive gallery at 1206 Cedar St (Mon & Thurs–Sun 11am–6pm; free).

Petrified Forest

Five miles west of Calistoga • Daily: summer 9am–7pm; spring & fall 9am–6pm; winter 9am–5pm; guided tours 11am, 1pm & 3pm • $12 • ☏ 707 942 6667, ⓦ petrifiedforest.org

The **Petrified Forest** is a popular local tourist trap, but there's little worth stopping here for unless you're a geologist or really into hardened wood. After an entire redwood grove was toppled during an eruption of Mount St Helena some three million years ago, the forest here was petrified by the action of the silica-laden volcanic ash as it gradually seeped into the decomposing fibres of the uprooted trees. It costs the same whether you guide yourself along the main trail or take in the **Meadow Walk** as part of a ninety-minute guided tour.

Mount St Helena

Daily 8am–sunset • Free

The clearest sign of the local volcanic unrest is the massive conical mountain that marks the north end of the Napa Valley, **Mount St Helena**, some eight miles north of Calistoga. The 4343ft summit is worth a climb for its great **views** – on a very clear day you can see Point Reyes and the Pacific Coast to the west, San Francisco to the south, the towering Sierra Nevada to the east and impressive Mount Shasta to the north. It is, however, a long, steep climb (ten miles round-trip) and you need to set off early in the morning to enjoy it, well equipped with water and snacks.

Sonoma Valley

On looks alone, the crescent-shaped **SONOMA VALLEY** beats Napa Valley hands down. This smaller, altogether more rustic stretch of land curves between oak-covered mountain ranges from the small town of **Sonoma** a few miles north along Hwy-12 to the hamlet of **Glen Ellen** and **Jack London State Park**, ending at the booming dormitory community of **Santa Rosa**. Sonoma Valley's **wineries** are generally smaller and more casual than their Napa counterparts, even though the Sonoma Valley fathered the wine industry from which Napa derives its fame. Colonel Agostin Haraszthy first started planting grapes here in the 1850s, and his Buena Vista Winery in Sonoma still operates today.

ROBERT LOUIS STEVENSON'S HONEYMOON HIDEAWAY

Mount St Helena and most of the surrounding land is protected and preserved as the **Robert Louis Stevenson Park**, though the connection is fairly weak: Stevenson spent his honeymoon here in 1880 in a bunkhouse with Fanny Osborne, recuperating from tuberculosis and exploring the valley – a plaque marks the spot where his bunkhouse once stood. Little else about the park's winding roads and dense shrub growth evokes its former notoriety, though it's a pretty enough place to take a break from the wineries and have a picnic. In Stevenson's novel, **Silverado Squatters**, he describes the highlight of the honeymoon as the day he managed to taste eighteen of local wine baron Jacob Schram's champagnes in one sitting. Quite an extravagance, especially considering that Schramsberg champagne is held in such high esteem that Richard Nixon took a few bottles with him when he went to visit Chairman Mao.

SONOMA WINERIES

Nearly fifty **wineries** are scattered across the Sonoma Valley but there's a good concentration in a well-signposted group a mile east of Sonoma Plaza, down East Napa St. Some are within walking distance but often along quirky backroads, so take a winery **map** from the tourist office and follow the signs closely. Tasting fees tend to be a tad lower than the Napa Valley's.

Bartholomew Park Winery 1000 Vineyard Lane ☎707 935 9511, ⓦbartpark.com. This lavish Spanish Colonial building is surrounded by some great topiary in the gardens and extensive vineyards. The wines are relatively inexpensive vintages that appeal to the pocket and palate alike. There's a good little regional history museum, which also provides an introduction to local viticulture. Tasting $10–20. Daily 11am–4.30pm.

Benziger Family Winery 1883 London Ranch Rd, Glen Ellen ☎707 935 3000 or ☎888 490 2739, ⓦbenziger.com. Beautiful vineyard perched on the side of an extinct volcano next to Jack London State Park. There are tram tours through the fields every half-hour (11am–3.30pm; $25) with an emphasis on viticulture, or a self-guided tour introducing trellis techniques. Tasting $20–40. Daily 10am–5pm.

Buena Vista Winery 8000 Old Winery Rd ☎800 926 1266, ⓦbuenavistacarneros.com. The oldest and grandest of the wineries, founded in 1857, whose wine has re-established a good reputation after some slim years. The tasting room, a restored state historical landmark, features a small art gallery. Tasting and tours $20–100. Daily 10am–5pm.

Chateau St Jean 8555 Sonoma Hwy, Kenwood ☎800 543 7572, ⓦchateaustjean.com. Attractive estate with an overwhelming aroma of wine throughout the buildings. There's a quirky tower to climb from which you can admire the view of the surrounding countryside. Special tastings with set times must be booked in advance. Tasting $15–75. Daily 10am–5pm.

Gundlach-Bundschu 2000 Denmark St, Sonoma ☎707 939 3015, ⓦgunbun.com. Set back about a mile away from the main cluster, Gun-Bun, as it's known to locals, is highly regarded. The popular tour and Cave tasting runs at 2.30pm Mon & Thurs–Sun and must be reserved. The winery also hosts various theatrical, cinematic and musical events throughout the summer. Tasting $20, Cave tasting & tour $40. Daily: June–Oct 11am–5.30pm; Nov–May 11am–4.30pm.

Mayo Family Winery 13101 Arnold Drive, Glen Ellen ☎707 938 9401, ⓦmayofamilywinery.com. Relatively new winery with a cosy feel and a friendly welcome, matching the small-time production of fewer than five thousand cases annually. It has another tasting room in Kenwood. Tasting $10–15. Daily 10.30am–6.30pm.

★**Ravenswood** 18701 Gehricke Rd, Sonoma ☎707 933 2332, ⓦravenswood-wine.com. Noted for their "gutsy, unapologetic" Zinfandel and advertising a "no wimpy" approach to the wine business, the staff at this unpretentious winery are particularly friendly and easy-going. Well known to locals for its summer barbecues. $18–50, tour $25. Daily 10.30am–4.30pm, tours at 10.30am.

Sebastiani Vineyards & Winery 389 4th St E, Sonoma ☎800 888 5532, ⓦsebastiani.com. One of California's oldest family wineries, only four blocks from central Sonoma, it boasts a smart hospitality centre, while the rest of the estate is slowly being returned to its original appearance. There's another tasting room on the central square at 103 W Napa St (☎707 933 3291). Tasting $20–50, tours $5. Daily 10am–5pm; historical tours at 11am.

Brief history

The area is known as the **"Valley of the Moon"**, a label that's mined by tour operators for its connection to former resident Jack London, whose book of the same name retold a Native American legend about how, as you move through the valley, the moon seems to rise several times from behind the various peaks. The area has long been a favourite with visitors: Spain, England, Russia and Mexico have all raised their flags in Sonoma, proclaiming it their own. The US took over in 1846 during the Bear Flag Revolt against Mexico in Sonoma's central plaza and annexed all of California.

Sonoma

Behind a layer of somewhat touristy stores and restaurants, **Sonoma** retains a good deal of its Spanish and Mexican architecture. There's more to Sonoma than historic buildings, however, and relaxing cafés, great restaurants, rare-book stores and a 1930s-era movie house ring the main plaza, making Sonoma a nice town to come

9

back to after a day in the vineyards. The town's charm emanates from the grassy square that acts as downtown's centrepiece, where visitors and locals alike linger over newspapers or lazy picnics. This is indicative of the town's welcoming and relaxed feel, although as a popular retirement spot with a median age of about fifty, it's not exactly bubbling with action.

Sonoma State Historic Park

Daily 10am–5pm • $3 combined entry to all sites • ☎ 707 935 6832, ⓦ sonomaparks.org

A number of historic buildings and relics stand in the sprawling **Sonoma State Historic Park**. The restored **Mission San Francisco Solano de Sonoma** was the last and northernmost of the California missions, established by nervous Mexican rulers fearful of expansionist Russian fur-traders. Half a mile west stands the **General Vallejo Home**, the leader's ornate former residence, dominated by decorated, filigreed eaves and slender, Gothic Revival arched windows. The chalet-style storehouse next door has been turned into a **museum** of artefacts from the general's reign.

Jack London State Historic Park

2400 London Ranch Rd • Daily 9.30am–5pm • $10/car • London's Cottage Daily noon–4pm • $4 • ☎ 707 938 5216, ⓦ jacklondonpark.com

Continuing north on Hwy-12, beautiful winding roads lead to the cosy hamlet of **Glen Ellen**, five miles from Sonoma, and more interestingly, **Jack London State Historic Park**. Half a mile up London Ranch Road past the Benziger Family winery, the state park sits on the 140 acres of ranchland the famed author of *The Call of the Wild* owned with his wife Charmian. A half-mile walk from the House of Happy Walls (see opposite) through the woods leads to the ruins of the **Wolf House**, which was to be the London ancestral home: "My house will be standing, act of God permitting, for a thousand years", wrote the author. But in 1913, a month before they were to move in, the house burned to the ground, sparing only the boulder frame. Mounted blueprints point out the splendour that was to be: the mansion contained a manuscript room, sleeping tower, gun room and indoor reflecting pool. Nearby lies London's final resting place – a red boulder from the house's ruins under which his wife sprinkled his ashes. Another trail near the House of Happy Walls (see opposite) leads past a picnic ground to **London's Cottage**, where he had died.

THE BEAR FLAG REVOLT

Sonoma Plaza was the site of the **Bear Flag Revolt**, the 1846 event that propelled California into independence from Mexico and then statehood. In this much-romanticized episode, American settlers in the region, who had long lived in uneasy peace under the Spanish and, later, Mexican rulers, were threatened with expulsion from California along with all other non-Mexican immigrants. In response, a band of thirty armed settlers – including the infamous John Fremont and Kit Carson – descended upon the disused and unguarded presidio at Sonoma, taking the retired and much-respected commander, Colonel Mariano Guadalupe Vallejo, as their prisoner. Ironically, Vallejo had long advocated the American annexation of California and supported the aims of his rebel captors, but he was nonetheless bundled off to Sutter's Fort in Sacramento and held there while the militant settlers declared California an independent republic.

The **Bear Flag**, which served as the model for the current state flag, was fashioned from a "feminine undergarment and muslin petticoat" and painted with a grizzly bear and single star. Raised on Sonoma Plaza, where a small plaque marks the spot today, the Bear Flag flew over the Republic of California for a short time. Three weeks later, the US declared war on Mexico and, without firing a shot, took possession of the entire Pacific Coast.

While far from a frontier town now, Sonoma once had a much wilder side and in fact gave the English language a slang word for prostitutes. Not long after the Bear Flag revolt, General Lee Hooker arrived, bringing along a group of ladies employed to cheer up the troops. The ladies soon became known as "Hooker's girls", and then simply "hookers".

House of Happy Walls
Just off the parking lot • Daily 10am–5pm • Free

The **House of Happy Walls** is a jewel of a London museum, housing an interesting collection of souvenirs the writer picked up travelling the globe. Manuscripts, rejection letters (more than six hundred before he was published for the first time), and the note explaining his and Charmian's resignation from the Socialist Party are among the exhibits.

Santa Rosa
Sixty miles due north of San Francisco on US-101 and about twenty miles from Sonoma on Hwy-12, **Santa Rosa**, the largest town in Sonoma County, sits at the top end of the valley and is more or less the hub of this part of the Wine Country. It's a very different world from the indulgence of other Wine Country towns, however; much of it is given over to shopping centres and strip malls. In an attempt to form a central pedestrian-only hub, **Historic Railroad Square** – a row of red-brick-façade boutiques – was created, but it lacks genuine character. With property prices higher than ever in the Bay Area, Santa Rosa is exploding with growth, making it both a dormitory community for San Francisco and site of the Wine Country's cheapest accommodation, with major chains located around town. It also has a decent selection of restaurants and bars.

Luther Burbank Home and Gardens
204 Santa Rosa Ave • Gardens daily 8am–dusk • Free • **Tours** April–Oct Tues–Sun every 30min 10am–3.30pm • $10 • ☎707 524 5445, ⓦ lutherburbank.org

You can kill an hour or two at the **Luther Burbank Home and Gardens**, where California's best-known horticulturist lived; the splendid gardens showcase some of his most unusual hybrids. The tour also includes his lavish home, with all its original furnishings, as well as the impressive greenhouse.

Charles M. Schulz Museum
2301 Hardies Lane • Mon–Fri 11am–5pm, Sat & Sun 10am–5pm, closed Tues in winter • $12 • ☎707 579 4452, ⓦ schulzmuseum.org • **Arena**: public skating times vary • $9.50, under-11s $7.50 • ☎707 546 7147, ⓦ snoopyshomeice.com

In Santa Rosa's northern suburbs, the **Charles M. Schulz Museum** is a paean to all things *Peanuts* in dedication to the famous cartoon's creator, Charles Schulz. There is the predictable barrage of memorabilia, among more interesting exhibits on the creative process. Just across the road from the museum, the **Redwood Empire Ice Arena**, better known as **Snoopy's Home Ice**, was built by Charles Schulz as a gift to the community.

Children's Museum of Sonoma County
1835 W Steele Lane • Mon & Wed–Sat 9am–4pm, Sun 11am–4pm • $10 • ☎707 546 4069, ⓦ cmosc.org

On the same block as the Charles M. Schulz museum, another great place to visit if you are travelling with young kids is the new **Children's Museum of Sonoma County**. This privately funded initiative has provided a wonderful space for kids under the age of 10 to engage in various creative and engaging activities from art to mini scientific experiments.

Safari West
3115 Porter Creek Rd, 5 miles northeast of Santa Rosa • Two to five tours daily, depending on the time of year • $83–115 • ☎707 579 2551, ⓦ safariwest.com

One enterprise few people would expect to find tucked away in the Wine Country is a full-blown **wildlife refuge**, yet spreading over four hundred acres of the pristine hills between the two valleys is **Safari West**. Set up in 1989 by Peter Lang, son of *Daktari* producer Otto, the refuge runs breeding programmes for hundreds of rare mammal and bird species. Three-hour African-style **jeep tours** take you through vast open compounds of herd animals, and you can wander at leisure past large cages of cheetah and primates or the leafy aviary, while expert guides supply detailed background on the inhabitants. You can even feed the giraffe, if you're lucky, or stay in genuine African luxury tents (see p.604).

9

ARRIVAL AND GETTING AROUND   THE WINE COUNTRY

BY CAR
If you avoid the rush-hour traffic, it's about an hour's drive from San Francisco to Napa or Sonoma. Good highways ring the region, and a loop of the two valleys is conceivable in a day or so. Consider working against the flow of traffic by taking in Sonoma and Glen Ellen first, before crossing the Mayacamas by way of Santa Rosa and dropping into Calistoga, St Helena and Napa.

BY BUS
Public buses There are limited public bus options from Golden Gate Transit (☎707 541 2000, ⓦ goldengate .org), Greyhound, Sonoma County Transit (☎707 576 7433 or ☎800 345 7433, ⓦ sctransit.com), Napa Valley's Vine bus system (Mon–Sat; ☎707 251 2800 or ☎800 696 6443, ⓦ ridethevine.com) and the Mendocino Transit Authority (☎707 462 1422 or ☎800 696 4682, ⓦ mendocinotransit .org). There are also direct connections to Napa from both San Francisco and Oakland airports with the Evans Airporter Shuttle (6–9 daily; 1hr 30min; $40 one-way; ☎707 255 1559, ⓦ evanstransportation.com).

Tours Another option for the car-less is to sign up for a guided bus tour from San Francisco with Gray Line (daily 9am; 8hr; $76; ☎800 472 9546, ⓦ grayline.com) or Blue and Gold (daily 9am; 8hr; $83; ☎415 773 1188, ⓦ blueandgoldfleet.com).

Destinations Santa Rosa to: Arcata (2 daily; 5hr 10min); Eureka (2 daily; 5hr 10min); San Francisco (hourly; 2hr–2hr 15min).

Napa to: Calistoga (every 30min–1hr; 1hr 20min); El Cerrito BART (12 daily; 1hr); Sonoma (6 daily; 40min); St Helena (every 30min–1hr; 55min); Yountville (every 30min–1hr; 30min).

Sonoma to: Napa (6 daily; 30min); Santa Rosa (hourly; 45min).

BY TRAIN
The 3hr Wine Train ($99–246; ☎707 253 2111 or ☎800 427 4124, ⓦ winetrain.com) runs several times daily from Napa's station at 1275 McKinstry St, east of downtown. The ten-car train of restored 1950s Pullman cars chugs up the valley to St Helena and back, taking in a couple of wineries and offering various dining options.

BY BIKE
If you don't want to drive all day, cycling is a great way to get around. You can rent a bike locally for around $25–75/day and $125–250/week. Most local firms organize tours, providing bikes, helmets, food and vans in case you get worn out. Both valleys are generally flat and the smaller parallel routes likely to be less clogged with traffic: try the Silverado Trail in Napa Valley and lovely Arnold Drive in Sonoma Valley. For the more athletically inclined, there's the Oakville Grade between Oakville in the Napa Valley and Glen Ellen in the Sonoma Valley, which has challenged the world's finest riders. Check with the Santa Rosa Cycling Club (☎707 544 4803, ⓦ srcc.com) for itineraries.

RENTAL COMPANIES
Getaway Bike Shop 2228 North Point Pkwy, Santa Rosa (☎800 499 2453, ⓦ getawayadventures.com).
Napa Valley Bike Tours 3259 California Blvd, Napa or 6500 Washington St, Yountville (☎707 251 8687, ⓦ napavalleybiketours.com).
St Helena Cyclery 1156 Main St, St Helena (☎707 963 7736, ⓦ sthelenacyclery.com).
Sonoma Valley Cyclery 20091 Broadway, Sonoma (☎707 935 3377, ⓦ sonomacyclery.com).

INFORMATION

Not surprisingly for such a tourist-dependent area, the Wine Country has a well-developed network of tourist information outlets, though the rivalry between the two valleys makes it next to impossible to find out anything about Sonoma when you're in Napa, and vice versa. The smaller towns usually have a tourist office, too.

Napa Valley Visitors Bureau 1310 Napa Town Center off 1st St in downtown Napa (daily 9am–5pm; ☎707 226 7459, ⓦ napavalley.com).
Sonoma Valley Visitors Bureau 453 1st St E on Sonoma Plaza (Mon–Sat 9am–5pm, Sun 10am–5pm;

☎707 996 1090, ⓦ sonomavalley.com).
Visit Santa Rosa 9 4th St (daily 9am–5pm; ☎707 577 8674 or ☎800 404 7673, ⓦ visitsantarosa.com), by Railroad Square.

ACCOMMODATION

Pricey hotels and bed-and-breakfast inns provide the bulk of the area's accommodation options, although there are some inexpensive motels in the more urban areas. During summer weekends, places are at a premium and prices can rise as much as fifty percent, so call ahead; from November to March, on the other hand, rates drop considerably, often by as much as half. Among the many accommodation services are Napa Valley Reservations (☎707 252 1985, ⓦ napavalleyreservations .com) and the online-only Sonoma Valley B&B Inns & Vacation Rentals (ⓦ sonomabb.com).

9

A BIRD'S-EYE VIEW OF THE WINE COUNTRY

The most exciting way to see the region is on one of the widely touted **hot-air balloon rides**. These usually lift off at dawn and last sixty to ninety magical minutes, winding up with a champagne brunch. The most established of the operators is Napa Valley Balloons (☎707 944 0228 or ☎800 253 2224, ☒napavalleyballoons.com), who fly out of Yountville. Other options in Napa include the slightly cheaper Balloons Above the Valley (☎707 253 2222 or ☎800 464 6824, ☒balloonrides.com). The crunch comes when you realize the price – at least $200 a head whichever company you use – but it really is worth every cent. Make reservations a week in advance, especially in summer, though with the increasing number of balloon companies, same-day drop-bys are a possibility.

If it's thrills you're looking for, consider taking to the air in a World War II propeller **biplane**. Vintage Aircraft Company, 23982 Arnold Drive, Sonoma (☎707 938 2444, ☒vintageaircraft .com), operates one- or two-person flights that take in both valleys. The basic choice is between the twenty-minute Scenic Flight ($175) and various forty-minute Explorer Flights ($295): add $50 to either for the extra thrill of some aerobatics.

NAPA VALLEY
NAPA

★**Candlelight Inn** 1045 Easum Drive ☎707 257 3717, ☒candlelightinn.com. Spacious mock-Tudor mansion with a pool in its lovely grounds and a luxurious interior, featuring rooms of varying sizes, all beautifully decorated. Friendly and informal atmosphere, with free drinks and snacks. **$189**

Napa Discovery Inn 500 Silverado Trail ☎707 253 0892, ☒napadiscoveryinn.com. This small, motel-style place has adequately furnished modern rooms and is well placed a short drive south of Napa and the Silverado Trail wineries. **$85**

YOUNTVILLE

Oleander House 7433 St Helena Hwy (Hwy-29) ☎707 944 8315, ☒oleander.com. Cosy and friendly B&B, with tastefully and simply furnished rooms, in a handy mid-valley location. Quiet enough despite being on the main road and not too far from restaurants and shops. Last-minute specials available. **$219**

Vintage Inn 6541 Washington St ☎707 944 1112 or ☎800 351 1133, ☒vintageinn.com. Huge luxury rooms, all with fireplaces, in a modern hotel complex, plus swimming pool and free bike rental. Handy for Yountville's many fine restaurants but vastly overpriced. **$445**

ST HELENA

El Bonita Motel 195 Main St ☎707 963 3216 or ☎800 541 3284, ☒elbonita.com. Old roadside motel done up to hotel standard in Art Deco style, with a pool and hot tub. Surrounded by a 2.5-acre garden, the rooms here come with microwaves and fridges. **$179**

Inn St Helena 1515 Main St ☎707 963 3003, ☒innsthelena.com. Luxury accommodation in the 1872 house once inhabited by Ambrose Bierce, a nineteenth-century author. Gourmet breakfast and evening wine with snacks included. **$259**

Wine Country Inn 1152 Lodi Lane ☎707 963 7077 or ☎888 465 4608, ☒winecountryinn.com. Set in stunning grounds on the hills above town, this fine B&B comprises of several buildings with luxury rooms of varying sizes, plus whole cottages. Pool and outdoor spa. **$369**

CALISTOGA

★**Calistoga Inn** 1250 Lincoln Ave ☎707 942 4101, ☒calistogainn.com. Relaxing, excellent-value rooms, with one bed and shared bathrooms, in a landmark building with its own lively restaurant and microbrewery right on the main street. There's an independent cottage on the ground floor. **$129**

Dr Wilkinson's Hot Springs 1507 Lincoln Ave ☎707 942 4102, ☒drwilkinson.com. Legendary health spa and hotel downtown. Choose from a variety of spacious, well-lit rooms with sparse furnishings, facing the courtyard or pool patio. **$180**

Luxe Calistoga 1139 Lincoln Ave ☎707 942 9797, ☒luxecalistoga.com. Luxuriously renovated old 1873 house with a wraparound porch, complete with five beautifully decorated, lavishly furnished and welcoming rooms, all with fireplaces. **$309**

SONOMA VALLEY
SONOMA

Andrea's Hidden Cottage 138 E Spain St ☎707 690 1034, ☒andreashiddencottage.net. Cute wooden cottage with a well-equipped kitchenette and simple but pleasant decor. It has a homely feel and is only a block off Sonoma Plaza. **$219**

★**An Inn 2 Remember** 171 W Spain St ☎707 938 2909, ☒aninn2remember.com. This wonderful B&B features elegantly restored rooms, an amazing breakfast and free bike rental, yet remains cheaper than many others. Some rooms offer a fireplace, private hot tub and patio. **$175**

9

Cottage Inn & Spa 302 1st St E ☎707 996 0719 or ☎800 944 1490, ⓦcottageinnandspa.com. A calm, beautifully decorated downtown B&B, with hot tub and a relaxing courtyard. One suite has a full kitchen, another a private patio. $180

Swiss Hotel 18 W Spain St ☎707 938 2884, ⓦswiss hotelsonoma.com. A 70-year-old landmark building situated right on the plaza, with a fine restaurant. The five cramped rooms have four-poster queen-size beds and views of either the garden patio or the plaza. $160

GLEN ELLEN AND KENWOOD

★**Gaige House Inn** 13540 Arnold Drive, Glen Ellen ☎707 935 0237 or ☎800 935 0237, ⓦgaige.com. Beautifully restored Queen Anne farmhouse in a quiet country setting. The splendid Zen suites boast individual Japanese gardens and oval granite tubs. No under-18s. $275

Jack London Lodge 13740 Arnold Drive, Glen Ellen ☎707 938 8510, ⓦjacklondonlodge.com. Modern motel near Jack London State Park, with comfy rooms and a pool. The friendly saloon is a popular local hangout. $134

Kenwood Inn & Spa 10400 Sonoma Hwy, Kenwood ☎707 833 1293 or ☎800 353 6966, ⓦkenwoodinn .com. Deluxe, beautiful and secluded Italian-villa-style B&B with a fireplace in all suites, some of which reach over $1000 in season. $475

Sugarloaf Ridge State Park 2605 Adobe Canyon Rd, 2 miles east of Kenwood ☎800 444 7275, ⓦreserveamerica.com. Set in a lovely wooded park towards the top of the valley, there is usually camping space except during summer, when you should make reservations in advance. Pitches $35

SANTA ROSA AND AROUND

Astro Motel 323 Santa Rosa Ave ☎707 545 8555, ⓦsterba.com/astro. No-frills motel, with compact but perfectly adequate rooms – some of the cheapest in the Wine Country – and conveniently located too. $70

Flamingo Resort Hotel & Spa 2777 4th St ☎707 545 8530, ⓦflamingoresort.com. One of the original 1950s resort hotels, with multiple wings radiating out from the huge swimming pool, it has been fully upgraded so that the rooms have all mod cons. $152

Hotel La Rose 308 Wilson St ☎707 579 3200 or ☎800 527 6738, ⓦhotellarose.com. Restored lodging in a century-old building on Railroad Square. Rooms are clean and nicely furnished, plus there's a decent bar. $149

★**Safari West** 3115 Porter Creek Rd, 5 miles northeast of Santa Rosa ☎707 579 2551, ⓦsafariwest.com. Luxury tents of varying sizes, imported from Africa to complete the safari experience (see p.601), hung on stilted wooden decks with views of the animals. $325

Spring Lake Regional Park Campground 5585 Newanga Ave ☎707 565 2267, ⓦparks.sonomacounty .ca.gov. Pitches at this spacious campground by a suburban lake must be reserved at least ten days in advance. There are also some cabins. May–Sept daily; Oct–April Sat & Sun. Pitches $30, cabins $79

EATING AND DRINKING

The Napa Valley has more than its fair share of excellent **fine dining** restaurants, many offering top California cuisine. The Sonoma Valley also has many fancy restaurants, particularly around the town of Sonoma and ritzy Glen Ellen. Humbler fare is available, too, especially cheap **Mexican food**. The consistent wine consumption during the day means nightlife is generally subdued but a few decent **bars** are dotted along both valleys.

NAPA VALLEY

NAPA

Cole's Chop House 1122 Main St ☎707 224 6328, ⓦcoleschophouse.com. This is the place to come for huge chunks of well-prepared red meat from $32. Very spacious inside and top service but the atmosphere is rather stilted. Mon–Thurs & Sun 5–9pm, Fri & Sat 5–10pm.

★**Downtown Joe's** 902 Main St ☎707 258 2337, ⓦdowntownjoes.com. One of Napa's most popular and lively spots for sandwiches, ribs and pasta for $10–25, with outdoor dining by the river and beer such as Tanric IPA brewed on the premises. The only place in town open till after midnight, with live music some nights. Daily 8.30am–1am.

Zuzu 829 Main St ☎707 224 8555, ⓦzuzunapa.com. Not the place to come if you're ravenous, as portions are modest in size for $5–15, but this popular tapas bar offers tasty fare such as *paella del día* and a good wine list in its trendy interior. Mon–Thurs 11.30am–2.30pm & 4.30–10pm, Fri 11.30am–2.30pm & 4.30–11pm, Sat 4.30–11pm, Sun 4.30–10pm.

YOUNTVILLE

Bouchon 6534 Washington St ☎707 944 8037, ⓦthomaskeller.com. Parisian chic and haute cuisine abound in this classy establishment by world-famous chef Thomas Keller, where mains are around $27–59, although there are cheaper brunch and late-night specials. Daily 11.30am–12.30am.

★**The French Laundry** 6640 Washington St ☎707 944 2380, ⓦfrenchlaundry.com. The ultimate place for a splurge. Another Thomas Keller establishment creates a nine-course tasting menu daily for a princely $310 each. Dress code. Daily: 11am–12.30pm & 5.30–9.15pm.

Mustards Grill 7399 St Helena (Hwy-29) ☎707 944 2424, ⓦmustardsgrill.com. Huge range of starters and main dishes like "famous Mongolian pork chop", which costs $33. Also does a range of gourmet sandwiches for around $12. Mon–Thurs 11.30am–9pm, Fri 11.30am–10pm, Sat 11am–10pm, Sun 11am–9pm.

ST HELENA

Tra Vigne 1016 Main St ☎707 963 4444, ⓦpizzeriatravigne.com. Now shifted to a new location, the gourmet pizzas for around $20 are the speciality here, although there are also great pasta dishes and flatbreads. Daily 11.30am–9pm.

★**Wine Spectator Greystone Restaurant** 2555 Main St ☎707 967 1010, ⓦciarestaurantgroup.com. Renowned Culinary Institute of America restaurant, where trainees concoct delicious dinners such as roast pork and wild halibut for $20–35. There's also a top-notch bakery. Tues–Sat 11.30am–2pm & 5.30–8.30pm.

CALISTOGA

All Seasons Bistro 1400 Lincoln Ave ☎707 942 9111, ⓦallseasonsnapavalley.net. Exquisite main courses such as crispy skin chicken breast with Dijon-truffle jus or Bohemian pheasant cost $24–30 in this upscale but relaxed bistro. Tues–Sun 11am–3pm & 5.30–10pm.

★**Brannan's Grill** 1374 Lincoln Ave ☎707 942 2233, ⓦbrannanscalistoga.com. Dishes like pan-seared duck breast and Alaskan halibut, plus a wonderful wooden interior, make this high-profile restaurant worth a visit. Main courses $25–40. Mon–Thurs & Sun 11.30am–9pm, Fri & Sat 11.30am–10pm.

Café Sarafornia 1413 Lincoln Ave ☎707 942 0555, ⓦcafesarafornia.com. Famous for delicious and enormous breakfasts and filling sandwiches, burgers and pasta for lunch. Expect queues around the block at weekends. All items under $15, many under $10. Daily 7.30am–2.30pm.

Puerto Vallerta 1473 Lincoln Ave ☎707 942 6563. Heaps of tasty and genuine Mexican grub can be consumed for under $10 in the shady courtyard of this simple taqueria, tucked in beside the Cal-Mart supermarket. Daily 8am–10pm.

Solbar 755 Silverado Trail ☎877 684 6146, ⓦsolage.aubergeresorts.com. Creative cuisine by chef Brandon Sharp in this resort restaurant a little out of town, where you can enjoy the likes of grilled zabuton of Snake River farm beef for $38 or take breakfast on the sunny patio. Daily 8am–9.30pm.

SONOMA VALLEY

SONOMA

★**The Girl & The Fig** 110 W Spain St ☎707 938 3634, ⓦthegirlandthefig.com. This renowned restaurant offers French dinners such as wild flounder *moulière* for $27, as well

as unusual appetizers and cheeses. Mon–Thurs 11.30am–10pm, Fri & Sat 8am–11pm, Sun 10am–10pm.

Hopmonk Tavern 691 Broadway ☎707 935 9100, ⓦhopmonk.com. Great place if you're aching for some quality ale in Wine Country. The brews, such as Rough Pumpkin Ale, go nicely with tasty bar grub for $12–17. Regular live music. Mon–Thurs & Sun 11.30am–9pm, Fri & Sat 11.30am–10pm.

La Casa 121 E Spain St ☎707 996 3406, ⓦlacasarestaurants.com. Friendly and festive Mexican restaurant just across from the Sonoma Mission, where house specialities – from standard burritos to Mexican Flag enchiladas – cost $10–20. There's a sunny outdoor patio too. Mon–Thurs & Sun 11.30am–9pm, Fri & Sat 11.30am–9.30pm.

Sunflower Café 421 W 1st St ☎707 996 6645, ⓦsonomasunflower.com. Located in a 150-year-old adobe, this trendy spot craftily combines elements of diner, espresso bar and wine bar. Most food items such as the smoked duck sandwich are $11–15. Café daily 7am–4pm; wine bar Fri–Sun 11.30am–4pm.

GLEN ELLEN AND KENWOOD

Café Citti 9049 Sonoma Hwy, Kenwood ☎707 833 2690, ⓦcafecitti.com. Small, inexpensive trattoria with great Italian food and an intimate, yet casual atmosphere. Lunchtime sandwiches and lots of salads and "create your own pasta" options anytime for $10–15. Mon–Thurs & Sun 11am–3.30pm & 5–8.30pm, Fri & Sat 11am–3.30pm & 5–9pm.

Glen Ellen Inn 13670 Arnold Drive, Glen Ellen ☎707 996 6409, ⓦglenelleninn.com. Husband-and-wife team (not called Glen and Ellen) cook and serve California-style gourmet dishes, such as mussels and garlic fries ($22.95), in a small, romantic dining room. Mon, Tues & Thurs–Sun 11.30am–9pm, Wed 5–8.30pm.

★**Yeti Restaurant** 14301 Arnold Drive, Glen Ellen ☎707 996 9930, ⓦyeticuisine.com. Sweet and welcoming Indian/Nepalese restaurant with a nice riverside wooden deck. Dishes such as chicken *saag* and lamb shank curry are in the $15–23 range. Daily 11.30am–3pm & 5–9.30pm.

SANTA ROSA

★**Bird & The Bottle** 1055 4th St ☎707 568 4000, ⓦbirdandthebottle.com. New Asian fusion restaurant with a modern interior and pleasant outdoor deck. The idea is to share small yet substantial plates like smoked black cod with horseradish, Korean barbecued half chicken and thrice-fried potatoes, ranging $6–26. Mon–Thurs & Sun 11.30am–9.30pm, Fri & Sat 11.30am–10pm.

Gary Chu's 611 5th St ☎707 526 5840, ⓦgarychus.com. Large helpings of high-quality Chinese food such as Szechuan lamb and prawns in lobster sauce for $11–14.

9

Tues–Fri 11.30am–3pm & 4–9.30pm, Sat 11.30am–10pm, Sun 11.30am–9pm. **Third Street Aleworks** 610 3rd St ☎707 523 3060, ⊛ thirdstreetaleworks.com. Frequent live music and hearty American grub like burgers and pizza for $12–15, washed down with microbrewed beer, are the order of the day at this lively joint. Mon–Thurs & Sun 11.30am–midnight, Fri & Sat 11.30am–1am.

The Sonoma coast

Hwy-1 twists and winds along the edge of the **SONOMA COAST** through persistent fog that, once burned off by the sun, reveals oyster beds, seal breeding grounds and twenty-foot-high rhododendrons. A spectacular introduction to the northern coast, Sonoma County's western rim is never short on visitors due to its proximity to San Francisco. But tourist activity is only intense at the height of summer, leaving these north-coast villages all but asleep for most of the year. One blessing that has slowed development, as wealthy San Franciscans continually cast their eyes towards the north for potential second-home sites, is the California Coastal Commission's policy of maintaining beach access for all. This keeps the architects at bay, making the Sonoma coast one of the few remaining undeveloped coastal areas in California; the southern third of the coast is almost entirely state beach.

Bodega Bay and around

Bodega Bay, about 65 miles north of San Francisco, is the first Sonoma County village you reach on Hwy-1. Pomo and Miwok tribes populated the area peacefully for centuries, until Captain Lt Juan Francisco de la Bodega y Quadra Mollineda anchored his ship in the bay and "discovered" it in 1775. Hitchcock filmed the waterside scenes for *The Birds* here; an unsettling number of his cast's descendants can still be found squawking down by the harbour. Not so long ago, a depleted fishing industry, a couple of restaurants and some isolated seaside cottages were all there was to Bodega Bay, but since San Franciscans got wind of its appeal, holiday homes and modern retail developments now crowd the waterside. There are **hiking** and **horseriding** trails around the dunes behind the beach, although they get crowded in summer.

North of Bodega Bay, the coastline coarsens and the trails become more dramatic. It's a wonderful stretch to hike, although the shale formations are often unstable and you must stick to the trails, which are actually quite demanding. Of Sonoma's thirteen miles of beaches, the finest are surfer-friendly **Salmon Creek Beach**, a couple of miles north of Bodega Bay and site of the park headquarters, and **Goat Rock Beach**, at the top of the coast. The latter offers the chance to get close to harbour seals.

Jenner

The tiny seaside village of **Jenner**, which marks the turn-off for the Russian River Valley, is a small, friendly place. **Russian River** joins the ocean in Jenner and a massive sand spit at its mouth provides a breeding ground for harbour seals from March to June.

Fort Ross State Historic Park

Daily: park sunrise–sunset; Fort Compound 10am–4.30pm • $8/car • ☎707 847 3286, ⊛ fortross.org

North of Jenner, the population evaporates and Hwy-1 turns into a slalom course of hairpin bends and steep inclines for twelve miles as far as **Fort Ross State Historic Park**, which houses the **Fort Compound**. At the start of the nineteenth century, San Francisco was still the northernmost limit of Spanish occupation in Alta California and from 1812 to 1841 Russian fur traders quietly settled this part of the coast, clubbing the California sea otter almost to extinction, building a fort to use as a trading outpost and growing crops for the Russian stations in Alaska. Officially they posed no territorial claims but, by the time the Spanish had gauged the extent of the settlement, the fort was heavily armed and vigilantly manned with a view to continued eastward expansion. The Russians traded here for thirty years until over-hunting and the failure of their shipbuilding efforts led them to pull out of the region.

Among the empty bunkers and storage halls, the most interesting buildings are the Russian Orthodox **chapel** and the **commandant's house**, with its fine library and wine cellar. At the entrance, a potting shed, which labours under the delusion that it's a **museum**, provides cursory details on the history of the fort, with a few maps and diagrams.

Gerstle Cove

Daily sunrise–sunset • $8/car • ☎ 707 847 3221, ⓦ parks.ca.gov

One of Sonoma County's most accessible and beautiful beaches, part of Salt Point State Park, is at **Gerstle Cove**, which includes a paved, wheelchair-accessible path from the cove to Salt Point, past kelp beds, wave-battered rocks and lounging harbour seals. The park's rainfall and habitat make mushrooms thrive, and Gerstle Cove is a popular place for **mushroom gatherers** to park their cars and begin foraging, which the park permits. Ask the ranger for the sheet of guidelines when you enter the parking lot.

Kruse Rhododendron State Natural Reserve

Just north of Salt Point and a little inland • Sunrise–sunset • Free • ☎ 707 847 3221, ⓦ parks.ca.gov

The **Kruse Rhododendron State Natural Reserve** is a sanctuary for 20ft-high rhododendrons, indigenous to this part of the coast and in bloom from April to June. The beaches on this last stretch of the Sonoma coastline are usually deserted, save for a few abalone fishermen, driftwood and the seal pups who rest here. They're good for hiking and beachcombing but stick to the trails. From here you pass tiny and inconsequential Stewart's Point before entering the Mendocino coast (see p.614).

ARRIVAL AND DEPARTURE   THE SONOMA COAST

By bus The only bus route that serves the Sonoma Coast is the once-daily MTA (see p.618) #95, which goes from Sonoma to Bodega Bay and then north via Jenner, Fort Ross and on into Mendocino County.

INFORMATION AND ACTIVITIES

Sonoma Coast Visitor Center 850 Hwy-1, Bodega Bay (Mon–Thurs 10am–6pm, Fri & Sat 10am–8pm, Sun 10am–7pm; ☎ 707 875 3866, ⓦ bodegabay.com).
Bodega Bay Surf Shack Pelican Plaza, 1400 Hwy-1 ☎ 707 875 3944, ⓦ bodegabaysurf.com. Rents out kayaks ($45/4hr) and surfing equipment ($16.95/day).

Chanslor Guest Ranch 2660 Hwy-1 ☎ 707 875 2721, ⓦ chanslorranch.com. For horseriding, this ranch offers a selection of rides, which range from a 35min wetlands jaunt ($30–50 per person) to 90min rides along Salmon Creek ($75–100).

ACCOMMODATION

BODEGA BAY
Bodega Coast Inn 521 Hwy-1 ☎ 707 875 2217, ⓦ bodegacoastinn.com. An extremely comfortable waterfront inn whose beautifully refurbished rooms come with fireplaces. **$179**
Bodega Dunes Campground Sonoma Coast State Park, 2 miles north of Bodega Bay on Hwy-1 ☎ 800 444 7275, ⓦ reserveamerica.com. At the base of a windy peninsula known as Bodega Head, this campground has picturesque sites and good shared facilities. Pitches **$35**
Bodega Harbor Inn 1345 Bodega Ave ☎ 707 875 3594,

ⓦ bodegaharborinn.com. The best-value inn in town, though predictably the cheapest rooms are those without ocean views. Also has some larger houses for rent. **$100**

JENNER
★**The Jenner Inn** 10400 Hwy-1 ☎ 707 865 2377, ⓦ jennerinn.com. Very salubrious rooms, cabins and cottages, all tastefully decorated, plus a stylish and highly rated restaurant are on offer here. **$128**
River's End Resort ☎ 707 865 2484, ⓦ ilovesunsets .com. The quaint cabins here all have small balconies from

9

which to admire the sunsets vaunted in the website's name. There is also a quality restaurant, closed on Wed. **$239**

FORT ROSS
Fort Ross Lodge 20705 Hwy-1 ☎707 847 3333, ⓦfortrosslodge.com. A welcoming place that provides well-equipped rooms, each of which has a private patio and barbecue, and some much pricier suites with hot tubs. **$149**
Timber Cove Inn 21780 Hwy-1 ☎800 987 8319,

ⓦtimbercoveinn.com. This inn offers a fair measure of luxury, with splendid ocean views from the costlier rooms and an intimate restaurant with outdoor seating. **$220**
Woodside Campground Salt Point State Park, 6 miles north of Fort Ross on Hwy-1 ☎800 444 7275, ⓦreserveamerica.com. This campground has a great location beside a rugged windswept beach, hence it's only open April–Oct. Pitches **$35**

EATING

BODEGA BAY
Lucas Wharf 595 Hwy-1 ☎707 875 3522, ⓦlucas wharfrestaurant.com. This restaurant with good views of the harbour specializes in crab (mid-Nov to June) and salmon (mid-May to Sept) dishes at around $20–25. Mon–Thurs 11.30am–9pm, Fri 11.30am–9.30pm, Sat 11am–9.30pm, Sun 11am–9pm.
★**Spud Point Crab Company** 1860 Westshore Rd ☎707 875 9472, ⓦspudpointcrab.com. Serving crab and wild king salmon caught by the owner and his son at market prices, this friendly family joint also has great sandwiches and hot dogs for $10 or less. Daily 9am–5pm.
Terrapin Creek Café 1580 Eastshore Rd ☎707 875 2700, ⓦterrapincreekcafe.com. Good relaxed spot just off Hwy-1, where you can enjoy oysters or scallops for

starters and mains such as pan-roasted Corvina sea bass for $30. Mon & Thurs–Sun 4.30–9pm.
Tides Wharf Restaurant & Bar Inn at the Tides 800 Hwy-1 ☎707 875 3652, ⓦinnatthetides.com. Upscale hotel restaurant with a fine vantage point for watching fishing boats unload their catch, while enjoying seafood or steak for $20–30. Mon–Thurs 7.30am–9.30pm, Fri 7.30am–10pm, Sat 7am–10pm, Sun 7am–9.30pm.

JENNER
Seagull Gifts & Deli 10439 Hwy-1 ☎707 865 2594. This place sells bagels, some Mexican dishes and wonderful clam chowder, all well under $10, on a deck along the river mouth. Shop for a souvenir once full. Daily 10am–9pm.

The Russian River Valley

Hwy-116 begins at Jenner and turns sharply inland, leaving behind the cool fogs of the coast and marking the western entrance to a relatively warm and pastoral area known as the **RUSSIAN RIVER VALLEY**. The tree-lined highway follows the river's course through twenty miles of what appear to be lazy backwater resorts but in fact are the major stomping grounds for partying weekend visitors from San Francisco. This part of Sonoma County is also the centre of the Farm Trails ecotourism effort (ⓦfarmtrails .org). The valley's seat, **Guerneville**, has the most nightlife and lodging, while **Healdsburg** serves as the gatekeeper for the **wine area**, bordering US-101 and the Dry Creek and Alexander valleys.

Guerneville

The main town of the Russian River Valley, **GUERNEVILLE**, came out some time ago. No longer disguised by the tourist office as a place where "a mixture of people respect each other's lifestyles", it is openly advertised as an **LGBT resort**, which it has been since the 1980s: a lively retreat popular with tired city-dwellers who come here to unwind. Gay men predominate except during **Women's Weekend** (☎707 239 4960, ⓦwomensweekend russianriver.com) in late May, when many of the hotels take only women.

If you don't fancy venturing along the valley, there's plenty to keep you busy in town. Weekend visitors flock here for the canoeing, swimming and sunbathing that comprise the bulk of local activities. **Johnson's Beach** (mid-May to early Oct daily 10am–6pm; free) on a placid reach of the river in the centre of town, is the prime spot, with canoes, pedal boats and tubes for rent at reasonable rates.

9

RUSSIAN RIVER FESTIVALS

During the first weekend after Labor Day, the Russian River Valley region hosts the **Russian River Jazz & Blues festival** (☎ 510 655 9471, ⓦ russianriverfestivals.com). Bands set up on Johnson's Beach by the river and in the woods in Guerneville for impromptu jam sessions as well as regular scheduled events. Gourmets will enjoy the **Russian River Food and Wine Festival** on the last Sunday in September.

Armstrong Redwoods State Natural Reserve

Armstrong Woods Rd • Daily 8am–1hr after sunset; visitor centre 11am–3pm • $8/vehicle • ☎ 707 869 2015, ⓦ parks.ca.gov

Guerneville's biggest natural asset is the magnificent **Armstrong Redwoods State Natural Reserve**, two miles north of town – seven hundred acres of massive redwood trees, hiking and riding trails and primitive campsites. The visitor centre can provide trail maps; take food and water and don't stray off the trails, as the densely forested central grove is quite forbidding and very easy to get lost in. A natural amphitheatre provides the setting for the **Redwood Forest Theater**, once used for dramatic and musical productions during the summer but now simply a fine spot for rustic contemplation.

ARRIVAL AND INFORMATION   GUERNEVILLE

By bus Sonoma County Transit (☎ 707 576 7433 or ☎ 800 345 7433, ⓦ sctransit.com) runs a fairly good bus service from Santa Rosa in the Wine Country to Guerneville (Mon–Fri 9 daily, Sat–Sun 4 daily; 1hr) and on to Monte Rio.

Chamber of Commerce & Visitor Center 16209 1st St (Mon–Sat 10am–5pm, Sun 10am–3pm [summer only]; 24hr information line ☎ 707 869 9000 or ☎ 877 644 9001, ⓦ russianriver.com).

ACCOMMODATION

Applewood Inn & Restaurant 13555 Hwy-116 ☎ 707 869 9093, ⓦ applewoodinn.com. Guerneville's most luxurious option, with superbly appointed rooms and suites, as well as a highly acclaimed gourmet restaurant and a spa. **$225**

Austin Creek State Recreation Area Campground Armstrong Woods Rd ☎ 800 444 7275, ⓦ parks.ca .gov. RV-free campground – which makes its wooded location all the more enjoyable – with basic facilities. Pitches from **$25**

Cottages on River Road 14880 River Rd ☎ 707 869 3848, ⓦ cottagesonriverroad.com. Set around a peaceful lawn, with a pool open April–Oct, these well-furnished cottages and studios welcome all comers. **$120**

★ **Creekside Inn and Resort** 16180 Neely Rd ☎ 707

869 3623, ⓦ creeksideinn.com. Extremely comfortable self-catering units in a rambling set of two-storey buildings amid the redwoods on the opposite side of the river. Swimming pool and upstairs hot tub. **$105**

Highlands Resort 14000 Woodland Rd ☎ 707 869 0333, ⓦ highlandsresort.com. This place caters primarily to the LGBT community and has a range of rooms and cabins, as well as camping facilities. Pitches **$20**, cabins **$70**, doubles **$90**

Johnson's Beach and Resort 16241 1st St ☎ 707 869 2022, ⓦ johnsonsbeach.com. The resort that runs the beach (see opposite) has simple, rustic and rather overpriced cabins and modest-sized tent pitches. Two-night minimum stay. Tents **$40**, cabins **$135**

EATING AND DRINKING

Betty Spaghetti R3 Hotel, 16390 4th St ☎ 707 869 8399, ⓦ ther3hotel.com. This lively hotel restaurant does filling pasta and meals like Italian pot roast for $19–29. The hotel bar is even livelier. Mon–Thurs & Sun 5.30–9pm, Fri & Sat 5.30–10pm; bar daily 11am–late.

Main Street Bistro 16280 Main St ☎ 707 869 0501, ⓦ mainststation.com. Serves pizzas, tasty tapas and more upmarket options such as herb-crusted prime rib for $23. There's nightly live jazz too. Mon–Thurs 3–11pm, Fri & Sat 3pm–midnight.

Rainbow Cattle Co 16220 Main St ☎ 707 869 0206, ⓦ queersteer.com. An LGBT hangout that gets livelier as

the night draws on. Organizes lots of parties and events. Daily 6pm–2am.

★ **Taqueria la Tapatia** 16632 Hwy-116 ☎ 707 869 1821. This is an excellent, authentic and cheap Mexican joint, with the usual brightly painted interior and a great range of filling tacos, tamales and burritos, mostly well under $10. Daily 11am–10pm.

Trio 16225 Main St ☎ 707 604 7461, ⓦ triorussianriver .com. Garishly painted grill serving sandwiches, some Mexican food and delicious baby back ribs for $19. Live music every night. Mon–Fri 3–10pm, Sat & Sun noon–10pm; bar till 2am daily.

9

Monte Rio

The small town of **Monte Rio**, four miles west along the river from Guerneville, is definitely worth a look: a lovely old resort with big Victorian houses that are constantly being refurbished. For years it has been the entrance to the 2500-acre **Bohemian Grove**, a private park that plays host to the San Francisco-based Bohemian Club. A grown-up summer camp, its membership includes a very rich and very powerful male elite – ex-presidents, financiers, politicians and their peers. Every year in July they descend for "Bohemian Week" – noted for its hijinks away from prying cameras in the seclusion of the woods.

ARRIVAL AND DEPARTURE
MONTE RIO

By bus Monte Rio is connected to Guerneville (10min) and all points to Santa Rosa (1hr 10min) by Sonoma County Transit (see p.602) route #20 (Mon–Fri 9 daily, Sat–Sun 4 daily).

ACCOMMODATION AND EATING

★**Highland Dell Resort** 21050 River Blvd ☎ 707 865 2300, ⓦ highlanddell.com. The classiest of Monte Rio's handful of places to stay is this expertly restored resort, with balconies overlooking the river. Its gourmet restaurant is highly praised. $99

Northwood Restaurant 19400 Hwy-116 ☎ 707 865 2454, ⓦ northwoodbistro.com. As well as good-value California cuisine for around $15, this popular place also does barbecue nights with pulled pork sandwiches for $10 and has karaoke every Saturday night. Daily 8am–11pm.

RUSSIAN RIVER VALLEY WINERIES

The Guerneville Chamber of Commerce (see p.609) issues an excellent *Russian River Wine Road* map, which lists all the **wineries** spread along the entire course of the Russian River – now numbering nearly a hundred. Unlike their counterparts in Napa and Sonoma, few of the wineries here either organize guided tours or charge as much for wine-tasting. Some of the wines are of remarkably good quality, if not as well known as their Wine Country rivals. By car, you could easily travel up from the Sonoma coast and check out a couple of Russian River wineries in a day, although the infectiously slow pace may well detain you longer.

Dry Creek Vineyard 3770 Lambert Bridge Rd, 4 miles northwest of Healdsburg ☎ 800 864 9463, ⓦ drycreekvineyard.com. This family-owned operation is well known for its consistently top-class wines – particularly the Cabernet Sauvignon and Chardonnay. Picnic facilities. Tasting $15–30; tour & tasting $30. Daily 10.30am–4.30pm; tours Mon–Fri 11am & 2pm.

Ferrari Carano 8761 Dry Creek Rd, 6 miles northwest of Healdsburg ☎ 800 831 0381, ⓦ ferrari-carano.com. One of the smartest wineries in the region, Ferrari is housed in a Neoclassical mansion with beautiful landscaped grounds. They specialize in Italian-style wines. Tasting $10–25 (waived with purchase), tours by appointment. Daily 10am–5pm.

HKG Estate Wines 6050 Westside Rd, over 5 miles south of Healdsburg ☎ 707 433 6491, ⓦ hopkilnwinery.com. Recently established, rustic winery with a traditional atmosphere but no snobbish attitude. Ironically, a plaque marks the spot where kilns used to dry the hops when this was beer country. Picnic area. Tour and tasting $15. Daily 10am–5pm.

★**Korbel Champagne Cellars** 13250 River Rd, 2 miles east of Guerneville ☎ 707 824 7000, ⓦ korbel.com. The bubbly itself – America's best-selling premium

champagne – can be found anywhere but the wine and brandy are sold only from the cellars and are of notable quality. The estate where they are produced is lovely, surrounded by hillside gardens covered in blossoming violets, coral bells and hundreds of varieties of rose. A microbrewery and upscale deli are also on the premises. Daily: May–Oct 10am–5pm; Nov–April 10am–4.30pm; tours April–Oct Tues–Sun 1pm & 3pm.

Porter Creek 8735 Westside Rd, over 5 miles east of Guerneville ☎ 707 433 6321, ⓦ portercreek vineyards.com. Small winery with a cottagey feel, producing only organic wines; Pinot Noir is a speciality. Tasting $15 (waived with purchase). Daily 10.30am–4.30pm.

Russian River Vineyards 5700 Gravenstein Hwy, Forestville, 5 miles from Guerneville along Hwy-116 ☎ 800 867 6567, ⓦ russianrivervineyards.com. One of the Russian River Valley's most accessible wineries, specializing in Zinfandels. The popular on-site restaurant *Stella's* (☎ 707 887 1562) serves Greek-inspired California dishes – dine on the patio with live jazz and views across the wildflower gardens. Tasting $15 (waived with purchase), tours by appointment. Daily except Wed noon–8pm.

Rio Villa Beach Resort 20292 Hwy-116 ☎877 746 8455, ⓦriovilla.com. Some of the larger rooms have fully equipped kitchens at this pleasant riverside boutique B&B with beautifully manicured grounds. **$160**

Village Inn 20822 River Blvd ☎707 865 2304, ⓦvillageinn-ca.com. Most of the rooms, which are all charmingly decorated in neutral colours, have balconies looking out through redwoods across Russian River. Also has an excellent restaurant. **$155**

Cazadero Highway

The lonely, narrow **Cazadero Highway** just to the west of Monte Rio makes a nice drive from the town, curving north through the wooded valley and leading back to Fort Ross on the coast. At the north end of the bridge over the Russian River in Monte Rio, **cyclists** can begin the world-renowned King Ridge–Meyers Grade ride, a 55-mile loop (and 4500ft of climb) that heads along the Cazadero Highway and into the hills, finally descending to the coast and Hwy-1. Contact the Santa Rosa Cycling Club (see p.602) for a complete itinerary.

Healdsburg

The peaceful modern town of **Healdsburg** straddles the invisible border between the Wine Country and the Russian River Valley and in a quiet way manages to get the best of both worlds. Romantic B&Bs have sprung up all over the area, including in the neighbouring village of **Geyserville**, and although the town's economic wellbeing is almost exclusively dependent on tourism, it still manages to maintain a relaxed, backcountry feel.

While **Veterans Memorial Beach**, a mile south of the pleasant plaza along the banks of the Russian River, is a popular spot for swimming, picnicking and canoeing in the summertime, there are also several dozen **wineries**, most of them family-owned, within a few miles of the town centre. The only cultural diversion in town is the **Healdsburg Museum** at 221 Matheson St (Wed–Sun 11am–4pm; free; ☎707 431 3325, ⓦhealdsburg museum.org), which displays local history through a decent collection of Pomo basketry, nineteenth-century tools and crafts and eight thousand original photos.

ARRIVAL AND INFORMATION   HEALDSBURG

By bus There's a good bus service on Sonoma County Transit (see p.602) between Healdsburg and Santa Rosa (18 daily; 50min).

Chamber of Commerce 217 Healdsburg Ave (Mon–Fri 10am–4pm, Sat & Sun 10am–3pm; ☎707 433 6935 or ☎800 648 9922, ⓦhealdsburg.com).

ACCOMMODATION AND EATING

Baci Cafe & Wine Bar 336 Healdsburg Ave ☎707 433 8111, ⓦbacicafeandwinebar.com. Barely a block from the green, wooded plaza, this trendy Italian joint offers a range of risottos, pasta dishes and mains such as veal osso buco for $32. Mon & Thurs–Sun 5–10pm.

★**Bear Republic Brewing Co** 345 Healdsburg Ave ☎707 433 2337, ⓦbearrepublic.com. Look no further than this welcoming spot for some fine local ale – try the hoppy Racer 5 – and suitably beer-themed bar food such as the hoppy burger for $14. Daily 11am–11pm.

Best Western Dry Creek Inn 198 Dry Creek Rd ☎800 222 5784, ⓦdrycreekinn.com. A fairly economic, if none too distinctive, option is this reliable chain, which has the usual neat and fairly spacious rooms, plus a few suites. **$149**

Madrona Manor 1001 Westside Rd ☎707 433 4231, ⓦmadronamanor.com. If you have the money to spend it's hard to beat this luxurious B&B in a Victorian-style mansion crowning a hilltop, with its meticulously maintained gardens and a gourmet restaurant. **$325**

Clear Lake

An alternative route to the northern coast along Hwy-29 from the Wine Country or via Hwy-20, if coming from the I-5 north of Sacramento, is through often-neglected **Lake County** and its centrepiece, **CLEAR LAKE**, the largest natural fresh-water lake in California.

9

With a surface area of 64 square miles and over a hundred miles of shoreline, the lake is renowned among anglers as the best **bass-fishing** territory in the country, and all sorts of water **activities** – windsurfing, waterskiing and boating – are available all around the lake. Mostly surrounded by rolling hills, the lake is dominated by the green twin cone of **Mount Konocti**, a 4500ft dormant volcano, which looms above its south shore. The largest city, conveniently named **Clearlake**, which occupies the southeast corner of the lake, has plenty of tourist facilities but is rather modern and faceless, so you're better off concentrating on the lakefront areas around **Lakeport** to the west and along the **North Shore**.

Brief history

With a basin that was lifted above sea level some fifty million years ago by the collision of the Pacific and North American crustal plates, Clear Lake is one of the most ancient lakes on the continent. The earliest inhabitants of its shores were the **Pomo**, attracted by the mild climate and abundance of fish, who traded peacefully with other tribes and remained here undisturbed until they were displaced by white settlers; now they number just two percent of the population.

Lakeport

The county seat of **Lakeport** is the older and prettier of Clear Lake's two towns, dating from the latter part of the nineteenth century, when settlers moved into the picturesque area as gold fever began to wane. Although the suburban sprawl along the lakefront gives the impression of a larger town, it's home to fewer than five thousand people. Downtown Lakeport still retains a good deal of Victorian charm, with the original 1871 brick courthouse standing imperiously on the gentle slopes of the grassy main square right in the heart of town. The building now houses the **Historic Courthouse Museum**, 255 N Main St (Wed–Sat 10am–4pm, Sun noon–4pm; $2; ☎707 263 4555). Exhibits concentrate on the area's native heritage, with a full-sized Pomo village diorama and a large collection of baskets, arrowheads and tools.

Clear Lake State Park

Six miles southeast of Lakeport • Daily sunrise–sunset • $8/vehicle • ☎707 279 2267, ⓦ parks.ca.gov

The nearest place of note to Lakeport is **Clear Lake State Park**, whose erratically opening visitor centre houses displays on the lake's cultural and natural history, as well as a 700-gallon aquarium of indigenous fish. The park also offers forest trails, a swimming beach and four developed campgrounds (see opposite).

Soda Bay

Right below Mount Konocti, in the protected waters between the park and Buckingham Peninsula, which almost spans the lake, **Soda Bay** is another haven for swimming and watersports. The eastern shore of the bay is blessed with soda springs, hence the name, which emanate from shafts over a hundred feet deep. Native American legend claims that the bubbling waters mark the spot where Chief Konocti's daughter Lupiyoma threw herself into the lake after her father and lover were killed in battle.

Mount Konocti

Majestic **Mount Konocti**, clearly visible from just about anywhere on Clear Lake's circumference, is a multiple volcano, estimated to have first erupted some 600,000 years ago but inactive for the last several thousand years. Indeed, geologists have declared large parts of it officially extinct. Its name comes from the Pomo words "kno" and "hatai", meaning "mountain" and "woman" respectively. As most of the mountain is under private ownership, visitor access was prohibited for many years until 2011, when the opening of **Mount Konocti County Park** (daily sunrise–sunset; free; ☎707 262 1618) granted access to the summit via a three- to four-mile trail.

North Shore
Some five miles north of Clearlake, Hwy-53 ends at Hwy-20, which continues northwest along the lake's **North Shore** past a series of small resorts under the shade of white oak and pepperwood trees. The first place you come to once the road hits the lake is Clearlake Oaks, which doesn't really merit a stop, so it's best to press on towards **Glenhaven**. There's more going on, however, up towards the lake's northwest corner, which also boasts the longest stretches of beach. Five miles beyond Glenhaven is the larger settlement of **Lucerne**, while several miles further on, where Hwy-20 prepares to leave the lake behind as the shoreline dips south towards Lakeport, the pleasant town of **Nice** is the best base on the North Shore.

ARRIVAL AND GETTING AROUND   CLEAR LAKE

By bus Lake Transit service (☎707 263 3334, ⓦlaketransit .org) runs frequent buses all around the lake every day except Sunday and also has connections (Mon–Sat 4 daily)

to Ukiah in neighbouring Mendocino County for longer-distance Greyhound and Amtrak Thruway services.

INFORMATION AND ACTIVITIES

Lake County Chamber of Commerce 875 Lakeport Blvd, Lakeport (Mon–Fri 9am–5pm; ☎707 263 5092 or ☎866 525 3767, ⓦlakecochamber.com).
Lake County Visitor Center 6110 E Hwy-20, Lucerne (summer Mon–Sat 9am–6pm & Sun 10am–5pm; rest of year Mon–Sat 9am–5pm & Sun noon–4pm; ☎800 525 3743, ⓦlakecounty.com).

Boating Disney's Boat Rentals, 401 S Main St, Lakeport (☎707 263 0969, ⓦdisneyswatersports.com), has a range of boats and jet-skis from $95/hr, plus kayaks and paddleboards from $30/hr.
Fishing To stock up on fishing gear, stop at Clear Lake Outdoors, 96 Soda Bay Rd, Lakeport (☎707 262 5852, ⓦclearlakeoutdoors.com).

ACCOMMODATION AND EATING

LAKEPORT
Chopsticks 185 N Main St ☎707 263 3310. Enjoy inexpensive Chinese food here; all the favourites from hot'n'sour soup to special chow mein are available for $15 or less. Mon–Thurs & Sun 11.30am–9pm, Fri & Sat 11.30am–10pm.
Konocti Vista Casino 2755 Mission Rancheria Rd ☎707 262 3279, ⓦkonocti-vista-casino.com. This modern yellow two-storey building is the only casino resort on the lake. The rooms are spacious and comfortable, plus there's a good café, RV park and marina. $89
Lakeport English Inn 675 N Main St ☎707 263 4317, ⓦlakeportenglishinn.com. This posh inn is the best of the B&Bs in the county seat, with lavishly designed rooms. Afternoon tea and scones included. $185
Park Place 50 3rd St ☎707 263 0444, ⓦparkplace lakeport.com. Serves filling pasta, burgers and steaks, as well as more inventive dishes such as honey mustard chicken breast, all for $10–20. Mon 11am–3pm, Tues–Sun 11am–9pm.

CLEAR LAKE STATE PARK
Clear Lake State Park campgrounds ☎800 444

7275, ⓦreserveamerica.com. Some of the most scenically situated camping spots, with reasonable facilities, are to be found in this park, plus some basic cabins. Pitches $35, cabins $65

SODA BAY
★**Edgewater Resort** 6420 Soda Bay Rd ☎800 396 6224, ⓦedgewaterresort.net. This excellent private resort offers tent and RV sites, as well as a few spacious, well-equipped family cabins. Pitches & RV $45, cabins $140
The Lakeside Inn 6330 Soda Bay Rd ☎707 279 1620. This cosy English boozer serves meat pies for only $9 and good ale; in fact it's an exact replica of its namesake in Southport, Lancashire, recorded in the *Guinness Book of Records* as the smallest pub in England. Food served Thurs–Sat 5–9pm, Sun 3–9pm; bar till 11pm.

MOUNT KONOCTI
Konocti Harbor Resort & Spa 8727 Soda Bay Rd, Kelseyville ☎707 279 4281 or ☎800 660 5253, ⓦkonoctiharbor.com. The biggest resort in the region, with accommodation ranging from motel-style rooms through beach cottages to a VIP suite that nudges $800 on

9

special-event weekends. Other facilities include a spa, marina, sports facilities, restaurants and a concert hall. $79

GLENHAVEN

Blue Fish Cove 10573 E Hwy-20 ☎707 998 1769, ⍟bluefishcove.com. A mile or so outside town are these rustic but nicely decorated cabins, where you can get great rates offseason. $90

Glenhaven Beach Resort 9625 E Hwy-20 ☎707 701 6000. Pleasant lakeside campground, with spacious and shady pitches. Inexpensive boat rental is also available here. Pitches $25

Sea Breeze Resort 9595 Harbor Drive ☎707 998 3327, ⍟seabreezeresort.net. This resort has quaint, nicely decorated cottages with carefully tended gardens. It is also nearest to the town's facilities. $99

LUCERNE

Fresh & Bangin Eatery 6244 E Hwy-20 ☎707 600 1275. New multi-cuisine restaurant that offers a wide menu of starters, sandwiches and larger meals with influences from the Mediterranean, Asia and good old American spuds. Most items $13 or less. Tues–Sat 11am–8pm.

Lakeview Inn 5960 E Hwy-20 ☎707 274 5515, ⍟lakeviewinnlucerne.com. This place offers some of the best-value rooms on the lake. Its outward appearance is motel-like but the rooms are classier and there is direct lake access. $69

NICE

The Boathouse 2685 Lakeshore Blvd ☎707 274 1100. Well-prepared fish and barbecued meat costs around $10–20, plus there is a good range of soup and starters. Outdoor patio with lake view. Mon–Thurs noon–10pm, Fri & Sat 11am–10pm, Sun 11am–9pm.

Featherbed Railroad Company 2870 Lakeshore Blvd ☎707 274 8378 or ☎800 966 6322, ⍟featherbedrailroad .com. This unique railway-themed establishment, where all the rooms are fashioned out of disused cabooses, is certainly the most unusual place to stay by the lake. $159

The Marina Grill 3707 E Hwy-20 ☎707 274 9114. Classic American-diner-style meals for around $15, as well as filling and inexpensive sandwiches, are served all day in this bright and breezy spot. Daily 11am–9pm.

Mendocino County

The coast of **Mendocino County**, 150 miles north of San Francisco, is a dramatic extension of the Sonoma coastline – the headlands a bit sharper, the surf a bit rougher, but otherwise more of the same. Sea stacks form a dotted line off the coast and there's an abundance of tide pools, making the area a prime spot for exploring the secrets of the ocean, either on foot or in diving gear. Surfers love it, too, for the waves and sandy beaches to be found between **Gualala** and **Albion**, and March brings out droves of people to watch migrating **whales**. Tourists tend to mass in charming **Mendocino** and gritty **Fort Bragg**, leaving the other small former logging towns along Hwy-1 preserved in the salt air and welcoming to visitors. The county also thrives as a location spot for the movie industry, having featured in such illustrious titles as *East of Eden*, *Frenchman's Creek*, *Same Time Next Year* and *The Fog*.

If you're already on the coast, you can continue to hug Hwy-1 all the way to Rockport when it turns east to join US-101, the last thirty miles constituting one of only two true wildernesses left on California's rim. The most direct route to Mendocino from the south, however, is to travel the length of the peaceful **Anderson Valley** by taking Hwy-128 north from US-101.

The southern Mendocino coast

The first seaside stop of note, once you leave Sonoma County on Hwy-1, is **Gualala**, which has developed into quite an artistic community, as well as a spot for holiday-makers due to its fine stretch of sand. A handy brochure locating the dozen or so **galleries** can be found at any one of them – try the central Dolphin Gallery (☎707 884 3896, ⍟gualalaarts.org) in Sundstrom Mall, directly off Hwy-1. Beyond Gualala the route is very appealing, as Hwy-1 climbs up through increasingly wooded hillsides that afford tantalizing glimpses of the crashing waves at the frequent bends. Eventually the road straightens out somewhat as it turns inland to become the main street of nondescript **Point Arena**, fifteen miles or so north. A turn on the north side of town leads two miles to the impressive **Point Arena Lighthouse** (summer 10am–4.30pm, rest of year 10am–3.30pm; $5, $7.50 including tower; ☎707 882 2809, ⓦpointarenalighthouse.com). Built in 1870 and rebuilt after the San Francisco earthquake of 1906, the landmark contains a small museum, and the 115ft tower is a great vantage point for viewing birds, whales and other ocean life.

Hwy-1 continues north through a mixture of coastal scrub and grazing land, rejoining the ocean around **Manchester Beach State Park** (daily 8am–sunset; free; ☎707 882 2463, ⓦparks.ca.gov), which has a largely deserted strand. Further on you reach the pretty village of **Elk**, which boasts an excellent driftwood-strewn beach and a couple of quaint but fairly pricey accommodation options. After that the road winds on through an extremely scenic stretch of cliffs counterpointed by sea stacks and crashing waves until it reaches **Albion**, a couple of miles north of the junction with Hwy-128, where the alternative inland route to Mendocino via the Anderson Valley reaches the coast. The small fishing village is only six miles south of Mendocino itself and has a couple of romantic places to stay.

ARRIVAL AND GETTING AROUND   THE SOUTHERN MENDOCINO COAST

By bus MTA's (see p.618) route #95 connects Point Arena to Gualala (1 daily Mon–Sat; 20min) and on into Sonoma County, while route #75 runs from Gualala up to Elk (1 daily Mon–Sat; 1hr) and through the Anderson Valley to Ukiah; this route connects at Navarro River to the #60 (2 daily Mon–Fri) to Mendocino (25min) and Fort Bragg (55min).

ACCOMMODATION AND EATING

GUALALA
St Orres 36601 S Hwy-1 ☎707 884 3303, ⓦsaintorres .com. The stunning main building of this complex is wooden, with domes reminiscent of St Petersburg. There are also cabins and cottages spread throughout the surrounding woods. Complimentary breakfast brought to the door and gourmet three-course dinners cost around $50. $140
The Surf Motel 39170 S Hwy-1 ☎707 884 3571, ⓦsurfinngualala.com. Many of the rooms and suites here have splendid ocean views. There are also self-catering units with fully equipped kitchens. Doubles $109, self-catering $119

MANCHESTER BEACH STATE PARK
Manchester Beach State Park Campground ☎800 444 7275, ⓦreserveamerica.com. Lots of individual pitches and some larger group sites are available at this wooded campground near the crashing waves. Pitches $35

ELK
Elk Cove Inn & Spa 6300 S Hwy-1 ☎707 877 3321, ⓦelkcoveinn.com. A range of mansion rooms, suites and cottages offering varying degrees of luxury and fine ocean views. Pamper yourself at the on-site spa. $155
Sacred Rock Resort 5910 S Hwy-1 ☎707 877 3422, ⓦsacredrockresort.com. Renamed but still co-run with the adjoining, hearty *Bridget Dolan's Pub & Dinner House*, all the accommodation options here are in delightful, newly refurbished seaside cottages. $159

ALBION
Albion River Inn 3790 N Hwy-1 ☎707 937 1919 or ☎800 479 7944, ⓦalbionriverinn.com. Perched on the edge of a cliff, with all the rooms except one facing the ocean. The inn also has a first-class restaurant, serving superb California cuisine with a spectacular wine list and top service. $195

The Anderson Valley

Running diagonally northwest for nearly twenty miles, from just south of its small main town of **Boonville** to within a few miles of the coast, is the fertile **ANDERSON VALLEY**, an amalgam of sunny rolling hills shaded by oaks and madrones that merge into dark redwood forest. Hwy-128, connecting US-101 near Cloverdale to the coast at Albion,

---

BOONTLING
The original **sheep farmers** of the Anderson Valley saw so few outsiders between the 1880s and 1920s that they developed their own language, **boontling**, snippets of which still survive today. A good sixth of this odd dialect was known as "nonch harpin's", meaning "objectionable talk", and largely referred to the then taboo subjects of sexual activity and bodily functions. You can see examples of boontling in the names of local beers and establishments, but if you want to know the full story, track down a copy of *Boontling, An American Lingo* in local stores or online.

9

ANDERSON VALLEY WINERIES

There are now around sixty **wineries** dotted along the Anderson Valley and the number increases year by year. The cooler temperatures, especially at the northwest end, which sees the coastal fogs roll in, are better suited mostly to white varieties such as Gewürtzraminer, Chardonnay and Riesling, but the hardy Pinot Noir fares equally well. For further details you can contact the Anderson Valley Winegrowers Association (☎707 895 9463, ⍟avwines.com). Most wineries, including those listed below, offer **free tastings** unless denoted otherwise and those that do have a fee usually charge less than their more commercialized cousins further south.

Foursight 14475 Hwy-128, just south of Boonville ☎707 895 2889, ⍟foursightwines.com. Small family winery that produces particularly excellent Sauvignon Blanc and Pinot Noir, as well as a mean Gewürtzraminer. Feb–Dec daily 10am–4.30pm.

Goldeneye Winery 9200 Hwy-128, just south of Philo ☎707 895 3202, ⍟goldeneyewinery.com. This offshoot of Napa's Duckhorn produces wines from the Pinot Noir variety exclusively, including an excellent rosé. Tasting $15–45. Daily 10.30am–4.30pm.

★ **Husch Vineyards** 4400 Hwy-128, almost 3 miles south of Navarro ☎800 554 8724, ⍟huschvineyards .com. Founded in 1971, this small family winery is the oldest in the valley, and you're assured of a warm welcome at its rustic tasting room. Produces no fewer than 21 wines. Daily: summer 10am–6pm; rest of year 10am–5pm; tours Mon, Wed & Thurs at 1pm & 3pm.

Lazy Creek Vineyards 4741 Hwy-128, 3 miles west of Philo ☎707 895 3623, ⍟lazycreekvineyards .com. Pinot Noirs are the speciality at this family winery with a small rustic tasting room. Mon & Fri–Sun 11am–4.30pm.

Navarro Vineyards 5601 Hwy-128, 3 miles north of Philo ☎800 537 9463, ⍟navarrowine.com. This small winery specializes in Alsatian-style wines, which it only sells directly to the consumer and select restaurants. It also concocts a wicked grape juice, so even the kids can enjoy a free sip or two here. Daily: summer 10am–6pm; rest of year 11am–5pm; tours at 10.30am & 2pm.

Roederer Estate 4501 Hwy-128, about 3 miles south of Navarro ☎707 8952288, ⍟roedererestate .com. One of the higher-profile Mendocino wineries, specializing in sparkling vintages. Tasting $10; tours by appointment $6. Daily 11am–5pm.

---

is the sole artery through the valley, which has a long-standing reputation as a magnet for mavericks: the original settlers were sheep farmers who developed their own language (see box, p.615). During the twentieth century, sheep farming gradually gave way to the cultivation of apples that, though many orchards still exist, they are fast being replaced by more lucrative **vineyards**, as the craze for California wine means that this area is becoming a northern annexe of the Wine Country, along with the **Yorkville Highlands**, the southeastern extension of the valley. Most of the Anderson Valley's existing wineries line Hwy-128 between the tiny settlements of **Philo** and **Navarro**; the former offers a few places to spend the night or have a meal, although it's all rather cutesy.

Anderson Valley Brewing Co

17700 Hwy-253 • Daily 11am–6pm, 7pm on Fri; tour daily 1.30pm, except Tues in winter • Tasting flight $5 • ☎707 895 2337, ⍟avbc.com

Apart from a growing reputation for quality wines, the area is also famous for the excellent **beer** produced at the **Anderson Valley Brewing Co**, just east of the junction with Hwy-128 on the south side of Boonville. Its Hop Ottin' IPA, an example of boontling (see box, p.615), and rich amber ales are especially delicious.

Boonville

Despite having a population of little over seven hundred, **Boonville** still easily manages to be the largest town in the Anderson Valley. Strung along its widened half-mile section of Hwy-128 are some quaint shops, a hotel and a few places to find sustenance.

Hendy Woods State Park

Signposted off Hwy-128 • Daily 8am–sunset • $8/car • ☎707 895 3141, ⍟parks.ca.gov

A great place to head for a picnic or leisurely stroll in the woods is **Hendy Woods State**

Park, three miles northwest of Philo. The park features hiking trails through two sizeable redwood groves, fishing on the Navarro River, and camping (see below).

ACCOMMODATION AND EATING   THE ANDERSON VALLEY

BOONVILLE

Boonville Hotel 14050 Hwy-128 ☎707 895 2210, ⓦboonvillehotel.com. The only choice in town in terms of accommodation is this grand nineteenth-century hotel, whose rooms vary considerably in price and luxury; the Casita is worth splashing out on. $145

The Buckhorn 14081 Hwy-128 ☎707 895 3224, ⓦbuckhornboonville.com. This favourite watering hole, revamped in modern Western style, has the town's only full bar and a range of grills and bar food for $15–20. Mon & Wed–Sun 11am–9pm.

Lauren's 14211 Hwy-128 ☎707 895 3857, ⓦlaurens goodfood.com. Apart from the hotel's spicy Mexican-influenced California cuisine, a fine range of Californian, Italian and Mexican food is to be had here for $12–20. Tues–Sat 5–9pm; also May–Oct Thurs–Sun 11.30am–2.30pm.

PHILO

Anderson Valley Inn 8480 Hwy-128 ☎707 895 3325, ⓦavinn.com. This welcoming inn is by far the best deal in the valley, with comfortable rooms decked in warm colours and a lovingly tended garden. $95

Libby's Restaurant 8651 Hwy-128 ☎707 895 2646. Friendly place which serves up excellent, inexpensive Mexican food such as tacos, tamales and big fat burritos for $10 or less. Don't miss the carnitas. Tues–Sat 11.30am–2pm & 5–8.30pm.

HENDY WOODS STATE PARK

Hendy Woods State Park Campground ☎800 444 7275, ⓦreserveamerica.com. This woody park has a mixture of hiker/biker and developed campgrounds, as well as some cabins. Hiker/biker pitches $5, developed pitches $35, cabins $55

Mendocino

As you head north, Hwy-1 passes the offshore kelp forests of Van Damme State Park before you reach the coast's most lauded stop, the decidedly touristy **MENDOCINO**. The quaint town sits on a broad-shouldered bluff with waves crashing on three sides; it's hard to find a spot here where you can't see the ocean sparkling in the distance. New England-style architecture is abundant, lending Mendo, as the locals call it, a down-home, almost cutesy air. Its appearance on the National Register of Historic Places and reputation as an artists' colony draw the curious up the coastal highway, and a fairly extensive network of B&Bs, restaurants and bars are more than happy to cater to their every need.

Brief history

Like other small settlements along the coast, Mendocino was originally a mill site and shipping port, established in 1852 by merchants from Maine who thought the proximity to the redwoods and exposed location made it a good site for sawmill operations. The industry has now vanished but the large community of artists has spawned craftsy commerce in the form of **art galleries**, gift shops and boutique delicatessens. This preservation didn't come about by accident. The state of California traded a block of old-growth forest with the Boise-Cascade logging company in exchange for the headlands surrounding the town. The **Mendocino Headlands** became a state park and Mendocino in turn became a living museum, with strict local ordinances mandating architectural design and upkeep.

Kelley House Museum

45007 Albion St • Mon & Fri–Sun 11am–3pm; walking tours Sat at 11am • Donation; tours $10 • ☎707 937 5791, ⓦkelleyhousemuseum.org

The **Kelley House Museum** has exhibits detailing the town's role as a centre for shipping redwood lumber to the miners during the Gold Rush, furnished with late nineteenth-century antiques. The Native American exhibit showcases artefacts from the local Pomo tribe. The staff also conduct **walking tours** of the town on Saturday mornings, though you could do it yourself in under an hour.

9

Mendocino Art Center and Theatre Company

45200 Little Lake St **Art Center** Daily 10am–5pm • ☎ 800 653 3328, ⓦ mendocinoartcenter.org • **Theatre Company** ☎ 707 937 4477, ⓦ mendocinotheatre.org

Chief among the numerous galleries is the **Mendocino Art Center**, which has a revolving gallery for mainly Mendocino-based artists, and runs workshops in ceramics, weaving, jewellery and metal sculpture. The **Mendocino Theatre Company** on the same premises puts on regular performances of both avant-garde and classic works.

Russian Gulch State Park

Two miles north of town • Daily 8am–sunset • $8/car • ☎ 707 937 5804, ⓦ parks.ca.gov

There's plenty to occupy you around town, with a long stroll along the headlands topping the list. At the west end of Main Street, hiking trails lead out into this mini wilderness, where you can explore the grassy cliffs and make your way down to the tide pools next to the breaking waves. The **Russian Gulch State Park** has bike trails, beautiful fern glens and waterfalls.

Van Damme State Park

Just south of town • Daily 8am–sunset • $8/car • ☎ 707 937 5804, ⓦ parks.ca.gov

Hiking and cycling trails weave through the unusual **Van Damme State Park**, which has a **Pygmy Forest** of ancient trees, stunted to waist-height because of poor drainage and soil chemicals. The coast of the park is punctuated with sea stacks and caves, carved by the pounding surf.

ARRIVAL AND INFORMATION

MENDOCINO

By bus Mendocino Transit Authority (MTA; ☎ 707 462 1422, ⓦ mendocinotransit.org) route #60 runs between Mendocino and Fort Bragg (4 daily Mon–Fri; 30min); two of these schedules run south to Albion and Navarro River for connections inland and further south along the coast.

Ford House visitor centre 735 Main St (Mon–Fri 11am–4pm, summer also Sat & Sun 10.30am–4.30pm; ☎ 707 937 5397, ⓦ visitmendocino.com). Located in one of many mansions built by the Maine lumbermen in the style of their home state, there are many historical exhibits, as well as the usual information.

ACCOMMODATION

Room rates are high in and around Mendocino but there are good-value deals to be found, especially at a couple of the lovely oceanfront B&Bs to the south around Little River. You can search for and book accommodation at no cost through Mendocino Coast Accommodations (☎ 800 262 7801, ⓦ mendocinovacations.com).

Brewery Gulch Inn Under a mile south of town at 401 N Hwy-1 ☎ 707 937 4752, ⓦ brewerygulchinn.com. Palatial luxury inn set on a grassy hill with a distant view of the ocean. The spacious rooms are beautifully furnished and decorated. Complimentary gourmet breakfast and light early evening meal in the huge, convivial lounge. $350

Joshua Grindle Inn 44800 Little Lake Rd ☎ 707 937 6022 or ☎ 844 567 4474, ⓦ joshgrin.com. Luxurious but intimate and friendly B&B, offering five standard and five deluxe rooms, which include excellent gourmet breakfasts. $179

★**Jughandle Creek Farm & Nature Center** 3 miles north on Hwy-1, just beyond Caspar ☎ 707 964 4630, ⓦ jughandlecreekfarm.com. Funky place with rooms, cabins and tent sites; prices quoted per person but there are discounts if you volunteer on the farm's ecological projects, plus special youth and student rates. Also has trails in the woods and nature-study programmes. Cash only. Pitches $20, rooms $45, cabins $50

★ **Little River Inn** 2 miles south of Mendocino on Hwy-1 at Little River ☎ 707 937 5942 or ☎ 888 466

MENDOCINO ACTIVITIES

Ninety-minute **sea-cave tours** of the coast off Van Damme State Park are available through Kayak Mendocino (daily at 9am, 11.30am & 2pm; $60; ☎ 707 937 2434, ⓦ kayakmendocino .com). **Kayaks**, **canoes** and **bicycles** can all be rented from Catch a Canoe & Bicycles, Too (☎ 707 937 0273, ⓦ catchacanoe.com), just south of Mendocino at the corner of Hwy-1 and Comptche–Ukiah Road.

MENDOCINO FESTIVALS

The first weekend in March brings the **Mendocino Whale Festival** (☎ 800 726 2780), a celebration of food and headland views of whales returning to the Arctic. Moviegoers will enjoy the **film festival** every May (☎ 707 937 0171, ⊚ mendocinofilmfestival.com), and music-lovers the two-week **Mendocino Music Festival** (☎ 800 937 2044, ⊚ mendocinomusic .com) in the middle of July; although the emphasis is largely on classical music and opera, some blues and jazz bands from all over the state also perform.

5683, ⊚ littleriverinn.com. Wonderful spot with views over a bay full of sea stacks. Accommodation ranges from cosy garden rooms to spacious seafront cottages. The restaurant/bar is excellent, too. **$275**

MacCallum House Inn 45020 Albion St ☎ 707 937 0289 or ☎ 800 609 0492, ⊚ maccallumhouse.com. The largest B&B in town, with a range of smart rooms in the grand main Victorian house, as well as luxury suites, cottages, and two off-site properties. Also has a fine restaurant and bar. **$169**

Mendocino Hotel 45080 Main St ☎ 707 937 0511, ⊚ mendocinohotel.com. Classy antique-filled rooms, the cheaper ones with shared bath, and some truly outstanding garden suites make this atmosphreic 1878 hotel a great choice. **$79**

Russian Gulch State Park & Van Damme State Park campgrounds ☎ 800 444 7275, ⊚ parks.ca.gov. Flanking Mendocino, both of these delightful state parks have proper developed campgrounds and more primitive hike/bike sites. Hiker/biker **$5**, developed sites **$35**

Sweetwater Inn & Spa 44840 Main St ☎ 800 300 4140, ⊚ sweetwaterspa.com. Some of the cosy, floral-patterned rooms have sweeping ocean views, and staying here entitles you to free use of the communal clothing-optional spa behind the property. **$130**

EATING AND DRINKING

Mendocino is renowned for its gourmet restaurants, some of which are in the accommodation listed above, but there are also a few cheaper cafés, as well as a couple of down-to-earth bars.

955 Ukiah St 955 Ukiah St ☎ 707 937 1955, ⊚ 955restaurant.com. High-quality main courses such as rosemary-scented lamb stew ($29) follow equally delicious starters such as duck and chickpea wontons in the elegant dining room. Thurs–Sun 6–10pm.

Café Beaujolais 961 Ukiah St ☎ 707 937 5614, ⊚ cafebeaujolais.com. The town's premier restaurant, whose founder wrote a book on organic California cuisine and which serves up a frequently changing menu of innovative main courses such as pan-roasted sturgeon fillet for around $23–35. Mon & Tues 5.30–10pm, Wed–Sun 11.30am–2.30pm & 5.30–10pm.

Dick's Place 45070 Main St ☎ 707 937 6010. Mendocino's oldest bar, with all the robust conviviality you'd expect from a spit-and-sawdust saloon, short of actually having sawdust on the floor or people spitting. Lots of sport on TV though. Daily 11.30am–2am.

Mendocino Café 10451 Lansing St ☎ 707 937 6141, ⊚ mendocinocafe.com. This homely little place serves a surprisingly eclectic mix of salads, pastas and sandwiches, as well as more adventurous dinners such as Brazilian fish stew for $26 and many Asian recipes. Daily 11am–9pm.

Patterson's Pub 10485 Lansing St ☎ 707 937 4782, ⊚ pattersonspub.com. Extremely friendly local joint with 28 beers on tap, cocktails and a fairly buzzing atmosphere. Chunky sandwiches and filling pasta dishes go for $13–18. Daily noon–2am.

Trillium Cafe 10390 Kasten St ☎ 707 937 3200, ⊚ trilliummendocino.com. A good choice for a filling lunch, as dinner main courses like the Mousse cioppino of mixed seafood cost around double at $24–30. Mon–Thurs & Sun 11.30am–2.30pm & 5.30–8.30pm, Fri & Sat 11.30am–2.30pm & 5.30–9pm.

Fort Bragg and around

A mere nine miles north of Mendocino, **FORT BRAGG** is very much the blue-collar flipside to its comfortable neighbour, although some of its trendier aspects have rubbed off. Still, for the most part, where Mendocino exists on organic food, art and peaceful ocean walks, Fort Bragg brings you the rib shack and tattoo parlour. Until not long ago the town sat beneath the perpetual cloud of steam choked out from the lumber mills of the massive Georgia Pacific Corporation, which used to monopolize California's logging industry and provide much of the town's employment. There was once a fort here, but it was only used for ten years until the 1860s, when it was abandoned and the land sold off cheaply.

RIDE THE SKUNK

You can take an amusing day-trip on the famous **Skunk Trains** operated by the Californian Western Railroad ($70 return; ☎ 707 964 6371, ⊛ skunktrain.com), which run twice daily during the summer months and once in the shoulder seasons from the terminus on Laurel Street in Fort Bragg, forty miles inland to the tiny halt at **Northspur** and back. It's fun to ride in the open observation car as it tunnels through mountains and rumbles across a series of high bridges on its route through the towering redwoods, taking almost three and a half hours to complete the trip. At Northspur you can connect with the tour from **Willits** (daily in summer, weekly in spring and fall; $59 return; ☎ 707 459 5248), on US-101 forty miles inland, which has interstate bus connections. There are also special-event trains at times like Easter, Christmas and Mother's Day, as well as other local festivals.

The otherwise attractive **Noyo Harbor** (south of town on Hwy-1) is these days crammed with an equal number of pleasure boats and diminishing commercial-fishing craft, as the town attempts to cash in on Mendocino's tourist trade. Indeed, its proximity to the more isolated reaches of the Mendocino coast, an abundance of budget accommodation, and a bevy of inexpensive restaurants make it a good alternative to Mendocino. There are few sights as such in town, but you could take a quick look at the historical exhibits of the **Guest House Museum** (June–Oct Mon 1–3pm, Tues–Fri 11am–2pm, Sat & Sun 10am–4pm; Nov–May Thurs–Sun 11am–2pm; $2; ☎ 707 964 4251, ⊛ fortbragghistory.org), in front of the train station at 343 Main St.

Glass Beach
At the end of Elm St

Spend a worthwhile hour or two rummaging on **Glass Beach**, a ten-minute walk north of downtown, below an attractive overgrown headland. Used as the town's dump until the 1960s, the disposed articles have been smoothed by the ocean into a kaleidoscopic beachcomber's paradise of broken glassware and crockery fragments.

Mendocino Coast Botanical Gardens
18220 N Hwy-1 • Daily: March–Oct 9am–5pm; Nov–Feb 9am–4pm • $14 • ☎ 707 964 4352, ⊛ gardenbythesea.org

A short drive or bus ride south of Fort Bragg will take you to the **Mendocino Coast Botanical Gardens**, where you can see more or less every wildflower under the sun spread across 47 acres of prime coastal territory. It's particularly renowned for the many varieties of **rhododendron** that bloom in April and May.

ARRIVAL AND DEPARTURE   FORT BRAGG AND AROUND

By bus Fort Bragg is connected by MTA buses (see p.618) to Mendocino and coastal points south on route #60, as well as Willits and Ukiah inland, for long-distance Greyhound services.

INFORMATION AND ACTIVITIES

Visit Mendocino County Office 345 N Franklin St (Mon–Fri 8.30am–5pm, Sat 10am–4pm; ☎ 707 964 9010 or ☎ 866 466 3636, ⊛ visitmendocino.com).

Boat trips All Aboard Adventures, which is down by the water at 32400 N Harbor Drive (☎ 707 964 1881, ⊛ all aboardadventures.com), organizes fishing and crabbing trips for $80 and whale-watching expeditions for $40 per person.

ACCOMMODATION

★**Beachcomber Motel** 1111 N Main St ☎ 707 964 2402, ⊛ thebeachcombermotel.com. Located just as the coast starts getting wilder again north of town, the smart and spacious rooms here enjoy splendid ocean views. Much better than the average motel, with a simple breakfast included. $149

Grey Whale Inn B&B 615 N Main St ☎ 707 964 0640 or ☎ 800 382 7244, ⊛ greywhaleinn.com. This quaint building covered in redwood clapboard has lovely, homely rooms of varying sizes, most with great views, as well as colourful grounds. $110

MacKerricher State Park campgrounds 3 miles

north of Fort Bragg ☎ 800 444 7275, ⓦ reserveamerica .com. Among 6 miles of coastal pines and sandy beach, the tent pitches here are shady and peaceful. Pitches $35
Surf Motel 1220 S Main St ☎ 707 964 3187 or ☎ 800

339 5361, ⓦ surfmotelfortbragg.com. One of the smarter of the many budget motels that line the southern approach to town, with nicely furnished and reasonably attractive rooms. $69

EATING AND DRINKING

Egghead's 326 N Main St ☎ 707 964 5005, ⓦ fortbraggrestaurants.com/eggheads. A good place for a big breakfast, this oviferous café lists 27 different omelettes on its menu, all for $10 to around $20 for Dungeness crab. Fine range of coffees too. Daily 7am–2pm.

Headlands Coffeehouse 120 E Laurel St ☎ 707 964 1987, ⓦ headlandscoffeehouse.com. Vegetarians can take refuge in the hearty Italian offerings (around $10) at this café, which also has live music every day and art exhibitions. Mon–Sat 7am–10pm, Sun 7am–5pm.

Jenny's Giant Burger 940 N Main St ☎ 707 964 2235, ⓦ fortbraggrestaurants.com/jenny-s-giant-burger. Usually full of earthy locals scoffing large hamburgers, all of which cost under $7, in an old-style place reminiscent of the Fifties. Daily 10.30am–9pm.

★**Mendo Bistro** 301 N Main St ☎ 707 964 4974, ⓦ mendobistro.com. This genteel option, upstairs in the converted old Union Lumber Store complex, serves excellent, imaginative international cuisine, including gourmet pasta dishes for $18. They also have a sleek downstairs bar called *Barbelow*. Daily 5–9pm; bar till late.

North Coast Brewing Co's Brewery Taproom 444 N Main St ☎ 707 964 2739, ⓦ northcoastbrewing.com. Stop in for one of the "handmade ales" at this award-winning brewery. You can also feast on pizza and various pub classics for around $20, plus there's live jazz every Fri & Sat 6–8pm. Mon–Thurs & Sun 11.30am–9.30pm, Fri & Sat 11.30am–10.30pm.

Piaci 120 W Redwood Ave ☎ 707 961 1133, ⓦ piacipizza.com. Tiny but extremely friendly place, which does good pizza and focaccia from $10 but also doubles up as a bar, with fine ales on tap. Mon–Thurs 11am–9.30pm, Fri & Sat 11am–10pm, Sun 4–9.30pm.

Leggett and around

As you head north from Fort Bragg, the next stretch of Hwy-1 is the slowest, continuing for another twenty miles of road and windswept beach before leaving the coastline to turn inland and head over the mountains to meet US-101 at **Leggett**. Redwood country begins in earnest here: there's even the first of several trees you can drive through (summer 8.30am–8pm; $5), though the best forests are further north.

Confusion Hill

Gravity House Daily: May–Sept 9am–6pm; Oct–April 9am–5pm • $5 • **Train ride** Summer daily 10am–5pm • $10 • ☎ 707 925 6456, ⓦ confusionhill.com

A short way past Leggett and just before you cross the Humboldt County line, you can pause briefly at kitsch **Confusion Hill** to see the "world's largest chainsaw sculpture", a totem pole hewn from redwood, which towers over 40ft above the parking lot. If that's not enough for you, the complex also includes the "mystery" Gravity House, a short Mountain Train Ride and the inevitable gift shop.

EATING   LEGGETT AND AROUND

Janice's Redwood Diner 67650 Drive Thru Tree Rd, Leggett ☎ 707 925 6442. All-American diner that dishes up hearty portions of breakfast standards and wholesome

lunch specials such as liver and onions, all for around $10 or less. Mon & Thurs–Sun 9am–2pm.

Humboldt County

Of the northern coastal counties, **HUMBOLDT COUNTY** is by far the most beautiful and also the one most at odds with development: the good folk of Eureka famously voted to bar chainstore-behemoth WalMart from erecting a huge waterfront outlet in 1999. This is logging land, and the drive up US-101 gives a tour of giant sawmills fenced in by stacks of felled trees. Yet Humboldt County also contains the largest preserves of

HUMBOLDT ON HIGH

Humboldt is perhaps most renowned for its "Emerald Triangle", which produces the majority of California's largest cash crop, **marijuana**. As the Humboldt coast's fishing and logging industries slide, more and more people have been turning to growing the stuff and new hydroponic techniques ensure that the potency of the ultra-thick buds is extremely high. It remains to be seen how the legalization of recreational marijuana in the election of November 2016 will affect the community and whether the majority of growers decide to go legitimate. What's certain is that production will continue apace. Meanwhile, subversive gifts and more innocent by-products of the region's industry can be obtained at The Hemp Connection, 412 Maple Lane, Garberville (Mon–Sat 10.30am–6pm, Sun 11am–4pm; ☎707 923 4851).

giant **redwoods** in the world. These "ambassadors from another time", as John Steinbeck dubbed them, are at their 375ft best in the **Redwood National Park**, which contains three state parks and covers some 106,000 acres of skyscraping forest. Both this and **Humboldt Redwoods State Park** are peaceful, otherworldly experiences not to be missed, though the absence of sunlight within the groves and the mossy surfaces can be eerie.

Locals worry that as more people discover the area, the rugged serve-yourself mentality here could quickly turn into a service economy. They still welcome outsiders but, beyond the few more touristic spots, do so on their own terms. The coastal highway's inability to trace Humboldt's southern coast formerly guaranteed isolation and earned the region the name of the **Lost Coast**. The area, while still isolated, is not quite as "lost" any more thanks to the construction of an airstrip in Shelter Cove and an infusion of hotels, restaurants and new homes.

Apart from the considerable areas given over to alternative agriculture (see box above), the county is almost entirely forestland. The highway rejoins the coast at **Eureka** and **Arcata**, Humboldt's two major towns and both jumping-off points for the redwoods.

As usual in this part of the state, **getting around** is going to be your biggest problem. Although Greyhound and Amtrak Thruway buses run as far as Arcata along US-101, they're hardly a satisfactory way to see the trees, and you'll need a car to make the trip worthwhile. **Hitchhiking** still goes on up here, and gaggles of locals gather at the gas stations and freeway entrances begging for rides. This is partly a throwback to the kinder decades when hitching was a normal practice on American roads but normal discretion should be exercised and remember that it is illegal on the freeway itself.

Garberville

A one-street town with a few good bars and hotels, **Garberville** is the centre of the cannabis industry (see box above) and a lively break from the freeway. Early every August, the town hosts the massive three-day **Reggae on the River** festival (☎707 923 4583, ☜reggaeontheriver.com), which attracts crowds from all over California and beyond. Weekend tickets cost at least $200, unless you take advantage of a hefty discount by the preceding October, and should be booked by early May, although a few day-tickets are made available on the gate.

ARRIVAL AND INFORMATION
GARBERVILLE

By bus The town has bus connections with Eureka on HTA (see p.627) and the train line at Martinez, with the twice-daily Amtrak Thruway service.
Chamber of Commerce In the Redwood Drive Center, 782 Redwood Drive (summer daily 9am–5pm; winter Mon–Fri 10am–4pm; ☎707 923 2613, ☜garberville.org).
Listings The *North Coast Journal* (☜northcoastjournal .com) details where to go and what to do in the area, as does the county website ☜redwoods.info.

ACCOMMODATION

Benbow Inn Several miles south of town at 445 Lake Benbow Drive ☎ 707 923 2124 or ☎ 800 355 3301, ⊛ benbowinn.com. This is a flash resort for such a rural location, with an upscale restaurant and golf course, and was being refurbished at the time of writing, though you can expect at least a couple of more moderately priced rooms to be available. $156

Benbow State Recreation Area Campground 7 miles south at 1600 US-101 ☎ 800 444 7275, ⊛ reserveamerica.com. A large number of shady tent pitches and good bathroom facilities are available at this lovely riverside location. Pitches $35

Humboldt House Inn 701 Redwood Drive ☎ 800 862 7756, ⊛ humboldthouseinn.com. This reliable Best Western franchise offers sizeable rooms, a circular swimming pool and is conveniently located right on the main drag. $145

EATING AND DRINKING

Even if you don't intend to stay in Garberville, at least stop off to sample some of the town's restaurants and bars, which turn out some of the best live bluegrass you're likely to hear in the state. Redwood Drive is lined with bars, cafés and restaurants.

Branding Iron Saloon 744 Redwood Drive ☎ 707 923 2562. Friendly bar with inexpensive drinks, simple snacks, a pool table and a small cover for its live music at weekends. Daily noon–2am.

★ **Cecil's New Orleans Bistro** 773 Redwood Drive ☎ 707 923 7007, ⊛ garbervillebistro.com. The area's best restaurant serves a delightful selection of Cajun favourites, from pork and okra gumbo for $7 to jambalaya pasta for $24, in a convivial dining room. Tues–Sat 5–9pm.

Treats Café 764 Redwood Drive ☎ 707 923 3554. Simple, spotlessly clean café that offers great sandwiches and other snacks for well under $10, plus ice cream and a range of soft drinks. Mon, Tues & Thurs–Sun 8.30am–6pm.

Woodrose Café 911 Redwood Drive ☎ 707 923 9191, ⊛ woodrosecafe.com. Serves mostly vegetarian food for $10–12, from salads to pasta, made from organic and locally grown ingredients. Also has organic beer and wine. Daily 8am–2pm.

Shelter Cove

From Garberville's neighbour Redway, the Briceland Thorn and Shelter Cove roads wind 23 miles through territory populated by old hippies and New Agers beetling around in battered vehicles. You eventually emerge on the aptly named **Lost Coast** at **Shelter Cove**, set in a tiny bay neatly folded between sea cliffs and headlands. First settled in the 1850s when gold was struck inland, its isolated position at the southern end of the **King Range** kept the village small until recent years. Now, thanks to a private airstrip, weekenders arrive in their hordes and modern houses are indiscriminately dotted across the headland. It's the closest settlement to the **hiking** and **wildlife** explorations of the wilderness around, which remains inhabited only by deer, river otter, mink, black bear, bald eagles and falcons.

A particularly fine spot to admire the ocean is from the **Cape Mendocino Lighthouse**, on Upper Pacific Drive (summer daily 11am–3pm; free; ☎ 707 906 1611), which was reopened to the public in 1998 after being relocated from the cape itself, much further north near Ferndale.

ACCOMMODATION   SHELTER COVE

Inn of the Lost Coast 205 Wave Drive ☎ 707 986 7521 or ☎ 888 570 9676. Perched on a wooded bluff on the north side of town, the huge rooms and suites here display a colourful modern design and all have ocean views. Fine restaurant, bakery and café all on the premises. $179

Mario's Marina Motel 533 Machi Rd ☎ 707 986 7595, ⊛ mariosofsheltercove.com. Humble-looking motel but the colourful rooms are perfectly adequate and it has a good restaurant and ocean views from its extensive grounds. It also rents out various items of seafaring equipment. $90

The Lost Coast loop

To the north of Shelter Cove the 24-mile **Lost Coast Trail** runs along clifftops dotted with half a dozen primitive **campgrounds**, most near streams and with access to black-sand beaches. Bring a tide book, as some points of the trail are impassable at high tide. Another trail takes you to the top of **King Peak**, which, at 4086ft, is the highest

9

point on the continental US shoreline. This is also the summit of the **King Range Natural Conservation Area**, which stretches along 35 miles of rugged coastline and covers a total of 68,000 acres from south of Shelter Cove northwards to the mouth of the Mattole River. Around twelve miles further north of the river, **Cape Mendocino** has the distinction of being the **westernmost point** of the lower 48 states.

Much of the Lost Coast is inaccessible by car but if do not have the time or leg power to hike, you can see parts of the lonely and atmospheric coastline by threading your way through the equally wild coastal hinterlands. From Shelter Cove, follow King Range Road north to Wilder Ridge Road, which continues north to **Honeydew**. From here Mattole Road snakes its way west, eventually issuing out on a beautiful ocean section before turning northeast and winding up in **Ferndale** (see below). The total driving distance is a good fifty miles and you should allow a couple of hours to cover it, not including any lengthy breaks.

Humboldt Redwoods State Park

Unrestricted entry • ☎ 707 946 2409, ⓦ humboldtredwoods.org

The heart of redwood country begins in earnest a few miles north of Garberville, along US-101, when you enter the **Humboldt Redwoods State Park**: over 53,000 acres of predominantly virgin timber, protected from lumber companies, make this the largest of the redwood parks – though it is the least used. Thanks to the Save-the-Redwoods League, which has been acquiring land privately for the park, it continues slowly to expand year after year. At the **Phillipsville** exit, the serpentine **Avenue of the Giants** follows an old stagecoach road, weaving for 32 miles through trees that block all but a few strands of sunlight. This is the habitat of *Sequoia sempervirens*, the coast redwood, with ancestors dating back to the days of the dinosaur.

The Avenue parallels US-101, adding at least thirty minutes to your travel time without stops, but there are several exits to the freeway if you're in a hurry. Pick up a free **Auto Tour** guide at the southern or northern entrances and, better still, stop at the **visitor centre** (see below). At sporadic points along the Avenue, small stalls selling lumber products and refreshments dot the course of the highway. There's a **Drive-Thru Tree** towards the southern end of the Avenue at Myers Flat ($5).

The Avenue follows the south fork of the Eel River, eventually rejoining US-101 at **Pepperwood**. Ten miles before this junction, Mattole Road peels off to the left and provides the best **backcountry** access to the towering trees, which most visitors neglect, as well as further access to the Lost Coast.

INFORMATION	HUMBOLDT REDWOODS STATE PARK
Visitor centre Halfway along the Avenue of the Giants at Burlington, a mile south of Weott (daily: summer 9am–5pm; rest of year 10am–4pm; ☎ 707 946 2263). This	place has fascinating interpretive exhibits on the redwoods, other flora and fauna, logging history, and the catastrophic flood of 1964.

ACCOMMODATION AND EATING

Humboldt Redwoods State Park campgrounds ☎ 800 444 7275, ⓦ reserveamerica.com. Three developed sites and a simpler environmental one, plus a couple of hike/bike sites, comprise your camping options within the park. Hiker/biker $5, developed sites $35

Riverwood Inn 2828 Avenue of the Giants, Phillipsville ☎ 707 943 3333, ⓦ riverwoodinn.info. A good, rustic place to stay, even if the rooms are a little tatty; the bar/restaurant occasionally showcases live bluegrass and other styles of music and serves meaty American grills, plus you're assured a friendly welcome from the locals. $80

Ferndale

Around fifteen miles north of Pepperwood, you should definitely detour a few miles west to **Ferndale**, unquestionably the Lost Coast's most attractive town, although with enough time on your hands an even better route is the stunningly scenic Lost Coast loop via Honeydew and Cape Mendocino (see opposite). Promoting itself unabashedly as "California's best-preserved Victorian village", Ferndale certainly has its charms – for once the appealing architecture is not just confined to one quaint street but continues for blocks on either side of Main Street in a picturesque townscape of nineteenth-century houses and churches. Indeed, the entire town, founded in 1852, has been designated a State Historical Landmark.

You can learn more about its history at the **Ferndale Museum**, 515 Shaw St (Tues–Sat 11am–4pm, Sun 1–4pm, closed Tues Oct–May; $2; ☎707 786 4466, ⒲ferndale-museum.org), by perusing the old newspaper cuttings, documents, photos and equipment that was once used in bygone occupations. The town's other claim to fame is as the finishing point of the annual Kinetic Sculpture Race from Arcata (see box, p.629). Ferndale also supports an active artistic community, so there are a disproportionate number of **galleries** and antiques shops to browse through.

ACCOMMODATION   FERNDALE

As you might expect, most of Ferndale's accommodation comes in the shape of stylish hotels and B&Bs, though the remote location keeps prices very reasonable.

★**Gingerbread Mansion** 400 Berding St ☎707 786 4000, ⒲thegingerbreadmansion.com. This dazzling piece of Victoriana is a riot of colour from its bright yellow exterior to the splendid lounge and various floral furnishings and wallpapers of its luxurious rooms. In-house spa. $165

The Hotel Ivanhoe 315 Main St ☎707 786 9000, ⒲ivanhoe-hotel.com. Claims to be the oldest hotel in town and the westernmost in the country. The four rooms vary greatly in size and there's a decent restaurant too. $95

Victorian Inn 400 Ocean Ave ☎888 589 1808, ⒲victorianvillageinn.com. The rather grand upper façade of the building conceals comfortable rooms above its classy lobby and lounge. Full breakfast at the hotel's famous restaurant (see below) is included. Entire four-bedroom rectory nearby also available. $139

EATING AND ENTERTAINMENT

Ferndale Pie Company 543 Main St ☎707 786 4444, ⒲ferndalepiecompany.com. Those with a sweet tooth will love the scrumptious pies here. The owners recently opened the *Ferndale Omelette Factory* a few doors down, good for an eggy brekky or lunch. Mon–Sat 7am–7pm.

Ferndale Repertory Theatre 477 Main St ☎707 786 5483, ⒲ferndale-rep.org. The main stage puts on mostly well-known touring productions, while the smaller Stage Two showcases more offbeat plays.

Poppa Joe's 409 Main St ☎707 786 4180. Old-fashioned diner that guarantees a warm welcome and dishes up down-home breakfasts and lunches. Most items on the menu are under $10. Daily 7am–3pm.

★**VI** Victorian Inn 400 Ocean Ave ☎707 786 4950, ⒲virestaurant.com. Ferndale's top restaurant serves quality California cuisine, such as braised beef short ribs bourguignon, for around $30, plus humbler sandwiches and great cocktails. Daily 7.30am–9.30pm.

Eureka and around

"Eureka", as is well known from the story of Archimedes, means "I have found it!" and, being the largest coastal settlement north of San Francisco, this expanding town would certainly displace a fair amount of water if dropped into the Pacific. Near the top of the north coast of California between the Arcata and Humboldt bays, **EUREKA** feels at first like an industrial, gritty and often foggy lumber-mill town, though its **fishing industry** carries the most economic weight, providing ninety percent of the state's catch of Pacific Ocean shrimp and Dungeness crab, as well as two-thirds of its oysters. Downtown Eureka is quite a mixed bag of neon-lit motels and chain restaurants, backing onto workaday rail- and shipyards, yet interspersed with some delightful Victorian architecture. It may initially strike you as somewhere just to pass through, but persevere and you will discover an appealing centre, dotted with cute B&Bs, an increasing number of galleries and restaurants and a number of worthwhile sights.

9

Old Town

Pretty, compact **Old Town**, whose main section is bounded by C, G, First and Third streets, at the edge of the bay, does its best to support a fledgling tourist economy. This area boasts an increasing number of vibrant restaurants, bars that would not look out of place in San Francisco, and galleries. The area is at its liveliest on the first Saturday of each month, when the galleries and boutiques throw their doors open for **Arts Alive!** night, when there are various live musical performances.

Visitors with children might be rewarded by dropping in at the **Discovery Museum**, 612 G St (Tues–Sat 10am–4pm, Sun noon–4pm; $5; ☎707 443 9694, ⊛discovery-museum .org), which has rotating hands-on art and science displays for youngsters. The collection of Native American art at the **Clarke Memorial Museum**, 204 E St (Wed–Sat 11am–4pm; donation; ☎707 443 1947, ⊛clarkemuseum.org), can't hold a candle to the stuff at the beautifully designed **American Indian Art & Gift Shop**, 517 5th St (Mon–Sun 10am–6pm; free; ☎707 445 8451, ⊛americanindianonline.com), which affords a rare opportunity for Native American artists to show and market their works in a gallery setting and an even rarer chance to get your hands on some incredibly good, inexpensive silver jewellery.

Carson Mansion

143 M St, at 2nd

The town's most iconic sight is the **Carson Mansion**, an opulent Gothic pile built in the 1880s by William Carson, who made and lost fortunes in both timber and oil. Unfortunately, it is now a private club and can only be enjoyed from the street.

Morris Graves Museum of Art

636 F St • Wed–Sun noon–5pm • Donation • ☎707 442 0278, ⊛humboldtarts.org

The **Morris Graves Museum of Art** has six galleries of modern paintings and a sculpture garden. As well as the permanent collection, it draws some quite prestigious temporary exhibitions and also runs regular interesting programmes and special events.

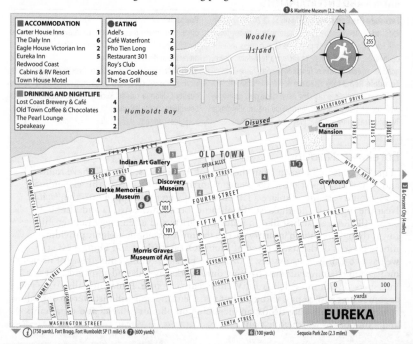

9

Fort Humboldt State Historic Park

3431 Fort Ave • Daily 9am–5pm, closed Mon Oct–May • Free • ☎707 445 6547, ⓦ parks.ca.gov

Just over a mile south of Old Town, **Fort Humboldt State Historic Park** provides visitors with a look at a restored army fort but not much else; disappointing, given that the army general and future president Ulysses S. Grant used it for a headquarters in 1853.

Sequoia Park Zoo

3414 W St • Daily 8am–5pm • $7 • ☎707 441 4263, ⓦ sequoiaparkzoo.net

A fine escape a couple of miles east of Old Town is the modestly sized **Sequioa Park Zoo**, which has a good range of creatures on view. The highlights are the red panda compound and otter tank, which includes a large plastic tube you can crawl through for a unique angle on their playful activities. There's also a colourful **Dahlia Garden** by the side entrance and a sizeable chunk of redwood forest behind the zoo in **Sequoia Park** itself, which is a great place for a stroll.

Samoa

A few minutes by car from Eureka across the Samoa Bridge, squashed against the Louisiana–Pacific plywood mill, the tiny company town of **Samoa** is the site of the last remaining cookhouse in the West. The **Samoa Cookhouse** was where lumbermen would come to eat gargantuan meals after a day of felling redwoods. Although the oilskin tablecloths and burly workers have gone, the lumber-camp style remains, making the cookhouse something of a unique dining experience for tourists (see p.628). There are also plenty of exhibits and old photos. Next to the cookhouse, the one-room **Maritime Museum** (mid-March to Nov Tues–Sat 11am–4pm; Dec to mid-March Thurs–Sat 11am–4pm; $5 suggested donation; ☎707 444 9440, ⓦhumboldtbaymaritime museum.com) is full of photos, maps and relics from the days when Eureka was a whaling port.

ARRIVAL AND INFORMATION

EUREKA AND AROUND

By bus Eureka has fairly limited transport links: Greyhound, 1603 4th St, connects Eureka to San Francisco twice a day but only goes as far north as nearby Arcata. For getting around town or up the coast as far as Trinidad and south as far as Garberville, Humboldt Transit Authority, 133 V St (☎707 443 0826, ⓦhta.org), operates buses every day except Sunday.
Destinations Arcata (Mon–Fri every 20–30min, Sat 11, Sun 6; 20–25min); San Francisco (2 daily; 7hr 20min–7hr

30min); Santa Rosa (1 daily; 4hr 55min–5hr).
By plane There are four flights daily to San Francisco and two daily to Portland and Redding from the California Redwood Coast Humboldt County Regional Airport at McKinleyville, 16 miles north. The airport is connected by local HTA buses (see above) to Eureka and Arcata.
Visitor centre 2112 Broadway, 2 miles south of downtown (Mon–Fri 8.30am–5pm; ☎707 442 3738 or ☎800 356 6381, ⓦeurekachamber.com).

ACCOMMODATION

The collection of motels that punctuate the town's two main thoroughfares make Eureka a reasonably economical base for exploring the redwoods to the north and south, although there is also an increasing number of far classier hotels and B&Bs.

★**Carter House Inns** 301 L St ☎707 444 8062, ⓦcarterhouse.com. All rooms are top quality within this enclave of four Victorian buildings arranged around a quiet junction, including the private $600-a-night Carter Cottage and the superb *Restaurant 301* (see p.628). Gourmet breakfast included. $208
The Daly Inn 1125 H St ☎707 445 3638, ⓦdalyinn .com. Imposing mansion built in 1905 for local magnate Cornelius Daly, which has been converted into a fine B&B with eight rooms and suites offering varying degrees of luxury. Excellent hot breakfasts. $130

Eagle House Victorian Inn 139 2nd St ☎707 444 3344, ⓦeaglehouseinn.com. As the name suggests, this stylish 1886 B&B re-creates the opulence and splendour of a bygone era with its range of lavishly presented rooms. Irish pub on the ground floor. $125
Eureka Inn 518 7th St ☎707 497 6093 or ☎877 552 3985, ⓦeurekainn.com. Occupying an entire block, this huge landmark hotel has been completely refurbished. The rooms are simply furnished and the massive lobby area remains a time warp in deep red. $124
Redwood Coast Cabins & RV Resort 4050 N US-101, 4

9

miles north of downtown ☎707 822 4243, ⓦredwood coastrv.com. This large site offers copious amenities, including a large pool, hot tub and sports facilities. Pitches $19, RV hookups $44, cabins $75

Town House Motel 933 4th St ☎707 443 4536, ⓦeurekatownhousemotel.com. The cleanest of the cluster of cheap motels heading north on US-101, with sizeable and adequately furnished rooms. Ideal budget base. $70

EATING

Eating options are numerous in Eureka, especially around Old Town, with seafood being a particular favourite because of fresh local catches.

Adel's 1724 Broadway ☎707 445 9777, ⓦadelsrestaurant.com. Basic meat-and-potato meals and salads for about $10–18 make this local hangout on the south side of town a good option. Daily 6am–10pm.

Café Waterfront 102 F St ☎707 443 9190, ⓦcafewaterfronteureka.com. A very reliable choice for delicious seafood and burgers, where the fancier main courses cost in the region of $20–30. There's also a full bar. Daily 9am–9pm.

Pho Tien Long 307 4th St ☎707 445 4735, ⓦpho-tienlong.com. Main courses such as the mouthwatering coconut shrimp go for $10–15, plus there's a range of pho soups at this authentic Vietnamese place. Daily 11.30am–8.45pm.

Restaurant 301 301 L St ☎707 444 8062, ⓦcarterhouse.com. The *Carter House Inns'* classy dining room serves sumptuous set menus and à la carte dishes for around $25–40. The cuisine is mostly California with a French touch, such as the fine duck confit, and you can choose from one of the

most extensive wine lists in the country. Daily 7.30am–10am, 11.30am–2.30pm & 6–10pm.

Roy's Club 218 D St ☎707 442 4574, ⓦroysclubrestaurant.com. The place to head if you want to try one of the Old-Town Italian restaurants, with main courses such as the spicy meatball pasta costing $20–25. Tues–Thurs & Sat 4.30–9.30pm, Fri 11.30am–2pm.

★**Samoa Cookhouse** Off Cookhouse Rd, Samoa ☎707 442 1659, ⓦsamoacookhouse.net. Eating massive portions of red meat at its long tables is pure entertainment; you're served as much as you can eat of the three daily fixed menus ($12–18) with a smile and a bit of history (see p.627). Daily 7am–9pm.

The Sea Grill 316 E St ☎707 443 7187, ⓦseagrillrestauranteureka.com. Classy grill that specializes in seafood such as cod Louisiana in the $20–30 range but also does great steaks and has the best salad bar in town, a meal in itself. Daily 5–9pm, bar till later.

DRINKING AND NIGHTLIFE

Eureka has a fair sprinkling of nightlife venues and some increasingly trendy bars. For full listings of what's on, check out the free weekly *North Coast Journal* (ⓦnorthcoastjournal.com).

★**Lost Coast Brewery and Café** 617 4th St ☎707 445 4480, ⓦlostcoast.com. Serves a superb range of beers and large, hearty meat and fish dishes for $10–18 to a rambunctious crowd of discerning microbrew drinkers and sports fans. Mon–Thurs & Sun 11am–10pm, Fri & Sat 11am–11pm.

Old Town Coffee & Chocolates 211 F St ☎707 445 8600, ⓦoldtowncoffeeeureka.com. Ranks as the coast's finest coffee shop, with its beautiful red-brick interior and top-notch roasts, plus beer, wine and cider. It's open until around 11pm and has fun open-mike nights. Mon–Wed &

Sun 7am–9pm, Thurs–Sat 7am–10pm.

The Pearl Lounge 507 2nd St ☎707 444 2017, ⓦpearlloungeeureka.com. The best example of old Eureka's new persona, this extremely chic joint, with sleek metal-and-glass bar and high-tech projection screen, is the spot to be seen with a cocktail. Live entertainment on Fri & Sat. Daily 5pm–2am.

Speakeasy 411 Opera Alley ☎707 444 2244. Small New Orleans-style bar with smooth music and hip decor, most stunningly in the toilets. Plenty of choice when it comes to beers, wine and cocktails. Daily 5pm–2am.

Arcata

ARCATA, only seven miles up the coast from Eureka, is far more immediately appealing, centred on a grassy central plaza that flies an Earth flag under those of the US and California. Beards and Birkenstocks are the norm in this small college town, with a large community of rat-race refugees and Sixties throwbacks, whose presence is manifest in some lively bars and the town's earthy, mellow pace. The beaches north of town are some of the best on the north coast, white-sanded, windswept and known for their easy hikeability and random parties. But think twice about diving headlong into the surf without a wetsuit, as the ocean in these parts is cold throughout the year.

Arcata Plaza

The main square, **Arcata Plaza**, is the focal point of the town's shops and bars, with everything you're likely to want to see and do within easy walking distance. In the middle of the square rests a statue of President McKinley. Originally intended for nearby McKinleyville, it fell off the train on the way and stayed put in Arcata.

Humboldt State University

1 Harpst St • Tours Mon–Fri at 10am & 2pm, Sat at noon • ☎ 707 826 4402, ⓦ humboldt.edu

Just east of the town centre, **Humboldt State University**, with its nationally known environmental education and natural resource management programmes, attracts a decidedly liberal student body, which contributes considerably to Arcata's leftist feel. If you're interested in the college's history and programmes, take one of the free student-led **tours**, which begin at the Plaza Avenue entrance.

Arcata Marsh and Wildlife Sanctuary

Wildlife Sanctuary At the foot of I St • **Interpretive Center** 569 South G St • Daily 9am–5pm; guided walks Sat at 2pm • ☎ 707 826 2359 • **Audubon Society walks** End of I St • Guided walks Sat at 8.30am • ⓦ rras.org

The **Arcata Marsh and Wildlife Sanctuary**, a restored former dump on 150 acres of wetland, is a peaceful place where you can lie on the boardwalk in the sun and listen to the birds. The Interpretive Center runs **guided wildlife walks**, as does the northwest chapter of the Audubon Society.

Arcata Community Forest

Redwood Park Drive

Those who don't have time to explore the Redwood National Park can visit the town's own second-growth **Arcata Community Forest**, a beautiful 575-acre spot with manageable trails and ideal picnic areas, accessible by going east on 14th Street to Redwood Park Drive.

ARRIVAL AND INFORMATION   ARCATA

By bus Greyhound buses only head south to Eureka and on to San Francisco from the stop at 925 E St; there's also a daily Humboldt Transit Authority (see p.627) link with Eureka. Going north, Redwood Coast Transit (see p.635) runs a daily service for $20 to Crescent City and on to Smith River.
Destinations Crescent City (2 daily; 2hr); Eureka (Mon–Fri every 20–30min, Sat 11, Sun 6; 20–25min); San Francisco (2 daily; 7hr 40min–7hr 50min); Santa Rosa (2 daily; 5hr 15min–5hr 20min).
Visitor centre Over a mile north of town just off US-101 at 1635 Heindon Rd (daily 9am–5pm; ☎ 707 822 3619, ⓦ arcatachamber.com).

ACCOMMODATION

Clam Beach County Park Campground 8 miles north of town on US-101 ☎ 707 445 7651. The nearest and cheapest campground, making it quite a party venue for dishevelled youngsters staying long-term. Toilets but no showers. Hiker/biker $10, pitch with car $20
Fairwinds Motel 1674 G St ☎ 866 352 5518, ⓦ fairwindsmotelarcata.com. This is the best of the motels available, with functional but well-maintained rooms. It's also walkable to the plaza in a little over 10min. $82

Hotel Arcata 708 9th St ☎ 707 826 0217, ⓦ hotelarcata.com. Right on the town's main square, this hotel exudes a quaint, old-fashioned charm with flock wallpaper and patterned carpets in its cosy rooms. $97
The Lady Anne 902 14th St ☎ 707 822 2797, ⓦ ladyanneinn.com. This B&B has rightly been an Arcata favourite for years, with three attractive rooms and two suites, one with a four-poster bed. $135

THE KINETIC SCULPTURE RACE

If you're around over Memorial Day weekend, don't miss the three-day **Kinetic Sculpture Race** (☎ 707 786 9259, ⓦ kineticgrandchampionship.com), a spectacular and somewhat left-field event in which competitors use human-powered contraptions of their own devising to propel themselves over land, water, dunes and marsh from Arcata to Ferndale.

9

EATING AND DRINKING

Abruzzi 780 H St ☎707 826 2345, ⓦabruzziarcata.com. Serves top-quality Italian dinners like herb-crusted Kurobuta pork loin with marsala cream for $30. There's also a huge selection of wines. Wed–Sun 5–9pm.

Café Brio 791 G St ☎707 822 5922, ⓦbriobaking.com. On the corner of the plaza, this is a great spot to enjoy a fine coffee, cake or baked snack, while watching proceedings in the square. Mon–Thurs 7am–5pm, Fri 7am–9pm, Sat 8am–9pm, Sun 8am–4pm.

Café Mokka Finnish Country Sauna and Tubs, 495 J St ☎707 822 2228, ⓦcafemokkaarcata.com. A relaxed place with live acoustic sets at the weekend. The hot tubs and sauna cabins in the garden cost $9.75/30min. Mon–Thurs & Sun noon–11pm, Fri & Sat noon–1am.

Humboldt Brews 856 10th St ☎707 826 2739, ⓦhumboldtbrews.com. Rough-and-ready joint offering twenty ales on tap and bar meals such as a basket of wings for $12. Also hosts regular gigs. Daily 11am–11pm, till 2am on show nights.

★**Jambalaya** 915 H St ☎707 822 4766, ⓦjambalayaarcata.com. This buzzing joint no longer actually serves jambalaya but its $20 pizzas and much cheaper burgers are supplemented by a nightly diet of R&B, jazz and rock bands. Mon & Tues 4pm–2am, Wed–Sat 4pm–2.30am, Sun 9am–2.30am.

Sushi Spot 670 9th St ☎707 839 1221, ⓦsushispotarcata.com. Does excellent sushi and sashimi, as well as hot Japanese dishes such as chicken katsu curry for $11.95 and fine veggie options. Good choice of sake and wine too. Mon–Thurs noon–9pm, Fri noon–10pm, Sat & Sun 4–9pm.

Wildflower Café and Bakery 1604 G St ☎707 822 0360, ⓦwildflowercafebakery.com. A vegetarian place turning out first-rate, cheap organic meals, such as cajun *seitan* for $10. Mon–Wed 9am–3pm & 5.30–9.30pm, Thurs–Sun 9am–3pm & 5.30–9.30pm.

McKinleyville

If you've got a car, take time to explore the coastline just north of Arcata along US-101. On the way, make a short detour east of the highway through the modern strip-mall town of **McKinleyville**, near Clam Beach, in order to see the world's tallest **totem pole**. The gaily decorated, 160ft ex-redwood stands proudly at the back of the McKinleyville Shopping Center, halfway along Central Avenue near the junction with City Center Road.

Trinidad and around

Around fifteen miles north of Arcata, **Trinidad** is a good place to eat or drink, nose around the small shops or just sit down by the sea wall and watch the fishing boats being tossed about in the picturesque harbour. **Patrick's Point State Park**, five miles north, sports an agate beach below rocky coastal bluffs; tours of a re-created Yurok village are conducted by appointment (☎707 677 3570), although you can wander alone at will.

Several miles further on, **Big Lagoon County Park** (☎707 445 7651; day-use $2) is a great place for camping (see below) and **kayaking** on the lagoon or its smaller sister **Stone Lagoon**; Kayak Zak's at 115336 US-101 (☎707 498 1130, ⓦkayakzak.com) rent single kayaks for $30 per hour, doubles for $40.

Moonstone Beach

Several miles south of Trinidad, **Moonstone Beach** is a vast, sandy strip that, save for the odd beachcomber, remains empty during the day but by night heats up with guitar-strumming student parties that rage for as long as the bracing climate allows.

ACCOMMODATION AND EATING   TRINIDAD AND AROUND

Big Lagoon County Park Campground Big Lagoon Park Rd, 7 miles north of Trinidad on US-101 ☎707 445 7651, ⓦco.humboldt.ca.us. This campground is pretty basic in terms of facilities but its 25 pitches enjoy a fantastic location between the ocean and the lagoon. Pitches **$20**

Emerald Forest 733 Patrick's Point Drive, 1.5 miles north of Trinidad ☎707 677 3554, ⓦemeraldforestcabins.com.

This privately administered slice of forest offers secluded luxury cabins, sturdily built and well furnished, as well as some RV and tent sites. Pitches **$35**, RVs **$40**, cabins **$179**

Lost Whale Inn 3452 Patrick's Point Drive, 4 miles north of Trinidad ☎800 677 7849, ⓦlostwhaleinn.com. One of the most romantic retreats along the entire coast, this luxurious and friendly B&B has an outdoor hot tub and access to a secluded little beach where seals frolic. $285

★ **Moonstone Grill** 100 Moonstone Beach Rd, Trinidad ☎ 707 677 1616, ⓦ moonstonegrill.com. One of the best restaurants on the north coast, with glorious ocean sunset views. Great seafood, including abalone for $58 and other fish under $30, as well as great steaks and vegetarian meals. Excellent cocktails too. Daily 7.30am–9.30pm.

Patrick's Point State Park Campground 5 miles north of Trinidad ☎ 800 444 7275, ⓦ reserveamerica .com. Reasonably secluded camping in this delightful wooded park in between the coastal highway and the ocean. Good facilities. Pitches $35

Seascape Pier Restaurant 1 Bay St, Trinidad ☎ 707 677 3762. Locals rave about this place for its menu of fresh

fish, steaks and pasta for $20–30, which taste all the more delicious given its waterfront location. Daily 7.30am–9.30pm.

Trinidad Bay Eatery 607 Parker Rd, Trinidad ☎ 707 677 3777, ⓦ trinidadeatery.com. A good solid place that dishes up chunky portions of fish and chips with Caribbean coleslaw for $17, as well as great ice cream. Mon & Tues 8am–4pm, Wed–Fri 8am–8.30pm, Sat & Sun 7.30am–8.30pm.

Trinidad Inn 1170 Patrick's Point Drive, 2 miles north of Trinidad ☎ 707 677 3349, ⓦ trinidadinn.com. This is a lovely motel in a quiet location, whose rooms are tastefully decorated in modern style. Some units have fully equipped kitchens. $100

Hoopa Valley Indian Reservation

The most interesting inland destination in Humboldt County is the **Hoopa Valley Indian Reservation**, around sixty miles from Arcata, the largest in California. The often violent confrontations that until not many years ago took place here between Native Americans and whites over fishing territory have been consigned to history, yet few take the time to check out the valley. Although some of the youth still hang around listlessly, the local casino provides income and the atmosphere is friendly enough. If you're here in the last week in July you should make an effort to catch the **All Indian Rodeo**, held southwest of the village. Otherwise it's enough to visit the **Hoopa Tribal Museum**, located in the Hoopa Shopping Center on Hwy-96 (Tues–Fri 8am–5pm, summer also Sat 10am–4pm; free; ☎ 530 625 4110) – full of crafts, baskets and jewellery of the Hoopa (aka Natinixwe) and Yurok tribes.

Willow Creek

The access point to the Hoopa Valley and nearest town with any facilities to speak of is **Willow Creek**, forty miles east of Arcata on Hwy-299. It is also the self-proclaimed gateway to **Bigfoot Country** (see box below) – indeed Hwy-96 north towards the valley is known as the "Bigfoot Scenic Byway". Near the Hwy-299/Hwy-96 junction, a statue of Bigfoot marks the entrance to the small **Willow Creek–China Flat Museum** (May–Sept Wed–Sun 10am–4pm; Oct Fri–Sun noon–4pm; rest of year by appointment; free; ☎ 530 629 2653, ⓦ bigfootcountry.net), which displays a modest collection of Native American quilts and settlers' possessions, plus the obligatory Bigfoot curios.

Rafting is popular on the Smith, Klamath and Trinity rivers near here. Among the numerous operators in the area, Bigfoot Rafting Company (☎ 530 629 2263, ⓦ bigfootrafting.com) offers guided trips from $69.

> ### THE LEGEND OF BIGFOOT
>
> Reports of giant 350- to 800-pound humanoids wandering the forests of northwestern California have circulated since the late nineteenth century, fuelled by long-established Native American legends, though they weren't taken seriously until 1958, when a road maintenance crew found giant footprints in a remote area near Willow Creek. Photos were taken and the **Bigfoot** story went worldwide. Since then there have been more than fifty separate sightings of Bigfoot prints, and it was near Willow Creek that the famous 1967 Patterson-Gimlin documentary, grainy footage of Bigfoot and all, was filmed. At the crossroads in Willow Creek stands a huge wooden replica of the prehistoric-looking apeman, who in recent years has added kidnapping to his list of alleged activities.

9

If you continue the extremely scenic route east on Hwy-299 from Willow Creek, you will eventually arrive in Weaverville (see p.651) and, further on, California's main north–south freeway, the I-5.

ARRIVAL AND INFORMATION   WILLOW CREEK

By car Take Hwy-299 east out of Arcata for 40 miles until you hit Willow Creek. To get to the Hoopa Valley reservation from here, take Hwy-96, the "Bigfoot Scenic Byway", north.

Chamber of Commerce 38919 Hwy-299 (summer only: daily 9am–5pm; ☏ 530 629 2693, ⓦ willowcreekchamber .com).

ACCOMMODATION AND EATING

Bigfoot Motel 39116 Hwy-299 ☏ 530 629 2142, ⓦ bigfootmotel.com. Referenced in the legendary song by The Jazz Butcher, the inevitably named town motel has decent-sized rooms, including some singles and larger kitchenettes. $88

Gonzales 38971 Hwy-299 ☏ 530 629 3151, ⓦ gonzalesmexicanrestaurant.com. Simple Mexican restaurant that serves up authentic grub, from soup, tacos and enchiladas to specials like *chimichanga* for $11. Daily 11am–10pm.

The Redwood National and State parks

Unrestricted access • Free

Way up in the top left-hand corner of California, the landscape is almost too spectacular for words and the long drive up here is rewarded with a couple of tiny towns and thick, dense redwood forests perfect for hiking and camping. Some thirty miles north of Arcata, **Orick** marks the southernmost end of this landscape, a contiguous strip of forest jointly managed as the **REDWOOD NATIONAL AND STATE PARKS**, a massive area that stretches up into Del Norte County at the very northernmost point of California, ending at the rather dull town of **Crescent City**.

The parks' 58,000 acres divide into distinct areas: **Redwood National Park**, southwest of the Orick area; the **Prairie Creek Redwood State Park**, south of the riverside town of **Klamath**; and the area in the far north around the **Del Norte Coast Redwood** and **Jedediah Smith Redwood** state parks, in the environs of Crescent City in Del Norte County. Together, they contain some of the tallest trees in the world: the pride of California's forestland, especially between June and September when every school in the state seems to organize its summer camp here. One word of caution: **bears** and **mountain lions** inhabit this area, and you should heed warnings (see box, p.44).

Orick and Tall Trees Grove

As the southernmost and most used entrance to the **Redwood National Park**, the Orick area is always busy. Its major attraction is **Tall Trees Grove**, home of one of the world's tallest trees – a mightily impressive specimen that stands at some 367ft. The best view of this giant and its companions is from the mostly dry riverbed nearby. Incidentally, the tallest tree in the world, recently measured at 379ft, stands in an undisclosed location, inaccessible to the public.

The most direct route to Tall Trees Grove is by driving to the main trailhead only a half-hour hike away but you first have to arrange access via a ranger at the visitor centre (see p.635), as there is a limit of fifty cars per day – this is only ever reached at major holiday weekends though. Otherwise, the lengthy alternative approach is by the 8.5-mile **Redwood Creek Trail** (permit needed if staying overnight in the backcountry) from near Orick: take a right turn off US-101 onto Bald Hills Road, then, six hundred yards along, fork off to the picnic area where the trail starts. The bridge, 1.5 miles down the trail, is passable in summer only.

Lady Bird Johnson Grove and the Coastal Trail

9

Further east another trail turns north off Bald Hills Road and winds for half a mile to **Lady Bird Johnson Grove** – a collection of trees dedicated to former US President LBJ's wife, a big lover of flora and fauna right up until her death in 2007. A mile-long self-guided trail winds through the grove of these giant patriarchs. On the western side of US-101, across from the entrance to the Redwood Creek Trail, begins the **Coastal Trail**, which follows the coastline and takes backpackers up the entire length of all three state parks.

Prairie Creek Redwood State Park

Elk Prairie $8/vehicle

Of the three state parks within the Redwood National Park area, **Prairie Creek** is the most varied and popular. Bear and elk often roam in plain sight, and you can take a ranger-led **tour** of the wild, dense redwood forest – check with the **Prairie Creek visitor centre** (see p.635) for details and informative displays. Whether you choose to go independently or opt for a tour, the main features of the park include the meadows of **Elk Prairie** in front of the ranger station, where herds of Roosevelt elk – massive beasts who can tip the scales over one thousand pounds – wander freely, protected from poachers. Remember that elk, like all wildlife, are unpredictable and should not be approached. There's a fee for vehicles to enter Elk Prairie itself but you can leave your car beside the road nearby and wander at will; if you're pressed for time, there are also some car-accessible routes through the woods.

Just south of the ranger station, on the east side of US-101, is the entrance to **Lost Man Creek**, an unpaved, 1.5-mile round-trip drive into an otherworldly grove of old-growth trees that passes by a cascade. To enter Prairie Creek Redwoods State Park, take the **Newton B. Drury Scenic Byway** off US-101 north of Lost Man Creek. A mile north of the ranger station, the magnificent **Big Tree Wayside** redwood, more than 300ft tall and, at over 21ft in diameter, one of the fattest of the coastal redwoods, overlooks the road. North of the Big Tree Wayside and before the byway rejoins US-101, the rough, gravel Coastal Drive branches off to the west following the Coastal Trail for 7.5 miles, leading to **High Bluff Overlook** and free camping (no water) at **Flint Ridge**.

Klamath and around

KLAMATH, in Del Norte County, isn't technically part of the Redwood area nor, by most definitions, does it qualify as a town, as most of the buildings were washed away when the nearby Klamath River flooded in 1964. Nonetheless, there are spectacular coastal views from trails where the Klamath River meets the ocean, famed salmon and steelhead fishing in the river itself, a few decent accommodation options (see p.635) and the Trees of Mystery (see below). Further south, where Hwy-169 peels off from US-101, the 725-year-old living **Tour Thru Tree** on Terwer Valley Road (daylight hours; $5) provides a cute photo opportunity.

Trees of Mystery

US-101 5 miles north of Klamath • Daily: summer 8am–7pm; rest of year 9am–5pm • $16 • ☎ 707 482 2251, ⊛ treesofmystery.net

For a bit of fun, head to the **Trees of Mystery**, where you cannot miss two huge wooden sculptures of Paul Bunyan and Babe, his blue ox. Taped stories of Bunyan's adventures emanate periodically from within the redwood stands and ethereal choral music greets you at the most impressive specimen of all, the **Cathedral Tree**, where nine trees have grown from one root structure to form a spooky circle. Enterprising Californians hold wedding services here throughout the year.

The steep entry fee is somewhat justified by an aerial **tram**, which takes you from the top of the foot trail over the forest canopy to 750ft **Ted's Ridge**. Here you're provided with binoculars to enhance your enjoyment of the ocean views to the west and tree-clad ridges and valleys to the east – from March to October, see if you can spot the oft-active osprey nest atop one distant redwood. Back down in the gift shop, the free **End of the Trail Museum** highlights artwork from a number of the region's Native American tribes.

Klamath Overlook

The most spectacular scenery in Klamath is not the trees but the ocean: take Requa Road about three-quarters of a mile up above the estuary to a point known as the **Klamath Overlook,** from where, once the fog has burnt off, there's an awe-inspiring view of the estuary meeting the sea and the rugged coastline to the south. From here you can pick up the Coastal Trail on foot, which leads north for ten miles along some of California's most remote beaches, ending at Endert's Beach in Crescent City.

Crescent City

The northernmost outposts of the Redwood National Park, the Del Norte and Jedediah Smith state parks, sit on either side of **Crescent City**, a rather forlorn place whose most attractive buildings were wiped out by a tsunami in 1964, leaving little to recommend it other than its budget accommodation and proximity to the parks. That said, the city is the halfway point on US-101 between San Francisco and Portland, Oregon, around 350 miles in each direction, and is therefore often used as a stopover.

Ocean World

304 US-101 S • Daily 9am–dusk • $12.95 • ☎ 707 464 4900, ⓦ oceanworldonline.com

Crescent City's most popular tourist attraction is **Ocean World**, an unmissably large complex on US-101 south of town, which has a limited range of fish and other sea creatures. The guided tours that run every fifteen minutes are informative and give you the opportunity to handle many of the inmates – if you fancy picking up a starfish or stroking a shark or sea lion, this is the place.

Battery Point Lighthouse

April–Sept daily 10am–4pm; Oct–March Sat & Sun 10am–4pm • $5 • ☎ 707 464 3089, ⓦ delnortehistory.org

Take an hour to visit the **Battery Point Lighthouse**, reached by a causeway from the western end of town; note that you can only tour it during low tides. The oldest working lighthouse on the West Coast, constructed in 1856, it houses a collection of artefacts from the *Brother Jonathan*, wrecked off Point St George in the 1850s. Because of this loss, the St George Lighthouse, the tallest and most expensive in the US, was built six miles north of Crescent City.

Main Museum

577 H St • May–Sept Mon–Sat 10am–4pm; Oct–March Mon & Sat 10am–4pm • $5 • ☎ 707 464 3922, ⓦ delnortehistory.org

The local history society maintains both this and the old-fashioned **Main Museum**, whose dusty interior contains some Native American artefacts, quilts, old musical instruments, a lens from the St George Lighthouse, historical displays and, most interesting of all, original cells from the building's earlier incarnation as the county jail.

Del Norte Coast Redwoods State Park

Open access • ☎ 707 465 7335, ⓦ parks.ca.gov

Seven miles south of Crescent City, **Del Norte Coast Redwoods State Park** is worth visiting less for its redwood forests than its fantastic beach area and hiking trails, most of which are an easy two miles or so along the coastal ridge where the redwoods meet the sea. From May to July, wild rhododendrons and azaleas shoot up everywhere, laying a floral blanket across the park's floor.

Jedediah Smith Redwoods State Park

9

Open access • ☎ 707 465 7335, ⊛ parks.ca.gov

Nine miles northeast of Crescent City, **Jedediah Smith Redwoods State Park** is named after the European explorer who was the first white man to trek overland from the Mississippi to the Pacific in 1828, before being killed by Comanche tribes in Kansas in 1831. Not surprisingly, his name is everywhere: no fewer than eighteen separate redwood groves are dedicated to his memory. Sitting on the south fork of the Smith River, the park attracts many people who canoe downstream or simply sit on the riverbank and fish. Of the hiking trails, the **Stout Grove Trail** is the most popular, a flat, one-hour walk leading down to a most imposing Goliath – a 345ft-tall, 20ft-diameter redwood.

If you're heading further east and are in no hurry, you could opt for the painfully slow but scenic six-mile route that follows Howland Hill Road from Crescent City through the forest to **Hiouchi**. Branching off this are several blissfully short and easy trails (roughly half a mile each) that are quieter than the routes through the major parts of the park. The **Little Bald Hills Trail** east of Hiouchi traces a strenuous ten-mile hike that should take about eight hours.

The apparent detour into Oregon on Hwy-199 to connect with I-5 back south is actually by far the quickest way to reach the interior of Northern California from the extreme north coast.

ARRIVAL AND GETTING AROUND

By bus Redwood Coast Transit (☎707 464 6400, ⊛redwoodcoasttransit.org) runs buses twice a day from Crescent City to Smith River, further inland, for $1.50 and

REDWOOD NATIONAL AND STATE PARKS

once a day down the coast to Arcata ($30). These will, if asked, stop along forested stretches of the highway; if you're lucky, you can even flag them down.

INFORMATION AND ACTIVITIES

Park visitor centres The Redwood National Park headquarters are at 1111 2nd St, Crescent City (daily: summer 9am–5pm; rest of year 9am–4pm; ☎707 464 6101, ⊛nps.gov/redw). This office is very helpful but the visitor centres and ranger stations throughout the parks are even better for maps and information, including up-to-date hiking conditions and the weather forecast. Most useful is the Thomas B. Kuchel Visitor Center (daily 9am–5pm; ☎707 465 7765), right by the southern entrance to Redwood National Park, before you get to

Orick, though it is slated to move to nearby Bald Hills Rd. Prairie Creek Visitor Centre (daily: summer 9am–5pm; rest of year 9am–4pm; ☎707 465 7354) is another helpful location.

Crescent City Visitor Centre 1001 Front St (summer Mon–Sat 9am–5pm, Sun 10am–4pm; rest of year Mon–Fri 10am–4pm; ☎800 343 8300, ⊛exploredelnorte.com).

Boat tours Klamath River Jet Boat Tours, 17635 Hwy-101 S, Klamath (☎800 887 5387, ⊛jetboattours.com), runs 2hr tours for $45 and can arrange guided fishing trips.

ACCOMMODATION AND EATING

Camping is your best bet. You can choose from the many developed, environmental, hiker/biker and primitive campgrounds spread throughout the parks. There are also a few motel/B&B recommendations in the scenic areas and, if all else fails, a host of motels around Crescent City. Eating options are fairly scant outside of Crescent City.

ORICK

Gold Bluffs Beach Campground ☎ 707 488 2171. You can camp here in the stomping grounds of elk. It's strictly first-come, first-served, so arrive early in the summer months. Pitches **$35**

Lumberjack Tavern (aka Hawgwild) 10 Hufford Rd ☎ 707 488 2108. This is a decent place for a game of pool, an ice-cold beer and a wild game dinner for $15–20, but it wins no prizes for decor. Mon–Thurs & Sun noon–11pm, Fri & Sat noon–midnight.

Palm Motel & Café 21130 US-101 ☎ 707 488 3381. Has functional but adequate rooms of varying sizes and a

covered pool, and serves cheap burgers and sandwiches in its attached café. **$70**

Redwood Adventures & Cabins 3 miles north of Orick ☎ 866 733 9637, ⊛redwoodadventures.com. This beautifully situated place offers superb eco-friendly cabins and a host of activities such as salmon fishing, horseriding, kayaking and guided hikes. **$289**

KLAMATH AND AROUND

★ **Historic ReQua Inn** 451 Requa Rd ☎ 707 482 1425, ⊛requainn.com. The sort of place you'd pay double for in a big city, the rooms here are all luxuriously appointed and

9

there is a superb restaurant, which does four-course dinners for $45. $119

Kamp Klamath 1661 W Klamath Beach Rd, 2 miles west of US-101 ☎707 482 0227. The place has shady tent sites with fewer RVs than many campgrounds and decent facilities on the south bank of the Klamath River, towards the river mouth. It even has friendly skunks in the back meadow. Pitches $29.50

Log Cabin Diner 301 Rte-169 ☎707 482 0400. Pickings are slim on the eating front around Klamath, especially in the evening, but this fine diner serves American standards till late afternoon for $10–15. Daily 8am–4pm.

Woodland Villa A mile and a half north of Requa ☎888 866 2466, ⓦ klamathusa.com. There are nicely equipped cabins with one to three bedrooms here in peaceful wooded surroundings, plus some deluxe kitchen suites. $90

CRESCENT CITY

★**Chart Room Restaurant** 130 Anchor Way ☎707 464 5993, ⓦ ccchartroom.com. The town's best restaurant offers the freshest fish and chips, good-value soups, sandwiches and burgers, plus pricier mains for $22–32. Tues 11am–4pm, Wed, Thurs & Sun 7am–7pm, Fri & Sat 7am–8pm.

Crescent Beach Motel 2 miles south of town at 1455 US-101 S ☎707 464 5436, ⓦ crescentbeachmotel.com. Right behind the beach with magnificent ocean views, the rooms here are brightly decorated and boast stylish modern furniture – definitely a cut above the average motel. $119

Fisherman's Restaurant 700 Hwy-101 S ☎707 465 3474. Great place for excellent, moderately priced seafood such as prawn and fresh fish dishes for around $15. The clam chowder is a winner. Daily 6am–8pm.

Light House Inn 681 Hwy-1 S ☎707 464 3993, ⓦ thelighthouseinncrescentcity.com. Pleasant, modern family-owned hotel with sizeable comfy rooms and suites. The complimentary breakfast lounge has a fireplace. $125

★**Thai House** 105 N St ☎707 464 2427. Thai and Vietnamese cuisine such as delicious stir-fries and curries, as well as baked fish, all cost in the $10–15 range. Mon–Thurs 11am–9pm, Fri & Sat 11am–10pm, Sun noon–9pm.

DEL NORTE COAST REDWOODS STATE PARK

Mill Creek Campground 2 miles east of US-101 ☎707 465 7335, ⓦ parks.ca.gov. Situated next to a lovely stream through the woods, this campground has a good number of shady pitches and clean bathrooms. No reservations – first come, first served. Pitches $35

JEDEDIAH SMITH REDWOODS STATE PARK

Hiouchi Motel 2097 Hwy-199 ☎707 458 3041 or ☎888 881 0819, ⓦ hiouchimotel.com. Simple motel with basic but adequate rooms, made cheerier by the patterned quilts and cheesy art. Also has a picnic area and gazebo. $70

Jedediah Smith Redwoods Campground Howland Hill Rd, off Hwy-199 ☎800 444 7275, ⓦ reserveamerica. com. This campground deep in the towering redwoods offers peaceful pitches and ample picnicking facilities. Hiker/biker $5, developed sites $35

Patrick Creek Lodge & Historical Inn 13950 Hwy-199 ☎707 457 3323, ⓦ patrickcreeklodge.com. The last place to stay in California on this route, with good single rates on the stylish rooms, plus spacious rustic cabins and an excellent but slightly pricey restaurant. $105

The Sacramento Valley

The **SACRAMENTO VALLEY** lays fair claim to being California's dullest region: a flat, largely agricultural corridor of small, sleepy towns and endless vistas of wheat fields and fruit trees. By far the best thing to do is pass straight through on I-5, which cuts an almost two-hundred-mile-long swathe through the region, enabling you to forge right ahead to the more enticing far north quite painlessly in half a day. If you're coming from San Francisco, save time by taking the I-505 byway around Sacramento. The most worthwhile place to halt is Chico, while Red Bluff and Corning also have a couple of things in their favour.

Chico and around

Charming little **CHICO**, right on Hwy-99 about midway between Sacramento and Redding and some twenty miles east of I-5 from the Orland exit, is a good stopoff if you don't want to attempt to cover the whole valley from top to bottom in one day, or if you're here to visit Lassen Volcanic National Park (see p.642) and want a choice of accommodation. It's home to **California State University Chico**, a grassy institution of laidback students renowned more for their devotion to partying than academic pursuits. Chico was once the grounds surrounding the mansion of General John Bidwell, one of the first men to cash in on the Gold Rush. As such, the city's traditional layout around a plaza, numerous college hangouts and surrounding expanse of parkland make it something of an oasis compared to the dusty fields and sleepy towns beyond.

Chico Museum

141 Salem St • Thurs–Sun 11am–4pm • Free • ☎ 530 891 4336, ⓦ chicomuseum.org

Chico doesn't have much by way of sights but strolling the leafy streets, college campus and shady riverside can be a relief after the monotonous drive up I-5. The 1904 **Chico Museum**, housed in the former Carnegie Library, contains three distinct parts: a permanent historical section, a reconstruction of a Taoist temple altar and a gallery for rotating shows.

National Yo-Yo Museum

320 Broadway St • Mon–Sat 10am–6pm, Sun noon–5pm • Free • ☎ 530 893 0545, ⓦ nationalyoyo.org

Those nostalgic for the innocent days of childhood will enjoy the **National Yo-Yo Museum**, where enthusiasts enjoy showing visitors around the thousands of exhibits and photos. Among the world's largest collection of yo-yos and associated memorabilia, pride of place goes to Big-Yo, which at 256lb is the largest working wooden yo-yo in history. The museum is actually dwarfed by the huge **toy shop** it shares premises with.

Bidwell Mansion State Historic Park

525, The Esplanade, the continuation of Main St **Mansion** Mon noon–5pm, Sat & Sun 11am–5pm; tours on the hour until 4pm • $6 • ☎ 530 895 6144, ⓦ bidwellmansionpark.com • **Park** Daylight hours • Free

Built in 1868, the three-storey **Bidwell Mansion State Historic Park** is an attractive Italian country villa filled with family paraphernalia, visited on 45-minute anecdotal

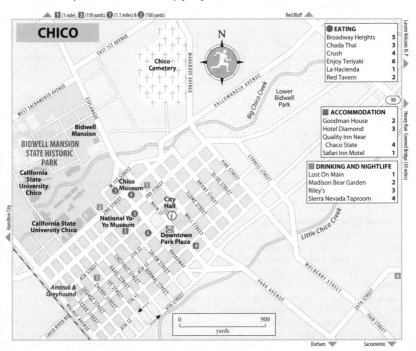

CHICO

EATING
Broadway Heights 5
Chada Thai 3
Crush 4
Enjoy Teriyaki 6
La Hacienda 1
Red Tavern 2

ACCOMMODATION
Goodman House 2
Hotel Diamond 3
Quality Inn Near
Chaco State 4
Safari Inn Motel 1

DRINKING AND NIGHTLIFE
Lost On Main 1
Madison Bear Garden 2
Riley's 3
Sierra Nevada Taproom 4

9

tours, though Bidwell Park is a more pleasurable place to spend your time. Extending from the centre of the town for ten miles to the northeast, this semi-wilderness and oak parkland is where the first Robin Hood film, starring Errol Flynn, was made. Students frequent the **swimming holes** on Big Chico Creek in the Upper Park, accessed by taking Vallombrosa Avenue all the way east, turning left into Manzanita Avenue, then right on Wildwood Avenue and on past the golf course.

Honey Run Covered Bridge

Ten miles outside Chico, south on Hwy-99 then east on Skyway to Humburg–Honey Run Road, the **Honey Run Covered Bridge** is one of the few remaining covered bridges in California. You can't drive on it, but its position in rugged Butte Creek Canyon over a riffling river leads to peaceful walking and swimming opportunities. Further east, the apple orchards of **Paradise** were used as a location for *Gone With the Wind*.

ARRIVAL AND DEPARTURE   CHICO AND AROUND

By train The Coast Starlight train, from Los Angeles to Seattle, stops once daily at the unattended station at 450 Orange St, though in the middle of the night in each direction. Destinations Dunsmuir (1 daily; 3hr 10min); Oakland (1 daily; 4hr 45min); Redding (1 daily; 1hr 20min); Sacramento (1 daily; 2hr 25min).

By bus Greyhound stops at the same transit hub as Amtrak, 450 Orange St.
Destinations Red Bluff (2 daily; 50min); Redding (2 daily; 1hr 30min); Sacramento (2 daily; 2hr 15min); San Francisco (2 daily; 5hr 40min–6hr 15min); Weed (2 daily; 3hr 10min–3hr 20min).

GETTING AROUND AND INFORMATION

By bike The trails in Bidwell Park are best appreciated by bike. You can rent a bike for $35/day from Campus Bicycles, right off the plaza at 330 Main St (☎ 530 345 2081, ⓦ campusbicycles .com); the shop also provides free maps for cyclists.
Chamber of Commerce 441 Main St (Mon–Fri 10am–4pm;

☎ 530 891 5556 or ☎ 800 852 8570, ⓦ chicochamber.com). Good for information on historical walking tours, mountain-bike trails and swimming-hole locations nearby.
Website To find out what's on, consult the free *Chico News & Review* (ⓦ newsreview.com), published every Thursday.

ACCOMMODATION

★**Goodman House** 1362 The Esplanade ☎ 530 566 0256, ⓦ goodmanhouse.net. Delightful ivy-clad B&B with cosy rooms full of European furniture and floral soft furnishings. The congenial owners provide a fine breakfast. **$139**
Hotel Diamond 220 W 4th St ☎ 866 993 3100, ⓦ hoteldiamondchico.com. Imposing edifice with a range of swish rooms and suites, as well as an elegant lobby, restaurant and bar. **$132**

Quality Inn Near Chico State 715 Main St ☎ 530 343 7911, ⓦ qualityinn.com. Decent chain motel two blocks from the plaza. Some of the simple rooms have fridges and all have coffee-makers. **$106**
Safari Inn Motel 2352 The Esplanade ☎ 530 343 3201, ⓦ safarichicomotel.com. Unbeatable prices at this pleasant motel, whose comfortable rooms are befitting of a far more expensive place. There's even a modest-sized swimming pool. **$69**

EATING

Chico does itself proud when it comes to food. If you happen to be in town on the second Sunday in September look out for the **Taste of Chico festival**.

Broadway Heights 300 Broadway St ☎ 530 899 8075, ⓦ broadwayheightschico.com. This modern upstairs establishment dishes up moderate California cuisine – dishes such as lemon rosemary chicken go for $15–20. Mon–Thurs 11am–8.30pm, Fri & Sat 11am–9pm, Sun 11am–5pm.
Chada Thai 117B W 2nd St. Down in the basement, this place offers authentic and predominantly vegetarian Thai cuisine at very affordable prices, especially at lunchtime. Most mains little over $10. Mon–Thurs & Sun 11am–9pm,

Fri & Sat 11am–10pm.
Crush 201 Broadway St ☎ 530 342 7000, ⓦ chicocrush .com. Stylish Italian restaurant which offers top-quality mains such as the spicy mussels "fra diavolo" for $20–25, as well as fine pizza and pasta dishes. Has an unusual late-night Happy Hour Thurs–Sat. Daily 3.30pm–midnight.
★**Enjoy Teriyaki** 450 Broadway St ☎ 530 298 7910. Simple, squeaky-clean restaurant offering a choice of Korean and Japanese favourites at great prices, such as eight *gyoza* pieces for $4.50 or a teriyaki, tempura, rice,

AN ALTERNATIVE PIT STOP

If you bypass Chico and enter Tehama County from the south on I-5, an alternative stop for gas and provisions is **Corning**, home of the celebrated **Olive Pit**, 2156 Solano St (☎530 824 4667, ⓦolivepit.com), just east off the interstate. This only-in-America store sells jars of olives, olive oil, garlic, almonds and pickles, while its café serves good burgers, sandwiches and ice cream as well. Martini-lovers can get bottles of olive-juice mixer, and a free tasting bar allows a trip around the world via olives – from Brine Greek wholes to Napa Valley Wine queens to French pitted and Sicilian cracked. The anchovy-stuffed greens are a must, and pint jars of all varieties go for around $5–8.

salad and miso soup combo for $13.50. Daily 11am–9pm.

La Hacienda 2635 The Esplanade ☎530 893 8270, ⓦlahacienda-chico.com. *Bon Appetit* and *Gourmet* magazines have done features on this Mexican restaurant's special pink sauce, known to locals as "Heroin Sauce" for its addictive, sweet flavour. Great margaritas too. Mon–Thurs & Sun 11am–8.30pm, Fri & Sat 11am–9pm.

Red Tavern 1250 The Esplanade ☎530 894 3463, ⓦredtavern.com. Quality California dishes such as grilled Mount Lassen steelhead are available for around $19–34 at this fairly upscale restaurant. Tues–Thurs 5–9pm, Fri & Sat 5–9.30pm, Sun 10am–2pm & 5–8pm.

DRINKING AND NIGHTLIFE

Being a California State University town, there are many excellent places aimed at the younger customer, as well as a handful of buzzing bars, featuring live music by national acts.

Lost On Main 319 Main St ☎530 892 2445, ⓦlostonmainchico.com. Popular student hangout that veers between chilled out open-mike or jazz nights, through more animated reggae and rock events, both live and DJed. Wed–Sat 9pm–2am.

Madison Bear Garden 316 W 2nd St ☎530 891 1639, ⓦmadisonbeargarden.com. Popular with beer-swigging students. Burgers, buffalo wings and other bar food is served, mostly under $10. Mon–Sat 11am–1.45am, Sun 10am–1.45am.

Riley's 702 W 5th St ☎530 343 7459, ⓦrileysbar.com.

Catch the ball game on one of the many TV screens and hang out with the enthusiastic students at the most popular sports bar in Chico. Mon–Sat 11am–late, Sun 9.30am–late.

★ **Sierra Nevada Taproom** 1075 E 20th St ☎530 893 3520, ⓦsierranevada.com. The taproom at one of the USA's most successful quality breweries, now distributed internationally, always has at least six beers on tap and a quality food menu. In-depth tours are available too. Taproom Mon–Thurs & Sun 11am–9pm, Fri & Sat 11am–10pm; tours daily 11am–5.30pm.

Red Bluff

The largest town in Tehama County is **Red Bluff**, 45 miles north of Chico on Hwy-99. Despite its favourable location on the Sacramento River, the town is better known as a gas-and-lodging stop before the fifty-mile drive into Lassen along Hwy-36 or the push north to Redding and Mount Shasta on I-5.

You may consider visiting the **Kelly-Griggs House Museum**, 311 Washington St (Thurs & Sun 1–3pm; donation; ☎530 527 1129, ⓦkellygriggsmuseum.org), where there's an exhibit on Ishi, "the last wild Indian". There are also a number of antiques shops to browse in, as well as Gaumer's, on the I-5 side of the bridge at 78 Belle Mill Rd (Mon–Fri 9am–5pm; free; ☎530 527 6166, ⓦgaumers.com), a jeweller's with an on-site **gemology museum**, displaying hundreds of precious stones, mining equipment, a lapidary workshop and a collection of corals and ammonites. The star exhibit is a sparkly 4ft-tall amethyst geode from Brazil.

ARRIVAL AND INFORMATION   RED BLUFF

By bus The Greyhound bus stops in front of the Salt Creek Deli at the junction of Hwy-36 and Antelope Rd (Hwy-99), on the twice-daily route between Redding (40min) and Chico (50min), but there is no public transport on into Lassen.

Chamber of Commerce 100 Main St (Mon–Fri 9am–4pm; ☎530 527 6220 or ☎800 655 6225, ⓦredbluffchamber.com).

9

Crystal Motel 333 S Main St ☎ 530 527 1021, ⓦ redbluffmotel.com. Considering this motel has some of the lowest rates to be found in California, it is surprisingly clean and well maintained. $45

Los Mariachis 604 Main St ☎ 530 529 5154, ⓦ redblufflosmariachis.com. Typically cheerful and colourful Mexican joint, where you can feast on breakfasts such as *chorizo con huevos* or all the usual main courses, like their great quesadilla supreme, all under $10. Mon–Fri 9am–9pm, Sat & Sun 9am–9.30pm.

Plumas County

Many visitors travelling between Lake Tahoe and the Lassen/Mount Shasta region bypass the Sacramento Valley altogether by using Hwy-89, which winds its way through sparsely populated and scenically exquisite **PLUMAS COUNTY**. It boasts no major set-piece attraction, but with only three traffic lights and constant vistas of pine-clad ridges, grassy valleys, sparkling lakes and trout-rich rivers, the county is rural California at its best. Geographically, it's significant as the meeting point of the lofty Sierra Nevada and volcanic Cascade mountain ranges.

The area was home to the hunter-gatherer **Maidu tribe** before white settlers flooded into the valleys when gold frenzy took hold in the mid-nineteenth century, followed by a substantial number of Chinese. The veins of the precious metal were never as rich as those to the south, however, so the prospectors left and the **timber** industry soon took over as the prime economy. That too has since gone into decline, leaving farming as the main source of income for the few inhabitants, along with a smattering of tourism.

Coming from the south, you pass through the golfing and retirement paradise of Graeagle before Hwy-89 combines with Hwy-70 to form part of the **Feather River National Scenic Byway**; this leads to the county seat and commercial hub of **Quincy**, whose Old Town merits a wander. Further north, Hwy-89 continues solo through the cattle-grazing land of the **Indian Valley**, past the lazy town of **Greenville** to the recreational area of **Lake Almanor**, within easy striking distance of Lassen Volcanic National Park, whose snowcapped peaks are visible in the distance.

Quincy

Nestled on the lower western slopes of the northernmost reaches of the Sierra Nevada mountains, **Quincy** is a pleasant town divided by a hill into two distinct halves. Modern and functional East Quincy is not especially appealing but the blocks surrounding West Main Street in Quincy proper present some fine examples of Victorian architecture and are worth a stop. Behind the grand old Neoclassical **courthouse**, which stands proudly near the junction where the highway through town veers from West Main Street into Crescent Street, you can visit the **Plumas County Museum**, 500 Jackson St (Tues–Sat 9am–4.30pm, Sun 11am–3pm; $2; ☎ 530 283 6320, ⓦ plumas museum.org). Inside you'll find informative displays on the area's Native American culture, the story of its settlement, and natural history, while the grounds contain an old buggy and an authentic 1890s gold-miner's cabin.

Greenville

Although it now depends more on cattle ranching and the felling of Christmas trees, sleepy **Greenville** still celebrates its mining heritage every summer with the **Gold Digger Days** festival on the third weekend of July. For the rest of the year it remains in its slumbers but its quietude and idyllic countryside setting still make a pleasant spot to break your journey. Though there's not much to see, just wandering along Main Street can give you a sense of the town's workaday past.

Lake Almanor

9

Lake Almanor, created in 1914 by the Great Western Power Company's damming of the north fork of the Feather River, stands at an elevation of 4500ft and covers 52 square miles, making it the largest of Plumas County's many lakes. This is also where the Cascades and the Sierras truly meet. The lake's clear blue waters reach a comfortable seventy-five degrees in summer, rendering it ideal for **watersports**. Numerous resorts ring the pine-forested shoreline and most rent equipment for water-based activities, from high-speed waterskiing to leisurely fishing.

Chester

At the northwest corner of Lake Almanor, the only town on its shores, **Chester**, is a relaxed place with a splendid setting and the lake's best selection of amenities. The small **Chester museum**, showcasing local history and displaying a fine collection of Maidu basketry, is inside the Plumas County library at 210 1st Ave (Mon–Wed & Fri 10am–1pm & 1.30–5.30pm, Thurs noon–5pm & 6–8pm, Sat 10am–2pm; free; ☎530 258 2742).

ARRIVAL, GETTING AROUND AND INFORMATION   PLUMAS COUNTY

By bus Although the most practical way to travel to and around Plumas County is by car, there is a bus service from Susanville via Chester to Redding and Red Bluff with Susanville Rancheria Public Transportation (Mon–Sat 1 daily; ☎530 257 1128) and a local bus service from Chester via Greenville (50min) to Quincy (1hr 30min) with Plumas Transit Systems (3–4 daily; ☎530 283 2538, ⓦplumastransit.com).

Chambers of Commerce The Quincy Chamber of Commerce is inside Plumas Bank at 336 W Main St (Mon, Wed & Fri 1–5pm; ☎530 283 0188, ⓦquincychamber .com); the Lake Almanor Area Chamber of Commerce is at 328 Main St, Chester (Tues–Fri 12.30–4pm; ☎530 258 2426 or ☎800 350 4838, ⓦchester-lakealmanor.com). Hours at both offices are rather sketchy in practice.

ACCOMMODATION

QUINCY

The Feather Bed 542 Jackson St ☎530 283 3000 or ☎844 275 8300, ⓦquincyfeatherbed.com. Located in a beautiful 1893 property in the old town, this is a comfortable and atmospheric B&B. **$110**

Gold Pan Lodge 200 Crescent St ☎530 283 3686. The best and most central of the several motels around town, with perfectly clean rooms and the usual cable TV channels. **$79**

Greenhorn Creek Guest Ranch 12 miles east of town at 2116 Greenhorn Ranch Rd ☎800 334 6939, ⓦgreen hornranch.com. The place to go for a Wild West experience – they specialize in packages including all meals and activities such as horseriding, fishing and hiking, but if it's not too busy you can stay on a room-only basis too. **$130**

GREENVILLE

The Hideaway 761 Hideaway Rd ☎530 284 7915, ⓦthehideawaymotelandlodge.net. Tucked in the woods behind town, this welcoming lodge has spacious motel-style rooms and some larger kitchenettes with a communal deck to eat on. **$85**

LAKE ALMANOR

All accommodation below is in counterclockwise order around the lake. For campers there are simple sites all over the lake that are usually let on a first-come, first-served basis, though some can be booked through the US Forest Service (☎800 280 2267, ⓦrecreation.gov).

Knotty Pine Resort 430 Peninsula Drive ☎530 596 3348, ⓦknottypine.net. Located on the peninsula that juts out from the north shore, the half-dozen large two-bedroom log cabins here are ideal for groups of four or five. **$180**

Lake Haven Resort 4379 Hwy-147, east shore ☎530 596 3249, ⓦlakehavenresort.com. A shady place offering great sunset views from its cabins of varying size, some of which have kitchenettes. Also has RV spaces. RV **$55**, cabins **$100**

★**Plumas Pines Resort** 3000 Almanor Drive W, Canyon Dam ☎530 259 4343, ⓦplumaspinesresort .com. Well equipped with motel-style rooms, cabins spaced out among the pines and RV slots, as well as decent food at its own grill with a pleasant outdoor deck. RV **$50**, doubles **$75**, cabins **$110**

CHESTER

Antlers Motel 268 Main St ☎530 258 2722, ⓦantlersmotel.com. This rather grand two-storey clapboard building is more appealing than the average

9

motel, as are the neat and tidy rooms within. Board games can be borrowed from the office. $69

The Bidwell House 1 Main St ☎530 258 3338, ⓦbidwellhouse.com. Great B&B with a range of delightful rooms, all beautifully decorated and the fancier ones with four-poster beds. The full breakfast includes gourmet omelettes. $100

North Shore Campground 2 miles east of town on Hwy-36 ☎530 258 3376, ⓦnorthshorecampground .com. The biggest campground on the lake, with ample tent pitches, RV slots and rustic cabins. Also does boat rental. Pitches $36, RV $46, cabins $119

EATING

QUINCY

Courthouse Café 525 W Main St ☎530 283 3344. Bang opposite – you guessed it – the courthouse, you can grab a filling breakfast of eggs and the works or a lunchtime sandwich for $10 or less. Daily 7am–2pm.

★**Pangaea Café & Pub** 461 Main St ☎530 283 0426, ⓦpangaeapub.com. This place offers an eclectic menu of salads, sandwiches, panini, sushi and Mexican favourites for $8–12.50. Also has a decent selection of beer and wine. Mon–Fri 11.30am–8.30pm.

GREENVILLE

Anna's Cafe 300 Main St ☎530 284 1998. Ample eggy breakfasts and huge burgers go for under $10 in this friendly, family-style joint. Mon–Wed & Sun 7am–2pm, Thurs–Sat 7am–2pm & 4.30–8pm.

Mountain Valley Pizza 116 Ann St (Hwy-89) ☎530 284 6680. All your favourite pizza toppings and varieties such as the tasty pesto chicken calzone for $10–20. Beer and ice cream available too. Daily noon–9pm.

LAKE ALMANOR

Carol's Café & West Shore Deli 2392 Almanor Drive W ☎530 259 2464. Of the reasonable restaurants dotted round the lake, this deli offers meat and fish main courses for under $20. Daily 7.30am–2pm & Sun 5–8pm.

Red Onion Grill 303 Peninsula Drive ☎530 258 800, ⓦredoniongrill.com. Good place for burgers and tacos for little over $10 and specials like the succulent filet mignon kebabs for double that. The bar is quite lively too. Wed–Sun 4–9pm, bar till late.

Tantardino's Pizzeria & Pasta 401 Ponderosa Drive ☎530 596 3902. Inside this humble clapboard building you can enjoy good hearty Italian pizza and pasta dishes for under $20, plus sandwiches and salads. Tues–Thurs 11.30am–8.30pm, Fri & Sat 11.30am–9pm.

CHESTER

Happy Garden 605 Main St ☎530 258 2395. Functional joint that dishes out huge portions of Chinese standards, from hot'n'sour soup to the meat-heavy special chow mein. Most main courses around $10. Daily 11am–9pm.

Kopper Kettle 243 Main St ☎530 258 2698. Good place to come for filling breakfasts or all-American fare such as chilli burgers and garlic fries or steak, mostly under $20. Good fruit pies too. Daily 8am–9pm.

Lassen Volcanic National Park and around

Always open · $10/vehicle/7 days, $5/hiker or biker

About fifty miles over gently sloping plains east from Red Bluff on Hwy-36, the 106,000 acres that make up the pine forests, crystal-green lakes and boiling thermal pools of the **LASSEN VOLCANIC NATIONAL PARK** are one of the most unearthly parts of California. A forbidding climate, which brings up to 50ft of snowfall each year, keeps the area pretty much uninhabited, with the roads all blocked by snow and, apart from a brief June-to-October season, completely deserted.

The national park lies at the southerly limit of the Cascades, a low, broad range which stretches six hundred miles north to Mount Garibaldi in British Columbia and is characterized by high **volcanoes** forming part of the Pacific Circle of Fire. Dominating the park at over 10,000ft is a fine example, **Mount Lassen** itself, which – although quiet in recent years – erupted in 1914, beginning a cycle of outbursts that climaxed in 1915, when the peak blew an enormous mushroom cloud some seven miles skyward, tearing the summit into chunks that landed as far away as Reno. Although nearly a hundred years of geothermal inactivity have since made the mountain a safe and fascinating place, scientists predict that of all the Californian volcanoes, Lassen is the likeliest to erupt again.

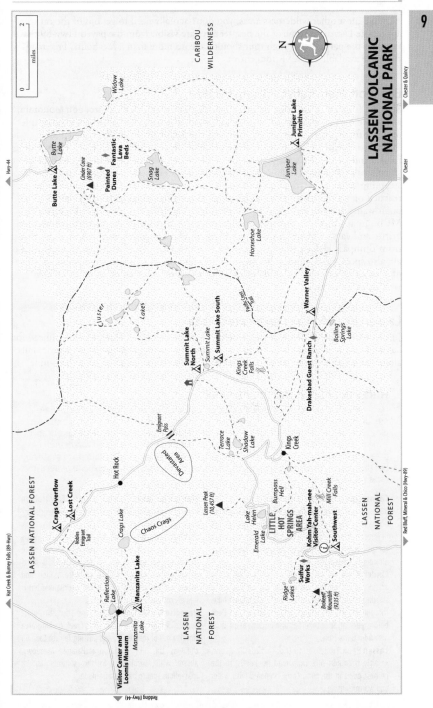

LASSEN VOLCANIC NATIONAL PARK

CARIBOU WILDERNESS

Widow Lake

Butte Lake

✕ Butte Lake

Cinder Cone (6907 ft) ▲

Painted Dunes **Fantastic Lava Beds**

Snag Lake

✕ Juniper Lake Primitive

Juniper Lake

Horseshoe Lake

Cluster Lakes

Pacific Crest Trail

✕ Summit Lake North

Summit Lake

✕ Summit Lake South

Kings Creek Falls

✕ Warner Valley

Drakesbad Guest Ranch

Boiling Springs Lake

Emigrant Pass

Devastated Area

Terrace Lake

Shadow Lake

Kings Creek

Hot Rock

LASSEN NATIONAL FOREST

✕ Crags Overflow

✕ Lost Creek

Nobles Emigrant Trail

Crags Lake

Chaos Crags

Lassen Peak (10,457 ft) ▲

Bumpass Hell

Lake Helen

LITTLE HOT SPRINGS AREA

Emerald Lake

Mill Creek Falls

Kohm Yah-mah-nee Visitor Center ℹ

✕ Southwest

LASSEN NATIONAL FOREST

Sulfur Works ↓

Ridge Lakes

Brokeoff Mountain (9235 ft) ▲

✕ Manzanita Lake

Reflection Lake

Visitor Center and Loomis Museum

Manzanita Lake

LASSEN NATIONAL FOREST

0 — miles — 2

N

Hwy-44

Chester & Quincy

Chester

Redding (Hwy-44)

Hat Creek & Burney Falls (89-Hwy)

Red Bluff, Mineral & Chico (Hwy-89)

9

Unlike most other wilderness areas, you don't actually need to get out of the car to appreciate Lassen, as some of the best features are visible from the paved Hwy-89 that traverses the park. A thorough tour should take no more than a few hours. Free road maps are available at the visitor centres.

Brokeoff Mountain to Bumpass Hell

Starting from the southwest entrance, you'll pass the trailhead to **Brokeoff Mountain**, a six-mile round-trip hike through wildflowers. The first self-guided trail is a couple of miles further up – follow your nose and the **Sulfur Works** can be reached via a 200ft boardwalk around its steaming fumaroles and burbling mud pots. The winding road climbs along the side of Diamond Peak before edging **Emerald Lake** and Lassen's show-stealer, **Bumpass Hell**, named after a man who lost a leg trying to cross it. This steaming valley of active pools and vents, bubbling away at a low rumble, can be reached on an undulating two-mile trail that eventually descends to a system of boardwalks that put you right in the middle of the stinky action. Recall the fate of Mr Bumpass, however, and stay on the trails; the crusts over the thermal features are brittle and easy to break through, leaving you, literally, in hot water. Across the road from Bumpass Hell's parking lot, the trails around the glassy surface of Emerald Lake are also spectacular, though in much quieter fashion; the lake itself resembles a sheet of green ice, perfectly still and clear but for the snow-covered rock mound which rises from its centre.

Lassen Peak to the Devastated Area

Just north of Lake Helen, the road reaches its highest point (8511ft) at the trailhead for **Lassen Peak**. It then winds down to the flat meadows around **Kings Creek**, whose trails along the winding water are popular for picnics. From road marker 32, a three-mile

---

HIKES IN LASSEN NATIONAL PARK

For a volcanic landscape, a surprisingly large proportion of the walking trails in the park are predominantly flat, and the heavily glaciated terrain to the east of the main volcanic massif is pleasingly gentle. Rangers will point you towards the **hiking routes** best suited to your ability – the park's generally high elevations will leave all but the most experienced walker short of breath, and you should stick to the shorter trails at least until you're acclimatized. For anything but the most tentative explorations, pick up one of the numerous hiking guides that detail the most popular hikes.

Chaos Crags Lake 3.5 miles round-trip; 2–3hr; 800ft ascent. From the *Manzanita Lake* campground access road, the path leads gently up through pine and fir forest to the peaceful lake. An adventurous extension climbs a ridge of loose rock to the top of Chaos Crags, affording a view of the whole park.

Cinder Cone 13 miles round-trip; 1 day; 800ft ascent. Check with the rangers for the best seasonal starting point for this, Lassen's most spectacular hike, through the Painted Dunes and Fantastic Lava Beds before reaching Snag Lake. Can also be done as a 4-hour hike from Butte Lake.

Lassen Peak 5 miles round-trip; 4hr; 2000ft ascent. A fairly strenuous hike from road marker 22 to the highest point in the park. Come prepared with water and warm clothing.

Manzanita Lake 1.5 miles; 1hr; flat. Easy trails on level ground make this one of the most popular short walks in the park.

Nobles Emigrant Trail 2.5 miles; 1–2hr; 200ft ascent. The most accessible and one of the more interesting sections of a trail forged in 1850 starts opposite the Manzanita Lake entrance station and meets Hwy-89 at marker 60. It isn't maintained but is heavily compacted and easy-going.

Paradise Meadows 3 miles round-trip; 3hr; 800ft ascent. Starting either at the Hat Creek parking area (marker 42) or marker 27, and passing Terrace Lake on the way, this hike winds up at Paradise Meadows, ablaze with wildflowers in the summer and a marvellous spot to pass an afternoon.

CAMPING IN AND AROUND LASSEN

During the few months of the year when conditions are suitable for camping, this is by far the best accommodation option (see p.646). Most sites in the park remain open from June to October. Remember that Lassen is **bear country**; follow the posted precautions for food and waste storage and make your presence known when hiking.

Primitive camping requires a free **wilderness permit** obtainable in advance from the park visitor centres and entrance stations. There is no self-registration and chosen sites must be a mile from developed campgrounds and a quarter of a mile from most specific sites of interest. In the surrounding **Lassen National Forest**, camping is permitted anywhere, though you'll need a free permit to operate a cooking stove or to light a fire; these are sometimes refused in the dry summer months. In addition, there are a couple of dozen private developed sites strung along the highways within thirty miles of Lassen, most charging between $10 and $35.

---

round-trip walk leads to the seventy-foot-tall **Kings Creek Falls**. At the halfway point you'll come to **Summit Lake**, a busy camping area set around a beautiful icy lake, from where you can start on the park's most manageable hiking trails. Press on further to the **Devastated Area**, where, in 1914, molten lava from Lassen poured down the valley, denuding the landscape as it went, ripping out every tree and patch of grass. Slowly the earth is recovering its green mantle but the most vivid impression is still one of complete destruction.

Manzanita Lake and the Loomis Museum

From the Devastated Area it's a gauntlet of pines to the northern entrance, site of tranquil **Manzanita Lake** and the **Loomis Museum** (summer daily 9am–5pm; rest of year Fri–Sun 9am–5pm; free), a memorial to Benjamin Loomis, whose documentary photos of the 1914 eruption form the centrepiece of an exhibition strong on flora and local geology – plug domes, composite cones and cinder cones.

McArthur-Burney Falls State Park

Sunrise to sunset • $8/vehicle • ☎ 530 335 2777, ⓦ burney-falls.com

Leaving Lassen, Hwy-44 heads forty miles west to Redding and I-5 or, alternatively, you can continue northwest on Hwy-89 one hundred miles to Mount Shasta, stopping halfway at the breathtaking **McArthur-Burney Falls State Park**. The park's centrepiece is a 129ft **waterfall**, unique for the way the water spills over the rim from two different levels. A paved trail leads to the misty pool at the base and a 1.5-mile steep loop takes you downstream and then back up the other side of the pool to a bridge over the falls' headwater. The Pacific Crest Trail passes alongside nearby **Lake Briton**, and paddleboats, canoes and rowboats can be rented at the park entrance. Plentiful **camping** is available among the black oaks.

GETTING AROUND AND INFORMATION

LASSEN VOLCANIC NATIONAL PARK

By car A car is a must for getting to and around the park, though during the winter, when the roads in the park are almost always shut down due to snow, a car won't do you much good either – snowshoes and cross-country skis take over as popular modes of transport.

Kohm Yah-mah-nee Visitor Center Just beyond the southwest entrance, 6 miles north of where Hwy-89 peels off towards Lassen from Hwy-36 (daily: summer 9am–6pm; rest of year 9am–5pm; ☎ 530 595 4480, ⓦ nps.gov/lavo. Park

rangers hand out free maps, offer detailed advice and issue backcountry permits. There is also a fine display on Lassen's natural wonders, a good café, a gift shop and a bookstore.

Manzanita Lake Visitor Center Manzanita Lake, just inside the north entrance (late May to Oct daily 9am–5pm; ☎ 530 595 4444 ext 5180); this is the older visitor centre, and incorporates the Loomis Museum (see above).

Provisions Camper Store, near Manzanita Lake Visitor Center, is the only place for provisions and gas within the park.

9

ACCOMMODATION AND EATING

Apart from the **cabins** mentioned below, the only way to stay inside Lassen is to **camp** (see box, p.645), but even in August night temperatures can hover around freezing so many people prefer to stay in one of the **resorts and lodges** that pepper the surrounding forest. To be sure of a room in the popular summer months, it pays to book well ahead. Apart from the food on offer at some of the accommodation options, there are hardly any independent **restaurants** in the Lassen area.

Butte Lake Campground In the far northeast corner of the park, accessed by Hwy-44 ☎877 444 6777, ⓦrecreation.gov. This campground can accommodate trailers and has a boat launch. 6100ft. Reservable. Pitches $15

Hat Creek Resort 12533 Hwy-44/89, Old Station, 11 miles northeast of the north entrance ☎530 335 7121, ⓦhatcreekresortrv.com. A complex of rentable trailers, yurts, motel units and fancier cabins with kitchens (two-day minimum stay), plus tent and RV sites. There is also a well-stocked deli. Closed mid-Nov to mid-March. Pitches $25, RV $36, doubles $89

Highlands Ranch Resort 41515 Hwy-36 E, 9 miles southeast of southwest entrance ☎530 595 3388, ⓦhighlandsranchresort.com. One of the few choices on this side of the park, this high-end resort offers a range of suites, many sleeping four people or more. Was in the process of taking over the cheaper *Childs Meadow* opposite at the time of writing. $229

JJ's Café 13385 Hwy-44/89, Old Station, 11 miles northeast of the park ☎530 335 7225, ⓦjjs cafeoldstation.com. Does filling breakfasts such as a lightly spiced corned beef hash with eggs, plus sandwiches and simple meals for lunch, all around $10 or under, plus weekend evening pizza for $15–20. Mon–Thurs & Sun 7am–3pm, Fri & Sat 7am–7pm.

Juniper Lake Campground In the far southeastern corner of the park ☎530 595 4480. There are some good hiking trails near this campground, as well as swimming in the lake. Drinking water must be boiled or treated. 6800ft. No reservations. Pitches $12

Lassen Mineral Lodge Mineral, 9 miles southwest of the southwest entrance on Hwy-36 ☎530 595 4422, ⓦminerallodge.com. Unspectacular base-rate rooms and considerably comfier family ones for not much more. There's a general store, restaurant and bar on site, as well as tent sites. Pitches $25, doubles $90

Manzanita Lake Campground Manzanita Lake ☎877 444 6777, ⓦrecreation.gov. By far the largest of the Lassen campgrounds and the only one with a camp store (8am–8pm), firewood for sale, 24hr showers (bring quarters) and a laundry. There are also surprisingly comfortable cabins. Rangers run interpretive programmes from here. Open late May to snow closure. 5900ft. Reservable. Pitches $29, cabins $65

Mill Creek Resort Mill Creek, 40271 Hwy-172, 8 miles south of the southwest entrance ☎888 595 4449, ⓦmillcreekresort.net. Set amid thick forest, there are cabins of different sizes and tent/RV spaces. Pitches $25, RV $40, cabins $70

Rim Rock Ranch Resort 13275 Hwy-89, Old Station, 11 miles northeast of the north entrance ☎530 335 7114, ⓦrimrockcabins.com. A collection of motel, B&B rooms and cabins of varying standards, the best sleeping up to six, dotted around a lush meadow. Closed Nov–March. Doubles $75, cabins $105

Southwest Campground By the southwest entrance on Hwy-89 ☎877 444 6777, ⓦrecreation.gov. Small tent-only campground with walk-in sites, water and fire rings. Open year-round. 6700ft. Pitches $10

★**Summit Lake Campground** Hwy-89 ☎877 444 6777, ⓦrecreation.gov. The pick of the Hwy-89 campgrounds, right in the centre of the park and at the hub of numerous hiking trails. It's divided into two sections: the slightly more expensive northern half can take trailers and is equipped with flush toilets, the southern half only holes. There's swimming in the lake for the steel-skinned. 6700ft. Pitches $15

Warner Valley Campground Off Hwy-89 in the south of the park ☎530 595 4480. This is a beautiful site but its distance from the road makes it only worth heading for if you're planning extended hiking in the region. 5700ft. No reservations. Pitches $16

Redding and around

At the heart of northern interior California, **REDDING** is often viewed simply as a hub for the region, without much to merit more than refuelling, grabbing a bite or changing transport. The region's largest city, with over 70,000 people, it's been a northern nexus since the late nineteenth century, when the Central Pacific Railroad came through. Today it remains a crossroads, bulging with cookie-cutter motels and diners that service traffic heading east to Lassen, west to Whiskeytown-Shasta-Trinity

National Recreation Area, north to Mount Shasta, and south to San Francisco. In recent years, however, the opening of a major museum and iconic new bridge across the central stretch of the Sacramento River have done more to detain passers-through. The one annual event that has long attracted substantial crowds is the **Kool April Nites** classic-car meeting (☎530 226 0844, ⊛koolaprilnites.com) in the second half of April, the only time you're likely to encounter problems finding a room. Redding's diminutive neighbour, **Shasta**, a once-lively gold-mining town just to the west, provides a historical counterpoint and seems a world away from the urban sprawl nearby.

Though fiercely hot in summer, the temperature drops forbiddingly in some of the surrounding areas in winter. Bear in mind that what looks like a mild day in Redding could turn out to be blizzard conditions at higher elevations only a few miles away.

Downtown

The old **downtown** is slowly being regenerated after years in the doldrums. One place to stop is the **Old City Hall Arts Center** at 1313 Market St (Tues–Thurs noon–5pm, Fri noon–6pm, Sat 11am–3pm; free; ☎530 241 7320, ⊛shastaartscouncil.org), which has rotating displays of works by local artists, and also has a performance space for

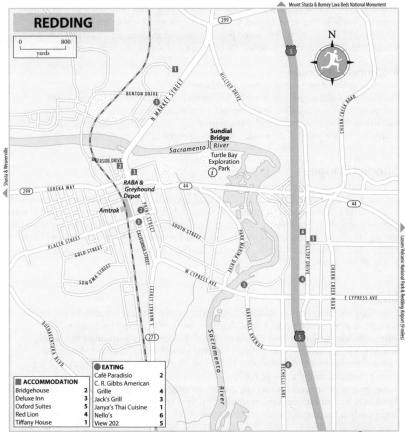

9

theatrical works. Even more attractive as a building is the beautifully restored Art Deco **Cascade Theatre**, 1731 Market St (☎530 243 8877, ⊛cascadetheatre.org), which hosts drama, concerts and films.

Turtle Bay Exploration Park

800 Auditorium Drive • June–Sept Mon–Sat 8.30am–5pm, Sun 9.30am–5pm; Oct–May Wed–Fri 9am–4pm, Sat & Sun 10am–4pm • $16 • ☎ 800 887 8532, ⊛turtlebay.org

The centrepiece of Redding's revitalization is the splendid **Turtle Bay Exploration Park**, an ambitious $64-million project. The glass-and-wood structure blends seamlessly into the riverside environment and contains permanent displays on the region's natural history, resources and Native American culture, including a full-scale replica of a bark-house. The skilfully crafted **Visible River** exhibit, which allows you to enter a simulated limestone cave and view local water-creatures in a 24ft tank, creates the impression that you're below a riverbank. The River Lab enables you to play with natural materials and learn by experience how processes such as erosion work, while the Exploration Hall and Art Gallery display changing cultural and artistic exhibitions.

A new outdoor addition to the park is **Paul Bunyan's Forest Camp**, which has a number of entertaining features including a play area, a summer butterfly enclosure, a parrot house, a turtle pond and a massive redwood log. The most enjoyable exhibit, however, is the **Interpretive Forest**, which displays various sylvan ecosystems of Northern California as well as some popular rescued animals, among them two foxes, a skunk and a porcupine. In summer there are animal shows at 11am and noon.

McConnell Arboretum

Summer 7am–dusk; rest of year 9am–5pm • $7, free with Turtle Bay entry

Another part of the grounds outside the Exploration Park, which can be visited independently, is the 220-acre **McConnell Arboretum**, which includes Mediterranean and other dry-climate flora, and a fascinating medicinal herb garden arranged according to the parts of the human body each plant treats.

Sundial Bridge

The central stretch of the river opposite the Exploration Park is dominated by the unique **Sundial Bridge**, designed by celebrated Spanish architect **Santiago Calatrava** and built in 2004. The gracefully curved and tapered 218ft mast at the northern end of this slim, translucent, glass-floored footbridge forms a sundial and has become a symbol for the region. From the bridge the newly extended **Sacramento River Trail**, designed for walkers and cyclists, now winds thirteen miles through savannah and wetland sections to the Shasta Dam.

Shasta

Huddling six miles west of Redding, the ghost town of **Shasta** – not to be confused with Mount Shasta (see p.653) – is about the area's only option for historic entertainment, and it's a slim option at that. A booming gold-mining town when Redding was an insignificant dot on the map, Shasta's fortunes changed when the railroad tracks were laid to Redding in the late nineteenth century. Abandoned since then, it remains today a row of half-ruined brick buildings that were once part of a runaway prosperity and literally the end of the road for prospectors. All roads from San Francisco, Sacramento and other southerly points terminated at Shasta; beyond, rough and poorly marked trails made it almost impossible to find gold diggings along the

9

Trinity, Salmon and Upper Sacramento rivers, so diggers contented themselves with the rich pickings in the surrounding area, pushing out the local Native Americans in a brutal territorial quest for good mining land.

Shasta State Historic Park

Main St • Unrestricted entry • **Courthouse Museum** Thurs–Sun 10am–5pm • $4 • ☎ 530 243 8194, Ⓦ parks.ca.gov

The **Shasta State Historic Park** straddles two blocks of Main Street (Hwy-299), and is less grand than it sounds, though it's a good place to stretch your legs before moving further west. Indistinguishable ruins of brick buildings are identified by plaques as stores and hotels, and the central area, not much bigger than the average garden, features miscellaneous mining machinery and a picnic area, along with a trail that loops around the back.

The centrepiece is the 1861 **Courthouse Museum**, full of mining paraphernalia and paintings of past heroes, though best are the gallows at the back and the prison cells below – a grim reminder of the daily executions that went on here. The miners were a largely unruly lot and in the main room of the courthouse a charter lays down some basic rules of conduct:

IV Thou shalt neither remember what thy friends do at home on the Sabbath day, lest the remembrance may not compare favorably with what thou doest here.

VII Thou shalt not kill the body by working in the rain, even though thou shalt make enough money to buy psychic attendance. Neither shalt thou destroy thyself by "tight" nor "slewed" nor "high" nor "corned" nor "three sheets to the wind," by drinking smoothly down brandy slings, gin cocktails, whiskey punches, rum toddies and egg nogs.

From The Miners' Ten Commandments

ARRIVAL AND DEPARTURE
REDDING AND AROUND

By bus The Greyhound station is at 1530 Yuba St (☎ 530 241 2070), integrated with the local RABA bus depot (☎ 530 241 2877, Ⓦ rabaride.com).
Destinations Chico (2 daily; 1hr 30min); Red Bluff (2 daily; 40min); Sacramento (4 daily; 2hr 40min–3hr 50min); San Francisco (3 daily; 6hr–7hr 50min).
By train The Amtrak station is at 1620 Yuba St. Trains in both directions stop here in the middle of the night.
Destinations Chico (1 daily; 1hr 30min); Dunsmuir (1 daily; 1hr 50min); Oakland (1 daily; 6hr 15min).
By plane There are three daily flight connections from SFO to Redding Municipal Airport (☎ 530 224 4321), plus one daily flight to Portland via Eureka. There's no public transport from the airport (though some hotels have shuttles).

INFORMATION

Visitor centre Visit Redding's small counter (☎ 530 225 4100 or ☎ 800 874 7562, Ⓦ visitredding.org) is inside the Turtle Bay Exploration Park shop (see opposite; same hours).
California Welcome Center Just off I-5 9 miles south of Redding at 1699 Hwy-273, Anderson (Mon–Fri 9am–5pm, Sat & Sun 10am–4pm; ☎ 800 474 2782, Ⓦ shastacascade .com). For broader information on the surrounding area and the whole of the northern interior and beyond, the Welcome Center has a huge collection of maps, information and displays, and is staffed by helpful outdoors experts.

ACCOMMODATION

Redding has worked hard to improve its image in order to tempt visitors to spend a day or two in its leafy urban environment before sampling the surrounding natural delights. Tourists tend to stay in the newer areas near the freeway rather than in the old downtown. **Motels** are concentrated along Redding's old main strip, Market St (Hwy-273), and Pine St, while the smarter chain **hotels** tend to be along Hilltop Drive, Redding's newer service area east of I-5. A few **B&Bs** are dotted around town.

Bridgehouse 1455 Riverside Drive ☎ 530 247 7177, Ⓦ reddingbridgehouse.com. This attractive B&B with sharply pointed tiled roofs and bright yellow walls contains four luxuriously appointed rooms. $129
Deluxe Inn 1135 Market St ☎ 530 243 5141. This cheapie is fine for a night but hardly lives up to its name, with rather poky rooms, although they have had a recent lick of paint, and lackadaisical service. $69
Oxford Suites 1967 Hilltop Drive ☎ 800 762 0133, Ⓦ oxfordsuites.com. This West Coast chain offers smart and comfy suites at good rates. You can drink your two free happy-hour beverages in peace by the pool. $109

9

Red Lion 1830 Hilltop Drive ☎ 530 221 8700, ⓦ redlion .com/redding. Large, modern, two-storey hotel with perfectly comfortable rooms and a decent-value buffet breakfast. Specials available most of the year. **$90**

★ **Tiffany House** 1510 Barbara Rd ☎ 530 244 3225,

ⓦ tiffanyhousebb.com. Run by a genteel and welcoming couple, the *Tiffany* is a plush yet good-value B&B in a converted Victorian house, with a pricier detached cottage behind. **$140**

EATING

Café Paradisio 1270 Yuba St ☎ 530 215 3499, ⓦ cafeparadisio.com. From its delicious starters like the $10.50 baked brie platter to main courses such as baked salmon for $19, this trendy place is guaranteed to hit the spot. Mon–Sat 11am–2pm & 5–10pm.

★ **C. R. Gibbs American Grille** 2300 Hilltop Drive ☎ 530 221 2335, ⓦ crgibbs.com. Top-quality restaurant with a variety of starters, burgers, pasta, pizza, plus seafood and meat mains for $17–36. Mon–Wed 11am–9pm, Thurs 11am–10pm, Fri 11am–11pm, Sat 4–11pm.

Jack's Grill 1743 California St ☎ 530 241 9705, ⓦ jacksgrillredding.com. Popular restaurant that prepares fine grilled steak, and shrimp and chicken dishes, for $18–40. Reservations not accepted, and though you'll probably have to wait for a table, it's well worth it. Mon–Sat 5–11pm.

Janya's Thai Cuisine 630 N Market St ☎ 530 243 7682, ⓦ janyasthaicuisine.com. This gem hidden behind a rather uninspiring strip mall frontage offers a huge menu, from spicy papaya salad to excellent stir-fries and curries, mostly $10–15. Tues–Fri 11am–2.30pm & 4–9pm, Sat & Sun 11.30am–9pm.

Nello's 3055 Bechelli Lane ☎ 530 223 1636, ⓦ nellosrestaurant.net. Good Italian cuisine specializing in veal and seafood dishes, as well as a range of pasta for around $15 – try the standout Manicotti cheese. Tues–Thurs 5–9pm, Fri & Sat 5–9.30pm, Sun 5–8.30pm.

View 202 202 Hemsted Drive ☎ 530 226 8439, ⓦ view202redding.com. This startling modern building that resembles a small museum is actually a fine restaurant where you can tuck into dishes like bacon-wrapped chicken for $26, or cheaper brunches. Mon–Thurs 11am–10pm, Fri & Sat 11am–11pm, Sun 10am–10pm.

Whiskeytown-Shasta-Trinity National Recreation Area

To the west and north of Redding lies the **WHISKEYTOWN-SHASTA-TRINITY NATIONAL RECREATION AREA**. Assuming the roads are open – they're often blocked due to bad weather in winter – this huge chunk of land is open for public use daily, year-round. Its series of three impounded **lakes** – **Whiskeytown**, **Trinity** and **Shasta** – have artificial beaches, forests and camping facilities designed to meet the needs of anyone who has ever fancied themselves as a waterskier, sailor or wilderness hiker. Sadly, during summer the area becomes completely congested, as windsurfers, motorboats, jet-skis and RVs block the narrow routes that serve the lakes. But in the low season, especially during the week, it can be supremely untouched, at least on the surface. In fact, there's an extensive system of tunnels, dams and aqueducts directing the plentiful waters of the Sacramento River to California's Central Valley to irrigate cash crops for the huge agribusinesses. The lakes are pretty enough, but residents complain they're not a patch on the wild waters that used to flow from the mountains before the Central Valley Project came along in the 1960s (see opposite). The only town of any size in this area apart from Redding is quaint, old-fashioned **Weaverville**, to the west of the lakes.

Whiskeytown Lake

Unrestricted access · $10 parking pass valid for one week · **Visitor Center** Daily 10am–4pm · ☎ 530 246 1225

Of the three lakes, **Whiskeytown Lake**, just beyond Shasta, is the smallest, easiest to get to and inevitably the most popular. Ideal for watersports, it hums with the sound of jet-skis and powerboats ripping across the still waters. Free **kayak tours** are organized in the summer (☎530 242 3462). The best place for **camping** and **hiking** is in the **Brandy Creek** area – a hairy five-mile drive along the narrow J.F. Kennedy Memorial Drive from the main entrance.

Trinity Lake
Unrestricted access • Day-use parking in some areas $5

After Hwy-299 has climbed over the wooded, 3213ft Buckhorn Summit, you can turn northeast on Hwy-3 around forty miles west of Whiskeytown to **Trinity Lake**, officially called Clair Engle Lake, but not locally referred to as such. This is much quieter, used by fewer in summer, and in winter primarily a picturesque stopoff for skiers on their way to the **Trinity Alps** area beyond, which in turn leads to the extensive **Salmon Mountains** range. There are several places to **stay** and enjoy the peaceful lapping waters. At its southern end, Lake Trinity squeezes through a narrow bottleneck to form the much slimmer and smaller **Lewiston Lake**, which can be reached by the backroad that cuts the corner between Hwy-299 and Hwy-3.

Weaverville
Sadly, many people don't bother to stop in the small Gold Rush town of **Weaverville**, 43 miles west of Redding, where Hwy-3 branches north to Trinity Lake, while Hwy-299 continues a further one hundred miles west to Eureka (see p.625) and the coast. The town's distinctive brick buildings, fitted with exterior spiral staircases, were built to withstand fires – indeed, the fire station itself is particularly noteworthy. The main draw, though, is the **Joss House** at 630 Main St (Thurs–Sun 10am–5pm; $4; ☎530 623 5284, ⓦparks.ca.gov), a small Taoist temple built in 1874 by indentured Chinese mine-workers. A beautiful shrine still in use today, it features a 3000-year-old altar and can be visited on a sadly uninspiring guided tour (last tour 4pm). Almost next door at no. 508, the **Jake Jackson Memorial Museum** (Jan–March Wed & Sat 11am–4pm; April & Oct Tues–Sat 11am–4pm; May–Sept daily 10am–5pm; Nov & Dec Wed–Sat 11am–4pm; $2; ☎530 623 5211, ⓦtrinitymuseum.org) exhibits artefacts from the Gold Rush. On the opposite side of the road look out for California's oldest still-functioning pharmacy, which stocks a brilliant selection of remedies in glass jars within original glass-and-wood cabinets.

Shasta Lake
East of the other two lakes and eight miles north of Redding is **Shasta Lake**. The biggest of the three lakes – larger than the San Francisco Bay in fact – it's marred by the unsightly and enormous **Shasta Dam**, 465ft high and over half a mile long, bang in the middle. Twice the mass of the Hoover Dam, it's the second largest dam in America, made of enough concrete to send a foot-square strip round the planet several times. Built between 1938 and 1945 as part of the enormous **Central Valley irrigation project**, the dam backs up the Sacramento, McCloud and Pit rivers to form the lake, the project's northern outpost. From Lake Shasta, I-5 crosses the world's highest double-decker bridge and races up towards Mount Shasta, an impressive drive against a staggering backdrop of mountains and lakes.

Shasta Dam
16349 Shasta Dam Blvd • Tours daily at 9am, 11am, 1pm & 3pm • Free • ☎ 530 275 4463, ⓦ shastalake.com/shastadam

From the Shasta Dam visitor centre, you can take one of the free hour-long tours of the powerhouse and into the dam, though security is tight and you cannot

9

take cameras or mobile phones with you. The historical and technical information given by the knowledgeable guides is interesting and the close-up views of the millions of gallons of water gushing down the face of the giant structure are memorable.

Lake Shasta Caverns

Daily 2hr tours: June–Aug every 30min 9am–4pm; April, May & Sept hourly 9am–3pm; Oct–March 10am, noon & 2pm • $26 • ☎ 530 238 2341 or ☎ 800 795 2283, ⓦ lakeshastacaverns.com

On the north side of the lake, the massive limestone formations of the **Lake Shasta Caverns** are the largest in California, jutting above ground and clearly visible from the freeway. The interior, however, conceals a fairly standard series of caves and tunnels in which stalactite and stalagmite formations are studded with crystals, flowstone deposits and miniature waterfalls. The admission price covers the short ferry journey from the ticket booth across an arm of Shasta Lake and the bus transfer on the other side.

INFORMATION

Whiskeytown Visitor Information Center Hwy-299 (daily: summer 9am–6pm; rest of year 10am–4pm; ☎ 530 246 1225, ⓦ nps.gov/whis). This is the place to pick up

WHISKEYTOWN-SHASTA-TRINITY

permits for primitive camping sites ($10) around the lake. **Weaverville Chamber of Commerce** 501 Main St (Mon–Sat 9am–5pm; ☎ 800 487 4648, ⓦ trinitycounty.com).

ACCOMMODATION

TRINITY LAKE

Old Lewiston Inn ☎ 530 778 3385, ⓦ theold lewistoninn.com. All the rooms at this old-fashioned inn are furnished with antiques and boast private entrances and wooden decks overlooking the river. **$125**

Pinewood Cove 45110 Hwy-3 ☎ 530 286 2201, ⓦ pinewoodcove.com. The cedar cabins here are sturdy and attractive, the larger ones having lofts. There are also sites for tents and RVs, plus boat rentals. Pitches **$28.50**, RV **$46**, cabins **$138**

Trinity Lake Resorts 45810 Hwy-3 ☎ 530 286 2225 or ☎ 800 255 5561, ⓦ trinitylakeresort.com. This resort is multifaceted and has well-appointed rooms, comfortable houseboats (minimum stay three nights) and an excellent restaurant. Boat rental available too. **$159**

WEAVERVILLE

Motel Trinity 1270 Main St ☎ 530 623 2129, ⓦ moteltrinity.com. Fairly standard but excellent-value motel, which has some rooms with jacuzzis for twice the price of basic ones. Small outdoor swimming pool. **$60**

Weaverville Hotel 481 Main St ☎ 530 623 2222, ⓦ weavervillehotel.com. Nicely refurbished 1861 building that still retains something of its Gold-era charm. Only one room has TV but some have claw-foot bathtubs. **$120**

SHASTA LAKE

Bridge Bay at Shasta Lake 10300 Bridge Bay Rd ☎ 800 752 9669, ⓦ sevencrown.com. This resort provides the only roofed accommodation right on the lake in the shape of motel rooms, suites, cabins and houseboats; you can also dine with a view of the water at the resort's *The CookHouse* restaurant. **$115**

★ Lakeshore East Campground Lakeshore Drive, off the first Lakehead exit from I-5 ☎ 530 275 8113, ⓦ shastatrinitycamping.com. Beautifully located on a steep bank overlooking the lake, this campground has spacious tent pitches, huge sturdy yurts, which can sleep five, and lots of picnic tables. The website lists dozens of other sites in the region. Pitches **$35**, yurts **$65**

EATING

WEAVERVILLE

★ La Grange Café 520 Main St ☎ 530 623 5325. Very friendly restaurant, whose bar is also the town's most convivial hangout, with a warm wood-and-brick interior. The creative traditional American cuisine includes the likes of juicy steaks, jambalaya and St Louis Nirvana ribs for $15–25. Daily 11.30am–9pm, later in summer.

Mama Llama Eatery & Cafe 490 Main St ☎ 530 623 6363, ⓦ mammallama.com. With its excellent $6–8

breakfasts and its range of quality coffees, teas and microbrews, this place is a top spot to browse the internet or the establishment's selection of books, music and gifts for sale. Mon–Fri 7.30am–5pm, Sat 8.30am–7pm.

Red Dragon 625 Main St ☎ 530 623 3000. Across from the Joss House – appropriately enough – the delicious Chinese and Thai dishes, such as the flavourful *pad ki mow*, served in the dark-red interior of this restaurant, cost $9–15. Mon–Sat 11am–9pm.

Mount Shasta

When I first caught sight of it over the braided folds of the Sacramento Valley I was fifty miles away and afoot, alone and weary. Yet my blood turned to wine, and I have not been weary since.

John Muir, on Mount Shasta

The lone peak of the 14,179ft **MOUNT SHASTA** dominates the landscape for a hundred miles all around, almost permanently snow-covered and hypnotically beautiful, but menacing in its potential for destruction: it last erupted over two hundred years ago but is still considered an active volcano. Summing up its isolated magnificence, Joaquin Miller once described it as "lonely as God and as white as a winter moon". Local lore is rich with tales of Lemurians – tall, barefoot men dressed in white robes – living inside the mountain, alongside their legendary neighbours

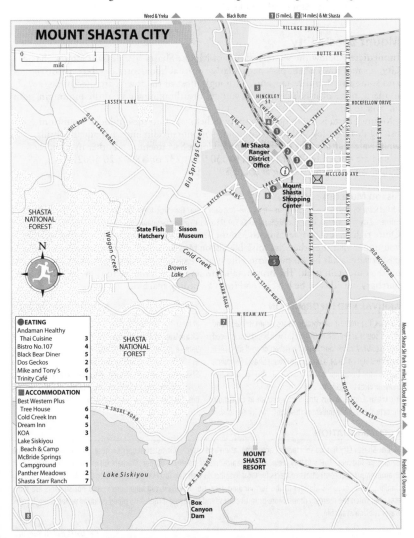

MOUNT SHASTA CITY

EATING
Andaman Healthy Thai Cuisine	3
Bistro No.107	4
Black Bear Diner	5
Dos Geckos	2
Mike and Tony's	6
Trinity Café	1

ACCOMMODATION
Best Western Plus Tree House	6
Cold Creek Inn	4
Dream Inn	5
KOA	3
Lake Siskiyou Beach & Camp	8
McBride Springs Campground	1
Panther Meadows	2
Shasta Starr Ranch	7

9

the Yaktavians, who are said to be excellent bell-makers. Such tales have lent the mountain a bit of a *Twilight Zone* reputation and numerous UFO sightings and otherworldly experiences have made Mount Shasta a centre of the American **spiritualism** movement. This prominence was heightened in 1987 when five thousand people arrived to take part in the good vibes of the Harmonic Convergence, an attempt to channel the energies of sacred power spots into peace and harmony. Not all is peaceful on the mountain, however, as hundreds of climbers annually attempt to ascend its icy heights, an activity that has resulted in deaths, usually from falls or the ever-changing weather.

The mountain is surrounded by satellite communities that can all make great bases for exploring the area, especially New Agey **Mount Shasta City**, the gourmet paradise of **Dunsmuir** and scenic little **McCloud**. The area also boasts other splendid natural assets, such as **Castle Crags State Park** and **Black Butte**.

Mount Shasta City

Immediately below the western slopes of Mount Shasta sits pleasant **Mount Shasta City**, a small town of shops – particularly spiritual bookstores (see box, p.656) – and some wonderful restaurants. Although most of the town's architecture is modern, none of it is high-rise, so you get breathtaking views of the mountain from all over town.

Mount Shasta is full of outfits hoping to help you into the outdoors, from trout fishing through dog sledding to, of course, mountain climbing. For aquatic thrills, **whitewater-rafting trips** on the churning Upper Sacramento and other rivers in the region are offered by River Dancers (☎530 925 0237 or ☎800 926 5002, ⊛riverdancers.com), starting at about $90 a day.

Sisson Museum

1 N Old Stage Rd · April & May Fri–Sun 10am–4pm; June–Aug daily 10am–4pm; Sept daily 1–4pm; Oct–Dec Fri–Sun 1–4pm; fish hatchery daily 8am–sunset · $1 suggested donation · ☎530 926 5508, ⊛mtshastamuseum.com

Quite rightly, few people come to Mount Shasta for its museums, but in bad weather you might visit the otherwise missable **Sisson Museum**, with a few examples of Native basketware, a fair bit on pioneering life in the region, and some more diverting material on the mountain itself. The brown, rainbow and eastern brook trout in the **fish hatchery** outside can be fed on food from a vending machine.

ARRIVAL AND INFORMATION   MOUNT SHASTA CITY

By bus The nearest Greyhound buses (from Redding and points south or Oregon in the north) will bring you to Weed (see p.659), 7 miles north. Half a dozen or so daily STAGE buses (☎800 247 8243) run to the Mount Shasta Shopping Center from Dunsmuir and Weed. STAGE also operates five daily services to McCloud.

By train Amtrak trains stop 9 miles south in Dunsmuir, unfortunately in the middle of the night; you'll have to wait at least 3hr for the first bus.

Chamber of Commerce 300 Pine St (daily: May–Sept 9am–4.30pm; Oct–April 10am–4pm; ☎530 926 4865 or ☎800 926 4865, ⊛mtshastachamber.com).

Siskiyou County Visitor Bureau ☎877 847 8777, ⊛visitsiskiyou.org. The Visitor Bureau has no office to visit, but this is the best resource for info on the whole county.

ACCOMMODATION

Mount Shasta City has no shortage of accommodation and reservations should only be necessary at weekends in the height of summer. The suitably New Age organization of spiritual author Amorah Quan Yin (☎530 926 1122, ⊛amorahquanyin.com) offers contacts for local lodging, as well as a fascinating insight into the Mount Shasta way of thinking. Campgrounds abound in the surrounding area, but few have full amenities – and hot showers are fairly essential when the mercury drops. More primitive sites tend to be free if there's no piped drinking water, though creek water is often available.

OPPOSITE MOUNT SHASTA >

9

MYSTICISM IN MOUNT SHASTA CITY

A disproportionate number of New Age **bookstores** and **gift shops** are sprinkled along North Mount Shasta Boulevard, providing the key to some of the town's more offbeat spiritual activities. Book Nook at no. 331 (📞 530 926 3338), for example, has a bulletin board and stacks of publications exhorting you to visit a sweat lodge or get in touch with the ascended masters. Soul Connections at no. 329 (📞 530 918 9533) has a huge collection of spiritual and mystical books, as well as groovy clothing, jewellery, crystals and other paraphernalia. Shasta Vortex Adventures, 400 Chestnut St (📞 530 926 4326, 🌐 shastavortex.com), is an interesting outfit whose primary business is providing personalized spiritual tours of the mountain, but they also offer other esoteric services.

HOTELS, MOTELS & B&BS

Best Western Plus Tree House 111 Morgan Way 📞 530 926 3101 or 📞 800 545 7164, 🌐 bestwestern .com. One of the more attractive and intimate members of the international chain, with an indoor pool, fitness centre and good restaurant. $160

Cold Creek Inn 724 N Mt Shasta Blvd 📞 530 926 9851 or 📞 800 292 9421, 🌐 coldcreekinn.com. Nicely refurbished motel, an easily walkable few blocks to downtown. Some of the simple but spacious rooms have mountain views. $99

Dream Inn 326 Chestnut St 📞 530 926 1536 or 📞 877 375 4744, 🌐 dreaminnmtshastacity.com. Very central and reasonably priced B&B, a block east of Mount Shasta Blvd, in a Victorian house with all the usual trappings. $80

★ **Shasta Starr Ranch** 1008 W.A. Barr Rd 📞 530 926 3870, 🌐 mountshastabedandbreakfast.com. A stylish ranch-house B&B with spacious rooms, a self-contained cottage, a hot spring and a great view of Mount Shasta. Now refurbished with all rooms en suite. $110

CAMPGROUNDS

KOA 900 N Mt Shasta Blvd 📞 530 926 4029 or 📞 800 736 3617, 🌐 koa.com. This fully equipped campground is a few blocks from downtown. Pitches $25, cabins $60

Lake Siskiyou Beach & Camp 4239 W.A. Barr Rd, Lake Siskiyou, 4 miles southwest 📞 530 926 2618, 🌐 lake siskiyouresort.com. The most picturesque campground in the area is this woodland option, where you can picnic, bathe and go boating. April–Oct. Pitches $22, cabins $69

McBride Springs Campground Everitt Memorial Hwy, 5 miles east 📞 530 926 4511, 🌐 fs.usda.gov. At a height of only 5000ft, this US Forestry Service campground tends to be open for most of the year. Toilets and drinking water. Pitches $10

Panther Meadows At the end of the Everitt Memorial Hwy, 14 miles east 📞 530 926 4511, 🌐 fs.usda.gov. This is the most useful of the primitive sites but its altitude of 7400ft makes it only suitable for the hardy, even in summer. Toilet but no drinking water. No reservations and closed in winter. **Free**

EATING

Andaman Healthy Thai Cuisine 313 N Mt Shasta Blvd 📞 530 926 5288. As the name suggests, there are plenty of veggie and even vegan options, as well as stalwarts such as pork green curry for $12–15. Mon–Fri 11am–2pm & 5–8pm, Sat & Sun 5–8pm.

Bistro No.107 107 Chestnut St, Mount Shasta City 📞 530 918 5353, 🌐 bistro107.com. Popular corner restaurant with a small wooden deck, where you can get gourmet burgers, panini and various specials for $10–20. Summer daily 11am–9pm; winter Mon & Thurs–Sun 11am–9pm.

Black Bear Diner 401 W Lake St 📞 530 926 4669, 🌐 blackbeardiner.com. The original location of this ever-growing family diner chain, a great place for heaped breakfasts or classic American dinners for $10–15. Daily 6am–10pm.

Dos Geckos 401 N Mt Shasta Blvd 📞 530 926 4843, 🌐 mexicanrestaurantmtshasta.com. Excellent build-your-own-burrito joint, with stunning views of the mountain from the patio. Everything on the menu is under $10. Mon–Sat 11am–3pm.

Mike and Tony's 501 S Mt Shasta Blvd 📞 530 926 4792, 🌐 mikeandtonysms.com. It may not look like much but this excellent Italian place specializes in home-made ravioli and gnocchi dishes for around $15. Great martinis, too. Mon & Thurs 5–9pm, Fri & Sat 5–10pm, Sun 10am–9pm.

★ **Trinity Café** 622 N Mt Shasta Blvd 📞 530 926 6200. The best place for quality international cuisine made from local produce. The menu changes weekly and fine microbrewed ales are available on tap. Most main courses are over $20. Tues–Thurs 5–8pm, Fri & Sat 5–9pm.

Dunsmuir

One example of how the Shasta area looked in the past can be seen in the hamlet of **Dunsmuir**, even quainter than Mount Shasta City. Situated nine miles south of Mount Shasta City on a steep hill sloping down from I-5, Dunsmuir's downtown was bypassed by the freeway, essentially freezing the community in time. Now it makes its living as a historic railroad town and the main drag, **Dunsmuir Avenue**, is lined with restored hotels and shops, many of them taking the train theme a bit too far; expect to see shopkeepers dressed as train engineers and business names like Billy Puffer Suites.

The waterfalls

Dunsmuir used to bill itself as a day-trip from Shasta, but now realizes that it has quietude and natural wonders of its own. Foremost among these are the Mossbrae and Hedge Creek **waterfalls**, along the Sacramento River Canyon, beautiful spots for walks and picnics.

To get to Mossbrae, drive north on Dunsmuir Avenue to Scarlet Way, crossing the bridge and railroad tracks to the parking area, then follow the walking trail along the

---

CLIMBING MOUNT SHASTA

Even if you're only passing through the region, you'll be tempted to tackle Mount Shasta. Ambling among the pines of the lower slopes is rewarding enough but the assault on the summit is the main challenge – and it can be done in a day with basic equipment and some determination.

PASSES AND PERMITS

This is not a climb to be taken lightly, and every year several deaths occur and numerous injuries are sustained through inexperience and overambition. The wise stick to the routes prescribed by the **Mount Shasta Ranger District Office**, 204 W Alma St (June–Aug daily 8am–4.30pm; Sept–May Mon–Fri 8am–4.30pm; ☎530 926 4511), which insists that you obtain a **summit pass** (also self-issued outside the office when closed and at the trailhead; $20) and enter your name in the **climbers' register** before and after your ascent. Those not planning to go above 10,000ft only require a free **wilderness permit**.

CONDITIONS AND EQUIPMENT

The mountain's isolation creates its own **weather**, which can change with alarming rapidity. In early summer, when most novice attempts are made, the snow cover is complete, making crampons and an ice axe a requirement to get a good grip; later during the season, as the snow melts, patches of loose ash and cinder appear, making the going more difficult and the chance of falling rock greater. Only at the end of summer, with most of the snow melted, is there a chance of climbing safely without equipment.

There are numerous **equipment rental agencies** in town, such as The Fifth Season, 300 N Mt Shasta Blvd (☎530 926 3606, ⊛thefifthseason.com), which has the following rental prices for trips up to three days: boots $38, crampons $23, ice axe $15, mountain tent from $75 and sleeping bag $38. They also provide a mountain weather forecast on ☎530 926 5555 and are the meeting place for **Shasta Mountain Guides** (☎530 926 3117, ⊛shastaguides.com), who arrange jeep trips up the mountain and conduct rock- and ice-climbing courses for all levels, as well as backcountry skiing trips, from around $125/day.

To be prepared for **storms** on the mountain, you'll want to bring extra food, stove fuel, a good wind-resistant shelter and plenty of warm clothing.

THE ASCENT

Even for fit, acclimatized climbers, the **ascent**, from 7000ft to over 14,000ft, takes eight to ten utterly exhausting hours. The easiest, safest and most popular way up is via **Avalanche Gulch** – just follow the footprints of the person in front of you. Drive up the mountain on the Everitt Memorial Highway to the **Bunny Flat** trailhead at 7000ft. A gentle hour's walk brings you to **Horse Camp** (7900ft), a good place to acclimatize and spend the night before your ascent – there's drinking water, toilet facilities and a knowledgeable caretaker who can offer good advice about your impending climb. The return trip is done in four or five hours, depending on the recklessness of your descent: Mount Shasta is a renowned spot for **glissading** – careering down the slopes on a jacket or strong plastic sheet – a sport best left to those proficient in ice-axe arrests, but wonderfully exhilarating nonetheless.

9

train tracks for a mile until you get to the railroad bridge; don't cross, but continue along the tracks through the trees and you'll see the falls ahead. Hedge Creek is accessible via the parking area at the North Dunsmuir exit on I-5

ARRIVAL AND INFORMATION
DUNSMUIR

By bus The five daily STAGE buses (see p.654) take only 15min to run between Dunsmuir and Mount Shasta City, from where they carry on to Weed and Yreka.

By train Amtrak trains stop at the usually deserted railway station, its last California halt before continuing

north to Oregon.

Visitors Bureau Suite 100, 5915 Dunsmuir Ave (summer Wed–Sat 9.30am–noon & 1–5pm; ☎530 235 2177 or ☎800 386 7684, ⓦ dunsmuir.com).

ACCOMMODATION

Cave Springs 4727 Dunsmuir Ave ☎530 235 2721, ⓦ cavesprings.com. Situated on the north side of the town, this place has a wide range of motel rooms and cabins, a couple of which have outdoor hot tubs overlooking the river. **$62**

The Dunsmuir Inn & Suites 5423 Dunsmuir Ave ☎530 235 4395, ⓦ dunsmuirinn.com. The building might be a bit of an eyesore against the green mountain backdrop but the rooms at this motel are clean, comfortable and cheap for the area. **$70**

Dunsmuir Lodge 6604 Dunsmuir Ave ☎530 235 2884, ⓦ dunsmuirlodge.net. This motel-style lodge in leafy grounds on the south side of town is freshly decorated and attractively furnished. **$79**

★ **Railroad Park Resort** 100 Railroad Park Rd ☎530 235 4440, ⓦ rrpark.com. The most unique lodging in the area, with most of its accommodations fashioned out of old railway cabooses, though there are also some cabins, tent sites and RV hookups. Popular dining-car restaurant too. Pitches **$29**, RV **$37**, doubles **$135**

EATING

Café Maddalena 5801 Sacramento Ave ☎530 235 2725, ⓦ cafemaddalena.com. Tasty Mediterranean evening meals like the scrumptious French cider-glazed king salmon go for around $20–25. Thurs–Sun 5–9pm; closed Jan to mid-Feb.

Cornerstone Bakery Café 5759 Dunsmuir Ave ☎530 235 4677. This is a good place for eggy breakfasts, sandwiches, including a few veggie options, gourmet burgers and a couple of pasta dishes. Most items $8–13. Daily 8am–2pm.

Dunsmuir Brewery Works 5701 Dunsmuir Ave, Dunsmuir ☎530 235 1900, ⓦ dunsmuirbreweryworks .com. Excellent new microbrewery, which offers a great selection of craft ales, quality sandwiches for under $10 and live music Fridays and Saturdays. Summer daily 11am–10pm; rest of year Tues–Sun 11am–9pm.

Pizza Factory 5804 Dunsmuir Ave ☎530 235 4849, ⓦ pizzafactory.com. About the only cheap place to eat in town, there's a diner feel here but it's basically a pizzeria, with minis going for under $10. Lots of toppings, like all-meat or pesto and garlic. Mon–Thurs & Sun 11am–9pm, Fri & Sat 11am–10pm.

Sengthong's Blue Sky Room 5855 Dunsmuir Ave ☎530 235 4770, ⓦ sengthongsrestaurant.com. Upscale but undoubtedly high-quality Southeast Asian cuisine, where some of the main courses, such as hot spiced prawns, cost over $20. Live jazz on Fridays. Mon–Fri & Sun noon–10pm, Sat noon–11pm.

Yak's 4917 Dunsmuir Ave ☎530 678 3517, ⓦ yaks.com. Canteen-style joint with colourful murals and grocery on one side. Huge portions of burgers, chilli fries and other greasy favourites for $13–15. Daily 11.30am–9pm.

Castle Crags State Park

13 miles south of Mount Shasta City, off I-5 • Daily 8am–dusk • $8/car • ☎530 235 2684, ⓦ parks.ca.gov

If you have time, explore the beautiful trails that climb four thousand feet up to the 225-million-year-old, glacier-polished granite crags at the aptly named **Castle Crags State Park**. The upper viewpoint of the often deserted, 6200-acre forested park is a great place to take a picnic and admire the jagged pinnacles that give the park its name.

McCloud

McCloud, a delightful little town with stunning views of Mount Shasta, can make a good base for the area, especially if you plan to spend much time in the Ski Park (see opposite). The only cultural diversion is the small **Heritage Junction Museum** at 320

Main St (May–Oct Mon–Sat 11am–3pm, Sun 1–3pm; donation; ☎ 530 964 2604), loaded with a haphazard collection of bric-a-brac, memorabilia and woodcutters' gear.

McCloud River Falls

Five miles east of McCloud on Hwy-89

There's not much to do in the town itself, but the nearby **McCloud River Falls** is a great spot for a picnic or gentle stroll. The falls, set amid thick woods, are divided into three distinct sections, each about one mile from the next and connected by a riverside walking trail but also accessible by road. If you're short of time, head for the more dramatic Middle Falls; at *Fowlers Camp*, near the Lower Falls, there's **camping**, often free because of the intermittent water supply, while the Upper Falls boast a lovely picnic area. Continuing southeast on Hwy-89, you'll eventually come to the more renowned and spectacular Burney Falls and, still further, Lassen Volcanic National Park (see p.642).

ARRIVAL AND DEPARTURE   MCCLOUD

By bus There are five daily STAGE buses (see p.654) from McCloud to Mount Shasta City (25min), from where they carry on to Weed and Yreka.

ACCOMMODATION AND EATING

Floyd's Frosty 125 Broadway ☎ 530 964 9747. A Fifties-style joint offering hefty burgers, thick shakes and ice cream. Most locals take their order away but there's plenty of seating. Daily 11am–7pm.

McCloud Hotel 408 Main St ☎ 530 964 2822 or ☎ 800 964 2823, ⓦ mccloudhotel.com. This hotel has lavishly refurbished rooms in a classily restored building and also boasts a fine restaurant, where a complimentary gourmet breakfast is served. **$145**

McCloud Timber Inn 153 Squaw Valley Rd ☎ 530 964 2893. The only motel in the vicinity, boasting an attractive location near the river and roomier-than-average lodgings.

The affable owner is a fount of local knowledge. **$79**

★ **Stoney Brook Inn** 309 W Colombero Drive ☎ 530 964 2300 or ☎ 800 369 6118, ⓦ stoneybrookinn.com. An excellent option, this inn has some rooms with shared bathrooms and particularly good single rates. Lavish breakfast and use of the spa facilities included. **$79**

White Mountain Cafe 241 Main St ☎ 530 964 2300, ⓦ mccloudmercantile.com. This attractive hotel restaurant is a good spot for eggy breakfasts and sandwiches or burgers for lunch, all under $10. Daily 7am–5pm.

Mount Shasta Ski Park

Near McCloud on Hwy-89 • Lift tickets Mon–Thurs $36, Fri–Sun $48; equipment rental: skis $25, snowboards $33 • ☎ 800 754 7478, ⓦ skipark.com

Mount Shasta Ski Park has yet to establish itself on the ski circuit, so its lift tickets and rental charges for ski and snowboard equipment are quite reasonable. On the lower slopes, keep your eyes peeled for the inedible **watermelon snow**, its bright red appearance caused by a microbe which flourishes here – think Frank Zappa, just change the colour.

Black Butte

Five miles north of Mount Shasta City, the largely treeless cone of **Black Butte** (2.5 miles; 2–3hr; 800ft ascent) offers a more modest alternative to climbing Mount Shasta. The switchback trail to this 6325ft volcanic plug dome is hard to find without the leaflet available from the Mount Shasta City Chamber of Commerce (see p.654).

Weed

A gateway town to Klamath Falls, Oregon and the Lava Beds National Monument, **Weed** can't compete with Mount Shasta City's hip charm, Dunsmuir's gourmet reputation or McCloud's cuteness. In a form of karmic justice, however, it gets the

9

better view of the peak during the summertime. Too bad the tourism board couldn't leave it at that, instead of dressing up the place as a "historic lumber town" with the groaner of a slogan, "Weed love to see you".

The only attraction in town, just off Main Street at 303 Gilman Ave, is the **Weed Historic Lumber Town Museum** (summer Mon & Wed–Sun noon–7pm; winter by appointment; donation; ☎ 530 938 0550, ⓦ siskiyous.edu/museum). Occupying the former courthouse, it outlines local history, primarily that of the lumber industry, and also contains a couple of fine old vehicles.

Just north of Weed, you can take Parks Creek Road to the top of the ridge, from where it's a ninety-minute hike along the **Pacific Coast Trail** to tranquil Dead Fall Lakes.

Living Memorial Sculpture Garden

Five miles outside of Weed, north on US-97 • Unrestricted entry • Donation • ☎ 530 938 2218, ⓦ weedlmsg.org

Out of town, on the way to Oregon and Lava Beds, the **Living Memorial Sculpture Garden** is an intriguing remembrance of the Vietnam War. Artist Dennis Smith has created ten metal sculptures illustrating different aspects of an American soldier's experience in the war. Surrounding the art are about 53,000 pine trees, one for every American killed in Vietnam. The trees, art, silence and position under Mount Shasta add up to a very moving experience.

Stewart Mineral Springs

4617 Stewart Springs Rd, off I-5 • Mon noon–7pm, Thurs–Sun 10am–6pm • Mineral bath $35, sauna $18; sauna free to residents • ☎ 530 938 2222, ⓦ stewartmineralsprings.com

After a day or two trudging around or up Mount Shasta, **Stewart Mineral Springs**, just north of Weed, provides welcome relief. Individual bathing rooms in a cedar and pine forest glade soothe your aches away. There are also two Karuk tribe sweat lodges on the premises, where regular ceremonies take place.

ARRIVAL AND INFORMATION   WEED

By bus The Greyhound office is at 628 S Weed Blvd (Mon–Sat 8.30am–4pm; ☎ 530 938 4454) and is also the nearest stop to Mount Shasta City. STAGE buses (see p.654) connect Weed with the other local towns.
Destinations Dunsmuir (5 daily; 40min); McCloud (5 daily; 50min); Mount Shasta City (9 daily; 20min); Yreka (11 daily; 40min).

Chamber of Commerce 34 Main St (Mon–Fri 9am–5pm; ☎ 530 938 4624 or ☎ 877 938 4624, ⓦ weedchamber .com).

ACCOMMODATION AND EATING

Hi Lo Motel & Café 88 S Weed Blvd ☎ 530 938 2731, ⓦ hilomotel.com. This motel is a notch or two above average, with neat and tidy rooms, as well as RV hookups. The café serves good snacks such as hash and eggs. RV $37, doubles $69

Glassy Junction 1886 Shastina Drive ☎ 530 938 1500. Simple Indian restaurant with padded seating in booths, where you can get wholesome North Indian items such as goat *saag* and fish masala for $10–14. Daily 10am–10pm.

Mt Shasta Brewing Company & Weed Alehouse 360 College Ave ☎ 530 938 2394, ⓦ weedales.com. The pub part of the brewery premises serves wraps, panini, pizza and hot dogs, as well as all the company's great ales. Ask for an informal tour. Daily noon–8pm, bar till late.

Stewart Mineral Springs 4617 Stewart Springs Rd, off I-5 ☎ 530 938 2222, ⓦ stewartmineralsprings.com. This delightful retreat (see above) has a range of inexpensive accommodation options, from camping pitches, through tipis and motel rooms and cabins. Pitches $35, tipis $45, doubles $80, cabins $100

Yreka

There's little to justify more than an hour or two in quiet, leafy **Yreka** (pronounced "why-REE-ka"), 25 miles north of Weed on I-5, but it makes a pleasant break. The reason most people used to come here was to ride the now defunct Yreka Western Railroad, better known as the **Blue Goose**, which fell foul of the financial crisis in 2008.

THE LAND OF THE MODOC

Until the 1850s Gold Rush, the area which now defines the Lava Beds National Monument was home to the **Modoc tribe** but after their repeated and bloody confrontations with the miners, the government ordered them into a reservation with the Klamath, their traditional enemy. After only a few months, the Modoc drifted back to their homeland in the Lava Beds and in 1872 the army was sent in to return them by force to the reservation. It was driven back by 52 Modoc warriors under the leadership of one **Kientpoos**, better known as "Captain Jack", who held back an army of US regulars and volunteers twenty times the size of his for five months, from a stronghold at the northern tip of the park (see p.664). Eventually Captain Jack was betrayed by a member of his tribe, captured and hanged, while what remained of the tribe was sent off to a reservation in Oklahoma, where most of them died of malaria.

Now there's not much to do apart from wander round the older backstreets, admiring the carefully preserved Victorian houses.

Siskiyou County Museum

910 S Main St • Tues–Sat 9am–3pm; outdoor section May–Oct Tues–Sat 10am–3pm • $3 • ☎ 530 842 3836,
Ⓦ siskiyoucountyhistoricalsociety.org

The **Siskiyou County Museum** deserves some attention for its exhibits on Native Americans, Chinese immigrants, trapping and gold mining, and for its rooms preserved in period style. The summer-only **outdoor section** is even better, with its historic buildings – church, houses and shops – transported here from around the county.

ARRIVAL AND INFORMATION   YREKA

By bus Yreka can be reached by STAGE bus (see p.654) from Mount Shasta City (9 daily; 1hr), Dunsmuir (5 daily; 1hr 20min) and McCloud (5 daily; 1hr 45min).
Chamber of Commerce 310 S Broadway (Mon–Fri

9am–5pm; ☎ 530 841 1078, Ⓦ yrekachamber.com) issues maps for a self-guided historic walking tour around Yreka's numerous Victorian homes.

ACCOMMODATION AND EATING

Baymont Inn & Suites 148 Moonlit Oaks Ave ☎ 530 841 1300, Ⓦ yrekainn.com. Modern franchise hotel in a quiet location, with comfortable, simply furnished rooms. Smart indoor pool and spa too. **$75**
Klamath Motor Lodge 1111 S Main St ☎ 800 551 7255, Ⓦ klamathmotorlodge.net. An independent lodge with small but pleasant rooms, close to amenities but far enough from freeway noise. **$53**
Natalee Thai Cuisine 1235 S Main St. A simple but very popular Thai joint, where you can get all the standard

dishes from pad thai through an array of stir-fries to tasty but not very spicy curries for $11–16. Daily 11.30am–9pm.
Nature's Kitchen 412 S Main St ☎ 530 842 1136. This café offers mostly organic food and drink, from fairtrade coffee to its mostly vegetarian sandwich selection (around $10), made from locally grown stoneground whole wheat. Some chicken and salmon options too. Mon–Fri 8am–5pm, Sat 9am–4pm.

Etna

A worthwhile twenty-mile detour south of Yreka along Hwy-3 takes you to charming, turn-of-the-century **Etna**. Its main claim to fame is the **Etna Brewing Company**, down the hill at 131 Callahan St, a tiny microbrewery which was revived in 1990 after seventy years of closure since Prohibition and has gradually been regaining a fine reputation as its brews begin to be distributed more widely. You can usually take an impromptu tour and the brewery's pub is wonderful (see p.662). While in Etna, check out the 1950s soda fountain in the Scott Valley Drugstore at the top of Main Street.

★**Etna Brewing Company** 131 Callahan St ☎530 467 5277, ⓦetnabrew.com. Great ales such as Double Crossed Imperial IPA are on tap to wash down the equally tasty pub grub, from sandwiches and burgers to the excellent tri-tip pork or beef steak for $18.50. Wed–Sun 11.30am–9pm.

Etna City Park Diggles St ☎530 467 5256. You can camp in the town park, but before doing so inform City Hall on the number given to make sure the sprinklers are not put on. Fees on a per-person basis. Pitches $10

Etna Motel 317 Collier Way ☎530 467 5388. Run by a welcoming couple, this basic but comfortable motel is the perfect place to crash out after a night in the town's brewery. $59

Lava Beds National Monument and around

After seeing Mount Shasta, you really should push on to the **LAVA BEDS NATIONAL MONUMENT**, which commemorates a war between the US and Modoc tribe on the far northern border of the state. Carved out of the huge **Modoc National Forest**, it's actually a series of volcanic caves you can explore and huge black lava flows with a history as violent as the natural forces that created them.

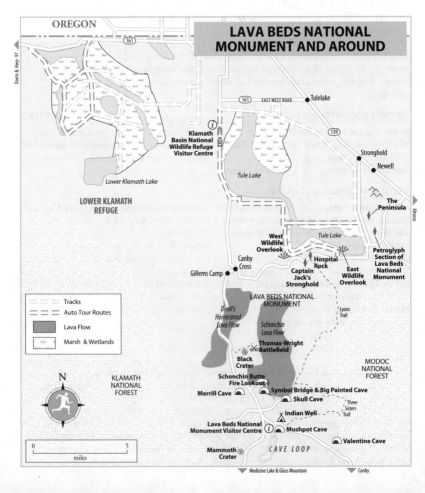

VOLCANIC SPELUNKING FOR BEGINNERS

To explore the Lava Beds, you can borrow torches from the visitor centre (see p.666) and begin your explorations of the caves just outside. Initially, though, entering the darkness alone can be an unnerving experience, so many people prefer to take the **free guided ranger walks** (summer daily). Two to three-hour morning walks (9am) leave from the visitor centre and explore little-known sections of the monument; afternoon tours (usually 2pm) are ninety-minute guided cave trips; and in the evening (around 8.30–9pm) rangers lead hour-long campfire talks and slideshows, which shift to Mushpot Cave in bad weather.

If you do go independently, you must abide by a few **rules**. Don't go alone, wear decent shoes and take at least two torches. Borrowed torches must be returned by nightfall to ensure no one goes missing. For night explorations (the caves remain open), you'll need your own light source. Hard hats are strongly advised and can be purchased or rented for $5 at the visitor centre.

Lava Beds is one of the most remote, forgotten and beautiful of California's parks, with pungent yellow rabbit-brush blooming around the burnt rocks in fall. It's in the heart of Modoc country (see box, p.661), a desolate outback where cowboys still ride the range, and where, as the territory of one of the last major battles with the Native Americans, there's still a suspicious relationship between the settlers and the native peoples.

Today the Lava Beds region is inhabited only by wild deer and three million migrating ducks, which easily outnumber the trickle of tourists that make it this far. To the west and north, the **Klamath Basin National Wildlife Refuge** spreads over the border into Oregon. This stop on the Pacific Flyway draws birders and hunters alike, hoping to catch sight of a rare eagle among the millions of migratory guests.

When you head south back towards Mount Shasta on US-97, your car will be stopped in otherwise dull **Dorris** by agriculture agents checking to see if you're transporting fruit or vegetables from out of state. Say "No" nicely and they might give you a colour map to welcome you to California.

Tulelake

The only **accommodation** near the park, and the one place to pick up supplies (the monument can only muster a drinks machine), is at **Tulelake**, fourteen miles north, which incidentally prides itself on being "the horseradish capital of the world". Apart from holding that honour, it's a pretty undistinguished place but does exude a certain sort of frontier appeal.

Tulelake-Butte Valley Fair Museum of Local History

800 S Main St • Mon–Fri 9am–5pm, also Sat 9am–5pm in summer • $3 • ☎ 530 667 5312

The one tourist attraction in town is the **Tulelake-Butte Valley Fair Museum of Local History**, in the expansive fairgrounds. This complex contains excellent displays on geological features, wildlife, history (especially the Indian Wars and World War II internment), Native American culture and current issues. The entry fee includes a one-hour interpretive **audio tour**. The fairgrounds host an enormous annual **fair** during the week following Labor Day in September.

The Monument and around

Open 24hr • $15/vehicle, valid for seven days • ☎ 530 667 8113, ⓦ nps.gov/labe

A day spent in the **Lava Beds National Monument** is akin to exploring the innards of a volcano, scampering down hollow tubes through which molten lava once coursed. The youngest of them were formed 30,000 years ago when volcanic upwellings sent molten,

9

EXPLORING THE LAVA BEDS

Most of the interest in Lava Beds lies around the visitor centre, where the largest concentration of caves can be visited on the short **Cave Loop** access road. For a confidence-building handle on your location in the 25 "developed" caves – less than a tenth of the known total – pick up the *Lava Caves Map* ($5.50) from the visitor centre. New ones are discovered all the time, so the possibilities are almost endless, but for the moment, the tried and tested caves below should satisfy.

Catacombs Cave On Cave Loop At over a mile long, this is the longest open tube in the monument, though you need perseverance, a slim body and a cool head to get anywhere near the end. The profusion of interconnecting passageways makes it one of the most confusing; keep track of whether you are heading up- or downhill.

Golden Dome Cave On Cave Loop The startling golden hues of the moist mossy roof lend the cave both its name and an otherworldly appearance.

Labyrinth Cave At the entrance to Cave Loop Striking geological features – lava pillars and lavacicles – and evidence of Native American habitation.

Mushpot Cave Right by the visitor centre near the start of Cave Loop The most developed of the caves, this provides a good introduction, is lit during centre opening hours and has interpretive panels highlighting key features.

Skull Cave About 2 miles north of Cave Loop Named after bighorn skulls found when the cave was discovered by early explorer E.L. Hopkins, this has the largest entrance of any of the lava tubes and contains ice all year round.

Symbol Bridge and Big Painted Cave 2 miles north of Cave Loop; 1.5-mile round-trip; almost flat No torch is needed to explore these two very worthwhile caves adjacent to each other, though one could come in handy. Some of the best examples of pictographs in the monument – tentatively dated between 1000 AD and 1500 AD – show up as different angles of sunlight catch the rocks beside the entrance. Respecting Modoc sensibilities, make two clockwise turns before descending into a large cave, open at both ends (hence the "bridge" name), in which zigzags, squiggles, sunbursts and human figures are depicted in grease and charcoal on a pumice-washed background. Make a single counter-clockwise turn on departure for Big Painted Cave, where the pictographs are less impressive. In the mid-1920s, J.D. Howard excavated a small tunnel at the very back of the cave to reveal an ice flow in a cavity 15ft down: with a torch you can scramble down there.

Valentine Cave About 2 miles southeast of Cave Loop Interesting because it combines various characteristic cave features, such as stalactites and catacombs. The ridges at the base of the walls leading down into the deep and wide chamber almost appear to be man-made, so even are their lines.

basaltic magma careering across the Modoc Plateau. As the magma came into contact with cool air, it solidified, leaving a flowing molten core feeding the expanding lava field downhill. In time, the magma flow stopped and the molten lava drained out, leaving the world's largest concentration of such hollow tubes – there were 746 at the last count in 2007. Most remain unexplored, but where the casing has collapsed, access is possible and you're free to scramble through (see box above). Some of the caves are so small that you have to crawl along on all fours, while others are an enormous 75ft in diameter. Some contain Native American **petroglyphs** – not to be confused with the names painted on the cave walls by J.D. Howard, one of the first white men to explore and name the caves.

The visitor centre

If caves don't do it for you, consider the other attraction of Lava Beds –its well-documented history. Begin at the **visitor centre** near the southern entrance for an exhibit on the Modoc War, including photos of its chief participants, including Modoc leader Captain Jack (see box, p.661), and scathing editorials from national papers condemning the US Army over its mission.

Captain Jack's Stronghold

In the northern reaches of the park is **Captain Jack's Stronghold**, a natural fortress of craggy lava flows and shallow caves on the shores of Old Tule Lake. When you arrive, pick up a trail book (50¢) from the parking lot and enjoy one of two well-narrated self-guided trails (one half a mile, the other 1.5 miles) through a war that in many ways typified the conquest of the West. When you get here you'll see how the Modoc managed to hide and move around through the passageways of the hills.

Canby Cross

Two miles west of Captain Jack's Stronghold, **Canby Cross** marks a turning point in the war, when Captain Jack, coerced by the man who would later betray him, drew a gun during a council and murdered US General Canby and a pastor.

Hospital Rock

Just northeast of Captain Jack's Stronghold, the shallow lava bowl of **Hospital Rock** marks the point where one Lt Sherwood, wounded by the Modoc, was unsuccessfully tended in a makeshift field hospital towards the end of the siege on the stronghold.

Mammoth Crater

Small volcanic craters, buttes, spatter cones and chimneys dot Lava Beds but the flows which produced most of the lava tubes came from **Mammoth Crater** on the southern perimeter of the monument, where a short path leads to a viewpoint overlooking the deep conical crater.

Medicine Lake

Underlying the most recent of Lava Beds' fabulous creations is a bed of basalt, the product of a huge shield volcano with a profile so flat it's barely noticeable. Its core is now filled by the subalpine **Medicine Lake**, ten miles southwest of Mammoth Crater. Formerly a Modoc healing centre, the only therapies on offer today are fishing and swimming from the cheap campsites along the north shore. It's accessible via an unpaved road closed November to mid-May.

Glass Mountain

More volcanic spectacle lies just west of Medicine Lake at **Glass Mountain**, made almost entirely of glassy, black obsidian – source of Modoc arrowheads – but covered in fluffy, white pumice quarried for stonewashing jeans. A short and fairly easy trail leads in from the road. Just beyond the monument's northeast corner, a small outlier known as the Petroglyph Section contains **Petroglyph Point**, a 300-yard-long cliff face made of "tuff", volcanic rock formed when lava flows hit Old Tule Lake. The soft rock offers some fine, but cryptic, examples of ancient art: shields, female figures and a series of small circles thought to represent travel. The crevices are home to various bird species, especially horned owls. Pick up an interpretive leaflet at the visitor centre (see p.666).

Newell

East of the Petroglyph Section, the road continues to Hwy-139 and the town of **Newell**, site of the **Tule Lake Camp**, where 110,000 people of Japanese descent, many of them American citizens, were interned without charge or trial between 1942 and 1946. There were as many as 18,000 inmates at any given time. Many of the camp buildings have been sold off to local farmers but the wood-sided police and military barracks remain and a simple plaque commemorates this disgraceful chapter and prays it will never be repeated. Nearby there was also a less well-known camp for internees of German and Italian origin.

Klamath Basin National Wildlife Refuge

Just to the north of Lava Beds along Hill Rd (Hwy-161) • Open daylight hours

The most rewarding excursion from the monument is to the **Klamath Basin National Wildlife Refuge**, on Hwy-161, leading to US-97 and spreading into Oregon. One of the last **wetlands** in California, with swathes of open water and emerging vegetation on

9

the shoreline, it attracts an estimated eighty percent of birds following the Pacific Flyway, the major migration routes from Alaska and northern Canada to Baja California in Mexico. In spring and fall, almost a hundred species are present and the population tops a million. Bald eagles appear from December to January, bringing out hundreds of photographers trying to navigate the snowy road. Spring is the best time for migratory birds and fall for waterfowl. The most accessible reaches of the reserve are the **Lower Klamath Refuge** and **Tule Lake**, an open body of water surrounded by reeds (*tule* in Modoc). Surprisingly, the best way of spotting the wildlife is by driving along designated routes: getting out of the car and walking scares the birds off.

ARRIVAL AND INFORMATION

By car Lava Beds is 160 miles northeast of Redding and inaccessible without a vehicle. The most tortuous but undoubtedly scenic route follows Hwy-89 to Bartle, then passes Medicine Lake; the approach via Hwy-139 is easier, but the best and fastest is from Weed, following US-97 through Dorris and then via Hwy-161 through the Klamath Basin National Wildlife Refuge.

Lava Beds National Monument visitor centre Just

LAVA BEDS NATIONAL MONUMENT

inside the southwestern entrance (daily: summer 8.30am–5pm; rest of year Mon 8am–5pm; ☏530 667 8113, ⦿nps.gov/labe). Pick up an excellent map of the monument and borrow a torch and hard hat here.

Klamath Basin National Wildlife Refuge visitor centre Hill Rd (Mon–Fri 8am–4.30pm, Sat & Sun 10am–4pm; ☏530 667 2231, ⦿fws.gov). This useful centre contains some informative displays.

ACCOMMODATION AND EATING

TULELAKE

Captain Jack's Stronghold 7 miles south of Tulelake on Hwy-139 ☏530 664 5566, ⦿cjstronghold.com. The area's best restaurant does excellent soups, salads, sandwiches, pasta and some international dishes like chicken teriyaki, all in the $12–20 range. Thurs–Sun 4–8pm.

Ellis Motel 2238 Hwy-139 ☏530 667 5342. This basic and extremely old-fashioned motel is cheaper than *Fe's* (see below) but is the only other option around town, otherwise it couldn't get away with charging this much. $55

★**Fe's Bed & Breakfast** 660 Main St ☏530 667 5145 or ☏877 478 0184, ⦿fesbandb.com. Very welcoming place with cosy rooms and a good breakfast to get you started. The knowledgeable owner also runs tours of the area. $80

Mike and Wanda's 423 Modoc Ave ☏530 667 3226. Fittingly rustic joint that churns out filling meals in the café and bar sections, plus a more expensive menu in the dining room in between, where steaks cost around $20. Mon–Thurs & Sun 7am–9pm, Fri–Sat 8am–10pm; bar till late.

LOWER KLAMATH REFUGE

Winema Lodge ☏530 667 5158, ⦿winemalodge .com. Right beside the refuge, this place has a mixture of motel-style and fancier lodge rooms, as well as RV slots. Continental breakfast is included and cheap lunches are available, but dinner is only possible for large groups. RV $35, doubles $85

CAMPING

All wilderness camping throughout the Lava Beds National Monument is free and no permits are necessary but campers must pitch at least a quarter of a mile from any road, trail or camping area and fifty yards from any cave. Be warned, though, that elevation throughout the park ranges from 4000 to 5700ft, so there's snow and freezing nights for much of the year, which can make camping uncomfortable.

Indian Well Campground 300m east of the visitor centre. This is the park's one developed campground, which has basic facilities. It cannot be reserved but you can check availability through the nearby visitor centre (see above). Pitches $10

Modoc County

Occupying the far northeastern corner of California, wild and rugged **MODOC COUNTY** is bordered by equally thinly populated areas of Oregon and Nevada and is about as remote as it gets. Despite covering an immense area, the total population is only ten thousand, the majority of whom reside in the county seat of **Alturas**. Outside of that modest settlement, the mostly high-desert region is home to a lot more wildlife – bobcats, mule deer, antelope, elk, mountain lions, wolves and birds such as sandhill cranes and bald eagles – than people, many of whom rely on cattle ranging and alfalfa cultivation for their livelihood. On the eastern side, the imposing **Warner Mountains** divide the rest of the county from **Surprise Valley**, home to several small communities within spitting distance of the Nevada state line.

Historically the area belonged to three native tribes – the Modoc, the Paiute and the Pit River tribes. The creation of the Emigrant Trail in the late 1840s, the main east–west route into Northern California, brought white settlers to the region in increasing numbers and into all-too-common confrontation with indigenous people. For the next six decades, a series of violent conflicts earned the region the title of **Bloody Ground of the Pacific**. The settlers gradually took over, though the area's control was successively bounced around between Utah Territory, Nevada Territory and California's Shasta and Siskiyou counties before Modoc County was created in 1874. It retains a frontier feel to this day and has the highest per-capita gun ownership in the state, so it's no surprise that most locals and many of those who find their way here tend to occupy themselves with outdoor pursuits like hunting.

Alturas and around

Out-of-the-way **ALTURAS** is about sixty miles southeast of Tulelake via Hwy-137 and then Hwy-299, which you can also take all the way up from the Burney Falls area. Coming from Lava Beds, the black craggy rocks gradually give way to the increasingly pine-forested hills of the **Modoc National Forest**, which surround the town on three sides.

Modoc County Historical Museum

600 S Main St • May–Oct Mon–Sat 10am–4pm • $2 • ☏ 530 233 2944

A glimpse into the region's turbulent past can be gained at the modest **Modoc County Historical Museum**, which occupies a modern building by the park; the displays concentrate on settler and Native American artefacts, as well as some of the county's natural history. Though many of its dozen blocks are modern, the town, with its position by the mountains and the clear relation of the people to the land, manages to exude a Wild West atmosphere.

Modoc National Wildlife Refuge

Two miles southeast of town • Daily 7am–sunset • Free • ☏ 530 233 3572 • Take the road between the Chamber of Commerce and the museum and turn right at the first main junction, after about half a mile

Spreading out over thousands of acres south of Alturas, the **Modoc National Wildlife Refuge** is composed largely of unspoilt grasslands, incorporating some wetlands, and is home to many avian species, among them sandhill cranes, tundra swans, teal, pintail ducks and warblers, as well as migratory visitors such as white-fronted geese, pelicans, cormorants and egrets.

Devil's Garden

Around twenty miles north of town, the **Devil's Garden** is a very different type of terrain, a densely forested plateau with more wetlands and a community of some four hundred **wild horses** – there are trails through the excellent hiking country but you should take a good map and be careful not to stray from the paths.

Goose Lake

A little further northeast from the Devil's Garden, accessible via US-395, lies **Goose Lake**, which straddles the Oregon state line. Good for fishing and other recreational activities, its largest settlement, on the east shore, is **New Pine Creek**, nearly all of whose facilities lie on the Oregon side – making it a good place to head to for cheaper gas.

9

Finally, nearby **Davis Creek**, just off US-395 towards the lake, is the site of numerous obsidian mines, and bucketfuls of the jagged black rocks can be carried away if you obtain a free permit from the Forest Service headquarters in Alturas.

ARRIVAL AND INFORMATION | ALTURAS AND AROUND

By bus Although you'll be pretty stuck without a car when you get here, Alturas does have bus links with Redding (2 weekly; 3hr 15min) via Burney Falls, and Reno (3 weekly; 4hr 15min) via Susanville, provided by Sage Stage (☎ 530 233 6410, ⓦ sagestage.com).

Chamber of Commerce 522 S Main St, Alturas (Mon, Wed & Fri 10am–1pm; ☎ 530 233 4434, ⓦ cityofalturas.org).

Modoc National Forest Service headquarters 225 W 8th St, Alturas (Mon–Fri 8am–5pm; ☎ 530 233 5811, ⓦ fs .us.gov/modoc). Provides a wealth of information on all the hiking, hunting, fishing and camping possibilities in the region, as well as some useful maps.

ACCOMMODATION AND EATING

Antonio's Cucina Italiana 220 S Main St, Alturas ☎ 530 233 5600, ⓦ antoniosalturas.com. Surprisingly smart yet casual Italian restaurant for such a remote area, serving filling pasta, pizza and sandwiches for under $15. Daily 11am–9pm.

★ **Niles Hotel** 304 S Main St, Alturas ☎ 530 233 3773, ⓦ nileshotel.com. Still a real throwback to the West's heyday, despite the recent refurbishment of some rooms, this venerable hotel offers comfort along with a touch of history. $80

Nuch's Thai Food 1001 N Main St ☎ 530 233 5650. Top-quality Thai food such as spicy *som tum* papaya salad and coconut curries for around $11–13 are served in a simple square dining room. Daily 11am–9pm.

Rim Rock Motel 22760 Hwy-395 N ☎ 530 233 5455, ⓦ rimrockmotelalturas.com. This out-of-town motel exudes a fittingly rustic air, with comfortably decorated rooms and views of the surrounding ridges. Equestrian activities available. $69

The Warner Mountains

Providing a dramatic backdrop to Alturas, the proud ridges of the **Warner Mountains**, snowcapped for two-thirds of the year and prone to snowfall in any month, exert a magnetic pull on the few outsiders who venture this far. The range is divided into north and south by the valley that carries Hwy-299 east through the mountains.

The road passes the **Cedar Pass Snowpark** (☎ 530 233 3323), where you can ski during winter weekends – all-day rope tow and T-bar tickets range from $8 to $20, and ski and snowboard rental is very cheap at $20–25 per day. It is, however, nearby **South Warner Wilderness**, part of the extensive Modoc National Forest, which presents the most fruitful territory for exploration. Here 77 miles of trails over more than seventy thousand acres of slopes, steeper on the east side than the west, offer excellent hiking opportunities. Get maps and details from the Forest Service headquarters in Alturas but make sure to carry provisions and all-weather gear. In the north, unpaved Route 9 ascends over the North Warners from US-395 near Goose Lake and climbs up over **Fandango Pass**, where the old Applegate Trail and Lassen forty-niner route converge. It's passable with care in a regular car and makes for a scenic alternative route east, with arresting views of Surprise Valley along the way.

Surprise Valley

On the sunrise side of the mountains, secretive **Surprise Valley** marks the border with Nevada and is hemmed in by more barren ridges to the east. Indeed, the fiercely independent types who live over here are said to feel more allegiance to the Silver State than the Golden State. Hwy-299 from Alturas ends in the pleasant small town of **Cedarville**, the largest in the valley, a modest claim though that may be. The only noteworthy sight is the re-created **pioneer village** of Louieville in the county fairgrounds, a couple of blocks east of Main Street. Among the venerable timber buildings are a church, a slaughterhouse and – here's the Wild West for you – two jails.

From Cedarville you can branch south to even quieter Eagleville or, better yet, head north past a couple of white alkali lakes to pay a brief visit to **Fort Bidwell**, home to a thriving community of 150 Paiute Native Americans. Here you can pop into their modern community centre (flexible hours) to see a collection of rocks, trophies and an original peace pipe.

INFORMATION   SURPRISE VALLEY

Chamber of Commerce Warner Realty, 517 Main St, Cedarville (Tues & Thurs 9–11am; ☎ 530 936 7822, ⓦ surprisevalleychamber.com).

ACCOMMODATION AND EATING

Country Hearth 551 Main St, Cedarville ☎ 530 279 2280. Open all day for a range of filling breakfasts, lunchtime sandwiches or snacks and hearty evening meals such as steaks for around $20, the name says it all. Mon–Sat 7.30am–8.30pm.

JnR Hotel 581 Main St, Cedarville ☎ 530 279 2449, ⓦ jnrhotel.org. The rustic outward appearance reinforced by the old wagon in the front yard gives way to surprisingly modern and well-appointed rooms. $58

Surprise Café 501 Main St, Cedarville ☎ 530 569 0740, ⓦ 2mysurprise.com. Serves up classic home-style breakfasts and lunches for $10 or less, but only drinks on Tuesdays and Wednesdays. Tues & Wed 8–11am, Thurs–Sat 8am–2pm.

★ **Surprise Valley Hot Springs** 5 miles east of Cedarville ☎ 530 279 2040, ⓦ surprisevalleyhotsprings .com. This resort is a real hidden gem, whose splendid themed suites each have a naturally heated outdoor tub and would cost double if the location was not so remote. $127

Contexts

History

To many people, California appears to be one of the least historic places on the planet. Seemingly unburdened by the past, it's a land where anything is possible, whose inhabitants live carefree lives, wholly in and for the present moment. Its very name, appropriately for all its idealized images, is a work of fiction, free of any historical significance. The word first appeared in a popular Spanish picaresque novel of the early 1500s, *Las Sergas de Esplandián* by García de Montalvo, as the name of an island, located "very near to the terrestrial paradise" and inhabited entirely by Amazons "without any men among them".

Native peoples

For thousands of years before the arrival of Europeans, the **aboriginal peoples** of California flourished in the naturally abundant land, living fairly peacefully in tribes along the coast and in the deserts and forested mountains. Anthropologists estimate that nearly half the native population then living within the boundaries of the present-day US were spread throughout what's now California, in small, tribal villages of a few hundred people, each with a clearly defined territory and often its own distinct language. Since there was no political or social organization beyond the tribe, it was not difficult for the colonizing Spaniards to divide and conquer, effectively wiping the natives out – though more died of epidemics than outright genocide.

Very little remains to mark the existence of California's Native Americans: they had no form of written language, relatively undeveloped craft skills and built next to nothing that would last beyond the change of seasons. About the only signs of the coastal tribes are the piles of seashells and discarded arrowheads that have been found, from which anthropologists have deduced a bit about their cultures. Also, a few examples of **rock art** survive, as at Chumash Painted Cave State Historic Park (see p.366), near Santa Barbara. Similar sorts of petroglyph figures were drawn by the Paiute Native Americans, who lived in the deserts near Death Valley, and by the Miwok of the Sierra Nevada foothills.

Discovery and early exploration

The first Europeans to set foot in California were Spanish explorers intent on extending their colony of New Spain, which, under the 1494 Treaty of Tordesillas, included all the New World lands west of Brazil and all of North America west of the Rocky Mountains. In 1535, **Hernán Cortés**, fresh from defeating the Aztecs, headed westward in search of a short cut to Asia, which he believed to be adjacent to Mexico. Though Cortés never reached what is now California, he set up a small colony at the southern tip of the Baja (or lower) California peninsula. Thinking it was an island, he named it Santa Cruz, writing in his journals that he soon expected to find the imagined island of the Amazons.

13,000BC	1542	1579
Natives begin inhabiting present-day California; their population reaches as high as 300,000 before settlement by Europeans	Spanish explorer Juan Cabrillo sees San Diego Bay and is the first person to call the uncharted area California	Sir Francis Drake claims "Nova Albion" for England upon landing near Point Reyes in the *Golden Hind*

The first explorer to use the name California, and to reach what's now the US state, was **Juan Cabrillo**, who sighted San Diego Bay in 1542 before continuing north to the Channel Islands, off the Santa Barbara coast. He died there six months later, persistent headwinds having made it impossible to sail any further north. His crew later made it as far as what is now the state of Oregon, but were unable to find any safe anchorage and returned home starving and decimated by scurvy. It was fifty years before another Spaniard braved the difficult journey: **Juan de Fuca**'s 1592 voyage caused great excitement when he claimed to have discovered the Northwest Passage, a potentially lucrative trade route across North America. It has long since turned out that there is really no such thing (de Fuca may have discovered the Puget Sound, outside Seattle), but Europeans continued to search for it for the next two hundred years.

English explorer **Sir Francis Drake** arrived in the *Golden Hind* in 1579, taking a break from his piracy of Spanish vessels in order to make repairs. His landing spot, now called Drake's Bay north of San Francisco, had "white bancks and cliffes" that reminded him of Dover. Upon landing, he was met by a band of native Miwoks, who feted him with food and drink, and placed a feathered crown upon his head; in return, he claimed all their lands – which he called Nova Albion (New England) – for Queen Elizabeth, supposedly leaving behind a brass plaque now on display in the Bancroft Library at the University of California, Berkeley.

Setting sail from Acapulco in 1602, **Sebastian Vizcaíno**, a Portuguese explorer under contract to Spain, made a more lasting impact than his predecessors, undertaking the most extensive exploration of the coast and bestowing most of the place names that survive. In order to impress his superiors, he exaggerated the value of his discoveries, describing a perfect, sheltered harbour, which he named **Monterey** in honour of his patron in Mexico. Subsequent colonizers based their efforts on these fraudulent claims, and the headquarters of the missions, as well as the military and administrative centre of the Spanish government, remained at Monterey, one hundred miles south of San Francisco, for the next 75 years.

Colonization: the Spanish and the Russians

The Spanish occupation of California began in earnest in 1769, with a combination of military expediency (to prevent other powers from gaining a foothold) and Catholic missionary zeal (to convert the Native Americans). It was that year when Father **Junípero Serra** and a company of three hundred soldiers and clergy set off from Mexico for Monterey – half of them by ship, the other half overland. **Gaspàr de Portola** led a land expedition that mistakenly pushed on as far as the San Francisco Bay Area, before realizing their mistake and turning back. They didn't find Monterey on the return journey either and regrouped with Serra back in San Diego.

In June 1770, after establishing a small mission and presidio (fort) at San Diego, a successful second expedition arrived at Monterey, where another mission and small presidio were constructed (see box opposite). During this time, the first towns, called **pueblos**, were established in order to attract settlers to what was still a distant and undesirable territory. The first was laid out in 1777 at San Jose, south of the new mission at San Francisco. Los Angeles, the second pueblo, was established in 1781, though neither had more than one hundred inhabitants until well into the nineteenth century.

1769	1770	1812
Travelling overland, Spanish explorer Gaspàr de Portola is the first recorded European to sight San Francisco Bay	The first Spanish mission in California is established in San Diego by Franciscan Father Junípero Serra	Russian fur traders establish the outpost of Fort Ross on the present-day Sonoma County coast

CALIFORNIA MISSIONS

Among the oldest European settlements in California, the state's 21 **missions**, established by Spain in the late eighteenth century, were built all along the coast, ostensibly to Catholicize the Native Americans – something they did with inquisitional fervour. In truth, each mission was accompanied by a pueblo, or secular settlement, and, most importantly, a presidio, or military fortress. Though masterminded by Franciscan Father **Junípero Serra**, most of the mission structures that survive today were built to the designs of Serra's successor, Father **Férmin de Lasuén**, who was in charge of the missions during the period of their greatest growth. By the time of his death in 1804, a chain of 21 missions, linked by the dirt path of **El Camino Real** ("The Royal Road"), ran from San Diego to Sonoma, north of San Francisco, ensuring that every mission was one day's ride or hard walk from the next; this proximity enabled easy commerce and communication along the chain. The missions flourished for more than one hundred years, converting and killing thousands of natives through a combination of forced evangelism and smallpox.

The complexes were broadly similar, with a church and cloistered residential structure surrounded by irrigated fields, vineyards and more extensive ranchlands. The labour of the Native American converts was co-opted: they were put to work making soap and candles, were often beaten and never educated. Objective accounts of the missionaries' treatment of the indigenous peoples are rare, though mission registries record twice as many deaths as they do births and their cemeteries are packed with Native American dead. Not all of the Native Americans gave up without a fight: many missions suffered raids, and the now-ubiquitous red-tiled roofs were originally a replacement for the earlier thatch to better resist arson attacks.

Eventually, when the missions were secularized under Mexican rule in 1834, much of the land was given not to the indigenous peoples, but to the Spanish-speaking *Californio* ranchers. The missions' chequered reputation lasted at least until the later Victorian era, when sentimentalist writer **Helen Hunt Jackson** gave them an idyllic gloss in her bestselling potboiler *Ramona* – a hugely influential book responsible for the current image of missions as charming outposts of quiet spirituality and quaintly austere architecture.

The largest and most populous settlement was San Luis Rey de Francia (see p.195) – its huge *lavandería*, or washing area, is now an impressive sunken garden – while arguably the most famous is San Juan Capistrano (see p.125), which welcomes migrating swallows every March. Visitors will find the most evocative, if not necessarily authentic, sense of early settler life at the restorations at San Antonio de Padua (see p.384) and La Purísima (see p.368).

One reason for Spain's military presence in California – which consisted of four presidios all told, with twelve cannons and only two hundred soldiers – was to prevent the expansion of the small **Russian** colony based in Alaska, which consisted mostly of trappers collecting beaver and otter pelts in the present-day states of Washington and Oregon. The two countries maintained friendly relations, and in any case, the Spanish presidios were in no position to enforce their territorial claims. In fact, they were so short of supplies and ammunition that they had to borrow gunpowder to fire welcoming salutes whenever the two forces came into contact. Well aware of the Spanish weakness, the Russians established the outpost of **Fort Ross** in 1812, sixty miles north of San Francisco. This further undermined Spanish sovereignty over the region, though the Russians abandoned the fort in 1841, selling it to John Sutter, a figure who features prominently in later California history (see p.676).

1841	**1846**	**1848**
The first Americans to migrate to California overland arrive via covered wagons over the Sierra Nevada mountains	The Bear Flag Revolt in Sonoma establishes the territory's independence from Mexico; three weeks later, the US assumes control	Gold is discovered in Coloma in the Sierra Nevada foothills, setting off the greatest voluntary migration in recorded human history the following year

The Mexican era

While Spain, France and England were engaged in the bitter struggles of the Napoleonic Wars, the colonies of New Spain rebelled against imperial neglect, with Mexico finally gaining independence in 1821. The Mexican Republic, or the United States of Mexico as the new country called itself, governed California as a territory. However, the fifteen distinct administrations it set up lacked the money to pay for improvements and soldiers needed to enforce the laws, so they were unable to exercise any degree of authority.

The most important effect of the Mexican era was the final **secularization** in 1834, after years of gradual diminution, of the Franciscan missions. As most of the missionaries were Spanish, under Mexican rule they had seen their position steadily eroded by the increasingly wealthy, close-knit families of the so-called Californios – Mexican immigrants who'd been granted vast tracts of ranchlands. The government's intention was to distribute half of the missions' extensive lands among Native American converts, but this was never carried out, and the few powerful families divided most of it up among themselves.

In many ways, this was the most lawless and wantonly wasteful period of California's history, an era described by **Richard Henry Dana** – scion of a distinguished Boston family, who dropped out of Harvard to sail to California – in his 1840 book *Two Years Before the Mast*. Most of the agriculture and cottage industries that had developed under the missionaries disappeared, and it was a point of pride among the Californios not to do any work that couldn't be done from horseback. Dana's Puritan values led him to heap scorn upon the "idle and thriftless people" who made nothing for themselves: for example, the large herds of cattle that lived on the mission lands were slaughtered for their hides and sold to Yankee traders, who turned the hides into leather which they sold back to the Californios at a tidy profit. "In the hands of an enterprising people", he wrote, "what a country this might be."

The first Americans

Throughout the Mexican and Spanish eras, foreigners were legally banned from settling, and the few who showed up – mostly sick or injured sailors dropped off to regain their health – were often jailed until they proved themselves useful, either as craftsmen or traders able to supply needed skills or goods. In the late 1820s, the first **Americans** began to make their way to California; males without exception, these new arrivals tended to fit in with the existing Mexican culture, often marrying into established families and converting to the Catholic faith. The American presence grew slowly but surely as more and more people emigrated, still mostly by way of a three-month sea voyage around Cape Horn. Among these was **Thomas Larkin**, a New England merchant who, in 1832, set up shop in Monterey, and later was instrumental in pointing the disgruntled Californios towards the more accommodating US; Larkin's wife Rachel was the first American woman on the West Coast.

The first people to make the four-month journey to California overland – in a covered wagon, just as in so many Hollywood Westerns – arrived in 1841, having forged a trail over the Sierra Nevada mountains via Truckee Pass, just north of Lake Tahoe. Soon after, hundreds of people each year were following in their tracks. In 1846, however, forty

1848	1850	1869
Following the United States' victory in the Mexican–American War, the Treaty of Guadalupe Hidalgo formally cedes California to the US	California becomes the 31st state in the US; four years later, Sacramento becomes its permanent capital	In a large part through the labour of Chinese immigrants, the transcontinental railroad is completed

migrants, collectively known as the **Donner party**, died when they became trapped in the mountains by early winter snowfall (see box, p.579). The immense difficulties involved in reaching California, either over land or by sea, kept population levels at a minimum, and in 1846, only seven thousand people, not counting Native Americans but including all Spanish and Mexicans, lived in the entire region.

The Mexican–American War

From the 1830s onwards – inspired by **Manifest Destiny**, the popular, almost religious, belief that the United States was meant to cover the continent from coast to coast – US government policy regarding California was to buy all of Mexico's land north of the Rio Grande, the river that now divides the US and Mexico. President Andrew Jackson was highly suspicious of British designs on the West Coast – he himself had been held as a (14-year-old) prisoner of war during the Revolutionary War of 1776 – and various diplomatic overtures were made to the Mexican Republic, all of which backfired. In April 1846, Jackson's protégé, President James Polk, offered forty million dollars for all of New Mexico and the California territory, but his simultaneous annexation of the newly independent Republic of Texas – which Mexico still claimed – resulted in the outbreak of war.

Almost all the fighting of the **Mexican–American War** took place in Texas; only one real battle was ever fought on California soil, at San Pasqual, northeast of San Diego, where a roving US battalion was surprised by a band of pro-Mexican Californios, who killed 22 soldiers and wounded another 15 before withdrawing south into Mexico. Monterey, still the territorial capital, was captured by the US Navy without a shot being fired, and in January 1847, when the rebel Californios surrendered to the US forces at Cahuenga, near Los Angeles, the Americans controlled the entire West Coast.

Just before the war began, California had made a brief foray into the field of self-government: the short-lived **Bear Flag Republic**, whose only lasting effect was to create what's still the state flag, a prowling grizzly bear with the words "California Republic" written below. In June 1846, American settlers in Sonoma Valley took over the local presidio – long abandoned by the Mexicans – and declared California independent, which lasted for all of three weeks until US forces took command.

The Gold Rush

As part of the Treaty of Guadalupe Hidalgo, which formally ended the war in 1848, Mexico ceded all of its Alta California territory to the US. Nine days before the signing of the accord, in the distant foothills of the Sierra Nevada mountains, flakes of **gold** were discovered by workmen building a sawmill along the American River at Coloma, though it was months before this momentous conjunction of events became known.

At the time, California's non-Native American population was mostly concentrated in the few small towns along the coast. Early rumours of gold attracted a trickle of prospectors and, following news of their subsequent success, men were flooding into California from seemingly everywhere by the middle of 1849 – eighteen months after the initial discovery – in the most madcap migration in world history. **Sutter's Fort**, a small agricultural community, trading post and stage stop which had been established

1870	1873	1890
With nearly 150,000 residents, San Francisco becomes the tenth most populous city in the US	The University of California's flagship campus opens in Berkeley	Sequoia, Yosemite and General Grant (now Kings Canyon) are established as the second, third and fourth national parks in the US, after Yellowstone

six years earlier by **John Sutter** on the banks of the American River, was overrun by miners, who headed up into the nearby foothills to seek their fortune. Some did – most didn't – and within fifteen years most of the gold had been picked clean. The miners moved on or went home, and their camps vanished, prompting Mark Twain to write that "in no other land, in modern times, have towns so absolutely died and disappeared as in the old mining regions of California".

Statehood

Following the US takeover after the defeat of Mexico, a **Constitutional Convention** was held at Monterey in late 1849. The men who attended were not the miners – most of whom were more interested in searching for gold – but those who had been in California for some time (about three years on average). At the time, the Territory of California extended all the way east to Utah, so the main topic of discussion was where to place the eastern boundary of the intended state. The drawing up of a state constitution was also important, since it was the basis on which California applied for admission to the US. This constitution contained a couple of noteworthy inclusions: to protect the dignity of the manually labouring miners, slavery was prohibited; and, to attract well-heeled women from the East Coast, California was the first state to recognize in legal terms the separate property of a married woman. In 1850, California was admitted to the US as the 31st state.

The Indian Wars

Though the US Civil War had little effect on California, white settlers and US troops fought many bloody battles throughout the 1850s and 1860s against the various Native American tribes whose lands the immigrants wanted. At first, the government tried to move willing tribes to fairly large reservations, but as more settlers moved in, the tribes were pushed onto smaller and smaller tracts. The most powerful resistance to the well-armed invaders came in the mountainous northeast of California, where a band of **Modoc** fought a long-running guerrilla war, using their superior knowledge of the terrain to evade US troops (see box, p.661).

Owing to a combination of disease and lack of food, as well as deliberate acts of violence, the Native American population was drastically reduced, and by 1870 almost ninety percent had been wiped out. The survivors were concentrated in small, value-deficient reservations, where their descendants still live: the Cahuilla near Palm Springs, the Paiute/Shoshone in Owens Valley, and the Hupa on the northwest coast. All are naturally quite protective of their privacy.

The boom years: 1870–1900

After the Gold Rush, **San Francisco** boomed into a boisterous frontier town, exploding in population from five hundred to fifty thousand inhabitants within five years. Though far removed from the mines themselves, the city was the main landing spot and supply town for ship-borne Argonauts (as the prospectors were called). Moreover, it was the place where successful miners went to blow their hard-earned cash on the

1906	1910	1913
A 7.8-magnitude earthquake strikes San Francisco and is followed by three days of raging fires	Angel Island, the West Coast's version of New York's Ellis Island, is opened to process (mostly Asian) immigrants	Following five years of difficult construction, the arrival of the Los Angeles Aqueduct opens the floodgates of Southern California development

1906 SAN FRANCISCO EARTHQUAKE AND FIRE

The earthquake that struck San Francisco in the early morning hours of April 18, 1906 was, at 7.8 on the Richter Scale, the most powerful to ever hit the continental US – before or since. The earthquake itself levelled hundreds of buildings, but by far the worst destruction was wrought by the innumerable post-quake fires caused by ruptured gas mains, collapsed chimneys and spontaneous combustion ignited by temperatures exceeding 2000°F. Conflagrations scorched the entire area west from the waterfront, north and south of Market Street, and west to Van Ness Avenue, where grand mansions were dynamited in a politically daring move to form a firebreak; all in all, over 75 percent of the city was toppled and/or torched. The damage and ensuing fallout was staggering: upwards of 3000 people perished and about three-quarters of the city's 410,000 residents were left homeless (many eventually resettling across the bay in Oakland), while 28,000 buildings were destroyed to the tune of $300–500 million worth of damage – one-third of California's taxable property at the time. In terms of loss of life, San Francisco's horrific 1906 calamities rank second only to the hurricane that devastated Galveston, Texas just six years prior.

whisky and women of the **Barbary Coast**, then the raunchiest waterfront in the world, full of brothels, saloons and opium dens. Ten years later, San Francisco enjoyed an even bigger boom as a result of the silver mines of the Comstock Lode in western Nevada, owned mainly by San Franciscans, who displayed their wealth by building grand palaces and mansions on Nob Hill – still one of the most exclusive addresses in the city today (see p.439).

The completion in 1869 of the **transcontinental railroad**, built using imported Chinese labourers, was a major turning point in the settlement of California. Whereas the trip across the country by stagecoach took at least a month and was subject to scorching hot weather and attacks by hostile natives, the crossing could now be completed in just five days.

In 1875, when the Santa Fe Railroad reached Los Angeles (the railroad company having extracted huge bribes from local officials to ensure the budding city wasn't bypassed), there were just ten thousand people living in the whole of **Southern California**, divided equally between San Diego and Los Angeles. A fare war developed between the Santa Fe and its rival, the Central Pacific, and ticket costs dropped to as little as $1 for a one-way ticket from New York. Land speculators placed advertisements in East Coast and European papers, offering cheap land for homesteaders in towns and suburbs all over the West Coast that, as often as not, existed only on paper. By the end of the nineteenth century, thousands of people, ranging from Midwestern farmers to East Coast elite, had moved to California to take advantage of the fertile land and mild climate.

Hollywood, World War II and after

The greatest boost to California's fortunes was, of course, the **film industry**, which moved here from the East Coast in 1911. The infant business was attracted by the state's temperate climate, in which directors could shoot outdoors year-round, and by the incredibly cheap land, on which large indoor studios could be built at

1923	1937	1941–45
Draped across the hills above Los Angeles' nascent film capital in large block letters, the "HOLLYWOODLAND" sign makes its high-profile debut; the last four letters are later dropped	The Art Deco span of the Golden Gate Bridge opens, elegantly connecting San Francisco with Marin County	Numerous wartime shipbuilding yards operate around San Francisco, Los Angeles and San Diego

comparatively little cost. Within three years, movies such as D.W. Griffith's *Birth of a Nation* – most of which was filmed along the dry banks of the Los Angeles River – were being cranked out by the hundreds.

Hollywood, a suburb of Los Angeles that was the site of many of the early studios, and which has ever since been the buzzword for the entire entertainment industry, has done the most to promote the mystique of California as a pleasure garden, disseminating images of its glamorous lifestyles around the globe. Los Angeles has since become established as an international centre for the music business as well.

This widespread, idealized image had a magnetic effect during the **Great Depression** of the 1930s, when thousands of people from all over the country descended upon California, which was perceived to be – and for the most part was – immune to the economic downturn that crippled the rest of the US. From the Dust Bowl Midwest, entire families, who came to be known as **Okies**, packed up everything they owned and set off for the farms of the Central Valley, an epic journey captured by John Steinbeck's bestselling novel *The Grapes of Wrath*, in the photographs of Dorothea Lange, and in the baleful tunes of folk singer Woody Guthrie. Some Californians who feared losing their jobs to the incoming Okies formed vigilante groups and, with the complicity of local and state police, set up roadblocks along the main highways to prevent unemployed outsiders from entering the state.

A Depression-era initiative to alleviate poverty and get the economy moving again was the government-sponsored **Works Progress Administration (WPA)** and its construction projects, which ranged from restoring the California missions and building trails and park facilities, to commissioning artworks such as the marvellous Social Realist murals on display in the interior base of San Francisco's Coit Tower.

Things turned around when **World War II** brought heavy industry to California, as shipyards and aeroplane factories sprang up, providing well-paid employment in wartime factories. After the war, most stayed on, and today several California companies still make up the roll call of suppliers to the US military and space programmes.

After World War II, many of the soldiers who'd passed through on their way to the battlegrounds of the South Pacific returned to California and decided to remain. There was plenty of well-paid work and the US government subsidized home purchases for war veterans; most importantly, an ambitious programme of **freeway and interstate highway construction** enabled land speculators to build new commuter suburbs on land that had been used for farms and citrus orchards.

The **1950s** brought prosperity to the bulk of middle-class America (typified by President Dwight Eisenhower's goal of "two cars in every garage and a chicken in every pot"), and California, particularly San Francisco, became a nexus for alternative artists and writers, spurring an immigration of intellectuals that, by the end of that decade, had manifested itself as the **Beat generation** – pegged far-out "Beatniks" by San Francisco columnist Herb Caen, in honour of Soviet space satellite Sputnik.

The 1960s and 1970s

California remained at the forefront of youth and **social upheavals** into and throughout the **1960s**. In a series of drug tests carried out at Stanford University – paid for by the CIA, which was interested in developing a "truth drug" for interrogation purposes –

1942–46	1945	1955
Tens of thousands of Californians of Japanese heritage (many holding US citizenship) are held in "War Relocation Camps"	The Charter of the United Nations is signed at the War Memorial Opera House in San Francisco	Disneyland opens in the Orange County suburb of Anaheim

unwitting students were dosed with **LSD**. One guinea pig was writer Ken Kesey, author of the highly acclaimed novel *One Flew Over the Cuckoo's Nest*, who soon secured a personal supply of the then-legal drug and toured the West Coast to spread the word of "acid". In and around San Francisco, Kesey and his crew, the Merry Pranksters, turned on huge crowds at **Electric Kool-Aid Acid Tests** – in which LSD was diluted into bowls of the soft drink Kool-Aid – complete with psychedelic light shows and music by the Grateful Dead. The acid craze reached its height during the **Summer of Love** in 1967, when the entire Haight-Ashbury district of San Francisco seemed populated by barefoot and drugged flower children.

Within a year, the superficial peace of Flower Power was shattered, as protests mounted against US involvement in the **Vietnam War**; Martin Luther King Jr and Bobby Kennedy, heroes of left-leaning youth, were both gunned down – Kennedy in Los Angeles after winning the California primary of the 1968 presidential election. The militant **Black Panthers**, a group of black radical activists based in Oakland, raised its profile significantly, and by the end of the decade, the "system", in California especially, seemed to be at breaking point, with the atrocities committed by **Charles Manson** and his "Family" in the state seemingly signifying a general collapse.

Antiwar protests, concentrated at the University of California campus in Berkeley, continued through the early **1970s**. Emerging from the milieu of revolutionary and radical groups, the Symbionese Liberation Army (SLA), a small, well-armed and stridently revolutionary group, set about the overthrow of the US, attracting media (and FBI) attention by murdering civil servants, robbing banks and, most famously, kidnapping 19-year-old heiress **Patty Hearst**. Amid much media attention, Hearst converted to the SLA's cause, changing her name to Tanya and – until her capture in 1977 – remaining underground and participating in the group's activities, which provoked national debate about her motives and beliefs.

California **politics**, after Watergate and the end of American involvement in Vietnam, seemed to lose its once-idealistic fervour, and popular culture withdrew into self-satisfaction, typified by the smug harmonies of Southern California musicians such as the Eagles, Jackson Browne and Fleetwood Mac. While the upheavals of the 1960s were overseen by California Governor Ronald Reagan, who was ready and willing to fight the long-haired hippies, the 1970s saw the reign of "Governor Moonbeam" **Jerry Brown**, under whose leadership California enacted some of the most stringent **anti-pollution** measures in the world. The state also actively encouraged the development of renewable forms of energy, such as solar and wind power, and protected the entire coastline from despoliation and development. The possession of under an ounce of **marijuana** was decriminalized (though it remains an offence to sell it), and the harvesting of marijuana continues to account for over $1 billion each year, making it the number-one cash crop in the number-one agricultural region in the US.

The 1980s and 1990s

The easy money of **1980s** Reaganomics and the so-called trickle-down economy, which unsurprisingly never quite trickled down to the state's poorest, ended in a messy downturn. Many saw this as a disgraceful but fitting finale to a decade when greed was elevated to a virtue. Los Angeles junk-bond king Michael Milkin was convicted of

1965	1967	1977
Underlying racial tensions escalate in Los Angeles as riots sear the Watts neighbourhood for six days in August; 34 deaths and over 1000 injuries result	The "Summer of Love" envelops San Francisco's Haight-Ashbury district in a hallucinogenic haze of peace, love and LSD	Designed by its namesake Bay Area company, the first Apple II home computer hits the US market

multibillion-dollar fraud, and the Savings and Loan banking scandals enmeshed such high-ranking politicos as California Senator Alan Cranston. Consequently, the **1990s** kicked off with a stagnant property market and rising unemployment.

In **Los Angeles**, the videotaped beating of black motorist Rodney King by officers of the local Police Department, and the subsequent acquittal of those officers, sparked off fierce **rioting** in April 1992. State and federal authorities, forced into taking notice of Los Angeles' endemic poverty and violence, promised all sorts of new initiatives, but achieved few concrete results. Race also dominated the protracted trial of black former football star **O.J. Simpson** – accused and finally acquitted of murdering his white ex-wife and her male friend – in 1994–95, splitting public opinion into directly opposed camps of black and white.

All these factors combined to make this era perhaps Southern California's bleakest since the Great Depression, and **natural calamities** – regional flooding, Malibu fires and mudslides and a cataclysmic 1994 earthquake – only added to the general malaise. Mike Davis's *City of Quartz*, despite flaws and inaccuracies, served as a secular bible for the time, an artfully written work based on the inevitable doom Los Angeles was facing. And with the city's chronic inter-ethnic hatred, natural disasters, bureaucratic inaction and general public pessimism, it seemed that Davis was probably right.

The latter half of the 1990s saw **Richard Riordan**, a multimillionaire technocrat who served as Los Angeles mayor from 1992 to 2000, preside over a major **revival** in the city's fortunes and a restructuring of its economic base – aerospace and automotive giving way to tourism, real estate and, as always, Hollywood. New property developments attempted to revitalize deprived areas, and even crime and violence tailed off marginally. However, these improvements probably owed more to the national economic upswing during the Clinton years than to purely local initiatives.

San Francisco also suffered in the early 1990s; on top of AIDS-related illnesses stretching health services, the area was hit by a series of natural disasters. The Loma Prieta **earthquake** in October 1989 devastated specific areas of the Bay Area, followed two years later by a massive **fire** in the Oakland hills, which burned over two thousand homes and killed 25 people – the third worst fire in US history.

But even more so than in Los Angeles, San Francisco's economic upswing turned the city around, replacing pre-millennium jitters with Information Age optimism. **Silicon Valley** industries boomed, with companies scrambling to find high-paid workers to fill their constantly growing rosters. San Jose, San Francisco's southern neighbour, surpassed the Golden Gate city in population, and even comparatively gritty Oakland began receiving a much-needed facelift. Still, not everyone in the Bay Area was happy with the apparent prosperity. **Gentrification** threatened to turn San Francisco from an artist-friendly province of activism into a playground and computer town for Silicon Valley's rich young things. Housing prices rocketed, and with tenancy at 99 percent, the situation began forcing out not only the city's poor, but its lower middle class as well.

The twenty-first century

The optimism that had overridden many concerns at the tail end of the old millennium soon took a pummelling once the new one started. The world's computers may not have gone belly-up at zero hour on Y2K, but the high-tech industry became the biggest

1978	1989	1991
Mayor George Moscone and Supervisor Harvey Milk (the US' highest-profile gay public official) are killed in San Francisco City Hall by former Supervisor Dan White	6.9-magnitude earthquake kills over sixty people, also collapsing a double-decker highway in Oakland and a section of the Bay Bridge	A firestorm scorches over 1500 acres in the hills of Oakland and Berkeley, killing 25 and causing $1.5 billion in damage

victim of a nationwide economic **recession** – the cause of it, in fact, according to many analysts. This immediately affected Silicon Valley companies, which saw billions wiped off their stock values and had to offload employees faster than they had hired them, though there was some recovery by the middle of the decade. On the other hand, the Bay Area's notoriously inflated **property prices**, which originally slowed for the first time in a decade with the high-tech bust, have continued to rise ever higher, especially in San Francisco itself.

After a series of embarrassing, Third World-type **power cuts** in 2001, the state was forced to fork out vast sums to import some of its shortfall in energy from other states. This and other areas of gross mismanagement led to widespread disaffection and a rare **recall** election (a vote of confidence, in effect) in October 2003, when Democrat Governor Gray Davis was replaced by Republican – not to mention Hollywood blockbuster actor and former bodybuilder – **Arnold Schwarzenegger**. The high-profile Governor's main remit was to balance the ailing **state budget**, and he set about it with a series of conservative measures to raise revenue, including hikes of day-use and camping fees in state parks, as well as cuts in welfare programmes and even the funding of tourism.

With the power crisis in mind, however, and environmentalists maintaining that there will not be a proper solution until serious money is invested in **renewable energy** sources, the "Governator" (as he soon became known, thanks to his roles in the Terminator films) broke with broader Republican policy and passed a series of green measures towards this end, making protection of the environment another centrepiece of his administration. Such measures, combined with the advantage of being married to a member of the Kennedy clan and a relatively liberal social platform (although he stopped short of supporting gay marriage), resulted in him being re-elected in 2006. His second term, however, was beset by continuing difficulties in controlling the state budget, which, compounded by the recession that started in 2008, reached a staggering deficit of almost $20 billion by the fiscal year 2011. As a result, and against the national trend towards the Republicans, **Jerry Brown**, following stints as State Attorney General and Oakland Mayor, won a fiercely contested race against former eBay CEO Meg Whitman to become Governor again in November 2010, nearly three decades since the end of his first two-term stint. Brown was re-elected in 2014 with 60 percent of the vote, and will serve until 2018.

California indeed remained a staunch **Democrat stronghold** against the swing back towards the right in the 2010 and 2014 Congressional elections. Having voted overwhelmingly for Barack Obama in the 2008 and 2014 presidential elections, the state returned Barbara Boxer and Dianne Feinstein to the Senate; Nancy Pelosi, meanwhile, despite losing her position as the first female Speaker of the House, was among the Californian representatives who at least held their seats (she was re-elected in 2016). In the 2016 presidential election, Hillary Clinton easily won the state (with over 60 percent of the vote) despite ultimately losing to Donald Trump. Democrat Kamala Harris replaced the retiring Boxer as senator.

In San Francisco and Berkeley, grassroots political **activism** underwent a renaissance in opposing George W. Bush's hardline domestic and international policies throughout most of the 2000s and a more recent burning issue across the whole state has been the ongoing battle over **gay marriage**. In November 2008, fifty-two percent of voters,

1992	1994	2002
Riots break out in Los Angeles upon the acquittal of four police officers accused of brutally beating motorist Rodney King; 53 are killed and over 2000 are injured	Centred in the San Fernando Valley community of Reseda, the 6.7-magnitude Northridge Earthquake kills 57	The Central Valley's annual agricultural output value crests $17 billion – eight percent of total US output

perhaps surprisingly, passed **Proposition 8** (the California Marriage Protection Act), which banned same-sex marriage by means of a constitutional amendment. The state's gay population and progressive sympathizers were outraged and campaigned vigorously for the act to be **overturned**, which it eventually was by US district judge Vaughn Walker in August 2010. Christian Conservatives immediately lodged an **appeal**, but a final decision deeming the controversial law unconstitutional was handed down in June 2013. Having been the first US state to legalize medical **marijuana** in 1996, California finally voted to legalize recreational use in the 2016 election.

In local politics, the most interesting developments have been at the southern end of the state. In 2005, Democrat and former union leader **Antonio Villaraigosa** was elected as LA's first Latino mayor in 133 years; his popularity led to re-election in 2009. Set against a background of rising national concern about illegal immigration, principally from Mexico, his success in two elections has emphasized the changing demographics of America and the power of the **Latino vote** (Eric Garcetti replaced Villaraigosa in 2013, becoming the city's first elected Jewish mayor). Meanwhile, in San Francisco, Democrat Ed Lee became the city's first Asian-American mayor in 2011. In this more conducive climate, the state's growing legions of legitimate immigrant workers have also been leading the way in **union organization**, which some believe could energize the national labour movement.

California has also been on the receiving end of extreme weather conditions, most likely attributable to climate change. These have mainly taken the form of **wildfires**, which have ravaged many different parts of the state in recent years, destroying hundreds of thousands of acres of forest and property and causing considerable numbers of casualties. There have also been disastrous spates of **flooding** in certain areas and ongoing drought in others, which has depleted water reserves.

Yet, despite these setbacks, California still manages to cling to its aura as a Promised Land of sorts. Barring any potential destruction wrought by the **Big One** – the earthquake that's supposedly destined one day to drop half of the state into the Pacific and wipe out the rest under massive tidal waves (see box opposite) – California seems set to continue much as it is, acting as the pot of gold at the end of the West's mythical rainbow, and as the place where the US forever reinvents itself.

2006	2015	2016
379ft Hyperion in Redwood National Park, on the state's north coast, is determined to be the tallest known tree in the world	With a Gross Domestic Product of $2.46 trillion – about the size of France – California possesses one of the largest economies in the world	In the elections, California votes to legalize recreational marijuana use

Environment and wildlife

Though popularly imagined as little more than palm trees and golden sand beaches, California is tough to top for sheer range of landscape. With glaciated alpine peaks and meadows, desolate desert sand dunes, and flat, fertile agricultural plains, it's no wonder that Hollywood film-makers have so often and so successfully used California locations to simulate distant and exotic scenes. These diverse environments also support an immense variety of plant and animal life, much of which – due to the protection offered by various state and national parks, forests, and wilderness areas – is both easily accessible and unspoiled by encroaching civilization.

California's landscape has been formed over millions of years through the interaction of all the main geological processes: Ice Age glaciation, erosion, earthquakes and volcanic eruptions. The most impressive results can be seen in **Yosemite National Park** in the Sierra Nevada, where solid walls of granite have been sliced and chiselled into unforgettable cliffs and chasms. In contrast, the sand dunes of **Death Valley National Park** are being constantly shaped and reshaped by dry desert winds, surrounded by foothills tinted by oxidized mineral deposits into every colour of the spectrum.

The major **ecosystems** of California are detailed below. The accounts are inevitably brief, as the area encompasses almost 164,000 square miles, ranging from moist coastal forests and snowcapped Sierra Nevada peaks to Death Valley, which is 282ft below sea level and receives an annual rainfall of two inches. These ecosystems are inhabited by a multitude of species. Native to California are 54 species of cacti, 135 species of amphibians and reptiles, over 400 species of birds and around 28,000 species of insects.

Some of the most fantastic **wildlife** is now extinct in its natural habitat: both the grizzly bear (which still adorns the California state flag) and the California condor (the largest North American land bird, with a wingspan of over 8ft) are no longer seen in the California wilds. Plenty of other creatures are still alive and thriving, however, from otters, elephant seals and grey whales seen along the coast, to chubby marmots – shy mammals often found sunning themselves on rocks in the higher reaches of mountains. Plant life is equally varied, from brilliant but short-lived desert wildflowers to ancient bristlecone pine trees, which live for thousands of years on the arid peaks of the Great Basin desert.

THE RING OF FIRE

Earthquakes – which earned Los Angeles the nickname "Shakeytown" – are the most powerful expression of the volatile unrest underlying the placid surface. California sits on the Pacific "**Ring of Fire**", at the junction of two tectonic plates. Besides the occasional earthquake – like the 1906 one which flattened most of San Francisco, or the 1994 quake which collapsed many buildings in Los Angeles' San Fernando Valley – this instability is also the cause of California's many **volcanoes**. Distinguished by their symmetrical, conical shape, almost all of them are now dormant, though Lassen Peak, in far Northern California, did erupt in 1914 and 1915, destroying much of the surrounding forest. Along with the boiling mud pools that accompany even the dormant volcanoes, the most attractive features of volcanic regions are the bubbling **hot springs** – pools of often-scalding water that flow up from underground. Hot springs occur naturally all over the state, and though some have now been developed into luxurious health spas, most remain in their natural condition, where you can soak your bones *au naturel* surrounded by mountain meadows or wide-open deserts. The best of these are listed throughout the Guide.

The coast

California's shoreline is composed of three primary ecosystems: tide pools, sand beaches and estuaries. The **Pacific Ocean** determines California's climate, keeping coastal temperatures moderate year-round. During spring and summer, cold and nutrient-rich waters produce cooling banks of fog and abundant crops of phytoplankton (microscopic algae); the algae nourishes creatures such as krill (small shrimp), which in turn provide sustenance for juvenile fish. This food chain offers fodder for millions of nesting **sea birds**, as well as harbour and elephant **seals**, California **sea lions** and whales. **Grey whales** (see box, p.533), the most common whale species spotted from land, were once almost hunted to the point of extinction, but have now returned to the coast in large numbers.

Pacific Grove (see p.400) is home to large populations of **sea otters**. Unlike most marine mammals, sea otters keep themselves warm with a thick, soft fur coat rather than blubber. The trade in sea otter pelts brought entrepreneurial Russian and British hunters to the West Coast, and by the mid-nineteenth century, the otters were virtually extinct. In 1938, a small population was discovered along the Big Sur coast, and with careful protection otters have re-established themselves in the southern part of the area. Using binoculars, it's easy to spot these charming creatures with their big rubbery noses and Groucho Marx moustaches, bobbing and resting on their backs while opening sea urchins with a rock, or sleeping entwined within a seat belt of kelp that keeps them from floating away. The bulk of the population resides between Monterey Bay and the Channel Islands, but – apart from Pacific Grove – the best places to see them are Point Lobos State Natural Reserve, 17-Mile Drive and Monterey's Fisherman's Wharf, where, along with sea lions, they often come to beg for fish.

Tide pools

To explore the **tide pools**, first check to see when the low tides (two daily) will occur. Be careful of waves, don't stray too far from the shore when the tide returns, and watch your step – there are many small lives underfoot. Miles of tide-pool-strewn beaches line the coast, with some of the best found in Pacific Grove, near Monterey. Here you'll find **sea anemones** (which look like green zinnias), hermit crabs, purple and green shore crabs, red sponges, purple sea urchins, starfish ranging from the size of a dime to that of a hubcap, mussels, abalone and Chinese-hat limpets – to name but a handful. You may also see black **oystercatchers**, their squawking easily heard over the surf, foraging for an unwary, lips-agape mussel. Gulls and black turnstones are also common, while during summer, brown pelicans like to crash-dive for fish just offshore.

The life of the tide-pool party is the **hermit crab**, which protects its soft and vulnerable hindquarters with scavenged shells, usually those of the aptly named black turban snail. Hermit crabs scurry around busily in search of a detritus snack, or scuffle with other hermit crabs over the proprietorship of vacant snail shells.

Many of the **seaweeds** you see growing from the rocks are edible. As one would expect from a Pacific beachfront, there are also palms – **sea palms**, with four-inch-long rubbery stems and flagella-like fronds. Their thick, root-like holdfasts provide shelter for small crabs. You'll also find giant **kelp** washed up on shore – harvested commercially for use in thickening ice cream.

Sand beaches

The long, golden **sandy beaches** for which California is so famous may look sterile from a distance. However, observe the margin of sand exposed as a gentle wave recedes, and you will see jet streams of small bubbles emerge from the holes of numerous clams and mole crabs. Small shore birds called **sanderlings** race among the waves in search of these morsels, and sand dollars are often easy to find along the high-tide line.

The most unusual sandy-shore bathing beauties are the **northern elephant seals**, which will tolerate rocky beaches but favour soft sand mattresses for their rotund torsos. The males, or bulls, can reach lengths of over six metres and weigh upwards of four tonnes; the females, or cows, are petite by comparison – four metres long, and averaging a mere two thousand pounds in weight. They have large eyes, adapted for spotting fish in deep or murky waters; indeed, elephant seals are the deepest diving mammals, capable of staying underwater for twenty minutes at a time, reaching depths of over four thousand feet, where the pressure is over a hundred times that at the surface. They have to dive so deeply in order to avoid the attentions of the great white sharks lurking offshore, for whom they are a favourite meal.

Elephant seals were decimated by commercial whalers in the mid-nineteenth century for their blubber and hides. By the turn of the twentieth century, fewer than one hundred remained, but careful protection has partially restored the California population, which is concentrated on the Channel and Farallon islands, at Piedras Blancas just north of San Simeon, and at Año Nuevo State Park.

Elephant seals only emerge from the ocean to breed or moult; their name comes from the male's long, trunk-like proboscis, through which it produces a resonant pinging sound that biologists call "trumpeting", which is how it attracts a mate. The beaches at Año Nuevo are the best place to observe this ritual, and every winter, bulls haul themselves out of the water here to battle for dominance. The dominant alpha male will do most of the mating, siring as many as fifty young pups, one per mating, in a season. Other males fight it out at the fringes, each managing one or two couplings with the hapless, defenceless females. During this time, the beach is a seething mass of tonne upon tonne of blubbery seals – flopping sand over their backs to keep cool, and squabbling with their neighbours while making rude snoring and belching sounds. The adults depart in March, while the weaned pups hang around until May.

Different age groups of elephant seals continue to use the beach at different times throughout the summer for moulting. Elephant seals are completely unafraid of people, but are huge enough to hurt or even kill you if you get in their way. Still, you're allowed to get close, except during mating season, when entry into Año Nuevo is restricted to ranger-guided tours.

Estuaries

Throughout California, many **estuarine** or river-mouth habitats have been filled, diked, drained, "improved" with marinas or contaminated by pollutants. Those that survive intact consist of a mixture of mud flats (exposed only at low tide) and salt marsh, together forming a critical wildlife area that provides nurseries for many kinds of invertebrates and fish, and nesting and wintering grounds for countless birds. Cord grass, a dominant wetlands plant, produces five to ten times as much oxygen and nutrients per acre as wheat.

Many interesting creatures live in this thick organic ooze, including the fat **innkeeper** (a revolting-looking pink hot-dog of a worm that sociably shares its burrow with a small crab and a fish), polychaete worms, clams and other goodies. The most prominent of estuary birds are the **great blue herons** and **great egrets**. Estuaries are the best place to see wintering shore birds such as dunlin, dowitchers, eastern and western sandpipers, and yellowlegs; peregrine falcons and osprey are also found here.

Important California estuaries include Elkhorn Slough (just north of Monterey), San Francisco Bay and Bolinas Lagoon, some fifteen miles north in Marin County.

Coastal meadows, hills and canyons

Along the shore, **coastal meadows** are bright with pink and yellow sand verbena, lupine, sea rocket, sea fig and the bright orange **California poppy**, the state flower. Slightly inland, **hills** are covered with coastal scrub, which consists largely of coyote brush. Coastal **canyons** contain broadleaf trees such as California laurel, alder, buckeye and oak, as well as a tangle of sword ferns, horsetail and cow parsnip.

Common rainy-season canyon inhabitants include four-inch-long banana slugs and rough-skinned newts. In winter, orange-and-black **Monarch butterflies** gather in large roosts in a few discrete locales, such as Bolinas, Santa Cruz and Pacific Grove. Coastal thickets also provide homes to weasels, bobcats, grey fox, raccoons, black-tailed deer, California quail and garter snakes. **Tule elk**, a once common member of the deer family, have also been reintroduced to the wild; good places to view them are near Tomales Point at Point Reyes National Seashore (see p.533), and inland at reserves near Bakersfield (see p.299) and in Owens Valley (see p.270).

River valleys

Like most fertile **river valleys**, the Sacramento and San Joaquin valleys – jointly known as the Central Valley – have both been greatly affected by agriculture. Riparian (streamside) vegetation has been logged, wetlands drained and streams contaminated by agricultural run-off. Despite this, the habitat that does remain is a haven for wildlife. Wood ducks, kingfishers, swallows and warblers are common, as are grey foxes, raccoons and striped skunks. Regular winter migrants include snow and Canada geese, green-winged and cinnamon teals, pintail, shovellers and widgeon. The refuges where many of these creatures live are well worth a visit, but be sure to watch for large numbers of duck hunters – the term "refuge" is a misnomer of sorts. However, most refuges have tour routes where hunting is prohibited.

Vernal pools are a valley community unique to California. Here, hardpan soils prevent the infiltration of winter rains, creating seasonal ponds. As these ponds slowly evaporate in April and May, sharply defined concentric floral rings come into bloom. The white is meadowfoam, the blue is violet-like downingia and the yellow is goldfields. Swallows, meadowlarks, yellowlegs and stilts can also be found here.

Forests

One of the most notable indigenous features of California's forests are the wide expanses of **redwood** (*Sequoia sempervirens*) and **sequoia** (*Sequoiadendron giganteum*) **trees**, both exhibiting the same fibrous, reddish-brown bark. Redwoods are the world's tallest trees, while sequoias (see box, p.316) have the greatest base circumference and are the largest single organisms on earth. Both species can live for over two thousand years, and recent research now indicates a maximum age of 3500 years for the sequoia. Their longevity is partially due to their bark: rich in tannin, it protects the tree from fungal and insect attack, while also inhibiting fire damage. In fact, fire is beneficial to these trees and necessary for their germination, so prescribed fires are set and controlled around them. The wood of the redwood in particular is much sought-after for both its resistance to decay and its beauty – near any coastal forest, you'll see signs advertising redwood burl furniture.

Redwoods and sequoias are the only surviving members of a family of perhaps forty species of tree which, according to fossil records, grew worldwide 175 million years ago. **Redwoods** are a relict species which flourished in a moister climate during the Arcto-Tertiary (just after the golden age of the dinosaurs); as weather patterns have changed, they have retreated to their current near-coastal haunts. Today, they are found in coastal pockets from the Oregon border to Big Sur – although you'll also encounter them as far inland as Napa Valley and the Oakland hills – and a tremendous battle between environmentalists and loggers is being waged over the remaining acres. **Virgin redwood forests** provide homes to unique creatures, such as the spotted owl and marbled murrelet.

The floor of the redwood forest is a hushed place with little sunlight, the air suffused with a rufous glow from the bark that gives the trees their name. One of the most common ground covers in the redwood forest is redwood sorrel, or oxalis, with its shamrock leaves and tubular pink flowers; ferns are also numerous. Birds are usually high in the canopy and difficult to see, but you might hear the double-whistled song of the varied thrush, or perhaps a chickadee's call. Roosevelt elk, larger than tule elk, also inhabit the humid northwest forests. Prairie Creek Redwoods State Park, near the Oregon border, is home to a large herd.

Sequoias are found on the western slopes of the Sierra Nevada, most notably in Yosemite, Sequoia and Kings Canyon national parks – though trees from saplings given as state gifts can be found growing all over the world. Juvenile sequoias – up to a thousand years old – exhibit a slender conical shape that, as the lower branches fall away, ages to the classic heavy-crowned figure with its columnar trunk. For its bulk, its cones are astonishingly small, no bigger than a hen's egg, but they live on the tree for up to thirty years before falling.

Sierra Nevada

In the late nineteenth century, the citizens' environmental movement was founded when John Muir fell in love with California's **Sierra Nevada** mountains, which he liked to call the Range of Light. Muir fought a losing battle to save Hetch Hetchy, a valley said to be as beautiful as Yosemite, but in the process the **Sierra Club** (see box, p.330) – and soon after, the National Park Service – was born, and the move to save America's remaining wilderness began in earnest.

The Sierra Nevada, which runs for much of the state's length, has a sharp, craggy, freshly glaciated look. Many of the same conifers can be found as in the forests further west, but ponderosa and lodgepole pines are two of the dominants, and the forests tend to be drier and more open. Lower-elevation forests contain incense cedar, sugar pine (whose eighteen-inch cones are the longest in the world) and black oak; in fact, the oaks, along with dogwood and willow, produce spectacular fall colour. The east side of the range is drier and has large groves of aspen, a beautiful white-barked tree with small round leaves that flutter harmoniously in the wind. **Wildflowers** flourish for a few short months here – shooting star, elephant's head and wild onions in early spring, asters and yarrow later in the season.

The dominant campground scoundrels are two sorts of noisy, squawking bird: Steller's jay and Clark's nutcracker. Black bears, who may make a raid on your camp, pose more danger to iceboxes than humans, but you should nonetheless treat them with caution. The friendly twenty-pound pot-bellied rodents that lounge around at the fringes of your encampment are **marmots**, who probably do more damage than bears: some specialize in chewing through the radiator hoses of parked cars. Always treat wildlife respectfully and manage outdoor dangers safely (see box, p.44).

Other common birds include mountain chickadees, yellow-rumped warblers, white-crowned sparrows and juncos; among mammals, deer, golden-mantled ground squirrels and chipmunks are plentiful.

The Great Basin

The little-known **Great Basin** stretches from the northernmost section of the state down almost to Death Valley, encompassing most of Nevada and stretching into nearby states such as Oregon and Utah. It's a land of many shrubs and few streams, with the streams that do exist draining into saline lakes rather than the ocean.

Mono Lake, reflecting the 13,000ft peaks of eastern Yosemite, is a spectacular example. Its salty waters support no fish but lots of algae, brine shrimp and brine flies, the latter two providing a smorgasbord for nesting gulls (the term "seagull" isn't strictly correct – many gulls nest inland) and migrating phalaropes and grebes. Like many Great Basin lakes, Mono Lake has been damaged through diversion of its fresh-water feeder streams, in this case to provide water for Los Angeles since the early 1940s.

Great Basin plants tolerate hot summers, cold winters and little rain. The dominant Great Basin plant is **sagebrush**, whose dusky green leaves are wonderfully aromatic, especially after a summer thunderstorm. Other common plants include bitterbrush, desert peach and juniper, as well as piñon pine, the cones of which contain tasty nuts that were a mainstay of the Paiute diet.

The **sage grouse** is one of the most distinctive Great Basin birds. These turkey-like fowl feed on sage during the winter and depend on it for nesting and courtship habitat. In March and April, males gather at dancing grounds called leks, where they puff out small pink balloons on their necks, make soft drum-banging calls and, in general, succeed in looking and sounding rather silly. The hens coyly scout out the talent by feigning greater interest in imaginary seeds.

Pronghorns are beautiful, tawny-gold antelope spotted regularly around the Great Basin; watch for their twinkling white rumps as you drive. Other Great Basin denizens include golden eagles, piñon jays, black-billed magpies, coyotes, feral horses and burros, black-tailed jackrabbits and western rattlesnakes. Large concentrations of waterfowl gather at Tule Lake in northeastern California, part of Klamath Basin National Wildlife Refuge Complex (see p.665), where hundreds of wintering **bald eagles** congregate in November before the fierce cold sets in.

Mojave Desert

The **Mojave Desert** lies in the southeast corner of California. Like the Great Basin, its vegetation consists primarily of drought-adapted shrubs – one of the most common being creosote, with its olive-green leaves and puffy yellow flowers. Certain areas of this higher-elevation (above two thousand feet) region are renowned for early spring wildflowers, when alluvial fans become covered with desert trumpet, gravel ghost and pebble pincushion. The quantity and timing of rainfall determines when the floral display peaks, but it's usually sometime between mid-February and mid-April in the lower elevations, and late April to early June (or even July) higher up. Besides shrubs, the Mojave is home to many interesting types of **cactus**, including barrel, cottontop, cholla and beavertail cactus, as well as many members of the yucca family. Yuccas have stiff, lance-like leaves with sharp tips, a conspicuous representative being the **Joshua tree** (see box, p.230), whose twisting, arm-like branches are covered with shaggy, upward-pointing leaf fronds that can reach to thirty feet.

Many Mojave Desert animals – including the kit fox, wood rat and various kinds of mice – conserve body moisture by foraging at night. The **kangaroo rat**, which hops rather than runs, has specially adapted kidneys that enable it to survive without drinking water. If you're lucky, you might catch sight of **bighorn sheep**, usually found in secluded canyons and on high ridges; **desert foxes**, a regular sight among sand dunes; and **coyotes**, which like to keep cool in the shade. Other high-desert animals include birds such as roadrunner, ash-throated flycatcher, ladder-backed woodpecker, verdin and Lucy's warbler, and reptiles like the Mojave rattlesnake, sidewinder and chuckwalla.

Film

In the early 1910s, attracted by the sunshine, cheap labour, low taxes and the rich variety of California landscapes, a handful of independent movie producers left the East Coast and the stranglehold monopoly of Thomas Edison's Motion Picture Patents Company, and set up shop in the small Los Angeles suburb of Hollywood. Within a decade, Edison's company was defunct and Hollywood had become the movie capital of the world, with Southern California the setting for everything from Keystone Kops car chases to Tom Mix Westerns, not to mention the odd biblical epic or historic romance.

Since then the list of **movies** set in California, and especially Los Angeles, has, unsurprisingly, become almost endless. What follows are those that make the most original use of California locations, and reflect the state's navel-gazing fascination with itself.

HOLLYWOOD DOES HOLLYWOOD

The Artist (Michel Hazanavicius, 2011). Showered with awards galore (including an Oscar for Best Picture), this exceptional romantic comedy-drama traces Hollywood's last days of silent films through the relationship of a fading silent-film actor and an early "talkies" starlet.

The Bad and the Beautiful (Vincente Minnelli, 1952). Bitter tale of the rise and fall of a ruthless Hollywood producer (Kirk Douglas), told in flashbacks by the star, writer and director he launched and subsequently lost.

Barton Fink (Joel Coen, 1991). Tinseltown in the 1940s is depicted by the Coen brothers as a dark world of greedy movie bosses, belligerent screenwriters and murderers disguised as travelling salesmen. Allegedly based on the experience of playwright Clifford Odets.

Ed Wood (Tim Burton, 1994). Loving tribute to the much-derided 1950s "auteur" of *Plan 9 from Outer Space* and *Glen or Glenda*. Gorgeously shot in black and white, with a magnificent performance by Martin Landau as an ailing Bela Lugosi.

Entourage (Doug Ellin, 2015). Based on the popular TV series (and, loosely, the life of actor Mark Wahlberg), this movie paints the ultimate fantasy of Hollywood sex, fame and wealth in the twenty-first century.

Good Morning, Babylon (Paolo and Vittorio Taviani, 1987). Two restorers of European cathedrals find themselves in 1910s Hollywood, working to build the monstrous Babylonian set for D.W. Griffith's *Intolerance*, in this story about the contribution of immigrants to early Tinseltown.

Hail, Caesar! (Joel and Ethan Coen, 2016). This ironic and somewhat bizarre send-up of 1950s Hollywood (based on real-life "fixer" Eddie Mannix) sees George Clooney's character kidnapped by a cell of Communist screen writers.

Hitchcock (Sacha Gervasi, 2012). Anthony Hopkins stars as the curmudgeonly and generally unlikeable Alfred Hitchcock during the making of *Psycho* in 1959. Filmed mostly in LA.

In a Lonely Place (Nicholas Ray, 1950). A glamourless Hollywood peopled with alcoholic former matinee idols, star-struck hat-check girls and desperate agents forms the cynical background for this doomed romance between Humphrey Bogart's hot-tempered screenwriter and his elegant neighbour Gloria Grahame.

The Player (Robert Altman, 1992). Tim Robbins is a studio shark who thinks a disgruntled screenwriter is out to get him; he kills the writer (at South Pasadena's Rialto Theater), steals his girlfriend, and waits for the cops to unravel the mystery. A wickedly sharp satire about contemporary Hollywood, with terrific celebrity cameos.

Singin' in the Rain (Stanley Donen and Gene Kelly, 1952). A merry trip through Hollywood set during the birth of the sound era. Gene Kelly, Donald O'Connor and Debbie Reynolds sing and dance to many classic tunes, including "Good Morning", "Moses", "Broadway Melody" and countless others.

A Star Is Born (David O. Selznick, 1937; George Cukor, 1954; Frank Pierson, 1976). The story of the rise of a starlet mirroring the demise of her Svengali. Janet Gaynor and Fredric March star in the early version (1937), Judy Garland and James Mason in the later. Both are worthwhile, while a 1976 remake with Barbra Streisand and Kris Kristofferson runs a distant third.

Sullivan's Travels (Preston Sturges, 1941). A high-spirited comedy about a director who wants to stop making schlock pictures and instead create gritty portrayals of what he believes real life to be. The first two-thirds are great, but the last third slogs along mawkishly.

Sunset Boulevard (Billy Wilder, 1950). Award-winning film about a screenwriter falling into the clutches of a long-faded silent-movie star. William Holden was near the beginning of his career, Gloria Swanson well past the end of hers. Erich von Stroheim nicely fills in as Swanson's butler, and even Cecil B. DeMille makes a cameo.

Who Framed Roger Rabbit? (Robert Zemeckis, 1988). Despite being a live-action/cartoon hybrid, this is a revealing film about 1940s LA, where cartoon characters suffer abuse like everyone else and big corporations seek to destroy the Red Car transit system.

LA NOIR

Chinatown (Roman Polanski, 1974). Jack Nicholson hunts down corruption in this dark criticism of the forces that animate the town: venal politicians, black-hearted land barons, crooked cops and a morally neutered populace. Great use of locations, from Echo Park to San Fernando Valley; an essential film about LA.

Devil in a Blue Dress (Carl Franklin, 1995). Terrific modern noir, in which South Central detective Easy Rawlins (Denzel Washington) navigates the ethical squalor of elite 1940s white LA and discovers a few ugly truths about the city's leaders – most of which he already suspected.

Double Indemnity (Billy Wilder, 1944). The prototypical film noir. Greedy insurance salesman Fred MacMurray collaborates with harpy wife Barbara Stanwyck to murder her husband and cash in on the settlement. Edward G. Robinson lurks on the sidelines as MacMurray's boss.

Gangster Squad (Ruben Fleischer, 2013). Loosely based on the LAPD'S fight against crime lord Mickey Cohen in the 1940s and 1950s, and almost entirely filmed on location in LA (notably City Hall and Union Station).

Heat (Michael Mann, 1995). It does star big names like De Niro and Pacino, but this crime drama, which also includes some stunning set pieces (such as a downtown LA shootout), is ultimately less than the sum of its parts.

Jackie Brown (Quentin Tarantino, 1997). A glorious return to form for Pam Grier, who, as a tough airline stewardess, plays the perfect foil for Samuel Jackson's smooth gangster. LA provides the gritty backdrop.

Kiss Me Deadly (Robert Aldrich, 1955). Perhaps the bleakest of all noirs, starring Ralph Meeker as brutal detective Mike Hammer, who tramples on friends and enemies alike in his search for the great "whatsit" – a mysterious and deadly suitcase.

The Killing of a Chinese Bookie (John Cassavetes, 1976). Perfectly evoking the sleazy charms of the Sunset Strip, Cassavetes' behavioural crime story about a club owner (Ben Gazzara) in hock to the Mob is just one of his many great LA-based character studies.

LA Confidential (Curtis Hanson, 1997). Perhaps the best of all the post-*Chinatown* LA noir films – a perfectly realized adaptation of James Ellroy's novel about brutal cops, victimized prostitutes and scheming politicians in 1950s LA.

The Long Goodbye (Robert Altman, 1973). Altman intentionally mangles noir conventions in this Raymond Chandler adaptation, which has Elliott Gould play Marlowe as a droning schlep who wanders across a desaturated landscape of casual corruption and bizarre characters.

One False Move (Carl Franklin, 1991). A disturbing early role for Billy Bob Thornton as a murderous hick who, along with his girlfriend Fantasia and psychotic colleague Pluto, murders people in a bungalow, then gets pursued by the LAPD and a small-town Arkansas sheriff.

The Postman Always Rings Twice (Tay Garnett, 1946). Lana Turner and John Garfield star in this steamy – and excellent – adaptation of the James M. Cain novel, first brought to the screen as *Ossessione*, an Italian adaptation by Luchino Visconti.

Touch of Evil (Orson Welles, 1958). Supposedly set at a Mexican border town, this noir classic was actually shot in seedy, decrepit Venice. A bizarre, Baroque masterpiece with Charlton Heston playing a Mexican official, Janet Leigh as his beleaguered wife, and Welles himself as a bloated, corrupt cop addicted to candy bars.

True Romance (Tony Scott, 1993). With a Quentin Tarantino plot to guide them, Patricia Arquette and Christian Slater battle creeps and gangsters amid wonderful LA locations, from cruddy motels to *Rae's Diner* in Santa Monica.

APOCALYPTIC LA

Blade Runner (Ridley Scott, 1982). While the first theatrical version flopped (thanks to a slapped-on happy ending and annoying voiceover narration), the recut director's version established the film as a sci-fi classic, involving a dystopic future LA where "replicants" roam the streets and soulless corporations rule from pyramidal towers.

Earthquake (Mark Robson, 1974). Watch the Lake Hollywood dam collapse, people run for their lives, and chaos hold sway in the City of Angels. Originally presented in "Sensurround!"

Escape from LA (John Carpenter, 1996). LA is cut off from the mainland by an earthquake and declared so "ravaged by crime and immorality" that it's been turned into a dead zone for undesirables. Sent in to stop the insurrection, Kurt Russell battles psychotic plastic surgeons in Beverly Hills and surfs a tsunami to a showdown in a netherworld Disneyland.

Falling Down (Joel Schumacher, 1993). Fired defence-worker Michael Douglas tires of the traffic jams on the freeways and goes nuts in some of the city's poorer minority neighbourhoods. A fitting reflection of the bleak attitudes of riot-era LA.

Mulholland Drive (David Lynch, 2001). A frightening take on the city by director Lynch, who uses nonlinear storytelling to present a tale of love, death, glamour and doom – in which elfin cowboys mutter cryptic threats, elegant chanteuses lip-sync to phantom melodies, and a blue key can unlock a shocking double-identity.

The Terminator (James Cameron, 1984). Modern sci-fi classic, with future California Governor Arnold Schwarzenegger as a cyborg assassin from the future sent to kill the mother of an unborn rebel leader. Bravura special effects and amazing set pieces here were succeeded by the director's 1991 blockbuster follow-up, T2: Judgment Day, as well as two additional films in the franchise and even a short-lived American television series.

MODERN LA

Boyz N the Hood (John Singleton, 1991). An excellent period piece that cemented the LA stereotype as a land of gangs and guns, starring Cuba Gooding Jr in his first big role, and Lawrence Fishburne as his dad.

Dogtown and Z-Boys (Stacy Peralta, 2002). Even if you have no interest in skateboarding, this is a fun, high-spirited look at the glory times of the sport in the mid-1970s, when a daring group of LA kids took to using the empty swimming pools of the elite as their own private skate-parks.

Erin Brockovich (Steven Soderbergh, 2000). Dramatization of the now infamous case brought against energy company PG&E for their contamination of the water supply at the Mojave town of Hinkley – much of the film was shot in LA or in and around Barstow.

L.A. Story (Mick Jackson, 1991). Though Steve Martin's wry satire on LA culture is 25 years old, some of the gags remain on point – the obsession with "half-caf, de-caf", 20-year homes being "historic" and refusing to get out the car and walk for even a two-block trip.

The Limey (Steven Soderbergh, 1999). Gangster Terence Stamp wanders into a morally adrift LA looking for his daughter's killer, and finds the burned-out husk of former hippie Peter Fonda.

Magnolia (Paul Thomas Anderson, 1999). A gut-wrenching travelogue of human misery. The San Fernando Valley serves as an emotional inferno of abusive parents, victimized children, haunted memories, plaintive songs, and a curious plague of frogs.

Mayor of the Sunset Strip (George Hickenlooper, 2003). Great, disturbing documentary about the titular character: a former stand-in for one of the Monkees, legendary DJ, lounge denizen, and apparent man-child who can't seem to get his life together, despite being pals with celebrities such as David Bowie.

Pulp Fiction (Quentin Tarantino, 1994). A successful collection of underworld stories presented in nonlinear fashion and set against a down-at-heel backdrop of LA streets, bars, diners and would-be torture chambers.

Short Cuts (Robert Altman, 1993). Vaguely linked vignettes tracing the lives of LA suburbanites, from a trailer-park couple in Downey to a wealthy doctor in the Santa Monica Mountains. A strong ensemble cast bolsters the intentionally fractured narrative.

Slums of Beverly Hills (Tamara Jenkins, 1998). Troubled teen Natasha Lyonne deals with growing pains in a less glamorous section of town, far from Rodeo Drive, where a pill-popping cousin, manic uncle, weird neighbours and her own expanding bustline are but a few of her worries.

Swingers (Doug Liman, 1996). Cocktail culture gets skewered in this flick about a couple of dudes who flit from club to club to eye "beautiful babies" and barter like Rat Pack-era Sinatras. Many LA locales are shown, such as the Dresden Room and The Derby.

To Sleep with Anger (Charles Burnett, 1990). An impressive look at LA's overlooked black middle class, directed with polish by a very underrated African American film-maker.

Tupac and Biggie (Nick Broomfield, 2002). Eye-opening documentary about the murders of rappers Tupac Shakur and Notorious B.I.G., both of whom the director suggests may have been the victims of hip-hop producer Suge Knight, along with rogue elements of the LAPD.

IF YOU'RE GOING TO SAN FRANCISCO ...

48 Hrs. (Walter Hill, 1982). Nick Nolte plays a hilariously gruff police detective opposite wisecracking convict Eddie Murphy (in his big-screen debut) in this entertaining action drama. Unique for its portrayal of San Francisco as a gritty, murderous world – no whimsical shots of colourful Victorian homes or the Golden Gate Bridge here.

Bullitt (Peter Yates, 1968). The classic portrait of San Francisco, presented at breakneck speed in cinema's most famous car chase, ripping up and down the city's steep hills at a frenetic, still-amazing pace – without the use of modern special effects.

The Conversation (Francis Ford Coppola, 1974). Opening with a mesmerizing sequence of high-tech eavesdropping in Union Square, Coppola's chilling character study of San Francisco surveillance expert Harry Caul is one of the best films of the paranoid Watergate era.

Dim Sum: A Little Bit of Heart (Wayne Wang, 1985). Set among San Francisco's Chinese community, Wayne Wang's appealing comedy of manners about assimilation and family ties is a modest and rewarding treat. His earlier sleeper *Chan is Missing* (1982) also shows a Chinatown tourists don't usually see.

Dirty Harry (Don Siegel, 1971). Based on the infamous case of the Zodiac Killer, Siegel's morally dubious, sequel-spawning thriller casts Clint Eastwood in his most famous role as a vigilante San Francisco cop. The first and best in a long series.

Escape from Alcatraz (Don Siegel, 1979). Though evocatively portrayed in *Bird Man of Alcatraz*, *Point Blank*, *The Rock* and many others, this is the ultimate movie about San Francisco's famously unbreachable offshore penitentiary. Starring Clint Eastwood (again) as a most resourceful con.

Fruitvale Station (Ryan Coogler, 2013). Michael B. Jordan stars in the role of Oscar Grant, a young African American shot dead by transport police in an Oakland BART station, in this critically lauded account of the final day of Grant's life. A rare cinematic peek into urban East Bay life, far from Hollywood's decades-long Bay Area fascination with San Francisco.

Gimme Shelter (Albert and David Maysles, 1969). Excellent documentary about the ill-fated Rolling Stones concert at Altamont, in which Hell's Angels were hired to provide their own version of "security". Its searing look at home-grown American violence and Vietnam-era chaos at the end of the 1960s includes an on-camera stabbing.

Greed (Erich von Stroheim, 1924). This legendary silent masterpiece about the downfall of Polk Street dentist Doc McTeague (based on the Frank Norris novel) was shot mostly on location in the Bay Area, and remains, even in its notoriously truncated version, a wonderful time-capsule of working-class San Francisco in the 1920s.

Invasion of the Body Snatchers (Philip Kaufman, 1978). Great remake of a classic 1956 paranoid chiller, in which aliens replicate by taking the shape of humans in the form of "pod people". This quite atmospheric and eerie

version is set in San Francisco – used to great effect – and has Donald Sutherland as the health-inspector protagonist.

Pal Joey (George Sidney, 1957). Based on the hit musical, this Frank Sinatra vehicle presents its title character as a womanizer with few limits, using Kim Novak and Rita Hayworth to his own ends, in the swinging city by the bay.

Petulia (Richard Lester, 1968). Julie Christie is dazzling in this fragmented puzzle of a movie about a vivacious and unpredictable married woman who has an affair with a divorced doctor (George C. Scott). Set against the wittily described background of psychedelic-era San Francisco, and superbly shot by Nicolas Roeg.

Play It Again, Sam (Herbert Ross, 1972). A strike in Manhattan led to one of Woody Allen's uncommon visits to the West Coast for this hilarious film about a neurotic San Francisco film critic in love with his best friend's wife and obsessed with Humphrey Bogart in *Casablanca*.

The Times of Harvey Milk (Robert Epstein, 1984). This powerful and moving documentary about America's first openly gay politician chronicles his career in San Francisco and the aftermath of his 1978 assassination. Based on the book by Randy Shilts (see p.695). Gus Van Sant's 2008 dramatic adaptation, *Milk*, won Sean Penn an Oscar for best actor.

The Towering Inferno (John Guillermin, 1974). Classic skyscraper-on-fire flick that ushered in the 1970s wave of disaster spectaculars, for better or worse, with this version featuring a cast of grizzled Hollywood old-timers and pulse-pounding action as a 138-storey building blazes away on the San Francisco skyline.

Vertigo (Alfred Hitchcock, 1958). Hitchcock's sombre, agonized, twisted love story is the San Francisco movie nonpareil, and one of the greatest films ever made. From James Stewart's wordless drives around the city to the film's climax at Mission San Juan Bautista, Hitchcock takes us on a mesmerizing tour of a city haunted by its past.

Zodiac (David Fincher, 2007). Pulse-pounder covering a lone cartoonist's search for the infamous Zodiac Killer of the late 1960s (who still hasn't been caught). Jake Gyllenhaal is good as the cartoonist; Robert Downey Jr is his usual brilliant and bizarre self as a crime reporter.

"WAY OUT" WEST

Beach Blanket Bingo (William Asher, 1965). A cult favourite – the epitome of sun-and-surf movies, with Frankie Avalon and Annette Funicello singing and cavorting amid hordes of wild-eyed teenagers.

Big Sur (Michael Polish, 2013). Artsy dramatization of the 1962 Jack Kerouac novel, based on his stays at Lawrence Ferlinghetti's cabin in Bixby Canyon, with much of the filming on location.

Bob & Carol & Ted & Alice (Paul Mazursky, 1969). Once-daring, but still-funny zeitgeist satire about wife-swapping and bed-hopping in hedonistic Southern California,

starring Natalie Wood, Robert Culp, Elliott Gould and Dyan Cannon as the titular foursome.

Boogie Nights (Paul Thomas Anderson, 1997). A suburban kid from Torrance hits the big time in LA – as a porn star. Mark Wahlberg, Julianne Moore and Burt Reynolds tread through a sex-drenched San Fernando Valley landscape in the disco years.

House on Haunted Hill (William Castle, 1958). Not the clumsy remake, but the ghoulish Vincent Price original, with the King of Horror as master of ceremonies for a scary party thrown at his Hollywood Hills estate – actually, Frank

Lloyd Wright's Ennis House (see p.83).

Modern Romance (Albert Brooks, 1981). Brooks – the Woody Allen of the West Coast – stars in this comedy about a neurotic film editor who dumps his girlfriend and instantly regrets it. Full of early 1980s LA signifiers, from quaaludes to jogging suits.

Point Break (Kathryn Bigelow, 1991). Pop favourite set in the surfer-dude world, with Keanu Reeves as a robbery-investigating FBI agent and Patrick Swayze as his rebel-surfer quarry.

Rebel Without a Cause (Nicholas Ray, 1955). Fine, brash colours and widescreen composition in this troubled-youth film, starring, of course, James Dean. A Hollywood classic with many memorable images, notably the use of the Griffith Observatory as a shooting location.

Repo Man (Alex Cox, 1984). Emilio Estevez is a surly young punk who repossesses cars for Harry Dean Stanton. Very imaginative and fun, and darkly comic.

Shampoo (Hal Ashby, 1975). Using LA as his private playground, priapic hairdresser Warren Beatty freely acts on his formidable, though nonchalant, libido. A period piece memorable for its washed-out look.

Valley Girl (Martha Coolidge, 1983). Early Nicolas Cage flick, in which he winningly plays a new-wave freak trying to woo the title character (Debra Foreman) in a clash of LA cultures. Good new-wave soundtrack, too.

OFF THE BEATEN TRACK

Bagdad Café (Percy Adlon, 1988). Inspiring fable about a German tourist who arrives at a dusty roadside diner in the Mojave Desert and magically transforms the place with her larger-than-life charm.

The Birds (Alfred Hitchcock, 1963). Set in Bodega Bay, north of San Francisco, Hitchcock's terrifying allegory about a small town that is besieged by a plague of vicious birds features indelible bird's-eye views of the Northern California coastline.

Citizen Kane (Orson Welles, 1941). In this pinnacle of American film-making, director Welles successfully copies the Baroque splendour and frightful vulgarity of William Randolph Hearst's legendary, prison-like palace near San Simeon on the Central Coast (see p.380). Here, it's called "Xanadu" and shot in San Diego's Balboa Park.

Faster, Pussycat! Kill! Kill! (Russ Meyer, 1965). Meyer's wonderfully lurid, camp, action flick unleashes a trio of depraved go-go girls upon an unsuspecting California desert. One-of-a-kind.

Fat City (John Huston, 1972). Stacy Keach and Jeff Bridges star in one of the last great films from Huston, a realistic, grim depiction of the lives of small-time Stockton boxers. Based on an equally acclaimed novel (see p.697).

The Graduate (Mike Nichols, 1967). Although usually identified more with youthful 1960s anomie than California per se, there are many evocative images in this generational comedy, including those of Berkeley campus life and suburban middle-class complacency.

High Plains Drifter (Clint Eastwood, 1972). Spooky Mono Lake is one of the bleak, disturbing settings for this tale of a mysterious gunslinger who comes back to a dusty burg to avenge a wrongful death – before drenching the town in blood and renaming it "Hell".

One-Eyed Jacks (Marlon Brando, 1961). Set, unusually for a Western, on the roaring shores of Monterey, where Brando tracks down Karl Malden – the bank-robbing partner who betrayed him five years earlier in Mexico – only to find him reformed and comfortably ensconced as sheriff.

Play Misty for Me (Clint Eastwood, 1971). Another Monterey movie – and Eastwood's directorial debut – this thriller about the consequences of a DJ's affair with a psychotic fan was shot in Eastwood's hometown of Carmel and on his own two hundred acres of Monterey coastland.

Riding Giants (Stacy Peralta, 2004). One of the best of the surfing documentaries, showing the glories of the sport (with modern, high-tech equipment), the life stories of some of its bigger names, and that perennial California backdrop of sun and waves.

Sideways (Alexander Payne, 2004). Two vino-slurping pals take a trip to the Central Coast's wine country, one of them seeking a last fling before he gets married, the other wallowing in shame and self-pity. The golden landscapes often resemble a two-hour ad by the California tourism board.

Some Like It Hot (Billy Wilder, 1959). This is the film some claim to be the best comedy ever. It is set around a luxurious Florida resort that's actually San Diego's own *Hotel del Coronado* (see p.188), itself dripping with swank beachfront elegance.

Three Women (Robert Altman, 1977). A fascinating, hypnotic and unique film in which Sissy Spacek and Shelley Duvall, co-workers at a geriatric centre in Desert Springs, mysteriously absorb each other's identity.

Books

No US state except perhaps New York can rival California for being the subject of more books – and for contemporary culture, it's clearly drawn the most ink. Most of California's stories tend to revolve around the Spanish Mission era, Gold Rush, movie industry, and modern politics and cultural mores. Los Angeles and San Francisco are predictably well covered, though other major cities appear much less often, with San Diego in particular yet to find an insightful chronicler comparable to Carey McWilliams (Los Angeles), Herb Caen (San Francisco) or Kevin Starr and Joan Didion (the entire state). The note "o/p" signifies an out-of-print title – which you may be able to find through one of the many secondhand-book merchants in and around Los Angeles, or online.

TRAVEL AND SPECIALIST GUIDES

Steve Grody *Graffiti LA*. If you're inclined to probe LA's poorer neighbourhoods, you might discover many of the colourful pieces of home-grown art depicted here, which the author dissects according to their ethnic, cultural, and (in places) gang affiliation.

Tom Kirkendall and Vicky Spring *Bicycling the Pacific Coast*. Excellent, detailed guide to bike routes running all along the Pacific Coast, from Mexico to Canada.

Eric Mahoney *Walking L.A.: 38 Walking Tours*. A bevy of fascinating treks through the city, from the well-trodden districts to obscure places off the radar of most locals and all tourists; well worth the journey.

Leonard Pitt and Dale Pitt *Los Angeles A to Z*. If you're truly enthralled by the city, this is the tome for you: six hundred pages of encyclopedic references covering everything from conquistadors to movie stars.

Ray Riegert *Hidden Coast of California*. Now in its eleventh edition, this detailed and compelling guide details the nooks and crannies along California's state beaches and parks, told from the perspective of a recreational enthusiast who tracks down all his favourite underrated beaches.

John R. Soares *100 Classic Hikes in Northern California*. An engaging presentation of wilderness hiking in the northern part of the state, from the Bay Area up to the Oregon border. Also good is the author's *100 Hikes in Yosemite National Park*.

Surfer Magazine's Guide to Southern California Surf Spots A handy, comprehensive reference to the best places in the state to ride the pipeline and find a killer break – fittingly, it's printed on waterproof paper.

HISTORY

Oscar Zeta Acosta *Autobiography of a Brown Buffalo; Revolt of the Cockroach People*. The legendary model for Hunter S. Thompson's bloated Dr. Gonzo, Oscar Zeta Acosta was in reality a trail-blazing Latino lawyer who used all manner of colourful tactics to defend oppressed and indigent defendants. Two vivid portraits of late-1960s California, written just before the author mysteriously vanished in 1971.

Mark Arax and Rick Wartzman *The King of California: J.G. Boswell and the Making of a Secret American Empire*. Essential reading for anyone interested in the real history of the state, focusing on how a family of Georgia farmers migrated to San Joaquin Valley and created the nation's biggest cotton empire – with hardly anyone noticing.

H.W. Brands *The Age of Gold*. Excellent introduction to

Gold Rush-era California, highlighting the immigrants from around the world who came to mine the ore, the unexpected fortunes of a lucky few, and the political and social repercussions of this unprecedented event – the first glimmer of the Gilded Age.

Gray Brechin *Imperial San Francisco: Urban Power, Earthly Ruin*. Long-overdue puncturing of myths about the City by the Bay, showing how dubious mining and financial schemes led to its rise, and how its history, strangely enough, parallels that of ancient Rome and other classical cities.

Vincent Bugliosi *Helter Skelter: The True Story of the Manson Murders*. The late 1960s wouldn't have been complete without the Manson Family, and here the prosecutor-author lays out the full story of the horrifying crimes carried out by the gang, inspired by their cult leader, formerly a Sunset Strip hippie and would-be pop songwriter.

Philip L. Fradkin *The Seven States of California: A Natural and Human History*. Part historical enquiry and part California road-trip travelogue, Fradkin's appealingly approachable writing is both journalistic and personal as he trundles through various regions, describing how California's singular combination of landscapes has influenced the behaviour of its residents. His more recent *The Left Coast: California on the Edge* traces a similar account along the state's nearly 1000-mile coastline.

John McPhee *Assembling California*. America's most versatile writer – McPhee has authored titles on such disparate subjects as tugboat captains, New England canoe-builders and the late tennis star Arthur Ashe – tackles the geology of California in his typically accessible style, drawing connections between the state's human and geological histories as he investigates each in depth.

Carey McWilliams *Southern California: An Island on the Land* (Gibbs Smith). The bible of Southern California histories, focusing on the key years between the two world wars and written by a lawyer and social activist involved in much of the drama of the time. Also excellent is McWilliams' broader *California: The Great Exception*.

Mark Reisner *Cadillac Desert*. An essential guide to water problems in the American West, with special emphasis on LA's schemes to bring upstate California water to the metropolis. One of the best renderings of this sordid tale.

Dennis Smith *San Francisco Is Burning: The Untold Story of the 1906 Earthquake and Fires* (o/p). An excellent, detailed examination – published on the one-hundredth anniversary of the event – of the infamous cataclysm, with a good mix of scientific and historical analysis and personal stories of some of the figures involved.

Kevin Starr *Golden Dreams: California in an Age of Abundance, 1950–1963*. The latest round of Golden State history from the state's pre-eminent chronicler, one in a series of eight such volumes. Of those, the best overall is *Material Dreams: Southern California Through the 1920s*, which covers the city's boom interwar years of celebrities and scandals.

POLITICS AND SOCIETY

James Conaway *Napa: The Story of an American Eden*. Compelling tale of how Napa Valley vintners attained international glory through clever science and down-and-dirty politics.

Mike Davis *City of Quartz*. The most important modern history of LA, in this case from a leftist perspective, vividly covering cops, riots, politicians, movies and architecture. Other volumes, *Ecology of Fear* and *Under the Perfect Sun* respectively, tell of LA's apocalyptic bent and of the corruption at the core of sunny San Diego.

Lisa McGirr *Suburban Warriors: The Origins of the New American Right*. The tale of how once-fringe right-wing activists in Southern California rose from the ashes of the 1960s to dominate state and, later, national politics, culminating with the presidency of Ronald Reagan and his acolytes.

Ethan Rarick *California Rising: The Life and Times of Pat Brown*. More than even Nixon or Reagan, Pat Brown was the most influential political figure for modern California, from building aqueducts and freeways to curbing racial discrimination. This impressive volume details the man and his empire-building legacy.

Bobby Seale *A Lonely Rage: The Autobiography of Bobby Seale* (o/p). One of the key founders of the Black Panther Party in 1966 Oakland bares all in this fascinating book, though it can be hard to find. Seale is still active in the Oakland area. Also worth checking out is *Angela Davis: An Autobiography*, chronicling the life of the famous California-based activist.

Randy Shilts *The Mayor of Castro Street: The Life and Times of Harvey Milk*. Overview of the life, career and martyrdom of one of America's most famous gay-rights advocates, presented as an emblem for the rise of identity politics and social activism in 1970s California.

Jeffrey Toobin *American Heiress: The Wild Saga of the Kidnapping, Crimes and Trial of Patty Hearst*. The most recent (2016) and definitely the most exhaustive and entertaining examination of the whole bizarre, twisted Patty Hearst episode, with especially illuminating details on the trial. Sex, politics and violence, it's all there. Check out also Toobin's *The Run of His Life: The People v. O. J. Simpson*.

ARCHITECTURE

Reyner Banham *Los Angeles: The Architecture of Four Ecologies*. The most lucid account of how LA's history has shaped its present form; the trenchant British author's enthusiasms are infectious.

Susan Cerny *Architectural Guidebook to San Francisco and the Bay Area*. Fine overview in text and photography of the key structures in the Bay Area, chronicling their historic and cultural importance, along with their architectural value.

David Gebhard and Robert Winter *Architectural Guidebook to Los Angeles*. For many years the essential guide to LA architecture, from historical treasures to contemporary quirks. Some of the quality has been lost with Gebhard's death, so try the 1994 edition (his last) for the best writing on Modernist structures.

Jim Heimann *California Crazy and Beyond: Roadside Vernacular Architecture* (o/p). Decades after its initial publication, this fun volume is still a favourite, and has now been updated to include the latest of the state's bizarre-chitecture, from diners shaped like hot dogs to wigwam motels, and the influence it has had nationally.

Randy Leffingwell *California Missions and Presidios*. Its attractive photos may draw the eye, but this valuable pictorial guide is best for its detailed story of the chequered history and architectural background of the state's signature spiritual/prison outposts.

Elizabeth Pomada *Painted Ladies Revisited* (o/p). One in a series of volumes on Victorian mansions (in San Francisco and beyond) that you'll see in bookshops throughout the region, and well worth a look as a photo glossy and architecture guide.

Elizabeth A.T. Smith *Case Study Houses: The Complete CSH Program*. An excellent compendium of essays, photos and articles about the Modernist homes of a pioneering 1950s design programme. A huge, expensive book, but essential for architecture buffs.

HOLLYWOOD AND THE MOVIES

Kenneth Anger *Hollywood Babylon*. Deliciously dark and lurid stories of sex scandals, bad behaviour and murder in Tinseltown, written by the *enfant terrible* of 1960s experimental film.

Jeanine Basinger *Silent Stars*. Great ode to still-famous and long-forgotten Hollywood figures of the silent era, with brief biographies that outline the careers of movie cowboys, vamps and sheiks. The same author's *The Star Machine* explains how the early studio system created movie icons out of unknowns – and how it kept its stars under a tight rein.

Robert Evans *The Kid Stays in the Picture*. Spellbinding insider's view of the machinations of Hollywood after the demise of the studio system, written with verve and flash by one of LA's biggest egos and, it turns out, most compelling authors – the head of Paramount when that company was at its modern peak.

Otto Friedrich *City of Nets*. Evocative descriptions of the major actors, directors and studio bosses of the last good years of the studio system, before TV, antitrust actions and Joe McCarthy had their way.

Ephraim Katz *The Film Encyclopedia*. The essential reference guide for anyone interested in the movies, providing valuable information on the old companies and countless studio-system bit players, along with more contemporary figures.

Jerry Stahl *Permanent Midnight*. When his employers heard that star scriptwriter Stahl (*Moonlighting*, and *Thirtysomething*) was spending his already huge pay cheque to support his heroin habit (among other indiscretions), they gave him a raise to cover the difference and keep him on the job. A gritty descent into Hollywood drug hell.

MUSIC AND CULTURE

Peter Ames Carlin *Catch a Wave: The Rise, Fall, and Redemption of the Beach Boys' Brian Wilson*. Fascinating study of the troubled genius behind one of California's most iconic rock bands, from his early days in working-class LA to global icon.

Erik Davis *Visionary State: A Journey Through California's Spiritual Landscape*. Quite a journey, indeed, focusing on the various cults, New Agers and Zen philosophers who have illuminated the state in recent decades, along with older shamans and showmen. Highlighted by evocative, tantalizing photographs.

Joan Didion *Slouching Towards Bethlehem*. One of California's best and most polarizing writers takes a critical look at 1960s California, from the acid culture of San Francisco to American tough guy John Wayne. In a similar style, *The White Album* traces the West Coast characters and events that shaped the 1960s and 1970s.

Barney Hoskyns *Beneath the Diamond Sky: Haight-Ashbury 1965–1970*. A vivid account of the glory days of 1960s psychedelia, with evocative pictures of seminal rock bands such as the Grateful Dead, Jefferson Airplane and Charlatans, and a narrative that describes how the hippie paradise was lost.

Walter Isaacson *Steve Jobs*. Few authors get under the skin of Silicon Valley like veteran writer Isaacson, whose biography of the Apple-founding visionary is likely to remain the definitive work for years to come.

Robert Koenig *Mouse Tales*. All the Disneyland dirt that's fit to print: a behind-the-scenes look at the ugly little secrets – from disenchanted workers to vermin infestations – that lurk behind the happy walls of the Magic Kingdom.

Kevin Nelson *Wheels of Change: From Zero to 600 MPH, the Story of California and the Automobile*. If you are a fan of the glorious epoch of auto worship – and salt-flat and drag racing, modified hot rods, car shows and other shrines to the mechanical beast – you'll love this sweeping overview of California's seemingly indispensable icon.

Danny Sugarman *Wonderland Avenue*. Publicist for the Doors and other seminal US rock bands from the late 1960s on, Sugarman delivers a raunchy, autobiographical account of sex, drugs and LA rock 'n' roll.

Tom Wolfe *The Electric Kool-Aid Acid Test*. Take an LSD-fuelled bus trip with Ken Kesey and his Merry Pranksters as they travel through mid-1960s California, before the counterculture was discovered and co-opted by corporate America.

FICTION AND LITERATURE

T. Coraghessan Boyle *The Tortilla Curtain*. Set in LA, this novel boldly borrows its premise – a privileged white man running down a member of the city's ethnic underclass – from Tom Wolfe's *The Bonfire of the Vanities*, and carries it off to bleak satiric effect.

Richard Brautigan *Trout Fishing in America*. A Washington-born writer often associated with the California Beat writers of the 1950s and 1960s, Brautigan's surreal work is overlaid with cultural references. His most successful book, *Trout Fishing in America*, although designed as a fishing handbook, stealthily creates a disturbing image of contemporary life. Part of a series of stories with a California theme that includes *The Pill Versus the Springhill Mine Disaster* and *In Watermelon Sugar*.

James Brown *The Los Angeles Diaries*. Difficult-to-stomach, but strangely compelling memoir about life in the dark underbelly of the state, awash in drug abuse, child molestation, arson, suicide and Hollywood striving. A memorable self-view from a talented author and screenwriter.

Charles Bukowski *Post Office*. An alcohol- and sex-soaked romp through some of LA's more festering back alleys, with a mailman surrogate for Bukowski as your guide. One of several books the author wrote exploring his encounters with the city's dark side.

James M. Cain *Double Indemnity*; *The Postman Always Rings Twice*; *Mildred Pierce*. Along with Raymond Chandler, Cain is one of the finest writers of dark, tough-guy novels. His entire oeuvre is excellent reading, but these three are the best explorations of LA's underside.

Michael Chabon *Telegraph Avenue*. One of America's most lauded contemporary writers set his 2012 novel in Oakland and Berkeley, around the intertwined lives of two California families, one black and one white, with the two protagonists owners of an old-school vinyl record shop (Chabon now lives in Berkeley).

Raymond Chandler *Farewell My Lovely*; *Lady in the Lake*; *The Big Sleep*. Famous books adapted into classic movies, but Chandler's prose is still inimitable: terse, pointed and vivid. More than just detective stories (centred on gumshoe detective Philip Marlowe), these are masterpieces of fiction.

Philip K. Dick *A Scanner Darkly*. Erratic, but brilliant author who evokes the mid-1990s split between the Straights, the Dopers and the Narks – a dizzying study of identity, authority and drugs. Among the pick of the rest of Dick's vast legacy is *Do Androids Dream of Electric Sheep?*, set in San Francisco, which gave rise to the film *Blade Runner*, set in LA (see p.690).

Joan Didion *Play It as It Lays*. Hollywood rendered in all its booze-guzzling, pill-popping, sex-craving terror. Oddly, the author went on to write the uninspired script for the third adaptation of *A Star Is Born*.

Dave Eggers *A Heartbreaking Work of Staggering Genius*. Technically a memoir rather than fiction, this remains the most haunting work from the San Francisco-based founder of literary journal *McSweeney's*; after both his parents die of cancer, Eggers and his siblings move to San Francisco to try and start a new life. Eggers' *The Circle* (2013) is a thought-provoking drama set amid the Californian internet boom.

James Ellroy *The Black Dahlia*; *The Big Nowhere*; *LA Confidential*; *White Jazz*. The LA Quartet: an excellent saga of city cops from the postwar era to the 1960s, with each novel progressively more complex and elliptical in style. The author's other LA-based works are also excellent – but start here.

John Fante *Ask the Dust*. The first and still the best of the author's stories of itinerant poet Arturo Bandini, whose wanderings during the Depression highlight California's faded glory and struggling residents.

F. Scott Fitzgerald *The Last Tycoon*. The legendary author's unfinished final work, on the power and glory of Hollywood. Intriguing reading that gives a view of the studio system at its height. The US edition features a reconstruction of what the finished version may have looked like.

Leonard Gardner *Fat City*. Poignant account of small-time Stockton boxing, following the initiation and fitful progress of a young hopeful and the parallel decline of an old contender. Painfully exact on the confused, murky emotions of its men as their lives stagnate in the heat of the San Joaquin Valley city and its surrounding countryside.

Molly Giles *Iron Shoes*. A sobering, but fascinating look into the life of a Northern California woman, busy caring for her dying mother while trying to juggle various absurd and dismal characters in her life.

Dashiell Hammett *Five Complete Novels*: *Red Harvest*, *The Dain Curse*, *The Maltese Falcon*, *The Glass Key*, and *The Thin Man*. Seminal detective novels featuring Sam Spade, the private investigator working out of San Francisco.

Chester Himes *If He Hollers Let Him Go*. A fine literary introduction to mid-twentieth-century race relations in LA, narrated by one Bob Jones, whose struggles mirrored those of author Himes, who later ended up living in Spain.

Helen Hunt Jackson *Ramona*. Ultra-romanticized depiction of mission life that criticizes America's treatment of Native Americans, all while glorifying the Spanish exploiters and showing the natives to be noble savages. A valuable period piece – perhaps the most influential work of fiction ever written about California.

Jack Kerouac *Desolation Angels*; *Big Sur*; *The Dharma Bums*. The most influential of the Beat writers on the rampage in California. See also his first novel *On the Road*, which features a little bit of San Francisco and a lot of the rest of the US.

Elmore Leonard *Get Shorty*. Ice-cool mobster Chili Palmer is a Miami debt collector who follows a client to Hollywood, where he finds that the increasing intricacies of his own situation are translating themselves into a movie script.

Ross MacDonald *Black Money; The Blue Hammer; The Zebra-Striped Hearse; The Doomsters; The Instant Enemy.* Following in the footsteps of Spade and Marlowe, private detective Lew Archer looks behind the glitzy masks of Southern California life to reveal the underlying nastiness of creepy sexuality and manipulation.

Armistead Maupin *Tales of the City; Further Tales of the City; More Tales of the City.* Lively and witty, if serpentine, these famed soap operas detail the sexual antics of a select group of archetypal San Francisco characters of the 1970s and early 1980s.

Henry Miller *Big Sur and the Oranges of Hieronymus Bosch.* Fans of Miller and travellers to the central coast may enjoy this autobiographical offering from the famously oversexed novelist, better known for his exploits in Paris via *Tropic of Cancer* – this tome describes his less frenzied life in Big Sur, where he resided for 18 years.

Walter Mosley *Devil in a Blue Dress; A Red Death; White Butterfly; Black Betty; A Little Yellow Dog; Bad Boy Brawly Brown.* Excellent modern noir novels that involve black private detective Easy Rawlins, who "does favors" from his South Central base. Mosley compellingly brings to life pre-riots Watts and, later, Compton.

Frank Norris *Novels and Essays.* One of the great naturalist writers presents a bleak, uncompromising view of the state at the turn of the twentieth century; *McTeague* has a San Francisco dentist face social struggle and his own violence, while *The Octopus* is an epic battle in San Joaquin Valley between railroad robber barons and heroic wheat farmers.

Kem Nunn *Tapping the Source.* One of the most unexpected novels to emerge from California beach culture – an eerie murder mystery set among the Californian surfing landscape of Orange County's seemingly idyllic Huntington Beach.

Thomas Pynchon *The Crying of Lot 49.* Pynchon's celebrated – and most readable – excursion into modern paranoia follows the hilarious adventures of techno-freaks and potheads in 1960s California; it also reveals the sexy side of stamp collecting. His later, lesser *Vineland* and *Inherent Vice* are set in Northern and Southern California, respectively.

Luis J. Rodriguez *Republic of East LA.* Stark, memorable tales of life in the barrio, where struggling romantics and working-class strivers face the inequities of class and race, and gang crime looms menacingly.

Theodore Roszak *Flicker.* In an old LA movie house, Jonathan Gates discovers cinema and becomes obsessed with director Max Castle – a genius of the silent era who disappeared via mysterious circumstances in the 1940s – leading Gates into a labyrinthine conspiracy with its roots in medieval heresy.

Danny Santiago *Famous All Over Town.* Coming-of-age novel set among the street gangs of East LA, vividly depicting life in the Latino community.

Budd Schulberg *What Makes Sammy Run?* Classic anti-Hollywood vitriol by insider Schulberg, a novelist and screenwriter whose acidic portrait of the movie business is unmatched.

Upton Sinclair *The Brass Check.* The failed California gubernatorial candidate and activist vigorously criticizes LA's yellow journalism and its underhanded practices. Sinclair also wrote *Oil!*, about California's 1920s oil rush.

Terry Southern *Blue Movie.* Sordid, frequently hilarious take on the overlap between high-budget moviemaking and pornography, with the author's vulgar themes and characters cheerfully slashing through politically correct literary conventions.

John Steinbeck *The Grapes of Wrath.* The classic account of a migrant family forsaking the Midwest for the Promised Land. Steinbeck's light-hearted but crisply observed novella, *Cannery Row*, captures daily life on the prewar Monterey waterfront, while his epic *East of Eden* updates and resets the Bible in Salinas Valley.

Robert Louis Stevenson *The Silverado Squatters.* Portrays the splendour of the San Francisco hills and the cast of eccentrics and immigrants who populate them, as well as the strange atmosphere of Silverado itself, a deserted former Gold Rush settlement.

Amy Tan *The Joy Luck Club.* Four Chinese women – new arrivals in 1940s San Francisco – come together to play mahjong and tell their stories. They have four daughters, divided between Chinese and American identities, who also tell tales from childhood and their often-troubled present.

Michael Tolkin *The Player.* A convincing look at the depravity and moral twilight of the film-making community, with special scorn for venal movie execs. Made into a brilliant film in 1992 by Robert Altman (see p.689).

Gore Vidal *Hollywood.* The fifth volume in the author's "Empire" series about emerging US power on the world stage, this one focusing on the movie industry, its interaction with Washington bigwigs and its boundless capacity for propaganda.

D.J. Waldie *Holy Land.* Strangely evocative memoir of growing up in the master-planned super-suburb of Lakewood in the 1950s, written in spare, haunting fragments by a poet who also happens to be the town's public information officer – though you'd never know it.

Evelyn Waugh *The Loved One.* The essential literary companion to take with you on a trip to Forest Lawn – here rendered as Whispering Glades, the apex of funerary pretension and a telling symbol of LA's postmortem status mania.

Nathanael West *The Day of the Locust.* The best book about LA not involving detectives: an apocalyptic story of the fringe characters at the edge of the film industry, which culminates in a glorious riot and utter chaos.

Small print and index

ABOUT THE AUTHORS

Nick Edwards In the decades since studying Classics and Modern Greek at Oxford, Nick has lived in Greece and the USA and spent a lot of time travelling, especially in India. Since 2008 he has been living with spouse Maria back in his native southeast London, where he can more easily follow his beloved Spurs, obscure psychedelic music and occasionally promote some Oneness.

Stephen Keeling has been traveling to California since his first trip via Greyhound bus in 1991, and has been covering the state for Rough Guides since 2013. He worked as a financial journalist and editor in Asia for seven years before writing his first travel book and has written several titles for Rough Guides. Stephen lives in New York.

ACKNOWLEDGEMENTS

Nick Edwards would like to thank the following for invaluable help: Richard Stenger of Humboldt Co; Dan Marengo and Barbara Hillman of Berkeley; Birgitt Vaughan and Tim Zahner of Sonoma; Heather Noll of Mendocino; Kelly Chamberlin of Half Moon Bay; Annora McGarry of Granlibakken; Sarah Winters of N Lake Tahoe; Lisa May of Shasta Cascades; and Christina Erny in Reno/Tahoe, as well as everywhere I stayed. Thanks to my friends who offered fine hospitality – Laramie and Wendi, Gail and Michael and Nicki and Eric – or just great company – Clint and Catherine, the rest of the Berkeley crowd and Charles H. Well done to Annie Shaw for brilliantly smooth editing and to all at RG HQ. Heartfelt thanks as ever to Maria for support from afar.

Stephen Keeling would like to thank: Brian, Sunshine, Chloe and Adele Fisher in San Francisco; fellow author Nick Edwards; Rachel Mills, Olivia Rawes and Ann-Marie Shaw in the UK for all their hard work and editing; and lastly Tiffany Wu, the world's greatest travel companion.

Rough Guide credits

Editors: Rachel Mills, Olivia Rawes, Ann-Marie Shaw
Layout: Pradeep Thapliyal
Cartography: Rajesh Chhibber, Richard Marchi
Picture editor: Michelle Bhatia
Proofreader: Karen Parker
Managing editor: Keith Drew
Assistant editor: Divya Grace Mathew

Production: Jimmy Lao
Cover photo research: Aude Vauconsant
Editorial assistant: Aimee White
Senior DTP coordinator: Dan May
Programme manager: Gareth Lowe
Publishing director: Georgina Dee

Publishing information

This twelfth edition published June 2017 by
Rough Guides Ltd,
80 Strand, London WC2R 0RL
11, Community Centre, Panchsheel Park,
New Delhi 110017, India
Distributed by Penguin Random House
Penguin Books Ltd, 80 Strand, London WC2R 0RL
Penguin Group (USA), 345 Hudson Street, NY 10014, USA
Penguin Group (Australia), 250 Camberwell Road,
Camberwell, Victoria 3124, Australia
Penguin Group (NZ), 67 Apollo Drive, Mairangi Bay,
Auckland 1310, New Zealand
Penguin Group (South Africa), Block D, Rosebank Office
Park, 181 Jan Smuts Avenue, Parktown North, Gauteng,
South Africa 2193
Rough Guides is represented in Canada by DK Canada, 320
Front Street West, Suite 1400, Toronto, Ontario M5V 3B6
Printed in Singapore
© Rough Guides, 2017
Maps © Rough Guides

Photo credits

All photos © Rough Guides, except the following:
(Key: t-top; c-centre; b-bottom; l-left; r-right)

1 Alamy Stock Photo: Sean Pavone
2 AWL Images: Adam Burton
4 Getty Images: Alan Copson
5 Alamy Stock Photo: LOOK Die Bildagentur der Fotografen GmbH
9 Alamy Stock Photo: ZUMA Press (t). **Getty Images:** Ronald J Stella (c); Bill Stevenson (b)
11 Alamy Stock Photo: Patrick Batchelder
13 4Corners: Justin Foulkes (t). **Getty Images:** Chad Ehlers (c); Simeone Huber (b)
14 4Corners: Giovanni Simeone / SIME
15 Getty Images: Walter Bibikow (t); Anders Blomqvist (b); Josh Edelson AFP (c)
16 Alamy Stock Photo: Ian G Dagnall (t); A. Denzer (b)
17 Alamy Stock Photo: Stephen Bay (bl); David Sanger Photography (tl)
18 Getty Images: Robert Ginn (c). **Robert Harding Picture Library:** Look / Hauke Dressler (b)
19 Alamy Stock Photo: Mediacolor's (b). **Getty Images:** Cavan Images (c)
20 Alamy Stock Photo: Greg Vaughn (tl). **Robert Harding Picture Library:** Eye Ubiquitous (b)
21 Alamy Stock Photo: Anthony Arendt (b). **Dreamstime.com:** Serrnovik (t)
23 Alamy Stock Photo: WILDLIFE GmbH (cr). **Dreamstime.com:** Tsyu87 (b). **Robert Harding Picture Library:** Thomas Stankiewicz (cl)
24 4Corners: Massimo Ripani
54–55 Getty Images: Bob Stefko
57 Robert Harding Picture Library: Andria Patino

99 Alamy Stock Photo: Bill Varie (b). **Robert Harding Picture Library:** Wendy Connett
137 Getty Images: Gavin Hellier (t)
150 Robert Harding Picture Library: Richard Cummins
153 Alamy Stock Photo: Jon Arnold Images Ltd
167 4Corners: Simeone Giovanni (b). **Robert Harding Picture Library:** Richard Cummins (t)
227 Robert Harding Picture Library: Moodboard (b)
252–253 Alamy Stock Photo: blickwinkel
294–295 Alamy Stock Photo: Steven Milne
297 Alamy Stock Photo: Witold Skrypczak
348–349 Getty Images: PHOTO 24
351 Dreamstime.com: Robert Bohrer
379 Robert Harding Picture Library: travelstock44 (b)
416–417 Getty Images: Ed Pritchard
493 Alamy Stock Photo: David Sanger Photography (t). **Getty Images:** Richard Cummins (b)
527 Alamy Stock Photo: Marvin Dembinsky Photo Associates (b); Frans Lanting Studio (t)
536–537 Alamy Stock Photo: Scott Sady / tahoelight.com
539 Robert Harding Picture Library: Russ Bishop
559 Alamy Stock Photo: Stephen Saks Photography (b). **Robert Harding Picture Library:** Michael DeFreitas (t)
586–587 Alamy Stock Photo: Gary Crabbe / Enlightened
589 Alamy Stock Photo: Marek Zuk
597 Robert Harding Picture Library: Walter Bibikow (b); Gary Moon (t)
655 Alamy Stock Photo: Chuck Pefley

Cover: Pacific Palisades, Los Angeles **SuperStock:** Citizen of the Planet

Help us update

We've gone to a lot of effort to ensure that the twelfth edition of **The Rough Guide to California** is accurate and up-to-date. However, things change – places get "discovered", opening hours are notoriously fickle, restaurants and rooms raise prices or lower standards. If you feel we've got it wrong or left something out, we'd like to know, and if you can remember the address, the price, the hours, the phone number, so much the better.

Please send your comments with the subject line **"Rough Guide California Update"** to mail@ uk.roughguides.com. We'll credit all contributions and send a copy of the next edition (or any other Rough Guide if you prefer) for the very best emails.

Index

Maps are marked in grey

Map symbols

The symbols below are used on maps throughout the book

▬▬ ▪ ▪ International boundary	🅵 Fuel station	⚡ Lighthouse	☐ Beach
▬▬▬ ▪ ▪ State/province boundary	ⓘ Information centre	✚ Windmill	☐ Park/forest
▬ ▬ ▬ Chapter-division boundary	@ Internet café	⊛ Watermill	🌲 Sequoia grove
Interstate highway	✉ Post office	↑ Wind farm	🌴 Oasis
41 US highway	⊞ Hospital/medical centre	◆ Point of interest	🌳 Tree
5 State highway	≈ Swimming pool	☼ Viewpoint/lookout	Swamp/marshland
▬▬▬ Railway	Building	∴ Ruins	Mountain range
— ⋅ — Ferry route	♦ Museum	⚔ Battle site	▲ Mountain peak
⁄⁄ Pass	⇨ Church (town maps)	⛏ Mining	Gorge
⋈ Bridge	✝ Church (regional maps)	⚡ Ski	Rocks
Pedestrianized road	⊞ Cemetery	⛳ Golf course	◠ Cave
‐ ‐ ‐ ‐ Path	🀄 Chinese temple	⬆ Immigration post	☇ Waterfall
✈ International airport	♠ Buddhist temple	◆ National park	∿ Spring
✈ Domestic airport/airfield	🏛 Stately home/palace	⊠ Gate/park entrance	⛲ Fountain/garden
Ⓜ MUNI	■ Tower	🏠 Ranger station	☺ Crater
Ⓑ BART	⏚ Observatory	⚠ Campground	◠ Arch
★ Transport stop	🐘 Zoo	卉 Picnic	☽ Sand dune
🅿 Parking	◯ Stadium	▬▬ Coastline	

Listings key

- ■ Accommodation
- ● Eating
- ■ Nightlife/drinking
- ● Shopping

A ROUGH GUIDE TO ROUGH GUIDES

Published in 1982, the first Rough Guide – to Greece – was a student scheme that became a publishing phenomenon. Mark Ellingham, a recent graduate in English from Bristol University, had been travelling in Greece the previous summer and couldn't find the right guidebook. With a small group of friends he wrote his own guide, combining a contemporary, journalistic style with a thoroughly practical approach to travellers' needs.

The immediate success of the book spawned a series that rapidly covered dozens of destinations. And, in addition to impecunious backpackers, Rough Guides soon acquired a much broader readership that relished the guides' wit and inquisitiveness as much as their enthusiastic, critical approach and value-for-money ethos. These days, Rough Guides include recommendations from budget to luxury and cover more than 120 destinations around the globe, from Amsterdam to Zanzibar, all regularly updated by our team of roaming writers.

Browse all our latest guides, read inspirational features and book your trip at **roughguides.com**.